THE DEVELOPMENTAL SCIENCE OF ADOLESCENCE

The Developmental Science of Adolescence: History Through Autobiography is the most authoritative account of the leading developmental scientists from around the world. Written by the scholars who shaped the history they are recounting, each chapter is an engaging and personal account of the past, present, and future direction of the field. No other reference work has this degree of authenticity in presenting the best developmental science of adolescence.

This book consists of autobiographical chapters by the following leading developmental scientists: Jeffrey Jensen Arnett, Robert Wm. Blum, Jeanne Brooks-Gunn, B. Bradford Brown, Marlis Buchmann, John Bynner, John Coleman, Rand D. Conger, James E. Côté, William Damon, Sanford M. Dornbusch, Nancy Eisenberg, Glen H. Elder, Jr., David P. Farrington, Helmut Fend, Andrew J. Fuligni, Frank F. Furstenberg, Beatrix A. Hamburg, Stephen F. Hamilton, Karen Hein, Klaus Hurrelmann, Richard Jessor, Daniel P. Keating, Reed W. Larson, Richard M. Lerner, Iris F. Litt, David Magnusson, Rolf Oerter, Daniel Offer, Augusto Palmonari, Anne C. Petersen, Lea Pulkkinen, Jean E. Rhodes, Linda M. Richter, Hans-Dieter Rösler, Michael Rutter, Ritch C. Savin-Williams, John Schulenberg, Lonnie R. Sherrod, Rainer K. Silbereisen, Judith G. Smetana, Margaret Beale Spencer, Laurence Steinberg, Elizabeth J. Susman, Richard E. Tremblay, Suman Verma, and Bruna Zani.

Richard M. Lerner is the Bergstrom Chair in Applied Developmental Science and the Director of the Institute for Applied Research in Youth Development at Tufts University, USA.

Anne C. Petersen is the Founder and President of Global Philanthropy Alliance and Research Professor in the Center for Human Growth and Development at the University of Michigan, USA.

Rainer K. Silbereisen is a Research Professor of Developmental Psychology and the Director of the Center for Applied Developmental Science (CADS) at Friedrich Schiller University in Jena, Germany.

Jeanne Brooks-Gunn is the Virginia and Leonard Marx Professor of Child Development and the Director of the National Center for Children and Families at Teachers College and the College of Physicians and Surgeons at Columbia University, USA.

THE DEVELOPMENTAL SCIENCE OF ADOLESCENCE

History Through Autobiography

Edited by

Richard M. Lerner, Anne C. Petersen,
Rainer K. Silbereisen, and Jeanne Brooks-Gunn

Psychology Press
Taylor & Francis Group

NEW YORK AND LONDON

First published 2014
by Psychology Press
711 Third Avenue, New York, NY 10017

Simultaneously published in the UK
by Psychology Press
27 Church Road, Hove, East Sussex BN3 2FA

Psychology Press is an imprint of the Taylor & Francis Group, an informa business

Library of Congress Cataloging in Publication Data
The developmental science of adolescence : history through autobiography / edited by Richard M. Lerner, Anne C. Petersen, Rainer K. Silbereisen, and Jeanne Brooks-Gunn.
    pages cm
Includes index.
1. Adolescent psychology. 2. Autobiography. I. Lerner, Richard M.
BF724.D464 2014
155.507—dc23   2013012639

ISBN: 978-1-84872-931-5 (hbk)
ISBN: 978-0-203-58166-7 (ebk)

Typeset in Times
by Book Now Ltd, London

Printed and bound in the United States of America by Publishers Graphics, LLC on sustainably sourced paper.

Contents

Contributors

Jeffrey Jensen Arnett
Clark University

Robert Wm. Blum
Johns Hopkins Bloomberg School of Public Health

Jeanne Brooks-Gunn
Columbia University

B. Bradford Brown
University of Wisconsin-Madison

Marlis Buchmann
University of Zurich

John Bynner
University of London

John Coleman
University of Oxford

Rand D. Conger
University of California, Davis

James E. Côté
University of Western Ontario

William Damon
Stanford University

Sanford M. Dornbusch
Stanford University

Nancy Eisenberg
Arizona State University

Glen H. Elder, Jr.
University of North Carolina at Chapel Hill

David P. Farrington
Cambridge University

Helmut Fend
University of Zurich

Andrew J. Fuligni
University of California, Los Angeles

Frank F. Furstenberg
University of Pennsylvania

Beatrix A. Hamburg
Mount Sinai Medical Center

Stephen F. Hamilton
Cornell University

Karen Hein
*Geisel School of Medicine at
Dartmouth College
Green Mountain Care Board, State of Vermont*

Klaus Hurrelmann
Hertie School of Governance

Richard Jessor
University of Colorado, Boulder

Daniel P. Keating
University of Michigan

Reed W. Larson
University of Illinois, Urbana-Champaign

Richard M. Lerner
Tufts University

Iris F. Litt
Stanford University

David Magnusson
University of Stockholm, Sweden

Rolf Oerter
University of Munich, Germany

Daniel Offer
University of Chicago

Augusto Palmonari
University of Bologna, Italy

Anne C. Petersen
University of Michigan

Lea Pulkkinen
University of Jyväskylä, Finland

Jean E. Rhodes
University of Massachusetts, Boston

Linda M. Richter
*Human Sciences Research Council and
the University of the Witwatersrand*

Hans-Dieter Rösler
University of Rostock, Germany

Michael Rutter
King's College London

Ritch C. Savin-Williams
Cornell University

John Schulenberg
University of Michigan

Lonnie R. Sherrod
Fordham University

Rainer K. Silbereisen
University of Jena, Germany

Judith G. Smetana
University of Rochester

Margaret Beale Spencer
University of Chicago

Laurence Steinberg
Temple University

Elizabeth J. Susman
The Pennsylvania State University

Richard E. Tremblay
University College Dublin and University of Montreal

Suman Verma
Panjab University, Chandigarh, India

Bruna Zani
University of Bologna, Italy

Appendix Contributors

Mary H. Buckingham
Tufts University

Robey B. Champine
Tufts University

Lisette M. DeSouza
Tufts University

Santiago Gasca
Tufts University

Kathleen N. Greenman
Tufts University

Maria K. Pavlova
University of Jena, Germany

Foreword

Although adolescence as the time between puberty and the age of majority comprises a mere single-digit percentage for most people the world over, it often constitutes the most critical and influential component of their lives. At this clearly formative stage future developmental trajectories are indelibly and variously shaped.

Never before in modern human history has this important, albeit fleeting, period been as threatened as it currently is by—contradictorily—a plethora of choices for some adolescents and the stark diminution of choices for many others, with rising levels of both social insecurity and economic uncertainty. We have witnessed youth in many countries—from Soweto to Tunis, from Beijing to London—representing the conscience and exuberance of idealism, taking to the streets clamoring for societal change, resulting in social change, even the fall of governments in some countries, and more repression in others.

The form and content of interaction and communication amongst youth, and particularly adolescents, have inexorably changed, portending an era of information overload sadly juxtaposed with alienation and deracination that are profoundly altering our behavior, especially the way in which we interact amongst ourselves and in the world. The highest rates of unemployment, poverty, and physical and psychological dislocation our world has seen, amidst the greatest technological advancement in history, only serve to underscore the largest levels of human redundancy, and create a confusing phalanx of harsh reality for adolescents struggling to find meaning and their own sense of belonging in many parts of the world.

This is an apposite time, then, for a unique and refreshing volume that considers this fascinating young discipline of adolescence through the autobiographical perspectives of its distinguished contributors. Representing the entire spectrum of adolescent science—from medicine, through sociology and criminology, to psychology—these erudite educators provide quintessential insights about their *raison d'etre* for engagement in the discipline and for doing what they have been so ably doing, through the confluence of time, place, and person interacting within the specificities of context to produce their substantiated understandings of adolescence. My own experience—of refusing to comply with racist oppressive dictates from the age of 15 years that shaped a struggle for human rights, including nine years in apartheid prisons—can relate to the validity of autobiographical historiography shedding novel perspectives on adolescent development.

This impressive volume should inspire new heights in the science, which should and must play a critical role in more effective future policy formulation. Such a role for science will help ensure that the omissions and commissions of adolescents are more appropriately catered for in society, that the ghosts of our past do not haunt our future, and that adolescence is restored to a positive, if tentative, and more wholesome experience that has lasting affirmative consequences for us all.

Saths Cooper, PhD
President, IUPsyS

Preface

The scientific study of adolescent development has burgeoned across the past four decades. Despite this growth, current scholarship does not address all the needs of the scholars, practitioners, or policy makers seeking to describe, explain, and optimize the course of the development of adolescents. We believe that present and subsequent cohorts of scholars will need to understand more about the history of the field. Such knowledge may provide rich depictions of past, contemporary, and likely future scholarship pertinent to the adolescent developmental period. Historical knowledge may also provide useful lessons about how to describe, explain, and optimize the life chances of the diverse young people of our world. To paraphrase philosopher George Santayana, if we want to gain from our successes and learn from our failures, we need to understand our history.

However, with few exceptions (e.g., Muuss, 1990; Steinberg & Lerner, 2004), the history of the developmental science of adolescence has not been a major scholarly topic. Accordingly the present book seeks to contribute to the understanding of the history of our field by integratively recounting the role of person, time, and place in creating the structure and evolution of the developmental science of adolescence. We have approached our task through bringing together leading scholars in the field to recount through autobiographical essays the development of their careers.

Autobiographical accounts have the asset of authenticity, although they do not provide complete objectivity. Such accounts need to be integrated with independent analyses that contextualize the autobiographer within the broader stream of scientific progress. However, presenting the history of the field through autobiography has the value of documenting the ideographic character of the life course and, in the present book, of the scientific careers of the colleagues who, across the past four decades, have shaped the developmental science of adolescence.

The chapters also underscore the fact that the study of adolescent development has been an increasingly more internationally collaborative endeavor across these decades. Accordingly, we bring together in this volume leading scholars from several parts of the world, both to provide significant sample cases of the international character of our field and, as well, to illustrate important variation in the nature and impact of time and place on the person.

Our authors are senior scholars, that is, scientists who are past the mid-points of their careers. By focusing on senior scholars of the developmental science of adolescence we provide a baseline for possible future volumes containing the autobiographical essays of the now still earlier-career scholars whose work continues to enhance understanding of diverse youth around the world. We focus on senior scholars for another reason. This publication occurs at a point in history when some major scholars who made significant contributions to the developmental science of adolescence across the last 30–40 or so years have passed away. The field and, of course, this book as well are diminished by the absence of their work, vision, and voice. Although we cannot include their autobiographical essays in this work, we have provided in an appendix brief synopses of the life and scholarship of several of the scholars who have passed away.

In sum, to the extent that scholars and students in the field of adolescence wish to appreciate its past, understand the breadth and depth of its present, and get purchase on directions for future scholarship, having top-tier scientists from around the world provide such specifications is an important approach, one that gives this book both a substantial level of authority and, as well, authenticity about how science is conducted within the actual lives of active scientists.

There are numerous people to thank for their roles in the preparation of this book. First and foremost we are indebted to the authors contributing to this project. Their scholarship and dedication to excellence enabled this work to be produced. We express our particular appreciation to Saths Cooper, the current President of IUPsyS, for writing the foreword to this book.

We are also grateful to Jarrett M. Lerner, the Managing Editor at the Institute for Applied Research at Tufts University, for his superb editorial work. His commitment to quality and productivity, his efficiency and judgment, and his resilience in the face of the tribulations of manuscript production, are greatly admired and deeply appreciated. The excellence of his editorial skills contributed mightily to the cohesiveness and clarity of this project.

We are grateful as well to the funding agencies, colleagues, and universities that supported us during the preparation of this book. Finally, we dedicate this book to our colleagues who have passed from our lives, and to our students who will succeed us as the leaders of the developmental science of adolescence throughout the succeeding decades.

Richard M. Lerner,
Anne C. Petersen
Rainer K. Silbereisen
Jeanne Brooks-Gunn

References

Muuss, R. E. (Ed.). (1990). *Adolescent behavior and society: A book of readings* (4th ed.). New York: McGraw-Hill.

Steinberg, L., & Lerner, R. M. (2004). The scientific study of adolescence: A brief history. *Journal of Early Adolescence, 24*(1), 45–54.

1

Introduction

*The History of the Developmental Science of Adolescence:
The Role of Autobiographical Perspectives*

RICHARD M. LERNER, ANNE C. PETERSEN, RAINER K. SILBEREISEN, AND JEANNE BROOKS-GUNN

The scientific study of adolescent development has burgeoned across the past four decades (Lerner & Steinberg, 2009). This growth has involved impressive increases in the quantity and quality of research devoted to this portion of the life span; marked increases in students seeking training in adolescent development; new investments by foundations and governmental bodies in addressing issues of health, education, employment, and civic engagement; and positive contributions to civil society of the 100 million individuals around the world who enter the adolescent decade each year (Lerner & Steinberg, 2009).

Scholarly resources such as handbooks and encyclopedias (Brown & Prinstein, 2011; Lerner & Steinberg, 2009) have grown to address the needs for knowledge about the development of adolescents (e.g., see Lerner & Steinberg, 2009, for a review). However, the availability of new scholarly resources does not meet all the needs of the scholars, practitioners, or policy-makers seeking to describe, explain, and optimize the course of the development of adolescents. Both present and subsequent cohorts of scholars who will carry the scientific study of adolescence into the future, and the practitioners and policy-makers who need to have evidence derived from such research to formulate appropriate actions to optimize the course of youth development worldwide, will need to understand more about the history of the field.

Such knowledge may provide both rich and detailed depictions of past, contemporary, and likely future scholarship pertinent to the adolescent developmental period. For instance, such knowledge may elucidate why the field is structured as it now is, explain why particular theories, methods, and substantive areas are of contemporary focal concern, and indicate what scientific issues have been resolved, what limitations of scholarship have been overcome, and what challenges exist for advancing science and its application. In short, the value of understanding the history of the developmental science of adolescence is that such knowledge provides lessons ("sample cases")

about how to best describe, explain, and optimize the life chances of the diverse young people of our world. To paraphrase philosopher George Santayana (1905), if we want to gain from our successes and learn from our failures, we need to understand our history.

However, to date, the history of the developmental science of adolescence has not been a major scholarly topic. A chapter by Muuss (1990), two chapters by Lerner and Steinberg (2004, 2009), two papers by Dubas, Miller, and Petersen (2002, 2003), and an article by Steinberg and Lerner (2004) were among the few recent discussions of this history prior to the present book. Accordingly, a key goal of the present work is to advance such historical scholarship. However, as we sought to formulate a plan to portray this history, we recognized that the methods of studying history, historiography, are varied. We needed to decide what approach may work best in understanding the history of the developmental science of adolescence.

Edwin G. Boring (1950, p. ix), in what is indisputably the most important and esteemed historical treatise in the social and behavioral sciences, the monumental *A History of Experimental Psychology* (1929, 1950), noted that Hermann Ebbinghaus, one of the 19th century pioneers of the science that was to be termed psychology, once observed that the field "has a long past, but only a short history." The same point is true for the field we term "developmental science," and as well for its areas of specialization, for instance, the developmental science of adolescence. The nature of the history of this field should be considered in selecting a methodological lens through which to view it.

Approaches to Recounting of the History of the Developmental Science of Adolescence

Adolescence is a term derivative of the Latin word *adolescere*, which means to grow up or to grow into maturity (Muuss, 1990). Muuss (1990) noted that the first use of the term adolescence appeared in the fifteenth century. However, more than 1,500 years before this first explicit use of the term, both Plato and Aristotle proposed sequential demarcations of the life span. In fact, Aristotle proposed stages of life that are not dissimilar from sequences that might be included in contemporary models of youth development (Lerner & Steinberg, 2009). He described three successive, seven-year periods (infancy, boyhood, and young manhood) prior to full, adult maturity.

About 2,000 years elapsed between these initial philosophical discussions of adolescence and the emergence within the twentieth century of the scientific study of this period of life, dated by the publication in 1904 of G. Stanley Hall's two-volume work on adolescence. The subsequent (at this writing) 109-year history of the scientific study of adolescence – a (relatively) short history, given the more than two-millennia span of interest in this age period – has been described by Lerner and Steinberg (2004, 2009) and Steinberg and Lerner (2004). One inference that is possible to draw from their historical reviews is that the developmental science of adolescence may be recounted accurately by describing the contributions of the set of scholars whose theoretically predicated empirical work and professional leadership shaped the field.

In fact, the rationale for reference to the work of such scientists as the basis for understanding the history of the structure and professional character of a scientific field, such as the developmental science of adolescence, has its foundation in Boring's *A History of Experimental Psychology* (1929, 1950). In discussing the nature of historiography, Boring reviewed several theories of history, bringing attention within social and behavioral science to the concepts of *zeitgeist* (spirit of the times) and *ortgeist* (spirit of the place) as ideas that speak to the role of the context in shaping the conduct of the scientists contributing to a given field. From these views, it is the context – time or place (Elder, 1998; Elder, Modell, & Parke, 1993; Elder & Shanahan, 2006) – that shapes the person. In turn, Boring contrasted such ideas with a view that suggests that it is the characteristics of the individual scientist that may create the *ortgeist* and may foster changes that contribute to the *zeitgeist*. In this view, it is the person who shapes the context.

Boring implies that these two views of the basis of historical change – the contextual and the personological – may not be mutually exclusive and, in so doing, forwards an idea that reflects contemporary ideas about human development. These are ideas that suggest that mutually influential relations between individuals and contexts provide the basis for systematic change across the life span and generations. As the person shapes the context, the context shapes the person. Examples of such ideas about bidirectional influences between individuals and their contexts are relational developmental systems models of human development (e.g., Overton, 2006, 2010, 2011; Overton & Mueller, 2012) and, more specifically, ideas about life-span (Baltes, Lindenberger, & Staudinger,

2006) and life-course (Elder, 1998; Elder & Shanahan, 2006) approaches to human development.

However, despite implying that person-context relations may be a basis for historical change, and perhaps because he was a psychologist, Boring traced the history of psychological science through recounting the contributions of scholars such as Johannes Müller, Pierre Flourens, Gottfried Leibniz, Gustav Fechner, Wilhelm Wundt, Franz Brentano, Hermann Ebbinghaus, Edward Bradford Titchner, William James, G. Stanley Hall, John Dewey, and numerous other European and American philosophers and scientists. Nevertheless, the stories he told of the genesis of the contributions of these scholars very much reflected the influences of both *ortgeist* and *zeitgeist* on their lives and their work. In essence, in Boring's (1929, 1950) account of the history of psychological science, person, time, and place all influenced the course of the history of a field (Elder, 1998).

In more recent accounts of the basis of change – at either individual or contextual levels or, especially, in regard to the relations among person, time, and place – another influence has emerged: Serendipity. As both Bandura (1982, 1998) and Lewis (1997) have explained, chance encounters, or serendipitous relations between individuals and contexts more generally (Napolitano, Bowers, Gestsdóttir, & Chase, 2011), play an important role in individuals' constructions of their lives and in historians' accounts of the bases of change in people and institutions, including fields of science. Indeed, in the sociology of science, Merton (1949/1957/1968), Merton and Barber (2004), and Barber and Fox (1958) have discussed the conditions under which personological characteristics of the scientist (for instance, self-regulatory processes, proclivity for risk-taking behaviors), and unexpected encounters with life or social events, anomalous laboratory findings, or chance meetings with people may combine to both shape the life of a scholar and the direction of a scientific field. Both life-course sociology and life span developmental psychology have also discussed such influences on individual and institutional history through the concepts of non-normative life or historical events (Baltes et al., 2006; Elder, 1998).

Integrating Person, Time, and Place in Recounting the History of the Developmental Science of Adolescence

Accordingly, we believe that it is useful to integrate the historiography approaches of Boring (1929, 1950), Bandura (1982, 1998), and others (Baltes et al., 2006; Barber & Fox, 1958; Elder, 1998; Lewis, 1997; Merton & Barber, 2004; Napolitano et al., 2011) to understand the role of person, time, and place in creating the structure and evolution of the developmental science of adolescence. Indeed, by focusing on the life stories of scientists we have a means to capture the unique integrations of person, time, and place that characterize all lives (Elder et al., 1993) and that may account for the insights, creative sparks, capitalization on serendipitous relations, and breakthroughs that characterize the work that may come to define the key facets of, and directions taken in, a scientific field.

We believe that this integrated historiography approach can be instantiated through autobiographical accounts. The confluence of person, time, and place can of course also be assessed by independent historians. However, autobiographical accounts have the asset of authenticity, although they do not necessarily provide complete objectivity. A complete historical overview of a field might, then, involve an approach that possesses the charm of authenticity that is tempered by independent analyses that contextualize the autobiographer within the broader stream of scientific progress. Clearly, then, our focus on autobiography does not involve the latter, tempering approach, and we therefore leave it to the reader or to other historiographers to supplement the approach we take in this book.

Nevertheless, we believe there is substantial value in the essays in this book. The chapters provide repeated evidence about the ideographic character of the life course and the scientific careers of the colleagues who, across the past four decades, have created as a separate field within the study of human ontogeny the developmental science of adolescence. We see how these colleagues interweave time and place, and often point to serendipitous relations, in accounting for the arc of their careers. These chapters reveal individual motivation and individual reflection, often as responses to serendipity. Together, the chapters underscore the varied paths that led these individuals to focus their scientific careers on the developmental science of adolescence.

For example, in Chapter 41, by Rainer K. Silbereisen, we learn that, had there not been a problem with teenage heroin users in Berlin at the time that he was searching for his first professorial position, he probably would not have entered into research on adolescence. In turn, without his personal relationships and interactions with people at the Max-Planck-Institute in Berlin he would not have subsequently met and established international collaborations with other scholars studying adolescent development, relationships that resulted in research grants and publications. These latter collaborations and achievements are part of the objective record available to independent scholars. However, the personal voice of Rainer Silbereisen grounds these features of his life and career in time and place as he experienced them.

Of course, just as person and context are embedded in time, so is this volume. As illustrated by the example drawn from the chapter by Rainer Silbereisen, the study of adolescent development has been an increasingly more internationally collaborative endeavor for more than three decades. Accordingly, we bring together in this volume leading scholars from several parts of the world, both to provide important sample cases of the international character of our field and, as well, to illustrate important variation in the nature and impact of time and place on the person.

Moreover, as will be evident from the group of scholars included in this book, we have focused on senior scholars, that is, we have included scholars who are, in the main, past the mid-points of their careers. This publication occurs at a point in history when some major scholars who made significant contributions to the developmental science of adolescence across the last 30 or so years have passed away. The field and, of course, this book, are diminished by the absence of their work, vision, voice. Although we cannot include their autobiographical essays in this work, we have provided in an appendix brief synopses of the life and scholarship of several of the scholars who have passed away. In turn by focusing on senior scholars of the developmental science of adolescence we provide a baseline for possible future volumes containing the autobiographical essays of the now still earlier-career scholars whose work continues to enhance understanding of diverse youth around the world.

Conclusions

By presenting in this volume the autobiographies of leading scholars from around the world whose lives have been devoted to the developmental science of adolescence, we believe that we offer an important and rich account of how person, time, and place combine to propel individuals across their lives and to shape what they do as scholars and as people. In taking this approach to presenting the history of this field, we believe that this book is unique within developmental science, generally, and certainly the developmental science of adolescence more specifically.

To the extent that scholars and students in the field of adolescence wish to appreciate its past, understand the breadth and depth of its present, and get purchase on directions for future scholarship, having top-tier scientists from around the world provide such specifications is a singular approach to this field of scholarship. We believe as well, that it is an important approach, in regard to both the level of authority of this work and the degree of authenticity it presents about how science is conducted within the actual lives of active scientists.

References

Baltes, P. B., Lindenberger, U., & Staudinger, U. (2006). Life span theory in developmental psychology. In R. M. Lerner (Ed.), *Theoretical models of human development* (pp. 569–664). Vol. 1 in W. Damon & R. M. Lerner (Eds.-in-Chief), *Handbook of child psychology* (6th ed.). Hoboken, NJ: Wiley.

Bandura, A. (1982). The psychology of chance encounters and life paths. *The American Psychologist, 37,* 747–755.

Bandura, A. (1998). Exploration of serendipitous determinants of life paths. *Psychological Inquiry, 9,* 95–99.

Barber, B., & Fox, R. C. (1958). The case of the floppy-eared rabbits: An instance of serendipity gained and serendipity lost. *American Journal of Sociology, 64,* 128–136.

Boring, E. G. (1929). *A history of experimental psychology*. New York: Appleton-Century-Crofts.

Boring, E. G. (1950). *A history of experimental psychology* (2nd ed.)., New York: Appleton-Century-Crofts.

Brown, B., & Prinstein, M. (Eds.) (2011). *Encyclopedia of adolescence*. New York: Academic Press.

Dubas, J. S., Miller, K., & Petersen, A. C. (2002). The study of adolescence during the latter parts of the 20th century. In W. Koops & M. Zuckerman (Eds.), *Are we at the end of the century of the child?* Cambridge, MA: Harvard University Press.

Dubas, J. S., Miller, K. & Petersen, A. C. (2003). The study of adolescence during the 20th century. *The History of the Family, 8*, 375–397.

Elder, G. H., Jr. (1998). The life course and human development. In R. M. Lerner (Vol. Ed.) & W. Damon (Ed.), *Handbook of child psychology: Vol. 1: Theoretical models of human development* (5th ed., pp. 939–991). New York: John Wiley.

Elder, G. H., Jr., Modell, J., & Parke, R. D. (Eds.) (1993). *Children in time and place: Developmental and historical insights*. New York: Cambridge University Press.

Elder, G., Jr., & Shanahan, M. J. (2006). The life course and human development. In R. M. Lerner (Ed.), *Theoretical models of human development* (pp. 665–715), Volume 1 of *The Handbook of Child Psychology* (6th ed.), W. Damon & R. M. Lerner, Editors-in-Chief. New York: Wiley.

Hall, G. S. (1904). *Adolescence: Its psychology and its relations to psychology. anthropology, sociology, sex, crime, religion, and education*. New York: Appleton.

Lerner, R. M., & Steinberg, L. (2004). The scientific study of adolescent development: Past, present, and future. In R. M. Lerner & L. Steinberg (Eds.), *Handbook of Adolescent Psychology* (pp. 1–12). Hoboken, NJ: Wiley.

Lerner, R. M., & Steinberg, L. (2009). The scientific study of adolescent development. In R. M. Lerner, & L. Steinberg (Eds.), *Handbook of Adolescent Psychology* (3rd ed., pp. 3–14). Hoboken, NJ: Wiley.

Lewis, M. (1997). *Altering fate: Why the past does not predict the future*. New York: Guilford Press.

Merton, R. K. (1949/1957/1968). *Social theory and social structure*. New York: Free Press.

Merton, R. K., & Barber, E. (2004). *The travels and adventures of serendipity*. Princeton, NJ: Princeton University Press.

Muuss, R. E. (Ed.). (1990). *Adolescent behavior and society: A book of readings* (4th ed.). New York: McGraw-Hill.

Napolitano, C. M., Bowers, E. P., Gestsdóttir, S., & Chase, P. (2011). The study and development of intentional self-regulation in adolescence: Theoretical foundations, research findings, and implications for the future. *Advances in Child Development and Behavior, 41*, 19–38.

Overton, W. F. (2006). Developmental psychology: Philosophy, concepts, methodology. In R. M. Lerner (Ed.), *Handbook of child psychology, Vol. 1: Theoretical models of human development* (6th ed., pp. 18–88). Editors-in-Chief: W. Damon & R. M. Lerner. Hoboken, NJ: Wiley.

Overton, W. F. (2010). Life-span development: Concepts and issues. In W. F. Overton (Ed.), *Cognition, biology, and methods across the lifespan*, Vol.1 of the *Handbook of life-span development* (pp. 1–29). Editor-in-Chief: R. M. Lerner. Hoboken, NJ: Wiley.

Overton, W. F. (2011). Relational developmental systems and quantitative behavior genetics: Alternative of parallel methodologies. *Research in Human Development, 8*, 258–263.

Overton, W. F., & Müller, U. (2012). Development across the life span: Philosophy, concepts, theory. In R. M. Lerner, M. A. Easterbrooks, & J. Mistry (Eds.), *Handbook of psychology: Developmental psychology* (Vol. 6, pp. 19–58). Editor-in-Chief: I. B. Weiner. New York: Wiley.

Santayana, G. (1905). *Reason in common sense* (Vol. 1). New York: Charles Scribner's Sons.

Steinberg, L., & Lerner, R. M. (2004). The scientific study of adolescence: A brief history. *Journal of Early Adolescence, 24*(1), 45–54.

2

Confessions of a Heretic

My Unlikely Career as a So-Called Psychologist

Jeffrey Jensen Arnett

Every work day, as I make the 10-second commute from the breakfast table to my home office, I am grateful for my life as an academic psychologist. To me, of all the ways that a person could pass through a lifetime, a career devoted to learning and to teaching others is surely among the best. I think of myself as fortunate heir to a long and venerable tradition of devotion to the life of the mind and the world of ideas, going back at least as far as Socrates, and to a comparable tradition of searching for the ultimate meaning of things, going back at least as far as the Buddha. Like me, both of them seem to have avoided ever having a normal job.

Yet, even though I call myself a developmental psychologist and that is what I am considered by others, I feel less comfortable in the more contemporary tradition of psychology. I love psychology as the exploration and creation of ideas about human life and human development. I love listening to people talk about how they understand their development, their relationships, and their beliefs, and integrating what they tell me into my own ideas about who we are and how we develop. I especially love learning about the ways of people in cultures other than my own, and the challenge of trying to see life from their perspective.

However, I am acutely aware that my way of approaching psychology is not the dominant way, which is much more quantitative, less cultural, and less focused on ideas and big questions than I would prefer. This awareness has often made me feel like a heretic within psychology. I have been amply rewarded by the field of psychology, yet I have never really felt like I belong here. Although

I greatly enjoy what I do, I have the persistent feeling of being an outsider and of wishing the field of psychology were different than it is. I would say that the main theme of my career is this status as an outsider and a dogged insistence on going my own unorthodox way.

Early Years: Other Aspirations

I was born in Detroit, Michigan, in 1957. I came to developmental psychology relatively late. As a kid, I imagined becoming a sports star (football or basketball) and then president. Not very original, or very realistic, but something more related to my actual future is that I was writing from an early age. I wrote my first "book" (complete with illustrations) at age 5 ("I Saw a Hill"), and by third grade I had written a short story about a dog named "Legs." So, a love of writing, and a literary way of writing, was evident in me from early on.

Psychology never crossed my mind in childhood or adolescence. I did take a psychology course in high school, but I don't remember much about it except that a hypnotist visited class one day. Alas, like most of my high-school courses, it demanded little of me and I didn't learn a thing.

I went to college at Michigan State University, a common path for someone growing up in suburban Detroit. Since I liked to write, I declared journalism as my major upon entering MSU. However, in my very first semester, one of my courses was introductory psychology, taught by Bertram Caron. He must have been about the last person in the country (if not the world) to be using Freud's *Introductory Lectures on Psychoanalysis* as the main text for an intro psych class. Of course, I didn't know that at the time. All I knew is that I loved it.

I didn't find the Oedipal tale plausible even then as the foundation of early development, but I found the idea of the unconscious fascinating and illuminating (and I still do). That same semester I was taking a wonderful short story course, in which we read *The Dead* by James Joyce, among other classics. From *The Dead* I absorbed the revelation that we can never truly know another person. From Freud I received an even more startling revelation: We never even know ourselves, because our most important motivations remain unconscious. Somehow these dual epiphanies were exhilarating rather than depressing or disorienting. They seemed to be essential keys to understanding an otherwise baffling world. I immediately changed my major to psychology.

The rest of my undergraduate psychology experience was considerably less exciting. I took great courses in economics, biology, chemistry, and history, but my courses in psychology left little impression. The only ones I remember at all are two I took in my senior year, on humanistic psychology and the psychology of religion, both taught by Benjamin Beit-Hallami, a visiting professor from Israel (and, I later learned, a major scholar in the psychology of religion). I loved both courses, and maintained an interest in both topics for many years afterward. In fact, I still have a great interest in the psychology of religion and include religious questions in all my interviews (although I am personally an agnostic).

I had my first experience with research my senior year, and it was not a pleasant one. I thought I might go into neuropsychology, which was even then (1980) an exciting and growing area, so I signed up as a research assistant in a project examining the role of the hypothalamus in hunger. My job was to anaesthetize rats, cut off the top of their skulls, insert an electrode, monitor the signals from the hypothalamus, then toss the rats in the garbage can. The poor rats! Whatever we learned from that dubious experiment, it can't have been worth their suffering, if you ask me. That was it for me and neuropsychology.

I graduated with no idea what I was going to do. I was aware I'd need to attend graduate school in order to go anywhere in psychology, but after that rat experience I didn't think I wanted to be a researcher, and the only other option seemed to be clinical psychology. I didn't want to become a clinical psychologist. I knew I was ill-suited to listening to people pour out their sorrows all day. The weight of those sorrows would soon break me.

Instead, I became a musician. During college I had taken up the guitar, and the summer after I graduated I played constantly. I played for the love of it, not with any idea of making a living off of it, but by the end of the summer, with no other job prospects in sight, I realized that I probably knew enough songs, and played and sang them well enough, to get paid for doing it. For the next 2 years I was a solo performer, playing and singing acoustic guitar songs (lots of James Taylor) in bars and restaurants. I didn't make a whole lot of money, but I didn't need a whole lot, as I had moved home after graduation and lived with my parents rent-free. And it was great fun, playing and singing all the time and actually getting paid for it. I had begun to write songs, too, and I poured a lot of my time and energy into writing and recording.

Meanwhile, I considered what to do next. I loved music, but I didn't have any intention of making a career out of it. I knew that if I did I wouldn't love it any more, eventually. I investigated the possibilities in psychology, by obtaining a book on graduate programs. I looked half-heartedly at clinical programs, but then I discovered something I had never heard of before, called *developmental psychology*. As described in the book, this was a branch of psychology that involved research on normal development, including intervention and prevention programs to enhance development. I knew instantly that this was for me.

It may seem odd that I first learned of developmental psychology only after graduating with a degree in psychology. It certainly seems odd to me now. How did I manage to get through a whole program in psychology without even knowing that developmental psychology existed? I guess the explanation is that this is what can happen when you are a student at a university that has (at the time) 45,000 other students and you are a psychology major among thousands of other psychology majors. I don't recall ever meeting with an advisor.

In any case, having discovered developmental psychology, I eagerly applied to graduate programs. Because I knew so little about the field, I didn't have a lot to say about what area I wanted to research. My application stated only some vague intentions of understanding the sources of problems by focusing on early development. Nevertheless, I was accepted at the University of Virginia and soon began the program there with great hopes and expectations.

Graduate School and Postgraduate Years: Still Searching

The developmental psychology program at the University of Virginia was (and still is) an excellent program, one of the best in the world. At the time I was there, it had many top developmental scholars, including Mary Ainsworth, Robert Emery, Mavis Hetherington, and Sandra Scarr. Still, I realize now that it was very conventional in its assumptions about development. The focus was entirely on early development—nothing on adulthood or even on adolescence—and on American children. The cultural issues that would later become the foundation of my own views of development were never mentioned and never occurred to me.

For my first 2 years I worked with Mavis Hetherington, as part of a big longitudinal study of stepfamilies. I was part of a graduate student team that coded videotaped interactions between parents and children. The videotapes were fascinating to watch. However, coding every "utterance" was tedious, and seemed to drain the life from the exchanges between parent and child. By the time we were done, all that was left was a series of numbers that was a mere shell of what we had watched. This was, I think now, the beginning of my disillusionment with traditional methodologies in developmental psychology.

By my third year I was tired of being a cog in a research machine, and looked around for other opportunities. Lucky for me, Sandra Scarr had just arrived as the new chair of the department, and we hit it off immediately. Sandra's approach to working with graduate students was the polar opposite of Mavis's. Like many prominent researchers running big projects, Mavis wanted a team of graduate students who would fit into all the different roles that would make the project go. Sandra, in contrast, wanted me to come up with my own idea for what to do, and that was a freedom I sought by now. I told her I was interested in doing something on early childhood, maybe related to day care, one of the many topics she had researched. She made a couple of calls, and soon I was set up to do an evaluation of day care quality on the island of Bermuda.

Yes, Bermuda. When I tell people this is where I did my dissertation research they usually respond with a smile and raised eyebrows, but it's not like I spent a lot of time snorkeling or lying on the beach. I worked from sunup to sundown every day during the week, visiting day care centers and rating the interactions between the caregivers and the children. On the weekends I sorted through the results of the previous week and prepared for next week. Nevertheless, I admit it was a glorious place to be for five weeks. By the time I returned home, I had all the data I would need for my dissertation.

My dissertation seems like a rather small thing to me now. Certainly there was no great originality to it, and no notable intellectual content. At that the time my main interest was in learning ways of enhancing the development of young children, and the dissertation focused on the practical issue of training caregivers so they would provide higher quality care. However, by the time I graduated, I realized it was not going to be enough for me to be involved in the practical application of research. I needed something intellectually meatier, something more creative and conceptual, something that would involve new *ideas*. But I did not know what that something would be.

I graduated in less than 4 years, and then as now the expected route was to find a postdoctoral fellowship and spend a few more years gaining research experience and publishing articles before seeking a tenure-track position at a university. However, I had no interest in following that route. Although I enjoyed my dissertation research, for the most part I didn't like what I had seen of research in developmental psychology so far. The dominant methods, especially questionnaires, seemed to me to hollow out rather than illuminate the human experience. The most esteemed status seemed to be to design a large study, obtain a multi-million dollar grant, recruit an army of graduate and undergraduate students, and wait for them to bring you the results after the people participating in the research had been reduced to mere numbers and displayed in a statistical model. I didn't believe this was the royal road to understanding human development, and I still don't. And I knew I didn't want to devote my life to it.

Well, then, what to do with my newly minted Ph.D.? I had taught a couple of courses in my final year as a graduate student, and discovered that I loved teaching. I sought and found a position at a liberal arts college, Oglethorpe University in Atlanta, where there was teaching galore—four courses a semester! I'm sure Sandra and my graduate student peers thought I was insane. Taking a teaching job like this must have seemed like a disastrous decision, or at any rate a decision that would put an end to any prospect of a research career. Who could find any time for research while teaching four courses a semester? But, not for the last time, choosing what appeared to be the unconventional, misguided, even bizarre path proved to be remarkably fruitful. In fact, going to Oglethorpe proved to be the turning point of my life, both personally and professionally.

At first it was all teaching, all the time. Preparing for, teaching, and grading four courses was all-consuming. However, by the beginning of my third year I had all my courses pretty well whipped into shape. I began to turn my attention to the possibility of doing research, but on what?

In one of my courses that year I had a student who was an avid fan of heavy metal music. He knew I was a musician, and after class he would sometimes try to persuade me of the musical virtues of heavy metal. I was skeptical of his argument—it is definitely not my kind of music—but I was fascinated by his devotion to the music. This was also a time (the late 1980s) when heavy metal was receiving a lot of negative media attention as a supposed peril to America's youth—all, I noted, without any basis in research. So, really just for fun, I decided to start interviewing heavy metal fans. I put up a sign in a music store offering a free heavy metal tape (this was before CDs, let alone iTunes) to anyone who would agree to be interviewed, and soon I had a substantial sample of young "metalheads."

What they had to say about the music surprised me. First, most of them were bright and thoughtful, a sharp contrast to the media image of metalheads as brutes and ignoramuses. They were deeply cynical about the adult world, and they loved heavy metal because of its blunt honesty in expressing that cynicism. Second, they saw heavy metal as great music and revered their heavy metal heroes as great musicians—again, a sharp contrast to the general portrayal of heavy metal as noxious noise. Third—and most compelling of all—when they talked about the effects of the violent music they loved, not only did none of them say it provoked them to violence, but many of them said that the primary effect of it was to *calm them down.*

I was excited to find something so unexpected and so contrary to what was generally assumed to be true. Even more exciting, however, and even more important for my future as a researcher, was that I had found a method, interviewing, that I loved and believed in. In contrast to the questionnaire and observational methods I had learned in grad school, interviews seemed to me to get to the heart of the human experience and account for the whole person. For the first time, a career as a researcher appealed to me.

Something else happened that year that was even more pivotal for my future. Although it was a "university," Oglethorpe was a small school, with barely over 1,000 students, and I was, personally, half the psychology department. Consequently, I came to know many of the students well, especially the psychology majors. One day a senior psych major, Lene Jensen, stopped by my office around the time she was to graduate. I knew her well from many classes she had taken with me, and we had enjoyed talking together about all sorts of topics, but I was totally surprised when she suggested we continue to meet and talk after she graduated. Twenty-three years later the conversations continue, and we are still happily together.

Lene has been the key to my life, as my marriage partner and as my partner in parenting our twins, Miles and Paris (now 13 years old). We have also been intellectual partners. She is the smartest and most thoughtful person I know, and we share a critique of the dominant methods in psychology, a critique we have no doubt developed together. The disparity between the scholarly approach we favor and the approach that dominates developmental psychology has been frustrating sometimes, but it has never been lonely because we have shared it together.

When we began living together she had already applied to graduate schools in psychology and philosophy, and at first we assumed our time together would be brief. In the fall she would head for graduate school in the Northeast or the Midwest, and I would remain in Atlanta. However, from day one we really, really, really liked living together, and by the time she was accepted into the human development program at the University of Chicago we were starting to think about ways to stay together. Serendipity intervened: I learned of a postdoc on adolescent development at the University of Chicago, applied for it and got it. This opportunity seemed to fit well with my new interest in adolescence, inspired by my interviews with heavy metal fans. Now I would be able to retrain as a researcher on adolescence, having learned nothing of the academic literature in the area as an undergraduate or graduate student.

Here was another unconventional career move that admittedly, as I look back on it, seemed to have rather slim chances of succeeding. Who would leave a fourth-year tenure-track academic position for an eight-month postdoc? What would you do at the end of those eight months? Nevertheless, I didn't hesitate. What I knew, unequivocally, was that I wanted to be with Lene, and that I didn't want to spend the rest of my career at a small college. (As with music, I knew that if I did nothing but teach for year upon year, I would stop loving it.) What would happen next, I had no idea. But I knew, from all my years as a musician, a student, and a penurious assistant professor, that I could live on very little if necessary.

Little did I know it when I arrived, but my period at the University of Chicago would be the formative intellectual experience of my career. The only reason I was there was because Lene was there. Yet it turned out to be just the place for me, too.

The human development program at the University of Chicago is unusual, in that it especially emphasizes the fusion of anthropology and psychology. At the time I was there the faculty included two eminent anthropologists, Richard Shweder and Gilbert Herdt. I had never read a thing in anthropology, but now that I was at the U. of C. I decided to read Herdt's ethnography of adolescence among the Sambia, a tribal culture in New Guinea. Herdt described a series of remarkable rituals that Sambia males undergo from middle childhood until their first child is born. Highlights include ritual nose bleeding (based on a fear of female menstrual blood) and a period of fellatio of older boys by younger boys (based on a belief that younger boys need to ingest semen in order to grow into manhood).

That ethnography challenged and rearranged my worldview in ways that still endure. I had never read anything like it. In the course of my conventional training in developmental psychology, I had absorbed the conventional assumptions that the purpose of psychology is to search for universal principles, and that this can be done by studying Americans and then generalizing to the rest of humanity—so much so that I didn't even think of them as my assumptions. The stunning contrast between adolescence among the Sambia and adolescence as I knew it in the United States convinced me that these assumptions were false. I saw that I would have to rethink everything I had learned and come to a new understanding of human development. It was thrilling to learn a cultural way of thinking that seemed to illuminate so much more than what I had learned so far.

My 8-month postdoc passed quickly, but I found another postdoc through the U. of C. and Northwestern University that extended for two more years. The new postdoc was run by Daniel Offer, a psychiatry professor at Northwestern and a major figure in adolescent research. Most postdocs involve working on someone else's data, but Dan let us do whatever we wanted as long as we were productive. There were about eight of us, half postdocs and half doctoral students at the U. of C., and we had freewheeling weekly meetings in which nothing was sacred. We all liked Dan, but we didn't hesitate to challenge him. I cringe when I think of just how much I challenged him—now that I'm the age he was then, I wish I had been more respectful!—but to his credit he welcomed it.

I'm also grateful for the freedom he allowed us. It was just what I needed in order to read widely and gain my footing in adolescence as a theorist and researcher. In thinking about possible research areas, I knew I didn't want to continue researching heavy metal fans. Fascinating as they were, I felt I had learned enough about them, and I didn't want to become known as "that heavy metal guy." What, then? Reflecting on my own youth, what stood out most was all the reckless things I did. (A quick, G-rated example: One college summer I hitchhiked 8,000 miles, from my Michigan home to Washington state, down to L.A.

and then all the way back.) I decided to study risk behavior in adolescence. Lene and I were planning to travel to Denmark that summer, and together we devised an ambitious plan to survey adolescents in nine schools in various regions, which also gave her a chance to show me around her home country. We eventually published the results in *Child Development* (Arnett & Balle-Jensen, 1993), and I'd call that my first notable empirical paper. During the same time, dissatisfied with the existing theoretical models of risk behavior, I decided to devise my own, and it was published in *Developmental Review* (Arnett, 1992a, 1992b), my first notable theoretical paper.

Emerging Adulthood and My Own Emergence

My postdoc idyll had to end eventually, and in 1992 I took a position at the University of Missouri in the Department of Human Development and Family Studies. Lene had finished 3 years of her doctoral program, including all her course work, so she was able to join me and continue her dissertation research there, on the cultural basis of moral development. I was once again uncertain about which research direction to pursue. I found the risk behavior area interesting, but it also seemed to me like it was already staked out, already thoroughly plowed over, again and again, with hundreds of researchers building on a corpus of decades of research, making it difficult for anyone new to be heard. I wanted to find uncharted territory, something no one had done before, something fresh that would inspire me to create something valuable and enduring.

Thinking again of my own development, I reflected on how I finally felt I had reached adulthood, at age 35. I had at last finished my long education, I had what seemed like my first "real job," I was engaged to be married, and Lene and I had bought a house. How, I wondered, do other people experience the transition to adulthood? How do they define adulthood, and how do they know when they've reached it?

I began interviewing people in their twenties, to find out. I didn't want to focus on college students, easy as that would have been at a big university, because few are above age 23 and even among 18–22 year-olds they represent only about half. Instead, I obtained alumni lists from local high schools and had research assistants look up addresses and phone numbers in the phone book (this was in 1992, before the Internet). Eventually we put together a sample of 18–29-year-olds that was diverse in educational levels and work statuses. Then and ever since, I have learned the most from the people who were of lower socioeconomic status (SES) because their experiences were so different from my own. I still remember a lot of those interviews vividly 20 years later, such as the one with the truck driver who had grisly tattoos all over his body and dreamed of owning a tattoo parlor.

In response to the question about what it means to be an adult, the answers fascinated and surprised me. I was expecting people to point mainly to transition events such finishing education, settling into a job, and getting married, not only because these were important in my own life but because these events had been the focus of a large literature on the transition to adulthood, mainly in sociology. Yet in interviews, people almost never mentioned them! Instead, the word "responsibility" came up over and over again, and nearly always in the context of responsibility for one's self rather than for others. Making independent decisions was next most frequent, and it was closely related to responsibility for one's self, in that both reflected individualistic values and signified the goal of becoming self-sufficient. Financial independence was third, and here again was the individualistic emphasis. Although unexpected at the time, those three criteria—accepting responsibility for one's self, making independent decisions, and achieving financial independence—have been remarkably consistent as the Big Three criteria for adulthood, for 20 years now in studies across SES groups, age groups, regions, and ethnic groups in the United States, and in countries all around the world (e.g., Arnett, 2003; Macek, Bejček, & Vaníčková, 2007; Mayseless & Scharf, 2003; Nelson, Badger, & Wu, 2004). Just as with my earlier finding about the cathartic effect of heavy metal music, it was exciting to discover something new and unexpected, and to be the first to describe what had previously been uncharted territory.

Another surprising finding of the interviews was the ambiguity in how they described their own progress to adulthood. Most people didn't give a simple "yes" or "no" answer when I asked them if they felt they had reached adulthood. Instead, their answers were usually multi-faceted; they felt like adults in some ways but not others. It was this answer that inspired the term *emerging adulthood,* to describe their sense of being no longer adolescent but not yet adult, on the way to adulthood but not there yet.

However, I was not yet ready to propose the idea that there was a new life stage of emerging adulthood in between adolescence and young adulthood. Instead, I was enjoying the interviews and focusing on learning more. Although my initial interest was in how people think about the meaning of adulthood, my interview covered pretty much everything, from family relationships to religious beliefs to hopes for the future. In 3 years I interviewed about 150 18–29 year-olds in Missouri. Then I had a fellowship year in San Francisco where I focused on African Americans and Asian Americans (as my Missouri sample had been almost entirely White). Like the rural low-SES Whites in Missouri, the African Americans and Asian Americans in San Francisco taught me much that was invaluable and indelible. I still remember many of the people I interviewed there, even where we met, what they wore, and their distinctive ways of expressing themselves.

Two other things happened during our time in San Francisco that made it a pivotal year. One was that I became involved as an expert witness in litigation against the major tobacco companies. How this happened, and what it was like, is a long story, perhaps worthy some day of an essay in itself, but there is not room enough to recount it here. For now let me simply say that it was unlike anything I've ever done, in both its rewards and its challenges. If you think academia can be cut-throat, try the legal world some time. It's set up to be adversarial, with one side clearly winning and the other clearly losing, and when billions of dollars are at stake, as in many tobacco cases, both sides go all out to win and have no compunction about chewing up and spitting out a few expert witnesses along the way. But I've loved it, partly because it appeals to the pugnacious side of my personality, and partly because of the exhilaration of fighting for a good cause against the Evil Empire of Big Tobacco, and often winning. Since the multi-state settlement in 1998, which imposed marketing restrictions and required the tobacco companies to pay $248 billion toward smoking prevention and treatment programs—the largest legal settlement in history—smoking among American high-school seniors has gone down nearly every year and is now barely half the rate it was then. I hasten to add, I have been only a bit player in the drama—the real heroes are the plaintiffs' attorneys, who took immense financial risks in what seemed at the time like a lost cause—but even so it has been a wonderful experience to be part of it, and I regard it as one of the most satisfying parts of my career.

The other big event of that year was that I wrote what became my first *American Psychologist* paper (Arnett, 1999). Since I became interested in adolescent research I had been struck by the oddness of the debate in the field over the concept of "storm and stress." On the one hand were the views of G. Stanley Hall, who originally applied the term "storm and stress" to the emotional and behavioral upheavals of the adolescent years, and Hall's successors today who were alleged to share Hall's alleged negative views of youth. On the other hand were today's adolescent psychologists, who had supposedly dispelled this negative stereotype and whose research had revealed the happy news that adolescents were doing just fine—no storm, no stress. It seemed to me that both sides were off the mark, and that the truth was both more complicated and more interesting.

After reading widely (including Hall's brilliant two volumes of *Adolescence*) and working on the paper for months, I submitted it to *American Psychologist*. Fortunately for me, it fell into the hands of a superb editor, Ann Masten. I'll always be grateful to Ann, and to the three anonymous reviewers, who recognized an amateur when they saw one but also perceived that there was the germ of a good idea in the paper that could potentially become a gem. To me this was the gold standard for the academic peer-review process: an attentive, insightful editor, and exacting but knowledgeable and fair reviewers, who, together, require and inspire the author to strive for excellence. When it works this way, it's an amazing and wonderful process.

Flapping Like Crazy: Becoming an Independent Scholar

Despite the fun of the year Lene and I had in San Francisco—or maybe because of it—as we returned to Missouri I felt deflated and dissatisfied. I had been granted tenure just before we left for San Francisco, and for most academics tenure is a major career milestone, a seal of accomplishment and a great relief for the security and stability it provides. However, it made me depressed and anxious. I was certainly happier to be awarded tenure than I would have been to fail to get it, but I didn't really feel like I had accomplished anything notable. Everything I had published seemed to disappear quickly in the vast ocean of the psychological literature after creating barely a ripple. Similarly, we liked our Missouri college town well enough, and we had a lovely home in a lovely neighborhood, but the town seemed smaller with each year, especially after our year in San Francisco.

Lene had now finished her dissertation, and during our San Francisco year she had completed a postdoc at the University of California-Berkeley, so she was ready to try the academic job market. She received an offer from the Catholic University of America in Washington, DC, and we had a decision to make. They had nothing for me, and there were no openings at other universities in the area. After a little but not much deliberation, we decided to go. I would leave my tenured Associate Professor position and leap into an unknown future.

This was another unusual decision, certainly, leaving a tenured position at a major university with no prospects in sight. However, like the earlier decision to leave Oglethorpe, it was not as difficult a decision as it may seem. First, Lene and I have always valued having an equal marriage, and after I had followed her to Chicago, and she had followed me to Missouri, it was my turn to follow again. Second, I wasn't giving up something I really valued. The security of a tenured position made me feel stultified, not secure. I was attracted to the prospect of having unbroken days for writing and research, without the obligation of teaching and the wasted time in committee work, and I thought the risks of my leap into the unknown might inspire higher accomplishments. "The prospect of being hanged in a fortnight concentrates the mind wonderfully," opined the venerable Dr. Johnson a few hundred years ago. I thought that might be true for me, in a less dire, more academic way. Maybe if I leapt into the abyss, I'd learn how to fly. At the very least, I'd be flapping like crazy.

I had been invited to write a textbook on adolescent development, and I accepted the offer. I still didn't have any real training in adolescence—my exposure to adolescent research at the U. of C. was unconventional, to say the least—and I figured that by writing a textbook I'd at last gain a thorough grounding in the field. Now that I had left Missouri, I'd be able to handle the immense time demands of writing a first-edition textbook. I also imagined that, if it sold well, I'd make enough income from the textbook that I wouldn't have to hurry to find another academic position. I could live as an independent scholar as long as I liked.

In 1998, during our first year in the DC area, I received word that my storm and stress paper had been accepted in *American Psychologist.* This was immensely inspiring to me. It made me feel I had at last broken into the top echelon in academia, and that psychology might be receptive to the kind of conceptual, big-idea papers I wanted to write. On the strength of this inspiration, I immediately began working on another paper intended for *American Psychologist,* this one a theoretical paper introducing emerging adulthood.

I had already been thinking of the age 18–25 period as emerging adulthood for years by this time, ever since I began my interviews in the early 1990s. I realized quickly that it didn't make sense to call them "late adolescents," as they were not going through puberty, not in secondary school, not minors under the law, and (mostly) not living at home. Nor did I find "young adults" appropriate, because this term had connotations of a more settled life stage lasting at least until age 40. I also rejected other terms that had been used occasionally such as "youth" (too vague) or "postadolescents" (defining them by what they were not). I had to call them *something,* at least in my head, and "emerging adults" seemed to fit as a new term for a new life stage that I viewed as developing only within the past half century.

I actually used the term *emerging adulthood* for the first time in an article published in 1994 in the *Journal of Youth and Adolescence,* at the end of a review paper on the transition to adulthood (Arnett & Taber, 1994). I used it again in 1998, at the end of a paper in *Human Development* on conceptions of adulthood (Arnett, 1998). However, both times I used it tentatively, as an afterthought at the end of a long paper, and no one seemed to notice. Now I was ready to shine a bright light on it and present it not just as a new term but as a theory of a new life stage, and I knew *American Psychologist* would be the place where it would have the best chance of gaining attention.

I wrote it quickly, having prepared the groundwork for years, and it zipped through the review process in short order and was published in 2000 (Arnett, 2000). I was happy to have it published, but I certainly didn't think that I had just published the paper that would change my life—as it did. I had grown accustomed to publishing papers that I thought were brilliant but that few other people seemed to notice. But this time it was different. It took several years, but gradually the paper gained momentum and came to be regarded as the spark that ignited the new field of emerging adulthood, even though it was really only a sketch of a theory and required a book (Arnett, 2004) to be developed fully. I think the timing was right, in that there were numerous other scholars who were fascinated by development during this age period but didn't have any term for it or any way of conceptualizing it. I proposed the idea that this

was a new life stage, and gave it a name that was new and distinctive, and soon many scholars who had an intuitive sense of this similar to mine embraced the idea. As I write this, in May 2013, that *American Psychologist* paper has been cited over 3,500 times, according to GoogleScholar, not just in psychology but in a wide range of fields.

Although not many people noticed the paper in the first months after it was published, one person who did became a crucial figure in the development of the field of emerging adulthood. Jennifer Tanner was a postdoctoral student at Penn State at the time. She was interested in relationships with parents during the transition to adulthood, and looking for a theory that would fit what she was seeing among the young people she was studying. She seized on the *American Psychologist* paper as the framework she was looking for, and contacted me with great excitement and eagerness to put it into action.

So began a remarkably fruitful collaboration that continues to this day. Although I proposed the initial idea, it is Jenn who is primarily responsible for developing emerging adulthood into an organized field of scholarship. It was Jenn who discovered the grant program through the *American Psychological Association* that provided the funding for the first conference on emerging adulthood, in 2003. It is Jenn who has been the driving force behind every biennial conference since then (the sixth conference was held in 2013). It is Jenn who is the main organizational force behind the newly established *Society for the Study of Emerging Adulthood* (SSEA; see www.ssea.org). I do not have the talents or the patience required for the kind of work involved in building an organization from the ground up, but Jenn does. We have very different personalities, but that is precisely what makes our partnership work. We develop ideas together, and Jenn is the one who translates the ideas into action.

In DC, I thrived on the independent scholar life. I didn't miss a thing about having an academic position. I had always preferred to do my writing and research mainly on my own, so I didn't miss having graduate students, and in any case Lene and I continued to be each other's main counsels in all our work. Now I had Jenn (and soon many others) as my collaborator in developing the emerging adulthood field. I sure didn't miss the politics and the committee work that are unavoidable in academic departments.

Being an independent scholar allowed me to take on a lot of new challenges and opportunities as they came my way. I became Editor of the *Journal of Adolescent Research* in 2002. I edited four encyclopedia volumes, two for the *International Encyclopedia of Adolescence* (Routledge) and two for the *Encyclopedia of Children, Adolescents, and the Media* (Sage), all four of which came out in 2007. I wrote another *American Psychologist* paper (Arnett, 2002) on an entirely new topic, the psychology of globalization. I worked on the second edition of my textbook *Adolescence and Emerging Adulthood: A Cultural Approach,* after the first edition came out in

2001 (Arnett, 2001). I continued to work as an expert witness in litigation against the tobacco companies.

In combination, this made for a full schedule, but it was also a flexible schedule, and this was especially valuable once our twins Miles and Paris were born in 1999. We had a nanny for 35 hours a week the first 2 years, and a wonderful child care program about 30 hours a week after that, but, as any parent knows, many an unexpected event can be expected in children's early years—from ear infections to snow days—and there has to be someone there to step in and take care of the kids. Lene and I were equal partners in parenting all the way, but I had the more flexible schedule because she was the one with the academic position.

I remain an independent scholar today. Lene and I moved to Clark University in 2006, after a fellowship year in Denmark, but I do not have a normal academic position there. My title is Research Professor, which means I teach one course per semester (at that level I really enjoy teaching) and have no committee responsibilities. I occasionally guide undergraduate and graduate students in research, but mostly I work on my own at home. I am happiest, and I think and write best, when I am working in my home office every day, with Lene as my mutual confidant, sounding board, and lunch partner.

My Uneasy Place in Psychology

If you were to look at the course of my career, say by scanning my CV, you might conclude that this has been the career of someone who has a comfortable place in academic psychology. Almost every article I've published has appeared in psychology journals. I am the editor of a journal that is classified as part of the psychology area. My book on emerging adulthood was published in the psychology section of Oxford University Press. My textbook on adolescence and emerging adulthood is used mainly in psychology courses. When I testify as an expert witness I draw mainly upon research and concepts from psychology.

Yet the truth is that I have never felt entirely at home in the field of psychology, and I have frequently experienced frustration with the dominant pattern of how scholarship is conducted in the field. For nearly my entire career, since my U. of C. days, I have felt like an unbeliever among believers, surrounded by people who share a view of how human development research should be done that I vehemently reject. I have touched on these issues earlier in this chapter, but let me now address three of them directly: the cultural narrowness of psychology, the sterility of the dominant methods, and the ill-conceived ideal for research programs.

Ever since the epiphany of my U. of C. days, when I read anthropological works on adolescence for the first time, I have considered myself a cultural psychologist. This means that I always see the psychology of human development in a cultural context. There are some biologically based universals in development, yes, but the differences among cultural groups are vast, and where people happen to have been born makes an enormous and decisive difference to the course of their development. To me the huge, enticing, inexhaustible question at the heart of psychological research is the question of how cultural beliefs and practices shape the raw material of biological development into an amazing array of patterns.

Yet this question is, at best, only in the margins of the field of psychology. Cultural psychology has risen in influence over the past 20 years, and is now widely recognized by other psychologists, but the mainstream of the field continues to flow on as if cultural psychology—and culture itself—did not even exist. In 2008 I published an *American Psychologist* article entitled "The Neglected 95%: Why American Psychology Needs to Become Less American" (Arnett, 2008). As part of that article, I performed an analysis of the nationality of authors, samples, and editorial board members in a wide range of major journals in psychology. The results were depressing, though unsurprising: the leadership and content of all the journals was entirely dominated by Americans, with little attention to cultural variation even within American society.

It's not that I have anything against Americans—I am, after all, an American myself—but it seems bizarre to me that a field that claims to be devoted to understanding the psychology of humanity should be satisfied with a focus on less than 5% of the human population. The basis for this narrowness, as I pointed out in the article, is mainly the dominant philosophy of science in psychology, which emphasizes the search for human universals rather than exploring the psychological basis of human cultural diversity. Now, with the surge of interest in neuroscience, the focus of psychology is likely to become even more focused on (alleged) universals and even more content to focus mainly on middle-class Americans. Along with a small cluster of culturally oriented colleagues, I spend a lot of my time and energy protesting this narrowness and advocating a more cultural and international approach to psychological research, but it often feels like howling at the moon. The moon is unperturbed.

The second aspect of my critique of psychology has to do with the dominant methods, specifically, questionnaires. My first experience with interviewing, in my study of metalheads, converted me permanently to a belief in the value of qualitative methods. I have used questionnaires as well, and I think the combination of questionnaires and interviews is especially fruitful. However, it is the interviews that have really taught me about human development. Questionnaires are rife with all sorts of assumptions about how people will respond to questions, and they presort people into categories determined by the creator of the questionnaire. I understand the necessity of this, especially in large-scale studies, but to me this approach is incomplete at best. Questionnaires provide the skeleton, but they need the flesh of interviews to come alive.

Yet in psychology, especially in adolescent psychology, large-scale questionnaire studies (with no qualitative component) are by far the dominant method. In the flagship journal of the Society for Research on Adolescence, the *Journal of Research on Adolescence,* qualitative studies are scarce. The overwhelming majority of articles published in the journal consists entirely of questionnaire data, as if questionnaires were some kind of gold standard of scientific merit. In the course of writing this chapter I examined the most recent issue of *JRA* (Vol. 21, No. 4, 2011) and recorded the methods used in each study: one was an experiment, two involved interviews, one used interviews and video-taped observations, and 12 were based on questionnaires. Articles on adolescents and emerging adults in other "top" journals such as *Child Development* and *Developmental Psychology* are also mainly questionnaire-based (although for infants and young children studies more often include experiments or observations). Increasingly, various questionnaires are stuffed into elaborate statistical models, the results depicted in figures with arrows extending from one questionnaire construct to another, supposedly unveiling the complex relationships among them.

Virtually no one seems to ask if the questionnaires are valid, if they are actually measuring what they purport to measure (internal reliability seems to be enough to satisfy editors and reviewers). Few people seem to notice that by the time the questionnaires chop people up into assumption-laden variables and grind up the variables in a statistical model there is no life left to them—only fragments and limbs but no human beings.

My third critique of psychology concerns the dominant model for research programs. The ideal in the field seems to be to run a large research enterprise. Graduate students are encouraged to begin grant writing early, and early career researchers are told that obtaining external funding is one of the expectations of most entry-level academic positions. Sometimes success in obtaining a large grant is even required for promotion to Associate or Full Professor.

But this emphasis locks psychological research into a scientific model that is highly questionable. In this model, the main function of the researcher is to obtain money, in the form of a large grant. The researcher, as "Principal Investigator," designs the study and writes the grant, often in collaboration with colleagues. If the grant is obtained, the researchers enlists graduate and undergraduate students to do the actual data collection, which usually consists mostly of having people fill out questionnaires. The only way the researcher ever has any contact with the participants in the study is in the form of numbers, as variables in summary statistics or statistical models. Then the researcher writes articles for scientific journals, drawing conclusions from the numbers—without ever having spoken to a single person who is the subject of the conclusions.

This strikes me as a misguided way to learn about human development. It is a model of scientific research drawn from other sciences, and maybe it works in biology or physics but it seems inadequate for studying human beings. The biologist can't know what it is like to be a fruit fly, and the physicist has no experience of being a quark, but all of us know what is like to be human. The most important asset, the most important research instrument, of scientists studying human development is their own essential humanity, their own insights and understandings wrought over a lifetime of their development. In interviews and in ethnographic research this humanity can be brought to bear, so that it illuminates and produces fresh insights and understandings. Without this, with only dead data from second-hand questionnaires, the results are sophisticated, complex, esoteric—and inert.

It is not questionnaires or statistics that I object to, per se, but the hegemonic dominance of quantitative methods, with anything qualitative—anything that involves listening to people and seeking to understand them as one person to another—shunted to the margins as "unscientific." I don't object to potato chips, either, but I wouldn't want to eat nothing but potato chips for breakfast, lunch, and dinner. In adolescent psychology it is pretty much all potato chips, all the time, and that is not good for the health of the field.

Final Reflections: The Heretic Finds a Home

Although I have had an unorthodox career in psychology, and my awareness of the difference between how I see things and how most research psychologists see things has often made me uneasy, I have no regrets about devoting my work life to the study of human development. At its best, as exemplified in the mixed-methods work of psychologists like Philip Hammack, Lene Jensen, Reed Larson, and Niobe Way, sociologists like Mark Regnerus and Christian Smith, and anthropologists like Susan and Douglas Davis, human development research can be illuminating and mind-expanding. It is their standard that I have sought to emulate, and it is the companionship of them and others that has kept me from feeling lonely as I have traveled my unconventional path.

I am critical of the dominant approach to scholarship in psychology, but other than my critique in "The Neglected 95%," I have sought to devote most of my energies to constructing rather than deconstructing, to building up rather than tearing down. In 10 years of serving as Editor of the *Journal of Adolescent Research,* I have given it a distinct identity as a journal where qualitative and mixed-methods research on adolescence and emerging adulthood is not only welcomed but highlighted (Arnett, 2005). In creating with Jenn Tanner the *Society for the Study of Emerging Adulthood,* I have sought to make it international and open to scholars from diverse disciplines with wide-ranging methodological approaches. My textbooks, the one on adolescence and emerging adulthood, as well as a recently published life span text (Arnett, 2012), have been written with a cultural approach, in the hope of encouraging new generations to think culturally about development from the very beginning of their careers.

The idea of emerging adulthood is my main claim to fame, and it has been amazing to see it grow in the past decade to become the basis of a new field in psychology. I receive email messages nearly every day from scholars all over the world who ask for information and want to be part of the new field. The idea has also reached a broader audience. When the *New York Times Sunday Magazine* published a cover story on emerging adulthood in August, 2010, suddenly the idea reached a general audience of millions. In the barrage of emails that followed (and continues to this day), and in many comments that I have received in speaking before various groups, I have had many people tell me that this concept helped them make sense of their lives or their children's lives. This response has reinforced my belief in the value and power of ideas. The reason I have tried to revive the reputation of life stages, which had become unfashionable in developmental psychology when I proposed emerging adulthood, is that I have seen over and over again how valuable they can be in helping people understand development, scientists and nonscientists alike (Arnett, Kloep, Hendry, & Tanner, 2011).

I suppose I will always be known as "that emerging adulthood guy," and it is a title I happily embrace. However, I do not believe that emerging adulthood is my last idea. Lately, I have been interviewing parents of emerging adults, mostly people who are in their late forties to early sixties, and it has provoked for me a lot of new thinking about their life stage (which also happens to be the stage that I, too, am now in). I think we are in need of a whole new model of life stages, one that is historically and culturally flexible. Stages gained a bad name in psychology because they were presented in the 20th century as universal (people everywhere experience the same stages) and uniform (people everywhere should experience them in essentially the same way). But if they are recognized as being historically and culturally variable, as helpful heuristics rather than natural facts, they can be extremely valuable for advancing our understanding of human development. That sounds to me like an idea worthy of some development of its own.

Despite my ambivalence toward psychology, I greatly enjoy being an academic psychologist. I love doing interviews, I love to write, and I love grappling with ideas and trying to create new ones. On the wall of my home office is a series of photographs of a monarch butterfly striving its way out of a chrysalis. That's the kind of challenge I feel every day, and there is joy and deep absorption in the strenuousness of it. Sometimes the result of my day's work looks like something quite other than an exquisite butterfly. Nevertheless, devoting myself to it is an honor and a privilege, and I hope to enjoy it for many years to come. The renowned EA troubadour John Mayer wrote these words in his twenties, but I'm hoping they could apply to the life stage I'm now in as well:

I'd like to think the best of me

Is still hiding up my sleeve.

References

Arnett, J. (1992a). Reckless behavior in adolescence: A developmental perspective. *Developmental Review, 12,* 339–373.

Arnett, J. (1992b). Socialization and reckless behavior: A reply to Jessor. *Developmental Review, 12,* 391–409.

Arnett, J. J. (1998). Learning to stand alone: The contemporary American transition to adulthood in cultural and historical context. *Human Development, 41,* 295–315.

Arnett, J. J. (1999). Adolescent storm and stress, reconsidered. *American Psychologist, 54,* 317–326.

Arnett, J. J. (2000). Emerging adulthood: A theory of development from the late teens through the twenties. *American Psychologist, 55,* 469–480.

Arnett, J. J. (2001). *Adolescence and emerging adulthood: A cultural approach* (1st ed.). Upper Saddle River, NJ: Prentice-Hall.

Arnett, J. J. (2002). The psychology of globalization. *American Psychologist, 57,* 774–783.

Arnett, J. J. (2003). Conceptions of the transition to adulthood among emerging adults in American ethnic groups. *New Directions in Child and Adolescent Development, 100,* 63–75.

Arnett, J. J. (2004). *Emerging adulthood: The winding road from the late teens through the twenties.* New York: Oxford University Press.

Arnett, J. J. (2005). The Vitality Criterion: A new standard of publication for *Journal of Adolescent Research. Journal of Adolescent Research, 20,* 3–7.

Arnett, J. J. (2008). The neglected 95%: Why American psychology needs to become less American. *American Psychologist, 63*(7), 602–614.

Arnett, J. J. (2012). *Human development: A cultural approach.* New York: Pearson.

Arnett, J., & Balle-Jensen, L. (1993). Cultural bases of risk behavior: Danish adolescents. *Child Development, 64,* 1842–1855.

Arnett, J. J., Kloep, M., Hendry, L. A., & Tanner, J. L. (2011). *Debating emerging adulthood: Stage or process?* New York: Oxford University Press.

Arnett, J. J., & Taber, S. (1994). Adolescence terminable and interminable: When does adolescence end? *Journal of Youth & Adolescence, 23,* 517–537.

Macek, P., Bejček, J., & Vaníčková, J. (2007). Contemporary Czech emerging adults: Generation growing up in the period of social changes. *Journal of Adolescent Research, 22,* 444–475.

Mayseless, O., & Scharf, M. (2003). What does it mean to be an adult? The Israeli experience. In J. J. Arnett & N. Galambos (Eds.), *New directions in child and adolescent development,* Vol. 100 (pp. 5–20). San Francisco: Jossey-Bass.

Nelson, L. J., Badger, S., & Wu, B. (2004). The influence of culture in emerging adulthood: Perspectives of Chinese college students. *International Journal of Behavioral Development, 28*(1), 26–36.

3

Robert Wm. Blum

An Autobiography

ROBERT WM. BLUM

The Early Years

The first recollection I have is the scent of a certain bathroom cleaner that was used years ago for tile. Over the subsequent years I have walked into post-War apartments (buildings built after WWI that is) and have smelled that same smell; and each time it brings back the same image of being an infant in a bathtub with my mom bathing me.

We moved into that apartment on East 86th St. in Manhattan before I was born, which was on an exceptionally snowy February evening in 1948. Of that I have no memory other than my parents recounting the story again and again. We stayed there until I was about two and then moved to 85th St. between Park and Lexington Avenues. For those whose image of the Upper East Side is of upscale boutiques, shops, and brownstones, the area where I grew up was quite different. It was mostly an immigrant community made up of Germans and Irish who had come to New York over the preceding century. My images are of dust and darkness, especially as we turned east for the EL (elevator trains) that ran on Third and Second Avenues and that obliterated the sun. We lived on 85th St. until I was twelve. Some of my images and recollections…

Mr. Reddy, the tailor, worked down the street; and once, I was playing in my dress pants, despite my mother's admonishments, and tore the knee. I secretly went to Mr. Reddy who sewed them up, charging me 25 cents (a significant sum for a 7-year-old). Horn and Hardart, a new type of restaurant in the 1950s, was on 86th and it was a big treat to go there for dinner. My sister, mother, and I would go. Nancy and I were each given a stack of nickels

(maybe 8 or 10) and we were able to retrieve the dinner from an endless source of gleaming white and glass vending machines which lined the walls and held foods of all types. The food was behind glass doors which slid open when I put a nickel in the slot. It was very exciting. The restaurant was the precursor to the vending machine. What an amazing treat for a kid: a whole restaurant that was a vending machine! There were other places on 86th St. but we weren't allowed to go—The Papaya King (which is still there) was off bounds because my mother alleged that it was dirty. The same was true for the 15-cents-by-the-slice pizza place which today sells the same slice for $3.75. The price of pizza was suspiciously linked, so it seemed, to the price of a trip on the subway. When I was eight I had saved up my allowance and one Saturday bought a slice and washed it down with a 10-cent drink from the Papaya King across the street. Heaven!

There were other memories as well of my early years: Saturday matinees at the RKO movie theater; music filtering through our open windows at home on warm spring days from the music school across the street, being infatuated with Davey Crocket and wearing a coon-skin hat to sleep; Sunday dinners with my family at Patsy's, Luchows, and a Chinese restaurant with a name that has faded from the recesses of my brain. Sunday Chinese food seemed to be a ritual much like going to synagogue on the High Holy days.

I started school at the age of four—less, I am sure, because I was a genius and more because my mother was ready to get me out of the house. As a consequence, I was always a year younger than my peers and very self-conscious about it. Mercifully I matured early. I went to PS6. In New York all public schools then started with PS. It was the neighborhood public school in the heart of the Upper East Side, which, even then, was the school of choice for those who did not want to send their children to private school. The school had an extraordinary number of luminaries who went there as children: Richard Avadon, Chevy Chase, J.D. Salinger and Lenny Kravitz to name a few…I didn't know any of them. When I was in the second grade we all walked in single file down Madison Ave. to the "new PS6" where, nearly 60 years later, it remains on 82nd St. and Madison Avenue. I stayed at PS6 for the rest of the year then left.

The Blum Family

My parents were very different from each other in temperament and background; what they had in common was that they were both first-generation American Jews, my mother's parents having come over from Austria and Poland and my father's from Russia. They also had a passionate commitment to education, to each other, and to our family. My father was the youngest of about five children—the exact number was never very clear to us as children. His parents died in the Great Flu Epidemic; and by the age of six he was orphaned. His aunt and uncle took him in and raised him as if he were their own. His older siblings were sent to orphanages … except for his 17- or 18-year-old sister. She moved in with her boyfriend; and the story is told that neither his aunt nor uncle ever mentioned her name again. How much contact my father had with his older siblings is very unclear as we rarely ever saw them and he almost never spoke of them.

Aunt Ray and Uncle Morris, who raised my father, were strict. Together with other relatives they had a small grocers business. Aunt Ray could read and write, Uncle Morris was totally illiterate and in fact, never learned to use the telephone. But they both had high expectations for little Morris, my Dad, and insisted he study. When the Depression came it had little financial impact on my father and his family, since they were not participants in the economic upswing of the Roaring Twenties. Moe, as my dad was known, went to Long Island University, then the University of Buffalo, following his two best friends into dentistry. He was the first member of his family to go to college, much less, professional school; and, as far as I know, none of his brothers or sisters chose that path. My dad spent most of the pre-war years studying—and delivering fruit and vegetables for his aunt and uncle when he was home.

My mother's story was substantially different. She was a child of advantage and a product of a liberal German Jewish tradition of many in her family income and social sphere. Her father, together with his brothers, owned a bank and she grew up on Riverside Drive in Manhattan, far away from the lower East Side and Queens neighborhoods of my father's childhood. The Barasch family had five children, one of whom died at a young age. My grandfather sold his bank before the crash, yet despite that good fortune they lost most of their money anyway in the years that followed. Gladys, a name you never hear today but that was popular in my mother's youth, went to Teachers College (today part of Columbia). She became an elementary school

teacher and before the War spent her summers traveling Europe and the Orient.

My parents were introduced to each other by an Army buddy who was dating my mother's sister. They married in the middle of the War before my father was sent to North Africa in the medical corps. My sister Nancy was born 2 years later in 1945. They rented the apartment on 86th St. and my father opened a dental office on Myrtle Ave. in Queens near where he grew up.

From the time they were married, it seemed that our family life centered around the Barasch family and my father's family was a distant thought and a less frequent presence in our lives.

Some of my childhood family memories:

- Spending numerous weekends and summers with my aunts, uncles, and cousins on my mother's side. We were exceptionally close—a closeness that continues to this day and extends to the next generation.
- Driving trips to Hershey, Washington, and Williamsburg with my parents and sister. When I was six or seven we were driving through Maryland and stopped at a diner for lunch. The sign on the front door said "Whites Only." I was stunned; I asked my parents what it meant; they explained as we moved on in search of another place to eat.
- Spending summers in Westport, Connecticut and Compo Beach, learning to ride a two wheeler, fishing off the peer and on Sundays having father/son (and subsequently daughter) soft-ball games. If it sounds like a sheltered and idyllic childhood—it was. It was there at the age of four I met David—my closest friend for the past 60 years.
- Sitting by an old mill in Silvermine, CT, watching my mother paint. My mother became an accomplished painter and subsequently a sculptor; and one of the lasting legacies is a house full of her art that surrounds my life.
- Leaving Westport on Labor Day to return to the city… and school.

The Riverdale Years

My transition to 3rd grade on to Riverdale Country School was memorable. I remember on the first day of school thinking to myself that the boy sitting next to me was the smartest kid I had ever seen. The next decade proved my initial assessment correct. Riverdale was in the Bronx about a 30-minute bus ride in each direction. It was a bucolic setting with fields and trees and a set of old school buildings that dated to the turn of the century when the school was founded. Some of the teachers were equally old. I remained there through my senior year. There are so many images and coming-of-age stories all linked with people and places. The school was an all boys' school. There was a girls' school a few miles and another world away. We had to wear ties and jackets from the 4th grade until we graduated and went to college. All my friends went to college.

Academics were always there, but not a major part of my life. That isn't to say I didn't study hard—I did. Academics did not come easily to me as it did to some of my classmates; and my mother's mantra still rings in my ears today: "I don't care what others are doing or that it is sunny, you will study until you know it." And I did…

But socializing was top priority. Growing up in New York City in the 1950s and 60s allowed for a degree of freedom not available to city kids today. By the age of 10 or 11 my friends and I would meet in "The Park" (aka Central Park) for touch football. Against the curbs of city streets we played "stepball," and occasionally despite my protests my mother would drag us to the Metropolitan Museum of Art for a dose of culture. Likewise, throughout the years my mother, sister, and I would go to Carnegie Hall to hear Leonard Bernstein conduct the New York Philharmonic, the Children's Concert Series. We moved through the City with surprising freedom as our neighborhoods were well defined and never felt the fear of urban violence despite the occasional time we would be robbed by bigger kids, sometimes with knives, sometimes just with their imposing size. It was simply a part of the cost of moving through the City.

When I was in the 5th grade I befriended a classmate, Jeff, whose mother was a "house manager" of one of the Broadway theaters. House managers ran the theater and they knew all the other house managers on Broadway. Jeff and I started going to plays together—sitting on the steps, standing in the back or if chairs were available sitting there. Between 1955 and 1963 I saw many major and at least as many minor plays on Broadway. And Jeff recognized everyone on the street. "Sir Lawrence," I recall him shouting once as we approached a total stranger, "I saw you the other night in 'Hamlet,' you were brilliant." I was left trying to figure out who Lawrence was.

Seventh grade began the social circuit with girls; and dance parties at people's houses became the norm. To this day every song of *The Four Seasons* recalls one of those parties…and girls. By the 8th grade I was "going steady" and by the 9th grade dancing had given way to making out. We would go to synagogue dances and, sometimes, each of the private schools would have a dance and invite the kids from the other private schools for a mixer. By the 10th grade I was taking girlfriends to bars in the Village to listen to jazz or singers like Marianne Faithfull and to drink. In the 1960s, as best as I can recall, New York City did not have a minimum drinking age, rather it seemed like there was a height requirement; and if you were tall enough to see over the bar you could order liquor. As I said before, I was an early maturer.

I also smoked in those years. I began smoking one cigarette a week I took from my parents when I was 10 or 11, smoking on the way to Sunday school. By the 10th grade I was smoking more but I was also involved with

sports—wrestling, football, and track (javelin); and while I did all those sports I was not very good at any. I hated the pain associated with football and the weight limits of wrestling. My other best friend, Johnny, was a really good athlete, and I would stay over at his place in Riverdale before Saturday meets. Repeatedly, his mother would prepare a delicious coconut cake for desert only to taunt me and then save me a slice for after the meet the next day. My javelin career ended one day in 10th grade when a new kid in school, Calvin, walked over picked up the javelin that he had never seen before, and threw it twice as far as my best toss. Calvin Hill went on to be a legendary running back for the Dallas Cowboys. By the 11th grade I had retired from organized sports.

Except for short road trips, my family did not travel during the school year, but starting in the 7th grade my father decided to take the first vacation of his life. We went to Europe. He was hooked on vacation and I thought that traveling was far more fun than camp or Westport. Throughout junior high and high school I spent most summers in Europe, first with my parents and then with study groups and finally hitchhiking on my own. By the time I graduated high school I had been from Stockholm to Istanbul; had studied in Pau, France, and in Jerusalem, and had spent two summers in Kenmere, Ireland, living with my childhood housekeeper and her family. They had a farm and lived in a house where the floor was packed earth, the kitchen had an open hearth for cooking and baking, and chamber pots were used instead of toilets. For a kid from New York, this was the coolest thing ever. My parents started me on a life of travel that has not stopped even today.

Lawrence Kohlberg once said that adolescents "are prophets of conventional wisdom" and that certainly was true for me. In high school we wore ties, white shirts, white socks and slacks. Politics were not much on my mind—or that of my friends—and social activism was being president of the social events club that organized school dances. Life was all Rock and Roll.

The one political event that did have a profound effect on me occurred on November 22, 1963. Much like September 11 or December 7, anyone alive back then vividly recalls where they were when they heard that President Kennedy had been shot. The whole school gathered in the school cafeteria where from a single black-and-white television, Walter Cronkite announced that the president was dead. I did not realize it at the time, but for many of my generation, it was the day the music died.

The College Years

I recall arriving at Lafayette College to the sound of the Rolling Stones *Can't Get No Satisfaction* blaring from some fraternity across the quad to the freshman dorm to which I had been assigned. Lafayette had not been where I wanted to go. Much like my high school, it was all male and was in remote town in Pennsylvania. My first months there are a bit of a blur, studying during the week and going back to New York on the weekends. One memory I do have was, shortly after arriving, some friends and I went to the State Liquor Store and each bought a pint of liquor. I bought Seagram's 7. During the course of the next few hours I got royally drunk, made it back to my room, passed out, and the next morning I was covered in vomit and blood (having cut my hand). I tried to sit up but the pain in my head was so severe that I crawled to the bathroom. Never since have I gotten so drunk—nor have I touched Seagram's 7.

I knew I wanted to go into medicine from long before I was in college and thought I would major in biology. Ever since I stopped wanting to be a fireman in the 2nd grade, I had wanted to be a doctor. In fact, the day I graduated from medical school, my parents gave me a laminated paper I wrote in the 3rd grade, "When I grow up…." That paper remains in my office.

By Thanksgiving of my freshman year we were informed that our dormitory was to be demolished and by the start of the winter term I had a roommate who had just transferred from Web Institute for Naval Architecture, an unusual college where 25 students are admitted annually, are charged no tuition or board, and half fail out by the end of the first year. Most who leave go to MIT or Cal Tech… but not Bill. Bill came to Lafayette.

He was the most eccentric person I ever knew—and the brightest. Some people brag that they don't study. Bill didn't brag—he just didn't study. And got all "A"s. He had no money. I remember one month his total out of pocket expenses were 42 cents. He came from a blue-collar Catholic family where his father was a union organizer. He was witty and sharp tongued, and for the rest of our lives we have remained connected. When I moved to Washington years later, he was there. When I moved to Minneapolis a few years later he showed up. There was no causal relationship. Pursuit of jobs and women led him to where I was living. A wonderful coincidence.

By the end of my freshman year I still wanted to pursue medicine but not biology; and as a sophomore, I declared my major to be English.

Another change began to occur during my freshman year—I began to become politicized. The Vietnam War was just starting to escalate in 1966; and at Lafayette we were required to take ROTC. Whether it was the military values ROTC espoused or the ROTC requirement I was required to meet, I was determined to end ROTC as a requirement. Together with a small band of friends, we organized a march, not in the magnitude of the marches occurring in New York or Washington but a demonstration anyway—30 or so students; and we were joined by a few faculty. We were water hosed; and when I met with the Dean of Students he said, "If you don't want to be water bombed don't demonstrate." Freedom of speech and freedom of attacks on demonstrators seemed somehow to peacefully coexist among my college's leadership. The administration's attitude made me all the more determined.

In the next year the war escalated and so did our demonstrations and our numbers. We disrupted ROTC and recruited more students and we began demonstrating against the war. By the end of sophomore year we experienced some success; ROTC was eliminated as a requirement; and I was on the Dean's List (not the one of which my parents would have been proud). I was on probation!

For the last 2 years of college I was accepted into the McKelvey Scholars Program with 19 other boys. Billy applied too. It was no surprise he got in; it was more surprising that I did. The program was located in a mansion off campus. We all had dinner and an academic program twice a week; and for the first time in my life I became a serious student. I loved Irish literature, taking a tutorial on James Joyce and writing my honors thesis on the plays of Eugene O'Neill. I remember lying on the couch in the beautiful living room of the house where I was living reading a play by J.M. Synge thinking to myself: "This is my *job*. Life can't get better than this!"

Since I still needed to complete all science courses for medical school and unable to do it all during the school year I went to Harvard for two summers. In the summer of 1968 I took a year of physics in 6 weeks with about 75 other kids and a professor from Stanford named Albert Baez. He was perhaps the finest teacher I had ever had. I recall the first day of class; he said, "It is your job to study and learn physics. It is my job to make it come alive." And he certainly did make it come alive. He was special in other ways as well. One week he announced that class was to be cancelled on Friday because he was going to Newport to hear his daughters perform. He invited the whole class to his home the following Monday for a barbecue.

Then the penny dropped. His daughters were Joan Baez and Mimi Farina. Mimi (together with her late husband Richard) was a well-known folk singer among aficionados; Joan was an icon. I had been going to Newport for years; and the Saturday concert was the central event. That summer night in 1968 Joan Baez and Bob Dylan were the headliners. And the following Monday after the barbecue, Joan and Mimi came downstairs and together with their parents played music for more than 2 hours. It was one of the highlights of my young life.

My senior year was filled with anti-war demonstrations, medical school applications, and interviews. I had known a white kid who was going to Howard Medical School; so I applied. Having lived most of my life in upper-middle-class settings, when I was offered an interview at Howard I jumped at it. After growing up in a bubble I wanted another type of experience where political activism and education intertwined.

I remember the interview as if it were yesterday for Lasall Lefall interviewed me. Dr. Lefall was a giant both in stature and status. Chief of Cardiovascular Surgery, he was amongst the best-known physicians at Howard; and I can still picture his looking down at me asking, "What does a white boy like you want coming to a place like this?" I can't remember exactly what I said but whatever

I said must have worked, because in the fall of 1969 I enrolled at Howard as one of five white boys in a class of 100.

I remember distinctly receiving my letter of acceptance to medical school. As I have previously recounted, by the time I was in college I had been smoking for nearly a decade. By the time I was a senior in college I was smoking 1–2 packs of cigarettes a day. The evening that I opened my admission letter to medical school I threw the pack I was smoking away and have not touched another cigarette since. How could I ever tell someone not to smoke if I were a smoker myself? What is interesting and typically adolescent is that I never viewed myself as a *smoker* in much the same way as a lot of my patients years later who did not use contraception did not consider themselves to be *sexually active.* In my own mind as long as I did not buy a carton of cigarettes I was not a smoker.

Before going on to medical school there was one other event worth mentioning. August 1969 was the Woodstock Music Festival, and my girlfriend Ann really wanted to go. I bought tickets. No one bought tickets to Woodstock; everyone just showed up. And together with the tens of thousands who showed up were the five of us who were ticket holders. While retrospectively one can romanticize the experience (and I certainly have retold the romanticized version repeatedly to my children), the reality was much more mixed. The music was nonstop; and everyone shared what food, blankets, and marijuana they had. It rained nonstop for 2 days and we were soaked and hungry with every concession having run out of food. We left the afternoon on Sunday before Jimi Hendrix sang his legendary version of "The Star Spangled Banner". We walked 5 miles to our car, found a motel, showered, dried off, and ate. In the fall, we parted ways—Ann went to veterinary school and I went to Howard.

Medical School Entry to Washington D.C and medical school was momentous. I had found a cute little place at 6th and C St. SE with a fellow college activist who was going to Georgetown Law. I arrived to the place before my parents showed up with the U-Haul. It was late summer and as I walked over to the park just to kill time until they arrived I saw a guy come running out of a bodega with a rifle chasing another man. I was a little shaken but thought it was a one-off event so I decided not to mention it to my folks. When they arrived we unloaded the car and U-Haul and were all set to leave when a man approached my mother, who was sitting in the passenger side of the car, and he shouted across the top of the car to my father who was standing outside on the other side, "Give me all your money or I'll blow her fuckin' head off." What my father could not see was that the man was holding a gun to my mother's head. My dad, being a little hard of hearing, replied, "What's that you said?" My mom, ever the New Yorker, said, "I have the money and if you let me reach down I'll get my

purse for you." The man agreed, my mom handed him the wallet, he ran off, we loaded up the car and u-hauled it out of there. That is how I came to live a 22nd and Massachusetts NW in Washington a block from the South Vietnamese embassy.

Howard University was a very different place than what I had anticipated. Expecting to find a hot bed of Black political activism, I quickly learned that if one is Black you don't make it into medical school as a radical. Rather, a number of my classmates grew up in the rural South where they had been singled out by their churches years before as having exceptional promise. Their church communities through college and now medical school supported these young men and women. They were their community ambassadors; and they were not about to risk it all for a political cause. They were going to be doctors! And everyone back home was watching.

I was a different story. By the winter of 1970 the war was in full force and demonstrations it seemed were a weekly occurrence in DC. I joined the Medical Commission for Human Rights, worked as a volunteer at medical stations during the demonstrations, owned a gas mask and felt I was contributing to the anti-war effort. Two events happened that spring that had a profound impact. One was the passing comment made by a hitchhiker I picked up one afternoon on the way to a demonstration. Turning to me he asked in an excited voice: "Since when have you been a radical? I've been one for six months now. It's so cool!" Cool was nothing I experienced at a demonstration. I had been to Woodstock, and demonstrations were no Woodstock; but I began to see many college students viewing protests as music festivals. Their shallowness was deeply disturbing.

And then in May 1969 the National Guard at Kent State University murdered four student protesters. To this day the photo of the dead students and the horror on the face of one survivor brings tears to my eyes. The country reacted with equal horror, and it seemed as if every college and university was closing down in support and sympathy. I called a class meeting to plead for Howard to close and join the demonstration. I gave an impassioned speech and discussion went back and forth when from the back of the room a diminutive young woman stood up and asked, "Orangeburg; do you remember Orangeburg?" I had no idea what she was talking about and said as much. She replied, "That's why we're not closing!" The place broke into applause; I slunk back to my seat subsequently to learn later that only a year before, in 1968, South Carolina state patrol officers fired into a crowd from Orangeburg State University protesting segregation. Three Black men were murdered and 28 injured including a pregnant woman. I was humiliated and humbled, but it did not stop there. My education at Howard went far beyond medicine. If it had not been for Howard, Orangeburg, would not have held the same meaning for me as Kent State.

Not 2 weeks after, hundreds of thousands of demonstrators poured into Washington to protest the Kent State killings, 2 students were killed and 12 injured by National Guard in a very similar circumstance at Jackson State College in Mississippi where they were protesting the Vietnam War. This time there was no outcry, no universities closed; there was no march on Washington.

Howard University closed that day the students were killed at Jackson State; and by the start of the new week all students were told to report for a mandatory week of Black Awareness. We did not have the luxury of remaining in the medical school; rather the entire routine of university life came to a full stop. I was sent to the School of Social Work. There I experienced the radicalism—and anger—I had not previously witnessed on campus. And there I came to view the marches and demonstrations as a luxury of a white, liberal upper-income elite.

That summer I applied to a new program established by the American Medical Student Association (AMSA) on American Indian reservations throughout the Southwest. I headed out driving across country alone and arrived into Tucson as the thermometer read 122°.

Together with a nursing and pharmacy student I was assigned to San Carlos Apache—a band of about 5,000 who live on the most arid and inhospitable land eking out a living as ranchers. The poverty was blinding, but for the first time in my life I saw resilience at a very profound and personal level. People, who in the face of extreme economic disadvantage could laugh, sing, and maintain their tribal language and ways. I returned the following summer to run this program and the next as we expanded it to the Dakotas, Wyoming, and Montana. It was through those experiences that my commitment to American Indian health was born. My plan was to complete my training and return to the reservation as a family physician. While that never happened, throughout my career I have always maintained a project on Native youth health concerns (Blum, 1992; Blum, Harmon, Harris, Bergeisen, & Resnick,1992; Blum, Potthoff, & Resnick, 1997; Borowsky, Resnick, Ireland, & Blum,1999; Cummins, Ireland, Resnick, & Blum, 1999; Pharris, Resnick, & Blum, 1997; Potthoff et al., 1998; Saewyc, Skay, Bearinger, Blum, & Resnick, 1998a; Story et al., 1997).

My plan to return to the reservation was derailed by a 4-year-old boy. During our clinical years at Howard we rotated through five hospitals; and I did my pediatrics at Bethesda Naval Hospital. There I met a 4-year-old boy with a terrible disease—rhabdomyosarcoma. I found myself staying hours with him and his parents after the day's work was done and I could have gone home. I figured if I enjoyed it so much I should explore pediatrics more, so I took additional electives. From those experiences pediatrics, and not family medicine, became my future.

A friend from AMSA was a student at the University of Minnesota and he encouraged me to visit. He was especially impressed with one professor—a pediatrician who ran the outpatient services. He was sure we'd hit it off, and he was right. I came to Minnesota to train under Bob ten Bensel. He remained my mentor for the next decade. But I am getting ahead myself since a few other events of note occurred before heading West.

One was meeting my future wife. In the winter of 1972 my childhood friend David and his wife, Karen, set me up on a date with a woman who was Karen's college roommate—Michael. The evening resulted in a bit of a mishap. Coming back from a party a driver ran a red light (Michael has always claimed the accident occurred because my eyes were on her not the road). She wound up in the hospital with a concussion, and I was left to explain to her parents at 1 a.m. what had happened. A call from a hospital room to one's future in-laws is inauspicious. Despite that start the relationship lasted … for the next 40 years. Michael had had a concussion and when she awoke, she had no memory of who I was. I stood by her bed in my short white medical jacket, belying the old saying that you have only one time to make a first impression.

We had planned to marry in June before starting my residency but it was cold in DC in January of my senior year when I saw the notice on the school bulletin board: "Clinical Externship: $6/a day." I came home and asked Michael if I should apply and try to get an externship in Hawaii. In mid-February I was accepted and a week later we were married in Philadelphia—a hurried wedding of sorts, so that we could spend the next 4 months in Maui as a married couple—not the last time in our lives that a travel opportunity influenced our decision-making.

I didn't know much about Hawaii or Maui but it sounded exotic and warm. At the Wailuku Medical Center I was introduced to my mentor, Marion Hanlon. Dr. Hanlon specialized in adolescent medicine, a specialty I had never heard of. I was not especially interested, but Maui was beautiful with palm trees, beaches, and all the coconuts and papayas we could gather and eat. Who was going to complain? Marion became a mentor and friend through the remainder of his life.

Residency and Public Health Training

My medical school friend who had encouraged me to go to the University of Minnesota also told me about *Jonathan,* a planned community 30 miles west of Minneapolis. Michael and I loaded our car in DC after returning from Hawaii and drove directly to Jonathan arriving at about 8 p.m. a day and a half later. There was a small townhouse complex that said *model* on it, and one of the neighbors saw us snooping. John Portnoy (a New Yorker) invited us in, offered us a drink, and called a neighbor who was a realtor. At nine in the evening we started looking at housing units. Michael, who had just completed her master's degree, was a freshly minted school psychologist. Over the course of the next 90 minutes we learned that the nearby school district was looking for a psychologist and that the realtor was on the school board. The next day he arranged for an interview and within a week we owned a 900 sq. ft. townhouse in Jonathan, and Michael was employed. My internship was about to begin.

We filed into the auditorium at Hennepin County Medical Center for orientation; and they handed us each white coats (it was one of the very few times in my clinical career I wore a white coat). Looking around the room I was stunned. I had never seen so many white faces with white hair and white coats in my life! In those years in Minnesota social mixing was when a Swede and Norwegian had lunch together. It was a far cry from Washington. Minneapolis is a very different place today.

As is true for most pediatric residents, despite my Hawaii experience, I saw my future as a clinician working with young children. Again, it was two patients who changed that trajectory, and again both had terrible diseases. John had leukemia and by the time I met him he was in his second or third relapse, meaning his disease had returned. All week he lobbied us to be allowed to go home to attend a little-league baseball team. We relented, and when he was at the game he talked the coach into letting him wear his uniform and sit with his team. Finally, he convinced the coach to let him have one time "at bat." He got a hit and rounded first and headed to second base. He slid into second.

I can't remember if he was safe or out, but I do remember that he got an overwhelming infection as a consequence. When your immune system is compromised it is very easy to get an infection. I was talking with him a few days later and asked him why he slid when he knew the risks. At first he joked and brushed me off, and then he said, "Because I wanted to decide how I was going to live my life." John died a week later at the age of 14; he had decided how he was going to live his life.

The second was a 15-year-old who I will call Clara, since I can't recall her real name. Clara had cystic fibrosis and was in the hospital for extended periods of time. I got to know her well. When I had some quiet time I would sit by her bed and we'd talk about her life—and mine, her fears and aspirations. I taught her self-hypnosis to manage the pain and have a degree of mastery in a world where 15-year-olds have little control, even when their lives are going well. She became so skilled that she was able to have bronchoscopy (a procedure where a tube is inserted in your airway) without analgesics. One day she told me she had to go home for the night, that there was something she had to do. She pleaded to be allowed to leave for just the night. We relented. The following morning her mom called me and told me at 3 a.m. Clara climbed into bed with her and died.

Neither Clara nor John could control their disease but they could decide how they chose to live and die. They taught me some of the most important lessons of my life about cherishing the moment. The Cheyenne have an expression among warriors, "Today is a good day to die." Not that they wanted death, but to live each day as if it were your last. That was Clara and John's legacy.

But they gave me other gifts as well. I began to see that as my peers backed away from teenagers, I was drawn to them. And as my peers avoided young people when they saw their health was deteriorating, I moved in closer. I developed a comfort with talking about death and dying, I studied with Elizabeth Kubler Ross, attended week-long workshops with her, and read everything she wrote on death and dying. It is hard for young physicians today to appreciate, but it was only a generation ago when today's childhood conditions were lethal diseases. Their experiences shaped my clinical research interest in adolescents with chronic conditions and for a decade in the 1990s I ran the National Center for Youth with Disabilities, as well as did research on transitioning to adulthood for youth with chronic conditions (Axtell, Garwick, Patterson, Bennett, & Blum, 1995; Blum, 1982, 1983, 1987c, 1987d, 1991b, 1991c, 1994, 1995, 1996a, 1996b, 2002a; Blum & Chang, 1981; Blum & Pfaffinger, 1994; Blum et al., 2000; Blum, Resnick, Nelson, & St Germaine, 1991; Dodgson et al., 2000; Garwick, Kohrman, Wolman, & Blum, 1998; Garwick, Patterson, Bennett, & Blum, 1995, 1998; Garwick, Patterson, Meschke, Bennett, & Blum, 2002; Harris, Blum, & Resnick, 1991; Joseph-Di Caprio, Garwick, Kohrman, & Blum, 1999; Kelly et al., 2002; Patterson & Blum, 1994, 1996; Patterson, Garwick, Bennett, & Blum, 1997; Payne et al., 1997; Remafed, Resnick, Blum, & Harris, 1992; Scal, Evans, Blozis, Okinow, & Blum, 1999; Stark & Blum, 1986; Suris, Resnick, Cassuto, & Blum, 1996; Wolman, Resnick, Harris, & Blum, 1994).

During my residency there were a number of people who had a profound effect on me beyond my patients, but one changed my career trajectory in a way I never anticipated. Paul Quie was a legendary infectious disease pediatrician, and early in my residency I had a 4-month-old patient who had a clinical disease that was a diagnostic quagmire. After an extensive evaluation it became apparent he had inherited from his father a genetic defect that made him prone to significant and recurrent skin and lung infections. We treated him and he was discharged from the hospital. I thought my job was done. Paul disagreed.

He insisted I write up the case for publication—something I had never done in my life—and he offered to work with me if I would take the lead. Not that it was something I wanted to do but I felt compelled because a person of Paul's stature had asked me to do so. I did write up the case and sent it to him for review. Paul was an infectious disease icon; he even had a disease named after him. He returned the paper the following Monday and best as I recall, the only thing he did not change in the draft manuscript was my name. Given the extensive edits, I suggested to him that he really should be the author. He looked at me and said, "I have no need for another publication; you do." I submitted it to *Pediatrics* and it was accepted within a week. I thought to myself that this academic work did not seem so hard; I could do it. It was the first time in my life I considered being an academician. The next paper I had accepted to *Pediatrics* was probably 20 years later! But Paul Quie taught me another important lesson that also shaped my academic career: "The more you give away, the more you get." This precept has guided my work with students and junior colleagues.

Another academic was also instrumental in shaping my trajectory. I met Gisela Konopka towards the end of my residency through a professor I had in public health. Gisa was the director of the University of Minnesota's Center for Youth Development and Research. She was a Holocaust survivor and in her late sixties when I first met her but she seemed to exude an appreciation of and a love for young people that I had not seen before. She defined adolescence as an *age of firsts*; she said we needed to understand the youth experience within the context of unfolding discoveries. Her research had been primarily qualitative working with incarcerated girls, listening to their stories, having them write poetry, and then publishing their poems. She would ask them, "If you could stand on the top of a building and shout something to the world, what would it be?" And she captured their worries, exuberance, and philosophy.

When I began my fellowship, Gisa offered me an office at her center. It was her last year on faculty and she had ample time to talk; I had ample time to listen. It was during that year her husband died of a heart attack; of the many stories that stand out, one is emblazoned in my memory. Gisa had been invited to be on a television program dealing with child abuse (a relatively new construct in American law). It was a week or so after her husband died. Despite her grief, she went.

During the show, the topic turned to discipline and the commentator started espousing an ethos of "spare the rod and spoil the child." "What you're talking about has nothing to do with discipline," Gisa said. "Let me tell you what discipline is. I woke up this morning and I had absolutely no interest in coming on this show. My husband died less than 10 days ago and I didn't want to be here. But I came here because it was the right thing to do." She paused. "Discipline is about doing the right thing even when it's not what you want to be doing. You can't beat that into a child."

Over the 25 years that followed I met with Gisa nearly every week. She became my children's grandparent while their grandparents were a thousand or more miles away; and on a very personal level I was the son she never had. When she died, we established the Paul and Gisela Konopka Chair in Adolescent Health at the University of Minnesota. Her photo remains on my desk as a constant reminder of the values she personified.

By the end of my clinical residency academic adolescent medicine was in my future. Dr. ten Bensel had moved to the School of Public Health at Minnesota where he headed Maternal and Child Health. He offered me a 2-year fellowship in community pediatrics with only one stipulation, that I get my MPH degree. Concurrently, I could put together a training program for myself in adolescent health. I spent time at the University of Minnesota's Institute for Child Development, Center for Youth Development and Research, and Department of Family Social Science. I structured clinical rotations in adolescent psychiatry, obstetrics and gynecology, and at community teen clinics. And I took course work for my master's degree.

But in truth, I had a jump start on course work since I started taking public health classes during residency as a change of pace from clinical work and for intellectual stimulation. I took courses while a resident but never did any of the work so by the time I started fellowship training in 1975 I had an extensive transcript but with all *incompletes*. By the time my fellowship ended 2 years later I had my master's degree, and had enrolled in a public health doctorate program (my advisor told me that *all* I had to do was clear up my incompletes, take the five prelims, write a thesis, and defend it). I way-underestimated what was involved. Before I signed on to get my doctorate, however, he did give me some good advice that I have repeated to others considering whether to pursue a doctorate: "Think about it now," he said. "Weigh the costs and the benefits of getting a doctorate. If you decide to go for it do not ever think about it again until you are done or you may never finish." There were a number of students in my cohort who quit after debating whether it was worth it or not. I have always been glad I did it; but as he advised, I never really thought whether it was worth it during my years as a student. The entire process was made easier because Michael was concurrently getting her doctorate. As it turned out we defended within a few weeks of each other and were awarded our diplomas at the same time (with our 1-year-old son in our arms). Thirty years later that son, Alex, followed a similar trajectory…went to Howard Medical School, became a pediatrician, and obtained a master's degree in public health.

The Adolescent Health Program

In 1976, in the midst of my fellowship, I was called by the department chairman and invited to meet with him. I had never been in the department chair's office; and I feared I was in trouble. He wanted to discuss a request for proposals for training in Adolescent Health that the Maternal & Child Health Bureau (MCHB) had just issued. Clearly, he knew no one else who was interested in adolescent health, so he asked if I wanted to write it. Without hesitation (or thinking) I said yes. It required collaboration among five schools across the university, so off I went, meeting with the Deans of Nursing, Social Work, Public Health, Psychology & Medicine. To say that I was a novice overstates my expertise. I had never written a grant before—as will become abundantly clear in a moment—and here were all these powerful people telling me what to do. "I published a paper on interdisciplinary teamwork" the Dean of Nursing told me, "be sure to include it in the grant." "I have a model for social supports," said the Dean of Social Work. And by the time I was done including everything all these people were advising, the proposal was over 750 pages long. Really! In 1976 the federal government required 26 copies of every grant. I can only imagine their horror when 20,000 pages showed up at the federal doorstep. The grant application became legendary at MCHB. Needless to say the grant was not funded; it was not ever read.

But to my surprise and delight the next year, out of the blue, Vince Hutchins called me. Vince, who became one of my heroes and mentors, was the director of the Maternal and Child Health Bureau; he informed me that MCHB would be issuing a new RFP (request for proposals) for two additional Adolescent Health Training programs. The requirement was that it did not exceed 50 pages: "Do you know what 50 pages is?" Dr. Hutchins queried. "I'm not sure but I know I can learn," I recall replying.

I defended my dissertation in early September, 1978, and 3 days later the training grant was awarded. I was a new assistant professor with a training program that was a sheaf of good ideas on paper. All that was left was to make it happen.

It is far beyond the scope of a chapter such as this to detail the first 25 years of the University of Minnesota's Adolescent Health Program, during which time I was the director. There are a few events and accomplishments worth highlighting.

The first was hiring brilliant staff and faculty. Karen Stutelberg was the assistant to the department chair and left that position the day the grant was funded; she retired 25 years later when I left for Hopkins. Michael Resnick—a public health doctoral student who was my thesis research assistant (and who I credit for getting me and Michael through our doctoral programs)—joined as Director of Research. Having a doctorally trained researcher as a regular faculty member was uncommon in a medical school department in 1980. Resnick joined as an assistant professor; today he is the Paul and Gisela Konopka Chair of Adolescent Health in pediatrics at the University of Minnesota. Mary Story joined as the program's nutritionist and became instrumental in creating the field of adolescent nutrition nationally. In 2011, she was inducted into the National Academies of Science, and is currently an associate dean at Minnesota's School of Public Health. Lyn Bearinger came first as a fellow and then joined as the faculty member in nursing; and like Mary Story did in nutrition, Lyn crafted the field of adolescent nursing. She is currently a professor of nursing at Minnesota and president of the International Association of Adolescent Health. Over the years others joined our group: Ken Winters, who went on to do landmark substance abuse treatment research; Dianne Newmark Sztainer, the country's leading adolescent obesity intervention researcher; and a group headed by Gary Remafedi that did some of the earliest work on LGBT (lesbian, gay, bisexual, and transgender) adolescents. Collaborations with Gary lead to my research with gay and lesbian youth (French, Story, Remafedi, Resnick, & Blum, 1996;

Remafedi & Blum, 1986; Remafedi, French, Story, Resnick, & Blum, 1998; Remafedi, Resnick, Blum, & Harris, 1992; Saewyc, Bearinger, Blum, & Resnick, 1999; Saewyc, Bearinger, Heinz, Blum, & Resnick, 1998; Saewyc, Skay, Bearinger, Blum, & Resnick, 1998b). With Mary Story and Dianne Neumark-Sztainer I explored a range of nutrition issues (French, Story, Downes, Resnick, & Blum, 1995; French, Story, Remafedi, Resnick, & Blum, 1996; Neumark-Sztainer et al., 1996, 1997a, 1997b; Neumark-Sztainer, Story, Resnick, & Blum, 1996, 1997a, 1997b; Neumark-Sztainer, Story, Resnick, Garwick, & Blum, 1995; Story & Blum, 1988; Story et al., 1991, 1994, 1997; Story, French, Resnick, & Blum, 1995; Neumark-Sztainer, Story, Resnick, & Blum, 1999) and with Lyn Bearinger I explored adolescent health service issues (Bearinger & Blum, 1987; Bearinger, Wildey, Gephart, & Blum, 1992; Blum & Bearinger, 1990; Resnick, Bearinger, & Blum, 1986).

But across 25 years at Minnesota's Adolescent Health Program my most enduring collaborator was Michael Resnick. It was with him that I launched the Minnesota Adolescent Health Survey, the Native American Youth Health Survey, the Alaskan Youth Health Survey, the Caribbean Youth Health Survey, and the health component of the National Longitudinal Survey of Adolescent Health. Over the 25 years of collaboration, we published over 40 manuscripts together. We were the Rogers and Hammerstein of adolescent health!

From its inception the Adolescent Health Program walked between being clinical and research focused. We held the bias that "clinical experience puts faces on data," and we were both domestic and international in our orientation. Over the years I was at Minnesota, fellows came from across the United States as well as from Spain, Portugal, Chile, Israel, Australia, China, Switzerland, New Zealand, and Argentina. And many of the international fellows lived in my home—some for 2 months and a few for up to 2 years. Not only was the program international but so too was our home! Our children became comfortable in a home where foreign students were coming and going at a regular pace.

Over the 25 years as the founding director of University of Minnesota's Adolescent Health Program, I recall many highlights, but there are a few that are worth singling out. In the early 1980s, Michael Resnick and I received a federal grant that was to have three components. The first was to use an established adolescent health survey instrument to collect school-based data on the health status of junior and senior high-school students in Minneapolis. While we had not done due diligence, we were sure such an instrument existed; and in addition, the survey was only the base-line component of the work we had planned. As it turned out, there was no such instrument; because of our commitments under the grant, we were compelled to develop one, which we did. The Minnesota Adolescent Survey collected data on over 17,000 young people, and it became the precursor to and prototype for the CDC's

Youth Risk Behavior Survey, which was launched in the mid-1980s (Blum et al., 1988).

Because of that work, I began to become identified with adolescent health survey research, and that became a major thread of my academic career. Over the ensuing years, Michael Resnick and I collaborated on numerous state-level surveys. In 1989, we surveyed over 14,000 American Indian and Alaskan Native youth on 56 reservations in what remains the largest survey of that population yet to be done. In 1994, we joined with the Carolina Population Center to launch what became the National Longitudinal Study on Adolescent Health (Add Health), and in 1997 we surveyed over 16,000 youths in 11 countries and territories of the English-speaking Caribbean. Large-scale domestic and international adolescent health survey research has continued to be a core part of my research (Bearinger, Wildey, Gephart, & Blum, 1992; Blum, 1987a, 1987b, 1990; Blum et al., 1988, 2003; Blum, Beuhring, Wunderlich, & Resnick, 1996; Lammers, Ireland, Resnick, & Blum, 2000; McGuire et al., 2002; Resnick et al., 1997; Resnick, Bearinger, & Blum, 1986; Resnick, Litman, & Blum, 1992; Sieving et al., 2001; Sieving, McNeely, & Blum, 2000).

By the mid-1980s, a theme was beginning to emerge from our data, suggesting a number of factors that appeared to be protective against risk involvement for youth. As a clinician, I was never surprised to hear that those who were reared in drug-abusing homes wound up using substances. And likewise, it was not a mystery to me that women born to teen mothers were themselves more likely to become teen mothers. But what was always intriguing was to see a young person who was reared in adversity escape the prophesy of his environment. What protected some young people from harm when their brothers and sisters were incarcerated, pregnant, or addicted? As a graduate student, I had studied at the Institute for Child Development and was very familiar with Norm Garmazy, Ann Masten, and other resilience researchers. I began to dig into the literature: Werner, Rutter, Cicchetti, and others.

Some of the answers began to emerge, not just from the literature but from the Minnesota and Native American Youth Health Surveys. But it was with Add Health that we made the deliberate decision to focus on protective factors for the seminal publication rather than generating, yet again, another report card on adolescent health. The protective roles of parent and school connectedness emerged, and it was from that work that a generation of research was spawned. This risk and resilience framework has guided my domestic and international research over the past two decades (Anteghini, Fonseca, Ireland, & Blum, 2001; Blum, 1991c, 1997, 2005; Blum & Ireland, 2004; Blum & Libbey, 2004; Blum et al., 2000, 2003; Blum, McNeely, & Nonnemaker, 2002; Guijarro et al., 1999; Loewenson & Blum, 2001; McNeely, Nonnemaker, & Blum, 2002; Mmari & Blum, 2009; Mmari, Blum, & Teufel-Shone, 2010; Nonnemaker, McNeely, & Blum,

2006; Ohene, Ireland, & Blum, 2004; Pilgrim & Blum, 2012; Resnick et al., 1997; Resnick, Harris, & Blum, 1993; Svetaz, Ireland, & Blum, 2000).

I had been on faculty in Minnesota for more than a decade when the opportunity arose (or it might be more accurate to say I created the opportunity) to go to Geneva to work at the World Health Organization. I wanted to have a sabbatical, and a friend of mine from Australia had just spent a couple of months there working on a project under Mark Belsey. Belsey had been a consultant to the project I ran on the San Carlos Apache reservation 15 years earlier. I wrote Mark, explained I was in adolescent health, and asked if he would connect me with the adolescent group in his unit. The connections with Jane Ferguson and Herb Friedman led to my sabbatical in Geneva in 1987–88. We lived in a small, very rural community in France on the backside of the Geneva airport; our two older children (Alex was ten and Jaime eight) went to the local village school where there were 65 children in the entire school. For them it was "Learn French or die." I worked from Monday through Friday noon and then the five of us took off and explored Europe. It was a glorious year; and by Thanksgiving our two older children were fluent. By the time I returned to the States, I had gained 10 lbs., was $20,000 in debt, spoke French, skied well, and had a new area of work in international adolescent health. It is a focus that continued throughout my years at Minnesota and since coming to Hopkins, has greatly expanded (Blum, 1991a, 2004, 2007, 2009; Blum & Ferguson, 2001; Blum & Ireland, 2004; Blum & Nelson-Mmari, 2004; Blum, Sudhinaraset, & Emerson, 2012; Fatusi, 2009; Fatusi & Blum, 2008; Guijarro et al., 1999; Le & Blum, 2009; Le, Blum, Magnani, & Hewett, 2006; Michaud, Blum, & Slap, 2001; Mmari & Blum, 2009; Ohene, Ireland, & Blum, 2004; Pelaez Mendoz, Rodriguez Izquiendo, Lammers, & Blum, 1999; Pilgrim & Blum, 2012, in press; Suris & Blum, 1993, 2001; Zabin et al., 2009).

For me, the value of such research has always been to provide the information that policy makers and program planners need to allocate resources, establish polices, and build effective programs. Thus, the translation of research has always been at the heart of what I have done; and from the very first survey research publication, we concurrently prepared high-quality reports that we would send 2 days before the publication was to be released in the journal to every policy maker and legislative aid we felt should receive the document (Blum, 1997, 2002b; Blum & Mmari, 2006; Blum & Rinehart, 2000; Blum et al., 1989, 1992; Blum, NcNeely, & Rinehart, 2002).

It would be disingenuous, however, to describe the years of accomplishment without sharing some of the less positive but equally memorable experiences. The first relates to the day I received my notice of grant award in 1978 for the Adolescent Health Training Program.

By the time the training grant was awarded, the interim department chair, who had encouraged my application and worked with me to obtain it, had stepped down, and the new department chair, who saw no value in this work, was firmly in place. When the notice of grant award came, he called me into his office for what I was sure was to be a celebratory meeting. Celebration was the farthest thing from his mind. He looked at me without as much as saying congratulations, and said, "I want your space; I want you to pack up everything and move." You need to understand that an institution makes a commitment for space when they apply for a grant; and the space (previously medical file storage space located next to the morgue) was the university's space commitment in the grant application. I turned to him and asked, "Where do you want me to move to? I have this new grant and will be hiring a staff." He responded that he really didn't care where I moved and I could take my grant and go elsewhere. I knew that was not a viable option and as quickly as it started, I saw my career in adolescent health coming to an immediate halt. The reality was that I had no place to go and absolutely nothing to lose. I turned to him and said, "Bill, this department and the university have made a commitment and I have absolutely no plan to leave my space without being physically forced to do so and if that occurs I will contest it in court." He flew into a rage and I responded by saying: "For me to sit here any longer is of little value." I got up and left quite convinced my days running this new training program had just ended. They hadn't. Later that afternoon he came down to my office, apologized and said I had the right to keep my space. At least I had a place to sit, but the central message for the next decade was to ask little from the Department of Pediatrics and they would ask little of me.

In the early and mid 1980s, adolescent medicine had neither status nor credibility in most medical centers, and that was certainly true at Minnesota. I remember when the clinical wards were being redesigned on pediatrics I made the case for building an adolescent medicine unit for those who were hospitalized between the ages of 12 and 19. Minnesota was a major treatment center for both cystic fibrosis and tumors; we often had upwards of 20 patients in that age bracket on the wards. As it stood, older adolescents could be placed in a room with a child 2–3 years of age. My plan was gaining some momentum when I was asked to present it to the "Clinical Chiefs" (i.e., the heads of all of the clinical departments such as orthopedics, neurology, and urology). I remember when I was done with my presentation one surgical specialist commented, "This is ridiculous. If we set up a ward for adolescents we might as well set up a ward for mothers-in-law." The room broke into laughter and applause, and my proposal went no further.

As adolescent health had little credibility within the institution, the promotion process was equally challenging for me. At every step along the academic ladder I ran into problems. When I went from assistant to associate professor I was denied promotion because a sufficient number of committee members felt the type of survey research I

did, as well as the focal areas of my research (especially teen pregnancy), was not sufficiently meritorious. The following year that hurdle was overcome because a sufficiently large number of external reviewers wrote letters to the contrary. Building a national network of colleagues proved critical to my academic career. Subsequently it has proven critical to my happiness.

My promotion to full professor proved even more complicated. My application had made it all the way through to the final departmental meeting of the promotions committee, where it looked like it was guaranteed. I was in clinic the morning the committee met, and was interrupted by the receptionist paging me to tell me I had a phone call. I was expecting the department chair to call (by that point in time the chair with whom I had initial conflicts had retired) and I was anticipating congratulations. Again, that was not the reality. Rather, he indicated that during the meeting of the promotions committee, one of the members brought forward a charge of academic malfeasance that had not arisen previously. The committee tabled its deliberations.

It was an extraordinary charge that consumed much of my time and all of my emotional energy over the next 3 months. I had a university attorney who investigated the charges; and to this day I remain eternally grateful to my assistants, Deb Seyfer and Linda Boche, who maintained obsessive records and copies of every piece of correspondence and every note, handwritten or typed, that ever came from my desk. Regarding this particular situation, they were able to produce a detailed paper trail that showed, without doubt, the groundless nature of the charges. A faculty member who I had dismissed from the department had brought the charges. Months later I was cleared of the allegations, my promotion reviewed, and at the age of 42 I was promoted to professor at the University of Minnesota.

I left Minnesota shortly after the Adolescent Health Training Program celebrated its 25th anniversary. There had been a set of both personal and professional considerations that factored into the decision to leave. First, I felt running any organization for 25 years was either long enough or too long; and I felt that the adolescent health group would benefit from a new vision and leadership. Second, our three children were grown and it was clear to both Michael and me they were moving East. By the time the opportunity to come to Hopkins arose, both of my parents had died; however, Michael's were still alive and were becoming increasingly frail. They lived on the East Coast and there was no chance that they, in their mid-eighties, would relocate to Minnesota.

But there were numerous work opportunities as well. I had never anticipated looking for a position; in truth, throughout my entire career I had only explored two other positions over the 30 years I was at Minnesota.

When I was invited to come to Hopkins to interview there were a number of things that made it compelling. Most importantly, I knew a number of faculty in the department. When I was offered the position I spoke with my department chair and dean at the University of Minnesota, and was deeply flattered by the opportunities they offered to try to retain me. I had seen this before in academia, and always felt it curious that one's stock increases only when one has a firm offer from elsewhere on the table. I have experienced through much of my career that the validation for my work lay more with colleagues from across the university and across the country than those within medicine and public health at Minnesota. The decision to relocate, however, was not a decision to leave, it was a decision to move to something new; for both Michael and me, with our youngest daughter Amanda having just having graduated from high school, it was like starting life over. It was a wonderful and exciting opportunity.

In the weeks preceding my departure there were parties and recognitions; many kind words were said; the *Minneapolis Star Tribune* wrote an article summarizing my work and contributions. All of these festivities were very flattering. About a week after the newspaper article was published I received a handwritten letter:

Dear Dr. Blum,

I read the article in the Star Tribune the other day and I don't know, but I think that you are the same Dr. Blum who I saw when I was 16 years old. There's no reason why you would remember me because you saw me only twice, two weeks apart at a community clinic. It was summer and I was up from Florida visiting my dad. I was due to return to my mother at the end of August and I was profoundly distraught. I didn't want to go but felt that I had no option. You spent a half hour with me that changed my life. You said that in fact I didn't know that I had no power because I hadn't even tested it. Because I was afraid to speak with my parents about wanting to stay with my father in Minnesota, I assumed that it couldn't happen. You suggested that if I didn't ask I would never know.

The letter went on to say she did speak with her parents and they decided to let her remain in Minnesota from where she graduated from high school. During her senior year her father was diagnosed with cancer and when she was a junior in college her father died. She said, "If you hadn't given me the courage to speak with my parents I never would have known my father." She was nearly 40 when she wrote the letter, had graduated from college, was married, and had two daughters. She concluded by saying, "Thank you. You never know when a few minutes changes someone's life."

And I would suggest that really is the message of working as a clinician in adolescent health care: "You never know when a few minutes changes someone's life." And it is a rare opportunity to hear 25 years later that you had that kind of impact.

The Hopkins Years

Our youngest, Amanda, graduated from high school on June 5. She was moving East to college. Alex was already in Washington in medical school; and our older daughter, Jamie, was in Boston pursuing a master's degree in social work with a goal of working with youth.

The evening of Amanda's graduation we threw a big graduation party; and the following day the movers backed up to our house, packed our furniture, and headed East. After 33 years, we bid farewell to Minnesota to assume our new life in Baltimore. For much of the preceding 6 months I had commuted between Minneapolis and Baltimore, getting to know the faculty and learning my way around both the city and the university.

My first impressions of Hopkins challenged my assumptions. While I was expecting Hopkins to be a high-powered Eastern university, I was only partially correct. It is high powered but the culture is much more Southern than it is Eastern in that interpersonal relationships are highly valued and cultivating relationships is central to academic as well as social success. While Minneapolis was subdued and reserved, Baltimore is boisterous and brash. While in Minneapolis people embraced you with a gentle tap on the back, in Baltimore, it is a bear hug. After 33 years of being among the diaspora, in Baltimore I felt I was home. We moved into the heart of the city, bought a terrific row house over-looking one of Baltimore's many harbors and my commute to work was reduced to 7 minutes.

I was attracted to the position at Hopkins for many reasons, but most centrally because I knew and had tremendous regard for many of those who would now constitute the faculty in the department I would chair. Even before relocating, I was installed as the inaugural William H. Gates Sr. Professor in a ceremony that coincided with the renaming of the School of Public Health to honor Michael Bloomberg. Bill Sr. was there, as was his wife Mimi. It was a great event attended by family, friends, and those who would become my close colleagues over the years that followed.

At the time I am writing this I have been chair of the Department of Population, Family and Reproductive Health for 7 years; in that brief period of time there are many images and stories, of which I will share a few.

When I had been at Minnesota I taught a course on adolescent health in the School of Public Health (though I was primarily based in the Medical School). I began each term by asking students to indicate what, if any experiences they had with adolescents. As I began my course at Hopkins I asked the same question, but the answers were very different from those I had previously experienced. One student responded, "I ran the adolescent HIV program for the Health Department in San Francisco for 5 years." Another indicated she had run adolescent reproductive health programs in Niger for Family Health International, and a third had worked at USAID. By the time the class was done sharing their experiences, I realized I had to revamp my course to build upon their exceptional experiential knowledge base. The students who I have had the honor to teach have themselves been extraordinary teachers.

One of the things I loved about attending on the clinical wards at Minnesota was that it compelled me as the supervising physician to have an ongoing and in-depth grasp of the clinical issues my patients faced. In much the same way, teaching has compelled me to read at a depth and breadth I have never had to do before. While my world at Minnesota had been focused on adolescent health (I used to joke that life began at 10 and ended at 24), now I adopted a life course framework. My teaching became equally expansive: Life Course and Health, Child Heath and Development, Adolescent Health, International Adolescent Health, and Leadership in Public Health are all courses I developed and continue to teach often together with colleagues. A particular joy is that for one, Child Heath and Development, I teach it together with my wife Michael, who brings child developmental expertise to the conversation. So too, we have had the opportunity to collaborate with other colleagues on a study of military children's experiences with relocation and parental deployment.

In addition to teaching, I have been able to take on research collaborations, some of which build on my previous work (e.g. the National Surveys of Youth Health in Vietnam, and a recent survey of adolescent health in seven territories of the Caribbean) and some are in new areas, such as the study of military children exploring the impact of both mobility and parental deployment (Blum, 2007, 2009; Blum & Mmari, 2006; Fatusi, 2009; Fatusi & Blum, 2008; Le & Blum, 2009, in press; Le, Blum, Magnani, & Hewett, 2006; Mmari & Blum, 2009; Pilgrim & Blum, 2012, in press; Zabin et al., 2009).

The opportunity for international research has expanded as well while here at Hopkins. Together with my colleague, Freya Sonenstein, I have launched a six-city study of 15- to 19-year-olds in the slums of New Delhi, Shanghai, Johannesburg, Ibadan, Rio de Janeiro, and Baltimore. That work is ongoing. I have been able to collaborate with the World Health Organization and faculty in my department to develop the adolescent component to the WHO Global Health Observatory, and with colleagues in Kenya, Egypt, India, Nigeria, and China I have been able to plan a new study that will look at the transition into adolescence in communities across the globe.

As a department chair, in addition to research and teaching I have numerous administrative responsibilities. The way I view those activities reflects a developmental evolution to my professional lens. Through my early years as an academic the greatest rewards came with new research opportunities and publications, but as I grew into a leadership role at the Center of Adolescent Health at Minnesota and as a department chair at Hopkins my reward structure has shifted. Today, while I still love all aspects of the academic venture, many of my greatest rewards come from creating an environment where my junior colleagues can flourish. Seeing them shine is probably my greatest professional reward.

But, as I tell people, I have both a day job and a night job. In 2006, the President of Johns Hopkins University asked me if I would take on an interim position as director of the Urban Health Institute. The president created the Urban Health Institute about 6 years before to serve as an interface between Hopkins and the East Baltimore community—one of the most economically impoverished neighborhoods in the United States. I remain uncertain why President Brody asked me to take on this position except that I had been his son's pediatrician when he was at Minnesota. That hardly qualified me for this new position, and at the time he asked I had been a resident of Baltimore for all of 2 years. I accepted that position reluctantly, assured I would do it for 6 months to a year. However, that has proven not to be the case. Rather, I fell in love with that work and with the East Baltimore community, in which Hopkins is embedded. While it is economically impoverished, in human resources it is brash, bold, and embracing, as I have previously described, and I found it invigorating. For the first time in my life, it has been an opportunity to take theory and apply it to practice. While the first years of my academic career had been focused on understanding the protective factors that make a difference in the lives of young people, now I had the opportunity to implement some of that learning, and we have seen some exciting successes.

For example, recently ground has been broken for a new state-of-the-art early child development center and school that will provide wrap around health, education and social services for children in the East Baltimore neighborhood from six weeks of age through the 8th grade. In addition, it will provide social supports to families, educational opportunities to parents and health services to all. We see this center as a prototype of what can be done to improve the outcomes for children and youth.

Another victory has been to shift the way Johns Hopkins Hospital provides health care to the community. Historically, the Urban Health Institute was responsible for running a "free clinic" which in truth was neither free, nor was it providing the quality of care I could support as the UHI director. After much discussion with university and community leaders, I closed the clinic to a hail of criticism from students, the media, and some in the community. The president of Johns Hopkins Hospital promised to "study" the situation and come up with an alternate plan. I was skeptical, for my years at Minnesota taught me that once something went to a "study group" it never emerged. That was not the case here.

A year later we announced The Access Partnership—a plan that assured everyone who lived within a two-zip-code area around Johns Hopkins Hospital would be guaranteed primary and all sub-specialty health care whether they are insured, underinsured, or an undocumented alien. The cost would be the purchase of a $20 identification card. Over the 4 years since the program has been initiated, it has expanded to seven zip codes; and while the Affordable Care Act holds the promise of making this type of program obsolete by 2014, it is today a unique and innovative program in that a major health care institution guarantees all health care services for nearly a quarter of a city's population.

Through the Urban Health Institute we have been able to engage the community in a process that rather than studying deficits will identify the human assets in the community. It is a process that rather than fixing problems will build capacity, and that rather than coming from the outside with solutions will work with community residents to strengthen their capacities and resources to address the priorities they identify. After a lifetime of studying what protects people from harm, the potential of empowering people to be the change they want to see happen is an exciting prospect.

Our vision is to transform the way Hopkins and the neighborhood in which we reside work together and in so doing improve the health and wellbeing of our neighbors. We see enough glimpses to know it is possible.

Conclusions

Not very long ago I was having breakfast with David Rubin, my childhood friend from age 4 in Westport, and he asked if I had given any thought to retirement. I am at an age where I see colleagues with whom I have worked for 25 years at the World Health Organization facing mandatory retirement, and I have colleagues in academia who have chosen to retire. I told David that while it has crossed my mind, I see too many opportunities on the horizon to give serious consideration to retirement now. I said, "I feel like I am in a race and have begun a sprint to the finish line." I don't quite know where that finish line is or when I will choose to slow the pace, but as anyone who has ever run a marathon knows, being in a group of runners is invigorating; and those with whom I run provide me with energy I did not realize I had. That has been my entire academic experience both at Minnesota and here at Hopkins. I have been able to run with the best, the brightest, the most creative people of the academic world, and I have been the beneficiary of that experience far beyond what I could have imagined.

References

Anteghini, M., Fonseca, H., Ireland, M., & Blum, R. W. (2001). Health risk behaviors and associated risk and protective factors among Brazilian adolescents in Santos, Brazil. *Journal of Adolescent Health, 28*(4): 295–302.

Axtell, S. A.M, Garwick, A. W., Patterson, J., Bennett, F. C., & Blum, R. W. (1995). Unmet service needs of families of young with chronic illness and disabilities. *Journal of Family and Economic Issues, 16*(4): 395–411.

Bearinger, L., & Blum, R. (1987). Adolescent medicine and psychiatry: Trends, issues and needs. *Psychiatric Annals, 17*(12): 775–779.

Bearinger, L. H., Wildey, L., Gephart, J., & Blum, R. W. (1992). Nursing competence in adolescent health: Anticipating the future needs of youth. *Journal of Professional Nursing, 8*(2): 80–86.

Blum, R. W. (1982). Death and decision making among Minnesota physicians. *Minnesota Medicine, 65*(8): 499–502.

Blum, R. W. (1983). The adolescent with spina bifida. *Clinical Pediatrics (Philadelphia), 22*(5): 331–335.

Blum, R. (1987a). Physicians' assessment of deficiencies and desire for training in adolescent care. *Journal of Medical Education, 62*(5): 401–407.

Blum, R. (1987b). Youths' views of health and health services. *American Academy of Pediatrics, Adolescent Health Newsletter, 8*(1): 19–24.

Blum, R. W. (1987c). Children with special needs come of age. *Minnesota Pediatrics,* (Fall): 3–4.

Blum, R. W. (1987d). Compliance in the adolescent with chronic illness. *Seminars in Adolescent Medicine, 3*(2): 157–162.

Blum, R. (1990). Adolescent medicine. *JAMA, "Contempo" issue, 263*(19): 2621–2623.

Blum, R. (1992). Native American youth: Poor health carries a powerful message. *Minnesota Medicine, 75*(7): 7–9.

Blum, R. W. (1991a). Global trends in adolescent health. *JAMA, 265*(20): 2711–2719.

Blum, R. W. (1991b). Overview of transition issues for youth with disabilities. *Pediatrician, 18*(2): 101–104.

Blum, R. W. (Ed.). (1991c). Vulnerability and resilience of children and their families. *Pediatric Annals, 20*: 455–511.

Blum, R. W. (1994). Children with special health care needs, executive summary and recommendations. *Journal of School Health, 64*(6): 221–222.

Blum, R. W. (1995). Transition to adult health care: Setting the stage. *Journal of Adolescent Health, 17*(1): 3.

Blum, R. W. (1996a). Compliance with therapeutic regimens among adolescent with chronic illness. *Israel Journal of Medical Sciences,* 325: 214–215.

Blum, R. W. (1996b). Growing up and moving on: Critical issues in and impact of life threatening illness on children and adolescents. *Israel Journal of Medical Sciences,* 325: 155–156.

Blum, R. W. (1997). Risco e resiliência. Sumário para Desenvolvimento de um Programa. *Adolescencia LatinoAmericana, 1*: 16–19.

Blum, R. W. (2002a). Introduction: Improving transition for adolescents with special health care needs from pediatric to adult-centered health care. *Pediatrics, 110*(6 Pt 2): 1301–1303.

Blum, R. W. (2002b). *Mother's influence on teen sex: Connections that promote postponing sexual intercourse.* Divison of General Pediatrics & Adolescent Health, University of Minnesota Adolescent Health Program.

Blum, R. W. (2004). Uganda AIDS prevention: A, B, C and politics. *Journal of Adolescent Health, 34*(5): 428.

Blum, R. (2005). A case for school connectedness. *The Adolescent Learner, 62*(7): 16–20.

Blum, R. (2007). Youth in Sub-Saharan Africa. *Journal of Adolescent Health, 41*: 230–238.

Blum, R. W. (2009). Young people: Not as healthy as they seem. *Lancet, 374*(9693): 853–854.

Blum, R. W., & Bearinger, L. H. (1990). Knowledge and attitudes of health professionals toward adolescent health care. *Journal of Adolescent Health Care, 11*(4): 289–294.

Blum, R., & Chang, P-N. (1981). A group for adolescents facing chronic and terminal illness. *Journal of Current Adolescent Medicine, 3*: 7–12.

Blum, R. W., & Ferguson J. (2001). International adolescent health: Realizing his vision: Herbert Friedman, Ph.D. (1936–2000). *Journal of Adolescent Health, 32*: 253–254.

Blum, R. W., & Ireland, M. (2004). Reducing risk, increasing protective factors: Findings from the caribbean youth health survey. *Journal of Adolescent Health, 35*(6): 493.

Blum, R. W., & Libbey, H. (2004). School connectedness-strengthening health and education outcomes for teenagers (executive summary). *Journal of School Health, 74*(7): 229–232.

Blum, R., & Mmari, K. (2006). *Risk and protective factors affecting adolescent reproductive health in developing countries: An analysis of adolescent sexual and reproductive health literature from around the world: Summary.* Geneva: World Health Organization.

Blum, R. W., & Nelson-Mmari, K. (2004). The health of young people in a global context. *Journal of Adolescent Health, 35*(5): 402.

Blum, R. W., & Pfaffinger, K. (1994). Myelodysplasia in childhood and adolescence. *Pediatrics in Review, 15*(12): 480–484.

Blum, R. W., & Rinehart, P. M. (1997). *Reducing the risk: Connections that make a difference in the lives of youth.* Division of General Pediatrics & Adolescent Health, University of Minnesota Adolescent Health Program.

Blum, R. W., & Rinehart, P. M. (2000). *Protecting teens: Beyond race, income and family structure.* Division of General Pediatrics & Adolescent Health, University of Minnesota Adolescent Health Program..

Blum, R. W., Beuhring, T., Shew, M. L., Bearinger, L. H., Sieving, R. E., & Resnick, M. D. (2000). The effects of race/ethnicity, income, and family structure on adolescent risk behaviors. *American Journal of Public Health, 90*(12): 1879–1884.

Blum, R. W., Beuhring, T., Wunderlich, M., & Resnick, M. D. (1996). Don't ask, they won't tell: The quality of adolescent health screening in five practice settings. *American Journal of Public Health, 86*(12): 1767–1772.

Blum, R. W., Geer, L., Hutton, L., McKay, C., Resnick, M. D., Rosenwinkel, K. et al. (1988). The Minnesota Adolescent Health Survey: Implications for physicians. *Minnesota Medicine, 71*(3): 143–145, 149.

Blum, R. W., Halcon, L., Beuhring, T., Pate, E., Campell-Forrester, S., & Venema, A. (2003). Adolescent health in the Caribbean: Risk and protective factors. *Am J Public Health, 93*(3): 456–460.

Blum, R. W., Harmon, B., Harris, L., Bergeisen, L., & Resnick, M. D. (1992). American Indian–Alaska Native youth health. *JAMA, 267*(12): 1637–1644.

Blum, R., Harmon, B., Harris, L., Resnick, M., et al. (1992). *The state of Native American youth health,* University of Minnesota Adolescent Program.

Blum, R. W., McKay, C., Resnick, M., Geer, L., et al. (1989). *The state of adolescent health in Minnesota,* University of Minnesota Adolescent Health Program.

Blum, R. W., McNeely, C., & Nonnemaker, J. (2002). Vulnerability, risk, and protection. *Journal of Adolescent Health, 31*(1 Suppl): 28–39.

Blum, R. W., NcNeely, C. A., & Rinehart, P. M. (2002). *Improving the odds: The untapped power of schools to improve the health of teens.* Minneapolis: Center for Adolescent Health, University of Minnesota.

Blum, R. W., Potthoff, S. J., & Resnick, M. D. (1997). The impact of chronic conditions on Native American adolescents. *Families, Systems, & Health, 15*(3): 275–282.

Blum, R. W., Resnick, M. D., Nelson, R., & St Germaine, A. (1991). Family and peer issues among adolescents with spina bifida and cerebral palsy. *Pediatrics, 88*(2): 280–285.

Blum, R., Sudhinaraset, M., & Emerson, M. R. (2012). Youth at risk: Suicidal thoughts and attempts in Vietnam, China, and Taiwan. *Journal of Adolescent Health, 50*(3, Suppl): S37–S44.

Borowsky, I. W., Resnick, M. D., Ireland, M., & Blum, R. W. (1999). Suicide attempts among American Indian and Alaska Native youth: Risk and protective factors. *Archives of Pediatrics & Adolescent Medicine, 153*(6): 573–580.

Cummins, J. R., Ireland, M., Resnick, M. D., & Blum, R. W. (1999). Correlates of physical and emotional health among Native American adolescents. *Journal of Adolescent Health, 24*(1): 38–44.

Dodgson, J., Garwick, A., Blozis, S., Patterson, J., Bennett, F., & Blum, R. W. (2000). Uncertainty in childhood chronic conditions and family distress in families of young children. *Journal of Family Nursing, 6*(3): 252–266.

Fatusi, A. B. R. (2009). Adolescent health in an international context: The challenge of sexual and reproductive health in sub-Saharan Africa. *Adolescent Medicine State of the Art Reviews, 20*(3): 874–886, viii.

Fatusi, A. O., & Blum, R. W. (2008). Predictors of early sexual initiation among a nationally representative sample of Nigerian adolescents. *BMC Public Health, 8:* 136.

French, S. A., Story, M., Downes, B., Resnick, M. D., & Blum, R. W. (1995). Frequent dieting among adolescents: Psychosocial and health behavior correlates. *American Journal of Public Health, 85*(5): 695–701.

French, S. A., Story, M., Remafedi, G., Resnick, M. D., & Blum, R. W. (1996). Sexual orientation and prevalence of body dissatisfaction and eating disordered behaviors: A population-based study of adolescents. *International Journal of Eating Disorders, 19*(2): 119–126.

Garwick, A. W., Kohrman, C., Wolman, C., & Blum, R. W. (1998). Families' recommendations for improving services for children with chronic conditions. *Archives of Pediatrics & Adolescent Medicine, 152*(5): 440–448.

Garwick, A. W., Patterson, J., Bennett, F. C., & Blum, R. W. (1995). Breaking the news: How families first learn about their child's chronic condition. *Archives of Pediatrics & Adolescent Medicine, 149*(9): 991–997.

Garwick, A. W., Patterson, J. M., Bennett, F. C., & Blum, R. W. (1998). Parents' perceptions of helpful vs unhelpful types of support in managing the care of preadolescents with chronic conditions. *Archives of Pediatrics & Adolescent Medicine, 152*(7): 665–671.

Garwick, A., Patterson, J., Meschke, L. L., Bennett, F., & Blum, R. W. (2002). The uncertainty of preadolescents' chronic health conditions and family distress. *Journal of Family Nursing, 8*(1): 11–31.

Guijarro, S., Naranjo, J., Padilla, M., Gutierez, R., Lammers, C., & Blum, R. W. (1999). Family risk factors associated with adolescent pregnancy: Study of a group of adolescent girls and their families in Ecuador. *Journal of Adolescent Health, 25*(2): 166–172.

Harris, L., Blum, R. W., & Resnick, M. (1991). Teen females in Minnesota: A portrait of quiet disturbance. *Women and Therapy, 11*(3/4): 119–135.

Joseph-Di Caprio, J., Garwick, A. W., Kohrman, C., & Blum, R. W. (1999). Culture and the care of children with chronic conditions: Their physicians' views. *Archives of Pediatrics & Adolescent Medicine, 153*(10): 1030–1035.

Kelly, A., Call, K. T., Staub, B., Donald, B., Wisner, C. L., & Nelson, A. F. (2002). Children with complex chronic medical conditions and special needs privately insured through an HMO. *Families, Systems & Health, 20*(3): 279–289.

Lammers, C., Ireland, M., Resnick, M., & Blum, R. (2000). Influences on adolescents' decision to postpone onset of sexual intercourse: A survival analysis of virginity among youths aged 13 to 18 years. *Journal of Adolescent Health, 26*(1): 42–48.

Le, L., & Blum, R. W. (2009). Premarital sex and condom use among never married youth in Vietnam. *International Journal of Adolescent Medicine and Health, 21*(3): 299–312.

Le, L., & Blum, R. (In press). Injury among youth in Vietnam; findings from two national, SAVY surveys. *Asian Journal of Public Health.*

Le, L. C., Blum, R., Magnani, R., & Hewett, P. (2006). A pilot of audio computer-assisted self-interview for youth reproductive health research in Vietnam. *Journal of Adolescent Health, 38*(6): 740–747.

Loewenson, P. R., & Blum, R. W. (2001). The resilient adolescent: Implications for the pediatrician. *Pediatric Annals, 30*(2): 76–80.

McGuire, M. T., Story, M., Neumark-Sztainer, D., Halcon, L., Campbell-Forrester, S., & Blum, R. W. (2002). Prevalence and correlates of weight control behaviors among Caribbean adolescent students. *Journal of Adolescent Health, 31*(2): 208–211.

McNeely, C. A., Nonnemaker, J. M., & Blum, R. W. (2002). Promoting school connectedness: Evidence from the national longitudinal study of adolescent health. *Journal of School Health, 72*(4): 138–146.

Michaud, P. A., Blum, R. W., & Slap, G. B. (2001). Cross-cultural surveys of adolescent health and behavior: Progress and problems. *Social Science & Medicine, 53*(9): 1237–1246.

Mmari, K., & Blum, R. W. (2009). Risk and protective factors that affect adolescent reproductive health in developing countries: A structured literature review. *Global Public Health, 21*: 1–16.

Mmari, K., Blum, R., & Teufel-Shone, N. (2010). What increases risk and protection for delinquent behaviors among American Indian youth? Findings from three tribal communities. *Youth & Society, 41*(3): 382–413.

Neumark-Sztainer, D., Story, M., French, S. A., Hannan, P. J., Resnick, M. D., & Blum, R. W. (1997a). Psychosocial concerns and health-compromising behaviors among overweight and nonoverweight adolescents. *Obesity Research, 5*(3): 237–249.

Neumark-Sztainer, D., Story, M., Resnick, M. D., & Blum, R. W. (1996). Correlates of inadequate fruit and vegetable consumption among adolescents. *Preventive Medicine, 25*(5): 497–505.

Neumark-Sztainer, D., Story, M., Resnick, M. D., & Blum, R. W. (1997a). Psychosocial concerns and weight control behaviors among overweight and nonoverweight Native American adolescents. *Journal of the American Dietetic Association, 97*(6): 598–604.

Neumark-Sztainer, D., Story, M., Resnick, M. D., & Blum, R. W. (1997b). Adolescent vegetarians: A behavioral profile of a school-based population in Minnesota. *Archives of Pediatrics & Adolescent Medicine, 151*(8): 833–838.

Neumark-Sztainer, D., Story, M., Resnick, M. D., & Blum, R. W. (1999). Lessons learned about adolescent nutrition from the Minnesota Adolescent Health Survey. *Journal of the American Dietetic Association, 98*(12): 1449–1456.

Neumark-Sztainer, D., Story, M., Resnick, M. D., Garwick, A., & Blum, R. W. (1995). Body dissatisfaction and unhealthy weight-control practices among adolescents with and without chronic illness: A population-based study. *Archives of Pediatrics & Adolescent Medicine, 149*(12): 1330–1335.

Neumark-Sztainer, D., Story, M., Toporoff, E., Cassuto, N., Resnick, M. D., & Blum, R. W. (1996). Psychosocial predictors of binge eating and purging behaviors among adolescents with and without diabetes mellitus. *Journal of Adolescent Health, 19*(4): 289–296.

Neumark-Sztainer, D., Story, M., Toporoff, E., Himes, J. H., Resnick, M. D., & Blum, R. W. (1997b). Covariations of eating behaviors with other health-related behaviors among adolescents. *Journal of Adolescent Health, 20*(6): 450–458.

Nonnemaker, J., McNeely, C. A., & Blum, R. W. (2006). Public and private domains of religiosity and adolescent smoking transitions. *Social Science & Medicine, 62*(12): 3084.

Ohene, S. A., Ireland, M., & Blum, R. W. (2004). Sexually-inexperienced Caribbean youth: Correlates of delayed sexual debut. *Journal of Adolescent and Family Health, 3*(4): 177–184.

Patterson, J., & Blum, R. W. (1994). La maladie chronique et le handicap chez les jeunes: Risques et adaptation. *Medicine et Hygiene, 52*: 1406–1409.

Patterson, J., & Blum, R. W. (1996). Risk and resilience among children and youth with disabilities. *Archives of Pediatrics & Adolescent Medicine, 150*(7): 692–698.

Patterson, J. M., Garwick, A. W., Bennett, F. C., & Blum, R. W. (1997). Social support in families of children with chronic conditions: Supportive and nonsupportive behaviors. *Journal of Developmental and Behavioral Pediatrics, 18*(6): 383–391.

Payne, W. K., 3rd, Ogilvie, J. W., Resnick, M. D., Kane, R. L., Transfeldt, E. E., & Blum, R. W. (1997). Does scoliosis have a psychological impact and does gender make a difference? *Spine, 22*(12): 1380–1384.

Pelaez Mendoz, J., Rodriguez Izquiendo, A., Lammers, C., & Blum, R. W. (1999). Abortion among adolescents in Cuba. *Journal of Adolescent Health, 24*(1): 59–62.

Pharris, M. D., Resnick, M. D., & Blum, R. W. (1997). Protecting against hopelessness and suicidality in sexually abused American Indian adolescents. *Journal of Adolescent Health, 21*(6): 400–406.

Pilgrim, N. A., & Blum, R. W. (2012). Protective and risk factors associated with adolescent sexual and reproductive health in the English-speaking Caribbean: A literature review. *Journal of Adolescent Health, 50*(1): 5–23.

Pilgrim, N., & Blum, R. W. (In press). Adolescent mental and physical health in the English-speaking Caribbean: A structured literature review. *Revista Panamericana de Salud Pública/Pan American Journal of Public Health.*

Potthoff , S. J., Bearinger L. H., Skay C. L., Cassuto N., Blum R. W., & Resnick, M. D. (1998). Dimensions of risk behaviors among American Indian youth. *Archives of Pediatrics & Adolescent Medicine, 152*(2): 157–163.

Remafedi, G., & Blum, R. (1986). Working with gay and lesbian adolescents. *Pediatric Annals, 15*(11): 773–783.

Remafedi, G., French, S., Story, M., Resnick, M. D., & Blum R. (1998). The relationship between suicide risk and sexual orientation: Results of a population-based study. *American Journal of Public Health, 88*(1): 57–60.

Remafedi, G., Resnick, M., Blum, R., & Harris, L. (1992). Demography of sexual orientation in adolescents. *Pediatrics, 89*(4 Pt 2): 714–721.

Resnick, M. D., Bearinger, L., & Blum, R. (1986). Physician attitudes and approaches to the problems of youth: A report from the Upper Midwest Regional Physicians Survey. *Pediatric Annals, 15*(11): 799–807.

Resnick, M. D., Bearman, P. S., Blum, R. W., Bauman, K. E., Harris, K. M., Jones, J., et al. (1997). Protecting adolescents from harm: Findings from the National Longitudinal Study on Adolescent Health. *JAMA, 278*(10): 823–832.

Resnick, M. D., Harris, L. J., & Blum, R. W. (1993). The impact of caring and connectedness on adolescent health and well-being. *Journal of Paediatrics and Child Health, 29*(Suppl 1): S3–9.

Resnick, M. D., Litman, T. J., & Blum, R. W. (1992). Physician attitudes toward confidentiality of treatment for adolescents: Findings from the Upper Midwest Regional Physicians Survey. *Journal of Adolescent Health, 13*(7): 616–622.

Saewyc, E. M., Bearinger, L. H., Blum, R. W., & Resnick, M. D. (1999). Sexual intercourse, abuse and pregnancy among adolescent women: Does sexual orientation make a difference? *Family Planning Perspectives, 31*(3): 127–131.

Saewyc, E. M., Bearinger, L. H., Heinz, P. A., Blum, R. W., & Resnick, M. D. (1998). Gender differences in health and risk behaviors among bisexual and homosexual adolescents. *Journal of Adolescent Health, 23*(3): 181–188.

Saewyc, E. M., Skay, C. L., Bearinger, L. H., Blum, R. W., & Resnick, M. D. (1998a). Demographics of sexual orientation among American-Indian adolescents. *American Journal of Orthopsychiatry, 68*(4): 590–600.

Saewyc, E. M., Skay, C. L., Bearinger, L. H., Blum, R. W., & Resnick, M. D. (1998b). Sexual orientation, sexual behaviors, and pregnancy among American Indian adolescents. *Journal of Adolescent Health, 23*(4): 238–247.

Scal, P., Evans, T., Blozis, S., Okinow, N., & Blum, R. (1999). Trends in transition from pediatric to adult health care services for young adults with chronic conditions. *Journal of Adolescent Health, 24*(4): 259–264.

Sieving, R. E., Beuhring, T., Resnick, M. D., Bearinger, L. H , Shew, M., Ireland, M., et al. (2001). Development of adolescent self-report measures from the national longitudinal study of adolescent health. *Journal of Adolescent Health, 28*(1): 73–81.

Sieving, R. E., McNeely, C. S., & Blum, R. W. (2000). Maternal expectations, mother–child connectedness, and adolescent sexual debut. *Archives of Pediatrics & Adolescent Medicine, 154*(8): 809–816.

Stark, T., & Blum, R. (1986). Psychosomatic illness in childhood and adolescence: Clinical considerations. *Clinical Pediatrics, 25*(11): 549–554.

Story, M., & Blum, R. W. (1988). Adolescent nutrition: Self-perceived deficiencies and needs of practitioners working with youth. *Journal of the American Dietetic Association, 88*(5): 591–594.

Story, M., French, S. A., Neumark-Sztainer, D., Downes, B., Resnick, M. D., & Blum, R. W. (1997). Psychosocial and behavioral correlates of dieting and purging in Native American adolescents. *Pediatrics, 99*(4): E8.

Story, M., French, S. A., Resnick, M. D., & Blum, R. W. (1995). Ethnic/racial and socioeconomic differences in dieting behaviors and body image perceptions in adolescents. *International Journal of Eating Disorders, 18*(2): 173–179.

Story, M., Hauck, F. R., Broussard, B. A., White, L. L., Resnick, M. D., & Blum, R. W. (1994). Weight perceptions and weight control practices in American Indian and Alaska Native adolescents. A national survey. *Archives of Pediatrics & Adolescent Medicine, 148*(6): 567–571.

Story, M., Rosenwinkel, K., Himes, J. H., Resnick, M., Harris, L. J., & Blum, R. W. (1991). Demographic and risk factors associated with chronic dieting in adolescents. *American Journal of Diseases of Children, 145*(9): 994–998.

Suris, J. C., & Blum, R. W. (1993). Disability rates among adolescents: An international comparison. *Journal of Adolescent Health, 14*(7): 548–552.

Suris, J. C., & Blum, R. W. (2001). Adolescent health in Europe: An overview. *International Journal of Adolescent Medicine, 13*(2): 91–99.

Suris, J. C., Resnick, M. D., Cassuto, N., & Blum, R. W. (1996). Sexual behavior of adolescents with chronic disease and disability. *Journal of Adolescent Health, 19*(2): 124–131.

Svetaz, M. V., Ireland, M., & Blum, R. (2000). Adolescents with learning disabilities: Risk and protective factors associated with emotional well-being. Findings from the national longitudinal study of adolescent health. *Journal of Adolescent Health, 27*(5): 340–348.

Wolman, C., Resnick, M. D., Harris, L. J., & Blum, R. W. (1994). Emotional well-being among adolescents with and without chronic conditions. *Journal of Adolescent Health, 15*(3): 199–204.

Zabin, L. S., Emerson, M. R., Nan, L., Chaohua, L., Ersheng, G., Minh, N. H., et al. (2009). Levels of change in adolescent sexual behavior in three Asian cities. *Studies in Family Planning, 40*(1): 1–12.

4

Person, Time, and Place

The Life Course of a Developmental Psychologist

JEANNE BROOKS-GUNN

Writing an essay about one's life or career is not easy. It feels as though one is being superficial and pompous at the same time. Furthermore, the story might not be interesting enough to hold the reader's attention. What parts are the most interesting or central to the narrative? Another annoying feature is that such an essay can focus so much on the self that the embeddedness of the self in a particular historical and contextual period is lost. At the same time, such a focus might not do justice to the relationships that were central to becoming a researcher and that sustained that research (two earlier autobiographical essays of mine were critiqued for spending too much time discussing others' influences on my work; Brooks-Gunn, 1990, 1996). Is the story about the person, or about the person as developing within a time and place and surrounded by others who define that time and place (as well as the person)? Clearly, social scientists who study lives over time think about such issues, especially if their work emerged in the tradition of life course and developmental theorists such as Glen Elder and Urie Bronfenbrenner, to name two of my major influences. Add to this a concern with how the self emerges in the context of relationships brings other theorists to the mix, such as George Herbert Mead and Merleau-Ponty. A dollop of sociologists who were concerned with how the self is defined by larger aggregates, such as neighborhoods (and how neighborhoods emerge as a function of the individual make-up of the neighborhood as well as the relationships among these individuals) with an interest in social stratification such as William Julius Wilson, and the earlier scholars from the Chicago School adds depth to the stew. And, let's not forget the importance of the genetic and biological influences in concert with the environment, in shaping one's personal characteristics, as evidenced by the writings of Sandra Scarr, Eleanor Maccoby, Harry Harlow, and Jerome Kagan. Finally, a late entry is the economic take on the emergence of self, especially family economic theory as presented by Gary Becker. Mix well, and add a few other ingredients, and my research trajectory emerges.

Another problem is that such an essay takes a linear view of a life. While that is how the life course is often studied, it is hard to take into account the experiences that were available (as well as those that were not), the take-up of some of these experiences (since some choice is involved), the rejection of some of these experiences (again, choice), and the likelihood that some chosen experiences lead to others. Economists talk about constraints and opportunities as well as information leading to the take-up (or not) of a particular experience. Sociologists look at how social stratification limits experiences for some. Life-course theorists use such terms as opportunities, constraints, turning points, knifing points, cascades, and recursive pathways to describe these phenomena. Psychologists consider the cognitive, emotional, and biological processes that underlie how individuals respond to various experiences and even how open individuals are to various experiences. They are often interested in changes in these processes as a function of development as well as experience and well as the individual differences seen across individuals within the same environment. Biologists are concerned with how experiences get under the skin and how experiences alter biological systems. Some of these phenomena include biological reactivity to events, different genetic sensitivity to environment events, cumulative stressors, and allostatic load. Of course, this description is quite simplistic, in that overlap occurs across disciplines. In fact, my career has been all about integrating insights from the various approaches to better understand development through time and place. However, disciplines seem to like their theories to be distinct. In a revision of an article for the *American Journal of Public Health*, our group attempted to outline a life course developmental theory (we were trying to show how the use of such a framework would enhance the exciting emerging work on differential genetic sensitivity to the environment (Mitchell et al., in press); two reviewers mentioned that the life course and the developmental frameworks were separate and should not be combined, which led to a mini-discourse on how the two differ rather than on how they are similar.

This chapter will be organized more linearly than it should, illustrating how one life course unfolded. Sections will be devoted to growing up (childhood and adolescence), becoming a researcher, establishing research directions and adding policy and prevention efforts, beginning new life-course studies and interventions, consolidating life-course developmental perspectives and policy interests, and considering biological and environmental intersections through genetics and epigenetics.

Overlapping personal events also enter here—getting married at a fairly young age (early twenties), goofing off with my husband by flying our 1947 Beechcraft Bonanza through the Caribbean, Central America, Canada, and Alaska as well as sailing and skiing a lot (twenties), spending lots of time with our extended family on the beach and in New York City (continues), building a house in the Sourland Mountains (outside of Princeton; thirties), becoming a parent at a fairly old age, moving to New York City for our son's preschool years (forties), juggling work and family, like everyone (continues), renovating a 150-year-old mini-Victorian cottage on a summer island off the coast of Maine and gaining a wonderful group of friends in the Squirrel Island Circle of Fire (forties), reconnecting with high school girlfriends (the dozen from the EGR Class of 65; early fifties), returning full-time to central New Jersey (fifties), building and decorating an addition to our house and cutting trees (continuous), shepherding our son through adolescence (fifties), sadly losing my husband much too early (forties), and experiencing college and emerging adulthood through my son's eyes.

Woven into the research narrative will be examples of unexpected opportunities (being introduced to a reproductive endocrinologist when just starting to study pubertal development, to a sociologist and a pediatrician when just thinking about other social reproductive events during adolescence, namely sexuality, pregnancy, and parenthood, to an economist when focusing on disadvantaged families over and above those who experienced an early pregnancy), to a demographer when conceding the intersection of poverty and single parenthood, to a criminologist, a child psychiatrist, and a statistician when thinking about the neighborhoods in which poor families and single parents live, and to a geneticist when adding DNA to a longitudinal birth cohort. In each of these cases, the introduction led to productive collaborations. All were at the time an add-on to an already rich research plate and all required learning about other disciplines. These decisions turned into cascades, leading to other opportunities and collaborations. The work on disadvantaged teenage mothers led to designing and evaluating programs for such families in Harlem at first and then nationally. Being involved in such program evaluations led

to being part of teams looking at federally funded programs (Early Head Start, current National Evaluation of Home Visiting), both of which serve teenage mothers as well as older disadvantaged mothers (Duggan et al., in press; Howard & Brooks-Gunn, 2009a; Love et al., 2005; Love et al., 2013).

Other events were knifing points. When I started to spend more time with larger data sets (ultimately going on to design multi-site or nationally representative longitudinal studies), time in the laboratory doing more intensive process-oriented work decreased dramatically, altering my research agenda forever. Another would be the decision to go to the University of Pennsylvania[1] given coordination of graduate school plans with my husband. At the time that I chose to go to Penn, it was unclear with whom I would work (ultimately training with Sandra Scarr and Michael Lewis, which turned out to be terrific experiences). No doubt my research would have been dramatically different if I had gone to another university and trained with other scholars.

Turning points would include the decision to leave a full-time research position at Educational Testing Service (ETS) in 1990 for a endowed chair (Virginia and Leonard Marx Professor of Child Development) and directorship of a newly formed center (National Center on Children and Families) at Columbia University's Teachers College (and eventually a professor-level position at Columbia College of Physicians and Surgeons), which offered a chance to train young research scholars and to focus more on policy relevant work. Another turning point would be the decision to take-up Sara McLanahan's offer (in the mid-1990s) to be a Visiting Scholar at Princeton University, when she moved there (after two decades, I am still a visitor with an office which is my sanctuary for writing and which is dangerously over-run with piles of papers). Yet another would be the decision to run a university-wide child and family policy center funded by the Provost at Columbia University with Sheila Kamerman and J. Lawrence Aber in the nineties as well. Later on, Sharon Lynn Kagan joined me as director of the center at Teachers College which I had started nine years earlier, which allowed for an expansion of our research policy endeavors and an education for me on pedagogy and financing.

Growing Up: Childhood

My childhood was in large part determined by the historical period in which I was raised. I was part of the first wave of the baby boomers. Like so many men of his age, my father returned from World War II, in his case a highly decorated Navy pilot from the Pacific Theater, determined to start a business and a family. Given that he grew up on a modest farm in Western Michigan and raised by his grandparents as his father died when he was a preschooler and his mother went to the "big" city (Grand Rapids) to work, his attending Northwestern University (he did not have enough money to travel to MIT where he had been given a scholarship) was born of grit and smarts (he earned money in college by playing poker). Unlike most women of her cohort, my mother had defied her conservative salesman father to get a master's degree in child development at the Merrill Palmer Institute in Michigan and then left a teaching job to join the Navy in the first cohort of women to do so. Recently, I discovered that two friends from her generation here in Princeton had been WAVES (the name for women in the Navy at the time). All three 90-somethings are still spunky and full of life.

After trying to set up an air cargo company in New York City (our lives would certainly been different if he had succeeded in terms of residence and income), my father became a contractor in Grand Rapids, building many housing developments (think small Levittowns) including probably the first integrated one in Western Michigan (which was soundly denounced at the time). Like so many other women of her generation who were employed during the war, my mother left the workplace and had four children. I was the eldest, born at a Naval Hospital as my parents were stationed in Washington, DC. She has described the transition as the most difficult of her life (from work that she loved to being at home, being in a strange city, having no friends there, having a husband who was struggling with a new company), no doubt compounded by my prematurity and what Tom Boyce today would term my high behavioral reactivity or Steve Suomi might characterize as being up tight (a phrase that he uses for some of his monkeys). I am still known as the high strung or the difficult one in my family.

In any case, my upbringing was indicative of a certain time and place—two parent families with multiple children, tidy neighborhoods and homes, good suburban schools, minorities segregated in the one poor section of town, almost no mothers in the workplace (I never saw a professional women with the exception of a few fantastic high-school teachers who had advanced degrees from the University of Michigan until I left for college), and, in the case of Western Michigan, a very conservative zeitgeist. Girls like me were adored by their fathers and were expected to achieve in school and go to a good college and then marry and settle down. That the achievement drive might lead to a desire for a career wasn't mentioned as a possibility (even though, years later, my mother admitted to me that she cried when she read *The Feminine Mystique*). Sometimes, it is hard to imagine what life was like then, given today's opportunities and women's rapid entrance into professional fields, nor how rapidly the context changed. When I become a Michigan Math Finalist, I wasn't even in advanced math courses and no one at my high school was willing to move me into them. Although one of the long-term (she had taught my mother and later tutored her when she took the GREs to apply to an MA program in her fifties), highly educated (advanced degree) women (single) teachers (she was called Ma) at the school cried when she talked about one of the guys in my class who was also a finalist (what a waste of a good mind) but no tears for me even though she adored me. How quickly the zeitgeist changes. Seven years younger than me, my sister was a math major at Dartmouth College.

Growing Up: Adolescence

Like a small group from my high school, I headed East for college. Connecticut College was a woman's college at that time, which was the right choice for me, I felt quite inferior to the students who had gone to private schools and East Coast suburban schools. I must have been at least 1 year behind everyone else (and I had gone to a good Midwest school); my freshman year was spent closeted in the library trying to catch up. And, a women's college was a safe place to do this and to tentatively speak out in class (I am not sure what would have happened to me if I had gone to Northwestern University my father's alma mater competing with men in the classroom). A disproportionate number of accomplished women had graduated from women's college in the 1950s and 60s compared with co-ed colleges (although of course these studies didn't have the type of controls for selection that we would have today). I met interesting women and had fantastic teachers, both men and women. I saw women professors leading fulfilling lives, both those who had children and those who did not. There is no doubt that I became a professor given these role models. At Conn College, I also fell in love with psychology from the first introductory course, through research methods, statistics, and then developmental psychology and finally several research papers and an honors thesis (one of my first little studies was on perceptions of stress as a function of exams and menstrual cycle, forecasting my interest in bio-behavioral processes as they interact with the environment, although I wouldn't have known how to say that then; another was on 3rd and 5th graders perceptions of ability and how ability contributed to their sense of self). I can never thank my professors enough for nurturing my interest and urging me to apply to graduate school. They are unsung heroes who trained three still-active academic women researchers.[2] I also loved the opportunity to separate my romantic and academic life with no distractions in the latter from the former during the week.

Becoming a Researcher

After college, I decided to get a master's degree at the Harvard University School of Education for a number of reasons. First, I was enamored with the social cognitive developmental theory of Lawrence Kohlberg and wanted to take courses with him. Second, I wasn't ready for a PhD program (or so I thought; what not being ready meant to me then is a total mystery). Third, and perhaps most important, was that I was dating a guy (eventually my husband) who still had a year to go in college and I didn't want to move too far away from him. The year was very rewarding although difficult. I had left a sheltered college nest where professors were warm and supportive to a major research university where being more assertive and confident was rewarded (not so easy when you had been schooled in Midwestern nice your entire life). Plus, the male graduate students were favored in subtle and not-so-subtle ways. Enter women's groups and women's studies as anecdotes. The learning that year was fantastic.[3] The potpourri of intellectual ideas would serve me well in the coming years.

I got more serious at the University of Pennsylvania, as my experiences with Scarr and Lewis led me to focus on development in young children. My interests were in social cognition as well as gender differences (more in socialization at the time than biology). My first experiment was an investigation of opposite-sex twins interacting with their mother in a playroom in order to look at differences in socialization as well as activity levels (Brooks & Lewis, 1974), given that I was a research assistant for Scarr on one of her studies on twins. Gender differences have continued to be an interest throughout my research career (Brooks-Gunn & Matthews, 1979), even though my views have become much more nuanced (i.e., looking at the intersection of biology and environment and looking at mothers and fathers as well as girls and boys) than they were (Brooks-Gunn, 1986; Browning, Leventhal, & Brooks-Gunn, 2005; DeKlyen, Brooks-Gunn, McLanahan, & Knab, 2006; Meadows, McLanahan, Brooks-Gunn, 2007; Mendle, Harden, Brooks-Gunn, & Graber, 2010; Nichols, Graber, Brooks-Gunn, & Botvin, 2006). As part of my mentorship with Lewis, we began a series of studies on social cognition in infancy and toddlerhood, studying how and when young children began to use social categories such as gender and age (Brooks & Lewis, 1976; Brooks-Gunn & Lewis, 1979; 1981) as well as the development of self-recognition as a specific aspect of social cognition (Brooks-Gunn & Lewis, 1984; Lewis & Brooks-Gunn, 1979; Lewis, Brooks-Gunn, & Jaskir, 1985). This developmental mostly cross-sectional work was embedded in genetic epistemology theory as well as social cognitive theory with a strong focus on the idea that the self (or person) only develops in relationship to others (time and place, although we tended to study place as relationships). I was thinking like a life span developmental scholar without knowing it as I finished my doctoral work in 1975.

Establishing Research Directions: The Thirties

My tenure as a Lewis graduate student segued into a position at ETS as a junior research scientist. The Lewis Lab was a dynamic place, perfect for applying what I had already learned about research—designs that were sound, addressed interesting questions, and provided credible answers (and were therefore publishable). We had a terrific group of graduate students, post-doctoral fellows, and visiting scholars,[4] as well as wonderful senior faculty in developmental psychology and in psychometrics.[5] Only in hindsight do I appreciate the gift of so many talented and devoted academics in one place at the time that I was learning my trade.

Three other collaborations began at this time which pushed my interests in social cognition, the person in the context of relationships, and gender further. The first

involved meeting Diane Ruble, then an assistant professor at Princeton University (ETS is located in Princeton); she was teaching a course on gender differences there just as I was at the University of Pennsylvania (in my case as part of Penn's new Women's Studies Program). Both of us had been struck by the paucity of information in general on girls' development and in particular reproductive events, which are both social and biological in nature. Events such as menarche, puberty, sexual behavior, pregnancy, and parenthood seemed to be discussed as medical matters, not universal (or almost universal) experiences of adolescents and young adult women. We started our work exploring social cognitions as well as stereotypes about menstruation (Brooks, Ruble, & Clarke, 1977; Ruble & Brooks-Gunn, 1979; Ruble, Boggiano, & Brooks-Gunn, 1982), moving on to menarche (Brooks-Gunn & Ruble, 1982; 1983). We were curious as to whether a person's social expectations and beliefs would influence reports of biological and behavioral symptoms associated with these physiological events as well as whether time and place would play a role looking at familial influences (Ruble & Brooks-Gunn, 1982). We wanted to know how adolescents and adult women incorporated the experiences of menarche and menstruation into their sense of self.

The second arose out of the first, as Ruble and I met Anne Petersen at a conference on gender issues in what turned out to be a path-breaking meeting organized by Jacquie [Parsons] Eccles (Ruble, Brooks-Gunn, & Clarke, 1980). With Petersen, I expanded my interest from menarche to pubertal events, considering their role in adolescent behavior, relationships, and moods (Brooks-Gunn & Petersen, 1984), organizing three conferences on puberty (Brooks-Gunn & Petersen, 1983; 1991; Brooks-Gunn, Petersen, & Eichorn, 1985) as well as editing a fourth volume with Petersen's graduate student and my post-doctoral fellow Julia Graber (Graber, Brooks-Gunn, & Petersen, 1996). One of my favorite moments was when our book, *Girls at Puberty*, was reviewed in *Science*. It seemed as though this field of study had arrived.

The third involved the continuation of my work with Lewis. We obtained federal funding to establish of an institute to study biologically vulnerable children. A joint venture with the Department of Pediatrics at St. Lukes-Roosevelt Hospital and Columbia University's College of Physicians and Surgeons allowed for a research laboratory to be built at the hospital on the Upper West Side of Manhattan (little did I know that I would continue at Columbia as a Professor later on). Our research portfolio included the study of low-birth-weight children and their families. It was the first time that I had worked with children considered at risk for developmental problems. And, we worked with families who were environmentally disadvantaged (given that the incidence of low birth weight is higher for poor, low-education, minority women) as well as thinking about how to ameliorate cognitive, linguistic, and emotional problems (Brooks-Gunn & Hearn, 1982). In the next decade, I would be involved in a multi-site intervention involving low-birth-weight children with Ruby Hearn, my co-author on that pediatrics review (The Infant Health and Development Program Staff, 1990).

Adding Longitudinal Studies and Experimental Evaluations

Now that I was spending more time at the hospital research laboratory in New York, I was introduced to other researchers as well as to policy scholars (in academia, the government, and foundations). A quartet of amazing opportunities arose, two focusing on my continuing interest in the social cognitive implications of reproductive events in adolescence and young adulthood and two targeting intervention strategies for vulnerable children and their families. While it seemed that my research was now poised to follow two somewhat independent themes, one focusing on children and the other on adolescence, these came together in the next decade through the addition of longer-term longitudinal studies and my interest in relationships as conceptualized as inter-generational exchanges.

The first was an expansion of the research on puberty and menarche with Michelle Warren, a reproductive endocrinologist at Columbia University which wonderfully, continues today. She had been studying delayed puberty, hypo-estrogen states, and osteopenia using classical dancers as a model, since they are expected to be quite thin and since dance is quite anaerobic (Warren, 1983). We designed a series of studies involving longitudinal follow-up of several groups of athletes as well as non-athletic girls, looking at a series of issues including the psychological significance of different pubertal events to girls (Brooks-Gunn, 1984; Brooks-Gunn, Warren, Samuelson, & Fox, 1986; Brooks-Gunn & Warren, 1988), the antecedents of delayed menarche (Brooks-Gunn & Warren, 1988; Graber, Brooks-Gunn, & Warren, 1995), the consequences of differential timing of puberty especially with respect to body image, dating, depression, eating disorders, and relationships with parents (Attie & Brooks-Gunn, 1989; Brooks-Gunn & Warren, 1985, 1989; Carlton-Ford, Paikoff, Oakley, & Brooks-Gunn, 1996; Gargiulo, Attie, Brooks-Gunn, & Warren, 1987; Paikoff, Brooks-Gunn, & Carlton-Ford, 1991; Paikoff & Brooks-Gunn, 1991), links between hormonal status, timing of puberty and girls' behavior and health (Brooks-Gunn, Graber, & Paikoff, 1994; Dhuper, Warren, Brooks-Gunn, & Fox, 1990; Warren, Brooks-Gunn, Hamilton, Hamilton, & Warren, 1986; Paikoff, Brooks-Gunn, & Warren, 1991; Warren et al., 1991). In collaboration with Julia Graber, Warren and I also initiated a longitudinal study of girls and boys, starting at age 10, when pubertal changes are just beginning to occur. In addition to examining HPG pubertal hormones, we also looked at the HPA axis, both in terms of hormonal profiles and in terms of response (measured by cortisol changes) to social, cognitive, and biological challenges. These pubertal studies continued into the next decade with new students and post-doctoral fellows (DeRose, Shiyko, Foster, & Brooks-Gunn, 2011; Foster, Hagan, Brooks-Gunn, 2008; Graber, Nichols, & Brooks-Gunn, 2010; Mendle, Harden, Brooks-Gunn, & Graber, 2010; 2012; Obeidallah, Brennan, Brooks-Gunn, & Earls, 2005; Sontag, Graber, Brooks-Gunn, & Warren, 2008; Tyrka et al., 2012).

The second was an extension of my interest in adolescent reproductive events to sexual behavior, pregnancy, and parenthood (Brooks-Gunn & Furstenberg, 1989; Furstenberg, Brooks-Gunn, & Chase Lansdale, 1989). I was fortunate to meet sociologist Frank Furstenberg, Jr. at a conference where we decided to follow-up his sample of teenage mothers from Baltimore 17 years after they had first given birth (Baydar, Brooks-Gunn, & Furstenberg, 1993; Brooks-Gunn, Guo, & Furstenberg, 1993; Furstenberg, Brooks-Gunn & Morgan, 1987; Furstenberg, Levine, & Brooks-Gunn, 1990; Guo, Brooks-Gunn, & Harris, 1996). In summary, the teenage mothers were not doing as poorly in their thirties as commentary at the time would have one believe; only one-quarter were on welfare continuously and one-quarter were doing quite well. Factors that predicted doing well included attendance at a school for pregnant teens, having lived with the family during the first years after the child's birth and then moving out (using the family as a secure base and as a support for the child while the mother finished school and starting working), and not having an early marriage and divorce. Since then we have used other data sets to look at the timing of leaving the family household and its association with maternal and child outcomes (Gordon, Chase-Lansdale, Matjasko, & Brooks-Gunn, 1997; Pope et al., 1993). At the same time, their offspring did not seem to be faring as well, leading us to think about the conditions of childhood that are related to lower educational attainment and achievement as well as behavioral problems, an interest that has continued today.

Being exposed to different disciplinary approaches to research; conducting a study on a sample which I had not seen in earlier waves; doing qualitative interviews with some of the adolescent offspring of the original teenage mothers; mastering sociological statistical techniques (with the help of our co-author Phillip Morgan); designing surveys for field staff to administer rather than my graduate students; participating in policy debates about the consequences of teenage parenthood; thinking about prevention strategies—I had a steep learning curve. It moved me into social science perspectives other than psychology (just as the collaborations with Warren provided me insight into endocrinology and health). I had caught the life-course bug, which moved me to larger life-course data sets (Brooks-Gunn, Phelps, & Elder, 1991; Chase-Lansdale, Mott, Brooks-Gunn, & Phillips, 1991). This meant that much of my work did not focus exclusively on the adolescent period, but began to include adolescence as one life stage (or two, if we consider the early years separately from the later years (in my reproductive framework, puberty and related school, peer and family events were the domain of early adolescence and sexuality, pregnancy, and parenthood of late adolescence).

Given my abiding interest in how parents influence their children over time and how family effects are transmitted across generations, I added a more psychologically oriented piece to the Baltimore Study in collaboration with Lindsay Chase-Lansdale. We obtained funding to observe some of the Baltimore families who had added a third generation, specifically a toddler born to one of the offspring of the original teenage mothers. We videotaped the grandmother (original teen mother), the mother, and the toddler in triads and dyads, in order to see if parenting practices were similar across generations (grandmother and mother individually with the toddler), which woman took a more active parenting role (when all three were together), and how the young mother resolved conflicts with her own mother (two adults together). We found some continuity in parenting (especially in harsher forms of parenting), high rates of detachment of the young mother in the triad situation, and large differences in self-representations, individuation, and autonomy in the youngest mothers during the mother–daughter conflict task (Chase-Lansdale, Brooks-Gunn, & Zansky, 1994; Wakschlag, Chase-Lansdale, & Brooks-Gunn, 1996). In general, the younger mothers' parenting behavior was either harsh or detached, a finding that we replicated in a much larger sample of poor mothers in Early Head Start (Berlin, Brady-Smith, & Brooks-Gunn, 2002) where we were able to control for many other familial characteristics.

Because of my work on the Baltimore study, I met Janet Hardy, a Professor of Pediatrics at Johns Hopkins University who had been one of the original investigators in the Collaborative Perinatal Study which was conducted in the early 1960s and had involved about 50,000 births across the country. Hardy and her colleague epidemiologist Sam Shapiro were going to follow-up the Baltimore sample of the larger Perinatal Study. I joined them as a co-investigator, helping design the almost 30-year follow-up survey of mothers and their children. I was much more confident this time around (thanks to Furstenberg). We published several articles on the consequences of teenage parenthood as well as the inter-generational continuity in early childbearing (Hardy et al., 1997; Hardy, Astone, Brooks-Gunn, Shapiro, & Miller, 1998). Since great longitudinal data sets have a very long life, I had the good fortune to use the Baltimore Perinatal Study with a post-doctoral fellow in the next decade, to look at associations between perinatal conditions and adolescent and adult outcomes (given my earlier interest in the biologically vulnerable infant who is born too early or too light; Nomura et al., 2009; Nomura, Rajendran, Brooks-Gunn, & Newcorn, 2008; Nomura et al., 2007).

The segue to research with low-birth-weight children was deliberate here, since I became involved in several projects related to perinatal health and child outcomes at this time, in large part due to my introduction to Marie McCormick, now a Professor of Pediatrics and Public Health at Harvard University. She involved me in a multi-site follow-up of low-birth-weight infants as their team did not have a developmental psychologist. Here, I learned about how epidemiologists do longitudinal research and how more public health and medical models are different, and complement, life-course sociology and psychology models. We focused on very-low-birth-weight children, given that more of them were surviving given medical successes in the neonatal intensive-care units (Klebanov, Brooks-Gunn, & McCormick, 1994a, 1994b; McCormick, Brooks-Gunn, Workman-Daniels, Turner, & Peckham, 1992; McCormick, Workman-Daniels, Brooks-Gunn, & Peckham, 1993).

McCormick and I were offered two other amazing research opportunities at this time, both of which were related to intervention. One focused on reducing the incidence of low-birth-weight births; it was a public health outreach model (with an economic incentive given to the outreach staff) to locate pregnant women who were not enrolled in prenatal care, which was based in Harlem Hospital (like St. Lukes-Roosevelt Hospital, one of the Columbia University affiliate hospitals). While a natural extension of my work with the urban poor in Baltimore, both teenage and old mothers were included (Brooks-Gunn et al., 1989; McCormick et al., 1987, 1989, 1990). The second opportunity involved the design and implementation of an early intervention program for premature, low-birth-weight infants (the Infant Health and Development Program), which was a randomized trial where the treatment group received home visiting in the first 3 years of life and a high-quality center-based program for the second 2 years of life. The eight-site intervention was very successful, as the treatment children had higher IQ and language scores and lower behavior problems at age 3 (The Infant Health and Development Program Staff, 1990). We have followed this cohort through childhood and adolescence, finding sustained effects (through age 18) for children whose birth weights were 2,000 grams or more (what we term heavier low-birth-weight infants; Brooks-Gunn et al., 1994; McCarton et al., 1997; McCormick et al., 2006). I learned a tremendous amount about randomized clinical trials from this experience. And, our group is still analyzing these data, looking at issues such as dose effects, differential efficacy of the home visiting and center-based aspects of the intervention, effects of interventions depending the counter factual, and engagement in the program (all non-experimental analyses by definition) (Hill, Brooks-Gunn, & Waldfogel, 2003; Hill, Waldfogel, & Brooks-Gunn, 2002; Klebanov, & Brooks-Gunn, 2006; Liaw, Meisels, & Brooks-Gunn, 1995) and have extended these propensity matching procedures to other data sets to ask similar questions (Lee, Zhai, Brooks-Gunn, Han, & Waldfogel, in press; Zhai, Brooks-Gunn, & Waldfogel, 2011; Zhai, Waldfogel, & Brooks-Gunn, in press). Cohort comparisons suggest that earlier evaluations of early childhood education might exhibit larger effects, since children who were in the control groups were much more likely to be cared for by their mothers (i.e., fewer mothers worked and there were fewer child-care opportunities, Brooks-Gunn, 2011). Our group is also attempting to understand how the child-care subsidy program works, in terms of who obtains subsidies, how obtaining a subsidy influences type and perhaps quality of child care, and whether children's outcomes are affected by subsidy receipt (Holod, Johnson, Martin, Gardner, & Brooks-Gunn, 2012, Johnson, Martin, & Brooks-Gunn, 2011; Ryan, Johnson, Rigby, & Brooks-Gunn, 2011). And, as stated previously, I am involved in Early Head Start Evaluation (Love, Chazen-Cohen, Raiches, & Brooks-Gunn, 2013) and the Home Visiting National Evaluation (Duggan et al., in press), with our center staff having coded over 6,000 parent–child interactions, which were videotaped in Early Head Start (Brady-Smith, et al., 2013; Fuligni et al., 2013; Fuligni & Brooks-Gunn, 2013).

As a complement to this prevention research with young children, Jody Roth, Margo Gardner, and I have been examining the influences of extracurricular activities and after school programs on outcomes of children and adolescents using various data sets (Gardner, Roth, & Brooks-Gunn, 2008; Roth, Malone, & Brooks-Gunn, 2010; Roth & Brooks-Gunn, 2003a; 2003b; Roth, Brooks-Gunn, Murray, & Foster, 1998). This work is not based on randomized trials.

Extending Life-Course Research and Prevention

Until this decade, my research on disadvantaged children and mothers (both biologically and environmentally, with the former more likely in cases of the latter) was contained to specific groups (low-birth-weight children, teenage mothers, urban poor (primarily Black) families). Meeting economist Greg Duncan was to enlarge my agenda to a wider spectrum of disadvantage as well as to larger, nationally representative samples of families. Duncan offered me the chance to learn about economic theory related to families, and we found common group between our two disciplinary approaches. He was already doing life-course research, directing the Panel Study of Income Dynamics (PSID), a representative panel of individuals drawn in the late 1960s and augmented as each individual entered a new household (through marriage, divorce, birth) such that extensive information is available on at least three generations within families (Brooks-Gunn, Berlin, Leventhal, & Fuligni, 2000). We decided to focus on family income (not surprising for an economist) with attention to other family characteristics such as parental education, age, and residence as well as a secondary interest in family structure. Using a series of data sets, we argued that low income was associated with achievement and educational attainment, especially if income was very low (deep poverty), persistent, and early (Brooks-Gunn, & Duncan, 1997; Duncan, Brooks-Gunn, & Klebanov, 1994; Duncan & Brooks-Gunn, 1997). These effects were modest, but withstood rigorous

attempts to control for other family characteristics (or selection; Duncan, Yeung, Brooks-Gunn, & Smith, 1998).

We extended our models to test the mediators of links between income (and education) and child outcomes, with a focus on cognitive stimulation in the home (Learning Stimulation Model), the purchase of goods to enhance child learning (Income Model), maternal depression and harsh parenting (the Family Stress Model). In general, the Family Stress model seems to be pre-eminent when looking at behavioral outcomes and the Learning Stimulation model when considering achievement (Klebanov, Brooks-Gunn, McCarton, & McCormick, 1998; Linver, Brooks-Gunn, & Kohen, 2002; Yeung, Linver, & Brooks-Gunn, 2002). We have extended the model (Johnson, Martin, Brooks-Gunn, & Petrill, 2008) to consider parental organization, chaos, and planfulness (a favorite study looked at effects of living in a clean house which lasted over several generations controlling for every possible confounder that existed in the PSID; Dunifon, Duncan, & Brooks-Gunn, 2001, 2004). This work parallels the "discovery" by economists that school attainment and wages are not solely determined by cognitive skills, and that what they term non-cognitive skills may play a role.

In a vein related to an interest in poverty, I became interested in employment and welfare receipt, as the first increases family income but possibly reduces parental time spent with children and as the second also provides cash but does so independently of parental work. Our group did a series of analyses looking at correlations and consequences of welfare receipt, as well as whether transitions on and off welfare are linked to child outcomes (Brady-Smith, Brooks-Gunn, Waldfogel, & Fauth, 2001; Brooks-Gunn, Klebanov, Smith, & Lee, 2001; Jackson, Brooks-Gunn, Huang, & Glassman, 2000; Smith, Brooks-Gunn, Klebanov, & Lee, 2000). When my son was born, I wondered whether working in the first year of life had any detrimental impacts. The National Longitudinal Study of Youth was used, which followed the children born to the women of that sample (Chase-Lansdale, Mott, Brooks-Gunn, & Phillips, 1991), finding modest links between early employment and cognition (Baydar & Brooks-Gunn, 1991). With Jane Waldfogel and others, I went to other data sets to see if the finding replicated, which it did with important caveats (somewhat similar to the links between income and cognitions). These modest findings appeared in White families but not Black families, they were restricted to early full-time employment (sometimes children of mothers who worked part time during the first year were faring best), and they did not extend to employment past 9 or 12 months (Berger, Brooks-Gunn, Paxson, & Waldfogel, 2008; Han, Waldfogel, & Brooks-Gunn, 2001; Hill, Waldfogel, Brooks-Gunn, & Han 2005; Brooks-Gunn, Waldfogel, & Han, 2002). To unpack these findings, we examined early employment links via structural equation modeling, which revealed that employment had beneficial effects based on its increase in family income and negative effects in terms of mothers' depressive symptoms (Brooks-Gun, Han, & Waldfogel, 2010; Chatterji, Markowitz, & Brooks-Gunn, 2013). In terms of children's wellbeing at age 7, these offsetting influences rendered employment in and of itself not significant.

At the same time that Duncan and I were investigating family income through a NICHD Research Network, we conducted some analyses attaching Census tract level data to the PSID and the IHDP (Brooks-Gunn, Duncan, Klebanov, & Sealand, 1993). We were invited to a Social Science Research Council (SSRC) meeting on the role of the neighborhood in the lives of children, youth, and families. The SSRC group began a series of analyses with extant data sets, which culminated in two edited volumes (Brooks-Gunn, Duncan, & Aber, 1997). I was sold on attempting to parse out effects of neighborhood and family influences as well as understand how each influenced the other.[6]

Later on, Tony (Felton) Earls, Rob Sampson, and Steve Raudenbush invited me to join their path-breaking work in Chicago, sampling neighborhoods and then recruiting families via canvas within processes had been done. The Project on Human Development in Chicago Neighborhoods was conducted in 80 neighborhoods (stratified by social class and ethnic mix) and several age cohorts were drawn (birth, 3, 6, 9, 12, 15, and 18 years), yielding a representative sample of Chicago children from the mid-1990s. Our group began analyses in the mid-2000s, with our work continuing to the present (Bingenheimer, Leventhal, Raudenbush, & Brooks-Gunn, 2005; Brooks-Gunn, Phelps, & Elder, 1991; Browning, Leventhal, & Brooks-Gunn, 2004, 2005; Lara-Cinisomo, Xue, & Brooks-Gunn, in press; Obeidallah, Brennan, Brooks-Gunn, & Earls, 2005; Riina, Martin, Gardner, & Brooks-Gunn, in press; Xue, Leventhal, Brooks-Gunn, & Earls, 2005).

Conclusion: Integrating Biology and Environment into Life-Course and Prevention Research

My most recent experience with a birth cohort study has been exciting and gratifying. Sociologist Sara McLanahan and economist Irv Garfinkel began the Fragile Families and Child Well-being Study in order to understand the life course of families in which the parents are unwed at the child's birth. Twenty cities were selected (16 from a stratified random draw of cities which varied on three dimensions—generosity of welfare benefits, stringency of child support regulations, and levels of unemployment). A sample of married couples was also drawn (Garfinkel, McLanahan Tienda, & Brooks-Gunn, 2001). The families were seen at birth (both mothers and fathers primarily in the hospital) and the parents were interviewed when the children were 1, 3, 5, and 9 years of age. Children were assessed at ages 3, 5, and 9 as well (and their home environments observed). Currently, we are busily working to raise money to continue the Fragile Families birth cohort into adolescence, atleast through age 15 and hopefully beyond. Given my long-term fascination with adolescents, the opportunity to start looking at childhood and adolescent trajectories along with maternal, paternal, and school influences is very gratifying. We are pleased that over one thousand researchers are currently using

the data, with even more likely to do so when the age 15 interviews are completed and on-line. And, we are doing analyses to tease apart influences of various environmental conditions (parental education, income, and employment, as well as family structure and instability at the household and neighborhood level; Waldfogel, Craigie, & Brooks-Gunn, 2010). Another question had to do with how parents' interactions with their children, their mental health, and their life stressors mediated or moderated influences of family characteristics and stability (Cooper, McLanahan, Meadows, & Brooks-Gunn, 2009; DeKlyen, Brooks-Gunn, McLanahan, & Knab, 2006; Meadows, McLanahan, & Brooks-Gunn, 2007; Ryan, Tolani, & Brooks-Gunn, 2009). We also considered how the mother–father relationship played out over time (Howard & Brooks-Gunn, 2009b), and what factors predicted continuing father involvement and co-parenting in families where the father was not physically present (Carlson, McLanahan, & Brooks-Gunn, 2008). More thought is now being given to the timing of family events, as well as changes in family circumstances in predicting children's health, school engagement and achievement, and behavior problems (Mitchell et al., in press).

None of the above is particularly surprising for a scholar of the life course and development today. The availability of such a rich data set, one that includes unwed couples and interviews with the fathers as well as the mothers is, though. In addition, a few birth cohorts, i.e., samples that have been first seen in the hospital; the other nationally representative sample—Early Childhood Longitudinal Study-Birth Cohort—first saw families when children were 9 months of age) in the United States follow children into adolescence and beyond (Brooks-Gunn et al., 2000).

One avenue of data collection has moved me in an unexpected direction, yet one very congruent with my previous work as a developmental psychologist. At the 9-year follow-up, we decided to collect DNA from the mothers and children during the home visit. We began working with Dan Notterman, a pediatric geneticist at the Pennsylvania State University, who provided seminars on genetics and DNA assaying techniques. I never expected to be learning about this topic, at least at this age. It was totally engaging to be, in a sense, back in the classroom as a student again (and a bit daunting; I still do not feel comfortable presenting our DNA data to a room full of biologists). And, of course, I am now learning about epigenetics, telomeres, and differential responses of different tissues to environmental events. The opportunity to look at the intersection of person and place via DNA is so exciting. After all, this interaction is a central feature of developmental psychological theory and was studied long before DNA assaying techniques. My work on hormonal changes during puberty, cortisol reactivity during early adolescence, and person characteristics as moderators of environmental effects all are based on notions of person by environment interactions. After all, my very first research publication involved twins. An article in the *Psychology Monitor* described me as "giddy with excitement" about the gene by environment interaction research. While I was not thrilled about the use of the term giddy to describe me, the feeling is genuine. I am loving this new research line (Mitchell et al., 2011).

Another new project involves the continuation of my interest in place as neighborhood and also as building unit. I am working with the New York City Housing and Preservation Development (HPD) on a multi-phase interdisciplinary study that will examine the impact of moving to city-sponsored subsidized housing on households across a range of incomes (not the poorest of the poor) and neighborhoods of residence, utilizing a randomized sample of households who apply and are eligible for subsidized housing through New York City's housing lottery system. Sociologist Elizabeth Gaumer is heading the HPD team and we are currently completing baseline intake for the lottery in the 12th building site. We hope to have over 2,000 families enrolled in the evaluation. A novel variant is that we are able to stratify the randomization, so that we will have a sample of families who move into the new buildings within their current neighborhood and another sample of families who move into the new buildings from a different neighborhood. This design allows us to separate out the effects of moving from effects of neighborhood, which the Moving to Opportunity evaluation (five-city, randomized trial of poor families in public housing who signed up to be randomized into three groups—stayers, movers with the usual section 8 voucher, and movers with a special voucher requiring moving to a neighborhood with low levels of poverty) was unable to do (Sabonmatsu, Kling, Duncan, & Brooks-Gunn, 2006), nor have other such demonstrations like the Yonkers Project (which moved families from projects to scattered site cluster housing; Fauth, Leventhal, & Brooks-Gunn, 2004). Doing a specific study of housing has been especially meaningful, since my father and brother built and managed low-income and affordable housing throughout Western Michigan.

And my interest in neighborhood as place continues with new analyses using the Project on Human Development in Chicago Neighborhoods with Chris Browning, Margo Gardner, and Martin and Tama Leventhal (Browning, Leventhal, & Brooks-Gunn, 2004; Browning, Burrington, Leventhal, & Brooks-Gunn, 2008; Gardner & Brooks-Gunn, 2009; Gardner, Roth, and Brooks-Gunn, 2009; Gardner, Martin, and Brooks-Gunn, 2012; Leventhal & Brooks-Gunn, 2011; Maimon, Browing, & Brooks-Gunn, 2010), particularly with respect to adolescent behavior. Rob Sampson is talking about a follow-up of these youth (about a decade since the last visit), which would really allow for an examination of long-term correlates of neighborhoods as well as of the timing of particular types of neighborhood residence on wellbeing. Speaking of follow-ups, I continue my interest in life course work as embedded in prevention research. The potential for seeing the children who received early childhood intervention from Early Head Start and from the Infant Health and Development Program also exists; given the interest in sustained effects (and the possibility of sleeper effects) in intervention, it is likely that these samples will be seen in late adolescence and adulthood. Now as a member of Larry Scheinhart's and Jim Heckman's team seeing the Perry Preschool children at age 50, the possibilities for collecting psychological, economic, criminal, and biological indicators of wellbeing are endless (although severely constrained by the length of time that respondents will put up with us researchers). In brief, I am still engaged in issues relating to the life course and development, albeit with slightly new twists. Our fields of inquiry keep scholars invested in learning and applying new methods and measures to the study of how individuals develop over time and place, and how the timing and accumulation of certain events lead to different life-course trajectories. Not only have I had the opportunity to be involved in amazing projects and to learn from my colleagues especially from different disciplines, but I have had the honor of being recognized for my work (or, our work) as well as being asked to consult on many policy and research issues. I look forward to being more active in the National Academies Institute of Medicine, the National Institute of Education, and the American Academy of Political and Social Science as I have been elected to these three invitational academies. Life-time awards from the Society for Research in Adolescence, the Society for Research in Child Development, the American Psychological Association, and the American Psychological Society have been such an honor as a developmental psychologist. And, a special thrill was being awarded an honorary doctorate from Northwestern University, which my father attended as a poor farm boy from Michigan. My research life is, and continues to be, a great ride.

Acknowledgments

It has been a pleasure to work on this volume with my incredible colleagues—Rich Lerner, Anne Petersen, and Rainer Silberiesen—all of whom have enriched my research, my theoretical thinking, and my life. And, to all of my students, colleagues, and mentors—nothing would have been accomplished without you. Whenever I am honored with an award, I always think that it ought to have gone to all of you as well. Clearly, a life of research (or anything else) takes a team that includes not only other scholars but administrative staff, grant officers, cleaning staff, finance wizards, travel agents (in the old days), computer-savvy friends, family, and IT folks, university deans, department chairs, policy makers, funders, nannies, and sometimes physical therapists (to repair the damage done by decades of lugging tons of paper around and sitting at disk-compressing desks for hours and hours) not to mention, in my case, the folks who keep my little boat running in the summer, who keep giving me new tips about GPS devices (it was easier with the compass and stopwatch) so I can get to the mainland with reliable computer access and more importantly, to my sweet sailboat. And, of course my beloved husband (now deceased), my beyond wonderful son, and my loving extended family who have encouraged me all along and who have put up with my multi-tasking for years with good grace. My gal pals have also been a welcome support (sisters and sisters-in-laws, the East Grand Rapids 12 from the Class of '65, the Squirrel Island Circle of Fire, and the Sourland Mountain neighbors), and their spouses and children.

Notes

1. Rather than University of Minnesota (John Flavell) or to Cornell University (Urie Bronfenbrenner)
2. Shelley Taylor, Rena Wing, and myself.
3. Kohlberg on social cognitive developmental theory, Pettigrew on discrimination and prejudice, Jencks on social stratification, and Whiting on cross-cultural child development and gender differences.
4. Including Marsha Weinraub, Nathan Fox, Candance Feiring, Deborah Coates, Carol Copple, Jeannette Haviland, Rod Cocking, Marci Hansen, Harry McGurk.
5. Including Walter Emmerick, Irv Siegel, Gordon Hale, Vicki Shipman, Roy Freedle, Sam Mesick, Howard Winer, Don Rock, Henry Braun.
6. From a life-course perspective, it is interesting that one explanation for the lack of early maternal employment-child outcome link for Black mothers is selection into the workforce; Black and White mothers who were working had different characteristics than those who were not; selection was greater for White than Black mothers, as the latter, being more likely to be single and poor, were more likely to enter the work force. Over time, these differences have probably narrowed, as more White women stayed in the work force after the birth of a child than in previous cohorts.

References

Attie, I., & Brooks-Gunn, J. (1989). The development of eating problems in adolescent girls: A longitudinal study. *Developmental Psychology, 25*, 70–79.

Baydar, N., & Brooks-Gunn, J. (1991). Effects of maternal employment and child-care arrangements on preschoolers' cognitive and behavioral outcomes: Evidence from the Children of the National Longitudinal Survey of Youth. *Developmental Psychology, 27*, 932–945.

Baydar, N., Brooks-Gunn, J., & Furstenberg, F. F., Jr. (1993). Early warning signs of functional illiteracy: Predictors in childhood and adolescence. *Child Development, 64*, 815–829.

Berger, L., Brooks-Gunn, J., Paxson, C., & Waldfogel, J. (2008). First-year maternal employment and child outcomes: Differences across racial and ethnic groups. *Children and Youth Services Review, 30*, 365–387.

Berlin, L. J., Brady-Smith, C., & Brooks-Gunn, J. (2002). Links between childbearing age and observed maternal behaviors with 14-month-olds in the Early Head Start Research and Evaluation Project. *Infant Mental Health Journal, 23*, 104–129.

Bingenheimer, J., Leventhal, T., Raudenbush, S., & Brooks-Gunn, J. (2005). Measurement equivalence and differential item functioning in family psychology. *Journal of Family Psychology, 19*, 441–445.

Brady-Smith, C., Brooks-Gunn, J., Tamis-LeMonda, C. S., Ispa, J. M., Fuligni, A. S., Chazan-Cohen, R. et al. (2013). Mothers' interactions with infants: A person-oriented, within ethnic group approach. *Parenting: Science and Practice, 13*, 27–43.

Brady-Smith, C., Brooks-Gunn, J., Waldfogel, J., & Fauth, R. (2001). Work or welfare? Assessing the impacts of recent employment and policy changes on very young children. *Evaluation and Program Planning, 24*, 409–425.

Brooks, J. & Lewis, M. (1974). Attachment behavior in thirteen-month-old, opposite-sex twins. *Child Development, 45*, 243–247.

Brooks, J., & Lewis, M. (1976). Infants' responses to strangers: Midget, adult, and child. *Child Development, 4*, 323–332.

Brooks, J., Ruble, D. N., & Clarke, A. (1977). College women's attitudes and expectations concerning menstrual-related changes. *Psychosomatic Medicine, 39*, 288–298.

Brooks-Gunn, J. (1984). The psychological significance of different pubertal events to young girls. *Journal of Early Adolescence, 4*, 315–327.

Brooks-Gunn, J. (1986). The relationship of maternal beliefs about sex typing to maternal and young children's behavior. *Sex Roles, 14*, 21–35.

Brooks-Gunn, J. (1996). Unexpected opportunities: Confessions of an eclectic developmentalist. In M. Merrens & G. Brannigan (Eds.), *The developmental psychologists: Research adventures across the lifespan* (pp. 152–171). Boston: McGraw-Hill.

Brooks-Gunn, J. (2011). Early childhood education: The likelihood of sustained effects. In E. Zigler, W. S. Gilliam, & W. S. Barnett (Eds.), *The pre-K debates: Current controversies and issues* (pp. 200–205). Baltimore, MD: Brookes Publishing.

Brooks-Gunn, J., Berlin, L. J., Leventhal, T., & Fuligni, A. (2000). Depending on the kindness of strangers: Current national data initiatives and developmental research. *Child Development, 71*, 257–267.

Brooks-Gunn, J., & Duncan, G. J. (1997). The effects of poverty on children. *Future of Children, 7*, 55–71.

Brooks-Gunn, J., Duncan, G. J., & Aber, J. L. (Eds.). (1997). *Neighborhood poverty: Context and consequences for children (Vol. 1). Policy implications in studying neighborhoods (Vol. 2)*. New York: Russell Sage.

Brooks-Gunn, J., Duncan, G. J., Klebanov, P. K., & Sealand, N. (1993). Do neighborhoods influence child and adolescent development? *American Journal of Sociology, 99*, 353–395.

Brooks-Gunn, J., & Furstenberg, F. F., Jr. (1989). Adolescent sexual behavior. *American Psychologist, 44*, 249–257.

Brooks-Gunn, J., Graber, J. A., & Paikoff, R. L. (1994). Studying links between hormones and negative affect: Models and measures. *Journal of Research on Adolescence, 4*, 469–486.

Brooks-Gunn, J., Guo, G., & Furstenberg, F. F., Jr. (1993). Who drops out of and who continues beyond high school?: A 20-year follow-up of black urban youth. *Journal of Research on Adolescence, 3*(3), 271–294.

Brooks-Gunn, J., Han, W.-J., & Waldfogel, J. (2010). First-year maternal employment and child development in the first seven years. *Monographs of the Society for Research in Child Development, 75*(2).

Brooks-Gunn, J., & Hearn, R. (1982). Early intervention and developmental dysfunction: Implications for pediatrics. *Advances in Pediatrics, 29*, 497–527.

Brooks-Gunn, J., Klebanov, P. K., Smith, J. R., & Lee, K. (2001). Effects of combining public assistance and employment on mothers and their young children. *Women and Health, 32*, 179–210.

Brooks-Gunn, J., & Lewis, M. (1979). "Why mama and papa?": The development of social labels. *Child Development, 50*, 1203–1206.

Brooks-Gunn, J., & Lewis, M. (1981). Infant social perception: Responses to pictures of parents and strangers. *Developmental Psychology, 17*, 647–649.

Brooks-Gunn, J., & Lewis, M. (1984). The development of early visual self-recognition. *Developmental Review, 4*, 215–239.

Brooks-Gunn, J., & Matthews, W. (1979). *He and she: How children develop their sex-role identity*. Englewood Cliffs, NJ: Prentice-Hall.

Brooks-Gunn, J., McCarton, C., Casey, P., McCormick, M., Bauer, C., Bernbaum, J. et al. (1994). Early intervention in low birth weight, premature infants: Results through age 5 years from the Infant Health and Development Program. *Journal of the American Medical Association, 272*, 1257–1262.

Brooks-Gunn, J., McCormick, M., Gunn, R. W., Shorter, T., Wallace, C. Y., & Heagarty, M. C. (1989). Outreach as case finding: The Process of locating low-income pregnant women. *Medical Care, 27*, 95–102.

Brooks-Gunn, J., & Petersen, A. C. (Eds.). (1983). *Girls at puberty: Biological and psychosocial perspectives*. New York: Plenum.

Brooks-Gunn, J., & Petersen, A. C. (1984). Problems in studying and defining pubertal events. *Journal of Youth and Adolescence, 13*, 181–196.

Brooks-Gunn, J., & Petersen, A. C. (Eds.). (1991). The emergence of depression and depressive symptoms during adolescence. *Journal of Youth and Adolescence, 20*(1 & 2).

Brooks-Gunn, J., Petersen, A. C., & Eichorn, D. (Eds.). (1985). Time of maturation and psychosocial functioning in adolescence. *Journal of Youth and Adolescence, 14* (3 & 4).

Brooks-Gunn, J., Phelps, E., & Elder, G. H. (1991). Studying lives through time: Secondary data analyses in developmental psychology. *Developmental Psychology, 27*, 899–910.

Brooks-Gunn, J., & Ruble, D. N. (1982). The development of menstrual-related beliefs and behaviors during early adolescence. *Child Development, 53*, 1567–1577.

Brooks-Gunn, J., & Ruble, D. N. (1983). The experience of menarche from a developmental perspective. In J. Brooks-Gunn & A. C. Petersen (Eds.), *Girls at puberty: Biological and psychosocial perspectives* (pp. 155–177). New York: Plenum.

Brooks-Gunn, J., Waldfogel, J., & Han, W.-J. (2002). Maternal employment and child cognitive outcomes in the first three years of life: The NICHD Study of Early Childcare. *Child Development, 73*, 1052–1072.

Brooks-Gunn, J., & Warren, M. P. (1985). The effects of delayed menarche in different contexts: Dance and non-dance students. *Journal of Youth and Adolescence, 14*, 285–300.

Brooks-Gunn, J., & Warren, M. P. (1988). The psychological significance of secondary sexual characteristics in 9- to 11-year-old girls. *Child Development, 59*, 1061–1069.

Brooks-Gunn, J., & Warren, M. P. (1989). Biological and social contributions to negative affect in young adolescent girls. *Child Development, 60*, 372–385.

Brooks-Gunn, J., Warren, M. P., Samelson, M., & Fox, R. (1986). Physical similarity of and disclosure of menarcheal status to friends: Effects of age and pubertal status. *Journal of Early Adolescence, 6*, 3–14.

Browning, C. R., Burrington, L., Leventhal, T., & Brooks-Gunn, J. (2008). Neighborhood structural inequality, collective efficacy, and sexual risk behavior among urban youth. *Journal of Health and Social Behavior, 49*, 269–285.

Browning, C., Leventhal, T., & Brooks-Gunn, J. (2004). Neighborhood context and racial differences in early adolescent sexual activity. *Demography, 41*, 697–720.

Browning, C., Leventhal, T., & Brooks-Gunn, J. (2005). Sexual initiation in early adolescence: The nexus of parental and community control. *American Sociological Review, 70*, 758–778.

Carlson, M. J., McLanahan, S. S., & Brooks-Gunn, J. (2008). Coparenting and nonresident fathers' involvement with young children after a nonmarital birth. *Demography, 45*, 461–488.

Carlton-Ford, S., Paikoff, R., Oakley, J., & Brooks-Gunn, J. (1996). A longitudinal analysis of depressed mood, self-esteem and family processes during adolescence. *Sociological Focus, 29*, 135–154.

Chase-Lansdale, P. L., & Brooks-Gunn, J. (Eds.). (1995). *Escape from poverty: What makes a difference for children?* New York: Cambridge University Press.

Chase-Lansdale, P. L., Brooks-Gunn, J., & Zamsky, E. S. (1994). Young African-American multigenerational families in poverty: Quality of mothering and grandmothering. *Child Development, 65*, 373–393.

Chase-Lansdale, P. L., Mott, F. L., Brooks-Gunn, J., & Phillips, D. (1991). Children of the NLSY: A unique research opportunity. *Developmental Psychology, 27*, 918–931.

Chatterji, P., Markowitz, S., & Brooks-Gunn, J. (2013). Effects of early maternal employment on maternal health and wellbeing. *Journal of Population Economics, 26*(1), 285–301. doi: 10.1007/s00148-012-0437-

Cooper, C. E., McLanahan, S., Meadows, S., & Brooks-Gunn, J. (2009). Family structure transitions and maternal parenting stress. *Journal of Family and Marriage, 71*, 558–574.

DeKlyen, M., Brooks-Gunn, J., McLanahan, S., & Knab, J. (2006). The mental health of married, cohabiting, and non-coresident parents with infants. *American Journal of Public Health, 96*, 1836–1841.

DeRose, L. M., Shiyko, M. P., Foster, H., & Brooks-Gunn, J. (2011). Associations between menarcheal timing and behavioral developmental trajectories for girls from age 6 to age 15. *The Journal of Youth and Adolescence, 40*, 1329–1342.

Dhuper, S., Warren, M. P., Brooks-Gunn, J., & Fox, R. (1990). Effects of hormonal status on bone density in adolescent girls. *Journal of Clinical Endocrinology and Metabolism, 71*, 1083–1087.

Duggan, A., Minkovitz, C., Chaffin, M., Korfmacher, J., Brooks-Gunn, J., Crowne, S. et al. (in press). Creating a national home visiting research network. *Pediatrics*.

Duncan, G. J., & Brooks-Gunn, J. (Eds.). (1997). *Consequences of growing up poor*. New York: Russell Sage.

Duncan, G. J., Brooks-Gunn, J., & Klebanov, P. K. (1994). Economic deprivation and early-childhood development. *Child Development, 65*, 296–318.

Duncan, G. J., Yeung, W. J., Brooks-Gunn, J., & Smith, J. R. (1998). How much does childhood poverty affect the life chances of children? *American Sociological Review, 63*, 406–423.

Dunifon, R., Duncan, G. J., & Brooks-Gunn, J. (2001). As ye sweep, so shall ye reap. *American Economic Review, 91*(2), 150–154.

Dunifon, R., Duncan, G. J., & Brooks-Gunn, J. (2004). The long-term impact of parental organization and efficiency. In A. Kalil & T. DeLeire (Eds.), *Family investments in children: Resources and behaviors that promote success* (pp. 85–118). Mahwah, NJ: Lawrence Erlbaum.

Fauth, R. C., Leventhal, T., & Brooks-Gunn, J. (2004). Short-term effects of moving from public housing in poor to affluent neighborhoods on low-income, minority adults' outcomes. *Social Science and Medicine, 59*, 2271–2284.

Foster, H., Hagan, J., & Brooks-Gunn, J. (2008). Growing up fast: Stress exposure and subjective weathering' in emerging adulthood. *Journal of Health and Social Behavior, 49*, 162–177.

Fuligni, A., Brady-Smith, C., Tamis-LeMonda, C., Bradley, R. H., Chazan-Cohen, R., Boyce, L. et al. (2013). Patterns of supportive parenting in the first 3 years of life: Correlates and consequences in low-income White, Black, and Latino families. *Parenting: Science and Practice, 13*, 44–57.

Fuligni, A., & Brooks-Gunn, J. (2013). Mother-child interactions in early Head Start: Age and ethnic differences in low-income dyads. *Parenting: Science and Practice, 13*, 1–26.

Furstenberg, F. F., Jr., Brooks-Gunn, J., & Chase-Lansdale, L. (1989). Teenaged pregnancy and childbearing. *American Psychologist, 44*, 313–320.

Furstenberg, F. F., Jr., Brooks-Gunn, J., & Morgan, S. P. (1987). *Adolescent mothers in later life*. New York, NY: Cambridge University.

Furstenberg, F. F., Jr., Levine, J. A., & Brooks-Gunn, J. (1990). The children of teenage mothers: Patterns of early childbearing in two generations. *Family Planning Perspectives, 22*, 54–61.

Gardner, M., & Brooks-Gunn, J. (2009). Adolescents' exposure to community violence: Are neighborhood youth organizations protective? *Journal of Community Psychology, 37*, 505–525.

Gardner, M., Martin, A., & Brooks-Gunn, J. (2012). Exploring the link between caregiver affect and adolescent sexual behavior: Does neighborhood disadvantage matter? *Journal of Research on Adolescence, 22*, 135–149.

Gardner, M., Roth, J., & Brooks-Gunn, J. (2008). Adolescents' participation in organized activities and developmental success two and eight years after high school: Do sponsorship, duration, and intensity matter? *Developmental Psychology, 44*, 814–830.

Gardner, M., Roth, J. L., & Brooks-Gunn, J. (2009). Sports participation and juvenile delinquency: The role of the peer context among adolescent boys and girls with varied histories of problem behavior. *Developmental Psychology, 45*, 341–353.

Garfinkel, I., McLanahan, S. S., Tienda, M., & Brooks-Gunn, J. (2001). Fragile families and welfare reform: An introduction. *Children and Youth Services Review, 23*, 277–301.

Gargiulo, J., Attie, I., Brooks-Gunn, J., & Warren, M. P. (1987). Girls' dating behavior as a function of social context and maturation. *Developmental Psychology, 23*, 730–737.

Gordon, R., Chase-Lansdale, P. L., Matjasko, J., & Brooks-Gunn, J. (1997). Young mothers living with grandmothers and living apart: How neighborhood and household contexts relate to multigenerational coresidence in African-American families. *Applied Developmental Science, 1*, 89–106.

Graber, J. A., Brooks-Gunn, J., & Petersen, A. C. (Eds.). (1996). *Transitions through adolescence: Interpersonal domains and context*. Mahwah, NJ: Lawrence Erlbaum.

Graber, J. A., Brooks-Gunn, J., & Warren, M. P. (1995). The antecedents of menarcheal age: Heredity, family environment and stressful life events. *Child Development, 66*, 346–359.

Graber, J. A., Nichols, T. R., & Brooks-Gunn, J. (2010). Putting pubertal timing in developmental context: Implications for prevention. *Developmental Psychobiology, 52*, 254–262.

Guo, G., Brooks-Gunn, J., & Harris, K. M. (1996). Parent's labor-force attachment and grade retention among urban Black children. *Sociology of Education, 69*, 217–236.

Han, W.-J., Waldfogel, J., & Brooks-Gunn, J. (2001). The effects of early maternal employment on later cognitive and behavioral outcomes. *Journal of Marriage and the Family, 63*, 336–354.

Hardy, J., Astone, N., Brooks-Gunn, J., Shapiro, S., & Miller, T. L. (1998). Like mother, like child: Intergenerational patterns of age at first birth and associations with childhood and adolescent characteristics and adult outcomes in the second generation. *Developmental Psychology, 34*, 1220–1232.

Hardy, J., Shapiro, S., Astone, N., Brooks-Gunn, J., Miller, T., & Hilton, S. (1997). Adolescent childbearing revisited: The age of inner-city mothers at delivery is a determinant of their children's self-sufficiency at age 27–33. *Pediatrics, 100*, 802–809.

Hill, J., Brooks-Gunn, J., & Waldfogel, J. (2003). Sustained effects of high participation in an early intervention for low-birth-weight premature infants. *Developmental Psychology, 39*, 730–744.

Hill, J., Waldfogel, J., & Brooks-Gunn, J. (2002). Differential effects of high-quality child care. *Journal of Policy Analysis and Management, 21*, 601–627.

Hill, J. L., Waldfogel, J., Brooks-Gunn, J., & Han, W.-J. (2005). Maternal employment and child development: A fresh look using newer methods. *Developmental Psychology, 41*, 833–850.

Holod, A., Johnson, A. D., Martin, A., Gardner, M., & Brooks-Gunn, J. (2012). Contracts, vouchers, and child care subsidy stability: A preliminary look at associations between subsidy payment mechanism and stability of subsidy receipt. *Child and Youth Care Forum, 41*, 343–356.

Howard, K. S., & Brooks-Gunn, J. (2009a). The role of home-visiting programs in preventing child abuse and neglect. *Future of Children, 19*(2), 119–146.

Howard, K. S. & Brooks-Gunn, J. (2009b). Relationship supportiveness during the transition to parenting among married and unmarried parents. *Parenting: Science and Practice, 9*, 123–142.

The Infant Health and Development Program Staff (Brooks-Gunn as member of Research Steering Committee) (1990). Enhancing the outcomes of low birth weight, premature infants: A multi-site randomized trial. *Journal of the American Medical Association, 263*, 3035–3042.

Jackson, A., Brooks-Gunn, J., Huang, C., & Glassman, M. (2000). Single mothers in low-wage jobs: Financial strain, parenting, and preschoolers' outcomes. *Child Development, 71*, 1409–1423.

Johnson, A. D., Martin, A., & Brooks-Gunn, J. (2011). Who uses child care subsidies? Comparing recipients to eligible non-recipients on family background characteristics and child care preferences. *Children and Youth Services Review, 33*, 1072–1083.

Johnson, A., Martin, A., & Brooks-Gunn, J. (2013). Child-care subsidies and school readiness in kindergarten. *Child Development*. doi: 10.1111/cdev.12073

Johnson, A., Martin, A., Brooks-Gunn, J., & Petrill, S. (2008). Order in the house! Associations among household chaos, the home literacy environment, maternal reading ability, and children's early reading. *Merrill-Palmer Quarterly, 54*, 445–472.

Klebanov, P., & Brooks-Gunn, J. (2006). Cumulative, human capital, and psychological risk in the context of early intervention: Links with IQ at ages 3, 5, and 8. *Annals of the New York Academy of Sciences, 1094*, 63–82.

Klebanov, P. K., Brooks-Gunn, J., McCarton, C., & McCormick, M. C. (1998). The contribution of neighborhood and family income to developmental test scores over the first three years of life. *Child Development, 69*, 1420–1436.

Klebanov, P. K., Brooks-Gunn, J., & McCormick, M. C. (1994a). School achievement and failure in very low birth weight children. *Journal of Developmental and Behavioral Pediatrics, 15*, 248–256.

Klebanov, P. K., Brooks-Gunn, J., & McCormick, M. C. (1994b). Classroom behavior of very low birth weight elementary school children. *Pediatrics, 94*, 700–708.

Lee, R. H., Zhai, F., Brooks-Gunn, J., Han, W. J., & Waldfogel, J. (in press). Head Start participation and school readiness: Evidence from Early Childhood Longitudinal Study-Birth Cohort. *Developmental Psychology*.

Leventhal, T. & Brooks-Gunn, J. (2011). Changes in neighborhood poverty from 1990 to 2000 and youth's problem behaviors. *Developmental Psychology, 47*, 1680–1698

Lewis, M. & Brooks-Gunn, J. (1979). *Social cognition and the acquisition of self.* New York: Plenum.

Lewis, M., Brooks-Gunn, J., & Jaskir, J. (1985). Individual differences in visual self-recognition as a function of mother-infant attachment relationship. *Developmental Psychology, 21*, 1181–1187.

Liaw, F., Meisels, S. J., & Brooks-Gunn, J. (1995). The effects of experience of early intervention on low birth weight, premature children: The Infant Health & Development Program. *Early Childhood Research Quarterly, 10*, 405–431.

Linver, M., Brooks-Gunn, J., & Kohen, D. (2002). Family processes as pathways from income to young children's development. *Developmental Psychology, 38*, 719–734.

Love, J. M., Chazan-Cohen, R., Brooks-Gunn, J., Raikes, H., Vogel, C. A., & Kisker, E. E. (2013). Beginnings of school readiness in infant/toddler development: Evidence from early Head Start. In S. Odom, E. Pungello, & N. Gardner-Neblett (Eds.), *Infants, Toddlers, and Families in Poverty.* New York: Guilford. (In press.)

Love, J. M., Chazan-Cohen, R., Raikes, H., Brooks-Gunn, J. (2013). What makes a difference? Early Head Start Evaluation findings in a developmental context. *Monographs of the Society for Research in Child Development.*

Love, J. M., Kisker, E. E., Ross, C., Raikes, H., Constantine, J., Boller, K. et al. (2005). The effectiveness of Early Head Start for 3-year old children and their parents: Lesson for policy and programs. *Development Psychology, 41*, 885–901.

Maimon, D., Browning, C. R., & Brooks-Gunn, J. (2010). Collective efficacy, family attachment, and urban adolescent suicide attempts. *Journal of Health and Social Behavior, 51*, 307–324.

McCarton, C. M., Brooks-Gunn, J., Wallace, I. F., Bauer, C. R., Bennett, F. C., Bernbaum, J. C. et al. (1997). Results at 8 years of intervention for low birth weight premature infants: The Infant Health Development Program. *Journal of the American Medical Association, 227*, 126–132.

McCormick, M. C., Brooks-Gunn, J., Buka, S. L., Goldman, J., Yu, J., Salganik, M. et al. (2006). Early intervention in low birth weight premature infants: Results at 18 years of age for the Infant Health and Development Program. *Pediatrics, 117*, 771–780.

McCormick, M. C., Brooks-Gunn, J., Shorter, T., Holmes, J. H., Wallace, C. Y., & Heagarty, M. C. (1989). Outreach as casefinding: Its effect on enrollment in prenatal care. *Medical Care, 27*, 103–111.

McCormick, M. C., Brooks-Gunn, J., Shorter, T., Holmes, J. H., Wallace, C. Y., & Heagarty, M. C. (1990). Factors associated with smoking in low-income pregnant women: Relationship to birth weight, stressful life events, social support, health behaviors, and mental distress. *Journal of Clinical Epidemiology, 43*, 441–448.

McCormick, M. C., Brooks-Gunn, J., Shorter, T., Wallace, C. Y., Holmes, J. H., & Heagarty, M. C. (1987). The planning of pregnancy among low-income women in central Harlem. *American Journal of Obstetrics and Gynecology, 156*, 145–149.

McCormick, M. C., Brooks-Gunn, J., Workman-Daniels, K., Turner, J., & Peckham, G. (1992). The health and developmental status of very low birth weight children at school age. *Journal of the American Medical Association, 267*, 2204–2208.

McCormick, M. C., Workman-Daniels, K., Brooks-Gunn, J., & Peckham, G. J. (1993). Hospitalization of very low birth weight children at school age. *Journal of Pediatrics, 122*, 360–365.

Meadows, S. O., McLanahan, S., & Brooks-Gunn, J. (2007). Parental depression and anxiety and early childhood behavior problems across family types. *Journal of Marriage and Family, 69*, 1162–1177.

Mendle, J., Harden, K. P., Brooks-Gunn, J., & Graber, J. A. (2010). Development's tortoise and hare: Pubertal timing, pubertal tempo, and depressive symptoms in boys and girls. *Developmental Psychology, 46*, 1341–1353.

Mendle, J., Harden, K. P., Brooks-Gunn, J., & Graber, J. A. (2012). Peer relationships and depressive symptomatology in boys at puberty. *Developmental Psychology, 48*, 429–435.

Mitchell, C., McLanahan, S., Brooks-Gunn, J., Garfinkel, I., & Notterman, D. (In Press). The influence and interplay of family instability and genes on children's prosocial behavior. *American Journal of Political Science.*

Mitchell, C., McLanahan, S., Brooks-Gunn, J., Garfinkel, I., Hobcraft, J., & Notterman, D. (in press). Genetic differential sensitivity to social environments over the life course: Implications for research and prevention. *American Journal of Public Health.*

Mitchell, C., Notterman, D., Brooks-Gunn, J., Hobcraft, J., Garfinkel, I., Jaeger, K. et al. (2011). Role of mother's genes and environment in postpartum depression. *Proceedings of the National Academy of Sciences, 108*, 8189–8193.

Nichols, T. R., Graber, J. A., Brooks-Gunn, J., & Botvin, G. J. (2006). Sex differences in overt aggression and delinquency among urban minority middle school students. *Journal of Applied Developmental Psychology, 27*, 78–91.

Nomura, Y., Halperin, J. M., Newcorn, J. H., Davey, C., Fifer, W. P., Savitz, D. A. et al. (2009). The risk for impaired learning-related abilities in childhood and educational achievement among adults born near-term. *Journal of Pediatric Psychology, 34*, 406–418.

Nomura, Y., Rajendran, K., Brooks-Gunn, J., & Newcorn, J. H. (2008). Roles of perinatal problems on adolescent antisocial behaviors among children born after 33 completed weeks: A prospective investigation. *Journal of Child Psychology and Psychiatry, 49*, 1108–1117.

Nomura, Y., Wickramaratne, P. J., Pilowskyb, D. J., Newcorn, J. H., Bruder, B., Davey, C. et al. (2007). Low birth weight and risk of affective disorders and selected medical illness in offspring at high and low risk for depression. *Comprehensive Psychiatry, 48*, 470–478.

Obeidallah, D., Brennan, R. T., Brooks-Gunn, J., & Earls, F. (2005). Links between puberty timing, neighborhood contexts, and girls' violent behavior. *Journal of the American Academy of Child and Adolescent Psychiatry, 43*(12), 1460–1468.

Paikoff, R., & Brooks-Gunn, J. (1991). Do parent–child relationships change during puberty? *Psychological Bulletin, 110*, 47–66.

Paikoff, R. L., Brooks-Gunn, J., & Carlton-Ford, S. (1991). Effect of reproductive status changes upon family functioning and well-being of mothers and daughters. *Journal of Early Adolescence, 11*, 201–220.

Paikoff, R. L., Brooks-Gunn, J., & Warren, M. P. (1991). Effects of girls' hormonal status on depressive and aggressive symptoms over the course of one year. *Journal of Youth and Adolescence, 20*, 191–215.

Pope, S. K., Whiteside, L., Brooks-Gunn, J., Keeleher, K. J., Rickert, V. I., Bradley, R. H. et al. (1993). Low-birth-weight infants born to adolescent mothers: Effects of coresidency with grandmother on child development. *Journal of the American Medical Association, 269*, 1396–1400.

Riina, E., Martin, A., Gardner, M., & Brooks-Gunn, J. (in press). Context matters: Links between location of discrimination, neighborhood cohesion and African American adolescents? *Journal of Youth and Adolescence.*

Roth, J. L., & Brooks-Gunn, J. (2003a). What exactly is a youth development program? Answers from research and practice. *Applied Developmental Science, 7*, 92–109.

Roth, J. L. & Brooks-Gunn, J. (2003b). Youth development programs: Risks, prevention and policy. *Journal of Adolescent Health, 32*, 170–182.

Roth, J. L., Brooks-Gunn, J., Murray, L., & Foster, W. (1998). Promoting healthy adolescents: Synthesis of youth development program evaluations. *Journal of Research on Adolescence, 8*, 423–459.

Roth, J. L., Malone, L. M., & Brooks-Gunn, J. (2010). Does the amount of participation in afterschool programs relate to developmental outcomes? A review of the literature. *American Journal of Community Psychology, 45*, 310–324.

Ruble, D. N., Boggiano, A., & Brooks-Gunn, J. (1982). Men's and women's evaluations of menstrual-related excuses. *Sex Roles, 6*, 625–638.

Ruble, D. N., & Brooks-Gunn, J. (1979). Menstrual symptoms: A social cognitive analysis. *Journal of Behavioral Medicine, 2*, 171–194.

Ruble, D. N., & Brooks-Gunn, J. (1982). The experience of menarche. *Child Development, 53*, 1557–1566.

Ruble, D. N., Brooks-Gunn, J., & Clarke, A. (1980). Research on menstrual-related psychological changes: Alternative perspectives. In J. E. Parsons (Ed.), *The psychology of sex differences and sex roles* (pp. 227–244). Washington, DC: Hemisphere.

Ryan, R., Johnson, A., Rigby, E., & Brooks-Gunn, J. (2011). The impact of child care subsidy use on child care quality. *Early Childhood Research Quarterly, 26*, 320–331.

Ryan, R. M., Tolani, N., & Brooks-Gunn, J. (2009). Relationship trajectories, parenting stress, and unwed mothers' transition to a new baby. *Parenting: Science and Practice, 9*, 160–177.

Sanbonmatsu, L., Kling, J. R., Duncan, G. J., & Brooks-Gunn, J. (2006). Neighborhoods and academic achievement: Results from the Moving to Opportunity Experiment. *Journal of Human Resource, 41*, 649–691.

Smith, J. R., Brooks-Gunn, J., Klebanov, P., & Lee, K. (2000). Welfare and work: Complementary strategies for low-income mothers? *Journal of Marriage and the Family, 62*, 808–821.

Sontag, L. M., Graber, J., Brooks-Gunn, J., & Warren, M. P. (2008). Coping with social stress: Implications for psychopathology in young adolescent girls. *Journal of Abnormal Child Psychology, 36*, 1159–1174.

Tyrka, A. R., Kelly, M. M., Graber, J. A., DeRose, L., Lee, J. K., Warren, M. P. et al. (2010). Behavioral adjustment in a community sample of boys: Links with basal and stress-induced salivary cortisol concentrations. *Psychoneuroendocrinology, 35*, 1167–1177.

Tyrka, A. R., Lee, J. K., Graber, J. A., Clement, A. M., Kelly, M. M., DeRose, L. et al. (2012). Neuroendocrine predictors of emotional and behavioral adjustment in boys: Longitudinal follow-up of a community sample. *Psychoneuroendocrinology, 37*(12), 2042–2046. PMCID:PMC3458171

Wakschlag, L. S., Chase-Lansdale, P. L., & Brooks-Gunn, J. (1996). Not just "Ghosts in the Nursery": Contemporaneous intergenerational relationships and parenting in young African American families. *Child Development, 67*, 2131–2147.

Waldfogel, J., Craigie, T.-A., Brooks-Gunn, J. (2010). Fragile families and child well-being. *Future of Children, 20*(2), 87–112.

Warren, M. P. (1983). The effects of undernutrition on reproductive function in the human. *Endocrine Reviews, 4(4)*, 363–377.

Warren, M. P., Brooks-Gunn, J., Fox, R. P., Lancelot, C., Newman, D., & Hamilton, W. G. (1991). Lack of bone accretion and amenorrhea in young dancers: Evidence for a relative osteopenia in weight bearing bones. *Journal of Clinical Endocrinology and Metabolism, 72*, 847–853.

Warren, M. P., Brooks-Gunn, J., Hamilton, L. H., Hamilton, W. G., & Warren, L. F. (1986). Scoliosis and fractures in young ballet dancers: Relationship to delayed menarcheal age and secondary amenorrhea. *New England Journal of Medicine, 314*, 1348–1353.

Xue, Y., Leventhal, T., Brooks-Gunn, J., & Earls, F. (2005). Neighborhood residence and mental health problems of 5–11-year-olds. *Archives of General Psychiatry, 62*, 1–10.

Yeung, J., Linver, M., & Brooks-Gunn, J. (2002). How money matters for young children's development: Parental investment and family processes. *Child Development, 73*, 1861–1879.

Zhai, F., Brooks-Gunn, J., & Waldfogel, J. (2011). Head Start and urban children's school readiness: A birth cohort study in 18 cities. *Developmental Psychology, 47*, 134–152.

Zhai, F., Waldfogel, J., & Brooks-Gunn, J. (in press). Estimating the effects of Head Start on parenting and child maltreatment. *Children and Youth Services Review.*

5

An Autobiographical Journey Through Adolescents' Social World

Peer Groups, Peer Influence, and the Effects of Electronic Media on Social Adjustment in College

B. Bradford Brown

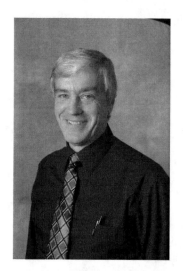

I suppose that my career as a developmental psychologist began during the fall of my junior year in college, the day that a revered professor of architecture pulled me into his office and said in a quiet but firm voice, "Bradford, you can't draw. You'll never make it in this profession." Reeling from that rejection, I began a desperate search for another major and another profession. Recognizing that I had been spending about as much time working with adolescents through volunteer organizations in the community as I had at my drafting table in the School of Architecture, I decided to pin my future on youth development. I set my sights on a degree in sociology because majoring in psychology would have cost me an additional year of undergraduate school. The scintillating lectures of Stephen Klineberg in social psychology (now at Rice University) and the mentoring of Robert A. Scott (retired from Stanford) helped to focus and give intellectual weight to my budding interests in adolescent development.

My senior thesis, a requirement of all Princeton undergraduates at the time, was a remarkably flawed and forgettable study, but two course projects set the stage for an impending intellectual journey. For one, I did an introspective analysis of one of my closest friendships, an awkward but candid evaluation of the progression of intentional and unintentional actions that led us from acquaintanceship to a much closer bond. The other, my first quantitative study, involved a simple but intriguing sociometric analysis of friendship patterns among members of the Princeton track team. I asked all of my teammates simply to list their three closest friends on the team, then proceeded to demonstrate

that principles of proximity applied even within the confines of a relatively small team: sprinters tended to befriend other sprinters, long-distance runners became closest to fellow distance runners, field events men hung around with others in field events.

Although none of these studies was particularly insightful, and certainly not publishable, they served two major functions. They piqued my curiosity about the nature and progression of peer relations across adolescence, and apparently, they were sufficiently intriguing to persuade faculty members at the University of Chicago to grant me admission to their graduate program.

In graduate school, the jagged path toward a profession continued with a series of twists of fate. The first began before I ever arrived on campus. I had applied and been accepted into a clinical psychology program, hoping to develop skills for working with adolescents. My interest in this career path was fueled by the experiences I had with young people during my undergraduate years, but I was markedly ambivalent about whether to pursue credentials as a clinician or a researcher. The decision was made for me when the American Psychological Association withdrew its accreditation of Chicago's clinical program just 2 months before I was scheduled to begin training. I was warmly welcomed to campus as a member of the new (and hastily constructed) "personality processes program." While the faculty members were scrambling to put together this new graduate program, I signed up for what proved to be one of the most inspiring classes I ever took—the first, indeed, the *only* course I ever had in adolescent development, taught by John Sims. John was a remarkably gifted teacher; his classroom overflowed with students enthralled by his theoretically rigorous exploration of this curious phase of the life span. He introduced me to psychodynamic theories of development, especially Erikson's (1950, 1968) work on adolescent identity development, and I dove into the material with more passion than I had experienced since my very first architecture class my initial semester in college.

At some point during his course, Dr. Sims asked me what I was doing in the personality processes program. It was his way of suggesting that I transfer into his department, the Committee on Human Development, where I could more easily focus my studies on adolescent development, under his direction. Enticed by a fellowship, I readily agreed. But the mentorship was short-lived. Sims was an enthralling teacher, but not as devoted a scholar, and the University declined to grant him tenure at the end of my second year in the program. Moreover, to the shock and disappointment of a small cadre of graduate students interested in adolescent development, the Human Development faculty decided that adolescence was not a legitimate stage of development, unworthy of a faculty line. We found ourselves adrift, and I found myself in the awkward possession of a pre-doctoral fellowship from the National Institute of Aging, intended to train a new generation of gerontology scholars. Full of Protestant guilt, I began redirecting my scholarly energies toward issues of adult development and aging. Learning from the likes of Bernice Neugarten, Bertram Kohler, Mort Lieberman, and William Henry was exciting, but the passion for studying adolescence would not die so easily.

I received a summer fellowship to work with esteemed psychoanalyst Daniel Offer, whose recent publication of his research on normal adolescent boys (Offer, 1969) was setting the psychoanalytic community on fire. In this work, Offer challenged Freud's depiction of adolescence as a time when inner turmoil was healthy and vital, demonstrating that a substantial majority of healthy adolescent males did not fit the "storm and stress" archetype of this era. This heresy, emanating from within the psychoanalytic community, spurred a dramatic reevaluation of the nature of adolescent development that is still being felt today through debates about the legitimacy of positive youth development perspectives, the plasticity of neural developmental processes, and the consistency of adolescent behaviors across cultural contexts. My interest was in whether Thematic Apperception Test (TAT) data from Offer's participants revealed insights about their friendships or romantic relations. Despite the assistance of Dr. Offer and noted TAT scholar William Henry (my academic advisor), I was too naïve an interpreter of TAT data to discover anything noteworthy; but the study gave me a deeper appreciation of qualitative research approaches and some of the inner dimensions of peer relationships. I probed some of these issues in a qualifying exam, for which I chose the topic of friendship, but Dr. Henry's departure to pursue a career in book editing not only left me again without an academic advisor but also in a department with no other faculty with even a remote interest in adolescent peer relations. A glimmer of hope came when James S. Coleman—whose treatise on the "adolescent society" (Coleman, 1961) remains one of the classic studies of adolescent development—was lured back to the University of Chicago faculty. It was dashed in my one and only meeting with him, in which he quickly dismissed

a fellow graduate student and myself with the pronouncement, "I'm no longer interested in that issue."

Fortunately, I landed in the research lab of Dr. Morton Lieberman, working on his longitudinal studies of psychosocial adjustment in adulthood and old age. From that project, my dissertation on help-seeking behavior among adults was derived, along with my only publication from graduate school work (Brown, 1978). Somehow, this was enough to persuade the good folks at the University of Wisconsin-Madison to offer me a position in the Human Development area of the Department of Educational Psychology, with the mission of revitalizing the adult development portion of their program. Arriving on campus in the Fall of 1979, I affiliated with the University's Institute on Aging, taught courses on adult development, and tried to attract new graduate students in that area. I began an earnest effort to establish a research program in adult development, initially partnering with a local nurse practitioner to conduct a study of how the absence of social network ties could be a factor in older adults' alcohol abuse (Brown & Chiang, 1983–84).

My heart, however, was still in adolescent development, so it is not surprising that I was struck by the results of an impromptu academic exercise while teaching an undergraduate course on adolescence during my second year on campus. To break the monotony of my lecture on peer relations to the 200-odd students, I invited six of them to come to the blackboard spanning the front of the lecture hall and record the names and a brief description of the major "crowds" in their high school. By chance, the reporters came from high schools that varied considerably in size, location, and demographic characteristics. Yet, there was remarkable overlap—as well as some individual uniqueness—in the types and features of crowds that students reported. This image of a variegated peer system stood in sharp contrast to the more common depiction of adolescents as a unified youth culture, coalescing in opposition to adult societal norms and expectations (Coleman, 1961; Brake, 1985; Feuer, 1969). It also departed from the standard depiction of "crowds" in adolescent textbooks, which featured Dunphy's (1969) portrait of a coalition of cliques, occasionally united to offer more effective opportunities to master the heterosocial skills expected of adults.

The insights emerging from this blackboard exercise piqued my curiosity. They stirred recollections of the different affinity patterns of segments of my undergraduate track team and the stereotypical image of each segment that helped to justify intra-team friendship patterns. Questions quickly flooded my thoughts. Do *all* schools display this differentiation of crowd types, and if so, how consistent are the types across institutions? Do all adolescents belong to a crowd, and if so, how do they become associated with one group as opposed to another? What purposes do crowds serve in adolescent development? Certainly, the primary purpose cannot be the socialization into heterosociality that Dunphy described or the rejection of adult values that Coleman claimed. Is this differentiated peer crowd system strictly a U.S. phenomenon? And beyond the questions about crowds, are there other central aspects of adolescent development that we have misinterpreted or misrepresented in the research literature? Offer (1969) exposed the fallacy of approaching adolescence as a necessarily tumultuous, conflict-ridden stage of life. What other false images of the period were lurking in the literature, especially in regards to adolescent peer relations?

Processes of Peer Influence

As I thought about the issue of lurking fallacies, the first to jump to mind was peer pressure, which was routinely demonized as the source of all evil action among teenagers. This was the era in which First Lady Nancy Reagan was urging all young people to "just say no" to drugs, by which she meant: say no to peers who were encouraging illicit drug use. This campaign unleashed a cadre of entrepreneurs selling drug prevention programs (the ill-fated DARE among them) with components such as "peer pressure proofing" or peer resistance education. I had my doubts that peer influence was truly so negative that it ought to be resisted at all costs, but the research literature on this issue was surprisingly limited. In fact, most developmental psychologist and even social psychologists had concerned themselves less with the social process of peer influence than with the individual characteristic of conformity dispositions or behavior. Experiments following the classic work of Solomon Asch (1951) demonstrated that adolescents were more likely than younger or older age groups to follow the lead of peers when evaluating ambiguous stimuli (Costanzo & Shaw, 1966; Iscoe, Williams, & Harvey, 1963), but these social psychological studies did not address decisions about the more unambiguous behaviors that young people routinely confronted in daily interactions with peers. Efforts to trace age differences in how youth indicated they would respond to peer pressure in realistic hypothetical situations came closer to the mark, again showing higher conformity dispositions in adolescence (Berndt, 1979; Bixenstine, DeCorte, & Bixenstine, 1976). Still, these studies dealt with conformity dispositions, not peer influence.

I decided that the best approach to this problem was to go "back to the blackboard," to ask young people directly to describe the nature of peer influences that they actually encountered. Through focus group interviews, my students and I discovered that adolescents perceived pressure from peers in a variety of life domains, not just regarding misbehavior, and not always in a negative direction. With generous grant support from the Spencer Foundation, we were able to trace age differences in perceptions of peer pressure (Clasen & Brown, 1985) and then to demonstrate that perceived pressures from peers as well as peer conformity dispositions had distinctive roles in young people's behavior patterns, but to different degrees in different domains of behavior (Brown, Clasen, & Eicher, 1986). The image of peer pressure emerging from our

study participants stood in stark contrast to the portrait proffered in "just say no" campaigns. The preponderance of peer pressure was oriented toward positive outcomes: finishing high school, getting along well with family members, and having strong friendships.

Although these studies hopefully helped to mitigate the negative image of peer influence in adolescence, they still focused exclusively on peer pressure as the mode of influence. Other scholars began demonstrating that peer pressure was not the exclusive or even the primary source of peer influence in adolescence (Adler & Adler, 1995; Dishion, Spracklen, Andrews, & Patterson, 1996). This finding dissuaded me from using the inventory of peer pressures that we had developed in subsequent studies of peer influence processes. Instead, in 2004 I decided to convene an advanced level seminar whose purpose was to derive a new, more comprehensive set of measures of peer influence processes. It took only about 3 weeks for us to recognize that such a task was premature because the field lacked a clear understanding of peer influence processes. We shifted our attention to a careful analysis of qualitative and quantitative studies of peer influence. With the help of several seminar participants I derived what I hoped to be a more comprehensive model of peer influence, stipulating the modes and motivations for influence as well as a set of moderating factors that could help to predict how an adolescent would respond to peer influence. This model (see Brown, Bakken, Ameringer, & Mahon, 2008) was meant to be a means of connecting various research studies that address different aspects of the influence process and its consequences, thereby helping to guide future research on the topic.

Our most recent explorations of peer influence, however, have called into question the efficacy of a general model of this phenomenon. At issue is whether peer influence manifests in sufficiently similar ways across different facets of adolescents' lives to lend itself to a general model. We are now beginning to explore in depth the processes of peer influence within the specific area of teen driving. Although traffic accidents represent the leading cause of death among U.S. adolescents and traveling with passengers seems to elevate the risk of accidents for teen drivers dramatically (Insurance Institute for Highway Safety, 2009), remarkably little effort has been expended to discern the ways in which peers have an impact on young drivers. Our initial efforts to document these influences have revealed modes of influence (e.g., distracting the driver or disrupting efforts to drive safely) that we failed to identify in our comprehensive model and that seem more specific to the context of an automobile. The challenge, however, is to produce concrete evidence of the effects of these passenger behaviors. As our work on this issue continues we hope to take advantage of new technologies that allow us to control driving conditions and assess teenagers' behavior in full-scale driving simulators or to capture their behavior as it occurs during actual driving using cameras mounted in cars.

Form and Function of Peer Crowds

Soon after initiating studies of peer influence processes, we also began to address the questions about crowds that arose from the blackboard exercise in my undergraduate lecture. The first step was to approach that exercise more scientifically. For a conceptual foundation for this work I turned initially to lessons learned in Dr. Sims' course back in graduate school—specifically, Erik Erikson's depictions of adolescence. Erikson (1968) described young people's efforts to gain a clearer sense of self as a process of "trying on" different identities until discovering one that fit with their sense of who they had been and were to become, one that also matched their self-image with their reputation in the eyes of others. For this to be true, there had to be a variety of identity prototypes available for adolescents to sample, as well as some freedom to move among prototypes over time. It also seemed reasonable to expect consensus among peers about the crowd to which a given adolescent belonged at a given point in time. Through pilot testing we identified major dimensions along which crowds tended to be differentiated, (e.g., styles of dress and grooming, typical weekend activities, attitudes toward school, extracurricular participation) along with the primary descriptors within each dimension. With our Spencer study participants we confirmed that each major crowd in the participants' schools had a distinctive profile on these dimensions, an identity prototype. Nevertheless, consensus on crowd features was not overwhelming, and some pairs of crowds were characterized similarly on several dimensions (Brown, Lohr, & Trujillo, 1990). Although these findings generally supported Erikson's theory, another important element emerged that was not predicted by Erikson, namely, our participants arranged the crowds into a status hierarchy.

The discovery of status as a major feature of the peer crowd system sent me back to my sociological roots in undergraduate school as well as would-be graduate school mentor James Coleman. In his classic study of Chicago area high schools, Coleman (1961) emphasized the influence of the leading crowd on the rest of a school's students, but he seemed to be unaware of the more fully articulated crowd system and the status hierarchy that arranged crowds within the system. Others, however, were quite cognizant of the impact of crowd status on student life. Ethnographers Ralph Larkin (1979) and Philip Cusick (1973) had already documented these crowd dynamics in the schools that they studied. Contemporaneous with our own study, David Kinney was completing a dissertation study that traced the metamorphosis of the crowd system across the middle and high school years. Kinney (1991) found that status differentiations among crowds emerged early in adolescence, then faded in significance across the high-school years, whereas the crowd system seemed to expand with the transition from middle to high school, then become murkier as the boundaries between crowds dissipated toward the end of high school. Although we

had discerned a more differentiated system of crowds than Kinney in the middle schools we studied, his other findings generally fit our observations. They prompted a new question: How do these structural arrangements and transformations of crowds serve the developmental needs of adolescents?

While we were puzzling through that issue we were also attempting to discern how easily adolescents could be classified into the crowds in their school. Contemporaneous with our own work, sociologists Herman and Julia Schwendinger (1985) were examining how adolescent group affiliations related to adolescents' delinquent activity. We modified their system for identifying crowds and crowd affiliations into a social type rating system in which a group of students who were diverse in their achievement orientations and school behavior but recognized as peer system leaders first identified the school's peer crowds and then indicated the crowd with which each of their classmates could be associated (Brown, 1979). Using this system, we identified members of major crowds, invited them to participate in our research study, then followed them for 3 years as they progressed through middle and/or high school.

Analyses of this sample revealed that adolescents recognized by their peers as members of various crowds generally behaved in accordance with the identity prototypes of their respective crowds (Brown, Mory, & Kinney, 1994). Moreover, perceptions of peer pressure varied in predictable ways among crowds, with the druggies, for example, perceiving more pressure to misbehave than other groups and the loners reporting relatively little pressure to conform to peer norms (Clasen & Brown, 1985). Without longer term longitudinal data (especially from childhood), we could not determine the extent to which similarities between adolescents' behavior and their crowd's behavioral profile were a function of selection or socialization, but our suspicion was that, just as in the case of friendship pairs (Kandel, 1978), both processes were at work.

With information from these and other analyses my graduate students and I finally felt comfortable formulating our own assertions about the developmental functions of the peer crowd system. We suggested that crowds serve as caricatures, channels, and contexts for adolescent development (Brown et al., 1994). The stereotypes associated with each crowd, collectively forming its caricature, provided an identity profile through which adolescents could evaluate (either through direct experience as a crowd member or vicariously through observation of members) an identity they might want to adopt. Equally importantly, however, crowds also helped to regulate social interactions in the increasingly complex social world of teenagers. As adolescents in the United States move from the relatively self-contained social world of an elementary school classroom to larger social systems in middle and high school, crowds serve as markers of individuals who are like or unlike them, both in terms of the identity elements of a given crowd and its position in the peer status system. Thus, they mark peers who are more or less reasonable candidates for friendship or romantic relationships. In other words, crowds channel adolescents toward associations with certain peers and away from affiliations with others. This was borne out in our sample when, with the exception of members of the normal crowd, adolescents drew a disproportionate share of their friends from members of their own crowd (Brown et al., 1994). These relationships were navigated within the context of the adolescent's crowd, we further argued, which featured distinctive norms and lifestyles. We illustrated this situation by documenting crowd (context) differences in the frequency and character of romantic relationships, the types of peer pressures reported, and the pattern of social activities in which adolescents engaged (Brown et al., 1994). Equally compelling evidence comes from other ethnographic work contrasting the quality of relationships in different crowds (e.g., Eckert, 1989; Finders, 1997).

Of course, by changing crowd affiliations—trying on different identities, in Erikson's terms—adolescents could alter their image among peers as well as the peer associates they could befriend and lifestyles they could follow. But it turns out that this element of Erikson's identity process is not so easily accomplished. Our study participants asserted that moving between crowds that shared similar identity prototypes was feasible, but successfully shifting to crowds with different images was unlikely (Brown, et al., 1994). There was a certain inertia in the crowd system, such that once one's reputation among peers was established it was difficult to change in more than subtle ways. We found that whereas two-thirds of 7th graders changed their professed crowd affiliation over the course of a year, this was true of only 40% of the 10th graders in our sample, and such changes were even rarer among older adolescents in the jock and druggie crowds (Brown, Freeman, Huang, & Mounts, 1992).

It is rather ironic that just as we were exploring the characteristics of adolescent crowds through scientific research, they exploded on the silver screen in a series of movies by someone soon to become famous for his depiction of teenagers: John Hughes. From *The Breakfast Club* to *Pretty in Pink* and *Weird Science*, Hughes captured the essence and angst of caricature, channel, and context that coursed through the reports of our own respondents. In *The Breakfast Club*, when Brian the brain asks preppie Claire whether or not the friendships that have blossomed among the group sharing a Saturday morning detention session would still be apparent Monday morning, Claire is bitterly rebuked by Bender, the delinquent, when she admits that they won't—especially in light of her obviously close relationship with Andy, the jock. However haughty or cruel Claire's response might seem, it was consistent with the views of our Spencer study participants, as well as those in other investigations of crowd affinities (Eder, 1985; Eckert, 1989).

Yet, there were complexities in the peer crowd system that neither Hughes nor we had adequately captured in our

work to date. To explore these factors we found it necessary to integrate Erikson's neo-psychoanalytic perspective on identity with principles from symbolic interactionist theories. Rethinking the modest consensus on crowd characteristics in light of arguments from social identity theory (Tajfel, 1974), we realized that the image an adolescent had of a particular crowd might depend on the adolescent's own crowd membership. Individuals within a given crowd (in-group members) should have a more positive image than those in a different crowd (out-group members). But we also speculated that "near-group" members (individuals affiliated with a crowd nearby in the status hierarchy or that shared several identity elements) would offer a more positive portrayal of the in-group than peers from more distant out-groups. These were precisely the dynamics that Margaret Stone found in her dissertation research (Stone & Brown, 1998, 1999). In other words, dissensus about the image of a given crowd seemed to be a manifestation of complex social identity processes.

As in John Hughes' films (and those of many other screenwriters since), our studies had concentrated on European American populations. Some scholars raised questions about the applicability of the crowd system to ethnic minority populations, whereas others identified crowd-like divisions in multi-ethnic populations (Larkin, 1979; Matute-Bianchi, 1986). Two new samples allowed us to explore this issue. The first sample, about which I will have more to say later, involved students in several high schools in the Midwest and West Coast. Would the crowd system give way to group differentiations along ethnic lines? Would it only apply to European American students? Would there be separate sets of crowds within each ethnic group? It turned out that, in these schools, the interest- and ability-based crowd types we had discovered previously were supplemented by ethnically oriented crowds, with ethnic minority youth distributed among ethnically based and non-ethnic crowds. The strongest predictor of their crowd affiliation (whether peer or self-rated) was the ethnic homogeneity of their friend network, but other factors—varying among ethnic groups—also played a part, sometimes reinforcing group stereotypes that could be a source of ethnic discrimination, other times affirming characteristics of a more positive ethnic identity for group members (Brown, Herman, Hamm, & Heck, 2008). But a closer look at specific ethnic groups can reveal within-group divisions that are at least apparent to adolescents of that ethnic background. For example, among immigrant Hmong youth, one of my graduate students discovered three distinctive crowd types, which were used by students to articulate the different balances of home and host culture that were central to their identity development (Nguyen & Brown, 2010). These two studies illustrated the ways in which different layers of the peer crowd systems could affect ethnic and general identity development in multicultural social contexts. Studies of racial prejudice stemming from social identity theory were somewhat informative, but not entirely consistent with our findings.

A third conundrum came from the discovery that adolescents did not always place themselves in the same crowd with which they were associated by peers—an important issue because so much of the research on peer crowds has been based on self-perceived rather than the methodologically and logistically more challenging peer ratings of crowds (Susman, Pokhrel, Ashmore, & Brown, 2007). Although consensus was stronger in older age groups, between a third and a half of adolescents associated by peers with a given crowd in our samples claimed membership in a different group, or no crowd at all (Brown, Clasen, & Neiss, 1987). Hardly any members of low-status groups such as loners, outcasts, or unpopulars assigned themselves to these groups. In earlier analyses we had found that adolescents who were regarded as outsiders (not members of any specific crowd) had varying levels of self-esteem, depending on whether they were happily independent of the crowd system or "wannabes," wishing to be part of a group (Brown & Lohr, 1987). We wondered whether the dissensus between self- and peer rated crowd affiliation might be a related strategy of impression management or self-esteem maintenance. Having found that self-esteem levels directly related to crowd status (Brown & Lohr, 1987), we reasoned that peer-rated high-status crowd members who affirmed their crowd membership would have higher self-esteem than those who denied this affiliation, but the opposite would be true for adolescents associated by peers with low-status crowds. Results of two separate studies supported these expectations, indicating that adolescents can blunt the psychological effects of being associated by peers with a low-status crowd by denying this reputation. In our data, however, these blunting effects were modest and did not clearly persist over time (Brown, Von Bank, & Steinberg, 2008).

A final problem was more challenging. Just as there was not consensus among adolescents on the defining characteristics of crowds, so, too there was disagreement about the crowd affiliations of adolescents. Individuals varied considerably in the proportion of peer raters who associated them with a particular crowd as well as the number of crowds that raters named for a given adolescent. Though young people could easily point to exemplars of each crowd, the boundaries of each group were blurry. Was it really reasonable to speak of jocks and druggies as concrete entities when what we were describing were reputations or images among peers, some feature of inchoate identities rather than the firmly bounded, interaction-based groups that characterized most work on social identity? One's position in the peer reputational system is inherently imprecise, a problem that has clouded the research on adolescent crowds for decades (Cross & Fletcher, 2009). One resolution is to think more in terms of image than group affiliation—of one's "jockishness" rather than being a jock. To operationalize this perspective one can use proportion scores (the percentage of raters who place a target adolescent in a given crowd) rather than categorical crowd assignments, which almost inevitably involve arbitrary decision rules. We took this approach in one study and affirmed that *degrees* of association (by peers) with various crowds differentiated adolescents' behavior patterns and several outcome measures (Brown, Lamborn, Mounts, & Steinberg, 1993), just as we had shown in previous categorically based analyses. This study, however, also marked a milestone in my moving to a broader perspective from which to consider the operation of the adolescent peer system.

Moving Beyond the Peer World to Parental Involvement

In 1985, two events occurred that changed the course of my scholarship and brought me back closer to my intellectual training in adult development and aging. First, the Wisconsin Center for Education Research won a major program project grant from the U.S. Department of Education to examine factors influencing secondary school achievement in the U.S. Second, as part of this project, I was asked to collaborate with Larry Steinberg, then a rising star in the world of adolescent research who had recently joined the U.W. faculty, on a critical review of research about factors outside of school that influenced adolescents' academic achievement. Our report was the genesis of a large-scale, longitudinal investigation of non-instructional influences on secondary school achievement, for which we joined forces with eminent senior scholar Sanford Dornbusch of Stanford University to examine the lives of over 12,000 youth in nine schools in the Midwest and West Coast. Commonly known as the Steinberg-Dornbusch study, the project generated scores of articles detailing the effects of parenting, peer relations, and experiences in employment and extracurricular activities on student achievement. For me, working closely with Larry and Sandy and watching them come to terms with conceptual and methodological issues was like a post-doctoral fellowship experience. We vigorously debated the features of various social contexts and the ways in which they combined to shape young people's achievement patterns.

My own particular interest was in the ways in which parenting practices affected adolescents' peer experiences. We found that specific parenting practices were associated with particular patterns of behavior, which in turn seemed to affect the type of crowd with which peers associated an adolescent (Brown et al., 1993). In other words, parents set adolescents on certain behavioral trajectories that helped to build their reputations and, consequently, association with specific peer crowds. Rather than viewing parents and peers as competing influences on adolescent development—a common perspective of many scholars—our data suggested that parenting behaviors might actually direct adolescents toward certain types of peer influence.

The findings suggested a rather distal and general connection between parents and peers, consistent with folk wisdom that parents seem to relinquish tight control over their child's peer relations as part of the heightened development of autonomy occurring in adolescence. Still involved with youth in the community, however, I did not sense that our study adequately captured the nature of parents' involvement. Do parents really step away from their child's peer interactions at this stage? The rich and detailed research literature on parental involvement in the peer relations of toddlers and children (Parke & Ladd, 1992) fell strangely silent when children crossed the threshold into adolescence. Our first, small-scale pilot investigation, involving parents from various socioeconomic strata and several ethnic backgrounds, suggested more of a transformation than abdication of parental involvement, but in ways that differed by demographic background (Brown, Hamm, & Meyerson, 1996). We witnessed how cultural norms of familism mitigated parents' withdrawal of oversight in Latino families, while greater emphasis on autonomy among higher economic European American families expedited parents' withdrawal. African American parents were more ambivalent, wanting to encourage independence but still concerned about poor choices of peer associates. Immigration status also seemed to be a factor, with immigrant parents often perplexed by the peer group norms their children were encountering and adopting from U.S. peers.

A further exploration of these intriguing initial findings awaited the arrival of a trio of graduate students who allowed me to reorganize my research lab to into a coordinated effort to examine the nature of parental involvement in adolescent peer relations within a multicultural context. Heather (Krein) Von Bank took the lead in deriving quantitative measures regarding parental involvement while Jackie Nguyen and Jeremy Bakken engaged in more qualitative efforts to understand the dynamics of involvement among recently immigrated Hmong and African American families, respectively. We derived a conceptual framework in which attitudes about what parents have a right to know were expected to relate to the actual behavior of both parent and child—the adolescent's actual disclosure patterns and the parent's information seeking. Our work was similar to studies by Judi Smetana and colleagues on the legitimacy of parental rule making (e.g., Smetana, 1988) but rather than adopting domain theory and considering a variety of areas in which parents could assert authority, we focused exclusively on peer relations and turned to adolescents to explain how they perceived their social world with peers.

In work that we are currently pursuing for publication, we have confirmed earlier focus group and pilot study findings (Krein & Brown, 2003) indicating that adolescents perceive four different realms of peer relations: activities with associates (where they are going, with whom, doing what, etc.), features of specific relationships (e.g., who they like as a romantic partner, whether or not they have a fight with a friend), positive characteristics of peers, and negative characteristics of peers. Adolescents believe that parents have a right to know more about certain aspects of their peer relations than others, and older youth tend to grant parents less of a right to know than younger adolescents. Attitudes in each area of peer relations are substantially correlated with the amount of information participants say they actually disclose to parents, and their attitudes are also consistently correlated with the strength of the parent–child (especially, mother–child) relationship as well as the extent of their interaction with peers (Chan & Brown, 2012). Parents also express more of a right to know about certain features of their child's peer relations than others, although they generally feel they are entitled to more knowledge than their children do. In each aspect of peer relations, parents' attitudes about what they have a right to know are substantially correlated with the degree of information they seek in that area.

These general patterns become more particular when viewed through a cultural lens. For example, African American parents expect to be told more about their child's peer relations than first generation Hmong parents do (Brown, Bakken, Nguyen, & Von Bank, 2007). Moreover, youth from these ethnic groups have a variety of strategies regarding disclosing information about peers, and although they zealously avoid outright lies to parents, they are also reluctant to engage in "full disclosure" (Bakken & Brown, 2010). The reasons underlying their decisions about disclosure are quite complex—sometimes strategic (considering how best to maintain the type of peer interactions they enjoy), sometimes developmental (efforts to assert more autonomy and personal responsibility), and sometimes interpersonal (trying not to worry or upset their parents unnecessarily).

The strategic nature of adolescents' disclosure of information sparked us to wonder whether parents are equally strategic in the information about peers that they seek. We developed a list of strategies that parents could employ to keep abreast of their child's peer interactions and relationships, then asked an ethnically and economically diverse set of parents to indicate the extent to which they used each strategy. Drawing some inspiration from Brian Barber's (2002) edited volume on intrusive parenting, we also asked a small sample of adolescents to rate the degree of intrusiveness of each strategy, then weighted parents' responses by these intrusiveness ratings. These findings also are being prepared for publication, but they indicate that mothers and fathers report equivalent levels of intrusive information seeking and are equally intrusive with daughters and sons. There are age and ethnic differences in levels of intrusiveness, but the most curious findings are that parents use more intrusive information seeking strategies when they have more positive relationships with their child (Brown & Chan, 2011).

As our work on parental involvement in adolescent peer relations continues, we plan to look more carefully at the factors underlying both adolescent disclosure and parent information seeking strategies. At this point, however, it seems safe to conclude that parents do not routinely relinquish their involvement in a child's peer relations when the child reaches adolescence, but move from a managerial role to a more negotiated level of involvement. We hope to explore these developmental trajectories longitudinally to see how they are affected by the child's relational history—for example, how entry into romantic relationships alters parental involvement. We also want to look more carefully at the strategies that parents employ to stay attuned to the child's peer interactions (perhaps without the child's awareness). Of course, a key area for more research is how parents' information seeking and children's disclosure patterns are related to important psychosocial outcomes, and how consistent these connections are across families of different ethnic or demographic backgrounds.

Peer Relations in an Age of Expanding Electronic Communication

For nearly a quarter of a century, my research focused almost exclusively on peer-related issues of early and middle adolescents. Now, toward the end of my career, I find myself complementing this work with a return to the issues that initiated the journey back in undergraduate school: friendship and social networking patterns of late adolescents in college. This new chapter in my research has been inspired largely by a new generation of graduate students (especially, Chia-chen Yang and Dong Liu), but also has been encouraged by the curious appearance of various electronic media at the dinner table, family computer, and bedrooms of my houseful of teenage offspring. The advent of chat rooms, instant messaging and social networking sites (especially Twitter and Facebook), multiplayer on-line games, and cell phones with ever expanding capabilities, has moved the current generation of adolescents into a social nexus in which close friends and distant acquaintances are never more than arm's length away. While parents struggle to figure out how these electronic media work, social scientists labor to understand how these electronic media have altered the nature of peer relations.

Initially, I was drawn to the issue of electronic media because they seemed to open up a new world of social relations for young people, with opportunities to encounter unknown peers halfway around the world as easily as well established friends down the block. The challenges of monitoring these electronic interactions were worrisome to many parents and continue to be a source of intriguing research. As teenagers drifted away from chat rooms and toward electronic media that facilitated connections with known peers, the interests in our research lab began to coalesce around the use of these media in the social context where the electronic revolution in social networking began: college undergraduates. We became particularly interested in how college students employ media to navigate the social transition to college—the need to rebuild their social network and determine which pre-college associates to retain in the network and which to dismiss.

In our initial work in this area, we have discovered rules of etiquette about which electronic media are appropriate at different phases of a relationship (Yang & Brown, in press). Especially for women, certain forms of electronic communication (e.g., Facebook chat versus a cell phone call) signal different levels of relationship; moving too quickly to more intimate forms may jeopardize a budding relationship. Concentrating on social networking sites, we have found that various motivations for using Facebook moderate the effects of Facebook usage on social outcomes and well-being among college students in the United States (Yang & Brown, 2013). For example, using Facebook to play Internet games was positively associated with social adjustment to college, but only among students motivated to seek new on-line relationships via Facebook. We also have evidence suggesting that self-disclosure on the Chinese equivalent of Facebook improves bridging social capital among Chinese college students, but does not affect bonding social capital (Liu & Brown, 2011). Our work on these issues draws from an integration of communications theories (media richness theory, uses and gratifications theory) and models emanating from social and developmental psychology (such as the theory of reasoned action). We perceive this theoretical integration across disciplines as a vital step in understanding the ways that social media may transform the nature of adolescent peer relations.

A major challenge in doing work on social media is that the media landscape changes more quickly than it can be carefully studied. Established media (e.g., chat rooms) fade in popularity, new media (e.g., Twitter) emerge, and adolescents migrate from one form of a given medium to another (e.g., from MySpace to Facebook). To help us think through the difficulties of doing research in this area, I have also joined forces with Patricia Greenfield of UCLA, an eminent scholar in the field of media use, to sponsor sessions at meetings of professional organizations (SRA, SRCD). We have led discussions of the emerging role of media in young people's social lives and of the best approaches to gaining a scientific understanding of this phenomenon. I have also had an opportunity to collaborate with international researchers on media issues. Recently, I assisted David Smahel, a noted scholar from the Czech Republic, in examining social media's role in more problematic behaviors such as Internet addiction (Smahel, Brown, & Blinka, 2012). We hope to continue such international collaborations as electronic media help to move the social world of adolescents to more of an international scale.

Final Thoughts: Missed Opportunities and Inspiring Collaborators

The work that we have done over the past three-and-a-half decades has been exciting, at least to me, but there also have been regrets over missed opportunities. Edward Laumann, a member of my dissertation committee, was also a pioneer of modern methods of social network analysis. I wish I could have spent time with him mastering these methods as they would have inspired more sophisticated research designs that could have helped us answer important questions about the connects between interaction- and reputation-based peer groups. A casual conversation with Wyndol Furman and Candice Feiring at the 1994 meetings of the Society for Research on Adolescence eventuated in a co-edited volume that helped to open up the field of romantic relations to more serious scholarship (Furman, Brown, & Feiring, 1999). I wish I had mustered the courage to follow these insightful scholars into a careful analysis of romantic relations and explore my interest in how romance was guided (and possibly obstructed) by the operations of the adolescent peer group. These are among the many opportunities I have missed to work effectively with outstanding scholars who have greatly advanced our understanding of the social world of adolescents.

On the other hand, I have had the privilege of working with a number of outstanding senior scholars (many already mentioned) as well as five generations of graduate students, who have been a steady source of ideas and inspiration. Mary Jane Lohr, Donna Rae Clasen, and Sue Ann Eicher helped to launch our studies of peer group structure and processes of peer pressure. A second generation of students guided our deeper exploration of these issues (Margaret Filkins, Harry Freeman, Jill Hamm, Tick-Ngee Sim, and Margaret Stone) and offered the first tentative glimpse of parents' role in peer processes (Amy Leventhal). I also was able to work closely with some of Larry Steinberg's outstanding students (Susie Lamborn, Nina Mounts) during this era. The next generation brought parental involvement more squarely in focus, with due attention to ways in which cultural factors shaped parenting behaviors (Leticia Alvarez and Patricia Quijada). Others of this generation continued work on peer crowds, with special attention to their role in problem behaviors such as drug use and sexual activity (Christa Klute and Wendy Theobald). A deeper, more culturally elaborated examination of parental involvement characterized the fourth generation (Jeremy Bakken, Jackie Nguyen, and Heather Von Bank). Their work continues in the current, fifth generation (Hsun-yu Chan), but is complemented by our study of electronic media and late adolescents' social adjustment to college (Dong Liu, Chia-chen Yang). Numerous undergraduates have also been part of our lab, which has come to be known as the Peer Relations Study Group. With colleagues such as these, I can look forward with excitement to the work yet to come.

References

Adler, P. A., & Adler, P. (1995). Dynamics of inclusion and exclusion in preadolesent cliques. *Social Psychology Quarterly, 58*, 145–162.

Asch, S. E. (1951). Effects of group pressure upon the modification and distortion of judgment. In H. Guetzkow (Ed.), *Groups, leadership, and men* (pp. 177–190). Pittsburgh, PA: Carnegie Press.

Bakken, J. P., & Brown, B. B. (2010). Adolescents' secretive behavior: African American and Hmong adolescents' strategies and justifications for managing parents' knowledge about peers. *Journal of Research on Adolescence, 20*, 359–388.

Barber, B. K. (Ed.). (2002). *Intrusive parenting: How psychological control affects children and adolescents*. Washington, DC: American Psychological Association.

Berndt, T. J. (1979). Developmental changes in conformity to peers and parents. *Developmental Psychology, 15*, 606–616.

Bixenstine, V.E., DeCorte, M. S., & Bixenstine, B. A. (1976). Conformity to peer sponsored misconduct at four grade levels. *Developmental Psychology, 12*, 226–236.

Brake, M. (1985). *Comparative youth culture*. London: Routledge & Kegan Paul.

Brown, B. B. (1978). Social and psychological correlates of help-seeking behavior among urban adults. *American Journal of Community Psychology, 6*, 425–439.

Brown, B. B. (1979). *Social type rating manual*. Retrieved from http://prsg.education.wisc.edu/.

Brown, B. B., Bakken, J. P., Ameringer, S. W., & Mahon, S. D. (2008). A comprehensive conceptualization of the peer influence process in adolescence. In M. J. Prinstein & K. Dodge (Eds.), *Understanding peer influences in children and adolescents* (pp. 17–44). New York, NY: Guilford Publications.

Brown, B. B., Bakken, J. P., Nguyen, J., & Von Bank, H. (2007). Sharing information about peer relations: Parent and adolescent opinions and behaviors in Hmong and African American families. In B. B. Brown & N. S. Mounts (Eds.), *Linking parents and family to adolescent peer relations: Ethnic and cultural considerations* (pp. 67–82). San Francisco, CA: Jossey-Bass.

Brown, B. B., & Chan, H-y. (2011, March). Keeping too close tabs?: Correlates of parents' intrusive information-seeking about adolescents' peers. In S. T. Hawk (Chair), *Parental privacy invasion during adolescence: Predictors, contexts, and consequences*. Symposium presented at the biennial meetings of the Society for Research in Child Development, Montreal, Quebec, Canada.

Brown, B. B., & Chiang, C. P. (1983–84). Drug and alcohol abuse among the elderly: Is being alone the key? *International Journal of Aging and Human Development, 18*, 1–12.

Brown, B. B., Clasen, D. R., & Eicher, S. A. (1986). Perceptions of peer pressure, peer conformity dispositions, and self-reported behavior among adolescents. *Developmental Psychology, 22*, 521–530.

Brown, B. B., Clasen, D. R., & Neiss, J. (1987, April). *Smoke in the looking glass: Adolescents' perceptions of their peer group status*. Paper presented at the biennial meetings of the Society for Research in Child Development, Baltimore.

Brown, B. B., Freeman, H., Huang, B. H., & Mounts, N. S. (1992, March). *"Crowd hopping": Incidence, correlates, and consequences of change in crowd affiliation during adolescence*. Paper presented at the biennial meeting of the Society for Research in Adolescence, Washington, DC.

Brown, B. B., Hamm, J. V., & Meyerson, P. (1996, March). Encouragement, empowerment, enmeshment: Ethnic differences in approaches to parental involvement with peer relationships. In B. B. Brown (Chair), *Buzz off or butt in?: Parental involvement in adolescent peer relationships*. Symposium presented at the biennial meetings of the Society for Research on Adolescence, Boston.

Brown, B. B., Herman, M., Hamm, J. V., & Heck, D. (2008). Ethnicity and image: Correlates of minority adolescents' affiliation with individual-based versus ethnically defined peer crowds. *Child Development, 79*, 529–546.

Brown, B. B., Lamborn, S. L., Mounts, N. S., & Steinberg, L. (1993). Parenting practices and peer group affiliation in adolescence. *Child Development, 64*, 467–482.

Brown, B. B., & Lohr, M. J. (1987). Peer group affiliation and adolescent self-esteem: An integration of ego-identity and symbolic interaction theories. *Journal of Personality and Social Psychology, 52*, 47–55.

Brown, B. B., Lohr, M. J., & Trujillo, C. M. (1990). Multiple crowds and multiple lifestyles: Adolescents' perceptions of peer group characteristics. In R. E. Muuss, (Ed.), *Adolescent behavior and society: A book of readings* (pp 30–36). New York, NY: Random House.

Brown, B. B., Mory, M., & Kinney, D. A. (1994). Casting adolescent crowds in relational perspective: Caricature, channel, and context. In R. Montemayor, G. R. Adams, & T. P. Gullotta (Eds.), *Advances in adolescent development, Vol. 6. Personal relationships during adolescence* (pp. 123–167). Thousand Oaks, CA: Sage.

Brown, B. B., Von Bank, H., & Steinberg, L. (2008). Smoke in the looking glass: Effects of discordance between self- and peer-rated crowd affiliation on adolescent anxiety, depression and self-feeling. *Journal of Youth and Adolescence, 37*, 1163–1177.

Chan, H.-y., & Brown, B. B. (2012, March). *Correlates of adolescent disclosure to parents about peers: The meditational role of "right-to-know" attitudes.* Paper presented at the biennial meetings of the Society for Research on Adolescence, Vancouver, BC.

Clasen, D. R., & Brown, B. B. (1985). The multidimensionality of peer pressure in adolescence. *Journal of Youth and Adolescence, 14*, 451–468.

Coleman, J. S. (1961). *The adolescent society.* New York, NY: Free Press of Glencoe.

Costanzo, P. R., & Shaw, M. E. (1966). Conformity as a function of age level. *Child Development, 37*, 967–975.

Cross, J. L., & Fletcher, K. L. (2009). The challenge of adolescent crowd research: Defining the crowd. *Journal of Youth and Adolescence, 38*, 747–764.

Cusick, P. A (1973). *Inside high school.* New York, NY: Holt, Rinehart and Winston.

Dishion, T. J., Spracklen, K. M., Andrews, D. W., & Patterson, G. R. (1996). Deviancy training in male adolescents friendships. *Behavior Therapy, 27*, 373–390.

Dunphy, D. C. (1969). *Cliques, crowds, and gangs: Group life of Sydney adolescents.* Melbourne, AU: Chesire.

Eckert, P. (1989). *Jocks and burnouts.* New York, NY: Teachers College Press.

Eder, D. (1985). The cycle of popularity: Interpersonal relations among female adolescents. *Sociology of Education, 58*, 154–165.

Erikson, E. H. (1950). *Childhood and society.* New York, NY: Norton.

Erikson, E. H. (1968). *Identity, youth, and crisis.* New York, NY: Norton.

Feuer, L. (1969). *The conflict of generations.* New York, NY: HarperCollins.

Finders, M. J. (1997). *Just girls: Hidden literacies and life in junior high.* New York, NY: Teachers College Press.

Furman, W., Brown, B. B., & Feiring, C. (Eds.) (1999). *The development of romantic relationships in adolescence.* London: Cambridge University Press.

Insurance Institute for Highway Safety (2009). *Fatality facts: Teenagers: 2008.* Arlington VA. Available from http://www.iihs.org/research/fatality_facts_2008/teenagers.html.

Iscoe, I., Williams, M., & Harvey J. (1963). Modification of children's judgments by a simulated group technique: A normative developmental study. *Child Development, 34*, 963–978.

Kandel, D. (1978). Homophily, selection, and socialization in adolescent friendships. *American Journal of Sociology, 84*, 427–436.

Kinney, D. A. (1991). "Dweebs," "headbangers" and "trendies": Adolescent identity formation and change within sociocultural contexts. Unpublished doctoral dissertation, Department of Sociology, Indiana University, Bloomington, IN.

Krein, H., & Brown, B. B. (2003, April). *Information management: What adolescents think parents have the right to know.* Paper presented at the biennial meetings of the Society for Research in Child Development, Tampa, FL.

Larkin, R. W. (1979). *Suburban youth in cultural crisis.* New York, NY: Oxford University Press.

Liu, D., & Brown, B. B. (2011, March). *Can self disclosure in social network sites benefit college students' social capital?* Poster presented at the biennial meetings of the Society for Research in Child Development, Montreal, Quebec, Canada.

Matute-Bianchi, M. E. (1986). Ethnic identities and patterns of school success and failure among Mexican-descent and Japanese-American students in a California high school: An ethnographic analysis. *American Journal of Education, 95*, 233–255.

Nguyen, J., & Brown, B. B. (2010). Making meanings, meaning identity: Hmong adolescent perceptions and use of language and style as identity symbols. *Journal of Research on Adolescence, 20*, 849–868.

Offer, D. (1969). *The psychological world of the teenager: A study of normal adolescent boys.* New York, NY: Basic Books.

Parke, R. D., & Ladd, G. W. (Eds.). (1992). *Family–peer relationships: Modes of linkage.* Hillsdale, NJ: Erlbaum.

Schwendinger, H., & Schwendinger, J. (1985). *Adolescent subcultures and delinquency.* New York, NY: Praeger.

Smahel, D., Brown, B. B., & Blinka, L. (2012). Associations between online friendship and Internet addiction among adolescents. *Developmental Psychology, 48*, 321–328.

Smetana, J. G. (1988). Adolescents' and parents' conceptions of parental authority. *Child Development, 59*, 321–335.

Stone, M. R., & Brown, B. B. (1998). In the eye of the beholder: Adolescents' perceptions of peer crowd stereotypes. In R. E. Muuss & H. D. Porton (Eds.), *Adolescent behavior and society: A book of readings* (5th ed., pp. 158–169). New York, NY: McGraw-Hill.

Stone, M. R., & Brown, B. B. (1999). Descriptions of self and crowds in secondary school: Identity claims and projections. In J. McClellan (Ed.), *The role of peer groups in adolescent social identity: Stability and change* (pp. 7–20). San Francisco: Jossey-Bass.

Susman, S., Pokhrel, P., Ashmore, R. D., & Brown, B. B. (2007). Adolescent peer group identification and characteristics: A review of the literature. *Addictive Behaviors, 32*, 1602–1627.

Tajfel, H. (1974). Social identity and intergroup behaviour. *Social Science Information, 13*, 65–93.

Yang, C.-c., & Brown, B. B., (2013). Motives for using Facebook, patterns of Facebook activities, and late adolescents' social adjustment to college. *Journal of Youth and Adolescence, 42*, 403–416.

Yang, C.-c., Brown, B. B., & Braun, M. T. (in press). From Facebook to cell calls: Layers of electronic intimacy in college students' interpersonal relationships. *New Media and society.*

6

Reflections on a Lifetime of Life-Course Research

Turning Opportunity into Passion

Marlis Buchmann

 As graduation from *Gymnasium*, the academic track of high school in the Swiss educational system, drew closer in the early 1970s, the impending choice of a major for my studies at the University of Zurich weighted heavily on me. With my interests as broad as they possibly could be and advisors offering little clues, I stumbled upon sociology. Given the political climate of the times, with the unrest of the late 1960s even striking conservative Switzerland, sociology appealed to me as a progressive choice and thus a an attractive subject to study. In retrospect, my interest in the functioning of society has most likely also been kindled by my experiences as an exchange student to the United States (upstate New York). This early year abroad definitely made me aware of how much beliefs and values, norms, and behaviors may vary from one country—or from one context—to the other. The desire to learn more about these societal differences and to better understand their causes and consequences made me go into sociology.

The studies of sociology at the University of Zurich at that time were very much focused on research experiences, "hands on," and "learning by doing." This approach was certainly challenging, particularly in the first years, as the largely "spoon-feeding" learning style experienced at the *Gymnasium* had not exactly prepared me for this type of study. It felt like jumping into cold water, struggling, and trying to survive. However, I also learned an important lesson for my future professional life: Research is a tough business and requires perseverance, stamina, and a long breath. Professor Peter Heintz, the founder of the Department of Sociology at the University of Zurich and the Department's chair at the time, had the fabulous ability of inspiring one's genuinely sociological thinking. Devoting his lifetime to the development of a theory

of world society, Peter Heintz managed to instill in his students a conception of the social world composed of multiple layers of stratified social levels, encompassing each other, interacting with each other, generating social tensions, and thus eventually change. This rather complex approach of thinking about the make-up of the social world—for sociology students in their early years rather perplexing at times—sharpened our intellect for what would later be framed as the *social embeddedness* (or *contextualization*) of agency. Although the research topics I was engaged in during my studies were light years away from the later-to-be-developed life-time research interests, the ways in which we were trained to think about society and its functioning provided us with indispensable conceptual tools for tackling research questions in novel sociological areas.

Against this background it was not surprising that my master thesis was a macro-analysis of differences in health expenditures between Swiss cantons, aiming to account for the economic, social, and political causes driving these differences. The units of this first independent piece of research of mine were contextual entities, Swiss cantons, and I was working with highly aggregated data. The groundwork that would spark my future interests in life-course research and human development was not a long time coming, however. Having just earned my master's degree and liking very much to do research, I was offered a research position at the Department of Sociology at the University of Zurich. The research project to which I was assigned was about the antecedents and consequences of delinquent and deviant behavior in youth, focusing on young people's early life-course trajectories and identity formation, the conditions of their up-bringing in the family, at school, and among peers. This study also traced the effects of being "labeled" a delinquent youth on the young people's further life course.

This research opportunity—encountered more or less by chance—introduced me to longitudinal analysis, life-course analysis, and behavioral outcomes related to events and transitions in the course of life. Most importantly, this project also caught my interest in the age groups of children and adolescents. The flourishing field of the sociology of the life course, promoting the idea that the life course is an institution of its own in modern society, greatly influenced my dissertation (Buchmann, 1983). There I showed how young's people life course is intertwined with their behavioral outcomes—above and beyond the influences that the family and its context of socialization may exert. While there certainly is "path-dependency" in the life course—earlier achievements or failures increase the likelihood of later accomplishments or lack of success—the questions of interest I pursued were also related to the circumstances and opportunities of breaking path dependency and thus beating the odds.

Consolidating Early Research Interests in International Contexts

Thanks to a habilitation stipend granted by the University of Zurich, followed by a post-doctoral grant of the Swiss National Science Foundation, I was able to further explore the intricate intertwinement between structural opportunities and individuals' capacity for action in various academic settings. In the second half of the 1980s I went to Paris and was a post-doctoral student at Pierre Bourdieu's *Centre de sociologie de l'éducation et de la culture* at the *Ecole des Hautes Etudes en Sciences Sociales* for some time. The first-hand exposure to another scientific culture in the social sciences sharpened my mind for contextual differences in academic traditions and in the ways in which salient scientific issues were approached. Hence, the idea was not farfetched that Pierre Bourdieu's theoretical outlook on the mechanisms of social reproduction, with its strong emphasis on the role of the family's and later one's own social position in shaping one's word views, visions, aspirations, and preferences, might have been influenced to a certain extent by the strongly stratified and rather hierarchical French society exhibiting, compared to other Western nations, less social mobility.

This thought inspired my ideas for the habilitation research project. If one aspires to stay in academia and to become a professor, the Swiss (and German) educational system expects you to earn this kind of a second PhD.[1] I hoped that a cross-national comparison of young people's entry into adulthood in France, the United States, and Switzerland would enable me to examine how differences in national contexts (i.e., institutional arrangements, structure of social inequality, cultural values, and beliefs) might shape young people's status transitions in different realms of life (i.e., education, labor market entry, leaving the parental home, and family formation) and their outlooks on life, expectations, and aspirations.

Continuing my post-doctoral studies at Stanford University (with John Meyer as my mentor) and the University of California at Berkeley (with Neil Smelser as my mentor), I gradually realized that I had to downsize my high-flying cross-national research project on the entry into adulthood if I wanted to earn my last educational degree within any reasonable amount of time.[2] The resolution to scale down my project was much facilitated by the visits at the Institute of Human Development at the University of California at Berkeley and the discussions with John Clausen (Clausen, 1993). I would learn so much about the Berkeley Growth Study, the Oakland Growth Study, and the Institute of Child Welfare Guidance Study, and I became fascinated by the time period these studies covered, probably making them the world's longest running studies of human lives. Consequently, I reread again Glen Elder's (1974) book *Children of the Great Depression*. The exposure to this research tradition deepened my interest in the ways in which social change would affect the dynamics of young people's life-course trajectories and their outlook on life, plans for the future, and strategies for action.

John Meyer at the Department of Sociology at Stanford University also encouraged me to think about the nature of the life course in modern society (Meyer, 1986, 1988). In my book entitled *The Script of Life in Modern Society: Entry into Adulthood in a Changing World* (1989), the product of my postdoctoral studies abroad, I laid out a conceptual framework of life-course analyses encompassing its macro- and micro side as well as its structural and cultural dimensions. At the structural level, a macro perspective of the life course focuses on the institutionalization of the life course, providing a set of rules and regulations that organizes individual life courses. At the cultural level, this perspective refers to the collective representations and ideologies of the life course predominant in the society of interest. A micro perspective, by contrast, acknowledges, at the structural level, the importance of the life course as an actual sequence of status and role transitions. At the cultural level, it takes into account the individuals' expectations, aspirations, and plans for their own lives. This framework was an attempt to contribute to a more theoretically informed life-course analysis by focusing "on the relation of social structure to individual choice in the life course" (Buchmann, 1989: 4) and to empirically test some hypotheses that could be derived from this framework.

In *The Script of Life* the empirical investigation was devoted to the comparison of the entry into adulthood of the 1960 and 1980 cohorts of white high-school seniors in the United States using data from *Project Talent* (1960 cohort) and *High School and Beyond* (1980). The book paid particular attention to the ways in which structural and cultural change had altered the timing and sequencing of status transitions to adulthood as well as young people's expectations, aspirations, and action strategies. Selecting these two cohorts of high-school seniors was an appropriate choice, as American society had changed profoundly and in many respects between the time when the older cohort went to high school and when the younger one did so. I argued that the nature of the transition to adulthood had changed from being a short period of transition accompanied by a highly normative sequence of transitions to a prolonged and less standardized transition period. I also made the argument that, not least as a result of the increasingly institutionalized and individualized life course, young people's action capacities, their expectations, and aspirations would become more important for successfully transitioning to adulthood. Perhaps, the most valuable aspect of this piece of research was to help stimulate scientific debates on the nature of the life course and life stages, particularly the life stage of youth, in late modern society and the role of agency in navigating life trajectories. Since the early 1990s, debates, predominantly in the European scientific community, revolved around questions of the individualization and destandardization of the life course (for review articles on these debates, see Brückner & Mayer, 2005; Kohli, 2007). In retrospect, my book was an early and empirically informed contribution to these debates.

Learning to Square Academic Duties with Precious Research Time

After my post-doctoral studies abroad, followed by the interlude of being a Visiting Professor for one year at the Center for European Studies and the Department of Sociology at Stanford University, I was appointed to a full professorship of sociology at the Swiss Federal Institute of Technology in Zurich (ETH)—also referred to as the MIT of Europe. This appointment was for the first chair of sociology at this institution of higher education. With the challenging (and definitely time consuming) task of building up the Department of Sociology at the ETH I scrambled for time to explore other aspects of the framework on the life course and social change developed in *The Script of Life*. Inspired by Karl-Ulrich Mayer's large-scale, multi-cohort life-course study that he had designed for Germany (Brückner & Mayer, 1998), my collaborators of the time and I set up a similar study for Switzerland, the Swiss Life History Study, comprising large representative samples of two birth cohorts of Swiss women and men born in 1949–51 and 1959–61, respectively, and residing in the German-speaking part of Switzerland. Data on the respondents' life trajectories was collected retrospectively in 1989, covering the entire educational career, labor market entry, early career development, further education participation, work experiences with IT, as well as the entire family trajectory. In this study, we extended our research interest beyond the transition to adulthood to early career development. Given my new academic home at a technical university, we focused our study on the ways in which rapid technological change, and the diffusion of IT and computer work, would affect labor market entry, the structure of occupational trajectories as well as work-related identities. The study design allowed us to examine these issues as the majority of the older cohort had entered the labor market and experienced early career development

before the rapid diffusion of IT, while the younger cohort started their careers with the ongoing rapid diffusion of this technology (see Sacchi, 2003). We argued that, if the widely held claim of the increasingly individualized and destandardized structure of the life course was indeed valid, occupational trajectories should exhibit a general trend toward greater variation and differentiation across cohorts (Buchmann & Sacchi, 1995a, 1995b). The findings from the Swiss Life History Study did lend support to our assumption. The sound empirical evidence proved useful as the tone of the discourse on these issues, particularly in the German-speaking countries, had often been quite ideological, lacking any empirical underpinning.

The preoccupation with the changing nature of labor market entry, employment careers, and occupational trajectories—the latter ones being particularly salient in the Swiss labor market characterized by segmentation along occupational credentials—led us to systematically explore, based on The Swiss Life History Study, how the alleged changes would shape women's trajectories regarding labor-market exits and reentries (Buchmann, Kriesi, Pfeifer, & Sacchi, 2002, 2003) and their continuous labor force participation (Buchmann, Kriesi, & Sacchi, 2004). Accelerated shifts in skill requirements coupled with less standardized patterns of occupational careers also begged the question of whether continuous (e.g., further or recurrent) education would become more important for occupational trajectories (Buchmann, König, Li, & Sacchi, 1999), women's and men's occupational mobility (Li, König, Buchmann, & Sacchi, 2000), and women's patterns of mobility out of female-dominated occupations as they are the less advantageous occupations (Li, Buchmann, König, & Sacchi,1998). Contributing the Swiss chapter to an international comparison of shifts in the transition from school to work, we investigated trends in educational opportunities and status-related entry into the labor-market for the two Swiss-born cohorts, examining the role of parental social background for successfully coping with this transition (Buchmann & Sacchi, 1998). Compared to other advanced industrial societies, the Swiss findings revealed the great and highly stable impact of parental social background on this transition, attesting to the strong social reproduction prevalent in Switzerland.

The Swiss Life History Study was (and still is; see below) a treasure trove for addressing innumerable research questions revolving around the many features of the changing nature of life-course trajectories in advanced industrialized countries. The purpose of this autobiographical account is certainly not to painstakingly report on the many and mostly interesting findings. I do want to point out, however, that they often did confirm the ways in which change in education, occupational structure, the labor market, and technology would affect work and employment trajectories, although the effects had often been greatly overestimated in the literature.[3] It is also worthwhile mentioning that the increasingly more prominent large-scale, multi-cohort studies in the 1990s, characterized by the recording of the precise timing of all the transitions and events in people's education, work, and family trajectories, allowed for the powerful application of event history analysis to life-course data. This development greatly advanced the methodology of life-course research. Despite these advances, I realized at some point that most studies based on The Swiss Life History data were a bit tilted to the structural level of analysis, asking how shifts in opportunity structures would affect the life-course outcomes of interest and examining the extent of social reproduction in these outcomes across generations.

The cultural turn

Against the background of the nicely laid out four-fold table of life-course analysis in *The Script of Life*, I felt the urge to contribute to those cells of the table I had neglected so far. Pretty familiar with the entire range of life-course literature by then, I was struck by the fact that the macro analysis of the life course at the cultural level had not received much attention at all. This approach to life-course analysis relates to questions of society's provision of collective representations and cultural codes about the life course and the person (i.e., actor) enacting his or her life trajectory. Profiting much from Ann Swidler's ideas of how culture works, published in her seminal article "Culture in Action: Symbols and Strategies" (1986), *The Script of Life* argued that cultural images were the backdrop against which individuals would devise their own lives, develop expectations, and aspirations. Acknowledging that such collective representations change only slowly, any attempt to study change in the cultural representations of the life course and the cultural imagery of the self would have to draw upon data able to capture long-term change.

I was particularly intrigued to think about what kind of data would allow me to tap the cultural dimension at the macro level and in historical perspective. More by chance than any purposeful intention I learned that Swiss newspapers had published personal ads, i.e., advertisements for seeking a (marriage) partner, since the later 19th century. I was immensely fascinated by reading the advertisements published in the late 19th and early 20th century and by comparing them to those written in the later 20th century. It took me a while, though, to realize that this type of data might be an excellent source for tapping the cultural code of personhood in the private realm of life and the cultural imagery of intimate relationships. In personal ads, women and men present in highly standardized ways who they are, providing information on those characteristics and features they think would make them attractive as marriage partners. We claimed that these women and men would draw upon the prevalent collective images of the culturally legitimated, appropriate person to present themselves, not least because they were expressing their views about themselves and the desired partner in the public realm of a newspaper with the intention of being successful in the marriage market (Buchmann &

Eisner, 1997a). As social scientists trained in quantitative research, my collaborators and I saw the potential of personal ads for developing quantitative indicators of long-term cultural change. We attributed this potential not only to the kind of cultural artifacts they represented, but also to the fact that they embodied everyday culture—as opposed to elite culture—and to their availability in large numbers. According to historical sources, personal ads were rather widespread practices for finding (marriage) partners, even in the late 19th and early 20th centuries. Accidentally and interestingly enough, we learned that our intention to construct indicators of long-term cultural change based on *advertisements* had a famous predecessor in sociology—Max Weber. At the first meeting of the German Sociological Association held in Frankfurt in 1910, Max Weber argued for a systematic investigation of cultural change, maintaining that

> we must examine the press ultimately to this effect: what does it contribute to the moulding of modern man? [. . .] To be frank, we shall have to start in a completely commonplace way to measure, with scissors and compasses, how the content of newspapers has changed with regard to quantity in the course of the last generation, not least in the advertisement section.

We took Max Weber's advice seriously and systematically collected more than 8,000 personal ads (80 randomly selected ads per year) that were published in two major Swiss newspapers between 1900 and 2000 (Buchmann & Eisner, 1997b). Developing an encompassing dictionary, we analyzed the ads with computer-aided content analysis. The size of our sample most likely makes our study the largest existing study on personal ads and perhaps one of the most extensive attempts to track long-term cultural change based on quantitative content analysis. Following Max Weber's suggestion, we interpret the content of personal ads as cultural artifacts that give us superb information about the *cultural models* of the private self prevalent in the society at large in a given time period. A quick glance at two ads will reveal how the presentation of the private self has changed over the 20th century. In the year 1901, we find a healthy young man who seeks a marriage partner in the upper-class newspaper *Neue Zürcher Zeitung* (English translation):

> Young man, 30 years old, completely healthy, with respectable, solid character, in secure position, seeks, in this way due to lack of suitable opportunity, a worthy, hard-working and merry 22–35 year-old daughter from a Swiss protestant and well-situated family for closer relationship with a view to an early marriage.

As if the author had attempted to condense Max Weber's Protestant Ethic to its extreme, he chose *diligence* and *restraint* to describe his inner qualities and virtues and those expected of his future wife. By this, he demonstrates how much his identity is rooted in the world of work. By contrast, a slim 34-year-old man with "pleasant appearance presents himself quite differently in the ad published in 1992 in the middle-class newspaper *Tagesanzeiger*:

> I, self-advertiser, (34/176/69kg), slim, pleasant appearance, have a variety of interests. I can offer you a lot and would like to share everything with you. Are you a pretty attractive young woman who enjoys life and is free for a common future? [. . .]

Not only has the world of work explicitly lost its dominant place in the cultural conception of the self—"my professional success means a lot to me, but not everything"—but the personal ad is also full of references to emotional qualities, such as empathy and sensitivity. The remarkable change in the inner qualities of the self that characterize these two personal ads, published almost a hundred years apart, was confirmed by our quantitative statistical analyses based on the full sample of 8,000 ads. We detected what we called the shift from the *obligated self*, a conception of the self deeply anchored in the "call of work duty," to the *expressive self*, revolving around one's self-actualization and the expression of one's unique, authentic, distinctive, and original qualities, (Buchmann & Eisner, 1997b, 1999). Although this general trend would hold for both women and men, we also found notable gender differences with women emphasizing appearance, attractiveness, and emotional qualities, whereas men would stress more social status and occupation (Buchmann & Eisner, 2001). At the level of collective representations, our study was probably the first one to garner much-needed empirical evidence of the widely postulated process of the increasing individualization in late modern society that would manifest itself particularly in the private self and in intimate relationships (see, for example, Giddens, 1991, 1992). To our surprise, the findings revealed that the cultural codes of personhood had already started to shift, much against the conventional wisdom, in the mid-1950s and coming into full bloom in the second half of the 1960s.

Venturing out to other unchartered research territory At about this time, I was again entangled between the twists and turns of job offers for academic positions. I had been offered a full professorship of sociology at the University of Zurich in 1995 and decided, after much thinking, to negotiate for a joint professorship of sociology at the ETH and the University of Zurich. At the same time, the Swiss National Science Foundation launched a large research program (at least by Swiss standards) with the aim of promoting social science research in Switzerland (Swiss Priority Program: Switzerland Towards the Future). As the program's research areas were broadly defined (e.g., social inequality in Switzerland, labor market, work careers), we seized the opportunity to align our research interests with those of the program. Having conducted many studies on school-to-work transitions and early career development (see above), my collaborators and I had often deplored a particularly

unfortunate lacuna in this area of life-course research. There was hardly any sound empirical research that would take the demand side of the labor market into account, testing hypotheses of how skill demand and employers' recruiting and hiring preferences would affect, for example, school-to-work transitions, early career development, women's employment trajectories, and status mobility across occupational careers. This lacuna was mostly attributable to the difficulties of measuring skill demand at the individual level. This level of measurement implies assessing job opportunities for individual labor force participants. Such a disaggregated measure was, however, a prerequisite for studying the ways in which occupation-specific skill demand, representing job opportunities for individual labor-force participants endowed with the requisite occupational qualifications, would impact employment and work careers. Intrigued by the great potential of advertisement data based on our research experiences with personal ads, we started to think about whether job ads could help to partially fill this gap.

In job ads, employers describe the ideal incumbent of the vacant position advertised, providing information on the company, the job title (i.e., occupation) and type of employment (e.g., full-time or part-time; fixed contract, etc.), the educational and other (formal and informal) requirements for the advertised job, the tasks to be fulfilled in the job, the work environment, and many other aspects of the job. We acted on the assumption that employers would especially rely on job advertisements as the preferred personnel recruitment strategy when a vacancy was hard to fill, be it due to a shortage of labor, scarcity of the particular skills in need, etc. Job ads would thus express the urgency of employers' skill demand. This feature was a highly desirable quality of job ads, when research interests would revolve around shifts in skill demand and the factors causing the change (Sacchi et al., 2005; Salvisberg, 2010) or in the ways in which variation in (occupation-specific) skill demand would affect outcomes in people's employment and occupational careers (e.g., skill-adequate labor market entry, risk of unemployment, salary, status mobility, etc.).

With the help of a substantial research grant from the above-mentioned program, we plunged ourselves into collecting job ads. Selecting a representative random sample of job ads published in newspapers and advertisers in the German-speaking part of Switzerland and dating back to 1950 (Sacchi, Salvisberg, & Buchmann, 2005), the database currently includes approximately 40,000 job ads with a total of over 60,000 vacant positions.[4] Matching the skill demand indicators with employment and work history data (from The Swiss Life History Study) annually and at the individual level, we examined how the business cycle, individual job opportunities, and structural characteristics of labor-market positions would affect transitions to self-employment (Buchmann, Kriesi, & Sacchi, 2009). Using a similar approach, the dissertation of one of my collaborators provided much-needed empirical evidence of the significance of individual job opportunities for women's labor-market exits and reentries (Kriesi, 2006). Another paper investigates the relationship between job opportunities and inter-firm upward, lateral, and downward status mobility in the Swiss occupationally segmented labor market (Buchmann, Kriesi, & Sacchi, under review). An ongoing dissertation project asks how young people's labor market entry is affected by the job opportunities they encounter. Of particular interest is whether poor job opportunities force young people to accept jobs for which their vocational training has not prepared them and how such skill-inadequate first jobs would affect early career development as well as their work identities.

The Opportunity to Bundle Up All My Research Interests

Another fortunate twist in my academic career happened in 2003 when the launch of a large national research program of the Swiss National Science Foundation, entitled Childhood, Youth, and Intergenerational Relationships in a Changing Society, coincided with the establishment of a new research center at the University of Zurich. It was the Jacobs Center for Productive Youth Development, a joint venture between the Jacobs Foundation and the University of Zurich. I was offered the position of director at this center. Assessing this attractive opportunity against my research interests and the prospect of setting up a large-scale longitudinal study on child and youth development, I came to the conclusion that this academic move would help me to put everything in place. I accepted the position and went about building up this new institution, already my second one, eager to vest this new center with a unique and distinctive research focus on child and adolescent development.

We defined the Center's mission as being the advancement of knowledge about the processes and mechanisms that generate social inequalities in children's and youth's early life-course outcomes, as well as their competence development. We attributed particular importance to *transitions* in the early life course, aiming at a fundamental understanding of how individual competences affect life-course transitions and, vice versa, how coping with these transitions would impact on the further development of competences.

From a sociological life-course perspective, transitions in the institutionalized life course assume great importance insofar as they mark the entry into novel spheres of social interactions characterized by their own social rules and demanding adjustment processes on the part of those who make the transition. The mastery of the transition is consequential for the future performance in the new social context and thus affects further development. We labeled the research program Early Life Course Transitions and Competence Development in order to portray the center's unique and truly interdisciplinary identity.

As this type of research requires a focus on longitudinal studies, the Jacobs Center for Productive Youth Development was the ideal institutional home. Longitudinal studies are always long-term and farsighted investments, with the scientific profits being reaped only after years. Fortunately enough, the research proposal I had submitted to the National Research Program, Childhood, Youth, and Intergenerational Relationships in a Changing Society, was successful, and we were rewarded with a huge grant (at least by Swiss standards in the social sciences) to set up a representative multi-cohort, multi-informant, longitudinal study on children's and adolescence life course and competence development.

The COCON study—the acronym for COmpetence and CONtext—is the first study of its kind for the German- and French-speaking parts of Switzerland. The study consists of representative samples of three cohorts, which each cohort representing a prototypical stage of childhood and adolescence: The cohort of 6-year-old children representing mid-childhood, the cohort of 15-year-old youth capturing mid-adolescence, and the cohort of 21-year-old people tapping late adolescence and early adulthood. Conducting the first survey in 2006, we aimed at following the cohorts of the 6- and 15-year-olds to the age of 21. Fortunately enough, we have managed to continue data collection for the past 7 years, collecting data in five survey waves, and hope to do so for many more years to come.

The multi-cohort, longitudinal design of the study has three major analytical interests. First, it allows us to investigate *intra*-individual development of competences and the unfolding of early life-course trajectories. As the COCON study includes representative samples of the respective cohorts, we can learn about typical early life-course trajectories and typical patterns of competence development. Second, *inter*-individual differences in competence development and life-course trajectories may be assessed, paying particular attention to the causes and consequences of these differences. Of major interest is how and to what extent children's and adolescents' social background and socialization contexts shape life-course trajectories and patterns of competence development. And finally, the research design is able to examine the effects of social change, asking whether early life-course trajectories and patterns of competence development alter as a result of the changing social and cultural contexts in which children and adolescents grow up.

A signature feature of the COCON study is its focus on the development of social competencies and the role of these competencies for achievements in children's and adolescents' life course.[5] These competences, broadly defined as the spectrum of competencies that regulate the quality of social interactions, have been under-researched from a longitudinal perspective. Given this lacuna, not much attention has been paid to the effects of social background, socialization contexts, and life-course transitions on the development of social competencies. Over the last years, we have attempted to systematically fill this gap. We analyzed how the development of these competences in pre-school age would affect the coping with the beginning school transition (Kriesi et al., 2012). We also looked at the joint effect of these competencies and the coping with the beginning school transitions on academic achievement in mid-elementary school (Buchmann & Kriesi, 2010) and asked whether gender would matter for explaining the role of competencies in these outcomes (Kriesi & Buchmann, forthcoming). Of major interest was also the importance of social competencies in the transition to vocational training after the completion of compulsory schooling. The findings show that social competencies do indeed play a role for the successful transition net of educational credential and grades (Bayard Walpen, 2013) as well as for earnings after labor market entry (Kriesi, under review).

A particularly promising aspect of the COCON study is its focus on children's and adolescents' moral and social-emotional development (Malti & Buchmann, 2010a). To our knowledge, COCON is the only study worldwide investigating longitudinally the various components of moral development as well as its individual and social antecedents and (mal)adaptive outcomes based on large, representative samples of children and adolescents. Specifically, our studies have focused on the development of moral emotions, such as guilt and sympathy, as well as its links to how children and adolescents reason about the moral conflicts that occur in everyday life (Malti & Buchmann, 2010b; Malti, Keller, & Buchmann, 2012). We showed how moral emotions and moral reasoning predict behavioral outcomes, including antisocial and prosocial behavior (Malti, Gasser, & Buchmann, 2009; Malti, Gummerum, Keller, & Buchmann, 2009; Malti, Gummerum, & Buchmann, 2007; Malti, Kriesi, & Buchmann, 2008). Other outcomes of interest were the development of sharing behavior in children and the role of sympathy and social acceptance (Malti, Gummerum, Keller, Chaparro, & Buchmann, 2012), the development of social justice values (Daniel, Malti, Dys, & Buchmann, 2013), and how emotions predict decision-making over an extended period of time (Krettenauer, Malti, Colasante, & Buchmann, 2013). Given our large representative samples, it was particularly intriguing to study the role of the most important social contexts (i.e., friendship, peer, and parent relationships) in developmental trajectories of moral emotions and moral reasoning (Malti & Buchmann, 2010a; Malti, Eisenberg, Hyunji, & Buchmann, 2013). Taken together, our findings have provided ample novel knowledge on how children and adolescents integrate emotions and cognitions in moral contexts, how this integrative process develops, and what the links between moral emotions with developmental psychopathology and positive mental health outcomes are. Particularly rewarding is that these findings have contributed to integrative developmental approaches to morality (see Malti & Killen, 2013; Malti & Ongley, in press).

Final Remarks

This autobiographical account may have given the impression that an academic's entire professional time was available for research. While we certainly know that this is not true, we do define ourselves through our research. Reflecting upon one's own research agenda, how it came about and developed through one's own life course is therefore perhaps the most interesting story to tell.

Going over the brief reflection on my life journey in academia made me aware how much it was shaped by chance and circumstance that initially were not totally under my control. However, the willingness, motivation, and capability to seize the opportunities that came about and "bend" them towards one's own research interests was probably the crucial factor for shaping my professional life trajectory.

As a social scientist I am well aware that the story recounted in my brief professional autobiography is a narrative—a selective one, saturated with retrospective re-interpretation. We emphasize particular aspects and neglect other ones. The final remarks are therefore the opportunity to highlight the underexposed or even neglected issues.

Academic careers certainly are individual achievements, but greatly nourished by an international network of colleagues who have an interest in your work, support your endeavors, and, most importantly, act as benevolent critics and thus push you forward. Again, whom you encounter always bears an element of chance. What you make out of these encounters is, however, in your own hands. I think I have never learned as much as by fortuitous encounters with colleagues interested in issues I was grappling with. This idea was never more apparent as when I had the opportunities to be a fellow at the Center for Advanced Study in the Behavioral Sciences at Stanford University. What greatly helped me to advance my various lines of research was the gift of having time away from the daily routines of academic life and discussing at length research matters with an interdisciplinary group of colleagues in a broader perspective. When I was at CASBS for the first time, I had the time to really think through and write the (successful) research proposal for the large COCON study. I made great strides in devising the story of the changing cultural imagery of the self over the 20th century based on our personal ads. I attribute this work mostly to the opportunity to read more widely and in areas I would not have thought of had I not greatly benefitted from the many illuminative discussions with co-fellows at the Center. Having known all the way along that this piece of research would pose daunting challenges, given the scope of its topic, it is on the right track, with several published papers, although the final product of a book has not seen the light of day yet.

And finally, the contribution to this volume would definitely not have seen the light of day if I had not been so fortunate to get another great opportunity to become a fellow at the Center for Advanced Study in the Behavioral Sciences. This is the place where things miraculously get done.

Notes

1. In the French educational system, the equivalent educational credential is called the Thesis of the State.
2. An auxiliary comment on the side: In the years to come, I encountered many opportunities to pursue this line of research although under different auspices. To name just two: Participating in a study involving a cross-national comparison of the transition to adulthood organized by Tom Cook and Frank Furstenberg, we explored how variations in institutional characteristics would affect young people's position and behaviors (Cook & Furstenberg, 2002; Breen & Buchmann, 2002). The invitation to write a review article on the transition to adulthood in Europe for the *Annual Review of Sociology* was the opportunity to emphasize the comparative component of the entry into adulthood across Europe (Buchmann & Kriesi, 2011).
3. Even a recent contribution to the Special Volume of *New Directions in Youth Development* in honor of Rainer Silbereisen (Buchmann & Malti, 2012) found, at least for Switzerland over the past 20 years, little change in women's choice of vocational training or studies and early career development. Despite young women's educational headways (in terms of number of years of schooling and credentials earned), they encounter serious difficulties in seizing the opportunities offered by global economic change due to persistent gendered constraints in education and the labor market.
4. Some years ago, we turned the database into a monitoring device of the Swiss labor market and started to include ads published in electronic media.
5. Economists usually refer to these competencies as non-cognitive competences.

References

Bayard Walpen, S. (2013). *Obligatorischer Schulabschluss – wie weiter? Zur Bedeutung von Kompetenzeinschätzungen für den Übertritt in eine nachobligatorische Ausbildung* [Completion of compulsory schooling – what next? On the importance of competence assessments for the transition to post-compulsory education]. Zürich: Seismo.

Breen, R., & Buchmann, M. (2002). Institutional variation and the position of young people: A comparative perspective. *Annals of the American Academy of Political and Social Sciences (AAPSS)* 580 (March): 288–305.

Brückner, E., & Mayer, K. U. (1998). Collecting life history data: Experiences from the German Life History Study. In J. Z. Giele & G. H. Elder, Jr. (Eds.), *Methods of life course research: Qualitative and quantitative approaches* (pp. 152–181). Thousand Oaks, CA: Sage Publications.

Brückner, H., & Mayer, K. U. (2005). De-standardization of the life course: what it might mean? And if it means anything, whether it actually took place? In R. MacMillan (Ed.), *The structure of the life course: Standardized? Individualized? Differentiated?* (pp. 27–53). Amsterdam: Elsevier.

Buchmann, M. (1983). *Konformität und Abweichung im Jugendalter: Eine empirische Untersuchung zur Biographie- und Identitätsentwicklung und abweichendem Verhalten Jugendlicher* [Conformity and deviance in youth: An empirical investigation of the development of biography and identity, and deviant behavior]. Diessenhofen: Rüegger.

Buchmann, M. (1989). *The script of life in modern society: Entry into adulthood in a changing world.* Chicago: The University of Chicago Press.

Buchmann, M., & Eisner, M. (1997a). The transition from the utilitarian to the expressive self. *Poetics, 25*(2/3): 157–175.

Buchmann, M., & Eisner, M. (1997b). Selbstbilder und Beziehungsideale im 20. Jahrhundert: Individualisierungsprozesse im Spiegel von Bekanntschafts- und Heiratsinseraten [Images of the self and ideals of intimate partnership in the 20th century: Processes of individualization in the light of personal ads]. In S. Hradil (Ed.), *Differenz und Integration: Die Zukunft moderner Gesellschaften* (pp. 343–357). Frankfurt am Main: Campus.

Buchmann, M., & Eisner, M. (1999). Freizeit als Element des Lebensstils und Mittel der kulturellen Distinktion: Bekanntschafts- und Heiratsinserate 1900–1996 [Leisure as an element of life style and a means of cultural distinction]. In C. Honegger, S. Hradil, & F. Traxler (Eds.), *Grenzenlose Gesellschaft?* (pp. 590–608). Frankfurt am Main: Campus.

Buchmann, M., & Eisner, M. (2001). Geschlechterdifferenzen in der gesellschaftlichen Präsentation des Selbst: Heiratsinserate von 1900 bis 2000 [Gender differences in the presentation of self: Personal ads: 1900–2000]. *Kölner Zeitschrift für Soziologie und Sozialpsychologie*, Sonderband 41: 75–107 Geschlechtersoziologie (Ed. B. Heintz).

Buchmann, M., König, M., Li, J. H., & Sacchi, S. (1999). *Weiterbildung und Beschäftigungschancen* [Continuous education and employment chances]. Zürich: Rüegger Verlag.

Buchmann, M., & Kriesi, I. (2010). Schuleintritt und Schulleistungen im mittleren Primarschulalter [Beginning school transition and academic achievement in mid-elementary school]. *Schweizerische Zeitschrift für Soziologie, 36*(2): 325–344.

Buchmann, M., & Kriesi, I., (2011). Transition to adulthood in Europe. *Annual Review of Sociology*, 37: 481–503.

Buchmann, M., Kriesi, I., Pfeifer, A., & Sacchi, S. (2002). *Half inside—half outside: Analyses of the labor market integration of women in Switzerland* [Halb drinnen—halb draussen: Zur Arbeitsmarktintegration von Frauen in der Schweiz]. Zürich und Chur: Rüegger Verlag.

Buchmann, M., Kriesi, I. Pfeifer, A., & Sacchi, S. (2003). Dynamics of women's employment careers: Labor market opportunities and women's labor market exit and re-entry. In W. Heinz & V. Marshall (Eds.), *Social dynamics of the life course: Transitions, institutions, and interrelations* (pp. 117–141). New York: Aldine de Gruyter.

Buchmann, M., Kriesi, I., & Sacchi, S. (2004). Labor market structure and women's paid work: Opportunities and constraints in the Swiss labor market. In J. Zollinger Giele & E. Holst (Eds.), *Changing life patterns in Western industrial societies* (pp. 165–188). Oxford: Elsevier.

Buchmann, M., Kriesi, I., & Sacchi, S. (2009). Labor market, job opportunities and transitions to self-employment. *European Sociological Review, 25*(5): 569–583.

Buchmann, M., Kriesi, I., & Sacchi, S. (under review). Status mobility in occupational labor markets: Occupational mobility chains and the role of job opportunities for upward, lateral and downward mobility in Switzerland.

Buchmann, M., & Malti, T. (2012). The future of young women's economic role in a globalized economy: New opportunities – persisting constraints. *New Directions in Youth Development*, Fall Issue, 135: 77–86.

Buchmann, M., & Sacchi, S. (1995a). Multidimensional classification of career data: An application to two Swiss birth cohorts. *Kölner Zeitschrift für Soziologie und Sozialpsychologie, 35*(3): 413–442.

Buchmann, M., & Sacchi, S. (1995b). Zur Differenzierung von Berufsverläufen: Ein mehrdimensionaler Kohortenvergleich. [Growing differentiation of occupational careers: A multidimensional cohort comparision.] In P. A. Berger & P. Sopp (Eds.), *Sozialstruktur und Lebenslauf* (pp. 49–64). Opladen: Leske + Budrich.

Buchmann, M., & Sacchi, S. (1998). The transition from school to work in Switzerland: Do characteristics of the educational system and class barriers matter? In Y. Shavit & W. Müller (Eds.), *From school to work: A comparative study of educational qualifications and occupational destinations* (pp. 407–442). Oxford: Oxford University Press.

Clausen J.A. (1993). *American lives: Looking back at the children of the Great Depression.* New York: Free Press.

Cook, Th. D. & Furstenberg, F. F. Jr. (2002) Explaining aspects of the transition to adulthood in Italy, Sweden, Germany, and the United States: A cross-disciplinary, case synthesis approach. *Annals of the*

American Academy of Political and Social Sciences, 580(March): 257–287.

Daniel, E., Malti, T., Dys, S., & Buchmann, M. (2013, in preparation). The development of moral emotions, moral reasoning, and social justice values from childhood to early adolescence.

Elder, G. H. (1974). *Children of the Great Depression.* Chicago: The University of Chicago Press.

Giddens, A. (1991). *Modernity and self-identity: Self and society in the late modern age.* Cambridge: Polity.

Giddens, A. (1992). *The transformation of intimacy: Sexuality, love, and eroticism in modern societies.* Cambdridge: Polity.

Kohli M. (2007). The institutionalization of the life course: Looking back to look ahead. *Research in Human Development, 4*(3–4): 253–571.

Krettenauer, T., Malti, T., Colasante, T., & Buchmann, M. (2013, under revision). The development of moral emotion attributions and decision-making from adolescence to early adulthood: A 6-year longitudinal study. *Developmental Psychology.*

Kriesi, I. (2006). *Beschäftigungsmöglichkeiten und Erwerbskontinuität von Frauen: Zur Bedeutung des Stellenangebots für Erwerbsunterbrechungen und Wiedereintritte ins Berufsleben* [Women's employment opportunities and continuous employment: The role of skill demand for labor market exits and reentries]. Chur/Zurich: Rüegger.

Kriesi, I., Bayard, S., & Buchmann, M. (2012). Die Bedeutung von Kompetenzen im Vorschulalter für den Schuleintritt [The role of competences developed in pre-school age fort he beginning school transition]. In Hupka-Brunner, S., Meyer, T., & Bergman, M. M. (Eds.), *Bildung – Arbeit – Erwachsenwerden* (pp. 160–180). Wiesbaden: VS Verlag für Sozialwissenschaften.

Kriesi, I., & Buchmann, M. (forthcoming). Beginning school transition and academic achievement in mid-elementary school: Does gender matter? In J. Eccles and I. Schoon (Eds.), *Gender differences in aspirations and attainment.* Cambridge: University of Cambridge Press.

Li, J. H., Buchmann, M., König, M., & Sacchi, S. (1998). Patterns of mobility for women in female-dominated occupations: An event-history analysis of two birth cohorts of Swiss women. *European Sociological Review, 14*(1): 49–67.

Li, J. H., König, M., Buchmann, M., & Sacchi, S. (2000). Influence of further education on occupational mobility in Switzerland. *European Sociological Review, 16*(1): 43–65.

Malti, T., & Buchmann, M. (2010a). Socialization and individual antecedents of adolescents' and young adults' moral motivation. *Journal of Youth and Adolescence, 39*(2): 138–149.

Malti, T., & Buchmann, M. (2010b). Die Entwicklung moralischer Emotionen bei Kindergartenkindern [The development of moral emotions in childhood]. *Praxis der Kinderpsychologie und Kinderpsychiatrie, 59*: 545–560.

Malti, T., Eisenberg, N., Hjunji, K., & Buchmann, M. (Under review). Developmental trajectories of sympathy, moral emotion attributions, and moral reasoning: The role of parental support.

Malti, T., Gasser, L., & Buchmann, M. (2009). Aggressive and prosocial children's emotion attributions and moral reasoning. *Aggressive Behavior, 35*(1): 90–102.

Malti, T., Gummerum, M., & Buchmann, M. (2007). Contemporaneous and one-year longitudinal prediction of children's prosocial behavior from sympathy and moral motivation. *Journal of Genetic Psychology, 168*: 277–299.

Malti, T., Gummerum, M., Keller, M., & Buchmann, M. (2009). Children's moral motivation, sympathy, and prosocial behavior. *Child Development, 80*: 442–460.

Malti, T., Gummerum, M., Keller, M., Chaparro, M.P., & Buchmann, M. (2012). Early sympathy and social acceptance predict the development of sharing in children. *PLoS ONE, 7*(12), e52017. doi: 10.1371/journal.pone.0052017.

Malti, T., Keller, M., & Buchmann, M. (2012). Do moral choices make us feel good? The development of adolescent's emotions following moral decision-making. *Journal of Research on Adolescence.* Early online publication, 4 December, 2012. doi: 10.1111/jora.12005.

Malti, T., & Killen, M. (2013; under revision). The role of emotions and judgments in morality: Developmental integrative approaches. *Child Development Perspectives.*

Malti, T., Kriesi, I., & Buchmann, M. (2008). Adolescent's prosocial behavior, sympathy, and moral reasoning. In F. Oser & W. Veugelers (Eds.), *Getting involved: Global citizenship development and sources of moral values* (pp. 131–146). Rotterdam: Sense Publishers.

Malti, T., & Ongley, S. (in press). The development of moral emotions and moral reasoning. In M. Killen & J. Smetana (Eds.), *Handbook of moral development.* New York: Taylor & Francis.

Meyer, J. W. (1986). The self and the life course: Institutionalization and its effects. In A. Sorensen, F. Weinert, & L. Sherrod (Eds.), *Human development and life course* (pp. 199–216). Hillsdale, NJ: Erlbaum.

Meyer, J. W. (1988). Levels of analysis: The life course as a cultural construction. In M. Riley et al. (Eds.), *Social structures and human lives* (pp. 49–62). Newbury Park: Sage.

Sacchi, S. (2003). Diffusion patterns of computer work in Switzerland. *Swiss Journal of Sociology, 29*(3): 433–452.

Sacchi, S., Salvisberg, A., & Buchmann, M. (2005). Long-term dynamics of skill demand in Switzerland from 1950–2000. In H. Kriesi, P. Farago, M. Kohli, & M. Zarin-Nejadan (Eds.), *Contemporary Switzerland: Revisiting the special case* (pp. 105–134). Houndmills: Palgrave Macmillan.

Salvisberg, A. (2010). *Soft skills in the labor market: Bedeutung und Wandel.* Zürich: Seismo Verlag.

Swidler, A. (1986). Culture in action: Symbols and strategies. *American Sociological Review, 51*(2): 273–286.

7

Journey to a Life-Course Perspective in Developmental Science

JOHN BYNNER

First Steps

Looking back on my intellectual career, there are two strands which have opened out through my life rather like the unfolding of a fan. They are not directly connected with psychology, but nevertheless established principles of enquiry—part epistemological, part moral, and part political—in my head which have never disappeared, if maybe mellowed, in places, over time. In this chapter I plan to pursue the intellectual journey through a series of strands of my thinking both arising from and driving the research I have done that have built out of the first two.

This is not a story about developing any grand psychological theory, more pursuing what Lee Cronbach (1975, p. 126) described as the more reasonable aspiration for the social scientist of assessing local events accurately, "to improve short run control," and developing explanatory concepts, "concepts that will help people to use their heads." In other words, our goal should be not only to add to understanding of human development and functioning, but by means of empirical evidence to contribute to their improvement (Lerner, Fisher, & Weinberg, 2000). There is, perhaps, no better way of putting it than the caution from Barbara Wootton (1959):

> The moral seems to be that it is in their role as the handmaidens to practical decisions that the social sciences can shine most brightly. Prediction may be a less ambitious goal than causation, but it is certainly more often within the reach of our present categories and techniques.
>
> (p. 324)

The last quotation also brings into the frame the names of significant people who have pointed the way to me by moving the subject on. Another such early influence was Hans Eysenck, external examiner for my Bristol first

degree and later for my London Birkbeck College PhD. His popular broadsides against unscientific psychological thinking, as exemplified by psychoanalysis, seemed at the time to be totally laudable correctives (Eysenck, 1953, 1957). It took me some time to recognize that one set of ideational rigidities can too easily be replaced by another closed system of belief of which Eysenck was no exception. Inevitably over a period of 50 years it is a selective picture, but I hope it gives more than just a flavor of the concerns that have dominated my career in social science and adolescent psychology.

So where do the two strands of this personal journey begin? I started my undergraduate career studying physics at the University of Bristol, where I soon realized that working in the physics laboratory was probably not for me. These doubts set me wondering whether one of my subsidiary subjects—philosophy, economics and psychology—might not be better instead. I chose psychology and managed to persuade those who held the purse strings to extend my funding for another year to complete an honors degree. Although physics as a subject had not absorbed my interest practically, the principles on which the subject stands could not have been bettered as preparation for the department I was entering. Bristol's psychology department had no doubts that the subject could, or should be, as much a science as physics and that scientific method applied to human development, functioning, and relationships was the only serious way to study it.

Behaviorism initially impressed, especially in its "purposive" form (Tolman, 1932), but soon gave way to neuro-physiology, cognitive psychology, and cybernetics. Ivor Pleydell Pierce and Frank George were the professors at the time and two books they promoted—one also acclaimed by Richard M. Lerner (see Chapter 26 this volume)—left a lasting impression. *The Organisation of Behaviour* (Hebb, 1949) made the connections between brain physiology and human action through the exciting concepts of the "Cell Assembly" and the "Phase Sequence." *Plans and the Structure of Behaviour* (Miller,

Galanter, & Pribram, 1960), introduced through the "TOTE" (test, operate, test, exit) mechanism the idea of continuous cognitive evaluation of action in the process of determining the action to take next.

The other experience at Bristol was outside science and psychology altogether. As something of a student activist I was elected to the office of Chairman of the Student Union's "Grants and Welfare" committee. The main task of the committee was distributing a small fund to help students who were in temporary financial difficulty. I also had my first exposure to survey data and survey research. My predecessor, as chairman, had conducted a survey of student attitudes to the university catering facilities for students. The data collected from a representative sample of students had never been analyzed and I was expected to do it. Engagement in the job was done somewhat reluctantly, but I soon came to realize the potential that both the survey and the analysis offered for improving a small part of student life.

The survey's potential resided not only in eliciting information but in the persuasive value of *concepts* grounded in *contemporary facts* about student catering in persuading those in control of the need for action that could improve it. I wove the findings into an argument for the importance, meaning, scope, quality, and location of catering facilities to the student's university experience, demonstrating how far short the present arrangements fell. Somewhat to my surprise the university authorities, rather than sidelining the report and its recommendations as to do with, perhaps, a personal agenda, took the ideas and the evidence, backing them very seriously. A program for action was established, recognizing that a university refectory is not only a place for eating but a space for socializing and communicating, and for resisting student isolation. I have never lost this realization of the value of evidence, nor the love of seeing it converted into action, not on the basis of facts or data alone, but through the explanatory concepts deployed in its interpretation. Concepts that shift perceptions and beliefs are to me where scientific excitement comes from.

Behavior and Identity

The heightened interest in policy and action, inspired by the catering facilities survey, may be one of my reasons in 1961 for deciding not to stay on at the university to do a PhD. Instead I joined a research team in what was then the Central Council for Health Education (CCHE) in a 3-year project to study the sexual behavior of young people (Schofield, Bynner, Lewis, & Massie, 1965). The context of the project was health education and the research was directed at what was perceived at the time as a massive rise in "venereal disease" among the youth population. The research approach was an interview-based survey carried out by a team of three with additional temporary help on random samples of young people in Leeds, Southampton, and London.

Data collection methods were inspired by the techniques developed in connection with the 1948 and 1953 *Kinsey Reports* on sexual behavior (Kinsey, Pomeroy, & Martin (1948, 1953) for collecting what at the time was seen by most young people as highly sensitive information. Embedded in a survey of attitudes and leisure activity, respondents were invited to deny, rather than assent to, each of a number of sexual acts in turn—"when did you first. . .?"—arranged in a hierarchy starting with kissing and finishing with intercourse. As the psychologist members of the team, my main responsibility was attitude measurement.

The research was tough and demanding involving interviewing young people aged 16–19 by appointment, some in a local office, often at home, sometimes almost within the hearing of their parents. A mystery that arose early on that inspired much of my interest and has done so ever since was the fact that boys reported sexual behavior at a level several times higher than the level reported by girls: such a mismatch could not possibly conform to reality. I began to realize that far less important to young people at this stage in their lives than giving facts about themselves was the impression they wanted to leave with others, including young adult interviewers. "Impression management" (Goffman, 1959) to convey masculine sexual prowess, as reflected in the number of sexual partners, was a key driver of a valued identity in the case of boys. For girls almost the complete opposite set of values prevailed. The aim was to appear both sexually attractive and potentially available, while not an easy conquest, with the risk of attracting the derogatory terms used by boys to describe girls, such as "easy," "cheap," or a "slag." At the time, before the "pill" and easy access to contraception, the overwhelming disincentive to being sexually active was the risk of pregnancy. But even in the era of the pill many of the same prohibitions prevail today, deeply rooted in longstanding cultural traditions, as driven by the perceived threat to family honor of girls' vulnerability to romantic advances and boys' unquenchable sexual drive.

The problem for the team was that the survey was intended to establish the facts of teenage sexual behavior and that is what, in my view, we were unable to do with complete confidence. The world of self-perception, if not deception, is the barrier many young people erect around themselves to stave off intrusion into their private lives and protect their true identities.

The thoughts stimulated by these observations soon converted into the desire to register for a Social Psychology PhD at Birkbeck College (part-time University of London institution for adults—21+). The topic was adolescent social and political attitudes and the research involved applying, in the analysis and interpretation of the survey's attitude data, the main ideas of Eysenck's theory of (adult) social attitudes (Eysenck, 1954), and his social attitude inventory. Pursuing his two-dimensional attitude model, "Toughness–Tendermindedness" (personality-based) and "Radicalism–Conservatism" (structurally, i.e., social class-based), I adapted the inventory for use with young people in the CCHE survey. The outcome was reformulation of the model in terms of what I called "Teenage Ethnocentrism–Teenage Integration," i.e., endorsement contrasting with rejection of a teenage "sub-culture" at variance with the mainstream culture of adult society; and "Teenage Progressiveness–Restrictiveness," i.e., rejecting as opposed to accepting official adult moral values.

Beginning the PhD coincided with the move shortly afterwards to my second job in 1964, research officer in the Government Social Survey (GSS), a government department now part of the Office of National Statistics. My boss was Aubrey McKennell, who I worked with in GSS until he left for a university post 4 years later. The subject this time was young people's smoking, one of a series of studies, directed by McKennell for the Ministry of Health and aimed at encouraging adults to give up smoking and discouraging young people from starting. *The Young Smoker* (Bynner, 1969a; McKennell & Bynner, 1969) was based on a survey of a sample of 5,601 boys aged 11 to 15; girls were not included because piloting showed that in this age group their smoking at the time was much rarer and could not be effectively studied without a substantially larger sample. The project enabled me to continue to pursue the theme of self-presentation as a major part of identity construction. A form of Osgood's "Semantic Differential" instrument was used (Osgood, Suci, & Tannenbaum, 1957), involving the rating of "the (typical) smoker," "non-smoker," self," and "ideal self," on 19 bipolar scales to identify the ways in which these images were perceived.

It was clear from the results of factor analysis of the ratings that smoking served as a significant identity marker. The first dimension, labeled *toughness,* and the second, less obviously *precocity/social maturity*, were seen as positive attributes of smoker identity in the eyes of other boys. That is to say, the toughness of a soldier or boxer to which most boys aspired as assessed from "the kind of boy you would like to be" was attributed, i.e., close in factor score, to "the kind of boy who smokes cigarettes" and some way from the score of the "kind of boy who does not smoke cigarettes". The other attribute, precocity, was more concerned with engagement in the social life of older teenagers, particularly those involving the opposite sex. Smoking would be admired as sophisticated and "cool" in such a group. Identifying with the "non-smoker" would then be seen as a denial of participation in this social life providing therefore a powerful disincentive to giving up.

Exactly in line with the experience of the student refectory survey, the *Young Smoker* turned out to be an influential report that had direct effects on health education policy. And the conclusions from it were converted into government messages to young people to discourage them from smoking and encourage them, if they did smoke, to give up. In theory this change in their smoking behavior should have not been very difficult to achieve, because by adult standards the amount smoked even by self-reported

"regular smokers," averaging only one cigarette a week, barely existed. However, the mere acknowledgement of the behavior at this level was a powerful discriminator not only in the boys' perceptions of the four identities but in a range of other teenage behaviors and attributes such as poor educational achievement. The power of the smoker identity was such that only advertising and promotional work that got right "under the skin" of young people in detaching smoking from their valued attributes, e.g., via role models presented as non-smokers, was likely to be effective.

The second addition to my intellectual luggage at GSS was a research project devoted to medical students that similarly involved managing identity but in a quite different way (Bynner, 1969b). Medical students are a particularly interesting population in which to study smoking because in the clinical part of their courses the students are increasingly likely to be confronted with its medical consequences. A study by Becker and Geer (1958), unrelated to smoking, threw light on the processes of attitude change that accompany the career of a student through medical school. Using participant observation they showed that medical students start their training with a very idealistic view of their future role as doctors. During the clinical period this idealism translates into heightened worries about their own health that converts increasingly into cynicism as the trainees come to realize the limitations of what they are able to do to help patients, especially those who are terminally ill. Once the students graduate there is a final readjustment, when a sense of realism takes over, i.e., they are able to detach their own personal lives and identities from the health issues they are confronting on a daily basis in their professional role as doctors, and come to see medicine as a career like any other.

The study for which I had responsibility compared samples of medical students at each of the 5 years of their medical training who were smokers with those who were non-smokers and with a third sample of non-medical students as a control group. As the students progressed through the course, a striking attitude change was apparent, paralleling that discovered by Becker and Geer. It was clear that in their smoking attitudes and behavior, preclinical students (the first 2 years of U.K. medical training) could hardly be separated from non-medical students. But in the first year of clinical medicine there was a striking rise in negative attitudes towards smoking, e.g., belief that smoking causes lung cancer, accompanied by a rise in the numbers giving up. This desire steadily converted into cynicism about the effectiveness of treatments for lung cancer and skepticism about the scientific case against smoking. By the time of graduation the students' attitudes had returned to their pre-clinical levels and for some there was even a return to smoking.

The project gave me my first glimpse of "life-course processes" of the kind that I have worked with ever since. That is to say, conflicting attitudes, beliefs, and behavioral norms, coupled with peer group pressure, have to be managed through the different stages of the medical training program. For the medical student, the continuing crisis of confronting people dying, together with his or her own vulnerability to illness, has to be resolved for the forging of "professional identity" to occur.

Analysis of cross-sectional survey data of this kind masks, of course, the possible interaction between age and cohort effects (Bynner, 2005a). That is to say, we cannot be sure that the changes in attitudes and behavior observed across the stages of the training are not products of the different years in which the students studied entered the program (cohort effect), rather than general properties of medical training itself. However, over the 5 years the training took, with no indication of a major overhaul during or preceding it, plus the convergence of the findings with Becker and Greer's, such interaction seems unlikely. It seems more plausible that medical training is accompanied by attitude shifts of the kind indicated.

The next project, based on a longitudinal survey, did not suffer from such age–cohort interaction difficulties, opening up in 1967 a new dimension of research experience, longitudinal study. My exposure to it was through the follow-up work to the U.K. Plowden Committee's 1963 investigation of English primary school education based on a representative sample survey of 7-year-old primary school children. At the urging of the survey's director, Gilbert Peaker, it was decided to carry out a follow-up survey 4 years later, focusing particularly on parents' attitudes to education and their aspirations for their children, now aged 11 (Bynner 1972). I came to realize from this study the great power of the time dimension in social scientific enquiry, not in any sense as a basis for *proving* causation, but by enabling the researcher to rule out certain kinds of plausible causal hypotheses, because they were contradicted by the sequencing of events.

Multivariate analysis (ordinary least squares regression) supported the hypothesis that parental aspirations were a key driver of primary school children's progress into secondary school, while taking account of parents' attributes such as educational level and the circumstances of the families involved. The alternative hypothesis that the children's progress was driving the parents' attitudes could be largely ruled out on the grounds that it showed the much weaker effect. At the same time, the fact that the reverse effect occurred at all, pointed to the process as dynamic with both effects working reciprocally to produce over time the positive outcome of continuous achievement or its opposite, decline: an example of "virtuous" as opposed to "vicious" circles (Rutter & Madge, 1976).

The English education system is premised on an assumed hierarchy of ability divided into a series of stages between childhood and adulthood through which achievement is shaped. Youth is the post-compulsory stage, relating in the UK to the period, post-16 and ending at age 19 years, by which time the transition to work is expected to have occurred, thus separating university student transitions from those of the population as a whole. The Plowden follow-up work brought home to me the poverty of this conception and the need for a much broader view of education as preparation for adulthood, including work, as a basis for heading off the alienation from schooling that many families and children clearly felt (Bynner, 1973). In contrast, the continental conception of youth extends to the mid-twenties, and beyond (Bynner, Chisholm , & Furlong, 1997). And for some countries, such as Germany, youth can last well into the thirties, as qualifications such as the *Habilitation*, which certifies readiness for a professorship, demand continuing (part-time) study up to this age.

My time at the Government Social Survey was an apprenticeship in survey methodology for learning the skills of the trade from an expert, Aubrey McKennell, with a record of path-breaking work in the study of attitudes to aircraft noise and in the measurement of psychological well-being. Rather in the role of the German *Meister,* McKennell inspired my interest in survey methods, and multivariate analysis of quantitative data and taught me how to use them. Structural Equation Modelling (SEM), initially through Confirmatory Factor Analysis (Jöreskog & Sörbom, 1979) soon became an essential part of my social science toolkit. But there was something missing for me in the framework of a government department devoted to projects to inform policy while at the same time having to meet the needs of a large-scale field force by keeping the interviewers in it permanently employed. I was fortunate in participating in programs of coordinated studies that enabled follow through of ideas from one survey to the next. But the office lacked an ambience of discussion and debate through which methodological principles and concepts, as a basis for action, could be exchanged, and on the completion of my PhD in 1970 I decided to move on.

Measurement and Evaluation

Almost by luck, through others' rejections of employment offers for a job in a largely unknown higher education venture, I was appointed as a lecturer in the Faculty of Educational Studies in the UK's Open University (OU), which was in its second year of operations. The OU was the complete opposite of GSS in most respects: rather like a large publishing house in which the production task was to produce, through a process of research review, exchange of ideas and debate, distance-teaching courses. Each course was available to adults (aged 21+ years), regardless of any prior qualifications, across the whole country and beyond, and comprised the collection of the required number of Units and half Units that added up to a university degree. There was no campus in the normal sense as student learning was done mainly at home, supported by the occasional face-to-face non-compulsory local tutorial (if accessible). For some courses there was also a 1-week summer school using the facilities of traditional universities during the summer vacation.

For the academic staff working at the OU, it soon became clear that the production of teaching materials alone was not sufficient to match professional aspirations. Research became an ever more important part of the workload, and PhD students were soon a feature of the campus. For the first few years I spent my time working in course teams each comprising academics, media experts (TV and radio producers), an education technology specialist, and a course assistant on the demanding, but highly stimulating, experience of course production. Chairing OU course teams proved invaluable experience that carried over subsequently in running research teams, especially in the multi-institution ESRC 16–19 Initiative, considered later. The group dynamics in the different contexts shared a lot in common.

The first course worked on was in education and child psychology, "Personality, Growth and Learning." The second that I subsequently chaired was "Methods of Educational Enquiry," to be replaced ultimately by the much broader and longer "Research Methods in Education and the Social Sciences and Education" and adapted in advanced form to become the OU's first distance-taught Master's degree. "Curriculum Evaluation and Assessment in Educational Institutions" followed. Each course took up to 4 years to write, after which it would be run for four more before review and revision or replacement by a new course designed from scratch.

Through working on Curriculum Evaluation and Assessment in Educational Institutions, coupled with an administrative role of chair of the university's Examinations and Assessment committee, measurement issues became an abiding interest, introducing me to Lee Cronbach's writings on psychometrics (Cronbach, 1951;Cronbach & Meehl, 1955; Cronbach, Gleser, Nanda, & Rajaratnam, 1972). The conceptual development they enshrined became an inspiration in relation to Cronbach's resolution of reliability and validity issues through the *Theory of Generalisability*.

Another influential component was the work of the Stanford Evaluation Consortium on new ways of looking at program evaluation (Cronbach, 1980). The case made there for viewing the evaluation of educational interventions as a matter of modeling the mismatch between the belief systems of policy administrators and the empirical realities of the program in action was particularly persuasive, rightly putting the randomized control trial in its proper place as a component of evaluation, not the whole story. Evaluation always needed to pay full regard to process and outcome in *variable contexts* ("external validity") and residual as well as explained variance, i.e., "off diagonal" special cases. This requirement demanded case study and the use of ethnographic and "action research" methods to run alongside, if not in place of, experimental enquiry as "illuminative" evaluators had argued (Hamilton, Jenkins, King, MacDonald, & Parlett, 1977; Parlett & Hamilton, 1977). The alternative view, in the tradition of Donald Campbell and colleagues, held tightly to the model of the "true experiment" (randomized control trial) not only as the scientific "gold standard" of sound evaluation but as a necessary condition for doing it (Campbell, 1969, Campbell & Stanley, 1966; Cook & Campbell, 1979). In reconciling the two positions, Campbell later acknowledged a role for what he called "qualitative knowing," i.e., recognition by participants of the program's value as an important validation tool (Campbell, 1978). Apart from its importance for program evaluation, Cronbach's approach and the debate with Campbell on the alternative "paradigm" had wider implications, as I argued, for psychological research methodology more generally (Bynner, 1980a, 1980b).

Models and Methods

My OU job became increasingly administrative, including taking on the role of Dean of the Faculty of Education Studies, with the effect that my empirical research was soon barely ticking over. This ended when, following in the footsteps of Aubrey McKennell, I was awarded a Fulbright Fellowship to work for a year in the Survey Research Centre of the Institute for Social Research (ISR) at the University of Michigan, sponsored by one of the ISR's original directors, Angus Campbell. Accompanied by my wife and two children aged 6 and 4, the experience was memorable in every respect with, apart from my project work, holiday trips to Canada, Washington, and the west coast via New Mexico, and full exposure to the U.S. pre-school and primary system. In ISR there was access to all the facilities of a top U.S. research institute in a university supplying first-class teaching while undertaking major, often government sponsored, research programs. Libraries were open all night, and there was 24-hour access to mainframe computing, 7 days a week, something unknown in the UK at the time. I took the opportunity to learn everything that I could about survey sampling, attitude measurement, and structural equation modeling (SRM) from ISR colleagues, Lesley Kish, Frank Andrews and Laura Klem, and continue to use what they taught me to this day.

My ISR project based in the Survey Research Centre was to join Jerry Backman and Patrick O'Malley in a re-analysis of the six-wave "Youth in Transition Survey" (YTS) focusing on the relationship between self-esteem and delinquency among high-school boys (Bynner, Bachman, & O'Malley, 1981). The work was done in response to a critique by Maurice Rosenberg of an earlier paper by Bachman and O'Malley (1977) on the theme of "Does self-esteem cause delinquency or delinquency self-esteem?" (Rosenberg & Rosenberg, 1978). We were able to show that rather than self-esteem declining in response to delinquent behavior, as argued by the Rosenbergs, it was actually the other way round. The longitudinal modeling over three waves of YIT data suggested that adjustment to poor educational performance that most of those with poor self-esteem had experienced could be compensated for by the status attached to delinquent behavior in the teenage culture operating outside school. So in other words, just like sex and smoking, the function of the behavior was less about explicit attributes of delinquency, e.g., in an economic or social sense than presentation of self in the maintenance and enhancement of identity in the peer group.

I was fortunate at this time to come across David Matza's book *Delinquency and Drift* (1964), demonstrating the way in which criminality is created, as much as resisted, by the judicial system. He argued that the system's prescriptions for reform of individual behavior are mediated by the social class of offenders, determining the way they are treated, i.e., in secure offender institutions (working-class young people) rather than in the family (middle-class young people). The consequence can be locking the former group, in more ways than one, into the downward trajectory of crime.

Structure of Personal Characteristics

Back in the OU, I drew on my Michigan experience to apply structural equation modeling methods in a program of analysis just beginning with my friend and colleague, David Romney, at the University of Calgary (Alberta). At the time, the work was more about teasing out more effective ways of understanding correlations between variables in survey data than adolescence specifically. But the methodology carried through into the later stages of my career when youth and adolescence became a major focus. It became clear, for example, that much of traditional theorizing about intelligence (IQ) was founded on a model of human attributes for which the method of analysis was incapable of producing anything else. Thus correlation data for cognitive ability/achievement test items subjected to "Exploratory Factor Analysis," originating in the work of the English psychologist, Charles Spearman, in the 1920s (Spearman, 1932) would inevitably point to a hierarchy of achievement with a common component, General Intelligence (G) lying at the heart of it.

The alternative (more egalitarian) conception from Louis Thurstone (1934, 1947) replaced G by a number of "oblique" (correlated) factors, reflecting "primary abilities" forming an optimum "simple structure" for the data. However, it was quite easy to reconcile the two by introducing the idea of "higher order factors." Factor analysis of the correlations among Thurstone's oblique factors reduced them ultimately to one, or in the case of attitudes, two.

None of the writers in this tradition contemplated the alternative possibility of cognitive abilities, or any other individual attributes, being ordered along a continuum in a sequence in which each could be conceptualized as a linear function of the others preceding it—described as a "simplex." Nor did they consider further possibilities, including the "circumplex," reflecting nearness of such attributes to each other in a circular structure (Guttman, 1954). From structural equation modeling of correlation data among "Richmond Test" scores for reading and math

abilities it was possible to assess which of such models fitted the data best. Two simplexes met the goodness of fit criteria, one for the reading tests in the order "vocabulary," "comprehension," "usage," "spelling," "capital letters," "punctuation," and the other for the math tests in the order, "concepts," "problems." Taking the modeling further, both linear sequences could be fitted to a model showing two sets of attributes arising from a single attribute, vocabulary, termed a "split simplex" (Bynner & Romney, 1985).

Rather than the static hierarchy produced by exploratory factor analysis, SEM offered the more rewarding conceptualization of a dynamic learning process in which levels of increasing cognitive complexity are achieved. The practical implication is that rather than matching teaching to the relatively fixed abilities with which children are typically believed to be endowed—a prescription for educational selection—better to adopt a positive developmental learning program building step-by step the cognitive competence of which all are capable.

Not surprisingly the split simplex, in place of a hierarchical factor model, produced hostile, if not outraged, reactions among some of the stalwarts in the area, including R. B. Cattell, H. J. Eysenck, and P. Kline, who responded to a discussion piece setting out alternative ways of modeling cognitive abilities. Cattell wrote, for example, "This is all awry," referring to "thirty years of serious research in America" as if that alone somehow validated the model he favored (Bynner, 1993a, 1993b; Cattell, Davies, Eysenck, & Kline, 1993). The emotion generated was in fact reflecting another aspect of psychological thinking that could only be described as an *ideological* commitment to a certain conception of human aptitudes as opposed to others (Richardson & Bynner, 1984). For Cattell the factor model of cognitive ability was seen as supplying irrefutable evidence for a natural hierarchy residing ultimately in genetic endowment, thereby supporting the structure of society that we find around us. As an embryonic developmental scientist, this was a conception I was increasingly coming to resist.

The experience made me come to realize that rather than liberating the human spirit from the shackles of Victorian hierarchical thinking some brands of psychology served to strengthen them through use of spurious evidence. In the words of philosopher of science Imre Lakatos, psychology creates "phony corroborations and thereby a semblance of 'scientific progress' where, in fact, there is nothing but an increase in pseudo-intellectual garbage" (1970, p. 176). Karl Popper turns the knife a little further: "In fact, compared with physics, sociology and psychology are riddled with fashions, and with uncontrolled dogmas. . . . how can the regress to these often spurious sciences help us. . .?" (1970, pp. 57–58). Ironically, some years later Cattell's name appears as co-author of a paper opening the door to structural equation models of cognitive abilities and personality characteristics including simplex and circumplex models (Boyle, Stankov, & Cattell, 1995).

The SEM methodology was applied to numerous other sets of attributes, including DSM III personality disorders in which the interpersonal disorders fitted a circumplex model and those that were more cognitively directed—a simplex (e.g., Bynner and Romney, 1989). The outcome was *Structure of Personal Characteristics* (Romney & Bynner, 1992), which drew attention to developmental process as a better way of looking at aptitudes and attitudes than static categorization.

The ESRC 16–19 Initiative

Towards the end of the period at the Open University in 1987, my research turned more directly to adolescent development, seen now less in terms of a biological ageing process subjected to environment influence and more as comprising the interactions of developmental transitions moderated and mediated by institutional structures, social relations and human agency in the different domains of life. Such transitions comprise: education to work; peer group to partnership to parenthood; pre-pubertal child to post-pubertal adolescent to adult citizen. The opportunity for pursuing this approach came through my appointment to coordinate a new program of research on young people in the UK, the *ESRC 16–19 Initiative* (Banks et al., 1992; Bynner, 1987, 1991a). The attraction of the program was that it provided the opportunity to combine my emergent developmental science perspective with action in the policy domain.

The end of the 1970s was something of a watershed in young people's experience of the transition from school to work. In the UK, psychologists Schaffer and Hargreaves (1978, p. 92) were still able to write: "Most adolescents join the labour market at 16 years: it is the normal life experience of the adolescent". The technological transformation of industry and the globalization that followed at the end of the 1970s changed the nature of employment, making many past skills and training redundant. The problems were intensified in the old industrial heartlands, such as those based on shipbuilding, coal mining, and steel, as businesses employing traditional production methods lost out to competition from better-prepared European competitors and the "Tiger Economies" of the far East (Ashton & Bynner, 2011; Ashton & Green, 1996).

The additional cap on job opportunities for young people was the worldwide economic recession that dominated the early 1980s, to be followed by another at the beginning of the 1990s. These upheavals in the economy added to young people's transition difficulties but especially among those with poor educational records. A major consequence was unemployment among young U.K. (age 16) school leavers in which only those with educational certification were relatively protected. Young women tended to fare better than young men in the sense that the flexible hours, including part time and home-working typical of the now IT-based office, accommodated them more easily. Others without the basic secretarial skills (business studies certification) usually needed for such a job frequently left the labor market early for the alternative career of motherhood.

The solution was seen by the (Thatcher) government at the time to lie in *youth training*. Rather than focus attention on the poor record of British business in investing in new infrastructure and plan for a new industrial future (Hutton, 1996), the problem was seen as lying in young people themselves who lacked the skills to be employable in the contemporary labor market.

The 16–19 Initiative was a 5-year research program starting in 1985 on the "economic and political socialization" of young people; that is to say, the ways in which young people were forming their adult identities under the conditions of the time. The importance of the local context was recognized in the decision to base the work in four economically contrasting labor market areas in Britain supplying the different "opportunity structures" through which young people made their way to adult work (Bynner, 1991a): *Liverpool*—high unemployment, long-term decline and reducing population arising from the collapse of the maritime industry; *Sheffield*—temporarily hit by the collapse of the light steels industry through competition from the Far East; *Swindon*—an old railway town transformed through IT-based industry and at the time the fastest expanding town in Europe; and *Kirkcaldy*—a mixed Scottish labor market combining traditional manufacturing industry like linoleum, some new tech developments, and agriculture. Four teams based in local universities had won the contracts to study the lives of two cohorts of 600 15–16-year-olds and 600 17–18-year-olds in each area—4,800 in all. Each cohort was to be followed from an initial questionnaire survey in 1987 for a further 2 years with repeated surveys in 1988 and 1989 spanning a total age range of 15–20. The program was innovative in combining perspectives from across the social science disciplines and education, including qualitative (case study) alongside quantitative survey methods.

Apart from the four U.K. labor markets, in the second year of the survey (1988), through a collaborative arrangement with colleagues—Walter Heinz (U. of Bremen), Klaus Hurrelman (U. of Bielefeld), Ken Roberts (U. of Liverpool) and Karen Evans (U. of Surrey) the study was extended cross-nationally (Bynner & Roberts, 1991; Bynner & Heinz, 1991; Evans & Heinz, 1994). Accordingly, 320 English respondents in Swindon and Liverpool were matched as far as possible with their German counterparts in terms of the occupational routes they were on—"academic/professional," "skilled," "partly skilled," and "uncertain." Young people in Bremen, a declining shipbuilding city, were matched with their counterparts in Liverpool. And similarly, young people in Paderborn, a declining railway town revived through new tech industry, were matched with young people in Swindon (the responsibility of the University of Surrey team). The key question addressed was: how does the experience and identity formation of young people pursuing routes to much the same kinds of occupations such as "fitter" or "hairdresser" differ between the two countries and in different labor market contexts?

The work was exceptionally challenging and illuminating in exposing me to issues of meaning and comparability that dominate the methodology of comparative research. Melvin Kohn's seminal paper on the subject arguing for the necessity of combining quantitative with historical case study and qualitative methods (Kohn, 1987) and Charles Ragin's argument for approaching comparative study as a "dialogue" between cases and variables (Ragin, 1987) were major influences on our approach. Later, Lynn Chisholm, a colleague at the time working for the European Commission, and I contributed our own prescriptions for optimum strategy in a paper on *Comparative Youth Transition Research* (Bynner & Chisholm, 1998). More recent reflections on the Anglo German study can be found in a paper presented at a developmental psychology session (convened by Rainer Silbereisen) for a conference in Jena, Germany, on research on the effects of German reunification (Silbereisen & Tomasik, 2010; Bynner, 2010).

The findings brought home the significance of a number of factors in the effects of economic transformation on the transition from school to work with both theoretical and policy implications. It is naive to think that the mere provision of what are presented as opportunities to access employment through training will change deeply ingrained cultural habits driven by values of recipients that fail to match policy expectations. Despite a general trend towards more staying on in education through the 1980s and 1990s arising from the lack of jobs and the introduction of the new and more accessible GCSE (General Certificate of Secondary Education) qualification, by the time of the first 16–19 Initiative survey (1987) half of the age cohort was still leaving education at the minimum age of 16 to find a job. Most were rejecting any training scheme they found themselves in at the first opportunity—"slave labour" as half the sample described it (Bynner, 1991b).

Early leaving was the tradition, particularly in Liverpool where opportunities for any kind of skilled job were outside most young people's experience; less so in Sheffield where the strong skills base associated with the steel industry was still largely intact and the economy was soon expanding. Kirkcaldy's slump was similarly temporary but with more patchy recovery through investment in new IT-based industry concentrated in some areas and not others. In Swindon, YTS barely took off at all with only IT training initially attracting much interest. In fact in the rapidly expanding local economy vocational qualifications, as acquired through YTS to certify employability, were worth little compared with the traditional, more academically oriented, qualifications. Young people qualified for university ("A-levels") were prized particularly, e.g., in financial services, because they were seen as both highly trainable and customer-friendly. Many local employers spent time actively discouraging such young people from continuing to university rather than entering employment where a whole package of career opportunities would be offered to them. The squeeze was at the bottom end on young people without qualifications. Leaving school at 16 and getting a job, without any type of certificate, was much more difficult, and casual work or unemployment was all that most of them could expect.

The situation could not have been more different in Germany. Although there were young people on these disadvantaged routes in training schemes or in casual jobs, these were in much smaller proportions in the population as a whole than in Britain. The assumed route for every school leaver not going to university, almost in the nature of a "rite of passage," was the "dual system" of apprenticeship. Apprenticeship comprised the 3 years of work-based training and offsite educational provision that 600,000 young Germans entered each year under the terms of a training contract. Government training schemes (some modeled at the time of the recession on English YTS) were established not to get young people into jobs but into apprenticeships, for without the certification gained from such training, prospects in the labor market were likely be bleak. The "social partners" (employers, trade unions, and local politicians) entrusted with running the system joined forces in ensuring that every young person gained the training and the certification of skilled status in a recognized occupation for which apprenticeship was available: the same standard as "A-Levels" in Anglo terms.

Apprenticeship as a prerequisite for adult work is so deeply embedded in German consciousness that its effect was to cast the young apprentice more in the role and accompanying identity as a student rather than employee. This self-image contrasted with that of adult worker, which is how British school-leavers, including apprentices, typically saw themselves. Clearly, any major shift away from this expectation in Germany—reinforced by the governance arrangements through social partnership—was unimaginable. Even though the economic transformation and recession had put the system under strain, with the 1,000+ occupations once recognized in Germany now reduced to 340, there was little real challenge to the principle that apprenticeship is an essential part of all young people's transition experience. In fact, many of the young Germans qualified for university entrance at a time of economic difficulty, as a form of "vocational insurance" (Bynner, 1999), were doing an apprenticeship first. The value was seen as in leading not only to a recognized occupation, which only about 50% of trainees entered after completion, but to the status of adult citizen in the German state (Bynner, 2011).

Youth and the Life Course

Towards the end of the 16–19 Initiative, and now in City University London as director, Social Statistics Research Unit, in 1989 I took over responsibility for the National

Child Development study, one of Britain's major longitudinal studies that began in 1958. The study is based on 17,000 individuals born in a single week in 1958 who have been followed up at regular intervals ever since, with a reasonably unbiased sample of 12,000 cohort members still participating (Bynner, Ferri, & Shepherd 1997; Ferri, Bynner, & Wadsworth, 2003; Bynner & Joshi, 2007; Wadsworth & Bynner, 2011).

Lying behind my interest in the job, and presumably the appointment, was a scoping study done for ESRC in 1984, to investigate why, despite the deposit of the NCDS dataset in the ESRC Data Archive at the University of Essex in 1983, little research use had been made of it since. The reasons were mainly technical, reflected in the daunting nature of accessing such a large and complex dataset in advance of the advent of modern IT and detailed documentation, which has largely removed such obstacles. The project also made me realize that the great potential of such a birth cohort study lies in making comparisons with other comparable longitudinal studies, of which there were two at the time: the earlier National Survey of Health and Development started in 1946 and run by the Medical Research Council since 1963, for which there is restricted access, and the more recent 1970 British Birth Cohort Study (Bynner, 2005a).

Through my friendship with Neville Butler—one of the great U.K. visionaries in foreseeing the potential value of birth cohort studies long before the technology was available to make proper use of them (Bynner & Goldstein, 1998)—in 1992 the opportunity came to take over the 1970 birth cohort study from the International Centre for Child Studies based in Bristol. Butler had founded the study and well into his late 70s still ran it. The study also brought with it funding from the Government's Adult Literacy and Basic Skills Unit to investigate the correlates of poor literacy and numeracy ("basic skills") among adults. The success of the project led to further funding to undertake a follow-up at age 37 of the 1958 cohort study. The aim this time was to investigate the origins of basic skills difficulties in the earlier cohort two thirds of whom in 1974 had been entering the labor market at age 16 in the traditional way. Although the program was addressed primarily at the needs of adults, their poor basic skills—representing a failure of the education system to facilitate acquisition of key attributes—it had much wider significance for understanding developmental processes and the differentiation of prospects that occurs in adolescence.

The job change and accompanying immersion in longitudinal data analysis corresponded with growing interest in the "life-course perspective" on human development (Elder & Shanahan, 2006; Elder & Giele, 2009; Giele, 2002; Heinz, 1991; Heinz, Huinink, & Weymann, 2009), which fitted well with the idea of a "trajectory of disadvantage" on which adults with poor basic skills are typically located. A lasting friendship had developed with Walter Heinz based on his inspirational contributions

to our Anglo-German project (Bynner & Heinz, 1991; Bynner, 2003) and subsequently with Glen Elder arising out of Heinz and Elder's shared interest in promoting life course study. This interest underpinned our ongoing collaboration, again inspired initially by Heinz, in stimulating ideas for a program of comparative research on the effects of the 2008 economic crisis, and its aftermath, on young people's transition to adulthood in Germany, England and the USA. The aim is to revisit hypotheses derived from Elder's classic work *Children of the Great Depression* (1999) about the differential effects of the economic collapse on families and young people at different ages. At the time of writing the components of the program for funding are being put in place.

Birth cohort studies are, by their very nature, multidisciplinary and holistic in the sense that the developing individual moves through a series of interacting domains or spheres of life including education, work, family, and community. These domains are experienced differently as the individual gets older and in response to societal (social, economic, and political) change. Activity in any one domain can at times be in harmony, or in conflict, with activity in another. Such tension continually needs to be resolved by young people in adhering to family rules and values when at home, while being in conflict with those shared by the peer group in leisure settings. And these values and norms—adult male "subterranean values" as Matza and Sikes (1961) describe them—may similarly be at variance with those in the setting of the school. Development through adolescence can be viewed as a process of reconciling these "focal conflicts" to achieve stable identity in adult life in which occupation becomes a central part (Coleman & Hendry, 1999).

In these terms, the idea of a largely socially constructed "youth stage" of the life course broadly, extending from the biological milestone of puberty in the early teens to the socially determined markers of independent adulthood in the mid to late twenties, had much salience for me. The youth stage encompasses the "career trajectories" comprising the transitions that young people make and their outcomes in the different life course domains—a central theme of the 16–19 Initiative (Roberts, 1984; Banks et al., 1992; Roberts & Parsell, 1989). The developmental processes involved underpin the "turning points" that may be critical in changing the trajectory's course (Robins & Rutter, 1990; Sampson & Laub, 1993; Schoon et al., 2002; Schoon & Bynner, 2003; Feinstein & Bynner, 2004, 2006). The perspective thus offers much in helping identify the key components of change in adolescents' contemporary situation and experience and the effect these are having on their developing identities.

Such writers as Ulrich Beck and Martin Baethge in Germany and Anthony Giddens in the UK (Baethge, 1989; Beck, 1992; Beck, Giddens, & Lash, 1994) stress increasing "individualization" of experience and increasing risk and uncertainty in the educational and occupation choices that have to be made in a contemporary world that through technological advance is changing so rapidly. This situation poses a formidable challenge to traditional concepts of socialization and paths to adult identity. A central feature of the change is the extension of the transition from education to work termed *post-adolescence* (e,g., Hurrelmann, 1989; Gaiser & Müller, 1989), demanding new forms of institutional arrangements in the education, training, and employment system for managing it. Some have questioned, however, whether the shift away from structural determinacy is as fundamental as these writers maintain. In the UK, at least, social class is still a major factor in life chances (Roberts, Clark, & Wallace, 1994; Furlong & Cartmel, 1997).

From the psychologist's perspective the emphasis will be placed more on such factors as environmental risk and such attributes as resilience as the agency response to determining how the life course proceeds (Schoon, 2006). The individualization thesis also needs to be aligned with Erikson's (1963), and later Marcia's (1966), psycho-social stages of identity development, "exploration," "foreclosure," moratorium," and "achievement," adapted to accommodate the extended transition from school to work (Fouad & Bynner, 2008) described by Jeffery Arnett as *Emerging Adulthood* (Arnett, 2000, 2004; Arnett, Kloep, Hendry, & Tanner, 2011). U.S. vocational psychologists have applied the stage concept to occupational identity formation, but they would place the final stage, moratorium, very much within the period that Arnett defines as Emerging Adulthood.

The proposition that a new psycho-social stage is needed to describe young people's development in their contemporary situation raises questions about the meaning of and delimiting descriptors for the adolescent period itself. As Arnett himself points out, G. Stanley Hall, the "father" of adolescence research, writing in 1904, actually saw the adolescent period as terminating around age 25. Restriction to a much shorter period post-puberty in the teens, was institutionally based—probably as much a product of convenience and practicality as any re-wiring of the psyche. Young people were tied to the (U.S.) education system until 18 (high-school graduation); hence easily accessible for research and the use of 18 as the delimiting age for adolescence.

The difficulty with the stages conception is that it to a certain extent de-contextualizes adolescent development. That that is to say, its normative connotations tend to downplay population heterogeneity structured by the socio-economic and other groupings to which young people relate (Bynner, 2000, 2001, 2005b; Bynner & Silbereisen, 2000; Hendry & Kloep, 2002). It is the differentiated and changing context associated with such groupings that needs to be taken into account if the shaping of teenage careers and adult identities is to be understood (e.g., Blustein, Devenis, & Kidney,1989; Savickas, 1985; Vondracek, Lerner, & Schulenberg, 1986). Central to this differentiation is access to resources.

Such resources can be usefully conceptualized in terms of the economists' term *capital*—namely an accumulating asset that can be transferred to others and invested and from which a financial return can be expected. The human capital identified with educational achievement and gaining qualifications during compulsory schooling (Becker, 1975) gives way in contemporary society to capital accumulation through life-long learning and occupational profile building by gaining experience in a variety of occupational roles.

The human capital concept is developed further in the idea of social capital acquired through membership of associational networks based on reciprocity and trust and increasingly under strain (Coleman, 1988; Putnam, 1999). It extends further still in the idea of "cognitive capital" (Bynner & Wadsworth, 2010) supplying the link to the wider set of agency attributes manifested finally in Jim Côté's "identity capital" (Côté 1996, 2002; Côté & Levine, 2002). This last form of capital, comprising such psychological attributes as adaptability, creativity, cognitive function, teamwork, and trust, coupled with self-efficacy, and motivation is, as Côté, convincingly argues, the distinguishing feature of effective functioning in "late modern" adulthood. His conceptualization offers a useful corrective to the narrowness of the stage-based approach to adolescent development and led to us joining forces in an attempt to recast the concept of emerging adulthood within a wider life course framework (Côté & Bynner, 2008).

Borrowing terms from one discipline to serve those of another can prove problematic, yet, at the same time, such borrowing may stimulate the new thinking that a perspective such as life-course study demands. Linked by our shared roles in leading a government-sponsored research center in the Institute of Education devoted to the "Wider Benefits of Learning," (Schuller et al., 2004), colleagues Tom Schuller, Leon Feinstein, and I attempted to dissect the issue in a discussion paper also linking to development economist Amartya Sen's (1992) more all-embracing concept of *capability* (Schuller, Bynner & Feinstein, 2004). Rather than focusing on capital assets as underpinning identity achievement, capabilities align with such psychological constructs as life plans as the foundation of "freedom to achieve wellbeing." That is to say, they combine individual and societal goals with the means of achieving them—the building blocks of successful transitions and a fulfilling adult life.

Social Exclusion and NEET

Relocation of the 1970 cohort study, alongside the 1958 cohort study, in 1998 to the Institute of Education, to establish the Centre for Longitudinal Studies, offered the opportunity to test and develop these ideas further. The Smith Institute, a London think-tank, commissioned a report for the first of a series of seminars in the Prime Minister's Office in 10 Downing Street, on the theme of *Obstacles and Opportunities on the Route to Adulthood* (Bynner, Joshi, & Tstsas, 2000). Another related project supported by the Joseph Rowntree Foundation followed,

Young People's Changing Routes to Independence (Bynner, Elias, McKnight, Pan, & Pierre, 2002). By comparing young people's trajectories up to the mid-20s across the 12 years separating the 1958 and 1970 cohorts it was clear that the traditional largely class-based routes to adulthood evident in the earlier cohort were being replaced by much more complex routes in which family and personal capabilities (financial, cognitive, social behavioral, and affective)—"life management" as described in the Nordic countries—had a much more significant role to play (Helve & Bynner, 1996, 2007).

Thus poor reading and math that had been little impediment to gaining employment for the 1958 cohort leaving school at 16 in the mid-1970s, was for the more recent cohort leaving school reaching age 16 in 1986 an attribute that now predicted a "patchwork" employment career (Bynner & Silbereisen, 2000), including extended spells of unemployment (Bynner, 1998). More significantly the 1970 cohort analysis identified psychological well-being, as reflected in the Malaise scale (a measure of depression), both as an outcome of poor educational attainment and as a precursor of time spent unemployed since age 16. There were signs of a vicious circle in train in which depression and poor self-esteem, arising from unemployment, reduced the prospects of employment, reinforcing negative affect even further.

The findings are best exemplified by the structural equation models that were estimated embracing significant predictors of unemployment captured by the full range of data collected for each cohort back to birth. The social-class-based route, dominated by the effect of class on educational achievement in the 1958 cohort, compared with the much more complex 1970 cohort routes, in which alongside social class and parents' poor educational record, their offspring's poor basic skills, failure to gain qualifications, leaving school early, number of jobs since leaving school, and malaise, all had a part to play in the prediction of the amount of time spent unemployed. Notably a social class effect from birth to unemployment persisted over and above all other potential mediators pointing to the possibility of a deep-rooted cultural component in the propensity to unemployment as well.

The consequence of the reshaping of U.K. youth transitions and the use of vocational training to make good the skills gap was the existence of a widening section of the youth population who were marginalized and effectively excluded from full participation in the labor market. Although overall, young people were staying on in education for longer periods, for a relatively fixed proportion of up to 30% there was early leaving and subsequent drift into unfulfilling, often part-time casual work, and unemployment. Such "scarring" effects signal poor employability attributes to potential employers, constituting a continuing obstacle to establishing an occupational career (Ellwood, 1982; Arulampalam, Gregg, & Gregory, 2001).

The 1997 Labour government took on the challenge of social exclusion by establishing a government unit devoted to the subject—the Social Exclusion Unit (SEU). The main task involved setting up 19 Policy Action Teams (PATS) to address different features of exclusion statuses and the processes leading to them ranging from drugs to teenage pregnancy and unemployment. As a member of PAT 12 on disadvantaged youth, I agreed to look at the life-course processes involved. The 1970 cohort study data was ideal to elucidate the origins and outcomes of lack of engagement with *education, employment* or *training* in the age period 16–18—increasingly described as NEET (Bynner & Parsons, 2002).

A number of features of NEET status were identified. First the NEET experience was likely to continue at the older age of 21, increasingly transforming into continuous unemployment. For the young women the division between occupational routes—employment or parenthood—became apparent with two-thirds of the NEET young women actually being young mothers. The others who had yet to become parents had much the same poor employment outcomes as boys. Another difference was that young women in the NEET situation showed at age 21 signs of damaged psychological well-being reflected in feelings of despair and hopelessness and lack of prospects. These outcomes were linked to prior circumstances and experiences that showed much the same pattern for both sexes—poor material conditions at home and lack of parent interest, especially in relation to daughters, being notable features. For boys, living in an inner-city house housing estate was also a strong predictor of NEET.

Other research carried out over this period reinforced the picture of mainstream development set against significant minority exclusion—an ever-widening gap—sometimes reinforced by public provision to ameliorate it. Thus analysis of data from the 1970 cohort on young people's out-of-school activity showed that youth clubs, rather than supporting educational progress among working-class young people, actually appeared to work against it (Feinstein, Bynner, & Duckworth, 2006). What appeared to be critical was the degree of "structure" in the activity on offer. Resonating with similar findings in Sweden (Mahoney, Stattin, & Lord, 2004), "hanging out" could simply encourage these young people to feed off each others' negative feelings about school in the strengthening of a "micro-culture" with its own anti-school norms and values. Organized games and community work, of the kind available to scouts and guides and in church clubs, worked against such a drift towards educational alienation. Participation, in sport, inside or outside a sports club, appeared best of all, however, because it showed the protective effects of a structured activity while also appealing equally across all the social classes. Middle childhood experience was the precursor of the marginalization that would become evident in adolescence leading to further analysis of the developmental processes involved (Feinstein & Bynner, 2004, 2006).

Another related project carried out at that time was a review for the Social Exclusion Unit of the *Impact of*

Government Policy on Social Exclusion and Young People (Bynner, Londra, & Jones, 2004). This drew attention to the distorting effects of age-based policies and provision for young people that, although administratively convenient, failed to match developmental need. A second project, partly arising from government concerns about NEET, comprised scoping and development work for a new cohort study of young people starting in year 9 (age 13–14 years)—subsequently launched in 2004 as the *Longitudinal Study of Young People in England (LSYPE)* (Bynner et al., 2004).

I learned from this work, but particularly the latter project, that the relationship between developmental science and policy is not always an easy one. The need for evidence to support ministers on the political battleground makes the historical nature of longitudinal data rarely ideal for the purpose; nor is the often very long-term nature of the conclusions to be drawn. Variables that may be central to the current policy interest may be irrelevant to that of development science and vice versa. A battle royal ensued, for example, over the inclusion of a question on birth-weight in LSYPE, a key life course predictor. The team barely won the argument and then only after spending much time producing a paper reviewing all the available evidence to prove birth-weight's worth as a factor in educational achievement and hence trajectory formation and later life chances.

Basic Skills

Another early priority of the incoming 1997 Labour government as part of the social exclusion agenda was to raise literacy and numeracy levels in the population. The working-group under the chairmanship of Klaus Moser, of which I was a member (DfEE, 1999) was established to review the evidence on the origins of poor basic skills and their role in exclusion from the labor market and effective functioning in other domains of adult life. The "Moser Committee" was charged with the task of formulating both the targets to be achieved and a program of effective practice for achieving them, "Skills for Life." The program included a research facility—the National Research and Development Centre for Adult Literacy and Numeracy (NRDC)—for which the Institute of Education won the contract and I became the first director. The continuing program of work on basic skills, now transferred to the NRDC, shifted the emphasis from the origins of skills difficulties towards their economic and social consequences. The focus was on the impoverishing effects of basic skills deficits not only on educational achievement and employment but on the more hidden benefits of learning in the social, emotional, and civic spheres that lay at the heart of civic responsibility and identity (Bynner, 2004; Bynner & Parsons, 2006, 2009; Parsons & Bynner, 2007; Reder & Bynner, 2009).

In subsequent work we extended the definition of basic skills to include IT access and proficiency in a U.K./U.S.

project on digital exclusion. We compared structural equation models of digital exclusion's relationship with lack of literacy and numeracy proficiency and employment for high-school dropouts in Portland Oregon with models for their matched counterparts in the 1970 cohort study in London and (urban) South-East England (Bynner, Reder, Parsons, & Strawn, 2010). The modeling pointed to the same developmental process in both countries of digital proficiency and employment preceding literacy proficiency. But large fluctuations in some model parameters in response to the changing economic circumstances in the two countries were also apparent. Thus the much earlier take-up of digital skills in Portland accompanied by a contracting labor market at the time needed to be set against the slower take-up in the English sample accompanied by a high demand for digital skills in an expanding labor market. In the Portland context, lack of digital capability was a major impediment to gaining and retaining employment. In the London context of expansion, apart from improving access to jobs, digital skills were at a premium for progression in employment, especially for men and for women access to higher level jobs. Lack of digital capability thus emerges as another of the ever-changing features of social exclusion.

Final Reflections

Reflecting on my career and where it goes next in "retirement mode," I see the challenge for developmental science residing in the globalizing pressures arising from accelerating technological change. The present economic crisis stemming from the banking collapse of 2008 is merely a blip in what is likely to be a continuing process of increasing fluctuation between "boom" and "bust." Those who pay the price are the "lost generations" who inherit the outcomes of economic catastrophe from those who created it. It therefore falls upon the older generation to supply the institutional structures and resources that offer the best prospects of securing young people's futures in a post-industrial world—provision that breaks free from the antiquated provision of the past. Coffield and Williamson (2011, pp. 28–29) offer the kind of liberated curriculum and learning structures for schooling to underpin the essential lifelong learning across the lifespan that is needed. Reporting the work of a Group commissioned by the Nuffield Foundation on 16–19 education, Pring et al. (2009) similarly lay out the themes of a model curriculum based on the principle of "what counts as an educated 18-year-old." The core components embrace economic value, but indirectly via the capabilities related to it and as part of a much broader spectrum of critical knowledge and awareness.

The argument in these prescriptions and repeated here with respect to youth transitions tends to focus on the central role of educational progress in overcoming the challenge of adversity in the achievement of a fulfilling adult identity. Acquisition of capabilities in mediating and moderating structural factors such as class and gender is seen as the key component of adolescent development rather than the more familiar internal psychological mechanisms such as "plans" and "control beliefs." This is not because of any belief that such agency mechanisms are unimportant. The emphasis on the role of individual and collective agency in life-course construction underlines their critical role. What is missing from a perspective that sees these mechanisms as the main, if not only, developmental driver is sufficient regard to the filtering structures and other contextualizing factors involved in their acquisition and distribution.

Human agency does not act in a vacuum. The individual is constrained by influences that are fundamentally social (i.e., relational) and structural in nature, the impact of which is also changing with time (Bronfenbrenner, 1979; Schoon, 2006). While young people's increasing postponement of commitments for the sake of education and career can be identified, this is not the case for all of them. Although during the school years some common features and a degree of homogeneity of experience can be assumed in most education systems, past the age of 16, life-course differentiation steadily increases, and structural factors, including social class, gender, ethnicity, and geographical location—which psychologists perhaps too easily overlook—increasingly make their place felt. Most importantly, these factors are not impermeable; nor are the interrelationships between them in any sense fixed. As Sampson and Laub (1993) showed in their reanalysis of the Gluecks' delinquency data the main predictor of desistence from a criminal career was marriage to a non-delinquent spouse. The presence of the temporal dimension further makes the point that each new generation is subject to a changing historical context in which the impetus is to maintain continuity while continually under pressure to shift in new directions (Bynner & Wadsworth, 2011). Teenage parenthood, which was the norm before the First World War, is now seen as an aspect of social exclusion. Psychology and history, therefore, are intimately related.

Developmental science, in which the life-course perspective is embedded, offers this comprehensive multidisciplinary account of critical factors in adolescent development in which identity in its active form converts into agency. Both are shaped by, and go to shape, adolescent lives in the context of an ever-changing socio-economic, cultural, and geographical landscape. Life-course study is thus part of a more general philosophical, if not ethical, commitment that grows stronger the older I get.

And this commitment takes me back to where this chapter began. While recognizing the relatively fixed biological basis of behavior, at least in species terms, static hierarchical models of human ability rooted in ideological beliefs about the natural order of things supported by restrictive methodology are a poor aid to understanding. As the evolutionary biologist Stephen Jay Gould (1981, p. 316) reminds us in *The Mismeasure of Man*, such perspectives that "blunted the hopes of millions" are a distortion of the scientific strategy that is needed.

Developmental science offers the more open prospect of formulating, testing, and reconceptualizing dynamic models of adolescent attributes and their development. We need sound conclusions about human action and its origins and consequences founded in evidence that offers realizable prescriptions for improvement. This idea applies not only to expanding opportunity, but to the reduction of inequality as well. The mission must be to improve the human condition rather than diminish it. And the means is interdisciplinary understanding to develop *concepts that work* as the intellectual engines of productive and equitable change accompanied by a methodology that is liberating rather than oppressive in matching scientific need. The longitudinal survey as a living observatory and potential laboratory, augmented by case study and ethnography, is the essential tool for meeting the challenges of a science that needs to adapt continually in response to social, economic, technological, and political change.

The student refectory in Bristol was a good place to start!

References

Arnett, J. J. (2000). Emerging adulthood: A theory of development from the late teens through the twenties. *American Psychologist, 55,* 469–480.

Arnett, J. J. (2004). *Emerging adulthood: The winding road from late teens through the twenties.* Oxford: Oxford University Press.

Arnett, J. J., Kloep, M., Hendry, J. J., & Tanner, J. J. (2011). *Emerging adulthood: Stage or process.* Oxford: Oxford University Press.

Arulampalam, W., Gregg, P., & Gregory, M. (2001). Unemployment scarring. *The Economic Journal, 111,* 577–584.

Ashton, D. & Bynner, J. (2011). Labour market, employment and skills. In M. E. J. Wadsworth & J. Bynner (Eds.), *A companion to life course studies: The social and historical context of the British birth cohort studies* (pp. 122–147). London: Routledge.

Ashton, D. & Green, F. (1996). *Education, training and the global economy.* Cheltenham: Edward Elgar.

Bachman, J. G. & O'Malley, P. M. (1977) Self-esteem in young men: A longitudinal analysis of the impact of educational and occupational attainment. *Journal of Personality and Social Psychology, 35,* 365–380.

Baethge, M. (1989). Individualization as hope and disaster: A socioeconomic perspective. In K. Hurrelmann & U. Engel (Eds.), *The social world of adolescents* (pp. 27–42). Berlin: de Gruyter.

Banks, M., Bates, I., Breakwell, G., Bynner, J. Emler, N., Jamieson, L. & Roberts, K. (1992). *Careers and identities.* Buckingham, UK: Open University Press.

Beck, U. (1992). *Risk society.* London: Sage.

Beck, U., Giddens, A., & Lash, S. (1994). *Reflexive modernization: Politics, tradition and aesthetics in the modern social order.* Cambridge: Polity Press.

Becker, G. S. (1975). *Human capital.* Washington, DC: National Bureau of Economic Research.

Becker, H. & Geer, B. (1958). The fate of idealism in medical school. *American Sociological Review, 23,* 50–56.

Blustein, D. L., Devenis, L. E., & Kidney, B. A. (1989). Relationship between the identity formation process and career development. *Journal of Counselling Psychology, 36,* 196–202.

Boyle, G. J., Stankov, L., & Cattell, R. B. (1995). Measurement and statistical models in the study of personality and intelligence. *Humanities & social sciences papers.* Paper 60. http://epublications.bond.edu.au/hss_pubs/60

Bronfenbrenner, U. (1979). *The ecology of human development; Experiments by nature and by design*. Cambridge, MA: Harvard University Press.

Bynner, J. (1969a). *The young smoker*. London: HMSO.

Bynner, J. (1969b). *Medical students' attitudes towards smoking*. London: HMSO.

Bynner, J. (1972). *Parents' attitudes to education*. London: HMSO.

Bynner, J. (1973). Parents' attitudes to education and their consequences for working class children. In J. Rushton & J. D. Turner (Eds.), *Education and deprivation* (pp. 7–22). Manchester: Manchester University Press.

Bynner, J. (1980a). Some problems with psychological research practice. *Bulletin British Psychological Society, 33*, 315–318.

Bynner, J. (1980b). Experimental research strategy and evaluation research designs. *British Educational Research Journal, 4*, 9–22.

Bynner, J. (1987). Coping with transition: ESRC's new 16-19 initiative. *Youth and Policy, 22*, 25–28.

Bynner, J. (1991a). Transition to work: Results from a longitudinal study of young people in 4 British labour markets. In D. Ashton & G. Lowe (Eds.), *Making their way: A comparison between education and training and the labour market in Canada and Britain* (pp. 171–195). Milton Keynes, UK: Open University Press.

Bynner, J. (1991b). Young people and training. *Education and Training, 32*, 22–25.

Bynner, J. (1993a) Factors versus processes in personal characteristics. *Education Sector Review, 17*, 48–53.

Bynner, J. (1993b). Author's reply to peer review of factors versus processes in personal characteristics. *Education Sector Review, 17*, 62–64.

Bynner, J. (1998). Education and family components of identity in the transition from school to work. *International Journal of Behavioural Development, 22*, 29–53.

Bynner, J. (1999). New routes to employment: integration and exclusion. In W. R. Heinz (Ed.), *From education to work: cross national perspectives* (pp. 65–86). Cambridge: Cambridge University Press.

Bynner, J. (2000). Social change and the sequencing of developmental transitions. In L. Crockett & R. K. Silbereisen (Eds.), *Negotiating adolescence in times of social change* (pp. 89–103). Cambridge: Cambridge University Press.

Bynner, J. (2001). British youth transitions in comparative perspective. *Journal of Youth Studies, 4*, 5–23.

Bynner, J. (2003). Transitions and biographies: The inspiration of Walter Heinz. In A. Bolder & A. Witzel (Eds.), *Bwerufsbiogrphien: Beitrage zu Theorie und Empirie iher Bedingungen, Genese und Gestaltunglewske*. Opladen: Leske + Budrich.

Bynner, J. (2004). Literacy, numeracy and employability: Evidence from the British birth cohort studies. *Literacy and numeracy studies, 13*, 31–48.

Bynner, J. (2005a). Longitudinal cohort designs. In K. Kempf-Leonard (ed.), *Encyclopedia of social measurement*, Vol. 2 (pp. 591–599). San Diego: Elsevier.

Bynner, J. (2005b). Reconstructing the youth phase of the life course: The case of emerging adulthood. *Journal of Youth Studies, 8*, 367–384.

Bynner, J. (2010). Youth transitions and changing labour markets: Germany and England in the late 1980s. *Historical Social Research (Historische Sozialforschung), 35*, 76–98.

Bynner, J. (2011). Youth transitions and apprenticeship: A broader view of skill. In T. Dolphin and T. Lamming (Eds.), *Re-thinking apprenticeship*. London: IPPR.

Bynner, J., Bachman, J. G., & O'Malley, P. (1981). Self-esteem and delinquency revisited. *Journal of Youth and Adolescence, 10*, 407–441.

Bynner, J. & Chisholm, L. (1998). Comparative youth transition research: methods, meanings and research relations. *European Sociological Review, 14*, 139–150.

Bynner, J., Chisholm, L., & Furlong, A. (Eds.) (1997). *Youth, citizenship and social change*. Aldershot: Ashgate Press.

Bynner, J., Elias, P., McKnight, A., Pan, A., & Pierre, G. (2002). *Young people's changing routes to independence*. York: Joseph Rowntree Foundation.

Bynner, J., Ferri, E., & Shepherd, P. (Eds.) (1997). *Twenty-something in the 90s: Getting on, getting by, getting nowhere*. Aldershot: Ashgate Press.

Bynner, J. & Goldstein, H. (1998). Three generations of children – an edited transcript of a video recording made in March 1982 of the then directors of the three major British cohort studies in conversation. *Paediatric and Perinatal Epidemiology: Special Issue in Honour of Professor Neville Butler, 12* (supplement): 1–14.

Bynner, J. & Heinz, W. R. (1991). Matching samples and analysing their differences in a cross-national study of labour market entry in England and West Germany. *International Journal of Comparative Sociology, 32*, 137–153.

Bynner, J. & Joshi, H. (2007). Building the evidence base from longitudinal data. The aims, content and achievements of the British Birth Cohort Studies. *Innovation, the European Journal of Social Science Research, 20*, 159–179.

Bynner, J., Joshi, H., & Tsatsas, M. (2000). *Obstacles and opportunities on the route to adulthood: evidence from rural and urban Britain*. London: Smith Institute.

Bynner, J., Londra, M., & Jones, G. (2004). *The impact of Government policy on social exclusion among young people*. Office of the Deputy Prime Minister, 04SEU 02461, London: Social Exclusion Unit.

Bynner, J., Londra, M., Plewis, I., Emler, N., Maung, N. A., Finch, S. et al. (2004). *Scoping study and development work for a new cohort study of young people (14 to 25): Longitudinal Study of Young People in England (LSYPE)*. UK Department for Education and Skills. www.dfes.gov.uk/rsgateway/DB/RRP/u013779/index.shtml

Bynner, J. & Parsons, S. (2002). Social exclusion and the transition from school to work: The case of young people not in education, employment or training (NEET). *Journal of Vocational Behaviour, 60*, 289–309.

Bynner, J. & Parsons, S. (2006). *New light on literacy and numeracy: Results of the literacy and numeracy assessment in the Age 34 follow-up of the 1970 cohort Study BCS70*. NRDC report, Institute of Education. www.nrdc.org.uk/uploads/documents/doc_849.doc

Bynner, J. & Parsons, S. (2009). Insights into basic skills from a UK longitudinal study. In S. Reder & J. Bynner (Eds.), *Tracking adult literacy and numeracy skills, findings from longitudinal research*. London: Routledge.

Bynner, J., Reder, S., Parsons, S., & Strawn, C. (2010). *The three divides: The digital divide and its relation to basic skills and employment in London, England and Portland Oregon*. NRDC report, Institute of Education. www.nrdc.org.uk/publications

Bynner, J. & Roberts, K. (Eds.) (1991). *Youth and work: Transition to employment in England and Germany*. London: Anglo German Foundation.

Bynner, J. & Romney, D. (1985). Intelligence: Fact or artefact. *British Journal of Educational Psychology, 36*, 13–23.

Bynner, J. & Romney, D. (1989). Evaluation of a circumplex model of DSMIII personality disorders. *Journal of Research in Personality, 23*, 525–538.

Bynner, J. & Silbereisen, R. K. (2000). Introduction: The life course and social change. In J. Bynner & R. K. Silbereisen (Eds.), *Adversity and challenge in life in the new Germany and in England* (pp. 1–16). Basingstoke: Macmillan.

Bynner, J. & Wadsworth, M. E. (2010). Cognitive capital: The case for a construct. *Longitudinal and Life Course Studies, 1*, 297–304.

Bynner, J. & Wadsworth, M. E. J. (2011). Generation and change in perspective. In M. E. J. Wadsworth & J. Bynner (Eds.), *A companion to life course studies. The social and historical context of the British birth cohort studies*. London: Routledge.

Campbell, D. T. (1969). Reforms as experiments. *American Psychologist, 24*, 409–429.

Campbell, D. T. (1978). Qualitative knowing in action research. In M. Brenner, P. Marsh, & M. Brenner (Eds.), *The social contexts of method* (pp. 184–209). London: Croom Helm.

Campbell, D. T. & Stanley, J. C. (1966). *Experimental and quasi-experimental designs for research*. Chicago: Rand McNally.

Cattell, R. B., Davies, R. B., Eysenck, H. J., & Kline, P. (1993). Peer review of "Factors versus processes in personal characteristics." *Education Review, 17*, 54– 59.

Coffield, F. & Williamson, B. (2011). *From exam factories to communities of discovery*. London: Bedford Way Papers, Institute of Education Press.

Coleman, J. (1988). Social capital in the creation of human capital. *American Journal of Sociology, 94*, supplement, 95–120.

Coleman, J. & Hendry, L. B. (1999). *The nature of adolescence*. New York: Routledge.

Cook, T. D. & Campbell, D. T. (1979). *Quasi-experimentation: Design and analysis for field settings*. Chicago: Rand McNally.

Côté, J. E. (1996). Sociological perspective on identity formation: The culture-identity link. *Journal of Adolescence, 19*, 417–428.

Côté, J. E. (2002). The role of identity capital in the transition to adulthood: The individualization thesis examined. *Journal of Youth Studies, 5*, 117–134.

Côté, J. E. & Bynner, J. (2008). Exclusion from emerging adulthood: UK and Canadian perspectives on structure and agency in the transition to adulthood. *Journal of Youth Studies, 11*, 251–268.

Côté, J. E. & Levine, C. G. (2002). *Identity formation, agency and culture*. Mahwah, NJ: Lawrence Erlbaum.

Cronbach, L. J. (1951). Coefficent alpha and the internal structure of tests. *Psychometrika, 16*, 297–334.

Cronbach, L. J. (1975). Beyond the two disciplines of scientific psychology. *American Psychologist*, February, 116–127.

Cronbach, L. J. (1980). *Evaluation for an open society*. San Francisco: Jossey-Bass.

Cronbach, L. J., Gleser, G., Nanda, H., & Rajaratnam, S. (1972). *The dependability of behavioural measurements*. New York: John Wiley.

Cronbach, L. J. & Meehl, P. E. (1955). Construct validity in the internal structure of tests. *Psychological Bulletin, 52*, 281–302.

DfEE (Department for Education and Employment) (1999) *A fresh start: Improving adult literacy and numeracy*. Report of the Working Group, Sudbury: DfEE Publications.

Elder, G. H. Jr. (1999). *Children of the Great Depression: Social change in life experience*. Boulder, CO: Westview Press.

Elder, G. H. Jr. & Giele, J. Z. (Eds.). (2009). *The craft of life course research*. New York & London: Guilford Press.

Elder, G. H. Jr. & Shanahan, M. J. (2006). The life course and human development. In W. Damon and R. M. Lerner (Eds), *Handbook of child psychology, Vol. 6: Theoretical models of human development* (pp. 665–715). New York: Wiley.

Ellwood, D. T. (1982). Teenage unemployment: Permanent scars or temporary blemishes. In R. B. Freeman & D. A. Wise (Eds.), *The youth labor market problem: Its nature causes and consequences* (pp. 349–390). Chicago: University of Chicago Press.

Erikson, E. H. (1963). *Childhood and society*. New York: Norton.

Evans, K. & Heinz, W. R. (1994). *Becoming adults in the 1990s*. London: Anglo German Foundation.

Eysenck, H. J. (1953). *Uses and abuses of psychology*. Oxford: Penguin Books.

Eysenck, H. J. (1954). *The psychology of politics*. London: Routledge & Kegan Paul.

Eysenck, H. J. (1957). *Sense and nonsense in psychology*. Baltimore, MD: Penguin Books.

Feinstein, L. & Bynner, J. (2004). The Importance of developmental trajectories in mid-childhood: effects on adult outcomes in the UK 1970 birth cohort. *Child Development, 75*, 1329–1339.

Feinstein, L. & Bynner, J. (2006). Continuity and discontinuity in mid-childhood: Implications for adult outcomes in the UK 1970 Birth Cohort. In A. Huston & M. Ripke (Eds.), *Developmental context of middle childhood: Bridges to adolescence and adulthood* (pp. 327–349). New York: Cambridge University Press.

Feinstein, L. Bynner, J., & Duckworth, K. (2006). Young people's leisure contexts and their relation to adult outcomes. *Journal of Youth Studies, 9*, 305–328.

Ferri, E., Bynner, J., & Wadsworth, M. (Eds.) (2003). *Changing Britain, changing lives: Three generations at the end of the century*. London: Institute of Education.

Fouad, N. & Bynner, J (2008). Work transitions. *American Psychologist, 63*, 241–251.

Furlong, A. & Cartmel, F. (1997). *Young people and social change: Individualization and risk in late modernity*. Buckingham: Open University Press.

Gaiser, W. & Müller, H. U. (1989) The importance of peer groups in different regional contexts and biographical stages. In K. Hurrelmann & U. Engel (Eds.), *The social world of adolescents* (pp. 27–42). Berlin: de Gruyter.

Giele, J. Z. (2002). Longitudinal studies and life-course research: Innovations, investigators and policy ideas. In E. Phelps, F. Furstenburg, & A. Colby (Eds.), *Looking at lives: American longitudinal studies of the twentieth century* (pp. 15–36). New York: Sage.

Goffman, E. (1959). *The presentation of self in everyday life*. New York: Doubleday.

Gould, S. J. (1981). *The mismeasure of man*. New York: Norton.

Guttman, L. (1954). A new approach to factor analysis: The Radex. In P. Lazarsfeld (Ed.), *Mathematical thinking in the social sciences* (pp. 258–348). Glencoe, IL: Free Press.

Hamilton, D., Jenkins, D., King, C., MacDonald, B., & Parlett, M. (Eds.) (1977). *Beyond the numbers game*. London: MacMillan Education.

Hebb, D. (1949). *The organisation of behaviour*. New York: Wiley.

Heinz, W. R. (1991). Status passages, social risks and the life course: A conceptual framework. In W. R. Heinz (Ed.), *Theoretical advances in life course research. Vol. I, Status passages and the life course* (pp. 9–22). Weinheim: Deutscher Studien Verlag.

Heinz, W. R., Huinink, J., & Weymamm, A. (Eds.) (2009). *The life course reader: Individuals and societies across time*. Frankfurt: Campus Verlag.

Helve, H. & Bynner, J. (Eds.). (1996). *Youth and life management*. Helsinki: Helsinki University Press.

Helve, H. & Bynner, J. (Eds.). (2007). *Youth and social capital*. London: The Tufnell Press.

Hendry, L. B. & Kloep, M. (2002). *Lifespan development: Resources, challenges and risks*. London: Thomson Learning.

Hurrelmann, K. (1989). A sociological perspective. In K. Hurrelmann & U. Engel (Eds.), *The social world of adolescents* (pp. 3–26). Berlin: de Gruyter.

Hutton, W. (1996). *The state we're in (revised edition): Why Britain is in crisis and how to overcome it*. London: Jonathan Cape.

Jöreskog, K. G. & Sörbom, D. (1979). *Advances in factor analysis and structural equation modelling*. Cambridge, MA: Abt books.

Kinsey, A. C., Pomeroy, W., & Martin, C. (1948). *Sexual behavior in the human male*. Philadelphia: Saunders.

Kinsey, A. C., Pomeroy, W., Martin, C., & Gebhard, P. (1953). *Sexual behavior in the human female*. Philadelphia: Saunders.

Kohn, M. (1987). Cross-national research as an analytic strategy. *American Sociological Review, 52*, 713–731.

Lakatos, G. (1970). Falsification and the methodology of scientific programmes. In G. Lakatos & A. Musgrave (Eds.), *Criticism and the growth of knowledge* (pp. 91–196). Cambridge: Cambridge University Press.

Lerner, R. M., Fisher, C. B., & Weinberg, R. A. (2000). Applying developmental science in the 21st century: International scholarship for our times. *International Journal of Behavioural Development, 24*, 24–29.

Mahoney, J., Stattin, H., & Lord, H. (2004). Unstructured youth recreation centre participation and anti-social behaviour development: Selection influences and the moderating role of anti-social peers. *International Journal of Behavioural Development, 28*, 553–560.

Marcia, J. E. (1966). Development and validation of ego identity. *Journal of Personality and Social Psychology, 3*, 551–558.

Matza, D. (1964). *Delinquency and drift*. New York: John Wiley.

Matza, D. & Sykes, G. (1961). Juvenile delinquency and subterranean values. *American Sociological Review. 26*, 712–719.

McKennell, A. C. & Bynner, J. M. (1969). Self images and smoking behaviour among schoolboys. *British Journal of Educational Psychology, 39*, 27–39.

Miller, G. A., Galanter, E. H., & Pribram, K. H. (1960). *Plans and the structure of behaviour.* New York: Holt Rinehart & Winston.

Osgood, C. E., Suci, G., & Tannenbaum, P. (1957). *The measurement of meaning.* Urbana, IL: University of Illinois Press.

Parlett, M. & Hamilton, D. (Eds.). (1977). Evaluation as illumination: A new approach to the study of innovative programmes. In D. Hamilton, D. Jenkins, C. King, B. MacDonald, & M. Parlett (Eds.), *Beyond the numbers game* (pp. 6–22). London: MacMillan Education.

Parsons, S. & Bynner, J. (2007). *Illuminating disadvantage: Profiling the experiences of adults with entry level literacy or numeracy over the life course.* NRDC Research Report, Institute of Education, London.

Popper, K. R. (1970). Normal science and its dangers. In G. Lakatos & A. Musgrave (Eds.), *Criticism and the growth of knowledge* (pp. 51–58). Cambridge: Cambridge University Press.

Pring, R., Hayward, G., Hodgson, A., Johnson, J., Keep, E., Oancea, A. et al. (2009). *Education for all: The future of education and training for 14–19 year-olds.* London: Routledge.

Putnam, D. (1999). *Bowling alone, the collapse and revival of American community.* New York: Simon and Schuster.

Ragin, C. (1987). *The comparative method.* Berkeley: University of California Press.

Reder, S. & Bynner, J. (Eds.) (2009). *Tracking adult literacy and numeracy skills: Findings from longitudinal research.* New York: Routledge.

Richardson, K. & Bynner, J. (1984). Intelligence: Past and future. *International Journal of Psychology, 19*, 499–526.

Roberts, K. (1984). *School leavers and their prospects.* Milton Keynes: Open University Press.

Roberts, K., Clark, S. C., & Wallace, C. (1994). Flexibility and individualisation: A comparison of transitions into employment in England and Germany. *Sociology, 20*, 31–54.

Roberts, K. & Parsell, G. (1989). Recent changes in the pathways from school to work. In K. Hurrelmann & U. Engel (Eds.). *The social world of adolescents* (pp. 369–392). New York: de Gruyter.

Robins, L. & Rutter, M. (1990) *Straight and devious pathways from childhood to adulthood.* Cambridge: Cambridge University Press.

Romney, D M. & Bynner, J. (1992), *Structure of personal characteristics.* New York: Praeger.

Rosenberg, F. R. & Rosenberg, M. (1978). Self-esteem and delinquency. *Journal of Youth and Adolescence, 7*, 279–291.

Rutter, M. & Madge, N. (1976). *Cycles of disadvantage.* London: Heinemann.

Sampson, R. J. & Laub, J. H. (1993). *Crime in the making: Pathways and turning points through life.* Cambridge MA: Harvard University Press.

Savickas, M. L. (1985). Identity in vocational development. *Journal of Vocational Behaviour, 27*, 29–327.

Schaffer, H. R. & Hargreaves, D. (1978). Young people in society: A research initiative by the SSRC. *Bulletin of the British Psychological Society, 31*, 91–94.

Schofield, M., Bynner, J., Lewis, P., & Massie, P. (1965). *The sexual behaviour of young people.* London: Longmans.

Schoon, I. (2006). *Risk and resilience: Adaptations in changing times.* Cambridge: Cambridge University Press.

Schoon, I. & Bynner, J. (2003). Risk and resilience in the life course: Implications for interventions and social policies. *Journal of Youth Studies, 6*, 1–31.

Schoon, I., Bynner, J., Joshi, H., Parsons, S., Wiggins, R. & Sacker, A. (2002). The influence of context, timing and duration of risk experiences for the passage from childhood to mid adulthood. *Child Development, 73*, 1486–1504.

Schuller, T., Bynner, J., & Feinstein, L (2004). *Capitals and capabilities.* Research Centre for the Wider Benefits of Learning Discussion Paper no. 1, www.learningbenefits.net/

Schuller, T., Preston, J., Hammond, C., Brassett-Grundy, A. & Bynner, J. (2004). *The benefits of learning: Impact of education on health, family life and social capital.* Basingstoke: Macmillan.

Sen, A. (1992). *Inequality re-examined.* Cambridge, MA: Harvard University Press.

Silbereisen, R. K. & Tomasik, M. J. (2010) Developmental action in changing contexts: Perspectives from six countries. *Historical Social Research (Historische Sozialforschung), 35*, 57–75.

Spearman, C. (1932). *The abilities of man.* London: Macmillan.

Thurstone, L. L. (1934). The vectors of the mind. *Psychological Review, 41*, 1–32.

Thurstone, L. L. (1947). *Multiple factor analysis.* Chicago: University of Chicago Press.

Tolman, E. C. (1932). *Purposive behavior in animals and men.* New York: The Century Co.

Vondracek, F. W., Lerner, R. M., & Schulenberg, J. E. (1986). *Career development: A life-span developmental approach.* Hillsdale, NJ: Laurence Erlbaum.

Wadsworth, M. E. J. & Bynner, J. (Eds.). (2011). *A companion to life course studies: The social and historical context of the British birth cohort studies.* London: Routledge.

Wootton, B. (1959). *Social science and social pathology.* London: Allen and Unwin.

8

Why Adolescence Matters

An Autobiography of a Psychologist

John Coleman

In the course of my career many people have asked me why I study adolescence. Adolescence is without doubt the Cinderella subject within developmental psychology. It gets less attention than other topics in the textbooks, in the curriculum and on research agendas. So why would someone want to spend their life studying this rather unpopular stage of the life cycle? Colleagues might suggest that the choice has something to do with my own experiences of the teenage years. Perhaps I am trying to understand my own "storm and stress." Or am I someone who simply never grew up? My own memories of adolescence are not unhappy ones, and I suspect that the reasons I study this topic are more to do with formative experiences in my early twenties than with any unresolved teenage trauma.

My Undergraduate Years

Two things happened which influenced the direction of my career. In the first place, I spent my undergraduate years studying psychology at McGill University in Montreal. Unlike the situation in the UK, Canadian universities have long summer vacations, and these made it possible for me to find unusual vacation work placements. I spent one summer on the Lower East Side in New York, working in a church project with Latino youth. The long, hot months of June, July, and August 1960 were taken up with attempting to keep the young people off the streets and out of trouble. In my second summer I got a job on a farm in Ontario, working with emotionally disturbed teenagers. These summers represented turning points in my career development, as I met inspirational adults, enjoyed myself hugely, and developed new skills. These experiences were also fundamental in later stages of my career, when I myself established a residential center in the UK.

Following graduation, I returned to England, determined to pursue postgraduate study in some aspect of child development. The second influential event occurred during the course of my PhD at University College, London. My supervisor had agreed to take me on as a postgraduate candidate on the condition that I would study the topic of aggression. She had four other students who were also working on various aspects of aggression. This was fine with me, as long as I could do something on children or young people. I came up with a proposal to study aggressive behavior in the playground among 10-year-olds. My supervisor was dismissive. "That's not good enough," she said. "Not much of a contribution to the literature in that!"

For some weeks I wandered unhappily around North London, convinced I would never make the grade in the research world. Finally I had an inspiration. Why not study aggression in two age groups, rather than one? By including 10- and 13-year-olds I would not only broaden the scope of the study, but I would also be able to look at that critical developmental phase—the beginning of adolescence. My supervisor grudgingly accepted the idea, and so began a lifetime of interest in this topic (Coleman, 1969a, 1969b).

Since that time I have worked with young people in a variety of settings, and in many different roles. I have carried out a range of research projects, in schools, in the community, in prisons, and in children's homes. I have worked as a clinical psychologist in adolescent units, and as the Director of a therapeutic community for very troubled teenagers. I have been the Director of an independent research center, and have held various academic positions, most recently as a Senior Research Fellow at the University of Oxford. In the chapter that follows I will describe some of these experiences, and how they have shaped my views of adolescent development.

A Trip to Florida

In 1964 I was one year into my PhD, and was beginning to feel what will be familiar to many doctoral students, a sense of frustration. Although my research was interesting, I was spending most of my time very much alone with my thoughts and my books, interspersed with short visits to school playgrounds where I was attempting to collect my data. I missed the atmosphere of North America, and wanted to recapture some of the excitement I had experienced in my undergraduate days. I went to the library in London and identified a selection of child development research centers across the USA. I wrote to them asking if they would take me on as an associate for a couple of months in the summer. It was a bold thing to do, and perhaps not surprisingly I received no replies! I was just about to pack my bags and go off to spend the summer with my family in France when I received a letter from a Professor Wally Kennedy at Florida State University. Yes, he replied, we would be happy to host you for the summer, as long as you are not too fussy about what you do!

The Kennedys were warm and hospitable, and made me very welcome during my visit to Tallahassee, a city I have not even heard of beforehand. One of the enduring memories of that time was of taking a boat on the weekends through the swamps and bayous of central Florida to the Kennedy's river house, built on stilts and sitting above the water and well away from the alligators. The Kennedys would invite a selection of students and colleagues for a couple of days in the wilds, and we would go fishing, eat wonderful food, and discuss psychology. What a way to spend a weekend!

I worked as an assistant in the clinic in the Psychology Department at Florida State that summer, helping with assessments, doing interviews, and doing basic statistics for some of the staff. I roomed with postgraduate students from Taiwan and Hong Kong, and learnt rudimentary Mandarin. It was all so completely different from London, and fired my enthusiasm for different approaches in clinical interventions with families. I began to think about family therapy, and to consider how to evaluate interventions in an ethical and rigorous manner. However, the most important lesson from that summer was a realization that it was possible to combine research and practice. I had never contemplated the possibility of a university department offering clinical services. This was a model that interested me greatly, since in England there appeared to be a rigid distinction between the academic world and the world of clinical practice. I was much influenced by my experiences at Florida State, and in much of my subsequent work I have tried to find ways of bringing the two worlds together.

Whitechapel, in the East End of London

Following the completion of my PhD I undertook a training to become qualified as a clinical psychologist. In those days, in the mid-1960s, training was not as regulated as it is today, and as long as one was working with an identified senior psychologist and completed 2 years,

involving experiences in two different settings, then that was considered sufficient. I was enormously lucky, in that I was able to spend most of my training on placement in a children's center at the Middlesex Hospital in central London, working jointly with pediatricians and psychiatrists. This provided me with an invaluable background in basic child and mental health, but it also introduced me to medical education, as the Middlesex was a teaching hospital as well as a center of excellence in my field.

I was even more fortunate in that this was a period of expansion in medical education in the UK, and a new department of psychiatry was being established at one of the oldest teaching hospitals in the capital—known as the London Hospital in the East End. New posts were being advertised, including one for a Lecturer in Clinical Psychology. I did not believe I had a chance, as I was too young for such a post, but I was encouraged by a colleague at the Middlesex to apply. At that time I had never even traveled to the East End, and I remember asking someone how to get there! I will never forget the moment when I stepped out of the tube station for the first time, to be met by the sights and sounds of the Whitechapel market. No-one could avoid being struck by the noise, the variety of colors, the crowds of every nationality, and the sense of having arrived in a vibrant and diverse community.

The new academic unit of psychiatry was headed by an unusual man, Desmond Pond, one of the earliest proponents of community child psychiatry. The post offered not only the chance to teach psychology to medical students and to do research, but also the opportunity to set up an innovative service for children and young people in this most deprived area of London. Again I was fortunate in the extreme to have the chance to work in this setting, and to be able to collaborate with a group of remarkable colleagues. It was not long before I was asked to appoint other lecturers in clinical psychology, and to plan a new service that would serve families in the East End. This was a time when the term "non-accidental injury" in relation to young children was becoming widely used. Many clinicians were wanting to address the needs of families, and to consider how to intervene early enough to prevent such things happening.

Whilst I continued to think about adolescence, and to retain an interest in this age group, I was asked to lead on the establishment of what become known as the London Pre-School Unit, a service for families with children under five who were considered to be at risk. This unit was supported by the establishment of another initiative, the formation of the Family Research Unit, and so the two centers were able to work together, a model that I continue to believe is an ideal one for demonstrating how research and practice can facilitate and enhance each other's efforts. When one looks back it seems like a golden age. Funding was available for such initiatives, and there was every encouragement from the community and from other professionals for work of this sort. Indeed it was considered exciting and innovative that, rather than remaining in the clinic waiting for families to attend, we should go into the community and reach out to families who otherwise would never get as far as the clinic door.

It was a time of rapid learning for me, and many of the principles of developmental psychology served me well in an applied setting. Through the use of video and a one-way mirror we helped parents to see their children in a different light. Behavioral concepts such as positive and negative reinforcement, and contingencies, were explained to mothers who had never thought of such ideas before. There was much discussion of theories of attachment, especially since writers such as Bowlby were influential in Britain at that time. Many of the mothers were depressed, vulnerable, and with a low sense of self-efficacy. This was the time when new attempts were being made to understand parenting, and to recognize some of the factors that contribute to abuse. Diana Baumrind, Mavis Hetherington, and others were beginning to write about parenting styles, and I remember it as a time when contributions from psychologists were welcomed by other clinicians.

Once the Pre-School Unit was established and running well I had time to turn my attention to my other research interest—adolescence. Following the completion of my PhD I had determined to take further the idea of a longitudinal study of this age group. My doctoral research had identified, not surprisingly, many interesting differences between the 10- and 13-year-olds, and it seemed to me that this would be a fertile field for further investigation. After much deliberation I decided to carry out a study of four age groups, 11-, 13-, 15-, and 17-year-olds. Although a longitudinal study was out of the question because of the time it would take, I was able to plan a cross-sectional study looking at the way concepts and experiences of relationships differed over this age span. This research culminated in my first book, *Relationships in Adolescence* (Coleman, 1974).

It was from this research that I formulated my focal theory of adolescent development. The findings came out at a time when there was heated debate over the question of "storm and stress" in adolescence. Many empirical studies had published evidence showing that the majority of young people coped reasonably well during this life stage, directly contradicting the notion that adolescence was a period of disturbance and turmoil. Thus these results posed a challenge to the theoretical positions of commentators such as Erik Erikson, most famously expressed in *Identity: Youth and Crisis* (1968). Erikson was one of the pre-eminent writers at this time, and with his notion of this stage as one of "identity crisis," he was seen as a champion of the "storm and stress" view. Yet empirical results did not support this idea, so how could one explain the disparities between theory and evidence?

A further question that fascinated me was how young people managed to adjust to the physical, emotional, and social changes that were a part of this developmental stage. If most coped reasonably well, and yet they had to face a considerable array of developmental challenges, how did they do this? My own findings showed that certain relationship issues came to the fore at different ages, so that, for example, concern over friendship choice peaked at one age, whilst anxieties about relationships with parents were more prominent at another age. As a result of this evidence I formulated a model that reflected this phenomenon. I called it the focal model, arguing that the majority of young people coped reasonably well with the challenges of this stage by focusing on different issues at different times, spacing out the problems and concerns they had to face. Where this was impossible, because of environmental or contextual factors, development was rendered more problematic. One other feature of the focal model that I wanted to highlight had to do with agency. Inherent in my model, I argued, was the notion that young people, by spacing out the issues, were expressing agency and showing how they were able to take control over their lives. This remains a central feature of my current thinking (Coleman, 2011), and I am glad to say has been picked up by many other writers and researchers over the years (e.g., Goossens, 2006).

A Therapeutic Community for Troubled Teenagers

Ever since I had worked on a farm treating disturbed adolescents during a summer vacation in Canada, I had wanted to continue my work with troubled teenagers. I had always dreamed of setting up such a facility in the UK, and from the mid-1970s I began to think seriously about whether such an enterprise might be possible. As a preliminary step to the setting up of a new community, I obtained research funding for a project on children in care, I joined the board of an organization engaged in providing services for troubled adolescents, and I spent a summer visiting residential facilities in the USA. This was a seminal experience, and helped me formulate how I would like to organize and run any center that was to be established in England. As part of my *tour d'horizon* I visited Boy's Town in Omaha, Nebraska, as well as a variety of other facilities including a "boot camp" in Illinois and a very "alternative" therapeutic community in Maine. What did I learn?

As I set out in my writing at that time (Coleman, 1980), I came to the conclusion that the theoretical model mattered less than other key features of any regime attempting to treat these young people. The three features I considered to be critical were effective leadership, care of the staff team, and equality among the different professional backgrounds of staff. I decided that, if staff were expected to provide support and nurturance to extremely deprived and needy teenagers, then the organization had to demonstrate that the staff themselves were to be nurtured too. I was also influenced at that time by a book called *The Other 23 Hours* (Trieschman, Whittaker, & Brendtro, 2009). In this book the authors argued that it was all very well for psychiatrists or other trained staff to come in to the residential facility and provide "treatment" for an hour a day, but it was really what happened during the rest of the day and at night time that mattered as much, if not more.

When I finally did leave my post in London and moved down to Sussex to establish a residential community these principles were enshrined in the ethos of the center. I had also retained my interest in the model that I had seen working in Florida many years previously, and I hoped to set up at Chalvington a center which would carry out training and research as well as providing a residential facility for the young people. This was a joint venture with other like-minded colleagues, and without their support Chalvington would never have become a reality. However, looking back now, I can see that our aspirations were very idealistic. The task of actually running a residential therapeutic center 24 hours a day, 7 days a week, appointing and managing staff, and persuading those responsible for very troubled and troubling young people to refer them to our new facility proved daunting in the extreme. Our finances became stretched, as referrals were at first slow to come in. Staff who had initially signed up to the principles of the therapeutic community became less committed as they experienced sleepless nights working with young people who had climbed on to the roof at three in the morning.

In the first year it sometimes seemed more like anarchy than a well-organized community, and the strain took its toll on all who were associated with this venture. Some thought that I had been naïve in imagining that it would be possible to put into practice the principles that I had developed on paper. I argued that it takes many years to establish a facility of the sort I had envisaged, and that we had to have faith and patience. Some of the goals had to be abandoned, so the research took a back seat, and there was less training than I had hoped for. However, the residential work began to take root, the education began to show results, and as more young people were referred the community began to settle down.

Funding was a continual challenge. When the plans had been drawn up, it was at a time when local authorities had sufficient finances to be able to send young people in care to new and innovative facilities, especially if they were open all year round, providing both education and treatment. However, during the 1980s local authority finances shrank, and it became more difficult to persuade local authorities to use Chalvington for their most troubled teenagers. Throughout the 1980s this proved the major obstacle to the work of the community. For much of the time the place was full up, taking in its total complement of 20 young people. However it was always hard to maintain the stability of the population, something that is essential for both staff and young people. Without the opportunity to establish long-term relationships it was always going to be a challenge to provide the therapeutic care that was Chalvington's key objective.

As the beginning of the 1990s there was a general move away from the type of provision exemplified by Chalvington. Many other therapeutic communities had to close due to lack of funding, and we were affected like everyone else by the pressures on local authorities. Even if social workers believed that a placement at Chalvington was the right choice for a particular teenager, they found themselves unable to make the referral because of policies which blocked such placements. In 1993, Chalvington closed its doors. It was a brave attempt to put into practice a model of therapeutic care that would address all the needs of some of the most troubled young people in the country. During the years it was open Chalvington helped more than 150 adolescents. Many of them have made good progress, and it is rewarding to hear from them about their families and their achievements. I have no regrets, but it was a hard lesson in the clash between ideals and reality!

The Trust for the Study of Adolescence

At the end of the 1980s, once I had stepped back from a direct management role at Chalvington, I began to think again about some of the other objectives that had been in my mind a decade earlier. I wanted very much to see a center established that pursued some of the objectives that had been put to one side at Chalvington. I wanted to see if it was possible to create an organization that did at least combine research and some sort of direct practical work, even if this was with adults living and working with young people, rather than with adolescents themselves. Many of my family and friends thought I should go back to an academic career, but I was still determined to pursue my ideals. Since I had already taken a path that lay outside the established institutional structures of the university world, I made the decision that I was not ready to go back to that sort of career.

Two factors made this possible. In the first place I had for some years been an advisor to the Prince of Wales' charities, known at that time as the Prince's Trust. I received a great deal of support from all the people associated with the Trust, and the Trustees were generous enough to provide a grant enabling me to set up the new center. The second factor that played a key role in this initiative was the encouragement of colleagues who believed in my vision. Some were brave enough to come and work with me, whilst others became members of a Board which provided the necessary framework for the project.

The Trust for the Study of Adolescence, or TSA as it became known, started work at the beginning of the 1990s. It was based in Brighton in Sussex, and had as its objectives to pursue research on adolescence, to provide training for professionals working with young people, and to offer support to parents of teenagers. It is important to say that there was no similar organization in Britain, nor as far as I was aware, in any other country. Whilst some university staff in the UK were carrying out research on this stage of the life course, funding was scarce, and at most there were one or two people in any academic institution interested in the topic of adolescence.

TSA grew from a handful of staff in the early years to a complement of 32 staff when I left in 2005. The first few years were hard-going, and we were often asked why we had established ourselves as an independent unit, rather than basing ourselves in a university setting. We were clear, however, that only by being independent would it be possible to combine research and practice in the way we wanted. We developed very close links with universities, especially those in the south of England, but retaining our autonomy enabled us to publish materials, run training courses, and concentrate on taking the evidence base to the public in a way that would have been impossible in an academic setting. In the early years we concentrated on projects that would raise our profile, as well as meeting our main objectives. Thus, for example, we developed educational materials for parents of teenagers, and we ran conferences on neglected topics such as young fathers, suicide in adolescence, and the experience of leaving care.

One question that dominated the early years of TSA was how to choose the topics upon which to focus. Within the field of adolescence there were clearly a wide range of areas to concentrate on, and we were often challenged to indicate our central interests. Many people expected that we would focus on educational topics, and carry out our work in schools, whilst others assumed that we were based in social work or counseling. In fact we made our choices based on a number of very different principles. We wanted to raise the general level of understanding of the teenage years, and address the predominantly negative stereotype of adolescence that is prevalent among the general public. We wanted to inform and educate people about this stage of life. We also wanted to influence government policy, so we chose topics, such as teenage pregnancy, that were either completely ignored by politicians or were misunderstood by those making policy decisions. However, we were also very much affected by the availability of financial support, so in our choice of work it was necessary to match a pragmatic approach with a set of principles about what was important.

Our work on adolescent suicide was a good example of this approach. One of the staff came to TSA with an interest in this, and she asked if she could run a short course on the topic. It so happened that a Prison Governor attended the course, and was impressed. He persuaded the Prison Service to support a number of workshops on adolescent suicide for prison staff, and that in turn led to our being asked to develop a wider training for all staff in young offender institutions in England and Wales on understanding adolescence. That was successful, and led to many approaches from other organizations. In addition TSA went on to carry out research on suicide among young people, and to develop training materials on suicide and self-harm (Coleman, 2006)

Not all of our work developed in this way, however. A different model is exemplified by the work we carried out on pro-social behavior. We were keen to highlight what is now known as an "asset model," or a strengths-based approach to adolescence, and to demonstrate that young people make significant contributions to society rather than being a drain on resources and a trial to their parents. We needed funding in order to carry out this work, but it was almost impossible to find suitable sources of grant money, and a number of our applications were turned down. We could have given up, and moved on to other topics, but there was a determination among staff and Trustees that this was a topic that should not be ignored. It took us 5 years to obtain funding, but finally a Swiss Foundation, the Johann Jacobs Foundation, indicated that they were willing to provide finance for research in this area. With their support we carried out two major studies on volunteering and campaigning among young people in Britain, work of which we were all very proud. This enabled us to publish academic papers on the topic as well as briefing papers for policy makers, and we also ran a number of conferences to highlight the findings (Eden & Roker, 2002)

Parenting was another area of work which was central to the development of TSA. I mentioned that we developed educational materials for parents, and in the early years we established a reputation for having some expertise in this area. When the Labour Government came to power in 1997 they wanted to introduce programs for parents of teenagers who were engaged in offending behavior. However, very little was known about interventions for parents of teenagers at that time in Britain, and TSA was asked by the Government to act as advisors. This was an exciting opportunity, and, as with the work on suicide, led on to many other related projects. TSA continued for a number of years to provide training and advice to local authorities, to custodial settings, and to practitioners themselves. We were also given the chance to carry out research on this topic, to develop videos and other training materials, and to work directly with groups of parents. We published a number of books on this subject, and our training materials are still being used a decade later in many parts of the country (Coleman and Roker, 2001; Roker and Coleman, 2007)

I retired from TSA in 2005, having reached the age of 65. It proved difficult to attract a new Director, and the two Assistant Directors—Debi Roker and Kevin Lowe— agreed to take over as Co-Directors. This is never easy, and they faced an uphill struggle to maintain funding levels. They each brought different skills to their work, and their commitment to TSA proved invaluable. They were able to continue some programs, as well as to develop new work on important topics such as the evaluation of interventions, and support for young fathers. Sadly, however, the global financial problems which followed the banking crisis of 2008, together with the change of Government in the UK in 2010, led to a reduction in funding for voluntary sector organizations, and TSA closed in 2011.

The establishment of TSA represented an important experiment in the social sciences. It showed that it is possible to forge a tangible link between empirical research and both policy and practice. Furthermore it did so by choosing a relatively unpopular subject—adolescence—as its main focus. It remains a puzzle to me that so few people recognize the importance of this stage of life. By any account the teenage years are of obvious significance for education, for the economic success of a country, for health and social services, and for family life. Why is it that adolescence is ignored in professional training, and accorded so little attention in academic circles? By establishing TSA my colleagues and I attempted to address this problem. We were able to show that there is a need for an organization that uses the skills and knowledge of researchers, working on a topic of universal significance such as adolescence.

Retirement to Oxford

As with most other colleagues who reach retirement age, I had no clear idea of what was going to come next. I hoped that I would be asked to do some consultancy, but beyond that I had not been able to formulate a coherent plan for my retirement. I was fortunate, therefore, to be asked to go to the Department of Health in London as a policy advisor for a period of 6 months in order to assist in the development of Government policy on the emotional health and well-being of young people. As a clinical psychologist I was only too familiar with psychiatric disorder, but I had given very little thought to the promotion of well-being. This was becoming a topic of great interest to Government at that period, and I learnt a lot from my time working in the civil service. However, the frustrations of policy making at this level soon began to weigh on me, and I found it hard-going. The contrast with my previous freedom at TSA, where I had been able to identify my own priorities, was striking, and I was not sorry to come to the end of my stint in the Department of Health.

At this point a colleague who I had known since my days in the East End of London took a hand in my fate! Ingrid Lunt was at that time the Director of Graduate Studies in the Department of Education at Oxford University, and it was as a result of her kindness and support that I was offered a post in this department. It was a remarkable opportunity, and enabled me to pursue my work on adolescence in a most congenial atmosphere. Here I have been able to teach, contribute to research, and most importantly, continue work both in the policy field as well as in the community. I have collaborated with a local Oxford charity to run workshops for parents of teenagers, and I have set up links with local teachers to raise awareness of the importance of understanding adolescent development. I have now been in Oxford since 2006, and at the time of writing there seems to be no end to the opportunities for continuing to study adolescence, and for trying to make research relevant to the world of practice and policy.

In addition to my enduring interest in parenting, four other themes have dominated my work during this period. In the first place I have wanted to provide a picture of adolescence based on statistical information already in the public domain. This initiative first started at TSA in the shape of a publication called *Key Data on Adolescence,* and has continued to appear on a biennial basis, most recently thanks to the Association for Young People's Health (Coleman, Brooks, & Treadgold, 2011). Second, I have not lost my interest in emotional health and well-being, and have managed to lecture and to publish on this topic (Coleman, 2009). Third, the subject of adolescent health has come to have a higher profile than was the case in previous decades, and I have very much enjoyed working to improve services for this age group and encouraging the need for more research on adolescent health (Coleman, Hendry, & Kloep, 2007). Finally, I have attempted to champion a positive perspective on this age group, and to do everything I can to promote a focus on resilience and on a strengths-based approach (Coleman & Hagell, 2007).

Conclusion

Whilst in many ways I have learnt an enormous amount during my career, it is true to say that many of the beliefs that motivate me now are no different from those that first inspired me in my early twenties. I believe that young people have significant strengths, as well as being wonderful companions. Sadly, adults too often see them as a threat rather than as a positive resource, thereby undermining many a good relationship. I also think there is still a serious job to be done in demystifying adolescence for parents and for professional adults who spend much of their working life with this age group. It is here that good research has such a valuable role to play. Adolescent behavior may appear puzzling and contradictory, but without too much effort it can be shown to make sense. I see this as a key task for social scientists, who have a responsibility to make empirical knowledge accessible to the public.

Of course the study of the adolescent years has changed beyond recognition since my early years as a psychologist. Research methods have continued to alter and to evolve, so that, for example, we can now draw on longitudinal data sets that did not exist in the 1960s and 1970s. There is more clarity about the empirical basis of evidence, and theoretical contributions are judged more rigorously today than was the case in the past. New techniques such as scanning have opened up the field of neuroscience, and behavioral genetics are making, and will continue to make, a major impact on developmental psychology. All this has influenced the study of adolescence, and it could be argued that, far from having solved all the puzzles, we are just at the beginning of a very exciting period of research in this field.

What I believe has changed less are the attitudes of the academic institutions to the importance of combining research with policy and practice. It is true that in the current Research Excellence Framework in the UK the concept of "impact" has been included, encouraging universities and other research centers to consider how their work will affect the communities they serve. Yet there is a long way to go before there is a genuine marriage between those who work directly with young people and those who carry out empirical investigations. When I work with parents of teenagers, or with teachers, there is a hunger for high-quality research evidence. Both professionals and the public want to know what research can tell us, and yet by and large as psychologists we have not done a good enough job at making this evidence widely available.

Finally, I would say that it is difficult to see why so few psychologists study adolescence. After all many of life's challenges occur during these years. From child to adult, the adolescent period represents one of the greatest psychological transitions we experience. Raising untold theoretical questions, it is a stage that offers ideal opportunities for original research. What makes it all worthwhile, however, is that working with adolescents is so very enjoyable.

References

Coleman, J. (1969a). Changes in TAT responses as a function of age. *Journal of Genetic Psychology, 114*, 171–178.

Coleman, J. (1969b). The perception of interpersonal relationships during adolescence. *British Journal of Educational Psychology, 39*, 253–260.

Coleman, J. (1974). *Relationships in adolescence.* London: Routledge and Kegan Paul.

Coleman, J. (1980). Central issues in the residential care of young people. *Journal of Adolescence, 3*, 175–186.

Coleman, J. (2006). *Teenage suicide and self-harm: A training resource for professionals.* Brighton, Sussex: Young People in Focus.

Coleman, J. (2009). Well-being in schools: Empirical measure or politician's dream? *Oxford Review of Education, 35*, 281–192.

Coleman, J. (2011). *The nature of adolescence* (4th ed.). London: Routledge.

Coleman, J., Brooks, F. & Treadgold, P. (2011). *Key data on adolescence* (8th ed.). Association for Young People's Health. www.youngpeopleshealth.org.uk

Coleman, J. & Hagell, A. (Eds.) (2007). *Adolescence: Risk and resilience.* Chichester: John Wiley.

Coleman, J., Hendry, L., & Kloep, M. (Eds.) (2007). *Adolescence and health.* Chichester: John Wiley.

Coleman, J. & Roker, D. (Eds.) (2001). *Supporting parents of teenagers: A handbook for professionals.* London: Jessica Kingsley.

Eden, K. & Roker, D. (2002). *Doing something: Young people as social actors.* Leicester: National Youth Agency.

Erikson, E. H. (1968). *Identity: Youth and crisis.* New York: Norton & Co.

Goossens, L. (2006). Theories of adolescence. In S. Jackson & L. Goossens (Eds.), *Handbook of adolescent development.* Hove, Sussex: Psychology Press.

Roker, D. & Coleman, J. (Eds.) (2007). *Working with parents of young people: Research, policy and practice.* London: Jessica Kingsley.

Treischmann, A., Whittaker, J., & Brendtro, L. (2009). *The other 23 hours.* Chicago: Aldine.

9

Rand D. Conger

An Autobiography

R<small>AND</small> D. C<small>ONGER</small>

In their instructions, the editors for this volume asked each author of a chapter to "… recount your scholarly career, from its inception to its current status, and … include a projection for the future development of your work." The initial task in response to these guidelines, of course, involves identifying the point of inception for one's scholarly career. For me, I would have to say that the beginning of my career started with the admonitions and support of my parents and it has developed since that time largely because of my good fortune in having significant interactions with a series of exceptional colleagues. Without the investments made by my parents and the influence of a number of scientific mentors and collaborators over the years, I would not have enjoyed the opportunities I have experienced in my work. Drawing on this perspective, the following pages consider the pathways I have followed in terms of the people most central to the experiences and decisions that have affected my scientific career and my goals for the future.

The Importance of Early Experiences

My parents raised five children without much money and under exceptionally difficult circumstances a good deal of the time. My father ended his education without graduating from high school and my mother received a high-school degree. Their married life began during the Great Depression of the 1930s and it was many years before my father got a regular job with the U.S. Postal Service. I cannot help but believe that my continuing interest in how families and children deal with their economic situations was first instigated by the financial hard times often experienced by my family. But despite the difficult era that marked the beginning of their marriage, my parents were

exceptional mentors and models for me in many important ways. They both placed a singular emphasis on hard work, meeting one's responsibilities in life, and commitment to family and children. They also were very bright and actively involved in discussions regarding the issues of the day. They encouraged all of their children to pursue higher education and invested the limited resources they had in fostering educational pursuits. Without their early efforts on my behalf, I would not have had the opportunity to enjoy the academic career that is the focus of this chapter.

But my initial forays in the world of adulthood were far from academic in nature. Following completion of high school in San Jose, California, I spent 2 years pursuing a degree in philosophy; however, this career path was far less attractive than an alternative trajectory involving the role of an itinerant musician. In my early twenties I left the university and played music more or less full time in the turbulent but exciting world of California during the 1960s. My enthusiasm for the life of a musician, working in venues ranging from coffee houses to college concert halls, far outweighed my interest in reading and writing in the pursuit of higher education. Alas, limited talent and opportunities as a professional guitarist eventually put a brake on any rise to stardom and I returned to school with the idea of completing a degree and getting regular work. Marriage and the arrival of two children during this period also necessitated a transition to a more lucrative line of employment.

I am convinced, though, that these early experiences as a starving artist were an enormous aid in the later development of my scientific career. Conducting research requires the ability to spend long hours studying the issues of interest, working through related problems, and sequestering one's self from the outside world for significant periods of time. These are exactly the traits that one develops as a practicing musician, and they have served me well over the years. In addition, the poverty often associated with the life of an artist provided further incentive for my eventual interest in understanding the role of economic hardship in daily life.

Back to the University

As the first step in my financial rehabilitation, in 1970 I enrolled in the BA program in sociology at Arizona State University with the hope that a degree would aid in my eventually finding regular work. That was the limit of my aspirations at the time. By good fortune, however, two extraordinary individuals led me to a much more rewarding career trajectory. First, Professor Richard Nagasawa, who was then an assistant professor of sociology, introduced me to the logic of science. In a series of fascinating courses, he charted the philosophical underpinnings of contemporary scientific inquiry and reviewed the underlying arguments for correlational and experimental research designs. These classes introduced me to the creativity and elegance of scientific research, and I was hooked.

Equally significant, Professor Peter Killeen, an assistant professor in psychology at the time, provided me with training in the application of specific theoretical ideas to the study of human and animal behavior. Peter had worked with Herrnstein and Skinner at Harvard during his graduate career and I was quite taken by the simplicity and power of the behavioral paradigm, which was remarkably effective in predicting the behavior of experimental subjects in response to environmental contingencies of reward and punishment. Through my work with Peter, I gained my first hands-on experience in conducting a research project with human participants. As a senior year project, we decided to evaluate the degree to which the "matching law" from behavioral psychology would predict human behavior in a discussion group setting. Up until that time, research involving this behavioral paradigm had been restricted to non-human, experimental models. In its simplest form, the matching law predicts that the proportion of individual behaviors will match the proportion of reinforcement they generate in the environment. This hypothesis is not straightforward inasmuch as it proposes that an individual will spend effort pursuing some activities that do not produce the maximum amount of available reinforcement. In the experiment we were able to demonstrate for the first time that discussion in a small group conformed to this behavioral principle (see Conger & Killeen, 1974).

The success of this initial study convinced me that I wanted to go on to graduate school and continue my training in the social and behavioral sciences. This work also taught me something about observing and recording behavioral interactions in a social setting, a methodology that has played a central role in my research throughout my career. My interest in the application of behavioral principles to social phenomena also helped identify the graduate program I wanted to attend. I applied and was accepted into the graduate program in the Department of Sociology at the University of Washington where a segment of that faculty was pursuing a line of work that they titled "Behavioral Sociology." Although my theoretical views and substantive interests have expanded well beyond this behavioral perspective across the years, this early work has continued to influence my thinking and my approaches to research methodology. I owe a great debt to Professors Killeen and Nagasawa, who played such a critical role in my decision to begin graduate study in 1972.

Graduate School

The sociology program at UW was, and continues to be, one of the best in the country. My initial interest in the program came from the theoretical and empirical work being pursued by Professors Burgess, Emerson, and Schmitt, who were developing social theories and conducting research aimed at understanding how contingencies of reinforcement and punishment shape the behavior of individuals and groups. Interestingly, these behavioral ideas mesh quite well with sociological interest in social structures, the social contingencies thought to play an important role in individual conduct. These scholars had an important influence on the types of research I eventually pursued. Many other faculty members also had a major impact on my professional development. For example, the program included an exceptional group of faculty members conducting research and training on advanced research methods. Professors Blalock, Costner, and Hargins were pioneers in the application of structural equation modeling to social research, an approach that is an important part of contemporary research methods. This methodological training has served me well for almost 40 years. There is not enough room in this chapter to mention all of the wonderful scholars in both sociology and psychology who influenced my early development at UW, but I profited greatly from their knowledge and commitment to social and behavioral science.

In addition to the training program itself, there were three additional experiences during graduate school that had a major impact on my future work. One involved a brief discussion with Professor Phil Blumstein while we were standing in the mail room of the sociology department. In form as a true believer in behavioral sociology, I was regaling Phil with all the reasons that the behavioral approach made sense as a sociological theoretical paradigm. My perspective could not have been further from Dr. Blumstein's on this subject, but he was very kind in his informal debate with a beginning graduate student. He simply concluded our discussion with the suggestion that it would seem ill-advised to throw out so much that is unique and important in human experience by adopting a singularly behavioral perspective. Of course he was right, and that simple observation motivated me to explore more vigorously other approaches to understanding the course of human development, as I have done in my research since that time.

The second most influential experience during graduate school actually involved a process that accounted in large part for the direction of my career from the 1970s to the present time. In 1974, I accepted a part-time position as a program evaluator for a human service organization in Tacoma, WA. The federal agency that supported this group (the Administration for Children, Youth and Families) became interested in more fundamental studies of the etiology of child abuse and neglect. By this time Professor Burgess had become my doctoral advisor and we decided to pursue a grant proposal for a basic study of child maltreatment with this agency. This proposal, and the study that followed once it was funded, set the direction for the rest of my career. Because Burgess moved to Penn State University during this time, we conducted the study in rural Pennsylvania. This project tested my ability to interview, observe, and encode information about children and families. We conducted the research in the homes of participating families including parents identified for engaging in abuse or neglect and parents with no histories of such problems. The basic approach we took in this study of visiting families in their homes, conducting extensive interviews and life histories, and observing the quality of family interactions in structured settings has characterized my approach to family and developmental research since that time. This study generated several papers concerned with the etiology of child abuse and neglect (e.g., Burgess and Conger, 1978; Conger, Burgess, & Barrett, 1979).

The third most crucial experience during graduate school involved the preparation for the child maltreatment study which was significantly influenced by the work of Gerald Patterson and John Reid at the Oregon Social Learning Center in Eugene. Both Burgess and I knew that we wanted to observe the quality of interactions in families as part of that study, but neither of us had ever done observational research with families. Patterson and Reid were pioneers in this area of study. They became two of my most significant mentors across the years, even though we never worked together in the same place. These researchers developed extensive coding systems for evaluating the way that family members treat each other and we borrowed heavily from their measurement methodology. What was truly remarkable was the generosity of these scientists. They shared grant proposals with me, were willing to talk with me on the phone, and always replied to the questions I raised with them. These early contacts led to visits to their research center which became a model for my later work. Simply put, Patterson and Reid had a fundamental impact on the way I developed my program of work and on the success I have had in pursuing issues of interest. With these graduate school experiences behind me and a doctorate in sociology on the books, I began my academic and research career.

Academic Appointments

Since completing my doctoral studies in 1976, I have been a professor at four different academic institutions: the University of Georgia (1976–81), the University of Illinois at Urbana-Champaign (1981–84), Iowa State University (1984–2001), and, currently, the University of California, Davis (2001–present). Looking at the roster of positions could make one wonder whether I can hold a job. My time in Georgia and Illinois was relatively short-term but important in terms of shaping the direction of my career. The longer periods in Iowa and California represent the periods of greatest scientific productivity and the clearest focus for my research agenda.

The University of Georgia, Athens (1976–81) As an assistant professor of sociology at UGA, I attempted to establish myself as an independent scientist concentrating on the study of families, children, and adolescents. My particular interest was how family stress, inter-parental relationships, and parenting practices affect the emotional and behavioral adjustment of offspring. Given my experience with the child maltreatment study in Pennsylvania, I knew that the work I wanted to pursue would require extramural support. In collaboration with Professor Ben Lahey in psychology and Professor Ray Yang in the Department of Child and Family Studies, we were able to secure funding for two separate grants, one from the National Institute of Mental Health and one from the state of Georgia, designed to extend the earlier research. We continued to employ the methodology developed in Pennsylvania, using extensive interviews and behavioral observations of families in their homes. Especially important, in Georgia we were able to study families from diverse ethnic backgrounds, an approach that was not possible in the earlier research with rural families in central Pennsylvania. The cumulative nature of this research is illustrated in an article that used data from all three studies, the first in Pennsylvania and the next two in Georgia, to demonstrate the similarity in findings across these different study populations (Conger, McCarty, Yang, Lahey, & Burgess, 1984a). This early report demonstrated my ongoing interest in the replication of findings in the social and behavioral sciences.

This work, among other experiences, illustrates some of the positive advances in my scientific trajectory at UGA. While there, I was able to solidify my research skills such that I became increasingly competent and confident in organizing community-based studies of families and children. In addition, my theoretical underpinnings advanced well beyond the behavioral paradigm alone and I began to incorporate a broader array of variables concerned with social cognition and emotional expression into my analysis of parenting and child development (e.g., Conger, McCarty, Yang, Lahey, & Kropp, 1984b). Many of these new directions grew out of interactions with a number of colleagues at UGA who pushed me to extend my scientific reasoning. These individuals included faculty members in sociology (e.g., Pat Horan and Terry Thornberry), psychology (e.g., Rex Forehand and Ben

Lahey), and child and family studies (e.g., Gene Brody and Ray Yang). And as a result of a 1976 paper on family influences on delinquency (Conger, 1976), I was invited to consult with Jerry Patterson and John Reid in Oregon, a visit that increased even more the significance of their work on my future research.

Despite these positive aspects of my time in Georgia, there were both professional and personal setbacks. Professionally, I became very uncertain about the exact direction that my work should take. Although I published several papers on topics such as delinquency, dysfunctional family processes, and observational research methods, the work failed to have a real programmatic quality or organizing base. Clearer direction in my efforts would not occur until after I left Georgia for other opportunities. Personally, my marriage of 14 years did not survive all the earlier transitions from musician to student to academic and I was divorced during my time at UGA. As events transpired, my 8-year old son, Zachary, stayed with me and my 12-year old daughter, Kim, moved elsewhere with her mother. To add to the turmoil, for some reason the Department of Human Development and Family Ecology at the University of Illinois, Urbana-Champaign contacted me to see if I would be willing to interview for their open position as department head. To this day I am not entirely clear why they elected to pursue an assistant professor as the next leader of their department. But they did, the interview must have gone well, and they offered me the position. Despite my trepidation about the ice and snow in the Midwest, the offer of promotion, tenure, and a very substantial salary increase convinced me to take the job. So with a young son in tow, in 1981 I headed for Illinois.

The University of Illinois (1981–84) As a department head at the U of I, I had the opportunity to significantly increase my understanding of both academic administration and the research enterprise at one of the nation's finest universities. Although I stayed at Illinois for only 3 years, the experience represents another fundamental turning point in my career. My interactions with some of the best university administrators in the United States gave me new insights into academic leadership, politics, and decision making. These experiences served me well both at the U of I and in later administrative positions. My time at Illinois also gave me the opportunity to learn from some of the best social and behavioral scientists in the country. In a very real sense, I received on the job, postdoctoral training in both administration and scholarship at the U of I. Without these experiences I doubt that my scientific career would have moved forward as it did in the following years.

During my time in Illinois, I had the opportunity to discuss the scientific enterprise with many faculty members who already were or have become leading scholars in their areas of research. In my department these discussions primarily involved interactions with Judy DeLoache and Leann Birch, whose ideas helped refine my perspective on the study of child development. Also from my department, Sonya Salamon gave me a new appreciation for the uniqueness of rural life in the Midwest. The insights she provided proved to be especially important during the next phase of my research in Iowa. Several sociologists also affected my thinking about the future direction of my work including Mike Gottfredson, Joan Huber, and John Mirowsky. Especially important was my growing recognition that my work would benefit from a more programmatic focus. Although the training that I received at the University of Washington was excellent, the mode of operation for many sociologists is to move from one research topic to the next with the idea that strong research methods can be applied to many different substantive issues, whichever issue is of interest at the moment.

Particularly telling in this regard were my interactions with three psychologists at the U of I: Steve Asher, John Gottman, and Ross Parke. Each of them has pursued a highly focused program of research in a small number of related areas. As I discussed their work with them and examined the approaches they took to identifying research questions, it became clear to me that my own program of work at the time was too diffuse and opportunistic. Rather than articulating a specific research theme and addressing it in a cumulative fashion, I had tended to move too often from one topic to another without allowing the focus of the next inquiry to grow naturally from the results of the previous study. The opportunity to consider approaches to research in discussions with these three scientists helped me to understand the need to take this more programmatic approach in my own efforts. Although this lesson was clear while I was at the U of I, application of the lesson occurred at a later time in a different academic home. Without a doubt the most important scientific advance I made at the U of I was increased understanding of the importance of taking a more cumulative approach to my program of research.

My time at Illinois, however, was largely committed to departmental administration; thus, I did not launch any significant new studies while in Illinois. Rather, I published a few papers based on the data collected earlier in Pennsylvania and Georgia (e.g., Conger, Brainerd, Birch, Friedberg, & Navarro, 1986). But my experiences at the U of I laid the groundwork for my research program once I left departmental administration. In terms of accomplishments as department head, the small department I led experienced increases in graduate and undergraduate enrollment and in research productivity. Moreover, we made some good new faculty hires that helped the department grow in positive directions. I felt that I had learned something about working with a group of faculty to develop and act upon a strategic plan that improved the usual markers of departmental success. These accomplishments as an administrator, for some reason, led me to believe that perhaps my most significant contributions to the academic world might lie in similar appointments at the college or university levels. With this idea in mind, in 1984 I applied for and received the position of Associate Dean for Research and Graduate Education in the then College of Family and Consumer Sciences at Iowa State University. Commendable performance in this type of position frequently leads to a deanship or more in an administrative career trajectory. That was my thinking at the time.

In addition to important professional activities, the move to Illinois provided several major improvements in my personal life. During this time I met Kathi Jewsbury, who worked for the Department of Children and Family Services for the state of Illinois. Despite her better judgment she agreed to sign on as a stepmother to my early adolescent son, Zach, and we married in 1982. Shortly thereafter, my daughter, Kim, came to live with us in Urbana. The quality of my life improved substantially as Kathi played a remarkable role in creating a real home and family life for the three of us. Since our marriage, Kathi went on to complete her doctoral studies in sociology and we now enjoy both family and profession in our lives together. In 1984, however, none of my immediate family members wanted to move to Iowa for the job I had taken. We were all depressed about leaving friends and colleagues in Illinois. So with great trepidation and concern that I was making one of the biggest mistakes in my life, we headed for Iowa.

Iowa State University (1984–2001) My time at Iowa State taught me how difficult it is to predict one's professional future. My plan was to spend perhaps 5–7 years at ISU, do a good job as an associate dean, and then seek a position as dean at another university. Real life dashed this simple formula for career development. First, I was not nearly as successful as an associate dean as I had been as a department head. Working across multiple departments with very different views of the academic enterprise did not mesh well with my impatience to see the College grow in terms of research productivity, graduate enrollments, and national visibility. It was like a clash of cultures that diminished my enthusiasm for administration and, I am sure, diminished the enthusiasm of many faculty members for my continuation in my administrative role.

Second, during the 1980s, Iowa was being battered by a terrible depression in the agricultural economy, the State's primary economic activity. Across the 99 counties in the State farmers were being forced off the land and many of the small town businesses that served farmers were going bankrupt. The downturn in rural areas rippled back into urban centers and depressed these economies as well. Several of my new colleagues and I realized that these adversities would have a major impact on the lives of the families and children who experienced them. We were especially concerned with identifying families who were either most vulnerable or most resilient to these enormous stresses in their lives. To pursue these issues, we applied

for and received several NIH grants to study the effects of these changes on families and children. Pursuing this line of research became my primary professional interest and, with that in mind, I resigned from my position as associate dean in 1989 and became a faculty member in the Department of Sociology. I also was invited to become the director for a new campus center concerned with the study of social and behavioral influences on the health of rural people. In fairly short order I had the opportunity to apply the lessons learned in Illinois about programmatic inquiry, and my research direction was set for the next decade.

Because of NIH interest in the implications of this economic downturn for the health of rural people, I was able to move from the relatively small-scale studies in Pennsylvania and Georgia, each of which had a sample size of less than 100, to much larger community-based research on several hundred families. I continued to use the same intensive measurement procedures as earlier involving observer ratings and interviews with multiple family members, but significant extramural support made it possible to recruit a much more representative sample of families from rural Iowa. During these years we obtained funding from the National Institute of Mental Health, the National Institute on Drug Abuse, and the National Institute of Child Health and Human Development to conduct a cohort study of approximately 550 early adolescents and their families who lived through the economic crisis of the 1980s. Some additional support in these efforts also was provided by the MacArthur Foundation Research Network on Successful Adolescent Development among Youth in High-Risk Settings.

Also important, NIMH supported a Center for Family Research in Rural Mental Health which I directed from 1990 to 2000. This center became part of a new Institute for Social and Behavioral Research which the university's Board of Regents approved in the mid-1990s. In addition to supporting research on families from rural and small urban areas, from 1992 to 1997 the Center also served as the primary site for a postdoctoral training program sponsored by NIMH. This new element of the work at ISU brought several outside collaborators and postdoctoral trainees into the overall research program. The outside collaborators represented some of the major figures in developmental, epidemiological, prevention, and family research (i.e., Brooks-Gunn, Burton, Cauce, Chase-Lansdale, Cox, Forgatch, Hauser, Kessler, Markman, and Suomi). Their association with the work at ISU provided a great deal of intellectual stimulation for our ongoing efforts at ISU and for my own continuing professional development.

Describing these research activities seems so simple, but their initiation and conduct was quite complex and involved the efforts of dozens of faculty scientists, postdoctoral trainees, graduate students, and research staff. In the beginning, so to speak, my colleagues and I at Iowa State profited greatly from the advice of several outside consultants who advised us on how to develop a compelling study of family life and child development during a historic financial meltdown. In particular, Del Elliott, John Gottman, Jerry Patterson, and Jon Rolf visited ISU in the late 1980s and helped us refine our research questions and methodologies. The team of investigators for the grants that eventually supported the research represented a diversity of interests necessary for the conduct of this complex study. My background conducting intensive investigations of highly stressed families contributed to the mix, and Glen Elder brought his special expertise gained from research on families going through the Great Depression of the 1930s. At Iowa State, Fred Lorenz provided statistical guidance for the program of research and Paul Lasley taught us much about unique features of rural life. Ron Simons and Les Whitbeck informed the assessment of adolescent maladjustment ranging from antisocial behavior to problems with substance use. In addition to the original investigators, many graduate students and postdoctoral trainees who began working with project data during the 1990s have gone on to have highly successful careers as professional researchers or faculty members in research universities including Chalandra Bryant, Ming Cui, Katherine Conger, Xiaojia Ge, Gordon Harold, Jan Melby, Laura Scaramella, Martha Rueter, and K.A.S. Wickrama.

By the end of the 1990s well over 100 papers had been published from this Iowa study and these papers have been cited thousands of times in the scientific literature. I feel quite gratified that, in collaboration with many gifted colleagues, I finally was able to develop a program of research that has made cumulative contributions to the study of family stress and resilience. Through the 1990s, findings from the research contributed to our understanding of the family economic stress process and the health of children and adults, the role of sibling relationships in development, family and community influences on child and adolescent competence and maladjustment, correlates of success and failure in marital and other romantic relationships, family problem solving processes, and the influence of family structure on child development. During this time, my primary contributions to this work related to the articulation and testing of the Family Stress Model of family economic hardship and the processes through which economic pressures affect parents and their children (e.g., Conger et al., 1992; Conger et al., 1993; Conger, Conger, Mathews, & Elder, 1999; Conger & Elder, 1994; Conger, Ge, Elder, Lorenz, & Simons, 1994; and Conger, Rueter, & Elder, 1999).

Especially gratifying, the Family Stress Model, which was developed to guide the Iowa project, drew significant support from study findings across the years of adolescence. The model proposes that economic hardship demoralizes parents through daily experiences involving the inability to meet basic material needs or keep up with normal expenses. This demoralization is expected to create conflicts in romantic relationships, disrupt effective parenting practices, and thus jeopardize the competent development of children and adolescents. In addition to drawing support from the Iowa study, similar findings have been reported from research involving urban as well as rural families, with ethnic minority as well as majority families, and in countries other than the United States (see Conger, Conger, & Martin, 2010). In fact, as part of the NIMH Center activities at Iowa State, in 1995 my colleagues and I launched the Family and Community Health Study, part of which involved an attempt to replicate findings from the Iowa study with over 800 African American families living in Iowa and Georgia. The results showed that the Family Stress Model predicted family response to economic pressure quite well in this very different study population (see Conger et al., 2002).

Simply put, the 17 years I spent at Iowa State were remarkably productive and gratifying. In collaboration with many bright and innovative colleagues, I was able to launch a program of studies that I would never have imagined possible when I initially started my academic career in Georgia. Because of space constraints, I have neglected naming many of the scientists who made this research possible, like Carolyn Cutrona, Meg Gerrard, Rick Gibbons, Danny Hoyt, Dan Russell, and Dick Spoth at ISU. Outside contributors included Gene Brody, Velma Murry, and Vonnie McLoyd, who played critical roles in the work with African American families. Also important were several university administrators who took interest in and provided occasional support for our efforts including two university presidents: Gordon Eaton and Martin Jischke. Indeed, to a significant degree it was the willingness of Iowa State administrators to take some financial risks in promoting this program of research that made it possible. Fortunately, these university investments paid off inasmuch as this program of work led to well over $60 million in extramural support through our research institute over a period of 10–15 years.

Despite this enormous support and my excitement over the research studies we were conducting, the long, cold Iowa winters finally wore me down. So when the opportunity arose to return to California where I had spent most of my youth, Kathi and I decided to move to the University of California, Davis in 2001. We accepted positions in the Division of Human Development and Family Studies and later I received a joint appointment in the Department of Psychology. Graciously, Iowa State University allowed me to continue in the role of Research Collaborator so that we could continue to conduct research with the original Iowa panel of 550 adolescents that began in 1989.

University of California, Davis (2001–present) After 17 years of fast-paced activity that involved developing new, community-based studies of rural families and children, creating a new research institute, and helping to conduct a postdoctoral training program, both Kathi and I were ready to slow down a bit and focus on being reasonably productive faculty members at UCD. We both had relatives in California and these new positions also allowed us to reconnect with our extended family members. Our daughter also got accepted to medical school at UCD, which was a welcome change as she had been living in New York. Our son had moved on to work in information technology in Denver. So we had visions of an idyllic, slower paced life in the sunshine of the golden state. Nothing could have been further from the reality that has evolved.

Indeed, for me the move to California led to new collaborations and opportunities that revitalized my interest in the work I had been and would be pursuing. Four general themes have evolved in this regard: (1) continuing research on the original Iowa panel and their transition to adulthood, (2) theoretical and empirical advances with regard to the association between economic circumstances and human development, (3) an increasing focus on ethnic diversity and culture, and (4) introducing biology into the equation. My work around each of these themes continues; thus, they represent not only what I have been doing during the past decade but also my plans for the future. And, of course, each theme includes important collaborators who have helped to make the work possible. I will briefly review each theme in turn.

The Iowa Study and the Transition to Adulthood
Through a good deal of persistence and good fortune, we have been able to get continuing support for the study of the original Iowa cohort of over 500 adolescents. These study participants averaged 12 years of age in 1989 and they now are in their mid to late thirties. Because we followed them across adolescence and their early adult years, they provide unique information regarding the factors that influence their long-term development and the development of their children who have become part of the ongoing study. Beginning in 1997, we began to assess the new families that the original cohort members established as they moved into their adult years. We used the same intensive measurement methodologies that we had used in their families of origin. Thus, we are now in a position to evaluate not only continuities or discontinuities in family life based on self-reports but also based on observations of actual family interaction processes.

Findings from this phase of the study have already led to exciting new information about the early antecedents of pathways to adult development. For example, we have shown that both early personality characteristics of adolescents and the quality of family interactions during adolescence affect the ability of participants grown to adulthood to function competently either as a parent or a romantic partner (e.g., Donnellan, Larsen-Rife, & Conger, 2005; Neppl, Conger, Scaramella, & Ontai, 2009). A primary focus of this work has involved early

determinants of later parenting behavior. A well-accepted view of both developmental scientists and the lay public is that parents learn how to raise children through their experiences as a child with their parents. Although research findings tend to support this view, the association between the quality of parenting in the first and second generations is fairly modest (Conger, Belsky, & Capaldi, 2009). Thus, a major issue in future research on intergenerational continuities in parenting involves the identification of conditions under which continuity is amplified or reduced. In a recent publication, for example, we have shown that the association between observed harsh parenting in the first and second generations in the Iowa study is not statistically significant if the co-parent models parenting behavior that is warm and supportive of the child (Conger, Schofield, & Neppl, 2012). Without the presence of this counter to a history of harshness, continuity is exacerbated.

Work on these issues continues and is increasingly being pursued by a new generation of scholars working on the project including Brent Donnellan, a former postdoc who is now a professor at Michigan State University; Tricia Neppl and Tom Schofield who are faculty members at Iowa State; and one of the original investigators, Fred Lorenz, at Iowa State. Through their efforts we hope to follow the original cohort members and their families well into middle age.

Socioeconomic Status and Human Development.
Through the late 1990s our theoretical and empirical research on SES and human development had focused primarily on the Family Stress Model, the proposition that economic disadvantage is disruptive to family relationships and child development. As noted earlier, this theoretical paradigm has been useful and hypotheses from the model have drawn support from numerous studies with very diverse populations. This perspective represents a social causation argument about the association between SES and human behavior. An opposite view involves the social selection argument that individual characteristics drive later economic success or failure; thus, the causal influence is from the individual to later SES rather than the reverse. As the participants in the Iowa panel have grown older, we now have the data to evaluate whether the social causation or the social selection view most adequately represent the experiences we see in real life.

When I came to UCD I had been trying to figure out how to simultaneously examine these two perspectives using data from our study. By good fortune, Dr. Brent Donnellan came to work with me as a postdoctoral trainee at that time. Brent is an expert on individual differences, and especially personality differences, and their development over time. He gave me a crash course in personality theory and research, leading me to believe that perhaps I was the postdoc and he was the mentor. Whichever was true, our earlier association has led to many collaborative efforts, one of which involved the development of what we called an "interactionist perspective" on the relationship between socioeconomic status and human development (Conger & Donnellan, 2007).

Basically, we argued that, when one expands the analysis across time and generations, both the social selection and social causation arguments will hold in an interactionist or transactional process. For example, in two recent papers we have shown that personality differences in adolescence predict socioeconomic status and family functioning during adulthood; however, these social circumstances independently affect later parenting and child development, consistent with the interactionist notion of reciprocity between the quality of the environment and individual characteristics (Martin et al., 2010; Schofield et al., 2011). K. Conger and her co-authors (2012) showed that this perspective also helps to explain the positive association between SES in first- and second-generation families. Plans for the future include important new tests of these ideas using data from the Iowa study and from other research populations as possible.

Ethnic Diversity and Culture One advantage of the move to UCD was improved access to highly diverse families. Indeed, the majority of children now being born in California are of Mexican rather than European origin. Thus, my new colleagues and I decided to extend the work I had done in Iowa by securing funds to study Mexican American families in California. This new investigation, the California Families Project (CFP), began in 2005 with a cohort of almost 700 fifth-grade Mexican American children and their families living in northern California. In this research we have used the same basic measurement methods involving interviews with parents and children and observational ratings of family discussions. The study continues as these children transition across the years of adolescence. Early in the process of developing the project we benefited greatly from interactions with Ana Mari Cauce, Melanie Domenech-Rodriguez, Nancy Gonzales, George Knight, Mark Roosa, and William Vega. The current team of investigators includes me and Emilio Ferrer, Richard Robins, and Keith Widaman from the Department of Psychology at UCD.

In addition to my earlier interests in family interaction processes, individual differences, and socioeconomic circumstances, this new work has brought the issue of culture to the fore and measures of culturally related values, priorities, and experiences were added to the core of measures used in the Iowa research. Although this work is still in development as we wait to have enough data to evaluate child and adolescent adjustment over time, already we have found support for the economic stress processes documented in earlier research (R. Conger et al.,

2012) and also for the importance of traditional cultural values in promoting healthy child development (Taylor, Larsen-Rife, Conger, & Widaman, 2012). We will be working hard during the coming years to identify social processes, cultural traditions, and individual characteristics of these families that promote competent child development even for families that oftentimes face enormous social and economic challenges.

Biological Issues A particularly exciting aspect to my work at UCD has been the addition of biological processes to my earlier interest in family relationships and human development. This work is too early in its infancy to provide a description of study findings, but I am sure these will come as the work develops over time. For the first of two projects, in 2010 my colleagues and I received support from NIH for a genome-wide association study of the over 2,000 family members in the original Iowa panel study: first generation parents, the cohort of second generation focal adolescents, a close-aged sibling of the cohort member, spouses and romantic partners of cohort members during adulthood, and the oldest child of the cohort member. The primary investigators for the study include me, Brent Donnellan and Michael Stallings at the Institute for Behavioral Genetics at the University of Colorado. Many other investigators associated with the Iowa study and who have already been mentioned are involved in this research. In addition, other colleagues from IBG are playing key roles in this investigation: Jason Boardman, Matt McQueen and Andrew Smolen. This year (2012) we are completing collection of DNA on all of these participants and data analysis will begin shortly thereafter. To our knowledge, this is the first family-pedigree study in the social and behavioral research literature. We hope to identify broad domains of genetic functioning that help to account for diverse pathways of development for study participants. Preliminary findings already have shown that certain genetic variants modify intergenerational continuities in positive and negative parenting and also affect response to the quality of interactions in romantic relationships. At this time these findings are undergoing editorial review. During the next few years this program of work will be a primary focus of my research.

In addition to this genetic research with the Iowa study, two colleagues at UCD, Amanda Guyer and Paul Hastings, took the lead on a grant designed to examine brain function and psycho-physiological processes related to adolescent development for participants in the CFP. This work will attempt to use multiple indicators of allostatic load to identify pathways through which study participants are made either more resilient or more vulnerable to the stresses and strains they often face in their lives. We expect to receive NIH support for this research beginning in 2012. Because the project has not yet begun, it is hard to anticipate the nature of the findings that will eventually be generated. However, we expect that the research will lead to new understandings of the interplay between biological, personal, social, cultural, and community factors that affect the course of human development. This work as well will be a primary focus of my research during the coming years.

Some Final Thoughts

Composing this autobiography has given me several insights on the course of my career and the people and opportunities that have shaped it. Certainly some of what I have written here has been a positive reinterpretation of events or experiences that others might characterize in a different light. Nevertheless, I think there are a few general observations from my experiences that others might find helpful. First, persistence may be the fundamental driver of developing a program of research that one finds satisfying and exciting. As I look back on the grants, the papers, and the work with colleagues, at least I can say that I gave my best effort in generating a program of research that made a contribution at some level to our understanding of families and human development. That realization has made these efforts worthwhile. Second, designing research efforts that have a potentially positive impact on both scientific understanding and on the broader community appears to increase the likelihood of generating support both from funding agencies and from universities. That has proved to be true for me in my work both in Iowa and in California.

Finally, I would encourage social and behavioral scientists who are initiating their careers to find the smartest colleagues possible and be willing to learn from them and work with them in advancing a program of research. My work certainly would not have prospered as much as it has without the benefit of collaborations with many people who helped to make up for my intellectual inadequacies in many areas of science. As I look back, I am very pleased that I have had opportunities and accomplishments that I never could have imagined when the journey began.

Acknowledgment

The programs of research discussed in this chapter have been supported by multiple agencies including the National Institute of Mental Health (MH051361, MH00567, MH19734, MH43270, MH59355, MH62989, MH48165), the National Institute on Drug Abuse (DA017902, DA05347), the National Institute of Child Health and Human Development (HD047573, HD051746, HD027724, HD064687), the Bureau of Maternal and Child Health (MCJ-109572), and the MacArthur Foundation Research Network on Successful Adolescent Development Among Youth in High-Risk Settings.

References

Burgess, R. L., & Conger. R. D. (1978). Family interaction in abusive, neglectful, and normal families. *Child Development, 49,* 1163–1173.

Conger, K. J., Martin, M. J., Reeb, B. T., Little, W. M., Craine, J. L., Shebloski, B. et al. (2012). Economic hardship and its consequences across generations. In V. Maholmes & R. B. King (Eds.), *Oxford handbook of child development and poverty* (pp. 37–53). New York: Oxford University Press.

Conger, R. D. (1976). Social control and social learning models of delinquent behavior: A Synthesis. *Criminology, 14*(1), 17–40.

Conger, R. D., Belsky, J., & Capaldi, D. M. (2009). The intergenerational transmission of parenting: Closing comments for the special section. *Developmental Psychology, 45,* 1276–1283.

Conger, R. D., Brainerd, D. W., Birch, L. L., Friedberg, P. J., & Navarro, L. A. (1986). Assessing the quality of family observations: A comparative analysis. *Journal of Marriage and the Family, 48,* 111–122.

Conger, R. D., Burgess, R. L., & Barrett, C. (1979). Child abuse related to life change and perceptions of illness: Some preliminary findings. *The Family Coordinator, 28,* 73–78.

Conger, R. D., Conger, K. J., Elder, G. H., Jr., Lorenz, F. O., Simons, R. L., & Whitbeck, L. B. (1992). A family process model of economic hardship and adjustment of early adolescent boys. *Child Development, 63,* 526–541.

Conger, R. D., Conger, K. J., Elder, G. H., Jr., Lorenz, F. O., Simons, R. L., & Whitbeck, L. B. (1993). Family economic stress and adjustment of early adolescent girls. *Developmental Psychology, 29*(2), 206–219.

Conger, R. D., Conger, K. J., & Martin, M. J. (2010). Socioeconomic status, family processes, and individual development. *Journal of Marriage and Family, 72,* 685–704.

Conger, R. D., Conger, K. J., Matthews, L. S., & Elder, G. H., Jr. (1999). Pathways of economic influence on adolescent adjustment. *American Journal of Community Psychology, 27,* 519–541.

Conger, R. D., & Donnellan, M. B. (2007). An interactionist perspective on the socioeconomic context of human development. *Annual Review of Psychology, 58,* 175–199.

Conger, R. D., Ebert-Wallace, L., Sun, Y., Simons, R. L., McLoyd, V. C., & Brody, G. H. (2002). Economic pressure in African American families: A replication and extension of the Family Stress Model. *Developmental Psychology, 38,* 179–193.

Conger, R. D., & Elder, G. H., Jr. (1994). *Families in troubled times: Adapting to change in rural America.* Hillsdale, NJ: Aldine.

Conger, R. D., Ge, X., Elder, G. H., Jr., Lorenz, F. O., & Simons, R. L. (1994). Economic stress, coercive family process and developmental problems of adolescents. *Child Development, 65,* 541–561. [Special issue on children and poverty.]

Conger, R. D., & Killeen, P. (1974). Use of concurrent operants in small group research: A demonstration. *Pacific Sociological Review, 17,* 339–415.

Conger, R. D., McCarty, J. A., Yang, R. K., Lahey, B. B., & Burgess, R. L. (1984a). Mother's age as a predictor of observed maternal behavior in three independent samples of families. *Journal of Marriage and the Family, 46,* 411–424.

Conger, R. D., McCarty, J. A., Yang, R. K., Lahey, B. B., & Kropp, J. P. (1984b). Perception of child, child-rearing values, and emotional distress as mediating links between environmental stressors and observed maternal behavior. *Child Development, 55,* 2234–2247.

Conger, R. D., Rueter, M. A., & Elder, G. H., Jr. (1999). Couple resilience to economic pressure. *Journal of Personality and Social Psychology, 76,* 54–71.

Conger, R. D., Schofield, T. J., & Neppl, T. K., (2012). Intergenerational continuity and discontinuity in harsh parenting. *Parenting: Science and Practice, 12,* 222–231. [Special issue on the arc of parenting from epigenomes to ethics.]

Conger, R. D., Song, H., Stockdale, G. D., Ferrer, E., Widaman, K. F., & Cauce, A. M. (2012). Resilience and vulnerability of Mexican origin youth and their families: A test of a culturally-informed model of family economic stress. In P. K. Kerig, M. S. Schultz, & S. T. Hauser (Eds.), *Adolescence and beyond: Family processes and development* (pp. 268–286). New York: Oxford University Press.

Donnellan, M. B., Larsen-Rife, D., & Conger, R. D. (2005). Personality, family history, and competence in early adult romantic relationships. *Journal of Personality and Social Psychology, 88*, 562–576. [Abstracted in *Clinician's Research Digest*, June, 2005.]

Martin, M. J., Conger, R. D., Schofield, T. J., Dogan, S. J., Widaman, K. F., Donnellan, M. B. et al. (2010). Evaluation of the interactionist model of socioeconomic status and problem behavior: A developmental cascade across generations. *Development and Psychopathology, 22*, 697–715.

Neppl, T. K., Conger, R. D., Scaramella, L. V., & Ontai, L. L. (2009). Intergenerational continuity in parenting behavior: Mediating pathways and child effects. *Developmental Psychology, 45*, 1241–1256.

Schofield, T. J., Martin, M. J., Conger, K. J., Neppl, T. M., Donnellan, M. B., & Conger, R. D. (2011). Intergenerational transmission of adaptive functioning: A test of the interactionist model of SES and human development. *Child Development*, 33–47.

Taylor, Z. E., Larsen-Rife, D., Conger, R. D., & Widaman, K. F. (2012). Familism, interparental conflict, and parenting in Mexican-origin families: A cultural-contextual framework. *Journal of Marriage and Family, 74*, 312–327.

10

A Stranger in Paradise

Fitting In, Managing Identities, and Reaching Out

James E. Côté

Introduction

The editors of this volume wanted me to tell my story—how Jim Côté became the Professor James Côté of today—and to do so in a creative fashion. I take up this charge with relish, but also with trepidation because part of my biography has required me to carefully control information about myself, in part by segregating various personal and professional audiences. One of the advantages of being a late-career academic, however, is that some things no longer matter, so I can now feel free to disclose information about myself to diverse audiences. Nevertheless, it is precisely that need for information control and audience segregation in my personal life that has provided some of the most valuable insights in my academic work on identity formation, and especially in developing the identity capital model. These real-world experiences taught me to require that any ideas and theories I endorse academically must pass my personal "sniff test," namely, that they make common sense and they are not so ill-defined as to ascend to some sort of intellectual Neverland.

The events leading to, and including, an academic career have been far from typical: working-class background, Catholic upbringing, prodigal phase leading to high-risk behavior and social exclusion, second-chance and redemption, nose-to-the-grind stone student, mentor-researcher-professor, inter-disciplinary gadfly, and trans-disciplinary conciliator. I was also the first in my bloodline to attend university, so was exceedingly unlikely to become a university professor. It would surely not have happened had I been a member of my father's generation.

As is the case in the lives of people from all walks of life, my winding trajectory into academia was strongly influenced by chance and circumstance, mixing a unique combination of religious denomination, social class, educational setting, academic discipline, and professional context. These experiences have shaped my scholarly contributions, which focus on identity formation, education–work transitions, and the transition to adulthood. As a sociologist, I have endeavored to understand societal contexts not as variables but in terms of the "big picture" that sets the parameters for people's lives, both in terms of opportunities (doors open to people of a given identity) and obstacles (doors closed because of another imputed identity). My commitment to understanding the impact of the larger societal context on peoples' potentials has necessarily involved challenging orthodoxies and taking political stances that are not always popular, but which I have felt morally obligated to do, often because of personal experiences and research-based insights.

Few people who will read this will know the whole story of the influences leading to the type of career I undertook and how I am spending its final chapter. Because the likelihood of my eventual professional accomplishments was remote given my starting point, I will begin with the present and work backwards in time. That is the perspective I have taken as I have contemplated writing this self-narrative, so I hope this rear-view mirror method helps readers understand why I have devoted my career to certain pursuits.

At the same time, there is always the trap of constructing one's past in a self-aggrandizing manner and I have been painfully aware of this possibility. Nevertheless, I hope that what I have to say will inspire others to try to "presume above themselves" and achieve their potentials. I also hope to inspire those whose academic destiny was prefigured by the good fortune of their birthright to give a hand up to those who might never have a chance to realize their potentials.

Late-Professional Career

As I entered what I call the last chapter of my career, I turned to more generative concerns, trying to give back to the profession and to help others in their intellectual journeys.

Following my promotion to full professor in the year 2000, I felt I had the latitude to become involved at an international level with several learned societies. That year, I began a 5-year term as founding editor of the new journal *Identity: An International Journal of Theory and Research* and served as President (2003–05) of the Society for Research on Identity Formation (SRIF). At the same time, I began the first of three 4-year stints on the Executive Board of the International Sociological Association's Research Committee (34) on the Sociology of Youth, which has culminated with the presidency of RC34 for the years 2010–14. In addition, I have taken on a 5-year term as an Associate Editor of the *Journal of Adolescence.*

These involvements have been tremendously rewarding: professionally by allowing me to influence the direction of two fields of study, and personally by putting me in the position where I can help younger colleagues publish their work and become more involved in learned societies.

The unusual thing about these involvements, however, is that they are in two large fields that have virtually no overlap other than the young age groups under study. In fact, there are serious tensions—even hostilities—between these two fields: one dominated by developmental psychologists and the other dominated by sociologists. But even within each of these disciplines, there are numerous disputes and tensions, some of which are academic and some of which are political (in the power-relations sense of the term). Moreover, the involvement with the identity journal and the Society for Research on Identity Formation (SRIF) mostly involves rubbing elbows with American colleagues, while involvement with the International Sociological Association involves about as much contact with European colleagues as it does with colleagues in Asia and Australia. I have lost track of the number of conferences I have attended during this period, but it is not unusual to travel from Canada to Europe three to four times a year, with an additional trip to Asia or another continent, and couple more trips to the United States. Many of these trips involve giving invited addresses or opening remarks at conferences.

Participating in such a diversity of events is extremely enlightening, but what is discussed at the psychology-based conferences in the United States often has little in common with what is discussed at the sociology-based conferences in other parts of the world; yet they are all about young people and the issues faced by young people today. With one foot in each discipline, my presentations are mostly social psychological, combining what I believe to be the best of both disciplines. This goes for my work on identity formation and higher education, as well as youth studies in general, the latter providing the overarching context for discussing the former.

In a recent keynote address to a large audience of European developmental psychologists in Lithuania (the European Association for Research on Adolescence; EARA), titled "Adolescent psychology and the sociology of youth: Toward a rapprochement," I laid out what I saw to be the principal differences between the psychological and sociological approaches to adolescence/youth. I ended with a plea for efforts to bridge the gaps between the two approaches by recognizing that each approach has its strengths and limitations but in ignoring the strengths of the other approach, we are limiting the impact that our collective efforts can have in bettering the lives of young people. Although the students in that audience seemed to be open to these ideas, the older members of the audience seemed not to be so pleased to have their disciplinary perspective put under scrutiny.

Although I have always been ever hopeful of breaking down disciplinary barriers, this disciplinary intransigence did not surprise me. This has been the general reaction I have encountered throughout my career: there is a general reluctance to understand human development in an interdisciplinary framework. In my specific fields, few scholars appear willing to consider identity formation (a social psychologically based endeavor) within the context of an increasingly difficult transition to adulthood (a sociologically based activity).

During this late-career period, I have continued to try to offer ways of understanding the compatibility of the psychological, social-psychological, and sociological perspectives, especially in the field of identity studies (Côté & Levine, 2002), but also in youth studies (Côté & Allahar, 2006) and higher educational studies (Côté & Allahar, 2007, 2011).

Mid-Professional Career

Receiving tenure and promotion to associate professor in 1990 opened the door for me to increase my focus on writing, especially undertaking larger projects that could culminate in book-length treatments of complex subjects. Although I have always found journal articles to be useful and writing them gratifying, they are by their nature limiting, especially in terms of attempting to link disciplinary perspectives. Too much of modern academia is based on partly spoken ideas, broken down to fit into the arid stories told in these articles. Books give authors much more latitude with which to link ideas from various perspectives and go into the depths necessary to build a body of ideas that can make sense of the many smaller projects that make their way into journal articles.

During this period, I was especially interested in the difficulties associated with the transition to adulthood, including among those who do not have the opportunity to attend institutions of higher learning—sometimes called the "forgotten half" (Allahar & Côté, 1998; Côté & Allahar, 1996; Côté, 2000). This work on the transition to adulthood attempts to correct a bias in much developmental work that "psychologizes" problems that more rightly can be seen as contextually significant, as the youth segment of the population has lost some of its social legitimacy and bargaining power, making young people's identity formation more difficult than it was in the past. This bias in adolescent psychology tends to glorify (Western) societal contexts, and blame those young people who encounter difficulties, when there is ample evidence that the transition to adulthood has become fraught with distinctive risks, especially for those unprepared by early family life and primary socialization. Fortunately, the positive youth development movement has done much to correct this bias (e.g., Lerner, 1995, 2000), but there is still much work to be done.

In the early 1990s, for example, I was able to take several years to investigate what was then a well-known controversy in anthropology involving Margaret Mead's (1928) seminal book *Coming of Age in Samoa*, which contrasted a benign "tribal" youth period with a more tumultuous "modern" one. I encountered this controversy obliquely, through its implications for the sociology of youth and the psychology of identity formation, links unbeknownst to most of those involved in the controversy and outside it. In addition to authoring several journal articles on the topic, I published my first book, *Adolescent Storm and Stress: An Evaluation of the Mead–Freeman Controversy* (Côté, 1994). Mead's daughter, Catherine Bateson, gave me full access to her mother's archives. Among other rare documents in these archives, the letters between Mead and her mentor, Franz Boas, are still available on a website I set up at the time (http://sociology.uwo.ca/mead/index.htm).

In the mid-90s, I co-authored another book that takes a macro sociological perspective on the extended transition to adulthood, criticizing both conventional psychological approaches and the more conservative sociological approaches (Côté & Allahar, 1996). This book attracted considerable attention from the Canadian public, in part because it was the first time many people had heard that something had changed in the way young people make their way to adulthood and that the causes of these changes could be traced to societal and economic causes. Subsequently, the article "A social history of youth in Samoa: Religion, capitalism, and cultural disenfranchisement" (Côté, 1997a) offered a critical perspective to the changing transition to adulthood. In this case, though, I brought Mead's 1920s work in Samoa up to date in terms of how the transition to adulthood has been adversely affected in societies that quickly Westernized in the 20th century.

During the 1990s, the publication of my work on identity capital began (Côté, 1996, 1997b), having been on the drawing board for some years before this. The value I see in this model is that it provides a way with which psychologists and sociologists might understand how young people can agentically manage the various elements of their identity—subjective, personal, and social—in ways that constitute a "portfolio" with which to make their way into a functional adulthood of their making. Identity capital resources are particularly important in societies where many identities are no longer ascribed (e.g., occupational identities), but where there is little structure to

replace the ascriptive processes, making the passage to adulthood less certain, even unwelcoming. To appreciate the identity capital model, however, it is helpful to have a working knowledge of developmental psychology—especially Erik Erikson's work—as well as sociological conceptions of identity construction and management and the presentation of self. Unfortunately, there is a small audience with this particular interdisciplinary combination of knowledge.

I also see the identity capital model as a reflection of my own lived experiences where I moved among various social contexts, and through certain barriers, especially social class ones. Doing so involves understanding how one is judged based on "who one is," and each social class has its own codes in terms of language, attitudes, and habits. Consequently, the ability to manage identities and present the self in a variety of contexts is very important. This skill involves a *personality process* that Erikson (1968) called ego strength, and others call agency. Additionally, it is crucial for the person to have a working knowledge of the *contents of identities* in differing situations for various audiences (e.g., pronouncing words differently to different audiences, knowing when to use formal and informal grammar, what attitudes and habits are esteemed by one audience but considered shameful by others).

Making the transition from the working class to middle-class professional life can be difficult, and subsequent life in the middle class is not necessarily a problem-free one in terms of managing deeply ingrained behavior and language patterns. Those who change social classes must learn many things as adults that are taken for granted by those whose primary socialization prepared them for their adult lives. Those who begin new lives in different social contexts are acutely aware of many things that others who have only known that one way of living take for granted. People with these experiences of contradictory class-location (or any cultural bi-location) should particularly appreciate the identity capital model.

Regrettably, many social scientists are unwilling to think outside of their "paradigmatic boxes." The biggest disappointment of my career has been in how little academics are willing to try to understand each other's work. This problem is certainly found in youth studies—broadly defined—involving a reticence to combine diverse perspectives and methods. I believe that the value of the identity capital model lies in helping economically and socially disadvantaged young people—those who do not have the benefit of an affluent background, coupled with parents who know how to pass on more intangible resources like effective impression management. It is indeed frustrating when something is so self-evident in terms of one's own personal experience and academic knowledge is not seen as such by others. Or worse, it is disheartening to be misunderstood as intending the opposite—to be seen as wanting to help only those who are advantaged by their backgrounds, a reaction commonly encountered in sociological circles when the prospect of "agency" is suggested.

Early Professional Career

During the late 1980s, I maintained my focus on identity formation within the context of the transition to adulthood, using my own personal experience as a source of insight.

For example, influenced by developmental contextualism (Lerner & Kauffman, 1985), I began work on a model of student development that eventually lead me to the identity capital model. This model of student development proposes that students' own personal efforts can help them to transcend or overcome structural barriers. In the current era, although Western societies continue to present barriers associated with social class and other forms of disadvantage, many institutions are open enough for some people to overcome those barriers by adapting their developmental efforts to compatible contexts. For example, higher-educational settings can be "open" in this sense, and my longitudinal research shows that in some cases one person's barrier can be another person's opportunity (Côté & Levine, 1997, 2000). The "openness" of these settings is selective, however, and the person's motivation and behavior can be all-important in determining how these settings are experienced and what benefits are derived from them. Specifically, my research suggests that those who approach their higher-education studies with the primary goal of enhancing their own personal and intellectual development do better in these contexts, and they experience those contexts and their mentors more favorably. Having spent the previous two decades doing this very thing in my own life, I was gratified to work it out theoretically and empirically. As noted, this research helped me to formulate the identity capital model, and the findings stand as an example of the developmental-contextual value of agentically applying specific resources to specific contexts.

I also conducted studies on the religious socialization of academics (Côté & Levine, 1992), finding that a significant proportion of professors—especially those in the humanistic disciplines—had experienced an intense primary socialization into a religion accompanied by a truncated trajectory toward the clergy. In Eriksonian terms (1958), the strong superego nurtured by an intense religious primary socialization can become transformed into an equally intense ego ideal as a result of an identity crisis. This was my experience, and apparently that of many of my colleagues, at least of my generation and the one preceding it.

My early years in academia were difficult at times, but I took solace in reading material like *Strangers in Paradise: Academics from the Working Class* (Ryan & Sackrey, 1985). That book helped me to understanding that many of the things I was experiencing were experienced by the other 20% of academics from working-class backgrounds. My adjustments during those years benefitted from the collegiality of Anton Allahar, also from the working class. We were able to talk through many things, sometimes into the wee hours of the night, and through these talks identified mutual interests that led us to eventually write five books together. His macro-sociological orientation coupled with my more social-psychological one helped us to frame issues in new and provocative ways.

Graduate School

I completed an MA in 1981 and a PhD in 1984. My recollection of the first day of my master's program is vivid. I had applied to a specific department because Orrin Klapp was on faculty (The University of Western Ontario, to which I later returned, and stayed, as a faculty member). He was then known for his book, *Collective Search for Identity* (Klapp, 1969). However, he was taking a sabbatical that year, so I was referred to Charles Levine to begin what became a career-long collaborative relationship and lifelong friendship. Levine was a relatively freshly minted PhD in 1977, and a couple of years later was to spend his first sabbatical at Harvard working with Lawrence Kohlberg, and the vibrant group of scholars studying there with Kohlberg. His academic adventure culminated with the influential co-authored book in which Kohlberg, Levine, and a colleague responded to Kohlberg's critics (Kohlberg, Levine, & Hewer, 1983).

I arrived in Levine's office that first day with my thesis proposal already written, based on the results of my Honors thesis. This began a series of in-depth discussions that continue to this day, in which we relentlessly work through the logic and underlying assumptions of the theoretical or empirical problem at hand. As a mentor, Levine was a logician's taskmaster, and by the time I had completed my master's thesis, I had enough theoretical material for the first few chapters of my PhD dissertation, which was influenced by another mentor, Michael Lanphier, a social psychologist who granted me the freedom to explore Erikson further and undertake an empirical study that laid the basis for work that was pursued for the remainder of my career. While doing my PhD, I also expanded my knowledge of the multivariate statistical techniques suitable for large samples and I was fortunate to have Paul Roazen in residence at that school, noted for his book *Erik H. Erikson: The Power and Limits of a Vision* (1976).

Like Erikson (1975), I found mainstream psychology too theoretically narrow and technique-oriented; in any event, my undergraduate academic record put me out of the running for acceptance in graduate psychology programs. Instead, I did both of my graduate degrees in sociology departments, where there was a greater tolerance for interdisciplinary work. Social psychology tends to be more broadly defined in sociology, as captured by the "three faces" model that James House (1977) described so well. Accordingly, I was free to fully explore Erikson's work (reading it *all*, some parts several times, making voluminous notes) as well as the neo-Eriksonian empirical work that was being published at the time. In the process,

I noticed a disjuncture between Erikson's theoretical accounts and the empirical attempts to operationalize them, leading me to launch a critique of the dominant empirical model that has since influenced my work as well as relations with colleagues favoring that model (i.e., the identity status paradigm; Marcia, 1964, 1980). In the end, I developed what I felt was a useful alternative interpretation of Erikson's work, by compiling his various postulates into a logically consistent and empirically testable form (Côté, 1984; Côté & Levine, 1987, 1988).

My progress through the master's degree was punctuated by a 2-year, full-time position as a psychometrist/research assistant in a child and adolescent psychiatric center. In that position, I saw first-hand the disturbances that can afflict those of these age groups. Reflecting my education in both psychology and sociology, I witnessed that many disturbances were obviously more than mere "labeling," while others were likely the products of family dynamics and other contextual influences. During this period, two additional resources were acquired. I honed my small-sample statistical and instrument-development skills and gained useful insights into how problematic behaviors were approached by the medical- and social-work models.

I took my doctorate at York University, jokingly referred to at the time as "the University north of Toronto" to underscore its inferior reputation in relation to the prestigious University of Toronto. It was considered the "working class" university in Toronto, built during the 1960s as part of Canada's push to massify its higher-education system. During that time, I cut my teeth on "big-city living" and mixing with people from diverse backgrounds: in my classes, with fellow students, and more generally in social circles. The academic standards at York University at the time would be considered "high" by current standards.

Undergraduate School

My undergraduate experience was transformative of my working-class worldview, but also provided an epiphany in terms of finding myself reflected in the theories I studied, especially Erikson's. I was fortunate to have the opportunity to attend an excellent liberal-arts university with caring professors who encouraged freethinking about moral and political issues. This was Trent University in Peterborough, Ontario, a school that was less than a decade old at the time and still had a good student–teacher ratio. It was perhaps at its peak historically and many of its graduates went on to outstanding careers in various fields.

Although I intended to major only in psychology, the excellent faculty in the sociology department at the time drew my interest and some were noted sixties' radicals, making for some very lively lectures and seminars. Consequently, I undertook a joint major in psychology and sociology (both departments were flexible enough to allow me to be the first to do so as a special request).

It was through the two types of courses that I discovered Erikson's work of identity formation, especially as it reflected my biography (e.g., Erikson, 1968; Erikson & Erikson, 1957), as well as symbolic interactionist works on identity maintenance and the presentation of self (especially Erving Goffman, 1959, 1963), helping me to make sense of how my own life was unfolding. Erikson helped me to work out my sense of meaning and direction, while Goffman helped me to understand how a stigmatized identity can hold one back, even in a self-imposed manner.

My Honors thesis constituted my first attempt to integrate systematically psychological and sociological perspectives on identity, and set the stage for much of my graduate work. It helped me to articulate how identity formation is a common thread of self-discovery and how a full understanding of identity formation and its maintenance has to be interdisciplinary, with sociological and psychological understandings coming together to tell a larger social-psychological story about: derailed trajectories, stigma, labeling, identity confusion and anxiety, exploration, fidelity, agency, goal-setting, delayed gratification, commitment, and yielding to a larger purpose.

But, getting through those 4 years to write that thesis was the culmination of countless inspirational experiences with mentors from both departments who spent their time nurturing my interests and abilities, especially Gary Reker (who generously stuck with me as my Supervisor of Studies for the full 4 years of my degree), Sandy Lockhart, Frank Nutch, Andy Wernick, and Paul Wong.

Early Influences

I was born in 1953 and raised in a small Canadian town (Gananoque, Ontario) in a working-class, Catholic family. Attending a Catholic primary school and being an altar boy constituted the first formative experiences outside my family. I often served daily morning masses, weddings and funerals, and of course the big Sunday masses. My school life was ordinary until one day when everyone in my grade six class was given a lengthy paper-and-pencil test. I recall finishing it early and, as I sat waiting the rest of the class to finish, wondered why they were taking so long.

After that day, there were major changes in how I was treated. Suddenly, I received special attention from the nuns who ran the school. I was entered into essay contests and kept after school hours to go over my work on these essays. I was also entered into public-speaking contests and regularly went to the local convent for elocution lessons. I soon realized that I was being preened for the priesthood.

In retrospect, and consistent with developmental contextualism, I attribute my path to academia and eventual occupation as a professor to these experiences, triggered by a single IQ test in the context of that time and place: the mid-sixties, grade six, and a Catholic school closely overseen by nuns. As noted above, as an academic, I was intrigued by this connection between early religious socialization and involvement in academia. In particular, I theorized that the professorial role is the equivalent of the "modern cleric" in certain ways, including providing moral–ethical leadership "from the pulpit" by reciting the "gospel" and through "epistles."

Whatever their symbolic relevance, these religion-based experiences, gave me the confidence to perform in public, and exposed me to role models of moral leadership. These school and church experiences stood in contrast to working-class family life where "little boys are to be seen and not heard."

However, in my early adolescence, the secure and normatively supported trajectory to the clergy was broken by a crisis of faith, undoubtedly associated with my development of formal operational thinking capacities. I recall that I began to ask questions in catechism class that made the nuns and priest uncomfortable, and I was told in the Principal's office that these questions set a bad example for the rest of class in terms of maintaining their faith. A deal was struck that if I held my tongue and "served out my time" as an altar boy until the end of grade eight, I would be left alone. However, I think the pattern had already been set for me to identify and question orthodoxies with the intent of exposing what the orthodoxies hid or obscured.

This religious identity crisis was resolved relatively quickly, but the structure of the moral character that had been instilled in me remained, as I searched for new moral content that was more meaningful to the world I saw around me.

Secondary school was a mixed experience. The public school I attended was large and impersonal, and without the nurturance of the small Catholic school setting I had attended at the elementary level. Like so many other teenagers, I found this type of experience quite alienating, with much of the curriculum unchallenging and without meaning. I excelled in certain subjects and was mediocre in others, depending on my interest in the subject and the quality of my relationship with the teacher of the course. There were no subjects available in the social sciences, so I focused my intellectual curiosity on the natural-science subjects available (physics and chemistry). To fill this void in school subjects touching on the meaning of life, in my spare time, I read books that my older brother had himself devoured (he had a similar experience with the Church, but rebelled much earlier and became a lifelong intellectually curious and eclectic reader). I recall reading a lot of science fiction, but also "heretical" non-fiction like *Worlds in Collision* by Immanuel Velikovsky (1950), and near the end of high school savored books like Henry David Thoreau's *Walden* (1910), R. D. Laing's *The Divided Self* (1960), *The Self and Others* (1961), and *Sanity, Madness and the Family* (1964), Eric Berne's *Games People Play* (1964), and Thomas Harris' *I'm OK, You're OK* (2004).

At the time (1970), Ontario schools had a Grade 13, which was supposedly a year of university preparation. The year before I had pre-enrolled in all of the available science courses, but after reading the above-mentioned books, I decided that I would rather pursue something in the social sciences. Given the few offerings available at that school, and the refusal of the administration to let me change my course selection anyway, I dropped out of school after a month.

What followed was a couple of years of experimentation, some involving travel (the type of wanderlust Erikson [1975] wrote about in his own autobiography), some involving trying my hand at several crafts, and some experimenting with the hippie subculture and the drug-taking involved. This latter experimentation wound me up in jail for a short spell (I was one of the first in the area "to be made an example of" by the police). Being thrown in with a large number of convicts, some of whom thrived on violence, certainly got my attention, and I still recall many of these experiences from 40 years ago as if they happened yesterday, but one in particular was pivotal.

This incident was a conversation during my first day in the county jail when I shared a cell with two brothers from my hometown. They would have been called "hoods" at the time. Although only a few years older than me, they were already hardened by street-fights, hard drinking, and petty theft. They came from a "bad family," which meant a home life of alcoholism and abuse. The local paper we were given to read in our cell had the story of my court case in which the pre-sentence report stated that because of my intelligence and minor role in the offense, I should get a lighter sentence. This stimulated a discussion with my cellmates about our future plans. They were headed for a hard and unpleasant life unless something changed for them, but I said that I was considering going to university. To my surprise, the older brother said something like "I hope you study something to make life easier for people like us." He said those words in a sincere and unthreatening manner, and I saw the gentle person inside the hard exterior. I said I would try, and that conversation has stayed with me since.

When first considering an eventual profession near the end of my undergraduate years, I considered going on to study criminology, but my inquiries with those who had followed that path suggested that I would have to set my ideals aside and take up the role of the heartless bureaucrat. The 1970s was also an era during which the public was becoming more hardened to crime and the old ideals of rehabilitation were being replaced with demands for retribution. Prisons in North America are now largely places where non-conformists from less privileged backgrounds are punished, and the abandonment of rehabilitation efforts has made the stigmatized identity of the "ex-con" a very difficult image to manage or eradicate.

Conclusions

The rest of the story worked out well for me because of a combination of chance events and relationships with several significant mentors. My life could have taken many directions, but in retrospect the checkered path it took was influenced at critical periods by significant identity-related experiences, just as Erikson explained in his writings, and why I found a "home" in his work. My experiences taught me that the motivation to learn from and take advantage of available resources is crucial. This is what I have attempted to capture with the identity capital model, with the hope of helping those who feel they are caught in circumstances beyond their control. At the same time, my hope is that psychologists and sociologists will learn how to build the bridges necessary to take this knowledge into the applied and policy realms.

References

Allahar, A. & Côté, J. E. (1998). *Richer and poorer: The structure of social inequality in Canada.* Toronto: Lorimer Press.

Berne, E. (1964). *Games people play.* New York: Ballantine Books.

Côté, J. E. (1984). *The identity crisis: A formulation and empirical tests of Erikson's theory of ego identity formation.* Unpublished doctoral dissertation, York University, Toronto.

Côté, J. E. (1993). Foundations of a psychoanalytic social psychology: Neo-Eriksonian propositions regarding the relationship between psychic structure and cultural institutions. *Developmental Review, 13,* 31–53.

Côté, J. E. (1994). *Adolescent storm and stress: An evaluation of the Mead–Freeman controversy.* Hillsdale, NJ: Lawrence Erlbaum Associates.

Côté, J. E. (1996). Sociological perspectives on identity formation: The culture-identity link and identity capital. *Journal of Adolescence, 19,* 419–430.

Côté, J. E. (1997a). A social history of youth in Samoa: Religion, capitalism, and cultural disenfranchisement. *International Journal of Comparative Sociology, 38,* 217–234.

Côté, J. E. (1997b). An empirical test of the identity capital model. *Journal of Adolescence, 20,* 577–597.

Côté, J. E. (2000). *Arrested adulthood: The changing nature of maturity and identity.* New York: New York University Press.

Côté, J. E. & Allahar, A. L. (1996). *Generation on hold: Coming of age in the late twentieth century.* New York: New York University Press.

Côté, J. E. & Allahar, A. L. (2006). *Critical youth studies: A Canadian focus.* Toronto: Pearson Education.

Côté, J. E. & Allahar, A. L. (2007). *Ivory tower blues: A university system in crisis.* Toronto: University of Toronto Press.

Côté, J. E. & Allahar, A. L. (2011). *Lowering higher education: The rise of corporate universities and the fall of liberal education.* Toronto: University of Toronto Press.

Côté, J. E. & Levine, C. (1987). A formulation of Erikson's theory of ego identity formation. *Developmental Review, 9,* 273–325.

Côté, J. E. & Levine, C. (1988). A critical examination of the ego identity status paradigm. *Developmental Review, 8,* 147–184.

Côté, J. E. & Levine, C. (1992). The genesis of the humanistic academic: A second test of Erikson's theory of ego identity formation. *Youth and Society, 23,* 387–410.

Côté, J. E. & Levine, C. (1997). Student motivations, learning environments, and human capital acquisition: Toward an integrated paradigm of student development. *Journal of College Student Development, 38,* 229–243.

Côté, J. E. & Levine, C. (2000). Attitude versus aptitude: Is intelligence or motivation more important for positive higher educational outcomes? *Journal of Adolescent Research, 15,* 58–80.

Côté, J.E. & Levine, C. (2002). *Identity formation, agency, and culture: A social psychological synthesis.* Hillsdale, NJ: Lawrence Erlbaum.

Erikson, E. H. (1958). *Young man Luther.* New York: Norton.

Erikson, E. H. (1968). *Identity: Youth and crisis.* New York: Norton.

Erikson, E. H. (1975). *Life history and the historical moment.* New York: Norton.

Erikson, E. H. & Erikson, K. T. (1957). On the confirmation of the delinquent. *Chicago Review, 10,* 15–23.

Goffman, E. (1959). *The presentation of self in everyday life.* Garden City, NY: Doubleday.

Goffman, E. (1963). *Stigma: Notes on the management of spoiled identity.* Englewood Cliffs, NJ: Prentice-Hall.

Harris, T. (2004). *I'm OK, you're OK.* New York: Harper.

House, J. S. (1977). The three faces of social psychology. *Sociometry, 40,* 161–177.

Klapp, O. E. (1969). *Collective search for identity.* New York: Holt, Rinehart, and Winston.

Kohlberg, L., Levine, C. & Hewer, A. (1983). *Moral stages: A current formulation and a response to critics.* Basel, Switzerland: S. Larger.

Laing, R. D. (1960). *The divided self: An existential study in sanity and madness.* Harmondsworth, UK: Penguin.

Laing, R. D. (1961). *The self and others.* London: Tavistock Publications.

Laing, R. D. & Esterson, A. (1964). *Sanity, madness and the family.* London: Penguin Books.

Lerner, R. M. (1995). *America's youth in crisis: Challenges and options for programs and policies.* Thousand Oaks, CA: Sage.

Lerner, R. M. (2000). *Positive youth development and civil society: A vision of youth development policy in the United States.* Paper presented at the Jacobs Foundation Conference on: "Adolescents into citizens: Integrating young people into political life." Marbach Castle, Germany, October 26–28.

Lerner, R. M. & Kauffman, M. B. (1985). The concept of development in contextualism. *Developmental Review, 5,* 309–333.

Marcia, J. E. (1964). Determination and construct validation of ego identity status. Unpublished Doctoral Dissertation, Ohio State University.

Marcia, J. E. (1980). Identity in adolescence. In J. Adelson (Ed.), *Handbook of adolescent psychology* (pp. 159–187). New York: Wiley.

Mead, M. (1928). *Coming of Age in Samoa.* New York: William Morrow and Company.

Roazen, P. (1976). *Erik H. Erikson: The power and limits of a vision.* New York: Free Press.

Ryan, J. & Sackrey, C. (1985). *Strangers in paradise: Academics from the working class.* Boston: South End Press.

Thoreau, H. D. (1910). *Walden.* New York: C. E. Merrill Co.

Velikovsky, I. (1950). *Worlds in collision.* New York: Macmillan.

11

My Research Life and Times

WILLIAM DAMON

The well-known claim that adolescence is a formative period for identity was certainly true in my case. It was during high school that I acquired an interest in research-based writing. As my interest in research and writing grew, I envisioned a career as an historian, journalist, or scientist of some kind. This was my first realistic career goal. Before that, my imagination had me employed as a deep-sea fisherman, a future baseball player, a military commander, and so on down a long list of young male fantasies. But once I had some experience with research and writing, these boyhood fantasies were replaced by a future vision that seemed just as exciting. The prospect of conducting research to discover something new, and then informing the world about it, struck me as an incredibly worthwhile and even powerful vocation.

I did not come upon this idea from any school courses that I took. When I first entered high school, coursework was the furthest thing from my mind. I had grown up in a down-at-the heels factory town that emanated a distinctly anti-intellectual ethos, and academic learning had little appeal to me. But then I had an experience during ninth grade that changed my attitude towards academic pursuits forever. This experience occurred because I joined my high-school newspaper. I did this in order to cover sports: I was too young as a freshman to make the school teams, but I enjoyed watching the games and hanging out with the older players.

As a rookie reporter, my first assignment was to cover a game that was of no interest to anyone. A group of Eastern European immigrants had formed an amateur soccer team and had requested a practice match with our junior varsity. Soccer was not even a major school sport back then, but it actually turned out to be an interesting spectacle, with the immigrant team demonstrating amazing skills that they had acquired in Europe. Still, that was not the story that captured my interest. I stayed around after the game to speak with the immigrant players. They spoke excitedly about coming to America, about the hard lives they had left behind, about what political freedom meant to them and their families, and about their hopes for themselves in this new land. All of this opened a world of cultural and historical understanding to me that went far beyond what I had ever heard about. When I wrote up this story for the newspaper about these immigrants' lives, my friends all read it and commented that they were fascinated by the story.

Subsequently, as I had more experiences of this kind, I had no trouble devoting myself to my school writing assignments. I was determined to learn the skills I needed to pursue this new purpose that I had discovered. My choice of a career as a researcher can be traced back to the satisfaction that I discovered while reporting for my school newspaper. Stepping aside from this autobiographical statement for a moment, I believe that there is a message here for school systems that curtail their extracurricular programs in order to focus single-mindedly on narrow instruction in testable skills.

My choice of psychology as my primary research field came about at the end of high school. Someone placed in my hands a copy of a book of selected papers by Edwin Boring called *History, psychology, and science* (Boring, Eds. Watson & Campbell, 1963). I do not recall anything specific from the book, but I do remember finding the mix of fields indicated by the title fascinating and compelling, and I liked the way Boring combined rigor with conceptual breadth. I determined at that point to become the same type of psychologist. I note with interest that Boring's historical treatment of psychological research was an inspiration for the present volume (Boring, 1929), and that Boring himself used autobiographical accounts to convey the ways that theoretical and research perspectives in psychology are formed (Boring, 1930).

After high school, the timing of my undergraduate study was fortunate: my college years (at Harvard) overlapped with its short-lived Department of Social Relations, which was set up to encourage cross-disciplinary exploration in the social sciences. Students had access to an array of brilliant scholars from many disciplines. My sophomore tutor was Talcott Parsons, my senior thesis advisor was Roger Brown, and I attended courses and lectures by Gordon Allport, Henry Murray, Erik Erikson, and David Riesman. My introduction to child development was a lively course by Jerome Kagan, and my introduction to cognitive science was Jerome Bruner's course in perception and cognition. It was a stimulating environment for social-science interchange, and I came away with an appreciation of many conceptual frameworks and diverse modes of inquiry. In addition to these renowned senior professors, I met a couple of graduate students who augmented my education in important ways. One was Douglas Carmichael, who told me to read *The language and thought of the child* (Piaget, 1928), and who also suggested that I apply to his alma mater, U.C. Berkeley, for my graduate study. The other graduate student I met while I was in college was Howard Gardner, who has been my friend and frequent collaborator ever since.

Graduate School

Late in my senior year of college, the great social psychologist and linguist Roger Brown called me into his office. Roger was my undergraduate thesis advisor and in many ways my role model for how a scholar could conduct careful research with a far-reaching and deeply humane vision. For an illustrious academic star, Roger was also amazingly considerate and gentle as an advisor to his students. But on this occasion he was not so gentle. Rather, he spoke with a tone of annoyance in his voice that was unique in all my experience with him. He had discovered that the committee on graduate admissions in Harvard's psychology department had turned down my application. He asked me, with uncharacteristic irritation, why I had made "made such a mess of" my application.

I knew what he was referring to. In my statement of academic purpose, I had concocted a plan to study "developmental sociology"—whatever that was (and I certainly did not know). I was imagining using insights from Jean Piaget, Erik Erikson, Erving Goffman, and Talcott Parsons (these were the people I was reading in those days) to charter human progress towards social harmony and personal fulfillment. It was, I am sure, a foolishly naïve statement. In my defense, I had produced that statement under the influence of Harvard's Department of Social Relations, a 1960s attempt at interdisciplinary social science that did not survive the harsher realities of academic discourse. Even in this heady atmosphere, my graduate application statement did not fly; and I was too clueless (or too stubborn) to take up Roger on an offer for me to submit a new statement. Fortunately for my aspirations, the University of California at Berkeley's psychology department decided to overlook whatever nonsense I wrote on its application

and accept me anyway. Most likely it did so because Roger Brown had written me a positive recommendation.

At Berkeley, I actually did manage to study how social and individual dimensions of development interact. This was much to the credit of my main professors (Jonas Langer and Paul Mussen), who not only were knowledgeable in their own areas of development but also tolerant of a student's desire to merge and expand areas. So much now is known about the dynamic interplay of developmental systems that it is hard to recapture how new this line of research seemed in the early 1970s. But I distinctly remember the puzzlement I encountered while seeking a dissertation committee for a topic that I was calling "social cognition." Of course I did not in any sense coin that phrase—it was in the wind, at the very least—but I had not been familiar with any previous uses of that term; and to the faculty with whom I spoke, the phrase sounded not only unfamiliar but possibly illusory. How quickly these things have changed.

While a PhD student at Berkeley, I started the research program that led to *The social world of the child* (Damon, 1977). The research program was an effort to uncover early forms of reasoning about central social relations such as friendship and authority and related moral concepts such as justice and sharing. Part of my agenda was to place these early forms of social and moral understanding in the context of children's cognitive capacities in general. The other part of my agenda was to determine how the development of social and moral understanding influences their conduct—and then, as later occurred to me, how interpersonal conduct can spur the growth of social and moral understanding. After publishing my graduate school work in *The social world of the child*, I extended the research program to include motivational and other goal-transformational processes during later periods of the life span, from adolescence through old age.

My Research Career After Graduate School

My research life has developed in three phases. The first phase, extending from the mid-1970s to the late 1980s, focused on social and self understanding during the first two decades of life. The bookends of this phase were *The social world of the child* (Damon, 1977) and *Self-understanding in childhood and adolescence* (Damon & Hart, 1988). The second phase of my research career focused on moral commitment throughout the life span, reflecting my growing belief that studies of social and self-cognition could not provide me with an adequate account of real-life human motivation and behavior. Accordingly, I joined some outstanding colleagues to examine the way social and moral goals operate in real-life settings and how these goals are sometimes transformed into enduring moral commitments. The bookends of this phase were *Some do care: Contemporary lives of moral commitment* (Colby & Damon, 1992) and *Good work: When ethics and excellence meet* (Gardner, Csikszentmihalyi, &

Damon, 2001). The third phase (and present) has focused on purpose, another goal-related construct, but a unique one in its extensivity. Purpose is an *ultimate concern* that can organize a variety of subordinate concerns: it can be a compelling reason for striving to meet shorter-term goals. My interest in purpose stemmed from my belief in its power to mobilize people to endure life challenges and pursue elevated achievements. I have studied the development of purpose in adolescence and adulthood, and I have explored the acquisitions of civic and entrepreneurial purpose in special detail. The beginning bookend of this period was *The path to purpose* (Damon, 2008); the final bookend is yet to come.

From time to time while carrying out these research agendas, I have taken on another absorbing scholarly task, editing collections of other scholars' writings. Two such engagements were especially significant: in 1978, I founded the sourcebook series *New Directions for Child and Adolescent Development*, which I continued editing for the next 25 years; and in 1998 I became editor-in-chief of *The handbook of child psychology*, fifth edition (followed by a co-editorship, with Richard Lerner, of the sixth edition in 2006). Although for myself I define my scholarly identity in terms of studies that I have done myself, others may believe that the value of these studies is eclipsed by the value of the work that I have done editing writings of others and thereby helping to advance and organize the field. This, of course, is not for me to say; nor is it a settled matter at the present time. For this reason, I offer here an account of my editorial contributions in addition to my research activities.

Studies in Social Understanding The research program that I began while a graduate student at Berkeley was aimed at uncovering the previously uncharted depths of social intelligence that young people use in their everyday lives. I had some inkling of this from summer jobs that I had in college as a day-camp counselor, and also from some visits that I made to a settlement house in New York City, where teenagers put on skits about the people they knew in their communities. From my observations in these settings, I could see that young people understood far more about their social worlds than anything that had been documented in psychological research.

At that time (the mid-1970s), there were two dominant characterizations of how social understanding develops during childhood and adolescence. The first was a well-known series of studies on "person perception" (the phrase that stood for social cognition in those days) (Livesly and Bromley, 1973). The bottom line of these studies was that, with development, the child's understanding of persons moves from the "overt" to the "covert:" early on, children think of people in terms of surface qualities such as physical looks, and as they get older, they perceive "inner" traits such as intentions and virtues. The second dominant view came from Kohlberg's moral judgment stage system (Kohlberg, 1976), which placed the origins of moral

cognition in the conception of power and authority that defined his Stage 1. In this view, children begin thinking about the social world as structured around the commands of authority figures such as parents and God, and they make judgments about right and wrong accordingly.

Although I respected both lines of work and learned much about investigatory methods from them, neither view seemed sufficient to me. The person perception studies were limited for two reasons: First, social understanding is largely a matter of thinking about *relations* and *transactions* between people, since these are what we experience first-hand, especially when young. A sole focus on thinking about what other people are like misses this relational view entirely. Second, I suspected that children knew more about the "inner" than they were given credit for, and that older people care more about the "outer" than the existing studies claimed. As for the Kohlberg stage system, it did not take much of an observer to realize that children's play-groups are full of moral behavior such as sharing, compassion, and a ready insistence on fairness. This observation had even made its way into the child psychology literature during its early field-work days, through studies by pioneering researchers such as Lois Murphy (1937). This, by the way, was the first of many times in my career that I have wondered why our field suffers from amnesia regarding important insights established in the past: other scientific fields seem more careful to build on established knowledge.

Over the next 15 years, I conducted a series of studies that chartered the growth of social concepts from early childhood through late adolescence. The concepts were relational in nature, and included friendship (Damon, 1977), authority (Damon, 1977, 1980), positive justice (Damon, 1977, 1980; Damon & Killen, 1982), social rules (Damon, 1977), and self (Damon & Hart, 1982, 1988), which, in the great tradition of William James and George Herbert Mead, we treated as a social concept. I conducted most of this research while a faculty member at Clark University, a vigorous beehive of developmental theorizing. My 15 years at Clark, initially as an assistant professor an eventually as full professor, department chair, and Graduate Dean, were among the most stimulating of my intellectual life: I still draw on the conceptual capital that I acquired in those days.

By the end of the 1980s, I had wound down this first phase of my research career, for a number of reasons. For one thing, the field's interest in developmental sequences was waning, especially with regard to cognitive capacities, and I was in accord with this change. In none of my studies had I been able to establish the exact nature of the link between understanding and interpersonal behavior, which left in doubt the value of describing social-cognitive sequences. I had worked at the edges of this problem, finding some weak associations between concepts of justice and sharing behavior (Damon, 1977), and examining how social interaction can lead to more advanced justice reasoning (Damon & Killen, 1982). But these minor efforts aside, I had left the mysteries of real-life social and moral conduct mainly unexplored. I decided to take on these mysteries more directly, using constructs like goals and commitment rather that those of understanding and reasoning as my main focus of analysis. This venture into the stuff of real-world conduct coincided with a major move that I made in 1989: I left Clark to become Chair of the Education Department at Brown University, and eventually Director of the Center for the Study of Human Development and University Professor at Brown. Although Brown lacked some of Clark's intellectual fervor and cutting-edge psychological work, it was an extremely congenial atmosphere for collaboration, and under the legendary leadership of Vartan Gregorian, it was a place where scholars were given the encouragement to expand their horizons.

Studies in Moral Commitment In 1987, Anne Colby and I received an invitation from SSRC (the Social Science Research Council) to meet with a committee on giftedness that SSRC had just established. The committee wanted to discuss with us whether there was such a thing as moral giftedness, and, if so, how it could be defined and studied. Anne and I had been fellow travelers on the moral science circuit for a number of years, and we were, not incidentally, also married; but we had never done any research together. Neither of us had thought much about the question of moral giftedness. The only paradigm in the field that might be used to address this at the time was Kohlberg's moral judgment stage system, which defined one higher stage of reasoning (Stage 6) that was so rare that it was actually omitted from Kohlberg's official coding manual. But elevated as this form of reasoning might be, Anne and I agreed that it was too cognitive in nature to provide a sufficient basis for anything as big-hearted as moral giftedness. For access to this question, we knew we would need to invoke concepts like courage, grit, compassion, and truthfulness, capacities that were intentionally dismissed in Kohlberg's theory as haphazard components of an unanalyzable "bag of virtues" (Kohlberg, 1971).

After some back-and-forth with the SSRC committee (members of whom included David Feldman and Howard Gardner), Anne and I received a $6,000 grant to conduct a study of people whom we decided to call "moral exemplars" (we worried that the "giftedness" label would give a nativistic bias to our work in this area). We used just about all of those funds to conduct a 2-year nominating study with 20 distinguished scholars from a range of disciplines and belief traditions. The nominators helped us define criteria and come up with names of living exemplars who met these criteria. On the basis of this lengthy procedure, we contacted potential subjects for the study and eventually found 23 exemplars who agreed to participate. At that point, at David Feldman's suggestion, we found a small foundation in California (the Institute for Noetic Sciences) that agreed to match our SSRC grant though some funds they had received from Lawrence Rockefeller to examine "the altruistic spirit." Thus on a total of $12,000 in grants—by far the smallest funding I have had for any

project since graduate school—we embarked on one of the most fruitful and meaningful efforts that either of us have had the fortune to engage in during our professional careers. The initial result of this effort was the volume *Some do care* (Colby & Damon, 1992); and the consequences of the project have lived on far beyond that, in my subsequent research on "good work," in the recent upsurge of interest in the exemplar methodology as a crucial research tool for positive psychology (Matsuba, King, & Bronk, in press), and (at this writing) in my present study with Anne on moral formation among extraordinary historical leaders of the 20th century.

The moral exemplar research that we published in *Some do care* yielded a number of surprises. We had gone into the study expecting to hear these extraordinary individuals—many of whom had lain their lives on the line for civil rights, social justice, and/or world peace—tell us about how they manage their fears and sustain their courage. But every one of our 23 subjects denied needing courage for what they did. Their common refrain was that they rarely experienced fear, because they felt that they had no choice other than to do what they knew was right. Such unanimity of response, even in a small sample, suggests that this finding was no anomaly. The responses indicated a degree of moral certainty that pre-empted normal concerns for personal protection and security.

This unexpected finding led us to look closely at the basis for our exemplars' certainty. Again to our surprise, a very high percentage of the sample (over 90%) cited faith in a higher power as the basis for their willingness to forgo personal concerns of security. For those with traditional religious views, it was faith in God's will ("the Lord will provide," was the way one exemplar put it). For others, it was faith in some other form of transcendent spiritual power. The reasons that this finding surprised us were: (1) the criteria that emerged from our procedure for nominating our exemplars were absolutely secular in nature; and (2) with few exceptions, the factor of faith had played only a minor part in research on psychological development at the time of our study. As an ancillary but also intriguing finding, the exemplars in our study who expressed faith demonstrated strong positivity about their lives' work, whereas the few who did not express faith sounded discouraged, cynical, and even despairing about what they had been able to accomplish. In our current research, Anne and I are trying to understand how this kind of faith and moral certainty (tempered by essential humility) are formed in the course of human development, and how these virtues work to promote noble behavior in challenging life circumstances (Damon & Colby, in press).

Two years after the publication of *Some do care*, I spent a sabbatical year at the Center for Advanced Study in the Behavioral Sciences at Stanford. During that year, I teamed up with Howard Gardner and Mihalyi Csikszentmihalyi to launch the Good Work Project. Our aim was to understand how certain creative and dedicated professionals manage to conduct work that is both excellent and ethical under conditions of pressure and/or negative incentives. Like many other observers, we perceived a trend in many professional fields towards commercialization and away from the public mission of the field. The result has been doctors who feel pressures to attend to rules of their HMO at the expense of their patients, lawyers who attend more to billable hour quotients than the needs of their clients, journalists who feel they need to write sensationalistic stories rather than do deep investigative reporting, and so on. We wanted to learn how some people successfully avoid or ignore such pressures. Our explorations took us into the fields of bio-science, journalism, business, philanthropy, and higher education, among others (Gardner, Csikzsentmihalyi, & Damon, 2001; Damon, 2004; Gardner, 1987; Damon & Verducci, 2006). To me, the single most striking finding from the Good Work studies was the clarity and intensity with which good workers from every field held on to their field's public mission. This finding led me directly into the third phase of my research career, studies in the formation of purpose, the personal correspondent to mission.

Interlude: Editing Assignments and Popular Books Before discussing this third (and thus far final) phase of my research life, I will discuss the other scholarly activities that have occupied major amounts of time and attention during my career. The first activity has been editing, which began in 1978, when Jossey-Bass publishers asked me to found a quarterly series of sourcebooks in child development. The resulting *New directions for child and adolescent development* was one of the great learning experiences of my life. During the 25 years of my editorship, the series opened up new approaches to many areas of the field, giving me at least a passing acquaintance with an enormous range of topics.

Based on my work with the *New Directions* series, I was offered the editorship of *The handbook of child psychology,* which for over 60 years had been the landmark organizer of research in our field. With an extremely talented group of co-editors (Richard Lerner, Robert Siegler, Deanna Kuhn, Nancy Eisenberg, Irving Sigel, and Anne Renninger), we produced a four-volume set that gave the *Handbook*'s grand tradition a forward-looking treatment similar to the *New Directions* series (Damon, 1998). It was a privilege to work with these co-editors, and over 70 distinguished authors, on this set of volumes; and I had one more opportunity to do this, with Richard Lerner then joining me as co-editor-in-chief (Damon & Lerner, 2006). I now plan to honor the *Handbook* tradition that has seen each of its three previous editors (Murchison, Carmichael, and Mussen) step down after producing two editions. Along with the closing of this chapter of my editing life, I also have passed along the editorship of *New Directions* to the very able hands of Lene Jenson and Reed Larsen.

The other absorbing scholarly activity that has accompanied my research career is the writing of trade books aimed at a general audience. I did not come up with this idea on my own. In the mid-1980s, a young editor from the Free Press who had heard me speak about children's morality asked me whether I would be interesting in writing an account of what was known in this area for a short book. It so happened that I had a draft manuscript on this subject that I had been unsuccessfully trying to sell to Harvard University Press. I revised the entire thing (always a useful move whenever possible) and sent it to Free Press, which put it out as *The moral child*. Much to my surprise, the book found a sizable readership, which included not just university faculty and students but also parents and other members of the public (somehow even getting a mention in *Vogue* magazine, of all unexpected places).

This experience whet my appetite for popular writing. In the mid-1990s, I published *Greater expectations* (Damon, 1995), which landed me on dozens of national media shows, including *Oprah* (to my bewilderment and near panic). That book made the case for raising young people with high standards for achievement and service. Nowadays this message sounds almost banal, but the 1990s were the heyday of the self-esteem movement, and in that overly indulgent climate, my book went enough against the grain to attract attention and controversy. *Greater expectations* went through several printings in hardback and paperback and remains by far my best-selling book. There is no way to know the book's contribution to public opinion, but I do know that the ideas and practices that it criticized have been on the wane in recent years. A follow-up book proposing a community-based strategy for educating young people with high standards was met with less interest (Damon, 1997). I was told by my publisher that this was because readers gravitate more to social critiques than to descriptions of possible solutions. The strategy that I proposed in that follow-up book (a "youth charter" of high standards that each community would work out in conversations between adults and young people) received some professional attention and was tried out in a few places, with modest success. But the strategy proved too labor-intensive for broad application. It also became too time-consuming for my own schedule after I relocated to Stanford, so I regretfully let this promising initiative drop.

Studies of Purpose The findings from the studies that my colleagues and I had done on moral commitment and good work impressed upon me the motivating power of a noble purpose (or "mission," as it was designated in our Good Work Project). The importance of purpose had been recognized in popular writings and spiritual teachings for centuries, and I spent some time searching through the "wisdom of the ages" on this matter. I found this philosophical and spiritual literature to be incredibly insightful and inspiring. Before settling on my own approach to this topic, I digested the highlights of what I had been reading into a short book of sayings and quotes, interspersed with essays that I wrote summarizing what was then known about how purpose functions in human life and how it develops over the lifespan. The eminent psychologist David Meyers did me the honor of writing an introduction to this little book, and we put it out as *Noble purpose* (Damon, 2003).

Then it was time for me to examine these philosophical and spiritual speculations in an empirical manner. Despite the ages-old recognition of purpose's central role in a well-directed life, the construct had been given surprisingly little attention in scientific study. There had been some interest in "meaning," mostly stemming from Victor Frankl's moving account of surviving the Holocaust by dedicating himself to the meaningful goal of preserving a manuscript (Frankl, 1946). In Frankl's writings, the constructs of meaning and purpose were used interchangeably, and the field had pretty much followed his lead on this use of terminology. Also, Frankl's main point about meaning and purpose was that they provide resilience under stress (Frankl started a school of psychotherapy called "logo therapy" that was derived from this insight). While I was strongly influenced by Frankl's seminal work, I believed that his vision needed to be expanded in two ways for the scientific study of purpose.

First, it was essential to distinguish the constructs of meaning and purpose. Meaning is a broad concept that includes anything that people consider to be personally significant. Purpose in part relies on meaning (if something is non-meaningful to the self, it will not trigger a sense of purpose), but purpose also implies an effort to accomplish something beyond the self. Thus we defined purpose as a stable intention to accomplish something *both* meaningful to the self *and* leading to engagement with the world beyond the self (Damon, Menon, & Bronk, 2003).

Second, even though it is true that resilience is a highly beneficial outcome of purpose, it is not purpose's only psychological benefit. Here I had been influenced by my participation in two like-minded intellectual movements that had recently captured the imaginations of many psychologists: positive psychology, heralded in by Martin Seligman and Mihalyi Csikszentmihayi, and positive youth development, for which Peter Benson, Richard Lerner, and I had been early advocates. Both movements urged an increased focus on people's strengths and "assets." In the two movements, there was a shared sense that the scientific view of human behavior had been distorted by an over-emphasis on problems, neuroses, conflicts, and other "deficits."

As one personal illustration of this, I remember the first day I entered the building that housed the Stanford Center on Adolescence. The walls of the corridor were lined with posters announcing the dread statistics on youth misbehavior: soaring rates of homicide, suicide, violence, drug use, and so on. After walking this gauntlet, one could not help feeling that young people today are little more than an object of concern and worry for our society, rather than a bright source of contribution. When I assumed the Center's directorship in fall 1997, my first act was to remove those posters. In the study on purpose that we launched in 2003, our focus was not just on what purpose enables us to endure but also what it enables us to achieve.

Our studies in youth purpose found many young people who were devoting their vast talents and energies to causes beyond themselves. Some of these causes were altruistic, as for example one 12-year-old boy who had already raised two million dollars for drinking wells in water-starved African villages. Other causes were aesthetic, such as inventing new jazz scales; others were religious, others scientific, and so on. We conducted case studies of young people who had demonstrated extraordinary purpose; and these "purpose exemplars" taught us many things about how purpose is formed during the adolescent years (Damon, 2008),

But such highly purposeful youth were the exception rather than the rule. In the sample that I wrote about in *The path to purpose*, only about 20% of young people ages 12-22 showed a clear sense of purpose (Damon, 2008). At the other end of the spectrum, about a quarter of the sample showed little interest in purposes of any kind. It was difficult even to talk with them about broader goals, because they were not looking for anything other than getting by day to day. Some of these youngsters were content with their purposelessness, seeming to enjoy the hedonistic opportunities that this state of mind offers (at least temporarily). Others were less comfortable in this state, feeling dejected, anxious, and/or apathetic. In the mid-range of our sample, between these purposeful and purposeless youth, we found a large group (55% of our sample) that had experienced occasional glimmers of purposeful activity but who had never sustained a commitment to any particular aspiration or goal. Some among this group we called "dabblers," because they were rotating from one interest to another without quite knowing why; others we called "dreamers," because they had visions of what they would like to become but no realistic sense of how to get there. (There were other patterns in our sample as well.) Generally these were capable and responsible youngsters who were diligently looking for ways to employ their considerable talents. But they had yet to find a cause that could sustain their efforts beyond disconnected, moment-to-moment engagements. With development, any or all of them may find purpose, but our longitudinal data revealed only small steps in this direction over a 3-year period. Purpose, if and when it arises, is a serious developmental milestone in life.

The most glaring gap that we found in purpose among today's youth was in the area of civic and political engagement. Although a good proportion of our sample expressed interest in community service, few showed any desire to pursue positions of civic and political leadership. Some had participated in campaigns or protest movements on specific occasions, but less than 1% of the sample saw politics as a field that they could imagine dedicating themselves to over time. For a democracy that requires new cadres of leaders in every generation, this disaffection from political aspirations among the young is clearly a troublesome concern. For this reason, I have turned my studies of purpose toward the subject of civic purpose, hoping to find ways to promote a renewed spirit of civic dedication in young citizens (Damon, 2012). Similarly, with a team of collaborators that includes Anne Colby, Richard Lerner, and Kendall Bronk, I am now examining the development of entrepreneurial purpose, hoping to find ways to expand the civic and vocational pathways available to young people from all backgrounds (Lerner & Damon, in press).

Looking Back Over the Changing Landscape of Ideas in Our Time

Anyone who toils in the vineyard of ideas comes under the influence of the intellectual context of his or her times. During the 1960s and 1970s, when I was forming my orientation to psychological research, grand theories were the order of the day, and they were hotly debated. What now appears to be just a heuristic, or a testable conceptual distinction, at that time often was a subject of intense ideological debate. Theories were considered to be entire worldviews that determined everything from the judgments that people make to the values they live by. Sometimes the tenor of the argument reached a fevered pitch. For example, during the Paris student revolts of the Vietnam era, Howard Gardner made the following observation about the theoretical position known as structuralism:

> ... the uprising of 1968 signaled a new shift in intellectual allegiance among the students .... 'Structuralism is dead' cried the students. Whether or not they had ever read a word of Piaget or Levi-Strauss, they sensed a tie between the philosophy of these men and the establishment they had come to despise.
>
> (Gardner, 1972, p. 214)

Even in scholarly journals, assumptions were fiercely contested; and abstract academic rhetoric took on an air that sometimes veered towards the apocalyptic. For example, just as I was finishing graduate school, I came across a critique of Kohlberg's moral development theory that amazed me. This early statement of a cultural perspective, published in the touchstone journal *Human Development*, concluded in the following manner:

> Perhaps our scientific search should be less for eternal verities and universal invariance than for alternative and creative modes of coping with the truly universal and eternal problems of justice and liberty .... The moral reasoning which we see actively applied today by the Western world, quite apart from high-minded professional philosophy, bids fair to destroy man .... We would do better to explore and analyze differences wherever found, to borrow and adapt, and to nurture invention and cultural mutation as it occurs, than to perpetuate the ideology of a suicidal world trying to reconcile its differences through the use of a theoretical framework ill-suited for containing and ordering real human diversity.
>
> (Simpson, 1974, p. 103)

This really was taking psychological theory seriously. The author was proposing that Kohlberg had devalued the perspectives of people living in non-Western cultures by claiming universality for a stage sequence that had been founded on Western philosophical assumptions and empirically validated by research with Western subjects. This raised, in the author's mind, the danger of a theoretical imperialism that could lead to cultural conflict and, ultimately, to world destruction. Nowadays it would be unusual to encounter a conclusion proposing a link between a particular theory of moral judgment and the fate of humankind, but at the time it almost seemed like a reasonable conjecture.

In some ways, such a concern with the "big picture" of ideology and theory had been a welcome change for American psychology, which was just emerging from a decades-long bout of what had been derided as "dustbowl empiricism." The field of child development was now moving past the lifeless agenda of simply cataloguing skills and behaviors of children at various phases of their growth trajectories, or of recording "a day in the life of the child" from dawn to dusk (Wright, 1960). The theoretical debates of the 1960s and 1970s brought excitement and drama to the field and added value to the research that scholars were choosing to do.

But theoretic discourse has its limitations too, especially if it becomes detached from the problems and data that the theories are intended to explain. The developmental literature of the 1970s was full of fine nuanced discussions contrasting universalism to contextualism, or comparing Piaget with Vygotsky, or behaviorism with cognitive science, or making the cases for biological, environmental, and/or interactionist explanations of behavior; but it was hard to use the insights generated by these discussions to answer common questions such as: How does TV (or the then-new computer or video games) affect learning during childhood and adolescence? What kinds of friendships do youngsters benefit most from? Why do many youngsters gravitate towards anti-social and destructive behavior? Where do adolescents find the goals and motives that shape their life choices? What variations in family patterns across time and social context influence the perspectives of the young? Do young people today have different challenges than children of previous generations? These are the kinds of questions that people outside our field seek answers to. It seemed to me that a more problem-centered and less theoretically driven type of research was needed to address such questions.

Moreover, the use of highly charged social and political ideology to shape psychological theory seemed to me incommensurate with the goals of open-minded scientific inquiry. Nor, on the other hand, could a return to sterile empiricism serve a constructive purpose. What seemed apparent at the time was that the profound conceptual work that had gone into building and critiquing developmental theories could be mined for its potential for helping us to understand the common problems of growing up.

I was by no means the only researcher who made this observation at the time. In 1975, my old mentor Roger Brown announced in a textbook that he wrote (with Richard Herrnstein) that "the days of the grand theory are over" (Brown & Herrnstein, 1975). For my own work, I decided to go with topics that represented problems of interest that could be addressed by an approach informed by available conceptual distinctions but not bound to any one theoretical or ideological system. At the same time, I was assuming that grappling with such problems would inform theory-building, so that the benefits of such an enterprise would flow in two ways, from theory to problem and back again. This remains my goal. In this way, as in many other ways, my research has grown out of the intellectual landscape of our times, although it is also true that I have conducted it in my own way.

References

Boring, E. G. (1929). *A history of experimental psychology.* New York: Appleton-Century-Crofts.

Boring, E. G. (Ed.) (1930). *A history of psychology in autobiography,* Vol. 4. Worcester, MA: Clark University Press.

Boring, E. G., Eds. Watson, R. I., & Campbell, D. T. (1963). *History, Psychology, and Science: Selected papers of Edwin Boring.* Oxford, England: Wiley.

Brown, R., & Herrnstein, R. (1975). *Psychology.* Boston: Little, Brown.

Colby, A., & Damon, W. (1992). *Some do care: Contemporary lives of moral commitment.* New York: The Free Press.

Damon, W. (1977). *The social world of the child.* San Francisco: Jossey-Bass. (German translation, 1983; Japanese translation, 1988.)

Damon, W. (1980). Patterns of change in children's social reasoning: A two-year longitudinal study. *Child Development, 51,* 1010–1017.

Damon, W. (1983). *Social and personality development: Infancy through adolescence.* New York: W.W. Norton. (German translation, 1988; Japanese translation, 1990; Chinese translation, 1992.)

Damon, W. (1995). *Greater expectations: Overcoming the culture of indulgence in our homes and schools.* New York: The Free Press.

Damon, W. (1997). *The youth charter: How communities can work together to raise standards for all our children.* New York: The Free Press.

Damon, W. (Ed.) (1998). *Handbook of child psychology: The fifth edition* (Vols. 1–4). New York: John Wiley and Sons.

Damon, W. (2003). *Noble purpose.* Radnor, PA: Templeton Foundation Press.

Damon, W. (2004). *The moral advantage.* San Francisco: Berrett-Koehler.

Damon, W. (2008). *The path to purpose: How young people find their calling in life.* New York: The Free Press.

Damon, W. (2012). Failing Liberty 101. *Educational Leadership, 69*(7), 22–28.

Damon, W., & Colby, A. (In press). *The power of ideals.* New York: Oxford University Press.

Damon, W., & Hart, D. (1982). The development of self-understanding from infancy through adolescence. *Child Development, 53,* 841–864.

Damon, W., & Hart, D. (1988). *Self-understanding in childhood and adolescence.* New York: Cambridge University Press.

Damon, W., & Killen, M. (1982). Peer interaction and the process of change in children's moral reasoning. *Merrill-Palmer Quarterly, 28*(3), 347–367.

Damon, W., & Lerner, R. (Eds.). (2006). *Handbook of child psychology* (6th ed., Vols. 1–4). New York: John Wiley and Sons.

Damon, W., Menon, J. L., & Bronk, K. C. (2003). The Development of purpose during adolescence. *Journal of Applied Developmental Science, 7*(3), 119–128.

Damon, W., & Verducci, S. (Eds.). (2006). *Taking philanthropy seriously: Beyond noble intentions to responsible giving.* Bloomington: Indiana University Press.

Frankl, V. (1946). *Man's search for meaning.* New York: Harper & Co.

Gardner, H. (1972). *The quest for mind.* New York: Random House.

Gardner, H. (Ed.) (1987). *Responsibility at work: How leading professionals act (or don't act) responsibly.* San Francisco: Jossey-Bass.

Gardner, H., Csikszentmihalyi, M., & Damon, W. (2001). *Good work: When excellence and ethics meet.* New York: Basic Books. (German, Spanish, Chinese, Portuguese, Romanian translations, 2001–2005.)

Kohlberg, L. (1971). From is to ought: How to commit the naturalistic fallacy and get away with it in the study of moral development. In T. Mischel (Ed.), *Cognitive development and epistemology.* New York: Academic Press.

Kohlberg, L. (1976). The study of moral development. In T. Lickona (Ed.), *Moral development and behavior.* New York: Holt, Rinehart, and Winston.

Lively, W. J., & Bromley, D. B. (1973). *Person perception in childhood and adolescence.* London: Wiley.

Matsuba, K., King, P., & Bronk, K. (In press). *Exemplar methods and research.* San Francisco: Jossey-Bass.

Murphy, L. (1937). *Social behavior and child personality.* New York: Columbia University Press.

Piaget, J. (1926). *The language and thought of the child.* New York: Harcourt Brace & Company.

Simpson, E. L. (1974). Moral development research: A case study of scientific bias. *Human Development, 17,* 81–106.

Wright, H. (1960). Observational child study. In P. Mussen (Ed.), *Handbook of research methods in child development.* New York: John Wiley and Sons.

12

How Personal Experiences Influenced My Research on Youth

Sanford M. Dornbusch

My memories of my early childhood are few, probably a function of having too few happy moments. My lack of memories may also be a result of my family being poor and not having a camera. There are only a few photographs of me or of the rest of my family during my early years, so there never were occasions in which old photos initiated discussions of past persons or events.

My earliest memory is my lying on a bed, drinking tea from a baby bottle, which must have seemed a treat. I was very young, about three. The location was a small apartment behind my grandfather's kosher butcher shop in a poor Bronx neighborhood. My parents had separated, and my mother and I had moved in with her loving parents. My grandparents migrated in 1888 to New York City, coming from a part of the Austro-Hungarian empire that is now in Poland.

A little later in my childhood, I recall my mother, my father, and I were in a judge's chamber. There was great tension in the room. The judge asked me questions about my feelings toward each parent, and I remember acting distant toward my father. I believe that my mother had carefully trained me to use "he" or "him" when discussing my father with the judge. This memory always makes me feel ashamed. My mother gained full custody of me, but I was to visit my father every Sunday.

My mother remarried when I was about seven. My stepfather, the son of Russian Jewish immigrants, had a well-paid blue-collar job delivering thousands of German-language newspapers via a horse-drawn wagon. After her remarriage, we rented a small apartment in an almost-new apartment house in Yorkville, the center of the German-American community in New York City. All the other buildings on our block were old and shabby, and their residents were poor. My mother tried to discourage the friendships I made on the street. She

would make comments about the neighborhood children like, "Even if he's poor, he could at least be clean. He has dirty ears."

I always did well in elementary school, but I recall very little of the early years. For first grade, I went to a school in the Bronx, but I don't remember much about it, even though I learned to read. One memory is being punished by having to sit under the teacher's desk. I recall the punishment but not the crime. When we moved to Yorkville, I entered PS 6, reputedly the best public elementary school in New York City. Even today, I read that Manhattan residents pay higher rents to live within its catchment area. My wife and I recently worked out my age in each grade in each school. To my surprise, it appears that my family lived in Yorkville, and I was in PS 6, for only 1½ years.

I don't remember any of my teachers or the other students at PS 6. My lack of recall may be related to the short time I spent in each grade. Every half-year, I would be assigned to the next grade, so that I was 1½ years younger than my classmates when I left PS 6. I remember an adult at school showing me the number 192 on my school records, saying it was my IQ. I didn't know, and still don't know, if that was true, but I accepted that skipping classes was part of my fate. I didn't enjoy it.

As Hitler began his march across Europe, the residents of Yorkville had mixed reactions. Our neighborhood became the headquarters of the German-American Bund, a pro-Nazi organization. Many other German-Americans were outraged by Hitler's policies. Members of both groups felt they did not want to display their German roots to the American public. Accordingly, many stopped buying German-language newspapers, and that was the end of my stepfather's job.

Dissatisfied with himself, my stepfather often made negative comments about my performing well in school. "You know where China is, but you can't tie your shoelaces," was a typical remark. I don't recall being bothered much by such jibes, perhaps because I knew how hurt he was by his long periods of unemployment and low-paying jobs.

We could no longer afford to live in Manhattan, so my mother, stepfather, kid sister, and I joined the rest of my mother's close relatives in a shared walk-up apartment in a poor Bronx neighborhood. It was hardly luxury living. There were two bedrooms and one bath for ten people. A prostitute occupied the apartment below us, but most of the neighbors were hard-working Irish, Italians, and Jews who were unable to get a decent job during the depression.

My big problem was where to sleep. The solution brought its own difficulties. My uncle and I shared a double camp cot. The only empty floor space big enough for the open cot was in the vestibule in front of the door to the apartment. But my divorced aunt Lillian was beautiful and had too many dates. Many times she returned after midnight, knocking lightly on the door to awaken us. We opened the door, closed the cot, let Lillian in, opened the cot, and tried to get back to sleep.

Under the terms of the divorce, my father was to pay 15 dollars each month, and I was to spend each Sunday at his home. He usually paid the required amount, and we had a weekly visit until I was about 12 years old. My father remarried and had two daughters for whom I was "big brother."

Each Sunday passed pleasantly, but I hated these visits. Why? Both my mother and father grilled me about life in the other household, and I hated being used as a spy in the enemy's camp. When, for unknown reasons, my father stopped his payments around 1938, I felt relieved because I no longer had to visit him. In 1991, 53 years later, I helped create empirical research that showed the negative effects of being "Caught between Parents" on children of divorce (Buchanan, Maccoby, & Dornbusch, 1991, 1996).

The public school associated with this poor neighborhood, PS 53, had a heterogeneous group of students and very capable teachers, all female and almost all Irish. Their high quality was a product of gender discrimination. Today, the females recruited into teaching may be far less talented, for women now have increased opportunities to enter more prestigious and higher paying occupations.

One friend at that school left a lasting impression. Red was a handsome Irish lad, about 15 years old while in 7th grade, who had been "left back" several times. He was tall and burly, looking like a man among children. Though I was only 10 years old, we liked each other. Red had a sweet personality, enjoying life and not concerned about his school performance. I was surprised by his solid practical intelligence. Perhaps my research on inappropriate tracking in schools had its origin in my puzzlement about the discrepancy between Red's abilities and his school performance (Dornbusch, 1994; Dornbusch, Glasgow, & Lin, 1996).

I know so little about a couple I adored, my mother's parents. Even though I lived with them for much of my childhood, I can't answer simple questions about their early life and marriage. They were happy to live in America and seldom reminisced about "the old country." My mother and her siblings were intent on assimilating to the American way of life, and they had no interest in the foreign background of their parents. Unfortunately, I was too young to appreciate the importance of understanding the background of the "old folks at home."

My grandparents' friends were all Jewish, but they remained appreciative of the American ability to incorporate diverse groups. When someone behaved badly, they were quick to say that there were good people and bad people among both Jews and *goyim* (non-Jews). I heard more negative ethnic and religious comments from my parents and their generation than I heard from my grandparents. They acknowledged their identity and history as Jews, but they didn't believe most Jewish religious doctrines.

Grandma and Grandpa were a happy couple and proud of their offspring. Since they were happy, this suggests that their children should have been more likely to make happy marriages. But their four children had eight marriages and only three offspring. What had gone wrong? I believe that my grandparents were too permissive as parents, so aware of their own status as "greenhorns" in their new America that they felt unsure as to the boundaries of behavior for young Americans. Their children lied to them about the usual standards for parental control, and they believed what they were told. Many decades later, I did research that showed the negative effects of permissive parenting (Dornbusch et al., 1985).

All the adults in our extended family expressed unstinting affection for all three offspring. Each child was viewed as wonderful in some ways. The evaluations of me as a student were high. I simultaneously felt confident in general and yet thought it unlikely that I could fulfill the family's grandiose dreams. I also knew that the members of this tight family group had few resources to help the next generation. For example, no member of my family had ever finished high school; my uncle had started high school, but he quit in order to be able to afford dating. My mother had been a good student, but she went to work after finishing eighth grade. My stepfather had completed only fourth grade.

At age 12, I enrolled in an extraordinary high school, Townsend Harris. Opened in 1840, it was the first public high school in New York City. It was the precursor of the City College of New York. Unlike teachers in other high schools in the city, Townsend Harris teachers were part of that college's faculty and paid more than teachers in the regular high-school system.

Admission was based solely on performance on a competitive test among students nominated by their elementary school. It was an all-male school, accepting 200 boys each semester. (Hunter High School was a comparable school for girls.) My elementary school selected three boys to take the entrance exam. When the other two students, whom I considered outstanding, were rejected, I realized how selective this school was and was surprised that I had been accepted.

All students at that school finished a 4-year curriculum in 3 years, and all took college-prep courses. Admission to City College of New York was guaranteed for all Townsend Harris graduates. Students had only a few course choices to make, such as the language they would take for 3 years and the language they would take for 2 years. I chose French and Spanish. During my later years at Townsend Harris, I learned that Latin was the language of choice for the boys from higher-status families.

I soon discovered that I was just an average Townsend Harris student. The numerous brilliant students made me feel relatively inadequate. What a change from my elementary school experience! At Townsend Harris I was an ordinary student, averaging a grade of 85 and graduating with no awards for anything. My academic self-esteem suffered a bit, but my teachers were usually excellent and taught me a lot. It was good for my soul that I was not at all special in this environment.

Because of my family's lack of education, when I had an academic problem, I was on my own. For example, I got a C in my first French course before I became aware that the gender of each French noun was important.

My high-school course in plane geometry was nearly a disaster. I got 53 on the midterm, a clear failure. Until then, I had never come close to failing a course. I am proud of the way I reacted: I tried to analyze what had gone wrong and develop a scheme for improvement. Plane geometry, I realized, consisted of a series of logical deductions, with later theorems proven by the use of earlier theorems and propositions.

Twice each day I traveled on the subway for 45 minutes to and from school. I decided to use that travel time for a simple remedial program. Let's say that, after the midterm, the class was assigned lesson 25. I would study lessons 1 and 25 on the subway that day. Continuing that pattern, I would do lessons 2 and 26 on the next day, and so on. I don't remember my final grade, but I think it was a low B. I do recall what was more important to me: my teacher's telling me that my improvement was impressive, even shocking.

Although that effort paid off handsomely, I did not always work hard for the rest of my life. Still, I did learn the importance of effort as a potential strategy. Other people say they learned from their mistakes. My wife, Barbara, says I learned from my improvement. My later research used effort-engagement behaviors, rather than self-assessment of effort, as a key factor in explaining academic performance in high school (Dornbusch, 1974; Massey, Scott, & Dornbusch, 1975).

In 1940, my family's economic situation improved, and we moved to a middle-class area in the Bronx. Previously, ten family members had occupied an apartment with two bedrooms and one bath. Now, in comparative luxury, we had seven family members in a three-bedroom, two-bath apartment.

I was 14, and I knew only one person in the new neighborhood: a Townsend Harris classmate. Yet, the situation changed rapidly. I would soon be meeting dozens of acquaintances every afternoon and evening at "the steps."

The steps were built to provide a way for pedestrians to walk up a steep incline to the Grand Concourse, the central boulevard of the Bronx. The area at the base of the steps was more than adequate for the daily gathering of some 80 to 100 youths.

There were subgroups within that mass of young people. I belonged to a clique of eight adolescents, the youngest in that clique. We were all good students. The age range was 3 years in our clique and 10 years in the larger group. The loiterers around the steps were never violent and were ethnically homogeneous. Almost everyone was Jewish, though, surprisingly, my first kiss was with a Catholic girl. Seldom did we arrange to meet. There were enough of us in both the larger group and our clique so that every afternoon and evening found some friends eager to discuss the news or to engage in horseplay.

In 1940, when I reached 14, the minimum age for employment, I sought work during the summer. My first job was delivering hats. A friend from Townsend Harris had learned that a large firm, Lowenstein and Co., needed delivery boys during a busy 2-week period. Since we both were breathing, we were hired. We were paid 30 cents an hour, the minimum wage during the depression. The work was easy, though always awkward and uncomfortable. After 2 weeks, we were fired.

I next worked in a large room packed with thousands of cheap dresses hung on three levels of scaffolding. I was one of three or four young men who would retrieve the dresses required for each order. We scampered like monkeys onto the metal support structures. I was slightly frightened every minute that I spent on the scaffolding. When the number of orders declined and I was fired, I was relieved.

When I was 15, now a high-school graduate, I went to an employment agency. A camera shop wanted a young clerk whom they would train. No experience was necessary. I was hired, but not for long. I knew nothing about cameras or film. After 2 days the manager explained that she expected a lack of experience, but I exhibited an unbelievable level of ignorance about photography.

Next, I served as a salesman in a large clothing store. My assignment was to sell boy's clothing. Never a clotheshorse, I tried hard to learn the basics. Most of the clerks were mature women, and they were extremely kind to me.

At the end of 2 weeks, the manager of the store called me in for an assessment. "You will hate me for this, but you are fired. I'm going to tell you why I'm firing you, and you will be upset. But years from now you will remember me and think what a nice man. For you are a terrible salesman, and, though you try hard and we all like you, you should avoid any job that requires salesmanship." I now think of him as a nice man.

At 16, unable to get and hold a job, I took some free college courses at CCNY during the period when I was too young to enlist. My family and I assumed that I would end up a businessman, so I took mostly business-related courses. An enjoyable course was an introduction to accounting. During its last meeting, a fellow student asked me, "What grade did you get?" "An A," I replied. "How would you like a job that pays 55 cents an hour?" Wow, a job at almost double the minimum wage (which had been my maximum wage to date)! How could I refuse?

During the depression, the position of junior accountant was coveted. A young man (few women then) who aspired to the status of Certified Public Accountant (CPA) had to serve an apprenticeship of 4 to 6 years under a CPA before taking the grueling test for admission to the guild of accountants. With business poor during the depression, a typical CPA had no need to hire additional junior accountants. Accordingly, during the depression, junior accountants secretly paid the CPA for the privilege of getting the needed experience.

It was now 1942, and the supply of junior accountants had suddenly disappeared. The military draft had created a shortage of young men in this occupation. The son of Morris B. Newman, CPA, was my classmate and a roving talent scout. I informed him of my eager acceptance, but I reminded him of my complete ignorance of real-life accounting. "No problem," he responded. "We'll always have an experienced accountant at the other end of the phone line. He'll answer every question."

The job was fun. Sometimes, when I asked a particularly stupid question, my telephonic advisor called me an idiot, but the number of my phone calls steadily decreased. I had about ten accounts to serve, nine of them small enterprises. My job was easy; I was usually doing simple bookkeeping.

My largest account was M. Bernstein and Co. "M" stood for Minnie, the wife of the owner-manager. He had been bankrupt too often, and all assets were in her name. Minnie's brother was the assistant manager, and he did most of the work. The company did dyeing and blending of furs and had about 15 employees.

At the end of M. Bernstein's fiscal year, I did a trial balance. The result shocked me. "How was business this year?" I asked the boss. He replied, "Terrible. Nobody liked our designs and blends." At this point, I announced the result of the trial balance. The company had made an enormous profit because their swollen inventory had doubled and tripled in value. The war had turned their poor sales performance into a shrewd investment. . The company's profit for the year was over $200,000, the equivalent today of about $3,000,000. The company immediately closed for the rest of the day.

Champagne was served to all. I concluded that, if there is a positive correlation between virtue and reward in this world, it must be remarkably low.

I had graduated from Townsend Harris High School in 1941, at age 15. Most of my male friends and acquaintances were 17 to 20, and soon almost all were drafted or had enlisted. When, on June 5, 1943, I celebrated my 17th birthday, I investigated various ways to enlist. I passed a test, got my crying mother to sign my enlistment papers, and joined the Army. I served in the Army for 1 year; then

I was in the Coast Guard for a year (Dornbusch, 1955); and I spent my third year in the Navy.

The story of my multi-service years is too complex to explain here. One feature of those years was the opportunity to meet and live with a remarkably diverse set of Americans. One who made me aware of the diversity of educational standards introduced himself to me as "Joseph Kendall Carr from Helper, Utah." This sailor at Navy Pier in Chicago was charming, full of life, eager for new experiences, witty, and funny. Yet, he was doing poorly in the elementary radio class that we were both taking. How could a guy who was that smart be unable to pass our weekly tests?

I don't remember how I broached the subject, but I did explain that I was startled by such low grades for a friend who was obviously so bright. He showed no reticence in answering me. "I can hardly read. I've never read a book in my life." He explained that in Helper, Utah, almost every male became a coal miner. The local schools didn't try to teach much to the students, and everybody was like him: fairly happy, a good worker, and unconcerned about the rest of the world.

Joseph Kendall Carr had passed the Navy's test for radar training, but the homework assignments were beyond him. Each day we had to read at least five or six pages in our textbook. Reading that much took him so long that he couldn't finish the required exercises. I volunteered to read the assignments to him, pretending that it wouldn't take me much additional time. Within a few days, he was passing the course.

My last meeting with Joseph Kendall Carr was so sad that I almost cry when recalling it. We were being transferred to different naval bases, and we would never meet again. He expressed pleasure at our brief friendship, but he also expressed a melancholy vision of his destiny. He said that he now knew why he was missing many of life's opportunities.

A second incident shocked me. During the war, I learned that many American schools had similarly low academic standards. One result was a widespread negative attitude towards reading and books. Since reading had been the source of my vicarious experiences during a difficult childhood and adolescence, reading was a central activity for me during my time in the armed forces. I read a lot; I read a wide variety of books; and I read fast. It seemed strange to me to be with intelligent soldiers and sailors who were not readers.

When I was stationed at Treasure Island in San Francisco Bay, I learned that my reading of books had a surprising interpretation. Like most sailors with liberty in San Francisco, I tried to meet some young females. One weekend I was extremely lucky. I somehow managed to find two attractive young women to join me for some pleasant hours in downtown San Francisco. We met several sailors from my outfit in the course of the evening.

I took the water taxi back to Treasure Island and got ready for bed. I was unpleasantly surprised when a couple of sailors truculently inquired as to what I had been doing with those two girls. I didn't think it was any of their business, but I responded mildly that we had had a good time together. Then they shocked me by asking, "But aren't you a homo?"

"No," I responded. "I like girls. What made you think I was a homo?"

"Well, several people have noticed that you have books in the bottom of your sea bag."

"That's because I like to read books," I explained. "When I ship out, I like to carry some of my favorite books with me."

Now that I was known to be heterosexual, I was able to overhear conversations within my unit about attacking and robbing homosexuals. This tactic was presented as a legitimate way to overcome a weekend shortage of cash. I said that I thought it was wrong to do this, but several sailors made it clear that, to them, homosexuals were not human. Some sailors told me I was a "weirdo" for both reading books and defending the rights of "queers."

After the war, I went to Syracuse University with the financial support of the G.I. Bill. Forced to choose a major while still in the Navy, my naïve choice of sociology was based on an error: I had read an interesting book, *The Making of Society*, in the Navy library and mistakenly thought it was a sociology text. I learned later that it was predominantly about anthropology. I was lucky, for I don't like to camp.

I was allowed to take one advanced sociology course in my first semester at Syracuse. I chose Primary Group Relations, a social psychology course taught by Robert E. L. Faris. The class was crowded, as were most courses. Faris was earnest and organized, but most of the students did not pay attention to his lectures. He spoke in a quiet monotone, seldom raising his voice, and he simply read his notes aloud for most of each hour. Seldom did he look up, which kept him from noticing that many of the students were reading books and newspapers or doing their homework.

I hated to accept this disappointing situation as normal, for I wanted to enjoy my major, or at least to learn something about it. Therefore, I moved my chair nearer to Faris's desk, so close that I could hear even a low mumble. That move changed my life. I took careful notes, and, when I read them later that evening, my attitude towards Faris changed. The material of the course was carefully organized and some of it was fascinating.

Halfway through the semester, Faris administered a midterm examination. It was a difficult essay exam, requiring the student to apply various aspects of the course to diverse situations. I got a 92 on that test and, in retrospect, it became the most important high grade I ever received. The next highest grade among my classmates was 59, which made my performance seem spectacular to Faris. Of course, the main reason for my being an outlier was that I often was the only student listening attentively to the lecture.

Bob Faris asked me to visit him during his next office hour. When he asked me my major, he was thrilled by my response. From that moment on, I had a helmsman for my career. He explained to me that I needed to prepare for graduate work in sociology. This was an unpleasant new thought. If I had known that graduate school was necessary, I would have selected some other career, such as law. Now I was on the road to an unexpected PhD degree. Looking back, I now wonder what future career I was contemplating. I had never wanted to be a social worker, so I must have had only a vague daydream about using sociology in some other occupation.

Faris immediately gave me the level of financial support that a star football player would receive, while simultaneously providing a speedy introduction to the role of a university teacher. He appointed me his teaching assistant. In addition, whenever he took a trip to an academic meeting, he would ask me to teach his classes and would pay me his salary as an associate professor for each day that I substituted for him. Sometimes I had to teach my fellow-students in a class I was taking, but my classmates were kind and gently teased me about my teaching performance.

When it was time for me to apply for graduate training in sociology, I naturally asked Bob's advice on where to send my application. His reply was, "Harvard, Chicago, Yale, and Columbia." I was unnerved by this all-star list and asked, "What school should be my fallback option?" Bob told me to forget about any fallback. I was shocked when all four schools accepted me. I decided to attend Chicago because Bob had studied there. Later, I understood why I was accepted by all those elite graduate schools. I didn't realize at the time that Bob Faris was a well-known sociologist, eventually elected President of the American Sociological Association, and that his glowing letter of recommendation opened all doors.

When I arrived at the University of Chicago, the rules for graduate students gave me the wrong incentives. In graduate courses, the main assignment and basis for grading was usually a term paper on a topic related to the course. There was no pressure to turn in the required paper at the end of the quarter. Indeed, faculty could not penalize students for late papers. If a grad student turned in the paper within 18 months, no penalty was exacted. But if the paper was one day or more beyond the 18-month deadline, the student flunked. Seldom did I finish a term paper in the quarter in which I was enrolled, and almost never was an incomplete paper handed in days before the statutory deadline.

I operated on the principle of the cornered rat. For 17 months after the end of each course, I would feel occasional anxiety and do no work. In the 18th month, I would think a bit about what I should write, but I postponed actual writing until the last few days before the F grade would be guaranteed. When I began to be serious, I would do nothing but work on the paper, often getting no sleep for 2 days. At the end of 2 or 3 days, I would finish, turn in the paper, and usually get an A. I hated the way I had behaved: long-term concern about the missing paper and a few frantic days of enormous tension. Yet, after each bout of painful self-assessment, I would continue the same pattern of lengthy delay and short-term hyperactivity.

In 1950, towards the end of my second year of graduate work at the University of Chicago, two major events occurred. One, on February 28, 1950, was my marriage to Barbara Farnham (whom I called "Red") on the third anniversary of our first meeting at Syracuse. The date was chosen for romantic reasons, but I spoiled things for her by noting the convenience of having to remember only one date.

There was a special moment in the wedding service when I was supposed to answer, "I do." I couldn't get any sound out. Perhaps the memory of my family's unhappy marriages had frightened me. At last, after a long pause, I managed to throatily whisper the magic words. They did dramatically change many aspects of my life, and some improvements came almost immediately.

I had started at Chicago in April 1948, and I had accomplished little before Barbara and I were married. I had finished only a few courses, had incompletes in many, and had just started my master's thesis. Marriage changed everything. I couldn't continue to loaf along, finding pleasurable alternatives to working on my thesis.

When I worked on my MA thesis and, later, my PhD dissertation, my task was made much easier by Barbara's presence. There were long hours of boring data analysis, and she just assumed that we would immediately do the necessary work together. All my habits of procrastination were broken (at least temporarily) by her calm acceptance that our efforts would be successful.

Thanks to Barbara's willingness to do thousands of divisions on the slow mechanical calculators we rented, we finished the work for my MA thesis and PhD dissertation. Both were on demographic topics. (Our months of calculations would today take less than a minute on a small computer.) Barbara always was willing to work, and her example shamed me into resisting the pleasant temptations of everyday life. She just assumed that I was a dedicated student, and she made me into one.

The second major event of 1950 was the strange route by which I got most of the money needed to stay in graduate school. My 3 years of support on the G.I. Bill were about to end. I desperately needed financial assistance, for the federal government would no longer pay my tuition, and there would be no monthly check of $110 for living expenses. Could I win a fellowship from my department? The answer was almost certainly negative. The Sociology Department was swollen with returning veterans, and there were only two fellowships for the entire group of two hundred graduate students. Nevertheless, though I knew my chance was slim, I applied for a University Fellowship.

One day our mail contained a one-page letter from the University of Chicago. Barbara and I were pleased when we read the first word, "Congratulations." As we read on, we were puzzled to learn that I had been appointed an Honorary University Fellow. What did that mean? The form on the reverse side of the letter listed my salary. I would be paid the number of dollars that was inserted into a blank space. Typed into that spot was a big, fat zero. Adding to our pain, the letter noted that I must promise to take no paid employment during the year of my fellowship. Nothing made any sense.

I raced to the Sociology office, looking for an explanation. The long–time secretary of the Department, a friend, knew all the departmental secrets. The faculty had agreed that I had done very well and probably deserved a fellowship, but there was no money left for me. Therefore, I would get an honorary fellowship. To keep me from starving, the Department informally instructed Professor Phil Hauser, former head of the United States Census, to create a job for me. He ran the Chicago Community Inventory, the University's center for demographic research. The hours of employment were to fit my academic schedule.

My duties as a research assistant at the Community Inventory were predominantly number crunching. Hour after hour I worked on calculators, manipulating data from the diverse communities that constituted the Chicago Metropolitan Area. The work was boring, but I developed familiarity with the various indicators of life in an urban area. We developed measures of age distributions, incomes, rents, educational levels, voting patterns, and other social statistics for each of the 75 community areas into which Chicago was divided.

Punching all those data into the calculator was laborious and seldom interesting. Yet, unknown to me, I learned a lot. So much information from the Census passed through my fingers that I developed a "feel" for results that were reasonable or extremely unlikely. I became able to spot my own errors in transcription. In later years, I was usually right when I said to my student and faculty collaborators, "I don't believe it. Let's do it over."

Each year at Chicago, Bob Faris wrote me and asked how I was doing. Each year I wrote him a truthful report about my difficulties in getting work done and my occasional successes. Near the end of my fourth year, as I was finishing my dissertation, I received only one job offer, a 1-year post as an acting assistant professor of sociology. Since I had not applied for the job nor been interviewed, I knew the basis for the offer. The letter came from the University of Washington in Seattle, a school that had recently hired Bob Faris as Professor of Sociology.

That year was 1952, long before "affirmative action" became a controversial standard for admitting students and hiring faculty. I was one of the many beneficiaries of an older recruitment device, "the old boys' network."

My wife and I loved our 2 years at Washington. The collegial atmosphere was great. I got the lowest salary of any faculty member in the entire University, and my acting appointment guaranteed nothing beyond the academic year. Yet, I wasn't worried. I wrote an elementary statistics book to get out of debt, had three research papers accepted, and received the highest possible teaching rating from my students. My faculty colleagues were very friendly, and I started a breakfast colloquium at which the graduate students and all the younger sociology faculty exchanged research ideas. Washington would surely want to keep me. If not, I felt I could always get another job (perhaps at a better salary).

Frank Miyamoto, an associate professor, and I collaborated on a small research grant of $400. We were studying empathy, and our project produced untrustworthy results. One morning, I thought of another way to use our data. In one day, we produced the first statistical study of the symbolic Interaction approach to the development of the self-concept (Miyamoto & Dornbusch, 1956). That trailblazing article got Frank promoted, and he later became dean of the liberal arts college at Washington.

In September 1954, I took a 1-year leave from the University of Washington to be one of the 36 Fellows at the newly established Center for Advanced Study in the Behavioral Sciences. At our first formal meeting, we sat in a large circle as each Fellow described his or her research ideas. I reported my dreams and then listened to my colleagues. When it was Al Hastorf's turn, he said, "I'll be working with Sandy Dornbusch. We have similar interests." I recall my internal reaction: "I don't even know this guy. He has his nerve, saying we will work together." We then spent the next 5 years on a joint research project and became friends and allies at Stanford for 45 years.

Near the end of the academic year at the Center, I received an offer to teach at Harvard as an Assistant Professor of Social Relations. Clyde Kluckhohn, a famous anthropologist who was a Fellow at the Center, had reported to his Harvard department that they should offer me the post. With no discussion, no interview, and no competition, the official offer arrived in the mail. Barbara and I had been poor but happy at Washington, and we wanted to return to that place where we had delightful friends and colleagues. Therefore, we were inclined to refuse this offer from America's most prestigious university.

Bob Faris, my mentor at Syracuse and Washington, phoned us his appraisal of the situation. He thought this was a fine opportunity for me, and he believed I should accept. The decision to leave Washington need not be final. The Department of Sociology at Washington would write me, promising that they would try to bring me back whenever I expressed a desire to return. With that informal guarantee in hand, Barbara and I decided to move to Harvard and assess the situation towards the end of each academic year.

We were not contented at Harvard. I was in charge of the only required course in Social Relations, an interdisciplinary introduction to methodology. I loved the course and my teaching colleagues, and the students appreciated our successful efforts to produce an interactive laboratory course. But that was the only collaborative venture at Harvard in which I participated. At the end of the first year, I said I was going to resign, and Social Relations

gave me a sabbatical to stay. At the end of the second year, Social Relations provided me with $20,000 for my research. Towards the end of my third year, I was told that the Department had run out of resources.

So, after 3 years at Harvard, I accepted the University of Washington's open invitation to come back as an associate professor. I drove our heavily loaded car to Seattle in September 1958, while Barbara flew with our two young sons. I met her at the airport, where she poured out her tale of the difficulties of flying with two young children. At that magical moment, I told her that I had just received an offer to become head of Stanford's new sociology department. It took about 30 seconds for us to agree that we were not going to move again so soon.

That immediate rejection was easy. We saw little reason to go to Stanford, whose two fine professors, Dick Lapiere and Paul Wallin, could not match the size and distinction of Washington's fifth-ranked Sociology Department. Of course, the horrors of moving were part of our current experience and played a supporting role in our decision.

The background of my move to Stanford provides an example of the difficulties Stanford faced in its recruitment efforts. I knew in 1958 that I was far from Stanford's first choice for head of Sociology. But it was not until many years later, while reading the files of Provost Terman, that I learned that I was Stanford's 14th choice. How did Stanford have to stoop so low as to end with me? And why was recruiting even me so difficult?

A committee sponsored by the Ford Foundation had suggested the breakup of Stanford's joint department of anthropology and sociology. Over a couple of years, 13 sociologists of some distinction were asked if they were interested in leading the new sociology department. All were over 40 and had tenure at good institutions. Almost all rejected early "feelers." A professorship at Stanford was simply not very attractive in those days. A somewhat desperate faculty committee, drawn from various departments, decided to invite a younger candidate, and, at age 32, I had been their choice.

Some months after I had rejected their offer, I visited Stanford for a meeting with Al Hastorf, the Dartmouth psychologist who had collaborated with me since our Center days. He was visiting Stanford on a 1-year fellowship. The Stanford Sociology Department learned that I was coming and asked me to talk about my research. I always accept such invitations. I did not know that the entire Sociology search committee was in the audience. To my pleasure and theirs, I gave a better-than-usual lecture. The next day I was told that the search committee's message to Dean Rhinelander was simply, "Get that kid."

I resolved to help the Stanford department even as I once again rejected the job. My intent was to soften administrative resistance to the future demands of the next potential leader. When I finally met with Dean Rhinelander, I handed him a list of 16 departmental needs. They ranged from increased library funds to support for trips to conventions, and from the appointment of four additional faculty to the building of research facilities. He read them in a couple of minutes and shocked me by saying, "Anything else?" That night, over the phone, Barbara and I decided to accept Stanford's offer.

Al Hastorf next influenced my life after he had also joined the Stanford faculty and we continued our joint work on social perception (Dornbusch, Hastorf, Richardson, Muzzy, & Vreeland, 1965). After serving as head of the Psychology Department, he was named Director of the new Boys Town Center for the Study of Youth Development. Al sought to create at Stanford a critical mass of researchers on adolescence. He immediately offered numerous faculty the money to pay for at least one research assistant. The only requirement was attendance at the Center's weekly research seminar. I said I couldn't accept the money—I had no interest in adolescent development. Al's response was, "I know you, Sandy. You'll feel guilty and search around for a research topic. I'm not worried. The money will bring you and others around."

Al's strategy worked. Soon, 25 diverse Stanford faculty from Education, Law, Medicine, and Humanities and Sciences were attending Al's seminar, collaborating across disciplinary lines, and providing constructive criticism. Within 2 years, Stanford was a major center for research on youth. That is how I got started on a program of research on adolescence, leading eventually to my being the first non-psychologist elected President of the Society for Research on Adolescence.

My first research topic at the Boys Town Center was not exciting: adolescent bed-wetting. Toby Gross, a professor of pediatrics, asked me to help her analyze data on enuresis in the National Health Examination Survey. We eventually published our research in a form accessible to pediatricians (Gross & Dornbusch, 1979, 1983). That early work led to considerable research on identifying early and late sexual maturation (Hammer, Kraemer, Wilson, Ritter, & Dornbusch, 1991), and the relation of sexual maturation to dating (Dornbusch et al., 1981, 1984b). We also wrote so many papers on growth, sexual maturation, and educational issues that we published a summary of our findings (Dornbusch, Gross, Duncan, & Ritter, 1987).

Finally, in a moment of pleasurable inspiration, I thought of using Thorstein Veblen's ideas in his 1899 book, *Theory of the Leisure Class*, to generate hypotheses that would help explain social class and gender differences in the desire to be thin among American adolescents. I used national data on sexual maturation and weight, and Veblen's ideas were strongly supported (Dornbusch et al., 1984a).

During much of the same period, I was doing research on the organization of public schools. I did not begin the pursuit of this topic because of a concern for the welfare of children. Instead, I studied schools because I couldn't gain access to post offices. Dick Scott and I were writing a book on evaluation processes in organizations (Dornbusch & Scott, 1975). To our pleasure, the five diverse organizations we were studying all produced findings in accord with our overarching theory. We then wanted to apply our theory to an organization whose structure was repeated in many branches. The best example we could think of was the United States Post Office, which had branch offices of varying size and complexity in heterogeneous communities.

I flew to Washington to discuss our project with the research director for the United States Postal Service. His response was short and not favorable. He reported to me that the Postal Service, the postal workers' unions, and the appropriate congressional committees all agreed that there was to be no research on personnel or personnel practices. Any attempt to study the operations of the post office would immediately lead to a strike. We shifted our attention to public schools.

The funds for our research on schools from 1968 to 1979 came from the Stanford Center for Research and Development in Teaching and Learning, where I was a research associate. Bob Bush, head of the Center, controlled the allocation of funds and loved our work. He permitted our wide-ranging efforts. Perhaps our central finding was the low frequency of evaluations of schoolteachers. They performed their tasks with such infrequent evaluations that they were dissatisfied with the evaluation process. Indeed, receiving negative evaluations from principals did not upset teachers. At least the principals were looking at the quality of the teacher's performances. To save space, I will note that I wrote some general papers that summarized our research on schools (Dornbusch, Glasgow, & Lin, 1996; Dornbusch & Kaufman, 2002).

We studied evaluation processes within schools, at first only the evaluation of teachers and principals. As I turned my attention to adolescent students, I again focused on processes rather than statuses. In particular, I wanted to understand the processes that led to divergent academic performances among ethnic groups and social classes. Sociologists tend to emphasize status differences, but I do not find such studies personally satisfying. I prefer processes as the subject of interest because they are more likely to be subject to change and directly affected by interventions. Thus, I preferred to study processes influencing the level of student effort rather than differences in income or community characteristics.

The first process that I studied among adolescents was family decision-making. While working on issues related to sexual maturation, I noticed that the National Health Examination Survey had excellent data on the relative influence of parents and adolescent in making various decisions of importance to the youth. After I worked with these data for a few months, I became convinced that they provided an excellent window into family processes as they affected the adolescent. To the best of my knowledge, no one had ever used the decision-making data collected by the government on a national sample of adolescents. What a waste!

We had information that characterized each of five areas of decision-making for each youth into Youth

Alone, Parent Alone, or Joint. Since American parents are aware that parental control must diminish as their child approaches adulthood, it is not surprising that Youth Alone decision-making increases as the adolescent gets older. In similar fashion, Parent Alone decision-making declines as youths age. Joint decision-making appeared in-between, as Parent Alone was reduced and Youth Alone gradually increased. Since we had thousands of adolescents in our sample, we calculated mean scores for adolescents of a specific age in months. Then we compared each adolescent's score with the mean for his or her age group, providing a measure of how relatively high or low the score was within adolescents of the same age and gender.

The results of these analyses provided strong support for the view that early Youth Alone decision-making was associated with poor school performance and deviance among adolescents. Much of the poor adjustment of adolescents from single-parent households was explained by the too early granting of autonomy by single parents. The single parent's lack of resources for monitoring the adolescent and desire that the youth learn early to be responsible are understandable bases for high Youth Alone scores. Yet, the negative results on adolescent functioning make this a dangerous strategy used too often by single parent households (Dornbusch et al., 1985; Dornbusch & Gray, 1988; Dornbusch, Herman, & Lin,1996; Dornbusch, Ritter, Mont-Reynaud, & Chen, 1990; Lamborn, Dornbusch, & Steinberg, 1996).

The Spencer Foundation supported my research program. As I started to publish my findings, Larry Steinberg and Brad Brown, both at the University of Wisconsin, found their research moving in a similar direction. They were funded by the National Institute of Mental Health. They proposed that we merge our two projects after getting approval from both sponsors. Everyone agreed, and the results were more than harmonious. I learned an enormous amount from my collaborators, especially from Larry. He had devoted his entire career to the study of adolescence, and he was both a colleague and a teacher to me. I was older (but not wiser), and I was also a comparative newcomer to the field.

As our joint efforts produced a succession of interesting papers on various family processes, I gave a presentation on our findings to a group of behavioral scientists at Stanford. I was displeased when Dick Scott, friend and collaborator, responded that I was reporting too many results. There must be, he said, a simpler way to summarize these processes. I was even more upset when I realized that he was right: I could think of a framework that included much of our research effort.

Diana Baumrind had developed an approach in terms of parenting styles. Her careful qualitative studies of the parenting of a relatively small number of young children produced a typology of parenting: permissive, authoritarian, and authoritative (Baumrind, 1978). When we applied it to our large-scale quantitative studies of thousands of high school students, we found that her typology explained much of adolescent educational achievement and deviance (Dornbusch, Ritter, Leiderman, Roberts, & Fraleigh, 1987). In California, there were so many permissive parents that we split them into two groups, indulgent parents (like my grandparents) and neglectful parents (Steinberg, Lamborn, Darling, Mounts, & Dornbusch, 1994).

We also used the typology to examine ethnic differences in achievement, since we had thousands of adolescents in our sample. Indeed, one of our ethnic analyses showed both the strength of Baumrind's typology and its limitations. We expected authoritative parenting to produce higher grades among adolescents than the other parenting styles. This was true in general. But was it true for all ethnic groups? We quickly observed a possible exception. Asian students, who did best in school among our four ethnic groups, came predominantly from families that were authoritarian in parenting style. Was authoritarian parenting of adolescents more effective than authoritative parenting among Asians?

No. Authoritative parenting, though infrequent, was the most successful style among Asians, with permissive parenting the worst style. These results were the same within each of the four ethnic groups (Steinberg, Dornbusch, & Brown,1992). The fine performance of most Asian students did not constitute a failure of Baumrind's typology; rather, it showed that other forces outside our model, probably cultural, were helping Asian academic achievement.

We published numerous papers on various topics related to Baurmrind's parenting styles. Examples of such topics included parental involvement in schooling (Steinberg, Lamborn, Dornbusch, & Darling, 1992), adolescent competence and adjustment (Lamborn, Mounts, Steinberg, & Dornbusch, 1991), and educational achievement (Dornbusch & Wood, 1990).

After our successful use of Baumrind's typology, I was invited to speak at a psychology convention at which Diana Baumrind was to be honored. When I gave my speech, she was more annoyed than pleased. I could understand her displeasure—she had worked so hard to develop careful measurements of the children in her relatively small sample, and we used quick-and-dirty methods to analyze questionnaires from thousands of adolescent students. I hope she eventually forgave us.

We cannot burden this autobiographical chapter with details of other types of studies I did on adolescents. I will, instead, briefly mention some research that indicates the extent to which I branched out to other aspects of the adolescent experience.

First, our studies of adolescent schooling led to publications intended to help schools and parents intervene to help students. The most general work is *Beyond the Classroom* (Steinberg, Brown, & Dornbusch, 1996). The emphasis in that book is on parents and peers, and on their influence on adolescent behavior in the classroom and after school hours.

Other papers were specifically designed to help home-school collaboration (Dornbusch, 1986: Dornbusch & Ritter, 1992). A paper on the same general topic (Dornbusch

& Ritter, 1988) received in 1989 the Distinguished Achievement Award of the Educational Press Association of America.

A Stanford undergraduate, Kristan Glasgow, applied some of our ideas to the issue of gender differences in mathematics performance. We were impressed by her work. We collaborated for several years and finally published a paper applying her attributional approach to our data. Her impressive finding was that female adolescents were more likely than males to attribute a poor performance in math to a lack of ability, not lack of effort. They did this in no other subject, and males attributed failure in all high school subjects primarily to lack of effort. This gender difference in attributions for failure in math helps explain the tendency for many females to avoid continuing contact with math courses and with occupations that continually use mathematics (Glasgow, Dornbusch, Troyer, Steinberg, & Ritter, 1997).

Sometimes the influences that shaped my research were unexpected. A Catholic researcher on adolescence approached me with the news that a Catholic archbishop loved my research. I had been doing research on adolescent moral choices (Dornbusch, 1987). Would I join him in examining the influence of Church, family and peers on moral decision-making among Catholic youngsters? Of course, I replied.

The results of the application of previous results to Catholic adolescents were mutually supportive. The perceived evaluations of particular moral choices by Church and by parents had little impact on the moral decisions of Catholic adolescents. The number of years of education in Catholic schools had no effect. Peer influences shaped the moral choices.

Yet, there was one surprising result. Catholic youths said that the evaluations of their parents were far more important to them than the evaluations of their peers. Why, then, did their choices reflect peer attitudes rather than parental attitudes?

We did the study all over again in another archdiocese. The explanation of the seeming discrepancy was simple: peers, more than their parents, were likely to know the choices that the adolescent made. Parental evaluations would matter greatly, but only if the parents learned about the actions of their child. Parental ignorance provided the setting for peer influence (Reinhardt, Meyer, & Dornbusch, 1981).

Among other topics we covered were the effects on education of ethnic differences in the amount of social capital (Valenzuela & Dornbusch, 1994; Stanton-Salazar & Dornbusch, 1995), developing a social process measure of adolescent deviance that combined the perspectives of social control and differential association (Erickson, Crosnoe, & Dornbusch, 2000), family and school factors that reduce adolescent deviance (Crosnoe, Erickson, & Dornbusch, 2002; Dornbusch, Laird, & Crosnoe, 1999), family influences on drop-out behavior (Rumberger, Ghatak, Poulos, Ritter, & Dornbusch, 1990), part-time

employment during adolescence (Steinberg & Dornbusch, 1991), and the relation of adolescent polydrug use to violence (Dornbusch, Lin, Munroe & Bianchi, 1999).

In this review of my research career, I have found a major lapse that I can only blame on myself. I never submitted for publication my presidential address to the Society for Research on Adolescence (Dornbusch, 1994). Therefore, I will take this opportunity to report the main findings of the research on tracking that I announced at that time. About 10% of all non-Hispanic White and Asian students were put in a high-school track that was lower than the higher track in which they were capable of performing well. Even worse, 20% of Hispanic and African-American students were placed in an inappropriately low track. This is an enormous waste of adolescent talent.

While I was doing this research on tracking, I had two searing personal experiences. The first came when I was visiting a local high school, honored as one of the best in the United States. I was accompanied on this tour by the head of the entire University of California system. The first class we were invited to watch was called "Algebra 0.5." What does "0.5" mean? we asked. The response was that these kids were too dumb or unprepared to take the first high-school course in algebra, and the goal of this course was to enable the students to take Algebra 1 during their sophomore year. The University of California executive was wiser than I: he asked the students in Algebra 0.5 to tell us their occupational goals. Some wanted to be models or basketball stars, but most gave traditional choices, such as lawyer, doctor, engineer, and teacher. My companion later pointed out to me that these students had no idea that taking this course meant that they were tracked to be ineligible for any 4-year college in California's state system. They were already relegated to the non-academic dump heap.

A few months later, I mentioned this experience in a large undergraduate course at Stanford. A hand shot up. "I was in Algebra 0.5," said a sloppily dressed Hispanic student. Startled, I asked how he had managed to even be considered for entrance to Stanford. He then told of his freshman experience in that excellent high school. He had been assigned to an English class where the first assignment was to read a few pages of J. D. Salinger's *Catcher in the Rye*. He misunderstood and read the whole book over the weekend. His teacher realized he had been misassigned and got him transferred to a more demanding course.

In mathematics, he had a different experience. Assigned to Algebra 0.5, he stayed for the entire term. After giving him an A grade, his teacher said that he really should not have been in that class. In order to finish the required high-school math courses for admission to a state college or university campus, he would have to take two separate math courses in his sophomore year in high school. He agreed to do that. He got high grades in both math classes, though he found the amount of work difficult. By successfully taking on that challenge, he managed to remain eligible for admission to a 4-year college. He did not appear resentful or surprised by these errors, products of stereotypes about Hispanic deficiencies in abilities and motivation.

Finally, I would like to note some general perspectives on research on adolescence that I have already published (Dornbusch, 1989; Dornbusch, Herman, & Morley, 1996; Dornbusch, Petersen, & Heatherington, 1991). In addition, I wish to suggest a broadening of the age groups subject to researchers concentrating on adolescence. Many years ago, the definition of pediatrics expanded to the study and treatment of adolescents. The reason for the change, I cynically suggest, was a decline in the birth rate; pediatricians needed more patients. For researchers on adolescence, my suggested expansion of the ages studied is based on public policy needs, not on sources of income or grants.

Just as the adolescent years reflect in part the processes of childhood education, adjustment, and functioning, the early years of adulthood are partially determined by the social capital, intellectual skills, and personality characteristics that have developed in the adolescent period of development. Near the time of my retirement, I urged researchers to examine the relation of processes in the adolescent period to adult initiation into the world of work and the assumption of new roles in the family (Dornbusch, 2000). The need for such longitudinal work across age groupings is increasingly evident.

References

Baumrind, D. (1978). Parental disciplinary patterns and social competence in children. *Youth and Society, 9*, 239–276.

Buchanan, C. M., Maccoby, E. E., & Dornbusch, S. M. (1991). Caught between parents: Adolescents' experiences in divorced homes. *Child Development, 62*, 1008–1029.

Buchanan, C. M., Maccoby, E. E., & Dornbusch, S. M. (1996). *Adolescents after divorce.* Cambridge, MA: Harvard University Press.

Crosnoe, R. C., Erickson, K. G., & Dornbusch, S. M. (2002). Protective functions of family and school factors on adolescent deviance: Reducing the impact of risky friendships. *Youth and Society, 33*, 515–544

Dornbusch, S. M. (1955). The military academy as an assimilating Institution. *Social Forces, 33*, 316–321.

Dornbusch, S. M. (1974). To try or not to try. *The Stanford Magazine, 2*, 50–54.

Dornbusch, S. M. (1986). Helping your kid make the grade. *The Stanford Magazine, 14*, 47–51.

Dornbusch, S. M. (1987). Individual moral choices and social evaluations: A research odyssey. In E. J. Lawler and B. Markovsky (Eds.), *Advances in group processes: Theory and research* (Vol. IV, pp. 271–307). Greenwich, CT: JAI Press.

Dornbusch, S. M. (1989). The sociology of adolescence. In W. R. Scott & J. Blake (Eds.), *Annual review of sociology* (pp. 233–259). Palo Alto, CA: Annual Reviews.

Dornbusch, S. M. (February 1994). Off the track. Presidential address at the biennial meeting of the Society for Research on Adolescence, San Diego, CA.

Dornbusch, S. M. (January, 2000). Transitions from adolescence: A discussion of seven articles. *Journal of Adolescent Research, 15*, 173–177.

Dornbusch, S. M., Carlsmith, J. M., Bushwall, P. L., Ritter, P. L., Leiderman, H., Hastorf, A. H. et al. (1985). Single parents, extended households, and the control of adolescents. *Child Development, 56*, 326–341.

Dornbusch, S. M., Carlsmith, J. M., Duncan, P. D., Gross, R. T., Martin, J. A., Ritter, P. L. et al. (1984a). Sexual maturation, social class, and the desire to be thin among adolescent females. *Journal of Behavioral and Developmental Pediatrics, 5*, 308–314.

Dornbusch, S. M., Carlsmith, J. M., Gross, R. T., Martin, J. A., Jennings, D., Rosenberg, A. et al. (1981). Sexual development, age, and dating: A comparison of biological and social influences upon one set of behaviors. *Child Development, 52*, 179–85.

Dornbusch, S. M. Carlsmith, J. M., Leiderman, P. H., Hastorf, A. H., Gross, R. T., & Ritter, P. L. (1984b). Black control of adolescent dating. *Sociological Perspectives, 27*, 301–323.

Dornbusch, S. M., Glasgow, K. L., & Lin, I. C. (1996). The social structure of schooling. *Annual Review of Psychology, 47*, 401–429.

Dornbusch, S. M., & Gray, K. D. (1988). Single-parent families. In S. M. Dornbusch & M. H. Strober (Eds.), *Feminism, children, and the new families.* New York: Guilford Press.

Dornbusch, S. M., Gross, R. T., Duncan, P. D., & Ritter, P. L. (1987). Stanford studies of adolescence using the National Health Examination Survey. In R. M. Lerner & T. T. Foch (Eds.), *Biological-psychological interaction in early adolescence.* Hillsdale, NJ: Lawrence Erlbaum Associates.

Dornbusch, S. M., Hastorf, A. H., Richardson, S. A. Muzzy, R. E., & Vreeland, R. S. (1965). The perceiver and the perceived. *Journal of Personality and Social Psychology, 1*, 434–440.

Dornbusch, S. M., Herman, M. R., & Lin, I. (1996). Single parenthood. *Society, 33*, 30–32.

Dornbusch, S. M., Herman, M. R., & Morley, J. A. (1996). Domains of adolescent achievement. In G. R. Adams, R. Montemayor, & T. P. Gullotta (Eds.), *Psychological development during adolescence: Progress in developmental contextualism* (pp. 181–231). Thousand Oaks, CA: Sage Publications.

Dornbusch, S. M., & Kaufman, J. G. (2002). The social structure of the American high school. In T. Urdan & F. Pajares (Eds.), *Adolescence and education*, Vol. 1. Greenwich, CT: Information Age Publishing.

Dornbusch, S. M., Laird, J., & Crosnoe, R. C. (1999). Parental and school resources that assist adolescents in coping with negative peer influences. In E. Frydenberg (Ed.), *Learning to cope: Developing as a person in complex societies*. Oxford: Oxford University Press.

Dornbusch, S. M., Lin, I. C., Munroe, P. T., & Bianchi, A. J. (1999). Adolescent polydrug use and violence in the United States. *International Journal of Adolescent Medicine and Health, 11*, 197–219.

Dornbusch, S. M., Petersen, A. C., & Hetherington E. M. (1991). Projecting the future of research on adolescence. *Journal of Research on Adolescence, 1*, 7–17.

Dornbusch, S. M., & Ritter, P. L. (1988). Parents of high school students: A neglected resource. *Educational Horizons, 66*, 75–77.

Dornbusch, S. M., & Ritter, P. L. (1992). Home-school processes in diverse ethnic groups, social classes, and family structures. In S. Christenson & J. C. Conoley (Eds.), *Home-school collaboration* (pp. 111–125). Silver Spring, MD: National Association of School Psychologists.

Dornbusch, S. M., Ritter, P. L., Leiderman, P., Roberts, D., & Fraleigh, M. (1987). The relation of parenting style to adolescent school performance. *Child Development, 58*, 1244–1257.

Dornbusch, S. M., Ritter, P. L., Mont-Reynaud, R., & Chen, Z. (1990). Family decision-making and academic performance in a diverse high school population. *Journal of Adolescent Research, 5*, 143–160.

Dornbusch, S. M., & Scott, W. R. (1975). *Evaluation and the exercise of authority.* San Francisco: Jossey-Bass.

Dornbusch, S. M., & Wood, K. E. (1990). Family processes and educational achievement. In W. J. Weston (Ed.), *Education and the American family: A research synthesis.* New York: New York University Press.

Erickson, K. G., Crosnoe, R. C., & Dornbusch, S. M. (2000). A social process model of adolescent deviance: Combining social control and differential association perspectives. *Journal of Youth and Adolescence, 29*, 395–425.

Glasgow, K. L., Dornbusch, S. M., Troyer, L., Steinberg, L., & Ritter, P. L. (1997). Parenting styles and adolescents' attributions and educational outcomes in nine heterogeneous high schools. *Child Development, 68*, 507–529.

Gross, R. T., & Dornbusch, S. M. (1979). Enuresis: A multi-handicapping condition. *Pediatric Research, 13*, 327.

Gross. R. T., & Dornbusch, S. M. (1983). Enuresis. In M. D. Levine et al. (Eds.), *Developmental behavioral pediatrics* (pp. 575–586). Philadelphia: W. B. Saunders.

Hammer, L. D., Kraemer, H. C., Wilson, D. M., Ritter, P. L., & Dornbusch, S. M. (1991). Standardized percentile curves of body mass index for children and adolescents. *American Journal of Diseases of Children, 145*, 259–263.

Lamborn, S. D., Dornbusch, S. M., & Steinberg, L. (1996). Ethnicity and community context as moderators of the relations between family decision making and adolescent adjustment. *Child Development, 67*, 283–301.

Lamborn, S. D., Mounts, N. S., Steinberg, L., & Dornbusch, S. M. (1991). Patterns of competence and adjustment among adolescents from authoritative, authoritarian, indulgent, and neglectful families. *Child Development, 62*, 1049–1065.

Massey, G. C., Scott, M. V., & Dornbusch, S. M. (1975). Racism without racists: Institutional racism in urban schools. *The Black Scholar, 7*, 10–19.

Miyamoto, S. F., & Dornbusch, S. M. (1956). A test of interactionist hypotheses of self-conception *American Journal of Sociology, 61*, 399–403.

Reinhardt, J. N., Meyer, L., & Dornbusch, S. M. (1981). *Who influences Catholic youth? The search retreat and the opinions of Catholic youth.* Washington, DC: National Catholic Youth Organization.

Rumberger, R. W., Ghatak, R., Poulos, G., Ritter, P. L., & Dornbusch, S. M. (1990). Family influences on dropout behavior in one California high school. *Sociology of Education, 63*, 283–299.

Stanton-Salazar, R. D., & Dornbusch, S. M. (1995). Social capital and the reproduction of inequality: Information networks among Mexican origin high school students. *Sociology of Education, 68*, 116–135.

Steinberg, L., Brown, B. B., & Dornbusch, S. M. (1996). *Beyond the classroom: Why school reform has failed and what parents need to do.* New York: Simon & Schuster.

Steinberg, L., & Dornbusch, S. M. (1991). Negative correlates of part-time employment during adolescence: Replication and elaboration. *Developmental Psychology, 27*(2), 304–317.

Steinberg, L., Dornbusch, S. M., & Brown, B. (1992). Ethnic differences in adolescent achievement: An ecological perspective. *American Psychologist, 47*, 723–729.

Steinberg, L., Lamborn, S. D., Darling, N., Mounts, N. S., & Dornbusch, S. M. (1994). Over-time changes in adjustment and competence among adolescents from authoritative, authoritarian, indulgent, and neglectful families. *Child Development, 65*, 754–770.

Steinberg, L., Lamborn, S. D., Dornbusch, S. M., & Darling, N. (1992). Impact of parenting practices on adolescent achievement: Authoritative parenting, school involvement, and encouragement to succeed. *Child Development, 63*, 1266–1281.

Valenzuela, A., & Dornbusch, S. M. (1994). Familism and social capital in the academic achievement of Mexican-origin and Anglo adolescents. *Social Science Quarterly, 75*(1), 18–36.

Veblen, T. (1899). *The theory of the leisure class: An economic study of institutions.* New York: Macmillan.

13

Following the Data (and Sometimes Theory)

The Career of a Socioemotional Developmental Scientist

Nancy Eisenberg

I was an adolescent of the 1960s. My college years in the late 1960s and early 1970s were during a time of considerable political unrest about the Vietnam War and civil rights for minorities in the United States. As an undergraduate at the University of Michigan, Ann Arbor, I was involved in some political activities and concerned with university and national civil rights policies, as well as the effects of the ongoing Vietnam War on both Americans and the Vietnamese. Given the emphasis on sociopolitical topics at the time, perhaps it is not surprising that I became interested in political attitudes and why others' needs and welfare are salient in the political thinking of some individuals but not others.

I have always been fascinated by what makes people who they are. In undergraduate school, I found psychology much more interesting than other subjects and was especially interested in issues to do with the development of social and political functioning and attitudes. Thus, when it was time to apply to graduate school, I applied to programs that included faculty studying social development and elected to work with Paul Mussen at the University of California, Berkeley. Paul was interested in, and was studying, individual differences in political orientations in early adulthood, as well as prosocial behavior (voluntary behavior intended to benefit another) in childhood and adolescence. Thus, our interests were a good match.

Most of the research I conducted in graduate school pertained, at least in part, to the development of humanitarian political attitudes. However, in one of my first term papers in graduate school, it became clear to me that to understand humanitarian attitudes, I would have to study the development and origins of other-oriented, prosocial behaviors and cognitions—behaviors such as helping, sharing, and comforting others—and their cognitive and socialization origins. Consequently, my interests quickly broadened to include

these topics. Moreover, as will be evident later, my interests contained to change and broaden as our data led me to new questions, conceptual speculations, and occasionally answers. It has been an stimulating and gratifying journey.

Prosocial Moral Reasoning and Prosocial Behavior

In both my master's thesis and dissertation, I studied political attitudes and multiple aspects of prosocial development, including reasoning about prosocial issues, helping behavior, and/or emotional reactions that are conceptually linked to prosocial functioning (e.g., empathy and sympathy). However, because of its likely association with political attitudes, the primary focus in these two early documents was on a cognitive aspect of prosocial functioning—specifically, prosocial moral reasoning.

I defined prosocial behavior as voluntary behavior intended to benefit another—for example, sharing objects, donating money, providing assistance with tasks, comforting behaviors, and working on projects or for organizations that benefit others. In contrast to actual prosocial actions, prosocial moral reasoning is a person's reasoning about dilemmas in which a story protagonist has an opportunity to assist others, but at a cost to the self, in a context in which the influence of laws, rules, and formal obligations is minimal. To assess prosocial moral reasoning, I developed a set of illustrated hypothetical vignettes for school-aged children and adolescents in which the story protagonist could help another person (usually, but not always, a child), but at a cost. For example, one dilemma is about a child who has an opportunity to assist a same-sex peer who is being bullied when doing so is likely to incur the bully's wrath. After hearing each vignette, children were questioned about what they thought the story protagonist should do and their reasons for the choice.

My work on prosocial moral reasoning was highly influenced by Lawrence Kohlberg's well-known research on moral judgment. However, I argued that Kohlberg's (1984) conception of moral reasoning was prohibition-oriented rather than oriented toward prosocial issues. In Kohlberg's moral dilemmas, the focus typically is on acts of wrongdoing such as murder, theft, or lying. Often Kohlberg's dilemmas pit one prohibited action against another; for example, in the well-known Heinz dilemma, respondents reason about the story protagonist's choice between stealing a drug to save his wife and the choice to allow his wife to die of cancer without the drug, both of which are behaviors viewed as negative and prohibited in our society.

Based on such dilemmas, Kohlberg initially delineated six stages of moral reasoning (organized in three levels) that he viewed as reflecting the development of changes in individuals' moral reasoning. He argued that his stages are invariant in sequence (i.e., development of the stages always proceeds in the same order) and universal across cultures. He also argued that each stage represents a totally new and unique way of thinking about moral issues, and that people seldom revert to using reasoning at a much lower level. Kohlberg apparently assumed that his stages of moral judgment were applicable to reasoning about the entire range of moral issues; however, when I began working on moral judgment, this assumption seldom had been tested.

As I started my work on prosocial moral reasoning, I hypothesized that there would be both similarities and differences between prohibition and prosocial moral reasoning. As one example, I expected other-oriented reasoning involving orienting to another's needs, perspective taking, and sympathy to be especially evident in prosocial moral reasoning and salient at a fairly young age for some children. In addition, I hypothesized that authority- and punishment-oriented reasoning, Kohlberg's stage 1, would be verbalized infrequently in children's prosocial moral reasoning because children seldom are punished for not helping or sharing, whereas they often are punished for wrongdoing and violating prohibitions.

Based on my PhD work and subsequent studies of children and adolescents, including a sample followed from age 4 to 5 into early adulthood, we delineated and assessed age-related changes in prosocial moral judgment. As can be seen in Box 13.1, my students and I found that preschoolers tend to use primarily self-oriented, hedonistic reasoning (e.g., "He shouldn't help because he might get picked on," or needs-oriented (i.e., primitive empathic) prosocial reasoning (e.g., "She should help because the girl's leg is bleeding and she needs to go to the doctor"). In elementary school, some children's prosocial moral reasoning occasionally begins to include concern with approval and enhancing interpersonal relationships (e.g., "Her family would think she did the right thing") or the desire to behave in stereotypically "good" ways (e.g., like a "nice" girl or boy). Beginning in late elementary school or later, some children explicitly state that they would take the other's perspective or sympathize. At these ages and sometimes later, they also begin to verbalize abstract moral principles and internalized affective reactions such as guilt (e.g., Eisenberg, Carlo, Murphy, & Van Court, 1995; see Eisenberg, 1986, and Eisenberg, Fabes, & Spinrad, 2006, for a review of some of the work).

BOX 13.1 Levels of Prosocial Moral Reasoning

Level 1: Hedonistic, self-focused orientation. The individual is concerned with his or her own interests rather than with moral considerations. Reasons for assisting or not assisting another include direct personal gain, future reciprocation, and concern for the other based on affection. (Predominant mode primarily for preschoolers and younger elementary school children.)

Level 2: Needs-based orientation. The individual expresses concern for the physical, material, and psychological needs of others even when those needs conflict with his or her own. This concern is expressed in the simplest terms, without clear evidence of self-reflective role-taking, verbal expressions of sympathy, or reference to such emotions as pride or guilt. (Predominant mode for many preschoolers and many elementary school children.)

Level 3: Approval and/or stereotyped orientation. The individual justifies engaging or not engaging in prosocial behavior on the basis of others' approval or acceptance and/or on stereotyped images of good and bad persons and behavior. (Predominant mode for some elementary school and high school students).

Level 4a: Self-reflective empathic orientation. The individual's judgments include evidence of self-reflective sympathetic responding or role-taking, concern with the other's humanness, and/or guilt or positive emotion related to the consequences of one's actions for others. (Predominant mode for a few older elementary school children and many high-school students.)

Level 4b: Transitional level. The individual's justifications for helping or not helping involve internalized values, norms, duties, or responsibilities. They may also reflect concerns for the condition of the larger society or refer to the necessity of protecting the rights and dignity of other persons. These ideals, however, are not clearly or strongly stated. (Predominant mode for a minority of people of high-school age or older.)

(Continued)

(Continued)

Level 5: Strongly internalized stage. The individual's justifications for helping or not helping are based on internalized values, norms, or responsibilities; the desire to maintain individual and societal contractual obligations or improve the condition of society; and the belief in the rights, dignity, and equality of all individuals. This level is also characterized by positive or negative emotions related to whether or not one succeeds in living up to one's own values and accepted norms. (Predominant mode for only a small minority of high-school students.)

Adapted from Eisenberg (1986).

In the later years of the longitudinal study, we followed the study participants into adulthood. When we examined age-related changes in percent of various types of prosocial moral reasoning from ages 15–16 to 25–26 years, hedonistic reasoning, which was relatively low, did not change with age; nor did higher-level abstract moral reasoning (although it did increase significantly from age 13–14 into later adolescence). Level 2 (rudimentary needs-oriented) reasoning did not change from 15–16 to 17–18 years, decreased sharply from age 17–18 to 21–22 years, and then leveled off; older adolescents and adults often tended to use more sophisticated types of other-oriented moral reasoning. In contrast, Level 4 (self-reflective, empathic orientation) reasoning increased with age from 15/16 to 21–22 years, primarily for females, and then dropped slightly in the mid-twenties. Surprisingly, the percent of stereotypic/approval oriented reasoning increased somewhat with age. Finally, there was a clear increase in the overall level of prosocial moral reasoning until age 21–22, and then it stabilized (Eisenberg et al., 2005a).

There were several notable findings in this body of work. For example, unlike for Kohlberg's prohibition-oriented moral reasoning, children and adolescents virtually never said they would help in order to avoid punishment or due to blind obedience to authorities such as adults. In addition, even 4- to 5-year-olds frequently appeared to orient to others' needs and exhibit what often seemed to be primitive empathic reasoning. As previously noted, this finding would not be expected from earlier discussions of work on Kohlberg's levels of moral reasoning. Furthermore, children's and especially adolescents' references to empathy-related processes such as taking the other's perspective and sympathizing were particularly common in prosocial moral reasoning. Moreover, similar to the findings of James Rest and some other researchers examining prohibition-oriented moral reasoning, but contrary to Kohlberg's assertions, we found that even people who typically used higher modes of level reasoning occasionally reverted to using lower level reasoning (such as hedonistic reasoning), especially when they chose not to assist the needy other.

The latter finding suggests that contextual variables influence when people use the various levels of moral reasoning in their repertoire. Consistent with this notion, in cross-cultural research, we found some minor differences in the reasoning of children from different cultures—differences that seemed to reflect concerns that were salient in their own cultures. For example, my Israel colleagues and I found that children who lived in communally oriented kibbutzim in Israel were particularly likely to emphasize reciprocity between people, whereas city children from both Israel and the United states were more likely than kibbutz children to be concerned with costs to themselves of helping (see Eisenberg, 1986, for a review).

Because individuals' moral reasoning differs somewhat across situations, we would expect only a modest relation between people's typical levels of moral reasoning and their tendencies to actually behave prosocially. This is what we have found. Children with a relatively high level of moral reasoning and other-oriented types of reasoning are more likely to act prosocially compared with their peers, especially those relatively high in hedonistic, self-oriented reasoning (that is, reasoning in which they focus on the costs to the self for helping). Also of interest (especially given my initial reason for studying prosocial functioning), we found a positive correlation between level of prosocial moral reasoning and children's and adolescents' humanitarian political attitudes and political liberalism (Eisenberg-Berg, 1976, 1979).

Fairly early into my career, I knew I needed to expand my research beyond prosocial moral reasoning in order to attain a better understanding of prosocial development. It seemed obvious that reasoning is only one of multiple factors affecting moral behavior, and that it is a weak influence in some contexts. One factor that seemed to be neglected in the study of prosocial behavior—and, at the time, in psychology in general—was emotion and its role in social and moral behavior. My work on prosocial moral reasoning suggested that children's orientation to others' needs and their own emotions (e.g., sympathy, guilt) affected prosocial responding. Moreover, influential theory and research by people in the 1970s such as Martin Hoffman, Marian Radke-Yarrow, and Carolyn Zahn-Waxler suggested that responding emotionally to others' feelings and needs frequently motivates comforting, helping, and sharing behaviors, even in very young children. Thus, I increasingly turned my attention to empathy-related responding in the 1980s.

Empathy: Conceptualization and Measurement

Although I was eager to study the role of empathy in prosocial development, I quickly discovered that it was more difficult than I expected to measure the construct. In the 1970s, there was a lack of differentiation among various emotional responses labeled as empathy and it was unclear if all types of responding would be expected to be related to prosocial behavior. Moreover, I found that the measures typically used to measure empathy at that time were problematic.

In regard to the first issue, the term *empathy*, when not used to refer to cognitive perspective taking, usually had been used to refer to most, if not all, types of emotional reactions that one might have when exposed to a person in need or distress. However, a person can feel a range of emotions to others' needs, including sadness, concern, distress, or even happiness. In the late 1970s, C. Daniel Batson, a social psychologist, started to discuss an important distinction among empathic responses relevant to predicting prosocial behavior—empathy and personal distress (see Batson, 1991). What Batson labeled as empathy is the same as what I would call sympathy, defined as an other-oriented response to another's distress or need, such as feelings of concern and sorrow for another. In contrast, Batson defined personal distress as a self-oriented, egoistic response to another's need, distress, or problematic situation—such as feelings of discomfort or anxiety when confronted with another's negative state or situation.

Batson argued that people who experience concern for another person (i.e., sympathy) are likely to be motivated to try to improve the other's condition, whereas people who experience personal distress would be expected to try to reduce their own aversive, negative emotion. If viewing or dealing with a distressed person is highly aversive, people are likely to try to avoid further exposure to the person. Batson further argued that personal distress can induce prosocial behavior, but primarily when assisting the other person is the quickest way to reduce one's own distress, such as when there is no easy way to escape dealing with him or her. However, when it is easy to avoid the person eliciting personal distress, Batson hypothesized that individuals experiencing personal distress will avoid rather than assist the person in distress or need. Thus, Batson argued that sympathy fosters altruistic behavior (prosocial behavior that is motivated by sympathy rather than concrete rewards or social approval), whereas personal distress is associated with egoistically motivated prosocial behavior and avoidance of the other person if possible.

In a series of creative studies with adults, Batson found that people induced to experience sympathy for a distressed individual tended to help even if it was easy to escape contact with the other person, whereas people induced to experience personal distress tended not to help when they could easily avoid doing so and others were unlikely to know whether they helped. However, it was unclear if the same pattern of findings would be obtained with children and if the distinction between personal distress and sympathy was meaningful in childhood. Thus, my goal was to assess children's empathy-related reactions to others in distress or need and to relate their reactions to their prosocial behavior.

Unfortunately, in the 1980s, there were not readily available, valid measures to assess sympathy and personal distress in children. In most of the prior work on empathy in children, empathy was assessed with a picture/story procedure. Children were told brief stories (often accompanied by illustrations) about others in emotionally evocative contexts (e.g., when a child loses his/her dog). Then children were asked "How do you feel?" or a similar question (often after being asked how the child in the story felt). Children who said that they felt an emotion similar to that which the story protagonist would be expected to experience (e.g., sadness in the lost-dog story) were coded as empathizing. There was no attempt to assess sympathy or personal distress. In early studies using this measure, we found that children's responses to this measure seemed to be affected by social desirability concerns and did not induce true affective responding. Moreover, in a meta-analytic review (a review combining the results from numerous studies), we discovered that responses on this measure were not related to children's prosocial behavior. In the same review, we found that children's reports of their empathy-related responding when they were exposed to enactments or films of needy/distressed others also were unrelated to their prosocial behavior. Thus, the validity of any self-report measure of children's empathy was in question. Moreover, in virtually none of the early studies of empathy were sympathy and personal distress assessed; thus, it was difficult to assess the hypothesis that it is sympathy, and not personal distress (and perhaps not even solely empathy), that motivates altruism.

In an effort to deal with these problems, we decided to try to assess children's empathy-related responding not only with their self-reports of sympathy and personal distress, but also with nonverbal procedures. First, we videotaped and coded children's facial reactions while they were exposed to empathy-inducing stimuli (e.g., films of needy or distressed people). Although a few other researchers had used facial measures of empathy-related responding, at that time no one, to our knowledge, had tried to differentiate between sympathy and personal distress using facial expressions. Therefore, we developed procedures for coding markers of other-oriented concern versus self-focused, distressed reactions when viewing others in need or distress.

In addition, we used psychophysiological measures. To do so was a daunting task because I knew nothing about physiological procedures or data. Moreover, psychophysiological equipment was expensive, but it was nearly impossible to obtain grant money to buy the equipment without demonstrating one's competence in using physiological methods.

Luckily, in a closet in the home economics department, my colleague and collaborator, Richard Fabes, found some old equipment for measuring heart rate. It was no longer manufactured and did not work. Against the odds, a gifted and prosocial colleague in my department, Dennis Glanzman, found a way to repair it so that we could try to collect some initial data. In addition, at a slightly later point in time, Joseph Campos, a developmental psychologist with expertise in psychophysiological measures, loaned us equipment for pilot testing and provided badly needed advice and consultation.

Based on the limited relevant psychophysiological research and theory, we hypothesized that sympathy, which involves an outward focus of attention, would be associated with the intake of information concerning the other person, interest in that person, and outward attention. Such information processing had been associated with heart rate deceleration in prior research. In contrast, when vicarious emotional responding results in an aversive reaction such as apprehension, anxiety, or discomfort (i.e., personal distress), it would be expected to be associated with processing of information relevant to one's own situation. Cognitive elaboration in the head, anxiety, and active coping with one's own emotion/situation had been associated with heart rate acceleration so it was reasonable to hypothesize that a self-focused, personal distress reaction would be associated with heart rate acceleration.

A few years later, we added skin conductance (previously called GSR or galvanic skin response) as a second physiological marker of personal distress. We hypothesized that people who are feeling personal distress experience a relatively high level of empathic arousal that they can not sufficiently regulate to bring down to a more tolerable level. Their high level of arousal is experienced as aversive so the individual is likely to focus on his or her own distress rather than on the other's needs and feelings. Therefore, I expected feelings of personal distress to be associated with high levels of skin conductance because skin conductance has been found to reflect (among other things) emotional arousal.

Because our ideas about facial and physiological markers of sympathy and personal distress were untested, we needed to assess the validity of our measures. Thus, we conducted a series of studies in which participants were likely to experience either sympathy or personal distress and then examined whether our measures differed across these conditions in the expected manner. For example, children or adults were exposed to parts of films about other people that were selected to elicit either concern for another (e.g., a film about a child with spina bifida) or personal distress (e.g., films about people in a frightening situation). Or study participants were asked to talk about situations in their past experience likely to elicit sympathy or distress.

In general, our findings supported the validity of our measures. Heart rate tended to accelerate during the evocative parts of film clips expected to evoke personal distress, and heart rate generally decelerated in response to the evocative parts of sympathy-inducing film clips. Similarly, skin conductance tended to be higher while participants watched distress-inducing as opposed to sympathy-inducing films. Moreover, heart rate generally was higher when people talked about distressing rather than sympathy-inducing events.

In addition, facial expressions associated with distress (e.g., nervous moving of the mouth, biting lips) and those associated with concerned attention (a marker of sympathy, including intense attention/interest, with the eyebrows over the nose pulled together and down, often accompanied by tilting one's head forward) differed across the films in the predicted manner. On average, children displayed more concerned attention as well as sadness in the sympathy-inducing situations and more distress in the distress condition. Adults exhibited less facial affect than did children in our studies so their facial expressions differed less across situations. Furthermore, when asked to report how the films or discussion procedures made them feel, both children and adults tended to report the expected emotions—distress in the distress situations and sadness and sympathy in the sympathy context. Thus, our findings provided support for the assumption that one could differentiate children's sympathy from personal distress using multiple methods (e.g., Eisenberg et al., 1988a, 1988b; Eisenberg, Fabes, Schaller, Carlo, & Miller, 1991a; see Eisenberg & Fabes, 1990, and Eisenberg et al., 2006, for reviews).

Testing Relations Between Prosocial Behavior and Empathy-Related Emotional Responses

These initial studies were conducted primarily to verify that our facial and physiological markers of sympathy and personal distress were valid measures of those constructs. Once we had a battery of measures of sympathy and personal distress, we could use those measures to test the relation between empathy-related responding and prosocial behavior. Specifically, in initial studies, we focused on the relation of children's and adults' sympathy versus personal distress to their subsequent prosocial behavior toward the people in the film or other individuals with the same problems or needs as the people in the film.

In a typical study, my colleague Richard Fabes, our students, and I had study participants watch sympathy-inducing film clips and then gave them an opportunity to help the person in the film. Prosocial behaviors varied across studies and included, for example, donating money for physical therapy or to a charity that helps people similar to those in the film, helping put crayons in packages for children in the hospital rather than playing with attractive toys, helping to assemble homework materials for a child in the hospital rather than enjoying recess, or adults' donating time to help a single mother with household tasks so she could visit her injured children in the hospital. To make study participants believe that the films depicted real-life events, we often told them that the film was a pilot news clip for a local university-based public television news program and that study participants were to evaluate the film in terms of its interest value.

While the study participants viewed the empathy-inducing film, we obtained physiological and facial data. After the film, we asked the participants to rate various adjectives to indicate how the film made them feel. Then, a bit later, study participants were provided with an opportunity to assist the person (or persons) in the film, generally in a context in which the experimenter seemed unlikely to know if the participants helped.

Across a series of studies varying in regard to the film and the helping situation, we found that people who exhibited higher heart rate acceleration and skin conductance during the most empathy-inducing segments of the film clip were less likely to assist the needy or distressed person(s) in the film than were other people. People who exhibited heart rate deceleration during the most evocative part of the films tended to provide more assistance. Higher levels of facial concerned attention and/or sadness (viewed as an index of empathic sadness that often leads to concern) tended to relate to higher levels of prosocial behavior, whereas facial distress was correlated with lower levels. The pattern of findings for facial measures was more consistent for children than adults, probably because adults are more likely to mask their emotions or found the films less evocative. Younger children's self-reported reactions to the films were relatively unlikely to predict their prosocial behavior whereas self-reported sympathy or personal distress more often predicted the prosocial behavior for older children and adults (see reviews in Eisenberg & Fabes, 1990; Eisenberg et al., 2006).

These findings had several interesting implications. First, it appears that children, like adults, experience both sympathy and personal distress and that these emotional reactions were related to their prosocial behavior. Moreover, consistent with Batson's research with adults, our findings indicate that whether or not people help others is a function of their specific emotional reaction (sympathy or personal distress) and not merely if a person responds emotionally in empathy-inducing situations. These findings, and other findings showing that enduring individual differences in children's, adolescents', and adults' typical levels of sympathy and personal distress (rather than solely their behavior in a specific situation) tend to be related to their prosocial behavior, suggest that sympathy and personal distress are likely to be important factors contributing to individual differences in prosocial behavior.

Temperamental/Personality Correlates of Predictors of Individual Differences in Empathy-Related Responding

Because of the clear individual differences we noted in children's and adults' empathy-related responding, and the association of these differences with prosocial actions,

I wanted to better understand variables that affected individual differences in sympathy versus personal distress, as well as factors associated with these individual differences. In thinking about and studying these issues, my research interests broadened to include the study of emotion beyond empathy and the self-regulation of emotion, as well their relations to individual differences among children in maladjustment and adjustment. Thus, my initial interest in empathy-related responding led to my use of psychophysiology to better measure the relevant constructs, and that body of work took me from the domain of moral development to the domain of emotions, self-regulation, and their relations to a broad array of developmental outcomes for children. It was a natural progression for me to move from studying moral development to socioemotional development as I tried to better grapple with both the conceptual issues and empirical findings from my research.

As noted previously, I hypothesized that the experience of sympathy, when derived from empathy, involves an optimal level of empathic arousal—one that is sufficiently arousing to induce concern for the other but not so intense that it is overwhelming and aversive. Conversely, I hypothesized that personal distress often is induced by empathic overarousal that is aversive and produces self-focused attention and an egoistic orientation. Our research in which high levels of skin conductance and heart rate were associated with markers of personal distress is consistent with this argument.

If this reasoning was correct, then it seemed plausible that individual differences in the tendency to experience emotions, especially relatively intense emotions, and also in the ability and tendency to regulate the experience of emotion, should relate to empathy-related responding. People prone to intense dysregulating emotions would be expected to be especially prone to person distress, although those high in self-regulation might be prone to sympathy regardless of whether they were prone to intense emotions or not (because they can modulate their emotions and maintain an optimal level of arousal).

In a series of studies we examined these issues. In general, we found that adults dispositionally prone to intense negative emotion (i.e., high on temperamental/personality negative emotionality, or intensity of negative emotionality) were prone to personal distress, although high levels of sadness were also associated with sympathy. In studies of children, high levels of negative emotionality (usually a variety of emotions combined) tended to be negatively related to sympathy. Moreover, both children and adults who were high in dispositional regulation were relatively high in sympathy (although for adults, sometimes only when controlling for individual differences in negative emotionality), whereas individuals low in dispositional regulation tended to be prone to personal distress (e.g., Eisenberg et al., 1994a, 1996a, 1998, 2007; Valiente et al., 2004; see Eisenberg et al., 2006). Thus, it appears that both emotionality and regulation play a role in individual differences in empathy-related responding.

In some of our early studies on prosocial behavior and sympathy, we obtained data suggesting that preschoolers who were more socially competent were prone to spontaneously enacting relatively costly prosocial behavior, and that sympathy was related to this sort of prosocial behavior. In addition, investigators (including my laboratory) had found that measures of empathy and/or sympathy, as well as prosocial behavior, tended to be positively related to social competence. Based on these empirical findings, as well as the conceptual argument that sympathy and prosocial behavior should contribute to the quality of one's social behavior, we started to view sympathy and prosocial behavior as instances of socially competent behavior. In addition, it made sense that self-regulatory skills would contribute not only to sympathy, but also to social competence and adjustment more generally. Thus, we started to examine relations of self-regulatory capacities to various aspects of socially competent functioning and maladjustment.

Self-Regulation and Children's Adjustment and Maladjustment

In an initial study of the relation of self-regulatory capacities to social functioning, we examined the relations of children's adult-reported attentional regulation to their adult- and peer-reported social competence (Eisenberg et al., 1993). We were impressed by the strength of the relations between these measures of children's regulation and their social competence. Moreover, we found that there were some relations between measures of self-regulation and children's actual real-life behavior when dealing with their own negative emotions (Eisenberg, Fabes, Nyman, Bernzweig, & Pinuelas, 1994b). From that point forward, I became increasingly interested in the nature and development of children's self-regulatory skills and the ways in which they predict diverse developmental outcomes.

Since that first study, we have examined self-regulation in four different longitudinal studies, with the study participants ranging from 18 months to adolescence. In general, we have found, consistent with an emerging body of work, that children and adolescents who are relatively well regulated (in regard to attention and/or behavior) tend to be more socially competent, prosocial, agreeable, and popular; are better behaved in the classroom, get along better with teachers, get higher grades at school; and are relatively low in externalizing problems (e.g., aggression, defiance, delinquent behaviors) and, at some ages and in some samples, internalizing problems (e.g., social withdrawal, anxiety, and depressive affect) (e.g., Eisenberg, Fabes, Guthrie, & Reiser, 2000a; Eisenberg et al., 2004, 2009b; Silva et al., 2011; Spinrad et al., 2006, 2007; see Eisenberg, Spinrad, & Eggum, 2010a, for a review of some findings). Moreover, we found that self-regulatory abilities were better predictors of many of these outcomes for those children prone to intense negative emotions. For emotional children, self-regulation is associated with better outcomes; regulation is somewhat less related to children's outcomes if they are not prone to intense negative emotions. This makes sense if one considers that children prone to negative emotions (or intense emotions) are likely to be in greater need of regulation (see, for example, Eisenberg et al., 2000a, 2000b).

We have also been interested in why there is an association between self-regulation and good outcomes for children—that is, in the processes that mediate these associations. For example, we have found that children who are better regulated tend to be higher in personality resiliency (e.g., the ability to deal with stress adaptively and flexibly) and, in turn, are more agreeable, popular, and lower in internalizing symptoms (e.g., Cumberland-Li, Eisenberg, & Reiser, 2003; Eisenberg et al., 2000a; Eisenberg et al., 2004; Hofer, Eisenberg, & Reiser, 2010; Spinrad et al., 2006). In addition, well-regulated children tend to exhibit more socially appropriate behavior and have fewer problem behaviors, and also have high-quality relationships with their teachers, which in turn predict better grades and a more positive attitude at school (Silva et al., 2011; Valiente et al., 2011). Thus, both personality resiliency and the quality of social behavior appear to mediate some of the effects of self-regulation on other desirable developmental competencies.

Another goal of my work has been to differentiate, conceptually and empirically, more effortfully controlled self-regulatory processes from those processes that involve control (inhibition) or the lack thereof (e.g., impulsivity) but which seem more difficult to control voluntarily. The work of a variety of investigators suggests that effortful regulation is situated most centrally in high-level cortical brain systems, whereas less voluntary approach and avoidance control systems are based in subcortical systems. There is not sufficient room to discuss this issue in its complexity, but suffice it to say that voluntary and effortful often provide some unique prediction of children's behaviors such as externalizing and internalizing problems and social competence, although by adolescence it appears that the effortful modes of self-regulation are the stronger unique predictors of level of externalizing problems than are measures of less voluntary impulsivity (undercontrol) or overcontrol (e.g., Eisenberg et al., 2004; Valiente et al., 2003).

In brief, we have found that self-regulatory skills, which develop quickly in the preschool years but continue to emerge into adulthood, are important predictors of a range of outcomes for children and adolescents, including not only sympathy, personal distress, and prosocial behavior, but also adjustment and maladjustment. Given these associations, understanding the origins of empathy-related responding and self-regulation is important.

Socialization of Empathy-Related Responding and Self-Regulation

Although hereditary factors clearly contribute to both empathy-related responding and self-regulation, it is also likely that socialization in the home contributes to these aspects of functioning. Thus, concurrently with our research on empathy-related responding and self-regulation, we have also examined the socialization correlates of individual differences in these capacities in children and adolescents. Space does not permit a detailed analysis of our findings so I provide only some examples. Again, our work on various topics such as empathy-related responding, prosocial behavior, adjustment, and regulation was interrelated in my mind and the findings in one domain of functioning often enriched our thinking about functioning in another domain.

Interestingly, some of the same parenting practices are related to both empathy-related responding and self-regulation, perhaps because of the role that regulation plays in empathy-related responding. For example, parents who display warm behavior when interacting with their children and tend to express positive emotion rather than harsh negative emotion in the home have children relatively high in sympathy and self-regulation (e.g., Eisenberg et al., 2005a, 2010b; Michalik et al., 2007; Valiente et al., 2004, 2006). Moreover, mothers who are warm but also direct their children's attention toward others when discussing empathy-inducing situations tend to have elementary school children who are sympathetic and helpful (Fabes et al., 1994). In addition, in adolescence, warm mothers who expressed positive emotion had children who were more positive and less negative when discussing conflictual issues with their mothers (Eisenberg et al., 2008). Furthermore, parents who report using authoritative parenting practices involving both warmth and an appropriate level of control (and disciplinary techniques such as reasoning) tend to have well-regulated children who are resilient to stress and socially skilled. Conversely, authoritarian parenting practices involving low warmth and high levels of control, especially the use of physical punishment, have been related to low regulation and resiliency (e.g., Eisenberg, Chang, Ma, & Huang, 2009a; Hofer et al., 2010; Zhou et al., 2004). Thus, the quality of parenting seems to matter for the development of both regulation and sympathy. However, the aforementioned studies, albeit often longitudinal (so that initial outcomes could be controlled when predicting outcomes from socialization), still involved correlational data so causal relations cannot be proved.

As might be expected, we also found that children's regulation seems to affect the quality of parenting behavior, at least in some contexts. For example, preschoolers who are better regulated seem to elicit more cognitively oriented information and questions from their mothers and fewer maternal directives (i.e., statements that simply tell the child what to do) in a teaching context two years later (Eisenberg et al., 2010c). Moreover, we found that mothers of well-regulated children, across time, reported fewer punitive responses to children's expressions of negative emotion, even when controlling for children's prior level of self-regulation (Eisenberg et al., 1999a).

In addition, we observed that a variety of emotion-related parental practices and teachings predict children's empathic responding and/or self-regulation. For example, in an early study, boys whose parents encouraged them to try to handle situations causing their own sadness or anxiety instrumentally (i.e., by taking concrete action) were likely to experience sympathy rather than personal distress in empathy-inducing contexts. Parents who teach sons to instrumentally deal with negative emotions and situations may be less likely to become over-aroused (and hence are better regulated) when experiencing vicariously induced negative emotion and, consequently, are more likely to experience sympathy (Eisenberg et al., 1991a). In addition, mothers who appeared to buffer their younger and/or emotionally vulnerable children from too much negative emotion when telling sad stories (by expressing some positive emotion themselves during the story telling) had more sympathetic and prosocial children (Fabes et al., 1994).

In addition, we have found that the ways in which parents deal with their children's emotions more generally are associated with both their regulation and sympathy. Parents who are restrictive in regard to children's expression of their own negative emotions such as sadness, anxiety, and appropriate anger tend to have children who are less skilled at coping, are less regulated, and more likely to experience personal distress rather than sympathy. For example, mothers who tried to get their sons to control the expression of emotions that were unlikely to injure another (e.g., their own sadness and anxiety) were high in facial and physiological signs of distress when viewing a sympathy-inducing film, but reported low distress in reaction to the film (Eisenberg et al., 1991a). Thus, these boys seemed to experience personal distress when confronted with others' distress, but did not want others to know their feelings. Children likely need to learn to acknowledge and manage their own feelings so they do not get overwhelmed by them.

Thus, these and other studies suggest that experiences in the home contribute to individual differences in children's and youths' empathy-related responding and self-regulation, although children also appear to affect parental behavior. Our findings suggest ways in which adults other than parents might affect children's and adolescents' regulation, empathy-related responding, and other aspects of their socioemotional functioning. In fact, based on the kind of findings discussed above, I have been involved in designing an intervention for promoting prosocial behavior and have assisted with an intervention designed to promote self-regulation and school readiness. Such work allows for the application of findings to real-world problems.

Recent Directions

Because of my broad interest in socioemotional functioning, as well as my students' interests, we have studied many other topics in addition to those discussed previously. These topics include the role of positive emotion in children's behavior, religiosity and coping, children's compliance, children's and youths' conflict behaviors, peer victimization, cross-group friendships, self-efficacy beliefs, the relations of cortisol responding and respiratory sinus arrhythmia (physiological regulation) to aspects of social behavior, shyness, and gender roles. Some of this research currently is in collaboration with my colleagues and friends in Rome, Italy; other work has been with colleagues in Brazil, Germany, Hong Kong, Indonesia, Israel, Norway, Poland, and other countries. One of the best perks of an academic career is the wonderful people one gets to meet, work with, and befriend as part of the job. It is a perk that many of us do not really anticipate when choose our line of work, but one of the most gratifying parts of my career.

Most recently, we have been examining the interaction of genes and environmental factors (e.g., the quality of parenting) when predicting children's maladjustment, compliance, and regulation (e.g., Sulik et al., 2012) and the interaction of respiratory sinus arrhythmia with demographic/family stress when predicting externalizing problems (Eisenberg et al., 2012). This is a natural extension of our work on socialization, self-regulation, and adjustment. One question leads to the next. But that is what is unique and exciting about being an academic involved in research.

Acknowledgment

Writing of this chapter was supported by a grant from the National Institute for Mental Health.

References

Batson, C. D. (1991). *The altruism question: Toward a social-psychological answer*. Hillsdale, NJ: Erlbaum.

Cumberland-Li, A., Eisenberg, N., & Reiser, M. (2004). Relations of young children's agreeableness and resiliency to effortful control and impulsivity. *Social Development, 13*, 191–212.

Eisenberg, N. (1986). *Altruistic emotion, cognition, and behavior*. Hillsdale, NJ: Erlbaum.

Eisenberg, N., Carlo, G., Murphy, B., & Van Court, P. (1995). Prosocial development in late adolescence: A longitudinal study. *Child Development, 66*, 1179–1197.

Eisenberg, N., Chang, L., Ma, Y., & Huang, X. (2009a). Relations of parenting style to Chinese children's effortful control, ego resilience, and maladjustment. *Development and Psychopathology, 21*, 455–477.

Eisenberg, N., Cumberland, A., Guthrie, I. K., Murphy, B. C., & Shepard, S. A. (2005a). Age changes in prosocial responding and moral reasoning in adolescence and early adulthood. *Journal of Research in Adolescence, 15*, 235–260.

Eisenberg, N., & Fabes, R. A. (1990). Empathy: Conceptualization, assessment, and relation to prosocial behavior. *Motivation and Emotion, 14*, 131–149.

Eisenberg, N., Fabes, R. A., Bernzweig, J., Karbon, M., Poulin, R., & Hanish, L. (1993). The relations of emotionality and regulation to preschoolers' social skills and sociometric status. *Child Development, 64*, 1418–1438.

Eisenberg, N., Fabes, R. A., Bustamante, D., Mathy, R. M., Miller, P., & Lindholm, E. (1988a). Differentiation of vicariously-induced emotional reactions in children. *Developmental Psychology, 24*, 237–246.

Eisenberg, N., Fabes, R. A., Carlo, G., Troyer, D., Speer, A. L., Karbon, M. et al. (1992). The relations of maternal practices and characteristics to children's vicarious emotional responsiveness. *Child Development, 63*, 583–602.

Eisenberg, N., Fabes, R. A., Guthrie, I. K., & Reiser, M. (2000a). Dispositional emotionality and regulation: Their role in predicting quality of social functioning. *Journal of Personality and Social Psychology, 78*, 136–157.

Eisenberg, N., Fabes, R. A., Miller, P. A., Fultz, J., Mathy, R. M., Shell, R. et al. (1989). The relations of sympathy and personal distress to prosocial behavior: A multimethod study. *Journal of Personality and Social Psychology, 57*, 55–66.

Eisenberg, N., Fabes, R. A., & Murphy, B. C. (1996a). Parents' reactions to children's negative emotions: Relations to children's social competence and comforting behavior. *Child Development, 67*, 2227–2247.

Eisenberg, N., Fabes, R. A., Murphy, B., Karbon, M., Maszk, P., Smith, M. et al. (1994a). The relations of emotionality and regulation to dispositional and situational empathy-related responding. *Journal of Personality and Social Psychology, 66*, 776–797.

Eisenberg, N., Fabes, R. A., Murphy, B., Karbon, M., Smith, M., & Maszk, P. (1996b). The relations of children's dispositional empathy-related responding to their emotionality, regulation, and social functioning. *Developmental Psychology, 32*, 195–209.

Eisenberg, N., Fabes, R. A., Nyman, M., Bernzweig, J., & Pinuelas, A. (1994b). The relations of emotionality and regulation to children's anger-related reactions. *Child Development, 65*, 109–128.

Eisenberg, N., Fabes, R. A., Schaller, M., Carlo, G., & Miller, P. A. (1991a). The relations of parental characteristics and practices to children's vicarious emotional responding. *Child Development, 62*, 1393–1408.

Eisenberg, N., Fabes, R. A., Shepard, S. A., Guthrie, I. K., Murphy, B. C., & Reiser, M. (1999a). Parental reactions to children's negative emotions: Longitudinal relations to quality of children's social functioning. *Child Development, 70*, 513–534.

Eisenberg, N., Fabes, R. A., Shepard, S. A., Murphy, B. C., Jones, J., & Guthrie, I. K. (1998). Contemporaneous and longitudinal prediction of children's sympathy from dispositional regulation and emotionality. *Developmental Psychology, 34*, 910–924.

Eisenberg, N., Fabes, R. A., & Spinrad, T. L. (2006). Prosocial behavior. In N. Eisenberg (Vol. Ed.) and W. Damon & R. M. Lerner (Series Eds.), *Handbook of child psychology: Vol. 3. Social, emotional, and personality development* (6th ed., pp. 646–718). New York: Wiley.

Eisenberg, N., Guthrie, I. K., Fabes, R. A., Shepard, S., Losoya, S., Murphy, B. et al. (2000b). Prediction of elementary school children's externalizing problem behaviors from attentional and behavioral regulation and negative emotionality. *Child Development, 71*, 1367–1382. doi:10.1111/1467-8624.00233

Eisenberg, N., Guthrie, I. K., Murphy, B. C., Shepard, S. A., Cumberland, A., & Carlo, G. (1999b). Consistency and development of prosocial dispositions: A longitudinal study. *Child Development, 70*, 1360–1372.

Eisenberg, N., Hofer, C., Spinrad, T., Gershoff, E., Valiente, C., Losoya, S. L. et al. (2008). Understanding parent-adolescent conflict discussions: Concurrent and across-time prediction from youths' dispositions and parenting. *Monographs of the Society for Research in Child Development, 73* (Serial No. 290, No. 2), 1–160.

Eisenberg, N., Michalik, N., Spinrad, T. L., Hofer, C., Kupfer, A., Valiente, C. et al. (2007). Relations of effortful control and impulsivity to children's sympathy: A longitudinal study. *Cognitive Development, 22*, 544–567.

Eisenberg, N., Schaller, M., Fabes, R. A., Bustamante, D., Mathy, R., Shell, R. et al. (1988b). The differentiation of personal distress and sympathy in children and adults. *Developmental Psychology, 24*, 766–775.

Eisenberg, N., Spinrad, T. L., & Eggum, N. D. (2010a). Emotion-related self-regulation and its relation to children's maladjustment. *Annual Review of Clinical Psychology, 6*, 495–525.

Eisenberg, N., Spinrad, T. L., Eggum, N. D., Silva, K., Reiser, M., Hofer, C. et al. (2010b). Relations among maternal socialization, effortful control, and maladjustment in early childhood. *Development and Psychopathology, 22*, 507–525.

Eisenberg, N., Spinrad, T. L., Fabes, R. A., Reiser, M., Cumberland, A., Shepard, S. A. et al. (2004). The relations of effortful control and impulsivity to children's resiliency and adjustment. *Child Development, 75*, 25–46.

Eisenberg, N., Sulik, M. J., Spinrad, T. L., Edwards, A., Eggum, N. D., Liew, J. et al. (2012). Differential susceptibility and the early development of aggression: Interactive effects of respiratory sinus arrhythmia and environmental quality. *Developmental Psychology, 48*(3), 755–768.

Eisenberg, N., Valiente, C., Spinrad, T. L., Cumberland, A., Liew, J., Reiser, M. et al. (2009a). Longitudinal relations of children's effortful control, impulsivity, and negative emotionality to their externalizing, internalizing, and co-occurring behavior problems. *Developmental Psychology, 45*, 988–1008.

Eisenberg, N., Vidmar, M., Spinrad, T. L., Eggum, N. D., Edwards, A., Gaertner, B. et al. (2010c). Mothers' teaching strategies and children's effortful control: A longitudinal study. *Developmental Psychology, 46*, 1294–1308.

Eisenberg, N., Zhou, Q., Spinrad, T. L., Valiente, C., Fabes, R. A., & Liew, J. (2005a). Relations among positive parenting, children's effortful control, and externalizing problems: A three-wave longitudinal study. *Child Development, 76*, 1055–1071.

Eisenberg-Berg, N. (1976). The relationship of political attitudes to constraint and prosocial moral reasoning. *Developmental Psychology, 12*(6), 552–553.

Eisenberg-Berg, N. (1979). The development of children's prosocial moral judgment. *Developmental Psychology, 15*, 128–137.

Fabes, R. A., Eisenberg, N., Karbon, M., Bernzweig, J., Speer, A. L., & Carlo, G. (1994). Socialization of children's vicarious emotional responding and prosocial behavior: Relations with mothers' perceptions of children's emotional reactivity. *Developmental Psychology, 30*, 44–55.

Hofer, C., & Eisenberg, N., & Reiser, M. (2010). The role of socialization, effortful control, and resiliency in French adolescents' social functioning. *Journal of Research on Adolescence, 20*, 555–582. doi: 0.1111/j.1467–9507.2009.00550.x

Kohlberg, L. (1984). *Essays on moral development: Vol. 2. The psychology of moral development.* San Francisco: Harper & Row.

Michalik, N., Eisenberg, N., Spinrad, T. L., Ladd, B., Thompson, M., & Valiente, C. (2007). Longitudinal relations among parental personality, emotional expressivity, youths' sympathy, and prosocial behavior. *Social Development, 16*, 286–309.

Silva, K., M., Spinrad, T. L., Eisenberg, N., Sulik, M. J., Valiente, C., Huerta, S. et al. (2011). Relations of children's effortful control and teacher-child relationship quality to school attitudes in a low-income sample. *Early Education and Development, 22*, 434–460. doi: 10.1080/10409289.2011.578046

Spinrad, T., L., Eisenberg, N., Cumberland, A., Fabes, R. A., Valiente, C., Shepard, S. A. et al. (2006). The relations of temperamentally based control processes to children's social competence: A longitudinal study. *Emotion, 6*, 498–510.

Spinrad, T. L., Eisenberg, N., Gaertner, B., Popp, T., Smith, C. L., Kupfer, A. et al. (2007). Relations of maternal socialization and toddlers' effortful control to children's adjustment and social competence. *Developmental Psychology, 43*, 1170–1186.

Sulik, M. J., Eisenberg, N., Lemery-Chalfant, K., Spinrad, T. L., Silva, K. M., Eggum, N. D. et al. (2012). Interactions between serotonin transporter gene haplotypes and quality of mothers' parenting predict the development of children's noncompliance. *Developmental Psychology, 48*(3), 740–754. doi:10.1037/a0026518.

Valiente, C., Eisenberg, N., Fabes, R. A., Shepard, S. A., Cumberland, A., & Losoya, S. H. (2004). Prediction of children's empathy-related responding from their effortful control and parents' expressivity. *Developmental Psychology, 40*, 911–926.

Valiente, C., Eisenberg, N., Haugen, R. G., Spinrad, T. L., Hofer, C., Liew, J. et al. (2011). Children's effortful control and academic achievement: Mediation through social functioning. *Early Education and Development, 22*, 411–433. doi:10.1080/10409289.2010.505259

Valiente, C., Eisenberg, N., Smith, C. L., Reiser, M., Fabes, R. A., Losoya, S. et al. (2003). The relations of effortful control and reactive control to children's externalizing problems: A longitudinal assessment. *Journal of Personality, 71*, 1179–1196.

Valiente, C., Eisenberg, N., Spinrad, T. L., Reiser, M. Cumberland, A., Losoya, S. et al. (2006). Relations among mothers' expressivity, children's effortful control, and their problem behaviors: A four-year longitudinal study. *Emotion, 6*, 459–472.

Zhou, Q., Eisenberg, N., Wang, Y., & Reiser, M. (2004). Chinese children's effortful control and dispositional anger/frustration: Relations to parenting styles and children's social functioning. *Developmental Psychology, 40*, 352–366.

14

Studying Lives in Changing Times

A Life-Course Journey

GLEN H. ELDER, JR.

Introduction

Scientific biographies in the social and behavioral sciences reflect changes taking place in society, its social institutions, and culture. This influence is expressed most often through family life, graduate education, and the transition to the first professional job. In my doctoral cohort of 1961, new PhDs in the quantitative social sciences were prepared for a career that drew heavily upon social survey methods. I followed this path in graduate studies at the University of North Carolina–Chapel Hill, with a specialization in social psychology that linked the Departments of Sociology and Psychology.

The 1960s brought dramatic change that would transform my thinking and career through a new type of research design that was gaining advocates at the National Institutes of Health (NIH) and among social scientists. This design moved beyond the cross-sectional survey so as to capture temporal change in people and in their environments. By the time I completed my doctorate, such projects had not yet occurred at the national level, but the momentum increased significantly across the decade. At century's end, this research design had proven its worth and was appropriately described as the "Hubble telescope" of the social sciences and as one of its greatest methodological innovations of the century (Butz & Torrey, 2006).

An early forerunner of this research innovation had been underway for several decades as longitudinal studies of children at the Institute of Human Development (then called Child Welfare) on the University of California campus at Berkeley. My first career appointment placed me in the middle of longitudinal studies at this internationally known research institute on child development. The resulting scientific biography describes a "turning point" in my career between the social survey world of graduate school and the temporal world of longitudinal research

at the Berkeley Institute of Human Development. This career change represented a turning point in method that I was not prepared for by graduate work and a postdoctoral fellowship even though methodological advances and training updates are commonplace for careers in social science. Nevertheless, early biographical experiences provide a frame for understanding how a seeming "product of the survey age" could become so involved in developing a temporal and contextual way of thinking about lives and human development in a longitudinal study.

I begin the chapter by focusing on what I consider the core "biographical influences" under "Impressions from Early Life"—the imprint of parents and family, the personal experience of social change, and the contributions of graduate studies and research. My transition to the Institute of Human Development comes next in "The Berkeley Years," a time span that extends, with some interruptions, from 1962 to 1974. This formative time involved mainly archival work and empirical studies based on longitudinal data. *Children of the Great Depression* (1974/1999) emerged from this research over nearly a decade of analysis, writing, and rethinking, along with numerous papers that contributed to it. The next section briefly considers markers of my contribution to the life-course perspective and its relation to developmental science. In closing, I offer some reflections on this life-course journey.[1]

Impressions from Early Life

Whenever I am asked what lies behind the fascination I have with human lives in a changing world, my first thought is to turn to parental influence. My mother was born in Buffalo (1905) to May and Gove G. Johnson, a minister over many years in the National Memorial Baptist Church of Washington, DC. She successfully resisted family wishes that she attend a woman's college and proceeded to graduate from the coeducational world of Denison College in Ohio. My father was born in 1901 to a farm couple of modest circumstances who ran a stock farm in Trumbull County near Youngstown, Ohio. He graduated from Ohio Wesleyan College. Both parents initially entered the field of high-school teaching, mother in English literature as well as coach of girls' basketball; and father in mathematics and coach of the boys' football team. They met through mutual friends and decided to marry even if it was "the valley of the Great Depression," 1932. I came along in 1934 and my brother 3 years later.

As my birth year suggests, I was too young to have lasting impressions from the Great Depression, but this was not the case for the onset of World War II. December 7, 1941 is etched in memories of family members quietly sitting around a Philco radio as they listened, stunned by the tragic news from Pearl Harbor. The radio news was always on during my family lunchtimes from school in 1942. That same year produced another kind of personal and family challenge, my serious encounter with poliomyelitis. In late August of 1943, we spent a day of swimming at a recreation area of Lake Erie. On the return home that night, I recall feeling hot and feverish. When I woke the next day, I could not move my legs. I remember trying to walk on the sidewalk beside my home in Berea (Ohio) and realizing that my legs were "stiff as a board." Before long I entered Cleveland City Hospital and was placed under the care of Dr. John Toomey in the "polio ward" with other children, some of whom were in iron lungs or in beds with leather straps on their legs. Because polio was considered an infectious disease, I could only talk to my parents from my window on the third floor over my 5-week stay in the hospital. Shortly after entering the hospital, I remember being wheeled into a brightly lit room with men in white coats where I received a large number of spinal injections. I was not told anything about my medical care at the time, but when I returned home I had full use of my legs and could play all my favorite sports, though I was very weak. I don't have any memory of the possibility that I might be crippled for life, but my parents were overjoyed by "the miracle." Some years after my parents died I discovered that I was blessed with the best possible care for a young patient with a case of poliomyelitis. In Dr. Toomey's obituary (January, 1950), he is placed "among America's greatest students of this disease" who developed many original methods of therapy that diminished the mortality risk and complications of the disease. The Unit for Contagious Diseases at the hospital is named the Toomey Pavilion in his honor.

Books always played an important part in our family life and especially in the life of my mother. But most importantly they were books about people's lives, both fictive and real. As a result, I acquired an interest in the biographies of historical figures and of people in diverse fields of work. Franklin D. Roosevelt was my only president up to age 10, and I read extensively about his life. Eventually, biographies became a favorite way for me to gain insight regarding events and processes in lives and changing times. This interest relates to a traditional method, the collection of qualitative life histories from members of studies, a technique used most effectively by Thomas and Znaniecki (1918) in their pioneering study of immigration from Europe to the United States, *The Polish Peasant in Europe and America*.

My father was also an influential force in my life, especially in showing me how to adapt to life change. To him, no obstacle was impossible to overcome. His time as a teacher and coach mainly occurred before I was born, and I was only 3 years old when he decided to take the Ohio Medical Boards in order to practice chiropractic medicine. This orthopedic practice became an extension of his interest in fitness training and continued for many years. During this time he explored the possibility of returning to his farming roots and he surprised us by making such a decision as the 1940s came to an end. At the time, I was a city kid with no experience in farming and my father was some 30 years removed from his father's farm. But he wanted to make this move before his sons left for college.

We discovered in May 1949 that the Elders were headed for life on a dairy farm in Northwestern Pennsylvania, and that the family would be driving there immediately. My parents asked me to stay on at the farm over the coming week so that work could proceed on the house. I agreed to do so even though I didn't know the neighbors and lacked a phone to call home. I don't recall feeling lonely. Instead I remember the "alone time" as a great adventure in exploring the fields, woods, and empty barns. But, I was totally unprepared for the extent of change between the Cleveland suburbs and the Pennsylvania farm——from urban to rural farm, 140 miles from Cleveland and 12 miles from the nearest small town of Titusville. In some ways, the transition resembled an immigrant's experience, except that we were not moving as links in a chain to a place occupied by family or friends. We did not know anyone around our farm and no one from our former community made the change with us. We were on our own in a very different culture.

The social discontinuities of this transition increased my awareness of the personal effects of disruptive change, an experience not unlike that of war mobilization in Cleveland. In both cases, families faced the challenge of doing things they had not done before and they were not always sure about how to do them. An effective response was essential and thus Clevelanders found a way to adapt effectively, and so did my parents. They were models of how to make the best of this life change. I eventually acquired a sense of being able to work things out that has been valuable when dealing with new situations. Childhood experiences of this kind shaped a way of thinking about the social world and people that I carried into college, graduate studies, and professional life——interest in the effect of social change on the lives of young and old.

The new farming experience led me to agricultural studies at Penn State in 1952. But, as so often happens, this early specialization was premature. By the end of the second year, interests had begun to crystallize on a social psychology of society's impact on people, such as in David Riesman's *The Lonely Crowd* (1950). Other appealing social psychologists included Theodore Newcomb, Muzafir Sherif, and Kurt Lewin, each one with a contribution to the social psychology of people in context. As I approached the completion of my undergraduate studies, my trajectory from agriculture to social science left me uncertain about the next step, whether graduate school or the workplace.

A speaker at Penn State, the Dean of Men at Kent State University (in Ohio), suggested an interim step that might help me think through such matters—a one-year staff appointment with residence in a student dormitory. The Dean had a doctorate in the field of sociology and so when I accepted his invitation, I also decided to enroll in the Sociology graduate program (fall, 1957) with the goal of an MA in a year. My eventual topic focused on a prominent issue among undergraduates in my dormitory, the factors that play a role in the academic and social adjustment of students. Reference group theory, as introduced to me by reading Robert Merton (1957), offered a way to think about this issue by addressing how individuals relate to membership and non-membership groups. I only had data obtained at a point in time and thus could not chart the changing reference orientations of students over time. My exposure to Merton's learned scholarship and eloquent prose in *Social Theory and Social Structure* (1957/1968) became an inspiration and model in graduate studies and beyond.

In the fall months of my time at Kent State, I explored doctoral programs in social psychology. Theodore Newcomb's interdisciplinary program at Michigan was attractive, but the University of North Carolina's Sociology Program soon became the most appealing option. At Carolina I could study social psychology with a major in Sociology and a minor in Psychology. The assistantship offer enabled me to work with Charles Bowerman on all stages of his National Institute of Mental Health study of adolescent parent–peer orientations using a large sample of 7th through 12th graders in central North Carolina and Ohio. After accepting the offer, I visited Chapel Hill with my Penn State bride-to-be, Karen Bixler, to work out matters of housing and employment. We married in New Jersey, just before driving down to our new home in Chapel Hill.

I soon discovered that the University of North Carolina provided an excellent match for my interests at the time. Departments in the College of Arts and Sciences actively encouraged cross-disciplinary associations through research consortia and institutes. The Alumni Building, then home to Sociology, was also the home of four other departments, the Institute for Research in Social Science, and Psychology's small group laboratory. The hot summer air in Alumni also indirectly exposed me to other disciplines and a serendipitous learning experience (Merton & Barber, 2004) when I escaped to an air-conditioned carrel in Wilson Library. Just across the aisle from my desk were shelves of books in developmental psychology, including the entire collection of monographs of the Society for Research in Child Development. It was not long before I began exploring the monographs. One by one they

came off the shelves, and slowly I acquired an education on the history of the Society for Research in Child Development—the early leading figures in the field, the pioneering child development institutes, and longitudinal studies. Marion Radke's (Yarrow) dissertation was especially interesting to me at this time. This exposure also included the Murchison *Handbook of Child Psychology* with a chapter by Kurt Lewin (1931). By the end of my doctoral work, I had an informal graduate-level education in developmental psychology, including issues that I would address decades later within the emerging field of developmental science.

This education was particularly helpful in the early stage of the adolescent project when I worked on a framework of developmental and social processes in adolescence relative to family, peer group, and school. Next on the agenda came the construction of a schedule for open-ended interviews with teenagers in a local high school. I conducted the interviews and found their typescripts to be invaluable stimuli for my thinking about young people and their development, and consequently for generating basic questions and response categories for the self-administered questionnaire survey. Well before Diana Baumrind's publications on authority relations, we devised measures of structured relations between adolescents and their parents that ranged from autocratic to democratic-egalitarian and permissive, laissez-faire. These structural patterns may well have been suggested by the group dynamic research of Lewin, Lippitt, and White (1939).

During the course of doctoral research I encountered the peer group studies of Urie Bronfenbrenner at Cornell University, and wrote to him about the adolescent study we were engaged in at the time. Before long, I received a substantial packet of publications and manuscripts from him with a note of encouragement on our work. This package included a paper reporting his Soviet peer group research as well as a fascinating essay that would soon have much greater relevance to my work at Berkeley's Institute of Human Development. It was entitled "Socialization and Social Class through Time and Space" (1958). Bronfenbrenner reported that studies of class and child-rearing from the 1930s made sense only when they were ordered by date of research, the survey's historical time. This exchange and others made Cornell's Department of Human Development an attractive place to visit after submitting my dissertation in the summer of 1961. I visited the Cornell Department of Human Development unannounced and discovered that Bronfenbrenner had just returned to the States from a trip to the Soviet Union. The Cornell possibility didn't materialize at that time, although it did nearly 20 years later when I became a professor in Bronfenbrenner's department.

As my social psychology crystallized during graduate school, it focused on socialization as a link between people and social structure. This static framework made sense with data from a cross-sectional survey, as on the adolescent project. My dissertation illustrated this point by investigating types of structured relationships between parents and adolescents and their association with aspects of socialization, from patterns of communication to methods of discipline (1961). A typology of structured relations between parents and youth formed the topic of my first presentation at the American Sociological Association in 1961. Subsequent papers investigated the explanatory communications of parents and their modification of structural effects in families. A 1-year postdoctoral fellowship from the National Institute of Mental Health enabled me to prepare additional papers from the Adolescent Project for publication. These were included in a monograph that was published with the revised dissertation chapters many years later (Elder, 1980b). Socialization was an established field of theory and research in social psychology during these years (Clausen, 1968), with explicit connections to the concept of life cycle. In a life cycle of generational succession, the young are socialized to maturity, give birth to and socialize the next generation, grow old and die.

The world of longitudinal studies was known to me only through monographs I had read as a graduate student. I never even imagined the Berkeley Institute of Human Development would become a career beginning, at least not until I was introduced to John Clausen in the spring of 1961 by Charles Bowerman, my dissertation advisor in the North Carolina graduate program of sociology. They were fellow graduate students and close friends in the pre-war Sociology Department at the University of Chicago home of the influential Chicago School of Sociology with its distinctive contextual perspective on people's lives (Abbott, 1999). Clausen had just become director of the Institute of Human Development and was in the market for a junior colleague who could collaborate with him on longitudinal studies at the Institute. I was enthusiastic about the job opportunity, and the chance to work with him on data records that depicted people over their lives. The precise timing of this offer with my job search illustrates well Bandura's perspective on "chance encounters in life (1982)."

The Berkeley Years

My career beginnings at the University of California at Berkeley occurred at a momentous time for the social and behavioral sciences on campus, as in the society at large. Leadership of the Institute of Human Development had just passed from psychologists who had founded it in the 1920s to sociologist John Clausen, trained in the traditions of the Chicago School of Sociology. The Institute had recently moved into the first floor of brand new Tolman Hall, the home of Psychology and the School of Education.[2] The Department of Sociology,[3] my other affiliation, had also undergone major change. Established in the mid-1950s under the leadership of Herbert Blumer, a distinguished social psychologist, the department had quickly become an assembly of internationally renowned faculty. These two worlds of faculty affiliation were some distance from each other on the campus and on academic ties, but their separation did not prevent me from bringing the disciplines together in my developmental social psychology and life-course studies.

Clausen has described his introduction to the Institute's enormous data archive as "somewhat overwhelming" (Clausen, 1999, xvii). The adolescent years included several parent interviews, interest questionnaires on the adolescents, personality and physical development inventories, and observational ratings by Institute staff and peers. The data transfer from the Institute's older facility to its new home in Tolman Hall still required some filing. On top of this, the Oakland study members had just participated in a middle-age (late 30s) follow-up. Coding and rating of the data were underway, but this work did not include a large part of my responsibility—data from the long interview, with its open-ended questions. The coding also did not apply to the development of a life record on biographical events and experiences, such as place of residence, education and work, military service, and family. The same kind of biographical history was needed on the parents. Records in the Oakland data archive did not enable a researcher to follow the life path of a study member.

I brought little relevant training to the Institute on the coding of open-ended interview data, and lacked a day-to-day supervisor to guide me in the design of an appropriate code book. However, Clausen believed I could manage this task and he gave me the freedom to devise a theoretical approach to the measurement task. His vote of confidence encouraged me to take charge of this operation. The Kent State research on the transition of young people to college and the Carolina study across the adolescent years underscored the relevance of an age-based theoretical model and so I began to search this domain for relevant sources.

Bernice Neugarten's intellectual role in the Committee on Human Development at the University of Chicago led me to her pioneering investigations of the meanings of age in the 1950s and early 1960s—the differential timing of a transition, social timetables and age expectations regarding appropriate behavior (Neugarten, 1996). In Neugarten's mind, the timing of status passages was not indicated by median age, but rather by relative age—by one's age in relation to the age of others. In a conventional or normative sense, some people marry relatively early, others at the expectable time, and still others do so very late in life. My immersion in Neugarten's thinking offered an appealing temporal slant on social psychology in what I now consider a developmental perspective. Her thinking eventually became a central component of my approach to the age-graded life course.

Other concepts of time and timing came from the link between the study member's birth year and historical time. Demographer Norman Ryder (1965) highlighted this link in his famous essay on birth cohorts in the study of social change. When each birth cohort encounters a major historical change, it is "distinctively marked by the career stage it occupies" (p. 846). The birth years of the Oakland cohort placed their childhood in the 1920s and their adolescence in the Great Depression. Oakland data on puberty documented maturation level and rate as concepts of ontogenetic time and timing. To think about ways of conceptualizing adult pathways, I turned to sociologist Harold Wilensky's code book on interlocking pathways in adulthood—family, work-life, and leisure. As a colleague in the Berkeley Department of Sociology, Wilensky encouraged me to take a look at how he measured adult pathways and I learned much from them, although his data were obtained from a community survey and could not document life changes.

With these age-based distinctions in mind, I began to assemble a life-record code book that included age at event information from each study member's data file in adolescence and another one on the adult years. The adolescent code book focused on family and parent life events including measures of event sequences based on the literature, such as work-life instability and parental marital history. The adult code book included life-history information on the study members' adult years, along with event sequences, such as a sequential typology of family and work roles. I obtained this information from a systematic reading of the Oakland long interview and proceeded to generate codes for the interview as well as for a life-history file at the Institute. Additional life-record information on the adult years of the study member was obtained from a mail-out survey questionnaire.

Data on the parents and family were drawn most heavily from the major parent interviews in 1932, 1934, and 1936 (all involving only mother). The interviews provided information on immigration status, nationality, educational level, number of children in the family, residence, usual occupation of father and mother, current employment, and work histories. The resulting overview revealed much change from year to year among the families, challenging the usefulness of single measurements at a point in time. The interviews provided information on total family income in 1929, before the economic collapse in the Great Depression, and in the worst year, 1933. By comparing these years, I could identify families that lost little if anything in the thirties and those that lost heavily, sometimes well over a third or half of their 1929 income. This serendipitous outcome led me to expand the scope of my study from careers to the impact of the Great Depression in lives. Social change had always been an interest of mine.

Income loss among the Oakland families was a likely source of the family problems that came to the attention of the Institute staff, such as the dissolution of families, and troubled children. I began to see Depression hardships as the engine of adversity in these families and the lives of their children. To make a case for research on this topic, I explored within the middle and working class of 1929 the effect of economic deprivation on family relationships, children's roles in the changing household economy, and the emotional health of family members. By the summer of 1965, my project report showed that mounting economic hardship exposed boys and girls to more family conflict,

household responsibilities, and parental health problems. Clausen found the results of considerable interest and cited them in one of his papers. But his leadership duties left too little time for him to collaborate on this research. He was also heavily involved in making the case for prospective longitudinal studies at federal agencies in Washington, DC. This period was an early stage of longitudinal studies and continuing educational efforts were needed. These leadership demands were frustrating to Clausen and me, but I valued the additional responsibility to move research along. And being more on my own enabled me to acquire a sense of self-direction in the new world of longitudinal and life-course studies.

All scientific careers are influenced by countless acts of mentoring across the years and I have acknowledged many of them in this chapter, but looking back over my half-century in the social sciences, it is clear that some developmental arrangements were not so considered at the time by my senior colleagues. One experience that stands out in my memory is John Clausen's inability to spend more time on a project he had planned for us to complete at the Institute of Human Development at Berkeley. His role as director of the Institute was all consuming. As a result, I was left with only general instructions on the big task at hand—the coding of data on a longitudinal sample. Though Clausen may have considered this a neglectful situation, I never thought of it in that way. Indeed, my open-ended assignment gave me a remarkable degree of freedom to develop ways of thinking and accomplishment.

This Berkeley experience brings to mind the earlier life situation I encountered when my father asked me to stay on our newly purchased farm by myself before my family's move from Cleveland. I never thought of this assignment as evidence of neglect. Though a city kid with no knowledge of farming, I remember the experience as both an adventure and a challenge. I may have repressed the downside of this time, but its rewards remain very real to me. In such experiences, I have discovered that it is not what people do for you, but rather it is what they leave you free to do.

I decided to pursue a more comprehensive study of the Oakland children's lives in the Great Depression and beyond, despite the many unknowns. As most scientists would agree, research often involves "doing something that no one has done before, [so] you don't always know how to do it or exactly what to do" (Barber & Fox, 1958, p. 136). When I had the Oakland project wrapped up as a book on Depression children, Clausen's foreword noted with much generosity that I brought substantial research experience and knowledge of adolescent development to the Oakland Study along with "insatiable curiosity and a prodigious amount of energy" (1999, p. xix). The Depression project required all I could muster for "on the job training."

To investigate the impact of drastic economic change on children's lives, I used family adaptations as a potential explanatory link, borrowing from Bakke's Depression study (1940). Three types of hypothesized adaptations were defined: (1) in the household economy—heavy loss of income called for new forms of economic maintenance that altered the social roles of family members, shifting responsibilities to mother and the older children; (2) in family relationships—father's loss of earning power increased the relative power of mother, reduced the level of parental control, and diminished the attractiveness of father as a role model; and (3) in social strains in the family, with increasing social ambiguity, family conflict, and emotional strain. These adaptations of processes were viewed in terms of the middle and working classes of families at the Depression's outset.

The duration of the Oakland study enabled me to design a study that could trace the Depression experience to outcomes in the dependency years of adolescence and then through young adulthood to mid-life. The first part of the project focused on the adolescents as they came of age in the Depression and assumed roles in the household division of labor, experienced change in family relationships, and were influenced emotionally by the changes. The next part began when the study members left high school and made the transition to adulthood, as marked by entry into college, the military, employment, and marriage. I assessed the Depression's effect in terms of educational and occupational attainment, marital and parental roles, and values. The final part of the study investigated the enduring effects of Depression hardship on emotional and physical health.

Initial investigations on a complex project can be both very encouraging and suggestive of additional work that needs to be done. I discovered this to be the case when I had completed all planned analyses and prepared drafts of chapters on the proposed topics. I tentatively entitled the manuscript *Children of the Great Depression* and sent it out for preliminary review. John Clausen was one of the readers. At the time I felt that I had not thought through the integration of all chapters into a life story that flowed smoothly. And I knew that I still had work to do in terms of the analytic structure and narrative of the chapters. One of the problems I faced involved the amount of technical detail—it disrupted the narrative flow of the chapters. The next draft, I concluded, would need to draw upon some published papers on the Oakland data file.

My misgivings about the manuscript were borne out by the reviews and I decided to set it aside for a while as I completed the papers for publication. The results of the reviews were disheartening, though deep inside I knew that I had an important story to tell and just needed the time to do the required work. The research I had done indicated that the big thematic outcome for the Oakland cohort would be resilience. The men and women from deprived families in the middle and working class had defied expectations by their accomplishments and health. By the age of 40, they ranked as well as the nondeprived, if not better, on occupational status. They had far more in common with the label of the "Greatest Generation" than with predictions of a "Lost Generation." This outcome

had much to do with the booming U.S. economy in the 1940s and 1950s, and with the extraordinary benefits that World War II veterans received—in education, housing, and health. I also concluded that it had much to do with the age of the Oakland participants when hard times occurred—they were too old to be seriously damaged by family disruptions and too young to feel the harsh consequences of a Depression labor market. Their age minimized exposure to such risks.

After several years at the university, I received a positive vote from the sociology faculty and encouragement to work toward the forthcoming tenure evaluation. However, a number of other issues eventually lured me back to a professorship at the University of North Carolina in 1967. The Berkeley campus was highly politicized during these years with the Free Speech Movement and this junior faculty member recalls the cross-pressures of senior faculty, administration, and undergraduate students. Positive affirmation was hard to come by. Thus news that my most esteemed member of the sociology faculty at Carolina, Rupert Vance, had urged his colleagues "to bring Elder back" was most welcome. Vance was past president of the American Sociological Association and a scholar who was widely admired for his pioneering demographic studies of the Southern region. When I was assigned by Kingsley Davis to launch my Berkeley teaching career with a course on urbanization and the city, a field for which I was not trained, I turned in desperation to Professor Vance and asked for guidance as well as a course syllabus. I credit Rupert Vance for my survival in this trial by fire.

My new focus on a "Children of the Great Depression" study led to a number of researchable questions that I explored when I returned to the University of North Carolina–Chapel Hill in 1967 for a professorship in the Department of Sociology. They ranged from the relevance of economic deprivation and other status changes for life chances and health to ways of addressing the generalization issue in a single cohort study. I achieved a comparative perspective by distinguishing between the relatively nondeprived and deprived families on each class level, but I needed another birth cohort to determine how exposure to the economic losses of the Great Depression influenced other birth cohorts. It was clear to me at the time that we had no reason to expect similar results from a younger or older birth cohort. As Norman Ryder made clear in his 1965 paper, birth cohorts are influenced differentially according to their life stage at the time of change.

The Berkeley Guidance sample seemed to be an ideal comparison cohort. The Study members were born at the end of the 1920s, nearly a decade later than the Oakland subjects, and the two studies were housed at the Institute of Human Development. They also came of age in the same larger community, that of the San Francisco Bay Area. John Clausen enabled me to gain access to the Berkeley data archive with the permission of its long-time director, Jean Macfarlane and her collaborator Marjorie Honzik. Data were available on 212 Berkeley study members up to age 40 and I found that I could measure economic deprivation (1929–33) on the study members' families by using income and other socioeconomic data. A National Science Foundation grant enabled me to spend a sabbatical year at the Berkeley Institute with a team of coders in 1972–73. In addition to John Clausen, two other directors of the Berkeley Institute—psychologists Paul Mussen and M. Brewster Smith—were very helpful on these projects and they continued to be special colleagues across the years.

Before launching this sabbatical year, I devoted a year to a complete revision of the manuscript of *Children of the Great Depression*. My thinking and research over several years had made a remarkable difference in this revision, but I will never forget the challenge of bringing the book together while teaching four courses and completing a chapter each month. In addition, I had three little boys and my wife Karen too much on the sidelines. In the first draft, I had "bits and pieces" of life-course thinking to draw upon. The analytic structure of the revised work brought out important features: (1) the age-graded model of the life course—historical, social and ontogenetic time; (2) the interdisciplinary and multi-level perspective on the life course with its linkages and contexts across levels of analysis; (3) prominent conceptual themes that became paradigmatic principles of the life course 20 years later; and (4) methods of working with archival longitudinal data, including recoding to create new variables. Longitudinal studies frequently outlive the purposes of their establishment many years earlier, and this was the case for the Oakland Study. I had adapted the data for new purposes with the goal of making the best of what we had.

The conceptual themes depict key elements of the lived experiences of the Oakland men and women who grew up in the 1930s. First of all, these lives were embedded in relationships with people, such as family, friends, and co-workers. "Linked lives" is the oldest principle of the life course. Second, the timing of events and social roles, whether early or late, influenced their impact. Life transitions that come earlier or later than usual make coordination difficult. Third, the lived experiences of the Oakland Study members were profoundly influenced by changing historical times and places, the central theme of the Great Depression research. Fourth, the Oakland Study members were actors with choices—human agency. People construct their lives by such choices even amidst the constraints of circumstances. And fifth, the study documented the study members "development and aging as lifelong processes."

During the final stage of preparing *Children of the Great Depression* for publication, I was influenced by a pioneering book on the socioeconomic life cycle of human populations, *The American Occupational Structure* (Blau & Duncan, 1967). Using a national retrospective life history survey, the authors drew upon population concepts (such as birth cohorts) to analyze social stratification and social mobility over phases of the life course (Elder, 1992). A sequel to this work (Duncan, Featherman, & Duncan, 1972) significantly enriched the status attainment process by investigating cognitive and motivational factors as well as career contingencies involving the timing of the first job, migration, marital disruption, and military service. Both studies reflect an early integration of the two major traditions in life studies—on role relationships, and age. They also represent a keen sensitivity to interdependent lives. By the mid-1970s, one of Featherman's doctoral students, Dennis Hogan, had extended the life-course model even further with emphasis on age grading by focusing his dissertation on event timing and sequences in the transition to adulthood (Hogan, 1981).

In final form as a book manuscript, *Children of the Great Depression* embodied distinctive intellectual themes of the early Chicago School of Sociology. Most importantly, it studied individual lives and their life histories within a particular time and place. Human lives are embedded in social contexts, from neighborhoods to communities. With this connection to the Chicago School in mind, I sent the manuscript for review to the University of Chicago Press in the summer of 1972 and within the year it was accepted. I had passed on a copy of the manuscript to John Clausen, whom I asked to write the book's foreword. Several weeks later, Clausen appeared at my Institute office door and commented on the chapters. He closed by saying "You know, Glen, this is going to be a classic!" That moment is vividly etched in my memory as a young assistant professor, and yet I really didn't grasp the significance of what he was saying. I remember only feeling relieved that the book was going to be published by a distinguished university press and that Clausen thought it would do well. A 2003 survey of the Society for Research on Child Development indicates that Clausen's prediction was on target. Participants in the survey rated *Children of the Great Depression* as the fourth "most fascinating study" in the field of child psychology since 1950.

When *Children of the Great Depression* was published in 1974, a decade had passed since the initial archival work and I realized that more than a significant book had emerged in the process. From a personal standpoint, it had motivated me to embark on a life-course program of theoretical and empirical work on studying lives in social pathways and changing times, often with attention to families as a link between such times and lives. Archival work on the Berkeley study enabled me to show that the effects of economic hardship in the Great Depression were more adverse for the younger Berkeley children than for the Oakland young people (the life-stage principle), and especially for boys. However, my research on military service in lives shows that the involvement of males in the military minimized this cohort difference (Elder & Caspi, 1990; Elder, 1999). Retrospective military histories on these cohorts provided data to show that their life-span resilience out of the Great Depression had much to do with their service in World War II and the Korean War (Elder, 1986).

In the 1990s, I returned to the subject of hard times with longitudinal investigations of the impact of a declining rural Midwest economy on young people and their families (Elder & Conger, 2000) and of poverty in the lives of inner city youth of Philadelphia (Furstenberg, Cook, Eccles, Elder, & Sameroff, 1999). Since the onset of the Great Recession in 2008, I have worked with European colleagues (Walter Heinz, University of Bremen; John Bynner, University of London) to organize research consortia in Germany, the United Kingdom, and the United States for the purpose of developing longitudinal investigations of the impact of this crisis on the lives of young people and their siblings.

Advances in Life-Course Theory and Research

Children of the Great Depression generated considerable interest across the social and behavioral sciences with its life-course perspective. For example, plans for the first volume of the *Annual Review of Sociology* included an essay on life-course studies, and I accepted the invitation to write it (Elder, 1975). An earlier chapter on this topic had been published (Cain, 1964), but it reflected the atemporal literature of the 1950s and earlier. I saw this invitation as an opportunity to give greater visibility to advances in longitudinal studies of age and the life course. Empirical studies relevant to the life course were still scarce, but notable research was available on the timing and order of life events, as well as on cohort-historical studies of people's lives, including *Children of the Great Depression*. The publication of this book and the *Annual Review of Sociology* essay encouraged the adoption of life-course distinctions in major longitudinal studies such as the Panel Study of Income Dynamics and the National Longitudinal Surveys. By shifting the focus from aggregate populations to the lives of individuals, the life-course paradigm totally "revolutionized demography" by the 21st century (Hogan & Goldscheider, 2003).

The launching of small-scale longitudinal studies as well as national studies (such as the National Longitudinal Survey of 1972) generated a good many conceptual and methodological issues. Frank Furstenberg's Baltimore project illustrates the pioneering character of small longitudinal studies in the 1960s and 1970s. I first met Furstenberg in 1968 at a National Institute of Health conference that was focused on Richard Jessor's multiethnic study. I had just returned to the University of North Carolina–Chapel Hill and Furstenberg (University of Pennsylvania) was exploring the possibility of following up teenage mothers from low-income African-American neighborhoods. They were members of a service program that was running out of funds. He added a matched sample of the former classmates of the teenage mothers who had not become pregnant in adolescence, and conducted interviews with both groups in 1970 and 1972. During this time, he became aware of my work on *Children of the Great Depression* and began to locate his study members within social history and their life course. In a major contribution, he creatively applied the concept of multiple interlocking career lines to the life-course adaptations of

unwed mothers (1976). But there were many times, as he has noted, when he wondered whether he would ever finish the project! This is surely a state of mind that is widely shared among investigators of lives over time. Nearly two decades later, I collaborated with Furstenberg, Thomas Cook, Arnold Sameroff, and Jacque Eccles on a study of Philadelphia families from the inner city (1999). This project emerged from a MacArthur Foundation network on youth in high-risk settings, chaired by Richard Jessor.

A network of social historians under the leadership of Tamara Hareven found the life-course perspective more dynamic and contextual than the life-cycle concept, and they appreciated the multiple meanings of age—historical through birth year, social in terms of age-graded expectations on timing and the order of life events, and social psychological according to age identity and health. Hareven invited me to meet members of this network at her home in Cambridge, Massachusetts, during the winter of 1975 and the meeting led to participation in a New Orleans workshop during the spring and a week-long conference at Williams College in the summer of 1976. Presentations by the historians drew upon 1880 census data on Essex County, Massachusetts. Though only cross-sectional, the data led to thoughtful papers that were published in a book entitled *Transitions* (Hareven, 1978). In *Family Time and Industrial Time* (1982), Hareven applied a life-course framework to her study of the rise and fall of the giant Amoskeag textile mill in the lives and families of Manchester, New Hampshire mill workers. These associations and activities paralleled my continuing longitudinal studies of the impact of social change on the life course as expressed through family adaptations.

By the mid-1970s, the interdisciplinary interests of the Social Science Research Council (SSRC) in New York City were addressing issues of the life course and human development. Sociologist Matilda White Riley, chair of a committee on this topic, invited me to join in 1977 and I was delighted to do so. At the time, members included psychologist Paul Baltes, a leading figure in the field of life-span developmental psychology. I had known Baltes since my visit to his Penn State program in 1973 and we had spirited debates across the years about our perspectives on human development, the differences and similarities—such as contextualism, developmental variance, and invariance. This good-natured exchange continued well into the 21st century, many years after he had moved to the Max Planck Institute in Berlin.

Another key member of the committee was M. Brewster Smith, whom I had known since his days at the Institute of Human Development. Smith was a supportive colleague in my junior role and a most helpful reader of *Children of the Great Depression* in manuscript form. He was also the faculty mentor who channeled a gifted senior at the University of California–Santa Cruz—Avshalom Caspi—to graduate studies with me in Cornell's Human Development program, 1980. Other members of the committee include sociologists Bert Brim, David Featherman,

John Meyer, Walter Muller, and Aage Sorensen, as well as psychologists Martin Seligman and Franz Weinert. Caleb Finch and George Martin represented the biological field. This committee continued under co-chairs Baltes and Elder into the 1980s with Matilda White Riley, now an Associate Director of the National Institute on Aging. At this time, the committee broadened its life-span frame toward child development and added prominent developmentalists—Judy Dunn, Mavis Hetherington, Richard Lerner, and Ross Parke. At the center of this large enterprise was Lonnie Sherrod, our incomparable SSRC staff member.

In these early years of the life-course approach to human development and aging, the SSRC committee played an important leadership role at the highest level. Sponsorship by the council gave national and international visibility to our central mission of advancing the field. This function was especially valuable for new PhDs who were just getting into this line of work. It played a mentoring role for them by inviting a small number to observe each meeting and to establish ties to members of the committee. In some instances, they were invited to participate in the discussions.

The significance of the SSRC's efforts to advance the life-course perspective has been noted by younger colleagues, such as Jeylan Mortimer (2008) at the Minnesota Life Course Center. In reflection on my role, she observed that

> Elder's involvement in the Social Science Research Council in the 1980s did much to further and legitimate the new interdisciplinary field of life course studies, drawing on the theoretical, conceptual, and methodological tools of multiple social sciences, but especially sociology, developmental psychology, and history. He continued this effort under the aegis of the National Research Council.
>
> (p. 221)[3]

The most important mentoring initiative of the committee involved the Panel Study of Income Dynamics (PSID). Researchers in early career were encouraged to submit short research proposals that applied a life-course design to PSID data for the purpose of investigating a research question. The best proposals were selected and funded by the committee for development into a presentation at the Belmont Conference Center outside of Baltimore. I chaired this project and edited the resulting volume, *Life Course Dynamics: Trajectories and Transitions*. The project generated fresh thinking about life-course models and advanced the use of longitudinal data in this type of research. This enterprise also had career implications for a majority of the authors who developed research careers that made use of the life-course perspective.

Some of the intellectual exchange associated with the Life Course Committee of SSRC occurred through cross-cultural conferences, such as one held in Heidelberg, Germany in April 1981. Sociologist Karl Ulrich Mayer from the University of Mannheim attended the conference

and I had a chance to spend a couple of hours with him in conversation about a large life-course project he was launching in Germany, called the German Life History Study (Brückner & Mayer, 1998). In order to obtain data about the prior lives of the respondents, the project used a retrospective life-history method in data collection. Prospective longitudinal data records to the 1920s were not available on birth cohorts in Germany owing to World War II. This meant that the development of such studies was limited to use of a retrospective method in data collection. German unification eventually became a major target of this research.

The Heidleberg conference occurred at the time of my expanding contacts with European social and behavioral scientists, particularly in Germany. This development reflected Paul Baltes' new affiliation with the Max Planck Institute in Berlin, along with the presence of Walter Muller (University of Mannheim) and Franz Weinert (Max Planck Institute) on the Life Course Committee. I met developmentalist Rainer Silbereisen at an SSRC conference in New York City and again during his visit with Urie Bronfenbrenner at Cornell (Silbereisen & Tomasik, 2008). He invited me to his Berlin conference and we began to establish scientific ties on the study of social change and human development. His initial work with Sabine Walper focused on the study of socioeconomic change and stress in children's lives, based in large part on the analytic framework of *Children of the Great Depression*. By the 1990s, the dramatic end of the wall separating West and East Germany led to Silbereisen's research project on the consequences of German unification. Twenty years later, German unification continues to be an important research issue. With Rainer Silbereisen's move to the University of Jena, his focus on social change and human development gained momentum and is continuing today through former students and colleagues in an impressive interdisciplinary program.

Another significant extension of my international collaboration occurred when sociologist Walter Heinz at the University of Bremen invited me (1989) to give the keynote address at a conference marking the initiation of his German Research Foundation program on status passages and risk in the life course. I revisited the program in the spring of 1999 to give a series of lectures and receive an honorary doctorate. This visit provided me with a chance to observe and appreciate its very significant impact on student training and research in a flourishing university. Bremen is located in a region that has lagged economically behind the southern regions of Germany, and many of the research projects addressed problems of disadvantage in the life course. From 1990 to the present, the University of Bremen has gained an increasingly prominent stature for advanced education in the field of social science and the life course. With the guidance of Walter Heinz and others, the University of Bremen has also become a key research center in an evolving three country study of the Great Recession and the life course of young people.

These European contacts heightened my awareness of distinctive differences between what has been called North American and European life-course studies. The former are characterized by a research focus on the individual in context, a perspective that applies to my research and conceptual perspective across the years. European studies, on the other hand, are more apt to focus on institutional effects as in studies of the welfare state. These institutional and policy effects are most evident in my study of changing manpower policy and deferments during World War II (Dechter & Elder, 2004). Such work on the life course emerged some 10–20 years later than the North American research.

At this time, the social change theme of the life course caught the eye of social scientists in Japan and China, prompting translation of *Children of the Great Depression* in both countries—by developmentalist Tokio Honda in Japan and sociologist Huang Ping in China. The SSRC responded to this interest by organizing a workshop at the East–West Center in Hawaii at the end of 1984 involving a group of American scholars and a Japanese research team headed by senior sociologist Kiyomi Morioka. Subsequent invitations from the Japan Society for the Promotion of Science (JSPS) in 1986, and the Japan Society of Developmental Psychology in 1977 led to my direction of life-course workshops in Tokyo. The JSPS visit was hosted by Yoriko Meguro of Sophia University, and the latter visit by developmentalist Tokio Honda. Connections with Chinese colleagues occurred through the Chinese Academy of Social Science in Beijing, led by Professor Huang Ping.

My perspective on the life course has always been interdisciplinary—the relation of historical context to social pathways and behavioral development. But this is a perspective constructed within my own mind—it does not require collaboration between practitioners of different disciplines. In what turned out to be the last major venture of the SSRC Life Course Committee, we proposed a project that would be based upon two-person teams made up of an historian and a developmentalist. The big question was whether the teams could develop a working relationship that integrates historical and developmental insights in a study of children's development. Historians are contextualists who trace the influence of the social environment to children's development, while developmentalists determine the nature of the social world in terms of the child. The latter ask about the social influences that make a difference in a particular outcome of a child's development. At the outset, we acknowledged these differences but believed that historical thinking would enhance the sophistication of studies of environmental effects on children. The cross-discipline teams identified collaborative projects which were then developed into papers for presentation. However, minimal contact between the two disciplines as well as their contrasting models posed major difficulties (Elder, Modell & Parke, 1993). Nevertheless, effective ways to combine elements of these intellectual fields did emerge from this long, challenging, and rewarding journey.

The cross-discipline interests and activities of the history–developmentalist network and the SSRC Life Course Committee were reflected in changes that were taking place in my professional career at the time. Two years after publication of *Children of the Great Depression* I moved a small research team from Chapel Hill to the new Boys Town research center on families and youth on the outskirts of Omaha, Nebraska. The purpose of this leave of absence was to assist the director in the development of a research center. While engaged in this project, I continued to investigate the lives of the Berkeley cohort members and engage in a systematic comparison of this cohort with the Oakland sample. During this appointment I had a chance to renew my friendship with Urie Bronfenbrenner when he visited the research center and I gave him an inscribed copy of *Children of the Great Depression*. This meeting also enabled me to express interest in his Cornell program. As my Carolina leave approached the end of its 2 years, I realized that I could not return to Chapel Hill in time, owing to the need to place members of the research group in academic posts. As a result, I began exploring professorships. After visiting the University of Chicago's Committee on Human Development and various sociology departments, family preferences favored the Cornell option as did my professional ties to Bronfenbrenner and a desire to become more fully involved in the field of human development.

My last year at Boys Town gave me time to complete a chapter for the first *Handbook of Adolescent Psychology* (Elder, 1980a) that viewed development across the early years to young adulthood from a multi-level life-course perspective. Consistent with the general theme of my work up to that point, I titled the essay "Adolescence in Historical Perspective." But judging from the studies at hand, the title should have been "adolescence without attention to historical context and the life course." As was the case for the Oakland and Berkeley longitudinal projects, most studies of adolescents in the 20th century had ignored the historical context of young people. And this neglect was no respecter of discipline. The pathways of adolescents and their developmental implications were also neglected, though some of this could be attributed to the scarcity of longitudinal studies. Only in the last decades of the century do we find empirical studies with a perspective that locates adolescents within the life course, as well as both historical time and place.

Bronfenbrenner's ecological perspective on human development nicely complemented my study of historical influences in the lives of parents and children. Ecological processes are expressed in historical change, as stated in one of the paradigmatic principles of the life course: "The life course of individuals is embedded in and shaped by the historical times and places they experience over their lifetime" (Elder, Johnson, & Crosnoe, 2003, p. 12). Unfortunately, I didn't fully appreciate this convergence between our research and writing at that time. However,

Bronfenbrenner did see this convergence as he worked on his now classic statement in *The Ecology of Human Development* (1979). During the months leading up to my Cornell transition, we had long phone discussions about his book and the issues he was addressing.

Time at Cornell was cut much too short by the health problems of my wife during the Ithaca winters, but it was in every way memorable and career shaping, thanks especially to Urie Bronfenbrenner and exceptional graduate students—Ann Crouter, Avshalom Caspi, Gerry Downey, Niall Bolger, and Elizabeth Colerick (Clipp), among others. Every year, Bronfenbrenner taught his course on the ecology of human development and I offered my seminar on the life course in the evening so that students could attend from other campuses. In my last year, the students in these seminars decided to bring everyone together in the College's large seminar room for a semester class that met every week. Neither Urie nor I were involved in planning or managing the enterprise. But it remains a special event among those who participated. Such initiative with Cornell faculty and students also played a role in establishing a life studies series of presentations and especially the Cornell Institute for Social and Economic Research during the early 1980s which is still in operation.

Another highlight of the Cornell years involved a student-led project that brought senior developmentalists to the campus for a conference on "persons in context: developmental processes." A team of students took the lead in designing the conference objectives, program, and participants. They had studied Bronfenbrenner's ecology of human development, and some had taken my seminar and collaborated with me on research papers. In a sense, the conference was designed to relate the two perspectives, but it extended well beyond to other research traditions as well, such as Gerry Patterson's innovative research on antisocial boys. In addition to this foundational work, the conference leaders applied successfully for funding, worked out the logistics and chaired the conference with great effectiveness. The final stage of this remarkable project moved the conference papers to revised manuscripts for an edited book that was accepted and published by Cambridge University Press as *Persons in Context* (Bolger, Caspi, Downey, & Moorehouse, 1988). Caspi has a chapter with me in this book (Elder & Caspi, 1988).

Leaving Cornell was difficult, but it was made easier by the interdisciplinary world of developmentalists at the University of North Carolina and Urie Bronfenbrenner's involvement with this developmental science community. I arrived on the campus with the hope that I would be able to contribute to a consortium on developmental studies. As far back as graduate studies, I admired the University of Chicago's Committee on Human Development and looked forward to the possibility of creating such an intellectual community. Within a year or so of my time at the university, I could recognize a path for this initiative—a visit to the developmental psychology program on campus to talk to Harriet Rheingold and Robert Cairns about organizing an interdisciplinary consortium on human development. In the process, I discovered that Cairns had been thinking along this line. After much discussion, we decided that the first step should be submission of a proposal for a training grant in developmental science for both predoctoral and postdoctoral students. This initiative marked the beginning of my intensive role in mentoring postdoctoral fellows who have become faculty in the life-course area. They include Robert Crosnoe, Steve Hitlin, Monica Johnson, Stephen Russell, Eliza Pavalko, Michael Shanahan (2008), and Andrea Willson, among others.

Sharon Landesman, director of the Frank Porter Graham Child Development Center at UNC–Chapel Hill, became an essential collaborator with Bob Cairns and me in our plan to develop a training grant. This proposal was funded by the National Institute of Child Health and Human Development in 1987 and became the foundation for a Carolina Consortium on Human Development with an interdisciplinary focus on developmental science. The funds only supported predoctoral and postdoctoral studies, but the Consortium had larger ambitions that led to a research center in developmental science in the early 1990s. Weekly Consortium seminars during each semester tended to follow a general theme that extended across disciplines. Faculty fellows were invited from nearby institutions and participants traveled as many as 100 miles round-trip to attend from nearby colleges and universities. All trainees were expected to attend and participate in the Monday evening seminars that were held in the large seminar room at the Child Development Center. Before long, the momentum of this intellectual adventure was producing a full house. All chairs were occupied around the seminar table and they were enclosed by an outer ring of students and faculty. There were even people seated in rows at the very end of the seminar table. I counted as many as 50 attendees on occasion. Frequently, the seminars were preceded by a light meal at a faculty member's house.

By the early 1990s, the Consortium fellows had decided to produce a collaborative statement on "developmental science," as well as essays to enhance broad understanding of this intellectual adventure. To do this, leading members of the Carolina Consortium (Cairns, Elder, Gilbert Gottlieb, and Peter Ornstein, among others) met at Breadman's, a well-known Chapel Hill restaurant, on a Saturday morning to work on the statement and discuss the contents of a book on developmental science. As stated in the book, developmental science represents "a fresh synthesis that has been generated to guide research in the social, psychological, and biobehavioral disciplines" (Cairns, Elder & Costello, 1996, p. 1). The collaborative statement and book affirm the premise that behavior develops in context and cannot be separated from it. Individual functioning occurs on multiple levels and is best understood accordingly. Moreover, "pathways of development are relative to time and place; they contribute to—and reflect—temporal changes in culture and society" (p. 1). With Bob Cairns' intellectual leadership, we produced a book manuscript on developmental science by 1995 that was published a year later by Cambridge University Press. Urie Bronfenbrenner introduced the book in his foreword as a "potential milestone" on the path to a "more powerful paradigm for the scientific study of human development" (p. ix). The Carolina Consortium and this book project gave momentum several years earlier to a successful NIMH proposal for a center on developmental science which today remains a lively community for interdisciplinary research and study.

Though based at Chapel Hill, this newly established Center for Developmental Science was conceived as a multidisciplinary community that included neighboring institutions, such as Duke and North Carolina Central University in Durham, North Carolina State University in Raleigh, and the University of North Carolina at Greensboro, some 60 miles away. The possibility of such a network came to my mind when I was pondering the move from Cornell back to Carolina. UNC–Chapel Hill was nested in the middle of research universities and the Research Triangle, a professional ecology that was most attractive to my dreams of a developmental community that included prominent sociologists as well, such as Linda George and Angie O'Rand at Duke. This concept of a developmental science network was soon implemented by Bob Cairns on the international level through summer institutes. David Magnusson and Lars Bergman at the University of Stockholm joined forces with Cairns in developing an initial collaboration along this line between the two universities, a network that was subsequently extended to other institutions, both in the United States and in Europe.

The synthesis achieved in *Developmental Science* (1996) corresponds in many respects to my objective in developing the life-course framework. An opportunity to discuss the life-course framework in a public forum occurred earlier in the 1990s when I received the Cooley–Mead Award (August, 1993) from the social psychology section of the American Sociological Association. In my address, I focused on the correlated emergence of life-course studies and the decline of socialization research. Consistent with my own experience, the inability of socialization studies to account for life-span development had shifted the focus to life-course studies across the life span with its defining paradigmatic principles of linked lives, historical time and place, human agency, and timing. Socialization represented a core social process across the life course rather than a framework for guiding studies of human development and aging.

In the course of this work, I turned to Urie Bronfenbrenner for a thoughtful assessment of this conceptual work on the life course, from the life-course principles in my Cooley-Mead address (published in 1994) to the life-course chapter in the *Developmental Science* volume (1996). Throughout our exchange, he insisted that I run for president of the Society for Research in Child Development (SRCD) so that I could give a presidential address to the membership

on the life course and child development. I did not believe that this presentation was needed, given my writings, but I soon discovered that an insistent Urie Bronfenbrenner was not to be denied. I joined the nomination committee for SRCD officers in 1995, but was notified shortly thereafter that I had been removed so that I could run as one of the two candidates for president. I was elected to serve as president in 1997, a time when the SRCD membership had grown well beyond its management resources. I confided to John Hagen, then executive secretary, that it was much more enjoyable to study drastic change, as I had, than to experience it with major responsibilities.

The biennial meeting of SRCD was held at the Washington Sheraton in early April and I prepared a presentation on the theme of "the life course as developmental theory" (Elder, 1998b). My objective was to emphasize the potential role of the life course as an explanatory link between changing times and developmental outcomes. More than a decade has passed since that time in Washington, DC, and I now fully appreciate Urie Bronfenbrenner's wise insistence that I run for president of SRCD and, if elected, give a presentation to the assembled membership on the life course and child development. In less than an hour, this presentation conveyed the essence of a life-course framework in studying child development and has since become a frequently cited paper.

John Clausen did not live long enough to see me give this address, but I had the special opportunity to write a foreword to his *American Lives* (1993), a book based on the Oakland and Berkeley men and women; and later on to celebrate this accomplishment in a panel discussion of the book amidst his family, friends, and colleagues. I knew about Clausen's interviews with study members, but we never had the kind of thorough discussions about the book that we had in the evolution of my work for *Children of the Great Depression*. Nevertheless, I knew from my Institute experience that he was most interested in the process by which people made choices that shaped their lives. This turned out to be the central theme of his volume, as exemplified by the concept of planful competence. On numerous occasions during my time at Berkeley, I would go to Clausen's office for a meeting and he would have a folder of a study member's interviews before him. Our initial discussion would focus on this case and related issues.

The growth of life-course research occurred without the benefit of a major chapter or book on life-course theory, methods, and research. But in 1996 the editors of the forthcoming 5th edition of the *Handbook of Child Psychology* had decided to include such a chapter in the volume on theory and invited me to be its author (Elder, 1998a). I didn't expect such an invitation but after some thought I concluded that the time had come for this kind of chapter. In the past I had worked on essays that focused on individual projects, such as the Oakland or Berkeley studies, or on specific concepts and problem foci, such as the historical influence of changing times and the role of human agency. But now I sensed that the field of life-course studies had reached a point where an integrative chapter on the life course and human development could be written. The empirical literature was now substantial in North America and Europe, and major conceptual advances had been achieved. The development and clarification of core concepts, such as pathways, trajectories, and transitions, provided a rich conceptual tool box. Most important was the emergence of paradigmatic principles that proved to be essential in defining the territory of the life course as a theoretical orientation. The process of developing a *Handbook* chapter became a developmental event in its own right and enabled me to think more broadly about the life course as theory, method, and research.

Many valuable lessons were learned from use of longitudinal data collected many years in the past to address very different questions. I found that all too frequently, explorations of such data archives have not been fruitful. First of all, the archive user must determine whether the particular data archive is relevant to investigating the research problem and the prospects for developing data codes that represent a better match for the issues at hand. An equilibration process should take place—changing the data to better fit the question through a recoding process, and reworking the question so that the data will have a better chance to address it. After a 1989 workshop on archival methods at the Murray Research Center in Cambridge, Massachusetts, two former postdocs, Eliza Pavalko and Elizabeth Clipp, joined me in preparing a small monograph that drew upon the workshop procedures that we had used over the years in making the best of the data at hand (Elder, Pavalko, & Clipp, 1993). The resulting monograph proved to be useful in my research projects and in the life-course projects of other investigators.

My next effort to provide methodological guidance for life-course research was to assemble authors who could address the methodological issues in the collection and use of qualitative and quantitative data as well as retrospective and prospective data. In *Methods of Life Course Research* (Giele & Elder, 1998), we addressed both measurement and analysis issues in this field of research. One of the best ways to master the methods of doing life-course studies is to follow expert practitioners as they carry out a study. With the collaboration of Janet Giele, we implemented this observation by recruiting expert practitioners for a book in which they walk readers through their research projects. The resulting volume was published in 2009 and consequently provides a picture of methodological change since 1998.

The 20th century came to an end for me with publication of a 25th anniversary expanded edition of *Children of the Great Depression* (1999). This volume includes an additional chapter on the paradigmatic principles of the life course and a comparative account of the importance of both the Great Depression and World War II on the lives of men and women in the Oakland and Berkeley cohorts. The 21st century began with publication of the first handbook on the life course in 2003 (Mortimer & Shanahan, 2003) and shortly thereafter with an update of my initial chapter on the life course and human development (Elder & Shanahan, 2006). Life-course studies had truly come of age.

A celebratory event for life-course studies was held before the annual meeting of the 2010 American Sociological Association in Atlanta. Two former postdoctoral fellows planned and organized the event—Robert Crosnoe (University of Texas–Austin) and Monica Johnson (Washington State), with support from many others, especially my administrative assistant, Terry Poythress. Crosnoe and Johnson had expressed the desire for such an event that would bring together my postdoctoral fellows and doctoral students across the years in honor of my contributions to this field. The initial thought that this could be a surprise quickly faded due to the realities of the event's size—two afternoon sessions, followed by a sit-down dinner. The first session focused on sociological perspectives, with presentations by Dennis Hogan (Brown University), Blair Wheaton (University of Toronto), and Mark Hayward (University of Texas–Austin). Eliza Pavalko (Indiana University) was the discussant. The second session dealt with life-course stages and contexts, with Jeylan Mortimer (University of Minnesota), Angela O'Rand (Duke University), Barbara Schneider (Michigan State), and Arland Thornton (University of Michigan). Richard Settersten (Oregon State University) served as discussant, while Michael Shanahan offered the closing remarks. Over 70 friends and former students attended the dinner. From beginning to end, this special day was filled with memories of a lifetime.

To broaden the event, Crosnoe organized a session with developmentalists at the 2011 Biennial meeting of the Society for Research in Child Development in Montreal, Canada. The event addressed life-course approaches to child development, and began with Vonnie McLoyd (University of Michigan) on interventions in parent and adolescent behavior. Jeanne Brooks-Gunn (Columbia University) focused on life-course applications in the Fragile Families Study; Aletha Huston (University of Texas–Austin) examined policy effects on human developments across the life course; and Richard Lerner (Tufts University) framed the session by discussing the life-course approach within the developmental system. The sociology celebration and the SRCD demonstration of life-course applications provided a fitting opportunity for me to encourage the younger generation to make life-course models work for them in their careers.

Life-Course Reflections and Prospects

Scientific careers are marked by choice points that may raise questions later on, such as why a certain option or pathway was pursued. In this autobiography, I asked how the early years through graduate school led me to a longitudinal study of lives and a contextual way of thinking about them. External forces shaped the world of my early years—the Great Depression, World War II, and family migration from city to farm. Their influence focused my attention on the personal effects of a changing world. Eventually, this social psychology became a specialty in graduate studies and subsequently channeled my interest to the Depression times of the Oakland study at the Institute of the Human Development.

I grew up in a world that collected survey information from people. And to some extent "time stands still" when people are only surveyed at a point in time. However, it is their lives that I found intriguing, thanks to my mother's biographies. Such books were everywhere in our home. By the time I entered high school, biographies had become a preferred type of book for me and I saw them as a rewarding way to learn about a particular time and place. In graduate studies, this orientation to lives tended to influence both my research questions and perspective. The questions were typically about life transitions. Thus my thesis focused on the transition of young people from high school to college, but I only had data on young people from a survey at a single point in time. My doctoral research also had data from only one survey.

Ideally, questions about lives are investigated with data from a prospective longitudinal study. Only a handful of these studies were underway in the United States when I completed graduate school, but it was my good fortune to have my very first academic appointment in the midst of such studies at the Institute of Human Development, with involvement in the Oakland Study. These study members were around 40 years of age when I arrived at the Institute in 1962 and I was 28, but my background in adolescent research was relevant for understanding their life course. What I did not have was expertise with longitudinal data, and this came eventually from "on the job" training through work with staff members. I also did not have a way of thinking about people moving through the transitions of life beyond merely a temporal perspective. However, my work with longitudinal data enriched this initial perspective on the life paths of people and their developmental processes.

These reflections bring to mind the similarities and differences between my career and that of Urie Bronfenbrenner, an influential mentor. Both of us launched our careers in a field-oriented social psychology that is known for its atemporal perspective, and then we moved toward a contextual framework across the years. We experienced major social disruptions in our early years with their implications for a contextual perspective: immigration from Russia to the United States for Bronfenbrenner, and migration from metropolis to farm for me. Our paths diverged after doctoral studies. Bronfenbrenner served in a special social science unit during World War II when surveys were the method of data collection in the field. Twenty years later, I moved to a world of longitudinal studies at the Institute of Human Development in Berkeley, California. Both of us have referred to these assignments as a "second phase of graduate-level studies." The temporality of the Berkeley research across changing contexts shaped my perspective in a major way. Bronfenbrenner did not have such experience in his early career and his theoretical model in *The Ecology of Human Development* (1979) does not feature a temporal perspective. I have often wondered whether our different early career experiences account for this dissimilarity.

The new wave of longitudinal studies in the 1960s–70s appears to be correlated in time with the emergence of life-span developmental psychology and the life-course perspective. Indeed, it is difficult to imagine either without the growth of prospective longitudinal studies. However, involvement in longitudinal studies cannot by itself explain the development of a contextual life-course perspective. After all, the staff at the Institute of Human Development had been involved in longitudinal studies for nearly 30 years by the early 1960s and they had largely ignored the pathways and historical circumstances of the study members' lives. I have noted that family background, as well as the personal experience of social change, had much to do with the contextual concept of lives that I brought to graduate school and my approach to longitudinal studies at the Institute——with a focus on "children of the Great Depression" and the impact of this event on their life course. Most of my subsequent studies have followed this model, linking types of social change to the life course and developmental processes, from military service and wartime influences to the impact of a rural economic depression and mounting urban poverty.

A half-century has passed since I embarked on longitudinal research at the Institute of Human Development and assembled a rudimentary perspective on the life course of Californians who grew up in the Great Depression. Since then, prospective longitudinal studies have become a popular research design around the world for studying the life course of individuals and their developmental path in changing times. Research applications of the life-course framework are now common across the social, behavioral, and medical sciences (Mayer, 2009).[4] Richardson, Hussey, and Strutz (2013, Figure 2) note that recent publications show a rapid acceleration of interest in the life course. The number of research articles in which the term life course (hyphenated or not) appears in the title or abstract has more than doubled between 2005 and 2010 to nearly 600 (ISI Web of Knowledge).

Comparable longitudinal data in different countries provide unusual research opportunities today to investigate societal variations and the boundaries of generalization. One example of this observation comes from my current work, a comparative study of the Great Recession's effect on the lives of adolescents and young adults. This research will also take into account notable variations *within* each country. Other research challenges have come from the increasing scope of inquiry across the life span and the pressing need to understand the linking mechanisms, and the investigation of the interplay of biological facts and the social life course.

During the early years of life-course studies in the 1970s, Frank Furstenberg urged me to follow a path of empirical studies instead of the exclusive path of theoretical work. That advice proved to be easy to implement because empirical inquiry had been a productive course of theoretical development on the Great Depression project. This was also the case when I turned my attention to military service and the life course of men, as well as the rural change and inner city projects. My exchange with Furstenberg brought to mind Marie Jahoda's thoughtful analysis of Paul Lazarsfeld's work style in a collection of essays that pay tribute to his career (Merton, Coleman, & Rossi, 1979).

Jahoda (1979) draws upon Isaiah Berlin's popular essay on Tolstoy (1953), *The Hedgehog and the Fox*, based upon text from Antiquity; "the fox knows many things, but the hedgehog knows one big thing" (p. 3). Jahoda concludes that Lazarsfeld was most definitely a fox, but historical circumstances moved him in the direction of a hedgehog. If as Jahoda asserts, hedgehogs tend to "emerge with one theory or one point of view" and "foxes help us understand the variety of the world in which we live" (p. 3), it seems that a large number of social scientists would probably combine the two styles. This is how I see my work. The hedgehog perspective involves my continuing efforts to develop a life-course framework or theoretical orientation and methodology, whereas my various empirical projects represent a lifelong effort to better understand the world in which we live and its influence on how we develop and age.

Notes

1. This chapter does not provide a biographical record of my major research projects and their publications. A narrative account of this life record has been published in a paper entitled "Families, Social Change, and Individual Lives" (Elder, 2001), along with a reference list that includes key publications. Other autobiographical essays are available on my website (http://www.unc.edu/~elder). An updated CV is also available there.

2. When I arrived at the Institute in August 1962, Jean Macfarlane was director of the Berkeley Guidance Study with assistance from Marjorie Honzik, and Nancy Bayley was engaged in research on the Berkeley Growth Study. John Clausen had taken charge of the Oakland Growth Study. Mary Jones, wife of the late Herbert Jones who had led the Oakland Study, was still actively involved in research with data from this archive. Jack Block (1961/1978), a well-known personality psychologist and author of the California Q Sort, was collaborating with Norma Haan in a longitudinal study of personality trajectories. The Q Sort data came from the Oakland and Berkeley Study members. M. Brewster Smith and Paul Mussen from the Berkeley Department of Psychology were actively involved in research and writing projects.

3. The Department of Sociology was chaired at the time by Kingsley Davis, a distinguished demographer. In addition to Davis and Clausen, Berkeley senior faculty in my world included Herbert Blumer, Guy Swanson, and Erving Goffman in social psychology; Seymour Martin Lipset and Reinhard Bendix in political sociology and comparative studies; Harold Wilensky in studies of work and family; Philip Selznick and Charles Glock in law and religion studies, respectively; and Neil Smelser in social theory, the youngest member of the group at age 32. As editor of the sociology flagship journal, *The American Sociological Review*, Smelser expertly guided me in the development of professional publications. Neil was especially important to me as a colleague and a friend.

4. Advisory groups and research networks continued this influential role of the SSRC. I met John Laub of the Henry Murray Research Center in Cambridge, MA, at an advisory group meeting in the late 1980s. With his colleague, Robert Sampson, he had just discovered the old Sheldon Glueck archive in the basement of the Harvard Law School. These data led to a pioneering life course project in the field of criminology. Our meeting also set in motion a career-long association of mutual encouragement (Laub & Sampson, 2008).

    The National Research Council and the MacArthur Foundation's research networks also brought social and behavioral scientists together in ways that advanced both life-course studies and developmental science through the research and collaborative projects of its members. For example, Jacque Eccles from the University of Michigan's Department of Psychology joined the MacArthur Network on youth in high-risk settings at the end of the 1980s, as did I, and we soon collaborated on projects in a life-course framework. Years later, she described her initial attraction to my contextual studies of human development, an early version of a life-course approach (Eccles, 2008).

5. In a letter addressed to me on May 4, 2011, Neal Halfon observed that:

    the past 20 years have witnessed an explosion of research on how health develops across the life course. This large, diverse, and growing body of research includes studies on the origins and development of chronic disease, neurodevelopmental research, a host of longitudinal cohort studies, and a range of child and adolescent development and intervention studies. . . . [The] importance and influence of the life course perspective is found in the new model that has been adopted by the Department of Health and Human Services for Health People 2020 and in the Maternal and Child Health Bureau's strategic plan.

Halfon's letter announced a design meeting for the organization of a Maternal and Child Health Life Course Research Network to facilitate the development of life-course studies that inform maternal and child health programs. See the first chapter in Kotch's *Handbook of Maternal and Child Health*, 3rd edition (Richardson et al., 2013), on the life-course perspective for the field of maternal and child health.

References

Abbott, A. (1999). The continuing relevance of the Chicago School. In *Department & discipline: Chicago Sociology at one hundred* (p. 70). Chicago: University of Chicago Press.

Bakke, E. W. (1940). *Citizens without work: A study of the effects of unemployment upon the worker's social relations and practices*. New Haven, CT: Yale University Press.

Bandura, A. (1982). The psychology of chance encounters and life paths. *American Psychologist, 37*(7), 747–755.

Barber, B., & Fox, R. C. (1958). The case of the floppy-eared rabbits: An instance of serendipity gained and serendipity lost. *American Journal of Sociology, 64*(2), 128–136.

Berlin, I. (1953) *The hedgehog and the fox: An essay on Tolstoy's view of history*. London: Weidenfeld & Nicolson.

Blau, P. M., & Duncan, O. D. (1967). *The American Occupational Structure*. New York: John Wiley & Sons.

Block, J. (1961/1978). *The Q-sort method in personality assessment and psychiatric research*. Springfield, IL: Charles C. Thomas.

Bolger, N., Caspi, A., Downey, G., & Moorehouse, M. (Eds.) (1988). *Persons in context: Developmental processes*. New York: Cambridge University Press.

Bronfenbrenner, U. (1958). Socialization and social class through time and space. In E. E. Maccoby, T. M. Newcomb, & E. L. Hartley (Eds.), *Readings in social psychology* (3rd ed., pp. 400–425). New York: Henry Holt & Company.

Bronfenbrenner, U. (1979). *The ecology of human development: Experiments by nature and design*. Cambridge, MA: Harvard University Press.

Bronfenbrenner, U. (1996). Foreword. In R. B. Cairns, G. H. Elder, Jr. & E. J. Costello (Eds.), *Developmental science* (pp. ix–xvii). New York: Cambridge University Press.

Bronfenbrenner, U. (2005). Ecological systems theory. Article 10 in U. Bronfenbrenner (Ed.), *Making human beings human: Bioecological perspectives on human development*. Thousand Oaks, CA: Sage Publications.

Brückner, E., & Mayer, K. U. (1998). Collecting life history data: Experiences from the German Life History Study. In J. Z. Giele & G. H. Elder, Jr. (Eds.), *Methods of life course research: Qualitative and quantitative approaches*. Thousand Oaks, CA: Sage.

Butz, W. P., & Torrey, B. B. (2006). Some frontiers in social science. *Science, 312*(5782), 1898–1900.

Cain, L. (1964). Life course and social structure. In R. E. L. Faris (Ed.), *Handbook of modern sociology* (pp. 272–309). Chicago: Rand McNally.

Cairns, R. B., Elder, G. H., Jr., & Costello, E. J. (Eds.). (1996). *Developmental science.* New York: Cambridge University Press.

Clausen, J. A. (1968). *Socialization and society.* Boston: Little, Brown.

Clausen, J. A. (1993). *American lives: Looking back at children of the Great Depression.* New York: The Free Press.

Clausen, J. A. (1999). Foreword. *Children of the Great Depression: Social change in life experience* (25th Anniversary ed., pp. xvii–xxi). Boulder, CO: Westview Press.

Dechter, A. R., & Elder, G. H., Jr. (2004). World War II mobilization in men's work lives: Continuity or disruption for the middle class? *American Journal of Sociology, 110*(3), 761–793.

Duncan, O. D., Featherman, D. L., & Duncan, B. (1972). *Socioeconomic background and achievement.* New York: Seminar Press.

Eccles, J. (2008). Agency and structure in human development. *Research in Human Development, 5*(4), 231–243.

Elder, G. H., Jr. (1975). Age differentiation and the life course. *Annual Review of Sociology, 1*, 165–190.

Elder, G. H., Jr. (1980a). Adolescence in historical perspective. In J. Adelson (Ed.), *Handbook of adolescent psychology* (pp. 3–46). New York: Wiley.

Elder, G. H., Jr. (Ed.). (1980b). *Family structure and socialization.* New York: Arno Press.

Elder, G. H., Jr. (1986). Military times and turning points in men's lives. *Developmental Psychology, 22*(2), 233–245.

Elder, G. H., Jr. (1992). Models of the life course. *Contemporary Sociology, 21*(2), 632–635.

Elder, G. H., Jr. (1994). Time, human agency, and social change: Perspectives on the life course. *Social Psychology Quarterly, 57*(1), 4–15.

Elder, G. H., Jr. (1996). Human lives in changing societies: Life course and developmental insights. In R. B. Cairns, G. H. Elder, Jr., & E. J. Costello (Eds.), *Developmental Science* (pp. 31–62). New York: Cambridge University Press.

Elder, G. H., Jr. (1998a). The life course and human development. In R. M. Lerner (Ed.), *Handbook of child psychology* (5th ed.), Vol. 1: *Theoretical models of human development* (pp. 939–991). New York: Wiley.

Elder, G. H., Jr. (1998b). The life course as developmental theory. *Child Development, 69*(1), 1–12.

Elder, G. H., Jr. (1999). *Children of the Great Depression: Social change in life experience* (25th Anniversary Edition). Boulder, CO: Westview Press. (Original publication 1974 by the University of Chicago Press.)

Elder, G. H., Jr. (2001). Families, social change, and individual lives. *Marriage and Family Review, 31*(1/2), 177–192.

Elder, G. H., Jr., & Caspi, A. (1988). Human development and social change: An emerging perspective on the life course. In N. Bolger, A. Caspi, G. Downey, & M. Moorehouse (Eds.), *Persons in context: Developmental processes* (pp. 77–113). New York: Cambridge University Press.

Elder, G. H., Jr., & Caspi, A. (1990). Studying lives in a changing society: Sociological and personological explorations. In A. I. Rabin, R. A. Zucker, R. A. Emmons, & S. Frank (Eds.), *Studying persons and lives* (pp. 201–247). New York: Springer.

Elder, G. H., Jr., & Conger, R. D. (2000). *Children of the land: Adversity and success in rural America.* Chicago: University of Chicago Press.

Elder, G. H., Jr., & Giele, J. Z. (Eds.). (2009). *The craft of life course research.* New York City: Guilford Press.

Elder, G. H., Jr., Johnson, M. K., & Crosnoe, R. (2003). The emergence and development of the life course. In J. T. Mortimer & M. J. Shanahan (Eds.), *Handbook of the life course* (H. Kaplan, series editor). New York: Plenum Publishing.

Elder, G. H., Jr., Modell, J., & Parke, R. D. (1993). *Children in time and place: Developmental and historical insights.* New York: Cambridge University Press.

Elder, G. H., Jr., Pavalko, E. K., & Clipp, E. C. (1993). *Working with archival data: Studying lives* (Vol. 07–088). Newbury Park, CA: Sage Publications.

Elder, G. H., Jr., & Shanahan, M. J. (2006). The life course and human development. In R. E. Lerner (Ed.), *Theoretical models of human development* (pp. 665–715) (Vol. 1: *The Handbook of child psychology,* 6th ed.), W. Damon, series editor. New York: Wiley.

Furstenberg, F. F., Jr. (1976). *Unplanned parenthood: The social consequences of teenage childbearing.* New York: The Free Press.

Furstenberg, F. F., Jr., Cook, T. D., Eccles, J., Elder, G. H., Jr., & Sameroff, A. (Eds.). (1999). *Managing to make it: Urban families and adolescent success.* Chicago: University of Chicago Press.

Giele, J. Z., & Elder, G. H., Jr. (Eds.). (1998). *Methods of life course research: Qualitative and quantitative approaches.* Thousand Oaks, CA: Sage.

Hareven, T. K. (1978). *Transitions: The family and the life course in historical perspective.* New York: Academic Press.

Hareven, T. K. (1982). *Family time and industrial time.* New York: Cambridge University Press.

Hogan, D. D. (1981). *Transitions and social change: The early lives of American men.* New York: Academic Press.

Hogan, D. P., & Goldscheider, F. K. (2003). Success and challenge in demographic studies of the life course. In J. T. Mortimer & M. J. Shanahan (Eds.), *Handbook of the life course* (pp. 681–691). New York: Kluwer Academic/Plenum Publishers.

Jahoda, M. (1979). PFL: Hedgehog or fox? In R. K. Merton, J. S. Coleman & P. H. Rossi (Eds.), *Qualitative and quantitative social research: Papers in honor of Paul F. Lazarsfeld* (pp. 3–9). New York: The Free Press.

Laub, J. H., & Sampson, R. J. (2008). Glen Elder's influence on life-course criminology. *Research in Human Development, 5*(4), 199–215.

Lewin, K. (1931). Environmental forces in child behavior and development. In C. Murchison (Ed.), *A Handbook of child psychology* (pp. 377–391). Worcester, MA: Clark University Press.

Lewin, K., Lippitt, R., & White, R. K. (1939). Patterns of aggressive behavior in experimentally created "social climates." *Journal of Social Psychology, 10*(2), 271–299.

Mayer, K. U. (2009). New directions in life course research. *Annual Review of Sociology, 35*, 413–433.

Merton, R. K. (1957). *Social theory and social structure: Toward the codification of theory and research.* Glencoe, IL: Free Press.

Merton, R. K., & Barber, E. (2004). *The travels and adventures of serendipity.* Princeton, NJ: Princeton University Press.

Merton, R. K., Coleman, J. S., & Rossi, P. H. (Eds.). (1979). *Qualitative and quantitative social research: Papers in honor of Paul F. Lazarsfeld.* New York: The Free Press.

Mortimer, J. T. (2008). From social structure and personality to life course sociology: Glen Elder's legacy at the University of Minnesota. *Research in Human Development, 5*(4), 216–230.

Mortimer, J. T., & Shanahan, M. J. (Eds.) (2003). *Handbook of the life course.* New York: Kluwer Academic/Plenum Publishers.

Neugarten, B. L., with a foreword by D. A. Neugarten. (1996). *The meanings of age: Selected papers of Bernice L Neugarten.* Chicago: University of Chicago Press.

Richardson, L. J., Hussey, J. M., & Strutz, K. L. (2013). A life course perspective on maternal and child health. In J. B. Kotch (Ed.), *Handbook of maternal and child health: Programs, problems, and policies in public health,* 3rd ed., Chapter 4. Sudbury, MA: Jones and Bartlett.

Riesman, D., in collaboration with R. Denney & N. Glazer. (1950). *The lonely crowd: A study of the changing American character.* New Haven, CT: Yale University Press.

Ryder, N. B. (1965). The cohort as a concept in the study of social change. *American Sociological Review, 30*(6), 843–861.

Shanahan, M. J. (2008). Glen H. Elder, Jr. and the importance of lived experience. *Research in Human Development, 5*(4), 195–198.

Silbereisen, R. K., & Tomasik, M. J. (2008). Berlin-Warsaw-Jena: A journey with Glen H. Elder through sites of social change. *Research in Human Development, 5*(4), 244–258.

Thomas, W. I., & Znaniecki, F. (1918). *The Polish peasant in Europe and America. Monograph of an immigrant group* (Vols. 1–5). Chicago: University of Chicago Press; Boston: Badger Press.

15

Reflections on a Life Course of Developmental Criminology

DAVID P. FARRINGTON

I was born in Ormskirk, Lancashire, in the North of England, in 1944, and went to the local state grammar school. My best subjects at school were math and chemistry, and I was fortunate enough to win a State Scholarship for my school examination performance at age 18 in math, physics, and chemistry. At that time, these Scholarships were given to the top 2,400 children in each age cohort (out of a total of over 670,000), of whom about 800 went to Cambridge University, 700 went to Oxford University, 400 went to London University, and 500 went elsewhere. Luckily, I got into Cambridge University after taking its entrance examinations. I started off doing math, physics, and chemistry, but eventually graduated in psychology, a subject which had fascinated me from an early age.

When I was 16, I had our local library order many of Freud's books and I read them avidly: *Psychopathology of everyday life, The interpretation of dreams* (of course I kept a notepad next to my bed and tried to write down my dreams when I woke up!), *The ego and the id, Totem and taboo, Civilization and its discontents, The future of an illusion* (see Wollheim, 1981). Public libraries were great! I was also inspired by Eysenck's books: *Uses and abuses of psychology* (Eysenck, 1953) and *Sense and nonsense in psychology* (Eysenck, 1956). However, Cambridge University focused very much on experimental psychology and the scientific method, and so I was soon taught that these idols had feet of clay!

Cambridge University

The greatest influence on my undergraduate career was a Lecturer in Psychology called Alan Watson. He supervised me in psychology and very conscientiously went through all my essays line by line. In supervisions, he would constantly say "How does this follow from that?" and "What do you mean by this?" He would challenge me to write more clearly and to be more explicit about what I wanted to say. Under his tutelage, my writing style and clarity improved enormously. Cambridge was great for me as an undergraduate because I felt that its stimulating environment enormously expanded my intellectual abilities.

After graduating in Psychology in 1966, I applied to do a PhD degree in Cambridge and, fortunately, was accepted. Alan Watson agreed to supervise my PhD, which tried to test different theories of human learning, focusing on the ability of Cambridge undergraduates to learn three-digit numbers. I had a very good memory for numbers myself and had always been good at mental arithmetic. The model of the Cambridge PhD was very much one of master and apprentice, and again I learned a great deal from Alan Watson about conducting and writing up experiments, reviewing the literature, etc.

My PhD thesis described 12 experiments that I carried out with Cambridge undergraduates. My meetings with Alan Watson were very stimulating, because we would take stock of the results obtained in the last experiment, then talk about the loose ends and new questions raised, and then plan the next experiment to address these new hypotheses. Actually, it was very reminiscent of the logical deductive methods I had used in chemistry, for example in trying to discover what an unknown substance was. It was very much the model of an experimental science. Nowadays, this work would fall within cognitive psychology.

Unfortunately, Alan Watson was very busy. He was a very clever man indeed, but he was Acting Head of the Psychological Laboratory in the mornings and Senior Tutor (Chief Executive Officer) of Fitzwilliam College in the afternoons and evenings. Consequently, our meetings were often in the Psychological Laboratory at 7.00 a.m. or in Fitzwilliam College at midnight. He read most of my drafts (and much else) in the middle of the night. Since he spent most of his time in teaching and administration, he rarely published anything and the one thing he did not do was teach me how to publish. Consequently, although my PhD thesis was accepted with no changes (a rare event) in 1969, I never published any of my 12 experiments in journals, which I should have done.

Over to Criminology

As I was coming to the end of my PhD, I was becoming disillusioned with experimental psychology. Much of it seemed rather irrelevant to real life, and I wanted to do something more socially relevant. At that time, I was interested in sociology and believed that it might have something to offer. Consequently, when I saw an advertisement in the Psychological Laboratory for someone to work as a Research Officer on a longitudinal study of delinquency, based in Cambridge, I applied for it, and was offered the job by Donald West in 1969. It suited me to stay in Cambridge, and I knew enough about longitudinal studies to know that they were unusual and interesting.

I knew nothing about criminology at the time. However, Donald West appointed me because of my statistical and computing skills. When I started my PhD in 1966, Alan Watson had encouraged me to learn Fortran programming, and so I knew how to analyze data using the computer, which was a fairly new thing at the time. The only other thing I did for my PhD thesis that has ever come in useful was to learn all about ROC (Receiver Operating Characteristic) curves (as applied to human learning and memory). ROC curves are extremely important in criminology in quantifying the strength of the relationship between a prediction score and a dichotomous outcome such as conviction or reconviction (see, e.g., Farrington, Jolliffe, & Johnstone, 2008).

Criminology was an alien environment. In 1969–70, British criminology was dominated by sociologists who were stridently anti-empirical and anti-scientific. They talked in impenetrable jargon (described as "gobbledegook" by a *Cambridge News* journalist in 1969) and were very critical of Donald's longitudinal study, which they regarded as an atavistic throwback to the work of the then-hated Gluecks (who were later revived by Sampson & Laub, 1993). However, I enjoyed working with Donald on this survey and thought that it was really fascinating. Donald was a very careful researcher. Like many psychiatrists, his first question was: "What is the evidence for that?" and I very much liked this. I think Donald's previous career as a parapsychology researcher had made him unusually careful. Whereas many criminologists accepted positive results rather uncritically, any positive results in psychical research were strongly challenged, which meant that it was important to be very careful and to think of and try to test possible alternative explanations of all findings.

I worked on soft money for 5 years, until I managed to get a permanent post in 1974. I really enjoyed the research but the financial uncertainties were troubling. Happily, I was appointed to a university teaching post in 1974, but

unhappily I then became Director of the MPhil Course in Criminology from 1975 to 1978. During this time period, I shouldered a heavy burden of university teaching and administration and also did a lot of college teaching. None of this was conducive to publishing journal articles.

The Cambridge Study in Delinquent Development (CSDD)

In the first few years of my career, I worked mainly on the CSDD, which is a prospective longitudinal survey (now from age 8 to age 56) of the development of offending and antisocial behavior in 411 London males mostly born in 1953. The CSDD began in 1961, and for the first 20 years it was directed by Donald West. As mentioned, I started working on it in 1969, and took over as Director in 1982. The CSDD has been funded primarily by the Home Office and secondly by the Department of Health. Results of the Study have been described in five books (Piquero, Farrington, & Blumstein, 2007; West, 1969, 1982; West & Farrington, 1973, 1977), in six summary reports (Farrington & West, 1981, 1990; Farrington, 1995, 2003b; Farrington, Coid, & West, 2009; Farrington et al., 2006), and in a total of about 200 publications (listed on my Cambridge Institute of Criminology website).

The original aim of the CSDD was to describe the development of delinquent and criminal behavior in inner-city males, to investigate to what extent this could be predicted in advance, and to explain why juvenile delinquency began, why it did or did not continue into adult crime, and why adult crime often ended as men reached their twenties. The main focus was on continuity or discontinuity in behavioral development, on the effects of life events on development, and on predicting future behavior. The CSDD was not designed to test any one particular theory about delinquency but to test many different hypotheses about the causes and correlates of offending, and many different mechanisms and processes linking risk factors and antisocial behavior. However, I did propose a developmental theory (Farrington, 2005) that has been independently tested in the Netherlands (Van Der Laan, Blom, & Kleemans, 2009).

Early Results of the CSDD

The boys were tested in their schools by CSDD psychologists at ages 8, 10, and 14, and their parents (usually the mothers) were interviewed about once a year by CSDD psychiatric social workers from when the boy was 8 until when he was 15. When I joined the CSDD in 1969, the interviews at age 16 were under way and the psychiatric social workers were coming to the end of their interviews with the parents. I was in charge of computerizing all the data, I carried out all the analyses that led to the book *Who becomes delinquent?* (West & Farrington, 1973), and I was very much involved in devising the interview at age 18, which was carried out in 1971–73.

Unfortunately, the then Director of the Institute of Criminology, Professor Sir Leon Radzinowicz, wanted all Cambridge research published in books in the Cambridge Studies in Criminology that he edited, and so he discouraged junior staff from publishing articles. Nevertheless, I published one article on school effects on delinquency (Farrington, 1972) that showed that the different official delinquency rates of the secondary schools were largely driven by their different intakes of boys from the primary schools at age 11, rather than by aspects of the secondary schools themselves. I also published an article on self-reported delinquency (Farrington, 1973) that focused on psychometric properties such as test—retest stability, concurrent validity, and (unusually) predictive validity. I showed that self-reported offending by unconvicted boys at age 14 predicted their future convictions in the next 3 years.

The main thrust of *Who becomes delinquent?* (West & Farrington, 1973) was to investigate which childhood risk factors measured at age 8–10 predicted juvenile convictions. The most important predictors included troublesome behavior (rated by peers and teachers), convicted parents (based on records), low nonverbal IQ (90 or less, based on the Progressive Matrices test), low family income, large family size (five or more children in the family), and poor parental child-rearing behavior (cold or rejecting parental attitude and harsh or erratic parental discipline; all rated by the psychiatric social workers based on interviews with parents).

The follow-up book *The delinquent way of life* (West & Farrington, 1977) focused on results obtained in the interviews at age 18, which was fully tape-recorded and transcribed. As always in the CSDD, attrition was low; 389 boys were interviewed out of 410 who were still alive at age 18 (95%). We always made tremendous efforts to secure interviews, because of our belief that the most interesting persons in any research on offending tend to be the hardest to locate and the most uncooperative. Surveys in which less than 75% of the target sample are interviewed may produce results that seriously underestimate the true level of criminal behavior. Generally, an increase in the percentage interviewed from 75% to 95% leads to a disproportionate increase in the validity of the results; for example, at age 18, 36% of the one-sixth of the sample who were the most difficult to interview were convicted, compared with only 22% of the majority who were interviewed more easily, a statistically significant difference (West & Farrington, 1977).

The main thrust of the 1977 book was to document the antisocial life-styles of the convicted boys at age 18. They tended to have unstable job records, to be sexually promiscuous, to spend time hanging about on the street, to take drugs, and to be heavy drinkers, heavy smokers, and heavy gamblers. Generally, we found that multiple risk factors led to multiple social problems, including delinquency (Farrington, 2002). Both in this book and in *Who becomes delinquent?*, we included many case histories to illustrate the statistical conclusions.

The delinquent way of life also tested a number of hypotheses about the intergenerational transmission of offending. It showed that criminal parents tended to have delinquent children, and that this relationship might have been mediated by poor parental supervision. The percentage of boys who were convicted did not vary according to whether the father was last convicted before or after the boy's birth, suggesting that there was no direct behavioral influence of criminal fathers on delinquent sons. There was no evidence that convicted fathers directly encouraged their sons to commit crimes or taught them criminal techniques. On the contrary, convicted fathers generally condemned their sons' offending. Hardly any convicted fathers co-offended with any of the Study males (Reiss & Farrington, 1991). However, controlling for self-reported delinquency, having a convicted parent increased the probability of a boy being convicted, suggesting that official processing may have been biased for boys coming from known criminal families.

In the CSDD, one of my main aims has always been to test alternative hypotheses about the intervening mechanisms between risk factors and delinquency. Numerous risk factors, such as having criminal parents, have been known for many years, but the precise mechanisms by which they have an effect on delinquency are not well understood. I have less often tried to test theories, but I did publish one of the first empirical tests of labeling theory, which argues that official processing has harmful effects. In agreement with the theory, I found that (between ages 14 and 18) boys' self-reported delinquency increased after they were convicted for the first time, compared with boys who were matched on self-reported delinquency at age 14 but not convicted (Farrington, 1977). Similar results were obtained between ages 18 and 21 (Farrington, Osborn, & West, 1978). The most important mediating factor seemed to be that first convictions led to an increase in hostile attitudes towards the police.

A fruitful collaboration with Leonard Berkowitz produced an article comparing individual and group fights at age 18 (Farrington, Berkowitz, & West, 1982). This article was based on tape-recorded unstructured accounts of physical fights. When the boy fought alone, his opponent was usually alone, he was usually provoked (e.g., the opponent stared at or insulted the boy or his girlfriend), and he usually started the fight. When the boy fought alongside others, he was usually fighting a group, he usually joined in to help a friend or because he was attacked, and the fights were likely to involve weapons, injuries, and police intervention. Fights often occurred when minor incidents escalated, because both sides wanted to demonstrate their toughness and masculinity and were unwilling to react to provocation in a conciliatory fashion.

In contrast to the relatively generous funding of the CSDD from 1961–74, initially by the Home Office and later by the Department of Health, the funding then declined during the remainder of the 1970s. Donald West was able to direct two further follow-up studies between

1974 and 1979 at ages 21 and 25, but not with the whole sample. At age 21, the aim was to interview all the convicted youths and an equal number of unconvicted youths, and 218 were interviewed out of a target sample of 241 (90%). At age 25, the aim was to interview only four special subgroups, (basically temporary versus persisting recidivists and unconvicted youths), and 85 youths were interviewed (West, 1982). I was not so centrally involved in these follow-ups as I had been in 1969–74, as I became bogged down in university teaching and administration.

I have always argued that within-individual analyses should be carried out to investigate the causes of offending (e.g., Farrington, 1988). If an individual commits more crimes during periods when a risk factor (e.g., unemployment) is present than during periods when the risk factor is absent, this is good evidence that the risk factor might be having a causal effect, because many other variables (e.g., individual, family, peer, neighborhood) are controlled. In contrast, most conclusions about causes in criminology are based on between-individual analyses, where for example an unemployed individual X is compared with a different employed individual Y. The great problem with between-individual analyses is that there are many uncontrolled variables. For example, unemployed individuals differ in many respects from employed individuals, and one of these other (unmeasured) variables may be responsible for any observed differences in offending between unemployed and employed individuals.

An explicitly within-individual analysis of the effects of unemployment on offending was carried out in the CSDD by Farrington, Gallagher, Morley, St. Ledger, and West (1986). Most of the boys left school at age 15, and this article investigated their convictions during periods of unemployment and employment between ages 15 and 18. The results were clear-cut: More offenses were committed during periods of unemployment. This was especially true of offenses leading to material gain, such as theft, burglary, robbery, fraud, and receiving, whereas other crimes, such as assault, threatening behavior, taking vehicles, vandalism, and drug use, were not more frequent during periods of unemployment. It was concluded that the causal mechanism was that unemployment led to a lack of money which in turn led to crimes of material gain. It was not the case that unemployment led to boredom or frustration, which in turn led to excitement-seeking crimes. Furthermore, the effect of unemployment only applied to those with the highest prediction scores for crime, suggesting that unemployment had a criminogenic effect especially on those boys with the greatest prior potential for offending.

Apart from height and weight, the most important biological variable that has been studied in the CSDD is heart rate (measured by the pulse rate). According to Raine (1993, pp. 166–172), one of the most replicable findings in the literature is that antisocial and violent youth tend to have low heart rates. This may be because a low heart rate reflects autonomic under-arousal, which leads to sensation-seeking, risk-taking, and aggression to increase

arousal. Alternatively, a high heart rate may be associated with anxiety, behavioral inhibition, and a fearful temperament, and more fearful people are less likely to commit violent acts. In the CSDD, extensive analyses were carried out on low resting heart rate at age 18 as a predictor and correlate of official and self-reported violence and teacher-reported aggression (Farrington, 1997). The relationship between low heart rate and these outcome variables held up after controlling for all other risk factors.

Ottawa and Washington

Two sabbaticals changed my life. After I finished my stint as Director of the MPhil Course, I spent a year (1978–79) in Ottawa in the Solicitor General's Department working on the Canadian Young Offenders Act. For this I have Irvin Waller to thank. When I went to Ottawa, I had published very little: a couple of books and about a dozen articles. In my year in Ottawa I completed 15 articles and, for the only time in my life, caught up with all the things that had been hanging around for years. From then on, I was able to learn from Alan Watson and publish lots and avoid administration like the plague.

The Solicitor General's Department was a large bureaucracy. On the first day, one of the people I met said "Welcome to the Titanic." My contract had been held up until the last minute because one Solicitor General (who was in favor of the Young Offenders Act) had to resign because he forged his girlfriend's husband's signature in order to get her an abortion, and then the next Solicitor General (who was worried about "a criminal code for juveniles") didn't want to have anything to do with this proposed Act. While I had had quite a bit of previous contact with the Home Office, it was very interesting to be close to the political and policy-making process.

Every month, I went to Montreal to collaborate with Marc LeBlanc. I stayed at the entrance to St. Joseph's Oratory and had to struggle up the hill every night to the University of Montreal to collect my computer printouts. In the winter, with the temperature around minus 15°F and with 2 feet of snow on the ground, it felt like climbing Mount Everest! I also struggled to read most of the excellent reports that Marc and his colleagues had written, since they were almost all in French at that time. I had studied French at school and could read French to some extent, but I spent a lot of time puzzling over tables (mainly I read the tables!) with the aid of a French dictionary. Still, I learned a great deal from this happy collaboration.

The first cross-national comparative study of the CSDD reported results obtained with the Eysenck personality inventory at ages 16–17 in London and Montreal (Farrington, Biron, & LeBlanc, 1982). The items that were most strongly related to official and self-reported delinquency in London were measures of impulsiveness such as "Do you often long for excitement?" and "Do you generally do and say things quickly without stopping to think?" The same items were significantly related to self-reported delinquency for both boys and girls in Montreal, suggesting that impulsiveness is the most important and replicable individual difference correlate of delinquency.

One of the papers I finished in Ottawa was a review of longitudinal studies in crime and delinquency that was published in Volume 1 of *Crime and Justice* (Farrington, 1979b). This was a very important publication, because it brought me to the notice of key American researchers such as Alfred Blumstein and Albert Reiss, who gave me detailed comments on the first draft that greatly improved the final version. It brought me into contact with Michael Tonry and Norval Morris, who also proved to be very important in fostering my career. In particular, it massively expanded my knowledge of American longitudinal and criminal career research. Also during my year in Ottawa, I travelled widely in the USA and visited leading American researchers who had previously visited Cambridge such as Leonard Berkowitz, Gilbert Geis, and James Short.

I soon decided that being on sabbatical leave was the best possible state, and so I applied for another sabbatical in 1981 to be a Visiting Fellow in Washington at the National Institute of Justice (NIJ). While at NIJ, I began my collaboration with Patrick Langan (Langan & Farrington, 1983) and further expanded my knowledge of American criminological research and researchers. NIJ in 1981 was initially rather demoralized by various threats of laying off staff by the new administration but in fact the tenure of James "Chips" Stewart as Director of NIJ proved to be the golden age of American criminological research in my opinion.

It was a golden age especially for longitudinal and experimental research, both of which I strongly advocated. While I was at NIJ, I completed a second *Crime and Justice* review of randomized experiments in criminology (Farrington, 1983b), which proved almost as influential as the first. NIJ funded many randomized experiments in the 1980s (e.g., Sherman, 1992). However, the 1980s were mainly memorable to me for the exciting development of longitudinal and criminal career research in the USA.

I found that the great thing about Americans was their optimism that everything was possible. When I advocated randomized experiments in the UK, the reaction was very negative: "You could never do it." Instead of thinking about all the problems, the reaction of American researchers was to say "Let's go for it." That is why I was delighted to be involved in so many exciting American research activities in the 1980s.

Longitudinal and Criminal Career Research in the 1980s

During the 1980s, the most influential American criminologists (at least with the federal government and leading foundations) were Alfred Blumstein, Norval Morris, Lloyd Ohlin, Albert Reiss, James Wilson, and Marvin Wolfgang. Happily, they all advocated longitudinal and criminal career research at this time. I was delighted to be a member of the

National Academy of Sciences (NAS) panel on criminal career research (chaired by Alfred Blumstein) in 1983–86, along with Morris, Reiss, Wilson, Wolfgang, and other luminaries such as Delbert Elliott, Rolf Loeber, and Lee Robins (Blumstein, Cohen, Roth, & Visher, 1986). I really felt that we were developing an exciting new paradigm and that we were pushing back the frontiers of knowledge (although Patrick Langan always chided me that I should say pushing forward the frontiers of knowledge!).

In 1982, the MacArthur Foundation decided that it wanted to advance knowledge about crime and set up a committee chaired by Norval Morris (and containing Lloyd Ohlin and James Wilson). This committee advised the Foundation to mount new longitudinal studies. The Foundation then set up a kind of architectural competition in which 20 researchers were invited to send in designs for a new longitudinal study. I was one of three persons who evaluated the 13 designs submitted. Three designs were chosen as "winners" to be discussed at a meeting in Chicago in 1983, but unfortunately the Foundation also invited the "losers" to the meeting, some of whom proceeded to lambast the "winners." The Foundation then decided that, if researchers could not agree among themselves, it would not be funding a new study.

Norval Morris saved the day in 1984 by persuading the Foundation to commission Lloyd Ohlin, James Wilson, and myself to write a book on *Understanding and controlling crime* outlining the design of a new study (Farrington, Ohlin, & Wilson, 1986). We advocated a new multiple-cohort longitudinal-experimental study. We proposed that four cohorts should be followed up, from prebirth to age 6, age 6 to age 12, age 12 to age 18, and age 18 to age 24, with experimental interventions implemented in the middle of each age range. One aim of this accelerated longitudinal design was to build up a picture of development from prebirth to age 24 in less than 10 years, by linking up comparable cohorts in the same large city.

In 1984–85, the Office of Juvenile Justice and Delinquency Prevention (OJJDP) funded a series of "executive sessions" on juvenile justice and juvenile delinquency organized by Mark Moore and James Wilson (e.g., Wilson & Loury, 1987). It was on the plane home from one of these sessions that James Wilson persuaded Pamela Swain of OJJDP that they should mount some new longitudinal studies. OJJDP put out a solicitation in 1986 and selected three new studies for funding, in Denver, Pittsburgh, and Rochester. Unusually, there was an emphasis on comparable data collection and replication. Happily, I was (and have continued to be) a co-investigator of the Pittsburgh Youth Study (PYS), along with Rolf Loeber and Magda Stouthamer-Loeber (see later). This has been a wonderful collaboration for me, as the PYS and the other two studies have really advanced knowledge in numerous ways. And I have come to realize that "Beautiful Pittsburgh" is not an oxymoron!

On my many visits to Pittsburgh, Alfred Blumstein and his wife Dolores were kind enough to put up with me in their house. Their hospitality was very warm and generous. Alfred has undoubtedly had a great impact on my professional life, and he has been a wonderful role model and mentor. He is an inspiring and stunningly brilliant researcher with an amazing ability to work up to about 4.00 a.m. on a regular basis. I once emailed both Alfred and Rolf at 9.00 a.m. in England (4.00 a.m. in Pittsburgh) and both responded at once! At that time, Alfred was just coming to the end of his shift and Rolf (who is a very early riser) was just beginning!

Sad to say, NIJ was rather upset when OJJDP mounted these three studies. There was always rivalry between the two agencies, and NIJ always regarded itself as superior. However, these three high-profile studies—considered to be the "jewel in the crown" of OJJDP's research program—threatened this assumption of superiority. Consequently, NIJ decided to collaborate with the MacArthur Foundation (who was now receptive to the idea, after our 1986 book) to mount a bigger and better longitudinal study.

NIJ and MacArthur funded the Program on Human Development and Criminal Behavior, led by Michael Tonry, Lloyd Ohlin and myself, from 1987 to 1989. We set up various working groups to plan a new longitudinal study and had numerous stimulating meetings culminating in the book *Human development and criminal behavior* (Tonry, Ohlin, & Farrington, 1991). Incidentally, this and many other key books of that time period were published in a Springer-Verlag series edited by Alfred Blumstein and myself and masterminded by a former student of mine, Robert Kidd. This was again a very happy collaboration. The 1991 book proposed a bigger and better multiple-cohort longitudinal survey with seven cohorts beginning prenatally and at ages 3, 6, 9, 12, 15, and 18.

Unfortunately, NIJ and MacArthur reacted to this book not by mounting the project but by suggesting that we should have several more years of planning meetings. At this point, Michael, Lloyd and myself decided that we were happy to pass the baton to Felton (Tony) Earls and Albert Reiss, who eventually (in the mid-1990s), along with Robert Sampson, mounted the seven-cohort study with over 6,000 participants (see Liberman, 2007). I preferred to spend time analyzing the data that had been collected in the CSDD and PYS rather than to spend more time planning a new study.

While the 1980s were an enormously exciting time for me, because I really felt at the cutting edge of incredible new developments, my effort was also enormous. For 3 years between 1987 and 1989, I crossed the Atlantic once a month on average. What with being away for a week and spending another week in preparation, all my British activities were compressed into 2 weeks every month. In 1 month (May 1989) I went back and forth to the USA three times for three successive weekend meetings, and on two of these weekends (in Boston) the hotel had a (false) fire alarm in the middle of the night which caused us all to stand outside in our night wear. While observing the likes of Albert Reiss and Lee Robins in pyjamas had a certain novelty, I was happy to withdraw from the NIJ–MacArthur initiative in order to have a less frantic life!

Developments in the 1990s

Unfortunately, my hopes of a less frantic life were not fulfilled, partly because my research became more and more diversified, and partly because of my service to scholarly societies. In 1990, I became President of the British Society of Criminology (BSC) for a 3-year term. I really don't know why I have agreed to be Chair and President of so many committees and organizations; these things seemed noble ventures at the time but usually consumed a lot of time that perhaps would have been better spent on research. I agreed to be Chair of the Division of Criminological and Legal Psychology of the British Psychological Society in 1983–85 because of my messianic zeal to advance the cause of psychological criminology, but in many other cases I am not sure why I agreed to take on these kinds of commitments; maybe I am not very good at saying no to people!

Anyhow, I had what still seems a good idea for my BSC Presidential address in 1990, which was to link up national victim survey, police, court, and prison data to put numbers and probabilities into the flow diagram from crimes committed to persons imprisoned. The first national British crime victimization survey was for the year 1981 and the third was for 1987, so by 1990 it was possible not only to put numbers in the flow diagram but also to track trends over a reasonable (6-year) time period.

Filling in the flow diagram for England and Wales was complicated enough, but I then decided to compare England and the United States in collaboration with Patrick Langan (see, e.g., Langan & Farrington, 1998). This required a huge amount of work to assemble comparable data for the two countries, and I made many trips to Washington. In 1992, we presented the first offense-specific national estimates for the flow of persons from offenses committed to offenders imprisoned (Farrington & Langan, 1992). One of our most important contributions was to include information on co-offending in our calculations, because (as an example) one million burglaries should not be directly compared to 50,000 persons convicted for burglary in a year to produce a probability of a burglar being convicted of 5%. If, on average, each burglary is committed by two offenders, it is necessary to compare two million offender–offense combinations with 50,000 convicted offender–offense combinations to produce a probability of a burglar being convicted of 2.5%, rather than 5%.

I also attended a number of meetings organized by Per-Olof Wikström in Sweden. Per-Olof had great ideas to integrate developmental, ecological, and situational theories and approaches. He was much more of a cross-national comparative researcher than I was (he had thought very deeply about all the issues arising), and so he suggested that we should compare the flow diagrams in England, the United States, and Sweden over time. After a lot of work, we compared all three countries between 1981 and 1991 (Farrington, Langan, & Wikstrom, 1994). We later extended the cross-national comparative study to eight countries between 1981 and 1999: virtually all countries with repeated large-scale national victimization surveys during this time period (Farrington, Langan, & Tonry, 2004).

As I said, my research diversified considerably in the 1990s, into shoplifting experiments (e.g., Farrington, 1999), bullying (e.g., Baldry & Farrington, 1998), and offender profiling (e.g., Farrington & Lambert, 1997), just to give a few examples. All of these seemed good ideas at the time, and I liked to pursue research that seemed interesting.

I also diversified geographically, for example publishing a paper on victimization in the Caribbean (Painter & Farrington, 1998) and on early predictors of childhood aggression in Mauritius (Raine, Reynolds, Venables, Mednick, & Farrington, 1998). Adrian Raine offered to fly me to Mauritius, since I was a consultant on his follow-up project, but I preferred to join him in sampling the night life in Santa Monica! I also spent time analyzing the Seattle Social Development Project, for example comparing self-reported and official delinquency careers (Farrington et al., 2003). I am a great admirer of David Hawkins and Richard Catalano and their wonderful array of intervention projects.

I was vice-chair of the National Academy of Sciences panel on violence (Reiss & Roth, 1993). This produced very good state-of-the-art reviews—especially in the three supplementary volumes—but was not as exciting as the criminal career panel, when we really thought that we were developing a new paradigm. Partly this reflected the personalities of the chairs. Alfred Blumstein was very much a convergent thinker who had almost to be wrestled to the ground to deflect him from moving in a straight line towards a solution. Albert Reiss, on the other hand, was very much a divergent thinker who could always think of some new interesting digression at a higher level of complexity. He really wanted to write an encyclopedia, not a report!

I also enjoyed collaborating with medical and public health researchers like Jonathan Shepherd of Cardiff and Frederick Rivara of Seattle (see, e.g., Rivara & Farrington, 1995; Shepherd & Farrington, 1993). I think criminologists have a lot to learn from medical and public health researchers, and these collaborations seemed to me to involve real science! I have also enjoyed collaborating with psychiatrists such as Jeremy Coid (e.g., Farrington & Coid, 2003) because of their commitment to hard scientific evidence.

Also, in the 1990s, I became the first (and so far only) President of the American Society of Criminology (ASC) based outside North America. I really enjoyed this and I have very happy memories of the meeting that I presided over in Toronto (and especially of the fabulous Royal Suite at the Royal York Hotel!). Of course, I felt that the

ASC was a bit like an ocean liner that could only be turned slightly and slowly. I was happy to keep a very successful society ticking over with few changes during my year of office, although I was very pleased to preside over the creation of a new Division of Corrections and Sentencing (see Turner, MacKenzie, & Farrington, 2010).

I was involved with Friedrich Lösel the founding of the European Association of Psychology and Law (EAPL), and became its President in 1997–99. I gradually had more and more contact with European psychologists, especially in Germany and Spain (see, e.g., Garrido, Farrington, & Welsh, 2006), and became increasingly aware of the high quality of psychological research in other European countries. The formation of the EAPL was intended to bring together previously isolated researchers, and we had a joint meeting with the American Psychology-Law Society in Edinburgh during my term as President. I also spent 5 years on the Scientific Advisory Board of the Netherlands Institute for the Study of Crime and Law Enforcement (NSCR), trying to persuade them to mount a "crime shuttle" longitudinal study (modeled on the space shuttle!) that could include various substudies after it got off the ground.

Later Results in the CSDD

After I took over as Director of the CSDD in 1982, I sought funding to follow up the whole sample again, and I managed to get funding from the Home Office in 1984–87 for a follow-up interview at age 32. At this age, 378 out of 403 men still alive (94%) were interviewed (Farrington, 1989). In general, success in tracing the men was achieved by persistence and by using a wide variety of different methods (Farrington, Gallagher, Morley, St. Ledger, & West, 1990). Searching in electoral registers and telephone directories, and visits to a man's presumed address, were the most successful tracing methods for the men who were not particularly elusive. Searches in the Criminal Record Office, National Health Service records, and leads from other men were most useful for the more elusive men. The key factor in obtaining the men's cooperation was probably the pleasantness of the interviewer in the first face-to-face meeting. As at age 18, the interviews enquired about accommodation, relationships, children, employment, illnesses and injuries, parents, smoking, drinking, drug use, physical fights, court appearances, and self-reported offending.

The next funding from the Home Office was obtained in 1993–94, to search the criminal records of the males and all their relatives (fathers, mothers, brothers, sisters, children, and female partners). These searches demonstrated that offending tends to be concentrated in families. While 40% of Study males were convicted up to age 40 in 1993, this was also true of 28% of their fathers, 13% of their mothers, 43% of their brothers, 12% of their sisters, and 9% of their wives or female partners The fact that the percentage of brothers convicted was similar to the percentage of Study males convicted suggests that the repeated interviews with the CSDD males had no effect on their likelihood of offending. There were on average 1.5 convicted persons out of 5.5 persons per family (or about 600 convicted persons out of 2,200 searched). While 64% of families contained at least one convicted person, only 6% of families accounted for half of all the convictions of all family members (Farrington, Barnes, & Lambert, 1996).

It was always difficult to secure funding for the CSDD, but major funding from the Home Office and the Department of Health was obtained in 1999–2004 by myself in collaboration with Jeremy Coid. This allowed another social interview with the men at age 48, plus a psychiatric interview that included the PCL-SV (a measure of psychopathy). Biological data were also collected, on height, weight, waist circumference, pulse rate, blood pressure, respiratory function, and testosterone. The men's female partners were also interviewed (based on advice from Terrie Moffitt). At age 48, 365 of the 394 men who were still alive (93%) were interviewed; a remarkable response rate in a 40-year follow-up study (Farrington et al., 2006).

Our most recent research involves following up the children of the Study males (Farrington, Coid, & Murray, 2009). Starting in 2004, attempts were made to interview all biological children of Study males who were aged 18 or older. Children were only targeted if their father had been interviewed, because of the requirement to seek his agreement to interviewing his child (in order to meet the standards of the South East Regional Medical Ethics Committee). In total, 518 out of 630 eligible children have been interviewed to date (82%). Therefore, the CSDD is one of the few projects including personal interviews with hundreds of people in three successive generations. I am currently seeking further funding to increase the percentage of children interviewed. This third generation study aims to advance knowledge about the intergenerational transmission of official and self-reported offending, drug use, psychopathy, sexual behavior, and educational problems.

A big effort to estimate the "scaling-up factor" from convictions to self-reported offenses was made in a final report to the Home Office (Farrington et al., 2006). On average, it was found that convicted males self-reported 22 offenses for each conviction. This scaling-up factor is very important for many reasons, including cost–benefit analyses. In most cases, evaluations of programs use official records to assess their success, but it is highly desirable to scale up any saving in arrests or convictions to a saving in offenses committed (see also Farrington, Jolliffe, Loeber, & Homish, 2007).

Many CSDD articles have investigated the extent to which childhood and adolescent features are related to specific outcomes, including intimate partner violence (Theobald & Farrington, 2012), bullying (Farrington, 1993b), criminal violence (Farrington, 2012), adult onset offending (Zara & Farrington, 2009), psychopathy (Farrington, Ullrich, & Salekin, 2010), early death and

disability (Shepherd, Shepherd, Newcombe, & Farrington, 2009), and illnesses and injuries (Shepherd, Farrington, & Potts, 2002). I have recently had many fruitful collaborations with Alex Piquero, investigating the link between offending trajectories and later outcomes such as early death (Piquero, Farrington, Shepherd, & Auty, in press) and psychopathy (Piquero et al., 2012).

Another within-individual analysis was carried out to investigate the effects of getting married. Convictions of Study males were followed up before and after their marriages, and they were matched with unmarried males on propensity scores (estimating the probability of getting married) and on prior offending. It is often believed that marriage to a good woman is one of the most effective treatments for male offending, and indeed we found that getting married led to a decrease in offending compared with staying single (Theobald & Farrington, 2009). Also, later separation from a wife led to an increase in offending compared with staying married (Theobald & Farrington, 2013).

A major problem with most criminological theories is that they do not make and test exact quantitative predictions. In the CSDD, we tested several mathematical models of the conviction careers of the Study males (Barnett, Blumstein, & Farrington, 1987). We found that models assuming that all offenders had the same frequency of offending were inadequate. In order to fit the data, we assumed that there were two categories of offenders, termed "frequents" and "occasionals," who differed both in their rates of offending and in their probabilities of desistance after each conviction. Both types incurred convictions at a constant (but different) rate during their criminal careers. Therefore, the individual age-crime curves were very different from the aggregate age-crime curve, which was largely driven by the prevalence of offenders rather than by the frequency of offending (Farrington, 1986).The two types of offenders had a similar average career duration.

We carried out a predictive test of this model (Barnett, Blumstein, & Farrington, 1989). The model was developed on conviction data between the 10th and 25th birthdays and aimed to predict reconviction data between the 25th and 30th birthdays. Generally, the model performed well, but it was necessary to assume that there was some intermittency (desisting and later restarting) of criminal careers. Some of the frequents ceased offending at an average age of 19 but then restarted after a period of 7–10 years with no convictions. This restarting may be connected to life changes such as losing a job or separating from a spouse. A recent book (MacLeod, Grove, & Farrington, 2012) reviews more recent attempts to formulate and test quantitative criminal career models.

Co-offending is an extremely important but neglected topic. For example, if offenses are committed by a group, incarcerating or rehabilitating one member of the group will not necessarily prevent them recurring. One of the first major studies of co-offending was carried out in the CSDD (Reiss & Farrington, 1991). This found that most juvenile and young adult offenses leading to convictions were committed with others, but the incidence of co-offending declined steadily with age. This was not because co-offenders dropped out but because the males changed from co-offending in their teenage years to lone offending in their twenties (just as they changed from excitement-seeking motives in their teens to utilitarian motives in their twenties: see Farrington, 1993a). Burglary, robbery, and theft from vehicles were particularly likely to involve co-offenders. Generally, there was some consistency in co-offending or lone offending between one offense and the next.

Co-offenders tended to be similar in age, gender, and race to Study males and lived close to their addresses and to the locations of the offenses. It was rare for Study males to offend with their fathers, mothers, sisters or wives, or with unrelated females. Co-offending with brothers was most likely when a Study male had brothers who were close in age to him. About one-third of the most persistent offenders continually offended with less criminally experienced co-offenders, and therefore appeared to be repeatedly recruiting others into a life of crime. Recruiting was especially common for burglary offenses.

As mentioned, while a great deal is known about key risk factors for offending, less is known about intervening causal processes. As an example of an attempt to investigate mechanisms linking risk factors and antisocial behavior, we tested different explanations of the relationship between broken families and delinquency (Juby & Farrington, 2001). Trauma theories suggest that the loss of a parent has a damaging effect on a child, most commonly because of the effect on attachment to the parent. Life-course theories focus on separation as a sequence of stressful experiences, and on the effects of multiple stressors such as parental conflict, parental loss, reduced economic circumstances, changes in parent figures and poor child-rearing methods. Selection theories argue that disrupted families produce delinquent children because of pre-existing differences from other families in risk factors such as parental conflict, criminal or antisocial parents, low family income or poor child-rearing methods.

It was concluded that the results favored life course theories rather than trauma or selection theories. While boys from broken homes (permanently disrupted families) were more delinquent than boys from intact homes, they were not more delinquent than boys from intact high-conflict families. Interestingly, this result was replicated in Switzerland (Haas, Farrington, Killias, & Sattar, 2004). Overall, the most important factor was the post-disruption trajectory. Boys who remained with their mother after the separation had the same delinquency rate as boys from intact low-conflict families. Boys who remained with their father, with relatives or with others (e.g., foster parents) had high delinquency rates. The results were similar whether convictions or self-reported delinquency were studied.

While a great deal is known about risk factors, there is now a great deal of interest in protective factors. In delinquency prevention, it is a more positive message to try to strengthen protective factors rather than to eliminate risk factors. Recently, we have made big efforts to study protective factors in the CSDD (Farrington & Ttofi, 2012). A protective factor is defined as a variable that predicts a low probability of offending among a group at risk, while an interactive protective factor is defined as a variable that interacts with a risk factor to nullify its effect. (Interaction effects in the CSDD were systematically investigated in an earlier paper by Farrington, 1994b.) Among troublesome boys, the most important protective factors were low extraversion, low neuroticism, parental harmony, few friends, and the mother having a full-time job. Among boys living in poor housing, the most important protective factors were good maternal discipline, parent interest in education, and low impulsiveness. Good parental supervision was an interactive protective factor because it reduced the probability of offending among troublesome boys but not among non-troublesome boys. Good child-rearing, small family size, and good maternal and paternal discipline had similar interactive protective effects for boys living in poor housing.

It is very important to investigate the extent to which results can be replicated in different places and times. We (Farrington & Wikström, 1994) investigated to what extent the criminal career results (up to age 25) in the CSDD were replicated in Project Metropolitan in Stockholm (focusing on working-class boys). Convictions in London were compared with police-recorded offenses in Stockholm. The cumulative prevalence curves were remarkably similar, as were the age of onset curves, average career durations, measures of continuity in offending and the growth in recidivism probabilities after each offense. In both London and Stockholm, an early onset predicted a long criminal career.

Another replication study compared the CSDD boys with 310 boys born 7 years later and living in the same small area of South London at age 14 (Farrington & Maughan, 1999). The younger birth cohort of London boys was more ethnically diverse. Unlike the CSDD boys, they were subject to police cautioning during their juvenile years, which was intended to divert young people away from court. Nevertheless, the cumulative prevalence of convictions was almost identical in the two studies. Since an additional number of the younger boys had been cautioned, it was concluded that cautioning had widened the net of recorded offenders.

The Pittsburgh Youth Study (PYS)

As mentioned, I have been a co-investigator on the PYS for the last quarter century. It has been a great privilege for me to collaborate with Rolf Loeber, Magda Stouthamer-Loeber, and their colleagues. The PYS is a prospective longitudinal survey of three cohorts each of about 500 Pittsburgh boys, first studied at ages 7, 10, and 13. It is noteworthy for the regular yearly data collected on the youngest cohort from ages 7 to 19 and on the oldest cohort from ages 13 to 25. The book *Violence and serious theft* (Loeber, Farrington, Stouthamer-Loeber, & White, 2008) gives a great deal of information about the PYS and reports studies of the prevalence and frequency and risk and protective factors for violence and serious theft.

The PYS has advanced knowledge in many different ways that are described in numerous articles. I have space here to describe only four studies. Other important articles have investigated the extent to which racial differences in violence were attributable to racial differences in risk factors (Farrington, Loeber, & Stouthamer-Loeber, 2003) and why some age cohorts were more violent than others (Fabio et al., 2006). The comparison of age cohorts showed the influence of large-scale social changes over time. The oldest cohort, whose teenage years coincided with a big increase in societal violence in Pittsburgh and the United States more generally, were much more likely to be serious and violent offenders than the youngest cohort, whose teenage years coincided with a big decrease in violence after the 1993 peak.

The first study compared results obtained in within-individual analyses and between-individual analyses (Farrington, Loeber, Yin, & Anderson, 2002b). We found that poor parental supervision predicted a boy's delinquency both between and within individuals, but that peer delinquency predicted a boy's delinquency between individuals but not within individuals. In other words, changes in peer delinquency within individuals (from one assessment to the next) did not predict subsequent changes in a boy's delinquency from one assessment to the next. This suggested that peer delinquency might not be a cause of a boy's delinquency but might instead be measuring the same underlying construct (perhaps reflecting co-offending). In contrast, poor parental supervision was predictive within individuals and therefore might be a causal factor. The message is that risk factors that predict offending between individuals may not predict offending within individuals, so that implications drawn from between-individual comparisons about causes and interventions may not be valid. These kinds of analyses can only be carried out in a study such as the PYS with numerous assessments repeated at regular intervals.

The book *Young homicide offenders and victims* (Loeber & Farrington, 2011) presented the first prospective longitudinal study of homicide offenders and victims. Out of 1,512 boys at risk, 37 were convicted of homicide and 39 were killed in their teens and twenties. The strongest childhood predictors of homicide offenders were social factors: coming from a broken home, living in a bad neighborhood, the family on welfare, and a young mother. In contrast, the strongest childhood predictors of homicide victims were individual factors: low guilt, low school achievement, and hyperactivity (as well as coming from a broken home). Racial differences in homicide offending and victimization were largely explained by racial differences in the prevalence of risk factors.

I have become increasingly interested in cost–benefit analyses, and the third study assessed the monetary cost to society of the (self-reported) crimes committed by the youngest cohort of boys between ages 7 and 17 (Welsh et al., 2008). It was estimated that the total cost of the more serious (index) crimes was $110 million (in 2000 dollars) or about $220,000 per boy. For the 34 "chronic offenders" who committed half of all crimes, the average cost per boy was of the order of $800,000. Similar analyses were carried out in the CSDD by Piquero, Jennings, and Farrington (2013).

We systematically compared childhood risk factors for court delinquency in the CSDD and in the PYS (Farrington & Loeber, 1999). Replicable risk factors included hyperactivity, impulsivity and poor concentration; low school achievement; poor parental supervision; parental conflict; an antisocial parent; a young mother; large family size; low family income; and coming from a broken family. It was interesting that these risk factors were replicable despite considerable social differences between London in the early 1960s and Pittsburgh in the late 1980s. For example, family size was greater in London and broken families and young mothers were more prevalent in Pittsburgh.

Where there were differences in results, these seemed largely attributable to different meanings of the risk factors. For example, maternal physical punishment was more important as a risk factor for delinquency in London, and low socioeconomic status was more important in Pittsburgh. However, maternal physical punishment included a cold, rejecting attitude in London, but it could be given in the context of a loving relationship in Pittsburgh; and low socioeconomic status in Pittsburgh took account of parental education, whereas in London it reflected only occupational prestige.

I have also been cochair with Rolf Loeber of four study groups: on serious and violent juvenile offenders (Loeber & Farrington, 1998) and child delinquents (Loeber & Farrington, 2001), both funded by OJJDP; on young adult offenders (Loeber & Farrington, 2012a), funded by NIJ; and on protective factors against youth violence (Loeber & Farrington, 2012b), funded by the U.S. Centers for Disease Control (CDC). These all involved several stimulating meetings over 2–3 years, as we discussed draft papers and moved towards a final report. We were very concerned to link up fundamental research on development and risk and protective factors with applied research on prevention and treatment. For example, in the NIJ study group on young adult offenders, we argued that there should be special legal provisions for offenders aged 18–24 because they were similar to juvenile offenders, partly because of societal changes that extended traditionally adolescent patterns of behavior into the mid-twenties (Farrington, Loeber, & Howell, 2012). I believe that such Study groups can be very valuable in advancing knowledge and setting policy and research agendas.

Intervention Research

I have been drawn more and more into intervention research in the last 15 years, rather than naturalistic longitudinal follow-ups. I have always been interested in interventions, and our OJJDP and NIJ study group books aimed to be relevant to practitioners and policy-makers as well as to scholars, by relating fundamental research on risk and protective factors to applied research on the effectiveness of interventions. Also, I have always advocated developmental or risk-focused prevention (e.g., Farrington, 1994a, 2007, 2010; Farrington & Welsh, 2010; Welsh & Farrington, 2010), and edited books on crime prevention (Farrington & Coid, 2003; Tonry & Farrington, 1995; Welsh & Farrington, 2006, 2012). In risk-focused prevention, knowledge about risk factors is used to select interventions designed to tackle these risk factors. In principle, knowledge obtained in intervention research could help in deciding which risk factors are causes, but in practice most interventions are multi-modal and it is difficult to disentangle the "active ingredients."

I have carried out a number of evaluations of the effectiveness of interventions. In particular, I directed a quasi-experimental evaluation of two U.K. "boot camps" for young offenders (Farrington et al., 2002a). One in the North of England combined military training with cognitive-behavioral skills training programs and a pre-release employment program, while one in the South involved only military training. We found that the Northern boot camp was effective in reducing recidivism but the Southern boot camp was not. We concluded that military training was ineffective in reducing recidivism, even though the boys liked the Army-style regime.

I also assisted in evaluating the "SNAP" (Stop Now and Plan) cognitive-behavioral skills training program for children aged 6–11 who were in trouble with the police in Toronto (Augimeri, Farrington, Koegl, & Day, 2007). A small-scale randomized trial showed that, compared with controls, the treated children decreased on the Delinquency and Aggression scales of the Child Behavior Checklist (CBCL) and also were less likely to have criminal records at follow-up. A later evaluation (Koegl, Farrington, Augimeri, & Day, 2008) concluded that there was a dose–response relationship between treatment intensity (the number of sessions) and the decrease in CBCL scores, and that effects were greater for girls and for older children (age 10–11), who may have been more cognitively advanced.

In 1998, Lawrence Sherman persuaded me to join the crime prevention program at the University of Maryland to help to update the very influential Maryland report on the effectiveness of crime reduction methods (see Sherman et al., 1997; Sherman, Farrington, Welsh, & MacKenzie, 2006). This was generously funded by Jerry Lee, who is perhaps the greatest benefactor that criminology has ever seen. Lawrence Sherman also created the Academy of Experimental Criminology to foster randomized experiments in criminology, and I was President of this from 2001 to 2003.

I have been delighted to learn the technology of systematic reviews and meta-analysis in the last few years,

and I agreed to be the founding chair of the Campbell Collaboration Crime and Justice Group in 2000 (Farrington & Petrosino, 2001; Farrington, Weisburd, & Gill, 2011). The aim of this Group is to carry out systematic reviews of the literature on the effectiveness of criminological interventions, and to make these reviews available to everyone (scholars, policy-makers, practitioners, the mass media, and the general public) on the internet. It is a noble cause that has consumed a huge amount of my time. However, I very much enjoyed chairing the steering committee meetings because the venture was exciting and worthwhile and the participants were very pleasant and stimulating. After 7 years as chair and then cochair, I stepped down in 2007 but have remained on the steering committee.

I have completed a number of systematic reviews and meta-analyses of the effectiveness of interventions, such as family-based programs (Farrington & Welsh, 2003), "Reasoning and Rehabilitation" (Tong & Farrington, 2008), mentoring (Jolliffe & Farrington, 2008), self-control programs (Piquero, Jennings, & Farrington, 2010), and parent training programs (Piquero, Farrington, Welsh, Tremblay, & Jennings, 2009). I also recommended criteria for evaluating methodological quality in evaluation research (Farrington, 2003c). I am now working with David Weisburd on an edited book, *Systematic reviews in criminology: What have we learned?*

I have also carried out a great deal of research on school bullying, in collaboration with my colleague Maria Ttofi. We completed a systematic review of the effectiveness of bullying prevention programs, and concluded that they were generally successful and reduced bullying by an average of about 20% (Ttofi & Farrington, 2011). As of May 2012, this was the most downloaded review from the Campbell Collaboration website, with over 54,000 downloads. We also completed systematic reviews showing the link between bullying perpetration and later offending and violence (Ttofi, Farrington, & Lösel, 2012; Ttofi, Farrington, Lösel, & Loeber, 2011b) and between bullying victimization and later depression (Ttofi, Farrington, Lösel, & Loeber, 2011a). I have also collaborated in research on bullying in young offender institutions (e.g., Connell & Farrington, 1996; Sekol & Farrington, 2010).

Inspired by Brandon Welsh, I have carried out a number of cost–benefit analyses of the effectiveness of interventions (see e.g., Welsh, Farrington, & Sherman, 2001). The argument that $7 is saved for every $1 expended on a program seems to be very persuasive with politicians and policy-makers who do not understand other measures of effect size. We showed that it was preferable to spend money on early intervention rather than on increased imprisonment (Welsh & Farrington, 2011).

My involvement in intervention research has also brought me into contact with several U.K. government ministers, from Kenneth Baker in 1992 to Tony Blair in 2006. I have invariably found them to be remarkably intelligent, and Tony Blair in particular was an incredibly humorous, self-deprecating, and likeable person. I was very impressed by his "Action Plan on Social Exclusion," launched in September 2006 (Cabinet Office, 2006), which coincided in many respects with the risk-focused prevention recommended in our book *Saving children from a life of crime* (Farrington & Welsh, 2007). I have also had quite a bit of contact with Ministers of Public Safety in Canada, who have been especially interested in results from cost–benefit analyses of interventions. However, I have generally avoided contacts with the mass media, because of their unpredictable tendency to distort reasonable messages. For example, when I talked to one newspaper reporter about the value of pre-school intellectual enrichment programs, this story was headlined "Reform Schools for Tiny Tots"! Similarly, I have avoided television appearances, although I did appear in the Inter-Regional Quiz of Great Britain (reaching the final!) at age 14.

Finally, there are many topics that I have not been able to discuss in this chapter because of lack of space. Most importantly, my collaborations with present and past PhD students have been crucial. I have already cited collaborative work with a number of my students, including Anna Baldry, Anne Connell, Christopher Koegl, Ivana Sekol, Delphine Theobald, Maria Ttofi, Sarah Van Mastrigt, and Brandon Welsh. I could have cited the work of many other former PhD students, including the very important research of Darrick Jolliffe in developing the widely-used Basic Empathy Scale (Jolliffe & Farrington, 2006), of Joseph Murray in studying the effect of parental imprisonment on children's internalizing and externalizing behaviors (Murray & Farrington, 2008), and of Lila Kazemian in predicting the residual duration of criminal careers (Kazemian & Farrington, 2006). While I have focused in this chapter on substantive results, I have also made some methodological contributions, for example in proposing a quantitative measure of specialization in offending (Farrington, 1986; Farrington, Snyder, & Finnegan, 1988).

A Future Research Agenda

Developmental and life-course criminology has changed enormously in the last 30 years, especially in its evolving focus on risk and protective factors and on the effects of life events (Farrington, 2000, 2003a). Looking forward, my main suggestion is that developmental criminology should aim to become more scientific. Sciences are based on systematic observation and experimentation, on testing quantitative predictions from theories, and on replication of key results. There are many key issues and questions that could and should be addressed, and many new studies that could and should be funded, but I will outline a few of my priorities, in no particular order.

First, a great deal of research in criminology relies on self-reports and interview data, but interviewees may have poor memories or may deliberately distort or conceal things. More valid information might be obtained from systematic observation of offending as it happens. For example, we (Buckle & Farrington, 1984, 1994)

systematically observed shoplifting and found that shoplifters tended to spend more time in a store, tended to look around a lot, and tended to buy goods as well as stealing them. We estimated the number of items stolen per 10 customer-hours in a store. I think that there should be more attempts to observe offending and to try to estimate how often (per unit time) different types of crimes are committed.

Second, most conclusions about causes in criminology are based on cross-sectional research which cannot establish time ordering or control adequately for unmeasured influences. There should be more efforts to carry out field experiments to investigate causes or immediate influences on offending. For example, we (Farrington & Knight, 1979, 1980) used the "lost letter" technique to investigate stealing. We left stamped, addressed, unsealed letters containing money (except in control conditions) and messages on the streets of London and observed members of the public pick them up. We experimentally manipulated the amount and form of the money and the nature of the apparent victim (e.g., male or female, young or old, rich or poor). We found that hardly anyone stole the money (compared with the control "no money" condition) when the apparent victim was a poor older female, whereas about 80% stole the money when the apparent victim was a rich younger male. Surely we could develop an experimental criminology (perhaps inspired by experimental social psychology: see Farrington, 1979a) of the causes of offending as well as an experimental criminology of the prevention and treatment of offending?

Third, there should be more prospective longitudinal studies of the development of offending, especially documenting relative continuity and absolute changes in behavior. Longitudinal research has many advantages over cross-sectional research (Farrington, 1979b), including establishing causal order and avoiding retrospective bias. In order to speed up results, accelerated longitudinal designs could be used. A key priority in criminology is to measure self-reported and official offending from childhood to adulthood (see Farrington, 1983a). This would require regular, repeated interviews at different ages, as seen to best advantage in the PYS.

In new longitudinal studies, there should be more efforts to study not only the development of offending but also situational factors that influence why offenses are committed. There needs to be more coming together of research on developmental and situational influences on offending, which have tended to be studied separately in the past (see Farrington, Sampson, & Wikstrom, 1993). Similarly, there should be more efforts in future longitudinal studies to measure biological and neighborhood/community influences on offending, because past research has tended to focus on individual, family, peer, school, and socioeconomic factors. There are many key issues that need to be addressed. For example, what mechanisms link hyperactivity/impulsiveness/attention deficit/low self-control/poor ability to delay gratification (etc.) to offending? How and why are anxiety and depression related to offending? To what extent do family factors predict offending after controlling for genetic influences? Why does offending vary with age, gender, and race? Are all these demographic relationships mediated by differences in risk factors? Are there demographic differences in the levels of risk factors or in the strength of relationships between risk factors and offending?

Fourth, while a great deal is known about risk factors for offending, there is a particular need to study protective factors in new longitudinal studies. Little is known about replicable protective factors. These can either be factors that predict a low rate of offending, factors that predict a low rate of offending in a risk category (e.g., low income), or factors that interact with a risk factor to nullify its influence, as mentioned above. Protective factors also need to be included in risk assessment devices and targeted in intervention programs.

Fifth, there is a special need to carry out quasi-experimental within-individual analyses in new longitudinal studies to investigate the effect on offending of life events such as leaving school, getting married, or becoming unemployed. The real strength of longitudinal studies lies in their ability to investigate within-individual change over time, but relatively few longitudinal researchers have used their data to do this. Within-individual analyses should be carried out to advance knowledge about causes (Farrington & Loeber, in press).

Sixth, more research is needed on co-offending. Many crimes, especially in the teenage years, are carried out with others, but there has been relatively little research on this topic. More research is especially needed on recruiters, defined as offenders who constantly commit crimes with younger, less experienced, or first offenders (Van Mastrigt & Farrington, 2011). These recruiters are prime targets for intervention because, if their behavior could be changed, this would have a disproportionate effect on the number of crimes.

Seventh, it is important to propose and test falsifiable theories that make quantitative predictions, which have rarely been made in criminology in the past. These could be based on criminal career models. It would be highly desirable for theories to predict the future course of criminal careers (numbers and types of crimes and duration in years). If criminological theories are to be scientific, they should make exact quantitative predictions. Also, it is crucial to compare and contrast the predictions of different theories in relation to empirical evidence (Farrington, 2006). I am planning to do more of this in the coming years, in collaboration with Tara McGee.

Eighth, there should be more randomized experiments to test the effectiveness of methods of preventing and treating offending. Unlike all other methods of evaluation, randomized experiments isolate the effect of the intervention by controlling for all measured and unmeasured variables. It would be desirable to carry out experiments not just on special types of offender treatment such as cognitive-behavioral therapy but also on mainstream sentences such as imprisonment, fines, probation, and community service (see, e.g., Killias, Gillieron, Villard, & Poglia, 2010). It should be possible to design intervention experiments to advance knowledge about criminological theories (Robins, 1992).

Ninth, it would be highly desirable to evaluate the impact of interventions within prospective longitudinal surveys, as advocated by Farrington, Ohlin, and Wilson (1986). There should be a number of measures, covering several years, then an intervention, then more measures, covering several years afterwards. It seems that no large-scale study of this kind has ever been carried out on offending using repeated interviews. Such studies could simultaneously advance knowledge about the development and causes of offending and about the effects of interventions. Also, the impact of interventions can be better understood in the context of pre-existing trends or developmental sequences, and the prior information about participants could make it possible to investigate interactions between types of persons (and their risk/protective factors and prior histories) and types of interventions (Farrington, Loeber, & Welsh, 2010). Long-term follow-up information after an experiment is highly desirable to show effects of an intervention that are not immediately apparent and to compare short-term and long-term effects and investigate developmental sequences that link them (Farrington & Welsh, in press).

Tenth, more attempts to replicate results over time and place in cross-national and cross-cultural comparisons are needed. Eleventh, more systematic reviews and meta-analyses are needed to determine the generalizability or external validity of findings. Twelfth, it is crucial to include cost–benefit analyses in evaluating interventions and in systematic reviews, in order to establish which interventions have the highest benefit:cost ratios. And it is especially important to communicate findings to policy-makers and practitioners so that the research has an impact. For example, I think that there should be a national agency to coordinate early prevention initiatives (Farrington & Welsh, 2007), and that there should be special court and correctional treatments for young adult offenders (Loeber & Farrington, 2012a). I have always been very concerned to communicate my findings and make them understandable to policy-makers, practitioners, and the general public. For this purpose, books are much more effective than articles in scholarly journals.

Looking back on my career, I have had the great luxury of being able to pursue my interests, which have been very wide-ranging, in Great Britain and North America. I have carried out research on many different topics, but my main interests have been in developmental criminology and early prevention. I have made big efforts to link up fundamental research on development with applied research on interventions. In developmental criminology, I am most proud of the 40-year CSDD follow-up and the 25-year PYS follow-up, both with very low attrition rates; of my research on co-offending in the CSDD and the prediction of homicide in the PYS; and of my attempts to identify mediating processes between risk factors and delinquency, and to study the effects of life events on offending using quasi-experimental within-individual analyses. I am also proud of my systematic observations of shoplifting and of my field experiments on stealing. In early prevention, I am most proud of my systematic reviews of the effectiveness of interventions, of my advocacy of risk-focused prevention, and of my influence on ministers in England and Canada, which in some cases has led to government initiatives that should have contributed more to the sum of human happiness than locking people up. And I have become an even greater advocate of the value of longitudinal and experimental research and of the combined longitudinal-experimental study.

Regarding advice to students or young faculty, I am torn between advising them to pursue whatever interests them (as I have) and advising them to specialize in one particular area. Perhaps I should have specialized more in developmental criminology. I would not advise students or faculty to "chase the bucks," although maybe that would be realistic advice in today's demanding climate. Other good advice is: Don't give up. Everyone has set-backs such as having a journal article or a grant proposal rejected, but the successful people are those who keep trying. Also, the most precious commodity is time, so it is highly desirable to maximize time available for research. And you can achieve a lot more (and learn a lot more) by collaborating than by research carried out alone.

In conclusion, many researchers seem to choose easy topics and easy methods that are guaranteed to produce results within a short time frame. I believe that it is more important to choose the more risky, challenging scientific methods that I have recommended in order to advance knowledge significantly, such as systematic observation, field experiments, longitudinal studies, randomized experiments on interventions, and the holy grail of the longitudinal-experimental study. And it is a lot more fun when you are convinced that you are really pushing back (or forward!) the frontiers of knowledge!

References

Augimeri, L. K., Farrington, D. P., Koegl, C. J., & Day, D. M. (2007). The SNAP Under 12 Outreach Project: Effects of a community based program for children with conduct problems. *Journal of Child and Family Studies,16*, 799–807.

Baldry, A. C., & Farrington, D. P. (1998). Parenting influences on bullying and victimization. *Legal and Criminological Psychology, 3*, 237–254.

Barnett, A., Blumstein, A., & Farrington, D. P. (1987). Probabilistic models of youthful criminal careers. *Criminology, 25*, 83–107.

Barnett, A., Blumstein, A., & Farrington, D. P. (1989). A prospective test of a criminal career model. *Criminology, 27*, 373–388.

Blumstein, A., Cohen, J., Roth, J. A., & Visher, C. A. (Eds.) (1986). *Criminal careers and "career criminals."* Washington, DC: National Academy Press.

Buckle A., & Farrington, D. P. (1984). An observational study of shoplifting. *British Journal of Criminology, 24*, 63–79.

Buckle, A., & Farrington, D. P. (1994). Measuring shoplifting by systematic observation: A replication study. *Psychology, Crime and Law, 1*, 133–141.

Cabinet Office (2006). *Reaching out: An action plan for social exclusion.* London: Cabinet Office.

Connell, A., & Farrington, D. P. (1996). Bullying among incarcerated young offenders: Developing an interview schedule and some preliminary results. *Journal of Adolescence, 19*, 75–93.

Eysenck, H. J. (1953). *Uses and abuses of psychology.* London: Penguin.

Eysenck, H. J. (1956). *Sense and nonsense in psychology.* London: Penguin.

Fabio, A., Loeber, R., Balasubramani, G. K., Roth, J., Fu, W., & Farrington, D. P. (2006). Why some generations are more violent than others: Assessment of age, period and cohort effects. *American Journal of Epidemiology, 164*, 151–160.

Farrington, D. P. (1972). Delinquency begins at home. *New Society, 21*, 495–497.

Farrington, D. P. (1973). Self-reports of deviant behavior: Predictive and stable? *Journal of Criminal Law and Criminology, 64*, 99–110.

Farrington, D. P. (1977). The effects of public labelling. *British Journal of Criminology, 17*, 112–125.

Farrington, D. P. (1979a). Experiments on deviance with special reference to dishonesty. In L. Berkowitz (Ed.), *Advances in experimental social psychology*, Vol. 12 (pp. 207–252). New York: Academic Press.

Farrington, D. P. (1979b). Longitudinal research on crime and delinquency. In N. Morris & M. Tonry (Eds.), *Crime and justice*, Vol. 1 (pp. 289–348). Chicago: University of Chicago Press.

Farrington, D. P. (1983a). Offending from 10 to 25 years of age. In K. T. Van Dusen & S. A. Mednick (Eds.), *Prospective studies of crime and delinquency* (pp. 17–37). Boston: Kluwer-Nijhoff.

Farrington, D. P. (1983b). Randomized experiments on crime and justice. In M. Tonry & N. Morris (Eds.), *Crime and justice*, Vol. 4 (pp. 257–308). Chicago: University of Chicago Press.

Farrington, D. P. (1986). Age and crime. In M. Tonry & N. Morris (Eds.), *Crime and justice*, Vol. 7 (pp. 189–250). Chicago: University of Chicago Press.

Farrington, D. P. (1988). Studying changes within individuals: The causes of offending. In M. Rutter (Ed.), *Studies of psychosocial risk: The power of longitudinal data* (pp. 158–183). Cambridge, UK: Cambridge University Press.

Farrington, D. P. (1989). Later adult life outcomes of offenders and non-offenders. In M. Brambring, F. Lösel, & H. Skowronek (Eds.), *Children at risk: Assessment, longitudinal research, and intervention* (pp. 220–244). Berlin, Germany: De Gruyter.

Farrington, D. P. (1993a). Motivations for conduct disorder and delinquency. *Development and Psychopathology, 5*, 225–241.

Farrington, D. P. (1993b). Understanding and preventing bullying. In M. Tonry (Ed.), *Crime and justice*, Vol. 17 (pp. 381–458). Chicago: University of Chicago Press.

Farrington, D. P. (1994a). Early developmental prevention of juvenile delinquency. *Criminal Behaviour and Mental Health, 4*, 209–227.

Farrington, D. P. (1994b). Interactions between individual and contextual factors in the development of offending. In R. K. Silbereisen & E. Todt (Eds.), *Adolescence in context: The interplay of family, school, peers and work in adjustment* (pp. 366–389). New York: Springer-Verlag.

Farrington, D. P. (1995). The development of offending and antisocial behaviour from childhood: Key findings from the Cambridge Study in Delinquent Development. *Journal of Child Psychology and Psychiatry, 36*, 929–964.

Farrington, D. P. (1997). The relationship between low resting heart rate and violence. In A. Raine, P. A. Brennan, D. P. Farrington, & S. A. Mednick (Eds.), *Biosocial bases of violence* (pp. 89–105). New York: Plenum.

Farrington, D. P. (1999). Measuring, explaining and preventing shoplifting: A review of British research. *Security Journal, 12*(1), 9–27.

Farrington, D. P. (2000). Explaining and preventing crime: The globalization of knowledge – The American Society of Criminology 1999 Presidential Address. *Criminology, 38*, 1–24.

Farrington, D. P. (2002). Multiple risk factors for multiple problem violent boys. In R. R. Corrado, R. Roesch, S. D. Hart, & J. K. Gierowski (Eds.), *Multi-problem violent youth: A foundation for comparative research on needs, interventions, and outcomes* (pp. 23–34). Amsterdam, Netherlands: IOS Press.

Farrington, D. P. (2003a). Developmental and life-course criminology: Key theoretical and empirical issues. *Criminology, 41*, 221–255.

Farrington, D. P. (2003b). Key results from the first 40 years of the Cambridge Study in Delinquent Development. In T. P. Thornberry & M. D. Krohn (Eds.), *Taking stock of delinquency: An overview of findings from contemporary longitudinal studies* (pp. 137–183). New York: Kluwer/Plenum.

Farrington, D. P. (2003c). Methodological quality standards for evaluation research. *Annals of the American Academy of Political and Social Science, 587*, 49–68.

Farrington, D. P. (2005). The integrated cognitive antisocial potential (ICAP) theory. In D. P. Farrington (Ed.), *Integrated developmental and life-course theories of offending* (pp. 73–92). New Brunswick, NJ: Transaction.

Farrington, D. P. (2006). Building developmental and life-course theories of offending. In F. T. Cullen, J. P. Wright, & K. R. Blevins (Eds.), *Taking stock: The status of criminological theory* (pp. 335–364). New Brunswick, NJ: Transaction.

Farrington, D. P. (2007). Childhood risk factors and risk-focussed prevention. In M. Maguire, R. Morgan, & R. Reiner (Eds.), *The Oxford handbook of criminology* (4th ed., pp. 602–649). Oxford, UK: Oxford University Press.

Farrington, D. P. (2010). The developmental evidence base: Prevention. In G. J. Towl & D. A. Crighton (Eds.), *Forensic psychology* (pp. 95–112). Oxford, UK: Blackwell.

Farrington, D. P. (2012). Predictors of violent young offenders. In B. C. Feld & D. M. Bishop (Eds.), *The Oxford handbook on juvenile crime and juvenile justice* (pp. 146–171). Oxford, UK: Oxford University Press.

Farrington, D. P., Barnes, G.C., & Lambert, S. (1996). The concentration of offending in families. *Legal and Criminological Psychology, 1*, 47–63.

Farrington, D. P., Berkowitz, L., & West, D. J. (1982). Differences between individual and group fights. *British Journal of Social Psychology, 21*, 323–333.

Farrington, D. P., Biron, L., & LeBlanc, M. (1982). Personality and delinquency in London and Montreal. In J. Gunn & D. P. Farrington (Eds.), *Abnormal offenders, delinquency, and the criminal justice system* (pp. 153–201). Chichester, UK: Wiley.

Farrington, D. P., & Coid, J. W. (Eds.) (2003). *Early prevention of adult antisocial behaviour.* Cambridge, UK: Cambridge University Press.

Farrington, D.P.,Coid,J.W.,Harnett,L.,Jolliffe,D.,Soteriou,N.,Turner,R. et al. (2006). *Criminal careers up to age 50 and life success up to age 48: New findings from the Cambridge Study in Delinquent Development.* London: Home Office (Research Study No. 299).

Farrington, D. P., Coid, J. W., & Murray, J. (2009). Family factors in the intergenerational transmission of offending. *Criminal Behaviour and Mental Health, 19*, 109–124.

Farrington, D. P., Coid, J. W., & West, D. J. (2009). The development of offending from age 8 to age 50: Recent results from the Cambridge Study in Delinquent Development. *Monatsschrift fur Kriminologie und Strafrechtsreform (Journal of Criminology and Penal Reform), 92*, 160–173.

Farrington, D. P., Ditchfield, J., Hancock, G., Howard, P., Jolliffe, D., Livingston, M. S. et al. (2002a). *Evaluation of two intensive regimes for young offenders.* London: Home Office (Research Study No. 239).

Farrington, D. P., Gallagher, B., Morley, L., St Ledger, R. J., & West, D. J. (1986). Unemployment, school leaving and crime. *British Journal of Criminology, 26*, 335–356.

Farrington, D. P., Gallagher, B., Morley, L., St Ledger, R. J., & West, D. J. (1990). Minimizing attrition in longitudinal research: Methods of tracing and securing cooperation in a 24-year follow-up study. In D. Magnusson & L. Bergman (Eds.), *Data quality in longitudinal research* (pp. 122–147). Cambridge, UK: Cambridge University Press.

Farrington, D. P., Jolliffe, D., Hawkins, J. D., Catalano, R. E., Hill, K. G., & Kosterman, R. (2003). Comparing delinquency careers in court records and self-reports. *Criminology, 41*, 933–958.

Farrington, D. P., Jolliffe, D., & Johnstone, L. (2008). *Assessing violence risk: A framework for practice.* Edinburgh: Risk Management Authority Scotland.

Farrington, D. P., Jolliffe, D., Loeber, R., & Homish, D. L. (2007). How many offenses are really committed per juvenile court offender? *Victims and Offenders, 2*, 227–249.

Farrington, D. P., & Knight, B. J. (1979). Two non-reactive field experiments on stealing from a "lost" letter. *British Journal of Social and Clinical Psychology, 18*, 277–284.

Farrington, D. P., & Knight, B. J. (1980). Stealing from a "lost" letter: Effects of victim characteristics. *Criminal Justice and Behavior, 7*, 423–436.

Farrington, D. P., & Lambert, S. (1997). Predicting offender profiles from victim and witness descriptions. In J. L. Jackson & D. A. Bekerian (Eds.), *Offender profiling: Theory, research and practice* (pp. 133–158). Chichester, UK: Wiley.

Farrington, D. P., & Langan, P.A. (1992). Changes in crime and punishment in England and America in the 1980s. *Justice Quarterly, 9*, 5–46.

Farrington, D. P., Langan, P. A., & Tonry, M. (Eds.) (2004). *Cross-national studies in crime and justice.* Washington, DC: U.S. Bureau of Justice Statistics (NCJ 200988).

Farrington, D. P., Langan, P. A., & Wikstrom, P-O. H. (1994). Changes in crime and punishment in America, England and Sweden between the 1980s and the 1990s. *Studies in Crime and Crime Prevention, 3*, 104–131.

Farrington, D. P., & Loeber, R. (1999). Transatlantic replicability of risk factors in the development of delinquency. In P. Cohen, C. Slomkowski, & L. N. Robins (Eds.), *Historical and geographical influences on psychopathology* (pp. 299–329). Mahwah, NJ: Lawrence Erlbaum.

Farrington, D. P., & Loeber, R. (In press). Establishing causes of offending: How can they be established? In G. J. N. Bruinsma & D. Weisburd (Eds.), *Encyclopedia of criminology and criminal justice.* New York: Springer-Verlag.

Farrington, D. P., Loeber, R., & Howell, J. C. (2012). Young adult offenders: The need for more effective legislative options and justice processing. *Criminology and Public Policy, 11*, 727–750.

Farrington, D. P., Loeber, R., & Stouthamer-Loeber, M. (2003). How can the relationship between race and violence be explained? In D. F. Hawkins (Ed.), *Violent crime: Assessing race and ethnic differences* (pp. 213–237). Cambridge, UK: Cambridge University Press.

Farrington, D. P., Loeber, R., & Welsh, B. C. (2010). Longitudinal-experimental studies. In A. R. Piquero & D. Weisburd (Eds.), *Handbook of quantitative criminology* (pp. 503–518). New York: Springer.

Farrington, D. P., Loeber, R., Yin, Y., & Anderson, S. J. (2002b). Are within-individual causes of delinquency the same as between-individual causes? *Criminal Behaviour and Mental Health, 12*, 53–68.

Farrington, D. P., & Maughan, B. (1999). Criminal careers of two London cohorts. *Criminal Behaviour and Mental Health, 9*, 91–106.

Farrington, D. P., Ohlin, L. E., & Wilson, J. Q. (1986). *Understanding and controlling crime: Toward a new research strategy.* New York: Springer-Verlag.

Farrington, D. P., Osborn, S. G., & West, D. J. (1978). The persistence of labelling effects. *British Journal of Criminology, 18*, 277–284.

Farrington, D. P., & Petrosino, A. (2001). The Campbell Collaboration Crime and Justice Group. *Annals of the American Academy of Political and Social Science, 578*, 35–49.

Farrington, D. P., Sampson, R. J., & Wikström, P-O. H. (Eds.) (1993). *Integrating individual and ecological aspects of crime.* Stockholm: Swedish National Council for Crime Prevention.

Farrington, D. P., Snyder, H. N., & Finnegan, T. A. (1988). Specialization in juvenile court careers. *Criminology, 26*, 461–487.

Farrington, D. P., & Ttofi, M. M. (2012). Protective and promotive factors in the development of offending. In T. Bliesener, A. Beelman, & M. Stemmler (Eds.), *Antisocial behavior and crime: Contributions of developmental and evaluation research to prevention and intervention* (pp. 71–88). Cambridge, MA: Hogrefe.

Farrington, D. P., Ullrich, S., & Salekin, R. T. (2010). Environmental influences on child and adolescent psychopathy. In R. T. Salekin & D. R. Lynam (Eds.), *Handbook of child and adolescent psychopathy* (pp. 202–230). New York: Guilford.

Farrington, D. P., Weisburd, D. L., & Gill, C. E. (2011). The Campbell Collaboration Crime and Justice Group: A decade of progress. In C. J. Smith, S. X. Zhang, & R. Barberet (Eds.), *Routledge handbook of international criminology* (pp. 53–63). New York: Routledge.

Farrington, D. P., & Welsh, B. C. (2003). Family-based prevention of offending: A meta-analysis. *Australian and New Zealand Journal of Criminology, 36*, 127–151.

Farrington, D. P., & Welsh, B. C. (2007). *Saving children from a life of crime: Early risk factors and effective interventions.* Oxford, UK: Oxford University Press.

Farrington, D. P., & Welsh, B. C. (2010). Preventing delinquency and later criminal offending. In J. M. Brown & E. A. Campbell (Eds.), *The Cambridge handbook of forensic psychology* (pp. 376–383). Cambridge, UK: Cambridge University Press.

Farrington, D. P., & Welsh, B. C. (In press). Randomized experiments in criminology: What has been learned from long-term follow-ups? In B. C. Welsh, A. A. Braga, & G. J. N. Bruinsma (Eds.), *Experimental criminology: Prospects for improving science and public policy.* Cambridge, UK: Cambridge University Press.

Farrington, D. P., & West, D. J. (1981). The Cambridge Study in Delinquent Development. In S. A. Mednick, & A. E. Baert (Eds.), *Prospective longitudinal research: An empirical basis for the primary prevention of psychosocial disorders* (pp. 137–145). Oxford, UK: Oxford University Press.

Farrington, D. P., & West, D. J. (1990). The Cambridge Study in Delinquent Development: A long-term follow-up of 411 London males. In H-J. Kerner & G. Kaiser (Eds.), *Kriminalitat: Personlichkeit, lebensgeschichte und verhalten* [Criminality: personality, behavior and life history] (pp. 115–138). Berlin, Germany: Springer-Verlag.

Farrington, D. P., & Wikström, P-O. H. (1994). Criminal careers in London and Stockholm: A cross-national comparative study. In E. G. M. Weitekamp & H-J. Kerner (Eds.), *Cross-national longitudinal research on human development and criminal behavior* (pp. 65–89). Dordrecht, Netherlands: Kluwer.

Garrido, V., Farrington, D. P., & Welsh, B. C. (2006). The importance of an evidence-based approach in the current Spanish policy for crime prevention. *Psicothema, 18*, 591–595.

Haas, H., Farrington, D. P., Killias, M., & Sattar, G. (2004). The impact of different family configurations on delinquency. *British Journal of Criminology, 44*, 520–532.

Jolliffe, D., & Farrington, D. P. (2006). Development and validation of the Basic Empathy Scale. *Journal of Adolescence, 29*, 589–611.

Jolliffe, D., & Farrington, D. P. (2008). *The influence of mentoring on reoffending.* Stockholm, Sweden: National Council for Crime Prevention.

Juby, H., & Farrington, D.P. (2001). Disentangling the link between disrupted families and delinquency. *British Journal of Criminology, 41*, 22–40.

Kazemian, L., & Farrington, D. P. (2006). Exploring residual career length and residual number of offenses for two generations of repeat offenders. *Journal of Research in Crime and Delinquency, 43*, 89–113.

Killias, M., Gillieron, G., Villard, F., & Poglia, C. (2010). How damaging is imprisonment in the long-term? A controlled experiment comparing long-term effects of community service and short custodial sentences on reoffending and social integration. *Journal of Experimental Criminology, 6*, 115–130.

Koegl, C. J., Farrington, D. P., Augimeri, L. K., & Day, D. M. (2008). Evaluation of a targeted cognitive-behavioral program for children with conduct problems – the SNAP Under 12 Outreach Project: Service intensity, age and gender effects on short and long term outcomes. *Clinical Child Psychology and Psychiatry, 13*, 419–434.

Langan, P. A., & Farrington, D. P. (1983). Two-track or one-track justice? Some evidence from an English longitudinal survey. *Journal of Criminal Law and Criminology, 74*, 519–546.

Langan, P. A., & Farrington, D. P. (1998). *Crime and justice in the United States and in England and Wales, 1981–96.* Washington, DC: U.S. Bureau of Justice Statistics (NCJ 169284).

Liberman, A. (2007) *Adolescents, neighborhoods, and violence: Recent findings from the Project on Human Development in Chicago Neighborhoods.* (Research in Brief). Washington, DC: U.S. National Institute of Justice (NCJ 217397).

Loeber, R., & Farrington, D. P. (Eds.) (1998). *Serious and violent juvenile offenders: Risk factors and successful interventions.* Thousand Oaks, CA: Sage.

Loeber, R., & Farrington, D. P. (Eds.) (2001). *Child delinquents: Development, intervention and service needs.* Thousand Oaks, CA: Sage.

Loeber, R., & Farrington, D. P. (2011). *Young homicide offenders and victims: Risk factors, prediction, and prevention from childhood.* New York: Springer.

Loeber, R., & Farrington, D. P. (Eds.) (2012a). *From juvenile delinquency to adult crime: Criminal careers, justice policy and prevention.* Oxford, UK: Oxford University Press.

Loeber, R., & Farrington, D. P. (2012b). Advancing knowledge about direct protective factors that may reduce youth violence. *American Journal of Preventive Medicine, 43* (2S1), S24–S27.

Loeber, R., Farrington, D. P., Stouthamer-Loeber, M., & White, H. R. (2008). *Violence and serious theft: Development and prediction from childhood to adulthood.* New York: Routledge.

MacLeod, J. F., Grove, P. G., & Farrington, D. P. (2012). *Explaining criminal careers: Implications for justice policy.* Oxford, UK: Oxford University Press.

Murray, J., & Farrington, D. P. (2008). The effects of parental imprisonment on children. In M. Tonry (Ed.), *Crime and justice*, Vol. 37 (pp. 133–206). Chicago: University of Chicago Press.

Painter, K. A., & Farrington, D. P. (1998). Criminal victimization on a Caribbean island. *International Review of Victimology, 6*, 1–16.

Piquero, A. R., Farrington, D. P., & Blumstein, A. (2007). *Key issues in criminal career research: New analyses of the Cambridge Study in Delinquent Development.* Cambridge, UK: Cambridge University Press.

Piquero, A. R., Farrington, D. P., Fontaine, N., Vincent, G., Coid, J., & Ullrich, S. (2012). Childhood risk, offending trajectories, and psychopathy at age 48 years in the Cambridge Study in Delinquent Development. *Psychology, Public Policy, and Law, 18*, 577–598.

Piquero, A. R., Farrington, D. P., Shepherd, J. P., & Auty, K. (In press). Offending and early deaths in the Cambridge Study in Delinquent Development. *Justice Quarterly.*

Piquero, A. R., Farrington, D. P., Welsh, B. C., Tremblay, R. E., & Jennings, W. G. (2009). Effects of early family/parent training programs on antisocial behavior and delinquency. *Journal of Experimental Criminology, 5*, 83–120.

Piquero, A. R., Jennings, W. G., & Farrington, D. P. (2010). On the malleability of self-control: Theoretical and policy implications regarding a general theory of crime. *Justice Quarterly, 27*, 803–834.

Piquero, A. R., Jennings, W. G., & Farrington, D. P. (2013). The monetary costs of crime to middle adulthood: Findings from the Cambridge Study in Delinquent Development. *Journal of Research in Crime and Delinquency, 50*, 53–74.

Raine, A. (1993). *The psychopathology of crime.* San Diego, CA: Academic Press.

Raine, A., Reynolds, C., Venables, P. H., Mednick, S. A., & Farrington, D. P. (1998). Fearlessness, stimulation-seeking, and large body size at age 3 years as early predispositions to childhood aggression at age 11. *Archives of General Psychiatry, 55*, 745–751.

Reiss, A. J., & Farrington, D. P. (1991). Advancing knowledge about co-offending: Results from a prospective longitudinal survey of London males. *Journal of Criminal Law and Criminology, 82*, 360–395.

Reiss, A. J., & Roth, J. A. (Eds.) (1993). *Understanding and preventing violence.* Washington, DC: National Academy Press.

Rivara, F. P., & Farrington, D. P. (1995). Prevention of violence: Role of the pediatrician. *Archives of Pediatrics and Adolescent Medicine, 149*, 421–429.

Robins, L. N. (1992). The role of prevention experiments in discovering causes of children's antisocial behavior. In J. McCord & R. E. Tremblay (Eds.), *Preventing antisocial behavior: Interventions from birth through adolescence* (pp. 3–18). New York: Guilford.

Sampson, R. J., & Laub, J. H. (1993). *Crime in the making: Pathways and turning points through life.* Cambridge, MA: Harvard University Press.

Sekol, I., & Farrington, D. P. (2010). The overlap between bullying and victimization in adolescent residential care: Are bully/victims a special category? *Children and Youth Services Review, 32*, 1758–1769.

Shepherd, J. P., & Farrington, D. P. (1993). Assault as a public health problem. *Journal of the Royal Society of Medicine, 86*, 89–92.

Shepherd, J. P., Farrington, D. P., & Potts, A. J. C. (2002). Relations between offending, injury and illness. *Journal of the Royal Society of Medicine, 95*, 539–544.

Shepherd, J. P., Shepherd, I., Newcombe, R. G., & Farrington, D. P. (2009). Impact of antisocial lifestyle on health: Chronic disability and death by middle age. *Journal of Public Health, 31*, 506–511.

Sherman, L. W. (1992). *Policing domestic violence: Experiments and dilemmas.* New York: Free Press.

Sherman, L. W., Farrington, D. P., Welsh, B. C., & MacKenzie, D. L. (Eds.) (2006). *Evidence-based crime prevention* (rev ed.). London: Routledge.

Sherman, L. W., Gottfredson, D., MacKenzie, D., Eck, J., Reuter, P., & Bushway, S. (1997). *Preventing crime: What works, what doesn't, what's promising?* Washington, DC: U.S. Office of Justice Programs.

Theobald, D., & Farrington, D. P. (2009). Effects of getting married on offending: Results from a prospective longitudinal survey of males. *European Journal of Criminology, 6*, 496–516.

Theobald, D., & Farrington, D. P. (2012). Child and adolescent predictors of male intimate partner violence. *Journal of Child Psychology and Psychiatry, 53*, 1242–1249.

Theobald, D., & Farrington, D. P. (2013). The effects of marital breakdown on offending: Results from a prospective longitudinal survey of males. *Psychology, Crime and Law, 19*, 391–408.

Tong, L. S. J., & Farrington, D. P. (2008). Effectiveness of "reasoning and rehabilitation" in reducing reoffending. *Psicothema, 20*, 20–28.

Tonry, M., & Farrington, D. P. (Eds.) (1995). *Building a safer society: Strategic approaches to crime prevention.* Chicago: University of Chicago Press.

Tonry, M., Ohlin, L. E., & Farrington, D. P. (1991). *Human development and criminal behavior: New ways of advancing knowledge.* New York: Springer-Verlag.

Ttofi, M. M., & Farrington, D. P. (2011). Effectiveness of school-based programs to reduce bullying: A systematic and meta-analytic review. *Journal of Experimental Criminology, 7*, 27–56.

Ttofi, M. M., Farrington, D. P., & Lösel, F. (2012). School bullying as a predictor of violence later in life: A systematic review and meta-analysis of prospective longitudinal studies. *Aggression and Violent Behavior, 17*, 405–418.

Ttofi, M. M., Farrington, D. P., Lösel, F., & Loeber, R. (2011a). Do the victims of school bullies tend to become depressed later in life? A systematic review and meta-analysis of longitudinal studies. *Journal of Aggression, Conflict and Peace Research, 3*, 63–73.

Ttofi, M. M., Farrington, D. P., Lösel, F., & Loeber, R. (2011b). The predictive efficiency of school bullying versus later offending: A systematic/meta-analytic review of longitudinal studies. *Criminal Behaviour and Mental Health, 21*, 80–89.

Turner, S., MacKenzie, D. L., & Farrington, D. P. (2010). Celebrating the American Society of Criminology Division on Corrections and Sentencing tenth anniversary. *Victims and Offenders, 5*, 199–202.

Van Der Laan, A., Blom, M., & Kleemans, E. R. (2009). Exploring long-term and short-term risk factors for serious delinquency. *European Journal of Criminology, 6*, 419–438.

Van Mastrigt, S. B., & Farrington, D. P. (2011). Prevalence and characteristics of co-offending recruiters. *Justice Quarterly, 28*, 325–359.

Welsh, B. C., & Farrington, D. P. (Eds.) (2006). *Preventing crime: What works for children, offenders, victims and places.* Dordrecht, Netherlands: Springer.

Welsh, B. C., & Farrington, D. P. (2010). Effective programs to prevent delinquency. In J. R. Adler & J. M. Gray (Eds.), *Forensic psychology: Concepts, debates and practice* (2nd ed., pp. 378–403). Cullompton, UK: Willan.

Welsh, B. C., & Farrington, D. P. (2011). The benefits and costs of early prevention compared with imprisonment: Toward evidence-based policy. *Prison Journal, 91*(3S1), 120–137.

Welsh, B. C., & Farrington, D. P. (Eds.) (2012). *The Oxford handbook of crime prevention.* Oxford, UK: Oxford University Press.

Welsh, B. C., Farrington, D. P., & Sherman, L. W. (Eds.) (2001). *Costs and benefits of preventing crime.* Boulder, CO: Westview Press.

Welsh, B. C., Loeber, R., Stevens, B. R., Stouthamer-Loeber, M., Cohen, M. A., & Farrington, D. P. (2008). Costs of juvenile crime in urban areas: A longitudinal perspective. *Youth Violence and Juvenile Justice, 6*, 3–27.

West, D. J. (1969). *Present conduct and future delinquency.* London: Heinemann.

West, D. J. (1982). *Delinquency: Its roots, careers and prospects.* London: Heinemann.

West, D. J., & Farrington, D. P. (1973). *Who becomes delinquent?* London: Heinemann.

West, D. J., & Farrington, D. P. (1977). *The delinquent way of life.* London: Heinemann.

Wilson, J. Q., & Loury, G. C. (Eds.) (1987). *From children to citizens, Vol. 3: Families, schools, and delinquency prevention.* New York: Springer-Verlag.

Wollheim, R. (1981). *Sigmund Freud.* Cambridge, UK: Cambridge University Press.

Zara, G., & Farrington, D. P. (2009). Childhood and adolescent predictors of late onset criminal careers. *Journal of Youth and Adolescence, 38*, 287–300.

16

My Turning Points in Adolescent Research

*From Internal Dynamics to External Opportunities to
Self-Governance of Development*

Helmut Fend

According to Sören Kierkegaard (1996, pp. 63, 161), life is lived forwards and understood backwards. In this sense a retrospective research biography often appears to involve a logical development. Various influences seem to supplement each other in a consistent way. In the process of biographical reconstruction the degree of intentionality in the developmental pathways taken is frequently overestimated. The role of chance and of fortunate happenings recede into the background.

With these warnings in mind I will attempt to undertake a reconstruction of my research in the developmental psychology of adolescence and the life span. Looking backwards, I was influenced by three research traditions:

- by the old endogenous European concepts of human development (Bühler, 1929/1967, 1932);
- by the discovery of contexts of development in cultural anthropology (Mead, 1939) and in the French historic perspective on changing societies (Braudel, 1958, 1985);
- by the Anglo-American pragmatism looking closely into the individual differences of growing up (Adelson, 1980).

My encounter with characteristic European concepts of development began with a book, which shaped my own adolescence and has again and again accompanied me in various transformations. This book, which was to occupy my mind over several decades in ever new functions, was Eduard Spranger's *The Psychology of Youth,* first published in 1924 and finally republished in the 29th edition in 1979 (Spranger, 1924). This range of time and degree of distribution demonstrates that it was the most important book on adolescence in the German-speaking countries until the seventies of the last century.

In my first encounter with this book it was already conceived as a corner stone in the curriculum for teacher training. Young teachers should be trained to better understand their clientele, especially the children in the phase of transition from childhood to adolescence. Because we as young students between 16 and 18 years old were still in the middle of this life phase, it became as an unintended side-effect a foundation enabling us to better understand our own life paths and our own inner turbulences.

What made this book so attractive for European youngsters? In a life phase marked by confusion it offered them an opportunity to generate order and to embed themselves securely within a cultural context. Youth is, as Eduard Spranger says, the time when the core self, which he termed the "king-ego," is discovered. It is the life phase in which a person for the first time examines who he is and who he could become. The "soul" senses its possibilities for perfection, as it was formulated later. The child still lives unseparated from the world; it is the adolescent who first sets himself off from a world taken for granted in childhood. The child is what he thinks, the adolescent thinks what he is and could be. Not only is the object of thinking reflected on, but also the origin of thoughts and feelings, the adolescent himself.

How can this active "construction"—as we would say today—of one's self come about? What is the "material" on which it is based? Spranger's answer was very helpful for educators and teachers. Individuation occurs when young people grow into a culture and into society by getting to know the cultural contents, the values of the culture, and integrating them into their own person. For Spranger these fields of value include scientific, religious, aesthetic, legal-political, technical, economic, and social ways of life of helping and philanthropy. By exploring the various ways of life a young person gradually discovers those which correspond to his own internal structure. This formative work on himself enables him to find the solution to the great life task of adolescence: the development of a life plan. Spranger believed he could see this process in his data base, which consisted of diaries of prominent people in arts, politics, science, and religion.

At this level of understanding Spranger's book became a helpful guideline and a model for many generations of German youngsters, enabling them to see meaning and a goal for their own development in times of confusion and indeterminacy.

It also had this effect on me and contributed to my decision to begin a course of studies in the humanities combined with a "bread and butter job" in teacher training, education, and psychology. At this time, I was already a young teacher in a small school high up in the mountains. Being infected with a concept the self-fulfillment, a feeling of incompleteness was inevitable. To close the gap, I intended to go to university. Because this decision did not result from family background but from an educational socialization process, in the eye of Eduard Spranger I could even serve as evidence for his speculations.

In this phase of my biography I was unaware that Spranger's book would accompany me in further transformations during the coming decades. It would turn out to be representative of a European branch of developmental psychology for which Boring (1957) has delivered a detailed description and critical commentary under the title "Gestalt psychology" (p. 587ff.). The core idea is presumably that human development is an endogenous developmental process, which proceeds by following laws of internal structure, in which the "Gestalt of the psyche" is transformed in accordance with inner laws.

Initiation into Continental Developmental Psychology

My initiation into scientific developmental psychology at the University of Innsbruck in Austria took place in a similar spirit. Here, too, I only realized in retrospect the psychological principles, which framed the scientific thinking about development. The key figure in this case was Lotte Schenk-Danziger (Schenk-Danzinger, 1987), who in the course of her career was the first assistant of Charlotte Bühler, who herself was financed by the American Rockefeller Foundation. Charlotte Bühler, the wife of Carl Bühler, founded the so-called Viennese School of Psychology (Schenk-Danziger, 1984), which was an international center of attraction for developmental psychology in the nineteen twenties and thirties. Charlotte Bühler originally wanted to study with Külpe, the well-known Gestalt psychologist of the Würzburg school (Boring, 1957, p. 397 ff.). This proved impossible on account of his early death, but the themes Bühler took up derived from Külpe's school. Charlotte Bühler was thus committed to the ideas of a Gestalt-like inner organization of consciousness, which is mediated through language and accessible through introspection. In this spirit, she was then to write a psychology of adolescence, probably the most widely disseminated alongside the work of Spranger.

Like Spranger, Charlotte Bühler assumed a Gestalt change from the child to the young person, which she—already sensing the concept of the life course—aspired to describe. But which empirical basis could be of service to her? Charlotte Bühler came after all from a context of psychology which defined science in relation to data. At the same time she came from a scientific tradition of psychology which attributed a high value to consciousness, thinking, and feeling and its systematic observation. And so she resorted to a data base containing the self-descriptions of personal thinking and feeling during youth: to *diaries* (Bühler, 1925, 1934). Starting from her own diary, she sought and accumulated a wonderful collection of diaries, a collection, which was tragically lost in the bombardment of Vienna. Only those diaries already published survived.

The diaries enabled her to undertake a wonderful analysis of consciousness. In them she found recurring themes such as the brooding preoccupation with the self, the often excessive self-observation, the working through of the first love, the search for life plans, the feelings of loneliness and longing (Bühler, 1921/1967).

This analysis of consciousness blended over to the idea of Gestalt change from childhood to adolescence (Bühler, 1929/1967), which she subsequently elaborated in the following way: What develops as something new out of childhood is above all the involvement with the self and the process of setting oneself apart from the hitherto taken-for-granted social world. This leads to new social attachments, to an orientation towards the opposite sex. In the emergence of this orientation, in the need for "complementation" Bühler saw the core of adolescence. This, she believed, is above all true of girls. In the case of boys she saw the development of life plans, the maturity to take rational action as the core aspect of the transition from childhood to adolescence.

These two examples of developmental psychology in the German-speaking countries from the 1920s to the 1960s reveal a way of observing human development, which focuses especially on *intra-individual* regularities coming from within. It shaped my own scientific socialization in this life phase.

This, however, was only one part of the scientific history of developmental psychology in the Vienna School. The other part consisted of an ever-increasing interest in the empirical analysis of the behavior and performance of children and adolescents. Experiments, observations, and tests already played a great role in the lectures of Lotte Schenk-Danziger, which I attended in Innsbruck, and in the observation seminars on infant behavior. In observing children, *inter-individual* differences and therefore variance in developmental processes came into focus.

Nevertheless attention continued to be paid to endogenously determined ideal-typical developmental processes. Consequently I continued trying to work on what was new in adolescence in comparison with childhood. For me, the key aspect was that the adolescent for the first time consciously positions himself in a relationship with himself and the world.

He no longer merely lives in the world; he is able to reflect on his relationship to the world. He can for the first time think systematically about the world and the different modalities of existence it offers; he unfolds a capacity for hypothetical thinking thereby imaging different worlds. Parallel to this development the libidinous attachment structure changes. Young people begin to attach themselves to persons of the same age and to romantic partners. At the same time the relationships of authority and autonomy in relation with their parents change. External control decreases and self-control increases accordingly. Changes in cognitive, motivational, and social relationship patterns go hand in hand. Contrasting the psychological Gestalt of adolescence with childhood and adulthood, adolescence appears as a unique mode of existence in the world (Fend, 1989).

The Antithesis: Contexts of Development

In the following years, starting 1965 with my dissertation (Fend, 1969) and cumulating in sociological work on the social history of growing up in modern Europe (Fend, 1988, 2000a), this endogenous perspective was overlaid and replaced by an antithetical view of human development.

My dissertation "Socialization and Education" was based on a paradigm shift in German research on human development. The starting point was the articulation of the *context* of human development. Although contexts had already been taken into account in endogenous perspectives, for example in studies on growing up in poverty (Hetzer, 1929), it was fully unfolded only in the sixties. The popularity of the writings of Margaret Mead (1939) played an important part in the process. She believed she could expose the inadequacy of the concept of the adolescent phase as an endogenously determined turbulent developmental period by comparison with the process of growing up in indigenous cultures, for example in Samoa. For her, inner development is not decisive; instead, the pathologies of Western civilization are responsible for the problems of youth, for sexual disturbances and deviant behavior.

The critical turn of cultural anthropology against biological vitalism, formulated in the 1930s by Ruth Benedict (1934), triggered off a new vision of human development. Applying this paradigm to growing up in Western cultures, it directed attention towards ways of growing up in different families, in different social classes, in rural and urban environments. My fascination with the diversity of the environments extended to beginning research on adolescence across geographical, social and cultural environments. *Socialization across space* became a new obsession. Empirically, I started to cast an eye on the environmental characteristics which can shape adolescents. The micro-worlds of the family, the school, and the peer group came into focus.

To extend the variance in contexts of development, I started to look into the history of environmentally based

opportunities of growing up. The perspective on socialization across space was thereby complemented with a historical perspective, with the analysis of *socialization across time*. The variance in the conditions of growing up seemed to be much more significant in a historical perspective than in a world-wide context. It also generated new theoretical perspectives. Contexts of growing up turned out to be closely interwoven with political, social, and cultural developments in society.

In French historical writing, centered on the periodical *Annales,* a perspective came to the fore, which called for the observation of long waves (*long duré*) in the development of society, lifestyles and mentalities in order to grasp fundamental changes. The French tradition of focusing on the history of scripts of life, mentalities and the *long duré* of opportunity structures (Braudel, 1958) significantly marked my thinking about contextual effects on the life course in the following years.

In this process it became highly visible, how the course of life as a whole and the developmental phase of adolescence in particular depend on institutional, social, and mental developments in societies. Youth as a life phase turns out to be a new phenomenon of the modern period, which is constituted particularly by the development of educational institutions and related economic and political changes. The modern script of life involves the active and rational mastery of tasks (Buchmann, 1989). Everyone is the architect of his own fortune; everyone is responsible for his own development. Although this normative assignment has deep religious roots in Christianity, it first became a right to individual self-fulfillment in the Enlightenment movement. The mental pattern of developmental opportunities and developmental tasks during the course of life was thus established (Havighurst, 1972). The most important inspiration for long waves in this time was for me Max Weber and his work on the sociology of religion (Weber, 1920).

Up to the nineteenth century, self-fulfillment and self-determination of one's own life, was still only a program. Real opportunity structures for self-determination developed as recently as during the last two centuries on the way of Western societies to the modern age. In my scientific biography tracing this historical process turned out to be a demanding and exciting path towards an understanding of developmental processes in adolescence in the context of modern societies. Against this background I wrote a social history of growing up (Fend, 1988) in which I attempted to reconstruct the long waves of living conditions for human development from traditional to modern society. Additionally, I was concerned with a detailed historical account of the changes in the living conditions of young people since Second World War.

The changes in living conditions from the perspective of the "long waves" in fact proved to be dramatic. Economic developments, urbanization, the reduction of infant mortality and the extension of life expectation, expansion of the educational system, secularization processes, and processes of state formation have led to unparalleled changes for the young. Traditional societies with close-knit social relationships, firmly established authority structures and high demands for child labor left only little scope for autonomous developmental processes. Some social historians have glorified these transparent, clearly arranged conditions in traditional societies, which pre-structured development (Brezinka, 1961). In their view, they offered security and stability. Others (Imhof, 1988) saw the negative sides more clearly: hunger, poverty, persistent risk of illness and death, oppressive social conditions, work overload—all configurations which permit autonomous development or even processes of identity formation in adolescence only to a very limited degree. It became vividly clear that what we today take for granted as adolescence, an autonomous life phase of about 10 years, has only emerged in the last three generations (Elder, 1992). Adolescence is nowadays characterized by zones of freedom for self-determination, which can be used individually.

In this historical and sociological perspective adolescence was conceived to be a social aggregate, which changed fundamentally in the course of history. Attempts were even made to reconstruct youth in antiquity (G. Bühler, 1991), in the Middle Ages (Winter, 1984) and in modern times up to the 20th century (Hoffmann-Nowotny, 1989). Of course the historical sources were mostly of a biographical and not seldom of a literary kind, but they nonetheless gave a vivid picture of the very restricted life circumstances, restrictions in traditional society and the corresponding virtues of subordination, modesty, obedience, and diligence.

Parallel to the changed aggregates of youth, the changed contexts of growing up became visible. In particular the changes in family structures attracted the attention of the social historians (Gestrich *et al.*, 2003). For research on adolescence it turned out that the historical formation of schooling was significant as developmental context, together with the accompanying peer context and the life worlds outside school.

These historical studies proved to be a real treasure trove for research on adolescence. The structure of the family in the modern age turned out to be of a unique quality, representing much more intense inner-familial structures of communication, more significant and closer emotional relationships and a greater openness for friendships. In recent years normative regulation has also undergone massive changes—from strictly determined authoritative standards to processes of negotiation and cooperation. Parents allow more freedom and place more emphasis on independence and personal responsibility. Parental expectations are nonetheless very high. They are directed, above all, towards good performance at school and a disciplined life style.

The socialization contexts of schools have also changed strikingly. In pre-modern societies the function of school as a means of imprinting religious concepts of life and the training of discipline was in the foreground.

Here too, authority and obedience and the unquestioning adoption of existing values and value systems were the focal points. Today, schools are contexts tuned to the acquisition of qualifications, in which individual efforts and individual choices within the educational system are at center stage (Fend, 1994b). The concept of adaptation has been transformed into a concept of investment. Effort is still of great significance but there has been a change in its function. It is no longer a sign of moral quality but the expression of individual investments. In this case too, a process of individualization has taken place (Fend, 2000a).

These configurations of modern expectations laid upon youth originate from long historical processes, which have occupied my attention in the framework of the sociology and social and cultural history of European educational systems. But the goal of these excursions was always the same: to use them as a background in order to better understand and carry out research on adolescence in modern contexts of growing up, with particular reference to academic socialization (Fend, 1992b).

The Adolescent as a Product of Himself: The Anglo-American Pragmatic Tradition of Empirical Research

Since my stay at the Institute of Education of the University of London and at the London School of Economics in 1965, I have been fascinated by Anglo-American pragmatism. The related epistemological positions have disciplined a tendency towards speculative approaches to human existence, which was still widespread in continental universities. It helped me to focus on evidence from empirical research and triggered attempts to develop research projects in the framework of quantitative social sciences. This led, together with my interest in contextualized human development to empirical research on the impact of school on personality.

It was also due to the influence of English pragmatism that the actions of individuals became the center of attention. Development was thus given back to actors, and placed on the individual responsibility of the actors involved. But I had been too strongly shaped by endogenous and contextual approaches to simply deny these theoretical traditions. But neither a model of *development without context* nor a model of *context without development* seemed to be adequate. In both the *individual activity* of persons is lacking. Young people have a *voice* of their own and actively pursue their own life projects. In the same way they are the creators of their own development, but not as free-floating individuals. They act within the boundaries of internal and external opportunities and restrictions.

But not only the developing person contributes actively to his development. The environment also contributes actively to the process of development. Parents in particular are by no means disinterested in the pubertal changes occurring in their children. On the contrary, they are highly involved and interested and try to help shape the development of their offspring. This makes *co-regulative* and *co-constructive processes* significant. At this third stage of my theoretical orientation development resulted from the complex interplay of inner developmental dynamics, contextual factors and the personal activity of the adolescent. Without taking into account internal readiness (endogenous preconditions), the demands of culture (exogenous offers) and active personal involvement (self-shaping) development during adolescence can't be conceptualized adequately.

For this understanding of the resultant developmental processes the concept of *developmental tasks* (Havighurst, 1972) proved to be very helpful. In these developmental tasks biological changes in the body of the adolescent, cognitive maturation processes and cultural ascriptions, expectations, and opportunities in socio-cultural environments all join together. The concepts of "coping" and of "development of action in context" (Silbereisen, 1994) turned out to be helpful in delineating developmental pathways. They were now embedded in psychological theories of action regulation in the cognitive, motivational, and volitional sense.

What proved to be the age-specific developmental tasks of adolescence? In the first place the ability to deal with one's own body is an evident task. "Learning to inhabit a new body" was the description given by my students to the complex processes which involve winning a positive relationship to one's own body and controlling the substantial hormonal processes. Here, new sexual impulses and their regulation are the focus of developmental work in adolescence.

In second place comes the reorganization of social relationships with parents, peers, and romantic partners. The child must develop into a being who is oriented towards a romantic partner. This reorientation begins in adolescence and lasts until mature parenthood. This difficult process of reorientation is supported essentially by peers, who come to play a central role at this stage of development.

The third developmental task requires substantial investments in time and effort from adolescents. The educational processes in this life phase aim toward building up competences which are highly relevant for future professions and hence for an independent economic existence. It is precisely in this field that the cultural, social, and economic resources of the family become relevant for adolescents in order to make optimal use of the opportunities for learning and the acquisition of qualifications.

With the increasing cognitive competence and the building up of systematic, hypothetical thinking, it is increasingly expected that adolescents become cognitively involved with the world. They should feel at home in the culture of a community and take on responsibility in the community.

These developmental tasks are finally combined in the building up of a new relationship of a person to himself, in building up a new identity.

In all these developmental fields adolescents are underway. They move out of the world of childhood and search for their own position, a conscious new place in the world, a placing in the multiplicity of possibilities open to them. The accelerated growth is hence always directed towards the future.

This pragmatic conception of developmental processes in adolescence opens up a huge field of research. It quickly becomes clear how great the inter-individual variations and the variations in intra-individual developmental processes are. The course they take is, furthermore, to a high degree group specific, running differently in minorities than in the mainstream of society.

With this focus on inter-individual difference the extremes in the distribution also become visible: the developmental risks. Therefore research on adolescence focuses on problem groups, involving either internalizing or externalizing problem behavior. This emphasis inspired a large number of empirical studies, which used to be presented at national and international congresses on adolescence and developmental psychology (SRA, ISSBD). New reference figures in this scientific community, new models for excellence in research on adolescence now became important: Rainer Silbereisen in Germany, Anne C. Petersen in America, Michael Rutter in Great Britain, and many others.

The empirical basis of my own research was the first large longitudinal study on adolescence in Germany. It started in 1979 with a first survey involving about 2,000 12-year-olds, followed up annually to the age of 16. The study also involved parents, teachers, and classmates. Thematically it was broadly based (Fend, 1989). It included indicators of cognitive development, ways of dealing with puberty (Fend, 1996), the development of relationships with parents and peers (Fend, 1993), cultural orientation and the organization of leisure time, academic investments (Fend & Schröer, 1985a), coping with school and relationships with teachers, civic involvement and civic knowledge, risk behavior and risk-taking developments (Fend, 1990a, 1992a), and the development of personality in the sense of identity-formation and of building up self-representations (Fend & Schröer, 1985b).

The inclusion of the proximal contexts of family, school and peers and of distal contextual characteristics such as social class, urban and rural areas was in keeping with the still significant contextual perspective in thinking about growing up.

This program sounds too demanding. But thanks to a competent team, large data sets and complex analysis were successfully dealt with. They provided the basis for several monographs, numerous articles in periodicals and contributions to congresses, unfortunately most of them serving a German-speaking audience (for English papers see above and Briechle, 1984, 1985; Fend & Prester, 1985). The resultant representative empirical account of the developmental processes in adolescence (covered in five monographs and one textbook: Fend, 1990b, 1991, 1994a, 1997, 1998, 2000b) was confronted with the classical conception of youth as a turbulent life phase. It came to me as a surprise that almost 70% experienced a continuous and emotionally positively colored development. The writing of diaries was indeed a phenomenon, which emerged in this life phase and then tended to disappear again. This classical characteristic of puberty was revealed, however, not in boys but in girls, including the ruminating cognitive processes and the problems of emotional regulation. Risk-taking increased in adolescence, the indicators being smoking, alcohol consumption, early sex, withdrawal of parental control. They indeed proved to be very significant, particularly when attention was paid to the timing of the initiation and the support of peers. At the same time it became evident that a polarization in the life paths of adolescents sets in. Some invest their efforts in academic achievement, whereas others distance themselves from academic pathways and focus on social investments, above all in membership to peer groups. Thereby, they distance themselves from adults. Conceptually, these tendencies could be covered with *investment theories*. Three questions came into focus: How do investments in school develop in adolescence, how is feedback on school performance reflected in self-representations, and how is the multiplicity in experiences of success and failure integrated into the personality structure. In searching for answers concepts of competence motivation research, attribution research, self-theories, and psychodynamic concepts were helpful.

Again it turned out that adolescents are not alone with these investments and their subsequent processing. How parents intervene supportively or punitively, how academic achievements are mirrored by teachers and interpreted by peers were questions to be dealt with in the study of adolescence. It became visible, how important in the eye of parents a successful school career of adolescents is and how deeply failure, above all, affects the family dynamics and the self of the child. In situations of failure, parents suffer just as much and may be even more than children and adolescents do. Failure leaves profound marks in the self-system of young people, particularly in regard to their self-esteem. Especially for unsuccessful sons the dominant way of coping was to maintain self-respect by de-evaluating school and thereby receiving support by their peers.

It became evident that the dynamic of adolescent development demanded a difficult balance. Investment in academic achievement, fulfilling expectations from parents and peers, and maintaining healthy self-representations are difficult to bring into productive relationships. The achievement system, the social system, and the self-system turned out to be the subsystems, which were to be re-organized in adolescence. The expectations of parents and peers, in particular, get out of balance during adolescence and must be renegotiated. The psychic reorganization of the libido, as psychoanalysis terms it, is overlaid in modern society by changes in the regulative powers of parents over their children and by new preferences for peers of the same and the opposite sex. The preference shifts in favor of peers are well documented, as are the zones of conflict and the concerns of parents. In the case of boys these are grouped, above all, around the issue of academic success and in the case of girls around the regulation of sexuality. We were able to analyze in detail the sufferings and the joys of parents, as we had included them in the survey directly.

All investments and all forms of coping ultimately join in the construction of new self-representations. But for young people what one is, could be, and will be is not fixed once and for all; it must be worked over and discovered in the process of identity formation. These processes of discovery and definition are then expressed in self-concepts and in self-evaluations weighed up against aspirations. From these processes, global self-acceptance or self-destructive thinking may result. They are accompanied by intensive emotions, which can blend into disturbances such as depression.

All in all, we were now able to unfold a rich picture of adolescence and to demonstrate its validity with both qualitative and quantitative data. This led to a new realistic view of adolescence, which was helpful to correct the old concept of turmoil as a general phenomenon of this life phase. Nevertheless, internalizing and externalizing problem behaviors could be identified, which are differentially manifested in various social segments or ethnicities and under varying opportunity structures—for example, in the case of youth unemployment and poverty. The close attention paid to these phenomena is highly justified in the light of personal and social costs involved.

Looking Beyond Adolescence: Life-Course Research

Nonetheless, research into the life-span of adolescence left me with a feeling of limitation. It resulted from the restriction to a specific period in life. What—so the obvious question—comes after the time of youth? Which processes during adolescence are of significance for the further mastery of life? What can be corrected later? What can destroy a good starting point?

Thanks to several happy circumstances I had the opportunity to contact and question our adolescents 20 years later, at the age of around 35. In a substantial effort of detective work we were able to find 85% of the former adolescents again, and with a highly sophisticated research design 83% ($N = 1527$) were persuaded to resume their participation in the study. We were thus in an excellent position to sketch their educational and occupational pathways, and their social life-lines from romantic relationships to parenthood. Developments in personality and risks to psychological and physical health could be followed up additionally. Even basic cultural and political attitudes were included. In this "LifE" (Lifelines into Early Adulthood) study, research results are subsumed under the concept of successful mastery of living.

With the resulting data sets developmental pathways to middle adulthood can be described and predicted from processes in adolescence and life events between adolescence and early adulthood. Productive coping with life in fields of occupation, social relationships, participation in society and personal self-fulfillment can be outlined over the whole range of interindividual differences and intraindividual processes can be accounted for. The interrelationships of internal antecedents, external opportunities, and restrictions, as well as personal investments and coping processes again play a crucial role in trying to understand development through the life course.

The first domain given attention to in the LifE study involves the educational and occupational life lines. The data provide ample evidence of the well known fact of inequality of educational opportunities. The interaction between family and educational institutions and the underlying mechanisms are revealed at all gateways in the educational and occupational career (Georg, 2004). Much to my dismay, going comprehensive up to the 10th grade—a very much disputed point in the public discussion on school reform in German-speaking countries (Glaesser, 2006, 2008)—does not really help in the long run. Nevertheless, the failure to fulfill parental educational aspirations can result in an intergenerational drama with long lasting psycho-social consequences. Boys are especially prone to resistance, deviant behavior, and low self-esteem. The LifE data also confirm the many-faceted consequences of the achieved educational status. Health behavior, risk behavior, unemployment (Glaesser, 2004), and income are tied to educational credentials and to the number of years spent in education.

Overall, for 70% of our sample the educational career was already fixed at the age of 12. They actually achieved what they aspired. The vocational careers were much more volatile. At the lower level of general educational achievement about 25% entered more than one vocational training. At the higher level, more than 60% took on two or more vocational training pathways. The resulting income is thus positively related to longer training (Weil, 2012).

The second domain outlined in detail in the LifE study concerns the social careers. This lifeline is much less institutionally guided, except at the stages of marriage or divorce. The social careers turned out to be complex social navigation processes but nevertheless following crucial initiation marks. They start with same- and especially opposite-sex friendships where the timing turns out to be predictive of later social risks. The subsequent timing of the termination of virginity turns out to be a precursor of the risk of divorce. It is connected with the initiation of frequent romantic relationships of a short duration, and the timing of leaving home. The next steps are institutionalized ones: marriage, parenthood, and possible divorce. In attempts to predict quality in marriage, satisfaction in parenthood and proneness to divorce the experiences in the families during adolescence turned out to be of major importance. The experience of parental divorce and dysfunctional families resulted in early mating, early termination of virginity, frequent changes of romantic partners and a higher risk of own divorce (Berger, 2011; Berger & Fend, 2006, 2008).

The impact of family experiences in adolescence as a protective resource provoked the intergenerational question of the continuity and intergenerational transmission of the quality of family life. The parent–child relationship over the life course became an important topic in the LifE study. Continuity could be observed but also important structural factors influencing positive transmission processes such as physical distance in living arrangements, and role transitions such as marriage and parenthood. Mother—daughter relationships turned out to be the major intergenerational bonds (Berger, 2012), much more than relationships to father (Berger, 2006).

Comparing adolescence and young adulthood gender specific pictures emerged: In adolescence girls are more successful than boys and they are easier to handle by parents. In early adulthood boys are better off and in a more comfortable position. For the girls the social responsibilities as daughters and as mothers are deeply connected with their wellbeing and prevent them from pursuing occupational careers. They keep the generations together. Young men in early adulthood detach themselves more from intergenerational bonds and strengthen their identity in occupational success.

The domains of educational, occupational and social transitions and their interlinkages kept us busy for a long time. Not only the related manifestations of coping and risk taking, but also the contextual influences and underlying personality development had to be considered. Personality development (self-representations, social competencies, cognitive competencies, achievement motivation) and influences of family background, peer context and school context on personality became topics of developmental analyses on their own (Sandmeier, 2004, 2007). The same holds true (Fend, 2004; Fend & Schröer, 1985c) for the analyses of risk behavior (alcohol consumption, smoking, unhealthy life-style) and for a rich or poor cultural life and civic engagement (Grob, 2004, 2007). Last not least, these developmental analyses were integrated into the overriding perspective of a successful life as seen from outside (occupational success, social success and responsibilities) and from inside (mental health, satisfaction and positive self-representations).

While I am writing this biography, the study has been continued with the now 45-year-olds and expanded into a generational study. This time the 12-18-year-old children of our former adolescent cohort were included. Again around 85% (parents and children) took part in the study. We are thus able to sketch the life courses of around 1,400 adults between the ages of 12 and 45 and to trace the intergenerational transfers to 600 children.

In looking back on my research biography, it is inevitable to reflect on personal shortcomings; it is as well inevitable to be confronted with parallels of the objects of the developmental research and the development of the subjects doing the research. Both are not exempted from getting older and being transformed in this process. One day we all have to leave the stage, handing over responsibility. Happily a young cohort of researchers is taking over to continue developmental research while inviting me to take part actively for some time come.

References

Adelson, J. (Ed.). (1980). *Handbook of adolescent psychology*. New York: J. Wiley.

Benedict, R. (1934). *Patterns of culture*. New York: Houghton Mifflin.

Berger, F. (2006). Father–child relations: Continuity and change from adolescence to adulthood—results from the German life-study. *Paper presented at the 3rd Congress of the European Society on Family Relations*, Darmstadt.

Berger, F. (2011). *Family experiences in childhood and adolescence as predictors of the course and quality of romantic relationships in adulthood*. Paper presented at the Biennial Meeting of the Society for Research in Child Development, Montréal.

Berger, F. (2012). Continuity and change in mother–child relations from adolescence to adulthood: Results from the German longitudinal life study. *Journal of Marriage and the Family* (submitted).

Berger, F., & Fend, H. (2006). *Predicting social transitions from adolescence to adulthood: Marriage, marital quality, and divorce*. Paper presented at the Biennial Meeting of the Society for Research on Adolescence, San Francisco.

Berger, F., & Fend, H. (2008). *Predicting marital quality from close relationships in adolescence: The contributions of parents, friends, and romantic partners*. Paper presented at the Biennial meeting for the Society for Research on Adolescence, Chicago.

Boring, E. G. (1957). *A history of experimental psychology* (2nd ed.). Englewood Cliffs, NJ: Prentice-Hall.

Braudel, F. (1958). La longue durée. *Annales, 4* (October–December), 725–753.

Braudel, F. (1985). *Der Alltag*. München: Kindler.

Brezinka, W. (1961). *Erziehung als Lebenshilfe* (2nd ed.). Wien: Österreichischer Bundesverlag.

Briechle, R. (1984). Level of moral judgement and political attitudes in adolescents. In G. Lind (Ed.), *Morality, Cognition, Education* (pp. 67–76). Konstanz: Universität Konstanz.

Briechle, R. (1985). *Conditions and development of antisocial attitudes*. Eighth Biennial Meetings of the International Society for the Study of Behavioural Development, Tours.

Buchmann, M. (1989). *The script of life in modern society. Entry into adulthood in a changing world*. Chicago: Chicago University Press.

Bühler, C. (1921/1967). *Das Seelenleben des Jugendlichen*. Stuttgart: Gustav Fischer Verlag.

Bühler, C. (1925). *Zwei Knabentagebücher*. Jena: Fischer.

Bühler, C. (1929/1967). *Kindheit und Jugend. Genese des Bewußtseins*. Göttingen: Hogrefe.

Bühler, C. (1932). *Der menschliche Lebenslauf als psychologisches Problem*. Göttingen: Hogrefe.

Bühler, C. (1934). *Drei Generationen im Jugendtagebuch*. Jena: Fischer.

Bühler, G. (Ed.). (1991). *Das Kind und seine Umwelt im Laufe der Zeiten. Eine Dokumentation. 1. Band: Die Antike*. Zürich: Verlag Hans Rohrer.

Elder, G. H., Jr. (1992). Adolescence in historical perspective. In J. Adelson (Ed.), *Handbook of adolescent psychology* (pp. 3–46). New York: Wiley.

Fend, H. (1969). *Sozialisierung und Erziehung*. Weinheim: Beltz.

Fend, H. (1988). *Sozialgeschichte des Aufwachsens*. Frankfurt a. M.: Suhrkamp Verlag.

Fend, H. (1989). *Patterns of development from childhood to adolescence in the light of classical European developmental psychology*. Poster at the 9th Biennial Congress of the Society for the Study of Behavioral Development. Jyvaskyla Finland.

Fend, H. (1990a). *Protective factors in risk development during adolescence*. Second Conference of the Society for Research on Adolescence, Alexandria.

Fend, H. (1990b). *Vom Kind zum Jugendlichen: Der Übergang und seine Risiken. Entwicklungspsychologie der Adoleszenz in der Moderne, Bd. 1*. Bern: Huber.

Fend, H. (1991). *Identitätsentwicklung in der Adoleszenz. Lebensentwürfe, Selbstfindung und Weltaneignung in beruflichen, familiären und politisch-weltanschaulichen Bereichen. Entwicklungspsychologie der Adoleszenz in der Moderne, Bd. 2*. Bern: Huber.

Fend, H. (1992a). *Gender differences in intra-individual change in depressive psychological functioning and patterns of social attachments to parents and peers from childhood to adolescence*. Third Conference of the Society for Research on Adolescence, Washington, D.C.

Fend, H. (1992b). *Social change in ecologies of growing-up in adolescence – secular changes in Europe*. Paper presented at the Symposium on Social Change and Adolescent Development, Penn-State University.

Fend, H. (1993). *Patterns of parent-peer-relationships and their psychosocial consequences in adolescence*. Twelfth Biennial Meetings of The International Society for the Study of Behavioural Development, Recife, Brazil.

Fend, H. (1994a). *Die Entdeckung des Selbst und die Verarbeitung der Pubertät. Entwicklungspsychologie der Adoleszenz in der Moderne, Bd. 3* (Vol. 3). Bern: Huber.

Fend, H. (1994b). The historical context of transition to work and youth unemployment. In A. C. Petersen & J. T. Mortimer (Eds.), *Youth unemployment and society* (pp. 77–94). New York: Cambridge University Press.

Fend, H. (1996). *Pubertal change, body-image, and psychosocial consequences in Swiss adolescents*. Paper presented at the 14th Biennial Meeting of the International Society for the Study of Behavioral Development, Quebec.

Fend, H. (1997). *Der Umgang mit Schule in der Adoleszenz. Aufbau und Verlust von Motivation und Selbstachtung. Entwicklungspsychologie der Adoleszenz in der Moderne, Bd 4*. Huber: Bern.

Fend, H. (1998). *Eltern und Freunde. Soziale Entwicklung im Jugendalter*. Bern: Huber Verlag.

Fend, H. (2000a). The cultural scripts of control and individualization: Consequences for growing up during adolescence in modern societies. In A. Grob (Ed.), *Society, control, and development*. Hillsdale, NJ: Lawrence Erlbaum Associates.

Fend, H. (2000b). *Entwicklungspsychologie des Jugendalters. Ein Lehrbuch für pädagogische und psychologische Berufe*. Opladen: Leske + Budrich.

Fend, H. (2004). *Smoking in adolescence and life course transitions*. Paper presented at the 18th Biennial Conference of the Society for the Study of Behavioural Development, Ghent.

Fend, H., & Prester, H. G. (1985). *Development of political competence: Its relation to party preferences in the federal republic of Germany*. Poster presented at the 8th Biennial Meeting of the International Society for the Study of Behavioural Development. Tours, France.

Fend, H., & Schröer, S. (1985a). *Family climate and self-cognitions as antecedents of depression in adolescence*, Paper presented at the 8th Biennial Meeting of the International Society for the Study of Behavioural Development. Tours.

Fend, H., & Schröer, S. (1985b). The formation of self-concepts in the context of educational systems. *International Journal for the Study of Behavioral Development, 8*, 423–444.

Fend, H., & Schröer, S. (1985c). School as a health-promoting community somatic stress, smoking and alcohol consumption in adolescence. In Kommission der Europäischen Gemeinschaft (Ed.), *Tagungsbericht vom Internationalen Symposium: Die Rolle des Lehrpersonals bei der Gesundheitserziehung* (pp. 43–88).

Georg, W. (2004). Cultural capital and social inequality in the life course. *European Sociological Review, 20*(9), 333–344.

Gestrich, A., Krause, J.-U., & Mitterauer, M. (2003). *Geschichte der Familie* (Vol. 1). Stuttgart: Alfred Kröner Verlag.

Glaesser, J. (2004). *Opportunities and risk factors in labour market entry: Results from a longitudinal study*. Paper presented at the Mobility and Transitions in the Youth Labour Market, Nürnberg.

Glaesser, J. (2006). Dropping out of further education: A fresh start? Findings from a German longitudinal study. *Journal of Vocational Education and Training, 58*(1), 83–97.

Glaesser, J. (2008). Just how flexible is the German selective secondary school system? A configurational analysis. *International Journal of Research & Method in Education, 31*(2), 193–209.

Grob, U. (2004). *Long-term prediction of civic involvement and hostility toward foreigners*. Paper presented at the 18th Biennial Conference of the Society for the Study of Behavioural Development, Ghent.

Grob, U. (2007). *The role of the parent–child relationship in the influence of parents and peers on hostile attitudes towards foreigners in adolescence and in early adulthood*. Paper presented at the 13th European Conference on Developmental Psychology, Jena.

Havighurst, R. (1972). *Developmental tasks and education*. New York: McKay.

Hetzer, H. (1929). *Kindheit und Armut*. Leipzig.

Hoffmann-Nowotny, H. J. (1989). The situation of young people in the context of socio-cultural change: Changing patterns of collective living and family structures. In H. Bertram, R. Borrmann-Müller, S. Hübner-Funk, & A. Weidacher (Eds.), *Blickpunkt Jugend und Familie. Internationale Beiträge zum Wandel der Generationen* (pp. 27–40). Weinheim: Juventa Verlag.

Imhof, A. E. (1988). *Die Lebenszeit. Vom aufgeschobenen Tod und von der Kunst des Lebens*. München: Beck.

Kierkegaard, S. (1996). *Papers and journals, translated by Alastair Hannay*. Indiana: Indiana University Press.

Mead, M. (1939). Sex and temperament in three primitive societies. In *From the south seas: Studies of adolescence and sex in primitive societies*. Oxford, UK: Morrow.

Sandmeier, A. (2004). *Self-esteem: Gender differences in stability and antecedents*. Paper presented at the 18th Biennial Conference of the Society for the Study of Behavioural Development, Ghent.

Sandmeier, A. (2007). *Relationships in family, peer group, and school and their influence on psychological health: Compensation across context?* Paper presented at the 13th European Conference on Developmental Psychology, Jena.

Schenk-Danzinger, L. (1984). Zur Geschichte der Kinderpsychologie: Das Wiener Institut. *Zeitschrift für Entwicklungspsychologie und Pädagogische Psychologie, 16*(2), 85–101.

Schenk-Danzinger, L. (1987). *Entwicklungspsychologie*. Wien: Österreichischer Bundesverlag.

Silbereisen, R. K. (1994). *Adolescence in context: The interplay of family, school, peers, and work in adjustment*. Berlin; Heidelberg: Springer.

Spranger, E. (1924). *Psychologie des Jugendalters*. Heidelberg: Quelle & Meyer.

Weber, M. (1920). *Gesammelte Aufsätze zur Religionssoziologie*. Tübingen: J.C.B. Mohr (Paul Siebeck).

Weil, M. (2012). *Mehrfachausbildungen. Wer sie macht und was sie bringen*. University of Potsdam, Potsdam.

Winter, M. (1984). *Kindheit und Jugend im Mittelalter*. Freiburg: Hochschulverlag.

17

From Ithaca to Los Angeles

Gaining Focus from Places and People

ANDREW J. FULIGNI

Looking back on a career likely creates an artificial sense of coherence to one's history. Yet, it is always best to tell a story, and mine describes how I came to focus on the key themes in my work: adolescence, family, social identity, and biobehavioral development. It is a story that has been written by the places in which I trained and worked and by the people who have shaped me as a scholar, and it begins when I first encountered the field of adolescence as a freshman at Cornell University.

A Focus on Adolescence

I entered Cornell in 1984 as a Human Development and Family Studies major, but I began to doubt that choice as my first semester drew to a close. The coursework was less than inspiring to me despite being taught by solid professors. Instead, my favorite class was a design course that tapped into the artistic interests I pursued in high school. Midway through freshman year, I was on the verge of following the encouragement of my design professor, switching majors, and considering a career in some type of design.

Ritch Savin-Williams and his course on Adolescent Development changed all of that in my second semester. A gifted lecturer, Ritch shared the wonderment, excitement, confusion, and passion inherent in the adolescent years. Consistent with the spirit of the department and the College of Human Ecology, Ritch taught the course from an interdisciplinary perspective that integrated basic biological development with the importance of social context. We read original texts that ranged from ethology and endocrinology to criminology and anthropology. Rather than plowing through a pile of content, he explored the ideas that make adolescence such a compelling period of life—autonomy,

independence, identity, family relations, peer influence, risk-taking, and sexuality. It helped to have students who had just experienced adolescence themselves, but the class had an energy that simply did not exist in my earlier classes.

As exciting as the class was, the clincher was my participation in an honors section of the course that inspired a love of research on adolescence. The section included only 5–6 students and we met weekly to discuss extra readings and debate key theoretical and empirical questions. When I look back on that honors section, I see how it was no different from the doctoral seminars and lab meetings that I lead today. We debated the merits of different theoretical approaches. We reviewed and critiqued original empirical articles. We designed studies to test competing explanations for adolescent behavior. All of this was done within a climate that was both challenging and supportive. At some point toward the end of the semester, I looked at Ritch and realized that one could actually get paid to do this sort of thing on a daily basis. I was hooked.

I spent the summers before my junior and senior years doing research with Ritch on the high-school students who stayed in the dorms and took college classes. These studies were the basis for my honors thesis which focused on teasing and ridicule among teens. The key finding from the study was that, whereas experiencing ridicule was unsurprisingly associated with poor mental health, being the recipient of playful teasing was linked to higher levels of self-esteem. We speculated that playful teasing, if it does not descend into harsh ridicule, is a marker of connectedness and acceptance among teenagers. Although never published, the study generated a lot of press and I found myself being interviewed on several radio stations, even being the guest on a call-in show from Canada.

Along with a love of research and a fascination with the adolescent period, I left Cornell with two key perspectives that continue to shape my work today. First, I came away with a belief in the importance of focusing upon normative development during the teenage years. In the 1980s, several scholars (including Ritch) began to challenge the dominant view of adolescence as a time of inevitable storm and stress. Good empirical studies of non-clinical and representative samples of adolescents began to show that although they faced many challenges, most teenagers managed to navigate the period successfully. I learned that in order to understand how and when things go wrong for adolescents, we must first understand what behaviors are normative and expected. This emphasis on normative development continues today with my work on adolescents from immigrant and ethnic minority backgrounds. In order to understand the challenges and difficulties faced by these teenagers, I believe, we must first understand how their normative patterns of development may be shaped by their immigrant and minority status.

Second, a student graduating from Cornell at that time could not help but be influenced by the ecological perspective of Urie Bronfenbrenner. I was fortunate to take an advanced course with him and I am not sure which was more memorable, his unique insights into human development or his dramatic late arrivals to class with wild hair and the frayed edges of his dot-matrix printout of notes trailing behind him on the floor. Each class focused on different sections of his classic book, *The Ecology of Human Development* (1979), and analyses of studies that best exemplified his person–process–context model of development. Although I did not believe that context drove everything in development, a view held by many of my fellow students and some faculty, I did come away appreciating the contribution of the cultural and social context to the adolescent period. For me, Bronfenbrenner provided a way to organize the social world such that one could be more precise when studying the role of contextual factors in development. It is fair to say that much of the research from my group over the years, particularly our repeated focus on mediating processes, has incorporated some form of the person–process–context model outlined by Bronfenbrenner in his original book.

A Focus on the Family

I did not start out with a focus on the family. My honors thesis on peer teasing and ridicule reflected my strong interest in studying peer relations during adolescence. Ritch was focusing on peers and friendships in his research and I naturally adopted the topic of my advisor's work. I actually discussed the role of peers in academic achievement in the personal statement of my application to graduate school. I was particularly interested in John Ogbu's thesis that negative peer influence could be one source of ethnic differences in educational motivation and success (Fordham & Ogbu, 1986).

Upon entering the graduate program in developmental psychology at the University of Michigan, I began to work with Jacquelynne Eccles on one of her longitudinal studies of the adolescence—the Michigan Study of Adolescent Life Transitions (MSALT). Working with fellow student

Bonnie Barber and others, we followed a large group of students from Southeastern Michigan by administering questionnaires and collecting school record data for multiple years in high school. I learned the bread-and-butter of conducting a long-term study of adolescents from Jacque and Bonnie. From driving to high schools at 5:30 in the morning to tracking students over time to hustling for grant support, I gained invaluable experience that I still use in my own longitudinal studies today. (I also learned about the risks of speeding to a school through rural towns of Michigan; most of the speeding tickets in my life were earned during data collection.) Perhaps my strongest memory from this time was a weekend at Jacque's house in Colorado, designing measures in the shadow of the Rocky Mountains in her backyard. The care we put into the design of each measure has stayed with me and I take particular pride in the quality of the measurement in our studies today.

My second-year project, called the 619 at Michigan because of the associated course number, was to address the question I posed in my graduate school application: did the differential influence of peers on achievement account for ethnic differences in high-school success during adolescence? As I explored the question further, however, I encountered two problems. The first was that there was not enough ethnic variation in the data for me to pursue the topic. As a result, I decided to focus on individual differences in peer influence in high school. The second problem was more significant—I could not come up with a reason *why* peers may be more or less influential for teenagers. Simply modeling the relative influence of peers and parents on high-school students seemed to be putting the cart before the horse.

Like a good developmental psychologist, I tried to think about early antecedents of why teenagers would place more or less importance upon their friends' views and opinions. It was then that I realized that Jacque's theory of Stage-Environment Fit could help. The theory argues that a lack of fit between early adolescents' need for autonomy and decision-making on the one hand and the learning environments of middle schools on the other hand produces declines in motivation and achievement during middle-school. I thought that the theory also could be applied to the family. Specifically, if the family environment did not fit children's increased need for participating in decision-making over the transition to adolescence, teenagers would turn away from parents and become more oriented toward peers.

The results supported the prediction. Employing longitudinal analyses, we found that children who did not perceive an increase in decision-making opportunities within the family across the transition to early adolescence tended to seek less advice from their parents and more advice from the friends about personal and future issues. They also oriented toward friends to such an extent that they were willing to forgo their parents' rules, their schoolwork, and their own talents in order to keep and be popular with their friends. My excitement about the findings were quickly dampened by the difficult time we had getting the paper published, my first experience with the grueling nature of the publishing process. We eventually succeeded and the paper is now one of my most highly cited publications (Fuligni & Eccles, 1993). I learned the value of persisting with your work and gained insight into the idea that difficulty in publishing may be positively related to the eventual impact of a paper.

This paper turned me into a family researcher. I was captured by the fundamental questions behind the issues I pursued in my 619 project. How do families accommodate an increasingly competent and mature adolescent? How do adolescents and families acknowledge the need for some measure of autonomy and self-reliance while still maintaining a connection to one another? As I was completing my 619, I become involved in the initial stages of research on peers with another faculty member, but I found myself returning to these questions. They simply grabbed me in a way that issues in the study of friendships and peers did not. The dialectic between independence and connection are fundamental to human relationships and strike to the core of the challenge facing families raising adolescents regardless of their cultural background or social circumstances. Although I did not realize it at the time, my take on these questions focused on the importance of children's contributions to the family. Wanting to participate in decision-making, even if it is about one's own self, is much more than a bid for autonomy. It is a desire to contribute, to play a role in the larger group. This desire is a well-established dynamic in larger groups and organizations but, in this case, the group is the family. It would not be until about 10 years later that I would come full circle and realize that this was my take on the family all along.

A Focus on Culture, Ethnicity, and Immigration

I had the good fortune to have a second advisor during graduate school, Harold Stevenson. One of the early founders of developmental psychology, Harold was a tremendous professional advisor who provided me with effective guidance in writing, public speaking, and navigating the political winds of academia. Harold's early work was on childhood learning and I joined his group as he was in the middle of a very successful turn of focus to international comparisons of teaching and learning. Projects included studies of cognitive development in Peru and ethnic differences in motivation and performance in the United States. But it was Harold's work on the achievement gap between the United States and Asia, done in collaboration with James Stigler and others, that gained the most attention. Done at a time of hand-wringing over the poor performance of American students on international achievement tests, Harold and his group provided a comprehensive portrait of the sources of academic differences between the United States, Japan, Taiwan, and China (Stevenson & Stigler, 1992). Explanations included the higher expectations of parents, a stronger belief in the role of effort over ability, and the purposive and intentional instructional practices of teachers.

I learned many lessons from that experience and some were so implicit that they are difficult to list. First and foremost, I suppose, is the time and care that is required in cultural research. One of the most vivid memories from my graduate career is sitting at the large round table in Harold's office, surrounded by bilingual speakers in Chinese, Japanese and English, developing interview protocols that would be appropriate in each language and culture. The meetings were endless. Two hours were spent on coming up with three questions to assess the same aspect of family relationships in the different societies. Constructs were debated and arguments broke out even among speakers of the same language. It was a long and hot summer around that table, but I realized that I never tired of thinking and debating issues of culture and child development. I learned much about East Asian societies and even my own American culture through the process (it was during this summer that I first heard the phrase that the value of cross-cultural work is that it makes "the strange familiar and the familiar strange").

I also learned a second lesson, this one about the limitations of research. Some concepts become so lost in translation that they cannot be compared across cultures. Better, it seemed to me after all of those hours around Harold's table, to choose a topic that one can confidently study across cultures and societies. Although interesting ideas about culture and child development are countless, ideas that can be empirically tested and well-defended are comparatively few.

A third lesson that I learned from my time with Harold was the value of studying both cultural beliefs and cultural practices. Many analyses of cultural differences stop at the level of cultural values and ideas, perhaps because they are simply so fascinating. For example, at first blush, the belief in many East Asian societies that individual effort is paramount for early school achievement seems not all that different from the American, Horatio Alger ideal of hard work. Yet close analysis of parenting, teacher practices, and school arrangements shows how much the American educational enterprise is focused on identifying the unique strengths and weaknesses of individual students—that is, a tremendous focus upon innate ability (Stevenson & Stigler, 1992).

The theme of assessing both beliefs and practices carries through to my work today, when we put tremendous effort into assessing the daily activities and experiences of adolescents from different ethnic and immigrant groups as well as assessing their attitudes and values (e.g., (Fuligni, Yip, & Tseng, 2002). Just as the link between individual values and behaviors can be tenuous at best, the connection between what cultures believe and what they actually do can be quite thin. And the disjuncture between the two can tell us even more about the nature of child development, particularly when cultural groups are forced to change and adapt (as in the case of the immigrant families, whom I eventually spent much of my early career studying).

I learned the lesson about the importance of focusing on cultural practices and behaviors directly with a paper on variations in adolescent time use between the United States, Japan, and Taiwan. The paper was rejected from a top journal outright, despite some fairly positive reviews, because the focus on time use was not compelling enough. Disappointed, I showed the reviews to Harold who responded in his typical blunt manner by saying, "That's just wrong." We crafted a response and appealed the decision, defending the importance of focusing on the activities in which adolescents spent their daily lives across societies. Direct, but respectful, our appeal won the day and the paper was eventually accepted and gets frequently cited even today (Fuligni & Stevenson, 1995). I tell this story to my students often because it exemplifies one of the most important professional lessons that I learned from Harold—fight for your science when you believe that it is strong and important. The review process is where the battles are fought and although appeals do not always succeed, well-reasoned arguments backed by solid science usually come out on top.

I applied the lessons that I learned about cultural research as I began to develop my dissertation ideas. Searching for a topic, I kept coming back to a disconnect between the theory that I had tested in my 619 project and what I had learned about East Asian cultures in my work with Harold. The basis for my 619 project was that relationship change in families was driven by adolescents' desire and need for greater autonomy and interdependence. Yet Japan and China are societies in which a core belief is that individuality and autonomy should be subsumed for the sake of the larger group, and in which respect for parents and elders is a cherished norm. How then, would parent–child relationships change during adolescence in these East Asian cultures? Perhaps what was considered to be a fundamental and normative developmental process was not truly universal. I was asking myself these questions at a time when mainstream developmental psychology was increasingly being critiqued for its focus on only Western and European American populations. The time, then, was ripe for a dissertation that compared a normative developmental process in different cultural groups.

My dissertation represented a blending of my work with both Jacque and Harold. The two key questions focused on variations in the transition to adolescence between those from European American and Asian backgrounds: (1) variations in academic motivation and achievement, and (2) variations in family relationships, specifically parent–adolescent conflict and cohesion. Consistent with what I had learned, I decided to measure both cultural beliefs and actual behaviors and outcomes. Given that I did not have the wherewithal to embark on a cross-national study, I decided to focus on ethnic differences among populations here in the United States. The key problem was that the only adolescents with Asian backgrounds living in Ann Arbor, Michigan, were the children of foreign graduate students. The 1990 U.S. Census data was available electronically for the first time, so I began to examine Asian representation throughout the country, moving from the state level down to the county and city level. Not surprisingly, California and the counties in the San Francisco area ranked at the top of the list of states and counties with high percentages of Asian individuals. But the thought of collecting my dissertation data on the other side of the country seemed daunting to the say the least. When I met with Harold to go over the pros and cons, he stopped me in mid-sentence and simply said, "Why not?" Coming from a man who had been conducting cross-national research for over a decade, it sounded like the most sensible statement. I often think about that conversation when I consider a particularly nutty and seemingly unfeasible project.

Up to this point, I had not thought much about issues of immigration and generational status and they were not part of my dissertation proposal. Yet for some reason, I decided to include questions about adolescent and parent birthplace in the questionnaire I administered to students who were before (6th graders) and after (8th graders) the transition to junior high school. Those two simple questions that were inserted as statistical controls, at best, unexpectedly sparked my post-graduate career.

The first paper that I wrote from the study focused on ethnic differences in achievement. I asked a friend from graduate school, Chen Chuansheng, to review a near-final version of the paper before I submitted it to a journal. Among his other comments, Chen noticed the generational difference in the regression analyses (generational status was a control variable) and asked if I had seen a recent paper by Grace Kao and Marta Tienda on the achievement of immigrant students (Kao & Tienda, 1995). After reading that paper, I realized that there was something much more interesting in the data than ethnic differences and I completely rewrote the paper to focus on the surprising success of foreign-born students. Arguing that my data provided a nice follow-up to the Kao and Tienda analyses that identified generational differences in a large, national sample, I emphasized how our ability to measure mediators and mechanisms in a small, community sample addressed unique, unanswered questions. I replicated the generational differences identified by Kao and Tienda and showed how they were mediated by higher parental aspirations, greater peer support for academics, and a greater value of academic success among first generation students (Fuligni, 1997).

That paper put me on a path to studying the adaptation and adjustment of children from immigrant families that has lasted 15 years. The timing was perfect. The United States and social scientists were waking up to the fact that we were experiencing a surge in immigration unseen since the early part of the 20th century. The existing research on immigration was focused primarily on the economic integration of adults, and only a handful of scholars were paying attention to children. The popular press, local service agencies, schools, and policy makers were clamoring for information on the "new Americans" and it was not hard to get attention for my research. Funding agencies became keen on supporting work on immigrant children and they had the means to do so during the economic boom of the mid-1990s. I managed to obtain grants from the William T. Grant Foundation and the National Institute of Child Health and Human Development, and I will forever be indebted to those agencies for providing me the support to begin my independent career.

The challenge that I faced was to how to position my work so that it could make a unique and valuable contribution to the emerging field of immigration. Knowing that it made little sense to try to repeat what was being done with large, national data sets or small, ethnographic samples, I decided to strike the middle ground by combining quality measurement of mechanisms and processes with community samples large enough for sophisticated quantitative analyses. And, as discussed before, I made sure to measure cultural beliefs, practices, behaviors. By capturing this middle ground, I could test mechanisms that were thought to underlie the broad patterns in demographic surveys as well as assess putatively key processes that were suggested by more ethnographic, qualitative studies. This approach, I believe, requires an interdisciplinary temperament. It requires the ability to understand work from disciplines as divergent as demography and anthropology and even more importantly, it necessitates being able to speak to those disciplines in order to communicate findings effectively. I learned some of these skills through my participation in the William T. Grant Foundation Faculty Scholars program, which involved individuals from a wide variety of disciplinary traditions. Holding the middle ground is not easy and I do not always do it well. People often want to force me into one disciplinary tradition or another and it can be difficult when my group's work does not fit the orthodoxy of a particular field, but I feel that this middle-ground stance is perhaps the best way that my work can make an impact on larger discussions about topics like immigrant adaptation and adjustment.

A Focus on Social Identity

Diane Ruble was one of my closest colleagues at my first academic position at New York University (NYU). She had coincidentally attended graduate school with Jacque Eccles, so there was a built-in connection from the start. While I was at NYU, Diane worked with Jacque and Kay Deaux, a social psychologist at the City University of New York (CUNY) Graduate Center, to obtain funding from the Russell Sage Foundation to support a research network on Social Identity and Institutional Engagement. I was fortunate to be part of this network which allowed me to be exposed to a more thorough treatment of Social Identity Theory (SIT) (Tajfel & Turner, 2001) than I had

obtained in my graduate courses. Being exposed to the work of social psychologists influenced by SIT and working with Diane propelled me to finally begin work on ethnic and cultural identity among Asian and Latino populations, a topic that I had avoided as much as possible. Up to that point, I honestly could not see that issues of ethnic identity would make much of a difference above and beyond the family dynamics that I had been studying. The Network, along with a collaborative study of young immigrant children with Diane and the budding interests of my graduate students, made me think otherwise and I added the study of the developmental significance of ethnic and cultural identity to my list of interests. This interest eventually led to several publications on the topic over the next 10 years or so (Fuligni, Kiang, Witkow, & Baldelomar, 2008; Fuligni, Witkow, & Garcia, 2005; Kiang, Witkow, Baldelomar, & Fuligni, 2010).

Yet my experience with the Social Identity Network had a more significant impact upon my core interest in family relationships. In the second study to emerge from my dissertation, there were no ethnic differences in either the levels or developmental changes in parent–adolescent conflict and cohesion (Fuligni, 1998). The results were counter to my hypotheses and I was reluctant to conclude that there were no variations in relationships across families with Asian, Latin American, and European backgrounds. Going back to the drawing board, my students and I conducted a series of focus groups with teenagers and looked more deeply into the literature. What emerged was the realization that rather having different dyadic relationships with their individual parents, adolescents from Asian and Latin American backgrounds had a fundamentally different orientation toward the larger family than did those from European backgrounds. The apparently greater closeness of these families was not emotional or dyadic in nature. Rather, it was a greater sense of identification with the larger group—a sense of "we-ness"—that went beyond how close adolescents felt to either parent or whether they even liked their parents. Family membership, therefore, functioned as a social identity for these youth.

The idea that family membership could serve as a social identity provided an effective way to organize my group's findings up to that point. We had begun to study adolescents' sense of instrumental obligation to the family—the sense of duty to support, assist, and respect the authority of the family (Fuligni, Tseng, & Lam, 1999). This sense of obligation, we believed, was a reflection of a social identification with the family as a group. Indeed, research on social identification in other groups such as workplaces suggests that identification leads to a greater willingness to support the group voluntarily. Two other aspects of SIT helped us to integrate our findings (Hogg, 2003). First, research suggested that when one identifies with a group, a key motivation is to try to become a "good" member of the group and being a good member of the group provides a sense of belonging, purpose, and well-being. This principle helped us to interpret why spending time helping the family is associated with feeling happy at the same time as feeling burdened, the former association being due to feeling like a good member of the family. Finally, work on SIT also has shown that group identification is heightened when the group feels under threat. This relation helps to explain why, contrary to many traditional ideas about acculturation and assimilation, adolescents from Asian and Latin American backgrounds retain a sense of obligation to the family across several generations. The challenges faced by being an ethnic minority in American society remains with these youth even when they are not immigrants.

Taking a social identity approach to the family, therefore, provided me with a clear theoretical viewpoint from which I could organize prior findings and generate new hypotheses (Fuligni & Flook, 2005). It also allowed me to go beyond what I felt were overly broad cultural explanations for the family relationships among adolescents from Asian, Latin American, and immigrant families. That is, contemporary adolescents in these families do not assist and support their families only because of long-standing cultural traditions regarding collectivism, familism, or filial piety. Those traditions may help to define the meaning of family identity, but basic psychological processes that exist even in arbitrary and "minimal" groups in laboratory studies function to both heighten family identification (e.g., ethnic minority families feeling under threat) and to sustain relevant behaviors (e.g., assisting siblings to be a good member of the family). These processes work at a group level to create greater family identification and assistance among teens from Asian and Latin American backgrounds, even if those teens are no more emotionally close to their parents than their peers from European backgrounds.

Excited by the potential of this approach, I continued to explore the different predictors and implications of family assistance over the years (Fuligni, 2001; Fuligni, Alvarez, Bachman, & Ruble, 2005; Fuligni & Pedersen, 2002; Fuligni et al., 2002; Telzer & Fuligni, 2009a, 2009b). An interdisciplinary approach was critical and we increasingly incorporated qualitative methods into our studies with the support of Tom Weisner, who developed an effective anthropological interview to study the daily routines and dynamics of family life. This addition was invaluable in rounding out the picture of the role played by family assistance in the daily lives of families for whom this support was a critical part of their social identity (Fuligni, Rivera, & Leininger, 2007). Consulting with Tom helped to broaden my disciplinary approach, but it also unexpectedly opened the door to my joining him at the Center for Culture and Health at UCLA.

A Focus on Biobehavioral Development

Moving to UCLA after 7 years at NYU was very difficult because it meant leaving several close colleagues who provided much support as I developed from a junior to a senior faculty member. I had always been treated well at NYU and it was good environment in which to start a career. Yet UCLA was attractive to me on several levels. It was a larger university that had a longer tradition of large-scale research support and infrastructure. The campus possessed more faculty members who studied families and children from different disciplinary perspectives. Issues of immigration were pursued at both universities, but regional differences in immigration flows meant that research on families with Asian and Latin American families had a greater profile at UCLA. Finally, and most importantly, my new position in the Department of Psychiatry and Biobehavioral Sciences and the Neuropsychiatric Institute (now the Semel Institute for Neuroscience and Human Behavior) provided me with the opportunity to be exposed to cutting-edge work in neuroscience and biobehavioral development. Add in a joint appointment in the Developmental Area in the Department of Psychology, and I felt that the move to UCLA would provide me the opportunity to learn new and different things about biobehavioral development while still remaining connected to my primary discipline.

I was unsure how the exciting developments that were taking place in the field of neuroscience were relevant for my own work until I sat in on a graduate course on biological approaches to behavior. Listening to a guest lecture by Matthew Lieberman on his social neuroscience studies of the self, I immediately was able to see how neuroscience could add to our understanding of the development of self and identity-related processes during the adolescent years. A graduate student, Jennifer Pfeifer, helped to tutor me in functional magnetic resonance imaging (fMRI) and collaborated with Matt and me on an interesting study that suggested that adolescents were more likely to recruit brain regions related to thinking about the views of others (i.e., mentalizing regions) when they evaluated themselves and their own abilities (Pfeifer et al., 2009). Adults used only regions related to self-processing in similar tasks. These findings were consistent with the idea that adolescents are more likely to incorporate others' opinions during their period of self-development, whereas adults are less likely to do so because they have a more mature, stable sense of self.

Matt and I next worked with Eva Telzer, another graduate student, on a second project that focused on the neural correlates of family assistance. We had been puzzling about how to examine the potentially meaningful and rewarding nature of helping the family within the brain. We then came across work by Jorge Moll, James Harbaugh, and others that suggested making donations to charities engaged similar mesolimbic reward-related regions in the brain as did receiving cash rewards oneself (Harbaugh, Mayr, & Burghart, 2007; Moll et al., 2006). This work was it. We adapted the paradigm used by Moll, which is a version of the Dictator Game in behavioral economics, and created a task in which individuals were presented with a series of financial offers that varied in terms of gains and costs to themselves and their family. Participants then decided whether to agree or decline such offers while having their brains scanned within an fMRI machine. The cash payouts were real and participants kept the money gained for themselves, and families were mailed their financial donations.

Our primary analyses focused on activation in reward-related regions when individuals made costly donations to the family (i.e., family gains money at a cost to the individual) as compared to accepting cash rewards for themselves (i.e., individual gains money at no cost to the family). Remarkably, Latino participants showed either similar or greater reward-related activation (e.g., ventral striatum, ventral tegmental area) when making costly donations to the family as compared to when they received cash rewards themselves (Telzer, Masten, Berkman, Lieberman, & Fuligni, 2010). The European American participants showed the reverse—greater mesolimbic reward activation when they received cash rewards than when they donated to the family. It was terribly exciting to see cultural and family patterns that I had been studying behaviorally for almost 15 years represented within the developing brain. The project stimulated additional papers and a new line of work led by Eva and in collaboration with Matt and Adriana Galván, a developmental neuroscientist at UCLA, on the implications of these family-related brain developments for risk-taking and other aspects of adolescent adjustment.

A second guest lecture in the same course on biological perspectives in behavior generated a second new line of research on daily experience and biological markers of health risk. Julienne Bower, a psychoneuroimmunologist, presented exciting findings about the protective effects of finding purpose and meaning on biological markers of inflammation and disease progression among those diagnosed with HIV (Bower, Kemeny, & Fahey, 2001). Again, the link with what we had been examining in our behavioral studies became clear. With the support of a seed grant from the Cousins Center for Psychoneuroimmunology and the collaboration of Julie, Michael Irwin, and Steve Cole, we collected intravenous blood from a subset of the participants in one of our longitudinal studies in which we obtained intensive measurements of daily experience throughout high school. We obtained results that were consistent with our previous behavioral findings that daily family assistance can be both challenging and meaningful: although youth who spent more time assisting the family showed elevated levels of inflammation, those who obtained a sense of meaning and role fulfillment from helping the family actually had lower levels of inflammation (Fuligni et al., 2009). Seeing the trace of culture and family under the skin propelled us to ramp up our work on biomarkers of health and with additional collaboration with Teresa Seeman, a noted biological epidemiologist, we recently launched a major study of the health risk of adolescents and families over the transition to adulthood. In addition to examining a wide variety of daily experiences, the study includes an intensive focus on sleep, a fundamental biobehavioral process in which

my group has become increasingly interested (Fuligni & Hardway, 2006; Gillen-O'Neel, Huynh, & Fuligni, in press).

Conclusions

It is strange to write an autobiography when the story is hopefully not yet finished. Yet, trying to find coherence in the past does bring into relief an underlying question that seems to have driven much of my work. Moving from peer teasing to assaying inflammatory markers in the blood seems as a great a distance as traveling from Ithaca to Los Angeles, but there exists a common concern with how adolescents' come to feel a sense of belonging in the settings of their everyday lives. I've never lost interest in the ways that teenagers from diverse cultural backgrounds and social settings establish that sense of belonging, whether through playful teasing, identifying with one's cultural background, or contributing to the family. I am particularly struck by how contribution, in particular, can establish a sense of belonging so powerful that it can be observed at the levels of culture, family, and biology.

I look forward to continuing to collaborate with and learn from my students, who have been central to my work but are too numerous to mention here. With them, I will continue exploring the unique ways in which adolescents find ways to contribute and belong.

References

Bower, J., Kemeny, M., & Fahey, J. (2001). Coping with HIV/AIDS: Finding meaning from HIV serostatus as a predictor of CD4 slope, AIDS diagnosis and mortality. *Brain Behavior, and Immunity, 15*, 138.

Bronfenbrenner, U. (1979). *The ecology of human development: Experiments by nature and design.* Cambridge, MA: Harvard University Press.

Fordham, S., & Ogbu, J. U. (1986). Black students' school success: Coping with the "burden of 'acting white'". *The Urban Review, 18*(3), 176–206.

Fuligni, A. J. (1997). The academic achievement of adolescents from immigrant families: The roles of family background, attitudes, and behavior. *Child Development, 68*(2), 351–363.

Fuligni, A. J. (1998). Parental authority, adolescent autonomy, and parent–adolescent relationships: A study of adolescents from Mexican, Chinese, Filipino, and European backgrounds. *Developmental Psychology, 34*, 782–792.

Fuligni, A. J. (2001). Family obligation and the academic motivation of adolescents from Asian, Latin American, and European backgrounds. In A. Fuligni (Ed.), *Family obligation and assistance during adolescence: Contextual variations and developmental implications, (New Directions in Child and Adolescent Development Monograph)* (pp. 61–76). San Francisco, CA: Jossey-Bass.

Fuligni, A. J., Alvarez, J., Bachman, M., & Ruble, D. N. (2005). Family obligation and the academic motivation of young children from immigrant families. In C. R. Cooper, C. T. G. Coll, W. T. Bartko, H. Davis, & C. Chatman (Eds.), *Developmental pathways through middle childhood: Rethinking contexts and diversity as resources* (pp. 261–282). Mahwah, NJ: Lawrence Erlbaum Associates.

Fuligni, A. J., & Eccles, J. S. (1993). Perceived parent–child relationships and early adolescents' orientation toward peers. *Developmental Psychology, 29*(4), 622–632.

Fuligni, A. J., & Flook, L. (2005). A social identity approach to ethnic differences in family relationships during adolescence. In R. Kail (Ed.), *Advances in Child Development and Behavior*. New York, NY: Academic Press.

Fuligni, A. J., & Hardway, C. (2006). Daily variations in adolescent sleep, activities, and mood. *Journal of Research on Adolescence, 16*, 353–378.

Fuligni, A. J., Kiang, L., Witkow, M. R., & Baldelomar, O. (2008). Stability and change in ethnic labeling among adolescents from Asian and Latin American immigrant families. *Child Development, 79*(4), 944–956.

Fuligni, A. J., & Pedersen, S. (2002). Family obligation and the transition to young adulthood. *Developmental Psychology, 38*(5), 856–868.

Fuligni, A. J., Rivera, G. J., & Leininger, A. (2007). Family identity and the educational progress of adolescents from Asian and Latin American backgrounds. In A. J. Fuligni (Ed.), *Contesting stereotypes and creating identies: Social categories, social identities, and educational participation* (pp. 239–264). New York, NY: Russell Sage Foundation Press.

Fuligni, A. J., & Stevenson, H. W. (1995). Time use and mathematics achievement among American, Chinese, and Japanese high school students. *Child Development, 66*(3), 830–842.

Fuligni, A. J., Telzer, E. H., Bower, J., Irwin, M. R., Kiang, L., & Cole, S. R. (2009). Daily family assistance and inflammation among adolescents from Latin American and European backgrounds. *Brian, Behavior, and Immunity, 23*, 803–809.

Fuligni, A. J., Tseng, V., & Lam, M. (1999). Attitudes toward family obligations among American adolescents from Asian, Latin American, and European backgroundss. *Child Development, 70*(4), 1030–1040.

Fuligni, A. J., Witkow, M., & Garcia, C. (2005). Ethnic identity and the academic adjustment of adolescents from Mexican, Chinese, and European backgrounds. *Developmental Psychology, 41*(5), 799–811.

Fuligni, A. J., Yip, T., & Tseng, V. (2002). The impact of family obligation on the daily behavior and psychological well being of Chinese American adolescents. *Child Development, 73*, 302–314.

Gillen-O'Neel, C., Huynh, V., & Fuligni, A. J. (in press). To study or to sleep? The academic costs of extra studying and sleep loss. *Child Development*.

Harbaugh, W. T., Mayr, U., & Burghart, D. R. (2007). Neural responses to taxation and voluntary giving reveal motives for charitable donations. *Science, 316*, 1622–1625.

Hogg, M. A. (2003). Social identity. In M. R. L. J. P. Tangney (Ed.), *Handbook of self and identity* (pp. 462–479). New York, NY: Guilford Press.

Kao, G., & Tienda, M. (1995). Optimism and achievement: The educational performance of immigrant youth. *Social Science Quarterly, 76*, 1–19.

Kiang, L., Witkow, M., Baldelomar, O., & Fuligni, A. J. (2010). Change in ethnic identity across the high school years among adolescents with Latin American, Asian, and European backgrounds. *Journal of Youth and Adolescence, 39*, 683–693.

Moll, J., Krueger, F., Zahn, R., Pardini, M., de Oliveira-Souza, R., & Grafman, J. (2006). Human fronto-mesolimbic networks guide decisions about charitable donation. *Proceedings of the National Academy of Sciences, 103*(42), 15623–15628.

Pfeifer, J. H., Masten, C. L., Borofsky, L. A., Dapretto, M., Fuligni, A. J., & Lieberman, M. D. (2009). Neural correlates of direct and reflected self-appraisals in adolescents and adults: When social perspective-taking informs self-perception. *Child Development, 80*, 1016–1038.

Stevenson, H. W., & Stigler, J. W. (1992). *The learning gap: Why our schools are failing and what we can learn from Japanese and Chinese education*. New York, NY: Summit Books.

Tajfel, H., & Turner, J. (2001). An integrative theory of intergroup conflict. In M. A. Hogg & D. Abrams (Eds.), *Relations: Essential readings. Key readings in social psychology* (pp. 94–109). New York, NY: Psychology Press.

Telzer, E. H., & Fuligni, A. J. (2009a). Daily family assistance and the psychological well being of adolescents from Latin American, Asian, and European backgrounds. *Developmental Psychology, 45*, 1177–1189.

Telzer, E. H., & Fuligni, A. J. (2009b). A longitudinal daily diary study of family assistance and academic achievement among adolescents from Mexican, Chinese, and European backgrounds. *Journal of Youth and Adolescence, 38*, 560–571.

Telzer, E. H., Masten, C. L., Berkman, E. T., Lieberman, M. D., & Fuligni, A. J. (2010). Gaining while giving: An fMRI study of the rewards of family assistance. *Social Neuroscience, 5*, 508–515.

18

How I Became a Developmentalist

Frank F. Furstenberg

How I Became a Developmentalist

I only realized I'd become a "developmentalist" after it happened to me. I set out to be a sociologist, but with time began to recognize how a developmentalist thinks, and ultimately realized that I had become a sociologist who studied development over the life course. I suppose that says something about how professional identities emerge and crystalize during an academic career. Unlike standard economic theory, which posits fixed preferences and rational choice, I, like most sociologists, believe that preferences are formed and expressed in social interactions, which in turn are shaped by the contexts in which those interactions occur.

My Training

My story begins in the late 1950s at Haverford College, a small liberal arts institution. In my sophomore year, I took a class taught by Ira D.A. Reid, a charismatic teacher who had come to Haverford a decade earlier after working with Charles Johnson and E.W. Dubois, two legendary figures in sociology. Dubois had founded *Phylon*, a journal of race studies, and Reid was a co-editor before joining the faculty at Haverford. The only African American at the college and one of the few black PhDs in the field at the time, Reid offered a riveting class on race, power, and social conflict. We read what might now be called "critical sociology," books of social commentary such as C. Wright Mills' *The Sociological Imagination* (1959), David Riesman's *The Lonely Crowd* (Reisman et al., 1961), and August Hollingshead's *Elmtown's Youth* (1949), among others. By the end of the semester, I had fallen in love with sociology, a love affair that continues to this day.

Immediately after graduation I went to Columbia University to study sociology. At that time in the early 1960s, Columbia was among the leading centers of the discipline. Robert K. Merton, Paul Lazarsfeld, Richard Cloward, and especially William J. Goode became my mentors—none of whom had any direct interest in human development or life-course sociology. Yet, each of these eminent figures left a strong mark on me that affected the way that I think about human development.

Merton (1949) was a brilliant sociological theorist who introduced a host of ideas into the field such as the "unanticipated consequences of purposive social action," "reference group theory," and, drawing on Durkheim, a theory of "anomie." Lazarsfeld, one of the originators of survey research in the social sciences, had completed path-breaking studies of Depression-era families and on the process of social influence (Stouffer & Lazarsfeld, 1937). He had studied in Austria under Charlotte Buhler, one of the first social psychologists, who was, in fact, an early developmental theorist. Richard Cloward had just published, with Lloyd Ohlin, *Delinquency and Opportunity,* on the effect of urban neighborhoods on the propensity to engage in delinquent behavior (Cloward & Ohlin, 1960). And William J. Goode, who became my principal thesis adviser, was at the height of his career, writing on numerous topics such as the process of divorce, the societal conditions that produce high rates of illegitimacy (as nonmarital childbearing was then called), and a monumental comparative study of family change (Goode, 1963).

During my first course at Columbia, a class in sociological theory, we were asked to write about a social theorist whose work was significant to us. W. I. Thomas, an important but now neglected figure in sociology, was my choice (Volkart, 1951). Thomas is best known for the sociological dictum, "If things are defined as real, they are real in the social consequences." He was a founder of the Chicago School of Sociology and an early developmentalist who studied the adjustment of immigrants, integrating macro and micro sociology. It was not by accident that I was drawn to his work.

In retrospect, I was learning many of the elements of life-course sociology and human development without ever knowing it. From the vantage point of hindsight, this is now evident to me, but at the time, it was not at all clear to me that I was acquiring a theoretical perspective that would implicitly and, later in my career, explicitly guide my future research agenda.

My thesis at Columbia examined how underprivileged youth on the Lower East Side of Manhattan responded to varying social opportunities in their families, schools, and neighborhoods. It drew on family-level data collected in the landmark study by Francis Fox Piven and Richard Cloward, "Mobilization for Youth" (Piven & Cloward, 1972). Specifically, I examined how social mobility was transmitted in families produced a distinctly minor contribution to understanding how and why some children from an early age were committed to getting ahead later in life (Furstenberg, 1971).

While I labored on my thesis, I was unwittingly drawn into another study that would turn out to be a more promising venture. In the summer of 1964, I began a study of teenage mothers in Baltimore (Furstenberg, 1999). I wandered into the research because my mother was a social worker with one of the nation's first comprehensive programs aimed at mitigating the effects of early childbearing. One day she called me for help. To receive continued funding, the hospital staff had to document the impact of an intervention designed to encourage young mothers to return to school and postpone a second birth until they were older. Knowing that I had taken a course on evaluation the year before, my mother insisted that I write some questions for the evaluation. Of course, I had no alternative but to help my mother out, and before I knew it, I had a second job as the program evaluator for this pioneering prenatal program at Sinai Hospital of Baltimore. Of course, if I had had any inkling that I was about to embark on a 30-year longitudinal study of teenage mothers and their offspring, I never would have dared to become involved!

But I did, and by the time I completed graduate school, I had conducted the first round of interviews in a survey of the pregnant teens and their parents, some of whom were randomly assigned to the special program and others who received routine prenatal and postnatal services. It was the first of what would be seven waves of interviews that spanned the lives of the teen mothers and their children from the mid-1960s to the mid-1990s. I confess that I hardly knew what I was doing, but in the 1960s, when social science was still in an early stage of professionalization, I was probably as well trained as most to conduct the evaluation of the Baltimore program. In any event, I bumbled along and managed to collect pretty good information on a cohort of nearly 400 young mothers, all of whom had their first child before the age of 18 (at the initial wave).

Launching a Career

By the time of the second wave of the study, I had completed my degree and had taken a job as an assistant professor of sociology at the University of Pennsylvania. I landed in a department where few of my colleagues had any interest in what I was doing. Back then, mentoring young faculty was not as common, and certainly not a required practice, as it is today. By this time, I had begun the laborious task of coding data and entering it on punch cards for computer analysis. I was fortunate to be the first generation of social researchers who made use of the computer for data analysis. I managed to complete several largely descriptive papers realizing that the value of the study would only accrue as I collected information on what happened to the teen mothers in the years following the birth of their first child. Gradually and without much forethought, the study was transformed from a straightforward evaluation to a longitudinal examination of the early adaptations of teen mothers and their families.

With some valuable assistance from the chair of the department, Vincent Whitney, I wrote a successful application in 1970 to do a third wave of interviewing that compared the teen mothers with their former classmates in an effort to examine the impact of early childbearing on further schooling, marriage, and additional childbearing. But my understanding of what the study was about remained largely theoretically and intellectually under developed, even as I forged ahead with data collection. It was by then certainly easier to collect data than to analyze it, much less to understand what I was discovering.

Writing was a torturous process for me in those days, as it is for many younger academics: I was still firmly convinced that I did not know what I was doing and therefore lacked "authority" to report my results. Nonetheless, I managed to get funded to do two more waves of data collection involving the young mothers and their offspring. The funding also allowed me to interview a substantial number of the men who had fathered the children. I was, however, unable to contact a large share of the nonresidential dads, many of whom were beginning to fade out of their children's lives. The information from the fathers, though fragmentary, turned out to be important to my later work on low-income fathers.

In 1972, I came up for tenure just 5 years after completing my PhD, as was the custom of the time. By then, I had received two sizable research grants, but I had produced a meager set of publications, only five of which were on the Baltimore study. I barely squeaked by in the tenure process, but the promotion gave me some badly needed time to think about what I was doing and where the project was headed.

Shortly after I was promoted, I had the good fortune to start working with a young social historian, John Modell, who was spending an extended post-doctoral position at Penn in the history department. John and I worked together on a paper on African American families in the antebellum period (Furstenberg, Herschberg, & Modell, 1975). We recognized almost immediately that we shared interests in the social organization of the life course and wrote another paper on the changing transition to adulthood (Modell, Furstenberg, & Herschberg, 1976). During this time, we both admired Glen Elder's new book, *Children of the Great Depression* (1974). We spent many hours discussing this seminal work, and each of us published a review of the work.

I had met Glen at a conference in the summer of 1969. He was among the first people to take a keen interest in the Baltimore study. Though only a scant 6 years older than I, he served as my first mentor at a critical stage in my career, reading my work and providing support and encouragement at a time in my life when I was professionally undernourished. In 1974, he invited me to Chapel Hill to give a colloquium on the study, one of the first occasions where I presented some of my findings. Glen was instrumental in helping me frame the study: He helped me to view premarital pregnancy as an ill-timed event, creating a deviation in what was then a rigid social timetable for becoming an adult in American society. Glen offered to write an introduction to the manuscript of my first volume on the Baltimore study, *Unplanned Parenthood: The Social Consequences of Teenage Childbearing* (Furstenberg, 1976). I really did not even think that I had written a book until I sent my "project report" to several professional friends, including Glen, Melvin Kohn, and Gladis Topkis, an editor at The Free Press who would eventually publish the book in 1976. Almost 10 years after I completed graduate school, I was beginning to get more than a glimmer of why I was examining the careers of teen mothers and their children. I was becoming a practitioner of life-course sociology!

I continued to read widely in areas of sociology that had not been part of my initial training at Columbia. I became enamored with the Chicago School tradition, especially the work of Everett Hughes and many of his students. One of these students was Howard S. Becker, who had already written a series of important articles on professional socialization, careers, and the importance of critical life events. Becker then and now was one of the leading practitioners of the Chicago School who drew on ideas advanced in the early decades of the 20th century by Herbert Mead and Charles Horton Cooley. Mead and Cooley saw social interaction in the family as a seedbed of social life. In a theory of symbolic interaction, they laid the theoretical groundwork for many of the classic studies of family and community influence on human development. Many of those ideas worked their way into my thinking about the consequences of unplanned life events and transitions, a continuous theme in my writings during the 1970s (Goode, Furstenberg, & Mitchell, 1970.)

My growing interest in the social organization of the life course led me to explore the topic of divorce and remarriage in the late 1970s. I vividly remember coming home on a flight a year or so after *Unplanned Parenthood* was published, seeing a motley group of bystanders holding a banner in front of a middle-aged couple stepping off the plane in front of me. The banner read, "Recycled Lovers." I remember thinking to myself in a rare moment of intellectual epiphany: "I should study the transition from divorce to remarriage!"

And so I did. Shortly, thereafter I met Graham Spanier, a young family sociologist at Penn State, who had done a study of divorce in Centre County, Pennsylvania. I proposed to Graham that we follow up his sample and examine the process leading from one marriage to the next. I reviewed virtually the entire literature on the topic and wrote a piece on divorce and remarriage, an underdeveloped area of work in the sociological literature. By then, I had become far more confident about applying the life-course framework to organize my research. Some years later, after we had worked out the study design and received a grant to follow up his sample, Graham and I completed a book entitled, *Recycling the Family* (Furstenberg & Spanier, 1984).

My growing interest in life-course sociology, I discovered, overlapped in large measure with an emerging field of scholarship in demography that is now known as "social demography." Demographers call the constellation of family changes that began in the 1960s to alter the form and function of the family the "Second Demographic Transition," and it was this transition that demographers and life-course sociologists were avidly studying in the 1970s as it was occurring in the North America and Europe. They were particularly interested in shifting gender roles, the rise of divorce, the growth of nonmarital childbearing, and declining levels of fertility. I suddenly discovered that I was a demographer of sorts as the field drew in many sociologists, like me, who had a strong interest in the sources and consequences of a rapidly changing family system. One of these social demographers was Andrew Cherlin, who shared my interest in divorce and remarriage.

Andy and I corresponded about our mutual interests in the late 1970s and agreed to meet at a conference of the American Sociological Association. I had by then begun to work with Child Trends, a research organization in Washington, on a second wave of the National Survey of Children, one of the first nationally representative studies to conduct interviews of children. Andy and I concocted the idea of graphing on a follow-up to the survey to study the impact of divorce on intergenerational relations. The result was a book we coauthored on grandparenthood, *The New American Grandparent* (Cherlin & Furstenberg, 1986). Throughout the late 1970s and the early 1980s, I continued my collaboration with Andy and a number of other colleagues and students on the consequences of divorce on children.

My interest in the development of the children in the Baltimore study and in the National Survey of Children overlapped. I was able to ask questions in both surveys that allowed me to look at the impact of divorce on children, a topic of growing interest to both social scientists and policymakers. The idea that I had was to view divorce as a process (rather than an event) that began long before the actual dissolution of marriage and continued to exert influence on children and family life after the divorce occurred. I speculated that that the nature of the divorce process and adaptation to the event would have differing impacts on children.

Divorce had been rising for more than a decade and there was growing discussion about whether the changes in family structure were imperiling the development of children. Drawn into this topic were some of the major figures in developmental science. At conferences and workshops, I became acquainted with many colleagues who were thinking about how changes in the family and the larger society were affecting children's lives and welfare, including Eleanor Maccoby, Mavis Hetherington, Robert Plomin, Judy Dunn, Larry Steinberg, Richard Lerner, and others, all of whom helped to educate me about child development in particular. By 1985, I made my first explicit attempt to bridge sociological and psychological development in a short essay to introduce a set of papers for a special issue of the journal, *Child Development* (Furstenberg, 1985).

The ideas I was advancing now drew on the stock of work that I had produced, which was itself a continuation of the intellectual tradition of a diverse set of developmentalists and life-course theorists such as Mead, Cooley, W.I. Thomas, C. Wright Mills, Urie Bronfenbrenner, Matilda Riley, Norman Ryder, Eleanor Maccoby, and, of course, Glen Elder. Each had examined human development as occurring at the intersection of historical events and times, social context, and the unfolding and shaping of developmental trajectories. The work combined elements of social history, demography, life-course sociology, and socio-psychological development. This body of ideas sought to understand how culture, history, demography combined to shape socialization processes and development in a diverse and often overlapping set of social milieus.

Entering Mid-Life

During the same period, I also worked with one of my greatest mentors, Orville G. Brim. Bert, as he was known, had been the head of the Russell Sage Foundation and the Social Science Research Council and was a leading impresario of developmental social science. In 1981 at a conference in Colorado, Bert brought together a small group of 15 or so younger developmentalists from a variety of disciplines. The topic was human development from birth to age 21. One of participants was Jeanne Brooks-Gunn, who at a frighteningly young age, was a prolific developmental psychologist. Brooke and I hit it off immediately, and it was she who proposed that we follow up the Baltimore sample. I thought it was a great idea and relished the idea of collaboration with a developmental psychologist.

Brooke and I began immediately to plan a 17-year follow-up that would focus on the Baltimore children. The teen mothers were now in their mid-forties and their oldest children, whom I had first interviewed in the early 1970s, were now the same ages as their mothers had been when the initial interview took place in the mid-1960s. All of the children had grown up in households that now would be described as "fragile families." The interviews in the early 1980s examined both how the mothers were faring in mid-life and how the course of their children's development had been shaped by their parents' turbulent lives. It was no easy feat to go back and find the families after so long a hiatus, but we managed to re-interview a surprisingly high number of families. For the first time, we also added a qualitative component to the study to try to capture some of the subjective experiences of both mothers and children.

As the teen mothers entered mid-life, so did I. My forties were a fruitful period: I was beginning to pull together overlapping strands of an expanded research agenda that for the first time explicitly brought together life-course sociology and developmental psychology that focused primarily on the reproduction of and escape from social disadvantage. Linking the generations, as we did, necessarily led to a crossing of disciplinary boundaries. Adding a young social demographer, S. Philip Morgan, to our team made it possible to employ some new methods to life-course research, which enabled us to examine how the mothers' adaptation to early childbearing influenced their children's developmental trajectories. This vein of study resulted in a second volume of the Baltimore study (Furstenberg, Brooks-Gunn, & Morgan, 1987a).

At about the same time that I launched the long-term follow-up of the Baltimore study, I was invited to join a committee of the National Academy of Sciences on Child Development and Public Policy. Among others, Urie Brofennbrenner was on the committee. In 1983, Urie invited me to go along with an interdisciplinary group of young scholars to the Soviet Union to discuss developments in social science. It was a remarkable team and included among others Michael Lewis, Rich Lerner, Robert Plomin, and Jeylan Mortimer. Jeylan's longitudinal studies of adolescent development were just beginning, and we discovered a huge overlap in interests as we both were by now, fellow developmental sociologists. Two decades later, Jeylan and I would work together on issues relating to the transition to adulthood.

The attention to public policy had been an underlying theme of my research from the very start, but it was now becoming a more prominent and explicit interest. For the first time in my career, I began to think seriously about how macro-level policies, and especially public policy in the United States, shaped the life course for young people, particularly those from less advantageous circumstances. As a result, I began to pay more attention to the child support system and the neglected role of men in the family (Furstenberg et al., 1987a; Furstenberg, Morgan, & Allison, 1987b; Furstenberg & Nord, 1985). It is hard to imagine now, but the vast majority of research on the family in the 1970s and 1980s was on the mother-and-child dyad. There was remarkably little research on men's adaptation to changing gender roles and, from my perspective, on how fathering occurred in divided families.

My work with colleagues at Child Trends had produced some of the earliest information on the paternal involvement among nonresidential fathers. In a paper that was admittedly an exercise in descriptive demography our team was able to show how patterns of paternal participation rapidly decayed after divorce. Men were largely connected to their children through marriage and their relationship to their mother's children. This package deal quickly dissolved when marriages ended (Furstenberg, 1981; Furstenberg, Nord, Peterson, & Zill, 1983). Many fathers were, in effect, swapping obligations to their biological offspring with obligations to new families formed by cohabitation and remarriage. Few of these men were actively engaged in decisions involving children from their first marriage (Furstenberg et al., 1987b).

In the mid-1980s, Andy Cherlin asked me to do a paper for a small working conference on men in contemporary family life at the Urban Institute. Change in the family was now becoming a topic of political and ideological concern in the popular media as well as among social science researchers. During the Reagan administration, disputes about the impact of family change had become heated because conservatives, especially after the "Moynihan Report," argued that family change was at the heart of the perpetuation of social disadvantage (Furstenberg, 2009). At the same time, the electric current of feminist ideas was provoking a great deal of discussion about whether changing gender roles were undermining family stability. Conservatives commentators blamed left-leaning social scientists, and feminists in particular, for "disturbing the nest." Yet, during this same period of the 1980s, there were glimmerings of a new movement toward greater paternal participation in domestic life resulting from the women's movement.

In a paper called "Good Dads/Bad Dads: The Two Faces of Fatherhood," I tried to bring together twin trends in paternal involvement, arguing for the first time that family change was playing out differently at the top and the bottom of American society (Furstenberg, 1988). This idea that inequality was creating very different family forms at the top and bottom of the social ladder remains a theme in my work today (Furstenberg, 2011). By the late 1980s, the trend toward growing inequality in the United States was already evident though its impact on the direction of family change was incompletely understood (Furstenberg, 1990).

In the late 1980s, I joined a research network of the MacArthur Foundation on adolescents in high-risk neighborhoods, first headed by Betty Hamburg, then President of the William T. Grant Foundation, and later by Richard Jessor, a developmentalist who had pioneered research on youth in social context. The MacArthur networks were an innovative strategy for promoting and supporting innovative interdisciplinary research on human development. This research network completed my graduate education in human development. In an ongoing research seminar with some of the leading developmentalists of the time, such as Glen Elder, Arnold Sameroff, Bob Haggerty, James Comer, William J. Wilson, Tom Cook, and Jacquelyn Eccles, several of us devised a study that examined development in Philadelphia neighborhoods with varying levels of opportunity and risk.

The study began with an intensive ethnographic examination of several different neighborhoods in Philadelphia (Furstenberg, 1993). This was followed by a survey of parents and youth. The aim was to understand how parents employed strategies to manage their children's dealing with schools and neighborhoods that provided different amounts of resources and dangers. *Managing to Make It,* the book that I coauthored with Cook, Eccles, Elder, and Sameroff in 1999, expanded notions of parental socialization by investigating parent practices used to manage the external world beyond the household. Socialization, we argued, was more than direct interaction between parents and children; parents also engaged in a different sort of socialization in their efforts to place their children in advantageous environments. We referred to those practices as "family management" to distinguish them from the face-to-face socialization that developmental psychologists had been studying for decades.

Becoming a Senior

My years on the MacArthur Network on Disadvantaged Youth in High-Risk Settings ultimately provided a bridge to my next large sociological venture that began as the Network was winding down in the mid-1990s. Without my really realizing it, I found myself becoming a senior figure in life-course sociology and demography. I spent the year at the Russell Sage Foundation in 1989–90. During my stay, I wrapped up my research on the impact of divorce on children's lives (Furstenberg & Cherlin, 1991). I also spent a great deal of time with Irwin Garfinkel and Sara McLanahan, who were beginning to think about and plan for the Fragile Families study that was to start a few years later. We talked endlessly about the links between public policy and child development, topics that I was writing about now more explicitly.

From time to time in an academic career, a researcher begins to sense when he or she needs a fresh topic. It was the mid-1990s, and I'd begun to write the results from the final wave of the Baltimore study. I wrote several chapters of a final book on the later lives of the women and the experiences of the children in their early twenties. However, I was so bored with what I had written that I threw away the chapters and abandoned the final book. I was in my fifties, and it was time for me to break into some new areas of developmental research. I had done scores of papers on divorce and teenage parenthood, and I was beginning to feel as though I had run out of fresh findings. It took a few years for me to discover rewarding new directions. As in the past, I found that new ideas required and emanated from an expansion of my professional networks.

During the decade of my fifties, I spent more time away from the University of Pennsylvania. I went twice to the Center for Advanced Study in the Social and Behavioral Sciences. It was a wonderful setting to think about the future direction of my research and complete unfinished pieces of my work. It was during my second stay at the Center that I sensed a new research direction. Significant economic and demographic changes in American society were altering the third and fourth decades of life, and in particular the set of demographic events that constituted the transition to adulthood. When John Modell and I had written papers 20 years earlier on this topic, we had stopped our investigations just at the point when the passage to adulthood was shifting from the post-war period, with its abundant manufacturing jobs. The subsequent shift to a knowledge-based economy that required more education and higher skill levels was on the horizon. With this shift, the entire landscape of early adulthood was being reshaped in ways that had been completely unimaginable when I had written the earlier papers. I spent my second stay at the Center putting together a volume of papers on this new stage of life with my colleagues Tom Cook, Rob Sampson, and Gail Slapp (Furstenberg et al., 2002).

By the time I left the Center in 1998, I had agreed to chair a new MacArthur Network, this one on Transitions to Adulthood and Public Policy. The Foundation and I assembled a group of leading younger developmental sociologists and psychologists together with several policy-oriented economists (for more information see www.transitions2adulthood.com). This research network was just the tonic I needed to break some new ground in human development beyond the adolescent years with a remarkably talented team of social scientists and policy experts.

The Network was officially established the following year and immediately began to prepare a descriptive volume on the new patterns of early adulthood that were emerging both in the United States and in economically developed nations throughout the world. With my colleagues on the Network, we began to map an agenda of research on development during the young adult years of life—the third and fourth decades of life that guided much of my work during the past decade. A key question was why adulthood was occurring later and how the postponement was affecting psychological development.

In 2003, we assembled a volume on our early findings that helped to stimulate interest in what appeared to be a new stage of life between adolescence and the adult years (Settersten, Furstenberg, & Rumbaut, 2005; Furstenberg, Kennedy, McLoyd, Rumbaut, & Settersten, 2004). My intellectual development as a life-course sociologist and demographer with a strong interest in the links between social structure, historical conditions, and human development had prepared me well to think about this emerging life stage. Early adulthood, much like adolescence a century earlier, was becoming a developmental period in the life course.

A generation ago, young people entered adulthood almost unconsciously as they moved into the labor force and established families in their late teens and early twenties. Choices also seemed predetermined because they were made at what now seem frighteningly early ages. Today, the process of assuming adult roles has become quite different, created by higher education and labor market conditions that dictate a slower passage into adult roles. This pattern of prolonged development is rapidly spreading throughout the world, changing the course of social maturation in many societies. As longevity has been extended, the years of investment in human development have expanded with profound consequences for individuals and social institutions.

Stable identities in all likelihood now develop later; the financial and emotional responsibilities of parents have been extended; and a variety of other social institutions are being challenged to adapt to this regime for growing up. With my colleagues on the Network, we have been reassessing the ways that institutions such as the family, higher education, the military, and the labor market are operating to respond to this new schedule (Berlin, Furstenberg, & Waters, 2010).

A later schedule for growing up appears to widen inequality for young people in large part because there is a vacuum of institutions for those who are not college bound. Low- and moderate-income parents are ill-equipped to guide their young adult children during this new stage of life because they lack the resources to support them in school or connect them to advantageous positions in the labor market. By contrast, youth from privileged families are better prepared and supported to move into tertiary education. Four-year colleges and universities are well designed to serve young adults if they are accessible and affordable. But, for a large segment of the population, entering these institutions that are now the principal pathway to economic success, poses a formidable challenge for public policy makers who seek to maximize human potential.

As I have in the past, my attention remains focused on the family. In my recent work, I have been examining how social stratification in the family creates very different childhood and adolescent experiences, which play out in the early adult years. With a team of collaborators, I have been looking more closely at families in the middle of the economic spectrum in different societies, trying to understand how public and private resources in different nations contribute to the development of children and young adults (Iversen, Napolitano, & Furstenberg, forthcoming). Cross-national comparisons are now becoming a more important component of my research. This strategy of examining how societies refashion institutions in the face of change has increased my attention to how macro-level processes affecting human development play out at the micro-level in families. In particular, how do different policy regimes insinuate themselves into intimate interactions within the family (or the school)?

Most recently, I joined yet another MacArthur Network that is examining how demographic shifts toward "an aging society" will require new institutional innovations in the next several decades (see www.agingsocietynetwork.org). The aging of the population will bring increased demands on the already overburdened family. Changes in one part of the population inevitably ripple through society to shake up the institutional status quo. Inevitably, demographic and economic changes work their way into family life, socialization, and ultimately generational replacement. Human development must be understood as an ongoing interaction between biology and changing social institutions, most immediately family and kin. Toward the end of my career, I continue to be fascinated by the challenge of understanding how social change occurs and how changing institutions can be shaped to enhance human potential.

Concluding Reflections

Over the span of five decades since I first realized that I wanted to be a sociologist, I can now look back with the advantage of hindsight and realize that my career has been shaped by a combination of aim and accident. Sometimes, I could hardly distinguish between the two when I experienced them. It is only in later reflection that I can see how they worked in tandem to shape my academic career. Academics refine and rationalize professional narratives such as I do in this essay by recognizing that both the elements of intention and chance figure heavily into the academics we become. It is through the interplay of intellectual themes, personal commitments, and career contingencies that we recognize who we want to become as scholars and how it happened.

My training at Columbia, my happenstance involvement in the Baltimore study, my early years in academia struggling to find an intellectual framework, and my good fortunate at locating mentors at critical stages in my career all figured importantly in my becoming a sociologist of the life course. I was not destined to be a developmental sociologist or a life-course demographer. How could I be when these social categories did not even exist when I entered the discipline? Looking back now, it makes sense that I discovered and eventually adopted these identities. I have been among the most fortunate of academics because I was able to find and fashion a life as a human developmentalist.

References

Berlin, G., Furstenberg, F. F., & Waters, M. (2010). Introducing the issue. *Future of the Children, 20,* 3–18.

Cherlin, A. J., & Furstenberg, F. F. (1986). *The new American grandparent: A place in the family, a life apart.* New York: Basic Books.

Cloward, R., & Ohlin, L. (1960). *Delinquency and opportunity: A theory of delinquent gangs.* Glencoe, IL: Free Press.

Elder, G. H., Jr. (1974). *Children of the Great Depression: Social change in life experience.* Chicago: University of Chicago Press.

Furstenberg, F. F. (1971). The transmission of mobility orientation in the family. *Social Forces, 9,* 595–603.

Furstenberg, F. F. (1976). *Unplanned parenthood: The social consequences of teenage childbearing.* New York: The Free Press (paperback edition, 1979).

Furstenberg, F. F. (1981). Remarriage and intergenerational relations. In R. W. Fogel, E. Hatfield, S. B. Kiesler, & E. Shanas (Eds.), *Aging: Stability and change in the family* (pp. 115–142). New York: Academic Press.

Furstenberg, F. F. (1985). Sociological ventures in child development. *Child Development, 56,* 281–288.

Furstenberg, F. F. (1988). Good dads–bad dads: Two faces of fatherhood. In A. Cherlin (Ed.), *The changing American family and public policy* (pp. 193–218). Washington, DC: Urban Institute Press.

Furstenberg, F. F. (1990). Coming of age in a changing family system. In S. Feldman & G. Elliott (Eds.), *At the threshold: The developing adolescent* (pp. 147–110). Cambridge, MA: Harvard University Press.

Furstenberg, F. F. (1993). How families manage risk and opportunity in dangerous neighborhoods. In W. J. Wilson (Ed.), *Sociology and the public agenda* (pp. 231–258). Newbury Park, CA: Sage Publications.

Furstenberg, F. F. (1999). How it takes 30 years to do a study. In E. Phelps, F. F. Furstenberg, & A. Colby (Eds.), *Looking at lives: American longitudinal studies of the twentieth century* (pp. 37–57). New York: Russell Sage Foundation.

Furstenberg, F. F. (2009). If Moynihan had only known: Race, class, and family change in the later 20th century. *Annals of the American Academy of Political and Social Science, 621,* 94–110.

Furstenberg, F. F. (2011). How do low-income men and fathers matter for children and family life? *Annals of the American Academy of Political and Social Science, 635,* 131–137.

Furstenberg, F. F., Brooks-Gunn, J., & Morgan, S. P. (1987a). *Adolescent mothers in later life.* New York: Cambridge University Press.

Furstenberg, F. F., & Cherlin, A. J. (1991). *Divided families: What happens to children when parents part.* Cambridge, Harvard University Press.

Furstenberg, F. F., Cook, T. D., Eccles, J., Elder, G. H., & Sameroff, A. (1999). *Managing to make it: Urban families and adolescent success.* Chicago: University of Chicago Press.

Furstenberg, F. F., Cook, T. D., Sampson, R., & Slap, G. (2002). Preface. Early adulthood in cross-national perspective. *Annals of the American Academy of Political and Social Science* (Special Edition), 580: 6–15.

Furstenberg, F. F., Hershberg, T., & Modell, J. (1975). The origins of the female-headed Black family: The impact of urban experience. *Journal of Interdisciplinary History, 7,* 211–233.

Furstenberg, F. F., Kennedy, S., McLoyd, V., Rumbaut, R. G., & Settersten, R. A., Jr. (2004). Growing up is harder to do. *Contexts, 3,* 42–47.

Furstenberg, F. F., Morgan, S. P., & Allison, P. D. (1987b). Paternal participation and children's well-being after marital dissolution. *American Sociological Review, 52,* 695–701.

Furstenberg, F. F., & Nord, C. (1985). Parenting apart: Patterns of childbearing after divorce. *Journal of Marriage and the Family, 47,* 893–904.

Furstenberg, F. F., Nord, C., Peterson, J. L., & Zill, N. (1983). The life course of children of divorce: marital disruption and parental conflict. *American Sociological Review, 48,* 656–688.

Furstenberg, F. F., & Spanier, G. B. (1984). *Recycling the family: Remarriage after divorce.* Newbury Park, CA: Sage Publications.

Goode, W. J. (1963). *World revolution in family patterns.* New York: Free Press.

Goode, W. J., Furstenberg, F. F., & Mitchell, L. (1970). *On the family, education, and war: Willard W. Waller.* Chicago: University of Chicago Press.

Hollingshead, A. B. (1949). *Elmtown's youth: The impact of social classes on adolescents.* New York: Wiley.

Iversen, R., Napolitano, L., & Furstenberg, F. F. (Forthcoming). Middle-income families in the economic downturn: Challenges and management strategies over time. *Longitudinal and Life Course Studies.*

Merton, R. K. (1949). *Social theory and social structure.* New York: Free Press.

Mills, C. W. (1959). *The sociological imagination.* New York: Oxford University Press.

Modell, J., Furstenberg, F. F., & Herschberg, T. (1976). Social change and transition to adulthood in historical perspective. *Journal of Family History, 1,* 7–32.

Piven, F. F., & Cloward, F. (1972). *Regulating the poor.* London: Tavistock Publications.

Riesman, D., Glazer, N., & Denney, R. (1961). *The lonely crowd.* New Haven, CT: Yale University Press.

Settersten, R. A., Furstenberg, F. F., & Rumbaut, R. G. (2005). *On the frontier of adulthood: Theory, research, and public policy.* Chicago: University of Chicago Press.

Stouffer, S. A., & Lazarsfeld, P. (1937). *Research memorandum on the family in the depression.* New York: Social Science Research Council.

Volkart, E. H. (Ed.). (1951). *Social behavior and personality: Contributions of W. I. Thomas to theory and social research.* New York: Social Science Research Council.

19

Exploring the Frontiers of Adolescent Psychology, Psychiatry, and Development

BEATRIX A. HAMBURG[1]

Introduction

The field of adolescent psychiatry as we know it today, with its foundation in adolescent psychology, was advanced by a handful of pioneers whose work was truly path-breaking in identifying and defining adolescence as a distinct period of development. Teenagers were no longer either big children or small adults; rather, they had finally been recognized as having a distinct developmental profile.

I was fortunate to be among that group of pioneers, and this chapter is a reflection on my personal exploration of the mysteries and challenges of understanding adolescent development. I began my journey in the 1940s at the Yale Medical School, known for its strengths in Pediatrics and Behavioral Sciences, and for its unique Child Study Center. It was a truly a time of new frontiers in adolescent medicine and the school's stimulating atmosphere inspired thought-provoking investigation.

When I first entered psychiatry, adolescence encompassed ages 10–20 and was generally treated as a single developmental era. Through my work, I soon realized that we could—and needed to—think of adolescence as having a trajectory that moved through three distinct phases—early, middle, and late—with all that that implied for medical and behavioral interventions and support.

At the time, adolescent research was focused on post-World War II populations of highly educated European teenagers in the later stages of adolescence. Notable scientists, including Anna Freud and Erik Erikson, truly helped the medical world focus on adolescence as a distinct phase—but their work, rooted in psychoanalysis, tended to be culturally and age-limited. Anna Freud, for instance, defined adolescents as having two main "instinctual" characteristics that distinguished them from adults: intellectualism and asceticism. The research of that period was largely based on retrospective reconstruction of childhood by adult patients. But these characteristics were difficult to apply to much of American youth, with their very different culture.

Erikson helped build needed bridges between the social sciences and psychoanalysis, and gave me much encouragement to do the same. But it was my dear friend, John Bowlby, who put me on the right path with his belief that to understand children and adolescents, scientists needed to study each population directly. And this is exactly what I and a number of my colleagues proceeded to do.

I had several specific research interests. One was in clearly identifying the distinguishing features of each phase of adolescence; another was in looking at the stressors and coping strategies for each phase; and lastly, in developing evidence-based interventions for adolescents, their families and schools that would provide effective support for youth in this sometimes tumultuous period in life. Though my work covered all phases of adolescence, I specialized in early adolescence with a keen interest in appropriate interventions.

For interventions to be useful, our field was challenged to adapt them to meet the evolving social and environmental contexts of American youth. Whole new contextual facets needed to be addressed to shape healthy coping strategies and learning environments. This included the reshaped and resized post-war nuclear family; the much greater role of schools in socializing youth; the rapid development and deployment of new technologies that demanded quick adoption by youth and adults alike; the shifts in adolescent biology; the advances in reproductive and public health medicine; the eruption of school violence, especially involving guns; the wide availability of illicit drugs and the declining age of substance abusers; and the numerous ethnic and social divides that create their own psychosocial pressures. In short, the myriad changes in America's social, scientific, economic, and technological environments kept this field dynamic—a very exciting environment for those of us who as scientists sought to understand adolescents and support them in their transition from children into adults.

Among the interventions that I explored and helped develop were those involving peer counseling. This was a wholly new concept as applied to prevention of bad outcomes in adolescents, especially with regard to substance abuse. I ran a highly successful pilot program in the schools near Stanford University, where I was based at the time. It was quickly and widely replicated. This model for training mentors and using them as peer counselors continues to be adopted in this country and abroad, with enduring success. Peer counseling, tutoring, and mediation (in conflict prevention) have wide applicability in formulating and utilizing coping strategies adapted to various needs and different cultures.

My work is best understood through some of the highlights of my published papers, some as sole author and some as co-author or editor. To review some of my earliest work and thinking in this field, I begin with a paper that focused on the special hurdles that youth face upon reaching junior high school.

Coping in Early Adolescence, the Special Challenges of the Junior High School Period (Hamburg, 1974) Coming of age in America is an increasingly lengthy, challenging, and fascinating process. We must look at adolescence as three distinct eras—early, middle, and late—each marked by characteristic tasks, challenges, and coping possibilities. There are distinguishing shifts in the biological, psychological, and cultural environments of each era, with further distinctions based on sex, ethnicity, and socioeconomic status. Prior to the Industrial Revolution there was little cultural intervention in adolescence—adult life began much earlier and was well aligned with the biological and maturational changes of puberty.

Psychiatrists in this field have generally focused on the transition into adulthood from late adolescence, with a special focus on males. The growing complexity and elongation of the adolescent period, however, call for a more comprehensive and multidimensional approach to understanding the transitions within each stage of adolescence. Further complicating matters, the boundaries of adolescence cannot be firmly fixed, given that there are extreme cases of both advanced and delayed development.

The beginning and ending eras of adolescence share a substantial change in status. While the beginning fosters a change in biological status and the end fosters one in psychological status, both shifts can result in significant disequilibrium. Each era is defined by a dominant theme—in early adolescence, it is pubertal change. I avoided the term "sexual change" used at the time as puberty also entails changes in growth, facial contours, fat distribution, pelvic proportions, and muscular-skeletal development. The net effect over time has been to extend the span of adolescence, as pubertal changes trend lower, while psychosocial changes extend the upper limits. While much research has now specified all of the

changes, my writing and presentations brought these concepts to many researchers.

The social setting of these biological changes, at least their beginnings, typically resides in junior high school, an environment originally designed to ease the transition from the self-contained classrooms and single teachers of grammar school to the larger population and campus, rotating classes, and multiple teachers that are later found in high school. Unfortunately, the establishment of these changes in middle school has not diffused this harsh transition; rather, it makes it 2–3 years earlier. Junior high school accompanies the significant pubertal changes in most girls, yet few boys, though both genders experience drastic changes in social status. Junior high school presents a significant increase in both quality and quantity of academic demands, accompanied by relationships with multiple teachers that are far less personal than those in grammar school. Though there are both advantages and disadvantages to this system, there is certainly discontinuity with the past.

Along with the significant biological changes, adolescence is also a time of major behavioral and social change. All of these changes carry significant implications for adolescent coping strategies. Psychological development is directly related to an individual's physical development. Importantly, the major physical changes in puberty have strong influence on the ways in which peers and adults alike perceive and treat adolescents, and the way in which the individual perceives him or herself. The timing of puberty has significant, differential consequences for boys and girls (Adams, 1964). Acceleration in growth brings distinct advantages for boys, but disadvantages for girls (Jones, 1963). Early-maturing boys are seen as more attractive and athletic; they enjoy enhanced heterosexual status and more leadership roles (Mussen & Jones, 1957). Late-maturing boys, whose skeletal development is 2 years behind their age cohorts, are treated in accordance with their more childish appearance, not their age. While individuals in this group showed more personal and social maladjustment at all stages of adolescence, the two groups did not differ in their needs for achievement and recognition. For girls, the advantage was reversed: Early-maturing girls were seen as submissive, listless, or indifferent in social situations, while late-maturing girls were seen as more outgoing, self-assured and as having leadership capability (Jones, 1963).

There are multiple clinical and research implications for each phase of adolescence. Adolescents could develop better coping skills if given appropriate knowledge in preparation, before the onset of puberty, including information about the wide range of normality and timetables for various manifestations of pubertal change. Broader public understanding of the different eras of adolescence helps support parents, especially in establishing guidelines. There is also a need to look at expanding the ways in which peer groups can be reliably used for constructive support, such as the peer counseling program established at Stanford by the author. Further investigation of gonadal hormones could help us better understand the moodiness of adolescence as well as the possible relation of gonadal hormones to aggressive behavior in males. Finally, there is a need for interdisciplinary research on the links between biological and psychosocial variables in early adolescence—this critical period of turbulence and potentiality deserves far more study than it has received.

Junior high school launches the early adolescent into the new world of teen culture and a wholly different school experience. New coping mechanisms are needed to meet the many psychosocial changes of early adolescence. With the sudden entry into their new role status, an early adolescent may feel the need to explore new behaviors, values and/or reference persons. Early adolescents from traditional families are generally well buffered and less subject to peer influence. In two class groups, though, there is sharp repudiation of parental values and guidance. In lower socioeconomic status families, common conditions of low parental involvement are highly correlated with low self-esteem and a heightened tendency for these early adolescents to seek support and guidance from their peers. In upper middle-class families, there may be a tendency to encourage independent decision-making and autonomy in a manner that is contraindicated by the needs of the young person for parental guidance. Most early adolescents are quite dependent on their environmental supports in attempting to anticipate and regulate responses to the challenges and tasks at hand.

Mid-adolescence largely takes place during the high-school years, from 15–18 years of age. It ends with graduation and the need for new adaptations suited to the impending task of finding a job or going to college, and likely separation from home and the nuclear family. The theme of this period is consolidation. There is a continued socialization into adolescent roles. There are, however, increasing social responsibilities and privileges, and the opportunity to work on familiar problems in greater depth. Adaptations are smoother in high school not only because tasks are less new and challenging but also because the coping assets within individuals are greater. Mid-adolescents are often interested in exploring the various facets of an issue, and can learn by debate and intellectual discussion in both academic and social settings. There is also a more highly critical use of the peer group, with less stereotypy and broader roles, and development of more mature sexual relationships, with mutuality and tenderness. The mid-adolescent makes many refinements to his or her self-image and sense of identity. This time period is one of substantial progress in laying the groundwork for the salient issues that will confront the late adolescent.

Late adolescence[2] follows graduation from high school and the end of the lengthy period of student life in secondary school. Autonomy is the key theme. Most of this population moves into an extended period of time in college, apprentice training, or at work. There is a chance to try out different modes of independent functioning and a renegotiated relationship with the family, with a goal of more mutual respect and equality. Commitment to work is an important task, as the late adolescent needs to identify and pursue a goal in which his or her talents are used, interests are focused and a sense of competency and personal confidence are established. With a move out of the family home and into the community, the individual defines himself or herself more broadly in relation to society. Finally, there is the challenge of sexual adjustment and intimacy, with the establishment of more mature, stable relationships.

Interventions that Work

It became quite clear, in my work with youth in the 1960s, that there was pressing need for new interventions that would address traditional developmental stressors as well as the new, rapidly evolving social stressors of the times— importantly, these interventions would need to be tailored to each of the three phases of adolescence. The interventions also needed to be rooted in the altered social environment for adolescents—where schools and peers play more important roles than in times past, with the increased expectations that schools would assume greater responsibility for both prevention of risky behavior and promotion of healthy life skills for a successful future.

One of my first experiments in this regard was with peer counseling. This effort was not without controversy given the severity of the issues for which early and middle adolescents might seek help: drug abuse—one of the most pervasive and immediate social stressors for this population; alienation; violence; sexual practices; and poor health behavior. Yet, we were able to engage parents, schools, school boards, and community organizations in this endeavor. With counselor training and oversight, this program rapidly proved itself, with mental health and other benefits to counselors and counselees alike.

Our approach soon became useful in providing comprehensive education and life skills as preventive health measures, cognitive skills in decision-making, and in creating learning environments for self-care and healthy choices. Effective interventions match developmental need with school, peer, and complementary programs. Additionally, we took into account the increasing influence of media, technology, sports, and popular icons on adolescent behavior and decision-making.

Peer Counseling in the Secondary Schools: A Community Mental Health Project for Youth (Hamburg & Varenhorst, 1972) The areas of major social concern for adolescents in the 1960s in secondary school were alienation, substance abuse, and violence. These problems are rooted in the myriad ways in which our complex technological society affects both individuals and their social environments. Schools wind up in the center of these issues. The modern American nuclear family—with its

small, mobile structure, often isolated from kinship ties—leaned on external support systems to meet the emotional and other needs of their adolescents. Schools, as powerful influences on adolescent socialization, came to fill this role: Parents expected schools to set and enforce standards and to educate their children about risky behaviors; teachers and counselors acted as surrogate parents; and peers became role models, bridging persons, and sources of useful information. Schools provide the ideal setting for organized peer counseling and other organizations could readily adopt these procedures.

Much work demonstrated the value of using students as counselors and tutors (Goodman, 1969; Lippitt & Eiseman,1969; Mattson, 1970; Rioch et al., 1963), showing that the intervention is of mutual benefit to both the student seeking help as well as to the one offering guidance. We developed a peer counseling program with responsibilities that included academic tutoring; helping with personal problems; teaching social skills; giving information about jobs, volunteer opportunities, and mental health resources; acting as role models; developing friendships; acting as a bridge to the adult world; and, ultimately, serving as agents of change in school environments. As part of their training, we exposed counselors to the full spectrum of student issues and backgrounds across the entire school district.

In terms of positioning the program, it was very important that it have strong positive connotations, and especially that it was clearly directed at all students, not just those who were considered "deviant, disturbed, or dumb," terms used at the time for special programs. Attracting normal students undergoing situational stresses would consolidate a positive image for peer counseling and preclude with a stereotype of pathology.

To assess feasibility, community acceptance and potential value, the pilot phase of the Peer Counseling Project was carried out from 1970–71 in multiple schools in Palo Alto. Mental health professionals worked closely together to help with the design, implementation, and oversight of the project. Building the groundwork for this path-breaking and potentially sensitive program involved numerous steps. Suggestions were solicited from a Planning Committee (comprising students, parents, teachers, counselors, staff, and project developers), the Superintendent of Schools, the entire guidance staff, all PTA groups, and all elementary school principals. Finally, we sought and gained approval from the School Board.

To launch the program, student counselors were recruited from across the school district of 12 secondary, junior high and senior high schools, with a total population of 7,000 students. The program sought peer counselors with these attributes: positive personal characteristics, a strong sense of responsibility, high dedication, and a feeling of involvement. A stringent training program was designed to weed out those who did not have these attributes.

The initial phase of training involved a large group exposure to the Life Career Game, both a decision-making simulation and an "ice-breaker" game; it revealed preliminary interest and aptitude among participants. At this point, 162 students proceeded to small group training. The curriculum was comprised of various fundamentals that addressed understanding people and interpersonal relations; relevant peer counseling topics; strategies in counseling; and a training practicum. Students participated in practice exercises, role playing, and group discussions.

Following small group training, each peer counselor—for an initial practicum—met independently with a small group of sixth-grade students, all facing the prospect of junior high within a few months. Each trainee also counseled a group peer, one-on-one. In final group sessions, ethical responsibilities were reviewed and discussed, and students examined the differences between counseling and advice-giving. This latter was one of the more challenging concepts to absorb, especially the right of the counselee to choose an individual course of action.

Out of the 162 students that entered the program, 155 went on to become Peer Counselors. There was a wide range in age, racial, and ethnic representation as well as in personality types and personal issues. The training program represented a significant experience in personal growth for the student participants, and at the end received very positive ratings. The pilot phase of the Peer Counseling Program filled a mental health need in the schools and demonstrated that acceptance for such programs by the community and schools could be achieved.

Education for Healthy Futures: Health Promotion and Life Skills Training (Hamburg, 1997) In contrast with historic views, we became aware in the 1960s of the necessity for school-based health education for adolescents, both to help them stay healthy and to prepare them for the myriad responsibilities of adulthood. This shift was partly due to greater recognition that health issues are more significant for this age group than previously assumed and that many of the illnesses associated with adolescents are preventable. Furthermore, the behaviors and lifestyles adopted in adolescence are determinants of adult morbidity and mortality. Consequently, new approaches to adolescent health education and life skills training programs became part of school reform in spite of ideological and financial constraints.

Many of the illnesses associated with adolescence do not have visible symptoms—the majority of health issues at this stage of life are psychosocial and/or related to health behaviors. We saw that about 25% of American youth engaged in smoking, drug and alcohol abuse, inappropriate sexual behavior, and injury-prone activities. Eating habits and substance abuse behaviors established at this age may lead to serious consequences in adult morbidity. The risks have been especially high for minority and disadvantaged adolescents. There was an urgent need for disease prevention and health promotion.

Young adolescents are immature at a time when they are exposed to novel, stressful challenges. Their developmental needs, fundamental to becoming healthy adults, include becoming a valued member of a group that provides mutual support; to become a cognitively and socially competent person with appropriate life skills; and to believe in a promising future. Preparation for mature adult roles and responsible citizenship requires competencies in social problem solving, conflict resolution, and the ability to evaluate powerful media messages. These developmental needs can be met within the school environment through integrated health education, life skills training, and the creation of supportive social networks. Therefore, we sought to provide, school-related, community-based experiences to help meet these needs.

Young adolescents, ages 10–14, face three major life challenges: the dramatic biological changes of puberty, the social system changes of middle or junior high school and the changes in their role status. This is a period of experimentation and risk taking; the ambiguity of their new roles and status test their self-confidence, leaving them insecure in their own beliefs, values, and judgments and, hence, highly susceptible to outside influences for better and worse. Finding the right role models is a challenge, especially in a world infused with popular entertainment and athletic figures whose behaviors are less than ideal archetypes for this age group. As early adolescents navigate this new world, they need strong adult mentors who can provide guidance as well as knowledge and information to counteract peer pressure to conform to maladaptive norms.

Our group in the 1960s and 1970s saw that the role of schools could become far more significant in providing structured support to help adolescents with their developmental needs—shifting from egocentric views of the world to more nuanced, complex thinking. We recommended:

- Teach the cognitive skills and critical thinking so students develop the basic competencies that employers seek in complex thinking, problem-solving skills, and teamwork. Schools can augment academic courses in conjunction with community organizations.
- Teach social competency as a life skill to help students develop mature, collaborative peer relationships.
- Teach decision-making skills to help adolescents make choices that are rationally based rather than emotionally driven, to shift from the concrete thinking of childhood to the more complex abstract thinking requisite to adult decision-making.
- Help youth and their families develop healthy social support networks. Multiservice schools that provide "one stop shopping" services for parents and children alike—with social and medical services, literacy training, community service programs and job referrals—have been especially successful in this regard but have biases to overcome.
- Provide comprehensive health education and life skills training based on known success factors. In this

realm, there must be multiple exposures to educational materials (Janis & Mann, 1977). Social learning theory (Bandura, 1995) highlights the power of learning through observation, imitation and practicing behaviors that are modeled by key persons in the adolescents' social environment. This can include peers, family and popular social icons.

Peer leadership has been especially successful in anti-smoking efforts that provide accurate factual and normative information, discussion of social pressures, assertiveness training and role playing to resist peer pressure. Botvin's work (Botvin & Eng, 1982) explicitly introduced life skills training (LST) as a new model in anti-smoking efforts. This multi-component, educational program based in social competency training was later successfully applied to other adolescent health behaviors including substance abuse and sexually transmitted diseases. The Midwestern Prevention Project (MPP) was the next iteration of LST, extending to 15 communities with a focus on changing community norms as an integral component to prevention of smoking and drug abuse (Pentz et al., 1989). It demonstrated that modifying socioenvironmental and social policy factors can have significant contributions to adolescent health outcomes.

Special attention must be given to high risk adolescents—those children from lower socioeconomic groups and minorities who often lack the life skills and social supports to manage the challenges of adolescence. These young people are disproportionately affected with the rising morbidity of youth: early unwanted pregnancy, sexually transmitted diseases, substance abuse, learning problems, and violence. To develop adequate life skills, this population needs structured, problem-focused sessions; a common basis for interaction; to be treated with respect and dignity; constructive peer influence; enhancement of ethnic pride. Two programs that have been especially successful in incorporating these features were developed and implemented by the Salvation Army and the Violence Prevention Project (Hamburg, 1990).

In addition to having the right core elements for health education and life skills training, the program's implementation and its evaluation each require careful attention. Six dimensions in effective implementation are: assessment of specific needs of the target population; selection of a program site that meets program needs but is also accessible and acceptable to the community; entry points that support collaborative work with the community; training the trainers; data collection and information management; and evaluation metrics that link outcomes to goals, with multiple measures. Program sites and entry points within most communities are social structures such as schools, faith-based organizations, housing projects, and community groups.

Key characteristics of effective programs included a serious commitment of classroom hours, substantial teacher training and program support resources. Programs that emphasized these features were especially successful (Connell & Turner, 1985; Connell, Turner, & Mason, 1985).

Since our early work, the knowledge base for health education and life skills training has advanced considerably. There are now programs for adolescent health education in schools worldwide, supported by the World Health Organization, the United Nations International Children's Education Fund and the Pan American Health Organization. But such accomplishments require persistent initiative to cope with political obstacles.

Applying the Phases of Adolescence to Managing Health Challenges

With a framework of the three stages of adolescence, I began looking at ways in which healthy, stage-appropriate coping strategies could be developed to manage health stressors and diseases.

A comprehensive approach to help patients and families can achieve lifelong coping responses. This includes the emotional, cognitive, and instrumental strategies to be considered and the team members who will make a difference in lifelong support for the individual with juvenile diabetes. Importantly, I highlight the characteristics of a good physician: one who will succeed in helping the patient and the family learn to manage the challenges of juvenile diabetes. These characteristics are valuable for any doctor–patient relationship.

Coping with Predictable Crises of Diabetes Most health care professionals, diabetic patients and families of patients have no clear model of psychosocial variables in diabetes care or principles for effective treatment and preventive interventions (Gore, 1978). A multivariate clinical model is presented here that is based on the constructs of crisis (Hamburg, Lipsett, Inoff, & Drash, 1980; Parad, 1965; Parad & Caplan, 1965), coping (Ahmed, 1981; Cohen & Lazarus, 1979; Kohlberg, 1969; Moos, 1977), and social support (Cassel, 1976; Cochran & Brassard, 1979; Dean & Lin, 1977; Gore, 1978; Gottlieb, 1981; Hamburg & Killilea, 1979; Mitchell & Trickett, 1980) with a developmental and life-course perspective. The opportunity of working at the National Institutes of Health in the 1970s was helpful in this formulation.

A diagnosis of diabetes falls into the category of life crises comprising unexpected events that threaten survival and/or one's values and lifetime goals. It is time-urgent and calls for a new set of coping strategies. Characteristics of this life crisis include a steep rise in anxiety, cognitive confusion, feelings of helplessness, withdrawal, and denial. Family and health care workers can have a profound impact in buffering the stress of this crisis and in contributing to improved health outcomes (Baumrind & Moselle, 1985; Johnston, 1985; Johnston, O'Malley, & Bachman, 1985; Kandel, 1985; Kovacs, Feinberg, Crouse-Novak, Paulauskas, & Finkelstein, 1984) as part of a patient's support network. Those diabetic

patients who withdraw from social contact are at higher risk for coping failure, experience worse personal and medical outcomes, and have significantly higher mortality (Berkman & Syme, 1979) than others with the disease.

Although most persons recover from the initial diabetes diagnosis and crisis in due course, prevailing notions of recovery needed revision. For instance, the period of inner distress is longer than once assumed; the impact of the initial crisis is something that is re-experienced multiple times over the course of a lifetime; the successive stresses of living with diabetes have a cumulative effect; prior coping successes and failures predict outcomes at later stages.

The patient, family, and physician must together develop a coordinated set of coping responses for the patient that address *emotional, cognitive,* and *instrumental* needs.

- Friends and family are essential in support that reduces anxiety and affirms a sense of worth. Their accepting attitudes help a patient gain mastery over the emotional response to an irreversible diagnosis.
- Cognitive strategies to help a patient develop the new skills and knowledge necessary for managing the demands of the medical regimen; continuously appraising options for next steps, and building on lessons learned to master new challenges.
- Dealing with the logistics of daily life and its exigencies.

Patients and their networks can engage in anticipatory coping for predictable crises, putting in place adaptations ahead of a crisis. Predictable crises in diabetes are medical and psychosocial, and are disease-specific, including emotionally distressing medical symptoms; hospitalization; responses to major complications; confrontation with significant therapeutic choices; failure to obtain desired therapeutic outcomes; and threat of imminent death. Doctor–patient–family communication in a clear, sensitive mode is essential.

At the time of diagnosis, familial stress may be widely communicated and felt by every family member; early attitudes and behaviors can influence the diabetic's therapeutic regimen so it is important that the family, as a unit, master the stress caused by the diagnosis and all that follows. The family and patient need help in dealing with the uncertainty of immediate outcomes, any parental guilt or anger, feelings of incompetence or helplessness, fears about future complications and early death, jeopardy to valued life goals, accepting the permanent changes that the disease implies for both patient and family. These stressors are difficult yet usually manageable in the context of biological–psychological integration. The physician has a central role in helping the family and patient address these concerns and in developing successful coping strategies to achieve positive therapeutic and family outcomes.

Parents and/or patients, no matter how intelligent or capable, will not absorb many of the details in the shock of the diagnosis. Some will then seek to master the circumstances through information seeking; others will be information "avoiders" who may need to be referred for counseling if disease management is at risk.

The physician needs to be a clear and confident leader from the outset who evaluates and interprets the clinical results and reports of allied medical personnel. Positive patient–physician interactions provide much needed social support for the patient and family and create a sound basis for the rational, compliant self-care that leads to good medical outcomes.

The physician's characteristics associated with desired outcomes (DiMatteo, Prince, & Taranta, 1979; Engel, 1981) are the following: adopts a "person" rather than "illness" orientation and is aware of developmental, psychological and sociocultural factors for that patient; establishes a relationship of trust, shows respect for family members, and has a nonauthoritarian, responsive mode of relating; works out mutual agreement with the patient on treatment goals and takes into account both medical and psychosocial needs; establishes a therapeutic team that includes the family, adjunct medical staff and physician as leader; emphasizes patient education, self-motivation, and responsibility; is aware of predictable crises and provides anticipatory guidance; and, finally, is alert to indicators for counseling or psychiatric referral.

Every developmental phase for the child is overlaid with the challenges of managing the illness. A young child, for instance, may view negative or painful experiences (e.g., injections) as a punishment for bad behavior and will try to make the situation better by compensating with "good" behavior. Going through puberty with diabetes can lead to uncertainty about sexual identity and body image (Schowalter, 1977). With developmental desire for independence may come exaggerated wishes for security and dependence, on the one hand, or hyperindependent, rebellious and risk-taking behavior, on the other.

Adolescents can benefit from peers who have been successful in coping with diabetes, for example, learning from them how to overcome a sense of alienation, to develop confidence in managing their illness and to see that some sense of normalcy is feasible. The mentors benefit as well, with a boost to their self-esteem. Importantly, parental peer groups are also effective, providing a needed resource for mutual support and shared learning about appropriate, successful mechanisms for relating to the challenges of a diabetic adolescent.

Parenting behaviors that reflect mutual agreement between the spouses and are consistent, directive, and reflect age-appropriate expectations of the child are associated with the best medical and developmental outcomes. Distortions of parenting, however, will lead to negative outcomes, which happens when parents go to extremes with either overly controlling or permissive behaviors. Additionally, there is a risk of sibling deprivation that can lead to health and behavior issues for the sibling(s), and can trigger additional feelings of guilt and pressure for the parents. With all this, marriages can be pushed to the breaking point.

As they become adults, diabetic patients face crises in education and occupational decision-making. There can be conflict in committing to long-term education or training; there may be disappointment and anger if the young adult experiences any discrimination based on having the illness. Marriage and children can bring on other developmental crises. There are the significant economic implications of having diabetes, including the inability to get health insurance. Generally, these economic burdens are underestimated for both adult patients and families of diabetic children, and cause significant psychosocial stress.

Fostering competent coping and promoting the adoption of health-enhancing behaviors are both possible and necessary in dealing with diabetes. Active coping processes can be developed and coordinated by patient, family, and health care professionals. Anticipatory coping will reduce feelings of helplessness and vulnerability and can lead to mastery and personal growth. Individuals demonstrate widely divergent levels of functional ability and personal satisfaction (Starfield, 1976), leading to multiple strategies and differing patterns of coping.

One major implication of this experience is the need for strengthening of behavioral pediatrics. At the time, this had achieved only modest attention, i.e., the linkage of pediatrics and behavioral science, especially in stress and coping. This led me to consider institutional changes that might strengthen this linkage and we pursued this under clinical and foundation auspices.

Violence and Adolescent Development

The fields of adolescent psychology and psychiatry have been challenged with the emergence of violence in schools—especially cases involving guns, which can cause widespread injury and death. It became evident, with early cases of individual violence in schools, that more attention needed to be given to causes and preventive interventions. This concern stimulated inquiry from the 1970s onward. We built a network of scholars interested in this subject, seeking deeper understanding and practical applications.

Violence in American Schools (Hamburg, Elliott, & Williams, 1998) After years of intervening studies and observations, I decided to draw together leading experts in youth violence for a major book on this subject. This book was published just prior to the shocking events at Columbine High School, events that galvanized a much greater public awareness of school violence. The experts who contributed to this book were drawn from the diverse academic disciplines and research traditions involved both in addressing underlying causes of youth violence and in developing evidence-based interventions to prevent or reduce it. Their fresh perspectives on *prevention* challenged current beliefs regarding society's response to this escalation in youth violence—specifically that there is little evidence that the typical harsh sentencing of youth offenders does anything to deter violence or rehabilitate these young people.[3]

One novel lens through which we examined school violence was development and human ecology—an approach that provided a whole-systems view of such outbursts and leads to successful mitigation by identifying integrated pathways to prevention. We saw five key components to this ecological–developmental framework for prevention: (1) the social ecology, including the family, peer groups, media and school; (2) the dynamic interaction between children and adolescents and their developmental ecology; (3) identifying the array of stakeholders who must collaborate for successful prevention; (4) recognizing the need for a *public health approach* to youth violence in which developmental psychology is crucial; (5) and finally, elucidating the elements requisite to successful intervention strategies and programs. These are difficult themes for understanding and social action, yet not beyond feasibility.

The first prominent theme, the ecology of family and social institutions, highlights the strong influence of social contexts on violent development. As a child grows older, there are increasingly larger spheres of social influence in his or her life including the family, peer groups, schools, the neighborhood, and interest and faith-based organizations. In different developmental phases, there are shifts in influence of these social contexts on an individual, with peer groups and the neighborhood taking on significantly greater importance in mid- and late adolescence.

Events in a parent's workplace can affect interpersonal and family relations, which in turn can influence neighborhood dynamics. Unfortunately, many of the social institutions directly responsible for preventing violence in youth have lost ground in providing the guidance and support to prevent or diminish it. Pressure on schools to compensate for these institutional failures increased. Given the increase in public health and safety issues associated with youth violence, and the growing complexity of psychological problems faced by adolescents, schools were expected to help students build strong practical skills in learning to live with others and in adapting to changing circumstances—assertiveness without violence; and pragmatic problem-solving in interpersonal disputes. We emphasized these orientations with a long-term view.

The social ecology of development is particularly salient in considering children who are raised in difficult or unsafe surroundings that can leave them without the psychological foundations to develop a sense of competence and self-worth. Furthermore, aggression in the home directly relates to aggression at school just as violence within communities affects a school's social climate. It was established that local crime rates were the strongest predictors of school violence. Many of the risk factors for becoming a victim of physical violence, especially from firearms, derive from behavioral and environmental factors that are external to the academic setting, such as one's access to and affinity for weapons.

There must be strong collaboration in establishing non-violent norms between the schools and families within a community; indeed it became clear that, the best "safe school" plans involve the full community, difficult as it may be to mobilize such efforts. Education of the public on these problems and emphasizes non-violent norms emerged as vital in serious efforts to diminish youth violence.

The second theme was that social contexts can shape the process of human development just as an individual's behavior can influence social settings. Children who witness violence, especially from firearms, can suffer from psychological trauma, which must be recognized and addressed constructively. Widespread concern for personal safety, whatever the reason, may reduce attendance, affect the quality of teaching, disrupt classrooms, and limit the availability of teachers before and after school. Further, expression of violence may reflect a youth's frustration or hopelessness in achieving the tasks expected of them in a given developmental phase. Violence often acquires a functional value towards accomplishing these tasks, and becomes a norm for changing status, asserting dominance, gaining power, enhancing material wealth, and resolving disputes—all outside the "normal" bounds of developmentally appropriate behaviors. Thus, school violence is truly toxic.

The third theme asserts the need for *collaboration* in effective *prevention*. Prevention involves building relationships among public and private institutions that affect a young person's life, and the collaboration among various organizations to develop prevention strategies that incorporate the many risk factors is of much practical importance. Not only must the adults from community organizations offering relevant social services be involved, but the youth themselves must have a voice. Taken together, we observed that this works best by monitoring local, state, and national levels to the extent possible. With widespread collaboration, there will be useful monitoring and dissemination of best practices. Finally, where collaborative community-wide movements can be constructed, the ability to improve children's lives has a much better chance of enduring success.

The fourth theme calls for a *public health approach to violence prevention*. The public health model emphasizes the community as is the case with disease prevention. Given the success of this model in reducing the burden of other preventable or controllable conditions, framing violence as a public health problem becomes an important strategy in violence prevention. This approach fosters changes in behavior on a community-wide level. It provides a scientific, multidisciplinary methodology for identifying effective means of prevention.

A significant public health consideration must also be addressed: The American school system was originally designed to match the work hours of its once agrarian and then industrial economy. As the world has moved into a post-industrial economy, many European and Asian school systems have extended their school days to match the changes in parents' work hours. This led us to recommend lengthening the school day, asking why our schools release children into unsupervised environments that bring such serious consequences to both our children and society, e.g., each of help in conflict resolution and unplanned, unwanted pregnancy.

There are three targeted areas for intervention strategies: systemic changes in schools, programs for individuals, and public policies. Schools can serve as multi-service centers, providing services to children and their families that are not otherwise available in the community; schools can help create *a culture of non-violence* and can serve as a safe haven in after-school activities; offer resources in stress management and crisis intervention. Programs geared to help individual children can focus on skill enhancement, e.g., anger management, social problem-solving, tutoring, and counseling. Schools practice interventions combining early childhood education and family support have demonstrated the ability to prevent aggressive behavior and violence. Children can learn to be assertive without violence and can develop the life skills of constructive achievement in and out of the classroom. Developing policies to help whole communities can address violence as a preventable health risk. We were cautioned about the cost of such initiatives but have then and ever since countered with the savings in human life, suffering, and economic loss if this approach is neglected.

Learning to Live Together (Hamburg & Hamburg, 2004)

In due course, I came to feel that these considerations should be explored with the best evidence in respect to a wider field of concern. My husband and I co-authored this book in 2004, drawing from our respective strengths in adolescent development and psychiatry, public policy, and prevention of violence—all based on the research literature and our experience in this field. We had the good fortune to work with world leaders and great scholars to fill the gaps in fostering child and adolescent development to overcome hatred and violence. Here are salient portions of the text that highlight the themes of my work and complement those in this chapter.

Cooperative Learning In the United States and abroad, rising immigration and refugee movements have brought ever greater diversity to schools. Racial, religious, and ethnic tensions and/or discrimination have followed this demographic shift into the school classrooms. Though expressions of intolerance in the United States are more subtle than 20 years ago, they still exist—and schools are on the frontline for identifying and reducing conflict related to this growing diversity in their student bodies.

One response of education has been the development of cooperative learning programs in which classrooms are re-organized into heterogeneous working groups. Importantly, groups are mixed in individual student achievement, gender, ethnicity, and socioeconomic status. This style of learning builds on the recognized benefits of peer-mediated interventions and alters the classroom dynamic from competition between winners and losers to collaborative achievement and motivated learning for all. Every student experiences some kind of success, and their efforts are manifestly respected. This became a powerful motivator for continued school achievement. Additionally, collaborative learning promotes healthy social behaviors and enhanced understanding of others' cultures. There has been careful, systematic research in this line of inquiry and good results. But the limit of public understanding and financial resources has put this work on a smaller scale then the problem requires.

Well-designed studies in secondary schools have compared cooperative and standard learning methods; more than two-thirds of these favored the cooperative learning methods. Student achievement is at least as high and often higher in the cooperative environment while also leading to improved interpersonal relations, strong motivation to learn, and enhanced self-esteem. All students are recognized for their diverse contributions and strengths in cooperative environments. These results hold true at all age levels in middle and high school, across all subjects and tasks.

These outcomes also support Allport's contact theory (Allport, 1954; Allport & Kramer, 1946; both cited in Amir, 1969) that students from diverse backgrounds who work together as equals not only form friendships but find it difficult to hold prejudices against one another. Working collaboratively to conduct complex tasks or solve problems broadens the cultural framework, and advances enduring friendships. Prejudices and negative expectations give ways to trust. When given the choice, students tend to select cooperative learning modes over competitive ones.

A mutual aid ethic is encouraged. Parents may initially be concerned about the potential for hindering individual advancement or about the effects of a disruptive student—while the latter is occasionally an issue, in general, these concerns are allayed by accomplishments and relationships. This is a good example of the value of superordinate goals. Such accomplishments are facilitated by school leadership and community support: mutual aid for mutual benefit.

School Mediation Programs Our early work on peer counseling spread to various modes and settings. Many colleges and universities created peer mediation programs to help resolve conflict in a manner acceptable to the students involved. This movement also spread throughout elementary and secondary schools. Students were trained in the principles of conflict resolution and were supervised in practice mediations. Evaluation of these programs found that student disputants felt that the process was fair and were usually satisfied with the mediated outcomes. A consistent finding has been that peer mediators themselves benefited from the training and enhanced self-esteem. Adapting mediation for parent–school conflict resolution has also been successful, leading to an improved school climate when and where applied.

Van Slyck, Stern, and Zak-Place (1996) showed that peer-mediated dispute resolution and the specific steps involved were compatible with the developmental tasks of adolescence, leading to skill development in active problem-solving and prosocial skills that can be applied to other similar settings across a lifetime.

Evidence suggests that these programs help reduce the level of violence in schools, and offer a much needed constructive alternative to suspension and expulsion for students who violate school norms. Individual, compassionate attention from teachers, peers, and school staff helps students learn to live together amicably.

Conditions Conducive to Improving Intergroup Relations Through foundations we headed, we each supported work to clarify these issues and make them understood in educational governmental and business communities. I served as president of the WT Grant Foundation (1992–98) and David as president of the Carnegie Corporation of New York (1982–97).

True integration in schools and communities is different from desegregation. Simply putting children together is not sufficient to achieve the development of positive relations between members of different groups. Building on Gordon Allport's (1954) contact hypothesis, there are three important elements that must be in place: equal status for members of all groups; cooperative interdependence; and explicit support by authority figures. Research suggests that multiethnic curricula of reasonable depth and of significant duration have a positive impact on intergroup relations, creating an equalizing effect among diverse school populations.

Why is this approach so powerful? For one, cooperation creates a crosscutting social identity: There is shared ownership of a group goal or product that diminishes bias. Having the opportunity to learn about an individual's personality traits, skills, and experiences leads to a discovery of similarities between oneself and the member of an "out-group." Stereotypes weaken as personal knowledge and bonds grow, and because individuals act in ways that contradict any stereotype. Additionally, it is increasingly apparent that introducing high expectations for group performance raises the achievement level for each student.

The support of authorities is also crucial to create positive changes in intergroup attitudes. The principal can model the desired behaviors and can make positive intergroup relations a priority for the school; he or she can also reward prosocial practices and behaviors, discouraging negative ones and clearly expressing an expectation of respect for others' rights and dignity. Teachers can enable, model, and foster similar behaviors in the same ways. Educators also can find ways to involve parents, as significant authority figures, in encouraging their children's participation in cooperative, intergroup activities. Over several decades, our interest in this approach fostered stronger efforts, new evidence and wider understanding.

This is an approach of world-wide utility if adequately supported—intellectually and financially—by relevant institutions.

Over Half a Century Reframing Adolescence and the Issues of Social Change

As social, technical, biological, and environmental contexts continued to evolve over the sixties and seventies, it was apparent that we needed new tools and perspectives to be able to support adolescents in their changing landscapes. It was not enough to recognize the three distinct phases; now we needed to delve deeper into the distinctions within each phase, especially within subgroups of adolescents. We needed clearer ways to identify those at higher risk and to implement interventions in public health and community-based programs, as evidence began to build that these were the most successful ways to help individuals and to build healthy, adaptive responses to social change. Moreover, we had reason to believe that further technology and changes would probably change the adolescent experience and therefore adaptability was of the essence. To do so called for placing adolescence in a wider context.

Adolescence: A Developmental Approach to Problems and Psychopathology (Petersen & Hamburg, 1986) Over the course of a lifetime, every individual undergoes a number of critical developmental transitions—periods in which significant changes occur within and/or outside of the individual. Adolescence is one of the most stressful among these. The number and nature of simultaneous changes and challenges seriously tax the adolescent's coping strategies, especially in the earliest stages; ineffective coping may lead to problem behavior or psychopathology. The various problems linked to adolescence as a phase of life can be traced to the particular developmental processes engaged at this time. Therefore, a developmental approach to adolescence is the most promising for advancing our understanding of this period and for developing helpful interventions.

In early adolescence, every dimension of growth and every important social context in which he or she functions brings change, making it a critical transition. The physiological changes of puberty are dramatic; cognitive change is equally significant. With the changes in appearance and thinking ability, the youth's psychological development and social development are also altered. His or her social ecosystem changes. The more anonymous setting of junior high schools, the growth in and importance of peer groups, as well as the changes in perceptions and expectations of the broader society, are all significant transformations.

The biological changes of puberty take 4–5 years to complete, and occur about 2 years earlier for girls than boys. Cognitively, adolescents begin to think in more abstract terms—they learn to "think about thinking." Kohlberg's

(1969) model for moral reasoning, for instance, mostly emphasized psychological development in males, involving the shift from mutuality, adherence to rules and the social order to individual responsibility and the related responsibilities of the larger society. In contrast to this rule-oriented model, a model for moral reasoning that focuses more on interpersonal relationships typifies female development (Gilligan, 1982). Personal development similarly advances from a self-protective stage through a conformist stage and finally into a more self-aware stage (Josselson, 1979).

With these changes, adolescents alter the way in which they interact within their social environments. They typically increase involvement with peers, and with greater emphasis on intimacy, shared thoughts and feelings as a basis of friendship. Conformity to peer pressure peaks in early adolescence while anxiety about friendships increases in intensity during middle adolescence.

Other significant social context changes occur at the family level, which may change in both structure and function. In terms of structure, the most common changes are divorce and a mother who rejoins the workforce. Functional changes are driven by the maturation of the adolescent who begins to demand more autonomy and an altered relationship with his or her parents. To varying degrees, parents comply, but interactions can be painful and full of conflict, especially as the young person unpredictably vacillates between child-like and more adult-like. Families differ in the amount of responsibility and trust they give the adolescent, which has large impact on their development. The biological changes elicit different perceptions of the young adolescent from his or her social environment, altering the dynamics of interactions with their broader social context.[4]

As peer groups expand in size and complexity, peer relationships become both more important and more differentiated; by mid-adolescence, romantic involvements increase. The shift in early adolescence from a supportive, primary-school environment to junior high schools, with multiple classrooms and teachers, especially challenges the coping resources of adolescents. The new school structure affects peer group interactions. Age-grouping creates dominant older age groups that become the role models for the younger age groups, establishing the behavioral norms, including risky and deviant behavior, e.g., drug use and sexual behavior.

In addition, the adolescent is heavily targeted as a consumer, with intense media campaigns that can affect cognition (Linn, de Benedictis, & Delucchi, 1982) as well as body image (Faust, 1983). Of special concern is the heavy promotion of products that promote risky behaviors—the sort of behavior that is highly attractive to many young adolescents.[5]

The sum total of all of these changes sorely tests every adolescent's coping strategies and ability to deal constructively with these new pressures, especially from their peers and the media. Generally, and rather remarkably, most adolescents do well. For most, the challenges

generate new resources and opportunities for growth; these youth develop individual responsibility for their behaviors and ultimately emerge from this testing period as healthy adults. Constructive social support systems, especially in school and at home, provide greater help in their adaptations. But for those who are overwhelmed, whose coping strategies are ineffective and do not withstand these tests, this is the time when serious problems and psychopathology arise—at school, in the home, and in the neighborhood.

Drug use has become a particularly characteristic transitional behavior for adolescents. A recent study found that roughly two-thirds of adolescents in the United States have used an illicit drug by the time they graduate from high school (Johnston, O'Malley, & Bachman, 1985), though certain specific drugs have lost favor, e.g., marijuana. Alcohol usage remains high among adolescents—by the time they graduate, 93% of seniors will have tried alcohol and 30% report that most or all of their friends get drunk at least once a week (Johnston, 1985). The number of adolescents who state that they use alcohol for psychological coping purposes has also continued to increase steadily (Johnston et al., 1985).

Few individuals begin using these substances in adulthood if they have not already initiated these behaviors in adolescence. Furthermore, the younger the age of initiation in use of illicit drugs, the more likely the individual is to develop a serious substance abuse problem and other adjustment problems (Kandel, 1985). Individuals who follow this path leave the usual developmental trajectory and therefore miss important healthy developmental experiences, for which there is no going back (Baumrind & Moselle, 1985). Thus, the scientific, medical, and public health communities are challenged with great responsibility and opportunity.

Unlike substance abuse, a behavior considered unhealthy for any age group, adolescent sexuality receives significant attention when its timing is considered premature. In the 1970s, there was a significant increase in teenage pregnancy, with premarital sexual experience among urban white women ages 15–19 rising 75%, from 23% in 1971 to 42% in 1979. Since then, there has been a major national effort to decrease adolescent pregnancy—and with notable success—e.g., the National Campaign to Prevent Teen Pregnancy.

Young people who engage in one deviant behavior are more likely to engage in other such behaviors. Delinquency, premarital sexuality and adolescent pregnancy, smoking, heavy drinking, illicit drug use, and impaired driving tend to co-occur in the same individual. These behaviors are less likely to arise in individuals who are religious, demonstrate higher school performance, and enjoy family stability with intact, respectful relationships.

In terms of adolescent psychopathology, about half the psychiatric disorders found in adolescence are continuations of or even spurts in earlier manifestations first appearing in childhood. There is a marked increase in depression and in bipolar affective disorders; an increase in completed suicide rates; the appearance of anorexia nervosa and bulimia; a peaking of antisocial disorder and delinquency in mid- to late adolescence, which is accompanied by an increased use of violence; nascent schizophrenia; and changes in phobias. With respect to pregnancy, special risks are associated with very early, unplanned, and unwanted pregnancies.

Antisocial behavior in adults is almost always preceded by such behavior in childhood. The incidence of depression appears to increase over the course of adolescence, and those who experience this earlier in life are at greater risk for more prolonged problems (Kovacs, Feinberg, Crouse-Novak, Paulauskas, & Finkelstein, 1984). Indeed, recent evidence suggests that individuals often manifest more than one disorder (Craighead, 1985). Less mature children lack an extensive resource of coping responses that could help resolve distress (Kovacs & Paulauskas, 1984).

Attention must be paid to *subgroups* of adolescents to understand the processes of development at this time. Investigation of only one group may say little about another. This is consistent with the emphasis on investigating groups at risk for problems as well as those appearing to be protected or resilient, as per Garmezy (1985) and Rutter (1983).

Prior social circumstances and environments may serve to strengthen or limit the individual's development of coping capacity. Maladaptive coping is less likely to facilitate healthy maturation in subsequent phases of development. This comes with serious consequences: developmental lag, specific developmental damage, and psychosocial maladjustment (Baumrind & Moselle, 1985). Here, prospective advances in genetics, behavioral sciences, and improved modes of communication—technically and interpersonally—offer much promise.

We can identify and develop tools and programs that help those who struggle with the profound challenges of this critical developmental transition. Whether the adolescent is able to cope adaptively and enhance subsequent developmental outcomes or jeopardizes future developmental outcomes depends on previous maturation in the individual, as well as the resources available to them within their social environment. This developmental framing provides us with a sound basis for enhanced understanding of adolescents and a foundation for interventions in addressing emotional–interpersonal problems and psychopathology. Research in this developmental framework has fostered progress in understanding, treatment, and prevention; it offers promise for the future.

Social Change and the Problems of Youth (Hamburg, 1975)

Rapid sociotechnical change was clear in 1961 when we joined the Stanford faculty and pursued evolutionary interests, anticipating changes in the next few decades that would have both opportunities and dangers.

Throughout the 1960s, a dominant theme and major concern worldwide was the "youth rebellion." There was wide despair over the turbulence of the decade, marked both by militant groups engaged in violent confrontations over social issues, as well as by large populations of passive "drop-outs"—alienated youth, many of them drug abusers.

Over the course of human history, as reflected in the written record, society has always been perplexed if not frustrated by the excesses displayed by its adolescent youth. Did the "youth rebellion" of the sixties just manifest the modern expression of a traditionally challenging developmental period? Or, did it constitute a true "generation gap"—perhaps foreseeing larger groups in the next century?

It is implicit in the concept of cultural institutions that ideologies, values, traditions, and beliefs are transmitted across generations. Culture is a dynamic concept. In the 20th century, it was generally believed that advances in technology played the prevailing role in initiating social change and was responsible for the challenges to behavioral coping in the face of drastic transitions.

The parental generation of sixties youth was born in the 1920s. They began life with a foundation of strong pride in family and country, adopted from their parents, and developed a certain toughness in coping with the depression and war of their era. Their generation went on to experience unheralded economic and material growth and benefit. More schools, hospitals, and libraries were built then than in any other time in American history. A new culture of the automobile and airplane was established, changing America in profound ways.

Economic development led to increased urbanization and the rapid expansion of suburbs, with their oases of comfortable homes for the middle class. Acquisition of material wealth and confidence in America's productivity fueled the affluent society. Moreover, there was a revolution of rising expectations founded partly on the belief that pluralism and equal opportunity would allow everyone to benefit in this rising tide. This combination of values and technology deeply influenced how this generation raised their children; yet there was apprehension in subsequent decades about a decline of the middle class and widening inequality.

In part, the changes of the 1960s were disruptive. Families became smaller, abandoned rural roots and flocked to growing urban centers or surrounding suburban settings, *leaving behind the supportive social networks* and stability of small towns. The growth of suburban populations led to greater social isolation, as well as age, race, educational and socioeconomic homogeneity—a new kind of segregation. Gender-based roles became more sharply divergent for many families, with fathers spending long hours either at or commuting to work, and mothers who were left with more responsibility for parenting. Benjamin Spock, and his "bible" on child-centered rearing fostered more permissive parenting attitudes in these families; children were raised to be independent rather than blindly obedient.

Youth are typically socialized by their parents and other significant adults, yet their behaviors and even some of their value orientations also shape those of the adults. Younger people are more likely to experiment with new technology— a factor that became very important in the post-war era and ever since. In terms of personal values, many parents credited their children with changing their attitudes to the controversial war in Vietnam. The youth scene of the sixties reflected the growing economy and increased standards of living, greater numbers of high-school graduates and a new world made possible by television, telephones, jet travel, and the advent of the computer with its powerful implication for future change in most aspects of society.

Yet, these were also children who no longer interacted, as in former small-town lives, with diverse adults from different walks of life, nor did they participate extensively in the adult settings in which they were a part. They became age-segregated, increasingly cut off from the support of and meaningful interactions with diverse adult role models as had existed for prior generations. TV and peer groups filled the vacuum.

In families, one of the most critical structural changes brought on by these technological and societal shifts was the dramatic increase in paternal deprivation. For the affluent, fathers worked long hours to "get ahead"; for the poor, fathers worked long hours, and sometimes two jobs, just to keep up. The impact on boys of this generation was especially significant, leaving many young males to rely on peers for guidance.

Removed from traditional family and social networks, families looked to schools to take on additional responsibility in the socialization of their children, to provide adult male role models and to educate children about drugs and sex. Formal and informal organizations attempted to meet the growth in non-familial demand for child and health care, special education, social needs, and recreation. Families became just one source of social values for the child, who no longer perceived the parents as dominant.

In summary, America shifted from a predominantly rural nation to one that was urban, industrialized, and continuing to change at a rapid pace with technological innovations that were leading to a post-industrial society. The effects of shrinking family size, isolation, and decline of parental authority had a pervasive bipolar distribution, i.e., in the upper and upper middle classes, on the one hand, and in the lowest socioeconomic groups, on the other.

The "baby boom" of the fifties brought a huge increase in the youth population. This surge of youth led to massive demands for public services, put huge pressure on the entire education system and provided business with a growing consumer market. Much attention has been paid to the rise in college enrollment in the sixties; little attention has been given to the even larger number of working youth: By 1970, this was nearly half again as large as the population enrolled in college.

Universities, however, were seen as providing the key to success in the new technological economy and a society based more on meritocracy than class; there was a surge in enrollment for which, despite plenty of advance warning, colleges and universities in the United States were ill-prepared. This created a tension on campuses for scarce resources—housing, class space—that may have primed the unrest that followed.

A hallmark of the sixties was the widespread outbreaks of student protests. The civil rights movement of the fifties was the paradigm for these protests. Students had learned about their political power and how to use moral issues as a means to attack "the establishment" as a whole. And they learned that a small minority can effectively shut down an idealistic institution, which is unlikely to use force to protect itself. The Vietnam War was the polarizing issue between youth and government in the sixties. Militant students dominated the scene.

These protests, however, were largely led by students from the elite schools, with their traditions of freedom with faculty support and guidance. Born in an era of affluence and the welfare state, protests were fueled by student expectations of equal rights and opportunity for all. The more militant students demanded changes that aligned with these values; passive students supported these goals even if they did not support their tactics. The University of California at Berkeley and the University of Wisconsin were the first sites of major student confrontations. At Berkeley, in 1963, sit-ins demanded equal employment rights for Negroes, leading to the formation of the Free Speech Movement. TV coverage was prominent and, along with modern mobility, contributed to the spread of protest movements from elite to other schools.

The contemporary context was primed for explosive results. Liberal colleges had worked hard to increase diversity in gender and race—the student bodies were more widely representative than ever before. The paradox of the time made the highly democratic institutions the targets of the greatest dissatisfaction and violence.

Nonetheless, in examining the key variables of social influences on behavior—cultural institutions, parental values and context, and the contemporary scene, the values of the students of the sixties do not fully represent a "generation gap." We can, however, identify a distinct gap between White and Black students. The Black student protest movement, also rooted in the civil rights movement, was reinforced by the failure of the White student movement to advance Black causes. Disillusioned Black students, who were the ones, after all, most affected and limited by racism were driven to organize their own protests.

The Black student population doubled in the sixties, due to vigorous policies in many schools of preferential admissions and generous scholarship aid. Some of these students were empowered, wanting to align themselves with the deprivations of those they left behind, demanding "Black power" and fueling the push for Black Studies programs, Black dormitories, and Black faculty and administrators. More militant protests against a racist society were quite violent—led by groups such as the

SNCC and Black Panthers. But many protesters adopted more constructive, goal-oriented tactics, promoting their vision for a just America, and achieving fairness through non-violent protest in the tradition of Mahatma Ghandi and Martin Luther King Jr.

There was little discussion of blue-collar youth—yet working-class youth were the majority of young people. Within this population, there were distinctive subgroups, each with its own values. Most Black college students were blue collar, but were more "conformist," reflecting the basic values of their families—they were not among the militant protesters, though most supported the goals of correcting racism and injustice in American society.

The one intergenerational difference in support for social change that has been documented is with respect to the role of women. The traditional view of women as homemakers and mothers give way to growing acceptance of women in the workplace, with wider options for work roles. Coupled with this was increased acceptance of the working mother—with younger generations more willing to accept that children would not be harmed with this shift.

No discussion of this era is complete without highlighting the liberation of women brought about by the birth control pill, and other means of controlling pregnancy. Pregnancy would increasingly be by choice—have more planned and wanted. Freedom in reproductive choice led to multiple freedoms in work and life choices for women nationwide.

Overall, this also helped launch a general acceptance of the principle of a range of choices in life style. This was buttressed, importantly, by the diversity promoted on television, a significant development for contemporary youth. TV diluted the influence of parents on growth, and contributed to cross-cultural transmission of values, beliefs, and attitudes.

Our research suggested that the "generation gap" idea was exaggerated. The families of America—no matter their socio-economic status—tended to transmit basic value patterns to their children, Children used parents as their comparative reference group in value orientation, while they look to peers as their normative reference group, which is emulated and supplies norms for overt behavioral styles. There is an integration here that most adolescents achieve.

Response to social change was more closely related to membership in a particular cultural subgroup than to age or generational lines and that within each group, there was continuity of values through the generations. The response to social change was a function of a subculturally determined readiness to adapt, but the family remained the core in guiding youth values. Thus, ingenuity in youth development existed side-by-side with continuing of basic values—i.e., variations on a theme. We could foresee further changes growing out of extraordinary technological and social changes.

Conclusion: Decades of Perspective on Adolescent Development

Our world transformation, much of it driven by expanded technological capabilities, provides an essential context for viewing adolescent development. Adolescence is now, in some very important ways, different than it was in our evolutionary past. Economic, scientific, technological, and social changes have had huge impacts on communities and on families. A new way of life has emerged in a few generations. These changes have had powerful effects on the experience of growing up. Today's children are in a very different situation than their parents or grandparents—in some ways better, in some ways worse. We need to clarify what is better and what is worse—and how to shift the balance from worse toward better.

Over the course of my career, in working with esteemed colleagues, we have tried to develop insights and innovations about adolescent development that draw upon basic research and clinical experience to improve their prospects. We felt that new information and ideas emerging in the field, not just from our own work, should be tested for further improvements and institutional innovations that could enlarge the scope of valuable initiatives. Let me summarize the arc of our work, in sequence.

In the early 1960s, as we broadened our experience with research literature and direct contact with many adolescents, we decided that adolescence should be more clearly recognized as a distinct phase of the life cycle, one involving considerable stress, the need for new coping strategies, and significant transformation. We became aware of the degree of human suffering in this phase of development and sought ways to relieve it. Likewise, we saw multiple constraints for future prospects of many adolescents, and sought ways to enhance their opportunities.

I gave a singular focus to early adolescence, roughly ages 10–14, marked by the onset of puberty and the frequent turbulence of the ensuing few years. Prior attention in psychology, psychiatry, psychoanalysis, and pediatrics largely focused on late adolescence in males and had blurred distinctions regarding the early, middle, and late phases of adolescence. This was a powerful stimulus to initiating studies of these phases as well as clinical observations. With my colleagues, I sought specific interventions to facilitate healthy adolescent development appropriate to each phase.

Most remarkable was the creation of peer counseling—with preparation, adult supervision, and thoughtful reflection by counselors and counselees alike. Success of this innovation spread to a variety of peer-mediated interventions: peer tutors, peer mentors, and peer conflict mediators. I have been delighted to see our original research and interventions with peer counseling adopted so widely and adapted to so many situations over the years.

At Stanford University, while heading Child Psychiatry, I helped create an interdisciplinary base for education in a field that had been narrow, rigid, and doctrinaire. This program undertook to integrate adolescent psychology with developmental psychology and anthropology in the context of child psychiatry involving clinical and social responsibilities. The interplay of these disciplines strengthened the knowledge base at a fundamental level and in due course improved diagnostic assessment and therapeutic intervention. In this context, we brought data and insights from these disciplines into child psychiatry and pediatric training at an earlier stage and more extensively than had been the educational pattern up to that time.

In the 1970s, President Carter appointed me as Director of Studies for the President's Commission on Mental Health. These studies influenced the field in many ways, e.g., the work on social supports as a systematic set of interventions useful in many settings, not only for adolescents but children and for adults.

Over the years, we have tried to stimulate interest in child and adolescent health policy through various institutions, especially Harvard University and the Institute of Medicine, National Academy of Sciences, where I served on various boards and IOM studies.

In the 1980s, I participated actively in the decade-long work of the Carnegie Council on Adolescent Development. One outcome was a thorough study of life skills training as a valuable array of interventions for adolescent development, building on the earlier work with President Carter's commission.

After serving for many years on the board of the WT Grant Foundation, I served 6 years as president. At the foundation, I expanded efforts in behavioral pediatrics, especially through programs such as the WT Grant Scholars Program.

Starting in these years, and continuing in the 1980s and 90s we undertook to clarify violence in American schools, and then preventing hatred and violence in childhood and adolescence altogether. Institutional innovations during these years were helpful in fostering this work, first as Chief of Child Psychiatry and Pediatric Liaison at Mount Sinai in New York and then as DeWitt Wallace Distinguished Scholar at Cornell Medical College. The interdisciplinary and even international cooperation greatly facilitated these efforts, including work on adolescent problems under the auspices of the Jacobs Foundation of Switzerland.

Throughout the profoundly stimulating research, clinical experience, and policy analysis of these years—and the facilitation of excellent institutions—my particular focus returned to the critical phase of early adolescence in its difficult, changing context.

The lengthening period of adolescence complicates the transition. In the past two centuries, control of infection and better nutrition in technologically advanced cultures have lowered the average age at which menstruation begins. At the same time, the social changes occurring during those centuries have postponed the end of adolescence and of dependence until later.

Although the human organism is reproductively mature in early adolescence, the brain does not reach a fully adult state of development until the end of the teen years, and social maturity lags well behind. Young adolescents make many fateful decisions that affect their entire life course, even though they are usually immature in knowledge, social experience, and cognitive development.

In early adolescence now, there is probably more ambiguity and complexity about what constitutes preparation for effective adulthood than was ever the case before. The version of adult life seen in the multiplicity of media creates a mix of reality and fantasy about adult life. This is complicated by the erosion of family and social support networks. Throughout most of human history, small societies provided durable networks, familiar human relationships, and cultural guidance for young people, offering support in times of stress and the skills necessary for coping and adaptation. In contemporary societies, such social networks have become more ambiguous or impersonal, often unreliable. There is easy access by adolescents to potentially life-threatening substances, weapons, and activities. Although these often appear to young people to be casual, recreational, and tension-relieving, their effects can endanger themselves and others.

Yet there are enduring human needs that enter into adolescent development. They must find a place in a valued group that provides a sense of belonging; identify tasks that are generally recognized by the group as having adaptive value and thereby earn respect when skill is acquired for coping with essential tasks; earn a sense of worth as a person; establish reliable, caring relationships with a few other people; find constructive expression of the curiosity and exploration that strongly characterize adolescence; find a basis for making informed, deliberate decisions, particularly those that have lifelong consequences; accept respectfully the enormous diversity of modern society, the individual differences among adolescents in size, shape, color, and rates of body and behavior change; and find ways of being useful to others.

Preventive approaches, including health education, life skills training, and the creation of social networks, can provide the foundation for promoting successful outcomes for almost all adolescents. In this way, the adverse impact of multiple risk factors concentrated in lower socioeconomic groups can be offset, and the likelihood of successful outcomes for mainstream youth can be enhanced. It is feasible to target health education and life skills training efforts at young adolescents in middle or junior high school. Early adolescence presents a major preventive opportunity because it is the time when attitudes, values, and behaviors are adopted that will characterize the health-related behaviors most crucial to adult health status and longevity.

The knowledge base for health education and life skills training has advanced considerably in recent decades. This can be translated into programs of health education and life skills of proven value to young adolescents. My work, along with that of my many peers and colleagues, has helped to clarify a substantial set of experiences, opportunities, and services that can make a large difference for the better in the lives of today's youth.

We have had to make judicious use of existing evidence while pressing for a stronger base of scientific evidence in the future. The low priority in science policy for research on adolescent development has been a costly mistake.

But the scope of the opportunities inherent in adolescent development, and advances in life sciences broadly conceived, give us a basis to reach higher in our aspirations. The central question is whether we can do better than we are doing now, and the answer is almost certainly yes. Looking back over the range of evidence and experience in our work, there are strong reasons to believe that we can provide better conditions in which adolescents can grow up healthy and vigorous, inquiring and problem solving, decent and constructive.

The Carnegie Council on Adolescent Development, on which I served for 10 years, emphasized:

> Wise investment in human and social capital is the most fundamental and productive investment any society can make. The vitality of any society and the prospects for its future depend in the long run on the quality of its people, on their knowledge, skill, and opportunities, as well as on the decency of their human and social relations.

It is in this spirit that our work has been conducted and our relations with adolescents have flourished.

Looking at our list of contributors to the volume, many are colleagues who have found my work stimulating and useful in their own work to which I am very grateful. They have built the field, given me strong encouragement, and I am deeply appreciative for their contributions in so many ways.

Thus, many scientists, scholars, clinicians, and educators have brought about the emergence of adolescent psychology in a way that is intellectually crucial and also provides relief of human suffering. So many good people have reached out to cooperate on research initiatives, grants, and meetings to make possible mutual aid in advancing the prospects of this field.

These are indeed topics of long-term significance: the importance of contextual factors within and across countries in the study of pubertal links with behavior; the long-term consequences of early puberty for mental health; pubertal influences as contingent on the peer group; teenage parenthood; peer counseling and mentoring programs; family conflict during early adolescence and paths to resolution; transitions into junior or middle school as a function of pubertal timing and social context—and more to come.

I worked with a remarkable group of people for 10 years in the Carnegie Council on Adolescent Development. We agreed on basic paths to meeting the essential requirements for healthy adolescent development. We concluded that all adolescents have enduring human needs that must be met if they are to grow up to be healthy, constructive adults: find a valued place in a constructive group; learn how to form close; durable relationships; feel a sense of worth as a person; achieve a reliable basis for making informed choices; know how to use the support systems available to them; express constructive curiosity and exploratory behavior; find ways of being useful to others; believe in a promising future with

real opportunities; master social skills; including the ability to manage conflict peacefully; cultivate the inquiring and problem-solving habits of mind for lifelong learning; acquire the technical and analytic capabilities to participate in a world-class economy; become ethical persons; learn the requirements of responsible citizenship; respect diversity in our pluralistic society (Carnegie Council on Adolescent Development, 1995).

Early adolescence—the phase during which young people are just beginning to engage in very risky behaviors, but before damaging patterns have become firmly established—offers an excellent opportunity for intervention to prevent later casualties and promote successful adult lives. This spirit of the shared formulation was fostered by my professional network in every way we could.

Notes

1. This chapter was written with the help of Carrie Hunter.
2. The average age of late adolescence has also dropped, now ranging from 15 to 19.
3. Readers will note that newer developments in the prevention of violence in schools still draw heavily from this body of work, despite the fact that it was developed in the 1990s.
4. Marked changes in bodily appearance—height, weight, sexual characteristics, and skin issues—alter social responses to the young person, especially among peers, parents, teachers, and other significant adults with whom they relate (Hamburg, 1974).
5. For instance, there is significant advertising specifically aimed at young teens that promotes a wide range of tobacco products, whether cigarettes, snuff, or chewing tobacco; others promote fruit-flavored alcoholic drinks.

References

Adams, J. F. (1964). Adolescent personal problems as a function of age and sex. *Journal of Genetic Psychology, 104*: 207–214.

Ahmed, P. (Ed.) (1981). *Living and dying with cancer.* New York: Elsevier.

Allport, G. W. (1954). *Nature of prejudice.* Cambridge, MA: Addison Wesley.

Allport, G. W., & Kramer, B. M. (1946). Some roots of prejudice. *Journal of Psychology, 22*: 9–39.

Amir, Y. (1969). Contact hypothesis in ethnic relations. *Psychological Bulletin, 71*(5), 319–342.

Bandura, A. (Ed.). (1995). *Self-efficacy in changing societies.* New York: Cambridge University Press.

Baumrind, D., & Moselle, K. A. (1985). A developmental perspective on adolescent drug abuse. *Advances in Alcohol and Substance Abuse, 4*(3/4): 41–67.

Berkman, L. F., & Syme, S. L. (1979). Social networks, host resistance, and mortality: a nine-year follow-up study of Alameda County residents. *American Journal of Epidemiology, 109*: 186–204.

Botvin, G. J., & Eng. A. (1982). The efficacy of a multi-component approach to the prevention of cigarette smoking. *Preventive Medicine, 11*: 199–211.

Carnegie Council on Adolescent Development (1995). *Great transitions: Preparing adolescents for a new century.* Concluding Report. Available at: http://carnegie.org/fileadmin/Media/Publications/PDF/GREAT%20TRANSITIONS.pdf

Cassel, J. (1976). The contribution of social environment to host resistance. The Fourth Wade Hampton Frost Lecture. *American Journal of Epidemiology, 104*: 107–22.

Cochran, M. M., & Brassard, J. A. (1979). Child development and personal social networks. *Child Development, 50:* 601–616.

Cohen, F., & Lazarus, R. S. (1979). Coping with the stresses of illness. In J. C. Stone, F. Cohen, and N. E. Adler (Eds.), *Health psychology—a handbook: Theories, applications and challenges of a psychological approach to the health care system* (pp. 217–254). San Francisco: Jossey Bass.

Connell, D. B., & Turner, R. R. (1985). The impact of instructional experience and the effects of cumulative instruction. *Journal of School Health, 55:* 324–331.

Connell, D. B., Turner, R. R., & Mason, E. F. (1985). Summary of findings of the school health education evaluation: Implementation and costs. *Journal of School Health, 55:* 316–321.

Craighead, W. E. (1985). *Adolescent depression and suicide.* Invited address presented at the meeting of the American Psychological Association, Los Angeles, CA.

Dean, A., & Lin, N. (1977). The stress-buffering role of social support. Problems and prospects for systematic investigation. *Journal of Nervous and Mental Disease, 165:* 403–417.

DiMatteo, M. R., Prince, L. M., & Taranta, A. (1979). Patient's perceptions of physicians' behavior: Determinants of patient commitment to the therapeutic relationship. *Journal of Community Health,* 4: 280–290.

Engel, G. L. (1981). The clinical application of the biopsychosocial model. *Journal of Medicine and Philosophy, 6:* 101–125.

Faust, M. S. (1983). Alternative constructions of adolescent growth. In J. Brooks-Gunn & A. A. Petersen (Eds.), *Girls at puberty: Biological and psychosocial perspectives* (pp. 105–125). New York: Plenum Press.

Garmezy, N. (1985). Stress-resistant children: The search for protective factors. In J. E. Stevenson (Ed.), *Recent research in developmental psychopathology* (pp. 213–233). *Journal of Child Psychology and Psychiatry*, Book Supplement No. 4. Oxford: Pergamon Press.

Gilligan, C. (1982). *In a different voice: Psychological theory and women's development.* Cambridge, MA: Harvard University Press.

Goodman, G. (1969). Companionship as therapy: the use of nonprofessional talent. In J. Hart & T. Tomlinson (Eds.), *New directions in client-centered psychotherapy,* Boston: Houghton-Mifflin.

Gore, S. (1978). The effects of social support in moderating consequences of unemployment. *Journal of Health and Social Behavior, 19:* 157–165.

Gottlieb, B. H. (1981). Social networks and social support. In B. H. Gottlieb (Ed.), *Sage studies in community mental health,* Vol. 4. Beverly Hills, CA: Sage Publications.

Hamburg, B. A. (1974). Coping in early adolescence, the special challenges of the junior high school period. In *American handbook of psychiatry*, Vol. 2 (pp. 385–397). New York: Basic Books.

Hamburg, B. A. (1975). Social change and the problems of youth. In D. A. Hamburg and H. K. Brodie (Eds.), *The American handbook of psychiatry,* Vol VI. New York: Basic Books.

Hamburg, B. A. (1990). *Life skills training: Preventive interventions for young adolescents* (working paper). Washington, DC: Carnegie Council on Adolescent Development.

Hamburg, B. A. (1997). Education for healthy futures: Health promotion and life skills training. In R. Takanishi and D. A. Hamburg (Eds.), *Preparing adolescents for the 21st century* (pp. 108–135). New York: Cambridge University Press.

Hamburg, B. A., Elliott, D. S., & Williams, K. R. (Eds.) (1998). *Violence in American schools: A new perspective.* Cambridge: Cambridge University Press.

Hamburg, B. A., & Killilea, M. (1979). Relation of social support, stress, illness, and use of health services. In *Selected readings in disease prevention: Report to the surgeon general on health promotion and disease prevention*, Part II. Washington, DC: National Academy of Sciences, Institute of Medicine.

Hamburg, B. A., Lipsett, L. F., Inoff, G. E., & Drash, A. L. (Eds.) (1980). *Behavioral and psychosocial issues in diabetes: Proceedings of the national conference.* DHHS Pub. No. (NIH) 80–1993.

Hamburg, B. A., & Varenhorst, B. B. (1972). Peer counseling in the secondary schools: A community mental health project for youth. *American Journal of Orthopsychiatry, 42*(4): 566–581.

Hamburg, D. A., & Hamburg, B. A. (2004). *Learning to live together: Preventing hatred and violence in child and adolescent development.* Oxford: Oxford University Press.

Janis, I., & Mann, L. (1977). *Decision making: A psychological analysis of conflict, choice and commitment.* New York: Free Press.

Johnston, L. D. (1985). *Some behavioral transitions in adolescence.* Invited presentation at a workshop on Adolescence and Adolescent Development, sponsored by the Committee on Child development Research and Public Policy, National Academy of Sciences, Woods Hole, MA.

Johnston. L. D., O'Malley, P. M., & Bachman, J. G. (1985). *Use of licit and illicit drugs by America's high school students 1975–1984.* DHHS Publication No. ADM 85–1394. Washington DC: National Institute on Drug Abuse.

Jones, M. C. (1963). Self-conceptions, motivations and interpersonal attitudes of early- and late-maturing girls. In R. E. Grinder (Ed.), *Studies in adolescence* (pp. 454–465). New York: Macmillan.

Josselson, R. (1980). Ego development in adolescence. In J. Adelson (Ed.), *Handbook of adolescent psychology* (pp.188–210). New York: Wiley.

Kandel, D. B. (1985). Effects of drug use from adolescence to young adulthood on participation in family and work roles. In R. Jessor (Chair), *Longitudinal research on substance use in adolescence.* Symposium conducted at the meeting of the International Society for the Study of Behavioral Development, Tours, France.

Kohlberg, L. (1969). Stage and sequence: The cognitive-developmental approach to socialization. In D. A. Goslin (Ed.), *Handbook of socialization theory and research* (pp. 347–480). Chicago: Rand McNally.

Kovacs, M., Feinberg, T. L., Crouse-Novak, M. A., Paulauskas, S. L., & Finkelstein, R. (1984). Depressive disorders of childhood: I. A longitudinal prospective study of characteristics and recovery. *Archives of General Psychiatry, 41:* 229–237.

Kovacs, M., & Paulauskas, S. L. (1984). Developmental stage and the expression of depressive disorders in children: An empirical analysis. In D. Cicchetti and K. Schneider-Rosen (Eds.), *Childhood depression* (pp 59–80). New Directions for Child Development, No. 26, San Francisco: Jossey-Bass.

Linn, M. C., de Benedictis, T., & Delucchi, K. (1982). Adolescent reasoning about advertisements. *Child Development, 53:* 1599–1613.

Lippitt, P., & Eiseman, J. (1969). *Cross-age helping program.* Ann Arbor: University of Michigan, Center for Research in Utilization of Scientific Knowledge.

Mattson, J. (1970). Peer counseling. *CAPS Capsule, 3:* 1–9. Ann Arbor: University of Michigan, Counseling and Information Center.

Mitchell, E., & Trickett, E. J. (1980). Task force report: social networks as mediators of social support. An analysis of the effects and determinants of social networks. *Community Mental Health Journal, 16:* 27–44.

Moos, R. H. (Ed.) (1977). *Coping with physical illness.* New York: Plenum Medical Book Co.

Mussen, P. H., & Jones, M. C. (1957). Self conceptions, motivations and interpersonal attitudes of late- and early-maturing boys. *Child Development, 28:* 243–256.

Parad, H. J. (Ed.) (1965). *Crisis intervention: Selected readings.* New York: Family Service Association of America.

Parad, H. J., & Caplan, G. (1965). A framework for studying families in crisis. In H. J. Parad (Ed.), *Crisis intervention: Selected readings* (pp. 53–72). New York: Family Service Association of America.

Pentz, M. A., Dwyer, J. H., MacKinnon, D. P., Flay, B. R., Hansen, W. B., Wang, E. Y. I., et al. (1989). A multi-community trial for primary prevention of adolescent drug use: Effects on drug use prevalence. *Journal of the American Medical Association, 261:* 3259–3266.

Petersen, A. C., & Hamburg, B. A. (1986). Adolescence: A developmental approach to problems and psychopathology. In *Behavior Therapy, 17:* 480–499.

Redmore, C. D., & Loevinger, J. (1979). Ego development in adolescence: Longitudinal studies. *Journal of Youth and Adolescence, 8:* 1–20.

Rioch, M., Elkes, C., Flint, A. A., Sweet Usdansky, B., Newman, R. G., & Silber, E. (1963). NIMH pilot study in training mental health counselors. *American Journal of Othropsychiatry, 33*: 678–689.

Rutter, M. (1983). Stress, coping and development: Some Issues and some questions. In N. Garmezy and M. Rutter (Eds.), *Stress, coping and development* (pp. 1–42). New York: McGraw-Hill.

Schowalter, J. E. (1977). Psychological reactions to physical illness and hospitalization in adolescence: A survey. *Journal of the American Academy of Child Psychiatry, 16*: 500–516.

Starfield, B. (1976). Measurement of outcome: A proposed scheme. In G. D. Grave and I. B. Pless (Eds.), *Chronic childhood illness: Assessment of outcome.* Fogarty International Center Series on the Teaching of Preventative Medicine, Vol. 3 (pp. 53–57). DHEW Pub. No. (NIH) 76–877.

Van Slyck, M., Stern, M., & Zak-Place, J. (1996). Promoting optimal adolescent development through conflict resolution education, training, and practice: An innovative approach for counseling psychologists. *Counseling Psychologist, 24*: 433–461.

20

Decisions and Directions

Making a Path Through Life

STEPHEN F. HAMILTON

Deciding what to do after college graduation was the third really hard decision in my young life. I majored in history at Swarthmore. Like many of my classmates, I often thought I would become a professor. But, while I envisioned myself as a good teacher, I had so many brilliant classmates that I feared, in comparison, I could be no more than an O.K. historian. I thought I could get some satisfaction from doing archival research but perhaps not enough to make it as big a part of my life as it would have to be in that profession.

Taking required courses taught me that I have to care about what I study to do really well at it. Reflecting on what fully engaged my interest and energy, I thought of two extra-curricular activities. In freshman year I had joined a group convened by students who wanted the college to create a summer program for disadvantaged secondary school students. With some private contributions and college approval, the program got underway. I did not apply to be a counselor because the pay was too little to make much of a dent in my college expenses. The pay improved the following year when the program was funded by Upward Bound, one of the new Great Society programs. I helped to write the proposal and then spent the next three summers with Upward Bound, directing the play the students performed for parents and friends at the end of the summer, and becoming head counselor. Senior year I directed the school-year program that we designed to provide tutoring and other support to participants.

The other activity was working with my friend, Lowell Livezey, to create a community organization in Chester, Pennsylvania, where most of our Upward Bound students lived. Chester is a declining industrial city on the Delaware River. Lowell was a social entrepreneur before the term was invented. He came up with the idea of bringing volunteers from the surrounding Philadelphia suburbs

for weekends of painting and fixing low-income housing in collaboration with Chester residents. He hoped the organization, the Chester Home Improvement Project, would become a force for solving community problems and that the work weekends and evening seminars would give people from outside the community a better understanding of poverty and discrimination. I walked, biked, and bussed around Chester asking local merchants for contributions, took my turn with hammer and paintbrush, and was principal author of the proposal that brought in federal money to establish a Community Action Program and to hire a local activist as director.

As an alternative to becoming a history professor, I considered career possibilities related to these activities. A speech on campus by Constantinos Doxiadis inspired me to consider city planning, and I read Lewis Mumford (1961) and some others. But education began to seem the best channel for me. As an educator I could remain grounded in the world of learning while also actively engaging with the issues that mattered to me. I could take on poverty and discrimination and still be around people who were intrigued by the question of why England never had a violent revolution and shared my love of Shakespeare.

Improving education is an essential component of the quest for equality of opportunity, though not sufficient by itself. In places like Swarthmore, more confrontational approaches were in favor at that time. Several of my classmates were among those arrested for participating in demonstrations in Chester. We debated whether it was more important to volunteer in the voting rights campaign in the South or to confront de facto segregation in Northern cities. What role did White people have in either of those struggles? Martin Luther King's call to link civil rights for Blacks to an inclusive anti-poverty movement was part of the answer to that question and a stirring challenge to the implicit assumption that eliminating racial discrimination would also reduce poverty. An extended campus visit by Gunnar Myrdal (1962) introduced me for the first time to the use of social science to aid understanding of these issues and guide action on them. (Swarthmore, as conservative about its curriculum as it is progressive in other ways, only added sociology to its course offerings in 1965.)

Early Years

The first hard decision I ever had to make was giving up basketball my junior year in high school so I could remain on the debate team. After a lot of inner turmoil I reasoned that I could be a debater and also play football and be on the track team, but if I played basketball I would have nothing like debate. It was the right decision. I missed playing on the state championship basketball team, but the football team also won the state championship that year. If I had given up debate my academic preparation would have been much weaker; debate taught me to do library research, construct an argument based on evidence, and speak persuasively.

The next hard decision was declining acceptance at Swarthmore because I thought their scholarship offer was too low. My mother, who became a teacher after my father died, had already supported my sister Jean through college and Joyce was graduating in the spring. Lyla was 2 years behind me. (Our oldest sister, Hazel Ann, married early and did not go to college.) To my great joy and good fortune, Swarthmore increased their offer and I matriculated. I became enamored with Swarthmore after Joyce, who later became a guidance counselor, gave me a list of Northeastern colleges and urged me to request their admissions information. Swarthmore looked like a place that valued a wide range of interests and activities, as I did. It was also a small co-educational institution, which I had decided I wanted after figuring out that I valued having girls as friends, and did not want to meet girls only at mixers. (I only learned that term later but had the idea.) Also, at the end of football season senior year I realized I didn't want to stop playing. I was not big or fast enough for a major team but thought I could play in what is now Division III. Swarthmore seemed like it would be an intellectually stimulating place that encouraged social engagement where I could also play football. It was.

My concern for social causes came from my parents. My mother told me once that she and my father planned to become missionaries to Burma after retiring. They came of age during the Great Depression and were staunch Roosevelt Democrats. They met at Colorado A&M (now Colorado State University). My mother grew up on a ranch in the Middle Park region of Colorado. My father came from the high plains of Northeastern Colorado. He became an agricultural engineer, specializing in irrigation and in soil and water conservation. He also became a lay minister in the Northern (now American) Baptist church. I have notes from a sermon in which he quoted Liberty Hyde Bailey (1919), founding dean of Cornell's College of Agriculture and now a patron saint of the ecology

movement. His work during the early years of my life had us living on cattle ranches in New Mexico, South Dakota, and Western Nebraska. The last move was one too many for my mother so he took a new job with the U.S. Department of Agriculture in Lincoln, Nebraska, where I went through the public schools. Had he died while working for a ranch owner rather than the federal government, my life would have been very different.

I never thought about it that way, but my decision to go into education could be seen as following in my mother's footsteps. Before my father was diagnosed with cancer she had decided to take courses to qualify as a teacher. She was slowed down when he became an invalid for 2 years and she worked as a secretary after his death. But she continued taking courses while teaching and caring for her family and 12 years later, before my senior year in college, she finished her Ed.D. and became a professor of education.

Becoming a Teacher

I entered the field of education by earning a master of arts in teaching (MAT) at Harvard. When my term paper for Dean Ted Sizer's history of education course grew too ambitious, he encouraged me to finish it the next semester as an independent study project. His course introduced me to John Dewey (1916), a philosopher who had actually run a school and who wrote about teaching and learning in relation to broad social issues in novel and insightful ways, if not always with great clarity. I wanted to be the kind of teacher Dewey envisioned in the kind of school he advocated and helped to create.

I confronted a fourth hard decision that year: what to do about the draft. I had been classified draft eligible with a 1-year deferment to continue my education. I tried to put together a convincing application for conscientious objector status, but found myself unable to claim that I was opposed to all wars or that my rather uncertain religion was the grounds for resistance. It was my country's policies and actions in Southeast Asia that I objected to. Refusing induction seemed likely to render me unsuitable for my chosen profession. Having grown up during the McCarthy Era, I assumed a prison sentence would exclude me from teaching. Canada beckoned but I could not imagine renouncing my citizenship. I wanted the United States to live up to its ideals, not to leave.

Sympathetic faculty helped me finish my 2-year program in a year and a summer, certifying me so that I could receive an occupational deferment if I worked in a district with a teacher shortage, which was not a great hardship because I wanted to teach in an urban district. My only regret was not having enough time learning to teach in a good school before trying my hand in a tougher place. Brookline, where I did my practice teaching, was such a school, but nothing, not even 3 years with Upward Bound, prepared me for Phelps Vocational High School for boys in Northeast Washington, DC. Students' reading levels clustered around fifth grade, which made high-school textbooks all but useless. My class roster might list 45 students, but I would seldom see more than 15 at a time. Of those, perhaps half came with some regularity. The others floated in and out, most disappearing by the end of the semester. Assigning homework was pointless.

Eventually I learned how to tell my students what to do so they knew I meant it. I was able to order textbooks with lower reading levels and to borrow a collection of supplementary books from the public library. I was given a classroom of my own and the bolted-down desks were replaced with desks I could rearrange. A summer program for teachers on Black history and literature at Howard University partly helped to compensate for the absence of that material in my education to that time. I returned the next summer as a teaching assistant. By my third year I was able to have my students engage in independent study activities, something I had not been able to manage before. But I also realized that even if I became the teacher I wanted to be I still would not make the impact I wanted to make. The D.C. schools were organized, I concluded, to keep teachers and other staff employed. Students' learning was far down the implicit priority list. I fantasized that students would be better off if all the schools closed and the money was disbursed to any groups that could put a plausible educational program together. After a few years it would be possible to identify the new schools that were working and to expand them. Others have since had a similar idea, but they acted on it by opening charter and other alternative schools. After aging out of the draft, I went back to Harvard, hoping to learn how to make changes that would matter.

The fifth big decision in my life was not hard at all. I married Mary Agnes Holzgrefe 10 months after our first meeting. She was teaching French and German in a Montgomery County, MD, middle school. Like me she had been inspired by accounts of British open classrooms (Featherstone, 1971), but she had worked out how to use those ideas and successfully taught both languages simultaneously to classes of 40 or more in which students worked individually or in small groups at activity centers. Although the district foreign language supervisor, after observing this beehive, told her she would return another day "when you are teaching," her excellence and creativity were recognized by an appointment to a committee led by the district's assistant superintendent for innovative practices, a title I coveted.

Becoming a Researcher

I applied to the Harvard Graduate School of Education's Ed.D. program in social studies, hoping to return to work with Stan Bolster and Don Oliver. After sending in my application I received a letter saying the program was ending and a new program, called Learning Environments, was taking its place. A description of the new program was attached with an invitation either to withdraw my application or to re-write my statement. I replied that I thought the statement I had already submitted was appropriate to the new program, which proposed to address learning not only in schools but in community settings as well. They agreed.

My first year of doctoral study introduced me to social science research. I was fascinated by Campbell and Stanley's *Experimental and Quasi-experimental Designs for Research* (1963). It was and remains a lucid explanation of how to generate evidence to answer your questions. In history this is cheating: You have to be satisfied with the evidence that has survived. The prospect of using research to illuminate some of the problems I cared about was exciting.

My fellowship through a U.S. Office of Education program called Training Teacher Trainers led me to work under the wise guidance of Peter Lenrow in the Cambridge Pilot School, an alternative school-within-a-school in the Cambridge public school system. With his encouragement, I became an observer at weekly staff meetings. I took copious notes and tried to understand the dynamics of the meetings and of the school.

I wanted to know how to improve existing schools and create new ones. A course with Chris Argyris introduced me to organizational behavior and development. Much of what I read was about failed attempts to implement change. Seymour Sarason's (1971, 1972) work was especially powerful, and I took a course from one of his students, Ira Goldenberg. Herbert Kelman's (1974) course on individual and social change gave me a firmer understanding of some useful principles and research and introduced me to social psychology. Reading about role theory, especially role conflict and ambiguity (Kahn, Wolfe, Quinn, Snoek, & Rosenthal, 1964), gave me the handle I needed. The concept of role links individuals with organizations. If organizations are to change or to function differently, then the roles of people in those organizations have to change.

My thesis was about Pilot School staff members' definitions of their roles (Hamilton, 1975). I called one set of staff members "role innovators" because they developed new and different roles not found in conventional schools. My friend, Rob Riordan, was known as "the school philosopher." In addition to being a highly respected teacher, he carried the flame of the school's founding ideals, not only reminding others of those principles, but also finding concrete ways to realize them. The art teacher began to work like an artist in residence, spending some of her time working at her art in the presence of students, in addition to giving instruction. The guidance counselor, inspired by the retreat I had organized for staff, and with Peter's constant advice, devised a plan for advising groups so that every teacher would participate in advising, with her counsel and support, thereby solving the problem she faced of not having enough time to be a counselor to all the school's students.

During the spring of my third year, in 1974, another decision loomed. Mary Agnes had enrolled in Learning Environments as a Certificate of Advanced Study student.

Federal student aid money was drying up so I took a part-time job as an evaluation researcher at the Education Development Center. I could keep working at EDC while I finished my thesis, but Mary Agnes was pregnant, to our great joy, and finding a better place to live than our basement apartment would mean moving to a distant suburb. The alternative was to accept the position I had been offered as an extension associate in Cornell's College of Human Ecology. Although I was uncertain about both the position and the nature of the college, housing costs were lower and we liked the prospect of being at a major university while living in a small city. We have been here ever since.

Cornell

Our son Peter was born in February 1975 and I completed my thesis soon after. My work was with 4-H educators around the state developing programs to give teenagers opportunities to take responsible roles in their communities. I focused on environmental improvement, local government internships, and cultural journalism——inspired by *Foxfire* (Wigginton, 1985). Cooperative Extension was a revelation to me. My next older sisters, Jean and Joyce, had been active in 4-H and I belonged to a short-lived club, but I had not known 4-H was connected to the University of Nebraska. The existence of a formal organization whose function was to link the knowledge of the land grant university with the people of the state offered a new career possibility. Instead of moving back and forth between a university position and school administration or trying to recreate Stan Bolster's career as a Harvard professor who taught half-time in the Newton public schools, I could hope for a university position that entailed real responsibilities off campus.

After completing my thesis, I assumed we would have to move to find a more appropriate position, but the professor I had been working with was granted tenure after considerable conflict and then decided not to stay. The department posted two assistant professor positions in adolescent development to take a combination of teaching, research, and extension responsibilities. I applied, saying I would like to combine extension with research, and I was hired.

Soon after, my distinguished colleague, Urie Bronfenbrenner, was invited to a conference organized by the National Institute of Education to explore diverse approaches to research on education. He asked me to co-author the paper about the ecological perspective he was then developing. I had read and commented on some of his draft material on the topic. He gave me some notes and we talked about the paper and then he turned me loose. I floundered. Not long before the paper was due, I gave him what I recognized as a mélange of incomplete ideas. I lacked both experience with this kind of writing and a conceptual framework for thinking about and discussing the issues. A week or two later, Urie completed a paper with both our names and gave me a copy. I recognized

some of my contributions, but he had neatly applied his ecological perspective to issues in education, a task that had eluded me. I then traveled to San Diego for a conference in which I met some luminaries in the field and some young scholars who later became prominent. I represented Urie's ideas to the best of my ability and returned feeling inspired by my first academic conference. Urie retained a few pages of my writing in his subsequent book, *The Ecology of Human Development* (1979), and credited me for them, my first published writing, in which I took great pride.

NIE subsequently commissioned me to write a review of research on experiential learning. I had a better idea of how to proceed this time (Hamilton, 1980). Dewey (1938) gave me the conceptual foundation I needed. The greatest challenge was the paucity of published research. Some unpublished evaluation studies were pertinent, but even good case studies of programs were rare. Yet I knew there was a great deal of practice wisdom in the field. People should publish, I concluded, because they have figured out and done things that others need to know about. Publication is not the opposite of perishing but a means of sharing knowledge with people who can benefit from it. I resolved to write about my work even when what I had to say was not decisive. I also recognized that one of my contributions would be syntheses, perhaps a remnant from my study of history where this kind of thinking and writing is more central than in the social sciences.

Germany

My approach worked well enough that my department chair, Phil Schoggen, regularly informed me of the senior faculty's favorable assessment of my research and extension work, which I managed to combine, for example by evaluating programs I designed. As a result, when the tenure review process got underway I allowed myself to consider what I might do next. The prospect of a sabbatical leave seemed wondrous. Imagine a job in which they give you time off to learn new things! I needed to take full advantage of the opportunity.

Having studied its history, I always wanted to spend time in Europe. Some of my classmates would share stories of their summer travels, but summers for me were a time to earn money, not spend it. Moreover, I thought if I ever got to go I would want to live in one place long enough to get to know it and the language too, not just be a tourist. So I began thinking about how I could get to Europe during my sabbatical.

By this time we had adopted our second son, Joey. Peter's birth had defied doctors' predictions so when another did not follow as planned, we found Joey. Babies contradicted my assumptions about the primacy of environmental influences. Peter emerged calm and observant. He cried almost not at all. Joey, at 7 months, was already a social creature, and had been since birth according to his foster mother. Our first weekend together, I took both boys to a story-reading at the library. Four-year-old Peter sat contentedly in my lap while Joey crawled around making contact with the other children and parents. Becoming a parent is miraculous, however, it happens. The experience gave me a stronger sense of my inability to control the things in my life that are most important and of gratefulness for all that is good that has happened that I could not make happen. Ben's birth 2½ years after we adopted Joey was more miraculous than most. I was surprised to end up as the father of three sons. Having grown up with four sisters and as "the man of the house" after the age of 9, I implicitly defined fatherhood as involving daughters.

Ben's irregular schedule slowed Mary Agnes's dissertation writing. With "only" two children and an untenured husband she had started working as a research associate for Ray Rist on data from the Youth Employment Demonstration Projects Act. He urged her to enroll as a doctoral student and use the data for her dissertation. She did and won a national prize for it, after finishing just in time for the five of us to move to Germany for a year.

I applied for a Fulbright Senior Research Fellowship in Germany because of its apprenticeship system. It was intriguing as an experiential component at the center of a formal educational system. I had observed a repeating cycle in the United States of people creating an experiential learning program that everyone agreed was wonderful, that was terminated as soon as budgets got tight. I wanted to find out how learning in the workplace was incorporated into the German educational system and how that part of the system worked. I had taken German in college, and then sat in on a class at Cornell to refresh and improve my skills. Another attraction was that Mary Agnes's father was born in Germany and her uncle still farmed the land that the family had worked for 1,000 years.

The Fulbright Commission generously allowed Mary Agnes to join me in a 2-month intensive German course in Regensburg, the first time, they told us, they had done this for a spouse. We then moved to Munich for the rest of the year. Peter thrived in his third-grade class, despite having to pick up the language without formal instruction. After some initial misses, we were able to find a wonderful Kindergarten for Joey and a playmate for Ben whose mother would switch off with Mary Agnes watching the two of them. Keeping the family going took most of Mary Agnes's time, leaving just a little time to pursue her professional interests.

My host at the University of Munich, Rolf Oerter, and his staff were extremely gracious and helpful, as were many other German scholars I met. I quickly learned that the topic I thought I had invented, the political socialization of German youth through apprenticeship, was a staple of German sociology. In fact, several major surveys had recently been completed. Reading reports of these and other studies gave me the big picture. Then I arranged to conduct a series of observations in schools and workplaces and interviews with apprentices, their teachers, and worksite supervisors. I had a great deal of assistance but

counted as one of the peaks of my linguistic accomplishments calling the owners of small auto repair shops on the telephone and securing their permission to observe and interview their apprentices.

As I had hoped, living in another country was stimulating, if sometimes stressful. Although I sometimes chafed at Bavarian formality—exemplified by the use of titles and seldom first names—I came to appreciate the respect it conveyed, which is directed disproportionately toward those titled Professor Doktor, as I was. Theory has a larger place in German social science. Evaluation research was not as prominent as in the United States. Germans seemed to place more weight on developing a theory that specified what was needed, assuming that if a program or practice embodied a strong theory then the results would follow as predicted. We in the United States are readier to try out many approaches and then assess which ones are working, irrespective of their theoretical bases, or lack thereof. German apprenticeship illustrates their proclivity for creating national systems. When we in the United States identify a social or educational problem, we generate a lot of programs, but we are not very good at building or rebuilding systems.

Youth Apprenticeship and School-to-Work

Coming home after a year and a month in Germany, I resumed my normal activities and began the project of turning my notes and memories from reading, observing, and interviewing into something informative to others. I gave talks, wrote an article (Hamilton, 1987), and finally got a book proposal together. It did not spark strong interest. One editor explained that readers would not be interested in Germany and advised making the book more about the United States. I followed the editor's advice partway by strengthening the comparative parts of the book. At the Free Press I found an editor who was willing to take on my project. Among her encouraging words were, "You may not have the last word to say on this topic, but it might be the first word." I began to think of my task with the book as adopting a lawyerly style of argumentation. I was trying to write the book that would be accessible to a wide audience while maintaining its scholarly substance. Academics advance as much evidence as they can and then tentatively suggest some inferences and conclusions, hemmed about with caveats and qualifications. Lawyers, who have to convince ordinary citizens, announce in advance the case they plan to make, then introduce different bits of evidence, returning with each bit to the claim they said they would prove and pointing out how they are proving it.

While I was trying to write a book that would stimulate efforts to try new approaches in this country, signs of weakness in the U.S. economy began to loom larger and people began to talk and write about the German economy's strengths, not only the Japanese. At the same time, the shrinking prospects of young people without a college education began to draw attention, most tellingly from the William T. Grant Foundation Commission on Work, Family and Citizenship. At the invitation of Sam Halperin, I drafted two chapters of the preliminary report, *The Forgotten Half* (1988), and wrote one of the working papers. I became a member of a group convened by Jobs for the Future that worked on promoting youth apprenticeship. What I had imagined as a solitary campaign was becoming a movement.

I also got invited to speak to various groups. Along with the favorable responses to my advocacy, I encountered some skepticism. Some said, "You can't do that here." And of course I agreed with them if by "it" they meant apprenticeship just as it is done in Germany. Others said, "We're already doing that," pointing to cooperative education, which is well established in engineering schools and in some universities, as well as in high-school vocational programs. Of course both objections cannot be true. In response to the latter claim, I began to distinguish small-scale programs with relatively short-term and mostly ad hoc sets of experiences from the German system that involved at that time about half of the appropriate age cohort for (usually) 3-year experiences that are formally specified by joint committees with representatives of employers, unions, and education and certified by tests that all apprentices must pass. A system is very different from a set of programs. The other objection, that it can't be done, could only be rejected by doing it, which I took as my next task.

When the book (Hamilton, 1990) was finally in manuscript form, the Majority Leader of the New York State Assembly, Jim Tallon, asked me to send the text and invited me to meet with him. I was impressed by the questions he asked and the mastery he demonstrated of the ideas in the book. I have difficulty enough as a professor keeping up with the reading I should do. I do not expect politicians to read in depth. He told me that he had always looked for ways to support economic development and human development but thought of them as two separate spheres. I had shown him how they are intertwined. He promised to help me advance the agenda I had laid out.

That agenda entailed creating a demonstration project to invent and try out an American-style youth apprenticeship. ("Apprenticeship American Style" was the title of one chapter in my book, suggested by Urie when he read a draft.) Jim secured state funding to support the project, generously telling me that it need not be located in his district. The Binghamton area proved fertile, though, in part because he also introduced me to business and education leaders who agreed to join in. The Pew Charitable Trusts also gave major support for the project thanks to the education program officer, Bob Schwartz.

Financial support made it possible to set up a local base at Cornell Cooperative Extension of Broome County and to assemble a staff. Mary Agnes became the leader of that staff. When I agreed to serve as department chair, I needed someone to put the project together and keep it running smoothly while I made frequent trips to meetings and conferences and tended to the department. I knew Mary Agnes was a good planner and attentive to details. I came to appreciate and admire her ability to make the details converge on the larger enterprise, which we designed together.

I accepted the chair out of a sense of obligation, believing it was my turn. Phil Schoggen had demonstrated that taking care of things regularly and conscientiously helps prevent big problems. My dean, Francille Firebaugh, was an admirable advisor and role model, but by the time she invited me to take a second term, I declined and felt relieved.

One other politician saw the book in manuscript form, the governor of Arkansas, Bill Clinton. I had suggested him to my editor as a possible blurb writer because of his support for youth apprenticeship in his state. Also, Sam Halperin had told me that Hillary Clinton had been the most active and productive member of the Grant Foundation Commission. Campaigning for president, Bill Clinton promised to support youth apprenticeship, and he followed through with the School-to-Work Opportunities Act of 1994. Mary Agnes and I were invited to bring some of our youth apprentices to attend the signing ceremony in the Rose Garden. Mary Agnes convinced the White House staff to invite the apprentices' parents as well, pointing out that they were an essential ingredient in our program.

Although the bill frequently referred to youth apprenticeship, and to building systems, the legislation gave states and districts options about the types of "work-based learning" their share of the funding would support. School officials could either invest in creating youth apprenticeships for a small number of students or send large numbers for field trips and job shadowing. With a few exceptions, they chose the latter. The permissive nature of the legislation unintentionally invited superficiality.

Another weakness was that the legislation was crafted in the spirit of Al Gore's "reinventing government" as a strategic investment that would leverage state and local funds that would continue after federal support ended. Successful examples of this strategy are rare, at best. Add to that the length of time needed to build systems, and the legislation seems in retrospect to have been inadequate in its conception.

School-to-Work began to lose momentum even under the Clinton administration. Campaigning for re-election, President Clinton advocated college for all. George W. Bush's election in 2000 doomed the initiative. The coup d' grace was delivered before he took office by Lynne Cheney (1998), who wrote an op-ed piece for the New York Times attacking School-to-Work for enabling the government to determine children's futures, usurping parents' responsibilities. The attack from the right was unexpected because George Bush senior had introduced legislation that was not as ambitious and failed to pass but was consistent with School-to-Work and because, until it was attacked, the initiative seemed to garner support from across the political spectrum. Ironically, labor union representatives were among the few skeptics. They seemed to fear that youth apprenticeship would diminish the small but respected registered apprenticeship programs that unions participate in. We supporters might have been better prepared to respond to partisan attacks if we had faced organized opposition while advocating for the ideas initially and implementing the legislation.

Some glimmers of renewed interest are now visible in both the underlying issues and the approach of promoting work-based learning (*Pathways to Prosperity*, 2012), but the mantra of college for all has clearly carried the day. With improved test scores the sole measure of quality, few school leaders are willing to send students out of the classroom to learn.

After carrying out our plan to turn over the youth apprenticeship demonstration project to a local institution, where it survives nearly 20 years later, Mary Agnes and I produced a booklet on system building for the School-to-Work Office (Hamilton & Hamilton, 1999). That aspect of the legislation was sorely neglected. We profiled serious efforts to build systems by school districts, regions, states, and corporations as illustrations of what that means and how it can be accomplished. The fact that the systems we described had been under construction before the legislation was passed confirmed the need for more time than the funding allowed.

Mentoring

As interest in and funding for youth apprenticeship faded, we turned to a component that was garnering increased attention, mentoring. One of our first professional partnerships was in connection with a demonstration mentoring program that a group of colleagues had initiated. We discovered that simply making a functional match was a serious challenge. We concluded that matches were more likely to take if mentors engaged their protégés in goal-directed activity, consistent with one of Urie Bronfenbrenner's principles (Hamilton & Hamilton, 1992). This led us to expect that our youth apprentices would find mentors in their workplaces not only among the adults assigned to teach them but also among others with whom they came into contact. With this in mind, we distinguished coaching from mentoring, defining the former as teaching young people how to do a specific job and the latter as teaching young people how to be a good worker and even how to live a good life, in addition to being a companion and supporter.

Our distinction did not catch on, so after turning the project over to others, we reverted to using the term, mentor, to mean the adult responsible for a youth apprentice's or intern's learning at work. With a grant from the U.S. Department of Labor, we were able to explore how adults teach youth at work and test whether we could improve their informal teaching. There we encountered again the challenges of conducting field research. Despite extensive questioning and screening, programs are not always what they say they are. And getting workplace mentors to attend training was a challenge in this project as it had been in our demonstration.

In 2003, Cornell created a new position, associate provost for outreach. I applied and was chosen to fill it. I got to work again with Francille Firebaugh, who was then vice provost for land grant affairs, and to work across the university on connecting its resources with the needs of people outside the academic community. The position also brought me back to my earlier focus on school reform because a great deal of outreach activity was aimed at K-12 education, especially in science (or science, technology, engineering, and math, or STEM, more broadly), but different groups' efforts were not coordinated. Outreach to schools was done primarily by faculty and staff, sometimes students, associated with research projects supported by NSF, NASA, and other funders who ask investigators to address "broader social issues." I was impressed by how many scientists care deeply about education before college and are willing to pitch in to help and are good at it. All of the efforts I learned about on curriculum development and professional development for teachers were worthwhile, but being scattered across departments and research institutes and supported on soft money, the whole amounted to less than the sum of its parts. I was able to make some progress toward coherence, efficiency, and higher impact, but, facing the financial crisis of 2008, the university eliminated the position and I returned to my faculty role full time—hardly a terrible fate.

Action Research to Support the Transition to Adulthood

Resuming my former activities proved more challenging than I had expected. As an administrator I was constantly looking for ways of bringing people together and helping others achieve their goals. As a professor I had to be selfish, concerned about how any activity would aid my own work. Switching back to that orientation was tough. Mary Agnes and I were fortunate to receive a new grant at just the right time. The Jacobs Foundation funded our proposal to engage in action research with four programs in Latin America that support the transition to adulthood of vulnerable youth.

This project grew out of a chapter we wrote on the need for new institutions, in addition to higher education, that support the transition to adulthood, which is not a biological change but a change in people's roles in institutions, especially families, schools, and workplaces. Our argument harked back to apprenticeship, which is an exemplary institution for this purpose, and continued a critique we had offered previously of treatments of "emerging adulthood" that take the life experiences of college graduates as normative (Hamilton & Hamilton, 2006). Mary Agnes and I had agreed to write a new chapter for the second edition of the *Handbook of Adolescent Psychology* about the transition to adulthood, emphasizing those who do not graduate from college (Hamilton & Hamilton, 2009). As the deadline drew near, we informed our editor, Rich Lerner, that the chapter was not coming. We said we did not have a good handle on it and would have to withdraw from the project. He extended the deadline and insisted that we could and should send him a manuscript. After some false starts, a rough manuscript emerged. While flying to California for the birth of our first granddaughter, we worked back and forth on the draft, probably driving the third person in our row of seats to distraction. Nia arrived late. Since there was nothing we could do to urge her along, we spent much of 5 days working on the chapter, finally sending it off to Rich just about the time we got the call to come meet our granddaughter. A few days later we got an e-mail from Rich with some minor suggestions and a lot of praise for the chapter. I was surely softened up emotionally at the time but I have never felt such relief and satisfaction at the acceptance of a manuscript.

Becoming a grandfather was even better. My joy recalled what I had felt when Peter was born and how I thought many times about how happy his Opa was. I recognized, after 30 years, that my vicarious joy for Mary Agnes's father was partly a displacement of the sense of loss I felt knowing my own father would never know his grandsons. Now I would be a grandfather for him too. Along with our two beautiful granddaughters, Nia and Elsa, I have two daughters-in-law who are such extraordinary women that I am proud to have sons they would marry.

Our project in Latin America was inspired in part by our wish to know more about the heritage of our daughters-in-law. Gueni was born in Mexico, Alicia in the United States to Mexican-born parents. Spanish is their first language. We worked with programs in Mexico, Colombia, and Argentina and took a more systematic approach to involving participants in the research, though it was perfectly consistent with the way we had been taught to do research at Harvard. We came to see ourselves as learning about "social inventions" and making those inventions more widely available. Both the methods and our findings are applicable in this country too, and we hope to build on them in both hemispheres (Hamilton, M.A., Hamilton, S.F., Bianchi, & Bran, 2013).

Translational research is a new banner I have taken up and a useful conceptual framework for what I have tried to do in my career. What is, at this writing, the newly created Bronfenbrenner Center for Translational Research is adapting the concept from medicine, where it is seen as moving basic research "from bench to bedside." Transferring the idea and the practices associated with it from a vast and richly funded domain is a serious challenge. I think of it as an umbrella concept that helps us see as a system the web of actual and potential connections between research and practice and then to strengthen that system so that our policies, programs, and practices are more effective at promoting human development. This systemic vision obviates the tired debates about qualitative vs. quantitative methods because different designs and methods are needed depending upon where one is working in the system, and, as always, what questions one wishes to answer. A key element in translational research is subjecting the system itself and the process of translation to empirical study. Research on implementation, dissemination, replication, etc., assumes a position of importance because it helps us understand how research might be more effectively incorporated into practice. From my perspective the process is bi-directional. In addition to learning from researchers, practitioners have lessons to teach researchers. Using action research and associated participatory approaches, practitioners, youth, and other stakeholders can conduct their own research, illuminating their local situation, learning that research is not a magic trick but a set of skills and a way of thinking that they can learn and use too. I think it is not too much to hope that research of this nature can also contribute to the accumulating body of knowledge.

Concluding Reflections

I know enough about history and the writing of history to know that stories about the past make far more sense in retrospect than they do to the people living the events at the time. I have tried for the reader's sake to tell a coherent story, but recognize that the reality was never so neat. Nevertheless, some themes emerge that seem genuine to me.

I have chosen to study some topics that are clearly related to my life experiences. I have seen experiential learning or service learning as important because many of my most powerful learning experiences occurred outside classrooms. Work experience in particular has been an interest because my summer jobs gave me a sense of adult life beyond the social circles of my family and most of my friends. By the time I went to Swarthmore I had been a ranch hand, busboy, surveyor's assistant, agricultural laborer, and factory worker. Some of my classmates liked to show their solidarity with the working class by wearing blue work shirts, like those I had worn out. Some fantasized about quitting school; I knew why I was there. Yet I also knew I could earn a living without a degree if it ever came to that. My experience in Upward Bound led me to education, not something I learned in a class.

I began studying mentoring opportunistically, after Urie, Steve Ceci, and Dale Blyth invited me to join and eventually take over a project they had started. My continuing interest in the topic surely reflects the central importance of mentors in my life, though I did not always recognize that at the time. After my father died, my mother wanted me to be around men, so she sent me for one summer to live with my father's brother, Uncle Howard, who managed a ranch in Nevada. I spent the next two summers with my father's sister and her family, working for my Uncle Cecil, who was a surveyor. I always resisted the idea that someone else was going to take my father's place. He could not be replaced and besides I carried him with me. But a series of men and some women have mentored me: my debate coach, Jack Mueller; Gil Stott at Swarthmore; Peter Lenrow; Urie Bronfenbrenner; Jerry Ziegler; Francille Firebaugh.

One more person deserves mention in this context. Brother David Steindl-Rast is a Benedictine monk who holds a Ph.D. in psychology and is a leading expert on Buddhism. Born in Austria, he has spent most of his career at a monastery not far from Ithaca, but has also given talks and led retreats around the world and published more than 20 books. After he began living in a retirement community in Ithaca, we began giving him rides to and from St. Catherine's. Eventually he joined us for holiday meals and meals on the spur of the moment, bringing a child-like enthusiasm to making cookies or savoring the tiniest serving of wine all through dinner. He is passionately engaged in current events and readily shares wisdom from the fathers of the early Christian church, St. Benedict, or the Dalai Lama, a personal friend of his, usually with a twinkle in his eye. Not being a Catholic—despite my mother's fear that I would convert after marrying one—I had no previous connection to the monastic tradition. Brother David's humility, wisdom, kindness, and centeredness exemplify what it means to be close to God, even to those of us who remain uncertain what God is. His friendship has been a great blessing in my life and my family's. It is for me an example of grace, unearned and undeserved yet given freely.

I am privileged to have had a career as a scholar trying to improve young people's learning and development. Fortunately my productive and satisfying professional partnership with Mary Agnes has worked seamlessly with our partnership in the family. It has been a good life, so far.

References

Bailey, L. H. (1919). *The holy earth*. Ithaca, NY: Comstock Publishing Company.

Bronfenbrenner, U. (1979). *The ecology of human development: Experiments by nature and by design*. Cambridge, MA: Harvard University Press.

Campbell, D. T., & Stanley, J. C. (1963/1966). *Experimental and quasi-experimental designs for research*. Chicago: Rand McNally.

Cheney, L. V. (1998). School-to-Work programs set students back. *New York Times*, February 3, Op-ed column.

Dewey, J. (1916). *Democracy and education*. New York: Free Press.

Dewey, J. (1938/1963). *Experience and education*. New York: Macmillan.

Featherstone, J. (1971). *Schools where children learn*. New York: Liveright.

The forgotten half: Non-college youth in America (1988). Washington, DC: Youth and America's Future: The William T. Grant Foundation Commission on Work, Family and Citizenship.

Hamilton, M. A., Hamilton, S. F., Bianchi, L., & Bran, J. (2013). Opening pathways for vulnerable young people in Patagonia. *Journal of Research on Adolescence, 23*(1), 162–170.

Hamilton, S. F. (1975). *Staff roles and the development of an alternative public school*. Unpublished doctoral dissertation. Harvard University Graduate School of Education.

Hamilton, S. F. (1980). Experiential learning programs for youth. *American Journal of Education, 88*, 170–215.

Hamilton, S. F. (1987). Apprenticeship as a transition to adulthood in West Germany. *American Journal of Education, 95*, 314–345.

Hamilton, S. F. (1990). *Apprenticeship for adulthood: Preparing youth for the future*. New York: Free Press.

Hamilton, S. F., & Hamilton, M. A. (1992). Mentoring programs: Promise and paradox. *Phi Delta Kappa, 73*, 546–550.

Hamilton, S. F, & Hamilton, M. A. (1999). *Building strong school-to-work systems: Illustrations of key components*. Washington, DC: National School-to-Work Office.

Hamilton, S. F., & Hamilton, M. A. (2006). School, work, and emerging adulthood. In J. J. Arnett & J. L. Tanner (Eds.), *Emerging adults in America: Coming of age in the 21st century*. Washington, DC: American Psychological Association.

Hamilton, S. F., & Hamilton, M. A. (2009). The transition to adulthood: Challenges of poverty and structural lag. In R. M. Lerner & L. Steinberg (Eds.), *Handbook of adolescent psychology* (3rd ed.), Vol. 2, *Contextual influences on adolescent development* (pp. 492–526). New York: Wiley.

Kahn, R. L., Wolfe, D. W., Quinn, R. P., Snoek, J. D., & Rosenthal, R. A. (1964). *Organizational stress: Studies in role conflict and ambiguity*. New York: John Wiley & Sons.

Kelman, H. C. (1974). Social influence and linkages between the individual and the social system: Further thoughts on the processes of compliance, identification, and internalization. In J. T. Tedeschi (Ed.), *Perspectives on social power*. Chicago: Aldine.

Mumford, L. (1961). *The city in history: Its origins, its transformations, and its prospects*. New York: Harcourt, Brace & World.

Myrdal, G. (1962). *An American dilemma: The Negro problem and modern democracy*. New York: Harper & Row.

Pathways to prosperity: Meeting the challenge of preparing young Americans for the 21st Century. Cambridge, MA: Pathways to Prosperity Project, Harvard Graduate School of Education. Accessed January 25, 2012 at www.gse.harvard.edu/news.../Pathways_to_Prosperity_Feb2011.pdf

Sarason, S. B. (1971). *The culture of the school and the problem of change*. Boston: Allyn and Bacon.

Sarason, S. B. (1972). *The creation of settings and the future societies*. Cambridge, MA: Brookline Books.

Wigginton, E. (1985). *Sometimes a shining moment: The Foxfire experience*. Garden City: Anchor Press/Doubleday.

21
Coming of Age

Karen Hein's Journey

KAREN HEIN

AIDS and Adolescents: Watching the Head, Not the Tail of the Whale in the HIV Epidemic

Will You Be My Doctor?

I was in the middle of a staff meeting in the house our Adolescent HIV/AIDS Program occupied in the Bronx near the hospital when they told me to take a call from an insistent patient. The house had no identifying features. The program was called the Adolescent Risk Reduction Program—no AIDS in the title so that the kids could come without anyone knowing the real reason. We opened our doors in 1987 but few people came in the beginning.

Few young people knew they were HIV infected or even at risk because AIDS was thought to be a problem only for gay men in their 30s–40s or for new born babies. We got our own building because we promised the president of the hospital that if he would assign it to us, I could get the Surgeon General of the United States to come for ribbon-cutting ceremony. At the time, many hospital administrators were reluctant to advertise the fact that they were treating people with AIDS, because irrational fear of contagion was pervasive. Blood and blood products used for transfusions were only beginning to be screened, so there was a degree of nervousness based on incomplete understanding about how and why the epidemic was expanding. We were getting ready for what we thought would be the next wave of the HIV epidemic—adolescents.

When we opened our program, we were ridiculed as being "The Emperor's New Clothes Clinic." We had no patients at all, but the "rationale for concern" had resulted in our being given $1 million grant from the Centers for Disease Control and Prevention based upon our arguments that were compelling about why and how the HIV epidemic had extended into the adolescent population. Most young people were unaware of their infection, most health care providers were unaware of the risk to young people and most attention and resources were given to older adults and babies (Hein, 1987). But our projections and rationale were correct. HIV had silently entered the adolescent population. We had a building, a program … but few patients. We were ahead of the curve. While others were focusing on where the HIV epidemic had surfaced, we were looking ahead to where it was going. We used the analogy of the breaching whale. Most people were focusing on the tail of the whale, while we were watching the whale's head to see where it was going, not where it had been.

"Hi. Will you be my doctor? No one here knows anything about what to do for me." Krista Blake was calling from Ohio. She was 16. She had AIDS. She was a good kid—lots of friends, editor of the yearbook, a cheerleader. After some unusual infections and pneumonia, she'd been diagnosed with AIDS by doctors at an academic medical center after her local doctor couldn't make sense of what was going on. She had an AIDS doctor but she was by far the youngest person and didn't like the way they treated her, ignoring all of the things that were most important to her and only concentrating on her blood counts and medications. Undoubtedly, the adult medical team viewed Krista as a problem patient. To them she was moody, difficult, hard to reach … a problem. What I heard on the telephone was a bright, determined young woman who was calling half way across the country to find a doctor who would understand what she was going through. Krista wanted to be able to talk and be heard as she confronted myriad issues about her life. Should she tell her friends? Should she sue her boyfriend for infecting her without admitting that he was living with HIV? Did he even know? Many doctors weren't even telling younger patients with hemophilia that they were likely to be infected with HIV and that they should be testing. Should she tell the school? Would they kick her out as they had done with three brothers in Florida because they had hemophilia?

Krista as a Resource in Providing Insight into the AIDS Generation Krista may have been a problem to her doctors in Ohio, but to me she was a tremendous resource.

Rather than being a problem, she represented the answer to the problem, the resource we needed not only to help her, but to figure out what we should be doing to help a generation of young people for whom the AIDS epidemic would define their passage from childhood to adulthood. Krista not only had the questions, she had the answers as well. Together we could sort it all out. Her questions became some of the research questions we began to systematically pose and answer. Explaining that it would be difficult to be her doctor given the hundreds of miles that separated us, I suggested that we continue talking and learn from each other the best way for her to live with HIV. For the next 5 years we talked, we met, gave presentations together, did press interviews and met each other's families. She stayed at our house. She dedicated her short, meaningful life to becoming an HIV/AIDS educator, giving a voice and face to the wave of the epidemic that wasn't fully recognized until she died.

AIDS in Adolescence: A Rationale for Concern

I was the founding director of the first comprehensive adolescent HIV/AIDS program in the country. We opened the program in 1987 after writing a paper for the Carnegie Corporation's Council on Adolescent Development entitled, "AIDS in adolescence: A rationale for concern" (Hein, 1988). We built the case for focusing on young people, the AIDS Generation. Whether infected or not, their lives would be forever changed by the happenstance of coming of age just as the epidemic was emerging into world consciousness. In the paper, our rationale for concern was based upon four arguments. Adolescents were at risk because of:

1. The prevalence of unprotected sexual intercourse and high-risk drug injecting practices, as well as the inadvertent HIV infection from blood or blood product transfusions before adequate HIV screening of the blood supply.
2. Their patterns of partner choice and spread of other sexually transmitted diseases, with higher potential of rapid, silent spread among adolescents, from adults to young people, among young people, and to babies born to adolescents.
3. The likelihood that HIV infected adolescents would mostly remain healthy for many years, only showing signs of AIDS when they were adults. The latency period from initial HIV infection to AIDS was, on average, 10 years so a young person infected at age 18 wouldn't be symptomatic or develop classic signs of AIDS until his or her late 20s.
4. The unique factors in the adolescent age group that deserved special attention. Some of them included the possibility of a different natural history of HIV when transmitted during adolescence instead of in adulthood or around the time of birth; the lack of health facilities for teenagers and the need for special considerations of

confidentiality, consent, access to treatment and age-appropriate tailoring of medication regimes; medical protocols; and the influence of adolescent physical, physiologic, psychological, and behavioral factors on the natural history, course, and outcome of HIV infection.

Krista Blake was right. Few health providers existed who could care for her in the late 1980s. Two years after we opened our doors, Gina Kolata's article on the front page of the Sunday *New York Times* about AIDS in adolescence in 1989 brought the facts about the epidemic to the consciousness of America (Kolata, 1989). In 1993, WHO confirmed our prediction, announcing that AIDS in adolescents was, indeed, the leading edge of the next wave of the HIV epidemic worldwide (Goldsmith, 1993).

Krista's Documentary Film, Before I Die During the same 5-year time period, Krista Blake, blond (sometimes redhead), blue-eyed high-school cheerleader, became a powerful force in communicating the special issues of HIV in adolescence to millions of people. When we presented together at Medical Grand Rounds, all of the questions were directed to her. Her boyfriend, who had hemophilia, either hadn't known or hadn't done anything to protect her from infection the few times they had intercourse. He died of AIDS but neither he nor his family ever acknowledged the cause. She helped parents imagine and acknowledge that their teenager might be at risk or even infected with HIV. She helped teachers get over their reluctance to be more explicit in discussions of HIV prevention.

Krista was featured on the cover of *Newsweek* magazine, enabling everyone to know that the epidemic touched the lives of all young people, of all people, whether or not they were personally infected or at risk, because they were living in the midst of an epidemic ("Teenagers and AIDS," 1992). She was also featured in a documentary entitled *Before I Die,* which ends with her funeral where her relatives read the letter she had written for that occasion explaining that her life's work was fulfilling as an HIV educator, even if her life was foreshortened, lasting only 21 years. I have stayed in touch with her family, exchanging holiday cards and letters. Krista's sister Holly completed college and graduate school in counseling. Her parents set up a fund to continue Krista's work and came to Washington, DC, when Krista's section of the AIDS Quilt was displayed on The Mall. At the time, I was the Executive Officer of The Institute of Medicine at The National Academies, and together we took photos of Holly sitting on the bronze lap of Albert Einstein in the sculpture garden outside the Academies' historic building facing the Viet Nam Memorial.

Krista's Lesson and Legacy Krista Blake and I were partners. She taught me that young people are the best spokespeople for issues facing adolescents. She taught me that often young people can talk about tough issues more directly and effectively sometimes than their parents or other adults. She taught me that answers to complex questions about illness, death, and life are best approached through teamwork, and that team needs to include the person or people most affected. Perhaps I taught her that she could carry out her life's work as an HIV educator by listening and encouraging her, by answering her questions or finding ways to formulate questions for others to answer.

Krista Blake encapsulates for me all of the reasons I was involved with adolescents and adolescent research. She is a prime example of the strength of assets-based youth development approach. Instead of dwelling on deficits or problems, she brings out the ways in which young people can thrive, not just survive. Her foreshortened life was full and complete in terms of her ability to be a resource to solve problems for herself and others, not a source of problems. Krista sought help in addressing her illness and the limitations it imposed, but her illness became a platform, a springboard from which she eloquently and effectively engaged with the people and world around her. I was lucky she called and asked me to be her doctor. She taught me a lot. Together we accomplished a lot. The rest of this chapter will explain why and how I entered and stayed in the field of youth development and the role of research in discovering and uncovering the valuable lessons I have learned from 40 years of working in partnership with young people (Hein, 2003).

Why Medicine … Why Adolescent Medicine … Why Adolescent Research

Environment and genetics contributed to my decision to become an adolescent medicine doctor. The "doctor" part was influenced strongly by both genetics and environment. I was (and am) energetic, determined, tall, inquisitive, bright enough, and extremely organized and focused. These genetic traits were rewarded by my school, my community, and my suburban family living on Long Island after World War II. My parents, first generation Americans, were born to Eastern European Jews. They were the first in their families to make it out of Brooklyn to Nassau County. They chose Great Neck, home of entertainer Eddie Cantor, opera singer Richard Tucker (nee Ruben Ticker), and writer F. Scott Fitzgerald (Goldstein, 2006). West Egg in Fitzgerald's novel, *The Great Gatsby,* was based upon Great Neck. Achievement through educational excellence was the mantra. Given my constitution and my proclivities, I was seen to be the Chosen One—the one out of four who would follow in my father's footsteps and become a doctor. I took my role seriously, studied hard, ignored the obstacles preventing most women from becoming all they could be, and excelled in nearly everything I was allowed to do. I wasn't allowed to have a Bat Mitzvah (no girls were permitted at that time) or allowed to play on many competitive team sports (there were few for girls) so I was a cheerleader (co-captain) and joined the swim club. I wasn't allowed to take mechanical drawing (boys only) so I took typing (luckily). I was a tomboy so I spent every non-school hour exploring the woods around our suburban development, riding my bike and playing with the guys. My father, a general practitioner, was the first chief of staff of a hospital that is now a major teaching affiliate of an academic health center. During my adolescence, it was our community hospital and I was a Candy Striper volunteer. My father's office was attached to our house by a ramp which we four kids loved to run up and down at full speed. I was intrigued by my father's office and explored its contents with great glee. There were two human fetuses in formaldehyde in jars. There were books used to explain contraceptive methods to my father's adult female patients. I could show my friends these treasures, including where exactly diaphragms were inserted and fit over the female cervix. My fate was sealed.

My mother was feisty. She was quite short, just 5 feet tall, blond (naturally and reinforced), blue eyed, and tough. Her primary role was to be the good doctor's wife. She, too, had wanted to become a medical doctor. She and my father talked about it and decided that one doctor was enough. Instead of becoming a doctor, she conveyed the message to me that I should do it for her. Instead she audited 2 years of medical school not for credit, saying that this would be the best way for her to learn medical terminology to help her in her role as doctor's wife. After we were all grown, she volunteered at a school for developmentally delayed children. She volunteered in the genetics lab at the hospital and later worked as a volunteer in Palm Springs' The Living Desert, demonstrating the tarantulas and snakes to school children during the winter months. Perhaps in another culture I would have been a shepherdess or even a shaman, drawing wisdom and sustenance from the living environment, plants and animals, but in Post-World War II Long Island, I became a medical doctor.

Coming of Age in the 1960s The news of JFK's assassination hit me hard as I was walking up Bascom Hill at the University of Wisconsin in Madison. Most of my friends marched, picketed, protested, and didn't become doctors. I sympathized with the causes and participated in anti-war activities locally, but getting through pre-med courses and becoming a doctor was my plan for contributing to the profound changes we thought were necessary in our society. We had no doubt that the force of our generation would change the country and the world. We were the answer to life's persistent questions, to turn a Garrison Keillor quote into our generation's mission. I worked in a research lab during college weighing guinea pigs for a high-altitude physiologist, Enrique Valdivia who was also the local undertaker. He invited me along to an autopsy, the first time I'd experienced being with a dead person, and certainly the first time I experienced dissecting one! I was riveted. The privilege conferred by being a doctor had nothing to do with status or salary; rather, I found honor in being at the most intimate, important moments in a person's life and connecting others with those moments and experiences. This was the motive for my becoming an adolescent researcher. It was a means to an end. Connecting people with each other in ways that enabled them to understand and feel united and empowered was the fuel behind my career choice.

Connecting People on the Outside with People on the Inside

I felt the privilege of being allowed into a place where the public was excluded. This ability to enter off-limit places has become a major theme in my professional life and career. Being a physician has allowed me to be inside intensive care units. Being a physician has been the way I spent time in jails for kids. Being a physician was my reason for spending 2 months in upcountry Liberia caring for people from 10 tribes alongside a famous missionary nurse, Esther Bacon, and a Lutheran missionary doctor. Being a physician was the reason I was given permission to enter Burmese refugee camps along the Thai border and Northern Kenya. Being a physician has been my excuse for being able to ask very personal questions to people I hardly know. Being a physician has enabled me to help deliver babies and sit with people as they die. Being a physician has enabled me to connect people with hidden places they ordinarily don't think about or care about. Being a physician has been the way I have enacted my adolescent desire to change the country and the world. By enabling others to know what is happening in hidden places, by connecting them with the people, my hope is that empathy will lead to action. My job was to become the connection of people on the outside with people on the inside. Adolescents were the first outside–inside connection.

Combining Medical Education with Social Activism

Combining my medical education with social activism took several forms. Knowing and doing weren't enough for me. The unknown was equally compelling. When I learned facts in medical school it raised questions in my mind. Why was one approach better than another? Would any of the interventions actually help people? How could we envision a system that was more equitable and effective in improving health and well-being? My questions were based upon my experiences. The actions weren't obvious. I didn't accept the current system or the ways care was being organized, delivered, or financed. There should be a better way. Research was the missing link. Terms like, "evidenced-based practice," "community-based participatory research," "comparative effectiveness research," and "outcome-oriented research" weren't yet invented, but the need for them was evident. My motivation for becoming a researcher was to find the right ways to engage others to change the way young people were perceived and to figure out ways to put young people into a role where their creativity, fresh views, and insights were valued and valuable. My experience as an empowered young person in the 1960s continues to be my motivation now that I am in my 60s!

White Coat, Clenched Fist

The book *White Coat, Clenched Fist* by my friend and colleague, Fitzhugh Mullan, encapsulates my personal transformation. The subject of *White Coat, Clenched Fist* is the role of the Student Health Organization (SHO) in transforming the lives of young health professionals through summer projects in the late 1960s in The Bronx (Mullan, 1976). The book was just republished in 2006 because of its enduring relevance. Students in the health professions are demanding experiences in global health, community-based care, and primary care, just as we did 50 years ago. My unusual career path, once an oddity among my colleagues, is of great interest to students as they recognize the contributions of other sectors to the health and well-being of adolescents and other segments of the population.

The summer I spent at Lincoln Hospital in the South Bronx through SHO was probably the single most influential experience in my early career. My first publication, "Boarder Babies at Lincoln Hospital" was the rough blueprint for the next five decades (Hein, 1968). My project required creating a list, a database of the children who were hospitalized at Lincoln Hospital in the middle of one of New York City's most devastated neighborhoods. The Boarder Baby Unit housed dozens of kids who were literally growing up in the hospital because their families couldn't take them home or because there were no facilities in the community to care for their needs. Some were born addicted to heroin. Some were simply abandoned or taken by officials in hopes of finding foster care or adoption placements. When I began, there were 30 boarder babies. During the summer, as a result of a strike by city social workers and nurses, I was able to reduce the census in the unit to just nine kids. As I wrote in this first publication, "There is no reason why this high rate of placement should not continue. Every incomplete form, every delay, every excuse, every mistake takes its toll on the children in the back of the surgery ward." This placement was not easy, however. I did this by assuming the role (somewhat illegally) of each health professional responsible for completing one part of the bureaucratic process—signing forms that needed to be updated monthly, arranging for transportation from the hospital to placement interviews, completing required medical examinations. It was a research project with the underlying questions: One, why are these kids here growing up in this hospital? Two, what's wrong with the system that the needs of these boarder babies can't be met to get them out of the hospital? And three, how could the system be altered to reduce the need for prolonged hospital stays or even eliminate the need for a Boarder Baby Unit completely? Shortly after our SHO summer projects ended, a group of doctors and community activists formed the Lincoln Collective and took over the administration of Lincoln Hospital. It was a wild experiment that included severing the affiliation contract with Albert Einstein College of Medicine. It polarized the community, the academic health center and the city, but it transformed the notion of who controlled the hospital.

Hospital as a Social Instrument At the end of the summer, we had a rousing meeting in Wappingers Falls with all of the SHO summer participants. The keynote speaker was Martin Cherkasky, MD, former President of the Montefiore Medical Center in the Bronx. Martin was truly a rebel with a cause (Levenson, 1984). He roared his message to us: without taking on the whole system, you can't be an effective doctor; without speaking up for those without voice, you are mute. That was it. I'd found my place in the House of Medicine. The house was indeed made of glass and I was looking outward beyond its walls as my way of making what happened inside relevant to the people on the outside.

Adolescent Medicine In and Out of Jail

My first paid job as an academic was in jail. I was Spofford Juvenile Center's Medical Director. After completing medical school and graduating from Columbia University's College of Physicians and Surgeons in 1970, I did my 3 years of internship and Pediatric Residency at Jacobi Hospital and Montefiore Medical Center in the Bronx. It had the reputation of having the smartest faculty, the most progressive, talented house staff, and the most innovative approaches to training. From the perspective of adolescent research, Spofford provided an important vantage point to document the health needs of a very marginalized population. Juvenile detainees were often viewed by the larger society as being neglected and abused kids in need of the best social services and health care available to make up for their lack of support in their earlier years.. The exact same young people were viewed by others as dangerous criminals who should be treated as adults, and punished, not rehabilitated or supported, despite their young age. The amount of barbed wire, protocols for visitors, and balance between rehabilitation or training versus punishment mentality swung back and forth, depending upon the political atmosphere in the city and in the country. For example, mayoral candidates would frequently make a well-publicized tour of Spofford either to point out the supportive services such as dental, psychiatric, and medical care, provided for kids who frequently had had no access previously to preventive care or medical treatment, or to blast the juvenile justice system that coddled dangerous criminals rather than holding them responsible for acts which would result in long prison sentences were they adults.

Shifting Political and Policy Context for Adolescent Research Law suits in the 1960s–70s had led to the identification of "status offenses," a legal definition of behaviors which were unique to young people because of their status as minors. These behaviors didn't constitute illegal activities in adulthood. Examples of status offenses were truancy or being "incorrigible" (uncontrollable according to adults). Offenders with serious charges were incarcerated with status offenders for many years. Spofford was

New York City's only detention center for juveniles. The census of 250 was often exceeded, as adolescents cycled through for an average stay of 2 weeks. Recidivism was common, so we had a form of interrupted continuous care as kids cycled through. The contract for their care was made between New York City's Department of Juvenile Justice and Montefiore Medical Center. It was one of the first such affiliation contracts in which services were provided by an academic health center, not the Corrections Department. The implication of this arrangement was that we defined our mission as caring for the kids while simultaneously documenting their unmet health care needs, as well as designing services and interventions based upon what those needs and problems were. Before clinical research publications at Spofford, there were few articles or systematic reports of the basics of health problems among detainees. There were no standards for the facilities that housed them. There was neither accreditation process for the health facilities nor much attention to the impact of services on the health outcomes. By crafting a contract with the tripod of service, research, and training as the basis of negotiation, the Spofford medical program was perfectly positioned to do ground-breaking work. The program was first established by Drs. Michael Cohen and Iris Litt, leaders in young adolescent medicine who had recently opened an Adolescent Division at Montefiore Hospital. Their philosophy was to bring services to where they were needed, so NYC's only juvenile detention center fit the bill.

Juvenile Detention: Another Boundary Issue for Physicians In the manuscript written to encourage physicians to care for incarcerated youth, we made the case for why physicians who care about the health of adolescents needed to go to where the kids were, rather than expecting them to go to hospitals or clinics for age-specific care (Hein et al., 1980). At the time there were few school-based services. Most teenagers were—and still are—cared for by family physicians. Some were cared for by pediatricians or obstetricians/gynecologists, but usually in their offices, not in a site where young people gathered. Experiments like The Bridge started as storefront free clinics then developed multi-service centers during the 1970s.

Spofford as a Sentinel Site for Emerging Issues in Youth By simply documenting the admitting diagnosis to the Spofford infirmary, we could detect emerging epidemics related to drug-use years before they were generally known to the larger medical community or country as a whole. For example, in the 1970s the number of detainees admitted to the infirmary with hepatitis skyrocketed. It was the sentinel sign for the emerging heroin epidemic which had only been reported sporadically among adults.

By analyzing the types of conditions diagnosed in the Spofford population we were able to codify their needs into four categories: (1) conditions associated with prolonged neglect and abuse (e.g., severe malnutrition, dental caries, improperly healed broken bones); (2) conditions associated with poverty (e.g., lack of correction of visual acuity problems, anemia); (3) Conditions created or exacerbated by institutional living (e.g., lactose intolerance due to the food service's insistence on serving milk at all meals, thereby exceeding many youngsters' low limit for lactose-containing foods, causing diarrhea, discomfort, and bloating in those affected); (4) conditions unique to juvenile detainees (e.g., handling of medical information and records when the courts requested use as evidence in court proceedings such as dental records to prove guilt if someone was bitten).

Adolescent Research as a Basis for Setting Standards

Publication of this systematic categorization of conditions was a first (Council on Scientific Affairs, 1990). It was the basis for designing the specific services and creating standards for juvenile detention facilities that followed ("Health Services to Adolescents in Adult Correctional Facilities," 1998). Legal and ethical dilemmas that surfaced around issues of consent, confidentiality, emancipated minor status, etc., caused us to establish weekly rounds with a lawyer and ethicist, as well as with epidemiologists and psychiatrists along with nurses, social workers, and doctors to address the panoply of issues confronted by the detainees. Two weeks of incarceration meant that we had a captive audience for various health-related group sessions, and screening of all detainees as well as treatment for heretofore neglected needs such as dentistry.

Spofford as a learning lab was vitally important not only to improving the health of the detainees, but establishing the whole field of prison medicine. Montefiore's Adolescent Medicine Division took over Riker's Island's Adolescent Remand and Detention Center (ARDC) based upon lessons learned at Spofford. Instead of a few hundred young people, Riker's ARDC had thousands of young adults (some of them Spofford graduates). Part of the success of various class action suits against prison facilities resulting in setting forth universally accepted standards of care and guidelines for care emanated from the efforts at Spofford (Operations Manual ICE Performance Based National Detention Standards, 2008).

In retrospect, I believe we had one of the first adolescents in the USA with HIV at Spofford. As a 16-year-old, he developed Mycosis Fungoides, a very rare cancer previously only diagnosed in elderly Italian men. He had extremely enlarged lymph nodes and a series of highly unusual infections. In retrospect these are criteria for AIDS, but at the time, we noted the highly unusual combination of conditions, and were able to have him evaluated and treated by specialists at the hospital. In 1973, we may have been treating one of the first adolescents with HIV. Fifteen years later, we opened the nation's first adolescent HIV/AIDS program at Montefiore Medical Center.

Perhaps the seed planted in the early 1970s germinated, grew, and came to fruition because of the type of systematic documentation and thinking that went into those early publications about the health needs of juvenile detainees.

We were already focusing on the head of the whale, not the tail.

Being a Reflective Practitioner

We were reflective practitioners, asking questions about the circumstances of the lives of young people incarcerated, enabling us to publish studies relevant not only to juvenile detainees, but to marginalized youth in other settings. Homeless young people, adolescents living on their own as emancipated minors or foster kids who had aged out of care and many other subgroups of adolescents deserve and needed the kind of comprehensive care we documented and created. Without the publications in peer-reviewed literature, our experience may have helped the relatively few teenagers sent to Spofford. The major impact on young people as a group was felt by those who read the studies and used them as a springboard for developing similar services and programs based upon a much wider understanding of the context of care. Currently, health systems research is the basis for much of the WHO and foundation-based funding to improve health of people in the country and the world ("Health Systems"). We were doing systems-based research and care 40 years ago as reflective practitioners and nascent health policy researchers.

From the Frying Pan into the Fire

New York Public Schools, Condom Availability, and Comprehensive Sex Education

The partnership between New York City's Juvenile Justice Department and Montefiore Medical Center's Adolescent Medicine Division presaged other significant partnerships between city or state actors and Montefiore Medical Center during my career, most notably with the New York City Board of Education during the subsequent decade when the HIV/AIDS epidemic was finally recognized for the tremendous impact it was having on the city, the nation, and the world. Once again, an enlightened group of administrators, in partnership with relevant stakeholders, took bold steps to use evidenced-based approaches to serious threats to the health and well-being of adolescents. Fast-forward to the 1990s, when Chancellor of New York City schools, Joe Fernandez, put his weight behind the expansion of HIV/AIDS education, including condom availability and comprehensive sexuality education.

HIV/AIDS Curricular Wars—Adolescent Research as Media Fodder

There are 450,000 high-school students and 1 million school children in New York. The Chancellor based his decision upon publications in the adolescent health field documenting the comprehensive approach rather than the growing trend towards "abstinence only" education. Defying threats to his job (and his and our lives) we crafted an HIV/AIDS curriculum for kindergarten through 12th grade. The rules of the AIDS Curriculum Advisory Committee were that majority ruled. The votes were almost always 5 to 4. Protests in support and in opposition to the curriculum and to condom availability were aptly documented on the front pages of the city newspapers.

The developmentally appropriate curriculum was approved by the Board of Education after months of rancorous debates, but the facts won out. The persuasion of people able to quote the literature on the subject won out over the cacophony of objections based upon parental rights and unfounded fear that education would lead to higher rates of unprotected intercourse. In partnership with researchers, The Board of Education looked at the outcomes of condom use and pregnancy rates in a comparable school system in Chicago, finding that condom use rates were higher and pregnancy rates were reduced when they were made readily available, as was the case in NYC (Guttmacher et al., 1997).

AIDS: Trading Fears for Facts In addition to all of the articles written in the peer reviewed professional, popular and grey literature, I co-authored a book, entitled *AIDS: Trading Fears for Facts—A Guide for Young People* with educator Teresa Foy DiGeronimo, published by Consumer Reports Books (Hein & Foy DiGeronimo, 1994). The cover was an original painting by artist Keith Haring who had not yet disclosed the fact that has living with HIV. The book was unusual for its time. On page 44 was a diagram of how to use a condom. At the time, the most explicit government publication on condom use showed a young man with a bare foot saying, "It's as easy as putting on your sock" but never mentioning the words penis, sex, or anything specific or explicit.

With Haring's memorable cover artwork, our little book was geared to young people and the adults who cared about them. It contained questions for young people to ask of their schools, summer camps, recreational programs, and families about aspects of confidentiality and consent for HIV testing, laboratory results, and services. In this way we were not only trying to empower the young people to have the information they needed, but to provide the same knowledge to their parents and other adults who cared for and about them. In addition, we highlighted stories of young people living with HIV, including Ryan White and David Kamens, who were devoting their lives to being HIV/AIDS educators. Recognizing that all young people were affected directly or indirectly by the epidemic we wanted to give each person reading the book a way to relate and help by either reducing their personal risk, or embracing a more knowledgeable compassionate reaction to those living with HIV.

Stigma, denial, and fear were the predominant emotions surrounding the HIV/AIDS epidemic during the early years. The incidence of HIV has hardly budged during the past two decades since the epidemic was documented (Hein, 1998). Our book was our way to present evidenced-based approaches and resources to young people in ways that helped them become a resource to their peers and to adults wanting to learn more. The book, with 5,000 volumes originally printed, finally went out of print after 100,000 volumes were sold and it was translated into four languages. We tried to fill the vacuum of age-specific literature for and about adolescents by writing a book that was specific, based upon evidence, and not shy about using explicit words and graphics so that young people could have access to accurate, timely information, in the absence of government or other national information because of the political climate in the late 1980s.

From an Idea to a Movement My own 15 seconds of fame came as a result of Earvin ("Magic") Johnson's public announcement that he was HIV infected. He was among the first celebrities and sports stars to make such a disclosure. He set up his Magic Johnson Foundation to bring attention to issues of children and youth in the epidemic. As a member of his Scientific Advisory Board, I helped him craft his messages, videos and projects using the latest information from the medical, behavioral and social science literature. With the new attention being paid to HIV in adolescence, I was suddenly propelled into the limelight. After initially being reluctant to be in the midst of the media frenzy, I agreed to do dozens of TV, radio, and print interviews because there were few physicians at that time willing and able to communicate with the public in a calm informed way. Just as our book had tried to do, I sought to help people separate fears from facts. Sometimes, I was put on a panel with opponents to AIDS education and comprehensive sex education or those who believed that HIV was transmitted casually, but my credibility as an adolescent researcher was what permitted my message to have traction. I was a doctor young people could confide in, parents could trust, and policy-makers could be reassured that I represented the evidence, not the emotion surrounding HIV.

Fast Forward from 1987 to 2011 The Montefiore Adolescent AIDS Program is still among the largest in the nation. There are some adolescents who became HIV infected during the perinatal period (either in utero or as very young infants) who, with excellent care and new medications, have survived into their teenage years. The Program, under the leadership of Dr. Donna Futterman, has continued to be productive in terms of publishing findings in peer-reviewed literature, participating in policy discussions on local, state, national, and international levels, and introducing innovative interventions in conjunction with strategic communications professionals around issues of condom use and routine HIV testing.[1]

The Role of Research in Making Sausage

After newly elected President Clinton announced his intention to make comprehensive health care reform his top-priority issue, I was accepted as a Robert Wood Johnson Health Policy Fellow in the 1993 U.S. Senate Finance Committee. The committee chair, Daniel Patrick Moynihan, was famous for his controversial but always erudite social commentaries including "Defining Deviancy Downward," his look at the role of Black families and Black men in the culture of poverty. The aphorism about Senator Moynihan was that he had written more books than most Senators had read!

Adolescents in Health Care Reform Legislation While I was the only Senate Finance Committee physician when I joined the Professional Staff, more physicians were added as we dealt with the incredible responsibility of being the committee with oversight of Medicaid, Medicare, and other central pieces of legislation. My responsibilities included serving as drafter of the provisions related to the benefits packages for various groups including children and adolescents. I also dealt with the dilemma of how to define what's "medically necessary" as a basis for what should be covered by health insurance, an extremely controversial topic which is still not resolved even after the recently passed overhaul of health insurance enacted by the Obama administration in 2010. My training meant that I paid particular attention to issues like consent, confidentiality for adolescent-specific services, their participation in clinical trials, etc.

The most significant achievement coming from my 15 months in the Senate Finance Committee was the passage of provisions for mental health and substance abuse parity. Key to our ability to gain acceptance of these provisions was Senator Moynihan's conviction that this was the right thing to do. We were able to produce evidence about the cost effectiveness of mental health and substance abuse treatment rather than relying on the opposition's unfounded fear that these services were a "bottomless pit" with no proven effectiveness. Although comprehensive health care reform legislation didn't pass, these provisions providing parity were enacted in a separate bill because of bipartisan support led by Senators Pete Dominici and Paul Wellstone's "Mental Health Parity and Addiction Equity Act of 2008." In this case, health services research, clinical research and policy research results provided the basis for key advocates to enact important legislation to improve the mental and physical health of Americans, including adolescents. Being an insider during a major legislative push enabled me to experience directly the power of research in informing policy and the law ... not always the case, but certainly noteworthy when it occurs!

The National Academies: Advising the Nation and the People Based Upon Evidence

After Congress failed to enact comprehensive health care reform legislation in 1994, I had caught Potomac Fever and wanted to stay in the place I felt was most likely to make the biggest difference in using research to inform policy. The position of Executive Officer of the Institute of Medicine (IOM) at the National Academies provided the perfect opportunity to contribute to this effort. My responsibilities included oversight for the 50+ reports of the IOM, as well as being part of the senior management team overseeing the 200+ reports of the National Research Council (NRC), the operating arm of the National Academy of Sciences (NAS) and the National Academy of Engineering (NAE) as well as the Institute of Medicine. In concert with the three elected Presidents of the Academies, and my counterparts in NAS and NAE, our team fostered joint ventures between the Academies, and provided administrative oversight for all of the 1,200 staff, the finances, meetings and products of The Academies. My scope went well beyond my background in adolescent health and development, but there were age-specific activities of the IOM and NRC.

During my tenure from December 1994 to June 1998, there were several noteworthy developments related to adolescent research. The Board on Children, Youth and Families was born out of the Board on Children, elevating the visibility and importance of research related to youth. Additionally, Michele Kipke was recruited as Board Director bringing special expertise in adolescent research to the staff leadership. We had become acquainted when she was a post-doctoral student in Health Psychology at Albert Einstein College of Medicine of Yeshiva University, which led her to the Adolescent HIV Program to conduct her research project for her dissertation on a specifically designed behavioral risk reduction intervention.

William T. Grant Foundation "Supporting Research to Improve the Lives of Young People"[2]

The William T. Grant Foundation is one of the few large independent foundations with a long track record in supporting research related to adolescent development. Shepherding the resources and shaping the mission articulated by William T. Grant in the 1930s is the responsibility of the President, Board and staff. William T. Grant, founder of a chain of highly successful department stores, expressed his desire to use the endowment to "further the understanding of people . . . that individual potential be more surely realized" (Cahan, 1986). He was prescient in recognizing the importance of the emerging behavioral and social sciences. The very first grants given by his nascent foundation were to "support knowledge." One of the early grants was to Harvard University, to better understand why the young men at Harvard succeed. That longitudinal study is still ongoing after over 50 years (Wolf Shenk, 2009)!

My tenure as President of this wonderful institution followed in the footsteps of two august physicians, Drs. Robert (Bob) Haggerty and Beatrix (Betty) Hamburg. Each had shaped the resources of the Foundation in important new ways. Bob Haggerty elevated the role of community in research, including such memorable publications as "Stress, Risk, and Resilience in Children and Adolescents: Processes, Mechanisms, and Interventions" (Haggerty, 1996). Betty Hamburg brought special attention to the mental health and development of young people during her tenure encapsulated by reports such as, *Children and Families in a Changing World: Challenges and Opportunities* (Hamburg, 1994).

Former Presidents Haggerty and Hamburg, current President, Robert (Bob) Granger, and I were committed to the support of the next generation of adolescent researchers through the William T. Grant Scholars (formerly Faculty Scholars) Program. During my tenure we appointed the 100th Scholar and had a reunion of all former scholars, their mentors, and the Scholars Selection Committee members to commemorate this signature foundation program. We also briefly partnered with the National Academies to award a prize to a site demonstrating research that made a difference conducted by multi-disciplinary teams working in close partnership with communities. By awarding this prize and by focusing the selection of Scholars to those conducting research related to our mission, we hope to bring the best and the brightest researchers into the field. The Scholars Program has recently been expanded to include community-based practitioners to hone their research skills in a program geared towards mid-career professionals.[3]

We believed that if people had a more positive opinion about youth in general, and the young people in their communities, then adolescents would have a better chance to live up to their potential. Since the 1980s, negative stereotypes of young people in general, and adolescents belonging to minority or marginalized populations specifically were the cause of many problems in the country and in the world. As a result, solutions to youth problems were often punitive, restrictive, and fear-based. We did not want to ignore the challenges faced by adolescents, but rather to balance concerns about risks and deficits with increased supports and opportunities (Hein, 1998-2002) (Figure 21.1).

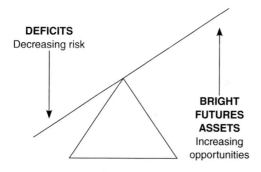

DEFICITS
Decreasing risk

BRIGHT FUTURES ASSETS
Increasing opportunities

FIGURE 21.1 Decreasing risk while increasing opportunity.

It was our hope that by reframing how the country viewed young people, we would have an opportunity to reshape the way the country viewed young people—not as the root of problems, but as a big part of the potential solution—youth as a resource, the Foundation's current mission.

The "positive youth development" or "assets model" underlay our efforts to reframe the view of young people. We were part of a growing wave of researchers, policymakers, and funders who were all promoting this more inclusive view. Simultaneously, the field of "positive psychology" was growing with the institution of new journals.[4] Other foundations, including Ford Foundation, Kellogg Foundation, Carnegie Corporation of New York, and the Surdna Foundation had major initiatives related to positive youth development, civic engagement, and youth leadership. Simultaneously, interest in the Himalayan Kingdom of Bhutan grew as the King promoted the 1970s-era "gross national happiness" (GNH) index, which replaced "gross national product" and, as his major development yardstick, aligned specific indicators of GNH with an assets model for the entire country ("Measuring GNH").

Another notable example of the "assets model" was the White House's "Conference on Teenagers: Raising Resourceful and Responsible Youth", chaired by Hillary Clinton.[5] A full day event held at The White House in 2000, the conference brought together a cadre of researchers in youth development, leaders of model programs, young people, and their families to highlight the synergy and connections between these sectors and the value of the assets model. Mrs. Clinton's decision to host this major event was influenced by her membership on the W. T. Grant Foundation's Commission on Work, Family, and Citizenship, whose findings on the 50% of American youth who did not go beyond high school had been previously distributed as "The Forgotten Half" (Haggerty, 1989). In focusing on this assets model, this White House Conference was unique. Others before and since have focused on the problems or deficits, as epitomized by the Bush-era White House conference on underage drinking.

Now, as the "Millennials" (young people born since the early 1980s) come of age and are more visible as young adults, there are ways in which both the assets model and deficit model are prominent simultaneously (Howe & Strauss, 2000).

We honor the contribution of our soldiers, both male and female, in the current wars in Iraq and Afghanistan. We reward the outstanding athletes of our time with accolades and high salaries. We marvel at the technological advances and phenomena of social media which have come from the imagination and skill of young entrepreneurs. Yet unemployment during the current recession among young Black males is above 50%; our current legislative initiatives to exclude undocumented immigrants and even prohibit American-born offspring of illegal immigrants from receiving college educational support is a stark contrast to the notion of enabling young people to live up to their potential.

From the USA to the Whole World: Global Health and Development

When I stepped down as President of The William T. Grant Foundation in 2003, I announced to the Board and staff that I wished to follow the words of Gandhi, "My life is my message." The implications of this choice mean that my life and my life's work are merged. We live in Vermont where I am shepherdess to a small herd of Cashmere Goats. Like Gandhi, I try to focus on life's basic elements, the making of yarn, cloth, books, paper as ways to make a meaningful life. My work in global health and humanitarian assistance is as a volunteer, without an institutional base, title or salary. I am an active member of the boards of marvelous organizations including The International Rescue Committee, ChildFund International and the ChildFund Alliance, The Robert Wood Johnson Foundation's Clinical Scholars National Advisory Committee, RAND Health Board and People in AID U.S. board among others. For instance, ChildFund International has an articulated theoretical framework, specific core program elements with specific evidenced-based core indicators of outcomes as part of their strategic plan (Kostelny & Wessells, 2008). Peter Benson's unparalleled contribution to the field of assets-based approaches to youth development is particularly noteworthy in light of his unexpected death in the fall of 2011. Peter's leadership of The Search Institute was stellar. I had the good fortune to welcome him to the William T. Grant Foundation staff as a Visiting Scholar during my tenure as President. He infused a sense of vitality, glee and energy into his (and our) work, providing a way in which people could value young people and quantify their invaluable contributions to communities and societies.[6]

All of these organizations base their programs on research, fosters research in their settings and recommends systems change and policy development based upon research. Each is geared towards identifying and supporting the next generation of leaders and in developing young people in their communities to succeed (Hein, 2009). The demographic pyramid of most developing countries is skewed towards children and youth, just the reverse of highly industrialized western nations. My focus has been resource-poor communities in these developing countries, particularly focusing on displaced or marginalized groups. In many situations, the medical principle of "do no harm" should be restated as "do better with what we know" (Hein, 2010). For the past 7 years, this philosophy has helped me focus on professionalizing humanitarian assistance (Walker, Hein, Russ, Bertleff, & Caspersz, 2010).

Looking Back … Looking Ahead …

My career path has been quite zigzagged. My journey has taken me through very different sectors, far from my comfort zone, away from traditional medicine as it is conceived and practiced in this country.

Medicine is my background. The world is my foreground. Adolescent research is the lens through which I have tried to make sense of the larger world for myself and in partnership with others, try to improve the conditions for young people and all people so that they might live up to their potential.

… And Back Again to the USA

Unexpectedly, in 2011, I found myself caught up in an incredible opportunity back in the USA. Newly elected Vermont Governor, Peter Shumlin, working with the State Legislature passed Act 48, a visionary comprehensive health care reform law which he signed in May 2011. The new law calls for universal access for all Vermont residents to a system of care that will be coordinated, comprehensive, evidenced-based and reward providers for value, not volume. It will be an "all payer" system in which public and private sources of revenue will be pooled then allocated by the Green Mountain Care Board in ways to improve the health of 162,000 citizens of the state. Reforms will include a new workforce plan, global budgeting, control of hospital costs, rate of rise in total health expenditures as well as determination of benefits. As one of the 5 members of the GMCB, I am now focusing on implementing this bold new law. It is our hope that this approach will not only help young people in Vermont, but actually help people of all ages in the state and hopefully, be a path forward for the nation.

Research in adolescent health and development has been the cornerstone of my career. In each of the five sectors I have worked (academia, government, think-tank, philanthropy, and global health and development), research principles, research questions, research methodology, and recommendations and policies based upon research have been my mantra. As a physician, I have been trained in the medical model, which has its limitations yet holds sway in our society for an approach to solving many intractable problems. It is my belief and experience that combining the best approaches in medical, behavioral, and social sciences, honoring the unique perspective each can bring—creating teams that draw upon the traditions and practices of a wide range of researchers, practitioners, and young people and the adults who care about them, is the best way to advance our knowledge and understanding. *Our mentoring goes both ways*—we to young people… and they to us.

Acknowledgment

The author wishes to express gratitude to Rachel Baras for her editorial assistance and her colleagueship and representing the best of the contributions and partnership between younger and older people.

Notes

1. For articles by Donna Futterman on this topic, see: www.einstein.yu.edu/home/faculty/profile.asp?id=1576&O=1&P=1.
2. For William T. Grant Foundation tagline, see: www.wtgrantfoundation.org/about_us.
3. For more information on the William T. Grant Foundation Scholars Program, see: www.wtgrantfdn.org/funding_opportunities/fellowships/william_t_grant_scholars.
4. See *Journal of Positive Psychology* at: www.tandf.co.uk/journals/journal.asp?issn=1743-9760&linktype=1.

5. For information on this conference, see: clinton3.nara.gov/WH/New/html/teenconf1.html.
6. To learn more about the Search Institute and the assets-based approach, please visit: www.search-institute.org/developmental-assets.

References

Cahan, E. D. (1986). *The William T. Grand Foundation: First Fifty Years, 1936–1986.* New York: The William T. Grant Foundation.

Council on Scientific Affairs. (1990). Health status of detained and incarcerated youths. *Journal of the American Medical Association, 263*(7), 987–991.

Goldsmith, M. (1993). "Invisible" epidemic now becoming visible as HIV/AIDS pandemic reaches adolescents. *Journal of the American Medical Association, 270*(1), 16–19. doi: 10.1001/jama.1993.03510010018004.

Goldstein, J. (2006). *Inventing Great Neck: Jewish identity and the American dream.* Piscataway, NJ: Rutgers University Press.

Guttmacher, S., Lieberman, L., Ward, D., Freudenberg, N., Radosh, A., & Des Jarlais, D. (1997). Condom availability in New York City public high schools: Relationships to condom use and sexual behavior. *American Journal of Public Health, 87*(9), 1427–1433.

Haggerty, R. J. (1989, December). Youth and America's future: The forgotten half. *Journal of Developmental and Behavioral Pediatrics, 10*(6), 321–325.

Haggerty, R. J. (Ed.). (1996). *Stress, risk, and resilience in children and adolescents.* Cambridge: Cambridge University Press.

Hamburg, B. A. (1994). *Children and families in a changing world: Challenges and opportunities.* Austin, TX: Hogg Foundation.

Health Services to Adolescents in Adult Correctional Facilities, National Commission on Correctional Health Care Board of Directors, May 17, 1998. Retrieved from www.ncchc.org/resources/statements/adolescents.html.

Health Systems. *World Health Organization.* Retrieved November 17, 2011, from www.who.int/topics/health_systems/en/.

Hein, K. (1968). Boarder babies at Lincoln Hospital. In S. Fisch & J. William (Eds.), *The Student Health Project of the South Bronx. Summer 1967* (pp. 138–144). New York: The Office of Economic Opportunity.

Hein, K. (1987). AIDS in adolescence: A rationale for concern. *New York State Journal of Medicine, 87,* 290–295.

Hein, K. (1988). *AIDS in adolescence: A rationale for concern.* Carnegie Council on Adolescent Development.

Hein, K. (1998, June 19). Aligning science with politics and policy in HIV prevention. *Science, 280*(5371), 1905–1906.

Hein, K. (1998–2002). President messages. *William T. Grant Foundation Annual Reports.*

Hein, K. (2003, June). *Spinning a tale, weaving a life.* Speech presented at the 2003 William T. Grant Scholars retreat.

Hein, K. (2009, June 11). *Kids over there – why should I care?: Helping children in developing countries thrive.* Albert P. Williams Memorial Health Lecture. Lecture conducted from RAND Corporation, Santa Monica, CA.

Hein, K. (2010, September). The competency of competencies. *Prehospital and Disaster Medicine, 25*(5), 396–397.

Hein, K., Cohen, M. I., Litt, I. F., Schonberg, S. K., Meyer, M. R., Marks, A. et al. (1980). Juvenile detention: Another boundary issue for physicians. *Pediatrics. 66*(2), 239–245.

Hein, K., & Foy DiGeronimo, T. (1994). *AIDS: Trading fears for facts – A guide for young people* (3rd ed.). Yonkers, NY: Consumer Reports Books.

Howe, N., & Strauss, W. (2000). *Millennials rising: The next great generation.* New York: Vintage Books.

Kolata, G. (1989, October 8). AIDS is spreading in teen-agers, a new trend alarming to experts. *The New York Times.*

Kostelny, K., & Wessells, M. (2008). The protection and psychosocial well-being of young children following armed conflict: Outcome research on child centered spaces in northern Uganda. *The Journal of Developmental Processe, 3*(2), 13–25.

Levenson, D. (1984). *Montefiore: The hospital as social instrument 1884–1984.* Vancouver, BC: Douglas & McIntyre.

Measuring GNH. *Permanent mission of the Kingdom of Bhutan to the United Nations in New York.* Retrieved November 17, 2011, from www.un.int/wcm/content/site/bhutan/cache/offonce/pid/7869

Mullan, F. (1976). *White coat, clenched fist: The political education of an American physician.* New York, NY: McMillan.

Operations Manual ICE Performance Based National Detention Standards (PBNDS). (2008). Retrieved from www.ice.gov/detention-standards/2008/.

Teenagers and AIDS. (1992, August 2). *Newsweek.*

Walker, P., Hein, K., Russ, C., Bertleff, G., & Caspersz, D. (2010, December). A Blueprint for professionalizing humanitarian assistance. *Health Affairs, 29,* 2223–2230.

Wolf Shenk, J. (2009, June). What makes us happy? *The Atlantic Monthly.* Retrieved November 17, 2011, from www.theatlantic.com/magazine/archive/2009/06/what-makes-us-happy/7439/.

22

Adolescents as Productive Processors of Reality

My Socialization Approach in Youth Research

KLAUS HURRELMANN

My access to youth research is characterized by socialization theory. Socialization refers to the development of a person's personality, and this is the result of the processing of both internal and external realities: Bodily and mental qualities and traits constitute a person's internal reality; societal and physical circumstances embody the external reality.

In the first section, I introduce this approach, report on its genesis, and comment on the principal insights. In the second section, I apply this approach to youth research and present ten epistemological "maxims" which are constitutive for my theoretical and empirical work. Finally, I give examples of theoretical and empirical research results which refer to the theoretical premises.

Theoretical Background: Socialization Approach

If I ask myself what the genesis of my comprehensive socialization approach could be, I arrive at two answers: First of all, my theoretical approach is influenced by personal biographical experiences from my youth. The second answer is that, during my academic training, this personal experience inspired me to further explore the psychological and sociological dynamics of puberty.

With regard to the first answer: At the age of 14, I had great difficulty with the developmental task of separation from my parents, specifically from my father. He was a strong and powerfully built man who had served as a sailor in the merchant navy. He thought I was too sensitive and soft and could not understand my interest in culture and politics. He gave me the impression that I was not a "real boy" in his eyes, so I looked for opportunities to prove him wrong and joined a group of classmates who shoplifted from department stores. I wanted to show my father that I was not as the careful "goody-goody" he

always accused me of being, so I stole some things. This was discovered and immediately reported to the police. The next day two police officers came to my school and I was arrested. Some weeks later, I had to appear before a juvenile court, where I was found guilty, and sentenced to several days in a remand home. As a result, I was expelled from school, and for the next two years, my family was visited by probation officers.

Concerning the effect of this on my academic studies, as a student of sociology and social psychology, I looked for scientific theories with which to explain developmental problems, and my personal experience told me that these theories had to establish a link between personality development and social living conditions. At that time in Germany, the field of sociology was still in its infancy, and it was U.S.-American social scientists and social psychologists who played a major role in my curriculum, among them George Herbert Mead, Talcott Parsons, Erik H. Erikson, Urie Bronfenbrenner, Albert Bandura, Robert J. Havighurst and—at a later time—Aaron Antonovsky. Through their work I found what I was looking for: the combination of sociological and psychological approaches to personality and explanations for developmental problems. Some years later, as an exchange student in Berkeley, I had the opportunity to elaborate on this theoretical approach. I also learned to appreciate the scientific culture of combining a sharp critical debate with the need finally to come to a constructive consensus. This approach has influenced me greatly in my scientific career and has made me look for theories that fit together.

Basic Questions of Socialization Theory Central to the theory of socialization is the tension between the individual and society. Two inter-related issues are of importance here:

- How does a society manage to socialize the people living within it and integrate them into its social structures?

- How do people living within this society manage to gain access to the freedoms necessary for their personal development and become autonomous individuals?

Influenced by my biographical experience, it was my personal mission to find comprehensive and at the same time conciliatory answers to these questions. My answers are found in the book *Social Structure and Personality Development. The Individual as a Productive Processor of Reality* (Hurrelmann, 1988), which is an attempt to develop a concept to connect relevant sociological and psychological approaches:

- Drawing from sociological theories, I have selected, among others, elements of the Theory of Symbolic Interactionism of George H. Mead; the Systems Theory of Talcott Parsons; and the Salutogenesis Theory of Aaron Antonovsky. All of these theories, which are based on social determinants of personality development, focus on how external reality is transferred to the interior of the personality.
- From psychological theories, I have, among others, taken the Psychosocial Development Theory of Erik H. Erikson; the Ecological Theory of Urie Bronfenbrenner; the Social Learning Theory of Albert Bandura and the Developmental Task Theory of Robert J. Havighurst. These theories are based on the bio-psychological determinants of personality development and discuss how these determinants can be reconciled with the demands of external reality.

The choice of these approaches was determined by the desire to combine micro and macro perspectives. The selected theories are concerned with analytical statements regarding both the aspect of the "individual" and that of the "society." They also have at their disposal a conceptual construct which is accessible on an interdisciplinary level. And last but not least, almost all of these theories have a common concept of human nature: They proceed from the assumption that personality development is an active process of dealing with internal and external demands (Hurrelmann, 2012).

Development of the Model of Productive Processing of Reality (PPR) Even though the individual sociological and psychological theories I have mentioned are extremely valuable, by their very nature they remain limited in their explanatory power as each approaches the phenomenon of human personality development from only one specific perspective: either from the perspective of the society, or from that of the individual. The core idea of my theoretical approach is, therefore, to link these individual theories and incorporate them into a comprehensive concept.

In order to provide a basic framework, I have developed a "meta-theoretical" model which is located beyond the individual theories. As a unifying and overarching

theoretical orientation I propose the Model of Productive Processing of Reality (PPR). The core assumption is that "personality does not form independently from society any of its functions or dimensions but is continuously being shaped, in a concrete, historically conveyed life world, throughout the entire space of the life span" (Hurrelmann, 1988, p. 42). The PPR model places the human subject in a social and ecological context that must be absorbed and processed subjectively. To achieve this, three central units of analysis have to be connected: Social and material environment as external reality; human organism as internal reality; personality dynamics and structure as managing of internal and external reality (Hurrelmann, 1983, p. 93; 1988, p. 45).

The Principal Assumptions of the PPR Model The following definition of "Socialization" is at the core of the PPR Model:

> *Socialization* refers to the personality development of a person. It is the result of the productive processing of internal and external realities. Bodily and mental qualities and traits constitute a person's internal reality; the circumstances of the social and physical environment embody the external reality. Reality processing is "productive" because human beings actively grapple with their lives and attempt to cope with the attendant developmental tasks. The success of such a process depends on the personal and social resources available. Incorporated within all developmental tasks is the necessity to reconcile personal individuation and social integration and so secure the I-identity.

This definition provides three important guidelines with regard to the theory of socialization:

(a) First of all, the definition understands socialization as a process of "personality development" : This refers to the individually specific and unique structure of bodily and mental traits, characteristics, and qualities. Personality development therefore also refers to the changes in fundamental elements of this structure which take place during the course of a lifetime. Human beings are environmentally conscious and adaptive entities, whereby they retain their basic personality structure, yet adapt their processing strategies according to the challenges they face in their personal history. In this way they construct their own life history.

(b) The definition also understands socialization as "productive" processing of reality: this presumes the lifelong active participation of individuals in the appropriation and processing both of natural predispositions and of social and physical environmental circumstances. Personality development is accordingly determined neither by inherited traits, nor by circumstance. Instead, it unfolds within the interplay of these two constants. The internal reality includes the bodily and the mental qualities; the external reality includes the conditions provided by the social and physical environment.

(c) The third guideline of the definition is that the ability to handle developmental tasks is a constant requirement of socialization: Each culture provides membership standards which, in the form of societal patterns and norms, determine the organization of its social institutions and environment. These include perceptions, desires, expectations, and attributes that are considered essential for active participation in society. When these have been adopted by an individual one can speak of his or her "social integration." Despite being socially integrated, each person remains a unique and distinctive personality, with concerns about not being totally monopolized socially ("individuation"). Thus, keeping the tension between integration and individuation in balance remains a lifelong task and a prerequisite for mental and physical health (Hurrelmann, 1989a).

These are the three principal assumptions which underpin my overarching socialization theory. The core idea is to combine macro and micro perspectives by bringing societal and psychological approaches into a single unit. The common assumption of the theories that are selected for the PPR Model is the proposition of a productive, structured acquisition of social and cultural conditions and their transfer into personal psychological characteristics of the individual personality.

Since this is an epistemological meta-theoretical model, complete empirical evidence cannot be achieved. The degree of empirical evidence is not the decisive criterion for the selection of the single theoretical approaches that go into the PPR model. Rather, it seems more important to provide a coherent body of theoretical concepts that can be used as a framework for the development of hypotheses for individual empirical research projects. I am convinced that the PPR model, though it has its origins in developed societies, can be transferred without any restriction to the conditions for personality development in less advanced societies. I am in favor of the hypothesis of a linear modernization of social structures and believe that the rules of personality development are universal.

Transferring the PPR Model to Youth Research

My theoretical contribution to youth research is to transfer the epistemological, meta-theoretical assumptions of the PPR model to adolescence. First, this requires the appropriate sociological and psychological theories necessary for an understanding of the adolescent phase of life to be selected; second, the empirical research questions and designs emanating from the model have to be defined (Hurrelmann, 1989b).

I first submitted a comprehensive study on the socialization theory of adolescence based on the PPR model in the mid-1980s. The latest edition of this theory appeared in 2012 in a book that I wrote in collaboration with Gudrun Quenzel (*Lebensphase Jugend*, Hurrelmann & Quenzel, 2012). The special feature of this book is that the epistemological assumptions of the PPR model have been condensed and are presented in the form of "maxims." These are meta-theoretical propositions that bundle and sum up various theoretical approaches of socialization-oriented youth research. The maxims also make the methodological strategies for youth research that result from these theoretical assumptions more accessible, and offer perspectives for future key areas of research. Ten maxims have subsequently been developed (Hurrelmann & Quenzel, 2012, p. 90):

First maxim: In adolescence, as in every phase of life, personality development emerges in the interplay between inherited traits and the environment. This then defines the basic framework for sexual and gender characteristics.

Second maxim: In adolescence the process of socialization, which is understood as the productive processing of both the internal and external reality, reaches an especially intense phase. This phase is of a pattern-building nature and has lifelong consequences. Productive reality processing presupposes the ability to cope with developmental tasks that are typical in adolescence.

Third maxim: Adolescents are creative designers of their own personalities. They possess competences which progressively expand towards an independent lifestyle.

Fourth maxim: Adolescence is characterized by a first-time biographical opportunity to develop an I-identity, which emerges in the creation of a balance between personal individuation and social integration, both of which exist in a relationship of mutual dynamic tension.

Fifth maxim: The socialization process in adolescence can take on crisis-laden proportions if adolescents do not succeed in reconciling and then inter-linking the demands of individuation and those of integration. In this event, the developmental tasks of adolescence are not resolved and cumulative developmental pressure arises.

Sixth maxim: In order for young people to cope with developmental tasks and create a balance in the dynamic tension between individuation and integration needs, they require not only individual coping skills ("personal resources"), but also social support services from the most important reference groups ("social resources").

Seventh maxim: Besides the family of origin, the most important socialization authorities which act as facilitators and supporters in the developmental process of adolescents are schools, training centers, peers, and the media. When the stimuli presented by these bodies complement and enhance one another, the effect on socialization is very positive.

Eighth maxim: Under modern historical, social, and economic conditions in developed societies, the adolescent phase of life must be identified as a distinct phase within the whole life course. This phase has lost its earlier character of being a transitional phase between childhood and adulthood.

Ninth maxim: Highly developed societies are distinguished not only by their rapid societal transformation, but also by large-scale social and ethnic diversity, and by ever-increasing economic inequality. These features also increasingly shape adolescence and lead to a partition in the life-world of adolescents.

Tenth maxim: The coping patterns of adolescents, who are dealing with developmental tasks, are shaped by whether they are female or male. During the last three to four decades, girls and young women are more successful than boys in this respect and thus increasingly have gained access to influential positions in society.

Each of the ten maxims is a potential point of departure for subsequent theoretical and empirical activities of youth research. In my own academic work—and strongly inspired by the biographical experiences I mentioned at the beginning of this chapter—I have focused on the issues discussed in the fifth maxim (coping with developmental tasks), the eighth maxim (the changing character of the adolescent phase of life) and the ninth and tenth maxim (socio-economic and gender diversity of socialization). In the following sections I give an overview of the main theoretical and empirical results of my work.

Adolescents as Productive Processors of Reality: Research Results

The Changing Position of Adolescence Within the Life Course As mentioned in the eighth maxim, in developed countries, adolescence is increasingly changing its former characteristic of being merely a transitional phase between childhood and adulthood. The demographic aging of the population not only alters the structure of the population with regard to age groups, it also has a significant effect on the shape and structure of life phases. From 1900 till the present day, in a time span of about three generations, life expectancy has increased continuously; and because of the decreasing birthrate, the percentage of members of the younger generation has decreased. At the same time the individual life phases have been repositioned (Hurrelmann & Quenzel, 2012, p. 17).

Most notable is the contraction of the two life phases childhood and adulthood; and the simultaneous redefinition of the life phases of the adolescent and senior citizen. Around 1900, the lifecycle consisted of only two phases: that of childhood and that of adulthood. Around 1950, two new life phases came into being: "adolescence" and the "senior citizen." More recently, these have expanded further, at the expense of the childhood phase, but with a particular effect on the adult phase. In contrast to the 1950s, adulthood is no longer a person's central life phase, but merely one amongst

many (Hurrelmann, 1994; Hurrelmann & Engel, 1990; Neubauer & Hurrelmann, 1996).

The Expansion of Adolescence as a Phase of Life The adolescent life phase has thus not only been newly differentiated within the last century, it has expanded continually. A significant reason for this has been the developments in the labor market and the resultant changes in the educational system. The greater the demand for increased qualifications, the longer the period of life spent in schools and colleges; consequently, the "youth" phase has become longer.

Young women and men do not typically take full social responsibility in the area of economic reproduction, but they do have the possibility of participating fully in other areas of society. This is especially true in respect of the consumer commodity market, the leisure industry, and the media sector, as well as with regard to private social relationships.

In all highly developed societies—because of a blend of limited economic independence and generous socio-cultural freedom—young people are being encouraged to create their own possibilities for social action and articulation in the areas of fashion, music, entertainment, media, leisure activities and in the development of relationships. Many young people become intensely involved in this period between childhood and adulthood when a social "moratorium" shields them from economic participation and other social obligations. They enjoy the independence of this period of shelter, which occurs at the time before they are absorbed into the status of responsible adulthood. The length of this moratorium has constantly expanded during the last century and has increased to an average period of 15 years (Hurrelmann 1994).

Biographical Management Requirements In the socially open and culturally diversified societies of today, young people are required to develop a personality structure that will enable them to respond to precarious societal demands, and to deal with rapidly shifting social, cultural, economic and ecological conditions. In this regard the following behavior patterns are functional:

- High behavioral virtuosity and great competence in the processing of problems. Young people are faced with the challenge of developing their own lifestyle and defining their own life plan at an early stage. Indeed, having to deal with the contradictory nature of social expectations and develop one's own identity within this difficult situation is a major characteristic of adolescence. The lack of synchronicity between the determinations of independence within the various areas of transition, and the differing value of the attained positions ("status inconsistency"), have to be endured and handled attentively (Hurrelmann, Engel, & Weidman, 1992a, 1992b).

- Today, a basic precondition for mastery of the adolescent phase of life is the ability to handle the uncertainty as to whether one will ever advance to adulthood, in the sense of full membership of society; or whether one will remain in the moratorium of youth. This implies living with the *structural insecurity* of whether one will ever attain a professional position, or whether one will have only short-term possibilities to work, or not even secure a place of work (Hurrelmann, 1984). This influences the decision regarding the future founding of a family. Consequently, the potential for biographical ambiguity, characteristic of a modern open and "individualized" society, is increased.

- Young people need a clearly structured self-concept of who they are and what they want to become. This is a prerequisite for managing to deal with the multiple demands for action, as well as with the contradictions inherent in gaining personal autonomy. In a highly individualized society, having a sense of what personal and social resources they have at their disposal, and of how they fit into society, can be a great benefit to young people. If such personal goals are available to them, they have the possibility of utilizing the enormous freedoms available today; and of optimizing their own personality development (Hurrelmann, 1990a, 1990b; Hurrelmann, Leppin, & Nordlohne, 1995; Nestmann & Hurrelmann, 1994).

Adolescence as a Paradigm for a Lifestyle During Adulthood The manner young people master everyday life has become a model for people in other life phases. The reason being that the youthful phase is no longer a transitional phase leading to "full maturity." Consequently, the way of coping with developmental tasks in adolescence is becoming increasingly typical for subsequent stages of life. In other words, living with uncertainty and disruptions, enduring restrictions to one's autonomy, and the constant effort to deal with "status inconsistency" has become characteristic of life for many adults today.

From a sociological perspective, young people are pioneers in the development of a lifestyle that responds to the latest cultural, economic, and social shifts in society. Young people intuitively refuse to follow the traditional patterns that shaped the lives of older generations. Today's open, dynamic, tension-filled life demands, necessitate reflexive action management. It is precisely this lifestyle orientation that is preferred by most young people (Hurrelmann & Quenzel, 2012, p. 50).

This orientation can be described as a blend between self-reference, sensitive behavior, and a somehow opportunistic attitude; requiring them to feel their way cautiously, while at the same time strategizing carefully. This can be described figuratively as *egotactic,* as here strong self-reference meets an evaluating cost–benefit attitude. A pre-determined and pre-planned sequence of actions is inadequate in the typical life situation of today's young people. They have to react unselfconsciously; yet respond openly and flexibly to rapidly shifting life conditions. Improvised lifestyle elements are at least as important as routinely experienced behavior patterns.

In this sense, individual young people have sole responsibility for the planning of their own lives. This includes a high degree of freedom regarding the way in which their lives are structured. Every one of these young people must grapple individually with the demands made on them regarding the way in which they live their lives, and concerning the manner with which they approach problems and find solutions. All these components will become increasingly important for their lives as adults. They will help contribute to a stronger intertwining of these two life phases than was the case in earlier times.

Coping with Developmental Tasks As mentioned in the fifth maxim, the adolescent phase of life is characterized by a tremendous density of age-specific challenges upon which the management of personality development in later life depends. Following the conceptual foundation laid by Robert J. Havighurst (1972), I subsequently define these challenges as *developmental tasks.* They define the age-based expectations of a society within a specific historical point in time. These expectations refer to societal norms and social role behavior, about which there is wide-ranging agreement within the respective cultures.

Developmental tasks, largely conveyed by the various agencies of socialization (family, kindergarten, school, peer group, media, etc.) are the focus of collective opinions as to what constitutes appropriate development and what can be understood as meaningful change within a specific age-period; and which can therefore be set as the goal for individual behavior. In this sense, developmental tasks can be seen as the implementation of the physical, psychological, social, and ecological demands made on the development of a personality in respect of socially and culturally accepted behavior patterns.

For further research, it is useful to differentiate between four central clusters of developmental tasks (Hurrelmann & Quenzel, 2012, p. 28):

(a) *Qualify:* The development of the intellectual and social competences necessary to meet performance requirements and societal demands as well as attaining the education and qualifications necessary in order to assume the social membership role of the professional.

(b) *Commit:* The development of a physical as well as a gender identity, the emotional detachment from parents, and the ability to make a commitment in order to assume the social membership role as the founder of a family.

(c) *Consume:* The development of social contacts and off-loading support strategies as well as the skills in dealing with economic opportunities, leisure activities, and media services, and so to assume the social membership role of the consumer.

(d) *Participate:* The development of an individual system of values and norms and the competence to participate politically, and so to assume a citizen's social membership role.

A psycho-biological and socio-cultural dimension can be distinguished in the developmental tasks that have to be mastered during these four phases of the adolescent phase of life.

The Psycho-biological Dimension of the Developmental Tasks The psycho-biological dimension of the developmental tasks can be described as follows:

(a) *The development of intellectual and social competences (qualify)*: This concerns the development of both the cognitive and the intellectual skills, and the societal behavioral means of acquiring knowledge and to act in a socially responsible manner. Once this dimension of the developmental task has been mastered, young people are able to deal confidently with performance requirements and societal demands. They are then capable of laying the foundations for the completion of their school education and their professional training (Petersen, Leffert, & Hurrelmann, 1993).

(b) *The development of a physical and a gender identity; and the capability to bond (commit)*: This is about accepting and actively participating in a changing physical and emotional makeup; the construction of a gendered identity; the emotional detachment from parents and the creation, depending on orientation, of a hetero- or homosexual long-term relationship that fulfills personal dreams and desires and which is the precondition for the later founding of a family.

(c) *Development of social contacts and off-loading support strategies (consume)*: The focus here is on the capability of forming close friendships and establishing ties with members of the same age group; developing an own lifestyle and a requirement-oriented handling of leisure opportunities and consumer choices. These competencies include the entire sector of luxury goods and stimulants as well as of drugs; all leisure time offerings and the productive use of media for the purpose of personal enjoyment and individual enrichment. All these skills serve to support the release of daily tensions and the regeneration of mental and bodily energies.

(d) *The development of an individual system of values and norms (participate)*: The focal point here is the unfolding of a personal lifestyle system of values and ethical principles that are in accordance with personal behavior and conduct, and which make a meaningful life orientation possible .

The Socio-cultural Dimension of the Developmental Tasks The socio-cultural dimension of the developmental tasks can be described as follows:

(a) *Acquire the competence to practice a profession as part of the societal membership role (qualify)*: Here the focus is on the development of cognitive and social capabilities, as well as of professionally relevant expertise, so that occupations and employment relevant to the society can be undertaken (Hurrelmann, 1987). If this dimension of the developmental task is fulfilled, and if there is a successful assumption of professional activity, the possibility of an independent source of livelihood is attained. This in turn leads to "economic reproduction" of one's personal existence and therewith of society.

(b) *Acquire the competence to found a family as part of the societal membership role (commit)*: The goal here is the emotional and social detachment from parents, which is the family of origin; and the establishment of close contacts to friends and members of the same age group; and the commitment to a loving, intimate relationship. A precondition for this is identification with one's own gender role, which is associated with the search for one's own individual sexual orientation. If this dimension of the developmental task has been fulfilled, there will be willingness, as well as an ability, to commit to a long-term relationship and loyal partnership, which may result in the founding of a family and to offspring. This then leads to the "biological reproduction" of one's own existence, and therewith of society.

(c) *Acquire the competence to become a consumer as part of the societal membership role (consume)*: The objective here is to practice an approach to dealing with all the possibilities offered by the commercial, leisure, and media sectors and their diverse relaxation, self-awareness, and entertainment programs in a manner that is independent, geared to one's own needs, interests, and financial limitations. The precondition is the secure knowledge of one's own needs; the strengths and weaknesses of their implementation; and an appropriate way of dealing with money. Young people, who accomplish this dimension of the developmental task, possess the ability to utilize consumption and leisure offers to their own benefit, and to run a home. They are also successful with regard to "mental reproduction," which is the recovery and the restoration of the creativity and productivity that has been depleted in other areas of their lives. This benefits the entire society.

(d) *Acquire the competence to participate in the economic membership role of a citizen (participate)*: The intention here is to acquire the capability to participate actively in the affairs of the social community. The precondition is the development of ethical, religious, moral, and political standpoints, and the capacity to act on them. Young people who achieve this dimension of the developmental task have at their disposal the competence to articulate their needs and interests in public; through civic participation, they also contribute to the strengthening of the society's self-monitoring capabilities, thus contributing to the social cohesion.

As this shows, the psycho-biological and socio-cultural dimensions of the four developmental tasks are closely related to one another. Mastering the psycho-biological dimension is the precondition for individuation; that is, the development of a young person's distinctive and unique personality. Mastering the socio-cultural dimension is the precondition for integration, which is the acceptance of a membership role in the community. Only when individuation and integration are interlinked with each other, will it be possible to develop an I-identity.

Time and Social Inconsistencies in the Coping Process In highly developed societies, the demands made with regard to the mastery of the four clusters of developmental tasks have become extremely complex. Due to the pluralization of value orientations and lifestyles, there are few defined social and cultural expectations as to how this mastery is to occur, so that the manner in which the tasks are to be mastered is left to the discretion of each young person. The standards according to which relevant social reference groups decide whether the developmental tasks have been achieved, are not stated explicitly, but must be inferred from the particular social context. To give an example: Which certificate and which grade in a particular educational system is regarded as a fulfillment of the developmental task, "qualify," depends on social background. Another example: Whether entering into a long-term homosexual partnership is regarded as the fulfillment of the developmental task "commit" will be decided by the particular socio-cultural environment.

These open structures demand a large degree of independent exploration of possibilities and opportunities from every young person; and a high capacity of self-determination (Chisholm & Hurrelmann, 1995). Today, there are also characteristic temporal and social variations in coping with developmental tasks. In each of the four clusters, mastering them occurs at varying points in time. Young people typically fulfill their developmental tasks in the areas of consumption and participation at an early stage. By contrast, fulfillment of the developmental tasks occurs very late in the area of committing to a long-term relationship and of founding a family; this also applies to the area of qualification and assumption of a professional role.

Due to the diverse nature of time patterns in the four clusters, there is an "inconsistency in social status." Here "status" refers to positions with specific social prestige. Young people simultaneously occupy positions with very different levels of prestige and have to endure the resultant tensions. The structural inconsistency between autonomy and the (lack of) ability to act is a typical characteristic of the adolescent phase of life (Engel & Hurrelmann, 1992; Hurrelmann & Engel, 1992; Hurrelmann, Engel, & Weidman, 1992a).

Status inconsistency is further increased, because in all four clusters of the developmental tasks there is a gap between the actual freedom of action and the legally permitted realization of such actions. For example, there is an early handling of money, but later legal competence; early economic activity as an unskilled worker, but much later professional activity; early sexual initiation, but much later founding of a family; an early contribution to a political association, but the official right to vote only at eighteen.

Problems with Regard to the Mastering of the Developmental Tasks According to my thesis, the more complex and differentiated societies become the less transparent and the less binding the rules for the participation of young people in social activities. Because of the open structure and the democratic constitution of our societies, legal rules lose their binding character. They only give rudimentary guidance with regard to when and under which circumstances young people should in fact play a part in the four different roles of adulthood which have been discussed.

Due to this situation, young people are expected to make the transition to adulthood according to their own rhythm and personally managed time sequence. Thus at the legally adult age of eighteen, young people have attained legal maturity; they are entitled to take legal action; to take responsibility for civil wrongs; can be held criminally accountable; may enter into marriage; and exercise both the active and passive entitlement to vote. The attainment of their majority does not, however, guarantee the transition to economic independence; and coming of age is seldom accompanied either by marriage or the birth of children. Conversely, at the age of fifteen young people may already commit to a long-term sexual partner relationship without, however, yet being legally "of age" (Hurrelmann & Hamilton, 1996).

Traditional societal perceptions of the transition from adolescent to adult are hardly suited to be part of a biographical point of reference. According to these ideas, young people attain "adulthood" when they have assumed one of the central membership roles that coincide with the four clusters of the developmental tasks. Young men or women are only said to have completed the adolescent phase of life when they perform *professional roles* as economically independent persons; *partner- and parent-roles* as responsible founders of families; *consumer roles* which include the utilization of the media; and the role of *politically active citizens* who act according to their own value systems.

In reality, these biographical points of reference can only be attained by a small number of young people in the adolescent phase of life. The social and chronological inconsistencies regarding the assumption of status already mentioned, coupled with growing unemployment, give rise to the situation that a growing minority of young people are not in a position to practice a profession (Hamilton & Hurrelmann, 1993). Currently, almost half of those belonging to the younger generation have decided against starting a family. Thus, according to traditional criteria, these young people are excluded from the status of "adulthood," and consequently also from full membership within society.

Inequalities in the Life Worlds of Adolescents One of my most interesting fields of research is concerned with the analysis of young people's differing pre-conditions in their ability to deal with today's lifestyle demands. The research of the last few decades has shown that socio-economic status and gender differences play a particularly important role here. The ninth and tenth maxims focus on this issue: Developed societies are distinguished not only by their rapid societal transformation, but also by large scale social and ethnic diversity and by ever-increasing economic inequality. These features increasingly shape the adolescent life phase and lead to unequal social worlds of adolescence (ninth maxim). The coping patterns of adolescents, who are dealing with developmental tasks, are shaped by whether they are female or male. During the last three to four decades girls and young women have been more successful than boys in this respect and thus have increasingly gained access to influential positions in society (tenth maxim).

Unequal Social Life Circumstances and Milieus In Germany, on the basis of regular representative surveys, we have the necessary data to construct historical time series of the evolution of inequality in adolescence (Shell Deutschland, 2002, 2006, 2010). The main research result shows that the vast majority of adolescents manage to cope with developmental tasks even under difficult cultural, demographic, and biographic circumstances. There is, however, a gradually increasing minority of almost 20% of the adolescent population who find it increasingly difficult or even impossible to cope. This means that almost one-fifth of the adolescent population is threatened by downward social mobility.

In Germany, as in most other countries, the social worlds of adolescents are disparate. The underlying reason for this is the high degree of social and ethnic diversity, and ever increasing economic disparity. In Germany about one in six young people is growing up in economically disadvantaged circumstances. The traditional equalizing mechanisms, including benefits provided by the social system, are not enough to compensate for this trend that has developed over the last 30 years. Responsibility for this is particularly lies with the high unemployment rate amongst the parents, which has led to families being unable to guarantee the living conditions regarded in this country as the societal norm for the "good life" (Hurrelmann, Rathmann, & Richter, 2011).

For young people from relatively poor families, therefore, the opportunities to participate in the consumption and leisure arenas are becoming fewer; and the consumption and lifestyle patterns touted in commercial promotions are unobtainable. The ability to "keep up" with their peer group and with the neighborhood, something which is constantly being tested, is at risk. The reaction is apparent in risk-behavior patterns, which range from aggression and violence to psychosomatic disorders and depression, culminating in the consumption of psychoactive substances and the manifestation of addiction (Hurrelmann, Engel, Holler, & Nordlohne 1988; Hurrelmann & Hamilton, 1996;

Hurrelmann & Loesel, 1990; Hurrelmann & Richter, 2006; Schulenberg, Maggs, & Hurrelmann, 1997).

In all instances, poor family circumstances and the parents' relational uncertainty reflects on parental contact with their children, resulting in feelings of inferiority and lack of self-confidence of the children. These young people are likely to be socially marginalized by their peer group. In other words, they are not then in a position to adjust their coping strategies in school, in peer groups, amongst friends or in public (Shell Deutschland, 2010).

Gender Differences in the Mastering of the Developmental Tasks Social inequality is equivalent to the important role played by gender inequality. Our research shows that, during the last three to four decades, girls, and young women have developed superior coping strategies in many more lifestyle areas than is the case with boys and young men. This has been found to be especially the case for the developmental task "qualify;" boys have not been able to keep up with girls, who have shown sustainable improvement in their performance record within the whole educational system (Quenzel & Hurrelmann, 2010).

Successful socialization—that is to say the productive processing of the interior and exterior demands of life—plays a decisive role in the person's intellectual achievement potential. Achievement does not solely depend on innate cognitive abilities, and intelligence. It is closely linked to how this potential is developed and nurtured. Here the psyche, the social environment, and the ecological life world come into play. Crucial basic parameters are set: in motivation and attitude to the self; in the social environmental conditions present in the parental home and in educational institutions; and in housing and ecological living conditions.

Our research indicates that young men are not as successful as young women in coming to terms with the everyday demands of internal and external reality. Young women additionally experience a more stimulating socialization environment than is the case for young men. Boys for example, learn from their peer group that reading, writing, and general linguistic adroitness are "unmanly," and unnecessary in their future profession. When young men have the sense that manliness can only be lived out within the peer group of their friends, i.e., outside school, this mindset leads to alienation from school and to a minimal investment in their attitude to education during class. Self-perception and an awareness of one's own capabilities are as important as the evaluation of academic performance. Boys tend to overestimate themselves: they believe they are capable of more than is, in reality, the case. This obviously decreases their educational success as they avoid making any particular effort and dismiss as "unmanly" exaggerated investments in perseverance and diligence (Quenzel & Hurrelmann, 2012).

Obviously, socialization and achievement are closely intertwined, and the result is that the educational success of boys, and therewith their ability to master the developmental task "qualify" is comparatively low. Ultimately, this is due to their adherence to a traditional understanding of their gender role. Boys with stereotypical perceptions of manliness tend to view academic achievements in school as negative because they are regarded as being "female." Stereotypically, being "unmanly" is equated with being effeminate—an attribute they desperately try to steer clear of. The consequences are clear: such boys are becoming completely alienated from school.

Summary

In the first section of this chapter, I have presented the origin and development of my theoretical orientation for my work in youth research. I have mentioned the crucial importance of some specific biographical experiences of mine for the "coloring" of my theoretical approach. The focus of my scientific work is to develop a comprehensive theory of socialization, and to offer it as the universal "grand theory" that explains the interplay of society and personality and which can be used in a variety of research areas. The epistemological Model of Productive Processing of Reality (PPR) guides the meta-theoretical orientation of the theory.

In the second section, I have tried to demonstrate how fruitful this approach is for theoretical and empirical youth research. I have explained in detail which epistemological and meta-theoretical assumptions are to be derived from the PPR model for theoretical and empirical youth research. I have finished by presenting ten "maxims," summarizing the epistemological and meta-theoretical concepts of comprehensive youth research.

In the final section, I have outlined in detail the results arising from research emanating from four of the ten maxims. As the chapter makes clear, the theoretical socialization orientation of youth research empowers research to link personality development in this key phase of the life course with social, cultural, demographic and economic conditions. I am deeply convinced that this approach is essential for interdisciplinary youth research world-wide.

References

Chisholm, L. & Hurrelmann, K. (1995). Adolescence in modern Europe. Pluralized transition patterns and their implications for personal and social risks. *Journal of Adolescence 18*, 129–158.

Engel, U. & Hurrelmann, K. (1992). Delinquency as a symptom of adolescent's orientation towards status and success. *Journal of Youth and Adolescence 21*, 119–138.

Hamilton, S. & Hurrelmann, K. (1993). The school-to-career transition in Germany and the United States. *Teachers College Record 96*, 329–344.

Havighurst, R. J. (1972). *Developmental tasks and education* (3rd. ed.) New York McKay.

Hurrelmann, K. (1983). Das Modell des produktiv realitätsverarbeitenden Subjekts in der Sozialisationsforschung. *Zeitschrift für Sozialisationsforschung und Erziehungssoziologie 3*, 91–103.

Hurrelmann, K. (1984). Societal and organizational factors of stress on students in school. *European Journal of Teacher Education 7*, 181–190.

Hurrelmann, K. (1987). The importance of school in the life course. *Journal of Adolescent Research 2*, 111–125.

Hurrelmann, K. (1988). *Social structure and personality development.* New York: Cambridge University Press (reprinted 2009).

Hurrelmann, K. (1989a). *Human development and health.* New York. Springer.

Hurrelmann, K. (1989b). Youth. A productive phase in human life. *Education 39*, 23–40.

Hurrelmann, K. (1990a). Health promotion for adolescents. Preventive and corrective strategies against problem behavior. *Journal of Adolescence 13*, 231–250.

Hurrelmann, K. (1990b). Parents, peers, teachers, and other significant partners in adolescence. *International Journal of Adolescence and Youth 2*, 211–236.

Hurrelmann, K. (Ed.). (1994). *International handbook of adolescence.* Westport: Greenwood Publishers.

Hurrelmann, K. (2012). *Sozialisation. Das Modell der produktiven Realitätsverarbeitung.* Weinheim: Beltz.

Hurrelmann, K. & Engel, U. (Eds.). (1990). *The social world of adolescents. International perspectives.* Berlin/New York: De Gruyter.

Hurrelmann, K. & Engel, U. (1992). Delinquency as a symptom of adolescents' orientation toward status and success. *Journal of Youth and Adolescence 21*, 119–138.

Hurrelmann, K., Engel, U., Holler, B., & Nordlohne, E. (1988). Failure in school, family conflicts, and psychosomatic disorders in adolescence. *Journal of Adolescence 11*, 237–249.

Hurrelmann, K., Engel, U., & Weidman, J. C. (1992a). Impacts of school pressure, conflict with parents, and career uncertainty on adolescent stress. *International Journal of Adolescence and Youth 4*, 33–50.

Hurrelmann, K., Engel, U., & Weidman, J. C. (1992b). Status insecurity and educational careers of adolescents in the Federal Republic of Germany. *International Perspectives on Education and Society, 2*, 81–107.

Hurrelmann, K. & Hamilton, S. F. (Eds.). (1996). *Social problems and social contexts in adolescence.* New York: Aldine de Gruyter.

Hurrelmann, K., Leppin, A., & Nordlohne, E. (1995). Promoting health in schools. The German example. *Health Promotion International 10*, 121–131.

Hurrelmann, K. & Lösel, F. (Eds.). (1990). *Health hazards in adolescence.* Berlin/New York: De Gruyter.

Hurrelmann, K. & Quenzel, G. (2012). *Lebensphase Jugend* (11th ed.). Weinheim: Juventa.

Hurrelmann, K., Rathmann, K., & Richter, M. (2011). Health inequalities and welfare state regimes. *Journal of Public Health 19*, 3–13.

Hurrelmann, K. & Richter, M. (2006). Risk behavior in adolescence. *Journal of Public Health 14*, 20–28.

Nestmann, R. & Hurrelmann, K. (Eds.). (1994). *Social network and social support in childhood and adolescence.* Berlin/New York: De Gruyter.

Neubauer, G. & Hurrelmann, K. (Eds.). (1996). *Individualization in childhood and adolescence.* Berlin/New York: De Gruyter.

Petersen, A. C., Leffert, N., & Hurrelmann, K. (1993). Adolescence and schooling in Germany and the United States. *Teachers College Record 94*, 611–629.

Quenzel, G. & Hurrelmann, K. (Eds.). (2010). Geschlecht und Schulerfolg: Ein soziales Stratifikationsmuster kehrt sich um. *Kölner Zeitschrift für Soziologie und Sozialpsychologie 62*, 61–91.

Quenzel, G. & Hurrelmann, K. (2012) The gender gap in education. *International Journal of Adolescence and Youth 18* (in press).

Schulenberg, J., Maggs, J., & Hurrelmann, K. (Eds.). (1997). *Health risks and developmental transitions during adolescence.* New York: Cambridge University Press.

Shell Deutschland (2002). *Jugend 2002.* 14. Shell Jugendstudie. (Conceptualization and coordination by Hurrelmann, K., Albert, M., & Quenzel, G.) Frankfurt: Fischer.

Shell Deutschland (2006). *Jugend 2006.* 15. Shell Jugendstudie. (Conceptualization and coordination by Hurrelmann, K., Albert, M., & Quenzel, G.) Frankfurt: Fischer.

Shell Deutschland (2010). *Jugend 2010.* 16. Shell Jugendstudie. (Conceptualization and coordination by Hurrelmann, K., Albert, M., & Quenzel, G.) Frankfurt: Fischer.

23

Problem Behavior Theory

A Half-Century of Research on Adolescent Behavior and Development

RICHARD JESSOR

A strong, overly zealous commitment to one's theory is important to scientific advancement.

Donald T. Campbell

Part I

Introduction *It all started in 1958.* An unexpected opportunity presented itself to become involved in a large-scale community study of an important social problem—alcohol abuse—in a marginalized group in American society, Native Americans. This chapter sketches the successive phases, from that point to the present, of the systematic development of Problem Behavior Theory, a theory increasingly employed in research on adolescent risk behavior by scholars in the USA and abroad. In a certain sense, the "biography" of that theory is the autobiography of my half-century of research and writing about the developmental science of adolescence.

In the time since my PhD in Clinical Psychology from Ohio State University in 1951, I had been teaching, doing clinical training, and conducting research studies with both college sophomores and laboratory rats at the University of Colorado. The reach of those activities was limited, and I was feeling disaffected about the current state of psychology and dispirited about the significance of my own classroom and animal studies. Psychology as a scientific discipline in the early 1950s was still struggling with the arid legacy of behaviorism which had banished subjectivity and meaning from consideration, while clinical work suffered from the general absence of socially relevant theory, relying instead on outmoded trait approaches or derivations from the formulations of psychoanalysis, both largely insensitive to the influence of the societal context on individual development and adaptation. Getting involved in the large-scale community study seemed a promising avenue to re-invigorate my scientific activity, to enlarge my conceptual perspective beyond the discipline of psychology

alone, to make my research more socially relevant, and to be able to focus on complex social behavior of societal significance. I decided to pursue the opportunity, and I helped write a grant application to the National Institute of Mental Health (NIMH) that was successful: 5 years of support and $300,000—large for that time. It was in designing and carrying out that research that what was to become Problem Behavior Theory was initially conceptualized and subjected to empirical scrutiny.

My alienation from conventional, discipline-focused, behavioral research had been growing ever since graduate school, fueled in part by an enriching involvement at Ohio State with Julian B. Rotter and his Social Learning Theory (Rotter, 1954) with its cognitive-social concepts of expectations and values and its contextual focus on the *psychological* situation. After joining the faculty at Colorado, I found myself challenging the behaviorist philosophy of science still dominating psychology, and I published several pieces critical of that perspective (e.g., Jessor, 1956, 1958). Along with colleagues, I also helped organize a symposium at Colorado on "Contemporary approaches to cognition" (Gruber, Hammond, & Jessor, 1957), one of the earliest volumes contributing to the so-called "cognitive revolution" in psychology which was just beginning to replace the behaviorist paradigm. But I had not yet been able to undertake the kind of research that would enable me to implement an alternative approach to inquiry about complex, human, social action; that was the opportunity that materialized with the 1958 grant award from NIMH. We were funded to carry out what came to be called "The Tri-Ethnic Study," and along with a team of collaborators that included Lee Jessor, a developmental psychologist, Ted Graves, an anthropologist, and Bob Hanson, a sociologist, we published our findings 10 years later in the volume *Society, personality, and deviant behavior: A study of a tri-ethnic community* (Jessor, Graves, Hanson, & Jessor, S. L, 1968). The social–psychological formulation of Problem Behavior Theory was first elaborated in that volume.

It seemed clear to me at the outset, in considering the opportunity provided by the NIMH grant award to undertake an alternative approach to social inquiry, that there would be a need to develop a coherent social–psychological theory, one that was problem-rather than discipline- focused (Kurt Lewin had long argued that basic research could, indeed, be accomplished in the context of studying applied problems). The theory would need to be multi-disciplinary, engage both person and environment, incorporate the perceived or phenomenal environment as well, and be attentive to the functions and goals of socially learned behavior. An ambitious and daunting agenda for a young scholar, to say the least!

In hindsight, I can think of three other important influences that helped to shape that agenda, beyond my felt disaffection with conventional psychological inquiry. First, I had been invited to spend the summer of 1954 as a member of a Social Science Research Council Interdisciplinary Summer Seminar on the topic of "occupational choice," along with two labor economists, two sociologists, and one other psychologist. The intense daily interaction across those summer months with colleagues from different disciplines—all of us intent on bringing understanding to such a complex, life-course process—taught me not only how to think beyond disciplinary boundaries, but the value and illumination of doing so. It had also provided me with the experience, for the first time, of delineating an interdisciplinary conceptual framework that incorporated, in logical fashion, constructs from the three disciplines involved. We published an integrative paper from that summer's work: "Occupational choice: A conceptual framework," (Blau, Gustad, Jessor, Parnes, & Wilcock, 1956).

A second major influence during the years leading up to the 1958 NIMH grant award was the formal establishment, in 1957, of the Institute of Behavioral Science on the University of Colorado campus, with participation of faculty and graduate students from multiple social science departments—anthropology, economics, political science, psychology, and sociology. Its establishment was the outcome of a growing recognition on the campus not only of the limitations of disciplinary research on human problems but of the explanatory benefits of transcending disciplinary boundaries. Having been an active participant in the deliberations and organizational planning that led up to our founding of the Institute, I was again exposed to the demands of interdisciplinary thinking and engaged again in cross-disciplinary interaction.

The third influence came from an enlarged understanding of the critical role of *theory* in guiding the research process and interpreting its findings. In my own field of personality research, much of measurement was employed opportunistically, relying on available instruments usually derived from popular views of personality variation, e.g., measures of introversion-extraversion. With the emergence, however, of attention to the requirements of "construct validity" (Cronbach & Meehl, 1955), the explanatory importance of deriving measures from theory,

measures that represented the logical properties of the constructs they were intended to assess, became salient. A critique of the widely used Taylor Anxiety Scale, challenging its lack of construct validity (Jessor & Hammond, 1957), had required extensive exploration of the nature of theory in the philosophy of science literature and of the role that an explicit nomological network plays in measurement and explanation. That experience, coupled with my earlier involvement in Rotter's theory-building efforts while I was still a graduate student at Ohio State, and my later participation in developing the occupational choice conceptual framework, all combined to reinforce an enduring commitment to engaging theory in social inquiry.

Together, these influences resulted in what I would now recognize as a "developmental readiness," after 7 years of conventional research, to undertake the kind of challenge that the Tri-Ethnic Study presented, and to make a "developmental transition" to what seemed to me then to be a new, socially meaningful, and conceptually more comprehensive kind of research. It turned out to be a life- and career-changing transition that, I'm happy to say, is still reverberating.

Constructing Problem Behavior Theory for "The Tri-Ethnic Study": The Initial Formulation
Although the original concern of NIMH was with understanding Native American alcohol abuse, it was the case that the rural community in southern Colorado in which the research was to be carried out was actually tri-ethnic in composition, made up not only of Native Americans, but of historically long-settled Hispanic residents, and of Whites or, as they were called then, "Anglos." The possibility of designing a *comparative* study of the three ethnic groups living in the same small community, rather than focusing solely on the Native American population, was methodologically attractive: It could make clear whether there were factors influencing Native American drinking behavior that were, indeed, unique to them or shared by the other two groups. Further, although the concern of NIMH was with excessive alcohol use, it was quite obvious that alcohol abuse was generally associated with a range of other normative transgressions, some of which, upon analysis, were oriented to similar goals or served functions similar to those that drinking behavior served, and which might, therefore, have similar determinants. Thus, it seemed theoretically important to cast a wide measurement net that assessed other problem behaviors, e.g., crime and violence, in addition to drinking, and—for construct validity purposes—that also assessed conforming or conventional behaviors, like church attendance and, for adolescents, school achievement and school club involvement.

The primary task confronted was to conceptualize the social environment and the person in terms that implicated each other and that were, at the same time, relevant to variation in problem behavior. That is, the task was to construct what Merton (1957) had termed a "theory of the middle range," a theory relevant to a circumscribed domain of social action—in this case, problem behavior—and that can guide empirical inquiry, rather than a "grand" theory of the sort that had, in the past, characterized so much of sociology (e.g., Parsons, 1937) and psychology (e.g., Hull, 1943; Skinner, 1938).

Conceptualizing the Social Environment Extensive exploration of the sociological and criminological literature, on the one hand, and intensive ethnographic experience in the tri-ethnic community, on the other, led to the conceptual differentiation of the social environment into three major structures of societal influence on the likelihood of occurrence of problem behavior—an *opportunity structure*, a *normative structure*, and a *social control structure*—with variables in each structure having directional implications for the occurrence/non-occurrence of problem behavior. Limited access to societally valued goals in the opportunity structure was posited to constitute *instigation or pressure* to engage in illegitimate means, i.e., in deviant or problem behavior, in order to achieve those goals. Greater exposure to dissensus in the normative structure—lack of agreement on appropriate ways of behaving, i.e., anomie—was posited to constitute *low normative control* against engaging in problem behavior; and greater access to engaging in problem behavior in the social control structure was posited to constitute *attenuated social control* against problem behavior. The balance of instigation and controls at any given location in society was hypothesized to determine the *rates or prevalence* of problem behavior at that location. From this theoretical perspective, differences in problem behavior among the three ethnic groups in the community would be due to differences in their positions in those three social environment structures. The indebtedness of this social environment formulation to the seminal contributions of Merton's concept of "anomie"

(1957) and Cloward and Ohlin's notion of "differential access to illegitimate means" (1960) is apparent and was gratefully acknowledged.

Conceptualizing the Person Although the social environment formulation could provide a grasp on the social determinants of between-group differences in levels or rates of problem behavior, it could not provide an account of the *intra*-group variation that exists at every social location; in order to achieve the latter, an *individual-level* account, a formulation about *persons,* was required. For conceptualizing person-level influences on the likelihood of occurrence of problem behavior, we sought structures of cognitive–social variables that could be seen as logically related to the social environment structures, i.e., as their conceptual analogues at the individual level. The value and expectancy concepts in Rotter's Social Learning Theory appeared to be apposite; "value-expectancy disjunction" at the person level was seen as analogous to limited access to societally valued goals in the opportunity structure and constituted, therefore, a *perceived opportunity structure* in the person. In the same vein, cognitive–social variables, such as "belief in internal versus external control," and "alienation," constituted a *personal belief structure*, analogous to the normative structure at the social environment level. Finally, variables like "attitudinal intolerance of deviance" constituted a *personal control structure* to serve, at the person level, as an analogue of the social control structure in the social environment.

The resultant of these conceptualizations was a sociocultural environment system of structures of variables relevant to problem behavior and a personality system of structures of variables relevant to problem behavior that, together, could account for *between-group variation* as well as *within-group variation* in problem behavior. The initial conceptual framework of Problem Behavior Theory for the Tri-Ethnic Study is presented in Figure 23.1 (Jessor et al., 1968, p. 132).

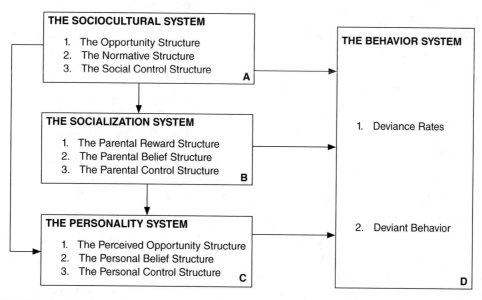

FIGURE 23.1 The over-all social-psychological framework for the study of deviance (Jessor et al., 1968, p. 132).

Collecting the Tri-Ethnic Study Data Interview and questionnaire measures of each of those variables were developed from the logic of their properties, i.e., from a construct validity perspective, and they were then employed in three converging studies carried out in the community, all testing the theory: (1) a stratified, random household interview survey of the adults in the three ethnic groups in the community—the Community Survey Study; (2) an in-school questionnaire study of all the adolescent students attending the community high school—the High School Study; and (3) an interview study of a random sub-sample of the parents of the high-school students who had participated in the questionnaire study—the Socialization Study. Our aim in mounting three converging studies on independent samples was to be able to minimize inferential ambiguity and to make a more compelling test, in an actual, complex field setting, of our social–psychological theory of problem behavior.

That the theory was an effective guide for research was evident in the consonant findings from all three studies. Theoretical predictors from both the sociocultural system and the personality system, taken together, yielded a substantial account of problem behavior variation. Those findings held across the three ethnic groups and across gender, as well. Overall, results were as theoretically expected, and they provided strong encouragement for our conceptual labors.

Revising Problem Behavior Theory for "The Socialization of Problem Behavior in Youth Study": The Intermediate Formulation The publication in 1968 of *Society, Personality, and Deviant Behavior: A Study of a Tri-Ethnic Community*, reported the first phase of the development of Problem Behavior Theory. My responsibility for that long-drawn-out enterprise definitively shaped the contours of my academic scholarship from that time forward. The 10 years of collaborative, interdisciplinary effort had been successful, the theory had been shown to be useful, the findings were illuminating, and the volume was well-received and, indeed, continues to be cited more than four decades later. An institutional outcome of the Tri-Ethnic research effort was the establishment, in 1966, in our Institute of Behavioral Science, of the interdisciplinary Research Program on Problem Behavior of which I became the founding director.

Despite its many strengths, however, particularly the conceptual mapping of both the social environment and the person in analogous terms relevant to problem behavior variation, and the theoretical coherence of the findings of its three converging studies, there was a fundamental shortcoming to the Tri-Ethnic work, namely, *it was cross-sectional in design*. The absence of time-extended data precluded inferences about causal direction or impact; remedying that limitation would require undertaking social inquiry that was *longitudinal* in design and that permitted the following of lives across extended and developmentally significant periods of the life course. An additional shortcoming was that, in assessing adolescents already in high school, it had elided the earlier adolescent life stage, a stage in which significant transitions occur or are prepared for. What seemed essential for a fuller grasp on adolescence was theory-guided longitudinal research that started earlier in the life course. A focus on the adolescent life stage and on adolescent behavior and development seemed the natural direction to pursue for the next stage of inquiry and for the further development of Problem Behavior Theory.

Even before the Tri-Ethnic book reached publication, however, a 1965–66 NIMH fellowship award enabled me to spend a full year learning about longitudinal research at the Harvard– Florence Research Project in Firenze, Italy, a unit that had been following three cohorts of boys since their early adolescence. The families of the boys all had their origin in southern Italy or Sicily, but the families of one cohort had migrated to Rome, the families of the second cohort had emigrated to Boston, and the families of the third cohort had remained in place. The year was extremely valuable for gaining a better understanding of how to follow young lives; it also provided an opportunity to interact with thoughtful developmental colleagues like Klaus Riegel and Douglas Heath, also resident that year at the Project, and it permitted me to carry out an interesting, cross-national, comparative study of drinking behavior in the three cohorts using selected psychosocial and behavior measures from Problem Behavior Theory (Jessor, Young, Young, & Tesi, 1970).

Armed with this experience, and in close collaboration with Lee Jessor, we began to plan a new longitudinal project that, while building on the accomplishments of the Tri-Ethnic Study, would revise and extend the theory to focus now on the behavior and development of young people during the entire adolescent stage of the life course. Two complementary, longitudinal studies of adolescents were designed, one beginning with middle-school adolescents, to be followed over four successive years (called the High School Study), and one beginning with college freshmen also to be followed over four successive years (called the College Study). Together, the two 4-year studies would span an age range from about 12 to 22, i.e., from early adolescence to late adolescence/early adulthood.

The cohort-sequential design for the middle schoolers involved lengthy, theory-derived questionnaires administered in school to initial samples of 7th-, 8th-, and 9th-grade students in the spring of each of the 4 years of the study, 1969–72, at the end of which they would be in 10th, 11th, and 12th grades, respectively. The simple longitudinal design used with the college freshmen also involved lengthy questionnaires administered in each of their four successive college years, 1970–73, at the end of which most would be in their senior year of college. Since this research took place at the end of the turbulent sixties and into the turmoil of the early seventies, the questionnaires included extensive sections on a variety of adolescent problem behaviors, including marijuana use, other, so-called "hard," drug use, alcohol use, delinquency, and for the first time, sexual activity, and also participation in militant protests; it also assessed involvement in a variety of conventional or pro-social behaviors, including academic effort and religious activity. The High School Study and the College Study were designed to permit testing Problem Behavior Theory cross-sectionally and longitudinally, and at earlier and later adolescent life stages. Unlike the tri-ethnic community, the setting for this proposed longitudinal study was a southwestern, largely White, middle-class, university community and its surrounding small towns, with only modest ethnic variation.

An application to NIMH in 1968 for support of a longitudinal project entitled, "The Socialization of Problem Behavior in Youth," was successful and, with later sponsorship by the National Institute on Alcohol Abuse and Alcoholism (NIAAA), yielded 7 years of funding. With the initiation of this new study, the second phase of the development of Problem Behavior Theory began. Nine years later, we published its findings in the volume *Problem behavior and psychosocial development: A longitudinal study of youth* (R. Jessor & S.L. Jessor, 1977).

Conceptualizing the Perceived Environment As with the Tri-Ethnic Study, the challenge was again to construct a theory of both the social environment and the person that had logical implications for the occurrence of, and intensity of involvement in, problem behavior. Given the relatively homogeneous nature of the new research community in terms of socio-economic status and ethnicity, and given that the focus was to be on adolescents, it seemed most informative in this study to explore and articulate the *perceived* environment rather than the social structural environment, as had already been done successfully in the Tri-Ethnic Study. The perceived environment is the environment as the adolescent sees it, the social environment that has meaning for the young person, an environment more proximal to action than the so-called "objective," social structural environment, and one that is consonant with such widely used concepts as "definitions of the situation" in sociology (Thomas, 1928) and "life space" (Lewin, 1935), "meaningful environment" (Rotter, 1954), and "phenomenal field" (Rogers, 1959) in psychology (for more on the perceived environment, see R. Jessor & S.L. Jessor, 1973). In this study, the social structural environment was dealt with in the more traditional way, i.e., demographically rather than conceptually, with several

indicators of socioeconomic status and family structure employed largely as analytic controls.

The perceived environment, then, is the environment the adolescent—placed by the questionnaire in the role of quasi-ethnographer—perceives about parents and friends and peers and teachers, their support and controls and influence, and their acceptance/non-acceptance of problem behavior. It was differentiated into a *proximal structure*, with variables that directly implicate problem behaviors, e.g., having friends who model problem behavior, and a *distal structure*, with variables whose link to problem behavior is indirect and follows only from the logic of the theory, e.g., parental support. Although proximal variables generally relate more strongly to problem behavior outcomes, such relationships are obvious and less interesting theoretically than the relations of distal variables which derive from and can strengthen theory.

Conceptualizing the Person The personality system for this project was delineated in essentially the same way as it had been for the Tri-Ethnic Study, with three structures of cognitive-social variables: one, the *motivational–instigation structure*, again mapped instigation or pressure to engage in problem behavior; and two, the *personal belief structure* and the *personal control structure*, again mapped controls against engaging in problem behavior. The measures employed were largely adapted from those devised for the earlier Tri-Ethnic Study, except for several new ones, such as a measure of social criticism, which was relevant to the new concern with militant protest behavior.

Shown in Figure 23.2 (from R. Jessor & S.L. Jessor, 1977, p. 38), the conceptual framework encompasses both an environment system and a personality system, as it did in the Tri-Ethnic Study, as well as a comprehensive behavior system, the latter with both a *problem behavior structure* and a *conventional behavior structure*. (As the figure shows, and as was the case with the Tri-Ethnic Study, there was also an effort to study various socialization processes as influences on adolescent behavior and development.) Despite revisions of the theory, the basic Problem Behavior Theory hypothesis remained the same: *Variation in the personality system and variation in the perceived environment system should each account for variation in problem behavior and, taken together, should provide a stronger account than either alone.* That hypothesis was tested in the two independent studies, the High School Study and the College Study, with both the cross-sectional data collected annually over the 4 years, as well as with the 4-year longitudinal data on each adolescent or young adult participant. Overall, the findings were impressive in their support of this later version of Problem Behavior Theory, the so-called "classical" version, published in the 1977 volume (for additional summary descriptions, see Costa, 2008; Donovan, 2005). In the

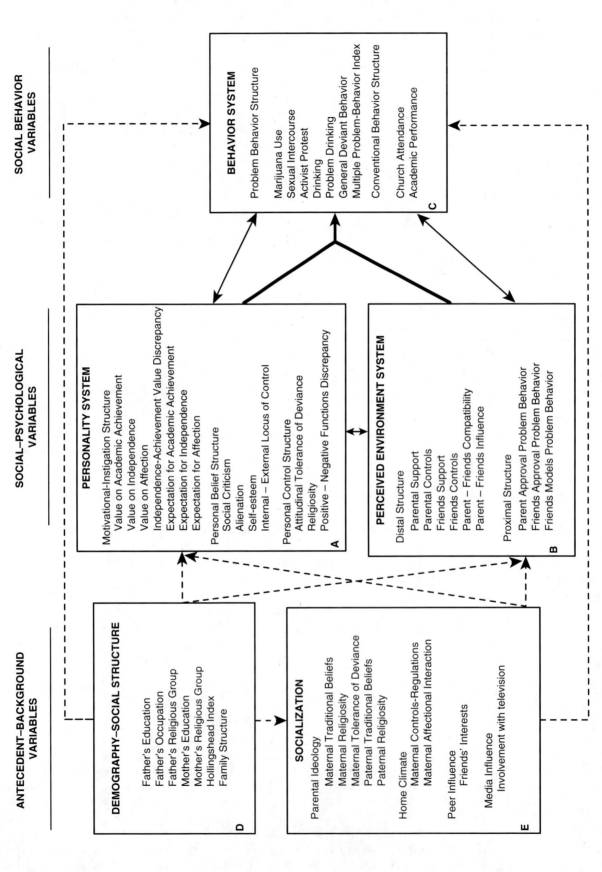

FIGURE 23.2 The conceptual structure of Problem Behavior Theory (R. Jessor, & S.L. Jessor, 1977, p. 38).

cross-sectional analyses, the theoretical account of variance in problem behavior was substantial, as much as 50% for some of the problem behaviors; in addition, the personality and perceived environment predictors were inversely related to the conventional or pro-social behaviors, demonstrating discriminant validity; and finally, the findings, though based on local samples in a particular local setting, were supported by a national sample survey of 13,000 high-school youth carried out about the same time that employed a number of our Problem Behavior Theory measures (Donovan & Jessor, 1978; Jessor, Chase, & Donovan, 1980; Rachal, Williams, & Brehm, 1975). From the cross-sectional findings alone, it was clear that Problem Behavior Theory provided a useful grasp on variation in adolescent problem behavior in both the High School Study and the College Study.

The research also generated several important problem behavior concepts that have since entered the literature. The concept of *problem behavior proneness* was employed as a theoretical summary term for the likelihood of engaging in problem behaviors, based on the set of personality variables and the set of perceived environment variables that, theoretically, are their predictors. It became possible to think of *personality proneness,* and *perceived environment proneness,* as well as overall *psychosocial proneness,* based on both systems of predictors taken together. Another important concept that emerged from this inquiry was the *problem behavior syndrome* in adolescence. The research provided consistent evidence that there was co-variation or co-occurrence among very diverse problem behaviors, i.e., that various problem behaviors were inter-related and tended often to have similar determinants and to fulfill similar functions. The notion of a *syndrome* challenged the allocation to different Federal agencies of responsibility for the separate problem behaviors—thereby partitioning the "wholeness" or integrity of adolescent behavioral individuality—and it highlighted the parochialism of the research tradition that focused on a single or isolated adolescent problem behavior alone. The concept of a problem behavior syndrome has since generated an outpouring of adolescent research that is still underway; a recent review for the National Academies of Science of the cumulated research on covariance of problem behaviors in adolescence musters persuasive support for the syndrome concept (Monahan & Hawkins, 2012).

While the cross-sectional findings were gratifyingly consonant with those of the Tri-Ethnic Study of high-school youth, the overriding concern of this later longitudinal inquiry was to examine the reach of the theory in accounting for *developmental change* across adolescence and into early adulthood. Toward that end, both descriptive and predictive analyses were undertaken with the longitudinal data. For the descriptive analyses, longitudinal "growth curves" were plotted across the 4 years of data,

not only for the various problem behaviors, but also for their personality and perceived environment predictors. Beyond intrinsic interest in the developmental change that the curves documented on those attributes across four data points, they also revealed a *theoretical consonance of developmental change* between the behaviors and their predictors over time, constituting an initial, although indirect, test of the developmental usefulness of Problem Behavior Theory. For example, in the High School Study, value on academic achievement declined significantly over the 4 years of measurement, value on independence increased, and intolerance of deviance decreased among the personality system predictors; among the perceived environment system predictors, parental controls decreased, while friends models for drinking increased. Each of these directions of developmental change is theoretically predictive of a developmental *increase* in problem behavior over the 4 years of measurement, and, indeed, that was the case for marijuana involvement and for delinquent behavior, among others. Further, they are consonant with a *decrease* in conventional behavior which was the case for the measure of church attendance. This theoretical consonance of parallel developmental changes in adolescence of both predictor and criterion measures was a novel developmental finding, one that was supportive, indirectly, of Problem Behavior Theory.

A more direct test of the usefulness of the theory in accounting for developmental change in adolescence entailed predicting differences in time of onset of problem behaviors hitherto never engaged in. These analyses generated another important new concept, namely, the concept of "*transition proneness.*" It was evident that, for many young people, engaging in problem behaviors such as drinking or smoking or having sex was a way of lodging a claim on a more mature status, i.e., of making a developmental transition. Since problem behaviors such as drinking or smoking or sexual intercourse are actually *age-graded behaviors*—behaviors that, while normatively proscribed for younger ages, are permitted or even prescribed for older ages, engaging in them for the first time can be a way of transgressing a norm, in this case an age norm, and thereby demonstrating that one is no longer a "kid." Problem Behavior Theory is designed to account for normative transgressions; that account should also apply to age norms, and the concept of "problem behavior proneness" therefore translates into or maps onto the developmental concept of "transition proneness," the likelihood of engaging in a transition- marking behavior. A number of tests of the notion of transition proneness were carried out in the High School Study where there were adequate samples of adolescents who had not yet initiated the problem behavior. What they demonstrated was the usefulness of the Problem Behavior Theory concept of transition proneness for predicting earlier versus later transition in regard to the onset of drinking, of marijuana use, and of becoming a non-virgin (Jessor, 1976; Jessor, 1987a; R. Jessor, Costa, S.L. Jessor, & Donovan, 1983; R. Jessor & S.L. Jessor, 1975; R. Jessor, S.L. Jessor, & Collins, 1972; S.L. Jessor & R. Jessor, 1975).

Overall, the longitudinal findings provided strong support for the developmental relevance of Problem Behavior Theory. They illuminated the developmental changes in those psychosocial attributes associated with, predictive of, and consequential upon the onset of transition behavior.

Extending Problem Behavior Theory Beyond Adolescence: "The Young Adult Follow-Up Study"

When the findings from the "Socialization of Problem Behavior in Youth Study" were published in the 1977 volume *Problem behavior and psychosocial development,* the second major phase in the evolution of Problem Behavior Theory came to a close. The High School Study and College Study participants, by the end of the longitudinal study in 1972 or 1973, respectively, had reached the ages of 16, 17, and 18 for the former, and 22 for the latter. To our great good fortune, the study of those same adolescents and young adults was to continue well into adulthood and to provide us with a unique opportunity to examine the applicability of Problem Behavior Theory to that later stage in the life course—young adulthood. With funding from NIAAA for "The Young Adult Follow-Up Study," we were able to launch a two-wave follow-up of our participants in 1979 and 1981; by 1981, the High School Study youth had reached the ages of 25, 26, and 27, and the College Study youth had reached the age of 30, all having navigated the transition to adulthood. The findings from this longitudinal inquiry about problem behavior in adulthood were published in the volume *Beyond adolescence: Problem behavior and young adult development* (Jessor, Donovan, & Costa, 1991), the third volume in the evolution and appraisal of Problem Behavior Theory.

In the interval since the fourth wave of data had been collected in 1972 and 1973, the longitudinal participants in our "Socialization of Problem Behavior in Youth Study" had scattered across the state, the nation, and even abroad. Locating them for follow-up was the initial challenge for the "Young Adult Follow-Up Study," a challenge that was met with extraordinary success: Almost all were located despite the significant passage of time, and fully 94% of both the High School longitudinal sample and the College longitudinal sample resumed their participation. Nearly all were out of school, most of the men and over half of the women were employed full-time, over half were married or in a committed relationship, and almost a third were raising families–evidence of the pervasive occupancy of the various roles of young adulthood. The two waves of data collected in 1979 and 1981 enabled examination

of the usefulness of Problem Behavior Theory in accounting for variation in problem behavior *within* young adulthood, and they also enabled exploration of developmental change *between* adolescence and this later time in the life course.

Several important contributions to developmental science emerged from this extended appraisal of Problem Behavior Theory. First, variance accounted for in problem behavior in young adulthood was as substantial as it was in adolescence—mostly better than 40%, but with some exceptions for particular problem behaviors—in both the 1979 and the 1981 data waves, providing thus another demonstration of developmental generality of the theory, i.e., its invariance across life stages. Second, the findings were similar to those obtained in adolescence in regard to the existence of a problem behavior syndrome, now evident in young adulthood, as well. A variety of analyses showed covariation across frequency of drunkenness, frequency of marijuana use, use of other illicit drugs, general deviant behavior, and cigarette smoking, and also showing that a single underlying factor could account for the observed correlations among those behaviors (Donovan & Jessor, 1985). Third, variation in problem behavior in 1981 was shown to be predictable from psychosocial proneness as far back as 1972/73, i.e., over quite a long developmental period; theoretical precursors in adolescence were able to forecast problem behavior in young adulthood. Fourth, with regard to developmental change in the theoretical predictors and the problem behaviors from adolescence into young adulthood, there is clear evidence of substantial *continuity* in change (Jessor, 1983); stability coefficients between Wave 1 and Wave 6 and between Wave 5 and Wave 6 were highly significant.

Two other important findings about youth development emerged from the Young Adult Follow-Up Study. Despite the observed stability of developmental change, the actual *direction* of change between the adolescent life stage and that of young adulthood "was unmistakably in the direction of greater conventionality" (Jessor et al., 1991, p. 276). This was especially noteworthy given that, for several of the variables, it was an actual reversal of the direction of developmental change observed *within* adolescence when it was toward greater *un*conventionality. Finally, we found that there was no evidence of a "spillover" effect, that is, that involvement in problem behavior in adolescence had compromised young adult outcomes in any other life areas—work, family, health, etc., or that it had "mortgaged the future" of these middle-class youth in any way.

These young adult findings added substantially to our understanding of the implications of the adolescent life stage for later development. They also strengthened our conviction about the developmental usefulness of Problem Behavior Theory in this later stage of the life course.

Part II

Expanding Problem Behavior Theory Beyond Problem Behavior In carrying out three, large-scale studies of adolescent problem behavior, both cross-sectional and longitudinal, our primary objective had been to innovate a conceptual framework—Problem Behavior Theory—and to establish its usefulness for advancing understanding of the adolescent life stage and the role played by problem behavior in adolescent adaptation and development. The three successive volumes that published the findings from those studies represented a cumulative corpus of work, over several decades, in support of that objective.

But there had been other objectives along the way, as well. A second objective had been to help promote an alternative style of social inquiry: a style that was problem-focused; that could enable strong inferences to be drawn from field or non-experimental studies; that was more comprehensive than what was generally seen in the literature, encompassing both person and environment and engaging a wide range of behaviors; and a style that transcended discipline- focused efforts and reflected what might best be called a *developmental behavioral science* approach (Jessor, 1993), an approach that is inherently interdisciplinary. Related to that objective is the fact that, in 1980, I was appointed director of the Institute of Behavioral Science, a position I held for over two decades, with responsibilities for overseeing a fairly large organized research enterprise with programs on population, the environment, political and economic change, and problem behavior (which I continued to direct, as well). That role required engagement with problem-based, interdisciplinary inquiry across a broad spectrum of the social and behavioral sciences, and it generated an even stronger commitment on my part to promoting developmental behavioral science as an approach to research.

Toward that end, and to celebrate the 25th anniversary of the Institute, I organized in the mid- 1980s a 2-year-long series of distinguished lectures on the current and future status of the various social science disciplines, and on such social problems as health, peace, and the environment. Beyond editing the volume *Perspectives on behavioral science: The Colorado lectures* (Jessor, 1991b), I tried in the final chapter, "Behavioral science: An emerging paradigm for social inquiry?" (Jessor, 1991a) to take stock across the lectures of whether a new trans-disciplinary paradigm was, indeed, emerging. Unhappily, I had to conclude that was not the case. That conclusion was not contradicted by a richly rewarding year spent, almost a decade later in 1995–96, at the Center for Advanced Study in the Behavioral Sciences at Stanford. The hold of the disciplinary organization of social–psychological research remains tenacious even today, nearly two decades later, despite the inherent necessity of an inter-or trans-disciplinary perspective when research is problem-based; see invited editorial, "Remarks on the changing nature of inquiry" (Jessor, 2005).

And a third objective was to promote greater reliance on theory in research and measurement. The theoretical or explanatory level of analysis, the level Kurt Lewin (1951), borrowing an analogy from genetics, termed the underlying *genotypic* level, not only provides for logical or systematic explanation, but it also yields greater generality than can be expected from analyses at the descriptive or *phenotypic* levels, which are necessarily parochial. We had already documented the generality of theoretical explanation in the Tri-Ethnic Study in which the theoretical variables showed similar explanatory value across the three ethnic groups despite their varied circumstances and mean-level differences on those variables. Theoretical generality had also been documented across gender and, in the Young Adult Follow-Up Study, across the developmental stage of young adulthood.

Problem Behavior Theory and Adolescent Health By the early 1980s, Problem Behavior Theory was becoming established and, indeed, beginning to be used by others to guide their own research. Although our third volume, *Beyond adolescence,* had not yet appeared, articles from that study were already being published (e.g., Donovan & Jessor, 1985; Donovan, R. Jessor, & L. Jessor, 1983; Jessor, 1983; Jessor, Donovan, & Costa, 1986; R. Jessor & S.L. Jessor, 1984). With all that as background, the ontogeny of Problem Behavior Theory's development entered a new phase, a phase that was characterized by an expansion of its application into additional domains of adolescent life beyond problem behavior alone.

Perhaps the most salient expansion was engagement of the theory with the domain of *adolescent health*. It had become quite clear to us over the years that many of the adolescent problem behaviors we were preoccupied with, e.g., smoking, alcohol abuse, and early or unprotected sex, could be viewed by those with a public health perspective not as normative transgressions, as we saw them, but as behaviors that compromised health, instead. It was evident, too, that even health-related behaviors that were not also problem behaviors were regulated by social and personal norms just as problem behaviors were, e.g., norms about healthy eating, appropriate exercise, or acceptable body weight, and in that regard it seemed our theory might well be apposite. An invitation by David Hamburg to participate in a conference at the Institute of Medicine served to precipitate an exploration of the applicability of Problem Behavior Theory to the domain of adolescent health (Jessor, 1978), and that led, subsequently, to preparing a chapter, "Adolescent development and behavioral health" (Jessor, 1984) for the volume *Behavioral health: A handbook of health enhancement and disease prevention,* edited by Matarazzo et al. From then on to the present day, concern for the adolescent health domain has threaded its way through our work in research and theory development and across very diverse settings in the United States and across the globe (Costa, Jessor, & Donovan, 1989; Costa, Jessor, Donovan, & Fortenberry, 1995; Donovan, Jessor, & Costa, 1991, 1993; Jessor, 1989; Jessor, Donovan, & Costa, 1990; Jessor, Turbin, & Costa, 1998a, 2010; Turbin, Jessor, & Costa, 2000; Turbin et al., 2006). Indeed, in 2002, I established and became the first director of the Research Program on Health and Society in our Institute of Behavioral Science, a position I continue to hold today. Sustaining this engagement with adolescent health, and illuminating its complexity for me, were various opportunities I had to participate in activities that implicated that domain of inquiry. Special mention must be made of service on the Carnegie Council on Adolescent Development for nearly a decade beginning in the mid-80s, which was a richly informative experience. Membership on the National Research Council's Committee on Child Development Research and Public Policy, as well as on its panels, including one on adolescent pregnancy and childbearing and one on high-risk youth, also helped to enlarge my outlook. Involvement in various projects of the World Health Organization, including a cross-national, comparative study of alcohol abuse in Zambia, Mexico, and Scotland, and preparing a presentation, "The health of youth: A behavioral science perspective" (Jessor, 1989), for WHO's 1989 Technical Discussions on the Health of Youth, sharpened my awareness of adolescent health issues in the developing world. And serving throughout the 1980s in advisory capacities for various agencies—NIAAA, NIDA, Health and Welfare, Canada—presented the challenge of linking social research on adolescent health to social policy.

A key contribution of Problem Behavior Theory to understanding adolescent health has been to demonstrate the embeddedness of health-related behaviors in a larger explanatory network of psychosocial and behavioral variables. Our research findings established that health behaviors were part of an adolescent's way of being in the world, i.e., part of a *lifestyle*. Health-enhancing behaviors, e.g., healthy diet, regular exercise, adequate sleep, and safety precautions, were shown to inter-relate or co-vary, as was true of problem behaviors; they were also shown to relate inversely to problem behaviors; and they were shown to reflect a general orientation of psychosocial conventionality. Variation in engagement in health-enhancing behavior related not only to proximal variables, such as value on health and attitudes and beliefs about particular health behaviors, variables that directly implicate the health behaviors, but also, and a more novel theoretical finding, to *distal* variables, such as religiosity, as well. These findings added support for the perspective that health behaviors are part of a larger way of being in the world, reflecting an organized, individual-level adolescent lifestyle.

Problem Behavior Theory and the Context of Disadvantage   In addition to its added concern for adolescent health behavior, Problem Behavior Theory also expanded in the 1980s to engage more deeply and directly with adolescent development under circumstances of disadvantage and in contexts of risk, a concern tangentially explored in the early Tri-Ethnic Study. Invited in 1985 by William Bevan to join an advisory group for the MacArthur Foundation's Program on Youth at Risk for Problem Behavior, I was appointed 2 years later as director of a new MacArthur Foundation Research Network on "Successful Adolescent Development among Youth in High Risk Settings," which emerged from the advisory group's deliberations. That began a decade of intense activity by the network members, more than a dozen of the leading scholars on adolescence from psychology, sociology, pediatrics, education, and psychiatry, to try to promote understanding of the process of "making it," i.e., how it is that adolescents growing up under severe conditions of adversity, disadvantage, and even danger nevertheless manage to "succeed": to stay in school and make progress, to avoid heavy engagement in problem behavior, to keep out of trouble with the authorities, to avoid too-early pregnancy or involvement with gangs, etc.

Studies were carried out by interdisciplinary teams of network scholars in inner city poverty neighborhoods in Philadelphia, New York, Chicago, and Denver, as well as in rural Iowa, where farm families had been exposed to the severe economic decline of the 1980s farm crisis. It was a heady experience, enthused with the notion of neighborhood impact on youth development, but also sensitive to other developmental contexts, especially the family and the school, and to individual-level characteristics. An *American Psychologist* article, "Successful adolescent development among youth in high–risk settings" (Jessor, 1993) provided an overview of the network's agenda and approach. Various papers were published from this endeavor, but its main contributions were three converging volumes: *Managing to make it: Urban families and adolescent success* (Furstenberg, Cook, Eccles, & Elder, 1999); *Children of the land: Adversity and success in rural America* (Elder & Conger, 2000); and *Good kids from bad neighborhoods: Successful development in social context* (Elliott et al., 2006). The MacArthur work resulted in significant advances in understanding about adolescent development in high-risk settings, especially in helping to right the balance from a preoccupation with negative outcomes to an emphasis on resources in both person and context, and on positive and successful development. It also revealed, importantly, that there was greater variation *within* neighborhoods than between neighborhoods, and that pure neighborhood effects were, after all, only modest. The MacArthur experience led, in my own work on Problem Behavior Theory, to a related paper, "Risk and protection in successful outcomes among disadvantaged adolescents" (Jessor, Turbin, & Costa, 1998b), which demonstrated the theory's usefulness in that domain.

Part III

Reformulating Problem Behavior Theory for Explaining Adolescent Risk Behavior: The Current Framework As the terms "risk" and "protection" in the title of that 1998 article suggest, Problem Behavior Theory had undergone something of a transformation beginning in the early 1990s. The new—and current—formulation extended the theory beyond problem behaviors alone to encompass the broader category of *risk behaviors*, all those behaviors that can compromise adolescent health and successful development. Toward that end, the theory's predictor or explanatory variables were "translated" into the language of risk factors and protective factors. Adoption of the new formulation was influenced by several things: the accumulated experience of expanding Problem Behavior Theory to apply to the domains of health and disadvantage; discovering that the theory also had reach into hitherto unexplored domains of risk behavior such as "risky driving" (Jessor, 1987b; 1989); and an awareness of the emergence of a new and relevant subdiscipline of *behavioral* epidemiology, which relied heavily on the concept of "risk factors" and "protective factors," factors that were congruent with many of our "instigation" and "control" theoretical predictors. The new formulation was designed to make Problem Behavior Theory more readily available to researchers in the health field and more useful for those interested in prevention/intervention, a constituency more familiar with the terminology of "risk" and "protection" than with constructs from our theory such as "problem behavior proneness."

In what was then for me a pivotal paper, "Risk behavior in adolescence: A psychosocial framework for understanding and action" (Jessor, 1991c), I undertook to create an overarching conceptual framework that could accommodate the variety of theories seeking to account for the broad domain of adolescent risk behavior, including Problem Behavior Theory. It articulated risk factors and protective factors in five different but interrelated domains of "causal" influence: biology/genetics; the social environment; the perceived environment; personality; and behaviors (Figure 23.3). In requiring specification of both risk and protective factors in each domain, it makes apparent the comprehensiveness and the complexity that a truly exhaustive account of variation in adolescent risk behavior would require. Problem Behavior Theory constitutes one particular derivation from that larger framework.

The incorporation of the concepts of risk behavior, risk factors, and protective factors in that larger framework stimulated some effort to clarify each. First, the concept of "risk behavior," behaviors that can have health-and life-compromising outcomes, avoids the confusion that has resulted from the pervasive employment of the term "risk-taking behavior" (with its unsupported corollary that adolescents are, therefore, "risk-takers"). The imputation of risk "taking" is analytically gratuitous when adolescents smoke or drink or have unprotected sex or eat junk food, and use of that term has tended to side-track and even preclude more appropriate explanatory efforts. Whether the deliberate taking of risk is entailed in any of those behaviors needs to be considered as problematic, something to be investigated rather than assumed. The term "risk-taking" has been a source of serious conceptual mischief and should be abandoned— except for those behaviors actually motivated by the conscious thrill of taking the risk involved. In addition, it is also important to recognize that although risk behaviors can compromise health and development, they can also achieve goals the adolescent values, such as a sense of autonomy, or peer approval, or being seen as more mature.

With regard to the concept of "risk factors," it is useful to differentiate the concept into risk factors for the *initiation* of a new risk behavior—its onset—and risk factors for the *intensification of involvement* in or commitment to that risk behavior, once initiated. Since so much of adolescent risk behavior is merely exploratory, the key societal concern has to be with risk factors for intense or committed or chronic involvement with them. With regard to "protective factors", conceptually their *protective* role operates *only when risk is present*. Importantly, in the absence of risk, protective factors play a *promotive* role conceptually, i.e., they provide support for positive, pro-social behavior and development. In addition, protective factors buffer or moderate the impact of exposure to risk factors, i.e., they interact with risk factors to reduce the likelihood of occurrence of risk behavior. It was the recognition of this latter, moderator role of protective factors that led us to shift Problem Behavior Theory from the additive regression model it had always relied on, in regard to instigations and controls, to an interactive model for the risk and protection relationship.

These considerations in mind, we reorganized the theoretical predictors in Problem Behavior Theory into structures of protective factors and risk factors drawn from the "causal" domains of the perceived environment, personality, and behavior. The protective factors that promote positive, pro-social behavior and thereby decrease the likelihood of engaging in risk behavior include: *models* for positive or pro-social behavior; personal and social *controls* against engaging in risk behavior; *social supports* for positive or pro-social behavior; and actual experience with *pro-social or health-enhancing behaviors*. The risk factors that, by contrast, increase the likelihood of occurrence of risk behaviors include: *models* for engaging in risk behavior; *opportunities* for engaging in risk behavior; personal *vulnerability* to engaging in risk behavior; and actual experience with *risk behaviors*. The re-formulated Problem Behavior Theory framework used in our

Risk and Protective Factors, Risk Behaviors and Risk Outcomes

Interrelated Conceptual Domains of Risk Factors and Protective Factors

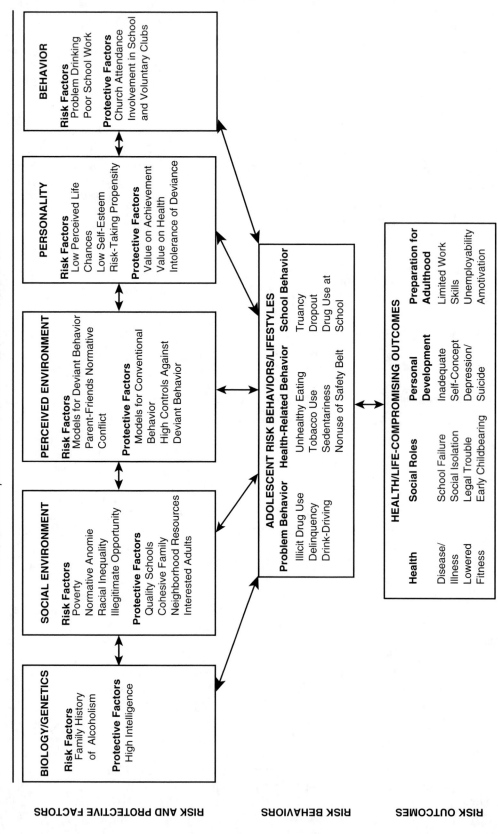

FIGURE 23.3 A conceptual framework for adolescent risk behavior (Jessor, 1991c, p. 602).

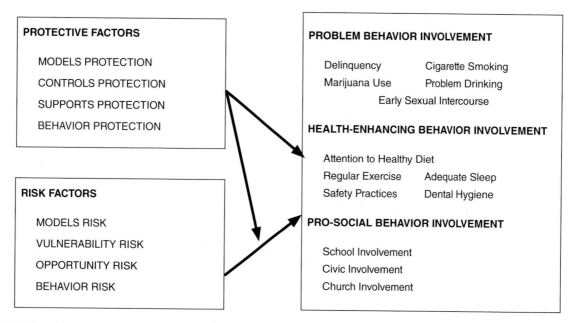

FIGURE 23.4 Problem Behavior Theory explanatory model for adolescent risk behavior.

research, in one version or another, since the mid-1990s is shown in Figure 23.4.

The framework illustrates the direct relation of protective factors and risk factors to risk behavior (the direct arrows), as well as the moderator effect of protection on the impact of exposure to risk (the indirect arrow). Both social context and personal variation continue to be represented in the framework. For example, Models Protection refers to perceived models in the adolescent's social environment—family, peers, school, neighborhood—for positive, pro-social, and health-enhancing behavior; Controls Protection refers to informal social controls from peers, family, neighbors, and teachers, as well as personal controls against risk behavior; Vulnerability Risk refers to low self-esteem, low perceived life-chances, and depression at the person-level, all enhancing the likelihood of engaging in risk behavior; etc. The particular variables from Problem Behavior Theory measured in each category of protection and risk can be seen in our various publications (Costa, Jessor, & Turbin, 1999, 2007; Costa et al., 2005; Jessor, Costa, Krueger, & Turbin, 2006; Jessor et al., 1995; Jessor et al., 1998a, b; Jessor et al., 2003; Jessor et al., 2010; Ndugwa et al., 2010; Turbin et al., 2006).

In its latest phase of development, then, the formulation of Problem Behavior Theory has expanded its reach beyond problem behavior to the larger domain of risk behavior in general, and it has brought social-psychological theory to bear in fields that had been largely descriptive, e. g., adolescent health and behavioral epidemiology, by translating its theoretical concepts into risk and protective factors.

Part IV

Problem Behavior Theory in the 21st Century: Establishing Cross-National Generality The past decade has seen the burgeoning of cross-national applications of Problem Behavior Theory in settings across the globe. The implications that these cross-national efforts have for the generality of findings when research is guided by theory are profound.

Our first systematic application of Problem Behavior Theory in a cross-national study had its origin in an unexpected contact from Professor Qi Dong, a distinguished developmental psychologist at Beijing Normal University, during my 1995–96 year at the Center for Advanced Study in the Behavioral Sciences at Stanford; familiar with my work, he thought it would be mutually beneficial if we could arrange a research collaboration on adolescent development. Intrigued by that possibility, and with funding a couple of years later from the Johann Jacobs Foundation, I organized an international workshop to plan a collaborative, cross-national study of adolescent health and development. The workshop brought together colleagues from Poland and Italy who were already using Problem Behavior Theory in their work, as well as Professor Qi and colleagues from China, and my research group from Colorado. Held in Italy in 1998, the workshop was successful in cementing the U.S.–China collaboration, and an application to the William T. Grant Foundation for a longitudinal research grant, "Adolescent risk behavior and development in China and the U.S.: A cross-national comparative study of risk and protection," was funded in 2000. Our Polish colleagues were ultimately unable to participate, and our Italian colleagues successfully carried out their own Problem Behavior Theory-guided study of Italian youth (Bonino, Cattelino, & Ciairano, 2005).

Most intriguing about the opportunity to test Problem Behavior Theory in The People's Republic of China was how pervasively different from the United States it was as a society and culture: a communist society, a society with a one-child family policy and an extremely low divorce rate, a culture of traditional respect for adults, a relatively lower prevalence of adolescent problem behavior, etc. Successful application of the theory in such a different societal context would provide compelling evidence of its generality. To insure that societal contrast, the study also included a city, Zhengzhou, in central China, which was less exposed than Beijing to Western influence. A comparative, school-based, longitudinal study of adolescent risk behavior was carried out in parallel in the two cities in China and in the city of Denver in the United States. Its findings have been reported in several U.S. publications (Costa et al., 2005; Jessor et al., 2003; Jessor et al., 2010; Turbin et al., 2006), as well as in publications in China.

Whether the analytic focus was on adolescent problem behavior, on pro-social behavior, or on health-enhancing behavior, there was strong support for the cross-national generality of the protection-risk explanatory model of Problem Behavior Theory. A substantial account of variation in risk behavior was provided by the same protective and risk factors in both countries, and for both genders, despite the large societal and cultural differences and despite differences in prevalence of the behaviors and in mean levels on the theoretical predictors. Of further importance, and as theoretically expected, protection was shown also to moderate the impact of exposure to risk in both countries. Just one important finding from this research: When the criterion was problem behavior, Controls Protection and Models Risk were the main predictors in both countries, but when the criterion was positive, that is, either pro-social or health-enhancing behavior, the important predictors shifted to Models Protection, Support Protection, and Vulnerability Risk, an entirely different pattern. Such findings attest to the value of differentiating both risk and protection and the necessity of considering such differentiation in prevention/intervention efforts.

Later, in collaboration with the African Population and Health Research Center in Nairobi, another cross-national study, with adolescents in the slums that surround the city, constituted the first application of Problem Behavior Theory in sub-Saharan Africa. In this contrasting setting from the U.S. contexts in which the theory had been developed, measures of the theory's psychosocial protective and risk factor variables again provided a substantial account of variation in adolescent problem behavior, and protection was again shown to moderate the impact of exposure to risk (Kabiru,

Beguy, Ndugwa, Zulu, & Jessor, 2012; Ndugwa et al., 2010).

Our studies in The People's Republic of China and in Kenya provided persuasive support for the cross-national applicability of Problem Behavior Theory. But the establishment of its generality by other, independent investigators makes that support even more convincing, and considerable literature has accumulated in recent years in that very regard. For example, Vazsonyi and colleagues (2008, 2010) report on their application of Problem Behavior Theory in cross-national studies, one using large, national probability samples of adolescents in Switzerland and The Republic of Georgia, and the other using convenience school samples from Hungary, the Netherlands, Slovenia, Spain, Switzerland, Taiwan, Turkey, and the United States. The former study supported the concept of a "problem behavior syndrome" in both societies, and confirmed that Problem Behavior Theory "has applicability across developmental contexts or societies" (2008, p. 562). The latter study concluded that: "The evidence appears to support great similarities in the relationships between risk and protective factors and the PBS [problem behavior syndrome] across the eight developmental contexts" (2010, p. 7). In another cross-national study, of early adolescent sexual initiation in Finland, Scotland, France, Poland, and the United States, Madkour et al. used Problem Behavior Theory as their framework; they conclude that "the fit of early adolescent sexual initiation within a PBT [Problem Behavior Theory] framework holds for multiple post-industrial national settings" (Madkour, Farhat, Halpern, Godeau, & Gabhainn, 2010, p. 397). By now, Problem Behavior Theory has been employed successfully in numerous other countries as well, ranging from Italy and the Netherlands (Ciairano, Kliewer, & Rabaglietti, 2009) to Ethiopia (Astatke, Black, & Serpell, 2000) to Iran (Aguilar-Vafaie, Roshani, Hassanabadi, Masoudian, & Afruz, 2011).

These consistent findings about the applicability of a theory devised and established in the United States to such widely differing societal and cultural contexts often startle or surprise, but as I indicated in an invited editorial, "Description versus explanation in cross-national research on adolescence," for the *Journal of Adolescent Health* when it published the 2008 Vazsonyi et al. paper, such generality is to be expected *at the theoretical level* (Jessor, 2008). Since a theory specifies underlying relations among variables, those relations should obtain in any context in which the theory can be applied—that is the nature of *explanatory* research. In considering the theoretical concept of "Support Protection," for example, its source may come from a single mother in a U.S. family or from an extended-kin group in China or from peers in the slums of Nairobi, but the theoretical relation of support protection to risk behavior should be the same in all three settings. It is this genotypic, explanatory role of theory that yields generality across phenotypic or descriptive differences in populations and contexts. Our studies have thus far supported the generality of the theory across ethnic groups, across gender, across life stages, across historically different U.S. cohorts (Donovan et al., 1999), and across widely diverse societies.

Concluding Reflections

The Problem Behavior Theory that has evolved from this half-century of cumulative work has, it is hoped, contributed to knowledge and understanding about adolescence along the way. As was true of the prior versions, its current protection/risk formulation is predicated on fundamental social–psychological processes that underlie behavior and shape the course of development both positively and negatively: social *models*; social and personal *controls*; social *supports*; contextual *opportunity*; personal *vulnerability*; and past engagement in risk, health, and pro-social *behaviors*. Although its early focus was on problem behavior, its applications to pro-social domains, including health-enhancing behavior, have been equally illuminating. This should not really be surprising; as the criminologist, Albert Cohen, pointed out: "A theory of deviant behavior not only must account for the occurrence of deviant behavior; it must also account for its failure to occur, or conformity" (1959, p. 463). This broader scope of Problem Behavior Theory is the legacy of a long-term, developmental behavioral science approach to inquiry.

That approach insists on the joint consideration of social environment and individual-level determinants of action. The distinguished personality psychologist, Henry Murray, asserted about the time that our work began that "no theoretical system constructed on the psychological level will be adequate until it has been embraced by and intermeshed with a cultural-sociological system" (1959, p. 20). From our early engagement with the socio-cultural system in the Tri-Ethnic Study to our recent concern for articulating risk and protective factors in the social contexts of daily adolescent life, we have sought to embrace the social environment in an interdisciplinary formulation for understanding adolescent behavior and development. And in documenting the unique variance added by the social environment measures to accounts based only on individual-level variables (Costa et al., 2005; Turbin et al., 2006), our findings have exemplified interdisciplinary research.

Complementing this engagement with the social environment has been our parallel interest in understanding the phenomenal world of the adolescent. From the very outset, the Tri-Ethnic Study was informed by extensive ethnographic explorations in the community; and in the three MacArthur volumes, ethnographic findings became an essential component of those studies. Indeed, the necessity to join qualitative with quantitative inquiry in order to achieve a deeper understanding of the impact of disadvantage on adolescent development quickly became apparent in the network, and toward that end, we organized a symposium on qualitative research that eventuated in an illuminating volume, *Ethnography and human development: Context and meaning in social inquiry* (Jessor, 1996; Jessor, Colby, & Shweder, 1996). It has been dismaying to continue to confront the intractable opposition of post-modernism in sociology and anthropology to quantitative work and the equally obstinate perspective of some quantitative social scientists about qualitative research; the volume bravely sought to overcome that polarity. We should be long past awarding honorific status to particular methods; methods serve as handmaidens to theory and problems.

As I look back now over more than five decades of research on adolescence, I'm most aware of how much remains to be accomplished. As successful as Problem Behavior Theory may have been—its social–psychological variables accounting in some cases for as much as half the variance in risk behavior—it is sobering to realize that fully half the variance remains unexplained; therein lies the challenge for the developmental science of adolescence in future years. One promising avenue to pursue in response to that challenge is engaging additional disciplines in the explanatory scheme. In this regard, it has been salutary to see the burgeoning attention to neuroscience and genetics in contemporary adolescent research. A caveat about following that course is in order, however; findings from those disciplines are too often considered as somehow more fundamental and more causal than findings at the social– psychological level, a kind of reductionist fallacy that can seriously skew scientific progress. Recent explanations of risk behavior based on the so-called "immature adolescent brain" or references to "addictive" behavior as a "brain disease"—especially in the absence of evidence about linking mechanisms—are two examples. In a long-ago article, "The problem of reductionism in psychology" (Jessor, 1958), I tried to argue against this tendency; more recently, Miller (2010) has addressed the issue in greater detail.

Another promising direction to pursue is gaining a deeper understanding of the social context of adolescent life. It is now clear to everyone that the standard demographic attributes—the so- called "social addresses"—are too distal to be helpful. Developing a more sensitive and differentiated theoretical language to describe the contexts of adolescent daily life, one that could better capture the learnings and rewards and opportunities and sanctions that exist in those settings, should yield a stronger grasp on the role of the social environment than we have yet achieved. Finally, probing more deeply the adolescent's phenomenology, getting at the quiddities of adolescent subjectivity, could certainly enrich understanding.

There is, of course, a sense of satisfaction in looking back at the contribution that Problem Behavior Theory has made to a developmental science of adolescence; at the same time, there is a continuing sense of excitement over addressing the challenges that remain for that still- emerging science.

Behind all scientific studies there is not only the drive to understand but the compulsion to persuade.

William Bevan

Acknowledgments

I am indebted to my students and colleagues who have, over the years, contributed immensely to the work described in this chapter. Many are named in the citations and references, but to all of them I am grateful for their ideas and their efforts. Three colleagues, Frances M. Costa, John E. Donovan, and Mark S. Turbin, deserve special mention and warm appreciation for their involvement in our most recent research.

References

Aguilar-Vafaie, M. E., Roshani, M., Hassanabadi, H., Masoudian, Z., & Afruz, G. A. (2011). Risk and protective factors for residential foster care adolescents. *Children and Youth Services Review, 33*, 1–15.

Astatke, H., Black, M. M., & Serpell, R. (2000). Use of Jessor's theoretical framework of adolescent risk behavior in Ethiopia: Implications for HIV/AIDS prevention. *Northeast African Studies, 7*, 63–68.

Blau, P. M., Gustad, J. W., Jessor, R., Parnes, H. S., & Wilcock, R. C. (1956). Occupational choice: A conceptual framework. *Industrial & Labor Relations Review, 9*(4), 531–543.

Bonino, S., Cattelino, E., & Ciairano, S. (2005). *Adolescents and risk: Behaviors, functions, and protective factors*. New York: Springer.

Ciairano, S., Kliewer, W., & Rabaglietti, E. (2009). Adolescent risk behavior in Italy and the Netherlands: A cross-national study of psychosocial protective factors. *European Psychologist, 14*, 180–192.

Cloward, R. A., & Ohlin, L. E. (1960). *Delinquency and opportunity: A theory of delinquent gangs*. New York: Free Press.

Cohen, A. K. (1959). The study of social disorganization and deviant behavior. In R. K. Merton, L. Broom, & L. S. Cottrell, Jr. (Eds.), *Sociology today: Problems and prospects* (pp. 461–484). New York: Basic Books.

Costa, F. (2008). *Problem behavior theory: A brief overview*. Available at: www.colorado.edu/ibs/jessor/pb_theory.html.

Costa, F. M., Jessor, R., & Donovan, J. E. (1989). Value on health and adolescent conventionality: A construct validation of a new measure in Problem Behavior Theory. *Journal of Applied Social Psychology, 19*(10), 841–861.

Costa, F. M., Jessor, R., Donovan, J. E., & Fortenberry, J. D. (1995). Early initiation of sexual intercourse: The influence of psychosocial unconventionality. *Journal of Research on Adolescence, 5*(1), 93–121.

Costa, F. M., Jessor, R., & Turbin, M. S. (1999). Transition into adolescent problem drinking: The role of psychosocial risk and protective factors. *Journal of Studies on Alcohol, 60*(4), 480–490.

Costa, F. M., Jessor, R., & Turbin, M. S. (2007). College student involvement in cigarette smoking: The role of psychosocial and behavioral protection and risk. *Nicotine & Tobacco Research, 9*(2), 213–224.

Costa, F. M., Jessor, R., Turbin, M. S., Dong, Q., Zhang, H., & Wang, C. (2005). The role of social contexts in adolescence: Context protection and context risk in the U.S. and China. *Applied Developmental Science, 9*, 67–85.

Cronbach, L. J., & Meehl, P. E. (1955). Construct validity in psychological tests. *Psychological Bulletin, 52*(4), 281–302.

Donovan, J. E. (2005). Problem behavior theory. In C. B. Fisher & R. M. Lerner (Eds.), *Encyclopedia of applied developmental science* (Vol. 2, pp. 872–877). Thousand Oaks, CA: Erudite.

Donovan, J. E., & Jessor, R. (1978). Adolescent problem drinking: Psychosocial correlates in a national sample study. *Journal of Studies on Alcohol, 39*(9), 1506–1524.

Donovan, J. E., & Jessor, R. (1985). Structure of problem behavior in adolescence and young adulthood. *Journal of Consulting and Clinical Psychology, 53*(6), 890–904.

Donovan, J. E., Jessor, R., & Costa, F. M. (1991). Adolescent health behavior and conventionality-unconventionality: An extension of Problem-Behavior Theory. *Health Psychology, 10*(1), 52–61.

Donovan, J. E., Jessor, R., & Costa, F. M. (1993). Structure of health-enhancing behavior in adolescence: A latent-variable approach. *Journal of Health and Social Behavior, 34*(4), 346–362.

Donovan, J. E., Jessor, R., & Costa, F. M. (1999). Adolescent problem drinking: Stability of psychosocial and behavioral correlates across a generation. *Journal of Studies on Alcohol, 60*(3), 352–361.

Donovan, J. E., Jessor, R., & Jessor, L. (1983). Problem drinking in adolescence and young adulthood: A follow-up study. *Journal of Studies on Alcohol, 44*(1), 109–137.

Elder, G. H., & Conger, R. D. (2000). *Children of the land: Adversity and success in rural America*. Chicago: University of Chicago Press.

Elliott, D. S., Menard, S., Rankin, B., Elliott, A., Wilson, W. J., & Huizinga, D. (2006). *Good kids from bad neighborhoods: Successful development in social context*. New York: Cambridge University Press.

Furstenberg, F. F. Jr., Cook, T. D. Eccles, J., & Elder, G. H. (1999). *"Managing to make it": Urban families and adolescent success*. Chicago: University of Chicago Press.

Gruber, H. E., Hammond, K. R., & Jessor, R. (Eds.). (1957). *Contemporary approaches to cognition*. Cambridge: Harvard University Press.

Hull, C. L. (1943). *Principles of behavior: An introduction to behavior theory*. New York: D. Appleton-Century Company.

Jessor, R. (1956). Phenomenological personality theories and the data language of psychology. *Psychological Review, 63*(3), 173–180.

Jessor, R. (1958). The problem of reductionism in psychology. *Psychological Review, 65*(3), 170–178.

Jessor, R. (1976). Predicting time of onset of marijuana use: A developmental study of high school youth. *Journal of Consulting and Clinical Psychology, 44*(1), 125–134.

Jessor, R. (1978). Health-related behavior and adolescent development: A psychosocial perspective. In *Adolescent behavior and health: A conference summary* (pp. 39–43). Washington, DC: National Academy of Sciences.

Jessor, R. (1983). The stability of change: Psychosocial development from adolescence to young adulthood. In D. Magnusson & V. L. Allen (Eds.), *Human development: An interactional perspective* (pp. 321–341). New York: Academic Press.

Jessor, R. (1984). Adolescent development and behavioral health. In J. D. Matarazzo, S. M. Weiss, J. A. Herd, & N. E. Miller (Eds.), *Behavioral health: A handbook of health enhancement and disease prevention* (pp. 69–90). New York: Wiley.

Jessor, R. (1987a). Problem-behavior theory, psychosocial development, and adolescent problem drinking. *British Journal of Addiction, 82*(4), 331–342.

Jessor, R. (1987b). Risky driving and adolescent problem behavior: Theoretical and empirical linkage. *Alcohol, Drugs, and Driving, 3*, 1–11.

Jessor, R. (1989). The health of youth: A behavioral science perspective. *Proceedings, Technical Discussions on "The Health of Youth."* Geneva: World Health Organization.

Jessor, R. (1991a). Behavioral science: An emerging paradigm for social inquiry? In R. Jessor (Ed.), *Perspectives on behavioral science: The Colorado lectures* (pp. 309–316). Boulder, CO: Westview Press.

Jessor, R. (Ed.). (1991b). *Perspectives on behavioral science: The Colorado lectures.* Boulder, CO: Westview Press.

Jessor, R. (1991c). Risk behavior in adolescence: A psychosocial framework for understanding and action. *Journal of Adolescent Health, 12*(8), 597–605.

Jessor, R. (1993). Successful adolescent development among youth in high-risk settings. *American Psychologist, 48*(2), 117–126.

Jessor, R. (1996). Ethnographic methods in contemporary perspective. In R. Jessor, A. Colby, & R. A. Shweder (Eds.), *Ethnography and human development: Context and meaning in social inquiry* (pp. 3–14). Chicago: University of Chicago Press.

Jessor, R. (2005). Remarks on the changing nature of inquiry. *Journal of Adolescent Health, 37*(1), 9–10.

Jessor, R. (2008). Description versus explanation in cross-national research on adolescence. *Journal of Adolescent Health, 43*(6), 527–528.

Jessor, R., Chase, J. A., & Donovan, J. E. (1980). Psychosocial correlates of marijuana use and problem drinking in a national sample of adolescents. *American Journal of Public Health, 70*(6), 604–613.

Jessor, R., Colby, A., & Shweder, R. A. (Eds.). (1996). *Ethnography and human development: Context and meaning in social inquiry.* Chicago: University of Chicago Press.

Jessor, R., Costa, F., Jessor, S. L., & Donovan, J. E. (1983). Time of first intercourse: A prospective study. *Journal of Personality and Social Psychology, 44*, 608–626.

Jessor, R., Costa, F. M., Krueger, P. M., & Turbin, M. S. (2006). A developmental study of heavy episodic drinking among college students: The role of psychosocial and behavioral protective and risk factors. *Journal of Studies on Alcohol, 67*(1), 86–94.

Jessor, R., Donovan, J. E., & Costa, F. (1986). Psychosocial correlates of marijuana use in adolescence and young adulthood: The past as prologue. *Alcohol, Drugs, and Driving, 2*, 31–49.

Jessor, R., Donovan, J. E., & Costa, F. (1989). Problem drinking and risky driving among youth: A psychosocial approach to a lifestyle pattern. In *Proceedings, International Conference on High Alcohol Consumers and Traffic* (pp. 137–152). Paris: INRETS.

Jessor, R., Donovan, J. E., & Costa, F. (1990). Personality, perceived life chances, and adolescent health behavior: An application of Problem Behavior Theory. In K. Hurrelmann & F. Lösel (Eds.), *Health hazards in adolescence* (pp. 25–41). Hawthorne, NY: Aldine/De Gruyter.

Jessor, R., Donovan, J. E., & Costa, F. M. (1991). *Beyond adolescence: Problem behavior and young adult development.* New York: Cambridge University Press.

Jessor, R., Graves, T. D., Hanson, R. C., & Jessor, S. L. (1968). *Society, personality, and deviant behavior: A study of a tri-ethnic community.* New York: Holt, Rinehart and Winston.

Jessor, R., & Hammond, K. R. (1957). Construct validity and the Taylor Anxiety Scale. *Psychological Bulletin, 54*(3), 161–170.

Jessor, R., & Jessor, S. L. (1973). The perceived environment in behavioral science: Some conceptual issues and some illustrative data. *American Behavioral Scientist, 16*(6), 801–828.

Jessor, R., & Jessor, S. L. (1975). Adolescent development and the onset of drinking: A longitudinal study. *Journal of Studies on Alcohol, 36*(1), 27–51.

Jessor, R., & Jessor, S. L. (1977). *Problem behavior and psychosocial development: A longitudinal study of youth.* New York: Academic Press.

Jessor, R., & Jessor, S. L. (1984). Adolescence to young adulthood: A twelve-year prospective study of problem behavior and psychosocial development. In S. A. Mednick, M. Harway & K. M. Finello (Eds.), *Handbook of longitudinal research. Vol. 2: Teenage and adult cohorts* (pp. 34–61). New York: Praeger.

Jessor, R., Jessor, S. L., & Collins, M. I. (1972). On becoming a drinker: Social-psychological aspects of an adolescent transition. In F. A.

Seixas (Ed.), *Nature and nurture in alcoholism* (pp. 199–213). New York: Annals of the New York Academy of Sciences.

Jessor, R., Turbin, M. S., & Costa, F. M. (1998a). Protective factors in adolescent health behavior. *Journal of Personality and Social Psychology, 75*(3), 788–800.

Jessor, R., Turbin, M. S., & Costa, F. M. (1998b). Risk and protection in successful outcomes among disadvantaged adolescents. *Applied Developmental Science, 2*, 194–208.

Jessor, R., Turbin, M. S., & Costa, F. M. (2010). Predicting developmental change in healthy eating and regular exercise among adolescents in China and the United States: The role of psychosocial and behavioral protection and risk. *Journal of Research on Adolescence, 20*(3), 707–725.

Jessor, R., Turbin, M. S., Costa, F. M., Dong, Q., Zhang, H. C., & Wang, C. H. (2003). Adolescent problem behavior in China and the United States: A cross-national study of psychosocial protective factors. *Journal of Research on Adolescence, 13*(3), 329–360.

Jessor, R., Van Den Bos, J., Vanderryn, J., Costa, F. M., & Turbin, M. S. (1995). Protective factors in adolescent problem behavior: Moderator effects and developmental change. *Developmental Psychology, 31*(6), 923–933.

Jessor, R., Young, H. B., Young, E. B., & Tesi, G. (1970). Perceived opportunity, alienation, and drinking behavior among Italian and American youth. *Journal of Personality and Social Psychology, 15*(3), 215–222.

Jessor, S. L., & Jessor, R. (1975). Transition from virginity to non-virginity among youth: A social-psychological study over time. *Developmental Psychology, 11*(4), 473–484.

Kabiru, C. W., Beguy, D., Ndugwa, R. P., Zulu, E. M., & Jessor, R. (2012). "Making it": Understanding adolescent resilience in two informal settlements (slums) in Nairobi, Kenya. *Child and Youth Services, 33*, 12–32.

Lewin, K. (1935). *A dynamic theory of personality: Selected papers.* New York: McGraw-Hill.

Lewin, K. (1951). *Field theory in social science: Selected theoretical papers.* New York: Harper & Row.

Madkour, A. S., Farhat, T., Halpern, C. T., Godeau, E., & Gabhainn, S. N. (2010). Early adolescent sexual initiation as a problem behavior: A comparative study of five nations. *Journal of Adolescent Health, 47*(4), 389–398.

Merton, R. K. (1957). *Social theory and social structure* (Rev. and enl. ed. ed.). New York: Free Press.

Miller, G. A. (2010). Mistreating psychology in the decades of the brain. *Perspectives on Psychological Science, 5*(6), 716–743.

Monahan, K. C., & Hawkins, J. D. (2012). *Covariance of problem behaviors in adolescence.* Paper presented at IOM Committee on the Science of Adolescence Workshop. Washington, DC.

Murray, H. A. (1959). Preparations for the scaffold of a comprehensive system. In S. Koch (Ed.), *Psychology: A study of a science* (Vol. 3, pp. 7–54). New York: McGraw-Hill.

Ndugwa, R. P., Kabiru, C. W., Cleland, J., Beguy, D., Egondi, T., Zulu, E. M. et al. (2010). Adolescent problem behavior in Nairobi's informal settlements: Applying Problem Behavior Theory in sub-Saharan Africa. *Journal of Urban Health, 88*(Suppl. 2), 298–317.

Parsons, T. (1937). *The structure of social action: A study in social theory with special reference to a group of recent European writers.* New York: McGraw-Hill.

Rachal, J. V., Williams, J. R., & Brehm, M. L. (1975). A national study of adolescent drinking behavior, attitudes, and correlates. (Rep. No. PB-246-002; NIAAA/NCALI-75/27). Springfield, VA: National Technical Information Service.

Rogers, C. R. (1959). A theory of therapy, personality, and interpersonal relationships as developed in the client-centered framework. In S. Koch (Ed.), *Psychology: A study of a science* (Vol. 3, pp. 184–256). New York: McGraw-Hill.

Rotter, J. B. (1954). *Social learning and clinical psychology.* Englewood Cliffs, NJ: Prentice- Hall.

Skinner, B. F. (1938). *The behavior of organisms: An experimental analysis.* New York: D. Appleton-Century Company.

Thomas, W. I. (1928). *The child in America: Behavior problems and programs*. New York: Alfred A. Knopf.

Turbin, M. S., Jessor, R., & Costa, F. M. (2000). Adolescent cigarette smoking: Health-related behavior or normative transgression? *Prevention Science, 1*, 115–124.

Turbin, M. S., Jessor, R., Costa, F. M., Dong, Q., Zhang, H. C., & Wang, C. H. (2006). Protective and risk factors in health-enhancing behavior among adolescents in China and the United States: Does social context matter? *Health Psychology, 25*(4), 445–454.

Vazsonyi, A. T., Chen, P., Jenkins, D. D., Burcu, E., Torrente, G., & Sheu, C-J. (2010). Jessor's problem behavior theory: Cross-national evidence from Hungary, the Netherlands, Slovenia, Spain, Switzerland, Taiwan, Turkey, and the United States. *Developmental Psychology, 46*(6), 1779–1791.

Vazsonyi, A. T., Chen, P., Young, M., Jenkins, D., Browder, S., Kahumoku, E. et al. (2008). A test of Jessor's problem behavior theory in a Eurasian and a Western European developmental context. *Journal of Adolescent Health, 43*(6), 555–564.

24

Adolescent Thinking in Action

Minds in the Making

DANIEL P. KEATING

Basic Questions

One key to a rewarding research career is selecting questions that are broad enough and personally significant enough to allow their pursuit in a sustained way. In the summer after 10th grade, I followed the social justice orientation of my Jesuit teachers at Loyola High School, volunteering in a literacy program in the heart of the Baltimore's impoverished inner city. Situated under the shadow of Johns Hopkins hospital, the school was attached to a missionary parish of the Josephite order. The students and nuns were all African-American. The pastor was Phil Berrigan, who, together with his brother Daniel, would soon become an icon of the anti-Vietnam War movement, most famously for pouring animal blood over draft files at a Selective Service office. Dan Berrigan later memorialized the ensuing trial of the "Catonsville Nine" in a stage play and book of the same name (Berrigan, 2004).

A suburban childhood and privileged schooling experiences had not prepared me for this summer teaching experience. The grinding poverty was obvious, even to a teenager dropped off in the morning and picked up at the end of the day. Getting to know the kids only reinforced this impression, with the predictable stories of family disruption, not enough food (a hot meal at breakfast and lunch was a big draw for having kids spend their summer in school), and a persistent fear about safety on the streets (a big draw for the parents to have their kids at school during the summer). Privilege and poverty seemed like a pretty good explanation for why my fellow high-school students were there as teachers while the kids we worked with were lacking basic literacy skills. Predictably, most of the kids were really struggling with basic reading and math. But not all of them—some stood out, not only grasping the basics but asking some penetrating questions along the way. Big differences among the kids in a uniformly

high-stress setting suggested that something more was going on, but I didn't really understand it.

In the next school year, there was another social project of a quite different nature. A group of us took a bus once a week to the Rosewood Training School just outside Baltimore. Begun as an asylum in the late 19th century, it had become a custodial institution for minors, with a range of developmental disabilities. Unknown to us, it had been cited time and again for poor or even inhumane patient care; also unknown to us was that almost all of the kids were destined to be in custodial "care" for life. What we observed was how excited the kids were to see us at each visit, and how starved for attention they were. It was a non-stop whirlwind from arrival to departure. I also remember thinking about some of the kids: Why are they here? Clearly, the majority had significant difficulties, but the most functional of the kids didn't seem all that different from some I had gotten to know in other places.

From our current clinical and scientific perspective, we know that nearly all these children could be successfully "mainstreamed" into regular classrooms, with special education support, and that custodial arrangements with minimal intervention for children with developmental disabilities are clearly iatrogenic. This recognition was later enacted, in 1975, into federal civil rights legislation as PL 94–142, now known as IDEA (Individuals with Disabilities Education Act). Some years after our weekly visits, the state of Maryland in fact closed the Rosewood facility, following court findings that they were failing to provide minimally adequate care.

These experiences shaped the questions that I began to pursue in graduate school and have continued as the touchstones for my professional work over the ensuing years: Why are people so different from each other? Why do people live in such different circumstances? What can be done to address disparities?

Getting Started

In March of 1973, during my second year in the graduate psychology program at The Johns Hopkins University, I attended the biennial meeting of the Society for Research in Child Development for the first time. At that time, developmental research was not my primary focus, nor was it a high-profile area within the department—which was true of many leading departments of psychology at the time. Behavioral learning (especially animal behavior), social psychology, quantitative methods and psychometrics, perception/cognition, and industrial/organizational psychology were all higher on the hierarchy. Given the current prominence, or even dominance of developmental psychology in many leading departments today, it is useful to note this history, because it provides a useful frame for understanding the directions of theory and empirical research over the subsequent decades.

This is not to say that a developmental Zeitgeist was absent. Confronting the local disciplinary pecking order was the intellectually and personally formidable Mary Ainsworth, whose translation of attachment theory into empirical reality was elevating the field of infant development to new heights at about the time I arrived at Hopkins. The personally formidable aspect is revealed in an anecdote (from a reliable eyewitness, so not apocryphal, I believe) about the erstwhile gender-segregated Hopkins faculty club, where women were not allowed to have lunch in the main room. There was a central table running the length of the room, at which (male) faculty were welcome to take any open seat. Professor Ainsworth brushed past the startled receptionist one day, took a seat, and simply announced, "Good afternoon, gentlemen." The protocol breach abruptly ended the practice.

Study of Mathematically Precocious Youth (SMPY)

My mentor at Hopkins was Julian Stanley, with whom I had the opportunity to help launch the Study of Mathematically Precocious Youth (SMPY), a ground-breaking and ongoing investigation of the nature of early-emerging high-level talent (Keating, 1976; Keating & Stanley, 1972; Lubinski & Benbow, 2006; Stanley, Keating, & Fox, 1974). A highly influential figure in psychometric theory, especially of measurement reliability, and in experimental and quasi-experimental designs (Campbell, Stanley, & Gage, 1963; Stanley, 1957, 1968a, 1968b), Stanley vigorously pursued the quest for effective educational accommodations for highly talented youth for the remainder of his career, spawning active programs at Hopkins, Duke, Iowa State, Vanderbilt, and elsewhere. Although somewhat paradoxical in light of my pre-graduate school interest in difficulties in development, my research on high-level talent and how to support it provided me with invaluable research tools and broadened my perspectives on development.

Immersed in this work as I was, my own interests began to move in a tangent to the educational measurement and intervention concerns that were central to SMPY—although not before completing a valuable apprenticeship in psychometrics and measurement (Keating, 1975a, 1975c, 1975d). An intellectually influential moment for me, which in hindsight is another indicator of the rapid

expansion of a developmental perspective more broadly, was a symposium at Hopkins presented by Jean Piaget in 1972 on the topic of creativity (Piaget, 1981). Two ideas from this talk stayed with me. First, he argued that it is important to understand the origins, pathways, and nature of creativity, rather than merely its manifestations. In other words, creativity, as with higher-order human functioning in general, deserves to be "unpacked." Second, he acknowledged that many would argue that differences in creativity are a matter for biology rather than psychology. He then noted that, even if true, this point merely moves the question of origins, nature, and pathways to a related domain, and still remains to be answered in those terms.

The SMPY research with its focus on exceptional ability and the developmental mindset fostered by Ainsworth were catalyzed for me by Piaget's approach into an overarching question that came to define the focus of my research interest: What makes people so different from each other? My initial interest arose from differences in abilities and talents, but has led during my career to ask the same question about differences in many domains beyond cognitive or academic competence, including social competence, emotional and behavioral problems, mental and physical health—which we have characterized with the omnibus term "developmental health" (Keating & Hertzman, 1999). Developmental health not only includes these multiple developmental outcomes, but also poses a working hypothesis: The origins and pathways of the multiple domains of developmental health share fundamental features.

This abbreviated personal history already points to some lessons learned about progress in research careers and research fields in general—and how they interact. A few framing observations are in order, because the biographical and autobiographical style is at odds with scientific argument. First, the weaving of an intellectual history is necessarily idiosyncratic, particularly in how one sees one's own work relative to questions of research and theory arising for the field as a whole. Second, the role of serendipity tends to be overshadowed in constructing a coherent story. Things often fit together better in retrospect than in the day-to-day. Finally, even beyond the unconscious reconstructive processes that lie at the heart of current models of everyday memory, autobiography evokes the creation of a narrative arc that entails omissions, emphases, and links in order to make it a story. The facts don't change, but how they fit together reflects an individual perspective.

Moving On and Moving Back to Basic Questions

At the start of a more independent pursuit of my basic questions, in the early 1970s, the nature–nurture war was on in full force both in academia and the political world, and the popular answers were simplistic: It's in the genes; it's in the environment. The arguments were wrapped in political and cultural conflicts as well, making a real dialogue hard to come by. The trajectory from this binary choice to our current realization that nature and nurture are fundamentally intertwined, and that the real scientific problem is working out the detailed mechanisms and processes of those interactions, captures in essence both my own intellectual history and the current, and highly appropriate, pre-eminence of developmental science in answering these core questions (Keating, 2011b)—as the following narrative seeks to illustrate.

One other lesson learned is likely apparent already, and will become more so. In addition to working on a question that is personally engaging, an equally important aspect of a research career is working with thoughtful and engaged colleagues: as mentors, as collaborators, and as students. The line of research on mathematically talented youth would not become my primary focus, although I have returned to it on various occasions (Keating, 1991, 2008), but the training and opportunities arising from my work with Julian Stanley have proved invaluable.

Precocious Formal Operations

To understand the underlying nature of major differences in cognitive performance, such as those revealed in SMPY (Keating, 1976), a leading candidate in the early 1970s was clearly the work of Piaget and his group in Geneva. Launched by the seminal 1958 work of Jean Piaget and Barbel Inhelder, *The Growth of Logical Thinking from Childhood to Adolescence*, which arose from Piaget's longstanding theoretical and empirical program on the development of logic and on genetic epistemology more generally (Piaget, 1950), research on adolescent cognition became a growth industry. This groundbreaking work focused on the development of propositional logic as the mature form of logical reasoning. In my dissertation, I posed the obvious question: Is high-level cognitive performance in early adolescence associated with, and perhaps driven by, earlier emergence of formal operations, the fourth and final stage of logical reasoning in Piaget's theory? Using tasks from Inhelder and Piaget's (1958) collection that were designed to assess formal operational reasoning, and similar tasks in a set of related studies, we found significant and substantial advancement of logical reasoning performance between groups of children and adolescents (11–14 years old) who were selected to be at or above the 98th percentile on school system-wide standardized mathematics assessments, compared with individuals between the 48th and 52nd percentiles (Keating, 1975b; Keating & Caramazza, 1975; Keating & Schaefer, 1975). The differences on the logical reasoning tasks were striking, with the younger, higher-scoring group outperforming the average-scoring group that was 2 years older.

The consistency of these findings, in the predicted directions, supported the idea that highly able early adolescents—as measured by standardized ability tests—were capable of performing very well on logical tasks of formal operations. But it raised the question of whether these findings showed early formal reasoning to be the source of individual differences in mathematical talent, or merely another way of measuring the same thing. My psychometric training led me to be wary of jingle-jangle fallacies: Constructs with the same name may not measure the same thing, and constructs with different names may not be really different. What might help to narrow the range of possible inferences from this set of findings? One option would be to see how general the associations were with precocity in formal operational reasoning.

As it happened, we already had a clue from the SMPY findings: While very high-level performance was statistically rare in the domain of mathematics (using a cutoff of 95th percentile or higher compared with college-bound high school seniors on the SAT-Mathematics entrance exam, while being no older than 14 years of age), similar performance was exceedingly rare on the verbal reasoning portion of the SAT, using a similar cutoff. This finding is not conclusive, of course, because the SAT-V included vocabulary knowledge as well as reasoning items, thus implicating the role of time to acquire word knowledge as a possible confound. But a similar contrast in performance between extreme scores among the early SMPY cohorts on tests of non-verbal reasoning (such as Raven's progressive matrices) and verbal analogies (such as Miller's Analogies Test) reinforced the idea that domain specificity was a component of the differences, rather than generalized reasoning precocity. We later tested this hypothesis more directly, by looking at the domain specificity versus generalizability of high ability in a different sample at similar ages (Matthews & Keating, 1995). The primary finding was that as one raises the cutoff for what counts as high ability, the proportion of individuals falling into more than one domain drops off rather quickly. In brief, intellectual precocity, especially exceptional precocity, tends to be domain specific rather than domain general.

This concern over domain specificity was not unknown in Piaget's work, of course, and was characterized by the term *decalage*, which had two aspects: Horizontal *decalage* referred to the observation that not all tasks with similar logical requirements would be performed equally well by an individual; vertical *decalage* referred to the observation that within a given task, an individual might progress more rapidly through more complex manifestations of it, perhaps because of a specific interest or focused effort, but not generalize that more advanced reasoning to different tasks. Perhaps more than any other feature of Piagetian theory, the concept of *decalage* illustrates the fundamental difference between psychometric methods and Piaget's *methode clinique*. In converting Piaget's genetic epistemology into a testable performance theory (sometimes referred to as the "North American question" by dubious Genevans), *decalage* may be seen as a correct observation, but one that fundamentally undermines the theory. If the development of reasoning entails a generalized cognitive reorganization, as the theory of genetic epistemology claims (Piaget, 1950), then this broad advancement should be observed without recourse to seemingly ad hoc corollaries (or "fudge factors" to return the favor of pejorative terminology, from North America to Geneva in this instance). The distinction here is between a structuralist theory of fundamental mental organization, which the tasks and observations are intended to illustrate, and a predictive performance theory, which would generate a set of testable hypotheses about how development proceeds, including how it leads to differences among individuals.

Putting on the Moves

One of the touted benefits of a classical education is to be compelled to read a fair amount of philosophy, and in its manifestation in Jesuit education (which I continued for my undergraduate years at the College of the Holy Cross) this expectation was combined with an equivalent amount of required courses in theology and scriptural exegesis. So the concept of "moves" becomes a habit of mind. This orientation has its modern (or more accurately, postmodern) equivalent in the intellectual movement known as "deconstruction" (more on this later), which contends that the actual nature of an argument can only be found by largely ignoring its surface features and uncovering what it is covertly arguing *against*. This approach loses its appeal when taken to an extreme, because it defies common sense that an argument is *only* about what it seeks to obscure. But in both the classical and the postmodern approach, making sense of a sustained argument in a field is greatly aided by paying close attention to the moves, both overt and otherwise, made by players in the contest of ideas.

In my own work and in the field of adolescent cognition more generally, there were four major moves in the study of adolescent cognition that arose more or less in parallel after the initial Piaget-inspired burst of research, and they impinged on each other: explicit testing of Piaget's theory of formal operational reasoning, construed as a performance model with testable predictions; consideration of alternative sources of the observable shifts in adolescent thinking, particularly arising from the componential model of human information processing (now subsumed within the broader field of cognitive science); a focus on the acquisition of expertise as a primary driver of cognitive shifts, with a particular emphasis on domain specificity observed in multiple cognitive functions; and what might be termed "genetic epistemology redux" in which a return to more basic questions about the nature, and limits, of reasoning became a focus.

Testing Formal Operations Throughout the 1970s, a dominant concern of research on adolescent cognition was testing various features of the theory of formal operations. More often than not, this work entailed a significant effort to spell out what empirical predictions were to be tested, because, as noted earlier, Inhelder and Piaget (1958) did not frame their approach as a testable set of specific predictions. As a consequence, studies with different assumptions, different empirical paradigms, and different outcomes proliferated. In a decision that proved to have longer-term consequences than I imagined at the time, I agreed to do a theoretical and empirical review of the accumulating literature on adolescent cognition (Keating, 1980). One long-term consequence is that I have frequently been asked to revisit this question, and have had trouble declining, judging from the ensuing reviews (Keating, 1990a, 1990b, 2004, 2011a, 2012).

A substantial literature on formal theory testing has continued to be generated, if at a decelerating pace, but most of the core issues have remained the same, as has the weight of empirical results. Three stand out, in my view: scaling of task difficulty; age of acquisition; and specificity of logical demands. My intent here is not to relitigate these disputes (see Keating, 2004 for a detailed review), but only to note that these central predictions of formal operations as a psychological theory of performance have not been confirmed (Keating, 2011a, 2012). On scaling, we should expect to find that tasks deemed to have higher-level logical demands should be more difficult overall than those with lower-level logical demands. In general, this finding is confirmed only at coarser levels of aggregation, with young children reliably worse than adolescents or adults. But in more precise comparisons, the scaling of performance on logical demands between older children and adolescents, or adolescents and adults, yields much more mixed results. It hardly needs noting that the reasons adolescents may outperform young children lie not only in their logical demands, thus predictions based on scaling logical difficulty would need to be relatively precise to avoid performance confounds.

A theoretically related expectation about the age of acquisition of various logical competencies has also fared poorly. In this vein, one of the early contributions was the work of Trabasso (1975) and his colleagues on the transitive inference task. Tom was one of a number of colleagues whose intellect and expertise I benefited from during my first tenured position at the Institute of Child Development at the University of Minnesota throughout the late 1970s. In what was to become a major paradigm in developmental studies, Tom altered the basic transitive inference task ("If A is greater than B, and B is greater than C, which is greater, A or C?") to get at the underlying logical demands while reducing other cognitive demands. This alteration aimed to reduce the memory demands through extended practice on the premises, before participants were asked to make the inferential leap. The core finding: Transitive inference performance was greatly enhanced among younger children, approaching that of adolescents or even adults. The Piagetian riposte was to argue that the extended practice sessions had reduced the logical requirements by building a spatial mental analogue from which the children could simply "read off." As I noted in an earlier review (Keating, 1990a), this counter-argument does not much help the stage theory defense: How do we know that adults performing the same task do not spontaneously construct a spatial analogue, and also "read off" the correct answer rather than using transitive logic?

Closely linked to this point is the more general issue of separating logical demands from other, theoretically unrelated task demands. One approach is that used by Trabasso, simplifying the non-logical task demands, and showing vastly better performance by younger children. A contrary approach is to maximize the logical demands so that non-logical skills are no longer useful, for example by using abstract or even counterfactual premises to ensure that the problems can be resolved only through logic. As one might expect, the opposite pattern of results generally ensued (Keating, 2004): Children were completely lost on such tasks, but then again, so were virtually all adolescents and the vast majority of adults. Simplification paradigms and purification paradigms lead to dramatically different performance patterns, but it is hard, perhaps impossible, to judge by some principled means which approach provides a cleaner test of the growth of logical thinking.

Human Information Processing: Componential Models

In thinking about moves in theory and research, we should not assume a linear path. There are many parallel lines of inquiry which impinge on each other. The work described above reflected the rapid growth on information processing approaches, whose application to developmental studies began as a trickle in the early 1960s and by the early 1970s had become a standard paradigm. Their value in testing Piagetian claims about reasoning performance was not their sole, or even primary goal. Instead, the overarching goal was to identify and test the central components of human cognitive activity (e.g., Neisser, 1967).

Drawing on this newer paradigm, and branching out from both the psychometric and the Piagetian traditions, a group of colleagues and students at Minnesota worked with me on a series of studies to look at the developmental and individual differences in information processing components (Keating & Bobbit, 1978), including attention allocation (Manis, Keating, & Morrison, 1980), long-term memory (Ford & Keating, 1981; List, Keating, & Merriman, 1985), arithmetic operations (Miller, Perlmutter, & Keating, 1984), search processing (Keating, Keniston, Manis, & Bobbitt, 1980), and mental rotation (Merriman, Keating, & List, 1985). Along with many researchers, we were interested in documenting general and specific growth parameters in processing components from childhood to adulthood (eventually aided by portable computer technology, enabling school-based research without a strenuous transportation and installation of a full-size tachistoscope for each data collection site!), and also observing the patterns of individual differences on these components. As predicted, older and psychometrically brighter children performed better, and the level of processing "precocity" was quite similar in magnitude to the psychometrically assessed differences.

We were also interested, however, in how well these components, for each of which there were significant associations with age and ability, would "add up" to give a reliable portrait of overall performance on complex tasks. In other words, is cognitive advancement on higher-order activity correctly viewed as merely or primarily the assembly of more basic components?

Looking at the pattern of results across our studies, and those of others, the evidence was not especially persuasive. In a multivariate validity investigation to address this directly, we found that componential recombination did not in fact explain as much variance in performance as would be expected (Keating, List, & Merriman, 1985). Others hypothesized that it was not the assembly of subcomponents that would account for variance in higher-order cognitive functioning, but rather more central drivers like general speed of processing (e.g., Kail, 1992) or increased mental capacity located in central conceptual structures (Case, 1991).

Several challenges to core processing-based accounts struck me then and now as not having been sufficiently addressed (Keating, 1984, 1996), but one in particular stands out. In general, the more narrowly focused the estimated parameters of processing were, by controlling for extraneous factors like practice, knowledge, motor response, and so on, the *less* variance in higher-order performance was accounted for, whether that variance was related to age or to ability. My concern with this approach was that it could be too easily conflated with a search for a G-factor of intelligence fully reducible to speed of neural function under exclusive genetic control, most explicitly argued by Eysenck (1986). I hasten to add that this view was decidedly *not* shared by my longtime Toronto colleague and collaborator Robbie Case, or by Rob Kail. Allow me to add another lesson learned through this work, namely to avoid overzealous prosecution of a theoretical position. We presented a critique (Morrison, Morrison, & Keating, 1992) of Kail's argument that general processing speed increases with development. In retrospect, we conflated the developmental variance attributable to this central factor with the variance in broader performance it accounted for. Kail (1992) rightly corrected this misinterpretation, and his position that speed of processing shows a general increase across childhood and adolescence subsequently converged with evidence from developmental neuroscience.

In 1985, while a visiting scientist at the Max Planck Institute (MPI) in Berlin—another serendipitous opportunity to learn much from a new set of colleagues, led by Paul Baltes—I had the occasion during a lunch conversation to ask Eysenck what theory guided the selection of stimuli for evoked potentials and of the EEG parameters that yielded the strong correlations with IQ that he had presented at an MPI guest lecture (respectively, a high-decibel square-wave tone at random intervals, and "string length" of the EEG signal up to 500 msec post stimulus). I was a bit taken aback with the answer that many stimuli and many parameters had been tried, but these yielded the best correlations. Subsequent event-related potential (ERP) research has made the picture much more complex, of course, but it was a startling insight into the scientific epistemology of essentialism. Given that the source of differences in cognitive performance is theoretically assumed to be a single driver (genetically determined G-factor, for Eysenck), then the goal is to keep searching until the tightest link can be found—not unlike seeking the configuration of factors that maximizes the odds ratio of a known diagnosis, like cancer.

Acquisition of Expertise In addition to the potential confounds among different parameters of information processing (attention, memory, reasoning, and so on) that complicated the task of identifying the sources of developmental and individual differences, a factor that garnered considerable research interest in the 1980s were the roles of learning, knowledge, and expertise. As shown in a number of studies (for example, Chi, Glaser, & Farr, 1988; Chi, Hutchinson, & Robin, 1989), basic processing differences between experts and novices were as large or larger than those associated with substantial age or developmental differences. A classic example was working memory for chess positions, in which early adolescent chess players far outperformed novice adults. This finding harkens back to the *decalage* and domain specificity concerns about reasoning performance, but extended these effects into quite basic information-processing parameters.

Following this basic paradigm, we also found substantial evidence for highly domain-specific expertise differences, not only in knowledge but in interactions of knowledge and context. In one study (Keating & Crane, 1990), we presented a set of proportional reasoning problems to late adolescents (college freshmen) in a standard mathematics test format, on which nearly all of them performed quite well. We selected a group that was at or near ceiling on this assessment, and then presented the mathematically identical problems in a different context involving comparisons of the proportions of physical objects, when their size and shape were allowed to vary. The core finding was that very few could in fact solve the same problems in the new context. We interpreted these findings as highlighting differences in the kinds of knowledge or expertise available to an individual, in this case that procedural or algorithmic knowledge can be quite different from conceptual understanding. Assessments of expertise, like those of reasoning or of processing components, appear to be highly sensitive to both the content being assessed and the context of its assessment. A similar finding on within-domain specificity showed that children's and adolescents' understanding of rights differed between self-determination rights, a more often researched aspect, or nurturance rights, focusing on what rights to parental or broader adult support minors should be able to expect (Ruck, Abramovitch, & Keating, 1998; Ruck, Keating, Abramovitch, & Koegl, 1998).

Genetic Epistemology Redux By the late 1980s, the cumulative evidence on the nature of cognitive development from late childhood through adolescence presented a complex picture whose resolution seemed increasingly hard to achieve. Lines of research on reasoning, on basic processing, on expertise, and on the sources of age and individual differences were generating intriguing snapshots, but were only rarely confronting each other. Within a given paradigm, the findings appeared, to me at least, to be adding complexity in many rich details, but not gravitating toward coherence.

During my time in Berlin, I took the opportunity to delve into a broader inquiry into the nature of thinking more generally, in the hope of getting a handle on the bigger picture. Perhaps inspired by the Continental setting, I was drawn to the work of Michel Foucault on the nature of knowledge (Dreyfus & Rabinow, 1982), and related developments in the "deconstructive turn." My take on this line of argument, as a developmental scientist, was that there was not—and could not be—a principled method of identifying which approach to understanding cognitive development should be "privileged" epistemologically (Keating, 1990c): the *structuralist* centrality of logical operations; the *empirical* assembly of basic processing components; *hermeneutic* inferences about the acquisition of expertise from a study of the individual's experiential and learning history; and not represented in adolescent research but an important alternative, a *phenomenological* stance that admits no need of a mediating cognitive system (e.g., Gibson, 1966).

At the same time, the abandonment of scientific scrutiny, because a privileged epistemological stance could not be established a priori, struck me as a path away from reality, not closer to it. Neither the linguistic play of deconstructive argument, in the style of Derrida, nor the negation of knowledge because it is fundamentally intertwined with power and privilege, in the style of Foucault, offered much hope for answering basic questions despite their utility as critical tools. They were assuredly not a promising route for acquiring knowledge that could be used to advance human development.

Also emerging in the broader intellectual environment at about this time was a different move away from essentialist thinking, toward dynamic systems thinking. Although the creative tension between structural and system approaches had been around for quite some time, the search for the essence of the closed structure had overshadowed the role of open systems approaches, including in Piaget's work (Keating, 1990c). The newer applications of dynamic systems theory offered a way to integrate across multiple approaches, without recourse to a predetermined "central driver" of development (Keating, 2004). The implication and promise of this move from essentialist to dynamic systems thinking is that reductionism can be understood as a useful though limited methodological tool, while the focus of investigation shifts to *how* the various elements of a system become coordinated during development as emergent properties (Keating, 1990c; Keating & Miller, 2000). The flipside of abandoning a search for a central driver is that it both enables and compels a search for ways in which multiple facets of cognitive development become coordinated over time (Demetriou, Christou, Spanoudis, & Platsidou, 2002; Keating, 2004).

Thinking in Action: Drilling Down and Ramping Up

Implementing dynamic systems approaches is undoubtedly more difficult than merely shifting how we think about development. Early precursors include the use of standard methods to expand the search for bidirectional influences, for example in taking both parenting practices and child characteristics into joint consideration. Although formal modeling is in the early stages, constrained by limitations in analytic tools, compared with the longstanding general linear model, and by the difficulty in effective modeling where the data density is insufficient (Keating & Miller, 2000), the implications of a shift in how the field approaches nearly all topics are none the less profound. Two of the implications stand out in my view. First, it provides an alternate approach to the search for essential drivers of development, focusing instead on the integration of multiple developmental contributions across multiple systems. Second, it draws attention to a search for the underlying mechanisms through which interactions across multiple systems actually transpire.

A major challenge to this approach arises from the fact that complexity increases exponentially as we consider multiple systems interacting with each other. Meeting this challenge requires that we maintain attention to the observed coherence and replicability of patterns in development at more macro levels. In other words, how do we embrace the paradox that burgeoning complexity at the level of mechanisms results nevertheless in strong coherence of developmental outcomes at both the individual and population levels?

We have been attempting to address this challenge in a research program that entails both drilling down to more detailed understanding of underlying developmental and biological mechanisms, and ramping up to more macro levels of developmental health outcomes to identify coherent patterns in individuals and populations that constrain accounts of adolescent development. What these approaches have in common is a methodology that focuses not on the underlying essence of adolescent thinking, but rather on what thinking looks like as it is manifested in action in the world. For me, this approach has the added advantage of a stronger concordance with my longstanding questions of disparities in developmental and health outcomes, and what might be done about them.

Drilling Down: Neurodevelopmental Mechanisms of Health-Risk Behaviors In adolescent developmental health, a dominant issue is the public health concern with behavioral misadventure, the largest contributor to mortality and morbidity during the second decade of life, specifically owing to the impact of health-risk behaviors. One prominent risk area is driving, in which the role of expertise and its interaction with the socio-emotional context are deeply implicated (Keating, 2007; Keating & Halpern-Felsher, 2008). This focus arises in part from research on adolescent decision-making, which has gravitated toward "dual process models" of cognitive activity. In this model, there are two sets of cognitive processes, one associated with effortful analytic reasoning, and the other of which relies on more heuristic processes—the latter of which are also characterized as experiential processing or instinctual processing. Dual process models have subsequently been applied to a wide range of adolescent cognitive functioning (Albert & Steinberg, 2011). Because analytic reasoning is effortful and heuristic processing appears to be the default, the former is less readily activated and requires specific circumstances to evoke it.

The difficulty lies in distinguishing between situations in which heuristic processes suffice from those in which a more conscious analytic effort would be beneficial. There is evidence that this balance of processing approaches may pose particular challenges for adolescents, because mature analytic skills are relatively recently acquired and thus even more effortful than they are for adults, and because the executive functions of inhibitory control and planning are not fully developed, making it difficult for them to identify situations in which decisions might be better if subjected to more careful cognitive processing. Even in relatively simple laboratory tasks of attentional focus such as anti-saccade, adolescent performance approaches adult levels, but at the cost of ongoing effortful monitoring (Luna et al., 2004). In addition, there is evidence suggesting that emotion and reward systems, affiliated with the limbic system of the brain, mature much more rapidly toward adult levels, compared with the slower growth of the prefrontal-cortex-supported executive functions, including self-regulation (Casey, Jones, & Somerville, 2011), suggesting a maturational mismatch of prefrontal and limbic systems that may place particularly acute pressures on the adolescent's cognitive system.

In recent work, we have begun to explore how best to build meaningful links among dual-process decision making models, neurodevelopmental bases of such models, and their relationship to health risks arising from behavioral misadventure. Initial results suggest that this integration is likely to encounter some significant challenges. One is the likelihood that not all risk behaviors originate from a reactive response that activates limbic over prefrontal systems. Some adolescents take risks on purpose, to obtain benefits that go along with them, and these adolescents show a *more* mature profile on neurocognitive tasks (Maslowsky, Keating, Monk, & Schulenberg, 2011). In a related study, we found that differential preferences for benefits relative to risks were a significant mediator of the relationship between sensation-seeking and risk behavior (Maslowsky, Buvinger, Keating, Cauffman, & Steinberg, 2011). It is important not to conflate faulty decision-making with disapproval of the decisions that are made (Keating, 1980). Of course, a planful decision to take a risk does not ensure the ability to manage the risk once undertaken, at which point a developmental maturity mismatch may become a key factor in navigating the situation.

At a more general level, it is likely that underlying biodevelopmental mechanisms will play a key role in future research on adolescent development. Two candidate mechanisms are neural sculpting and epigenetic modification of gene function (Keating, 2011b, 2011c). The first is a direct mechanism, known also as synaptic pruning. Early adolescence is a period of rapid synaptic overproliferation, after which there is substantial pruning that "wires together what fires together." As in early child development, this biological embedding of the lived lives of adolescents has profound implications not only for adolescent behavior, but also for life-course developmental health (Boyce & Keating, 2004; Keating, 2011c; Keating & Hertzman, 1999). A second mechanism, less direct but potentially more far-reaching, involves epigenetic mechanisms through which genes can listen to the physical and social environment by means of chemical modification of the regulator or promoter segment of the gene (through DNA-methylation or histone modification). It may reach farther because it appears to operate at any point of development and because of its ability to transmit the epigenomic alterations to subsequent generations (Szyf & Bick, 2012). Clearly, we are moving further and further away from the old controversy of a nature versus nurture dichotomy, but we now encounter the even more challenging task of elucidating exactly *how* nature and nurture interact (Keating, 2011b, 2011c).

Ramping Up: Population Developmental Health As suggested above, drilling down to find underlying biological and developmental mechanisms will almost surely increase the complexity of potentially important processes, often exponentially. What constrains this work in a way that allows meaningful investigation, by focusing on the most promising candidate mechanisms? The strongest constraint, in my view, is the highly robust and replicable patterns of developmental health outcomes: longitudinally within individuals; in the distributions of individual outcomes across societal factors; and in an even larger aggregation, comparative population indicators across countries or other jurisdictions (Keating, 2011c). Underlying mechanisms that cannot be strongly linked, at least theoretically, to known patterns of population developmental health afford much less promise for interdisciplinary integration.

We have pursued studies of population developmental health for some time, focusing on both early childhood and adolescent development (Boyce & Keating, 2004; Keating, 2011c; Keating & Hertzman, 1999; Keating, Siddiqi, & Nguyen, 2013; Miller, Jenkins, & Keating, 2002; Siddiqi, Hertzman, Keating, & Kawachi, 2013).

The animating idea for much of this work is that there are extensive social disparities in a wide range of outcomes we have aggregated as developmental health, and that those patterns are socially patterned in similar ways across outcomes. These disparities may be based on gender, as in a set of studies on the "math filter" exclusion of girls more often than boys, a filter that can be somewhat modified by intervention (Shapka & Keating, 2003) but that is observed to be similar in a number of different countries (Watt et al., 2012). A focus drawn from the field of population health more broadly is the pervasiveness of social gradients, in which individuals from more advantaged socioeconomic circumstances fare better than those less advantaged. The potential for the importance of biological embedding—both from neural sculpting and epigenetic modification—makes it a prime candidate mechanism.

A contrary view would hold that social gradients may primarily reflect more enduring genomic factors, reinforced by a combination of social mobility and assortative mating. This idea is situated within a large controversy, of course, but one major counterargument would arise from findings that social gradients are reliably different across societies, and are stable across time. We recently reported investigations of this possibility (Keating et al., 2013; Siddiqi et al., 2013). We focused on indicators of adolescent health and development, where national indicators were available such that social gradients could be estimated across the time period of the "neoliberal era," which brought substantial societal changes in the direction of more market control, but did so differentially in different societies. We hypothesized that countries we deemed as highly resilient (maintaining more equitable income distribution, maintaining human development investments, greater social coordination of market forces) would fare better in terms of adolescents' population developmental health (PDH) over this period (roughly 1980 to 2010), compared with countries that did not follow those policies. We found that highly resilient countries had significantly more positive changes on a PDH index based on changes in both mean performance *and* steepness of the social gradient for educational achievement, self-reported health, and social participation (in school or working in the 15- to 19-year-old range), such that better outcomes and shallower social gradients were more characteristic of high resilient societies.

In sum, social policies and practices are associated with country differences in adolescent PDH, including parallel changes in both, suggesting a strong societal role in health and development. This regularity provides a clear opportunity to unpack these patterns in terms of the underlying developmental and biodevelopmental mechanisms (Keating, 2011c; Keating et al., 2013).

What Next? Paradoxical Opportunities

What lies ahead for the study of adolescent development will be shaped, in my view, by the opportunities and challenges offered by confronting a series of related paradoxes: complexity and coherence; nature and nurture; individuals and populations; drilling down and ramping up. It seems less and less likely that some magic bullet containing the resolution to these paradoxes will be found. Instead, working across and seeking integration of multiple research traditions and disciplines will allow a more comprehensive and dynamic picture to emerge. This broader approach will require a shift in thinking, in research paradigms, and in the training of the next generation of researchers. In the end, however, the answers generated are far more likely to be useful for policy and practice, because they will not depend on a particular disciplinary or epistemological stance, and will have had to confront the realities of development that emerge in biology, in individual behavior, in populations, and in society.

References

Albert, D., & Steinberg, L. (2011). Judgment and decision making in adolescence. *Journal of Research on Adolescence, 21*(1), 211–224.

Berrigan, D. (2004). *The trial of the Catonsville Nine.* New York: Fordham University Press.

Boyce, W. T., & Keating, D. P. (2004). Should we intervene to improve childhood circumstances? In S. Ben-Shlomo & D. Kuh (Eds.), *A life course approach to chronic disease epidemiology.* Oxford: Oxford Univeristy Press.

Campbell, D., Stanley, J. C., & Gage, N. (1963). *Experimental and quasi-experimental designs for research.* Boston: Houghton, Mifflin and Company.

Case, R. (1991). *The mind's staircase: Exploring the conceptual underpinnings of children's thought and knowledge.* Hillsdale, NJ: Lawrence Erlbaum Associates.

Casey, B. J., Jones, R. M., & Somerville, L. H. (2011). Braking and accelerating of the adolescent brain. *Journal of Research on Adolescence, 21*(1), 21–33.

Chi, M. T. H., Glaser, R., & Farr, M. (Eds.). (1988). *The nature of expertise.* Hillsdale, NJ: Erlbaum.

Chi, M. T. H., Hutchinson, J. E., & Robin, A. F. (1989). How inferences about novel domain-related concepts can be constrained by structured knowledge. *Merrill-Palmer Quarterly, 35*, 27–62.

Demetriou, A., Christou, C., Spanoudis, G., & Platsidou, M. (2002). The development of mental processing: Efficiency, working memory, and thinking. *Monographs of the Society for Research in Child Development, 67* (1, Serial No. 268).

Dreyfus, H. L., & Rabionow, P. (1982). *Michel Foucault: Beyond structuralism and hermeneutics.* Chicago: University of Chicago Press.

Eysenck, H. J. (1986). Inspection time and intelligence. *Personality and Individual Differences, 7*(5), 603–607.

Ford, M. E., & Keating, D. P. (1981). Developmental and individual differences in long-term memory retrieval: Process and organization. *Child Development, 52*, 234–241.

Gibson, J. J. (1966). *The senses considered as perceptual systems.* Boston: Houghton-Mifflin.

Inhelder, B., & Piaget, J. (1958). *The growth of logical thinking: From childhood to adolescence.* New York: Basic Books.

Kail, R. (1992). Evidence for global developmental change is intact. *Journal of Experimental Child Psychology, 54*(3), 308–314.

Keating, D. P. (1975a). Possible sampling bias in genetic studies of genius. *Educational and Psychological Measurement, 35*, 657–662.

Keating, D. P. (1975b). Precocious cognitive development at the level of formal operations. *Child Development, 46*, 476–480.

Keating, D. P. (1975c). Testing those in the top percentiles. *Exceptional Children, 41*, 435–436.

Keating, D. P. (1975d). The study of mathematically precocious youth. *Journal of Special Education, 9*, 45–62.

Keating, D. P. (Ed.). (1976). *Intellectual talent: Research and development.* Baltimore, MD: The Johns Hopkins University Press.

Keating, D. P. (1980). Thinking processes in adolescence. In J. Adelson (Ed.), *Handbook of adolescent psychology* (pp. 211–246). New York: Wiley.

Keating, D. P. (1984). The Emperor's new clothes: The "new look" in intelligence research. In R. Sternberg (Ed.), *Advances in the psychology of human intelligence* (Vol. 1, pp. 1–35). Hillsdale, NJ: Erlbaum.

Keating, D. P. (1990a). Adolescent thinking. In S. Feldman & G. Elliott (Eds.), *At the threshold: The developing adolescent* (pp. 54–89). Cambridge, MA: Harvard University Press.

Keating, D. P. (1990b). Adolescent cognition. In R. M. Lerner, A. C. Petersen, & J. Brooks-Gunn (Eds.), *The encyclopedia of adolescence.* New York: Garland Publishing.

Keating, D. P. (1990c). Structuralism, deconstruction, reconstruction: The limits of reasoning. In W. F. Overton (Ed.), *Reasoning, necessity, and logic: Developmental perspectives* (pp. 299–319). Hillsdale, NJ: Erlbaum.

Keating, D. P. (1991). Curriculum options for the developmentally advanced: A developmental alternative for gifted education. *Exceptionality Education Canada, 1*, 53–83.

Keating, D. P. (1996). Central conceptual structures: Seeking developmental integration. *Monographs of the Society for Research in Child Development, 61*(1–2, Serial No. 246).

Keating, D. P. (2004). Cognitive and brain development. In R. Lerner & L. Steinberg (Eds.), *Handbook of adolescent psychology.* New York: Wiley & Sons.

Keating, D. P. (2007). Understanding adolescent development: Implications for driving safety. *Journal of Safety Research, 38* (2), 147–157.

Keating, D. P. (2008). Developmental science and giftedness: An integrated lifespan framework. In F. Horowitz, D. Matthews, & R. Subotnik (Eds.), *The development of giftedness and talent across the life span.* Washington, DC: American Psychological Association.

Keating, D. P. (2011a). Cognitive development. In B. B. Brown & M. Pearlstein (Eds.), *Encyclopedia of Adolescence.* Netherlands: Elsevier.

Keating, D. P. (Ed.). (2011b). *Nature and nurture in early child development.* New York: Cambridge University Press.

Keating, D. P. (2011c). Society and early child development: Developmental health disparities in the nature-and-nurture paradigm. In D. P. Keating (Ed.), *Nature and nurture in early child development.* New York: Cambridge University Press.

Keating, D. P. (2012). Cognitive and brain development in adolescence. *Enfance, 3*, 267–279.

Keating, D. P., & Bobbitt, B. (1978). Individual and developmental differences in cognitive-processing components of mental ability. *Child Development, 49*, 155–167.

Keating, D. P., & Caramazza, A. (1975). Effects of age and ability on syllogistic reasoning in early adolescence. *Developmental Psychology, 11*(6), 837–842.

Keating, D. P., & Crane, L. L. (1990). Domain-general and domain-specific processes in proportional reasoning. *Merrill-Palmer Quarterly, 36*, 411–424.

Keating, D. P., & Halpern-Felsher, B. L. (2008). Adolescent drivers: A developmental perspective on risk, proficiency, and safety. *American Journal of Preventive Medicine, 35*(S), 272–277.

Keating, D. P., & Hertzman, C. (Eds.). (1999). *Developmental health and the wealth of nations: Social, biological, and educational dynamics.* New York: Guilford Press.

Keating, D. P., Keniston, A. H., Manis, F. R., & Bobbitt, B. L. (1980). Development of the search processing parameter. *Child Development, 51*, 39–44.

Keating, D. P., List, J. A., & Merriman, W. E. (1985). Cognitive processing and cognitive ability: A multivariate validity investigation. *Intelligence, 9*, 149–170.

Keating, D. P., & Miller, F. K. (2000). The dynamics of emotional development: Models, metaphors, and methods. In M. D. Lewis & I. Granic (Eds.), *Emotion, development, and self-organization: Dynamic systems approaches to emotional development* (pp. 373–392). New York: Cambridge University Press.

Keating, D. P., & Schaefer, R. A. (1975). Ability and sex differences in the acquisition of formal operations. *Developmental Psychology, 11*(4), 531–532.

Keating, D. P., Siddiqi, A., & Nguyen, Q. (2013). Social resilience in the neoliberal era: National differences in population health and development. In P. Hall & M. Lamont (Eds.), *Social resilience in the neoliberal era.* New York: Cambridge University Press.

Keating, D. P., & Stanley, J. C. (1972). Extreme measures for the exceptionally gifted in mathematics and science. *Educational Researcher, 1*, 3–5.

List, J. A., Keating, D. P., & Merriman, W. E. (1985). Differences in memory retrieval: A construct validity investigation. *Child Development, 56*, 138–151.

Lubinski, D., & Benbow, C. (2006). Study of mathematically precocious youth after 35 years: Uncovering antecedents for the development of math-science expertise. *Perspectives on Psychological Science, 1*(4), 316–345.

Luna, B., Garver, K. E., Urban, T. A., Lazar, N. A., & Sweeney, J. A. (2004). Maturation of cognitive processes from late childhood to adulthood. *Child Development, 75*, 1357–1372.

Manis, F. R., Keating, D. P., & Morrison, F. J. (1980). Developmental differences in the allocation of processing capacity. *Journal of Experimental Child Psychology, 29*, 156–169.

Maslowsky, J., Buvinger, E., Keating, D. P., Cauffman, E., & Steinberg, L. D. (2011). Cost-benefit judgment mediates the relationship between sensation seeking and risk behavior among adolescents. *Personality and Individual Differences, 51*(7), 802–806.

Maslowsky, J., Keating, D. P., Monk, C. S., & Schulenberg, J. S. (2011). Planned versus unplanned risks: Neurocognitive predictors of subtypes of adolescents' risk behavior. *International Journal of Behavioral Development, 35*(2), 152–160.

Matthews, D. J., & Keating, D. P. (1995). Domain specificity and habits of mind: An investigation of patterns of high-level development. *Journal of Early Adolescence, 15*, 319–343.

Merriman, W. E., Keating, D. P., & List, J. A. (1985). Mental rotation of facial profiles: Age-, sex-, and ability-related differences. *Developmental Psychology, 21*, 888–900.

Miller, F. K., Jenkins, J., & Keating, D. P. (2002). Socioeconomic status, parenting practices, and childhood disturbance. In J. D. Willms (Ed.), *Vulnerable children: Findings from the National Longitudinal Study of Children and Youth.* Edmonton: University of Alberta Press.

Miller, K., Perlmutter, M., & Keating, D. P. (1984). Cognitive arithmetic: Comparison of operations. *Journal of Experimental Psychology: Learning, Memory, and Cognition, 10*, 46–60.

Morrison, G., Morrison, S. R., & Keating, D. P. (1992). On estimating processing variance: Commentary and reanalysis of Kail's "Developmental functions for speeds of cognitive processes." *Journal of Experimental Child Psychology, 54*(3), 288–307.

Neisser, U. (1967). *Cognitive psychology.* East Norwalk, CT: Appleton-Century-Crofts.

Piaget, J. (1950). *Introduction à l'épistémologie génétique.* Vol. 1: *La pensée mathématique.* Vol 2: *La pensée physique.* Paris: Presses Universitaires de France.

Piaget, J. (1981). Creativity. In J. McC. Gallagher & D. K. Reid (Eds.), *The learning theory of Piaget and Inhelder* (pp. 221–230). New York: Brooks-Cole.

Ruck, M. D., Abramovitch, R., & Keating, D. P. (1998). Children's and adolescents' understanding of rights: Balancing nurturance and self-determination. *Child Development, 64*(2), 404–417.

Ruck, M. D., Keating, D. P., Abramovitch, R., & Koegl, C. (1998). Adolescents' and children's knowledge about rights: Some evidence for how young people view rights in their own lives. *Journal of Adolescence, 21*, 275–289.

Shapka, J. D., & Keating, D. P. (2003). Performance, persistence, and engagement in mathematics and science: Effects of a girls-only curriculum during adolescence. *American Educational Research Journal, 40*, 929–960.

Siddiqi A., Hertzman C., Keating D. P., & Kawachi, I. (2013). Population health in a neoliberal era: Assessing social resilience through comparison of Canada and the United States. *International Journal of Health Services, 43*(2), 193–216.

Stanley, J. C. (1957). Psychometric methods. *Journal of Educational Psychology, 48*(8), 552–553.

Stanley, J. C. (1968a). An important similarity between biserial r and the Brogden-Cureton-Glass biserial r for ranks. *Educational and Psychological Measurement, 28*(2), 249–253.

Stanley, J. C. (1968b). Maximum possible Kuder-Richardson Formula 20 coefficients for test scores from constant, rectangular, and rectangular-normal distributions of difficulties of dichotomously scored zero-chance-success items. *Proceedings of the Annual Convention of the American Psychological Association, 3*, 185–186.

Stanley, J. C., Keating, D. P., & Fox, L. H. (Eds.). (1974). *Mathematical talent: Discovery, description, and development.* Baltimore, MD: The Johns Hopkins University Press.

Szyf, M., & Bick, J. (2012). DNA Methylation: A Mechanism for embedding early life experiences in the genome. *Child Development.* (Epub ahead of print).

Trabasso, T. (1975). Representation, memory, and reasoning: How do we make transitive inferences? In A. Pick (Ed.), *Minnesota Symposium on Child Psychology* (Vol. 9, pp. 135–172). Minneapolis: University of Minnesota Press.

Watt, H. G., Shapka, J. D., Morris, Z. A., Durik, A. M., Keating, D. P., & Eccles, J. S. (2012). Gendered motivational processes affecting high school mathematics participation, educational aspirations, and career plans: A comparison of samples from Australia, Canada, and the United States. *Developmental Psychology.* (Epub ahead of print.)

25

Studying Experience

Pursuing the "Something More"

REED W. LARSON

I grew up in Falcon Heights, Minnesota, a suburb then on the outer edge of the Twin Cities. There was a wood and open space behind our house, with plenty of room to roam. My friends and I climbed trees, dug tunnels, enacted battles, swung on rope swings, and played ball. We built go-carts, snow forts, and rafts to float in the marsh at the end of the street. My favorite time of year was early spring when the snow melt created large pools of cold clear water. We dug streams in the snow to drain the water and damns in the street to create lakes. Then we would breach the damns and enjoy watching the torrent of water racing toward the marsh.

Some of these activities were inspired by my dad, Curt Larson, who was a farm kid and child of the Depression. He could build or fix anything with carpentry, wire, or the lashing techniques he'd learned in the navy. If the first solution didn't work, he'd try another. His larger projects began with a drawing on graph paper. This ingenuity led him to a career in engineering, as a professor of hydrology and civil engineering at the University of Minnesota. Dad provided patient encouragement and support for my junior-high-school science projects, which won modest district awards. Dad's career focus on the dynamics of water later fed my interest in the psychological concept of "Flow," developed by my graduate school mentor, Mihaly Csikszentmihalyi.

My mother, Miriam Johnson Larson, was artistic and literary. While Dad was trying to fit data to equations, Mom was interested in capturing the nuances of human experience with prose and paint. In high school she had won a national prize for a short story. She was patient in reading drafts and providing feedback on my high-school papers. Although my language skills were weaker than my math skills, she helped me develop the craft of writing.

In my grad school applications, I wrote that I was driven to the social sciences by my desire to reconcile my dad's empirical scientific approach with my mother's artistic interests. At the time it seemed like a clever way to start an essay, but in fact, it became a major theme of my professional career.

Childhood

I started kindergarten in a one-room schoolhouse. It was friendly, but I resented the intrusion on my freedom. After 2 weeks, I decided to quit. The next day when the bus was coming, I wrapped my arms around a tree in the backyard and refused to be pried away. It was a credit to my parents that they allowed me an extra year of independence.

The next year, my attitude toward school was not much different, but I slowly adapted. The benefit of the 1-year delay was that I was older than others in my class and, though I was an average student (receiving mostly "Ss," for Satisfactory, rather than "Os" for Outstanding), I emerged as a leader. I remember in 1st grade how I lined up 20 to 30 boys for instructions prior to our swooping towards an attacking group of 2nd-grade boys.

Being older also made me the most popular boy with the girls in my class—the kind of responsible boy their mother wanted them to like. That status ended in 6th grade when my family spent a year at Stanford so Dad could complete his Ph.D. The California 6th graders were much more sophisticated than I. The girls cared less about their mothers—and me. Some of the boys carried condoms in their wallets, and I didn't understand what they were for.

Navigating Adolescence

My childhood was in the 1950s, a time of comfortable conformity. My adolescence was in the 1960s, a time of tumult and social change. Mom became interested in the civil rights movement and (along with my future mother-in-law and others) helped create a civil rights commission for our small white suburb. The deed on our lot said that the property could not be sold to "Negroes," "Indians," and others. Commissions like this made small steps in eliminating legal barriers to residential segregation, and stimulated local conversations about race and racism. My older brother, whom I greatly admire, also worked for civil rights. After completing a year at Yale and another at the University of Chicago, he dropped out to resist the draft, oppose the Vietnam War, and work for societal change. Concern with social justice was a family theme.

I was more introspective than my brother and, while I identified with the social justice causes of the time, my adolescent quest was played out on a narrower and more personal stage. In high school and at various times in my life I have taken leadership roles, but at other times I have chosen to step back. I'm not that shy but have generally preferred participation in smaller life worlds that allow me more autonomy. As a junior in high school I was elected Treasurer of Student Council, and did well. But, though next in line for President, I decided not to run. I also dropped out of a close group of friends, preferring to spend Friday and Saturday nights at home doing art work, writing, and trying to read serious books.

During this period I started reading existential psychology, not too much Sartre or Heidegger, but more accessible authors, like Albert Camus, Rollo May and R.D. Laing—also every novel by Dostoyevsky and Hermann Hesse. A key phrase of the existentialists was "existence precedes essence." To me this meant that human experience was more complex, unique, and meaningful than could ever be captured by generalities. Intellectuals can try—after the fact—to describe human life with universal concepts or scientific laws, but that effort inevitably gives short shrift to the enormous variations and layers of meaning that make up human experience.

The primacy these authors gave to individual experience served my identity explorations and those of many in my generation. I experimented with art, poetry, and dance. In late adolescence I hitch hiked to Mexico and traveled to Europe. I loved jazz. Unlike Bill Clinton, I not only used pot, I inhaled and was intoxicated by the flights of imagination and insight it provided.

I also had an identity crisis during this period—a spiral into the abyss. My reading (and isolation) led me to the conclusion that logic had no way of establishing meaning in life. As Camus wrote, life is absurd. Although I had not read Erik Erikson's book on identity, I experienced a textbook case of the symptoms he described, including periods of metaphysical terror. Once again, my parents were caring and patient. But I would accept no help from them. Fortunately, meaningful relationships during this period helped pull me out of this void.

College and a Clash of World Views

I entered the honors program in psychology at the University of Minnesota in the fall of 1969. In an era of youth revolt against our elders, psychology—not sociology or economics—was the most popular major. My goal was studying what I labeled "philosophical social psychology." I wanted to address deep questions about humans' experience as social and psychological creatures.

I was appalled, then, to learn that psychology at Minnesota explicitly rejected the study of experience. Behavior was all that mattered. Skinner had been at Minnesota only a few years earlier, and my introductory classes focused on the basic "laws of learning" developed from research on pigeons and rats. Human behavior was "nothing but" a product of these reductionist laws. Essence was all that mattered; existence was not important. Although a few of my professors acknowledged the possibility of "something more," there was little or no discussion of relationships, emotions, and certainly not subjective experience.

Dustbowl empiricism ruled. One moralizing psychology professor taught us that all beliefs not established by research were "overbeliefs." They were to be treated as false until proven otherwise. In retrospect, my Minnesota training sensitized me to the importance of evidence—and "standards of evidence." But this obsession with trying to define a bright line between truth and falsehood struck me as harsh—and naïve—like locking oneself up in a small closed box. Fortunately course work in anthropology, philosophy, history, literature, and a thrilling class on Piaget kept me excited.

I was determined to pursue a deeper and more humanist course of study. Graduate programs in Human Development appeared to be more open-minded than psychology programs, and I was offered a fellowship at the University of Chicago's Committee on Human Development. Chicago was a place where theoretical inquiry—the life of the mind—was noble and respected. I was especially interested in adolescence, which I saw as an exciting period for philosophical social psychology—as a time of conscious awakening.

Graduate School: Finding a Niche

In the fall of 1974 I packed all my possessions in my Dodge and headed for grad school. As the Chicago skyline came into view I remember shouting that I would *not* let work consume me. I would not compromise my personal life to a career! I lost that battle. But it was because the University of Chicago offered me opportunities that I found enthralling. Human Development was an interdisciplinary program which recognized that human lives entail many levels. The faculty favored mixed methods research, and didn't let rigid methodological strictures inhibit them from asking important questions.

I was happy as a fish in water. In Salvatore Maddi's personality class, I was able to present the arguments of behaviorists, while critiquing their folly. In another class, Richard Shweder attacked the essentialistic notion of personality traits, arguing they were cultural constructs that were mainly in the eyes of the beholder (research has since proven that the Big Five personality traits *do* have explanatory value; McAdams & Olson, 2010). I was not sure I would ever have much standing as a scholar, but that was not a major concern. In a survey for our student newsletter, I reported, half seriously, that my goal was to become a professor at "an isolated small rural college or university."

Though interested in adolescence, my fellowship was in Adult Development and Aging, and I had the chance to work with Robert Havighurst and Bernice Neugarten, early leaders in this new field. My first (and I think most-frequently cited paper) was a review article on the predictors of life satisfaction in the elderly—an essentialistic enterprise if there ever was one (Larson, 1978). My conclusion from 30 years of research merely confirmed ancient wisdom that "health, wealth, and love" are the biggest predictors of happiness. But I had my dad's scientific mind and enjoyed ordering statistical findings. Furthermore "satisfaction" or what I called "subjective well-being," though reductionistic, was about experience. In the conclusion of the article, I had the extreme joy of writing, "these statistics do not describe a determinate course for individuals. They refer to aggregates. At best they suggest broad contours for the *complex historic path of a person's life*" (Larson, 1978, p. 177, emphasis added).

The best part of graduate school was my mentor, Mihaly Csikszentmihalyi. "Mike C." was (and is) humble, open-minded, wise, accepting, and friendly—the perfect non-authority figure for a child of the 1960s. He was just publishing a book with a powerful theory of the subjective experience of motivation (Csikszentmihalyi, 1975). His research with rock climbers, artists, and surgeons showed that they often experienced an optimal state of deep concentration, intrinsic motivation, and enjoyment, which he called *flow,* from engaging with the difficult challenges of their work. The research also suggested that people can, at least partly, create the conditions for getting into this optimal state. What better way to start one's career: with a theory of how to make challenging work deeply enjoyable!

This state of flow is important, including to adolescents, not only because it is enjoyable and self-motivating. Research shows that it alters consciousness in ways that facilitate effective, creative, self-controlled thought, and that people in flow engage in work they are doing at deeper meta levels (Larson & Rusk, 2011). What was really stimulating for me was that this was an empirically derived theory that was not reductionist. The properties of the state of flow could be studied with scientific methods, yet the concept did not take human agency out of the picture. To the contrary, the state of flow is a *catalyst* for self-determined, emergent, and original thinking—including potentially for teens' developmental thinking and learning.

Another marvelous gift from Mike was that he saw our mission as a creative enterprise. *Work is play.* Mike was not wedded to an overly serious, moralistic view of methodology. There are many possible truths, which can be examined from many perspectives. We need to try multiple methods and approaches. What's important is not just the "*p* < .05" but how important the question is, the elegance of the ideas, and how well the findings fit to lived experience. Mike was ready with quotes from Einstein and other great thinkers on how they viewed their work from a similar playful perspective.

As a result, I came to see my role as principally that of an explorer looking for theoretically promising findings and ideas. I have great respect for the hard labor of scientists devoted to building an edifice of firm truths. I have taken that role in review articles. But I am more comfortable out on the edge. In Vygotsky's terms, I see my role as stretching the field's zone of proximal development: pushing the envelope, helping generate provocative ideas and empirically based theory for others to build on, if they find them useful. Rather than dismiss exploratory findings as "overbeliefs," I see them playing a critical role in generating theory that can scaffold further understanding. I also see exploratory methods as a vehicle for us to think systematically about the huge domain of important issues that we may never be able to test with the dominant ham-fisted research methods of our field.

Development of the Experience Sampling Method

During this period Mike and our research team were developing an exciting new mixed-methods research technique. The Experience Sampling Method (ESM) is a procedure for systematically exploring exactly what interested me: lived experience. The method involves asking people to carry a signaling device, and report on and rate what they are doing, thinking, and feeling when it signals them at randomly selected moments across waking hours. We obtained samples of experience on 30–50 representative moments over a week, first from dozens, then hundreds, of youth (Csikszentmihalyi & Larson, 1987).

The ESM provided many rich snapshots of life: a boy getting pumped up on rock music before school, a girl distraughtly watching a fist fight between friends; many occasions of eating dinner with family, sitting in class, hanging out with friends. In reading through a youth's reports over a week, one could see the variety of experiences that made up her or his life—the nuances and complexities. I had no illusions that we were getting people's *full* experience at each moment. True existentialists might not have approved.

But this method was a dream come true for scientific exploration of daily life. The thousands of reports we obtained provided a database that could be mined to study dozens of topics: to look for patterns in how youth spent time, the people they spent it with, and how numeric ratings of their emotions and other subjective states differed from one context to another (and from one person to another). In contrast to the survey research on life satisfaction, the ESM allowed fine-grained statistical analysis of daily experience.

Solitude One of the first findings that jumped out at me—as a person with an active interior life—was the large portion of time teens spent alone. The European American youth in our first studies reported being alone an average of 25% of their random self-reports. This percentage was surprising, given that adolescents are viewed as such social creatures. For my master's thesis and then dissertation, I wanted to know what goes on during this alone time: What do teens do and feel? How do these solitary experiences relate to their mental health? Are their experiences of time alone as powerful as mine were?

No one had studied this large solitary part of adolescents' lives. In my one conversation with Urie Bronfenbrenner I suggested that time alone should be recognized as a significant "microsystem" in teens' lives—a suggestion he did not endorse. But my dissertation findings, reported in the *New York Times*, confirmed what I had found in my master's thesis: that this segment of adolescents' lives appeared to play an important role in some teens' well-being. In measured doses, solitude provided a lonely but restorative retreat that—like a bitter medicine—had a net positive relationship to their average emotional state (Larson, & Csikszentmihalyi, 1978, 1980). My later ESM studies replicated this preliminary picture with another sample of European American adolescents (1990, 1997), but not with samples of African American teens and middle-class youth in India. To be clear, these findings were correlational, and they didn't get at the deeper issues of identity and meaning that were part of my teenage solitude. Nonetheless they suggested that for some Euro-American adolescents, time alone might serve as an opportunity—another kind of "catalyst"—for constructive developmental experience.

Adolescent Emotionality In the Dostoyevsky novels I loved, youth were possessed by strong emotions. Another finding that jumped out from the ESM data was how much teens' emotions swung between emotional extremes, often within hours or minutes. There was a hot debate in the 1960s and 1970s about whether adolescence was a period of turmoil. Sigmund and Anna Freud, Erikson, and others argued that emotional tumult was not only inevitable, it was *necessary* for youth to become healthy adults. But research by Daniel Offer and Michael Rutter had recently contradicted this theory. They found that this tumult is experienced by only a minority of adolescents and this minority *was more not less likely* to have continuing problems in adulthood.

I had the opportunity to contribute to this debate. We had the first systematic data from teens on what emotions they experienced *in the moment* during their daily lives. My analyses found that teens' emotional states had significantly wider variance than adults' (Larson, Csikszentmihalyi, & Graef, 1980). This was confirmed in two additional ESM studies with teens and their parents, including one we conducted years later in India (Larson & Richards, 1994; Verma & Larson, 1999). But, while these data indicated that teens can be emotionally labile, their emotional swings didn't look like the "emotional turmoil" described by others. For most youth, these extremes did not appear to be driven by the inner torment of Dostoevsky's characters or Anna Freud's patients. They were reactions to the ordinary events of teenage life. For the 1980 article I created the first of many graphs charting the ups and downs in a youth's emotional states over a week. This one showed how a young man's swings were due to being elated from skipping school on a beautiful spring day, then wincing in pain after banging his knee dunking a basketball; enjoying a party on Saturday night, and being distressed by a teacher's negative attitude. Surely there may be developmental factors amplifying these swings, but most of youth's emotions did not appear to be directly attributable to inner turmoil—rather to the novel and rich experiences of adolescent life.

An important discovery for me was that adolescents experienced more extreme emotions, not only at the negative end of the scale, *but also at the positive end*. This was true in all three studies comparing teens and adults. Further, having frequent positive emotions was *not* related to problems (Larson & Ham, 1993). As I'll discuss later, I think some of these frequent positive emotions reflect important, active conscious developmental processes. Research shows that positive emotions can be an opportunity to "broaden and build" (Frederickson, 2001).

My *own* strong positive emotions during this work were attributable to having my cake and eating it too: to capturing the nuanced variety of adolescents' experiences, as well as having the "hard data" to identify meaningful patterns—and to get the results published.

Being Adolescent The culmination of my graduate and post-doctoral period was the publication of a book, *Being Adolescent*, with Mike (Csikszentmihalyi & Larson, 1984). We used ESM data to provide a descriptive picture of the "daily ecology of adolescent experience." If that sounds ambitious, that is what we intended. Bronfenbrenner had introduced the metaphor of "ecology" for thinking about the contexts of young people's lives. What could be more important than describing the ecology of adolescents' daily activities, relationships, and emotions? We didn't cover all of Bronfenbrenner systems; and the data came from only 75, mostly white, youth in a middle-working class suburb. Nonetheless, description (though often neglected) is valuable. The book was frequently cited in textbooks and used in college classes.

Mike provided the theory and creative big-picture perspective for the book. The data came from an ESM study that Patrick Mayers and I had conducted for our dissertations. My contribution was doing the statistical analyses and drafting many of the empirical chapters. Along the way, I developed new ways of graphing ESM data to show underlying regularities in experiences. I also delighted in using youth's descriptions of specific moments to show the richness and variety behind these regularities. When the editor told us a book on adolescent experience *had to* include sex, I was able to find examples, including one where two youth reported having sex with each other—but reported quite different feelings (p. 161).

The biggest story in the book was the pronounced disjuncture between the two largest parts of adolescents' lives. During free time, especially with friends, our teens reported being more motivated and happy, but were less likely to feel challenged or report deep attention. In contrast, during class and schoolwork, the pattern was opposite: They were more likely to be concentrating and feel challenged—but they were not motivated by the challenges; boredom was frequent. Our discovery of this disjuncture, of course, was not that surprising. It resonated with my generation's critique of schools and our parents' suspicion of our friends. But showing it with systematic *in vivo* data, I think, made it more real.

For Mike it was a travesty that so many teens reported boredom in schoolwork. He (along with other scholars) had concluded that humans have a built-in system of intrinsic motivation designed to facilitate challenging work and learning—flow. What a waste to have an education system that does not take advantage of this.

For me a striking additional finding (repeated in subsequent ESM studies; Shernoff, 2013) was that the one context in which teens reported experiencing high levels of motivation, attention, and challenge—all at once—was organized youth programs: sports, arts, and clubs. This finding was to inspire a major shift in my research 20 years later.

Generativity: Charting Adolescents' Daily Experience

But at this point, my focus was taking advantage of the tremendous opportunities provided by the ESM, as well as establishing a career.

Career Steps Let me back up a little. I finished grad school in 1979 then took a 2-year post doc in a program at Chicago's Michael Reese Medical Center run by Daniel Offer, Anne Petersen, and Bert Cohler. Dan was an important influence, having demonstrated that the typical adolescent is much more healthy and well-adjusted than most clinicians and adults thought. As my post doc finished, I was invited to take Anne Petersen's position as the Coordinator of the post doc program and, then, as Director of the Laboratory for the Study of Adolescence at Michael Reese.

Although the faculty at Chicago had been good at supporting development of creative ideas, they were less concerned with supporting career development. (At my graduation, a faculty member told my dad, a professor of engineering, that they were not a *mere* professional training program.) My first 10 articles were published without one rejection. But no one had been pushing me to submit this new exciting research to prestigious journals.

In my new position, counseling post docs, I started to figure out how important this kind of thing was. Offer encouraged me to apply for grants. After two rejections, on the third try I obtained NIMH funding to conduct a large ESM study of young adolescents. We drew on Anne Petersen's model of a large bio-psycho-social study and she graciously let us use many of her survey measures as a complement to the ESM data. Maryse Richards, one of Anne's students, became a vital partner in this study (and subsequent NIMH-funded ESM studies). We had an excellent team for The Young Adolescent Study (YAS), and were able to collect ESM data from a normative sample of 483 randomly selected 5th–9th graders (a total of over 16,000 self-reports!). YAS began in 1985, the same year I moved to the University of Illinois in Urbana (that "isolated" rural University I'd envisioned). I commuted weekly to conduct the study from Michael Reese.

When the data became available, we had 15 years of flow writing articles that delved into this fund of 16,000 moments in young adolescents' lives. Because we covered so many topics, it is difficult to concisely convey what was exciting about each, but let me give an overview.

Mental Health and Daily Experience NIMH's primary concern is mental health, and Maryse, I, and our students had a mandate to understand the "emotional ecology" of adolescents' mental health problems. How are stress, depression, and other problems manifest in—or generated by—teens' hour-to-hour experiences? A first discovery from YAS was that adolescence itself appeared to be associated with a downward shift in teens' range of states: 8th and 9th graders reported *more* frequent negative and *fewer* extreme positive states than 5th and 6th graders (Larson & Lampman-Petraitis, 1989). These age differences were evident across contexts of daily life (Larson & Richards, 1989). An important related discovery was that this shift was more strongly related to an individual's experience of stress than to puberty (Larson & Ham, 1991; Richards & Larson, 1993). I still think that adults' tendency to attribute teens' moods to "raging hormones" tells us more about adults than it does about adolescents (although much of the action may well be in *interactions* of biology and experience).

But this downward shift did not mean that most teens are glum. The average daily emotional state of the teens in our study was positive. It was just somewhat less positive than earlier. Nonetheless this shift—and its underlying causes—mattered to mental health. Youth with more frequent negative states were more likely to manifest symptoms of depression, have weight and eating disorders, and other problems (Larson, Raffaelli, Richards, Ham, & Jewell, 1990; Richards, Casper, & Larson, 1990).

But what caused what? What made some youth experience more negative emotions than others? We were too busy exploring all the other opportunities provided by the data to start new research on this. But much later, a brilliantly designed ESM study conducted by Jennifer Silk and colleagues suggested what one of the causal mechanisms might be (Silk, Steinberg, & Morris 2003). Their research provided evidence that depressed adolescents responded to negative emotion with disengagement, avoidance, rumination, and impulsive behavior—responses that appeared to perpetuate negative emotional states. This was an excellent illustration of how the dynamics of immediate experiences (in combination with other bio-psycho-social factors) might contribute to larger mental health and developmental patterns.

Developing a Strategy to Get Findings into Print Most successful scholars develop a signature gig they use to keep the publications coming. In developmental psychology, people often identify a new concept and create a measure to go with it. They build a career by applying these across different issues and populations. My gig was being "the beeper man." I developed a strategy—including statistical techniques, language, and a recipe of sorts—for formulating a scientific story from the ESM data. I then combined the farm kid scientific ingenuity of my dad, with skills from my apprenticeships in writing that stretched from Mom to Mike C.

What was my strategy? Many other people using the ESM were not having the same success. Daily experience is complex and nuanced—that's why I liked it; but as a result, ESM data are incredibly messy to analyze. People had difficulty trying to meet the demanding assumptions of statistics yet also say something important. However, these assumptions should not be a straitjacket. You are not struck dead if you violate one. Statistics are a tool to be used (Abelson, 1995). I developed ways to do the best that was possible (with the methods at the time) to show the patterns in the data, be honest about what I was doing, and try to directly address any threats to the validity of findings (Larson & Delespaul, 1991). The results section of our articles typically started with the most solid analysis, usually descriptive patterns that were evident across all the youth in the study. The middle steps were then the key findings. My biggest pleasure was that (having done these prior steps) reviewers allowed us to put in one or two more creative and provocative analyses at the end. One example was a graph constructed to show the sequence of emotional catharsis that bulimic young adults reported before, during, and after an episode of binging and purging (Johnson & Larson, 1982).

With this strategy, I became a wayfarer who moved from writing articles in one subfield of adolescence to another (family, stress, TV watching, eating disorders), as well as trying to invent a few of my own (time alone, the weekend). For each article, I read as much as I could in the subfield to identify "problems" within it that our ESM data could address. My Chicago training gave me the audacity to believe I could enter almost any domain of study and find something valuable to contribute with

our experiential data. I never established membership in any particular topic area, but I got my articles accepted in major journals and was invited to write chapters in many different domains. People seemed interested in the findings! Lived experience was something they found meaningful.

Contexts as Experiential Systems A fundamental insight originating from my work on time alone was that the different contexts of adolescents' lives were each associated with a distinct profile of experiential possibilities. Time alone was associated with loneliness but, in limited doses, was also related to greater well-being. This idea of context as a unit of study was not original: Roger Barker, John and Beatrice Whiting, and others were concerned with describing contexts as "activity systems," interactional systems, and "opportunity structures." What the ESM allowed us to add was data on the emotions and psychological states associated with different contexts. Happily, we found that many of the patterns of psychological states reported in a given context were replicated across studies, sometimes across cultures. For example, in every study watching TV is associated with lower motivation, concentration, and emotion.

A context of adolescent experience that I gave much attention to was the family. It was the topic of several articles and a second book, *Divergent Realities*, with Maryse Richards (Larson & Richards, 1994). Across ESM studies of American youth, their average emotional states with their families was not as happy as time with friends, but it was happier than time alone and in class. Being with family members was not nearly as fun as being with friends. This may be one of the reasons that the amount of time spent with family fell off greatly from ages 10 to 18 (Larson, Richards, Moneta, Holmbeck, & Duckett, 1996). Our book contains numerous illustrations of many, mostly petty, daily aggravations these teens experienced with family that seemed to compromise their experience. (One bright spot was that the average American teen felt more important and calm, also less nervous and embarrassed, when with family than in other contexts. Family appeared to provide a secure base.)

But culture makes a difference. My colleague, Suman Verma, collected ESM data on 100 8th graders in India; and we found that their daily experiences with their families were strikingly different. They spent much more time with their families than our American 8th graders, and their emotional states when with their parents were nearly as positive as when with their friends. The article we wrote on these findings describes how cultural differences in value systems are likely contributors to this contrast (Larson, Verma, & Dworkin, 2003).

Our different studies allowed us to tell a distinct story about the experiential patterns and dynamics associated with numerous other daily contexts. My findings on peer interactions suggested how the experiential properties of interactions with peers might make them susceptible to "runaway positive feedback dynamics" (Larson, 1983). We discovered that the later hours of Friday and Saturday nights were associated with a trend toward increasing excitement but decreasing experience of control. We also found that in the Unitred States (but not in India) romantic relationships were the most frequent explanations give for both extreme positive and negative emotions (Larson, Clore, & Wood, 1990).

The End of a Good Run The culmination of this period of my career was an article in *Psychological Bulletin* that reviewed research on "How children and adolescents spend time across the world" (Larson & Verma, 1999). The article reviewed ESM and diary research on time budgets. It was based on the concept that different activity contexts (e.g., chores, schoolwork, media used, active leisure) each represent a distinctive "developmental niche":

> Each engages participants in a milieu of rules, scripts, and goals (Gallimore, Goldenberg, & Weisner, 1993; Whiting, 1980), and each is associated with differing emotional and motivational experiences (Csikszentmihalyi & Larson, 1984). Each also engages participants' attention in a distinct life world of information, such as the world of housecleaning knowledge or the world of popular songs and musicians. … [C]hildren's participation in an activity context is associated with a distinct set of socialization experiences. (p. 702)

In the article, we marshaled evidence identifying what developmental opportunities and liabilities appeared to be associated with time spent in different activity contexts. This included those suggested by my many ESM studies. Then we reviewed how time spent in each activity context varied across nations. The idea was that the amount of time children spent in a given "developmental niche" is a measure of the dosage of its opportunities that they receive.

This theoretical project was exciting. But it could also be caricatured as a board game view of human development. If a teen spends more time in a given context, he or she is statistically more likely to accumulate *X* benefits and *Y* liabilities. But, of course, this model overlooks tremendous variability within a given context, cultural differences, and person-by-situation interactions. The article suggested some of the "broad contours" of children and teens' daily experiences, which is important. But so much was left out.

The truth is that I was getting restless with what I could learn with the ESM. I could have kept developing my career as the "beeper man." New hand-held computers provided better ways of signaling and recording people's experiences. The development of HLM provided stronger means for modeling the data. There were emerging vistas in bio-medical research and in each domain of research that I could have kept taking deeper. But the lens would

have been the same—examining patterns of experience (means, correlations) related to contexts and individual difference variables. I wanted something more. Although I don't regret my 25 years of ESM work, the nuanced complexity of experience was getting too much of a back seat. I was at a career stage where I wanted to go further out on the edge.

From Numbers to Narratives: Adolescence as an Age of Awakening

When my son, Renner, was about 16 months old, he walked into the room, pulled up his pant legs to his thighs, and with sheer bliss, declared his latest epiphany as though it would change the world: "KNEES!!!" Many of the adolescents and emerging adults I have studied and known (including Renner and my daughter Miriam) experienced similar blissful epiphanies on a regular basis—at a deeper level. These epiphanies are less often the pre-operational excitement that, "Jeez, something has a name!" They are more profound: discovering other minds, insights into how the world works, and into new levels of the self. This may partly explain why teens have frequent positive moods: They are awakening to new horizons. This is why I had chosen adolescence. I wanted to study this.

This awakening, I think, is attributable to adolescents gaining the potential for new operations that are more powerful and flexible than Piaget imagined (Kuhn, 2009). Research in cognitive science, social development, brain science, and other areas all converge in demonstrating that adolescence is an age period when new "meta" capacities start to emerge for deeper levels of thought and action—an "executive suite" of diverse and generative cognitive tools (Kuhn, 2009; Smetana, 2010; Steinberg et al., 2006). These include new powers of agency—skills for self-regulation, self-change, and working toward goals.

But this awakening doesn't happen at once. It is not like a computer upgrade. I side with those who think it occurs though a lot of small steps in the contexts of daily life (e.g., Fischer & Bidell, 2006). The epiphanies often relate to specific experiences: She/he loves me; I'm a good actress; when I hold back my anger I don't get into these messes; my mom has some cool things to say; if I apply myself I can make things happen. To be sure not all these epiphanies are cheery—these new cognitive potentials can make teens more sensitive to pain, worry, and hurt (Larson & Asmussen, 1991). This includes encountering the abyss of doubt that Erikson described (and I experienced); also the raw reality of entrenched social injustice. Nonetheless, for me, the "positive" in research on positive adolescent development is about this tremendous potential for learning and self-change (Larson, 2000).

To fully understand this awakening, I felt it essential that my research employ open-ended qualitative interviews with youth. I wanted to start with discovery methods to learn about youth's epiphanies. My dad playfully joked with me: "If you can't measure it, it doesn't exist." But adolescent positive development is much more than a variable; it entails learning about multi-leveled complexity. I wanted to learn about youth's conscious process of developing and creatively applying their new cognitive tools to real-life complexities. (Of course development involves much more than conscious process. But we can't leave it out, can we?)

For me, organized youth programs were an ideal setting to study adolescents' development of their new potentials. They are contexts in which teens take on challenging work (Heath, 1999); and, as my ESM research had found, they are contexts in which youth report high levels of motivation and attention. Teens in programs appear to experience a state of intrinsic motivation in which their skills are pitted against challenges. Adults in programs typically play a supportive rather than directive role. Fortunately, the William T. Grant Foundation had developed an interest in after-school programs, and was willing to take a risk on my research.

I won't try to describe all the glimpses we are getting of youth's awakening experiences. But I think we are opening new vistas for understanding youth programs—and hopefully for the broader field of adolescent development.

A basic conclusion I've come to is that the developmental challenges adolescents face are far greater than we appreciate. The problems they need to solve to become functioning adults are ill-structured, messy, and multi-layered. For example, although emotions at first seem to adolescents like they are windows to one's true self, in real-world scenarios they can also steer you in wrong directions. *Teens face a difficult task of sorting out the many complex layers of emotion* (Larson & Brown, 2007). A second example: Although young adolescents begin to spot contradictions and hypocrisy in adults, under the right conditions older teens start to grasp how adults are often dealing with competing pressures at multiple levels in their lives: Being between two rocks and three hard places is part of the human condition, and you need to learn to manage this. Our society's negative view of adolescents, I think, is due to a fundamental attribution error. We see their behavior and attribute it to some flaw in their personality. We fail to appreciate the complexities of the issues and situations they must learn to navigate (Larson, 2011).

Our new research is observing how youth in programs start to develop skills for dealing with these multi-level complexities. They are learning strategic skills for planning a project that include tools for navigating the competing demands and paradoxes of human life (Larson & Angus, 2011). They are learning skills and dispositions for responsibility that include learning to persevere when an obligation becomes much more difficult and gnarly than you ever expected (Wood, Larson, & Brown, 2009). They are learning tools to understand, manage, and use the abstract, surreal dynamics of emotions (Rusk et al., in press). Our research provides glimpses of adolescents' awakening as conscious beings trying to understand and navigate an enormously complex world.

Reflections

Any story of a life is inevitably simplified, and that is true here. In telling my story I have left out so much: my sabbatical in India, the study group I ran on "Adolescence in the 21st Century" (Larson, Brown, & Mortimer, 2002), my term as President of the Society for Research on Adolescence, and my current excitement in studying the expertise of youth practitioners (Larson, Walker, Rusk, & Diaz, invited). I also cut out many important complexities—choices, pressures, mistakes, anxieties—at each step of the story. If I had the skills of a novelist, I would have tried to stack together more of these simultaneous narratives.

In rereading this account, it is clear that I have had a privileged and blessed professional life. My dad was a professor (as was my father-in-law), so I grew up in the trade. I had a very supportive life partner, Sharon Irish, who was gracious in accepting my absorption in work. Our family did not have to deal with poverty, prejudice, or the kind of major traumas that disrupt careers. I have had wonderful students and colleagues, including Marcela Raffaelli who has been a key collaborator at two points in my career. My program in Human and Community Development at the University of Illinois and my department heads provided freedom to do the research I wanted, without pressure to conform to the narrower strictures of a given discipline and—later in my career—allowed me to avoid dealing with the Procrustean demands of NIH.

Further, my grad training, Mike C., and the ESM provided me the gift of strong tools to be creative, play, and work on the edge. This allowed me to take risks and to avoid the suffocation I would have felt being an expert on a single topic. I also benefited from my own self-sufficiency, which I credit to my parents' patience and humble Midwestern perspective. I made decisions– at many points –not to be driven to try and rise to the top: to my level of incompetence. I want recognition, but I don't. I wanted that job at Stanford, but I didn't. I promote my work, but I know that I may sometimes be wrong.

Did I use my privilege and these gifts in the best way I could? I have devoted effort to social justice issues— leading an SRA committee on diversity, research on low income adolescents, writing on street children and global structural inequality. But I have also been quite self-absorbed in the business of writing article after article.

Are there lessons in my story for others? Career choices are inevitably loaded with ambiguities and unknowns. I could have devoted myself to research in an established area, and who knows where that would have led. It is essential to our field that many people take that path, but I may not have been successful at it. In retrospect, my seemingly risky decision to pursue ESM research was a sound one, partly because I had a background that provided me with tools to create order out of messy data.

It was scary when I shifted from my established gig doing ESM research to doing qualitative grounded theory research on adolescents' conscious experiences. Would I ever get published in *Child Development* again? My "stock value" within the field peaked in 2000. The shift to using methods that have less prestige in the field has meant less recognition and fewer citations. To our field's credit, however, journals (including *Child Development*) have been more receptive to our qualitative work than I expected. (Warning to younger scholars: I have been able to succeed in this shift because I built on a career's worth of accumulated knowledge and skills.)

But I love being able to study youth's direct accounts of their experiences—to be able to understand their genius in learning to solve the complex developmental challenges they face. I also love doing research that is directly relevant to youth practitioners. Further, I feel a strong mission to expand the perspective of our field. It is critical that we study adolescent problems, but it seems at times that this research is so dominant that it feeds negative public stereotypes that taint and harm all youth. Further, our almost exclusive focus on statistical modeling has the invidious effect of suggesting that adolescents are not conscious and creative, but rather passive beings, influenced by variables in predictable mechanical ways. Something is wrong with this picture! The last 30 years of research has revealed incredible new information about how ingenious infants can be. It is time we do the same for adolescents.

References

Abelson, R. P. (1995). *Statistics as principled argument.* Hillsdale, NJ: Erlbaum.

Csikszentmihalyi, M. (1975). *Beyond boredom and anxiety.* San Francisco: Jossey-Bass.

Csikszentmihalyi, M., & Larson, R. (1984). *Being adolescent: Conflict and growth in the teenage years.* New York: Basic Books.

Csikszentmihalyi, M., & Larson, R. (1987). The experience sampling method. *Journal of Nervous and Mental Disease, 175,* 526–536.

Fischer, K.W., & Bidell, T. R. (2006). Dynamic development of action and thought. In W. Damon & R. M. Lerner (Eds.), *Handbook of child psychology* (6th ed.), Vol. 1 (pp. 313–399). Hoboken, NJ: Wiley.

Fredrickson, B. L. (2001). The role of positive emotions in positive psychology: The broaden-and-build theory of positive emotions. *The American Psychologist, 56,* 218–226.

Gallimore, R., Goldenberg, C., & Weisner, T. (1993). The social construction and subjective reality of activity settings: Implications for community psychology. *American Journal of Community Psychology, 21*(4), 537–559.

Heath, S. B. (1999). Dimensions of language development: Lessons from older children. In A. S. Masten (Ed.), *Cultural processes in child development: The Minnesota symposium on child psychology, 29,* 59–75. Mahwah, NY: Erlbaum.

Johnson, C., & Larson, R. (1982). *Bulimia: An analysis of moods and behavior. Psychosomatic Medicine, 44*(4), 341–351.

Kuhn, D. (2009). Adolescent thinking. In R. M. Lerner & L. Steinberg (Eds.), *Handbook of adolescent psychology* (3rd ed.), Vol. 1 (pp. 152–186). Hoboken, NJ: Wiley.

Larson, R. (1978). Thirty years of research on the subjective well-being of older Americans. *The Journal of Gerontology, 33*(1), 109–125.

Larson, R. (1983). Adolescents' daily experience with family and friends: Contrasting opportunity systems. *Journal of Marriage and the Family, 45*(4), 739–750.

Larson, R. (1990). The solitary side of life: An examination of the time people spend alone from childhood to old age. *Developmental Review, 10,* 155–183.

Larson, R. (1997). The emergence of solitude as a constructive domain of experience in early adolescence. *Child Development, 68*(1), 80–93.

Larson, R. (2000). Towards a psychology of positive youth development. *American Psychologist, 55*(1), 170–183.

Larson, R. W. (2011). Positive development in a disorderly world: SRA Presidential Address. *Journal of Research on Adolescence, 21,* 317–334.

Larson, R. W. (In press). Studying experience: Pursuing the "something more". In J. Brooks-Gunn, R. M. Lerner, A. C. Peterson, & R. K. Silbereisen (Eds.), *The developmental science of adolescence: History through autobiography.* New York: Psychology Press.

Larson, R. W., & Angus, R. M. (2011). Adolescents' development of skills for agency in youth programs: Learning to think strategically. *Child Development, 82,* 277–294.

Larson, R., & Asmussen, L. (1991). Anger, worry, and hurt in early adolescence: An enlarging world of negative emotions. In M. E. Colton & S. Gore (Eds.), *Adolescent stress: Causes and consequences* (pp. 21–41). New York: Aldine de Gruyter.

Larson, R., Brown, B. B., & Mortimer, J. (Eds.). (2002). Adolescents' preparation for the future: Perils and promise [special issue]. *Journal of Research on Adolescence, 12*(1), 1–166.

Larson, R. W., & Brown, J. R. (2007). Emotional development in adolescence: What can be learned from a high school theater program. *Child Development, 78,* 1083–1099.

Larson, R., Clore, G., & Wood, G. (1999). The emotions of romantic relationships: Do they wreak havoc on adolescents? In W. Furman, B. B. Brown, & C. Feiring (Eds.), *Romantic relationships in adolescence* (pp. 19–49), New York: Cambridge Press.

Larson, R., & Csikszentmihalyi, M. (1978). Experiential correlates of solitude in adolescence. *The Journal of Personality, 46*(4), 677–693.

Larson, R., & Csikszentmihalyi, M. (1980). The significance of time alone in adolescent development. *Journal of Current Adolescent Medicine, 2*(8), 33–40.

Larson, R., Csikszentmihalyi, M., & Graef, R. (1980). Mood variability and the psycho-social adjustment of adolescents. *Journal of Youth and Adolescence, 9*(6), 469–490.

Larson, R., & Ham, M. (1993). Stress and 'storm and stress' in early adolescence: The relationship of negative events with dysphoric affect. *Developmental Psychology, 29*(1), 130–140.

Larson, R., & Lampman-Petraitis, C. (1989). Daily emotional states reported by children and adolescents. *Child Development, 60,* 1250–1260.

Larson, R., Raffaelli, M., Richards, M. H., Ham, M., & Jewell, L. (1990). The ecology of depression in late childhood and early adolescence: A profile of daily states and activities. *Journal of Abnormal Psychology, 99,* 92–102.

Larson, R., & Richards, M. (Eds.). (1989). The changing life space of early adolescence [Special Issue]. *Journal of Youth and Adolescence, 18*(6), 501–626.

Larson, R., & Richards, M. (1994). *Divergent realities: The emotional lives of mothers, fathers, and adolescents.* New York: Basic Books.

Larson, R. W., Richards, M. H., Moneta, G., Holmbeck, G., & Duckett, E. (1996). Changes in adolescents' daily interactions with their families from ages 10 to 18: Disengagement and transformation. *Developmental Psychology, 32*(4), 744–754.

Larson, R. W., & Rusk, N. (2011). Intrinsic motivation and positive development. In R. M. Lerner, J. V. Lerner, & J. B. Benson (Eds.), *Advances in child development and behavior: Positive youth development* (pp. 89–130). Oxford, UK: Elsevier.

Larson, R., & Verma, S. (1999). How children and adolescents around the world spend time: Work, play, and developmental opportunities. *Psychological Bulletin, 125*(6), 701–736.

Larson, R., Verma, S., & Dworkin, J. (2003). Adolescence without disengagement: The daily family lives of Indian middle-class teenagers. In T. S. Saraswathi (Ed.) *Cross-cultural perspectives in human development: Theory, research and applications* (pp. 258–286). New Delhi: Sage.

Larson, R., Walker, K. C., Rusk, N., & Diaz, L. B. (Invited). Understanding youth development from the practitioner's point of view: A call for research on effective practice. *Developmental Science*, special issue.

McAdams, D., & Olson, B. (2010). Personality development: Continuity and change over the life course. *Annual Review of Psychology, 61*, 517–542.

Richards, M., Casper, R., & Larson, R. (1990). Weight and eating concerns among pre- and young adolescent boys and girls. *Journal of Adolescent Health Care, 11*, 203–209.

Richards, M. H., & Larson, R. (1993). Pubertal development and the daily subjective states of young adolescents. *Journal of Research on Adolescence, 3*(2), 145–169.

Rusk, N., Larson, R., Raffaelli, M., et al. (In press). Positive youth development in organized programs: How teens learn to manage emotions. In C. Proctor & P. A. Linley (Eds.), *Research, applications, and interventions for children and adolescents: A positive psychology perspective*. New York: Springer.

Shernoff, D. J. (2013). *Optimal learning environments: Maximizing the engagement of youth in schools*. New York: Springer.

Silk, J. S., Steinberg, L., & Morris, A. S. (2003). Adolescents' emotion regulation in daily life: Links to depressive symptoms and problem behavior. *Child Development, 74*, 1896–1880.

Smetana, J. (2010). *Adolescents, families, and social development: How teens construct their worlds*. Malden, MA: Wiley-Blackwell.

Steinberg, L., Dahl, R., Keating, D., Kupfer, D. J., Masten, A. S., & Pine, D. S. (2006). The study of developmental psychopathology in adolescence: Integrating affective neuroscience with the study of context. In D. Cicchetti & D. Cohen (Eds.), *Developmental psychopathology* (2nd ed., Vol. 2, pp. 710–741). New York: Wiley.

Verma, S., & Larson, R. (1999). Are adolescents more emotional? A study of the daily emotions of middle class Indian adolescents. *Psychology and Developing Societies, 11*(2), 179–194.

Whiting, B. B. (1980). Culture and social behavior. *Ethos, 8*, 95–116.

Wood, D., Larson, R. W., & Brown, J. (2009). How adolescents come to see themselves as more responsible through participation in youth programs. *Child Development, 80*, 295–309.

26

Taking the Boy out of Brooklyn

Time, Place, and People in the Development of a Developmental Scientist

RICHARD M. LERNER

 Brooklyn, New York. Today, the location elicits images of twenty-somethings sitting in sea-side cafes sipping French wine. They peer at the Manhattan skyline composed of the buildings within which their jobs in finance, the arts, or entrepreneurial endeavors are embedded. Brooklyn in 2013 is a place of in-migration, a setting within which individuals and young families aspire to live.

Brooklyn was not always this place, and certainly not for people growing up there in the 1940s and 1950s. I was born in February, 1946 in Beth-El Hospital (now Brookdale Hospital), on Linden Boulevard, in an East Flatbush neighborhood located just on the cusp of Brownsville. My parents, Sara and Max(well) Lerner, younger brother (Robert), and I lived in Apartment 3A at 1088 Willmohr Street, on the corner of East 95th Street. We were one block north of Brooklyn's Church Avenue. In addition to being the (obvious) location of numerous churches, the avenue was famous for being the setting of the 1944 Frank Capra comedy, *Arsenic and Old Lace*, which starred Cary Grant. It was famous as well for its trolley line, which became the last such route of this vehicle in a borough once defined by these conveyances. The original name of the Brooklyn Dodgers was "The Trolley Dodgers" because the ubiquity of these vehicles constituted obstacles to the pedestrians of Brooklyn.

However, the leisurely progression of the trolley car along its route was becoming increasingly unsuitable for the pace of life of the communities in a borough that was growing increasingly crowded with young families having the need to get on with their lives, lives that had a different aspiration than emblematic of many of the people living in Brooklyn today.

The aspirations of my family and the families of my friends and relatives were to get out, to leave their crowded tenement apartments and to attain the financial means to make it to the fabled Jewish Mecca in the east: Long Island. This land (I was told) was one of single family homes, expansive lawns of grass, and attached garages to hold the family car.

Despite the long hours they worked, most of the adults I knew had little hope that they themselves would ever have the income to leave Brooklyn. However, they had more than the hope that their children would have an exodus marked by such acquisitions. They had the unshakable belief that this transition would occur. And they knew the mechanism that would enable this transformation in financial status and quality of life: Education.

My early recollections of family life, especially at dinners at the apartment of my maternal grandmother and grandfather, Lillian and Samuel Goldfarb, and my mom's three brothers and their wives, Milton and Ruth, Daniel and (his first wife) Claire, and Norman and (his first wife) Eleanor, was that I (and, later, my brother and the cousins who were born after us) would become a doctor (which meant a "real doctor" to my family—a physician or, failing that, a dentist).

The problem with my becoming a doctor was that I was not a very ambitious student. Although I loved to read and had an interest in a lot of things, these foci were not necessarily ones that would prepare me for medical, dental, or even law school. I loved baseball, reading comic books, listening to music, drawing and coloring, and watching the cartoons and Flash Gordon and other serials on television.

My immersion in these pastimes must have had some positive impact. During the 1950s, all 6th-grade students were tested for entry into a special, accelerated learning program, termed "special progress" (SP). Instead of spending three years in junior high school (Grades 7–9), SP students went from 7th to 9th grade. I was shocked to learn that I had passed the test, and that I was being invited to select entry into either SP1 (where one studied French as part of the curriculum) or SP2 (where Spanish was the language focus). Because some friends in the neighborhood who had also passed the test had opted to study French, I chose to enter 7SP1 the following fall. Now, seemingly overnight, I was going to be regarded as a promising student!

Junior High School and High School

P.S. 252, Arthur Somers Junior High School, was only a half block from my apartment on Willmohr Street. The school was located on East 95th Street in the direction of Lenox Road. Yet, when I entered the gray brick building in September, 1959 I came into what was a new world for me.

My fellow 7SP1 students came from neighborhoods beyond the borders of Willmohr Street, and bore wondrous tales of life in adjoining but unexplored by me neighborhoods in East New York and Brownsville. However, the traveling I did with these new classmates involved moving together from room to room around the huge Somers building. We had different teachers for the several subjects assigned to us and a home room teacher that kept track of our attendance and progress. Except for our class in hygiene, taught to the boys by one of the gym (physical education) teachers, we stayed together as a group every day, and would continue to stay together through the 9th grade. We were told that we were exceptionally bright students, from whom great achievements were expected. We were told as well that we were going to be treated like high-school students, and that we were expected to come to every class with our homework completed and ready for the pop quizzes that we could expect to encounter in all of our classes (with the exception of gym).

I really liked the status of being in the SP class. When my classmates and I walked through the halls of Somers the other kids acknowledged us as the really smart ones. In a neighborhood marked by families having invariantly high academic expectations of all of its children, these attributions were hard to keep from going to one's head.

However, I had no trouble staying humble. I quickly established myself as an "underachiever," as someone consistently falling below academic expectations. Despite the fact that I was almost a year younger than the rest of my classmates (because of school admission rules, my February birth allowed me to start kindergarten with all the children who had been born between March, 1945 and February, 1946), I was an early maturer and one of the tallest boys in my grade. My size helped me get chosen first in after-school softball games, and I soon became someone who excelled in my cherished pastime—in all its myriad forms: Little League and Babe Ruth League hardball, softball, and the borough-defining instantiation of the game, Stick Ball. In turn, my early transition into puberty gave me a new focus to distract my attention from my studies: Girls!

Across my 2 years of junior high school, I cannot recall that I had even one distinctive academic achievement. And, while I got taller and thinner (despite my early mature status, I ended up a bit more than 6 feet tall), and improved on my baseball skills, especially my hitting, I also cannot recall any distinctive romantic relationships. I did expand my sports repertoire to include basketball and touch football and, although I was never excellent in either sport, my size helped me play at above average levels. I do recall trying hard to be popular, which included trying to have a girlfriend—whatever that might have meant to a 13-year-old boy in 1959. However, in this domain, I viewed myself as below average.

However, I had a positive outlook. I had just been Bar Mitzvah'ed and was proud of this transition. I had some good friends from both SP classes who would be my convoy of social support as we moved together into the 10th grade. Things would definitely be better in high school in regard to sports and dating.

Only not so much. Samuel J. Tilden High School (named after the only person who—to that point in history—had had won the popular vote for the Presidency of the United States but lost the election in the Electoral College) was located on Tilden Avenue, between East 57th and East 59th Street, just a block away from Kings Highway. The building occupied two city blocks. What I had regarded as the huge edifice of Somers would have fit comfortably in one part of one wing of Tilden. Nevertheless, despite its size, the school required three different scheduling sessions to accommodate the more than 5,000 students in Grades 10–12 attending it. Tilden would one day gain visibility as the high school from which Chris Rock and the Reverend Al Sharpton graduated. However, in the early 1960s our most famous graduate was our football star, Ronny Blye, who became a running back for Notre Dame and then the New York Giants and the Philadelphia Eagles.

I thirsted to be popular. I of course had not the prescience to know of the future work of Brad Brown (e.g., Brown & Larson, 2009) about peer groups, but I concluded that the only pathway for me to become popular was to become an athlete. Naturally, given that I regarded myself as a star baseball player, I saw the Tilden Baseball Team as my path to popularity.

I quickly learned my first lesson in individual-context relations. At Somers, I was one of the best baseball players in the neighborhood, able to hit long flies onto the roof of the tenement that provided the left field wall of the Somers schoolyard (and softball field). However, in my try-outs for the Tilden team, my bat speed was insufficient to catch up with the fast balls thrown by the varsity pitchers and, when they threw curve balls, I was totally befuddled. About the only thing I did well during this otherwise dismal performance was succeeding in wind sprints, especially those that occurred toward the end of the series that the coach had us perform. Apparently, I had more than average endurance in running. Who knew?! Nevertheless, I went home feeling shell-shocked about my failure at baseball. However, reflecting the compensatory processes of intentional self-regulation that I would study decades later (e.g., Gestsdóttir & Lerner, 2007, 2008), by the next morning I had formulated Plan B. I would try out for the Tilden Track Team.

I succeeded at track, finding a "starting" place in middle-distance events, such as the 880-yard and the 1,000-yard races and distance medley relays. I quickly grew to love track and, even after my competitive days ended (after my freshman year in college), I kept running, and now jog as part of my daily exercise routine. My success in track (I won varsity letters in both my junior and senior years) gave me entry to the crowd of "jocks," which intermingled freely with the "populars" (Brown & Larson, 2009) at Max's Kosher Pizzeria and other hang-out spots, and afforded opportunities to meet, date, and at points even go steady with some of the popular girls (I was for a short time during my senior year going steady with one of the Tilden Cheerleaders). My life, then, was quite full. Track practice and track meets (cross-country in the fall, indoor track in the winter, dual meets in the spring, and borough- or city-wide competitions throughout the year) occupied me every almost day of the year. I made almost-nightly visits to Max's. And then there was my sporadic dating, and my part-time job as a delivery boy for Hymie's Grocery Store on Church Avenue, between East 95th and East 96th streets, that I needed to maintain to support my "dating habit." These priorities left little time for other activities, such as homework.

Behaving consistent with my designation as an "underachiever," I graduated from Tilden with an overall average of 75 (or C+). My academic record did include some high grades, particularly in the few honor courses within which I was placed—which were mostly Honors English. However, in courses I did not enjoy, for instance, French, I made little effort to succeed and, once, I failed a French course and had to attend summer school to make it up.

Nevertheless, I had committed myself to a career by my senior year. My fellow track team member, Alan Unger, and I decided to become high-school physical education teachers and track coaches (and owners of a summertime camp in the Catskill Mountains). This decision meant I had to go to college, a destination I had always anticipated moving toward (given the socialization I received from my family). Now I had my own reason to attend, one beyond the fact that such an educational level was simply expected of me and I was too obedient or concrete to even contemplate another direction for my life.

However, I wanted to stay close to home and therefore I aspired to attend college in Brooklyn. My first choice was Brooklyn College, part of the City University of New York (CUNY) and therefore a free (no tuition) school. Free was exactly within my budget. My parents had no money to pay the tuition charges at private schools, such as Long Island University, which had a campus in "downtown" Brooklyn. However, I did not have the grades to get into Brooklyn, and so my only free college option was to somehow get into one of the other campuses of CUNY. My SAT scores were pretty good and so I had a chance of gaining admission to Hunter College in the Bronx (now Lehman College). Two of my Somers SP friends, with academic profiles similar to mine, had been admitted to Hunter. I therefore made it my first choice on the form I submitted listing the CUNY schools that I wished to have consider me.

A few weeks later I received an acceptance letter! Soon, in September, 1962, I was now going to embark on a great adventure and another new world. I had been west of Brooklyn a few times, to New Jersey, when my Uncle Danny and his wife Claire had moved to open up a camera store. I also visited my maternal grandparents during their summer stays in the Catskills, and therefore must have been a passenger in cars or buses passing through the Bronx on the way there. But now I would be a regular visitor to the borough of the Bronx—a ride of over 90 minutes on the Woodlawn–Jerome Avenue subway to Bedford Park Boulevard West, miles north of Yankee Stadium and just minutes from the border of Westchester County and the state of Connecticut! The growth of my geographic horizons seemed to now know no bounds.

Hunter College in the Bronx

My first steps onto a college campus stunned me. Hunter College in the Bronx was situated on a 30+ acre campus. It could hold several Tilden High Schools on it. I could not really believe that I was going to be a part of such a vast educational setting. However, I was now a college freshman, I had registered for my courses, and I had ample opportunity to learn what the northbound, New York City Woodlawn–Jerome train was like at early morning hours, and the southbound, Utica Avenue train was like in the evenings.

During my first year in college, these train trips became my ersatz dorm rooms: I slept, ate, and did homework during the 3 hours of commuting I did each day. I worked harder at my studies in college than I did in high school, but it seemed not hard enough. I completed my freshman year with a GPA less than 3.0. Having a part-time job, plus participation on the freshman track team, proved sufficiently time-consuming to keep me from my putting in a lot of study time beyond the hours spent on the subway. Nevertheless, I thought that my freshman grade point average was more than adequate for the physical education major I would declare at the beginning of my sophomore year.

Registration for my fall semester sophomore classes went smoothly. I was able to get into a popular major course in physical education: Games of High Organization, which included baseball, basketball, and badminton (!). However, a series of non-normative life events (Baltes, 1983), starting with my experience in this course, changed the direction of my life.

As I walked into the first class meeting of Games of High Organization, I immediately noticed three things. First, there were only guys in the room. Second, all of the students other than me were wearing sweat clothes (I was dressed in the "uniform" of my era—jeans, a tie-dyed sports shirt, and penny loafers with Clorox-bleached sweat socks). Third, I was the only one in the class with a neck.

Then the instructor (who had been my freshman track coach) began the lecture. He reiterated the title of the course and announced that he would begin by teaching us about baseball. His remarks, as I recall them, went something like this: "There are four bases in baseball. The first is called first base, the second is called second base, the third is called third base, but the fourth is not called fourth base. It is called "home plate." What? Was he kidding? I thought that this must be a joke, and a smile broke out on my face. I looked around at my classmates to see who else might be starting to laugh. However, everyone else had their heads down and were busily taking notes!

I had not gone to college to take a course like this. The small level of academic self-regard I may have had bubbled over into a quick decision. If this class was what a major course in physical education was like, I was wasting my time. I would change my major and explore a new life course. However, I had no idea what it might be.

I went to the bursar's office and got a copy of the Hunter College Bulletin. I would find my new major in it and, as I rode the subway home that evening, I sat next to my friend Bernie and paged through the list of departments and the descriptions of the majors. Art. I loved to draw and paint, and my mom had been a professional artist for a time, but I knew I really had no talent. Chemistry. No. I had not liked it in high school and thought it involved only memorization of the periodic tables of the elements. English. I had loved English in high school. And I loved to write. However, my freshman writing instructor, Dr. Roberts, told me that I had no talent as a writer and his opinion was reinforced by the feedback I received from the professor of the English literature course I had taken. History seemed to have some interesting classes, but there also seemed to be a lot of requirements about centuries or civilizations about which I did not have any interest. On and on, and then I came to something I knew absolutely nothing about: Psychology. The courses had titles such as, *Psychology of Personality*: "Hey, I have a good personality," I thought. *Social psychology*: "I love parties and I did want to date more." The *Psychology of Sex*: "Sold!"

I turned to my friend Bernie. "I am going to be a psychologist," I announced. "Lerner," you are an idiot," he replied immediately. "You don't know anything about the subject. I don't think you ever heard of it before five minutes ago. Who do you think you'll be? Sigmund Freud?" (In retrospect, I am amazed that, and have no idea how, Bernie knew Freud's name.) "Hey," he announced loudly to anyone on the train car who was not already in earshot, "This crazy guy here thinks he is going to be the next Sigmund Freud." "Lerner," he then said in a voice directed only to me, "don't be stupid, man. Major in something that will get you a job. Nobody gets a job teaching psychology in public schools."

I was pissed by his mocking me and by his condescending advice. The next morning—more to prove Bernie wrong, and to show him that I gave his advice no credibility, than to pursue something I was sure I would like—I went into the registrar, changed my major to psychology, and dropped Games of High Organization. I picked up an open section of Psychology 101, which fit into the rest of my schedule and that would meet for the first time later that day. I would not have missed anything in the course.

The class was a course taught by Dr. Benjamin B. Wolman and the book he assigned was by someone named Ernest R. Hilgard (*Psychology*, 3rd ed., 1962). I bought a used copy of the book for $5.70 (the book sold new for $7.50), and went off to find a place on campus where I could begin to read it. It was the first psychology book I ever touched, opened, or read. It is still on the shelf of my office at Tufts University. I was not yet 18 years old and, because of stubbornness and bravado, I told myself I would be a psychologist—although I really had no idea what that meant.

Benjamin Wolman was a psychoanalyst who had studied with Freud himself. The section I had chosen was a small class, about 30 students. Wolman told us we were responsible for knowing the book, and that we would be tested on its contents. However, he would not lecture about the chapters he assigned. Instead, he would lecture only about two topics: The work of Freud and the work of a person whose name was new to me: B. F. Skinner. Wolman explained that the ideas of Freud and Skinner framed what was in his view the two major approaches within then contemporary psychology. He said that if we sought to understand psychology we needed to appreciate the nature and implications of the ideas of these two people, and how their ideas, and the bases of their ideas, shaped theory and research.

It would not be until years later, when as an assistant professor writing what would be the first edition of my first book, *Concepts and theories of human development* (Lerner, 1976), I fully comprehended the intellectual gift that Wolman gave his students that semester. There, in the fall of 1963, I was being exposed to ideas that, relatively soon afterward, Willis F. Overton and Hayne W. Reese (Overton & Reese, 1973, 1981; Reese & Overton, 1970), would explain were the organismic and the mechanistic metamodels that framed much of developmental science in the 1960s and 1970s. My interest in these two metamodels, in metamodels more generally, and in the importance of related philosophical concepts, such as paradigms (Kuhn, 1962, 1970) and world hypotheses (Pepper, 1942), has framed my scholarly work across five decades (e.g., Lerner, 1976, 1978, 1988, 1991, 1996, 1998, 2002, 2006, 2010, 2011, 2012). My enrollment in this course was completely serendipitous. Wolman's section was still open at the moment I abandoned my intended career as a physical education teacher and adopted the unknown one of a psychologist. And it happened to fit into my schedule. I sometimes wonder if another section with another instructor would have been available, what my subsequent career path might have been. I'll never know.

The passion with which Wolman talked about psychology, and the intimate relation he had with his field, captivated me. I had never seen someone so engrossed in the world of ideas and so comfortable and facile at talking about abstract concepts. This world of ideas attracted me. I wanted to have his passion. I wanted to demonstrate to him that I could master every bit of information he conveyed or assigned. I knew how to train hard for track. I knew what it took to be a varsity athlete. I had demonstrated commitment, stick-to-itiveness, and enthusiasm in this arena of my life. I believed that I could transfer these skills to my work in psychology and, now, having selected mastery of psychology as my goal, I once again used in this new arena of my life the intentional self-regulatory skills I would study decades later in other youth (e.g., Gestsdóttir & Lerner, 2007, 2008; Lerner, Lerner, von Eye, Bowers, & Lewin-Bizan, 2011). Seemingly abruptly, then, I became a serious student of a field that just a few weeks before I did not even know existed.

In December, on my third attempt I passed my road test and obtained my driver's license. My friend, Joel Berman, told me about a guy his father knew who was selling his 1956 Oldsmobile for only $250.00. I bought it and, after placing new plates on it, proudly parked it in front of my home and offered my mom, dad, and brother a chance to take a ride with me. My mom and brother agreed. My dad told me he would ride with me on some other occasion. He would.

On Friday evening we happened to eat dinner together as a family. I announced that, now, after owning a car for 3 days, I was going to go to Long Island that evening to visit a friend who I had met at Hunter. My dad became upset with me. He pointed out that snow was forecast and that I was a new driver, had never driven to Long Island, and had never driven in snow. He said that I was too inexperienced to drive at night such a long way in the snow. He said I should stay home. He was of course perfectly correct. However, I was 2 months shy of my 18th birthday and my adolescent egocentrism (Elkind, 1967) led me to insist that I could easily make the trip and that he was foolish to worry. We argued.

However, after a few minutes of increasingly heated back and forth, I noticed something funny. "Hey, Dad," I said, "Your right lower eyelid is curled up." What's going on?" My mother looked at his eye and became hysterical. "Max, Max, what's wrong?," she screamed. In a quiet voice, much in contrast to the voice level he had been using with me just a few moments earlier, he said, "I don't know. I don't feel well."

"Do you think you need to go to the hospital," I asked. "Yeah . . . Can you take me?"

I helped my dad down the three flights of stairs from my apartment. I led him to the passenger side of the front seat of my car. My mom got into the back seat. My brother stayed with my Uncle George and Aunt Rose, who lived across the hall. I drove the eight blocks from our apartment building to the Emergency Room entrance of Beth-El Hospital.

This ride was the only one I would ever give to my father. He had had a stroke. His condition worsened. He died 3 weeks later. He was 54 years old.

The night after the funeral, people visited us in our apartment. The overflow of guests were in my uncle and aunt's apartment. My mom's three brothers, Milton, Dan, and Norman, asked me to join them in George's and Rose's kitchen. They were seated at the table and they asked me to sit down with them. I didn't. I told them I preferred standing. Dan did the talking. My mom was not working and, now, with my dad gone, there would be no income coming into the house, he reported. One of them explained that they did not have the resources to replace my father's income. One of them (I cannot recall who) concluded that my only choice was to quit college and get a job to support the family. Milton's wife, Ruth, could get me a full-time job as a stock boy in a new S. H. Kress dime store that was opening up in Canarsie, another Brooklyn neighborhood. It was now up to me, and only me, they stressed.

I became angry and for the first time in my life talked back to my uncles who, until that moment, I revered. Yes, it was up to me, I agreed, and said that I would take the job Ruth had for me. However, I would not drop out of college. I would, instead, combine college and as many hours of employment as Kress would give me in the evenings and on weekends (they were opened until nine every night and all day on Saturdays and Sundays). They seemed shocked by my adamancy. They reminded me that I was on my own, that they could not help. I said I understood completely and returned to my apartment.

Now, in addition to having to prove my friend Bernie wrong, I had something to prove to my family. However, the stakes were higher now. I couldn't fail my mother or brother.

The rest of my sophomore year and the following three semesters were a period of continuous work—school, studying, and "stockboying." I decided that if I was going to be a psychologist, I needed to go to graduate school. And, because of my family situation, I needed to get there as quickly as possible. I took 18 credits (six courses) a semester, enrolled in summer school after my sophomore and junior years, worked at least 30 hours a week at Kress, and trained myself to "pull an all nighter" two evenings a week, even when I did not have a test or a paper to prepare. I was able to graduate from Hunter in 3½ years, in January 1966. I was a month away from my 20th birthday.

Although my time at Hunter was short, I was able to have the opportunity to learn a great deal from several professors. Two, in particular, were mentors and, as well, responsible for my accepting admission to the then relatively new doctoral program in psychology at the City University of New York (CUNY), which involved classes at several of the campuses of the university (Hunter, Park Avenue; Brooklyn College, City College, and Queens College) but was administered at the Graduate Center, which was then located on West 42nd Street, between Fifth and Sixth Avenues just across from Bryant Park.

Virginia Staudt Sexton taught me to love the history of psychology and, as well, was my instructor for experimental psychology. She required students to design and conduct a study as the final project for the course, and the one I conducted, on semantic conditioning and generalization, resulted in my first conference presentation (at the meetings of the Eastern Psychological Association) and my first publication (Lerner, 1968a). In turn, Charles Knehr, taught the advanced introductory psychology course, and framed it by presenting work of D. O. Hebb (1949, 1958). I thought that Charles Knehr was the smartest person I had ever met, and I became a groupie of his. I sat in the front row of every course he offered, and watched as he chain smoked cigarettes as he sat and lectured to the class. He lit his new cigarette from the end of his old one. He then tossed the old one, with the butt still smoldering, onto the floor between his feet. As he continued to lecture, he moved his right foot around on the floor until his shoe found the butt; he then crushed it with the sole of his shoe. This process was repeated several times in each 50-minute class; it was not atypical for Professor Knehr to go through a half pack of filterless cigarettes.

I asked Professor Knehr if he would allow me to do an honors thesis under his direction. He agreed. I did a laboratory study of the span of apprehension, based on a tachistoscopic procedure that he had developed. I was able to publish two articles based on this work (Lerner, 1968b, 1969).

I would not fully comprehend for several years the significance of Professor Knehr's discussions and my readings of Hebb's (1949) ideas. However, these discussions of the "conceptual nervous system" (Hebb, 1955), of cell assemblies, phase sequences, and the ratio of association fibers to sensory fibers that differentiated organisms varying in the final level of behavioral stereotypy or plasticity they attained across their ontogeny, would shape much of my thinking about the nature of the developmental process, especially when I recognized the links between the ideas of Hebb (1949) and the work of comparative psychologist, T. C. Schneirla (e.g., 1956, 1957; Tobach & Schneirla, 1968), that I would encounter a few years later in graduate school.

However, during my undergraduate days I thought that Hebb was a physiological psychologist because of his ideas and so, when I applied to the CUNY doctoral program in psychology, I indicated that I was most interested in concentrating in this area. Although Professor Knehr did not teach in the CUNY graduate program, Professor Sexton did. Therefore, when CUNY offered me a $3,000 stipend and free tuition as a National Defense Education Act (NDEA) Title IV fellow and allowed me to begin graduate school in mid academic year, I accepted this offer and turned down the one given to me by New York University (which involved less money and the need to wait until fall, 1966 to start graduate school). Consistent with my continuing geographic bias, I only applied to graduate programs in New York City.

Moreover, I could select Hunter College, Park Avenue, as my "home" campus, and take many of my classes there. My home school would keep me to a great extent at home, in at least the same college, if not the same campus. By the time of my 20th birthday, I was a doctoral student at CUNY. I was going to be a physiological psychologist and enter into a career of laboratory research and teaching. I believed that everything was set and my road ahead was certain and fixed.

The Genesis of a "Basic" Developmental Researcher

And then I encountered the concept of development. I don't think I ever seriously thought about the concept of development until my first year of graduate school, even though I had taken a very interesting undergraduate course in child psychology with Joseph Church, where I read the first edition of his textbook with Joseph Stone, *Childhood and adolescence: A psychology of the growing child* (Stone & Church, 1957).

In February 1966, the CUNY doctoral program in psychology at CUNY was relatively new. Although I had indicated to the CUNY faculty that I intended to concentrate in physiological psychology, there were no hard lines drawn among physiological, comparative, conditioning and learning, social, or developmental program areas. One could move from one concentration to another, at least in the beginning period of one's studies; only clinical psychology, which was based at City College of CUNY, was walled off from students freely entering it. I took courses across all areas of the program other than clinical.

My first course in physiological psychology was with Stanley Novak. I enjoyed the course a lot, perhaps because the material seemed like an extension of the ideas and facts I had learned from Charles Knehr. However, by the time I had completed my second course in physiological psychology (with David Rabb, at Brooklyn College), I knew this concentration was not for me. Focusing almost completely on work derived from studying the giant squid axon, and framed by Professor Rabb through discussions of batteries and the physics of electricity, I found the area too remote from understanding human functioning. Had I had the word "reductionism" in my vocabulary at the time I would have used it to point to the reason I felt alienated from Professor Rabb's approach to psychological science. As Sam Korn—who would become my mentor—would latter explain to me, there was a tendency in the psychology of the mid to late 1960s to try to learn more and more about less and less until, Sam quipped, one knew everything about nothing. Professor Rabb told my classmates and me that his approach to the field was the only one that constituted rigorous science. However, I did not become interested in psychology to study batteries and electricity. I wanted something else.

Fortunately, I re-encountered Hebb but, now, through exposure to the theory and research of Schneirla. Through the instruction of Elizabeth Gellert and, most importantly, Sam Korn, I learned that Hebb (1949) was actually presenting a theory of development, of how, through interactions between the organism and its experiences, the brain and, ultimately, behavior became organized. I began to understand that the process of development enabled the actualization of the potential for plasticity in brain organization and behavioral function that Hebb discussed (Lerner, 1976, 1984, 1986).

Although I knew I had a lot to learn and was often overwhelmed by it, motivated by Sam Korn's gentle prodding, I was also growing in my intellectual excitement about what I was learning. Through studying Dale Harris's (1957) classic edited volume *The Concept of Development,* I was exposed to some of the key philosophical issues involved in understanding development—for example, teleology, organicism, and the unity-of-science, or mechanistic and reductionist, perspectives (Nagel, 1957). In addition, this book introduced me to the ideas of Heinz Werner (1957), Robert Sears (1957), and—most important to me—T. C. Schneirla (1957). One section of Schneirla's chapter in the 1957 Harris book gave me not only the basic idea to test in my dissertation, but also arguably the only good idea I have ever had and, perhaps, the one idea that has framed all of my research.

In a section of his chapter entitled "Circular functions and self-stimulation in ontogeny," Schneirla (1957, pp. 86–89) explained that individuals are, in effect, in relationships with themselves over the course of their development. On the basis of their characteristics of individuality, individuals evoke differential reactions in other organisms; these reactions provide feedback to the individual and constitute a significant portion of the experience that promotes the development of further individual distinctiveness for the organism. In essence, then, by influencing those who influence him or her, the person becomes a source of his or her own development (Lerner, 1982; Lerner & Busch-Rossnagel, 1981; Lerner & Walls, 1999). As such, the integration of action—the relation of the organism on the social context and of the context on the organism—becomes the focal process of development (Brandtstädter, 1998, 1999; Brandtstädter & Lerner, 1999).

I was unaware at the time that, by drawing on Schneirla's (1957) ideas about circular functions, I was aligning myself with a group of scholars, primarily Germans, who were developing what I later understood were action theories of human development. These scholars, for instance Paul and Margret Baltes (1990), Jutta Heckhausen (1999), and Jochen Brandtstädter (1998), focused on the concept of *developmental regulations*, the rules governing the course of human development. Their key idea was that these rules involved the integration of action—of the individual on the context and the context on the individual. These integrative relations (represented as individual ←→ context relations) were the fundamental process of life; and when the bidirectional relations were mutually beneficial, when they supported the positive maintenance and healthy perpetuation of both components of the relation, both the individual and the context, they were *adaptive developmental regulations* (Brandtstädter, 1998, 2006).

Years later, I would turn my attention to how the adolescent contributed to these adaptive developmental regulations, either through relatively automatic physiological processes (e.g., involving hypothalamic functioning or circadian rhythms) or intentional means, that is, via intentional self-regulation (Gestsdóttir & Lerner, 2008: Lerner, Freund, DeStefanis, & Habermas, 2001). However, meeting, and getting to know the work of Paul and Margret Baltes, would be the means through which I saw the connections between the idea of circular functions and German action theory. I would not meet Paul and Margret for several years and so, at this point in my graduate education, I just recognized that studying circular functions would be both of great interest to me and, at the same time, an innovative approach to addressing processes that seemed (albeit vaguely to me, at the time) to go beyond the nature–nurture controversy. However, I was not clear about how to study these circular functions in children and adolescents. Schneirla had studied mostly army ants and cats. Was there any way to approach this topic with humans?

Sam's tutelage in these ideas led me to switch my concentration from physiological to developmental psychology and to ask Sam to be the chair of my doctoral committee and my dissertation advisor. I told him of my interest in circular functions, and he was glad to know of my interest. Sam had received his Ph.D. from Herbert Birch, a psychologist at NYU and, as well, a pediatrician on staff at NYU Medical Center. Birch, in turn, had received his Ph.D. from Schneirla, when Schneirla was on the faculty of NYU. Therefore, as an intellectual "grandchild" of Schneirla, Sam was glad that one of the "children" to whom he would give intellectual birth wanted to follow in the Schneirla tradition. Now all I had to do was to figure out how to accomplish this task while studying children and adolescents.

I was taking one of my last courses in graduate school—a seminar in personality development in childhood and adolescents. The text for the course was authored by Boyd R. McCandless: *Children and Adolescents: Behavior and Development* (1961). McCandless was discussing the work of Harvard physician, William Sheldon (1940, 1942). Sheldon claimed that he had identified three basic body types in men, endomorphs (whose bodies were dominated by adipose tissue), mesomorphs (whose bodies were marked by strong musculature) and ectomorphs (whose bodies were thin and linear). Sheldon claimed that the genes that gave men their body types also gave them their temperaments. However, McCandless, who was a social learning theorist, cited a 1954 article by Brodsky that found that there were different social stereotypes associated with drawings of adult male endomorphs, mesomorphs, and ectomorphs. He suggested that the existence of these stereotypes might serve to differentially socialize men with different body builds and, as a consequence of this conjecture, he claimed that social learning, and not nature-related variables, could account for links between body type and temperament, or personality more broadly.

McCandless did not suggest precisely how the presence of social stereotypes translated into different personality development, but I had an idea—perhaps the only good idea I have ever had in my career: Circular functions were involved. I suggested that if children, adolescents, and adults, with different body builds elicited differential (and stereotyped) reactions from the people in their social world, these reactions could feed back to the individuals and channel them into stereotype-consistent behaviors. I thought such social channeling might be especially true if the people possessing these different body builds had the same social stereotypes as found generally in society. Conducting the longitudinal research necessary to verify this process was not feasible for a dissertation. However, as a start, I could present the model and assess part of it. I could see if children, adolescents, and (young) adults of different body builds had the same stereotypes about body build–behavior relations. In short, for my dissertation, I used the circular functions idea to frame a study of the role of individual differences in male children's, adolescents', and young adults' body builds for their social stereotypes about body build–behavior relations and, in turn, for their self-reported personality and social development.

The results of the research were consistent with the Schneirla-influenced theoretical model I had developed (Lerner & Korn, 1972), and work on this topic was my initial foray into testing my "one good idea," that individuals, through their effects and actions on the context, could contribute to circular functions that provided a source of their own development. I saw this individual ←→ context relational process as not being a nature or a nurture one but, instead, as a matter of exchanges between person and context that constituted a "third source" of development. Indeed, my response to the first question asked of me in the oral defense of my dissertation (by Joe Glick, then the head of the developmental psychology program at CUNY) —"What do you hope to accomplish with the line of work you have set upon through your dissertation research?"— was "I want to solve the nature–nurture controversy." Joe and some other faculty members at the defense laughed at my response. However, Sam just smiled and nodded approvingly. (In 1989, when I won a Ph.D. Alumni Special Achievement Award from CUNY, Joe Glick came up to me after the ceremony to offer his congratulations. Quite generously, he told me that he and other colleagues at CUNY were very proud of my record of research and, especially, of my contributions to developmental theory. I reminded Joe of our exchange at my defense. He said he did not recall the incident.)

It is important to add that, although my dissertation was obviously successfully defended, it is prophetic that a key objection of the CUNY psychology doctoral faculty to my proposal to do this research as a dissertation was that the topic was not *psychological* in nature. Although Sam Korn did not ever tell me which colleague or colleagues raised the objection to the proposed focus of the research, he did say that when the faculty met to discuss my defense of the proposal, one objection was that the topic seemed more sociological or anthropological than psychological.

At the time, given the perhaps understandable lack of objectivity by a graduate student interested primarily in completing his doctoral degree, I objected to and in fact dismissed this criticism. Had not Boyd R. McCandless (1961, 1967, 1970)—the then (founding) editor of the new APA journal, *Developmental Psychology*—not only discussed but in fact sponsored analogous dissertation research (see Staffieri, 1967)? However, in retrospect, there was a good point being made by this comment—at least insofar as the traditional personological approach to psychological development is concerned.

However, I didn't dwell too long on the assertion that my work crossed the boundary of psychology and came perilously close to drawing on ideas from—and perhaps even being relevant to—other disciplines. I had to devote my attention to being a professor as well as to completing my dissertation, and deep reflection about the implications— theoretical, empirical, or professional—of engaging ideas from multiple disciplines was not a high priority for me. During my last year of graduate school, the desire to earn money and, as well, to move out of my apartment with my mother and brother, led me to go on the job market.

I had several interviews and in fact received a few offers. One was at Northeastern University in Boston, where I was offered a 9-month salary of $10,000 and the opportunity to live in what seemed to me to be a city that offered both intellectual and social excitement. Another offer was at Eastern Michigan University, in Ypsilanti, Michigan, a town that bordered Ann Arbor, and offered the exotica of living somewhere in the green zone depicted in the famous poster of the Steinberg *New Yorker* cover—between Jersey and the Pacific Ocean (the poster still hangs over my computer table in my study at home). I had no idea where Michigan was (or even how to spell it), but my Uncle Milton, who had fought in D-Day and therefore was a man of the world, told me that if I drove over the George Washington Bridge and continued west I would eventually see a sign for Michigan (probably around Nebraska or Kansas, he speculated). I went for the job interview (flying to Detroit Metro Airport) and was thrilled to receive an offer of $12,000 for a 9-month contract! Plus, since I was ABD, the Department Chair, Sam Karson, told me that I would get a bonus of $900.00 when I finished my Ph.D.

How could I forgo such wealth?! A thousand dollars a month was more money than I ever dreamed of making. I accepted the offer, shipped all my books by U.S. mail to the Eastern Michigan University Psychology Department in Ypsilanti, put all of the rest of my belongings into the new, 1969 red, Volkswagen Beetle I had just purchased for $900.00 (it was so inexpensive because I took a model off the lot that had no radio in it), and following my Uncle Milton's directions drove west to Michigan.

I arrived a few days later, with the Discussion section of my dissertation still to complete but also with the expectation that, aside from this detail, I would be now be launching a successful life as a professor.

Seven Years in Ypsilanti

I found an apartment in Ann Arbor and, after responding to an ad that read "Three rooms of furniture for $300.00" and a couple of trips to the local K-Mart for dishes, glasses, knives, forks, spoons, and a few other implements I recalled being in my mother's kitchen, I occupied a now fully furnished and functional one-bedroom apartment along with an assigned parking space in front of the door to the building in which I lived. I had one other purchase to make, however. I bought a color TV so that I could watch, in style, the 1969 Mets play the Baltimore Orioles in the World Series. The investment—more than the cost of my furniture—was worth it. I had predicted that the Mets would win in four games and, after they lost the first encounter, I was proven correct. I stayed in the apartment for 2 years and then, with the bonus I received when I completed my Ph.D., I bought a townhouse located by the North Campus of the University of Michigan.

At Eastern Michigan University (EMU), I was given a five-course teaching load: introductory psychology (in both semesters), a master's level graduate course in the psychology of adjustment (whatever that was), and two developmental courses—one in child development and the other in adolescent development. I was stumped about the latter course. Other than for the chapter in the McCandless (1961) book that led to my dissertation research, and the few other chapters in his text that discussed adolescence, I knew nothing about this age period. None of my colleagues had any ideas about how to teach the class—I was the only developmental psychologist in a department dominated by clinical psychologists—and I knew of no textbooks to use. Having to make a decision quickly, I settled on an edited book by James Adams (1968), *Understanding Adolescence: Current Developments in Adolescent Psychology.*

I became very friendly with my Department Chair, Sam Karson, and he and his wife, Dorothy, sort of adopted me. Along with their two children, Michael and Linda, I found myself invited to family dinners, especially over the holidays. They did not want me to spend such times alone and, even when I had a steady girlfriend, they still made me part of their social world.

Although he was a clinical psychologist and had no real interest in developmental topics, Sam taught me a lot about being a professional and about career development. Looking back, I think I stumbled into a 7-year post-doctoral experience, because this was the length of time I remained at EMU and, although promoted to associate professor with tenure along the way, I realize now that Sam always regarded me more as his post-doc (and, perhaps as well, as a second son) than a junior colleague. Somehow I didn't mind. I loved his company—usually—and I learned a great deal from him, substantively and professionally.

Sam was a "quantitative" clinician. He had been a consultant for the Federal Aviation Administration and was in charge of screening applicants to serve as air traffic controllers for their psychological fitness. He was a colleague of Raymond B. Cattell, and he used the Cattell 16-PF (Cattell, Eber, & Tatsuoka, 1970) for this screening. His relationship with Cattell and, as well, his interest in multivariate statistics, earned Sam membership in an elite scholarly organization, the Society for Multivariate Experimental Psychology (SMEP). I was a good statistics student in my graduate courses, but my knowledge of statistical methods extended only through analysis of variance and regression. Sam exposed me to multivariate methods and, in particular, factor analysis. He pushed the Psychology Department to have a critical mass of statistical methodologists on the faculty and, about a year after I joined EMU, he hired a new Ph.D., John Knapp, who had been a student of one of his SMEP colleagues. John had received his Ph.D. from the University of Denver, studying with John Horn. Sam told me that Horn was one of the two great former students of Ray Cattell. Naturally, I asked who the other former student was. "John Nesselroade," he replied. I had not heard the name before.

John Knapp and I became close friends as well as good colleagues. Not only did John, and another terrific methodologist in the EMU department, Stuart Karabenick, teach me a great deal about statistical procedures but, as well, we began to co-author research. Knapp taught me how to use the statistical packages that were then beginning to become available. These were the days when I was actually doing my own data analysis and, as I tell my students now, I was using SPSS (Statistical Package for the Social Sciences) when it had only one "S" in it.

A year after John joined the department, we launched a search for a junior-level social psychologist. John recommended a person who had just completed his Ph.D. in the Psychology Department of the University of Denver: Peter Benson. Peter was brought in for an interview and was impressive. He was a dynamic speaker and presented what were then innovative interests, in spiritual development and the psychology of religion, in ways that made several faculty members, including me, see the importance of these topics for their own work. Peter was offered the job and he accepted. Although I was not able to convince him—at the time—to join me in research on adolescent development, we both found a common interest in the study of helping behavior. Peter and I, along with Stu Karabenick and another faculty member, Steve Vincent, published several papers on helping behavior and one—on helping behavior shown at the Detroit Metro Airport to people who differed in their physical attractiveness (Benson, Karabenick, & Lerner, 1976)—caught the attention of the media and was even turned into a question on a television game show, *Hollywood Squares.*

Peter did not stay at EMU long. After a couple of years he, and his wife Tunie, left Ypsilanti for Peter to take a position at a Quaker-affiliated institution, Earlham College, in Richmond, Indiana. I was sorry to see him leave, and hoped that our paths would cross again. Years later they did and, once we met again, we remained close friends and colleagues until his untimely death on October 2, 2011.

I also followed up on Sam's reference to John Nesselroade, and this exploration changed my life. It enabled me to integrate my burgeoning understanding and skills in multivariate statistical methodology with my training in developmental psychology. However, the approach to developmental psychology I was beginning to take was one that I had not encountered as a graduate student. Nesselroade was working with two colleagues, Paul B. Baltes and K. Warner Schaie, at West Virginia University, and their theoretical and methodological approach to human development was, even in the early 1970s, rapidly changing the lens through which ontogeny was understood and studied.

Now, at about this time in my years at EMU I found that a lot of publishers' representatives knocked at my office door. I was teaching high enrollment courses and these representatives wanted me to consider adopting the texts their companies published. I got a lot of free books through these encounters—both samples of the books they wanted me to adopt and other books they published in which I had an interest. I must have met dozens of these sales people but two in particular not only became friends but, as well, became important influences in my life—and led me to a life-long association with Baltes, Nesselroade, and Schaie!

One publisher's representative, for Academic Press, was an engaging and high-energy person who filled my small office with ideas and energy about the future of psychology. His name was Larry Erlbaum. Although he had no books to offer me for course adoption, he asked to meet me because he was interested in getting to know people who might be entertaining ideas about writing or editing books that would change the field. He asked, "Are you writing anything or considering writing anything." I reflected for a moment and said something along the lines of, "Well, now that you ask, I think there is a need for a text that takes a new approach to child development. Most of the books that exist, even the very good ones, such as Mussen, Conger, and Kagan (1969), emphasize study after study and spend very little time taking about the theories that, at least in ideal situations, should frame these studies. What do you think about a book that would emphasize the concepts and theories that frame the study of human development?" Larry answered that he thought such a book was needed, but that he was not (then) looking for books at the introductory level. He said, prophetically as it turns out—since the third edition of my graduate text, *Concepts and theories of human development* (2002), was published by Lawrence Erlbaum Associates (LEA)—-that if I decided to write the book at an advanced or graduate level we should talk again. Over the years we of course talked scores of times and I was privileged to author or edit about a dozen books published by LEA and, as well, launch and edit two journals that were published by his company (*Journal of Research in Adolescence* and *Applied Developmental Science*, which I still edit, with Celia B. Fisher, at this writing).

The second publisher's representative, for Addison-Wesley, was Stuart Johnson. Stuart was quiet but nevertheless engaging and, like Larry, he was incredibly smart. He also seemed more of a professorial type than a sales person. He actually read broadly in the field within which he was publishing (and, I learned, in almost any other field I happened to discuss with him), and he loved to engage me in deep discussions about the literature I was reading. When he asked me the inevitable question about whether I was writing anything or had a plan to write anything, I replied in essentially the same way as I had to Larry Erlbaum. However, Stuart (I learned about 2 years later) misinterpreted my responses as meaning that I was going to write a book that competed with Mussen, Conger, and Kagan (1969), albeit taking a somewhat different approach to the discussion of concepts and theories of human development. He asked me to prepare a brief prospectus about the book and soon, although by this point I was a relatively new Ph.D. (I finally completed my doctorate during my second year at EMU) and was still an untenured assistant professor, I signed a contract with Addison-Wesley to write an undergraduate textbook in child development, albeit one that would put theory in the foreground of the discussion.

Writing this book enabled me to interact with the literature of human development, if not with the people generating it. I was isolated from other developmental psychologists at EMU. When I moved to my townhouse I discovered that I shared a backyard with and was very friendly with John Hagen of the Psychology Department of the University of Michigan. We became social friends at that point in our lives, however, and I really had no professional association with John or with other developmental psychologists at Michigan, Wayne State, or Michigan State. Therefore, I had no network in developmental psychology with whom to exchange ideas about the chapters of the book. I wrote the book in relative isolation and, when I completed a full draft in 1973, I sent it to Stuart Johnson for him to obtain reviews.

A few reviews came back after a few months. One was devastating. I had written a chapter dealing with the nature–nurture issue in regard to intelligence and had raised some questions about the quality of the data about the resemblance of IQ scores of identical twins reared together and separately. I of course discussed the publications of Cyril Burt, whose work with such twins was regarded as the providing the best data about the heritability of intelligence. I was not smart enough to raise all the questions about the accuracy of the data that, soon afterward, Leon Kamin (1974) would raise in a book published by Larry Erlbaum's then relatively new company. I certainly did not have any idea of the scandal that would occur when Hearnshaw (1979) published his biography of Sir Cyril. However, I did note that the hereditarian interpretations of Burt's data could just as easily be turned into evidence of the power of the environment, both in utero and after birth. In the face of data that could be interpreted in these distinct ways, I used the ideas of Anastasi (1958) to suggest that we were asking the wrong questions about the nature and nurture of intelligence and, although I had not yet encountered the foundational theoretical work of Willis (Bill) Overton (e.g., 1973), I suggested that the correct question was one that asked how nature and nurture variables interacted dynamically in the development of intelligence.

This argument made the reviewer furious. The reviewer asked "Who is Richard Lerner?" The reviewer said that he/she had never heard of him and that none of his/her colleagues had heard of him either. The reviewer went on to note that I had no standing in science to question the work of Cyril Burt and that my ideas were patently absurd. The reviewer recommended that Stuart reject the book. The reviewer concluded that I was a poor scholar (stronger adjectives were actually used) and that it would be a huge embarrassment for Addison-Wesley to publish the book.

I was crushed. I offered to withdraw the book but, for some reason, Stuart said that I should just revise the chapter and resubmit the manuscript. He would then get another review. However, I was paralyzed. For the first (and only time) in my life I could not write a thing. I had absolutely no confidence in my ideas and, with no other developmentalists around, I had only sympathetic colleagues to talk with. Sam Karson, John Knapp, and Stuart Karabenick lent supportive ears and, about 6 months later, I decided that I would just delete the offending material from the manuscript and submit a revised manuscript to Stuart Johnson. (Those readers familiar with the second and third editions of the book, however, know that this material is now a prominent feature of the book; Lerner, 1986, 2002.)

More than 6 months went by before I heard from Stuart about the book's fate. There was good news and bad news. The good—actually wonderful—news was that the new reviewer he commissioned—Sheldon (Shep) White from Harvard—loved the book. He compared it favorably to the then recently published book by Jonas Langer (1969) and said that, although he did not know me, he believed that the ideas I was presenting were innovative and important. He urged Stuart to publish the book!

I was thrilled. However, Stuart then dropped the other shoe. When Shep compared my book to the Langer (1969) book, Stuart realized—apparently for the first time—that the text he had in his possession was not going to be a competitor of introductory child development texts. Instead, it was going to be an upper-level undergraduate or graduate book—a much smaller market than he anticipated. He explained that Addison-Wesley could not invest as much money in the production of such an upper-level book as it could an introductory book. Therefore, other than for a photo of a child with Down Syndrome, there would be no other photos in the book, which would be printed with small font and in black and white. I wanted to have pictures of the various theorists whose work I discussed in the book, but with no photo budget I asked if

Stuart would allow me to commission an artist to draw likenesses of the theorists based on publically available photos. Stuart's response was that if the artist "worked cheap," I could explore such an option.

As I was ruminating about this dilemma in my child development class one day, a student raised her hand and said she was an artist and would be interested in trying her hand at the task. Her name was Kathy Gendron and her drawings of the theorists I discussed, plus her abstract design for the cover of the book, are truly magnificent (and she worked for $5.00 a drawing—a budget that even Addison-Wesley found acceptable). I think her work gave the book a quality that was distinct, indeed memorable—a view shared by many of the colleagues whose drawings appear in the book. Several years later, when Graham Spanier and I were completing our adolescent development text for McGraw Hill (Lerner & Spanier, 1980), Kathy's work so impressed our editor that she was hired to draw chapter openings for the book. She was paid much more this time and, as well, used her work in the two books to launch her career as a graphic designer.

The production of the book was a slow process (it did not appear until 1976) and my work on it (for instance, reading copy-edited manuscript, and reviewing galley and then page proofs) extended across much of 1975. Addison-Wesley was in no rush to get into print a book that they now anticipated would have small sales and, perhaps, a short shelf life.

In retrospect, I think the slow production schedule was a great benefit to me.

In 1974, Sam Karson invited John Knapp and me to be guests at a meeting of SMEP, which was to be held on the campus of Educational Testing Service (ETS) in Princeton, New Jersey. I knew that most of the presentations were going to be over my head, but I could not pass up the opportunity to meet some of the scholars about whom I had only read. The conference involved staying in Princeton for two nights, but I told Sam I would go only for one night and then get back to Michigan to keep a date I had with a woman I was seeing at the time.

There was a plenary dinner the first evening of the conference and Warner Schaie was the dinner speaker. I did not have the chance to meet him that evening but I still remember the gist of his talk, which was more about career development than methodology. Warner said that really good ideas come rarely to a scientist and that, when one comes, a scientist should seize upon it and then pursue it relentlessly. In short, he said that a key to success was, first, recognizing that an idea is such a career-shaping one and, second, effectively using the idea as a frame for one's scholarship. He then explained that his one good idea was "cohort effects," and the rest of the talk illustrated why it was a good idea and how he had continued to use it as a basis for his research.

As I have explained, during my graduate student days, I had seized on my own "one good idea," that is, circular functions, which was not even my own idea at all but, instead, was the brain child of T. C. Schneirla (1957). Nevertheless, I had been at least smart enough to see the brilliance and some of the implications of Schneirla's idea, and was able to extend it to the study of children and adolescents. In any case, despite my one good idea belonging to Schneirla, I felt enormously affirmed by Warner's talk. I believed that I was on the correct path. I shared my reaction with John Knapp, and told him that now all that I needed to do was figure out how I would expand on the circular functions idea to build my career. I told him I was not quite certain how to accomplish this end but, as chance would have it, in a few moments a path would open up that would lead me in precisely the necessary direction.

After the talk, people began to return to their rooms. John Knapp and I were filing through one of the doors leading to the staircase. Sam happened to be standing by this exit, and he stopped me. He said that he had been looking for me because a colleague wanted to meet me. He was standing next to a tall man, whose physique suggested that he was once a lineman for a major football team (I learned later that he had been a Marine). However, he had a warm, friendly face and was smiling broadly. "Rich," Sam said, "I'd like you to meet John Nesselroade."

My conversation with John was short. I was struck by what I later came to know well: his soft style and his generosity. He told me how eager he had been to meet *me*! He said it was great to be able to put a face to a name. I think I blathered on for a bit about what a fan I was of his work and how it had influenced me so much, and that I was writing this book that included a major section on his research with Schaie and Baltes …. He gently interrupted me. "Are you going to be here tomorrow?" he asked. "Well, I was thinking of getting back to Michigan tomorrow morning," I replied.

"It would be great if you could stay through some of the day tomorrow. My colleague, Paul Baltes, will be here tomorrow and I know he was hoping to meet you as well."

Before I could answer, John Knapp jumped in and assured John Nesselroade that it would be no problem for me to stay on. "No problem," I reiterated. "Great," John replied. "I will introduce you to Paul tomorrow."

John Knapp and I were sharing a room and when we got back there, John was even more excited than I was. John Horn had of course told John Knapp all about his fellow Cattell student, John Nesselroade and, from the very beginning of graduate school, the only methodologist that Knapp had read more about than Cattell and Horn was Nesselroade. He knew too of all the work that Nesselroade, Baltes, and Schaie had done together and, in fact, in the sections of my book devoted to their work, Knapp was the only person I knew who could critique the material for accuracy. Knapp was surprised but also impressed that Nesselroade and Baltes would reach out to me, and he assured me that they were probably interested in recruiting me to Penn State, where they had both recently moved—Nesselroade as a professor and Paul as both professor and head of the department of Individual and Family Studies (IFS) in the College of Human Development.

I hoped that Knapp's interpretation of these events was true, but I could not really imagine that either Nesselroade or Baltes was aware of my work or, even if Sam had told them about me, a hypothesis that Knapp generated and that I agreed was likely, that they would be interested in my research. I had published by this time several articles, and some of them were in *Child Development* and *Developmental Psychology*. However, the work was not reflective of a life-span approach. It was not longitudinal. The statistical analyses were relatively simplistic, compared to those used by Baltes, Nesselroade, and Schaie. And the people I studied were children and adolescents—not the adult and aged groups studied by Baltes, Schaie, and Nesselroade.

Nevertheless, when I met Paul the next morning, he made it seem as if he was a bigger fan of my work than my mother or grandmother. He referred to several of my papers and, in turn, seemed genuinely flattered that I had sections about his work, and the work of Nesselroade and Schaie in "this book" that I told him I was finishing. Our conversation closed with a request from Paul that I put him on my "mailing list" for distribution of future publications. I promised I would and asked that he include me on his mailing list as well. He promised he would do so and promised as well that he would stay in touch with me.

He kept his word. I was entering my sixth year at EMU and had been promoted to associate professor with tenure. I wanted to move on from EMU and have a chance to work in a department that was more research focused than the one I was in and that trained doctoral students. I applied for an associate professor position in the School of Public Health at Johns Hopkins. Then I received a call from John Nesselroade. He told me that Penn State was searching for two beginning associate professor positions in child development. One was in cognitive development and the other was in personality and social development. He was the chair of the search committee and he explained that he was calling to ask me to apply. He said that both he and Paul thought I would be a good candidate for the personality and social development position. Needless to say, I applied.

I was called for an interview for the Johns Hopkins position and, a couple of weeks after I returned home, I was offered the job. Everyone at EMU was genuinely excited for me. To move from EMU to Johns Hopkins was an incredible leap. All of my colleagues knew I would accept the position, and Sam and Dorothy Karson began to plan my going-away party.

However, I had qualms about the position at Johns Hopkins. Yes, this was a top-tier university and a wonderful opportunity. However, I worried that I would be moving away from developmental psychology, especially because, once again, the program I would be in would have very few colleagues in my area. In addition, the job I really wanted was the one at Penn State. Working with Baltes and Nesselroade would be a dream come true.

I had a few days left before I had to give Johns Hopkins my decision. I was working at home and the phone rang. It was John Nesselroade again. He had bad news. Because of financial problems in the College of Human Development, the dean of the College, someone named Don Ford, had cancelled the searches. John wanted me to know about this situation, especially because, he reported, I would have been invited in for an interview. I told him that I was disappointed about the cancellation but felt honored to know that I would have been invited.

John then gave me a ray of hope. He told me that Dean Ford had said that if the financial situation improved he would re-authorize the searches for next year. John explained that there was no guarantee that such a possibility would in fact materialize. In addition, he further cautioned me that, even if the searchers were reopened and I applied again, there was no guarantee that I would make the short list again and be invited to interview. I asked how likely he thought it was that the searches would be reopened. He said he just did not know. He could not give me an estimate of the probability. Nevertheless, I thanked him for the call and we hung up.

I am not a gambler. Once, in 1979, driving cross-country from Penn State to Palo Alto, my wife, Jackie, and I stopped in Elko, Nevada. The lobby of the motel had a nickel slot machine. I deposited a nickel and pulled the lever. I lost. I had never gambled before and my loss in Elko stopped me from further gambling. I have never gambled since that day.

However, as soon as I hung up the phone with John, I made a decision that was the biggest risk of my life. I decided to turn down the offer at John Hopkins and remain at EMU for a seventh year—all because of the hope that Don Ford would reauthorize the searches, that my application would once again result in an invitation for an interview, and that I would be given the job. I knew that my decision could mean that I might spend the rest of my career at EMU. However, the chance to work at Penn State with Baltes and Nesselroade, as low probability as it might have been, was too attractive to ignore.

I took the risk. It was the best decision I ever made in my life. There were two reasons.

Jacqueline Rose Verdirame

It was the first day of classes in the fall semester of 1975. I was in my office and, as usual, the door was open. Cheryl Hilburn knocked and asked if she could come in. She had been an undergraduate student in a couple of my courses and was very smart and motivated. She had applied to our Department's general master's program and was readily admitted. Cheryl asked if I was going to be given a research assistant by Dr. Karson, as she knew I had been in the past. Sam used some of the Department's general funds to support research-active faculty by giving them the money to support a half-time research assistant. Sam had given me such assistance for the past several years. I told Cheryl that I assumed that I would again be assigned a research assistant, and Cheryl asked if she could be considered for the position.

I told her that the decision was Dr. Karson's, but I would certainly ask him. She said she understood. A few minutes after she left I walked down the hall to Sam's office. I knew that Sam would have no preference for who he assigned to me, and that if there was someone I requested he would in all likelihood honor my request. Lynn Sharrock was an undergraduate work-study student and, that day, she was serving as Sam's receptionist. Lynn was then a friend (she had dated Sam's son, Michael, and I often met her when I visited the Karsons' home). She remains a friend today.

I asked Lynn if Sam was in and if I could see him for a few minutes. She said she didn't think he was too busy and that I could just knock on his door. However, as I began to walk past her desk and towards Sam's office, she asked if I was going to ask Sam if Cheryl Hilburn could be assigned as my research assistant. When I replied that I was on the way to make this request she said that she had just met another of the new students, Jackie Verdirame, and advised me to request her. She said "She is smart, from New York, and really pretty. You'll love her!" Yes. This is what she said! I took Lynn's advice. I asked Sam that Jacqueline Verdirame be assigned to me. He agreed, but asked that, in return, I hand out the syllabus in a class wherein the regular instructor was ill. This class was required of all new master's students and so my new research assistant was definitely going to be in the group.

When I got to the class I distributed the syllabus and said that I thought it was a good idea to go around the room and have the students briefly introduce themselves. A woman in a salmon-colored pants suit was sitting at the back of the left-most set of seats. She was the sixth person to talk. "I'm Jackie Verdirame," she announced. "I'm from Queens, New York. I came here to study in the clinical master's program." I was stunned by how attractive she was, but I managed to contain myself.

When introductions were over, I took the elevator back to the sixth floor. Most of the students also came to the sixth floor. They had been told that any teaching or research assignments they would be given would be posted outside the main office and they were eager to learn of their positions. I walked past the front office and was about to turn right to go down the hallway to my office when I heard someone calling "Dr. Lerner! Dr. Lerner!" I turned to see the woman in the salmon-colored pants suit walking quickly towards me. She explained that she had been assigned to me as a research assistant, and I explained that I knew of the assignment and tried to remain detached and professional in demeanor.

However, then she said "I guess it was because of my statistics. Is that right?"

"Huh? What do you mean?" Was I that transparent? Had Lynn spilled the beans?

"Well I am interested in clinical, not development. So it must be that the reason that I was assigned to you is because of all the statistics courses I took as an undergraduate. My background in statistics must be why Dr. Karson thought I could help you with your research."

"Yes. Of course. That is why." I breathed a silent sigh of relief. I asked her to stop by my office when she had a chance in the next day or two so that we could get started on working together.

That was 37 years ago, in the fall of 1975. On July 24, 1977 Jackie and I were married (at a country club in Roslyn, Long Island). At this writing we are still working together. I am not certain that any of our three children—Justin (born May 19, 1980), Blair (born January 22, 1983), and Jarrett (born January 12, 1987)—are familiar with this story. But it is the story of how I met their mother!

The Interview

I was working at home one morning, finally reviewing the page proofs for *Concepts and theories of human development*, when John Nesselroade called. The job at Penn State had indeed opened up again and I of course had applied for it. John was calling to invite me in for an interview!

The interview took place on December 5, 1975, on the day of the death of Boyd R. McCandless. Boyd, whom I never met, was an important person in my career nevertheless. As I have explained, he was the author of the 1961 text that gave me the idea for my dissertation and, as (founding) editor of the journal, *Developmental Psychology*, he published in 1969 (in the inaugural volume of the journal) the first paper I ever published in an APA journal, an article that served as a "pilot" for my dissertation and that was one of the several studies I discussed in my colloquium that day (Lerner & Gellert, 1969). In addition, several of Boyd's former students—Shep White, Hayne Reese, Lew Lipsitt, and Dave Palermo—were mentors, collaborators, and friends who promoted my work and shaped my career. In so many ways, Boyd McCandless was a major influence in my career and life.

On the evening of my interview, John and his wife Carolyn hosted a reception. Several faculty members and I sat in the Nesselroades' family room, the fire roaring, and enjoying drinks and hors d'oeuvres. The faculty were talking about all the mimeographed memos from Paul Baltes that appeared on a regular basis in their mail boxes. One faculty member joked that he was so deluged by memos on a daily basis that he took to reading only a few random selections each week. Several folks laughed, but one of the younger faculty members did not. It was Graham Spanier, a sociologist who had graduated from Northwestern University, and was then a relatively new assistant professor in the department. Graham said, with complete earnestness, that he read each of the memos and usually wrote Paul a reply to each on the same day! There was a pause in the conversation for a brief moment, and then the laughter began again. "Only you would do this Graham," someone said. "Yes," someone else agreed, "and there beats the heart of a born administrator!"

How prescient. Graham would become the professor-in-charge of the Department's undergraduate program and, a few years later, he became associate dean for undergraduate programs in the college. Soon thereafter he left Penn State to become Vice Provost for Undergraduate

Programs at SUNY–Stony Brook and then he became Provost at Oregon State University. This job was followed by his being named Chancellor for the University of Nebraska–Lincoln and then, in the spring of 1975, he was named to be the 16th President of The Pennsylvania State University.

He served with distinction until he resigned on November 9, 2011, during the initial public outcry associated with the child abuse indictments of former Penn State assistant football coach Jerry Sandusky. Graham, and his wife Sandra (Sandy) Spanier, became dear friends to both Jackie and me. They are two of the finest, most decent, generous, and loving people we know.

At the end of my interview, Paul mentioned that he would appreciate seeing the page proofs of my *Concepts and theories* text, which I told him and other Penn State faculty would be published in early 1976. He made this request almost as an afterthought during my exit interview with him. This style was classic Paul Baltes: I understood that he, John Nesselroade, and the other Human Development and Family Studies (HDFS) faculty would not want to hire someone who would then publish a book that would be an embarrassment to the Department. However, Paul did not want to elevate his reading and evaluation of my book as a condition of employment. I promised him I would send him a copy of all page proofs as soon as I returned to Michigan.

About a week after the proofs arrived, I received a call from Paul. He offered me the job. I would be appointed as Associate Professor of Human Development and Family Studies and given a 9-month salary of $19,000. The tenure I had achieved at EMU would not carry over to Penn State, however. I would need to go up for tenure once again. But Paul and I agreed I could do so immediately upon arrival. I figured that folks would not want to fire me just a few months after they had hired me, and so giving up tenure did not seem to be a gamble at all. I accepted the job offer.

The risk I had taken in turning down the offer at Johns Hopkins paid off. I met the love of my life and I had been given my dream job. And with an income that, by teaching summer school, would put me in the $20,000+ bracket, I considered myself rich!

The Pennsylvania State University

I moved to State College, PA in the summer of 1976. I drove to town with Jackie, in my 1972 green, four-door Chevy Impala. My friend, Jed Pendorf, followed me in the U-Haul I had rented to bring the furniture from my two-bedroom, Ann Arbor townhouse to State College. The first thing that I did when we arrived was direct Jed to back up the truck into my two-car driveway, so that we could move my furniture from the van into the garage and then into the house. I signaled him to keep on moving back and he promptly crashed into the basketball hoop that was overhanging the garage. It broke off. Three minutes into home ownership and I already needed to call for repairs!

The next morning, Jed returned to Michigan. That evening, Jackie and I decided to go to downtown State College which then (and now) was constituted by two streets—West College Avenue and West Beaver Avenue—running between South Atherton Street (Route 322) and (about) Shortlidge Road. The College of Human Development was on the University Park campus, next to the intersection of South Pugh Street and West College Avenue. We were walking south on College Avenue and as we approached the corner of Pugh Street, I saw Paul Baltes walking in our direction. He was accompanied by a young, attractive woman with dark hair. I introduced Paul to Jackie and, in turn, he introduced me to Lynn Liben.

This woman was the "star" that Paul and John had told me they hoped to get to round out their recruitment in child development. I would represent the area of personality and social development and Lynn would represent cognitive development. We were both hired as beginning associate professors—Lynn from the University of Rochester (where she was on the faculty with such developmental psychology luminaries as John Flavell, Arnold Sameroff, Michael Chandler, and David Elkind) and me from EMU. We shook hands and I was impressed by her warmth and friendliness. She was clearly happy to meet Jackie and me. She said that she was looking forward to working with me and was excited to learn more about my work. She sounded completely sincere and genuine. She was!

I settled in quickly at Penn State, and I did get to work. In the fall of 1976 Paul had a faculty meeting to present his vision of the substantive foci of the department and his aspirations for its future. He wrote on the board several areas of expertise that he believed were represented in IFS. For instance, he wrote *family studies*, and he listed in this category Graham and our colleague Ted Huston; *human development intervention*, and he listed Bernie and Louise Guerney, Anthony and Judy D'Augelli, Steve Danish, and Fred Vondracek; *cognitive development*, and he listed Lynn and (in *adult development and aging*) Dave Hultsch; and *early childhood education*, and he listed Don Peters and Sherry Willis. Finally, he wrote life-span development on the board. He listed himself, John Nesselroade, and Rich Lerner.

I raised my hand to speak. "Paul," I said, "there must be a mistake. I study personality and social development in childhood and adolescence."

"No, Rich," Paul countered. "You are a life-span developmental psychologist. You just don't know it yet."

As I found to be invariantly the case, Paul was correct. I didn't yet know what I was. However, Paul had read *Concepts and theories of human development* and concluded that the only differences between his approach to development and mine were the age levels on which we focused, the methodological rigor involved in my research, and the label I attached to myself. Strategically, he wanted someone to work on portions of the life span other than the adult years, so that he could begin to disentangle what was then an unnecessary linkage between the

ideas associated with life-span development and the age levels associated empirically with the use of these ideas (which, to that point, were virtually exclusively the second half of the life span). In regard to my needing to understand and use multivariate and change-sensitive designs, measures, and statistical procedures in my research, Paul knew that John and he could easily train me. And, indeed, I began to undergo a continuing education "course" in developmental methodology that was taught to me by them and then, in later years, as well by my dear colleague and friend Alexander von Eye. The course continues through this writing, but with Paul's passing the new instructor on this team is Peter Molenaar, who arrived at Penn State well after I departed. I could not have better or more patient instructors!

Insofar as the label I used to describe myself and my work, I adopted the description Paul assigned to me. At first, it seemed a poorly fitting suit. It seemed way too big for me. However, with Paul's mentorship I grew into it.

Paul had a grand strategy for transforming developmental psychology from a disciplinary-based field focused in infancy and childhood, and one believing in the causal primacy of early experience (as either the time during which genetically based biological changes emerged to determine the course of life *or* as the ontogenetic period within which the environment exerted a preeminent and plasticity-constraining influence on subsequent life) into the multidisciplinary field of developmental science. The field he envisioned would be framed by ideas that stressed the continual interplay of biological and environmental variables. These ideas saw individuals not as passive recipients of the genes that blueprinted their behavior and development, or of an environment that modeled them (recall here Skinner's famous statement, in *Beyond Freedom and Dignity* [1971, p. 211], that "a person does not act upon the world, the world acts upon him"). In turn, these ideas saw individuals as active agents (producers) of their own development, and viewed the resulting relative plasticity (that is, potential for systematic change) in the structure and function of behavior and development as the basis for the potential for change across the life span. Paul's strategy was multifaceted and long term. It involved working with like-minded scholars, such as sociologists Glen H. Elder, Jr., Orville G. (Bert) Brim, and Matilda White Riley, in joint publications, in organizing committees and subcommittees of the Social Science Research Council, in holding conference at Penn State and symposia at key meetings of developmental scholars, such as those of the Society for Research in Child Development (SRCD) and the International Society for the Study of Behavioral Development (ISSBD), and in recruiting to Penn State faculty members who would crystallize and extend the life-span perspective he was developing.

I was a part of his plan, and I was and am honored by and grateful for the confidence he placed in me. His vision for the field became my vision. I know I took some directions in my work about which he may not have been completely happy. For instance, I don't think he was ever fully comfortable with my thorough rejection of the model of genetic influence found in behavior genetics (e.g., Lerner, 1992, 2002). For example, in a chapter by Baltes, Lindenberger, and Staudinger (2006), in Volume 1 of the sixth edition of the *Handbook of Child Psychology*, which I edited, Paul continued to struggle to find some use for this egregiously conceptually flawed and empirically counterfactual approach to understanding the role of genes within the relational developmental system. Nevertheless, I believe that, in the end, when I last saw him in the summer of 2006 (I visited him in June, in Berlin, and although he was gaunt, ashen, and weak, he still was warm, witty, engaging, and replete with enthusiasm for a new line of work he and former student, Alexandra Freund, were developing on *Sehnsucht*, or life longings), he was proud of my work and of the foundational role he played in shaping it and my career.

From the first days of my arrival at Penn State, Paul helped build my career by opening doors through which I ran with great enthusiasm. For instance, he believed that the model of development I presented in *Concepts and theories* needed to be integrated with a more sophisticated and nuanced understanding of the ecology of individual development, as levels of organization that were constructive parts of the life course. As a relatively traditionally trained developmental psychologist, I had tended in my research to act *as if* the multiple levels of the context were settings within which individual processes of development unfolded. Paul, teaming me with Graham Spanier to hold a conference that would integrate our respective ideas about human development, gave me an intellectual means for beginning to see the ecology of human development not as composed of variables that could be reduced to psychogenic processes but, instead, as part of a dynamic developmental system wherein relations among levels were the basis of developmental change.

Graham and I held a conference at Penn state in April 1977 (a conference that Graham and I began to plan almost as soon as I set foot on campus in the fall of 1976). From that conference the first of three books Graham and I would do together emerged, *Child Influences on Marital and Family Interaction: A Life-Span Perspective* (Lerner &Spanier, 1978). With the publication of this book I announced in print that I was a life-span human developmentalist. This book included a chapter by my mentor, Sam Korn, derived from his work with the NYU psychiatrists, Alexander Thomas and Stella Chess (a chapter co-author), on temperamental individuality in early childhood and its impact on family functioning In addition, the book contained chapters by colleagues who would share with me across subsequent decades a commitment to framing research within theoretical models that underwent various labels, for example, dynamic interaction (Lerner, 1978), contextual dialectic (Lerner, 1982; Lerner & Busch-Rossnagel, 1981), developmental systems (Ford & Lerner, 1992), development contextual (e.g., Lerner, 2002), and now

relational developmental systems (Lerner, 2006; Lerner & Overton, 2008; Overton, 2010, 2011, 2012; Overton & Lerner, 2012; Overton & Mueller, 2012). For instance, chapters by Michael Lewis (and Candice Feiring) and by Michael Lamb were the first steps of collaborations that have lasted, now, more than 30 years.

Graham and I extended our collaboration into bringing a life-span perspective to our respective fields, developmental psychology and family relations, in a textbook we co-authored, *Adolescent Development: A Life-Span Perspective* (Lerner & Spanier, 1980). In addition, since I was a relative novice in the study of adolescent development, Lynn Liben prevailed on her former University of Rochester colleague, David Elkind, to write a foreword for the book. David, who, years later (beginning in 1999) would become my colleague in the Eliot-Pearson Department of Child Development, wrote a generous piece and helped legitimize Graham and me to colleagues in the field of adolescence. The book was well received, both by people in the field of adolescent development and, as well, people who were interested in understanding if the life-span perspective could in fact be used to elucidate periods of ontogeny prior to the adult years. Indeed, one reviewer underscored this relevance by stating that the book could have been titled "The life-span view of human development: The sample case of adolescence." Mission accomplished, in Graham's and my view!

The relational developmental systems model of development involved in both of my first two books with Graham emphasized that the fundamental process of human development involved mutually influential relations between the developing individual and the changing features of his or her multi-level context. This ecology included culture and history and, as such, made sociocultural institutions a part of the basis for all individual behavior and development. This ecology also imbued the role of temporality and of historical events in all levels of organization within which the individual and the context were embedded. As such, the mutual actions of the individual on the context and of the context on the individual (individual $\longleftrightarrow$ context relations) enabled the individual to influence the context (the people and social institutions, such as the family, school, or community) that was influencing him or her. These relations, made the person's location in time and place a critical shaper of the life course (Elder, 1980, 1998; Elder & Shanahan, 2006). Using what I had learned from Paul in regard to field building, I teamed with a singularly impressive graduate student, Nancy Busch-Rossnagel (now Dean of the Graduate School of Fordham University) to edit a book, *Individuals as producers of their development: A life-span perspective* (1981), to bring forward theory and research about the ideas of individual $\longleftrightarrow$ context relations. The book was dedicated to Paul and to John Nesselroade, and included a generous foreword by Bert Brim.

My first years at Penn State were focused not only on research and publications but, as well, on networking. Shortly after I arrived at Penn State, Paul took me out for a drink. He said that a key challenge I had was that very few people knew who I was or what I did. He gave me good advice about how to build a network—advice that I follow to this day and pass on to my own students. Whenever I met someone—at a conference or colloquium, or on a visit to our campus—I followed the meeting with a brief note. I told them that I was glad to have met them and, if I had promised to send along a paper, I enclosed it along with my note. If I had asked for the person to send me something, I told them that I was looking forward to receiving the piece and that I hoped that they would keep me on their mailing list. And, if no exchange of information was involved in our discussion, I simply said that I looked forward to future professional meetings. No matter what the substance of the conversation had been, I sent a follow-up note. Today, with email being a ubiquitous form of communication, these notes are much easier to send than they were in the 1970s. During that time, I typed each letter on my office typewriter and, after typing the envelope as well, I used the U.S. Postal Service to build my professional network.

In early 1979, Paul told me about a summer institute for young scholars that was going to be held at the Center for Advanced Study in the Behavioral Sciences (CASBS), which is located on a hill overlooking the campus of Stanford University in Palo Alto, California. Paul had been a CASBS Fellow the prior year, and had told me how wonderful the place was—in regard to both intellectual stimulation and physical beauty. I was eager to visit there, if only for the 6-week-long period of the workshop. The focus of the summer institute was on morality and moral development. Although my work did not directly pertain to this focus, I was nevertheless selected to participate. Jackie and I drove cross country to get to Palo Alto in time for the start of the workshop, which was led by two former CASBS Fellows, Dennis Krebs, a psychologist who had become devoted to the then still relatively new field of human sociobiology, and Robert Simon, a moral philosopher.

Because many 1978–79 Fellows were still in residence during the summer months encompassing the time of the workshop, workshop participants had to double up in vacant studies. My roommate (in Study 15) was a then social learning theorist, J. Philippe Ruston. Philippe of course became an ardent sociobiologist. Another participant was Anne Colby who, at that time, was Larry Kohlberg's major collaborator. She, and her husband, Bill Damon, and Jackie and I have been close friends and collaborators since this time. Other participants included Dale Miller, Bill Puka, and Nancy Eisenberg. Nancy's mentor, Paul Mussen, although certainly not a young scholar, was a former CASBS Fellow and, because of the topic of the workshop, made the drive from UC Berkeley to Stanford quite often in order to participate in the group's discussions. In effect, he joined Dennis Krebs and Bob Simon in leading the workshop.

Shortly after I returned to Penn State after the end of the workshop, I received a call from the CASBS Director, Gardner Lindzey. Gardner was a giant in the field of psychology, then a living legend. He was a leader in social psychology, the co-author, with Gordon Allport and Phillip Vernon, of the *Study of Values* (1960), and the co-author, with Calvin Hall, of the most important textbook in the area of personality at that time, *Theories of personality* (1957). Gardner told me that the Center was interested in having early career scholars become Fellows and that the summer workshops were one vehicle for identifying suitable young scholars. He told me that the leaders of the workshop had identified me and one other participant (who, I learned later, was Dale Miller) as people suitable to be awarded fellowships. Would I like to come to the CASBS to be a 1980–81 Fellow? Needless to say, I accepted!

My year at the CASBS is a highlight in my career. I was privileged to have in my class Edward (Ned) Jones, Herb Abrams, Dale Miller, Phil Kendall, Art Goldberger, and Hazel Markus, who introduced us to her then boyfriend, Bob Zajonc. Ruth (Toby) Gross was also in my class. She introduced me to her colleague, Iris Litt, who has remained a friend and collaborator since then.

One day at lunch, Toby began to tell me about some new research she had encountered about endorphins. She asked me if I had read about this work. I replied that I was not familiar with the term. Harkening back to the only word I had in my vocabulary that was similar, I asked if the term had anything to do with endomorphs! Patiently, Toby began that day a conversation about brain chemistry that turned into a multi-week, mini-tutorial for me. We delved into both brain structure and function, and I began to see how the work she exposed me to bore directly on the ideas of plasticity that were figuring prominently in my thinking about the relational developmental system and interdependencies among the levels of organization, ranging from the biological through the cultural and historical. Through the catalytic conversations I had had with Toby, an idea for a book about the sources and implications of plasticity began to crystallize. A few years later the book, *On the nature of human plasticity* (1984), was published. Although the data about genetic, brain, behavioral, and contextual plasticity that I reviewed in the book are now out of date, recent research on evolutionary biology, epigenetics, and neuroscience (Lerner & Benson, 2013a, 2013b) provide even stronger support for the main point of the book, that is, that the basic process of human life and development involves mutually influential relations—developmental regulations—between an active individual and his or multilevel and changing context. Simply, as Glen Elder (1998; Elder, Modell, & Parke, 1993) has emphasized, the course of life is composed of the fusion of person, time, and place.

People, time, and place were changing at Penn State as well. Paul Baltes had left the university to join, beginning in 1980 and continuing through his death on November 7, 2006, the Max Planck Institute for Human Development in Berlin, where he served as Director of the Center of

Life-span Psychology. Paul invited me to conferences at the Max Planck. One of the conferences, "Individual Development and Social Change: Explanatory Analysis" (Nesselroade & von Eye, 1985) was chaired by John Nesselroade and a relatively new Ph.D.—Alexander von Eye, who had joined the Max Planck after completing his doctorate with Jochen Brandtstädter. This conference began my career-long collaborations with Alex and with another young developmentalist I met at the conference: Rainer Silbereisen.

The faculty of HDFS were worried, to say the least, that the energy and vision that Paul had provided would be lost. However, the Department prospered, due in large part to the fact that we were able to bring Anne C. Petersen to Penn State as our new chair. I believe that Anne may have been the only person in the world who could succeed Paul Baltes and both solidify and extend the life-span development "brand" and success of the department. Her accomplishments were remarkable. She brought to the Department scholars with expertise in a wider range of disciplines than had been present before (e.g., biology, on the one hand, and anthropology, on the other). She furthered our commitment to diversity, both substantively (e.g., in regard to gender and to racial and ethnic diversity) and in regard to our role in the communities we served. She garnered the attention and admiration of the life-span scholars from around the world by bringing K. Warner Schaie to Penn State to fill the slot that Paul had vacated. She integrated superb developmentalists from other parts of the College, notably Jack Wohlwill, into HDFS. She enhanced the international composition of our faculty and our success at grantsmanship.

I had first met Anne when, in the late 1970s, while serving as a member of the Human Developing and Aging Study Section of NIH, I chaired a site visit team that traveled to Michael Reese Hospital in Chicago and met with Anne and her colleague, Dan Offer. The group was greatly impressed by Anne's work and we recommended with great enthusiasm (and as high a priority score as I have ever seen) that she be funded. We thought we were meeting a scientific star on the rise, and time has proven this impression more than correct. Anne's career has been marked by both singular scholarly leadership in the student of adolescent development around the world and administrative and organizational leadership of key scientific organizations and scholarly associations in the United States and internationally. As did Paul and John, Anne generously gave me numerous opportunities to both advance my work and, in turn, to extend it in new directions.

For instance, with our colleague, Jeanne Brooks-Gunn, we edited what was then the first *Encyclopedia of Adolescence* (Lerner, Petersen, & Brooks-Gunn, 1991) and then, in her role as President of the then relatively new Society for Research in Adolescence (SRA), she named me as the founding Editor of its journal, the *Journal of Research in Adolescence* (*JRA*), which I edited—along with my two co-editors, Doris Entwisle and Stuart T. Hauser—from 1991 through 1996. However, a third opportunity that Anne gave me would be even more career shaping: She gave me the opportunity to become an applied developmental scientist!

In the late 1980s, Fred Vondracek had a beginning-of-the-new-academic-year cocktail party at his home and, not being one to pass up such events, I attended. One of the new assistant professors in the department, Rick Birkel, a clinical child psychologist trained at the University of Virginia, came up to me to chat. I had not had any social contact with Rick up to that point and was surprised when he began the conversation by saying how much my theoretical work had shaped his own ideas about intervention with children and families. I was puzzled, I said, and remember saying to him that I was engaged in theory-predicated basic research and was not interested in applications. Rick then made a bold statement, especially when one recognizes that he was an untenured assistant professor talking to a tenured full professor. He said that I didn't understand the implications of my own theory.

I asked him, in as polite a tone as I could muster, what these implications were. He replied that my ideas about plasticity across the life span, which I believe came about from the interrelations between individuals and their contexts, meant that if one could change those interrelations, one could capitalize on plasticity and promote healthier or more positive development in youth and their families.

After a few moments of reflection I decided that Rick had an important point. "I think you may have something there." Mick Smyer, another clinician in the Department, just happened to be standing a few feet away from Rick and me. I asked him to join our conversation and reiterated the exchange Rick and I just had had. Mick agreed that Rick's idea was good.

I asked if he would like to join Rick and me for coffee sometime soon. Mick agreed, and a few days later we began to meet to talk about Rick's insight. The paper that came out of these conversations, "Applied developmental psychology as an implementation of a life-span view of human development," was published in the *Journal of Applied Developmental Psychology* (Birkel, Lerner, & Smyer, 1989). It marks my first foray in applying developmental theory in the service of promoting positive human development and serves as the intellectual dividing line between all that I was doing before that date and all that has come after it.

However, even with the publication of this paper, I was not certain how I could transform my own career in the direction Rick, Mick, and I outlined in the paper. I was a scholar of child and adolescent development, an expert in the study of youth and families. I guessed that I could contribute not only to better knowledge about youth development but, as well, to using that knowledge to make development better for young people. But I could not figure out how to take this second step. What, precisely, would I do? I did not see a specific pathway forward for me. However, it was Anne who saw opportunities for me to use my new focus to advance scholarship in the study of adolescence.

Celia Fisher of Fordham University and John Murray of Kansas State University had organized a National Task Force in Applied Developmental Science. Representatives from several scholarly organizations were to meet at Fordham's Lincoln Center, New York City campus to define the field of applied developmental science and to formulate guidelines for graduate education in the applications of developmental science across the life span. Organizations sending representatives to the meeting included the American Psychological Association (APA), the Gerontological Society of America (GSA), the International Society for Infant Studies (ISIS), the National Black Child Development Institute, the National Council on Family Relations (NCFR), and the Society for Research in Child Development (SRCD). Anne, as President of the Society for Research on Adolescence (SRA) wanted representation at this meeting and, based on my article with Rick Birkel and Mick Smyer, she appointed me as SRA representative.

This meeting changed my career and life in many ways. Most obviously, it allowed me to be present at the meeting that defined this new area of specialization in developmental science and, as such, to bring the life-span perspective and the ideas about the relational developmental systems-derived conception of plasticity into the discussion. I argued that there was considerable theory-predicated research across the life span indicating that optimism was warranted about the potential to change in positive directions the course of individual $\longleftrightarrow$ context relations. These ideas played a prominent role in the article that derived from the meeting of the task force (Fisher et al., 1993). In addition, this meeting launched what is now a quarter-century-plus collaboration with Celia Fisher. In addition to the 1993 article, we published the first text in the field, *Applied Developmental Psychology* (Fisher & Lerner, 1994) and, later, the first encyclopedia in the field, *Encyclopedia of Applied Developmental Science* (Fisher & Lerner, 2005). Perhaps most important, we launched (with Rich Weinberg) in 1997 a new journal, *Applied Developmental Science*, which Celia and I continue to edit through this writing.

Another way in which the meeting changed my life was meeting Don Wertlieb there. Don, a faculty member in the Eliot-Pearson Department of Child Development at Tufts University, became a strong supporter of the goals of applied developmental science. He noted at the Fordham meeting, and again in a chapter on graduate education in applied developmental science that he wrote with David Henry Feldman (1996), that Eliot-Pearson was already training its graduate students in applied developmental science. Indeed, the doctoral program at Eliot-Pearson was a program in applied child development. Don and I "bonded" at the meeting at Fordham and, a few years later, when, as chair of the Eliot-Pearson Department, he

convinced Drs. Joan and Gary Bergstrom to endow a chair in applied developmental science within Eliot-Pearson, we renewed our relationship.

There was another way that Anne enabled me to bring my interest in the application of developmental science to the study of adolescence, and this instance of her support and mentoring eventually led, about a decade later, to the most important empirical work of my career. Anne was now Dean of the College of Health and Human Development at Penn State, and she had been working with David Hamburg, who was then the President of the Carnegie Corporation of New York, to find a project that would integrate theory-predicated research and application in the study of adolescent development. The project was given the acronym PRIDE: Policy, Research, and Intervention for Enhancing Development in Early Adolescence. Through Anne's vision and leadership, the foundation gave the College a grant for this work, and Anne catalyzed a university-wide effort that involved about 80 scholars, from multiple disciplines across five Penn State colleges and 21 departments to undertake the work of PRIDE. As reflected in the words associated with this acronym, this work involved a coordinated plan of activities involving research (which Anne asked me to lead), the design, delivery, and evaluation of a program of interventions, professional development activities, and policy analysis and engagement (Petersen, 1993). Another product of this project was a book, *Early Adolescence: Perspectives on Research, Policy, and Intervention*, which I edited (Lerner, 1993).

In planning PRIDE, David and Anne had agreed that it would be crucial to gain the cooperation of the 4-H program, which was part of the Penn State College of Agriculture. David noted that the programs that 4-H delivered were not typically based on good developmental research but, nevertheless, the programs of 4-H reached millions of youth across the nation. He and Anne believed that PRIDE was an opportunity to link 4-H programs with a stronger evidence base and, as well, to create a model for 4-H educators to collaborate with scholars from across the university. Fortunately, Wayne Schutjer, the director of 4-H programs at Penn State at the time, agreed completely with the ideas of David and Anne regarding the opportunity for model building that the PRIDE project represented. However, to overcome what had been a long-standing separation between 4-H educators and researchers from outside the College of Agriculture, Wayne though that it would be strategic if I accepted a partial appointment within the 4-H program. Anne agreed, and 10% of my time was supported by the 4-H program in the College of Agriculture. I was the first Penn State faculty member in 20 years with such an appointment.

Anne had another strategic idea. She thought it would be useful to ask Richard (Dick) Sauer, the then President of the National 4-H Council, to serve on the advisory board that she was empanelling for PRIDE. Dick agreed to serve and at meetings of the advisory board that I attended we struck up more than an acquaintance. We became good friends. Dick invited me to visit the National 4-H Council campus, which is located at 7100 Connecticut Avenue in Chevy Chase, Maryland. He thought that the work that I was doing with PRIDE could in fact help 4-H programs across the nation become more attuned to the science of youth development.

On my first visit to Council he introduced me to two people who, through this writing, remain dear friends and close collaborators. Wendy Wheeler was the director of the Innovation Center at National 4-H Council and Dick asked her to work with me in organizing a series of talks about the science of youth development. I would deliver these talks at 4-H state meetings across the United States. Wendy and I launched this work together and, in 1995, it resulted in a book sponsored by National 4-H Council that was published by Sage Publications and distributed to 4-H leaders and programs across the United States.

The second person Dick introduced me to was Don Floyd. Don, it was rumored, was being groomed to succeed Dick as President, when Dick retired (which he planned to do a few years later). As I write this chapter, Don in turn is now planning to retire from the Presidency of National 4-H council in about a year, after more than 15 years of extraordinary, visionary leadership.

My first conversation with Don involved his expression of enthusiasm for the efforts I was making to integrate research about youth development with youth development programs such as 4-H. He said that he believed that researched-based practice must be the standard for youth development programs to prosper in the future. I agreed, and said that I thought that 4-H was uniquely situated to be a model for such practice. He said that he hoped we could work together in this effort. Little did I know that this statement was more than a hope. It was his intention—as I would learn early in 2001.

Through my collaboration with 4-H on the PRIDE project and, then, in the talks about youth development theory, research, and application across the nation that Wendy was organizing for me, my work in the youth development field must have become known to leaders at other land-grant universities. In any case, one morning, Jackie and I were sitting in our living room in State College. We were now living at 124 Sandy Ridge Road, on the corner of Crandall Drive, in a then relatively new subdivision just across Valley Vista Drive and the Park Forest area where we had first lived. We had built this house and it had everything we wanted in a home and, as well, a huge backyard where our three young children had an elaborate swing set and climbing area. They also had great friends and good schools. We also had good friends and superb colleagues, and we were professionally happy. Jackie, who had graduated from Penn State in 1980 with her Ph.D. in Educational Psychology, and had completed a post-doctoral position at Stanford during my year at the CASBS, had been hired into a tenure-track position in HDFS and now, in the spring of 1991, was a tenured associate professor and was planning to go up for full professor the following year.

We also had had great students. For instance, I chaired the doctoral committees of Patricia East, Nancy Galambos, Wendy Gamble, Karen Hooker, Jasna Jovanovic, Lauren Jacobson, Mary Ann Kacergis, Kathleen Lenerz, Patricia Mulkeen, Christine Ohannessian, Marion Palermo, Bernadette Riedy, Jacqueline Schwab, Judy Shea, Gwendolyn Sorell, Rachna Talwar, Jonathan Tubman, and Michael Windle. I had also served on the committees of several other superb developmental scientists, for instance, Nancy Busch-Rossnagel, Roger Dixon, Laura Hess, Margie Lachman, John Schulenberg, Ellen Skinner, and Ron Spiro, to name just a few. Moreover, being at Penn State had given me the opportunity to form close collegial relations with top-tier developmental scientists at the University and many of the leading developmental scientists throughout the United States and in Europe.

So, when the doorbell rang that morning we were not contemplating anything other than our next years at Penn State. The person at the door had a special delivery package for me. It was from Dr. Julia R. Miller, Dean of the College of Human Ecology at Michigan State University. There was a letter, and associated literature, that described a new initiative centered around a revitalization of the College's Institute for Children, Youth and Families, and supported by a large grant from the W. K. Kellogg Foundation. The Institute would lead a university-wide effort to integrate research and programs aimed at enhancing the healthy, positive development of diverse children, adolescents, and families. The 4-H programs at Michigan State would, along with the office of the Vice Provost for University Outreach, work with the Institute to bring faculty and communities together to apply good developmental science to promote positive development. The letter concluded that I had been identified as a person who could lead these efforts and asked that I contact the head of the Search Committee, Associate Dean Mary Andrews, to discuss this invitation to interview for the position.

Jackie and I concluded that it could not hurt to just call Mary Andrews to learn a bit more about this position, which Jackie and I agreed sounded like an exciting opportunity for me to instantiate everything I was writing about and had been working on in the PRIDE project. A few days later I made the call.

Michigan State University

When I called Mary Andrews I learned more about the position of Director of the Institute for Children, Youth, and Families and that, because of the university-wide status of the Institute, I could have tenured appointments in several departments—Family and Child Ecology, in the College of Human Ecology; Psychology, in the College of Social Sciences; Educational Psychology in the College of Education; and Pediatrics and Human Development, in the College of Allopathic Medicine. In addition, I learned that Jackie was in the process of being contacted about coming to Michigan State as a full professor in the Department of Psychology. Both Jackie and I thought that the opportunities for bringing our work to new levels were too attractive to pass up, and so we accepted the offers to move to Michigan State. We arrived in the late summer of 1991.

In addition to the professional opportunities, we liked the idea of moving to a more urban area. Although not a big city, the greater Lansing area, of which East Lansing and the Michigan State campus were parts, had a population of about 400,000, which was about 10 times the size of State College.

I enjoyed enormously my 5 years at Michigan State University (MSU). Although it lives in the shadow of, or at least in constant competition with, the University of Michigan, it is really a unique institution. I have never experienced a university where there is greater evidence for the presence of and commitment to the land-grant spirit, of scholarship in the service of the welfare and positive development of the individuals, families, communities, and businesses of the state. The president of MSU at that time, John DiBiaggio, was a charismatic, visionary leader and his articulation of the land-grant vision was compelling, and infused throughout the institution.

Time and place aligned perfectly for me, therefore, and I approached my leadership of the Institute for Child, Youth, and Families (ICYF) with great enthusiasm. I learned a great deal and had some positive accomplishments. However, one thing I learned was that I am not good at administration. I had wonderful role models and mentors at MSU—chiefly Julia Miller, the Vice Provost for University Outreach, Jim Votruba, and Lou Anna Simon, then the Provost and now the President of MSU. In addition, I had been privileged to work with superb administrators at Penn State—Paul Baltes, Don Ford, Anne Petersen, and Graham Spanier. Nevertheless, my strengths (such as they were) involved scholarly leadership and not administrative skills or creativity. However, with the support of Julia and Jim and, as well, several superb colleagues, for instance, Larry Schiamberg, Hiram (Hi) Fitzgerald, Bob Zucker, Francisco (Chico) Villarruel, Bob Griffore, Tom Luster, Pat Terry, Chuck Ostrom, Marvin McKinney, Harriette and John McAdoo, and Alex von Eye (who left Penn State and joined me at MSU), and several excellent students, Nancy Hill, Domini Castellino, Linda Juang, Melissa Freel, and Daniel Perkins (my one MSU Ph.D., in 1995), we did accomplish a great deal in regard to applied developmental science.

One colleague in particular was a major influence on my thinking and research: Carl Taylor. Carl, a criminologist by training, is one of our nation's leading experts on youth gangs. Carl and I, together with John McAdoo, designed a longitudinal study of strengths and bases of positive development among gang and non-gang involved African American male adolescents living in Detroit. Borrowing a term from the research of Emmy Werner (Werner & Smith, 1992), we termed the study "Overcoming the Odds" and—with generous grants from the William T.

Grant foundation—we launched the study shortly before I left MSU in 1996. Unfortunately, by the time the funding for the project was secured, John had passed away. Carl and I remain grateful for his collaboration, vision, and collegiality. With the brilliant methodological contributions of Alex von Eye, Carl and I were able to transform the interview data that Carl collected into compelling evidence that both the gang and the non-gang involved youth had strengths and resources in their social worlds that, when combined with their individual strengths, provided pathways for their positive development (Lerner, Taylor, & von Eye, 2002; Taylor et al., 2002a, 2002b).

My longitudinal research with Carl was my first empirical exploration of the concept of positive youth development (PYD), an idea I encountered shortly after I arrived at MSU. Jim Votruba told me about a new foundation that has been established by a huge grant (of $60 million) from the W. K. Kellogg Foundation to a person whom, in 1991, I had not yet heard about: Rick Little. With the grant, Rick had launched the International Youth Foundation (IYF), and opened offices for it in Battle Creek, just across the street from the Kellogg foundation. Jim said that a lot of the ideas that Rick Little seemed to be promoting sounded a lot like those I was also discussing, and he urged me to visit Rick.

If there is a dictionary that has the terms "charismatic leader" and "social entrepreneur" in it, then there are no words needed to define these terms. A photo of Rick Little will suffice! When Rick and I met he explained that the goal of IYF was to use its resources to establish what in effect would be partner, community foundations in nations around the world to support the positive development of youth. He also said that he had developed a conception of what positive youth development was, based on his interviews with about 300 scholars and practitioners around the world. He recounted that hundreds of words were used by these people to describe their conception of PYD. However, Rick had been able to coalesce these words into four superordinate terms, each beginning with a "C:" Competence, Confidence, Connection, and Character. Although my training in psychometrics led me to be wary of the validity of any "arm chair factor analysis," Rick's description of the process he undertook to extract these four terms from his interviews was reasonable. In the absence of any empirical work on the concept of PYD, I adopted his Four Cs as a temporary working definition of a concept that I was convinced was predicated on an important and relatively unique strength-based vision of adolescence—instead of a deficit view of the period, which tended to define positive development in youth as the absence of "bad" attributes, such as risk/problem behaviors (e.g., smoking, drinking, unsafe sex, drug use, or bullying).

I saw the real-world applicability of Rick's working definition of PYD when, about a year after my meeting him, the Kellogg Foundation appointed me as one of five consultants to travel to the partner foundations that IYF was establishing, so that we could assess the quality and impact of IYF's efforts to support community-based programs that promoted the Cs. Over the 5 years of this consultantship, I learned an enormous amount of information about the diversity of ways in which people from around the world could effectively pursue efforts to enhance the lives of the young people of their respective nations. As well, I learned that there was a remarkable commonality among youth and adults around the world in their aspirations for health and positive development. The Cs that Rick devised were at a level of abstraction sufficiently general to enable people from around the globe to exchange ideas about and examples of programs promoting PYD.

Accordingly, I saw that Rick's Four Cs provided an important, new vocabulary to talk about this strength-based vision and I left my meeting with him with the intent of "someday" seeing if there was any empirical validity for the Four Cs concept. I also left my meeting with Rick with a key question about the bases of PYD: Given my relational developmental systems perspective, I wondered what individual and ecological variables combined to create the individual ←→ context relations pertinent to the positive development of youth. Dan Perkins led me towards an answer.

Dan came into my office one afternoon and asked me if I had ever heard of someone named Peter Benson and Search Institute. "Yes," I replied, and told Dan about Peter and me being colleagues for a short while at EMU many years before. I also told Dan that I had heard that Peter had left academe and taken a job at a community-based research institute, Search Institute, which had been founded by the Lutheran Brotherhood. However, I admitted, other than for this information, I did not know anything about what either Peter or Search Institute were doing.

Dan explained that Peter was leading Search Institute in survey research that sought to identify the presence in the lives of America's youth of the individual and ecological resources needed for their positive development. Peter termed these resources for healthy behavior and development "developmental assets," and his hypothesis was that if these assets were integrated across the adolescent years, then positive development would occur (Benson, Scales, Hamilton, & Semsa,, 2006; Benson, Scales, & Syvertsen, 2011). Peter had included in the survey that Search was using with large national samples of diverse youth items indexing both individual and ecological assets (eventually 20 in each category) and eight indicators of "thriving," his term for PYD. Dan had gotten the permission of Peter to use the portion of the Search Institute data set derived from Michigan youth, and Dan proposed that he employ this data set in his dissertation. I agreed and, with Alex von Eye as Dan's second advisor, Dan undertook and successfully completed a dissertation describing the presence of developmental assets in the lives of Michigan youth.

The dissertation was also the vehicle for me to become reacquainted with Peter Benson. We had hardly seen each other since our days at EMU but now, in the context of Peter's work on developmental assets and my interest in Rick's ideas about PYD we began to talk, to meet, and to imagine ways we could collaborate. I began to discuss with Peter ways in which research could integrate developmental assets and the "Cs" of positive development.

Although Peter's terms for PYD did not align with those used by Rick Little, I saw that their implicit theoretical model—their theory of change—was identical: If the strengths of youth (their individual developmental assets, in Peter's terms) were integrated across adolescence with ecological assets, then he likelihood of PYD (thriving) would be enhanced. I recognized that this model was consistent with my ideas about individual ←→ context relations and, in particular, about adaptive developmental regulations, being the fundamental process of healthy, positive development. Peter wanted to retain his current focus on surveying American youth in regard to the presence of developmental assets, and so we put on the back burner any plans for a longitudinal study testing the integrative theory of change that I suggested.

Nevertheless, in the mid-1990s I made one attempt to integrate Rick's and Peter's ideas. Peter had organized a meeting in June, 1995 in Aspen, Colorado and he invited several researchers, NGO leaders, and foundation staff to attend. The purpose was to explore and potentially integrate ideas regarding the growing interest in PYD. Although Rick Little was not able to attend the meeting, Karen Pittman, who was then a Vice President at IYF, attended. During the meeting, Karen and I suggested that we should use the concept of PYD, as operationalized by Rick's Four Cs, to speak of the desired outcomes of the presence of developmental assets in the lives of youth. The group liked the idea (although, to be candid, I saw a clear reluctance by Peter to embrace it) but, nevertheless, there was some hemming and hawing among the group. Several participants suggested that something seemed to be omitted from the Cs of competence, confidence, character, and connection. Wasn't there more to positive development than just these four attributes? Since the Cs were at that time just an invention by Rick, I thought I could move the discussion towards consensus regarding the Cs if I took the concerns about something being missing as a "friendly amendment" and invented another C. I had thought for some time that caring, or compassion, was an additional attribute of a positively developing young person. I believed it reflected a concern for the welfare of others, for social justice. I "nominated" caring as the Fifth C.

The group (including Peter) liked the idea, and so we left the Aspen meeting with "Five Cs" now defining the still-to-be-measured concept of PYD. Karen went along with the group, saying only that she would run this new "C" by Rick to see what he thought.

Rick's answer came at the 1996 meeting of SRA. Karen and I were on a symposium together and, during the Q & A session following it, I recounted the story of the bases of the Five Cs. Karen spoke next and she said that

Rick was willing to go along with these Five Cs but, in turn, he had his own friendly amendment to add. As Karen explained it, Rick thought that if a young person was competent, confident, positively connected to others, had good character, and cared about others, then he or she would be motivated, indeed would feel compelled morally and even spiritually, to make a positive difference in his or her family, school, community, and ultimately his or her society. He or she would "Contribute" to making these components of the world better. Rick suggested, then, that a "Sixth C," Contribution, would emerge in a young person who developed high levels of the Five Cs.

I think that everyone in the audience and on the panel during this SRA convention session left with the conviction that there were now six Cs being discussed as part of the PYD perspective that was emerging. This conviction was ideological, and not empirical. Nevertheless, I talked and wrote more and more about both Rick's Cs of PYD and Peter's developmental assets, but recognized that these discussions would remain only useful as conversation points until the longitudinal research needed to test the model was conducted. However, my guess was that the money needed to conduct such research would run into millions of dollars and, I assumed, unless some angel dropped down and made such money available to me, it was not likely that I would be able to conduct the research to match my rhetoric about what was beginning to emerge as the "PYD perspective."

It would be several years before I actually encountered such an angel, in the form of Don Floyd. However, what led me in his direction in regard to this research was a final set of activities in which I was engaged during my time at MSU.

From a relational developmental systems perspective in general, and from the perspective of the burgeoning PYD model I was developing, to best promote positive development all individuals, groups, and institutions in the context should integrate their resources. They should collaborate or form partnerships to promote positive development. This contention is based on the ideas that, if the relations in the developmental system are the bases of human development, then it may be feasible to promote positive development by having individuals and institutions within the system act in a collaborative manner, combining their strengths to enhance the lives of youth.

Although land-grant institutions were developed (through the original Morrill Act of 1862) to be institutions that used their assets and resources to promote positive individual, family, and community development, my MSU colleagues and I were aware that—even with the commitment of our institution to its land-grant roots—we could do more to forge university–community collaborations in support of youth and families. Moreover, across the Big 10 universities there was a growing interest in elevating the scholarship of knowledge application (to use Boyer's, 1990, term) to be as valued and rewarded as other forms of scholarship. However, outreach activities,

including what Julia Miller and I termed "outreach scholarship" (Lerner & Miller, 1998; Miller & Lerner, 1994), remained at the periphery of interest among most faculty members at both land-grant universities and at other public and private universities. Accordingly, and harkening back to my work with the PRIDE project, Lou Anna Simon and I organized conversations and, eventually, an edited book to provide a vision for greater investment by universities and their faculty in community-collaborative, outreach scholarship supporting youth and families (e.g., Lerner & Simon, 1998).

I published several other pieces about outreach scholarship during my time at MSU (e.g., Lerner et al., 1994; Miller & Lerner, 1994; Villarruel & Lerner, 1994) and, through the lectures I gave around the United States that were sponsored by the National 4-H Council, my views about outreach scholarship were apparently becoming known. One morning, sitting in my MSU office, I received a call from Mick Smyer, who was now the Dean of the Graduate School and Associate Vice President for Research at Boston College (BC). As a Jesuit institution, BC was devoted to serving its community through the application of scholarship and the then President of BC, Father J. Donald Monan, wanted to create a center for child, family, and community partnerships. Mick said as well that the School of Education had two openings, one was an endowed chair, the Anita L. Brennan Professor of Education, and the other was for a full professor in the School's Counseling, Developmental, and Educational psychology Department. Mick asked whether Jackie and I would be interested in moving to Boston and take on these positions.

Our children were at an age when moving would be hard, especially for Justin, who was going to be a junior in high school in the fall of 1996. However, living in Boston would place us closer to both Jackie's family, in Queens and New Jersey, and my mom, in Brooklyn. In addition, once again, the professional opportunities seemed too good to not consider. We visited BC twice before we accepted the positions. With the complaints of our children persisting unabated, we nevertheless moved to Boston in the summer of 1996.

Boston College

My move to the Boston area and to BC was nothing like I had anticipated. In many ways, this move was the most disastrous step in my personal and professional life. After several house hunting trips to the Boston area, Jackie and I decided that Wayland, a town about 18 miles west of Boston, provided the two things we needed for our family: Good schools (as I noted, Justin was going into his junior year of high school, and Blair was going to start high school, while Jarrett was going into 4th grade) and a house that we could afford. However, we learned that afford in the Boston area meant "barely afford."

In addition, the allergens in Boston were different than those in Pennsylvania and Michigan. Jackie developed allergies that changed her voice completely (she recovered eventually, after about a year). In turn, it took several months for the Executive Vice President at BC, Frank Campanella, to allocate the money to order furniture for my office or to put on the BC payroll the staff or graduate student I had offered positions to. Although they tried to help, neither Mick, by then a new Dean, Mary Brabeck, nor the Academic Vice President, Father Bill Neenan, were able to expedite this paperwork and so, for the first few months of my time at BC I worked at a makeshift desk and with a borrowed computer.

My Overcoming the Odds grant with Carl Taylor, and another grant that I was negotiating with the Jacobs Foundation, to support training doctoral students from developing nations in my lab and then having them bring applied developmental science back to either their countries or to other European, Asian, etc. countries, were the bright spots in my scholarly life. These activities kept me moving forward during this stressful time. I also had some wonderful colleagues at BC who were supportive of my work—for instance, Penny Hauser-Cram, Maureen Kenny, Liz Sparks, Brinton Lykes, Mary Walsh, and Ellen Winner, as well as Mick Smyer and Mary Brabeck and a few terrific students—Imma DeStefanis, Selcuk Sirin, Kim Howard, Laurie McCubbin, and Katie Barton.

With these BC colleagues and students and, as well, with my collaborators across the United States and internationally, I was able to remain fairly productive. For instance, I completed my work editing Volume 1, *Theoretical models of human development* (Lerner, 1998), of the 5th edition of the *Handbook of Child Psychology*, for which Bill Damon provided overall editorial leadership (Damon, 1998). In addition, Liz Sparks, Laurie McCubbin, and I wrote a book, *Family diversity and family policy: Strengthening families for America's children* (Lerner, Sparks, & McCubbin, 1999), that extended my ideas about the application of developmental science to family policy. Jochen Brandtstädter and I (Brandtstädter & Lerner, 1999) edited a book that brought together an international group of scholars to present theory and research pertinent to different action theoretical models of individual ←→ context relations. In addition, Jackie and I, joined by several of our former doctoral students—Domini Castellino, Laurie Hess, Jasna Jovanovic, Chris Ohannessian, and Dan Perkins—put together a set of six books of readings, each pertinent to a different substantive area within the study of adolescent development (e.g., Lerner & Lerner, 1999). Yet, despite this productivity, I was unhappy. The institutional support I needed to build a strong laboratory focusing on the application of developmental science pertinent to the positive development of youth was just not present.

Nevertheless, Bill Neenan tried to make me happy. He prompted the BC magazine to do a feature story about my work and, as well, he always made a point of inviting me to the numerous social events held at the university. However, one day, this generosity took a wrong turn. Bill introduced me to a guest as "Rich Lerner, our Jewish endowed professor." I was taken aback. When I reminded him that I was not a professor of theology but a member of the School of Education faculty, he said he of course knew that fact. However, his slip of the tongue crystallized that I was a "stranger in a strange land" and that I needed to find a new academic home.

However, Jackie was prospering in the Department and our children, after an initial period of intense animosity towards Jackie and me (mostly me) for taking them away from their Michigan friends, were thriving, and enjoying their new lives in Wayland. Even Justin decided that he loved living in Boston. Accordingly when, early in my second year at BC, I received a call from Don Wertlieb, telling me that Eliot-Pearson was launching a search for the Bergstrom Chair in Applied Developmental Science and asking me if I was interested in applying, I said no. I said that I was not happy at BC but that I did not want to leave it just yet. I felt that I needed more time to try to fit in before I left. I told Don that I thought my colleague, Marc Bornstein, who had grown up in Boston, would be a terrific candidate for the Bergstrom Chair. I urged them to pursue him.

They did. Eventually, Marc was offered the job. However, for several reasons he turned it down and so, early in my third year at BC (the 1998–99 academic year), I received another call from Don. Joan Bergstrom was growing impatient with the Eliot-Pearson Department. If they did not fill the position soon, she said she might withdraw her money. She urged the Department, and the co-chairs of the search committee, Fred Rothbaum and Jayanthi Mistry, to re-contact me and "make me an offer I could not refuse." By this time, I could not find a way to reconcile saying no to exploring an opportunity to leave BC but to stay in Boston. Had Jackie and the children not been doing so well I might have tried to return to Michigan State. However, I did admire the Eliot-Pearson Department and Tufts University. In addition, John DiBiaggio had left Michigan State and was now the President of Tufts. I imagined that my goals in applied developmental science would not only mesh with the faculty and students of Eliot-Pearson but, as well, might fit with John's interests in university–community collaboration.

In December, 1998 I interviewed at Eliot-Pearson. I thought the day went very well. I enjoyed my meetings with faculty, students, and staff and, as well, I thought my colloquium was well received. After the day ended, the search committee took me to dinner at the Rialto Restaurant in the Charles Hotel in Cambridge. Joan Bergstrom joined the group for dinner. Joan had been an Eliot-Pearson undergraduate student, and she then went on to get her doctorate in education from the University of Massachusetts-Amherst. She was a professor at Wheelock College and, as well, a businesswoman and entrepreneur. Joan founded two Massachusetts companies that developed curriculum and educational materials for children's out-of-school-time activities, "Children's Out-of-School Time" and "The

Activities Club." She also was the co-founder of Workplace Connections, which creates family friendly programs and promotes child-care settings in the workplace. In addition, Joan founded the Center for International Education, Leadership, and Innovation at Wheelock, through which she coordinated the college's international programs. I sat next to her at dinner and although I am certain we all talked with all the other people at the dinner table, I can only recall my conversation with Joan. She was incredibly smart, engaging, and warm.

At the end of the evening I stood up to leave (since I was a local, I had brought my own car to the restaurant). Joan excused herself as well, telling the rest of the group that she would walk me to the door and then return. When I got to the door with her I discovered another of her attributes that I admired. She was open and direct. There were no hidden agendas with her. She asked me if I would take the job if it was offered to me.

I could have replied with a statement that would have given me plenty of wiggle room, for instance, "Well it depends on the details of the offer," or some statement like that. Instead, I said, "Yes, if I can count on you to help me succeed." "Yes," she said. "You can." She was true to her word. She remained my chief collaborator, supporter, and mentor through her untimely death on April 6, 2010 at the age of 69.

A few days later, I received a call from the then Chair of the Eliot-Pearson Department, Francine Jacobs. I was offered the job. After a brief conversation with the then Dean of the School of Arts and Sciences, Susan Ernst, the details of the offer were finalized. I left BC in August, 1999 and moved across the Charles River to Tufts University. For the first time since 1977, when Jackie came to Penn State as a doctoral student, she and I were no longer associated with the same university. Through this writing she has remained at BC and I am completing my 14th year at Tufts.

Tufts University

Fran Jacobs, Don Wertlieb, David Henry Feldman, Fred Rothbaum, Maryanne Wolf, Ann Easterbrooks, Jayanthi Mistry, David Elkind, Kate Camara, Calvin (Chip) Gidney, Sylvia Feinberg, and George Scarlett, now my new colleagues in the Eliot-Pearson Department of Child Development, were warm, supportive, and incredibly welcoming. In fact, the collegiality and sense of common purpose within Eliot-Pearson reminded me a great deal of the HDFS Department at Penn State. I felt I was at home!

I brought two grants with me to Tufts. One was the W. T. Grant Foundation-supported "Overcoming the Odds" project with Carl Taylor and the other was the Jacobs Foundation-supported project allowing me to recruit international students for training in my lab, which was located just a few hundred yards down the street from the Eliot-Pearson Building.

Since doctoral students are recruited in the early months of a calendar year in order to begin their training in the late summer/early fall of the year, I had not been a Tufts faculty member when student selections were made. I had money to support several research assistants, but I did not have any people to place into the positions. Fran Jacobs came to the rescue. She said that there were two students who had been admitted to the master's program but whom she believed could become doctoral students if they were appropriately mentored. One student was from Bosnia—Aida Bilalbecovic—and the other was from Boston (and a former Tufts undergraduate)—Deborah (Deb) Sadowski. They were both quite impressive.

Aida had been a third-year medical student in Bosnia when the dangers of ethnic cleansing led her and her brother to flee to the United States. (Her parents remained in Bosnia and survived.) Somehow, Aida ended up in Iowa as a refugee with no proof of her academic credentials. She started college all over again (and graduated from Coe College), and was now beginning her master's program at Tufts.

Deb had left Tufts for a career in the business world and had become a Certified Financial Analyst (CFA). However, as a Tufts' triple major—in Child Development, Psychology, and Spanish—she wanted to return to the academic world and had enrolled in the master's program as a start.

Neither Aida nor Deb knew me or had heard anything about me. However, they were both eager to gain research experience and, after I told them about my current work and my plans, they signed on. Aida and Deb became my first two research assistant at Tufts.

They were soon joined by Elizabeth Dowling and Pam Anderson. Elizabeth was actually a Ph.D. student but, after being admitted to the Eliot-Pearson doctoral program on the basis of her interest in early childhood education (she was a former kindergarten teacher) she decided that her interests were actually more aligned with my interests in promoting positive development among diverse youth. She was intrigued by the Overcoming the Odds project and so she too joined my group. Pam's story was a bit different. She was not certain that she wanted to get a Ph.D., but she was certain that she wanted to use her knowledge and skills in studying child development to work in community settings or programs aimed at enhancing the lives of diverse youth. My interests in applied developmental science attracted her to my lab and so she joined Aida, Deb, and Elizabeth.

As my lab was getting organized, Joan, as well as her husband, Dr. Gary Bergstrom, an MIT-trained economist and the founder of Acadian Asset Management, a Boston-based investment management company which, in the 1980s, began with zero assets and now manages over $65 billion for clients from over 20 countries, got busy introducing me to their friends in the greater Boston area. They also welcomed Jackie and me into this network, as friends as well as professional colleagues. Joan and Gary wanted their friends to know about the work that I was conducting and planned to conduct at Tufts and to have them join in the

Bergstroms' efforts to support my lab. Towards the end of my second year at Tufts, Gary suggested that it would be more attractive for people to support an academic entity that had a name that was catchier than "Rich's lab." Although I thought that I was through with heading institutes or centers (given my experiences at both Michigan State and Boston College), I suddenly found myself the director of the Applied Developmental Science Institute (ADSI) at Tufts. Neither the acronym nor the full name of the lab had meaning to most people encountering these terms. In addition, both Joan and Gary felt that a name was needed that reflected what I actually did as a scholar, and applied developmental science was just too vague.

Gary came up with a name: The Institute for Applied Research in Youth Development. I loved it, and so did other people, both at Tufts and in the community—although the acronym for the institute (IARYD) was meaningless and hard to say. In any event, I was now the Director of this Institute but, to anyone who would listen beyond my telling them the tag line for the institute—"We seek to find out what goes right in the lives of youth"—I explained that this entity was just another name for Rich's lab.

However, whether an institute or a lab, we were growing exponentially, for reasons I will explain next. I needed someone to help me manage the business end of the lab and, Deb, who had finished her master's degree and was now married (to Scott Bobek), had just the right set of knowledge and skills to be the Managing Director of the Institute. She knew the literature of developmental science and, especially, the literature from which I drew my ideas. She knew business. She knew Tufts. And she knew how to manage me! So, with Deb Bobek as my partner ADSI became IARYD and we set upon a path that involved conducting longitudinal research pertinent to the positive development of diverse youth.

Why were we growing so quickly? The answer begins with a phone call I received from Don Floyd late in 2000. As best as I can remember this call, it involved Don asking me how much would it cost to do a study of positive youth development. I told Don I could not give him an amount without knowing the question about positive youth development he wanted to address, how PYD would be measured, how many youth were going to be studied, how old they would be, where and how the sample would be obtained, how many times they would be measured, and what else would be measured. However, Don did not want to get into these details and asked me to give him a number.

"Okay. A million dollars!" I pulled this number out of the air.

"Great. That's all I needed," Don said. "Speak to you later." He hung up.

Then, about 6 months later, I received another call from Don. He said, "Hi Rich. Great news. I got you the money. In fact, I got you a bit more. I was able to get $1.3 million!"

I did not immediately remember Don's earlier call. "What money?," I said.

"Don't you remember?," he asked. "For the study of positive youth development. I got you $1.3 million from Phillip Morris. When can you get started?"

Looking back, both Don and I agree that it would have been much better for the design and launch of the study if we had taken a more conventional route to proposing and reviewing the ideas for the study. However, Don "wanted to strike while the iron was hot," and thought it best to capitalize on the enthusiasm by the leadership of the Philip Morris smoking prevention group for the idea of the study. In turn, since the generous funding that Don and Philip Morris, which evolved into the Altria Corporation, provided only supported the pilot year of work and the first two waves of what became an eight-wave longitudinal study, the subsequent funding we received was vetted in more conventional ways. Moreover, in addition to these reviews for continuation funding that, eventually, totaled about $7 million in direct costs, we empanelled a group of advisors that provided continual input about and evaluation of our work.

Over the years, the composition of this board changed. However, Alex von Eye, of Michigan State, generously served as chair of the group across the more than 10 years of work associated with the project. Other members of the Board were Dale Blyth, University of Minnesota, Lynne Borden, University of Arizona, Connie Flanagan, then of Penn State and now of the University of Wisconsin, Suzanne LeMenestrel, U.S. Department of Agriculture (and a Penn State doctoral student during Jackie's and my time at Penn State), Daniel Perkins, who, after graduation from Michigan State, became a professor at Penn State (where Jackie and I first met him as an undergraduate student), Mike Rovine, also of Penn State, and Linda Jo Turner, of the University of Missouri and also the National 4-H Council. Therefore, our Board reflected Jackie's and my roots in land-grant universities. Although only a small proportion of the participants in the study, which would eventually include 7,000 youth from 42 states, had ever participated in 4-H, we wanted to be certain that the perspective of the land-grant system of 4-H had voice in the study. Don wanted the study to be about the youth of America and not only about 4-H youth. The only stipulation he put on the conduct of the study was that I, as PI—and eventually Jackie as well, who, after the pilot year of the project, joined the project as its Scientific Director—do the best work we were capable of doing. Don never asked anything of us other than this devotion to good science and, insofar as information that might be learned, good or bad about the impact of participation in 4-H on PYD, he maintained the view—to all the constituencies he served and, as well, to the folks at Altria—that he could learn something valuable from the findings, no matter what they were. In my experience, his vision and integrity are singular and, coupled with the generosity and commitment to the vision for the project that the people of Altria (for instance, Jennifer Hunter, Megan Witherspoon, and Ed Largo) shared with Don, the support for conducting good science that Jackie and I received was extraordinary.

To launch the study, Don, Alex von Eye, and I thought it would be useful to have a face-to-face meeting of the Advisory Board and the team I was assembling at Tufts. Our agenda was to finalize the plans for the design of the study and the measurement model that we had been discussing through email. We met at the National 4-H Council on September 10, 2001. It was a beautiful day in the greater Washington, D.C. area, mild, bright, and sunny, without a cloud in the sky. The next day promised to equally as clear and mild and so, although I flew back to Boston's Logan Airport that evening, some of the colleagues attending the meeting decided to stay in D.C. for one more day and then return home on the evening of September 11, 2001.

Of course they never were able to fly out of D.C. on that day that everything changed for America and, arguably, the world. However, then, and now, I see the fact that I was given the opportunity to conduct a study that sought to measure and identify the possible bases of positive development among the diverse youth of the United States as a serendipitous but somehow very appropriate project to have evolved out of a meeting framed by one of the most negative experiences in the history of the children, youth, families, and communities of America.

For much of my time at Tufts, the conduct of the 4-H Study occupied a huge share of my professional life, at least insofar as my empirical work was concerned. Jackie and I were blessed by smart and creative students who either carved their Ph.D. research from the measurement model of the study, added new variables to it, or—even if their dissertation work pertained to other projects ongoing in the Institute—nevertheless contributed to the quality and productivity of the project. Each of my four original graduate research assistants—Pam Anderson, Aida Bilalbegovic (now Balsano), Elizabeth Dowling, and Deb Bobek, who completed her doctorate while also serving as the Managing Director of the Institute—worked on the 4-H project, as did Michelle Boyd, Aerika Brittian, Kristen Fay, Steinunn Gestsdóttir, Helena Jelicic, Sonia Koshy, Yibing Li, Alicia Lynch, Lang Ma, Sophie Naudeau, Christina Theokas, and Amy E. Alberts Warren. At this writing, three other students—Kristina Schmid Callina, Megan Kiely Mueller, and Christopher Napolitano—will be completing their Ph.D. degrees in 2013 using at least part of the 4-H Study data set as a basis for their dissertations.

A key reason that the 4-H Study, and the other projects in the lab, were so productive—the 4-H Study alone has resulted in more than 100 publications at this writing—was that the students and I had exceptional colleagues in the Institute. After she completed her doctorate, Deb Bobek left the lab, and became Director of Visitor Education in the New England Aquarium in Boston. She was succeeded by Heidi Johnson, who has been both an administrative leader and a source of wisdom about the nature of grantsmanship and academic life. I have had a series of three superb assistants, Holly Maynard, Nancy Pare, and Dee Pratti and, in turn, I have had several wonderful people serve as the Managing

Editor of the Editorial Office of the Institute: Lisa DeFonzo, Jennifer Davison, Lauren White, Leslie Dickenson, and, at this writing, Jarrett Lerner (my son).

Undoubtedly, however, a key to the scholarly success of the Institute was Erin Phelps. I had been a friend of Erin's for decades and, in 2004, she left the Murray Research Center at Radcliffe College to join me in directing IARYD. Until June, 2009, when Erin had to leave Tufts permanently because of her worsening medical condition, we worked together on the 4-H Study, co-authored several scholarly publications, and—most important to both of us—shared in the training of the incredibly talented doctoral students that I have explained were vital parts of the work of the lab. Erin also joined several other colleagues and me from across the United States in organizing the Society for the Study of Human Development (SSHD), which is an organization predicated on adopting a lifespan/life-course approach to the study of human development. Erin served as its first Executive Secretary and then became the Editor of its flagship journal, *Research in Human Development* (*RHD*). Erin stepped down from her editorship when she left the Institute. She passed away on February 16, 2012.

One of the many great contributions that Erin made to the Institute was helping us diversify our "portfolio" of grants. Erin was instrumental in our successfully receiving our first grant from the John Templeton Foundation (JTF). In many ways, the now several projects in the Institute that have been, and at this writing are, supported by JTF represent a significant but theoretically predicated evolution of the work we had undertaken in the 4-H Study.

As I have explained, the theory of change tested in the 4-H Study specified that when the strengths of youth were aligned with the ecological assets in their lives, then PYD, marked by the Five Cs, would develop and that, in turn, when these Cs developed, youth would become Contributors to their social worlds (the "Sixth C" of PYD, based on Rick Little's "hypothesis") and, as well, the likelihood of engagement in problem/risk behaviors would decrease (J. Lerner et al., 2012; Lerner, Almerigi, Theokas, & Lerner, 2005; Lerner, von Eye, & Lewin-Bizan, 2009; Lerner, von Eye, Lerner, Lewin-Bizan, & Bowers, 2010, Lerner et al., 2011; Lerner, Lerner, & Benson, 2011). Our 4-H research had found that there was good empirical evidence for the measurement of PYD as indexed by the Five Cs and that, as well, PYD predicted, both within and across the years of adolescence, Contribution (or, among older youth, a more differentiated construct, Active and Engaged Citizenship [AEC]). Moreover, this research has found that these links between PYD, Contribution (or AEC) and risk/problem behaviors were maximized when, as predicted, the internal strengths of youth were aligned with ecological resources, such as (indices of) authoritative parenting, mentoring, or participation in youth development programs (such as 4-H, Scouting, Boys & Girls Clubs, YMCA, or Big Brothers/Big Sisters). The strengths of youth, their "internal developmental assets" in the terms of Peter Benson (Benson, Scales, Hamilton, & Semsa, 2006; Benson, Scales, & Syvertsen, 2011), included the intentional self-regulation (ISR) attributes of selection, optimization, and compensation that I discussed earlier (Freund & Baltes, 2002; Gestdóttir & Lerner, 2008) and, as well, constructs such as hope for the future (Schmid et al., 2011), school engagement (a context-specific ISR construct, in our view; Li & Lerner, 2011), and spirituality.

As explained by Pamela Ebstyne King (2012; King, Carr, & Boitor,, 2011), spirituality is a construct that involves cognitions and feelings associated with the idea of transcendence, of wanting to "go beyond the self," to invest yourself in an ideology (e.g., a religious institution) or a cause (e.g., protecting the ecology) that allowed you to pursue a meaningful, positive purpose in life (Damon, Menon, & Bronk, 2003), to "plant trees under whose shade you would never sit." With such a conception of spirituality, it was clear to us that a next step in our PYD research would be to ascertain the links between the orientation towards Contribution and youth spirituality. Indeed, in all the talks I had heard Rick Little give about the spark that would put young people on a life journey that would be marked by healthy and positive development, he had pointed to the very variable that I was now setting out to study: spirituality. Therefore, once again, it seemed that my research career could be fairly characterized by one in which I was merely attaching numbers to Rick Little's great ideas.

Erin and I believed that this research idea would be of interest to JTF, given the emphasis that Sir John Templeton had placed on discovering new spiritual realities in life. In addition, we were interested in ascertaining the links among spirituality, PYD, Contribution (or generosity, in the terms preferred by JTF), and the other youth strengths that we studied—and in particular ISR. We thought that ISR would be of particular interest to the Foundation in that Sir John presaged much of the contemporary interest within developmental science in self-regulation (e.g., see Geldhof, Little, & Colombo, 2010). Indeed, in summarizing his ideas about self-regulation or self-control, Sir John (2012) had noted that when one rules one's mind, then one rules one's world.

I had learned of the John Templeton Foundation through Peter Benson and Bill Damon, who were both members of the JTF Board of Advisors. They told the Vice President of the Foundation, Dr. Arthur Schwartz, that my work would be of interest to JTF. Arthur invited me to be a guest at a JTF Board meeting that was held in Palo Alto. We "clicked" at the meeting and soon afterword Arthur nominated me to Sir John and to Foundation President John M. (Jack) Templeton, Jr. to serve on the Board. Sir John and Jack approved my nomination and I joined the board the following year, for my first of two 3-year terms of service on the Board.

In a subsequent meeting with Arthur, I told him about the idea I had for a study of PYD and spirituality, and he liked it. With his guidance, I obtained a grant, "The role of spiritual development in growth of purpose, generosity, and psychological health in adolescence." The three years in which we undertook this project resulted in our being able to build a network of senior and junior scholars interested in the spirituality–PYD relations. For example, among the senior scholars we involved in this project were Jeff Arnett, Marina Bers, Bill Damon, Jacque Eccles, David Henry Feldman, Elena Grigorenko, Lene Jensen, Carl Johnson, Palema Ebstyle King, Sara Lazar, Ofra Mayseless, Tomas Paus, Rob Roeser, George Scarlett, Lonnie Sherrod, Carola Suarez-Orozco, Margaret Beale Spencer, and Wei Zhang. Some of the then junior scholars who participated in the project were Jenni Menon Mariano, Na'ilah Nasir, Guerda Nicolas, Selcuk Sirin, and Heather Urry. In addition to several pilot studies that were derived from the project and, as well, three dissertations—by Mona Abo-Zena, Sonia Koshy, and Amy Warren—there were two books (Lerner, Roeser, & Phelps, 2008; Warren, Lerner, & Phelps, 2012). In the first book, which was dedicated to Sir John, Peter Benson wrote the foreword and Bill Damon contributed a chapter (with Jenni Menon Mariano). In the second book, also dedicated to Sir John, Rick Little wrote the foreword and Pam King wrote the afterword.

One of the several things I learned from my work on this JTF-supported project was that some of the key constructs within the PYD model were identical to the attributes of character of central concern to Sir John—for example, attributes such as diligence, entrepreneurship, future mindedness, generosity, and purpose. Accordingly, in the past several years Jack Templeton, and the superb group of Vice Presidents and Program Directors he has assembled—for instance, Mike Murray, Barnaby Marsh, Kimon Sargeant, Daniel Green, Sarah Hertzog, and in particular Craig Joseph—have generously supported the work of the Institute, to pursue in several different projects the nature and bases of character development and, in particular, the formal and informal educational experiences that may promote it.

For instance, in collaboration with Bill Damon, Anne Colby, and the Stanford Center for Adolescence that Bill directs, we are conducting the first-ever longitudinal study of the individual and ecological bases of the development of entrepreneurship in late adolescence and young adulthood. In addition, we are studying the way in which the Williamson School, a 3-year junior college in Media, PA, fosters among deserving but socioeconomically disadvantaged young men the values of faith, integrity, diligence, excellence, and service, character attributes that correspond with many of those included by Sir John in the JTF charter (e.g., diligence, future mindedness, generosity, and honesty). Although most educational programs focus separately on either character, moral, or civic education, the Williamson Schools is one prominent exception, and we seek to determine if its educational model has the potential to have a positive enduring impact on socioeconomic sectors of our society often bereft of hope and positive purpose. In addition, we are collaborating with the Cradle of Liberty Council of the Boy Scouts of America to assess if and how their model of youth programming enhances the character development, the academic attainments, and the community contributions of participating youth.

As I indicated earlier, one facet of the work we have been doing with JTF that reflects the wisdom of Sir John regarding controlling one's mind involves our research on ISR as a key strength of youth. With the collaboration of Craig Joseph, we have been able to disseminate our findings regarding intentional self-regulation, and this dissemination has attracted the interest of other funders. For instance, we have been able to garner support from the Thrive Foundation for Youth, a Palo Alto Foundation created through the philanthropy of Bob and Dottie King and their family, to translate our findings about the role the ISR attributes of selection, optimization, and compensation in promoting PYD into tools for mentors in youth development programs to use to enhance both intentional self-regulation and positive development among their program participants. In a project led by my colleague, Dr. Ed Bowers, we have been able to develop rubrics for both the attributes of ISR and PYD that we study, and these materials, as well as guide books for mentors and videos illustrating the successful use of ISR skills in the lives of diverse youth, have been validated as useful for the enhancement of positive behaviors among youth participating in different youth-serving organizations.

Of course, collecting data from the conduct of grant-supported research would not be able to continue unless the Institute was able to publish the results of its work. Over the almost 14 years I have completed at Tufts, the colleagues, students, and staff have been superb collaborators in such dissemination. Since 1999, when I arrived at Tufts, the Institute has produced more than 350 publications, including books, chapters, and articles. In addition, we have made more than 150 scholarly presentations at conferences, workshops, and colloquia.

One instance of this dissemination in which I have been particularly privileged to participate involves editing some of the key handbooks in developmental science. In 2006 Bill Damon and I collaborated, as co-Editors-in-Chief, in the four-volume 6th edition of the *Handbook of Child Psychology* (Damon & Lerner, 2006). In addition, Larry Steinberg and I collaborated to edit both the second and the third editions of the *Handbook of Adolescent Psychology* (Lerner & Steinberg, 2004, 2009). In turn, Fran Jacobs, Don Wertlieb, and I collaborated in editing the four-volume *Handbook of Applied Developmental Science: Promoting positive child, adolescent, and family development through research, policies, and programs* (Lerner, Jacobs, & Wertlieb, 2003). In 2010, I was also Editor-in-Chief of the two-volume *Handbook of Life-Span Development* (Lerner, 2010). The volume editor for the first volume of this work was Bill Overton, and the volume editors for the second volume were Michael Lamb and Alexandra Freund. In 2010, I also co-edited a handbook produced in memory of the late Gilbert Gottlieb, *The Handbook of Developmental Science, Behavior and Genetics* (Hood, Halpern, Greenberg, & Lerner, 2010).

Finally, as I complete this chapter and the book it is in, I am also completing my co-editing of the *Handbook of Developmental Systems Theory and Methodology* (Molenaar, Newell, & Lerner in press). With both of these projects are in press, I will turn my attention to what I suspect may be my last major edited work. I will be Editor-in-Chief of the four-volume, 7th edition of the *Handbook of Child Psychology*. However, I have elected to rename the work the *Handbook of Child Psychology and Developmental Science*. With my volume editors, Bill Overton and Peter Molenaar (Vol. 1), Lynn Liben and Ulrich Mueller (Vol. 2), Michael Lamb and Cynthia Garcia Coll (Vol. 3), and Marc Bornstein and Tama Leventhal (Vol. 4), I hope to frame the work presented in the 7th edition within a relational developmental systems, life-span perspective.

After all, all those years ago Paul Baltes wrote down on a blackboard that, although I studied children and adolescents, I was a life-span developmentalist. I have done pretty well so far in following Paul's advice, and so I think I will keep at it at least one more time.

Conclusions

I have been incredibly fortunate in meeting the right people at the right time and in the right places. I have had wonderful role models and mentors, superb colleagues and students, and dedicated and creative staff. I owe them so much. Without them I would not have the opportunity to tell my story in this book.

I also have a wonderful family. Most of all I have a wonderful wife. She has been my muse, my chief collaborator, and my truest friend. Without Jackie Lerner there would be no Richard Lerner of any note.

Now that I am approaching my 67th birthday, people are asking me more and more often if I plan to retire. My answer is a simple no. I cannot imagine spending my time doing anything I love more than teaching and research. As long as I am capable of doing a good job, I will keep going. Jackie and our children would, in any event, be the first to tell me if I was not up to the task any longer. Besides, Jackie has said repeatedly "For better and for worse, but not for lunch." I better stay at my lab, then. I want to keep her happy so that she'll keep me around.

Acknowledgment

The preparation of this chapter was supported in part by grants from the John Templeton Foundation, the National 4-H Council, and the Thrive Foundation for Youth.

References

Adams, J. F. (Ed.). (1968). *Understanding adolescence: Current developments in adolescent psychology.* Boston: Allyn & Bacon.

Allport, G. W. Vernon, P. E., & Lindzey, G. (1960). *Study of values.* Oxford: Houghton Mifflin.

Anastasi, A. (1958). Heredity, environment, and the question "how?" *Psychological Review, 65,* 197–208.

Baltes, P. B. (1983). Life-span developmental psychology: Observations on history and theory revisited. In R. M. Lerner (Ed.), *Developmental psychology: Historical and philosophical perspectives* (pp. 79–111). Hillsdale, NJ: Erlbaum.

Baltes, P. B., & Baltes, M. M. (1990). Psychological perspectives on successful aging: The model of selective optimization with compensation. In P. B. Baltes & M. M. Baltes (Eds.), *Successful aging: Perspectives from the behavioral sciences* (pp. 1–34). New York: Cambridge University Press.

Baltes, P. B., Lindenberger, U., & Staudinger, U. M. (2006). Life span theory in developmental psychology. In R. M. Lerner (Ed.), *Theoretical models of human development,* Vol. 1 of *Handbook of child psychology* (6th ed., pp. 569–664). Editors-in-chief: W. Damon & R. M. Lerner. Hoboken, NJ: Wiley.

Benson, P. L., Karabenick, S. A., & Lerner, R. M. (1976). Pretty pleases: The effects of physical attractiveness, race, and sex on receiving help. *Journal of Experimental Social Psychology, 12,* 409–415.

Benson, P. L., Scales, P. C., Hamilton, S. F., & Semsa, A., Jr. (2006). Positive youth development: Theory, research, and applications. In R. M. Lerner (Ed.), *Theoretical models of human development,* Vol. 1 of *Handbook of child psychology* (6th ed., pp. 894–941). Editors-in-chief: W. Damon & R. M. Lerner. Hoboken, NJ: Wiley.

Benson, P. L., Scales, P. C., & Syvertsen, A. K. (2011). The contribution of the developmental assets framework to positive youth development theory and practice. In R. M. Lerner, J. V. Lerner, & J. B. Benson (Eds.), *Advances in Child Development and Behavior, 41,* 195–228.

Birkel, R., Lerner, R. M., & Smyer, M. A. (1989). Applied developmental psychology as an implementation of a life-span view of human development. *Journal of Applied Developmental Psychology, 10,* 425–445.

Boyer, E. L. (1990). *Scholarship reconsidered: Priorities of the professoriate.* Princeton, NJ: The Carnegie Foundation for the Advancement of Teaching.

Brandtstädter, J. (1998). Action perspectives on human development. In R. M. Lerner (Ed.), *Theoretical models of human development,* Vol. 1 of *Handbook of child psychology* (5th ed., pp. 807–863). Editor-in-chief: W. Damon. New York: Wiley.

Brandtstädter, J. (1999). The self in action and development: Cultural, biosocial, and onotgenetic bases of intentional self-development. In J. Brandtstädter & R. M. Lerner (Eds.), *Action and self-development: Theory and research through the life-span* (pp. 37–65). Thousand Oaks, CA: Sage.

Brandtstädter, J. (2006). Action perspectives on human development. In R. M. Lerner (Ed.). *Theoretical models of human development,* Vol. 1 of *Handbook of child psychology* (6th ed., pp. 516–568). Editors-in-chief: W. Damon & R. M. Lerner. Hoboken, NJ: Wiley.

Brandtstädter, J., & Lerner, R. M. (Eds.). (1999). *Action and self-development: Theory and research through the life-span.* Thousand Oaks, CA: Sage.

Brodsky, C. M. (1954). *A study of norms for body form-behavior relationships.* Washington, DC: Catholic University of America Press.

Brown, B., & Larson, J. (2009). Peer relationships in adolescence. In R. M. Lerner & L. Steinberg (Eds.), *Handbook of adolescent psychology* (3rd ed.), Vol. 2: *Contextual influences on adolescent development* (pp. 74–103). Hoboken, NJ: Wiley.

Cattell, R. B., Eber, H. W., & Tatsuoka, M. M. (1970). *Handbook for the 16PF.* Champaign, IL: Institute for Personality & Ability Testing.

Damon, W. (Ed.). *Handbook of child psychology* (5th ed.). Hoboken, NJ: Wiley.

Damon, W., & Lerner, R. M. (Eds.). *Handbook of child psychology* (6th ed.). Hoboken, NJ: Wiley.

Damon, W., Menon, J., & Bronk, K. C. (2003). The development of purpose during adolescence. *Applied Developmental Science, 7*(3), 119–128.

Elder, G. H., Jr. (1980). Adolescence in historical perspective. In J. Adelson (Ed.), *Handbook of adolescent psychology* (pp. 3–46). New York: Wiley.

Elder, G. H., Jr. (1998). The life course and human development. In R. M. Lerner (Ed.), *Theoretical models of human development,* Vol. 1 of *Handbook of child psychology* (5th ed., pp. 939–991). Editor-in-chief: W. Damon. New York: Wiley.

Elder, G. H., Modell, J., & Parke, R. D. (Eds.). (1993). *Children in time and place: Developmental and historical insights.* New York: Cambridge University Press.

Elder, G. H., Jr., & Shanahan, M. J. (2006). The life course and human development. In R. M. Lerner (Ed.), *Theoretical models of human development,* Vol. 1: of *Handbook of child psychology* (6th ed., pp. 665–715). Editors-in-chief: W. Damon & R. M. Lerner. Hoboken, NJ: Wiley.

Elkind, D. (1967). Egocentrism in adolescents. *Child Development, 38,* 1025–1034.

Fisher, C. B., & Lerner, R. M. (Eds.). (1994). *Applied developmental psychology.* New York: McGraw-Hill.

Fisher, C. B., & Lerner, R. M. (Eds.). (2005). *Encyclopedia of applied developmental science.* Thousand Oaks, CA: Sage Publications.

Fisher, C. B., Murray, J. P., Dill, J. R., Hagen, J. W., Hogan, M. J., Lerner, R. M. et al. (1993). The National Conference on Graduate Education in the Applications of Developmental Science Across the Life Span. *Journal of Applied Developmental Psychology, 14,* 1–10.

Ford, D. H., & Lerner, R. M. (1992). *Developmental systems theory: An integrative approach.* Newbury Park, CA: Sage Publications.

Freund, A. M., & Baltes, P. B. (2002). Life-management strategies of selection, optimization and compensation: Measurement by self-report and construct validity. *Journal of Personality and Social Psychology, 82,* 642–662.

Geldhof, G. J., Little, T. D., & Colombo, J. (2010). Self-regulation across the life span. In M. E. Lamb & A. M. Freund (Eds.), *The handbook of life-span development,* Vol. 2: *Social and emotional development* (pp. 116–157). Editor-in-Chief: R. M. Lerner. Hoboken, NJ: Wiley.

Gestsdóttir, S., & Lerner, R. M. (2007). Intentional self-regulation and positive youth development in early adolescence: Findings from the 4-H Study of Positive Youth Development. *Developmental Psychology, 43*(2), 508–521.

Gestsdóttir, G., & Lerner, R. M. (2008). Positive development in adolescence: The development and role of intentional self regulation. *Human Development, 51,* 202–224.

Hall, C. S., & Lindzey, G. (1957). *Theories of personality.* New York: Wiley.

Harris, D. B. (Ed.). (1957). *The concept of development.* Minneapolis: University of Minnesota Press.

Hearnshaw, L. S. (1979). *Cyril Burt, psychologist.* New York: Cornell University Press.

Hebb, D. O. (1949). *The organization of behavior.* New York: Wiley.

Hebb, D. O. (1955). Drives and the C. N. S. (conceptual nervous system). *Psychological Review, 62,* 243–254.

Hebb, D. O. (1958). *A textbook of psychology.* Oxford: Saunders.

Heckhausen, J. (1999). *Developmental regulation in adulthood: Age-normative and sociocultural constraints as adaptive challenges.* New York: Cambridge University Press.

Hilgard, E. R. (1962). *Introduction to psychology* (3rd ed.). New York: Harcourt, Brace, & World.

Hood, K. E., Halpern, C. T., Greenberg, G., & Lerner, R. M. (Eds.). (2010). *The handbook of developmental science, behavior and genetics.* Malden, MA: Wiley Blackwell.

Kamin, L. J. (1974). *The science and politics of IQ.* Potomac, MD: Wiley.

King, P. E. (2012). Afterwod. In A. E. A. Warren, R. M. Lerner, & E. Phelps (Eds.), *Thriving and spirituality among youth: Research perspectives and future possibilities* (pp. 333–342). Hoboken, NJ: Wiley.

King, P. E., Carr, E., & Boitor, C. (2011). Religion, spirituality, positive youth development, and thriving. *Advances in Child Development and Behavior, 41,* 161–195.

Kuhn, T. S. (1962). *The structure of scientific revolutions*. Chicago, IL: University of Chicago Press.

Kuhn, T. S. (1970). *The structure of scientific revolutions* (2nd ed.). University of Chicago Press.

Langer, J. (1969). *Theories of development*. New York: Holt, Rinehart & Winston.

Lerner, J. V., Bowers, E. P., Minor, K., Lewin-Bizan, S., Boyd, M. J., Mueller, M. K. et al. (2012). Positive youth development: Processes, philosophies, and programs. In R. M. Lerner, M. A. Easterbrooks, & J. Mistry (Eds.), *Handbook of psychology*, Vol. 6: *Developmental Psychology* (2nd ed., pp. 365–392). Editor-in-chief: I. B. Weiner. Hoboken, NJ: Wiley.

Lerner, R. M. (1968a). Semantic conditioning and generalization. *Psychological Reports, 22,* 1257–1260.

Lerner, R. M. (1968b). Brightness constancy and the span of apprehension. *Perceptual and Motor Skills, 26,* 442.

Lerner, R. M. (1969). Note on Knehr's Span of Apprehension Test. *Perceptual and Motor Skills, 29,* 887–891.

Lerner, R. M. (1976). *Concepts and theories of human development*. Reading, MA: Addison Wesley Publishing Company.

Lerner, R. M. (1978). Nature, nurture, and dynamic interactionism. *Human Development, 21,* 1–20.

Lerner, R. M. (1982). Children and adolescents as producers of their own development. *Developmental Review, 2,* 342–370.

Lerner, R. M. (1984). *On the nature of human plasticity*. New York: Cambridge University Press.

Lerner, R. M. (1986). *Concepts and theories of human development* (2nd ed.). New York: Random House.

Lerner, R. M. (1988). Kontextualismus und Person-Kontext-Interaktion aus der Life-Span Perspektive. [Developmental contextualism and person-context interaction: A life-span perspective.] *Schweizerische Zeitschrift fuer Psychologie, 47,* 83–91.

Lerner, R. M. (1991). Changing organism–context relations as the basic process of development: A developmental contextual perspective. *Developmental Psychology, 27,* 27–32.

Lerner, R. M. (1992). *Final solutions: Biology, prejudice, and genocide*. University Park: Penn State Press.

Lerner, R. M. (Ed.). (1993). *Early adolescence: Perspectives on research, policy, and intervention*. Hillsdale, NJ: Erlbaum.

Lerner, R. M. (1995). *America's youth in crisis: Challenges and options for programs and policies*. Thousand Oaks, CA: Sage Publications.

Lerner, R. M. (1996). Relative plasticity, integration, temporality, and diversity in human development: A developmental contextual perspective about theory, process, and method. *Developmental Psychology, 32*(4), 781–786.

Lerner, R. M. (Ed.). (1998). *Theoretical models of human development*, Vol. 1 of *Handbook of child psychology* (5th ed.), Editor-in-chief: W. Damon. New York: Wiley.

Lerner, R. M. (2002). *Concepts and theories of human development* (3rd ed.). Mahwah, NJ: Lawrence Erlbaum Associates.

Lerner, R. M. (2006). Developmental science, developmental systems, and contemporary theories of human development. In R. M. Lerner (Ed.), *Theoretical models of human development*, Vol. 1 of *Handbook of child psychology* (6th ed., pp. 1–17). Editors-in-chief: W. Damon & R. M. Lerner. Hoboken, NJ: Wiley.

Lerner, R. M. (Ed.). (2010). *Handbook of life-span development*. Hoboken, NJ: Wiley.

Lerner, R. M. (2011). Structure and process in relational, developmental systems theories: A commentary on contemporary changes in the understanding of developmental change across the life span. *Human Development, 54,* 34–43.

Lerner, R. M. (2012). Essay review: Developmental science: Past, present, and future. *International Journal of Developmental Science, 6,* 29–36.

Lerner, R. M., Almerigi, J., Theokas, C., & Lerner, J. V. (Eds.). (2005). Positive youth development. *Journal of Early Adolescence, 25*(1).

Lerner, R. M., & Benson, J. B. (Eds.). (2013a). *Embodiment and epigenesis: Theoretical and methodological issues in understanding the role of biology within the relational developmental system*, Vol. 1. London: Elsevier.

Lerner, R. M., & Benson, J. B. (Eds.). (2013b). *Embodiment and epigenesis: Theoretical and methodological issues in understanding the role of biology within the relational developmental system*, Vol. 2. London: Elsevier.

Lerner, R. M., & Busch-Rossnagel, N. A. (Eds.). (1981). *Individuals as producers of their development: A life-span perspective*. New York: Academic Press.

Lerner, R. M., Freund, A. M., De Stefanis, I., & Habermas, T. (2001). Understanding developmental regulation in adolescence: The use of the selection, optimization, and compensation model. *Human Development, 44,* 29–50.

Lerner, R. M., & Gellert, E. (1969). Body build identification, preference, and aversion in children. *Developmental Psychology, 1,* 456–462.

Lerner, R. M., Jacobs, F., & Wertlieb, D. (Eds.). (2003). *Handbook of applied developmental science: Promoting positive child, adolescent, and family development through research, policies, and programs*. Thousand Oaks, CA: Sage Publications.

Lerner, R. M., & Korn, S. J. (1972). The development of body build stereotypes in males. *Child Development, 43,* 908–920.

Lerner, R. M., & Lerner, J. V. (Eds.). (1999). *Theoretical foundations and biological bases of development in adolescence*. New York: Garland.

Lerner, R. M., Lerner, J. V., & Benson, J. B. (Eds.). (2011). *Positive youth development: Research and applications for promoting thriving in adolescence*. London: Elsevier.

Lerner, R. M., Lerner, J. V., von Eye, A., Bowers, E. P., & Lewin-Bizan, S. (2011). Individual and contextual bases of thriving in adolescence: A view of the issues. *Journal of Adolescence, 34*(6), 1107–1114.

Lerner, R. M., Lerner J. V., von Eye, A., & Lewin-Bizan, S. (Eds.). (2009). Foundations and functions of thriving in adolescence: Findings from the 4-H Study of Positive Youth Development. *Journal of Applied Developmental Psychology, 30.*

Lerner, R. M., & Miller, J. R. (1998). Developing multidisciplinary institutes to enhance the lives of individuals and families: Academic pitfalls and potentials. *Journal of Public Service & Outreach, 3*(1), 64–73.

Lerner, R. M., Miller, J. R., Knott, J. H., Corey, K. E., Bynum, T. S., Hoopfer, L. C. et al. (1994). Integrating scholarship and outreach in human development research, policy, and service: A developmental contextual perspective. In D. L. Featherman, R. M. Lerner, & M. Perlmutter (Eds.), *Life-span development and behavior* (Vol. 12, pp. 249–273). Hillsdale, NJ: Erlbaum.

Lerner, R. M., & Overton, W. F. (2008). Exemplifying the integrations of the relational developmental system: Synthesizing theory, research, and application to promote positive development and social justice. *Journal of Adolescent Research, 23*(3), 245–255.

Lerner, R. M., Petersen, A. C., & Brooks-Gunn, J. (Eds.). (1991). *Encyclopedia of adolescence*. New York: Garland.

Lerner, R. M., Roeser, R. W., & Phelps, E. (Eds.). (2008). *Positive youth development and spirituality: From theory to research*. West Conshohocken, PA: Templeton Foundation Press.

Lerner, R. M., & Simon, L. A. K. (Eds.). (1998). *University–community collaborations for the twenty-first century: Outreach scholarship for youth and families*. New York: Garland.

Lerner, R. M., & Spanier, G. B. (Eds.). (1978). *Child influences on marital and family interaction: A life span perspective*. New York: Academic Press.

Lerner, R. M., & Spanier, G. B. (1980). *Adolescent development: A life-span perspective*. New York: McGraw-Hill.

Lerner, R. M., Sparks, E. S., & McCubbin, L. (1999). *Family diversity and family policy: Strengthening families for America's children*. Boston, MA: Kluwer Academic Publishers.

Lerner, R. M., & Steinberg, L. (Eds.). (2004). *Handbook of adolescent psychology* (2nd ed.). New York: Wiley.

Lerner, R. M., & Steinberg, L. (Eds.). (2009). *Handbook of adolescent psychology* (3rd ed.). Hoboken, NJ: Wiley.

Lerner, R. M., Taylor, C. S., & von Eye, A. (Eds.). (2002). *Pathways to positive development among diverse youth. New directions for youth development: Theory, practice, and research.* San Francisco: Jossey-Bass.

Lerner, R. M., von Eye, A., Lerner, J. V., Lewin-Bizan, S., & Bowers, E. P. (Eds.). (2010). The meaning and measurement of thriving in adolescence: Findings from the 4-H Study of Positive Youth Development. *Journal of Youth and Adolescence, 39*(7).

Lerner, R. M., & Walls, T. (1999). Revisiting individuals as producers of their development: From dynamic interactionism to developmental systems. In J. Brandtstädter & R. M. Lerner (Eds.), *Action and self-development: Theory and research through the life-span* (pp. 3–36). Thousand Oaks, CA: Sage.

Li, Y., & Lerner, R. M. (2011). Developmental trajectories of school engagement across adolescence: Implications for academic achievement, substance use, depression, and delinquency. *Developmental Psychology, 47*(1), 233–247.

McCandless, B. R. (1961). *Children and adolescents: Behavior and development.* New York: Holt, Rinehart & Winston.

McCandless, B. R. (1967). *Children: Behavior and development.* New York: Holt, Rinehart & Winston.

McCandless, B. R. (1970). *Adolescents: Behavior and development.* Hinsdale, IL: Dryden Press.

Miller, J. R., & Lerner, R. M. (1994). Integrating research and outreach: Developmental contextualism and the human ecological perspective. *Home Economics Forum, 7,* 21–28.

Molenaar, P. C. M., Lerner, R. M., & Newell, K. (Eds.) (In press). *Handbook of developmental systems theory and methodology.* New York, NY: Guilford.

Mussen, P. H., Conger, J., & Kagan, J. (1969). *Child Development and Personality.* New York: Harper.

Nagel, E. (1957). Determinism in development. In D. B. Harris (Ed.), *The concept of development* (pp. 15–24). Minneapolis: University of Minnesota Press.

Nesselroade, J. R., & von Eye, A. (Eds.). (1985). *Individual development and social change: Explanatory analysis.* New York: Academic Press.

Overton, W. F. (1973). On the assumptive base of the nature–nurture controversy: Additive versus interactive conceptions. *Human Development, 16,* 74–89.

Overton, W. F. (2010). Life-span development: Concepts and issues. In W. F. Overton (Ed) *Cognition, biology, and methods across the lifespan.* Vol. 1 of *Handbook of life-span development* (pp. 1–29). Editor-in-chief: R. M. Lerner. Hoboken, NJ: Wiley.

Overton, W. F. (2011). Relational developmental systems and quantitative behavior genetics: Alternative of parallel methodologies. *Research in Human Development, 8,* 258–263.

Overton, W. F. (2012). Evolving scientific paradigms: Retrospective and prospective. In L. L'Abate (Ed.), *The role of paradigms in theory construction* (pp. 31–65). New York: Springer.

Overton, W. F., & Lerner, R. M. (2012). Relational developmental systems: Paradigm for developmental science in the post-genomic era. *Behavioral and Brain Sciences, 35*(5), 375–376.

Overton, W. F., & Müller, U. (2012). Development across the life span: Philosophy, concepts, theory. In R. M. Lerner, M. A. Easterbrooks, & J. Mistry (Eds.), *Handbook of psychology,* Vol. 6: *Developmental psychology* (pp. 19–58). Editor-in-chief: I. B. Weiner. New York: Wiley.

Overton, W. F., & Reese, H. W. (1973). Models of development: Methodological implications. In J. R. Nesselroade & H. W. Reese (Eds.), *Life-span developmental psychology: Methodological issues* (pp. 65–86). New York: Academic Press.

Overton, W., & Reese, H. (1981). Conceptual prerequisites for an understanding of stability-change and continuity-discontinuity. *International Journal of Behavioral Development, 4,* 99–123.

Pepper, S. C. (1942). *World hypotheses: A study in evidence.* Berkeley: University of California Press.

Petersen, A. C. (1993). Foreword. In R. M. Lerner (Ed.), *Early adolescence: Perspectives on research, policy, and intervention* (pp. xi–xii). Hillsdale, NJ: Erlbaum.

Reese, H. W., & Overton, W. F. (1970). Models of development and theories of development. In L. R. Goulet & P. B. Baltes (Eds.), *Life-span developmental psychology: Research and theory* (pp. 115–145). New York: Academic Press.

Schmid, K. L., Phelps, E., Kiely, M. K., Napolitano, C. M., Boyd, M. J., & Lerner, R. M. (2011). The role of adolescents' hopeful futures in predicting positive and negative developmental trajectories: Findings from the 4-H Study of Positive Youth Development. *The Journal of Positive Psychology, 6*(1), 45–56.

Schneirla, R. C. (1956). Interrelationships of the innate and the acquired in instictive behavior. In P. P. Grassé (Ed.), *L'instinct dans le comportement des animaux et de l'homme.* Paris: Mason et Cie.

Schneirla, T. C. (1957). The concept of development in comparative psychology. In D. B. Harris (Ed.), *The concept of development: An issue in the study of human behavior* (pp. 78–108). Minneapolis: University of Minnesota Press.

Sears, R. R. (1957). Identification as a form of behavioral development. In D. B. Harris (Ed.), *The concept of development.* Minneapolis: University of Minnesota Press.

Sheldon, W. H. (1940). *The varieties of human physique.* New York: Harper & Row.

Sheldon, W. H. (1942). *The varieties of temperament.* New York: Harper & Row.

Skinner, B. F. (1971). *Beyond freedom and dignity.* New York: Knopf.

Staffieri, J. R. (1967). A study of social stereotype of body image in children. *Journal of Personality and Social Psychology, 7,* 101–104.

Stone, L. J., & Church, J. (1957), *Childhood and adolescence: A psychology of the growing child.* New York: Random House.

Taylor, C. S., Lerner, R. M., von Eye, A., Balsano, A. B., Dowling, E. M., Anderson, P. M. et al. (2002a). Stability of attributes of positive functioning and of developmental assets among African American adolescent male gang and community-based organization members. In R. M. Lerner, C. S. Taylor, & A. von Eye (Eds.), *New directions for youth development: Theory, practice, research: Pathways to positive development among diverse youth* (Vol. 95; G. Noam, Series Ed.) (pp. 35–55). San Francisco: Jossey-Bass.

Taylor, C. S., Lerner, R. M., von Eye, A., Balsano, A. B., Dowling, E. M., Anderson, P. M. et al. (2002b). Individual and ecological assets and positive developmental trajectories among gang and community-based organization youth. In R. M. Lerner, C. S. Taylor, & A. von Eye (Eds.), *New directions for youth development: Theory, practice, research: Pathways to positive development among diverse youth* (Vol. 95; G. Noam, Series Ed.) (pp. 57–72). San Francisco: Jossey-Bass.

Templeton, J. M. (2012). *The essential worldwide laws of life.* Philadelphia, PA: Templeton Press.

Tobach, E., & Schneirla, T. C. (1968). The biopsychology of social behavior of animals. In R. E. Cooke & S. Levin (Eds.), *Biologic basis of pediatric practice* (pp. 68–82). New York: McGraw-Hill.

Villarruel, F. A., & Lerner, R. M. (Eds.). (1994). Promoting community-based programs for socialization and learning. *New Directions for Child Development, 63.* San Francisco: Jossey-Bass.

Warren, A. E. A., Lerner, R. M., & Phelps E. (Eds.). (2012). *Thriving and spirituality among youth: Research perspectives and future possibilities.* Hoboken, NJ: Wiley.

Werner, E. E., & Smith, R. S. (1992). *Overcoming the odds: High risk children from birth to adulthood.* Ithaca, NY: Cornell University Press.

Werner, H. (1957). The concept of development from a comparative and organismic point of view. In D. B. Harris (Ed.), *The concept of development* (pp. 125–148). Minneapolis: University of Minnesota Press.

Wertlieb, D., & Feldman, D. H. (1996). Doctoral education in applied child development. In C. B. Fisher, J. P. Murray, & I. Sigel (Eds.), *Applied developmental science: Graduate training for diverse disciplines and educational settings* (pp. 121–141). Norwood, NJ: Ablex.

27

Doing "Good Time"

Iris F. Litt

As far back as I can recall, I knew I would be a doctor like my father. Neighbors in our Brooklyn apartment building describe seeing me at 2 years of age with my doll carriage telling all who would listen that my doll had pneumonia and I was treating her with sulfadiazine and aspirin. I often accompanied my father on house calls and, when old enough, even carried his bag up those long flights of brownstone stairs, awaiting the stories and cookies that would greet us at the top. The plight of his patients was of more than intellectual interest as their lives and health impacted on the ebb and flow of ours.

Because I always knew I'd be a doctor and assumed my role-model father shared that view. Imagine how shocked I was when he exploded upon hearing (for what couldn't possibly have been the first time) that I would be pre-med in college. "Medicine is no career for a woman!" he bellowed. "You should be a teacher like your mother and then you could be home for your children in the afternoon and summers, etc.". I was devastated! No, he was never grooming me for a career as a doctor, he protested. He took me to his office and on house calls because he enjoyed my company, etc., etc. For me, despite the disappointment, there was no turning back.

The next challenge was the reality that medical schools limited the enrollment of women to less than 10% of any class. They believed that women would not complete the training, would drop out to raise a family and, in so doing, would take the place of a "more deserving" male.

The engagement ring on my finger when interviewing was surely not an asset. The interviewers (all male) had no qualms about (or legal restrictions against) telling me that I was at high risk for fulfilling that prophecy. Rather than getting angry, it just heightened my resolve to prove that I was as competent as the men. I was not alone in this

reaction, which was shared by my female pre-med classmates. What I could not abide, however, was the tone of ridicule that greeted me during these interviews: "How dare I waste their time" was the prevailing attitude back then in 1960. Being Phi Beta Kappa at Cornell University and having an excellent record of extracurricular and community activities carried no weight. All of this notwithstanding, I was accepted at all the schools to which I applied. I chose to go to the State University (of New York- Downstate) because the nominal tuition was affordable to newlyweds.

Having graduated from college in January of my senior year (with medical school not starting until the following September) and newly married, I took a temporary position as a teacher of General Science to Junior High School students in Brooklyn. That experience opened my eyes to the joys of working with teenagers. I set my sights on doing that as a physician, despite the fact that no discrete field of adolescent medicine yet existed. Pediatrics was the closest and logical choice and I decided to become a pediatrician, the first step away from the only path I knew, my fathers'. I found that being a female medical student was a mixed blessing. Fewer than 20 of us in a class of 200 meant that I was often in the spotlight. Fortunately, I did well academically and had a number of opportunities as a result. The first of these was an offer of a summer job to work as a lab assistant on the research project of a professor of rheumatology. Pipetting the days away led me to conclude that I would never do research. Seeing no examples of clinical research meant that this option was entirely unknown to me. What a loss!

One night, while in medical school, my father alerted me to a talk by a physician from Harvard focused on a new field called "adolescent medicine"! The speaker was J. Roswell Gallagher, the pioneering school physician who had recognized the importance of providing age-appropriate health care to teens. To discover that others shared my interest and, more importantly, were training physicians, was validating and gave me hope that I could fulfill my dream. Reality later intervened and, owing to having a child and a husband bound to New York, I was never able to go to Boston to train with Dr. Gallagher.

Getting a good pediatric residency in New York proved another challenge as New York Hospital (my first choice) had already taken their "one woman." I was, however, elated some weeks later when they called to tell me that they had decided to break tradition and take another! Of course I was required to sign a contract stipulating that I would remain for 3 years, even if my husband was transferred out of town. Only later did I learn that none of the men was required to do likewise. Being on duty every weekday, every other night, and every other weekend for 18 months until the schedule "improved" to every third night proved exhausting, especially as I became pregnant in the first year after 4 years of marriage. Having a supportive husband and a loyal daytime nanny got us through.

In my last year of residency, I began to search for an opportunity to work with teens, only to find that there had not yet been a southerly migration of adolescent medicine. Later that year I was elated to learn that an adolescent medicine program was to begin at Montefiore Hospital of the Albert Einstein Medical School in the Bronx. My elation was short lived as Michael Cohen, its director, had no funds to hire me. I was resigned to accept a position in a general pediatric practice at that institution with the hope that I might develop a link to that program from within.

To my delight, months later, Michael called and told me that he now had funds for a half-time salary and offered me a job. The only hitch was that the salary had resulted from a contract just signed with the City of New York to establish and operate a health-care program for its Juvenile Detention Centers. I would have done anything to have the chance to help create this new program and work with Michael, a bright, energetic and creative man a few years older than I who was in the process of teaching himself about adolescent medicine, having been trained as a Pediatric Gastroenterologist. It wasn't until I arrived at Spofford Juvenile Detention Center, a locked, massive, walled building housing 10,000 "delinquents" per year that I realized the magnitude of the task I had so easily assumed.

Juvenile Detention and Prisons

The contract between the city of New York and Montefiore Hospital was the outcome of a Grand Jury investigation into the death of a teenager at the Center that concluded that the health care was seriously deficient. I would have used stronger language as there was, in fact, almost no health care delivered there. A per diem physician reportedly left the engine of his car running during his daily visits and there were no medical records, procedure books, etc. Worst of all, those confined to the infirmary were locked in their cell-like rooms with no access to toilets or mechanism for contacting the nurse on duty. We inherited a demoralized and poorly trained nursing staff who were suspicious of the hospital's (and, by extension, my) motives for coming. This situation was especially problematic owing to the racial strife in the city at the time and the clear racial differences between the nurses and correctional staff and that of the physicians. To make matters worse, our arrival was preceded by rumors that "the white hospital was coming to perform medical experiments on the Black and Hispanic inmates."

Naïve and idealistic, I had expected that the arrival of a high-quality medical screening and treatment program for youngsters who had not previously had any medical care would be greeted with open arms. I rapidly learned otherwise. Not only were there grievances brought against me by the nurses' union owing to my insistence that the patients not be locked in infirmary cells and by the union representing the couriers who objected to bringing "dirty" specimens (e.g., stool and urine) to the medical center for analysis; I also was the target of opposition from the Pediatric Residents from Montefiore who were required to rotate through the facility for part of their adolescent medicine training. They protested that they had chosen Pediatrics in order to care for "innocent" babies, not "hardened criminals." The fact that there was a New York City election looming a few months after the programs' commencement didn't help, as every political candidate opened his campaign on the steps of the detention center decrying the conditions, including medical care, in the institution. Even Margaret Meade, then a member of New York's Citizens Committee for Children, toured the facility and greeted my description of the high-quality medical program there by saying that anything anybody did to make the place better was evil because the only solution was to shut the place down.

An unexpected blow was also dealt by the Juvenile Court judges. They had learned that our extensive screening process had revealed a high rate of abnormal liver function tests among these young drug users. The fact that most of these represented chemical hepatitis, rather than the infectious variety, was lost on them. We learned about this situation when we read in the local newspaper that the Center was about to be shut down because of a "hepatitis epidemic" since Montefiore arrived. Following many hours of conversation with the Chief Judge, not only did they rescind the order, but recognized the tremendous value of the medical screening/care provided. But our problems with them did not end there—they began remanding juveniles to the detention center for the sole purpose of obtaining medical care!

Shell-shocked initially, I eventually weathered these events. In fact each of these setbacks challenged one's creativity and led to a number of solutions that eventually strengthened the program: for example, remodeling of the infirmary to provide for more dignified conditions and protection of nurses, setting up analytic laboratories at the Center that later provided opportunities for teaching patients and training laboratory technicians, and eventually replacing the city nurses with superb Montefiore nurses. The ability to collect health data on this underserved population allowed us to develop community-based services and to work with the city administration to design programs.

For the youngsters detained at the facility, contact with pediatricians, I believe, provided more than medical care alone. For many of them, this was their only non-adversarial contact with an authority figure who cared about them and their health.

Recognition of a vast range of health problems in the detained population, largely because of lack of access to health services previously (Hein et al., 1980; Litt, 1983; Litt & Cohen, 1974), underscored the need to establish resources within the facility: for example, the finding of widespread dental problems led to the development of an on-site dental program with a training component. Similarly, the greater than anticipated need for radiology services resulted in a built in x-ray suite with a training program for x-ray technicians. When John Lindsay, the then Mayor of New York proclaimed that there was no drug problem in teens in the city in 1969, we were able to refute his claim with the data we had collected at the Center (Hein, Cohen, & Litt, 1979; Litt & Schonberg, 1975). This refutation led to his establishing a high-level committee to develop resources. The most remarkable outcomes involved the Pediatric Residents who, through later surveys, revealed that in retrospect, they found their rotation at the juvenile detention center the most rewarding of all their training experiences (Litt & Cohen, 1978)! By coincidence, as I write this, I have just received an email message from one of them who states: "I've had an incredible career, the past 25 years or so devoted to prison and jail health care. Looking back, your rotation at Spofford in 1971 headed me in the right direction."

The other unexpected outcome of the experience was the change in my thinking about a research career. Having previously only seen bench-lab researchers in medical school and residency, I was unprepared for what happened to me at Spofford. There were so many clinical issues that presented themselves (how to treat barbiturate withdrawal in 14-year-olds, what does heroin do to the liver, why do girls taking heroin stop menstruating, etc.) for which there were no answers in the literature at the time. The need to get the answers led me to the lab, the only place where such answers might be found (Litt, Colli, & Cohen, 1971). I then realized that "research" meant generation of new knowledge and my career as a researcher was launched.

After 5 years, with the Program running smoothly and a system of training and health data collection firmly in place, the City of New York showed its approval by asking if the medical center (read "I") would help them to set up health services at the Rikers Island Prison. While the details of an island-wide program were being discussed, it was decided that the Division of Adolescent Medicine and I would replicate the Spofford program at the Adolescent Remand Center at Rikers (for 16–20-year-old males) as a prototype of the future island-wide program. As familiar as I had become with guards, keys, and high walls, and

even many of the inmates previously detained at Spofford, I didn't think anything could surprise me. I was wrong …

A tour of the existing infirmary at Rikers revealed conditions that made Spofford look like a country-club by contrast. Despite the formidable physical and psychologic barriers to delivery of excellent health care that existed in these detention facilities, we found a way to achieve our goals and to develop what became a model for other such institutions. Sharing our findings in the peer-reviewed medical literature, in testimony before the U.S. Senate and N.Y. State commissions, etc. led to the development by various national bodies (including the American Academy of Pediatrics) of Standards for Care in Prisons and Detention Facilities.

Society for Adolescent Medicine

J. Roswell Gallagher, the Father of Adolescent Medicine, clearly focused the medical community on the special health needs of adolescents. His background as a boarding school physician paved the way for developing ambulatory services for this age group at the Children's Hospital at Harvard in the 1950s. He later started the first training program for physicians interested in specializing in the health care of teenagers. Many of his Fellows built upon the training and experiences in Boston and established adolescent medicine programs tailored to their unique environments. They also began the process of research on this age group. These physicians, mainly medical school faculty, recognized the importance of sharing their experiences and research findings. Out of this grew the Society for Adolescent Medicine (SAM) of which I was a Charter Member in 1968. SAM (as it was known until 2010 when its name was changed to SAHM—the Society for Adolescent Health and Medicine) grew and attracted health professionals and behavioral scientists who shared an interest in teens. It was exhilarating for me to participate in this growth and, ultimately, to become its 13th President in 1982. (On a personal note, my husband, Dale Garell, was the Society's 3rd President.)

Service to SAM spanned my entire career. In 1990, I became the second Editor-in-Chief of its then bi-monthly journal, *The Journal of Adolescent Health Care.* I was pleased to guide the journal through its growth to a monthly publication, a name change (to *Journal of Adolescent Health*), and an exponential increase in impact factor over the 14 years of my leadership. For me, the enormous workload (in addition to my "day job," see below) was amply rewarded by the excitement of knowing what was new and interesting in the field, as well as by the opportunity to shape the literature to some extent through the mechanism of "calls for papers" on a topic of my choosing. It was enjoyable to write a monthly Editorial, the only time in my academic career that I didn't need peer review! It was my chance to share thoughts about adolescent medicine and the world of adolescents, about work-force issues (e.g., asking the question of why, given the shrinking availability of abortion providers, adolescent medicine doctors shouldn't get trained to provide this service). I was so pleased that my Editorials were preserved in a book presented to me at the time of my retirement as Editor.

I was profoundly touched to have been awarded the Society's Outstanding Achievement Award in 1992. Another meaningful honor bestowed upon me by SAM was the establishment of the "Iris F. Litt Visiting Professorship" to support the travel of a leading adolescent health researcher to an institution that had successfully competed to receive her/him.

The American Board of Pediatrics

It is hard to believe that until 1981 when I was invited to join this august body as an Examiner, that only two of its nearly 200 members were women. The prevailing attitude had been that women were not willing or able to travel to the examination sites owing to their obligations at home. This was clearly paternalistic and inherently unfair, given the fact that more than half of the candidates for Board certification/recertification are/were women at the time. I am grateful to Laurence Finberg, my first Chair, and a former President of the ABP, for bucking the trend and having the confidence that I would make a contribution to this critically important organization. My tenure at the Board included membership on the "Board of the Board" (i.e., the Board of Directors) from 1989 to 1995, as well as my representation of the Board on the Certifying Committee of the Committee on Child and Adolescent Psychiatry of the American Board of Psychiatry. Undoubtedly, my most significant contribution come out of my membership on the "New Subspecialties Committee of the Board" during the time that the proposal from SAM to create a Sub-Board in Adolescent Medicine was presented, argued, and approved. I then sat on the committee that wrote the first examination for certification in this new subspecialty.

Stanford University and the Department of Pediatrics / Division of Adolescent Medicine

Throughout the years at Montefiore, I structured my days so that I would spend mornings at the prison/detention center and afternoons at the medical center, each informing and supporting the other. It didn't take long for me to notice the differences among the teens in the two settings. No, not the obvious ones, but rather things like the fact that those who I saw in the correctional setting had been self-administering all sorts of drugs/substances without apparent concern about any possible adverse effects, whereas those in the traditional setting were often brought to my attention because of their unwillingness to take prescribed medications, often for life-threatening conditions. Not only was I fascinated by these differences but also by the larger issue of health behavior among teenagers.

In 1976, I was invited to move to Stanford University to establish a Division of Adolescent Medicine by Dr. Ruth T. Gross who was then Director of General Pediatrics. Dr. Gross, a distinguished pediatric hematologist and the first women to hold an Endowed Chair at Stanford University, had found herself increasingly intrigued by social and behavioral issues over the years. This interest led her to design the groundbreaking "Infant Health and Development Program" of the Robert Wood Johnson Foundation in 1983.

I welcomed the move to Stanford University as the long-awaited opportunity to work in an environment where I could learn from, and collaborate with, colleagues in the behavioral sciences to better understand the complexities of adolescents' health behavior and, hopefully, to begin to motivate change. I chose to focus on medication "adherence," the teenagers' willingness/ability to follow physicians' prescriptions. Not only was Stanford University home to some of the leading psychologists, sociologists, educators, legal scholars, etc. but all of them who were interested in adolescents had come together the year before my arrival and formed the Boys Town Center for Adolescent Research. Imagine that every Thursday morning for 2 hours, I sat around a table with the likes of Sandy Dornbusch, Merrill Carlsmith, Lee Cronbach, Eleanor Maccoby, Alberta Siegel, Michael Wald, etc. to share my research, hear about theirs, and receive feedback. The other invaluable bonus of these connections was that I had access to their students (undergraduates and graduate students), many of whom became my research assistants. Stanford University's Human Biology Program, an interdisciplinary and, at the time, innovative and successful program that taught an integrated approach to the science of people, immediately connected me with its curriculum and opportunities to teach undergraduates. When the funding from the Omaha Boys Town ended, the center evolved into the Center on Adolescence. I was fortunate to have been a member of the search committee for its director, under the expert leadership of Eleanor Maccoby, that chose Bill Damon.

At Stanford University School of Medicine, I established the Division of Adolescent Medicine (in 1976) whose mission was to provide interdisciplinary and excellent health care to teenagers, to teach medical students, pediatric and (later) child psychiatry/psychology interns and residents and fellows in adolescent medicine, and to foster cutting-edge research into the many unanswered questions about the health and biology of adolescents. The Program was initially part of the Division of General Pediatrics, became free-standing in the early 1980s. The "laboratory" for these activities was primarily the outpatient department, the "psychosomatic" inpatient unit, and for about a decade, a separate medical adolescent inpatient unit.

At Stanford University, as had been the case at Albert Einstein/Montefiore, I chose to study the problems of the teens who were our patients. I continued my interest in their health behaviors, especially with regard to adherence with prescribed medication, including contraceptives, and, later, as an increasing number of patients appeared with weight loss and related phenomenon, became immersed in the study of eating disorders. With regard to the former, I was fortunate enough to identify both existing data (collected for other reasons) and interested collaborators to begin this research. The first of my descriptive studies was, accordingly, about teens adherence to medication for rheumatoid arthritis, a good model for many chronic diseases (Litt, Cuskey, & Rudd, 1980). This paper began a series of studies about other chronic disease and contraceptive medication adherence, many of which were first-authored by our fellows (e.g., DuRant, Jay, Litt, Linder, & Shoffitt, 1984; Friedman, Litt, Henson, Holtzman, & Halverson, 1981; Friedman et al., 1986; Jay, DuRant, Litt, Linder, & Shoffitt, 1984; Litt, 1985; Litt & Cuskey, 1981; Litt, Cuskey, & Rosenberg, 1982; Litt, Jay, & DuRant 1984; Neel, Jay, & Litt, 1985; Neel, Litt, & Jay, 1987). Insights gained through these studies led to development of interventions designed to improve adherence (e.g., Friedman & Litt, 1987; Jay, DuRant, Litt, Shoffitt, & Linder, 1984).

Another exciting opportunity presented itself the summer of my arrival at Stanford. William Dement, the "Father of Sleep Research" and his Fellow, Mary Carskadon, had just completed 2 months of data collection based on somnographic tracings from teenagers in residence at Sleep Camp. Their goal was to describe developmental changes in sleep patterns during the second decade of life. After painstakingly reviewing these tracings (before the days of computers—they filled rooms!) they were dismayed to find no differences, despite the range of ages of the subjects. My contribution was to point out the importance of using Stage of Pubertal Development (a.k.a. "Tanner Stages") as the independent variable. We did the appropriate staging and, lo and behold, important developmental differences in sleep patterns emerged! Increased daytime sleepiness and delayed sleep latency were seen between Stages 3 and 4 (Carskadon et al., 1980).

The importance of using pubertal development as the independent variable, rather than chronologic age proved to be important in many studies of both physiologic and psychologic development. Unfortunately, just about the time that colleagues in the social sciences began to adapt it, schools were becoming increasingly wary about physical examination of genitalia/breasts on their premises. To address such concerns, my colleague/then Fellow Paula Duncan (then "Duke") and I devised a study which showed that teens could be taught to evaluate their own stage of pubertal development using standardized drawings (Duke, Litt, & Gross, 1980).

In the late 1970s, I compared notes with my child psychiatrist colleague, Hans Steiner, and found that he, too, was seeing more young women with weight-loss, unexplained by chronic or acute traditional medical diagnoses. We decided to join forces and set up a clinic for interdisciplinary evaluation and treatment of anorexia nervosa and bulimia. Together, we learned about these illnesses that had not yet been well-described, understood, or diagnosed

in this age-group, especially in the pediatric literature. We developed a treatment program, both in- and out-patient (as dictated by the severity of the patient's condition) that had excellent results and became a model of care. The collaboration for clinical care evolved into collaborative research (Steiner, Mazer, & Litt, 1990; Steiner, Smith, Rosenkranz, & Litt, 1991).

Another unanticipated outcome was the opportunity to train each other's students/residents/fellows in the perspectives of our respective disciplines. Collaborations were also forged within the department of pediatrics, especially with Laura Bachrach, an endocrinologist and, at the time, an emerging expert in bone growth and development in teens. Together with Debra Katzman, who was then a Fellow in Adolescent Medicine, we pursued my hunch that teens with anorexia nervosa would have low bone density (Bachrach, Guido, Katzman, Litt, & Marcus, 1990; Bachrach, Katzman, Litt, Guido, & Marcus, 1991). Of interest is the realization that there were no normative data for bone density in this age group at the time and, in order to test the hypothesis, we had to gather such data. Those findings proved as interesting to me as those for the patients! We learned, among other things, that bone density peaked in late adolescence and was correlated with BMI.

I have always derived great pleasure from mentoring younger people, and my passion for it has grown over the years. I am particularly proud of the generations of Adolescent Medicine Fellows I have trained who are now national and international leaders in their own right, mostly in academic medical centers, with some in government or philanthropy. With regard to the international, graduates of our Programs (i.e. from Stanford and Montefiore) direct adolescent medicine programs in France, Spain, Korea, and Thailand, as well as Canada where, at one time, I was able to claim that I had trained all the directors of Canadian adolescent medicine programs! It has also been gratifying to co-mentor trainees from other disciplines (e.g., Psychiatry, Psychology, Anthropology, etc.), an opportunity facilitated by the openness to collaboration of my colleagues in other schools at Stanford University.

Institute for Research on Women and Gender I was surprised when the search committee for the Directorship of Stanford University's Institute for Research on Women and Gender contacted me in 1990 as their first choice for the position. Having always conceptualized my body of research under the heading of "Adolescent Medicine," I had never thought about the fact that it had actually focused on the health problems of *female* adolescents. The experience of considering (and eventually accepting) this invitation was one of the most intellectually stimulating of my career. Having previously considered "feminists" in negative terms (owing to my ignorance), I would not have wanted to be counted as one. In fact, my son Bill (now a public interest lawyer), as co-editor of UCLA's *Women's Law Journal*, later teased me that he became a feminist before I did! Not only did my subsequent experience and education change my attitude about the term as well as my own feminist life-script (receiving lower pay for equal work, balancing work/child rearing, achieving despite quotas and other barriers etc.), but it also enlightened me about how little we knew about health problems of women of all ages.

From that time on, my research has been informed by that experience, and I became more intellectually curious and open, thanks to the work of my new colleagues who were researchers from the humanities and social sciences who studied fields as diverse as feminist history of the American Revolution to the writings of 15th-century French writer, Christine de Pisan. I served as Director (a half-time rotating position) for 7 years while continuing to direct the Division of Adolescent Medicine and serving as Editor-in-Chief of *The Journal of Adolescent Health* (*JAH*). The position also offered me the opportunity to broaden the scope of research of some colleagues in the School of Medicine who, like me, had never considered the issue of gender in their research. For example, one of my psychiatric colleagues had not previously analyzed his data on depression on the basis of gender. Once he did, he discovered important differences which are now well-known. During that time, I authored *Taking Our Pulse: The Health of America's Women* (Litt, 1997), a developmental approach to the state of knowledge about the subject at the time. I also taught a course in Stanford's Continuing Studies Program, as well as one for undergraduates interested in the health problems of women. Upon completion of my term as Director, the Institute's Board established the *Iris F. Litt Fund* to support research on women's issues of Stanford faculty. I am so pleased that it continues to do so.

Center for Advanced Study in the Behavioral Sciences at Stanford University Although eligible for a sabbatical leave in 1982, I was denied this privilege because there was no one to assume my clinical responsibilities, as I was the sole faculty member of the Adolescent Medicine Division. I will be forever grateful to Dr. Ira Friedman (subsequently and currently the Director of the Student Health Service (Vaden) at Stanford University) who came to my rescue. He had been a fellow in our Program in the late 1970s and was seeking new settings when he agreed to take over for me in 1984. I was quite fortunate at that time to have been invited to become a Fellow at the Center for Advanced Study in the Behavioral Sciences on the Stanford campus (although not part of Stanford University at that time). The opportunity to spend my sabbatical years (as a Kaiser Foundation Fellow) was unique, especially for a physician in this milieu of behavioral scientists. With the distinguished psychologist, Gardner Lindsay, as the Director, the rules were few: Work on anything you wished but come to lunch and the weekly seminar, one of which you would be required to present. There were 48 of us that year. Everyone, I later learned, initially dreaded lunch, fearful that they would have nothing in common

with the others from different disciplines and with different vocabularies. None of us could have anticipated how quickly and enjoyably common ground was found and the learning curve for us all, meteoric!

I spent the year collaborating (long-distance) with Victor C. Vaughan III, M.D., the distinguished pediatrician, long-time Associate Editor of the *Nelson Textbook of Pediatrics*, former Chair of Pediatrics at Temple University, President of the American Board of Pediatrics, etc. Together we wrote *Child and Adolescent Development: Clinical Implications* (Vaughan & Litt, 1990), with him writing the half about children and I, about adolescents. (The collaboration was so successful that we later married!)

In the summer of 2009, I was invited back to the Center, by this time a Stanford University research center, to become its Director. I was honored and agreed to accept the invitation while a search for a permanent Director was begun. I remained for 18 months and enjoyed the experience "from the front of the house." The Center had, in my days as a Fellow, appeared to have run itself—as Director, I learned otherwise. While the administrative, personnel, and fund-raising responsibilities consumed most of my time, the intellectual stimulation of interacting on a daily basis with such a wide range of people from so many disciplines working on fascinating projects more than compensated me for my efforts. I also undertook the conceptualization and completion of the Center's first ever Strategic Plan in anticipation of the arrival of the Center's 10th Director in its 55-year history, Stephen Kosslyn, a prominent cognitive psychologist from Harvard who arrived in January of 2011 to relieve me. He stepped down in March of 2013 and I am, again, the Director (interim).

The Stanford Center on Longevity In 2002, I was asked by Stanford's Provost, John Etchemendy, to join a task force to explore interest among Stanford's faculty in participating in a proposed new research Center, the Stanford Center on Longevity to be led by Laura Carstensen, an accomplished life-span psychologist. For me, the invitation underscored my belief that many of the health problems of the elderly have their origins (and/or can be prevented) by attention during childhood and adolescence. The Center was established in 2006 and I continue to serve on its Advisory Board.

The Stanford Center for Research in Disease Prevention Also as a result of earlier collaborations with behavioral scientists, I was very fortunate to be invited to participate in research at this unique resource, the Center for Research in Disease Prevention at Stanford University. There, in the late 1980s we designed and launched a prospective study to examine the antecedents of eating disorders in a population of 5th graders who we followed prospectively, after designing an intervention to prevent their developing these disorders. Although we realized that we had begun the study too late for prevention, the results were most informative (Hammer et al., 1991; Killen et al., 1993, 1994a; Wilson et al., 1991, 1992). As well, we learned that eating disorders were not only found in affluent White teens, as suggested by the literature at the time, but were rising in incidence in low socioeconomic Latinas and Asian-Americans (Robinson et al., 1996). Very importantly, we also learned about the role of early onset of puberty in increasing the risk of eating disorders, as well as other affective disorders (Hayward et al., 1992, 1997; Killen et al. (1992, 1994b, 1997).

The culmination of my career at Stanford University was my receipt of an Endowed Professorship in 2002, the Marron and Mary Elizabeth Kendrick Professor of Pediatrics. This professorship was particularly meaningful, as I had been told at the time of receiving tenure that I was likely the first, but certainly the last, faculty member at Stanford's School of Medicine to do so as a clinical researcher!

Foundations

My career has involved engagement with several private foundations.

The Robert Wood Johnson Foundation (RWJF) has been a *leitmotif* of sorts throughout my academic career. In the mid-1970s they selected our program at Stanford University to be one of the sites of their innovative General Pediatric Academic Development Program with the late Ruth Gross as the PI. This award provided funding for our Fellowship program and placed us in a network of other institutions and their leaders who shared our interest in research in behavioral issues of children and adolescents.

In 1990, I was invited by the late John Eisenberg to join the National Advisory Committee (NAC) of the new RWJF Generalist Physician Faculty Program. The Program was conceived as a mechanism for elevating the visibility of Primary Care faculty and contributing to the research in the field of Generalism, broadly defined. The NAC included pediatric leaders such as Evan Charney and Tom Boat, but also introduced me to a new group of national leaders in the fields of internal medicine and family medicine, ably led by the group's Chair, Ken Shine (President of the Institute of Medicine at the time). The NAC had the responsibility of selecting Scholars, mentoring them, and having them participate in an annual meeting at which their research was presented.

In addition, I was asked to conduct an internal evaluation of the Program, which resulted in its funding being continued by the Foundation for 5 years longer than initially planned. The Program ended in 2003 and was replaced by the RWJF Physician Faculty Scholars Program (PFSP), which I was asked to direct. This Program differed from its predecessor in that it was open to junior medical school faculty from all disciplines, not only the generalists. It provided only 3 years of support. It featured the successful components of the Generalist Program (e.g., annual meeting and mentorship), but added a career development curriculum (delivered through the internet); there was also a formal networking component and a more formal program of mentorship by the NAC. Although its funding ended in the summer of 2012, it has already been successful in accelerating the academic trajectory and publication productivity of the participants, addressing important issues of health care delivery, prevention of adverse health behaviors, and development of innovative strategies for addressing important health problems through their research. It has also served as a model for other academic career development programs. A number of academic faculty in Adolescent Medicine became scholars in these Programs.

While designing and planning the PFSP for the Foundation, I also was National Director for its long-standing Robert Wood Johnson Clinical Scholars Program for 2 years. This is a Fellowship level Program in which participants spend 2 years at one of four sites at medical schools around the country and become involved in interdisciplinary research about health services delivery, prevention, health policy and/or community-based participatory research.

W. T. Grant Foundation In 1998, I was invited by the then President, Betty Hamburg, to join the Selection Committee of the Faculty Scholars Program of the W.T. Grant Foundation, a longtime leader in philanthropic support for research on youth development. I had the pleasure of serving in that capacity until 2003 under three presidents: Betty Hamburg, my former Fellow, Karen Hein and, her successor, Robert Granger.

The Institute of Medicine (IOM)

It was most humbling to have been elected to the prestigious Institute of Medicine of the National Academy of Sciences in 1995. The thrill of my election was equaled only by that of participation in its committees. The care that goes into the composition of these committees, the concern with achieving balance and avoiding any actual or appearance of conflict of interest or bias, the superb staff/research support, and the standards for assuring accuracy is unparalleled in the scientific/policy world, especially impressive given the controversial and important topics addressed. Over the years, I have participated in a number of these committees and generated publications ranging from understanding toxic shock syndrome, to sleep research, and health care needs of lesbians. In each case, the invitation for my participation was grounded in an appreciation of the importance of the special issues for adolescents.

International World

The ability to influence the field of adolescent health around the world through the training of a number of Adolescent Medicine Fellows over the years has been described above. Another, more direct relationship has developed with pediatricians in Thailand who have made great strides over the past decade in establishing services for teens under the auspices of Mahidol University and the leadership of Dr. Subharee Tongudia and Dr. Deo. I now serve as Advisor to the Royal College of Pediatrics, Committee on Adolescents.

Synthesis

Erik Lander put it best when he said: "You live your life prospectively and tell your story retrospectively, so it looks like everything is converging" (Kolata, 2012). It is only as I look back that I appreciate the myriad of contextual, historic, and cultural issues that have influenced the choices I have made and the opportunities I have had over this almost half-century of my work with adolescents reviewed here.

In the late 1960s when I began my adolescent medicine career, I did not do so in a vacuum. New York City was seething with racial strife and the city's juvenile detention center in which I set up health care services proved a microcosm in which otherwise routine medical services were daily examined through the lens of distrust and suspicion. As a naïve 27-year-old, I was often baffled by the misunderstandings that arose. The first Grand Rounds I gave at nearby Lincoln Hospital found the entrance to the lecture hall barred by machine-gun bearing Black Panthers in military garb! Finding myself in a hostage-taking lockdown in Rikers Island Prison during my pregnancy with my son, Bob, was surely frightening but gave me unprecedented (for a middle-class young woman) access to the minds and feelings of an entire segment of both correctional officers and detainees, again played out against a background of racial conflict.

The entire country was experiencing frustration with the seemingly out-of-control behavior of adolescents—rising rates of drug use and pregnancies, as well as criminal activity. Largely out of fear, legislation was passed and funding became available for establishing clinics and hospital facilities with the hope that the medical profession could do something about these problems. This funding made it possible for a number of medical centers, Montefiore included, to build special units for adolescent patients. At the time, there were no data about health problems of this age group and it came as a great surprise to many that once they were brought together and examined as a group, that we discovered a myriad of physical, as well as the expected emotional, health problems. For example, certain cancers (e.g., osteogenic sarcoma, testicular cancer) were unique to the adolescent age group and others had a higher incidence in this age group (e.g., thyroid cancer). Having "captive" populations of teens also provided an opportunity to discern patterns of physical development and their interaction with psychologic development and disease states.

Today this linkage is obvious, but it is important to remember that prior to this time, teens generally avoided coming to doctors and neither their parents or physicians had any reason to advise them to do otherwise. Guided by the discoveries made on hospitalized teens and those in legal detention, we and others began to reach out to teens in community settings, knowing that they would be unlikely to come to traditional health care settings. For example, programs were set up in schools (leading to the now commonplace practice of having school-based clinics) to provide both screening, treatment, and health education. The National Job Corps is another example from the 1970s of the effectiveness of bringing together health services with education and career training in a community setting which has provided a model for care for teens.

These early experiences not only informed our understanding of teenagers and our ability to provide needed services but their impact was felt more broadly. For me, they guided my subsequent embrace of interdisciplinary collaborations as essential to my research but also my appreciation of the need for community involvement, not only in design of services but also in the formulation of research.

My career has been even more fulfilling and rewarding than I could have ever imagined when I chose to become a physician—surely nothing like that of my earliest role model, my father. I have had reason to reflect on my unique journey and the challenges of being a woman in the early years of gender bias in academic medicine on the occasion of my selection to be included in the National Library of Medicines project: "The Changing Face of Medicine: Celebrating America's Women Physicians" (National Library of Medicine Exhibit, 2002).

As I transition to retirement, I will continue my involvement with the next generation of academic physicians as a mentor. I look forward to more time with my wonderful family, especially Abigail (age 3) and Mira (now 9 months) and I am so thankful that I never had to choose between a family and a career. In fact, in retrospect, I realize that each enriched the other. I surely learned a lot about adolescents when my sons entered that category and they, in turn, have said how much their adolescent experience was shaped by the fact that I was "in the business!"

I will also enjoy more time to pursue my passion for creating glass art!

References

Bachrach, L. K., Guido, D., Katzman, D. K., Litt, I. F., & Marcus, R. (1990). Decreased bone density in adolescent girls with anorexia nervosa. *Pediatrics, 86*(3): 440–447.

Bachrach, L. K., Katzman, D. K., Litt, I. F., Guido, D., & Marcus, R. (1991). Recovery from osteopenia in adolescent girls with anorexia nervosa. *Journal of Clinical Endocrinology & Metabolism, 72*(3): 602–606.

Carskadon, M. A., Harvey, K., Duke, P. M., Anders, T., Litt, I. F., & Dement, W. C. (1980). Pubertal changes in daytime sleepiness. *Sleep, 2*(4): 453.

Duke, P. M., Litt, I. F., & Gross, R. T. (1980). Adolescents' self-assessment of sexual maturation by Tanner staging. *Pediatrics, 66*(6): 918.

DuRant, R. H., Jay, M. S., Litt, I. F., Linder, C. W., & Shoffitt, T. (1984). The influence of psychosocial factors on adolescent compliance with oral contraceptives. *Journal of Adolescent Health Care, 5*(1): 1–6.

Friedman, I. M., & Litt, I. F. (1987). Adolescents' compliance with therapeutic regimens: Psychological and social aspects and intervention. *Journal of Adolescent Health Care, 8*: 52–67.

Friedman, I. M., Litt, I. F., Henson, R., Holtzman, D., & Halverson, D. (1981). Saliva, phenobarbital and phenytoin concentration in epileptic adolescents. *Journal of Pediatrics, 98*(4): 645–647.

Friedman, I. M., Litt, I. F., King, D. R., Henson, R., Holtzman, D., Halverson, D. et al. (1986). Compliance with anticonvulsant therapy in epileptic youth: Relationships to psychosocial aspects of adolescent development. *Journal of Adolescent Health Care, 7*: 12–17.

Hammer, L. D., Wilson, D. M., Litt, I. F., Killen, J. D. Hayward, C., Miner, B. et al. (1991). Impact of pubertal development on body fat distribution among White, Hispanic, and Asian female adolescents. *Journal of Pediatrics, 118*: 975–980.

Hayward, C., Killen, J. D., Hammer, L. D., Litt, I. F., Wilson, D. M., Simmonds, B. et al. (1992). Pubertal stage and panic attack occurrence in sixth- and seventh-grade girls. *American Journal of Psychiatry, 149*(9): 1239–1243.

Hayward, C., Killen, J. D., Wilson, M., Hammer, L. D., Litt, I. F., Kraemer, H. C. et al. (1997).The psychiatric risk associated with early puberty in adolescent girls. *Journal of the American Academy of Child & Adolescent Psychiatry, 36*(2): 255–262.

Hein, K., Cohen, M. I., & Litt, I. F. (1979). Illicit drug abuse among urban adolescents: A decade in retrospect. *American Journal of Diseases of Children, 133*: 38.

Hein, K., Cohen, M. I., Litt, I. F., Schonberg, K., Meyer, M. R., & Marks, A. et al. (1980). Juvenile detention: Another boundary issue for physicians. *Pediatrics, 66*(2): 239–245.

Jay, M. S., DuRant, R. H., Litt, I. F., Linder, C. W., & Shoffitt, T. (1984). Riboflavin, self-report, and serum norethindrone: Comparison of their use as indicators of adolescent compliance with oral contraceptives. *American Journal of Diseases of Children, 138*: 70–73.

Jay, M. S., DuRant, R. H., Litt, I. F., Shoffitt, T., & Linder, C. W. (1984). Effect of peer counselors on adolescent compliance with use of oral contraceptives. *Pediatrics, 73*(2): 126–131.

Killen, J. D., Hayward, C., Litt, I. F., Hammer, L. D., Wilson, D. M., Miner, B. et al. (1992). Is puberty a risk factor for eating disorders? *American Journal of Diseases of Children, 146*: 323–325.

Killen, J. D., Hayward, C., Wilson, D. M., Taylor, C. B., Hammer, L. D., Litt, I. et al. (1994a). Factors associated with eating disorder symptoms in a community sample of 6th and 7th grade girls. *International Journal of Eating Disorders, 15*(4): 357–367.

Killen, J. D., Robinson, T. N., Haydel, K. F., Hayward, C., Wilson, D. M., Hammer, L. D. et al. (1997). Prospective study of risk factors for the onset of cigarette smoking. *Journal of Consulting and Clinical Psychology, 65*: 1011–1016.

Killen, J. D., Taylor, C. B., Hammer, L. D., Litt, I. F., Wilson, D. M., Rich, T. et al. (1993). An attempt to modify unhealthful eating attitudes and weight regulation practices of young adolescent girls. *International Journal of Eating Disorders, 13*: 369–384.

Killen, J. D., Taylor, C. B., Hayward, C., Wilson, D. M., Haydel, K. F., Hammer, L. D. et al. (1994b). Pursuit of thinness and onset of eating disorder symptoms in a community sample of adolescent girls: A three-year prospective analysis. *International Journal of Eating Disorders, 16*(3): 227–238.

Kolata, G. (2012). Power in numbers. *New York Times, Science Times,* January 3: D1.

Litt, I. F. (1983). The physician and imprisoned youth. *Pharos 46*(3): 15–19.

Litt I. F. (1985). Know thyself: Adolescents' self-assessment of compliance. *Pediatrics, 75*: 693–696.

Litt, I. F. (1997). *Taking our pulse: The health of America's women.* Stanford University Press.

Litt, I. F., & Cohen, M. I. (1974). Prisons, adolescents, and the right to quality medical care: The time is now. *American Journal of Public Health, 64*: 894–897.

Litt, I. F., & Cohen, M. I. (1978). Training in adolescent health as viewed by pediatric house officers. *Journal of Medical Education, 53*: 608–609.

Litt, I. F., Colli, A. S., & Cohen, M. I. (1971). Diazepam in the management of heroin withdrawal in adolescents: A preliminary report. *Journal of Pediatrics, 78*: 692–696.

Litt, I. F., & Cuskey, W. R. (1981). Compliance with salicylate therapy in adolescents with juvenile rheumatoid arthritis. *American Journal of Diseases of Children, 135*(5): 434–436.

Litt, I. F., Cuskey, W. R., & Rosenberg, A. (1982). The role of self-esteem and autonomy in determining medication compliance among adolescents with juvenile rheumatoid arthritis. *Pediatrics, 69*(1): 15–17.

Litt, I. F., Cuskey, W. R., & Rudd, S. (1980). Identifying adolescents at risk for noncompliance with contraceptive therapy. *Journal of Pediatrics, 96*(4): 742–745.

Litt, I. F., Jay, M. S., & DuRant, R. H. (1984). Compliance with therapeutic regimens. *Journal of Adolescent Health Care, 5*(2): 124–136.

Litt, I. F., & Schonberg, S. K. (1975). Medical complications of drug abuse in adolescents. *Medical Clinics of North America, 59*: 1445–1452.

National Library of Medicine Exhibit (2002). Changing the face of medicine: Celebrating America's women physicians. Available at: http://www.nlm.gov/changingthefaceofmedicine/physicians/biography_161.html

Neel, E. U., Jay, M. S., & Litt, I. F. (1985). The relationship of self-concept and autonomy to oral contraceptive compliance among adolescents. *Journal of Adolescent Health Care, 6*: 445–447.

Neel, E. U., Litt, I. F., & Jay, M. S. (1987). Side effects and compliance with low- and conventional-dose oral contraceptives among adolescents. *Journal of Adolescent Health Care, 8*: 327–329.

Robinson, T. N., Killen, J. D., Litt, I. F., Hammer, L. D., Wilson, D. M., Haydel, K. F. et al. (1996). Ethnicity and body dissatisfaction: Are Hispanic and Asian girls at increased risk for eating disorders? *Journal of Adolescent Health, 19*(6): 384–393.

Steiner, H., Mazer, C., & Litt, I. F. (1990). Compliance and outcome in anorexia nervosa. *Western Journal of Medicine, 153*: 133–139.

Steiner, H., Smith, C., Rosenkranz, R. T., & Litt, I. F. (1991). The early care and feeding of anorexics. *Child Psychiatry and Human Development, 21*(3): 163–167.

Vaughan, V. C., & Litt, I. F. (1990). *Child and adolescent development: Clinical implications.* Philadelphia: W.C. Saunders.

Wilson, D. M., Killen, J. D., Hammer, L. D., Litt, I. F., Vosti, C., Miner, B. et al. (1991). Insulin-like growth factor-I as a reflection of body composition, nutrition, and puberty in 6th and 7th grade girls. *Journal of Clinical Endocrinology & Metabolism, 73*: 907–912.

Wilson, D. M., Stene, M. A., Killen, J. D., Hammer, L. D., Litt, I. F., Hayward, C. et al. (1992). Insulin-like growth factor binding protein-3 in normal pubertal girls. *Acta Endocrinologica, 126*: 381–386.

28

Individual Development—a Transformation Process

A Longitudinal Program

DAVID MAGNUSSON

Introduction

This chapter presents my ideas for how to study individual development as a transformation process. I hope that they can be helpful to researchers planning to conduct longitudinal research. The main vehicle for outlining these ideas is a description of a longitudinal research program that I initiated and led for more than 30 years, namely Individual Development and Adaptation (IDA). It is presented in some detail, and includes the process of IDA's initiation and planning. The theoretical and empirical implications of the carrying out of the program for research on the adolescent period are discussed at the end of the chapter. Because my early experiences and educational background have been decisive for how IDA was designed and implemented, some personal information is also included.

Personal Background

Upbringing Conditions My upbringing environment was a small farm in the highlands of southern Sweden. I was born as the second son with an older brother, two younger brothers, and a younger sister. My parents were warm and social people with a high respect for education, not because it meant a higher social position, but rather that it had a high value in itself.

The way we lived and worked on the farm has meant a lot for me, not only in my private life but also in my scientific work. The way we constantly collaborated, with the focus on the work that had to be done, founded my view of myself and my place in society. What nowadays is considered leisure time, was for us totally filled with work. The seasons determined the work that had to be done, whether it was spring, summer, autumn, or winter. What we could decide was how we could do the work.

The cultural code that dominated the home of my upbringing was old-time religious practice, and this code formed a mental world of self-confidence, integrity, and responsibility. The cultural code of the village built a world of mutual trust and respect for other individuals and for common rules. It was a world that is nowadays infrequent as an upbringing environment for children and youngsters.

The economic conditions for farming in the village were limited. I assume that some people would feel sorry for the children, who had to grow up under such poor conditions. Let me emphasize, I could not imagine a more positive environment to grow up in, and not only for social reasons. From some of the basic rules for successful farming, I learned some of the basic rules for successful scientific work. For example, the necessary prerequisite for a final good harvest was a careful matching of soil for the seed one wanted to cultivate, constructive collaboration, and the need for long-term planning, considering the conditions under we worked.

Although the cultural codes for family and village life contributed to a secure and positive upbringing, the later successive adjustments to environments with other, sometimes conflicting cultural codes was not without problems, both in my personal social life and in my professional life. With due consideration, my experiences show the enormously strong power of the socialization process during the first years of life.

When I began my schooling in 1932, at the age of 7, the local school was situated in another village. Sometimes the school children were transported by car, other times we had to walk about 3 miles, mainly through the forest. This walk offered a lot of experiences about nature and the way its life changed with the seasons.

Among other experiences, I remember one with long-term implications for my social and professional life. In the forest I learned that ants always built their anthills with consideration to the direction of the sun. One morning, parts of an anthill had collapsed. Some days later, the anthill was totally repaired. When I arrived at the school, I asked the teacher a question that I still wonder about: "How does each ant know, where it shall locate the specific needle that it has just found, so that the total result of all ants' achievements will become a functioning ant-hill and not a heap of needles?" From history I had learned how people with good intentions killed each other for "the sake." In the long run it taught me first that in a functioning society all members are equally important, no one is more important than the other, and second, each member can best contribute to a good society by participating in constructive collaboration with other members in the position he/she has adapted to.

Compulsory basic education lasted for 6 years. In 1938, I applied for entrance to the secondary school. It was situated in the neighboring small town about 3 miles from my home village. At that time the entrance examination took several days and consisted of written and oral examination in basic subjects.

Personal Experiences in Teaching Children and Youngsters Scientific endeavors are triggered by the desire to find an answer to a particular question. The research being undertaken, within the framework of the IDA program, seeks answers to questions that are rooted in a realistic and true-to-life analysis of the lifelong individual process that one wishes to comprehend and, if possible, explain.

My interest in the issues that engage the IDA program stems from my early experience of children of various ages. After completing the 4-year teacher-training course at the college for elementary school teachers in Linköping in 1946, I worked until 1952 as a primary school teacher in a small town in Småland. There I taught an unselected class of boys and girls whom I followed from their third to seventh school year. My time at that school ended with a class of boys and girls at the age of 9–10 years of age. During several years I also taught voluntary evening classes for youngsters and adults.

On a leave of absence, I studied in Stockholm for a year (1952–53) at the Erica Foundation's institute for remedial teaching. This period of study entailed attending lectures and seminars, as well as making observations and reporting therapy with children with specific disturbances.

After a year as a primary school teacher in Solna (1953–54), combined with studies at the University of Stockholm, I worked half time in Solna as a school psychologist. Half of my time was devoted to being head teacher for a small group of 14–15-year-olds who had difficulty in keeping up with an ordinary class. These tasks gave me important insights into the uniqueness of individual development during childhood and adolescence, not least the part played by the family in the transformation process. This period was during the introduction of school psychology in Sweden; as the only psychologist I was responsible for 9,000 pupils. One of my functions was to attend the child and youth guidance unit (PBU) once a fortnight to report and obtain comments on an acute case among my pupils.

Conclusions My experiences as a primary school teacher and school psychologist were of direct importance for the planning and implementation of the IDA project:

1. When I welcomed 26 pupils, who were 9 years of age, in 1946 they seemed to me to be a largely homogeneous group, though obviously differing in height, weight, and appearance. However, I soon arrived at what for a teacher and scientist is a vital insight: each child is a unique, indivisible whole in continuous interaction with the individually unique environment in which it acts and grows up. Looking back, I realize that when I tried to understand a child or a teenager, I never thought in terms of variables.
2. When the pupils were about 11 or 12 years old, I noted that some of the girls turned into young women with developed bodies, while others the same age were still children. I also saw that this difference had consequences for how they behaved in general, for instance in their relationships with boys and other elements of their environment.

Two conclusions of importance for scientific research on the transformation process of a girl or a boy could be drawn: (1) the way in which each individual functions in a particular situation and the content and form of his/her transformation process are unique; and (2) in order to understand and explain an individual's behavior in a particular school environment, as well as how this affects his/her transformation process, it is necessary to follow individuals over time.

When in my professional life I sought answers to questions that arose from the behavior of a particular pupil, I was surprised to find that the relevant research had largely disregarded the two circumstances that I referred to above. The literature was filled with cross-sectional studies of certain variables or constellations of variables at a group level with no consideration for the unique aspects of the pupils' mental and behavioral responses to the educational and environmental demands on behavior and learning.

University Teaching When I started to teach at the department of psychology in Stockholm in 1958 and later supervised graduate students, the earlier experiences prompted questions. Two circumstances colored my university entrance. One was Gösta Ekman, the department's head and sole professor, who was internationally known for his research, which focused on methods for measuring basal cognitive processes. The other circumstance was the general perception of research as being rooted in traditional theories and models from the natural sciences. There was a tacit understanding that psychological research should aim for what J. B. Watson (1913) formulated in his presentation of behaviorism, namely "to predict and control behavior," and that experiments were science's proper empirical method for achieving this end. These two aspects of the scientific process provided the implicit foundation for perceiving psychology as a natural science. In that tradition I wrote the textbook *Test teori* (Magnusson, 1961). The Swedish version was translated into more than a dozen other languages (see, e.g., Magnusson, 1967).

International Contacts

From the start of IDA, international contacts and collaborations with leading scientists and research groups played an important role. They have continuously contributed to mutual exchange of information in both directions.

Study Trip to the USA Crucial for my research, including the planning and implementation of IDA, was that in 1963 the Council for Social Science Research provided funds for a study trip to the USA. This trip enabled me to attend the international congress in Washington and then visit internationally established scientists, particularly those involved in developmental psychology and in methods for psychological research. The international congress in Washington yielded two matters of decisive importance for the evolution of IDA. One was a long discussion with the person in charge of Project Talent, a longitudinal research venture that had been set up in the United States in 1960 in response to the Soviet challenge in space research. The other was my first encounter with Saul B. Sells, one of the pioneers of interactionism; our meeting initiated a life-long collaboration.

My stay in the USA in the late summer of 1963 gave me opportunities to discuss research in developmental psychology with Harold Seashore and Robert Thorndike II in New York, Raymond B. Cattell and Joe McV. Hunt at Champagne-Urbana, Illinois, J.P. Guilford in Los Angeles, and Paul Horst in Seattle, all of them internationally leading researchers in psychological theory and method. These discussions were exceedingly fruitful, particularly those with Joe McV. Hunt, a former president of the American Psychological Association (APA) whose book *Intelligence and Experience* had introduced Piaget's ideas in the USA. After a talk at the hotel, where I was staying, he invited me to a continuation at his home; two days of talking later he stood up and declared, "Go home and do it!" This laid the foundation for a life-long professional affinity and personal friendship.

These encounters were crucial for my future: the subjects that engaged me were acceptable as research in an international perspective!

Planning and Preparing Data Collections

After a thorough perusal by the head of a division at the Swedish National Board of Education, in spring 1964, the Board decided to support the longitudinal research program, known initially as the Örebro Project. The first data collection was carried out in the spring 1965, after intense planning in the previous autumn.

A scientifically grounded understanding of individual transformation processes calls for a meticulous analysis not only of individually specific processes, but also of the contextual conditions for these processes. Such an analysis provides the necessary foundation for the choice of research strategy, research methods, and the use of statistics. The important preparatory work took various forms.

Preparatory Empirical Studies One of a number of useful measures of children's and adolescents' development is teachers' ratings of pupils. When such ratings of pupils of the same chronological age but from different classes are combined, the statistical processing is complicated by different sources of error. One problem in planning IDA was that girls and boys in mixed classed would be rated by male and female teachers, respectively. A preliminary study in 1961–62, using data from a school district in Stockholm, tested whether there were any systematic differences between male and female teachers in their assessments of the behavior of pupils of the opposite sex. The results played a decisive role in the formulation of the instructions to teachers for their ratings in IDA. These assessments proved to be very valuable for the analyses of the different aspects of individual transformation processes.

An important aspect of the individual transformative process is each child's and adolescent's self-perception. A preliminary study of the value of self-ratings in the pattern of individual personalities was undertaken and reported in the departmental report series.

Group of Founders Planning during the autumn of 1964 and the early part of 1965 was managed by a working group consisting of myself, Anders Dunér, and Rolf Beckne. Anders Dunér had a broad theoretical knowledge of individuals' developmental processes, theoretical insights into and understanding of methodological problems at all levels, and varied experience of children of different ages. He played a central part in the management of IDA, not least during the vital phase of planning and initiation. His experience as a teacher and headmaster in a local school system for years helped to make the cooperation with all those involved realistic. Thanks to his post as principal school psychologist in the community in which the data collections were performed and as the head psychologist in the school system, in which we planned to implement the program, Rolf Beckne played a significant part in the planning and implementation of the program.

The team's work involved analyzing the overall issues and their consequences for the formulation of specific questions, as well as for relevant research strategies and methods for the study of such questions. At regular meetings we discussed general theoretical frameworks, specific issues, forms for collaboration with researchers in key fields (medicine, sociology, and criminology), forms for cooperation with local and government authorities, school health care, the medical profession, parents, and the press. The work was documented in mimeographed reports presenting the initial planning of the project.

Local Authorities After due deliberation it was decided that the collection of data on school children and their home conditions could best be arranged with Örebro Municipality. My conversations in Washington in 1963 with Project Talent's administrator were worth a great deal when making this decision. He advised against a nationally representative sample and suggested instead that we study all the pupils in a municipality that would have a sufficiently large number of youngsters for studies of special samples. Subsequent developments proved that this was a wise advice, not the least because one of the benefits was the positive and constructive attitude of all those concerned.

Local Planning—Working Group Our combined experiences from schoolwork indicated that the success of what we planned depended a great deal on cooperation with all those concerned. Other longitudinal studies that were being planned at the time had been discontinued because of insufficient preparation of contacts with the school, parents, and representatives of society.

In order to create a favorable climate for the program, in autumn 1964 I arranged a number of meetings with the head of the local education authority, the senior school medical officer, representatives of the parent and teacher associations, and the two local newspapers in Örebro. As a result, a local working group with representatives of the parties concerned was formed at an early stage. The members included someone from the National Board of Education, the chairman of the local school board, the head of Örebro's local education authority, Örebro's senior school medical officer, the chairman of the parents association, and representatives of the teachers at each level.

The working group was very active throughout the planning period and the data collections. Its members examined, commented on and approved each step in the data collections, the instruments for this work, and the kind of information that the pupils and parents were given prior to each data collection. The same information was given to the journalist at each of the local newspapers who was covering the research program.

The Press During one of my visits in Örebro in autumn 1964 I met the two local newspapers' editors-in-chief. We agreed that both papers would first receive information about the program's overall aims and organization and then regular information about each planned data collection and its purpose. They in turn undertook to delegate a member of their staff as the recipient of all information from the program and as the person who would inform anyone who happened to inquire. This step turned out to be of major, if not decisive importance. Some other contemporary research projects that were at least partly based on teachers' ratings of pupils of various ages ran into trouble, because what pupils told their parents, often due to misunderstandings, prompted the latter to complain

in letters to the press and the authorities. The information that parents received prior to each data collection in IDA meant that we avoided such misunderstandings. On one occasion parents did turn to one of the newspapers to complain about the content of a questionnaire, whereupon the journalist, who handled IDA information, was able to put the matter straight. A single such misunderstanding that could not be cleared up in time would have been sufficient to ruin the program.

It may be worth noting that one of the editors-in-chief got in touch and suggested I should write an article about our agreement for one of the national papers. In his broad experience of the media world, the way we managed information was unique in the interplay between research and the press. As he saw it, researchers divulged as little as possible in order to avoid a public discussion that they either could not, or did not, want to handle. To him, what we were doing was an innovation in relations between academia and the press and it ought to be made public.

Frame of Reference for the Collection of Data—a Holistic View

My own experiences as a school teacher and as a school psychologist, together with my stay at the Erica Foundation, laid the ground for the planning of the data collections in IDA, *the holistic view* of individual functioning and development. The scientific world that I met when I entered the university was dominated by the paradigm fetched from experimental psychology. The questions were concentrated on pieces of cognitive models. On the person side of individual functioning and development, the *variable* was the most important concept. In my experiences I had never thought about a youngster in terms of variables. The unwillingness to discuss problems related to youngsters' real world was a surprise. My propositions and questions were met by some with open scorn and called "scientific prostitution."

In 1969 I was appointed professor of psychology at Stockholm University and chairman of the department of psychology. At that time, there was only one professorship of psychology at the University. Because supplied teachers had filled the position of chairman for more than 4 years, there were two important long-term problems to be solved, when I entered the position in 1969—the lack of higher positions as professor and the lack of suitable localities, particularly for advanced laboratory work. Very competent scientists worked without optimal organization for scientific collaboration; accordingly, strengthening the scientific competence through new professorships, and increasing the local space for the department became the most important tasks.

My interpretation of the goal of psychology as a scientific discipline guided my work as a chairman of the department. In my mind, *the goal of scientific psychology was and is to understand and explain why and how the individual, as an active, integrated psychobiological and social human being in continuous interaction with his/ her proximal and distal environment, functions currently and develops over time* in a transformation process. This holistic view was discussed in terms of *a person-oriented approach* (Magnusson, 2003).[1]

The holistic view was adopted in general terms from the beginning in the planning and implementation of the data collections in the IDA program. Hereby, the ground was laid for empirical studies of developmental issues that were in tune with important new propositions for measurement models that could match the character of the processes of central interest to us.

Collection of Data

As mentioned above, the first data collections were carried out in late spring 1965; they are described in more detail in Magnusson, Dunér, & Zetterblom (1975). Göran Zetterbom made an important contribution to that work before moving to an administrative post in the Office of the Chancellor of Swedish Universities. The following account summarizes the collections and considers some aspects of the database.

The first data collection involved the pupils in three grades and their parents:

Grade 3:	1,025 pupils
Grade 6:	960 pupils
Grade 8:	1,259 pupils

In the Swedish school system at that time, children started school at the age of seven. Accordingly, at the time of the first data collection in 1965, a majority of the pupils in the three cohorts were approximately 10, 13, and 15 years old, respectively.

Study Groups

1. *The main group.* The pupils in Grade 3 at the time of the first data collection in 1965—the youngest of the groups—constituted and still are the research program's main group. This group was subsequently followed with extensive data collections, focusing on teenage problems, in 1968 and 1970, when a majority of these pupils were 13 and 15 years old, respectively. The main group is still being followed.
2. *The pilot group.* The group of pupils, who were around 13 years old at the time of the first data collection, was followed by collecting new data 3 years later. Accordingly, the database contains information about two cohorts in their early teens, an important phase of development.
3. Data for the Grade 8 pupils, who were about 15 years old at the time of the first collection in 1965, were not collected later. Data for this group only served and still may serve under specific conditions for control of cohort effects.

4. *Biomedical sample.* A sample of around 240 boys and girls (later men and women) from the main group was obtained in order to supplement the main database with data that had to be collected individually, above all data for aspects of the transformation process that could not be covered in the main collections. The biological studies concerned cognitive processes and electrophysiological cerebral activity (EEG), the collection and analysis of urine samples for the study of adrenaline excretion, and tests of physical strength and lung capacity. The data from the sample were first obtained in connection with the second extensive collection of data in 1968, when the pupils of the main group were around the age of 13. The sample has been followed together with each new collection of data for the main group. Detailed presentations of the data collection process were given in Magnusson (1988).

Sources of Information Information about the individuals was obtained from the pupils themselves, their parents, teachers, authorities (register data), school medical officers, and school psychologists. In every case the collection was preceded by a discussion in the local working group. The data are stored with strict confidence and limited access. All the participants have been informed about the content of the database, how data have been made non-identifiable, and how they are used.

Situation-Specific Assessments While traditional methods could be used to study certain aspects of the individual transformation process, in other cases they did not suit our purpose. A good example is the study of individual teenage behavior connected with cultural values and codes. With reference to my concurrent research program, Holistic Interactionism, new instruments were developed for such studies (see Magnusson, 1999; Magnusson & Törestad, 1993). Instead of the usual practice of using general questions about values, for instance "Is stealing acceptable?," questions were formulated in terms of situational behavior, for instance "Bob/Mary is in a store and can conceal a pocket calculator in his/her coat without getting caught," followed by questions concerning the pupil's own behavior, how he/she expected peers to behave and react, and the expected reactions of parents, etc. The pupils' responses to a series of questions of this type—indicating their own situational behavior, peers' expected behavior, and parents' expected reactions to ten situations of relevance to teenagers—yielded important individual information.

Upbringing Conditions In the first data collection the parents—with an exceptionally high response rate (98%)—provided information of fundamental importance for the studies at an individual level, which was the program's objective. These data were essential for elucidating the role that parental values, as manifested for example in various forms of social engagement, may play in an individual's developmental process.

Register Data An important addition to the data provided directly by the participants consisted of extracts from various registers: on crime, obstetrics, psychiatry, and alcohol abuse. All the participants have been informed about access to these data.

Access to Data IDA's database is a result of careful planning in accordance with a general theoretical approach and the intention of collecting data from the same individuals over a period of more than four decades. As evaluators with different perspectives have pointed out, this research affords unusually valuable possibilities for studying questions of importance in developmental psychology. Under these circumstances it is natural that, given an agreement with IDA's management, the data in the IDA database can be made available for research after due discussions with the leaders of the program.

In traditional research in developmental psychology, statistical methods are commonly chosen for answering questions without the choice of method being preceded by a thorough analysis of the developmental processes that are to be understood and explained. This tradition is partly sustained by the superficial sense of credibility and meaningfulness that the use of data and statistics imparts (see, e.g., Sorensen, 1998). In this tradition IDA's database would very soon be ruined and useless for scientifically planned and implemented analyses. Therefore, access to IDA data has to be limited by specific restrictions to preserve the database's scientific quality.

Final Points

The data collections to date are presented in a report by Lars Bergman (Bergman, 2008). Virtually every data collection, from the first, extensive one in 1965 onwards, went smoothly in accordance with the planning that preceded it. The data, which have been regularly collected and stored in ways that the local working group was fully informed about, have been preserved intact.

In connection with each data collection, information about what had been planned was distributed to teachers, parents, and the press. The meetings that had been held with the local working group contributed to the formulation of this information. In the occasional public discussions of conditions for and the value of longitudinal studies, IDA's open way of presenting the research program has been seen as important. This approach has provided a ground for the positive attitude that has characterized every assessment of the project. The way in which all individual data in the database are protected so that the participants' identities cannot be revealed has contributed to the positive reception. In the late 1980s, when longitudinal research was being debated in the Swedish parliament, an otherwise critical member cited IDA as a model for how such research ought to be prepared, implemented, and reported.

Running Research Activities

Seminars For a long time, continuous discussions in the regular weekly research seminars at the Department of Psychology at Stockholm University were important elements in the planning and implementation of the entire program. These sessions, which began at an early stage, dealt with the general theoretical and methodological issues that arose as the program took shape. There were frequent discussions of graduate papers and dissertations. The seminars were also an opportunity for visiting scholars to present their research. In this way and by participating in the regular discussions, they helped to keep us aware of the international research perspective. Regularly we invited representatives of other scientific disciplines of interest for a scientific study of individual development. For example, Professor David Ingvar spoke about modern knowledge of brain functioning, Professor Uno Lindberg presented microbiological research on embryonic development, and Professor Birgitta Tullberg gave a talk on modern genetic theories about the dichotomy of inheritance and environment.

The regularity of the seminars and the breadth and depth of their treatment of important issues, usually with contributions by highly competent scientists, made the sessions increasingly popular. A growing number of participants came from practical fields, for example school medical officers, or from other scientific disciplines. The seminar room was quite often filled to capacity and we had to use the corridor as well.

Publications Studies using IDA data have regularly been reported in different ways. Since the beginning of the 1960s, one of IDA activities has been to present preliminary results in project reports, then to publish them in the usual international journals or books.

Directing Research In that the individual information covered an increasingly long section of the individual transformation process, the available data became more and more extensive and complex. After each round of data collection, a new, sizeable body of data had to be incorporated in the existing database without revealing the participants' identity.

In the late 1980s the responsibility for specific parts of the program was allocated to active colleagues so that the planning and implementation of data collection, and the utilization of available data, could be kept in line with the holistic approach behind the program's theoretical scientific framework. By way of informing all participating researchers and funders, including scientists abroad and visiting researchers, the structure of the theoretical background and the current allocation of responsibilities were summarized in a brochure: *The Laboratory for Longitudinal Research on Individual Development.*

Within the framework of the holistic approach, which was my responsibility, the specific responsibilities were assigned as follows:

- *Socialization and antisocial development:* Håkan Stattin, currently professor of psychology at Örebro University.
- *Personality and psychobiology:* Britt af Klinteberg, currently professor emeritus of psychology at Stockholm University, affiliated with Karolinska Institutet.
- *Alcohol and drug abuse:* Tommy Andersson, currently assistant professor and lecturer at Umeå University.
- *Methodological and empirical aspects of a person-oriented approach to individual development:* Lars R. Bergman, from 1994 Professor of behavioral science research methodology at Stockholm University.

The Database A central task in the implementation of the research program is to arrange for all the collected information—specific for each individual or otherwise relevant for the study of individual development—to be assembled in a database. Examiners in various contexts have underscored the database's scientific value for future studies of individual development. For many years Lars Bergman played a central part in building up the database, from the time when each collection of data was being planned to the database's organization and accessibility. For almost three decades the daily, time-consuming and sometimes unenviable task of adding new data to the existing base and keeping, in an efficient and meticulous way, the base accessible for scientists with various interests, has been in Ola Andersson's hands. Without Lars Bergman's leadership and Ola Andersson's conscientious efforts, the extremely complex and vast database could easily have been abused and come to resemble a heap of pine needles rather than a functional anthill. During Lars Bergman's time of responsibility for the IDA database, Petter Zettergren has served as a member of his working group.

International Links

It takes time for a longitudinal program to yield its scientific harvest. Time is, of course, a fundamental dimension for the implementation of such a program. This role of time puts a premium on the ability of those concerned to plan for the long run. In this context, recurrent international contacts with scientists, research teams, and institutions became increasingly important as time passed and the program became internationally established and recognized.

Visiting Scientists Material assembled in a longitudinal research program, that is scientifically sound and sustainable, becomes increasingly valuable as time passes. For different reasons, scientists of varying rank, from PhD students to internationally established scholars, came to the research program for a shorter or longer stay. Visiting scientists have been valuable participants in our seminars and daily discussions.

Besides the presentation of the research program in scientific journals, natural components of international cooperation have been presentations at local and international seminars and my work as a member of research committees in various countries. Participation in seminars, symposia, and congresses provided natural opportunities to meet other scientists, exchange ideas, and share information about developments in various fields.

International Research Collaboration As a member of scientific committees at research institutions in Berlin, North Carolina, Penn State, and Michigan, I obtained information not only about current research results but also about plans and ideas at the cutting-edge of research. At the same time, I was in a position to inform leading centers of research about our work in IDA. For many years, I enjoyed particularly close personal contacts, among others, with Paul Baltes at the Max Planck institute in Berlin, Jack and Jeanne Block at Berkely, Robert and Beverly Cairns at the Center for Developmental Science in North Carolina, Richard Jessor in Boulder, Colorado, Richard Lerner, Anne Petersen, and John Nesselroade at Penn State, Jeanne Brooks-Gunn at Teachers College, and Larry Pervin at Rutgers University. Through these contacts, a mutual exchange of scientists gave us a continuous flow of information about the current international state of research at the same time as we were able to spread information about what was happening at IDA.

Finland and the Baltic States One of our earliest collaborations with longitudinal research programs abroad was with the program that Professor Lea Pulkkinen initiated and led for a long time in Jyväskylä, Finland. Pulkkinen's program soon found its place in the informal international network that evolved in the 1980s and 1990s (see, e.g., Pulkkinen, Virtanen, af Klinteberg, & Magnusson, 2000). This cooperation has been sustained in various forms under Lars Bergman's guidance. He has also overseen the development of cooperation with the Baltic states, in particular with Lithuania. Among other things, this collaboration has led to visits by scientists and to work on doctoral dissertations presented at Stockholm University.

Eastern Europe Regular participation in symposia that were organized by scientists from Eastern Europe, was interesting and valuable, not least for our mutual scientific exchange. Developmental psychology was the dominant theme. The meetings were organized locally and this arrangement caught on in East and West Germany, Poland, Bulgaria, Austria, what was then Czechoslovakia, and Russia.

The origin of this lively collaboration with East European scientists was an invitation to a symposium in Czechoslovakia in 1973. The collaboration, which continued for decades, took two forms. One consisted of regular invitations to the seminars in these countries in the 1970s and 1980s, which enabled me to follow their research in various fields and present what IDA was doing. The other was the active collaboration that IDA co-workers established with the research institute of the Russian Academy of Science (NAUK). Close cooperation with Boris Lomov at the Academy and with Andrej Brushlinsky and Tatjana Ushakova at its research institute stimulated my own thinking and scientific output. One indication that IDA's scientific quality was appreciated was my election as a foreign member of the Academy. In that NAUK is one of Europe's oldest and most respected academies of science, this election could be seen as a token of international recognition of our work.

Empirical Research Collaboration While some of the symposia, for natural reasons, were marked by the political situation in East European countries, they still provided opportunities for fruitful scientific exchange. Among other things, I learned a great deal about the historical background of modern psychological research, including studies in developmental psychology, much of it less well known to western scientists. In 1994, my coworkers and I presented our longitudinal research program during a visit to the department of psychological research at the Academy of Science in Moscow. Supported by the Swedish Academy of Science, one of IDA's staff, Britt af Klinteberg, initiated a program of collaboration with the Russian department's researchers, an activity that continued for many years.

One of our studies is noteworthy in this context. Eva Chinnapah, a senior scientist with roots in Czechoslovakia and with knowledge of differences in childhood cultural environments, contributed to a multicultural follow-up of IDA's data from the teenage period. The Swedish data had indicated that teenage behavior was strongly influenced by environmental cultural codes. A study about this issue was undertaken in a small eastern town in the Czech Republic, where traditional conservative cultural codes still applied. In this cultural environment the teenage girls' behavior in relation to the opposite sex was considerably more restrained than that of their Swedish counterparts. Studies of this type are naturally of great importance, above all the data from the person-oriented approach on which the IDA research program is based. With reference to the focus of this volume on the adolescent period of individual development, this result is of special interest and shows the importance of further cross-cultural studies. Such studies play an important role for the discussion of distal environmental factors in the individual transformation process.

The European Science Foundation (ESF) was founded in 1974 by academies of science and research councils in Western Europe; their counterparts in Eastern Europe have also been members since the fall of the Berlin wall. I became Sweden's representative in ESF's Council in 1983 and one of three vice presidents in 1986. Over the years, ESF has been active and successful in organizing various forms of cooperation between research teams in Europe and this collaboration has been arranged most cost-effectively.

In September 1984, the research ministers of West European governments met in Paris to consider the promotion of scientific cooperation at the European level. They concluded that the best forum for discussing and initiating such plans would be a body dominated by scientists. ESF responded to the challenge and invited all its member countries to submit proposals for scientific networks. Later in 1984, after a discussion with Kerstin Niblaeus, Under-Secretary of State at the Swedish Ministry of Education and Research, and with a colleague of hers, to discuss possible Swedish initiatives, I was asked to draft a proposal for a European network for longitudinal research. I did so and the result was presented to ESF as a possible Swedish contribution.

An independent committee perused all the proposals that ESF received and ranked them for scientific quality and European relevance. The Swedish proposal was well received and a decision was made establish the first official network: The European Network for Longitudinal Research on Individual Development. The research councils in 11 European countries accepted the invitation to participate in this network and agreed to cover its costs. As chairman, I then led the most competent committee I have ever worked on; its members included leading scientists from fields of importance for an understanding of the individual developmental process: psychology, biology, psychiatry, and criminality.

The cooperation in this network produced eight volumes, published by the Cambridge University Press, and setting out theoretical and methodological analyses of longitudinal research in various fields. Lars Bergman was a prominent participant in a symposium on method. Bertil Törestad, another long-term colleague, made an important contribution as an organizer and coordinator of the symposia. Another product of the network was a published account of all the current longitudinal programs in Europe; they totaled around 500 projects. As proposed by the committee, the future task of updating this report was handed over to a European research center in Trier, Germany.

Links with the United States As a member of the Board of Trustees for the Social Science Research Council in the USA since 1991, I was able to promote European social science research cooperation with the USA. As I was also a member of the Swedish Academy of Science and chaired its social science class, it helped to widen our outlook on international research.

The work of the network under ESF had an international impact and highlighted Europe's leading role in the theory and methodology of longitudinal research. This leadership was evident from a growing interest in setting up new longitudinal research programs, for instance in the form of Euro-American networks.

Summary Two aspects of international cooperation have had decisive effects on our work. One is frequent participation in international symposia and seminars. The other is visits by scientists at every level, from PhD students to internationally prominent persons, who stayed at our department for various durations.

Finances

As mentioned earlier, the approach on which IDA is based did not find favor with experimental psychologists, in Sweden or elsewhere. Some educationists, for instance, considered that the project's aims belonged to their research territory. In 1977, a fairly new Swedish journal on research into education published an assessment of IDA by a reputable educationist professor, whose main field was statistical methodology. He was extremely critical of IDA and concluded that cross-sectional studies would yield the same scientific results more quickly and at considerably less cost.

This article had immediate consequences. I was summoned to the director-general of the National Board of Education who told me that unfortunately the Board could no longer fund IDA. The reason he gave was the article in question and the professor's reputation as a scientist.

To obtain future financial support for IDA, the application for money was sent to the Swedish Council for Planning and Coordination of Research. Shortly before my application was considered, I incidentally met the Council's chairman, who had just read the application and considered that we had a good case. From then on, IDA was funded mainly by the Council and the Bank of Sweden Tercentenary Foundation.

There was a period when IDA benefited greatly from a decision that research programs that are dependent on long-term funding would be guaranteed a continuous flow of funds subject to certain controls. If it is to yield the return that meets the necessary scientific standards, such research cannot be discontinued for a time and then resumed when funds become available again.

Coworkers

The extent to which a longitudinal program functions properly and the quality of its results depend on many people's competence and efforts. The inputs to IDA have naturally varied over time. Many of those who have been involved in the program are easily identified from their authorship of the papers that have been published in scientific journals or reported in the program's internal series. Most of those from the early decades are also presented in Magnusson (1988). Others who have made important, sometimes crucial, contributions are liable to be overlooked. At least some of those without whose efforts IDA

would not have become what it is today are mentioned below. Graduates at various levels displayed great enthusiasm and commitment in the choice and development of relevant methods for the study of teenage problems, and thereby contributed to the database's content of important data for the study of individuals' development processes during that period.

Neither would IDA have attained its present position without the program's secretarial staff. They have been important, not least of all for our international contacts. During the first 16 years of the program these contacts were one of Barbro Svensson's responsibilities and she saw to it that they became increasingly lively. This responsibility was taken over in 1986 by Luki Hagen as head of the secretariat. In recent decades, Viera Dornic has been in charge of financial supervision and the accounting of research grants. The responsibility for the present overview was taken by Jelena Corovic.

Scientific Assessments

A research program such as IDA is dependent on continuous funding. This support has entailed reports of the program and its theoretical foundation, which in turn has consequences for the choice of sources of information, methods for data collection, and methodological approach; for grounding the program in the local school system and society; and for our applications for research funds. When it came to examining the applications for funds, those who have helped to finance the program—mainly the National Board of Education in its day, the Bank of Sweden Tercentenary Fund and the Council for Planning and Coordination of Research—have turned to national and international specialists. The results of the assessments have been consistently favorable, and in some cases very favorable.

Evaluations As mentioned earlier, the program's results have been presented in, for example, volumes with the common title *Paths Through Life*, published by Erlbaum and Associates. The second volume, Stattin and Magnusson (1990), was reviewed in *Contemporary Psychology* by Richard Lerner, a distinguished scientist in developmental psychology, and one of his coworkers. They summarized their opinion of the research program as follows:

> In sum, the research project from which this book is derived should be the standard citation for a data set exemplifying the developmental contextual view of human development. To the extent that this research is the exemplar of the importance of what may be a new theoretical paradigm—not only for developmental psychology but for the study of human behavior in general (cf. Bandura, 1986)—Magnusson's IDA project may be the single most important longitudinal study of this century.
>
> (Lerner & Schwab, 1991)

What Have We Learned? Concluding Comments on the Study of Individual Development as a Transformation Process

The holistic approach to individual development was fundamental right from the start of the IDA project. This approach was based on my experience as a school teacher and a school psychologist, as well as on my experience with the Erica Foundation. It is reflected in the breadth and depth of the information about individuals that is stored in the IDA database.

During IDA's life, important contributions have been made to the arsenal of appropriate models and methods for the study of individual developmental processes. For the scientific use of the IDA database, these propositions have increased the possibilities of answering central questions concerning individual development as *a transformation process*.

Here I will draw attention to the most important propositions that are relevant in the application of the IDA database for the study of the individual transformation process. For all propositions, the consequences are important for a proper choice and application of measurement methods with reference to the character of the phenomena under investigation.

General views

Questions and Generalizations In a recent article in *Scientific American*, the biologist Stuart Firestein (2012) emphasized the importance for progress in scientific work of formulating relevant questions. For progress in the research process, questions are more important than answers. Let me add: If our questions are to contribute to real progress, a prerequisite is that they are based on careful and correct analyses of the phenomena we want to understand (Magnusson, 1992). This belief was what motivated the breadth and depth of the planning and implementation of the IDA database with reference to a holistic view of individual functioning and development.

A central element of the scientific research process is *generalization*. Psychology is the only scientific discipline in which the target for generalization in the interpretation of results from studies on specific issues is the integrated human being (Magnusson, 2011).

Two Worlds for Generalization In the book *This Is Biology*, Mayr (1997) emphasized the distinction between *the physical, inanimate world* and *the living world* as different universes of phenomena for scientific investigation and emphasized the different demands they make on theory, research strategies, and methodologies. This distinction has had clear implications for the planning and implementation of IDA. First, from a holistic perspective, we have tried to obtain important information about individual functioning from both worlds. Each of them requires its own measurement model for true scientific analysis. Second, the distinction between the two worlds of phenomena has been

maintained in the application of measurement models and methods. The importance of this distinction and its maintenance was made clear by Mayr (1997), who noted that, in the 1920s, biology refrained from using methods involved in the study of the physical world and, as a consequence, developed successfully as a scientific discipline. As researchers in psychology, we have more to learn from biology, as a discipline concerned with the living world, than from physics. Accordingly, we should take the experiences from the history of biology seriously, if we want to contribute to progress in psychology as a scientific discipline.

Individual Development—a Holistic Transformation Process A modern conception sees individual development as a holistic *transformation* process. This characteristic has clear-cut consequences for virtually every theoretical and empirical step in the research process. The psychological intention behind the transformation process was aptly formulated by Fentress (1989), who noted that the child or animal refines across its development facets of its functioning. This refinement involves integrating formerly isolated characteristics into new configurations. Such integration creates new opportunities for receptivity to the world and, at the same time, diminishes other formats for interaction. Together these changes establish a unique individuality for the organism (Fentress, 1989).

Theoretical Frame of Reference—a Holistic View At the most general level, the IDA program rests on the following proposition: The goal for psychology as a scientific discipline is to contribute scientifically valid knowledge about the functioning and development of the individual as a unique, integrated psychobiological and social human being in a continuous dynamic process of interaction and interdependence with his/her close and distal environments. That formulation constitutes a holistic approach to scientific psychology (Magnusson, 1999). With reference to a holistic view, the planning and implementation of data collections have contributed to the construction of a database that is appropriate and meets the requirements for the application of modern measurement models.

Optimal generalization from results of studies on specific elements of the integrated psychobiological and social human being presupposes that empirical studies of human functioning and development have a holistic frame of reference. Such a frame of reference is essential if generalizations from results of specific studies are to be scientifically valid. A fundamental proposition is that the total functioning of an individual is built on the interdependence of sub-processes in the way described by Fentress (1989). At each level of the total process, each active element is functionally coordinated with other elements at the same level of the total process. At each level of the total process, each involved system is functionally coordinated with all other relevant systems, so as to enable the whole organism to fulfill its goal.

The importance of a holistic view as a frame of reference for the formulation of specific questions and for the interpretation of empirical results is nicely illustrated by the work of Darwin (1859). His theory of evolution laid the foundation for the enormous progress of research on the living world. This work exemplifies how a general frame of reference helps to avoid the fragmentation that otherwise hampers real progress in scientific psychology (see e.g., Scarr, 1981).

Two Perspectives: Adaptation and Transformation When planning and implementing research on individual functioning and development within a holistic frame-work, it is necessary to observe a fundamental distinction between (a) understanding how the human being functions in single, specific situations in current processes of *adaptation* to situational conditions, and (b) understanding how the individual develops over time in a process of *transformation*.[2]

These two objectives are not irreconcilable. Integrated in a holistic frame of reference, both are necessary for understanding the unique constancy of the individual—the person-oriented approach (Bergman & Magnusson, 1997; Magnusson, 2003). An individual's current psychobiological and social functioning are dependent on the foregoing transformation process in which all elements are involved; at the same time, it forms the platform for the character of the individual's further transformation process.

Planning, performing, and generalizing in the IDA program have focused on the developmental perspective. Understanding developmental processes in a scientifically valid way, as an integrated transformation process, requires specific types of questions, a matching research plan, and its own frame of reference for the generalization of results from studies on specific issues.[3]

Two points are essential for the planning, implementation, and interpretation of studies on single issues: (1) functionally, the two perspectives are integrated—an individual's way of functioning at a certain point in time is built on the character and content of the earlier transformation and forms, at the same time, the conditions for the individual's further development; and (2) in both a current and a developmental perspective, an individual adapts to situational conditions and interacts with contextual conditions across time, in terms of processes. Accordingly, the measurement models that are adequate in each of the two perspectives for the planning and implementation of research are basically different.

A Longitudinal Perspective I have previously related how a well-known researcher in education tried to stop further financing of the IDA program. His main argument was that the results that the program yielded could have been obtained much more quickly and at less cost with a series of cross-sectional studies. Superficially, at the data level, this kind of argument has been put forward in various contexts. The unscientific nature of the criticism is evident in the light of the view that individual development is constituted as a transformation process. The importance of a cross-disciplinary, longitudinal

approach in research on individual development was emphasized in the series of volumes from the European Science Foundation network published by the Cambridge University Press (see, e.g., Magnusson & Caesar, 1993).

Chronological Age as a Measure of Individual Maturation One of the most important aspects of the individual transformation process is at what stage in the individual's life span a certain event occurs. Frequently, in statistical analyses, chronological age is used as the independent variable in studies of the relation between maturation and certain events in an individual's life. Interindividual differences with respect to chronological age, for example during puberty, have decisive implications for the planning, implementation, and interpretation of studies on, and understanding of, specific aspects of the individually unique life-span development (see, e.g., Bergman, Magnusson, & El-Khouri, 2003; Gustafson & Magnusson, 1991). It is important to bear in mind that chronological age is simply a measure of how many times the Earth has orbited the Sun since a particular individual was born. Research on puberty, its onset in the individual life-span process, and its role in the individual transformation process, provides an illustration of the role which chronological age plays in studies of individual development (see Stattin & Magnusson, 1990). For a further discussion of this issue, see Wohlwill (1970).

Latent Variables and Statistical Analyses A conversation years ago with a well-known scientist from a neighboring discipline illustrates the misunderstanding of the character of latent person variables, i.e., arbitrary person variables, derived from observations and interpretations of actual individual behavior. His use of the concept of intelligence caused me to say: "Your proposition presupposes that intelligence exists, but as I see it, it does not. What does exist is observations of individual acts, which in the context in which the observations are made, might be judged and called intelligent."

This example illustrates the misunderstanding and misuse of reified hypothetical variables in empirical psychological research. The literature, be it in books or in journals, contains numerous illustrations of analyses of data for reified variables that represent phenomena which have neither clear-cut boundaries nor clear-cut contents.

The problem connected with the use of latent variables in theoretical and empirical research was illustrated in an empirical study using IDA data (see Magnusson, Andersson, & Törestad, 1993). By partialing out the effect of other frequently used person variables in the prediction of adult problems documented in official registers, not one of the single variables demonstrated a unique prediction coefficient above 0.10. That is, the unique contribution from each of the single predictor variables to the total variance of the distribution of data for adult registered problems was less than 1% (Table 28.1).

TABLE 28.1
The Uniqueness of Single Personality Variables in Statistical Analyses

Independent Variable	Correlation	
	Point-Biserial	**Semi-Partial**
AB	.221	.025
MR	.236	.036
CD	.262	.048
LSM	.259	.030
DIS	.248	.079
SA	−.180	−.018
PR	.055	−.049

Note: The table presents point-biserial correlations and semi-partial correlations between the independent variables and the dependent variables (registered alcohol abusers, aged 18-24). Data for the five variables: aggressive behavior (AB), motor restlessness (MR), concentration difficulties (CD), lack of school motivation (LSM), and disharmony (DIS) were based on teacher ratings. Data about school achievement (SA) was based on school grades, and peer rejection (PR) was based on peer ratings from friends.

With reference to a holistic view on personality research, the issue is more carefully discussed in Magnusson (2003), "The person approach: Theory, measurement models, and research strategy."

Recent Development of Adequate Measurement Models and Methods Since the start of IDA, new basic propositions have been launched concerning research in general—some of them specific for psychology as a scientific discipline—for which the IDA database provides good conditions for application. In totality, the conditions for psychology as a scientific discipline have become more fruitful and it is up to us as researchers to use them for further real scientific progress (see, e.g., Magnusson, 2011).

Statistics in the Living World The scientific goal of expressing the lawfulness of individual transformation processes is basically different in the two worlds (see Crick, 1988). In the living world, the lawfulness of processes cannot be formulated as it can in the natural sciences. The best we can do is identifying the *principles* underlying psychological processes and the *mechanisms* through which they work.

Statistics and the Person-Oriented Approach Because the target for generalization in psychological research is the individual as a unique psychobiological and social being in constant interaction with his/her environment, a basic principle is that generalizations to individuals cannot be made from empirical results at the group level (see Molenaar, Huizinga, & Nesselroade, 2002). This principle calls for the development and application of measurement models and methods which match the character of the transformation processes; that

is, the *person-oriented approach* (see Bergman et al., 2003; Magnusson, 2003).

Chaos Theory and the Holistic Frame of Reference The holistic approach in terms of "chaos theory" has had a strong impact on the scientific study of processes in the physical world. In a discussion of chaos theory, Prigogine and Stenglers summarized this proposition for the physical world by saying "the description of elementary behaviors is not sufficient for understanding a system as a whole" (Prigogine & Stenglers, 1984, p. 8; see also Gleick, 1987). This point is equally valid for understanding phenomena in the living world.

The central tenet that the process of a system cannot be understood by summing research results from sub-elements also holds for research on the individual transformation process. The study of a specific problem should be planned, implemented and interpreted with reference to the characteristics of the integrated human being, that is, applying a holistic approach. This point was underlined in the paper "Back to the phenomena" (Magnusson, 1992).

Summary Comment Together, these propositions are mainstays for all empirical research in psychology as a scientific discipline. It is important for further progress that they are considered in the planning, implementation, and interpretation of single studies. In the history of the IDA program, the general attitude to these propositions has evolved from rather vague general terms to what it is today. This process has entailed a great deal of work on methodological issues, mainly under the leadership of Lars Bergman (see, e.g., Bergman et al., 2003; Magnusson, 1988).

Adolescence The general focus of this volume is the adolescent period of individual life. Girls and boys enter this period as children and leave it as adults. A special role in the individual transformation process during adolescence is played by the transformation with respect to biological aspects of the total organism; that is, *puberty*. The adolescent period, during which a person goes through a transition from boy to man or from girl to woman, involves a strong transformation process of mental and biological person-bound factors in the person-environment interaction process. The characteristics of transformation processes through which this change happens differ from the characteristics of the process before and after adolescence. Since this transformation process, which contains the integrated person–environment interaction process, has important implications for the rest of individuals' lives, it has been an object of special analyses in the IDA program (see Magnusson, 1988).

Adolescence: A Limited but Important Period of the Life-Span Process The adolescent transformation period occurs (a) at different ages for girls and for boys (about 2 years earlier for girls than for boys) and (b) with large interindividual differences within each sex (Tanner, 1981). This difference can be observed in any unselected school class during the chronological age for adolescent transitions. For a correct study of this period of individual life it is necessary to bear in mind that individual adolescence is not a certain point in time, valid for all individuals with respect to chronological age. Among other things, this point invalidates the frequent use in empirical research of chronological age as the measure of individual maturation during the adolescent period.

One of the clearest and most significant manifestations of individual puberty is the change in relation to the social environment's cultural codes. The usual way of measuring age as a chronological phenomenon in terms of months and years—if you will, the number of times the Earth has orbited the Sun since a person was born—is a handy yardstick of individual development but does not tell us much.

Considering how a girl's developmental process tends to vary with her chronological age at menarche, it is surprising that chronological age is still such a dominant measure of the individual transformative process. Research on puberty, its beginning in the individual life-span process and its role in the individual transformation process, provides an illustration of chronological age in studies of individual development (see Stattin & Magnusson, 1990). Using chronological age as a measure of individual maturation will introduce a certain amount of error variance in the matrix of data. In order to avoid the abuse of chronological age, in the IDA program, age at menarche is used as a more relevant measure. A girl's memory of that event has turned out to be a rather reliable measure of the transformative development processes.

A Holistic Process Adolescent transformation is a holistic process, involving mental and biological aspects of the integrated individual and his/her social and physical aspects of the environmental context of which the individual is an integrated, intentional, and active part. Studying this process empirically, unique for each individual, entails particular demands for scientific analyses.

Cross-Cultural Differences Margret Mead's observations (see Mead, 1934) of youngsters in archaic cultures are informative as long as they are interpreted as characteristics of how adolescent transmission occurs in a societal context, stamped by its special cultural codes. But the integrated transformation process in cultures with old-time cultural codes differs from that in societies with modern cultural codes, as illustrated in the study in Czechoslovakia described on page 325 in this chapter. Accordingly, one should be cautious about generalizing observations from one culture to another.

Results obtained in western countries are treated all too frequently as norms that hold for individual functioning and development in all cultures. Results for other cultures that differ from those obtained from western cultural contexts are sometimes regarded as deviations from this norm, in spite of the fact that rather the deviations may contain important information about the role of cultural elements in the process under investigation.

Summary (a) The unique character of the individual dynamic maturation process and (b) the interindividual differences with respect to the age of puberty invalidate the scientific application of chronological age as an independent variable in the application of linear regression models.

Final Statement

The application of a holistic frame of reference, the availability of a carefully planned and implemented longitudinal database, and access to advanced measurement models in the IDA program, have made and will continue to make it possible to analyze and discuss important and frequently used theoretical concepts and empirical questions concerning individual development in terms of a unique transformation process.

Acknowledgments

The research presented here was made possible by financial support from the SwedishRiksbankens Jubileumsfond.

A research program such as the one which is the focus of this chapter involves many persons with alternate duties. Some of them have been noticed in the text. All of them and also some who have not been presented by name, have made the positive outcome of the program possible. To all of them I give my sincere thanks. Here I want particularly to thank Lars Bergman and Anders Dunér for their long time responsibility for fulfilling the original plans and for enriching the intellectual quality of the program. In 1997, Lars took the full formal and scientific responsibility for IDA. The continuous support by Bernard Devine and his help with the computational work has meant much for a long time. I also want to thank Jelena Corovic for her generous help with the preparation of the final manuscript. From this year the responsibility for the IDA program has been taken over by Henric and Anna-Karin Andershed at the Örebro University. I wish them all good for the future.

Notes

1. The concept of interaction in this definition has a different meaning from its use as a statistical concept. As a concept in the proposition that individual development is a transformation process, the more appropriate metaphor is that it resembles a river in which all elements are involved in a holistic, dynamic, and interdependent process at each moment of the process. At each moment of observation, the direction and strength of the stream depend on the characteristics of the shore.
2. Most of the relevant theoretical issues brought up in this chapter are not new (see, e.g., Lewin, 1935). The available space does not permit a representative list of references. Accordingly, in accordance with the purpose of the volume, most of the references here are restricted to my own research. Relevant references can be found in Magnusson (1988) and in handbooks on developmental psychology (e.g., Lerner, 2006).

3. The holistic view is not new. In *Oeconomia Naturae* from 1749, about balance in nature, the Swedish naturalist Carl von Linné proposed about species that "such a relation exists between all parts, that if just one disappeared, the whole would not last" (Broberg, 1978, p. 29).

References

Bergman, L. R. (2008). Short description of the longitudinal research program Individual Development and Adaptation (IDA). *IDA Internal Report*.

Bergman, L. R., & Magnusson, D. (1997). A person-oriented approach in research on developmental psychopathology. *Development and Psychopathology, 9*, 291–319.

Bergman, L. R., Magnusson, D., & El-Khouri, B. M. (2003). Studying individual development in an interindividual context: A person-oriented approach. In D. Magnusson (Ed.), *Paths through life*, Vol. 4. Mahwah, NJ: Erlbaum.

Broberg, G. (1978). *Carl von Linné: Om jämvikten i naturen. [Carl von Linné: About balance in nature.]* Stockholm: Carmina.

Crick, F. (1988). *What mad pursuit: A personal view of scientific discovery.* New York: Basic Books.

Darwin, C. (1859). *On the origin of species by means of natural selection or the preservation of favored races in the struggle for life.* London: Murray.

Fentress, J. C. (1989). Developmental roots of behavioral order: Systemic approaches to the examination of core developmental issues. In M. R. Gunnar & E. Thelen (Eds.), *Systems and development* (pp. 35–75). Hillsdale, NJ: Erlbaum Associates.

Firestein, S. (2012). What science wants to know: An impenetrable mountain of facts can obscure the deeper questions. *Scientific American,* March 28, 7.

Gleick, J. (1987). *Chaos: Making a new science.* New York: Penguin Books.

Gustafson, S. B., & Magnusson, D. (1991). Female life careers. In D. Magnusson (Ed.), *Paths through life*, Vol. 3. Hillsdale, NJ: Erlbaum Associates.

Lerner, R. M. (2006). Theoretical models of human development. In W. Damon & R. M. Lerner (Eds.), *Handbook of child psychology* (3rd ed.), Vol. 1. New York: Wiley.

Lerner, R. M. & Schwab, J. (1991). On the importance of being pubescent. *Contemporary Psychology, 36*, 288–289.

Lewin, K. (1935). *A dynamic theory of personality: Selected papers.* London: McGraw-Hill.

Magnusson, D. (1961). *Test teori*. Stockholm: Almqvist & Wiksell.

Magnusson, D. (1967). *Test theory*. Hillsdale: Addison-Wesley.

Magnusson, D. (1988). Individual development from an interactional perspective: A longitudinal study. In D. Magnusson (Ed.), *Paths through life*, Vol. 3. Hillsdale, NJ: Erlbaum Associates.

Magnusson, D. (1992). Back to the phenomena: Theory, methods, and statistics in psychological research. *European Journal of Personality, 6*, 1–14.

Magnusson, D. (1999). Holistic interactionism: A perspective for research on personality development. In L. A. Pervin & O. P. John (Eds.), *Handbook of personality: Theory and research.* New York: The Guilford Press.

Magnusson, D. (2003) The person approach: Theory, measurement models and research strategy. Special Issue of *New Directions for Child and Adolescent Development, 101*, 3–23.

Magnusson, D. (2011). The human being in society: Psychology as a scientific discipline. *European Psychologist, 17*, 21–27.

Magnusson, D., Andersson, T., & Törestad, B. (1993). Methodological implications of a peephole perspective on personality. In D. C. Funder, R. D. Parke, C. Tomlinson-Keasy, & K. Widaman (Eds.), *Studying lives through time: Personality development* (pp. 207–220). Washington, DC: APA.

Magnusson, D., & Caesar, P. (1993). *Longitudinal research on individual development: Present status and future perspectives.* Cambridge University Press.

Magnusson, D., Dunér, A., & Zetterblom, G. (1975). *Adjustment: A longitudinal study.* Stockholm: Almqvist & Wiksell.

Magnusson, D., af Klinteberg, B., & Stattin, H. (1994). Juvenile and persistent offenders: Behavioral and physiological characteristics. In R. D. Ketterlinus & M. E. Lamb (Eds.), *Adolescent problem behaviors: Issues and research* (pp. 81–91). Hillsdale, NJ: Lawrence Erlbuam Associates.

Magnusson, D. & Törestad, B. (1993). A holistic view of personality: A model revisited. *Annual Review of Psychology, 44*, 427–452.

Mayr, E. (1997). *This is biology: The science of the living world.* Cambridge, MA: The Belknap Press of Harvard University Press.

Mead, M. (1934). *Mind, self and society.* Chicago: University of Chicago Press.

Molenaar, P. C. M., Huizenga, H. M., & Nesselroade, J. R. (2002). The relationship between the structure of inter-individual and intra-individual variability: A theoretical and empirical indication of developmental systems theory. In U. M. Staudinger & U. Lindberger (Eds.), *Understanding human development* (pp. 339–360). Dordrecht, The Netherlands: Kluwer Press.

Prigogine, I., & Stengers, I. (1984). *Order out of chaos: Man's new dialogue with nature.* Bantam Books.

Pulkkinen, L., Virtanen, T., af Klinteberg, B., & Magnusson, D. (2000). Child behavior and adult personality: Comparisons between criminality groups in Finland and Sweden. *Criminal Behaviour and Mental Health, 10*, 155–169.

Scarr. S. (1981). Comments on psychology: Behavior genetics, and social policy from an anti- reductionist. In R. A. Kasschau & C. N. Cofer (Eds.), *Psychology's second century: Enduring issues* (pp. 147–187). New York: Praeger Publishers.

Sorensen, A. (1998). Theoretical mechanisms and the empirical study of social processes. In P. Hedström & R. Svedberg (Eds.), *Social mechanisms: An analytical approach to social theory* (pp. 238–266). Cambridge, MA: Cambridge University Press.

Stattin, H., & Magnusson, D. (1990). *Pubertal maturation in female development.* In D. Magnusson (Ed.), *Paths through life,* Vol. 2. Hillsdale, NJ: Erlbaum Associates.

Tanner, J. M. (1981). *A history of the study of human growth.* Cambridge: Cambridge University Press.

Watson, J. B. (1913). Psychology as the behaviorist views it. *Psychological Review, 20*, 158–177.

Wohlwill, J. F. (1970). The age variable in psychological research. *Psychological Review, 77*, 49–64.

29

Growth and Development

The Interrelationship of Personal Experiences and Scientific Endeavors

ROLF OERTER

Childhood and Adolescence

I spent my childhood and adolescence in a small village near Schweinfurt, an industrial city in the middle of Germany. Early adolescence is a crucial period in one's life and for me it coincided with the demise of the Nazi Regime and the occupation of Germany by the Allied Forces. For me, therefore, the advance of the American army and the eventual surrender of our village to them by the local priest was a critical life event. When, the next morning, the other children and I observed the newly arrived GIs, we were surprised by how anxiously they proceeded through the village. While we stood in the middle of the street observing what was going on, the soldiers took cover moving forward cautiously from house to house. However, the GIs quickly won the friendship of the children through chocolate and chewing gum. My first impression of Americans was that they were open minded, friendly, loud, humorous, nonchalant, and having a lot of sex. As my brother and I were the only ones in the village who spoke a little English, we occasionally served as interpreters, but found it hard to cope with more difficult messages. America was for all of us the Promised Land with its abundance of food, wonderful big cars, and lots of clothing. One of the GIs jokingly invited me to the States; for him only a joke, but for me an exciting prospect. I mention these details because it was the first suggestion that there might be a connection between wealth, happiness, and democracy. It was also during adolescence that I made up my mind to at some point live in America.

My first contact with American culture was through an America House—these *Amerika Häuser* were built in post-World War II Germany as places for Germans to learn more about America, and for America to spread a positive message about the West. There I became acquainted with American literature and discovered German authors, such as Thomas Mann; it was then that I read *Josef und seine*

Brüder. I also heard real jazz music for the first time—considered "decadent" by the Nazis, it had been banned—which lead to my attempting to play it myself.

When economic improvement in Germany occurred in the 1950s and 1960s, the picture of America became more realistic. Americans even began to prefer German cars. I became more and more curious to see what America was really like, but it would take tens of years until my curiosity was satisfied.

Only 20 years later, my naïve early impression of an American changed when I met an American psychologist working on verbal associations at the psychological institute of Wuerzburg where I studied Psychology. He was introverted, polite, quiet and modest, just the opposite to my GIs of 1945/46.

Becoming a Teacher and Cultivating My Hobby

During adolescence music was the center of my life. I taught myself to play the piano and as such reached a remarkably good level. However, due to the war, I wasn't able to receive a good musical education so that my dream of becoming a serious musician was illusory.

Since I could not follow a career as a musician, I chose the occupation I was most familiar with: teacher. My father was the only teacher in our small village and it seemed to me logically to take the same job. I have to confess that this decision was also related to my low self-esteem. Therefore, I was amazed to find myself at the top of the class after the first teacher examination. Already at this time, my friends and colleagues suggested that I should study psychology. However, in the early fifties it was not easy to earn one's living, so I decided to teach and put the idea of studying psychology on the back burner.

Instead, I used my free time to attend the conservatory in Würzburg. This was a wonderful time for me. The young musicians enrolled there shared my love of music and we played together in many concerts. Each of us had to perform in private at the conservatory, as well as at public events. In my last public concert I performed the

Humoresque by Robert Schumann, a piece with many parts that takes about half an hour to perform, but I think it was then that I realized that this was as good as it would get and that I would never reach more than amateur status; I decided to put a stop to my music career. Nevertheless, the time at the conservatory shaped my whole life. I learned not only to play piano professionally, but also harmony and counterpoint, improvisation, and composition. These competences would prove to be invaluable for my later engagement in music psychology.

After my second teacher examination in 1955, I was offered a position at a boarding school. Since this job offered the possibility of studying psychology at the University of Würzburg, I accepted. I began to attend the university with my friend Lothar Katzenberger, who chose the same career. During this time, my friend and I used our musical capabilities to arrange cultural evening events. We recruited fellow students with musical and other talents and combined them to present parodies of well-known operas, sketches, songs, pantomimes, and zippy dialogues, amongst other things. From then on the two pillars of my life, psychology and music, accompanied me into old age.

After some years studying, I married in 1958 and one year later my first son was born. After the arrival of my second son, I was the only bread-winner in the family and had to earn sufficient money to keep us all. So I continued working as a teacher, but also continued my studies at the university. Family life, a fulltime job, and studying were a challenge, but I was happy and motivated in all three domains. In 1960, I finished my studies as a psychologist with an MA and immediately started work on my Ph.D. dissertation. Besides psychology, my doctoral studies included the study of music science and philosophy—the former much to my surprise—I had never thought I would need music science for my profession. As the subject of my dissertation I chose "the development of attitudes during adolescence." This was the beginning of a long series of research on adolescence. I received my Ph.D. in 1963 and my dissertation was published in 1966 (Oerter, 1966).

During this time, I still worked as a teacher, so that, altogether, I spent 11 years in practical work with adolescents. This experience had a substantial influence on my later theoretical thinking about adolescence and the resulting empirical research.

Psychology Becomes My Main Occupation

Besides my preoccupation with developmental psychology, I became interested in attitude research, which was not very popular in Germany at that time. However, I was fascinated by the models of attitude change, such as Festinger's (1957) theory of cognitive dissonance, and by models of structural balance (Heider, 1958; Rosenberg & Abelson, 1960; Brehm & Cohen, 1962). In the same year that I finished my doctoral studies, my first publication appeared: Suggestive effects of group members with

extreme positions on the other group members (Oerter, 1963). One year later a second article was published: "Cognitive dissonance and educational influence" (Oerter, 1964). Both studies were theoretically based on the new models of attitude change that had just appeared in the United States.

In autumn of 1963 I became an assistant professor in Munich. I had to give lectures and seminars for students studying education. I was also invited to give lectures about developmental psychology for practicing teachers. I traveled around South Bavaria telling teachers about the new results in developmental psychology. My mentor and advisor of a small publishing company proposed that I should write a book about developmental psychology. I finished the book within 1 year and gave it the title *Modern developmental psychology* (Oerter, 1967). At this point in time, developmental psychology in Germany was not well connected internationally and was oriented towards the German philosophical school of phenomenology. In my book, I included up to date research results from the United States and Great Britain, as well as Piaget's and Inhelder's theories and results. Jean Piaget was at that time completely unknown in America. John Flavell was the first to arrange the translation of Piaget's work. As a consequence, my textbook comprised more research and theoretical approaches than contemporary American textbooks. I sympathized with the publisher, who took the risk of printing a book by a completely unknown young fellow, but very unexpectedly within half a year the first printing was sold out. Colleagues working in the field, like Heinz Heckhausen and Ferdinand Merz, made critical comments and suggested themes that should have also been included in the book. The new editions of the book incorporated the proposals of my colleagues and the textbook became a bestseller. Since then, every new edition is updated to include new findings from developmental psychology.

Shortly after this book was published, I was invited to present my results on the psychology of thinking. This was a new field, even in America where the cognitive revolution had just begun and behaviorism still dominated. Four hundred teachers listened to my lecture and I began to recognize how important cognitive processes were for teachers, as well as for students. I decided to write a textbook about the psychology of thinking, a really naïve decision that did not take into account the newness of cognitive psychology as a field of research. Nevertheless, available research presented enough useful information. The book included aspects of the traditional German psychology of thinking, concept formation, strategies of thinking, thinking and values, and last but not least, a chapter on creativity. Creativity research was at this time predominately being done in the United States. American politicians were alarmed by the "Sputnik shock" (1957) and began to believe that creativity in research might be an important aspect of the arms race. The Soviet Union's focus on improving creativity disturbed everyone with the result that research on creativity started simultaneously in many places in the States. So, brand-new results from the early sixties were also included in my chapter. The book about thinking (Oerter, 1971) was also a success and was even used in Japan, where a German-speaking colleague told me years later that he had used my book for lectures and seminars at the University of Osaka.

As mentioned earlier, between 1963 and 1968, I began to work on the measurement of values and attitudes. On the basis of attitude research and the then *en vogue* theories (e.g. cognitive dissonance, cognitive–affective balance), I used the paradigm of compliance in an activity that is contrary to one's own beliefs (Brehm & Cohen, 1962). Since I was unsatisfied with the simple form of attitude measurement, which simply involved posing questions with answers given via a Likert scale, I tried to define value structures as deeply anchored systems. To do this I used factor analysis (P-sort) on the judgments of subjects who had to evaluate 40 professions by 24 characteristics (kind, polite, fair, honest, strict, healthy, etc.). So for each subject a factor structure before and after treatment was calculated. It turned out that, contrary to the main stream of attitude research, subjects showed a boomerang effect. The boomerang effect is a concept used in attitude research when an influence on attitude change has the opposite effect to that which was intended. Results and a broad theoretical introduction including the main positions of attitude research were published in a book. It was also part of my "habilitation," which in Germany is the exam one needs to be eligible for a university professorship. This book was the first publication in Germany to introduce actual research on attitude and on theories of attitude change (Oerter, 1970). While the two other books offered information for a broader audience, the book about structure and change of values was of special interest for researchers working in this field.

It was not my original intention to connect traditional German psychology with the actual state of research in America and Great Britain, but as a matter of fact, my contributions in the sixties and early seventies helped German psychology to take a step towards the state of international research. Thus, my individual scientific development paralleled, at least partially, the development of German psychology.

Professor at the University of Augsburg

In 1968 I was appointed by the federal state of Bavaria as a full professor at the University of Augsburg with the task of educating future teachers. Teacher education was particularly important to me, since my own experience as a teacher motivated me to improve teacher education at universities. I was the head of the institute of educational research, which provided the optimal opportunity of combining our research findings with teaching. While at Augsburg, a series of publications appeared where my coworkers Heinz Mandl, Barbara Hanke, Jan-Bernd Lohmoeller, and Achim Zimmermann presented their research findings.

In the late sixties the Head Start initiative and the models of new preschool education reached Europe, and eventually also Bavaria. The government provided lots of financial support for the establishment of preschool education and I was appointed by the Bavarian government as head of the Bavarian project group, which was responsible for developing programs for preschool education. My co-workers and I developed plans for an Institute of Early Education with about 50 researchers and staff. The Department of Education of Bavaria agreed, the institute was founded and began to work. However, it quickly became evident that the values and scientific goals of the institute did not match the politics of the Department of Education or the conservative majority who dominated the state government at that time. The work was blocked more and more by conflicts. Since the institute was part of the Department of Education, the secretary prescribed goals and prohibited scientific activities that were not in accordance with the political goals of the government. So, after a short period of time, I resigned and was relieved to again have time for my own research. Twenty-five years later, I had the honor of giving the invited keynote lecture at the 25th anniversary of the Institute of Early Education.

Despite my resignation as the head of the institute, my engagement in early education continued. Early education experts in West Germany developed a big project that focused on producing multimedia materials for kindergarten children and teachers. We collected information about new approaches to preschool education in many European countries, as well as in the United States, and produced films about developmental topics, such as socialization, self-regulation, and group dynamics in kindergarten. The materials were implemented and evaluated. The main result can be summarized as having achieved a change in the concept of the child by the kindergarten teachers. After implementing the program, the child was seen as more mature, self-determined, and as a person to be respected. The whole research was published in a book by Bernd Lohmoeller and me (Oerter & Lohmoeller, 1978).

After I finished my books about thinking and values, I thought that developmental psychology was something of my past, but everyone still labeled me as a developmentalist. As a consequence, I began working simultaneously in different domains. One domain was the psychology of thinking. Eva and Michael Dreher and I began to study thought processes with ecological validity. We constructed organizational tasks and presented them to different age groups, ranging from early adolescence to young adulthood. The theoretical approach behind this enterprise was the integration of psychology of thinking, ecological psychology, and developmental psychology, the results of which were published as a book (Oerter, Dreher, & Dreher, 1977).

Establishing the New Developmental Psychology in Germany

In 1975 I experienced an influential life event: the Meetings of the Society for Research in Child Development (SRCD) in Denver. Hellgard Rauh, who had already visited the United States several times and had participated in scientific meetings there, organized a German group of psychologists to attend the Denver event; I was one of those involved. This meant I was already 44 years old when I visited America and was able to meet American researchers in person for the first time. All of the German participants had a great time, both scientifically as well as personally at the conference. From then on, I had regular contact with my American colleagues. We organized meetings, published together and I became friends with many of them. This contact was intensified by a specific event in Germany, the International Seminar for Developmental Psychology (ISEP) in Herl, near Trier, in the South-West of Germany. The Volkswagen Foundation funded a three-week workshop in which many famous American developmentalists participated. This seminar was the final step in reaching international standards for developmental psychology in Germany. The participants were young scientists who afterwards began research projects, many of them in cooperation with American colleagues, on the topics of the seminar. So Denver and Herl were connected with each other; Denver was the motivating starting point and Herl was the decisive enterprise for developmental research in Germany. I was a co-organizer of the seminar and mentor to one of the four groups with a focus on development in adolescence. ISEP also offered an opportunity to gather the best minds of developmental psychology in Germany for a new up-to date textbook about developmental psychology. This enterprise was as a great success. The textbook edited by Leo Montada and me (Oerter & Montada, 1982) appeared in six editions, the last appearing in 2008.

Intermezzo in Tbilisi

Another important life event for me was the international conference on learning held in Tbilisi, Georgia, in 1976. Since colleagues from the East could not travel to the West, conferences were arranged in Eastern countries. Each country was represented by only one member. The participant from the USA was Bob Glaser and I was the German representative. The focus of the conference was less on discussing scientific progress and more on providing an opportunity for the Eastern and Western representatives of psychology and pedagogy of learning to meet. Tbilisi is the capital of Georgia and enjoyed some advantages with regard to freedom of life in the Soviet Union. We visited an exhibition where I remember one painting in particular. This showed the globe captured by two greedy hands from east and west, one representing the Soviet Union and the other the United States. This artistic liberty in the middle of the Soviet Union was amazing.

Ecological Perspective of Development

It was not only my work about thinking with Eva and Michael Dreher that used an ecological approach; I took the developmental context into account in all areas of my research.

The turning point from an isolated view of individual abilities, skills, motivation and emotion towards an ecological perspective of development had several outcomes. One was the lifespan perspective that had been presented long before by Charlotte Bühler (1933) and which I reintroduced in Germany with a book entitled *Development as a Life-long Process* (Oerter, 1978). Another result was the organization of an international symposium about ecology and development in Konstanz 1977. The results of the symposium were published in a book entitled *Ecology and development* (Walter & Oerter, 1979).

In 1977, at the biennial conference of the German Society of Psychology, I took the concept of developmental task from Havighurst's work and introduced the idea of using it as a developmental approach that combines the individual and environment. Indeed in the coming years there was a flood of studies and publications about developmental tasks with a focus on adolescent development. Certainly, the concept would have succeeded without my introduction of this new take on an old idea, but the process was accelerated through my presentation. The idea seemed so important that I was invited by Paul Baltes to write a chapter in the series *Life-span development and behavior* (Oerter, 1986a).

The ecology of human development had a final, late result: the book *Coping in adolescence* (Oerter, 1985). Adolescence was understood not only as governed by internal rules and laws, rather it was also understood in the context of specific environments. For example, apprentices were interviewed about their understanding and attitudes towards work. The answers were compared with objective structures of labor in western societies. Labor is the medium through which the worker exchanges his/her work power and abilities for money. However, the majority of interviewees attributed labor as having an identity-forming function. Work was not only a necessary condition for survival and to earn money, but was also important for self-esteem and for one's own identity. A minority of adolescents reduced work to the Marxist position of selling one's own work-force. A cross-cultural comparison of adolescents' conceptualization of work is published in English (Oerter, 1986b).

A Brief Theoretical Digression

Behind all this work of the seventies and early eighties was a theoretical approach which related the environment (culture) and individual in a systematic way. The approach started from an action theory, which took the relation between subject and object as a basic entity. The terms "subject" and "object" are defined as in philosophy. It is assumed that every action (to which thinking as imaginative acting also belongs) is related to an object (which comprises physical objects, persons, as well as mental object like knowledge and psychological expressions). All objects in this meaning are human constructions. Under this perspective both culture and individual can be described by the formula $S \rightarrow O$. We perceive culture as a universe of (physical, mental, psychological) objects. The subject as the constructor of objects remains hidden. For example, if we use a cup for drinking, the toolmaker who realized the idea of the specific form of a cup is not in our mind, but without this actor we would not have a cup to use. This fact can be illustrated by our formula as: $(S \rightarrow) O$.

While from a cultural perspective the constructor of the object remains hidden, we perceive subjects as entities without objects. They march around separated from their environment. However, a subject can only be defined through his/her objects, may it be knowledge, or relations toward family and friends, or even the desire for future objects. If we illustrate this fact by our formula, it becomes: $S (\rightarrow O)$. Nevertheless, culture and the individual can be described by the same formula. Now we are able to define culture as the "objective structure" and individual knowledge and action capacities as the "subjective structure." Both objective and subjective structures are regulated by the principle of isomorphism.

In mathematics, isomorphism is a one-to-one correspondence between two sets that preserves mutual relationships between elements of the sets. Since we define both culture and the individual through the same subject–object relationships, we can describe individual as well as cultural development by the principle of isomorphism. In ontogenesis, the individual gradually improves his/her subjective structure towards the objective structure. He or she becomes an expert within the culture. Adults are to a certain degree experts of their culture, whereas children are novices (Rogoff, 1986). In this context, expertise means that the adult has reached a certain level of isomorphism with the objective structure (represented by culture). However, individuals as members of a culture also contribute more or less to changes of the objective structure. New inventions, new scientific knowledge, and new artistic work produce changes in cultures, i.e., changes in the objective structure. In this process, culture adapts via isomorphism towards individual structures, so that a specific segment of the objective structure becomes isomorphic with a subjective structure. The process of isomorphic regulation is reversed. Needless to say, perfect isomorphism between the subjective and objective structures will never be reached. Experts approach isomorphic structures within a specific domain, but every member of a culture must reach a certain level of isomorphism, otherwise he or she could not survive. The advantage of this approach is that development can be more precisely described in terms of levels of isomorphism. For example, music development in children follows the principle of isomorphism exactly: with every step in their musical development, the child/adolescent reaches higher levels of isomorphism with the music structure of our culture. For a description of the theory in English see Oerter (1991).

Cross-Cultural Research

As a consequence of my conceptualization of the relationship between culture and individual, I became more and more interested in cultural psychology. In particular, the idea of conducting studies in cross-cultural psychology emerged during the 1983 ISSBD Meetings in Munich, which I had the honor and pleasure of organizing. At this conference I met colleagues from many countries, including third world countries. Among others, I met Kuswiratri Setiono from Bandung, Indonesia, and discussed with her some ideas about cultural studies. Also, following the conference, I was able to spend a sabbatical in the United States, where I worked mainly with Urie Bronfenbrenner at Cornell University in Ithaca, New York, but also with Michael Cole in La Jolla, California. Both of these psychologists had a strong impact on my theoretical orientation, as well as on my further research. Urie Bronfenbrenner introduced me to systemic thinking; Michael Cole stressed respecting other cultures and introduced me to a new methodology with regard to cultural research. Bronfenbrenner's (e.g. 1977) methodological perspective regarded human development as embedded in systems. To view people as elements in a system means a change in perspective. It depends on the system how and where individuals develop, and development is understood as movement through different systems.

So I drifted away from my abstract theory of objective and subjective structures and began to look for a more concrete question. I found it within the concept of human nature. Everybody has a kind of philosophy about what humans are and should be. Eva and Michael Dreher had already developed an interview about subjects' understanding of adulthood (see for example Dreher & Oerter, 1986), which contained questions concerning the three main societal roles; family, job, and social, as well as questions about responsibility, the meaning of life, and happiness. A final question asked about the respondent's own development during the past years. Along with the interview, we included a second method in our cross-cultural studies, namely the presentation of two dilemma stories. One dilemma dealt with the family–job relationship and the other introduced a conflict between alternative careers. The stories contained a dialectical contradiction that could not be resolved through preference for one alternative. Via a guided interview, respondents dealt with different aspects of the dilemma and showed either relativistic thinking (tolerated different views of the scenario) or dialectical thinking (finding a synthesis of the given contradictions). In all countries included in our studies, subjects were in either late adolescence or early adulthood. These laborious and time-consuming methods were preferred because the subjects could elaborate on their individual cognitive structures and, in the case of the dilemma stories, their way of thinking (e.g. dialectical thought). The main goal of this research was to see if a universal concept of a human being existed among people beyond culture-specific features. In a globalized world, it becomes increasingly important to find a shared understanding of human nature in order for communication between varying cultural groups to function. Indeed, we found similar structures in the conception of human beings in very different cultures, ranging from the USA and Germany, to Japan, Indonesia, and the Quechua-Indians in Peru. Five universal levels of understanding human beings seem to exist within individuals from different cultures. They change from surface structure to deep structure, and from simple structure to complex structure. These structures can be briefly labeled as: humans as actors, humans as bearer of psychological characteristics, autonomous identity, mutual identity, and socio-cultural identity. Since these levels correspond to age, they can also be understood as developmental levels. Results from Japan, Korea, China, Indonesia, Europe, Peru, and the United States provide evidence that, during development, the five universal levels take on culture-specific features. The main differences exist, as to be expected, between eastern collectivistic and western individualistic cultures. A series of publications documented this research (e.g. Oerter, 1995; Oerter & Oerter, 1995; Oerter, Oerter, Agostiani, Kim, & Wibowo, 1996).

Music Psychology—a Late Fulfillment of an Early Interest

In the early 1980s, one of my students, Herbert Bruhn, accompanied me to the subway station. Along the way I discovered that he was also a musician and was interested in music research. Based on my own musical background, I immediately became interested and suggested that he should write his PhD about music psychology. He agreed and this was the beginning of a long cooperation in a new field. We planned to edit a handbook of music psychology. In Germany at this time, music psychology was in a similar position as the rest of psychology was in the sixties, whereby it had developed mainly within the country and did not really consider international developments. My first advice, therefore, was to include the actual international state of affairs. This led to our editing a handbook together, *Music psychology*, the first edition of which appeared in 1985 and contained articles by leading international scientists in music psychology (Bruhn, Oerter, & Rösing, 1985). Later we published a pocket book on the same topic but in a completely reworked edition (Bruhn, Oerter, & Rösing, 1993), and, finally, we edited an encyclopedia of music psychology (two volumes, Vol. I: Stoffer & Oerter, 2005; Vol. II: Oerter & Stoffer, 2005).

My own research on music psychology focused on improvisations of preschool children. Analysis of their performance showed a remarkable parallel to composition of artists including characteristics like repetition, variation, and structuring. One investigation dealt with adolescents and their preferences for specific bands and music groups. Contrary to our assumption, the choices of music groups did not concentrate on a few famous groups but showed a widespread range of different music groups as favorites. As already mentioned, music psychology is related to my own biography. With my contributions to

music psychology, I consummated a late integration of a juvenile hobby and a scientific career.

Psychology of Play—an Ethological Approach

The study of adolescent action in particular situations is similar to ethological research in biology. Just as animals are observed in their natural environment, adolescents are observed in their "natural" environment. For example, a research group around Rainer Silbereisen presented observations based on adolescents' behavior in the streets and department stores (e.g. Noack, 1990). However, human ethology is much more complex. A complete application of the ethological method would mean that the behavior of adolescents is completely registered and described in terms of subject-environment relationships.

Nevertheless, I was fascinated by the possibility of observing behavior in natural settings and the simultaneous sub-ordering of observations under a theoretical system, in this case under an action-theoretical approach with the general formula $S \rightarrow O$, as described earlier. I finally found a domain where this goal could be reached: children's play. Play normally includes the acting subject, objects, a specific environment, and specific sets of action. Therefore, play represents the complete range of subject-environment relations. So we began to videotape natural play scenes, developed a manual for their description, whereby we used a kind of action grammar in analogy to the language grammar, and related observations to an action theory. The method delivers action structures which can be compared with regard to similarity and complexity. To give a brief impression of this idea, I present two simple examples (Figure 29.1).

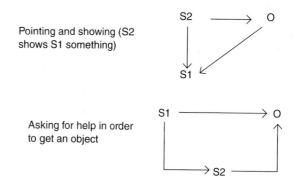

FIGURE 29.1 Two examples for an action grammar: showing and asking for help. Arrows pointing toward S mean 'appropriation,' arrows pointing away from S toward O or another S mean "reification." Reification is given when a subject produces or manipulates an object. Appropriation refers to processes of perception and learning, but also to taking possession of something.

Subjects were mainly children from 1½ to 6 years. The investigation also included a longitudinal study with children from 6 months to 3 years. Most of the videos showed natural play scenes without any intervention, analogous to ethological observations of animals. However, in order to get information about the meaning of the observed play behavior, parents, siblings, and the filmed child were often interviewed. The result of all this work was presented in the book *Psychology of play* (Oerter, 1993). This presents an action theory of play in which a superordinate action level is introduced that represents the meaning of the play which lies "behind" or "above" regulating the overt action. In other words, all play has a theme or a motif that promotes the overt play action. All themes or motifs reflect particular issues, such as: developmental tasks (e.g., toilet training), traumatic experiences (e.g., a stay in hospital), power (e.g., playing superman), social relations and conflicts (e.g., rivalry between siblings), attachment versus independence (e.g., approaching and removing with a play boat from the father's position) or wishes that cannot be fulfilled (e.g., driving a car).

Even though the focus of the research was the play of children between 1½ and 6 years, we also videotaped play behavior of adolescents. Among other things, we analyzed a sophisticated game called "The Black Eye" (*Das Schwarze Auge*). In this game, fantasy figures like warrior, elf, dwarf, and magician act according to fixed rules. The whole game is regulated by the game master, who tells the actors the outcome of their actions. Analysis was done in different directions. So we developed flow diagrams of action sequences, e.g., of an attack. We analyzed group dynamics, which showed a strong emotional involvement and a transfer in social interaction of participants outside the game, for example, participants felt ashamed or proud of their game actions also in real social interactions outside the game. In general, we observed three main characteristics of the game: strong group attachment, extremely hostile environments, and always new and unexpected features introduced by the play master.

"The Black Eye," which is quite similar to multiplayer online computer games, involved the adolescents for weeks and months so that they came to live in a second reality. This phenomenon is also found in computer games.

Of course, I was also confronted with the question of how play is related to learning. Articles and lectures at different places discussed the issues of play learning, incidental learning through play, and play attitudes for learning.

Old Age—Integrity Versus Despair

During this latest phase of my life, I realized that throughout my life I often acted like an adolescent. I never stopped being curious, initiating new approaches, and was rebellious against the mainstream. Even so, I feel comfortable with Erikson's eight life conflicts, especially with the last one, which is my current life stage, entitled integrity versus despair. In my view, integrity dominated in my scientific life, which means that there was a continuous development and improvement of knowledge. Indeed, my personal history of science and its development can be described as less shaped by contradictions than as a continuous broadening and growing of knowledge. Therefore it seems natural to try to integrate all of the scientific experiences across my life. A forthcoming book attempts to accomplish this. It deals with the interrelationship between evolution, culture, and ontogenesis. I hope to present a better understanding of human nature, an issue which was for me as a psychologist always the center of my research. In this way, the book might also become a synthesis of my life's work.

References

Brehm, J. W. & Cohen, A. R. (1962). *Explorations in cognitive dissonance*. New York: Wiley.

Bronfenbrenner, U. (1977). Toward an experimental ecology of human development. *American Psychologist, 12*, 513–531.

Bruhn, H., Oerter, R., & Rösing, H. (Eds.). (1985). *Musikpsychologie – Ein Handbuch in Schlüsselbegriffen*. München: Urban & Schwarzenberg.

Bruhn, H., Oerter, R., & Rösing, H. (Eds.). (1993). *Musikpsychologie – Ein Handbuch in Schlüsselbegriffen*. Reinbek: rohwolt, Taschenbuch.

Bühler, Ch. (1933). *Der menschlichebLebenslauf als psychologisches Problem*. Leipzig: Hirzel.

Dreher, E. & Oerter, R. (1986). Children's and adolescents' conceptions of adulthood. The changing view of a crucial developmental task. In R. K. Silbereisen, K. Eyferth & G. Rudinger (Eds.), *Development as action in context* (pp. 109–120). Berlin: Springer.

Festinger, L. (1957). *A theory of cognitive dissonance*. New York: Row Peterson.

Heider, F. (1958). *The psychology of interpersonal relations*. New York: Wiley.

Noack, P. (1990). *Jugendentwicklung im Kontext. Zum aktiven Umgang mit sozialen Entwicklungsaufgaben in der Freizeit*. München: Psychologie Verlags Union.

Oerter, R. (1963). Die Suggestivwirkung von Gruppenmitgliedern mit extremer Position auf die Gruppe. *Psychologische Rundschau, 14*, 275–285.

Oerter, R. (1964). Kognitive Dissonanz und erziehliche Beeinflussung. *Psychologie und Praxis, 8*, 108–118.

Oerter, R. (1966). *Die Entwicklung von Werthaltungen während der Reifezeit*. München/Basel: Ernst Reinhardt.

Oerter, R. (1967, 1987, 21. Aufl.). *Moderne Entwicklungspsychologie*. Donauwörth: Auer.

Oerter, R. (1970). *Struktur und Wandlung von Werthaltungen*. München: Oldenbourg.

Oerter, R. (1971). *Psychologie des Denkens*. Donauwörth: Auer.

Oerter, R. (1978). *Entwicklung als lebenslanger Prozess*. Hamburg: Hoffmann Campe.

Oerter, R. (Ed.). (1985). *Lebensbewältigung im Jugendalter*. Weinheim: VCH Verlagsgesellschaft.

Oerter, R. (1986a). Developmental task through the life span: A new approach to an old concept. In P. B. Baltes, D. L Featherman, & R. M. Learner (Eds.), *Life-span development and behavior* (Vol. 7, S. 233–269). Hillsdale, NJ: Erlbaum.

Oerter, R. (1986b). Cognitive development in adolescence: A cross-cultural study of the conceptualization of work. In F. Klix & H. Hagendorf (Eds.), *Human memory and cognitive capabilities. Mechanisms and performances* (Vol. 1, pp. 437–447). Amsterdam: Elsevier.

Oerter, R. (1991). Self-object relations as a basis of human development. In L. Oppenheimer & J. Valsiner (Eds.), *The origin of action: Interdisciplinary and international perspectives* (pp. 65–100). New York: Springer.

Oerter, R. (1993). *Psychologie des Spiels*. München: Quintessenz.

Oerter, R. (1995). Persons' conception of human nature: A cross-cultural comparison. In J. Valsiner (Ed.), *Child development within culturally structured environments* (Vol. 3, pp. 210–242). Norwood, NJ: Ablex.

Oerter, R. & Lohmöller, J. B. (1978). Die Erprobung des Medienverbundes 'Vorschulerziehung im Ausland.' *Av forschung, 19*, 101–139.

Oerter, R., Dreher, E., & Dreher, M. (1977). *Kognitive Sozialisation und subjektive Struktur*. München: Oldenbourg.

Oerter, R. & Montada, L. (Eds.). (1982). *Entwicklungspsychologie*. München: Urban & Schwarzenberg.

Oerter, R. & Oerter, R. M. (1995). Zur Konzeption der autonomen Identität in östlichen und westlichen Kulturen. Ergebnisse von kulturvergleichenden Untersuchungen zum Menschenbild junger Erwachsener. In G. Trommsdorff (Ed.), *Kindheit und Jugend in verschiedenen Kulturen* (pp. 153–173). Weinheim: Juventa.

Oerter, R., Oerter, R., Agostiani, H., Kim, H.-O., & Wibowo, S. (1996). The concept of human nature in East Asia. Etic and emic characteristics. *Culture & Psychology, 2*(1), 9–51.

Oerter, R. & Stoffer, Th. (Eds.). (2005). *Enzyklopädie der Musikpsychologie* (Vol. 2). Göttingen: Hogrefe.

Rogoff, B. (1986). Adult assistance of children's learning. In T. E. Raphael (Eds.), *The contexts of school-based literacy* (pp. 27–40). New York: Random House.

Rosenberg, M. J. & Abelson, R. P. (1960). Cognitive, affective and behavioral components of attitude. In C. I. Hovland & M. J. Rosenberg (Eds.), *Attitude organization and change*. New Haven, CT: Yale University Press.

Stoffer, Th. H. & Oerter, R. (Eds.). (2005). *Musikpsychologie, Bd. 1: Allgemeine Musikpsychologie*. Göttingen: Hogrefe.

Walter, H. & Oerter, R. (Eds.). (1979). *Ökologie und Entwicklung. Mensch-Umwelt-Modelle*. Donauwörth: Auer.

30

The Life and Academic Journey of an Empiricist[1]

DANIEL OFFER

Although I am 82 years old and long past adolescence, words my beloved grandfather spoke to me when I was a teenager still resound in my mind: "Tommy (my childhood name)," he said, "now that I finally know something about pediatrics, I must leave." Ludwig Ferdinand Meyer, MD, indeed knew something about pediatrics—as a young researcher in Berlin, Germany, he had discovered the role of potassium in infant diarrhea, thus radically improving every child's chances of surviving infancy.

Today I feel much as I imagine my grandfather did then. I have no immediate plans to leave, but hopefully I know something about adolescence. And, like my grandfather before me, I now have an opportunity to share some random thoughts about my career as a research scholar with younger generations. I hope these ideas and reminiscences will be useful to those of you who find yourselves on a similar path. However, let me begin my account at the beginning.

My Beginnings

I was born Thomas Edgar Hirsch on December 24, 1929, in Berlin, Germany, into a distinguished family that had lived for many generations within the walls of the old city. Throughout her life, my mother Ilse proudly displayed the centuries-old document that granted this privilege to her Jewish ancestors. As the first child of Walter Hirsch, MD, and his wife Ilse, and as the first grandchild of Ludwig Ferdinand Meyer, MD, and his wife Lotte, I had been preceded by three generations of physicians. I was showered with love.

In the early 1930s, my family watched as Hitler, Nazism, and virulent anti-Semitism arose in Germany. Ludwig, the chief of pediatrics at Berlin University, and Walter, an assistant professor of pediatrics, were ardent German citizens who had served their country honorably in World War I. Yet both lost their positions when Hitler became chancellor and immediately barred all Jews from government positions. I did not help the situation. As a 3-year-old, I enjoyed marching about the playroom shouting "Heil Hitler!" and saluting—with the wrong arm.

With the domestic situation deteriorating, Ludwig and Walter traveled to Palestine in 1934 to see what opportunities might exist for them there; Ilse, Daniel's mother, was an ardent Zionist and had argued for emigration to Israel rather than to the United States. So, in the spring of 1935, urged by their gentile friends and convinced that it was time to leave Germany, my family flew from Berlin to Trieste, then boarded a ship for Haifa. As Amos Elon (2002) writes, "The rich had the fewest problems:" My family escaped with their china, crystal, silver, and furniture. Ludwig and Lotte Meyer settled at 29 Idelson Street in Tel Aviv in a house that would later be recognized as a treasure of the Bauhaus school of design. My baby brother Michael, my parents, and I moved into a small flat at 15 Gaza Road in Jerusalem, then only a sleepy backwater town of forty thousand without even a single traffic light. So on a warm September day in 1936, I headed off to school for the first time, wearing the *lederhosen* that I would quickly exchange for khaki shorts.

Despite the curfews, the water rationing, Arab terrorist attacks and the stresses of World War II, I believe I had an idyllic youth. My life was filled with Boy Scouting, rummaging for antiquities in the hills around Jerusalem, and playing with my rambunctious friends. In the 6th grade, I wore braces on my teeth, took lessons in social dancing, and, with future cabinet minister and Knesset member

---

[1] The Editors note with sadness that professor Daniel Offer died on May 13, 2013.

Yair Tzaban, experimented with cigarettes on the roof of the shed that stood behind my family's apartment building. I kept a large map of Europe and eagerly followed the Allied war effort. When I was 14, I overheard my parents and grandparents making plans to flee Palestine for New Zealand with only the clothes on their backs, if necessary, in the event that El Alamein fell to the Afrika Korps of the German Army. Each year I visited my brother Michael at Michael's boarding school in Kibbutz Beit Alpha in the Galilee, a community so thoroughly socialist that, at bath time, I was embarrassed and delighted to find myself in the shower with both boys and very grown-up girls. A third child, my brother Juval, was born in 1937.

In February of 1948, all 30 boys and girls of my senior high-school class at the Hebrew Gymnasium were dismissed in order to enter the army and begin training for the war that was certain to begin as soon as the state of Israel was declared. I was chosen for the Palmach ("strike force"), the commando units that for years after the war would furnish the young state of Israel with its military, political, and cultural leaders. It was then, during my 6 weeks of basic training at a base near Tel Aviv, that I legally changed my name from Tommy Hirsch. I rejected the name Tommy because it was the nickname for the British during the British Mandate of Palestine, and Hirsch because it was German. I renamed myself Daniel Offer, proudly claiming my identity as a citizen of Israel.

The state of Israel was declared on May 14, 1948, and, as expected, the armies of six Arab nations attacked the following day. I was stationed in the Negev, and I was sure that I would not survive the war—my only weapon was a 20-pound Canadian rifle, a virtual antique. The War of Independence lasted 6 weeks. Although I was not athletic, I was nonetheless very fast. This ability served me admirably, both as a scout and as a member of a submachine gun unit. One of my most profound memories of the war is of Egyptian planes strafing my camp site. As I ran to safety and dove into a trench, a young friend, a girl who could not move as quickly as me, was shot and killed. After that I fought in the battle of Rouchama, helped take Beersheva, then headed south with my unit to participate in the liberation of Eilat, the last battle of the war.

I spent the second year of my army service in the medical corps. Then, in 1950, after my discharge from the Israel Defense Forces, I spent one semester at Hebrew University, where I studied physics and typed a Hebrew translation of Gogol's *Dead Souls* for my future stepfather, the poet and writer Yitzchak Shenhar.

Israel did not have a medical school in 1950. And because my father and grandfather wanted me to receive the best possible preparation for a medical career, they recommended that I go abroad for my undergraduate studies. This experience would of course be followed by a medical education. So with a letter of acceptance from the University of Rochester in hand, I sailed from the port of Haifa in the summer of 1950. My most vivid memory of my arrival in America was

of the food. Having come from a young country where both the quality and quantity of food were very limited, I was a skinny young man suddenly in a world of plenty. On arriving in New York, I was met by friends of my family. When we stopped at a supermarket and they asked me to select a steak, I picked out a nice, small steak thinking that it was intended for the whole family. I was shocked when my host then picked out four additional steaks for dinner.

My 3 years at Rochester were an education in more ways than one: for the third time in my mere 20 years I had to adapt to another culture and master yet another language. When, cleverly, the university placed the three freshman foreign students in a room together, I found myself living with a German and an Englishman. The Brit and I quickly formed an alliance. I enjoyed classical music. Luckily, Rochester is the home of the Eastman School of Music— an ideal place to be. (To this day, when my wife hears a piece of music and says, "Name that tune in five notes," I can usually name both the composition and the composer.) And I did like a good prank: When the university required students to wear jackets and ties to dinner on the weekends, my friends and I did just that but left off our shirts.

The Emergence of an Empiricist

After 3 years at Rochester I came to the University of Chicago to attend medical school. I published my first paper, "Psychosomatic Aspects of Ulcerative Colitis" (Offer, 1958), while still a student, an early indication of the research career that lay ahead. Following medical school, I did a year of internship at the University of Illinois in Chicago where I formed a relationship with the Institute of Juvenile Research that continues to this day.

While still an intern I interviewed for a residency in the department of psychiatry at Michael Reese Hospital and Medical Center in Chicago, a nationally renowned department that had distinguished itself in research, training, and patient care. The interview for the residency was a stressful one. I walked into a conference room in which 12 august psychiatrists were poised around a large table. When the department chairman, Roy Grinker, commented, "You don't look like a commando," I quickly replied, "I was a very special commando." When Roy then asked, "What kind?" I answered, "A Jewish commando." I was accepted for training and began my residency on July 1, 1958.

In the summer of 1960, Jack Wineberg, then director of the Illinois State Psychiatric Institute, had his eyes open for a bright and eligible young psychiatrist who would be suitable marriage material for the daughter of friends. He invited both Jay Hirsch, MD, and me to a large party at the home of Judith Baskin, a lovely young woman, who took an immediate liking to me. We married in July of 1961 and children soon followed: Raphael in June of 1963 and Tamar in February of 1965.

My career began to soar with the publication of several books derived from my research. In 1963, I realized very little was known about the development of normal (i.e., non-patient) adolescents. I was fortunate to receive 8 years of federal grants to study the psychological development of normal adolescents. In the first phase of the study, 73 incoming freshman boys were selected from two suburban Chicago area high schools and followed for 8 years. The major finding for the high-school phase was that stability, not turmoil, was the overriding characteristic of normal adolescents. This finding contradicted the then current notion of normal development: all adolescents go through major turmoil as they move thru the high-school years. The 4 years of the post-high-school phase of the study substantiated this finding. The two books that resulted from the adolescent studies were *The Psychological World of the Teenager: A Study of Normal Adolescent Boys* (Offer, 1969), and *From Teenage to Young Manhood: A Psychological Study* (Offer & Offer, 1975).

In turn, during my work on the Offer Longitudinal Study, I became interested in how mental-health professionals viewed normality. Working with Melvin Sabshin, we defined the four perspectives of what constitutes normal behavior. They are: normality as health, as utopia, as average, and as process. Two books resulted from this work, a first and a second edition: *Normality: Theoretical and Clinical Concepts of Mental Health* (Offer & Sabshin, 1966, 1974).

My studies of normal adolescents did not mean that I was no longer interested in deviant and disturbed adolescents. In fact, I undertook a 5-year study, 1969–74, of psychiatrically disturbed juvenile delinquents. This was a study to analyze the makeup of this population and how society can best help them. My colleagues and I were in charge of an inpatient unit for this population at the Illinois State Psychiatric Institute, a setting which allowed for an in-depth study. A book resulted from the study: *The Psychological World of the Juvenile Delinquent* (Offer, Marohn, & Ostrov, 1979).

All this professional accomplishment and joy was coupled with personal sadness when Judith was diagnosed with breast cancer. Tragically, she died at the age of 36 in May of 1976. I suffered a double loss: She had been my partner not only in life but in research as well.

I found myself living a bittersweet existence. Although in 1977 I achieved a lifetime goal of becoming chairman of psychiatry at Michael Reese, I was a solitary man raising two young children alone. Always a respecter of data, I turned to Edward Goldfarb, MD, a Reese psychiatrist renowned for his "little black book." To my great good fortune, Eddie recommended me to Marjorie Kaiz, then a young widow with an 8-year-old daughter, Susan.

Marjorie and I met in January of 1979 and I courted her, not with flowers and candy, but with copies of my books! Fortunately, she nevertheless found me to be charming, interesting, and fun, and we married in August of that year. And, when I became Marjorie's husband, I became a father for the third time when I adopted my daughter Susan.

Our years together have gone much too quickly. Our children have grown and prospered. Each has achieved a graduate degree, married a fine partner, become the parent of two children, and acquired a mortgage. They telephone us frequently from their homes in Sunnyvale, California; London, England; and Mercer Island, Washington. We watch with great pleasure as our five granddaughters and one grandson travel the well-worn paths of human development.

Most surprising to me has been the discovery that once again I have a wife who is a research partner. It took me a while to accept her unconventional credentials— a bachelor of science degree from the Medill School of Journalism at Northwestern University—but just as I had mentored more than seventy 70 fellows in adolescent psychiatry, I mentored her.

During 1996 and 1997, 94% (67 individuals) of the original sample in the Offer Longitudinal Study were reinterviewed at age 48. Two subjects had died of natural causes. The original finding held. All were well-adjusted late middle-aged individuals. The major finding was the discovery that well-adjusted adults do not remember their adolescence accurately. The data showed there is no correlation between what our subjects as adults thought and felt about their adolescence and what they actually thought and felt when they were adolescents. *Regular Guys: 34 Years Beyond Adolescence*, written with Eric Ostrov (Offer, Offer, & Ostrov, 2004), is the product of our collaboration.

Lessons Learned and Advice Given: The Shaping of a Career in Research

If you, like me, end your career a researcher, then you probably started out in life as one too. As I look back on my own journey, I can see that an intense desire to explore has always been an important part of my being. Perhaps I was born with this drive: According to my mother Ilse's diary of my early childhood, I was a curious child, always asking a lot of "why" questions. And inquiry was certainly a part of everyday life as I was growing up; my father and grandfather were pediatric researchers, and I eavesdropped on academic discussions throughout my childhood.

In my high-school years, I undertook my first real research project—the classification of my prized insect collection. I also collected arrowheads and antiquities that I found on my hikes around Israel (then Palestine). To this day, I fondly display these collections in my home on Mercer Island, Washington.

My trajectory toward research continued at the University of Chicago Medical School (1953–57) where I pursued a number of research-related electives and published my first scientific article. But it was during my residency in psychiatry at Michael Reese Hospital and Medical Center (1958–62) that my future career became most evident. I published five papers during my time there and discovered how much I truly enjoyed the research experience. Looking back, I realize now how very fortunate I was that my natural abilities were nurtured throughout my childhood, adolescence, and young adulthood by my family and teachers. I have also been blessed with mentors and talented co-authors along the way, among them both of my wives.

Destined though I may have been for an academic life, it was not an easy road. When I completed my psychiatric residency, I watched as many of my peers began their clinical practices and teaching careers at salaries that were often five times that of a typical researcher. Any worries they may have had about meeting the monthly bills could be addressed by simply adding more patients to their practices. Grants, on the other hand, were and still are far more difficult to obtain. As my medical school colleagues traveled to their weekend homes, I reviewed data in my small townhouse, enduring, as all researchers must, the exhausting processes of evaluation and revaluation that accompany every grant application.

Is there anything one can do to make this career easier? First, you must be certain that research is the career that suits you best. And ideally you should enjoy the entire process: forming the research question, collecting and analyzing the data, and writing up your findings. And while each stage has its challenges, writing seems to be the task that researchers find the most difficult. I have seen excellent researchers struggle with writing for years and even end their careers because of this issue. This outcome is particularly unfortunate when an individual has collected an extraordinary data set that he or she is simply unable to prepare for publication. An effective way to overcome the difficulty of writing, including the daunting blankness of your first page, is to create a detailed outline of your paper, and then to write from this outline. You must also accept the fact that a first draft is exactly that—a first attempt. You should expect to rewrite your papers several times.

You should also be completely aware of other challenges you will face, especially loneliness. An academic researcher leads a solitary life: You begin with a question that you alone choose and to which you alone seek the answer; you slowly, methodically, and tirelessly work toward an answer that in the end may not be the one you expect or want. Longitudinal research presents its own hardships: You must wait for years, sometimes more than a decade, for your answers. But even without immediate gratification from your work, the wait is well worth it. Of the many satisfactions of research, the greatest, without a doubt, is the discovery of new knowledge. It is immensely rewarding to see that your work influences and eventually modifies current theory. In my case, the ultimate achievement is watching my research find its way into real-life clinical settings where it actually helps adolescents obtain better mental health care.

One advantage of clinical work is the esteem and gratitude of patients; transference or not, your patients hold you in high regard and take your observations seriously. The researcher, on the other hand, faces the exact opposite situation: Peers critically evaluate your research on its own merit, an unfeeling and sometimes painful process focused only on whether or not you have proved your hypothesis. If you have not, you may return to many more

months of work or you may even decide to abandon your project for another one. Either way, you may feel sorry for yourself, but no one else does.

Another stumbling block can be the doctoral training experience itself. Over the years I have seen students bury themselves in their research, sometimes taking as long as 12–15 years to complete a thesis. I believe that the optimal time for completing a PhD is 5 years. Remember, you need only demonstrate to the university that you have mastered the research process—you can always leave your original work for later when you have your degree in your hand. In addition, if you have a thesis adviser with whom you do not get along, or if you see that he or she does not have your best interests at heart, ask for a new adviser. This simple change has helped any number of students.

There are many wonderful things about academic life. I have especially enjoyed my relationships with peers from all over the world, many of whom have become cherished lifelong friends. I first began to enjoy this aspect of my career when I became one of 30 researchers to receive a Career Investigator grant from the National Institute of Mental Health. From 1963 to 1968, to encourage the cross-fertilization of our ideas, all 30 of us met once a year for long weekends in Colorado. By presenting our work to each other and receiving feedback, we created a community of like souls whose camaraderie strengthened our dedication and affirmed our research careers. When I taught at the University of Chicago and at Northwestern University, I always encouraged my students to attend and present at meetings in their field so that they too could develop these important bonds—antidotes for the inevitable isolation that accompanies a career in research.

In mid-career, I had another extraordinary opportunity to join with peers from a multitude of fields. From 1973 to 1974, I was a fellow at the Center for Advanced Studies in the Behavioral Sciences at Stanford University. The center offers fellowships to about 30 individuals from a variety of disciplines—the social, psychological, and political sciences, as well as from medicine, history, linguistics, and biology. During my year of residency at Stanford, a year in which I was free to work on whatever I wished, I often mingled and socialized with the other fellows. Once again, the loneliness of research was alleviated by fulfilling relationships with my fellow academics.

Another positive aspect of academic life is the healthy dose of narcissistic delight one gets from seeing one's work in print. It was enormously gratifying to me, for instance, to enter the public library in Melbourne, Australia, and to find that it had copies of almost all of my books, and that the most recent one had been taken out only a week prior to my visit.

I have been most fortunate to work with both of my wives: Judith Baskin Offer to whom I was married from 1961 until her death in 1976; and Marjorie Kaiz Offer whom I married in 1979—two exceptionally bright women who, perhaps because they were untrained in research, brought fresh and creative perspectives to our work. (It is important to remember the words of Albert Einstein: ("Imagination is more important than knowledge.") For 14 years Marjorie and I collaborated on a follow-up study of a group of adolescents I originally studied from 1962 to 1971.

In spite of what Louis Pasteur wrote about it ("Luck prefers the prepared mind."), luck will certainly play a role in your career. Early in my research career, I needed advice from a statistician about a test I was developing called the Offer Self Image Questionnaire. When I sought out Kenneth Howard, PhD, then a senior researcher at the Institute for Juvenile Research at the Chicago campus of the University of Illinois, he referred me to a young colleague. But when this fellow's advice turned out to be incorrect and I returned to Ken in dismay, Ken felt so guilty that he personally became my consultant. This gesture evolved into a collaboration that lasted 37 years until Ken's death in 2000, and produced no less than four books and 40 scientific articles.

What was extraordinary about our collaboration was the dedication we both felt to academic research. We met every Friday throughout those 37 years. Fridays became our sacred research days and nothing stood in their way— not clinical emergencies, administrative duties, nor teaching responsibilities. Ken was the methodologist and statistician, and I was the empiricist and the theoretician. And while luck played a role in our finding each other, we were both prepared to make the most of our chance encounter. Since 2000, Fridays have not been the same for me.

Conclusions

Perhaps now is the time to give you some bits of advice. First, it is important to set aside some time every week for research. Inevitably, psychiatrists and psychologists fill up their research time with the exigencies of daily life. And even though they tell themselves that they will one day make the time, they never do. The lesson here is that time for research must be ironclad. Otherwise, it simply evaporates.

Second, it is important that young researchers "keep their eyes on the prize," as my wife Marjorie likes to say. Keep focused and do not give up. My first book, *Normality* (Offer & Sabshin, 1966), was submitted to no less than seven publishers before Basic Books accepted it for publication in 1965. What a long and painful but ultimately worthwhile journey that was; *Science* gave *Normality* an excellent review, a rare thing indeed.

Third, beware of the media, which can be both seductive and destructive. Watch out in particular for the journalist who is merely fishing for copy. My rule of thumb has been to speak only about matters on which I am truly expert. On the other hand, I also recommend that you not be snobbish about the media. Years ago the *National Enquirer* interviewed me about my research and subsequently published a very accurate article about normal adolescence. Hopefully a new audience learned that troubled teenagers are not just being "adolescent," but need professional help.

My next bit of advice is about writing. Your writing should be clear, concise, and so free of academic jargon that a scholar in any field can understand it. Remember that the really talented researcher can communicate what he has learned to anyone. I know this is not the trend today but it should be every scholar's gold standard.

Finally, I would like to point out that opportunities for scholarship exist everywhere. For the past 13 years I have been a dialysis patient due to renal failure. This has not prevented me from teaching, doing research, publishing, and exploring the world, however. I have been dialyzed in no less than 43 clinics around the world—"suds factories," as Marjorie and I have nicknamed them. While we have had many unusual experiences associated with dialysis, none can compare to the sessions that took place on a 2-week cruise from Buenos Aries, Argentina, to Santiago, Chile. For 3 hours every Monday, Wednesday, and Friday, I found myself in a tiny room with a fellow patient, Ahmed, who had been born and raised in Cairo, Egypt. He too had come to America for his education; he had a PhD in engineering from Stanford and had built a career in the United States. And he too had fought in the 1948 war—but on the side of Egypt. We were two souls tethered to the same life-giving machine at the end of the world, and we had some very interesting conversations.

During these years I have learned a great deal about chronic illness in general and about renal failure in particular. When Marjorie and I discovered that there was virtually nothing in print to guide dialysis patients and their families through this sometimes daunting process, we, along with our daughter Susan Offer Szafir, decided to write a book for the general public. *Dialysis Without Fear* the result of our work together, was published by Oxford University Press (Offer, Offer, & Szafir, 2007). The book presented me with opportunities to interview nephrologists, social workers, nurses, technicians, and dieticians, as well as patients and their families. My hope is that our findings have provided help and encouragement to the more than 400,000 Americans who currently cope with renal failure.

If it is true that the value of a life can be measured by what one bequeaths to posterity, then I believe I will leave behind three important legacies by which future generations may evaluate my life: First, there are my publications—18 scientific books and monographs, sixty-seven scientific articles, and three psychological tests and interpretive manuals. Second, are my three children and six grandchildren. Third, is my participation in the founding of the state of Israel, a dream that lay dormant for 2,000 years and came to fruition in the time of my youth.

In March of 2006, Springer, one of the world's foremost scientific publishers and the publisher of the *Journal of Youth and Adolescence*, held a reception to honor me for my role as the founding editor of the *Journal* and for my 35 years as its editor-in-chief. This elegant event was held at the bi-annual meeting of the Society for Research in Adolescence in San Francisco and was attended by my then 10-year-old grandson, Ron Offer Yehoshua, and his parents. Ron was the only child there and he had fun taking photographs of everyone and listening carefully to all the speeches. After the talks were completed, his father asked him, "Do you know what your grandfather did?" "Yes," Ron replied, "he invented adolescence." "Not quite," he was lovingly told.

So these are my current musings about my long, fulfilling academic journey. Would I do it all over again? In a heartbeat.

References

Elon, A. (2002). *The pity of it all: A portrait of the German-Jewish epoch, 1743–1933*. New York, NY: Picador.

Offer, D. (1958). Psychosomatic aspects of ulcerative colitis: A review. *Illinois Medical Journal, 114*(4), 159–163.

Offer, D. (1969). *The psychological world of the teenager: A study of normal adolescent boys*. New York, NY: Basic Books.

Offer, D. Marohn, R. C., & Ostrov, E. (1979). *The psychological world of the juvenile delinquent*. New York, NY: Basic Books.

Offer, D., & Offer, J. L. (1975). *From teenage to young manhood: A psychological study*. New York, NY: Basic Books.

Offer, D., Offer, M. K., & Ostrov, E. (2004). *Regular guys, 34 years beyond adolescence*. New York, NY: Springer.

Offer, D., Offer, M. K., & Szafir, S. O. (2007). *Dialysis without fear: A guide to living well on dialysis for patients and their families*. New York, NY: Oxford University Press.

Offer, D., & Sabshin, M. (1966). *Normality: Theoretical and clinical concepts of mental health*. New York, NY: Basic Books.

Offer, D., & Sabshin, M. (1974). *Normality: Theoretical and clinical concepts of mental health* (2nd ed.). New York, NY: Basic Books.

31

Autobiography Through Adolescence

Augusto Palmonari

 I have worked as researcher and professor of the University of Bologna since the beginning of the 1960s, and for many years even in precarious positions. "Will power and commitment to the cause!" says the Non-Existent Knight in Italo Calvino's novel of the same title. My interest in adolescence-related thematics was born out of my work in the field with adolescents rather than in the lab. Experimental research and many studies, for what they are worth, came later on. When I received the invitation to collaborate in this prestigious academic volume I felt honored, though uncertain of whether I would be up to such a dignified task. On the other hand, I pondered on the real occurrences that have marked my career and here I am, giving it a try in the hope of not becoming too much of a bore.

The academic interests I have nurtured throughout my career from a strictly academic point of view are connected with the developments of social psychology in Europe. In parallel with the abovementioned domains I grew an interest for a wide range of issues concerning adolescence. It might sound strange that a social psychologist should deal with this particular stage of human development, but I hope it will become clearer in the next paragraphs, the particular way I engaged with this issue. I hasten to clarify that while owing my interest in social psychology to my studies and personal encounters I had with H. Tajfel, S. Moscovici, and W. Doise on various academic occasions, I see my research on adolescence as originating in my pre-university experiences, in particular my engagement with the young Catholics' association. It was in this particular habitat that I found the reasons for participating in social life and discovered the importance (or rather the duty for whom inhabits a democratic society) of social engagement. As early as the beginning of my university studies I was very keen on deepening my knowledge on socialization processes involving adolescents and engaged in courses organized by various summer schools. I also studied many works, in Italian as well as in French, that spoke about social engagement oriented to the creation of a social community. In those years I also discovered the importance of living an intensive group life, made of true friendships founded on shared ideals.

The personal life experience as a member of that particular association certainly influenced my later choice of studies after high school: I decided to enrol in the Faculty of Medicine of University of Bologna because I saw in the medical profession an important gateway for helping and alleviate suffering, especially with the less advantaged. Moreover, the fact that in the small town near Bologna where I was born and grew up there was a psychiatric hospital led me to plan completing my medical studies with a major in psychiatry. Thus, my university studies were remarkably cast in a voluntary framing, which at the same time marked their limits: I perceived my education as being more aimed at contributing to my growing on the professional edge rather than at improving my knowledge and cultural background. Of the university courses, the ones that actually interested me were mainly those that I regarded as useful to serving particular social causes.

My interest in psychology had already overridden that for psychiatry as early as the third year of my medical studies: At that time I was attending the lectures in fulfillment of the principal course on human physiology. I recall the professor going through very rapidly the part concerning the functioning of sensory organs in order to elaborate in-depth on issues of a more psychological nature: perception in the framework of Gestalt theory, emotions and their impact on perceptual and memory processes from the New Look perspective, aggression theory from Freudian thought, and the frustration–aggression model. All these topics were absolutely new to me and convinced me that psychology was the right field of study to pursue if I were to fulfill my motivation for helping others in need.

Once a medicine graduate (1960), I came to an agreement with my psychology professor to attend, on an unpaid voluntary basis, the Institute that was being set up at the University of Bologna. At the same time I continued to follow psychiatric clinical practice in order to acquire a specialization that would enable me to hone a formally recognized profession (thus reassuring my family who was sustaining me financially) in case my personal projects regarding psychology would not come to fruition.

The necessity of earning my living and being able to afford a rented room in Bologna became pressing in the meantime (it was 1963 and I was 27 years old). The Institute of Psychology where I was working several days a week in order to learn how to do research was not able to offer me any formal (and thus paid) position. However, I was offered other types of part-time professional consultancy jobs in applied domains of interest, such as the treatment of adolescent deviance, the long- term institutionalization of children and adolescents in need, and the professional training of adolescents (14 and 18 years old) prematurely introduced to working contexts. I worked with enthusiasm on these issues although they were not of strictly academic interest. Nevertheless, such engagement with the adolescence related problems played a decisive role in my future work.

Along with my progressive integration in the academic domain of psychology which passed from a purely voluntary basis to a more institutional one (in 1968 I was given a Lectureship in Social Psychology), I started working in collaboration with other young volunteers of the Institute of Psychology on research on institutionalized minors and apprentice adolescents. Yet again, the experience of working in groups proved to be very fruitful.

In my and my collaborators' opinion, the research was aimed at documenting real situations of social malaise and identifying the conditions necessary for making a change. It was not our impression that we were doing research that could be useful for academia. A qualitative turn came about following a seminar organized by the European Association of Social Psychology in order to promote social psychology in the University of Bologna. The seminar revolved around a key-lecture of Henry Tajfel, at the time (1975) one of the most influential leading figures of European social psychology. On that occasion we presented our work to Tajfel and specifically expressed our desire to conduct research in social psychology. Much to our surprise our interlocutor attributed an unexpected value to what we had already accomplished (with regard to the integration of formerly institutionalized adolescents in small living units housed in city apartments) to the point of considering our work as highly relevant for research on the genesis of rules in natural groups. In this regard, he suggested that we read the work of the Sherifs. Starting from that episode our relationship with Tajfel became very intensive, on the personal as well as professional level. We adopted his ideas on group relations in order to frame our studies on adolescent group dynamics and interpret the findings we would gather in successive years in light of his theory of social identity.

In other terms, we started then to feel like real social psychologists, conscious of having to learn everything from scratch but also encouraged by the fact that we had identified a significant area of research. I will try, at this point , to describe the research and studies conducted in collaboration with young colleagues who had started working with me (Carugati, Casadio, Lenzi, Palmonari, & Ricci Bitti, 1973).

Re-Socialization Processes in Institutionalized Adolescents

The socio-cultural climate, within which I was working on this topic, typified the 1960s and early 1970s: The fight against formal institutions (a case in point being the closure of the Psychiatric Hospital of Gorizia by Franco Basaglia based on sound theoretical and humanitarian grounds) was raging and was on the agenda of many social actors, professionals of our sector being at the forefront. During that time we contributed to drafting innovative solutions for residential services for children and adolescents in need. Until then, there were only formal institutions for youngsters (Goffman, 1961). In our city and in the wider region there were many such facilities hosting inmates (a term taken by Goffman) from various regions of Italy. The local authorities then took the decision to shut these facilities down, one after another, and set up support plans for facilitating the return home of the majority of children and adolescents. However, this solution could not be applied to everyone. Therefore, the Institute of Psychology was asked to draft a project aimed at shaping new prototypes of community life as an alternative to formal institutions. In charge of the project our team suggested to the local authorities the creation of small living units of girls and boys (6–7 each), each unit to be housed in a city apartment under the care of three educators and be given the necessary financial means for everyday expenses. The members of each unit would attend the public schools of the city.

The project was approved and five living units were created. The reference criteria for the functioning of the unit were the following:

- Educators could rely on the supervision of one member of our work group.
- Their activities with the guests were inspired in principle, as well as in practice, by the democratic style operationalized by Lewin, Lippit, and White (1939) in their well-known study on leadership styles. Our participation in the project also foresaw that the original criteria be reformulated and tailored to specific situations.

In the five living units that we supervised by means of direct observation at different times throughout the day, nondirective interviews and focus group discussions with educators, we noticed that adolescents manifested a behavioral pattern which mirrored their typical everyday life in the total institutions they came from (lasting approximately 6–8 weeks); a phase of intensive personal disorganization, otherwise known as "crisis" (lasting approximately 3 months); and a phase of personal reorganization characterized by the discovery of shared rules of living together and of an opening to the outside world (lasting until the end of the project).

A Short Comment on These Three Phases

During their long stay in residential institutions, adolescents had acquired a very rigid lifestyle, totally regulated by forces beyond their power. It is natural that they used the very same style in order to integrate into the new environment; however, they quickly became aware that the new setting offered many novelties compared with the previous one: They could move freely around the apartment; there was no rigid control; the educators seemed available to their proposals; they could refuse to eat the food they did not like; they could go to school unaccompanied. The crisis phase emerged as they became fully conscious of the different psychological atmosphere of their living unit compared with the one before.

The crisis was considered a group phenomenon, since all the guests placed in the various apartments displayed disorganized behavior: They ate at unusual times; for brief periods some of them feed exclusively on fruit and sweets; they slept the whole day; they made terrible noise during the night. At the same time, they searched for physical contact with the adults often by sitting on their lap and dressing in their clothes, and needed to be continuously reassured about the normality of their own physical development.

During the crisis phase the emotional strength and the availability of contact provided by the adults was decisive: Their patience always allowed for adolescents to express themselves freely although in infantile ways, paving the way for a new reorganization effort to emerge. One by one the guests accepted the idea of discussing amongst them about shared rules of living together, how to manage the money at their disposal or organize the functioning of the apartment in the best possible way. After some time they also agreed to reflect upon their personal histories, attitudes towards their families of origin, and their experiences as institutionalized children. It was as if they were discovering that it was possible to make personal projects for the future.

Then we tried to interpret the process that had been activated in the described situations. Lewin et al.'s (1939) research on leadership styles shows that during a group's transition from an authoritarian to a democratic style of leadership there is a phase of confusion due to the loss of reference points previously provided by authoritarian rules. The advantages of the democratic life style are discovered only after some time has passed. The case of our groups was that of a transition from institution life which was regulated in an authoritarian way to that of the living units in a city apartment characterized by democratically

inspired principles of relationships. Therefore, the crisis phase was a reaction to this transition; the disorganized behavior displayed by the guests occurred as they were trying to "take charge" of the new reality, importantly after a long period of adaptation to their previous institutional life. Disorganized behavior was in general followed by a phase of new equilibrium, described by the protagonists themselves as "a new life," "an opening to the world" (Carugati, Emiliani, & Palmonari, 1975).

The regularity of the sequence of events described above led us to believe that the three phases were not accidental but represented a real personal change. Berger and Luckmann (1966) maintain that a process of personal change is characterized by: A subjective feeling of total transformation, in the sense that the individual has the feeling that a change is taking place in their own world; a marked change in the value attributed to reality, so much so that things that were important before become irrelevant, whereas others previously considered of no apparent value are given the highest priority; the creation of intense affective relations with significant others (in our case with educators). The crisis phase we observed corresponded to that of disintegration of the subjective reality of the adolescents. De-socialization was followed by a phase of re-socialization into a new set of values. After the crisis phase the units we studied discovered the necessity of creating rules of living together in a community where members do not reciprocally annihilate one another. In the 1975 meeting with H. Tajfel in Bologna, we illustrated these results specifically stating that our work concerned the strict documentation of a social intervention. Tajfel himself analyzed our findings very carefully and situated them in reference to the work of the Sherifs on group norms creation. This helped us gather courage and present our research in a Small Group Meeting of EAESP which took place in Poland, in 1977. Moreover, we presented the results of our intervention in various meetings in Italy promoting an interpretation based on the *three-phase model* which was applied in various settings to set up residential initiatives for children and adolescents in need, as an alternative to institutionalization practices. (Carugati, Emiliani &Palmonari, 1984)

Adolescents: Imperfect Identities

In this line of research we were inspired by the work of Lewin, in particular his paper titled "Field Theory and Experiment in Social Psychology" (1951), specifically the part concerning adolescence. A center for professional training of apprentice adolescents requested my personal collaboration in understanding the reasons underlying passive behavior and lack of motivation for work that many apprentices manifested. Thus I began to analyze the perception of self, the motivational system and the temporal perspective of two groups of adolescents: Apprentices and students of the same age. I found a series of differences between the two categories of youngsters. Whereas students were able to define their own position with regard to diverse social realities (public institutions, politics, professions, banks, etc.) and were conscious of the necessity to gain a cultural background with a view on the future, apprentices, on the other hand, were totally absorbed by their everyday life exigencies (the work, sustaining the family, recreational events), so much so that they did not find any time to reflect on their future, or the importance of professional training and relations with their social reality.

Consequently, my colleagues and I decided to investigate more in-depth the reasons behind such marked differences via a differential study of apprentices and students. Sociological studies had already highlighted the importance of factors such as social class and generational difference in terms of cultural background in order to differentiate the behavior of groups of adolescents towards social engagement, the capacity to define a personal life project, and the relations with social institutions and politics. Our objective was more that of analyzing how adolescents, apprentices, and students organized the relations between representations of self and the main social categories. We asked participants (a group of male students and a group of male apprentices of the same age) to choose from a list of behaviors and personality traits those that were more characteristic of the following social categories: adult men, adult women, young male students, young female students, young male workers, young female workers, young males in general, young females in general. Each participant was requested to state whether each of the items also applied to himself. We found the following results: The representation of self played a central role for all participants and was defined in similar ways by both groups, whereas the representations of other categories (adults and youngsters, men and women, etc.) were very different. We nevertheless observed an important difference in the definitions provided by apprentices and students. Whereas the latter evaluated the distance between themselves and the respective in-group (students) as smaller than that between self and the out-groups (the abovementioned categories), apprentices evaluated the distance between self and the in-group as important and, at least as more accentuated than the distance between self and the out-group of students.

Apart from this there was evidence that while students defined members of their own group as *youngsters*, they did not recognize the category of apprentices as similarly constituted by youngsters but perceived them as more similar to adults. Moreover, apprentices defined the proper group as made of youngsters whose prototype they recognized in the category of students. In short, all adolescents participating in our research elaborated a practically identical representation of self but highlighted a difference between students and apprentices when the representations of self were placed in reference to the categories youngster/adult and young student/young apprentice. In intergroup theory terms, students identified with their own in-group, whereas the apprentices identified more with one of the out-groups.

The perceived differences between apprentices and students were further investigated by means of a questionnaire administered to the same participants examining their motivation for achievement viewed in relation to time perspective. Students saw a continuity of past–present–future, and perceived the future as a privileged place where engagement in the present could lead to consistent modifications of the self as well as of the external reality. On the other hand, apprentices did not seem to capture the continuity between past, present, and future, and experienced the present, that is, their present situation, as frustrating. They too, had the expectation that in the future their present problems would be solved but because of the discontinuity between the present and the future, such expectation was experienced unrealistically. For them it was as if all had to happen immediately through a radical transformation of reality and under the urgency of the subject's emotional needs. Moreover, the urge to get possession of prestigious goods as a way of compensating the frustrations of actual life conditions was more accentuated amongst apprentices compared with students. Perhaps these data can be read in connection to the lack of flexibility of the category of the possible which allows one to define articulate expectations about the future in a more or less realistic way.

Tajfel's Social Identity theory was particularly relevant for the interpretation of these research data; we also made ample reference to Social Representation Theory of Moscovici (1976/1961, 2008) in order to make sense of participants' representations of the present and the future. Additionally, the experience and knowledge gained through the research process served as a basis for the work we conducted on adolescents' identity development processes. Moreover, it had us convinced of the relevance of studying the adolescence with reference to multiple social categories that adolescents belong to in different historical moments (not just student adolescents but also apprentices, not just Italian but also immigrant adolescents of diverse nationalities and religions; see Palmonari, Carugati, Ricci Bitti & Sarchielli, 1979, 1984).

The Importance and Spreading of Adolescent Peer Groups

The authors that while studying adolescence have paid most attention to the interdependence of social, personal, and cultural factors until now are Muzafer and Carolyn Sherif (1964, 1969; Sherif, 1984). I will not spend time on illustrating the importance of their contribution. Nevertheless the contribution of the Sherifs has shown that thanks to peer groups, adolescents have the possibility of experimenting with new social roles, of facing significant events (the first intimate relations, schooling difficulties, work situations), and of discussing with others the discoveries they make in the actual reality in which they live. The leap towards peers is a clear signal that a balance shift in the system of self is taking place: The principal reference is shifted from adults to peers, at least with regard to the activities and life experiences that are not dominated by adults.

Mapping the Presence of Adolescents Peer Groups in an Urban Territory

After having long discussed the work of the Sherifs, in particular their proposed device for the systematic observation of *natural groups of adolescents,* we decided to adopt a modified version that fit our socio-cultural context with the aim of identifying existing groups of adolescents and understanding their social functioning. We framed our work accordingly, conscious of the fact that field research on peer groups requires a particular attention to the Italian context specificity: The importance attributed to family; the various notions regarding the education of children; the degree of freedom of movement granted to them; the organization of schools and duration of studies.

We adopted the following procedure:

- knowledge of the physical and cultural habitat of the area of intervention;
- identification of the most common types of youth groupings, be they organized formally or defined by spontaneous encounter exigencies;
- identification of the habitual settings of such group encounters;
- interviews with key persons present in the territory such as teachers engaged in cultural and extra-curricular activities, coaches of sport groups, heads of formal groups, be they religious or else, local police officers, owners of coffee shops or other gathering places for adolescents.

This preliminary information allowed us to access the territory from the bottom and identify groups active in a given area. At a first stage we tried to identify the groups of adolescents that were active in three blocks of the city of Bologna: We wanted thus to make a mapping of the present groups in the given territory. We identified various groups of adolescents, boys as well as girls that met on a regular basis, at least three times a week in a public park, on a street corner, in front of the school or the coffee shop. The groups were of different sizes (from 6–8 to 12–15 adolescents) with a larger number of boys than girls. In the three neighborhoods considered we noticed that apart from the informal groups of adolescents there were also formal groups, namely groups that were led by an adult who was responsible for guiding the group towards achieving its objectives. Public opinion in general gives a lot of importance to the formal groups (be they of religious or sport affiliation) which are considered as essential to the education of adolescents. Conversely, there is general distrust of informal groups, their members are often perceived as doing nothing, as being losers and often considered as similar to, or identified with deviant groups. The field studies of Sherif had already falsified

this belief; our data showed that among informal groups only some of them engaged in deviant behaviors, whereas the majority of these informal groups served important socialization functions for their adolescent members.

Our first field research served as an inspiration for a more intensive research on groups (formal and informal) operating in working-class and middle-class neighborhoods of the cities of Bologna, Salerno, and Torino. We wanted to verify whether informal groups were distributed in the same way in various cities of Northern, Central, and Southern Italy and whether there was an equal participation of girls. The results showed a great distribution of groups, a greater number of informal groups than formal ones, and active participation of girls in all types of groups. Additionally, we noticed that the spontaneous association of peers during the central phase stage of adolescence (14–19 years) is a phenomenon observed in all social strata, equally concerning student adolescents as well as working or unemployed adolescents. The importance attributed to the group decreases in the years of emerging adulthood as interpersonal and romantic relations become more relevant (Amerio, Boggi-Cavallo, Palmonari, & Pombeni, 1990; Crocetti & Palmonari, 2011).

Peer Groups' Everyday Life

Our team established direct contacts with a number of adolescent members of the identified groups for the purposes of the abovementioned research and other field studies conducted with the same methodology. We organized thematic group meetings where we asked adolescents to reflect on the history of their group, on their family experiences, on problems they faced in school or work. During these encounters we were quick to differentiate among adolescents who belonged to spontaneous (informal) groups and those in more formal ones. The latter included mainly students of middle- and upper-class families and the number of girls was higher than that of boys. In the former, a representation of all the social classes was found. Also the members of these groups were students, as well as workers and unemployed, and boys as well as girls. Informal groups were frequently homogenous with regard to their members' social conditions.

Group life in adolescence is guided by a number of fundamental rules, the first being that of keeping one's promises and never betraying the trust of friends. Other rules concern the attitude of the group towards behaviors that are considered problematic within the group, such as heavy drug use or other deviant behaviors (e.g., bullying). Some groups consider even light drug use as an inappropriate way of dealing with personal problems and that it should generally be avoided.

Adolescents refuse those who try to impose themselves as leader, even though this does not mean that there is no differentiation in positions and roles within the group. There are frequent cases of members who are able to safeguard the unity of the group even in conflicting situations. In others, there are members, mostly male, who are so competent that they win over the admiration of friends. Almost always these are competences related to everyday life actions, like repairing a motor bike or operating electronic devices. In fact, the group creates its proper cohesion thanks to such small experiences which are actually experienced collectively. This awareness leads to the need for getting together on a daily basis.

Formal groups reveal a higher complexity of rules compared with informal groups. Very often a distinction is made between principles on the one hand, which are the same for all and which everybody should respect, and norms on the other, for which compliance is left to the individual's personal choice. All formal groups that we interviewed considered lack of commitment and failure to take charge of the activities of the group as serious forms of transgression. In order to be accepted by others it is necessary to prove one's continuous and assiduous commitment to the group, also in conformity with school or work exigencies.

The measures taken by various groups towards members that violated rules revealed a generally democratic style: The strategies most commonly used involved discussion and helping the group member to reconsider the mistake committed, regardless of the person's age or type of group in question. Nevertheless, various assessments of the importance of rules were made. In general, girls were more firm than boys in rejecting all forms of transgression. Adolescents coming from underprivileged social-class families seemed to show an enhanced disposition towards transgression, but at the same time they reacted more strongly to rule violations (even by physically attacking the transgressor). Those belonging to more privileged classes instead favored verbal reproaches more than physical violence.

Obviously a first-hand interpretation of such differences would require consideration of cultural and socialization factors, of family life context that beyond and prior to the group life provide adolescents (whether male or female, educated or not) with diverse models of behavior. To summarize, it can be said that the totality of the rules that every group creates for itself is linked with the values and socio-cultural systems to which the group refers. Respect for such rules grounds the very life of the group itself and makes possible its continuation: The stronger the internal cohesion of the group and individuals' identification with it, the greater the malaise felt by the adolescent upon its breach (Palmonari, Pombeni, & Kirchler, 1990).

Different Kinds of Interaction Among Peer Groups

We were able to verify that the given adolescents were well acquainted with diverse youth aggregations present in their territory. Certainly everyone knew better the story of their group, but also knew a lot about the proximate and the similar ones. Therefore everyone was able to identify in the constellation of groups operating in the larger territory those that they would never want to be part of and that were perceived as very different from their own.

The groups most often perceived as "most different" from their own were the political youth groups. This was an intriguing finding indeed given that many sociological studies highlighted that, at least in Italy, adolescents are not interested in politics. (It seems that at present, and from the distance of 10 years, the picture is slightly changing; however, we do not have concrete data in this regard.) Apart from these data, the *informal groups* on the one hand, and the *formal groups of a religious affiliation* on the other, constituted two opposing poles. Members of informal groups considered religious groups as very different from their own, whereas members of religious groups considered those of informal groups as most different from their own way of being. Members of sport groups instead, which is another example of formal grouping, considered both religious groups and informal groups as the very different from their own. As we could examine through interviews with members of these groups such differences are certainly related with ways of behavior and value systems that members of the given out-groups showed.

Peer groups thus represent social systems in which adolescents feel personally implicated. Even though they seem fragile from the organizational point of view, like many informal groups that have a duration of no longer than a couple of years, groups draw their own vitality from their members' daily interactions, which makes possible the elaboration of more or less shared representations (Kirchler, Pombeni & Palmonari, 1991).

However, it needs to be noted that a limited but relatively stable number of adolescents (boys and girls) that participated in our research (approximately 7%) maintained that they did not have any kind of relations with friends of their own age: The interviewees often related such a fact to a psychological difficulty in establishing friendship relations. Sentiments of loneliness and malaise originated in such difficulty. Clinical psychology has thoroughly investigated such phenomena, treating them in some cases as typical of adolescence in general. We, however, did not examine the processes underlying such malaise.

Peer Group and Family

We are aware that peer groups do not constitute the only socialization habitat of adolescents: Family and school in the majority of cases play a very important role in this sense. In these regards we conducted field research: After establishing collaborative relations with members of seven groups of adolescents (three formal and four informal groups) which used to gather in a public garden of a neighborhood of Bologna, we asked them to think about difficult situations they had actually experienced, emotionally relive those situations, and describe them in detail to the researcher. Afterwards, we asked about the actions they had taken to overcome such situations of tension and pain. We asked if they had found support in friends from the group, or family or other adults. Results showed that there was no counteracting effect between the support given by the family and that of the peer group. If the problems in question referred to difficult choices related to school, work, or future, it was the family that provided the strongest support; if problems referred to difficulties in interpersonal or intimate relations, it was the group that offered the most efficient support. These findings allowed us to conclude that effective integration in the peer group does not constitute a threat to adolescents' good relations with their family (Pombeni, Palmonari, & Kirchler, 1990).

We replicated the same research in three Italian cities, with a sample of 1,600 adolescents responding to a questionnaire drafted on the basis of answers given by the participants of the previous research. The gathered data showed that the possibility of identifying both with their own family and peer group allowed adolescents to enhance their proper self-esteem and elaborate a positive representation of self (Palmonari, Kirchler, & Pombeni, 1991). Moreover, adolescents who identified both with the family and with the peer group were able to distinguish the type of support they could expect from diverse social entities. The procedure that we came up with to identify the groups of adolescents that were present and active in a given urban territory was then adopted in various settings, mainly by local social services in order to establish contacts with the same groups as well as to draft recreation and community projects for adolescents.

Adolescents' Peer Groups and Intergroup Dynamics

Starting from mid-1980 we tried to establish a close link between our applied studies on adolescent groups and Tajfel's intergroup relations theory. With reference to social identity theory, we studied the influence of group membership on the definition of self-concept. The focus was on the type of ingroup, whether formal or informal, and on the relationship with other types of peer groups, even out groups perceived as most different from one's own group. The most surprising result of our research was that the type of group did not influence on the definition of self. Members of formal groups perceived their self and their social environment in much the same way as adolescents belonging to informal groups. We tried to interpret our results referring to the self-categorization theory of Turner, Hogg, Oakes, Reicher, and Wetherell (1987). Turner holds that it is the relationship between the participant and his/her group, rather than the characteristics of the group per se which influences redefinition of the self-concept, the concept of the in-group, and the wider social field. In fact, according to our findings, identification with one's own peer group was a fundamental variable which proved to be more important than the type of organization of the peer groups. The results highlight that the definition of self, the concept of in-group, and that of out-group are independent

of the type of group one joins, be it formal or informal. However, our results are only partially in line with self-categorization theory. High identification with the in-group does not necessarily lead to high differentiation between in-group and out-groups. On the other hand, low identification was not related to smaller perceived distance between in-group and out-groups. On this issue, the possibility of interpreting data with the co-variation model, as proposed by Deschamps (1982), seems to be prevalent (Palmonari, Pombeni, & Kirchler, 1992).

Going a step further, we pursued a line of research aimed at studying social functions of adolescents' peer groups (Palmonari, Rubini, & Graziani, 2003). According to Social Identity Theory, identification with a social group is mainly motivated by the need for positive self-esteem. Individuals, in fact, strive to achieve a positive social identity which derives largely from favorable comparisons made between the in-group and relevant out-groups. But several authors have shown that other motivations may be at the basis of relations between group membership and social identity (Hogg & Abrams, 1993; Brewer, 1993). Deaux, Reid, Mizrahi, and Cotting (1999), in particular, hypothesized the existence of several identification functions besides self-esteem enhancement.

Taking into account the results gathered by Deaux et al. (1999), we assumed that there can be specific motivations leading adolescents to join different types of peer groups. We found that besides the self-esteem enhancement, adolescent peer groups perform different social functions: They give members relevant information to understand themselves and their social milieu (self-insight and social understanding), provide them with help and support (cooperation and cohesion), and give them the possibility to enjoy themselves along peers sharing similar interests (amusement). In addition they allow members to evaluate themselves (downward comparison) and their social groups (intergroup competition and comparison) and offer them the opportunity to try new roles and behaviors (leadership) and establish interpersonal (social interaction) and romantic relationships (romantic involvement). The group membership functions were differentially endorsed by formal and informal peer groups. Sports members underlined the importance of the amusement that characterized group activities; religious ones seemed to be motivated by the need to know themselves and their social reality; political ones stressed the relevance of intergroup competition; and informal ones emphasized the importance of intra-group comparison. Interestingly, in-group cooperation and self-esteem were strongly emphasized by all different peer groups (Graziani, Rubini, & Palmonari, 2006, 2007). Our findings show that while adolescent peer groups are not all alike, they are able to serve different functions for their members and that this is strongly related to in-group identification.

We then decided to focus our attention on informal groups. As previously shown, these spontaneous associations are out of the control of adults, do not have formally explicated goals, and meet on the street or on the corners of public parks. For these reasons, they are often considered by common sense as deviant groups. If common sense were correct, given the spread of adolescent informal groups in our cities, the situation with the public order would be much more serious than what it actually is. Through an additional questionnaire we examined the perception of members of 15 informal groups involved in our research, of the integration–segregation of their own group in the given social context, as well as the frequency with which they engaged in blatantly deviant acts (such as drug use, shoplifting, and fights). Based on the frequency of the reported deviant acts we were able to distinguish the predominantly deviant from the non-deviant informal groups. Results show that whereas membership in non- deviant groups is linked with the need for social self-insight, members of deviant groups emphasize the importance of intergroup competition and comparison. This highly competitive attitude of the group towards others active in the area correlated with relationships characterized by a perception of segregation from the own social context. In fact, adolescent members of deviant groups declared having more difficult relations with significant others (such as parents, teachers, or other adults such as neighbors or local police officers), so much so that in many cases it borders a feeling of isolation and almost social segregation. It is important to note that of the 15 informal groups taken into consideration, only five of them manifested obvious signs of deviance, risk factors that serve as precursors to engagement in fully fledged delinquent behavior. We hold that, with the above-mentioned results we provided useful elements for public opinion to take a much more aware stand with regard to the multiplicity of functions and behaviors that informal groups of adolescents can perform.

At this point we posed ourselves a further question: Do members of informal groups feel part of a group in the same way as their peers who are members of formal groups? In fact, in the case of the latter there are external factors, be they institutional or organizational, that affect the cohesion of the entity, whereas the same does not hold for informal groups. According to Lewin, "the group constitutes a dynamic whole which is different from the sum of its parts …. Conceiving of a group as a dynamic whole includes a definition of group which is based on interdependence of the members" (1951, p. 146). What allows one, then, to perceive an aggregate of individuals as a dynamic totality?

Campbell (1958) coined the term *entitativity* to explain how individuals are able to perceive invisible entities such as social groups. Only many years later, Hamilton and Sherman (1996) rediscovered this notion, focusing their attention on the differences of information processing and in impression formation processes regarding simple individuals versus groups. Many other studies followed. With reference to the various adolescents' groups considered we were interested in investigating to what extent the perception of entitativity plays a role in the perception

of different groups, be they formal or informal. So, we decided to examine the perception of group entitativity in adolescents' peer-groups (Rubini, Moscatelli, Paselli, Graziani, & Palmonari, 2004). In general terms, the results revealed that all the groups were perceived by their members as equally characterized by a high level of entitativity. This result can be explained by the different factors acting as antecedents of the group entitativity perception in the different typologies of groups. But we wanted to focus our attention mainly on the in-group versus out-group perspectives in perceiving group entitativity. The results obtained showed that the comparison between the ratings of in-group and out-group entitativity suggest interesting implications with regard to the difference between these two ways of thinking about a group. In fact, whereas in-group members tended to consider their own group as highly entitative, they also tended to consider the out groups as less entitative than their own group.

While the great majority of the studies concerning group entitativity seems to imply that this perceptual phenomenon is only guided by cognitive processes, the documented in-group versus out-group discrepancy enables us to hypothesize that some motivational factors can intervene on group perception when the in-group versus out-group comparison is at stake. In other words, we advanced the idea that group entitativity is not only a cognitive representation of one's own group or of out-groups, but it is also a powerful way of intergroup differentiation. This can explain why one's own group is systematically perceived as more entitative than the out-group. Thus, we can maintain that entitativity is a shared cognitive representation loaded with value and at the same time it serves as a means of intergroup differentiation, which needs to be further explored.

During adolescence, the institutional framework of the society assumes a particular importance. The sensation of distance and extraneousness that the institutional world produces in adolescents may, on first contact, be overcome only if they perceive the need to respect the norms and rules that are valid for everyone to the aim of becoming part of the greater society in a fulfilling way. In order to achieve this, social actors, particularly the youngest ones and all the newcomers to a certain social system have to know and be willing to understand the rules governing the system itself so as to adapt their own behavior accordingly (Berger & Berger, 1975). The position that adolescents adopt with regard to the formal system may be termed "orientation towards institutional order' (Emler, Reicher, & Ross, 1987; Reicher & Emler, 1985). The attitudes and behaviors that adolescents adopt in order to relate to the formal system are a communicable component of one's own identity. On their basis the observers build up the public reputation of other people (Emler & Reicher, 1995).

We tried, with our research, to illustrate how adolescents' orientations in this regard are shaped to a considerable extent by their experiences with the school system and by their interactions with peer groups. In this respect we considered different aspects of adolescents' school experience, taking into account the pivotal role of school socialization in shaping the general orientations of individuals towards institutions. We also looked at the interplay between school experience and peer group membership in influencing attitudes and behaviors towards social institutions. Before concentrating on these links, we analyzed how the institutional framework of the society assumes a particular importance during adolescence, which are the components of institutional orientation, how it develops, and what sort of implications it has in terms of the social identity it communicates (Moscatelli & Roncarati, 2006; Rubini & Palmonari,1995, 2006; Ravenna & Rubini, 2006).

To Conclude

Throughout my career I have dealt with social psychological issues that have been of a significant importance to me, although marginal to some extent with respect to the discipline's mainstream (Palmonari, Cavazza, & Rubini, 2002). In this chapter I tried to give an account of this by focusing on the social psychological dimensions of adolescence. Certainly, I also dealt with issues usually found in textbooks on adolescence. I myself edited, in collaboration with several colleagues, an Italian textbook on adolescence, the third edition being now freshly printed for psychology and social science students (Palmonari, 1993, 1997, 2011).

Moreover, following a long period of joint study on issues such as representation of self and time perspective, together with colleagues H. Rodriguez Tomè and F. Bariaud (Paris), S. Jackson and H. Bosma (Groningen), and B. Zani (Bologna). I participated in the founding of the European Association for Research on Adolescents (EARA), which was created as a result of three foundational seminars organized biannually in Paris (1988), Groningen (1990), and Bologna (1992). At present, EARA constitutes a reference point for whoever conducts research on adolescents in Europe. Every 2 years it organizes a congress gathering participants among associates and many other researchers. It has established fruitful relations of collaboration with the Society for Research on Adolescence regularly organizing Summers Schools for PhD students. In the 2008 Congress taking place in Turin, Italy, H. Bosma and I were conferred the EARA Honorary Lifetime Membership Award.

What about my future projects? In fact, as a retired professor I have mostly focused in this chapter on my past work. Does this mean that I am not contemplating new research? Many ideas are brewing in my head, although I do not know whether I will be able to translate them all in research or intervention projects. I am ever more convinced that adolescence needs to be approached from diverse and trans-disciplinary perspectives: A decisive step ahead would be the systematic articulation of combined insights from developmental psychology and social psychology in order to address more in-depth the

problematic relating to development processes of the second decade of life, in our complex societies; moreover, the need for a more in-depth investigation of the link between friendships amongst peers (there are plenty of studies on "the best friend") and group participation.

Some examples of studies that I foresee designing in this prospective:

- Which developmental tasks, that are different for boys and girls, emerge in the multicultural settings where individuals grow up?
- What criteria do we need to adopt in order to adequately meet the psycho-affective needs of minors and adolescents who cannot count on the support of their own family as they grow up? (See the case of minors from Africa, Asia, and Latin America immigrating alone to our countries.)
- How can we prevent and deal with both intergenerational and intercultural conflicts which have become so frequent at present?
- How can we find innovative ways that combine insights from pedagogical and socio-psychological science in order to address problems such as drug addiction, youth deviance, and youths' lack of commitment to social issues?
- How can we achieve such a shared representation of adolescence that departs from ethnocentric conceptions which still have a strong hold in today's societies?

In order to address such relevant issues there emerges the need to design training programs for adults and youngsters that involve communities and offer individuals the possibility of participating in crucial moments of social life, thus creating a shared language. Last but not least, it is urgent to spread competences on the possibility of conducting, with appropriate methodologies, longitudinal research programs aimed at decoding the fundamental passages of adolescent growth in diverse cultures.

References

Amerio, P., Boggi-Cavallo, P., Palmonari, A., & Pombeni, M. L. (1990). *Gruppi di adolescenti e processi di socializzazione* [Adolescent groups and socialisation processes]. Bologna: Il Mulino.

Berger, P. L., & Berger, B. (1975). *Sociology: A biographical approach.* New York: Basic Books.

Berger, P. L., & Luckmann, T. (1966). *The social construction of reality: A treatise in the sociology of knowledge.* Garden City, NY: Anchor Books.

Brewer, M. B. (1993). Social identity, distinctiveness, and in-group homogeneity. *Social Cognition, 11,* 150–164.

Campbell, D. T. (1958). Common fate, similarity, and other indices of the status of aggregates of persons as social entities. *Behavioral Science, 3,* 14–25.

Carugati, F., Casadio, G., Lenzi, M., Palmonari, A., & Ricci Bitti, P. (1973). *Gli orfani dell'assistenza: Analisi di un collegio assistenziale per minori* [The orphans of welfare: Analysis of a welfare juvenile institution]. Bologna: Il Mulino.

Carugati, F., Emiliani, F., & Palmonari, A. (1975). *Il possibile esperimento* [The possible experiment]. Rome: A.A.I.

Carugati, F., Emiliani, F., & Palmonari, A. (1984). Resocialization processes in instituzionalized adolescents. In W. Doise & A. Palmonari (Eds.), *Social interaction in individual development* (pp. 231–245). Cambridge: Cambridge University Press.

Crocetti, E., & Palmonari, A. (2011). Le fasi adolescenziali e giovanili nello sviluppo psicosociale [Adolescent and youth phases in psycho-social development]. In A. Palmonari (Ed.), *Psicologia dell'adolescenza* (pp. 53–66). Bologna: Il Mulino.

Deaux, K., Reid, A., Mizrahi, K., & Cotting, D. (1999). Connecting the person to the social: The function of social identification. In T. R. Tyler, R. M. Kramer, & O. P. John (Eds.), *The psychology of the social self* (pp. 91–113). Mahwah, NJ: Lawrence Erlbaum.

Deschamps, J. C. (1982). Social identity and relations of power between groups. In H. Tajfel (Ed.), *Social identity and intergroup relations* (pp. 85–98). Cambridge: Cambridge University Press.

Emler, N., & Reicher, S. (1995). *Adolescence and delinquency: The collective management of reputation.* Oxford: Blackwell.

Emler, N., Reicher, S., & Ross, A. (1987). The social context of delinquent conduct. *Journal of Child Psychology and Psychiatry, 28*, 99–109.

Graziani, A. R., Rubini M., & Palmonari, A. (2006). Le funzioni psicosociali dei gruppi adolescenziali [Psycho-social functions of adolescent peer groups]. *Psicologia Sociale, 1*, 157–174.

Graziani, A. R., Rubini, M., & Palmonari, A. (2007). Nei gruppi conosciamo noi stessi: le funzioni dei gruppi adolescenziali [Within groups we know ourselves: The functions of adolescent peer groups]. *Età Evolutiva, 88*, 31–41.

Goffman, I. (1961). *Asylums: Essays on the social situation of mental patients and other inmates.* New York: Doubleday Anchor.

Hamilton, D. L., & Sherman S. J. (1996). Perceiving persons and groups. *Psychological Review, 108*, 336–355.

Hogg, M. A., & Abrams, D. (1993). Towards a single process: uncertainty reduction model of social motivation in group. In M. A. Hogg & D. Abrams (Eds.), *Group motivation: Social psychological perspectives* (pp. 173–190). New York: Harvester-Wheatsheaf.

Kirchler, E., Pombeni, M. L., & Palmonari, A. (1991). Sweet sixteen … Adolescents' problems and the peer group as a source of support. *European Journal of Psychology of Education, 6*, 393–410.

Lewin, K. (1951). Field theory and experiment in social psychology: Concepts and methods. In D. Cartwright (Ed.), *Field theory in social science: Selected theoretical papers.* New York: Harper & Row. (Reprinted from *American Journal of Sociology* (1939*), 44*, 868–897.)

Lewin, K., Lippit, R., & White, R. K. (1939). Patterns of aggressive behaviour in experimentally created "social climates.' *Journal of Social Psychology, 10*, 271–299.

Moscatelli, S., & Roncarati, A. (2006). Famiglia e scuola: Rapporti e percezione di giustizia [Family and school: Relationships and perception of justice]. In F. Garelli, A. Palmonari, & L. Sciolla (Eds.), *La socializzazione flessibile. Identità e trasmissione dei valori tra i giovani* (pp. 253–287). Bologna: Il Mulino.

Moscovici, S. (1976). *La psychanalyse, son image et son public*, 2nd revised ed. Paris: PUF (1st ed., 1961).

Moscovici, S. (2008). *Psychoanalysis: Its image and its public.* Cambridge: Polity Press.

Palmonari, A. (Ed.). (1993, 1997, 2011). *Psicologia dell'adolescenza* [Psychology of adolescence] (1st, 2nd, & 3rd ed.). Bologna: Il Mulino.

Palmonari, A., Carugati, F., Ricci Bitti, P., & Sarchielli, G. (1979). *Identità imperfette.* Bologna: Il Mulino.

Palmonari, A., Carugati, F., Ricci Bitti, P., & Sarchielli, G. (1984). Imperfect identities. A socio-psychological perspective for the study of the problems of adolescents. In H. Tajfel (Ed.), *The social dimension*, Vol. 1 (pp. 111–133). Cambridge: Cambridge University Press.

Palmonari, A., Cavazza, N., & Rubini, M. (2002). *Psicologia sociale.* Bologna: Il Mulino.

Palmonari, A., Kirchler, E., & Pombeni, M. L. (1991). Differential effects of identification with family and peers on coping with developmental tasks in adolescence. *European Journal of Social Psychology, 21*, 381–402.

Palmonari, A., Pombeni, M. L., & Kirchler, E. (1990). Adolescents and their peer groups: A study on the significance of peers, social categorization processes and coping with developmental tasks. *Social Behaviour, 5*, 33–48.

Palmonari, A., Pombeni, M. L., & Kirchler, E. (1992). Evolution of the self-concept in adolescence and social categorization process. *European Review of Social Psychology, 3*, 285–308.

Palmonari, A., Rubini, M., & Graziani, A. R. (2003). The perceived importance of group functions in adolescent peer-groups. *New Review of Social Psychology, 2*, 62–67.

Pombeni, M. L., Palmonari, A., & Kirchler, E. (1990). Identification with peers as a strategy to muddle through the troubles of the adolescents years. *Journal of Adolescence, 13*, 393–410.

Ravenna, M., & Rubini, M. (2006). Adolescenti e coetanei: Evoluzione dei rapporti di gruppo [Adolescents and peers: Development of group relationships]. In F. Garelli, A. Palmonari, & L. Sciolla (Eds.), *La socializzazione flessibile. Identità e trasmissione dei valori tra i giovani* (pp. 289–310). Bologna: Il Mulino.

Reicher, S., & Emler, N. (1985). Delinquent behaviour and attitudes to formal authority. *British Journal of Social Psychology, 24*, 161–168.

Rubini, M., Moscatelli, S., Paselli, M., Graziani, A. R., & Palmonari, A. (2004). Ingroup-outgroup perspectives in perceiving group entitativity. *New Review of Social Psychology, 3*, 55–64.

Rubini, M., & Palmonari, A. (1995). Orientamenti verso le autorità formali e partecipazione politica degli adolescenti [Orientation towards formal authority and political participation of adolescents]. *Giornale Italiano di Psicologia, 22*, 757–775.

Rubini M., & Palmonari A. (2006). Adolescents' relationships to institutional order. In S. Jackson & L. Goossens (Eds.), *Handbook of adolescent development* (pp- 264–283). Hove, NY: Psychology Press.

Sherif, C. W. (1984). Coordinating the sociological and the psychological in adolescent interaction. In W. Doise & A. Palmonari (Eds.), *Social interaction and individual development.* Cambridge: Cambridge University Press.

Sherif, M., & Sherif, C. W. (1964). *Reference groups: Exploration into conformity and deviation of adolescents.* New York: Harper and Row.

Sherif, M., & Sherif, C. W. (1969). Adolescent attitude and behaviour in their reference groups. In J. P. Hill (Ed.), *Minnesota symposia on child psychology*, Vol. 3. Minneapolis: University of Minnesota Press.

Turner, J. C., Hogg, M. A., Oakes, P. J., Reicher, S. D., & Wetherell, M. S. (1987). *Rediscovering the social group: A self-categorization theory.* Oxford and New York: Blackwell.

32

Researcher as Bumblebee

Developing a Science of Adolescence Integrating Biology, Using Rigorous Research Methods, and Including Girls

ANNE C. PETERSEN

Life, for me, has been a set of fascinating serial paths or chapters, driven not so much by a singular vision than by curiosity, ambition, and tremendous opportunities largely provided by social change, as well as much good luck. I think of myself as a bumblebee, spreading "pollen" in the form of new and good ideas and findings, in this case for research on adolescence. While I have contributed some modest discoveries, I believe that facilitating the exchange of scientific ideas and results has been my greatest contribution to the study of adolescence.

This chapter aims to draw out those aspects that seem to have influenced my direction and the results for my career as a researcher of adolescence. The topics listed in the title reflect themes that began my research career, and that have been interwoven throughout it. I also humbly recognize the roles of recollection and selective memory in writing autobiographically (cf. Cohler, 1982).

The Early Years

My childhood was spent in a little town in Minnesota (about 8,000 people then, smaller now). While this region was later declared a poverty area during the U.S. "Great Society" era of President Johnson's efforts to reduce poverty, it was rich in many ways. I will highlight a few of these in this section.

My father was a high-school football coach and later athletic director who also taught Minnesota history and government. My mother was not college-educated, of Norwegian immigrant parents. Both had high expectations for all three of their children—I was the middle child—that we would at least complete college and do our very best in school. My older brother excelled in athletics (as was expected of him) and did well enough in school, but with

strong test performance and mediocre course achievement. His minimal investment in school achievement enabled me to have a niche (e.g., Feinberg, McHale, Crouter, & Cumsille, 2003). I taught myself to read before beginning school, which caused my elementary school to recommend that I be advanced in grade, something my parents rejected. The creative teachers gave me extra projects and asked me to tutor students with learning difficulties in my early elementary years. I did very well in courses throughout elementary and secondary school. Given that this was the "Sputnik" era (i.e., the period of U.S. competition with Russia on space exploration), we experienced enriched science and mathematics, even in our school. This played a key role in my future, with one example being a new mathematics teacher who came in my senior year of high school. He told me that I could not expect my usual A grade unless I did extra research projects. I was delighted and really enjoyed learning new mathematical content and ideas. I'm certain that this enhanced science and math work played an important role in boosting my achievement test scores (SATs) in mathematics to a nearly perfect level (and significantly above my verbal scores).

One difficult aspect about growing up as a girl in those times was the strong gender stereotyping. My father was very traditional, and while he expected and supported high academic achievement from me, he didn't seem to value other roles I played. Girls' competitive sports stopped with the end of elementary school (except for physical education courses). This was a great disappointment to me as I was quite good in neighborhood games and competitions, which I continued. In sixth grade (about age 12 years and the last year of our elementary school), the culminating spring track events included both boys and girls competing together; I did very well—which seemed to come as a surprise to the teachers and which gave me the sense I was not "supposed" to excel in sports (or at least not excel more than the boys). The only other "athletic" role was to be a cheerleader—something I enjoyed in both high school and college. My father made it clear that he didn't value the role of cheerleaders when he denied our request to join the team bus to attend a basketball game when we were unable to fill a bus of student fans. (With hindsight, he might also have been worried about a few girls with all the boys, and perhaps especially since my boyfriend was the team captain.) None of us had much awareness of these societal issues at the time, so I interpreted his action personally.

My brother was 3 years older, and away at college during most of my high school but generally I attribute to him the "toughening" he instilled in me, with continual competition and occasional mild torture (in the form of experiments he would try out on me—like giving me electric shocks when I touched his bedroom door handle following his invitation). With hindsight, I learned from him how to be competitive, including in tough neighborhood games, and persistent despite interpersonal harassment.

The neighborhood where we grew up included many children who organized games and plays in nice weather, and building snow forts and ice skating in the winter. I even enjoyed ice fishing with my father on the open ice. Neighborhood football and basketball games were always being played. (Because I was away in the summers, I missed out on baseball but did play on a summer girls' softball team a couple of summers in our vacation home town.) One of my fondest memories of adolescence was an evening winter party that included skating long distances on a creek, cooking over a fire, and singing campfire songs; it was a magical evening!

Another feature of growing up in a small Midwestern U.S. town was "undermanned" schools (e.g., Barker & Gump, 1964) which provided ample opportunities for experimenting with diverse roles in childhood and adolescence. Our teachers—being still in the days when teaching was one of the few professions available to women—were generally outstanding. And at all levels, we had the full range of extracurricular opportunities. We had unusually rich opportunities in music due to a local benefactor who brought outstanding music performances to our little town. This also increased the quality of music teachers we enjoyed. I was able to participate in several choral and orchestral groups, that increased in number and diversity through school. In addition, I was active in theater, student council, all-school events like dances. One high-school teacher told me that I was the student to go to if something needed to get done.

My childhood was further enhanced by spending summers in a tourist area in northern Minnesota. My father felt that he had the best of all possible worlds—teaching/coaching for 9 months and fishing for the other three—as a fishing guide on a beautiful large lake. I rehabilitated an old sailboat my father had purchased from a camp that was closing, and finally learned to sail it by tacking as well as running by reading a book after my father informed me that he wasn't going to tow me back across the lake again. I also loved to fish, until my fish-cleaning brother went

away to college and my father refused to clean my fish. (It didn't occur to me at the time that I was participating in gender-stereotyped behavior by thinking that cleaning fish was yucky!) So I had fun and learned responsibility. These summers also provided exposure to people from throughout the Midwest United States and sometimes beyond, stimulating curiosity about different schools, different practices, and different ideas.

Ethnic diversity was not extensive in the Midwest at that time, with most of the population of Euro origin. My summers, however, were spent on an Ojibwe (then called Chippewa, but now more formally known as Anishinaabe) Native American reservation. During my first decade plus, I recall weekly pow-wows, and really enjoyed the dancing and drumming. During childhood, I had many Ojibwe friends and enjoyed participating in cultural traditions such as "ricing"—the harvesting of wild rice from canoes. By mid-adolescence, these friends increasingly disappeared. I didn't understand what had happened at the time but have learned much more subsequently; I have continued my interest and support of tribal youth to this day. (For example, I was appointed in the 1990s by President Clinton to his Board of Advisors on Tribal Colleges and Universities.)

My childhood was generally quite rich and stimulating, and growing up in a small town was safe because neighbors watched over all the children. As an adolescent, I didn't always appreciate the fact that I could do nothing I shouldn't be doing without my parents knowing rather quickly. My brother was also ready to tell our parents about anything he learned I was doing. So my experience with wild boys in fast cars was short-lived!

In many ways, I experienced an ideal childhood—safe, stimulating, and full of learning. That is not to say there weren't traumas but these were at a pace and intensity that generated growth and learning rather than overwhelming defeat. I am grateful that I had such an opportunity and look back on those years with fondness.

Becoming a Researcher

While my high-school years included the usual science-fair experience, I didn't otherwise experience much research until college. I was recruited to the University of Chicago (UC) through a special (and short-lived) program for students from small Midwestern towns, and became a mathematics major in a small undergraduate student body within a much larger graduate student body, the majority of the latter focused on research. While this was prior to the current emphasis on undergraduate research in the United States, research was a strong component of UC education, with basic sources (rather than textbooks) the core of the curriculum. The greatest benefit of my undergraduate experience at UC was learning to learn.

Following college, I became a mathematician and computer systems intern at the National Security Agency (NSA). I wanted a break from academe (and to start repaying my college loan) and was attracted by the opportunity to work with the nation's largest computer system, following stimulating work at the UC Institute for Computer Research in my senior year of college. Although the NSA training was outstanding and exciting, I stayed only 1 year because I was disappointed by the limited challenge of the work (presumably related to the workforce transition the Agency was then undergoing). I returned to Chicago to marry a college classmate and work at the UC Biomedical Computer Facility on research projects as a computer programmer.

My self-driven research career began with graduate school, where I simultaneously pursued a PhD in Measurement, Evaluation, and Statistical Analysis (MESA) in the Department of Education (Social Sciences Division) with full funding and an MS in Statistics (Physical Sciences Division). From the start I was in demand as a statistical consultant on research projects, providing further research experience plus additional income. My familiarity with UC gave me an advantage relative to my classmates, especially knowing I could explore any seminars and classes across the University, without paying additional tuition, as long as I satisfied degree requirements. My PhD professor, R. Darrell Bock, steered me toward research methods in human development and his male student who started with me toward quantitative areas. While I was irritated by the sex stereotyping at the time, with hindsight, it was a good direction for me and contributed to my enthusiasm to pursue my own research questions.

Why Adolescence?

There were no courses on adolescence in either of my graduate programs. So how did I decide to do research in the area for my doctoral dissertation? Given my interest in sex differences (which I discuss below), puberty seemed a likely stimulus for sex-divergent development in cognition during adolescence, at the time a hot topic in sex differences research. While I considered pursuing a doctoral dissertation in collaboration with a young pediatric endocrinologist who was studying puberty (building from the field discovery of accurate blood assays of sex hormones), gathering a clinical sample in a reasonable timeframe was problematic. Exciting endocrine research yielding what we believed were better measures of puberty stimulated the emergence of the scientific study of biological change in and under the skin relative to developmental change in adolescence (e.g., Grumbach, Grave, & Mayer, 1974; Tanner, 1969).

Instead I used data from the Fels Growth Study (e.g., Kagan & Moss, 1962) to study puberty based on hormone-influenced physical characteristics and pubertal timing (Petersen, 1973, 1976). The pubertal timing measure was based on a parameterization of longitudinal growth data developed with colleagues (Bock et al., 1973). This method used height data to identify the components of growth, finding two components: prepubertal linear growth and the pubertal growth spurt which also curtailed the linear growth, thus reaching final adult height. Age at peak height velocity, one of the model's variables, proved to be an excellent index of pubertal timing, having strong correlations with menarche and similarly reliable and valid for both boys and girls. My doctoral dissertation tested the hypothesis that extent of physical androgyny (i.e., less extremely masculine or feminine physical characteristics) in both boys and girls was related to better spatial ability relative to fluent production, a hypothesis that was supported. The pubertal timing hypothesis was not supported in these data (Petersen, 1976).

These initial studies established an identify for me as an emerging researcher of adolescence, a trend continued by my first faculty position as a research associate (assistant professor 1972–76, associate professor 1976–82) in the Psychiatry Department of the Medical School at UC. I began with the Woodlawn Project working with social psychiatrist Sheppard Kellam and sociologist Margaret Ensminger, among others on the follow-up study of Woodlawn adolescents who had been studied longitudinally in the early years of elementary school (e.g., Kellam, Ensminger, & Turner, 1977). This research taught me much about the fields of psychiatry and sociology, as well as about the fundamental importance of respect for community strengths in studying adolescents.

After 3 years on the Woodlawn study, I took the position as Director of the Laboratory for the Study of Adolescence at Michael Reese Hospital and Medical Center, a teaching hospital of UC (continuing my faculty position at UC). The psychiatry department at Michael Reese was headed by distinguished researcher of adolescence, Daniel Offer (e.g., Offer & Offer, 1975). With Offer, I wrote a proposal for a training grant upon arrival. We were awarded a grant from NIMH for a Clinical Research Training Program on Adolescence. The faculty, including Dan Offer, Bert Cohler, Mike Czikzentmihalyi (the latter two from the Committee on Human Development, UC) among others, together with the pre- and postdoctoral fellows—Maryse Richards, Lisa Crockett, Reed Larson (all of whom went on to lead the field of adolescence, among many other fellows)—were an outstanding group from whom I learned tremendously, and I became longtime colleagues and friends, and collaborators with some.

Daniel Offer provided significant writing opportunities (e.g., Offer & Petersen, 1977a, b), as well as time for me to read the extant literature on adolescence. Offer also introduced me to Joseph Adelson, editor of the first *Handbook of Adolescent Psychology,* in which I had a few chapters, including what is likely my most highly cited theoretical article, "The Biological Approach to Adolescence" (Petersen & Taylor, 1980), which helped launch the field. I was also invited around this time to write a cover story on puberty in the popular magazine *Psychology Today* (Petersen, 1979a).

My first research grant, *A Developmental Study of Adolescent Mental Health* (NIMH 1979–93), was written and awarded shortly after arriving at Michael Reese, for a longitudinal study of adolescence, testing the hypothesis that all aspects of adolescent development were linked to the timing and developmental changes of puberty. Several major theories at the time considered developmental changes as stages—such as Piaget's cognitive development (e.g., Inhelder & Piaget, 1958), Kohlberg's moral development (Kohlberg, 1969), Erikson's identity development (e.g., Erikson, 1968), among others. It seemed reasonable then to hypothesize that these developmental changes were linked to biological change in adolescence. With hindsight (e.g., Petersen & Leffert, 1995), that wasn't such a reasonable hypothesis given that (almost) all young people go through puberty but the accumulating evidence on stage theories generally, and cognitive and psychosocial developmental outcomes specifically, made clear subsequently that not all young people reach "complete" development, mostly because the theories were based on narrow populations (e.g., Camerena, Stemmler, & Petersen, 1994; Keating, 1990; Spencer & Dornbusch, 1990). We also had results demonstrating the linkage among aspects of cognitive and psychosocial development (e.g., Jarcho & Petersen, 1981).

The NIMH grant (aided by the late Vicky Levin, NIMH mentor to so many developmental scientists over about four decades) also permitted significant measure development which was necessary for the field to advance (e.g., Petersen, Tobin-Richards, & Boxer, 1983): a revision downward to early adolescence of the Offer Self Image Questionnaire: SIQYA—Self-Image Questionnaire for Young Adolescents (Petersen, Schulenberg, Abramowitz, Offer, & Jarcho, 1984); and a new and still very popular measure for pubertal development: the Pubertal Development Scale (PDS; Petersen, Crockett, Richards, & Boxer, 1988), since by then few schools employed school nurses who had been the ones taking annual height and weight measures required for age at peak height velocity used in my earlier research and in the many U.S. growth studies of the first half of the 20th century (e.g., Jones & Mussen, 1958; Mussen & Jones, 1957), among other measures from the study (e.g., Galambos, Petersen, Tobin-Richards, & Gitelson,1985). Although the study's primary hypothesis, that developmental change in adolescence was driven by puberty, was not supported, we gained significant knowledge about the relationship of puberty and especially pubertal timing to psychosocial development (discussed extensively below), among many other significant results (some discussed below). For example, in 1984, an entire issue of the *Journal of Early Adolescence* was devoted to the early adolescent portion of the study (e.g., Petersen, 1984; Crockett, Losoff, & Petersen, 1984; Richardson, Galambos, Schulenberg, & Petersen, 1984; Schulenberg, Asp, & Petersen, 1984), contributing to building the knowledge base on early adolescence.

Another involvement that grounded me in adolescence was the launching of the Society for Research on Adolescence in 1984. Herschel Thornburg organized a couple of meetings in Tucson, AZ (where he was on the faculty at University of Arizona) earlier in the 1980s. I participated in those meetings, and participated in discussions about building a scientific society. That was fortuitous for me and other emerging scientists at the time. I was privileged to become SRA's third President.

Also important in the 1980s for the field of global adolescence was the launching of the Jacobs Foundation in Switzerland, a foundation focused on research on adolescent development. David Hamburg and I were the two U.S. participants in the initial meeting in the late 1980s. The other younger scholar was Rainer Silbereisen, already an adolescent development colleague, and now longtime friend. My long relationship with the Jacobs Foundation was an early and continuing source of global interests and relationships.

These early years of my career were an exciting period for my growth and achievements. A capstone publication for my role as an adolescent researcher was the invitation to write the very first review article on adolescence in the *Annual Review of Psychology* (Petersen, 1988). I took this responsibility very seriously, as it not only had implications for me as a researcher but also for the field of research on adolescence.

Two additional subsequent contributions to the field of adolescence more generally are seen with papers on the importance of adolescence for education and for adolescent health. As to education, I engaged in several activities including one by the Carnegie Corporation of New York on the education of young adolescents (e.g., Carnegie Council on Adolescent Development, 1989), a special issue of the *Journal of Research on Education* focused on research on adolescence and education (e.g., Epstein & Petersen, 1991; Petersen & Epstein, 1991), plus several additional articles focused on educational practice and policy (e.g., Petersen & Dubas, 1992; Petersen, Hurrelmann, & Leffert, 1993). In the area of adolescent health, I participated in an extensive effort of the Carnegie Corporation of New York on adolescent health that resulted in a major volume (e.g., Crockett & Petersen, 1993; Hamburg, Millstein, Mortimer, Nightingale, & Petersen, 1993; Millstein, Petersen, & Nightengale, 1993a, b) and other publications (e.g., Petersen, Leffert, Graham, Ding, & Overby, 1994; Petersen, Leffert, & Graham, 1995). David Hamburg was President of the Carnegie Corporation of New York at this time, and Beatrix Hamburg, his wife, and pioneering researcher of early adolescence and preventive interventions with adolescence, played a key role in Carnegie's efforts on adolescence.

From my early background, I moved on as researcher and academic, also taking administrative positions in academe, government, and philanthropy. I discuss the latter roles toward the end of this chapter but first review my research according to dominant themes over time: sex/gender differences, puberty, self-image and depression, and the less dominant themes of research methods and policy. More than one issue, of course, was likely to be included in any single piece of research. Coding my roughly 225 publications (including chapters but excluding reprints) for the (single) primary theme yields 29% focused more generally on adolescence (and more recently, youth) throughout my career, 26% on puberty or biological change (starting in the late 1970s until now but peaking in the 1980s), 22% on self-image (late 1970s and early 1980s) and later depression (primarily 1990s), 19% on sex (or gender) differences (starting in the late 1970s until now and steadily over the 1980s and '90s), and 3% each in methods (dominant initially in the 1970s and sporadically subsequently as a primary issue, but more typically integrated into substantive publications) and policy (mid-1990s on). The "bumblebee" role was most strongly related to conferences and meetings, since many of the related publications were edited books which are mostly unread. Regrettably I haven't tracked key meetings on my curriculum vitae. (At some point I made the unwise decision to reduce the length of the CV by focusing only on recent presentations, and did that successively through key years, losing my presentation record in the ether.) What is clear without a written record, however, is that as I took on other administrative roles, my participation in scientific meetings declined. My bumblebee days were over, alas, or at least dramatically diminished. Would I have done things differently in my career had I been aware of the implications?

Sex Differences

The Women's Movement emerged while I was in graduate school, and I fully embraced it—co-founding two consciousness-raising groups, one focused on research on women and the other among friends, with lots of reading and discussion in both groups. I was very curious about gender issues generally, with a specific interest in understanding the achievement difference in math and statistics—major strengths and interests of mine—since these were "male" fields in which women were thought to be incapable (e.g., Maccoby & Jacklin, 1974). The Women's Movement stimulated an explosion of research on women and girls, previously neglected. My research in the 1970s was more focused by these considerations than by the emergence of biology in psychosocial research, but both lines of work proceeded in parallel, and issues of women and girls, typically considering males as well for comparative purposes, continue to be important for me.

The topic of sex differences in the scientific literature focused initially on persuading scientists that females were essential in a sample if the intent was to generalize to humans (e.g., Maccoby & Jacklin, 1974; Guttentag & Secord, 1983). Another theme of research emerging from the women's movement, and embraced by me, largely focused on minimizing differences (and emphasizing androgyny), as well as surfacing female strengths such as interpersonal relationships (e.g., Chodorow, 1978; Gilligan, 1977). Even during the 1970s, those who felt they were trapped in bodies of the "wrong" sex disagreed with those who were minimizing the importance of gender. This latter voice has prevailed in current times (e.g., Meyerowitz, 2002), with gender identity now largely a self-defined construct, and almost no weight given to biology (especially insofar as it can be modified surgically or hormonally).

A key mentor for me in the sex differences area was the late Carol Jacklin (e.g., Jacklin, 1981, 1989; Maccoby & Jacklin, 1974), whom I met at a major conference while a graduate student. After she had given an invited address, I asked to talk with her (an action I was to repeat subsequently with those whose work I admired, an approach I've strongly urged my mentees to pursue). While I never published with Carol (her primary research area was infancy), we frequently discussed science and policy of sex differences research, and we remained lifelong friends.

My first invited conference was at Smith College in 1976. Jacque Parsons (later Eccles) organized a conference entitled *The Psychobiology of Sex Differences* (Parsons, 1980). Most of the presenters were junior women and 85% of the chapters were first-authored by women, highly unusual for the time. Just as the volume title reveals much about thinking at the time, the volume sections are also revealing: psychosexual neutrality, sexuality, women's reproductive system and life cycles, and cyclicity and menstruation. My talk was in the lead section, entitled "Biopsychosocial Processes in the Development of Sex-related Differences" (Petersen, 1980). This was a notable and subsequently important group of colleagues to me and the field.

Also in the late 1970s, I collaborated with Michele Wittig, whom I met through the emerging psychology of women field. We published an edited book (Wittig & Petersen, 1979), *Sex-Related Differences in Cognitive Functioning: Developmental Issues*. We noted (Petersen & Wittig, 1979) that an extensive review had not yet been devoted to cognitive functioning, and that the bias in the volume was biological, with only 25% of the book devoted to sociocultural factors; we made the choice of chapter content based on the research to date and because most social and behavioral scientists were less familiar with the methods and findings of biological research.

Many of our chapter authors were women, something the publisher questioned as evidence of being polemical; fortunately we succeeded in persuading him that we were scientists, and that the distribution was appropriate since most of the researchers in this field were women. Because of the status of the field at that time, many of the chapters were reviews of extant literature, with limited new data. Among the data chapters was one I wrote on sex difference in cognition (Petersen, 1979b), including my dissertation results (Petersen, 1973) and reviewing recent research of others (Broverman, Broverman, Vogel, & Palmer, 1964; Fennema & Sherman, 1977; Klaiber, Broverman, Vogel, Abraham, & Cone, 1971; Waber, 1976, 1977).

A small team of us at Michael Reese (including some of the pre-and post-doctoral fellows in our adolescent training grant mentioned earlier), obtained a grant, *An*

Intensive Study of Factors Related to Sex Differences in Cognition from the Spencer Foundation (1979-81). Among the key findings from that research were: (1) regardless of performance, boys expected that they would do better on cognitive tasks than girls expected, both prior to and following taking the tasks, much stronger sex differences than any found with actual performance (Gitelson, Petersen, & Tobin-Richards, 1982); (2) many results showing sex differences in the cognitive factors predicting ego functioning, for example, with interpersonal reasoning for girls and physical-mathematical reasoning and verbal intelligence for boys (e.g., Hurtig, Petersen, Richards, & Gitelson, 1985); and (3) an analysis of the role of parenting in creating differences between boys and girls found that mothers influenced the self-esteem and especially ego development of boys more than girls, with fathers playing little role with either though self-esteem was higher in both boys and girls whose other-sex parent was perceived to be warm and supportive (Richards, Gitelson, Petersen, & Hurtig, 1991).

Sex differences were also examined in the NIMH study mentioned earlier. Only the results with cognition or achievement will be mentioned in this section. Kavrell and Petersen (1984) examined the cohort-sequential longitudinal data from early adolescence in that study and found significant effects showing that: (1) the sexes did not differ in IQ and achievement overall, and there was an effect of time measured by grade in school (increases in mathematics and total achievement, and a sex × time interaction effect in reading); (2) course grades showed a main effect of sex, with linear effects showing declines in all courses, and most courses showing a quadratic effect suggesting that performance dropped most rapidly from grades 6 to 7; and (3) sex role identification showed sex differences (in the expected directions) but neither masculinity nor femininity was related to achievement, for either boys or girls.

Two other studies with the NIMH study sample examined achievement. In the first (Roberts, Sarigiani, Petersen, & Newman, 1990), we found that (1) the link between achievement and self-image was more positive for boys than girls and (2) gender differences increased developmentally providing modest support for the gender intensification hypothesis (Hill & Lynch, 1983), with the correlation between self-image and achievement decreasing for girls and increasing for boys, and with some specific variations from the hypotheses. In the second study, Roberts and Petersen (1992) found that, in general, a young adolescent's orientation toward academics, social aspects, and athletics influenced different patterns of achievement over the years of early adolescence, and different relationships between social self-image and school achievement. The results suggested that there are psychological disincentives for the pursuit of excellence in science and mathematics for those who are socially or athletically oriented. The results were more consistent for girls than for boys, but generally obtained for both.

Galambos, Almeida, and Petersen (1990) used the NIMH study data to directly test the *gender intensification* hypothesis, proposed by Hill and Lynch (1983) and linking the emergence of sex differences to puberty which could influence increased identification with ones' gender. The results did not find a link with pubertal timing but did find evidence of increasing gender divergence in masculinity and attitudes toward women's roles.

Another major collaboration of mine in the area of sex differences research was that with Marcia Linn. In the early 1970s, encouraged by Elizabeth Fennema, a researcher of sex differences in mathematics, I initiated an organization focused on Research on Women in Education, with the first meeting in 1976 and continuing to this day as a Special Interest Group within the American Educational Research Association. Through this group, I met Marcia Linn, with continuing collaborations and friendship. We wrote three articles together, all focused on meta-analyses of the research on sex differences in aspects of cognitive performance (Linn & Petersen, 1985a, b, 1986). These analyses helped resolve many of the debates of the time, but of course left others unresolved.

Colleagues told me early on that I would never be respected as a scientist if my research focused solely on women, gender, and sex differences. Of course my research was never that narrowly focused, but the message was heard by me. I made a deliberate attempt to expand my networks and scientific topics, though the topic holds continued importance for me personally.

Puberty

My longtime collaboration with Jeanne Brooks-Gunn began at the Smith conference, mentioned above. Together we began to jointly plan conferences and working groups focused on puberty, thus developing this field. It was a very exciting, highly productive time, and I still treasure my collaborations with Brook, now a long-time friend.

While our joint collaborative workshops and symposia began in the late 1970s, our first publication was *Girls at Puberty* (Brooks-Gunn & Petersen, 1983a), which followed an exciting conference held at the Salk Institute sponsored by the Johnson & Johnson Company (enabling us all to have high-quality figures prepared by them, something usually too costly at the time, especially for early career scholars). We note in the Introduction to the volume (1983b, p. xix), that puberty had been historically the most frequently mentioned distinctive characteristic of the transition from childhood, but it had not been studied systematically. We also noted that the social significance of puberty was its link to emerging sexuality, with other aspects of the importance of puberty typically ignored. The focus on girls was determined by the sponsor (who manufactures menstrual products); we also endorsed this focus conceptually because of the usual neglect of girls in research, as highlighted by the sex differences field just discussed.

My contributions in this volume were focused on cognition (Petersen, 1983a) and the psychological significance of puberty (Tobin-Richards, Boxer, & Petersen, 1983). The chapter on cognition reviewed past research but also presented new research from our group (Herbst & Petersen, 1979, 1980) funded by the Spencer Foundation (mentioned earlier), as well as that of other researchers (e.g., Carey, Diamond, & Woods, 1980; Epstein, 1978; Newcombe, Bandura, & Taylor, 1983; Waber, 1977) on the role of brain development, especially lateralization. My analysis in the chapter is that the results on brain lateralization were inconsistent across studies, a common result early in a research area. At the same time, there was some consensus that puberty disrupted the cognition of girls. I used this analysis from earlier research to develop a model for testing factors that might influence cognitive changes at puberty. I tested the model with data from the NIMH study, specifically testing the hypothesis that there is a disruptive effect of puberty causing a decline in cognitive performance for girls, primarily due to changes in physical appearance. Because we failed to find the hypothesized decline in performance for girls, we did not test the complete model, and concluded that the result obtained in other studies may be a weak one, appearing only when extreme (i.e., very early and very late) pubertal timing samples were used. We tested the model again with broader constructs of cognitive achievement (Kavrell & Petersen, 1984), again failing to support the pubertal disruption hypothesis.

The second chapter from our research group in the Brooks-Gunn and Petersen puberty volume (1983a) also tested a hypothesis with data from the NIMH study. The hypothesis derived from past research from our group and others was that there would be different patterns for the psychosocial meaning of physical maturation for boys and girls (Tobin-Richards, Boxer, & Petersen, 1983). Specifically, we expected that for boys the pattern would be linear, with earlier maturation related to more positive body image and feelings of attractiveness, and for girls, we expected more a more complex curvilinear pattern with on-time development the most positive. We also expected that weight would be more strongly related to perceptions of puberty for girls than boys. The results supported the hypothesis for boys, with a couple of additional findings: (1) on-time maturation was intermediate between early and late timing, demonstrating that the relationship is strictly linear and not just a difference between early and late, and (2) facial hair was the aspect of pubertal maturation that showed the strongest relationships to psychosocial variables, suggesting that it is the most visible and therefore salient aspect for young adolescent boys, though all indicators of pubertal maturation operated together. For girls, the hypotheses were also supported; in addition, the results suggested that (1) while being on-time in maturation showed the most positive relationships with body image and feelings of attractiveness, being late was better than being early; (2) both perceptions of and satisfaction with weight were important correlates of body image for girls, and weight-related variables constitute a second

factor of puberty change for girls, with neither result found for boys. The results were discussed relative to increased sexual responses of others to post-pubertal girls, and the complex social consequences.

My second major collaboration (involving conferences and symposia and resulting in a publication) with Brooks-Gunn focused on timing of pubertal maturation (which was emerging as the most potent aspect of puberty related to psychosocial development), and culminated in two special issues (sequentially) of the *Journal of Youth and Adolescence* in 1985 (Brooks-Gunn, Petersen, & Eichorn, 1985a, b). Our team also included Dorothy Eichorn, distinguished colleague from the growth studies at UC Berkeley, a key researcher in maturational timing research from the earlier growth studies (e.g., Eichorn, 1973). Two special issues were required because the highly enthusiastic group had important new data to report. This effort resulted from a 1983 meeting of the Social Science Research Council on Life-Span Development and Early Adolescence, at which discussions kept returning to the issue of maturational timing effects, particularly with new results that built from but were not entirely consistent with the earlier growth study results on the topic. The co-editors of the volume then received funding for a SRCD Study Group, including funds from the Child Development Foundation and the WT Grant Foundation, to focus on early adolescence as a key transition in the life course, and especially on new theories, conceptual frameworks, and measures for the role of maturational timing.

The SRCD Study Group brought together an interdisciplinary group of psychologists, sociologists, endocrinologists, and pediatricians who were currently examining maturational timing effects. The group discussed findings, explored discrepancies among current studies and earlier research, and developed conceptual frames for interpreting the differences. The newer generation of life-span developmental studies had been grounded in the landmark methodological work of Baltes and colleagues (e.g., Baltes, 1968; Nesselroade & Baltes, 1974), identifying the importance of age, historical era, and non-normative influences for life-span development. Elaborating further and based on the research of my group, I identified four age-graded factors at early adolescence: chronological age (life experience), biological age (maturation and pubertal age in adolescence), cognitive age (intellectual capacity), and grade in school (accumulated knowledge) (Petersen, 1987). As one example, the paper from our research group in this volume (Petersen & Crockett, 1985), compared the effects of pubertal timing and grade-in-school on five adjustment constructs (school achievement and four scales of the Self-Image Questionnaire for Young Adolescents). There were twice as many significant grade effects as pubertal timing effects, with no interactions (but some gender differences). These results, together with others in the special issue, suggest that all potential influences on development need to be considered, especially given population and culture differences, different school structures, asynchronous individuals (advanced on one timing measure and delayed on another), and the like. Using chronological age as a proxy for anything important in adolescence makes no sense (and yet continues as the major practice to this day). Most heartening about this effort was that many theories/conceptual models were being tested with data, often in more than one study. It was a highly productive effort.

Many other papers from the NIMH study focused on puberty. For example, Crockett and Petersen (1987) examined data on menarcheal age relative to other aspects of adolescent development. Two major theoretical models (and their variations) were examined: a generalized maturation model which posits that aspects of maturity are generally synchronous and a pubertal disruption model in which puberty enhances or detracts from the developmental course. Analyses with many psychosocial and cognitive variables suggested that there were few effects of menarcheal age on psychosocial and cognitive development, but those that were found suggest support for: (1) the generalized maturation model with most aspects of cognitive development; (2) pubertal disruption with emotional tone; and (3) perimenarcheal enhancement with verbal abstract reasoning, impulse control, and family relationships. Thus, the analysis yielded no strong support for a single model.

Crockett and Petersen (1987) reviewed findings from our studies on the relationship of pubertal change to psychosocial development in early adolescence, seeking to address two questions: (1) What aspects of psychosocial development are affected? (2) What are the pubertal mechanisms causing these effects? This chapter presented new analyses on pubertal status effects and summarized results reported elsewhere on pubertal timing effects. Pubertal status effects were studied within grades, to unconfound the two variables. Similarly, because girls develop earlier than boys, analyses were done separately for the two sexes. Effects replicated across grades include: satisfaction with appearance (especially for girls, and involving especially lower satisfaction with weight with higher pubertal status; boys were more satisfied with appearance with increased pubertal status), moods (more effects for boys, involving more Impulse Control and better Emotional Tone with increased pubertal status), peer relationships (both boys and girls reported more positive romantic relationships with increased pubertal status, with slightly stronger effects for girls; few replicated results were found for same-sex relationships), and relationship with parents (effects only found for girls, with decreasing quality of relationship with increased pubertal status, with improved relationships reported for post-pubertal girls in 8th grade (roughly 14 years old). No consistent effects of pubertal status were found with cognitive performance or school achievement. The authors concluded that strong consistent pubertal status effects seem limited to those areas more closely linked to physical changes of puberty. Pubertal timing effects were more pervasive and generally indicate that being deviant in timing—such as with early timing for girls and later timing for boys (making each group very deviant for the whole peer group of boys and girls given the 2-year-earlier puberty for girls)—has the strongest effects. All of these effects implicate the social circumstances within which puberty is experienced, rather than biological effects of the change.

Dorn and colleagues (1988) used the NIMH study data to examine the relationship of pubertal status to intrapersonal changes. We found that girls who were more physically mature reported less satisfaction with their appearance, and especially weight, with the reverse effect for boys. Boys also showed the same kind of linear effect with impulse control and emotional tone (scales from the SIQYA), effects not seen with girls.

Richards, Boxer, Petersen, and Albrecht (1990) examined community differences in the NIMH study to test hypothesized effects on girls when more rather than fewer school-related activities were offered. These effects were found in strong community by sex interactions, and were attributable to the greater availability of activities for girls in one community. Sports were offered for boys in schools in both communities, and no community difference was found for boys. The results emphasized the importance of offering activities for both boys and girls in early adolescence, if both are to thrive and develop positively.

Dubas, Graber, and Petersen (1991b) examined the effects of pubertal status and pubertal timing on school achievement in the NIMH study. Results indicated that during early adolescence, late-maturing boys had the lowest school achievement, while late-maturing girls showed the highest achievement in school courses. Beliefs about one's ability to achieve—achievement orientation—did not explain these results. Very few long-term effects of puberty on high-school achievement measures were found.

Several papers from the NIMH study examined methodological issues of puberty. Earlier I mentioned the papers on the Pubertal Development Scale (Petersen et al., 1988), with additional research by our group and others on diverse and global samples (e.g., Robertson et al., 1992; Silbereisen, Petersen, Albrecht, & Kracke, 1989). The PDS remains a valid and popular measure of puberty (e.g., Dorn et al., 2006). Early development work on that scale was also reported by Petersen Tobin-Richards, and Boxer, (1983).

Dubas, Graber, and Petersen (1991a) examined longitudinally, adolescents' self-ratings of timing of puberty and how these perceptions related to an objective measure of pubertal timing, pubertal status, and feelings about their pubertal timing during 7th, 8th, and 12th grades. The results showed moderate consistency in self-reported pubertal timing across adolescence. Perceptions of pubertal timing at 12th grade were predicted by both objective pubertal timing and 8th-grade perceptions. Furthermore, the direct comparison of perceived timing with an objective timing measure indicated that perceptions became more accurate by 12th grade. Feelings about pubertal timing were related to perceived timing but not to the objective measure of pubertal timing. These results suggest that actual and perceived timing are overlapping but distinct timing measures that reflect different biological and psychosocial processes.

Self-Image and Depression

Influenced by working with Daniel Offer in the 1970s, I wrote about (e.g., Petersen, 1977a, b; Petersen, 1981; Petersen, Offer, & Kaplan, 1979) and conducted several studies of self-esteem and self-image (reviewed below). In addition, as mentioned earlier, my students and I created a downward extension of the Offer Self Image Questionnaire, the Self-Image Questionnaire for Young Adolescents (SIQYA; Petersen et al., 1984), a measure that continues to be used for the adolescent decade and into young adulthood.

Self-image was measured in all my studies with the SIQYA, and reported in many papers (e.g., Abramowitz, Petersen, & Schulenberg, 1984; Hurtig & Petersen, 1990). For example, one study (Sarigiani, Wilson, Petersen, & Vicary,1990) compared data from two studies, one from a suburban community and the other rural, and found that self-image was lower among adolescents in the rural community, with similarly lower education plans among other indicators of aspiration.

A related construct to self-image is psychological well-being, which I first worked on with the Kellam group on the Woodlawn Project. One paper on the *How I Feel* used in that research demonstrated the reliability and validity of the measure with the population of black adolescents in the Woodlawn Project (Petersen & Kellam, 1977).

My research shifted over the 1980s to focus more specifically on adolescent depression, integrating prior research on sex differences and puberty. This shift was stimulated by an emphasis by NIMH away from developmental studies to studies of specific mental disorders. In addition to measures we were already using, such as the SIQYA and specifically the Emotional Tone Scale, we added the Kandel Depression Scale (Kandel & Davies, 1982), as well as the TOYS, an epidemiological interview based on the NIMH Diagnostic Interview Schedule.

Our research presentations (e.g., Kennedy, 1989; Petersen & Ebata, 1986, 1987b), as well as articles (Ebata, 1987; Kennedy & Petersen, 1991; Petersen & Ebata, 1987a; Petersen, Bingham, R., Stemmler, & Crockett, 1991; Petersen, Ebata, & Sarigiani, 1987; Petersen, Sarigiani, & Kennedy, 1991) began to focus intensively on understanding why girls more than boys reported increased depression during early adolescence (e.g., Kandel & Davies, 1982; Nolen-Hoeksma, 1987). A summary article of this research (Petersen et al., 1991) tested a developmental model for the emergence of the gender difference in depression over adolescence. The research supported the hypothesis that girls became more depressed in adolescence because they experience more challenges, specifically early pubertal time and synchronous pubertal timing and school change (becoming pubertal before or during school change was worst, and much more likely for girls than boys), together with experiencing negative family events (a variable that showed different results for boys and girls, with boys showing a steeling effect of negative family events and girls showing a negative result, perhaps because of other cumulative effects). Effective coping skills moderated the negative effects of challenges in early adolescence. This research was the first longitudinal study of the emergence of sex differences in depression over adolescence, and the first to test a comprehensive model of all the factors hypothesized to influence the emergence of sex differences in depression.

In the late 1980s, Jeanne Brooks-Gunn, Bruce Compas, and I organized a WT Grant Foundation Consortium on Depression in Childhood and Adolescence that included a wonderful multidisciplinary group of colleagues including such leading researchers as Norman Garmezy and Michael Rutter. This group influenced all of our thinking, and involved an invited summary publication in *American Psychologist* (Petersen et al., 1993) based on a report for the Carnegie Council on Adolescent Development (Petersen, Compas, & Brooks-Gunn, 1992). These major papers brought together extant knowledge about depression in adolescence as well as effective treatments and interventions, and policy implications.

One other major study was funded by the W.T. Grant Foundation in 1988: *Coping with Early Adolescent Challenge: Gender-Related Mental Health Outcomes* (Petersen, 1988).This psychoeducational intervention study was conducted in a working-class community in Pennsylvania and focused on improving depression among young adolescents (Rice, Herman, & Petersen, 1993). Although the intervention had few effects, we published major articles on coping (e.g., Herman-Stahl & Petersen, 1996, 1999; Herman-Stahl, Stemmler, & Petersen,1995) and made several presentations on variations in mood based on frequent sampling using pagers (often called "beepers") (Petersen, 1999, 2000) with two articles published (Ding, Davison, & Petersen, 2005; Barber, Jacobson, Miller, & Petersen, 1998) and one article on diurnal variations in preparation (Barber and others). Herman-Stahl and colleagues (1995) found that young adolescents who used approach coping (i.e., engaging in cognitive or behavioral strategies to modify stressors) were less depressed than those who used avoidant coping (i.e., denying or ignoring stressors) and those who switched over time to avoidant coping became more depressed. Herman-Stahl and Petersen (1996) found that coping style, mastery, optimism, and support resources were all important for reducing depression and navigating through stressful life events. The same authors (1999) further found that feelings of self-efficacy and mastery together with positive relationships with parents appeared to reduce the depression levels 1 year later in early adolescence.

Methodology Research

Beginning with my degrees in mathematics, statistics, and research methods, and my early methodological publications from my graduate school years (e.g., Bock et al., 1973; Bock & Petersen, 1975; Wainer & Petersen, 1972), my career reflects continued though less intense interest in these topics. Development of new measures was mentioned earlier, specifically the SIQYA—Self-Image Questionnaire for Young Adolescents (Petersen et al., 1984), the PDS—Pubertal Development Scale (Petersen et al., 1988), and the AWSA—Attitudes toward Women Scale for Adolescents (Galambos et al., 1985).

In addition, my research group conducted several methodical studies related to the measurement and understanding of puberty (Dubas, Graber, & Petersen, 1991a, b; Petersen, 1983b; Petersen et al., 1983). Crockett, Schulenberg, and Petersen (1987) compared the validity of self-report to objective data including course grades, height, and weight; the results revealed some systematic bias in self-reports but overall concluded that self-reports could typically be considered reliable and valid.

Additional methodological studies include one on the problem of missing data, a problem inherent in longitudinal studies. From the beginning of our longitudinal studies, we were imputing missing data. Bingham and others (1999) examined the validity of our method, and compared it with other imputation methods that had been developed subsequently; our method fared reasonably well. We also concluded that it certainly would have been easier to use an off-the-shelf computer program to impute missing data, rather than our home-grown program, but nothing else was available when we began the research.

We used several different methods to study growth and change in our longitudinal studies, initially relying on multivariate analysis of variance with several between-subjects factors such as gender and community, and testing within-subject patterns by fitting polynomials based our hypotheses for change. As my students learned newer approaches, our study analyses used these as well. For example, Ding and colleagues (2005) used multidimensional scaling to study growth and change using "beeper" data on moods from the WT Grant Study. Stemmler and Petersen (2005) used latent growth curve modeling based on structural modeling on data from the NIMH study to test hypotheses about the development of depressive affect for boys compared with girls, finding that the hypothesized risk factors predicted depressive affect for girls but not boys. Stemmler and Petersen (2011) used the same method to examine the relationship of drug use and other "norm-violating" behavior to developmental changes in adjustment over the adolescent decade among girls; the findings revealed that both drug use and norm-violating behavior compromised the usual positive trends in adjustment over adolescence.

Policy

My interests in policy were escalated with my role as the Deputy Director/Chief Operating Officer of the National Science Foundation (NSF), a position nominated by President Clinton and U.S. Senate confirmed. I could not renew my research grants while in that kind of an appointment at NSF, which effectively ended my active research career. I was increasingly called upon for policy perspectives on a variety of science issues. A policy frame also emerged in my writing about adolescence, as well as from my leadership roles in scientific societies and as a member of the Institute of Medicine (National Academies) serving on or chairing various IOM/NA committees and Boards.

Drawing from my experience at NSF, I wrote a couple of articles on the opportunities and challenges of considering policy changes benefitting adolescents and youth. Both of these articles were initially presentations in conferences. In Petersen (2006), I discussed general principles of policy development and then used examples from adolescent research on delinquency as a very important policy target to demonstrate more and less effective policy analyses and approaches. Petersen (2009) built from the 2006 paper (and the many presentations related to it) to make a stronger case for the importance of incorporating policy analysis into basic research if policy impact is one aim of the research. With my presidency of the International Society for the Study of Behavioral Development, I have been increasingly asked to write from a global perspective (e.g., Petersen, 2011, 2013). The global perspective on research on adolescent development has brought me full circle: serving as a bumblebee in persuading colleagues that since all science is global (e.g., Suresh, 2012), developmental science must be also. We have much to learn from our colleagues globally about the course of and influences on development over adolescence and youth.

Developmental Science on Adolescence

This review of my research contribution to the field was the first I've done, and was illuminating as well as humbling. My research groups made many important contributions in key areas: (1) stimulating significant research on the role of puberty in adolescent development; (2) stimulating increased understanding about the causes of the emergence of depression in adolescence, and especially differences between boys and girls. In addition, we contributed key measures essential for the development of the field. I hope to yet play a stimulating role for research on adolescence viewed globally.

What was humbling was realizing that my opportunistic "random walk" approach came with a cost: the near absence of periodic stock-taking of what we'd accomplished and what threads/important hypotheses deserved further research. Based on periodic conversations with colleagues about abandoning these hypotheses—which began with a chance conversation on an airplane with one of my statistics professors about all the statistics research I'd begun but didn't complete to publication, I'm guessing that this is not an unusual pattern for researchers. But it is unsettling nonetheless. The realization that this is the first review I've ever done of my research is similarly surprising, and disappointing.

Another humbling realization emerging from this review of my research is that many primary research results were reported in chapters in edited books. (And I was only able to access a few of my publications in edited books. All of the journals are now available online, while few books are available online without paying for copies.) I knew from early on in my career that such edited books were seldom read. (While I was an active researcher, impact factors were not yet prevalent; this practice makes even clearer the importance of publishing on journals, and especially highly rated, more frequently read journals.) What is most disappointing about this realization is that it served my students poorly, since they also were not publishing in the best publications.

At the same time, my research results were heavily disseminated by me and my students while we were active, through our many talks at scientific meetings. So I have no doubt that we influenced thinking among our colleagues at the time. Would we have had more impact publishing results primarily in the best journals? Would our impact have had more longevity? The study can no longer be done. The assumption of impact factors is that the place of publication does matter, and the impact factor has now become a cause of publishing primarily in the highest quality, most read journals thus obviating the study of the question. Another question is whether we have less effect on the scientific record because of the nature of search functions being able to access journals (since they have been digitized) and not edited books; the answer is likely to be that we have had less effect. Alas.

Other Career Roles

Although I did not make a conscious choice to leave research behind, my other roles and responsibilities increasingly distracted me from doing research. With hindsight, I wish I'd been more aware of what I was doing. At the same time, I really enjoyed the opportunities I had to explore other roles, and aspects of myself. Realistically, all of life involves doing some jobs primarily for money, while those of us who are lucky might have other jobs that yield pleasure. Doing research was certainly a labor of love. Other roles were more mixed, but interesting in their own ways.

While I was completing my doctoral research, I took a position at the MacArthur Foundation, initially as a consultant reviewing proposals that were submitted before guidelines for the Foundation were written, and ultimately as Associate Director of the Health Program (1980–82), partnered with John Conger, director of the Health Program who was located in Denver, Colorado. He was a wonderful colleague in this work, and also recruited me to co-author his adolescent textbook (Conger & Petersen, 1984). While that textbook collaboration taught me a great deal about adolescence, it also persuaded me that I didn't have enough experience teaching undergraduates to be a good textbook author. While at MacArthur, I had

the opportunity to work with many important scientists such as Board members Jerome Wiessner, Jonas Salk, and Murray Gell-Mann, as well as health scientists such as Norman Garmezy, Michael Rutter, Jerome Kagan, among others through the networks we created—a really exciting structure to develop! David Hamburg was the Science Advisor to the Health Program and became an important mentor to me, along with his wife Betty; both of them provided much learning and many opportunities to me. They have continued to be dear colleagues and friends. The MacArthur Foundation experience was also highly valuable in my learning about philanthropy, something I knew I wanted to return to after developing myself as a researcher.

Colleagues at the Pennsylvania State University Department of Individual and Family Studies (IFS) recruited me in 1982 from my positions in Chicago to be Department Head and Professor. These recruiting colleagues included Rich Lerner, who has been a lifelong colleague, collaborator, and dear friend; Graham Spanier, who sweetened the recruitment by flying my husband and me from Pittsburgh to State College in his plane; and Liz Susman, who answered questions about women at Penn State, and also became a collaborator, colleague, and lifelong friend. I replaced Paul Baltes who had reframed and powerfully strengthened the department, prior to returning to Germany to be a Max Planck Institute Director; Paul was a valuable mentor and dear friend through Penn State and subsequent ventures, such as the development of the Jacobs Foundation. He created a department I wanted to be part of, and I was willing to take an administrative role to do it. Once I felt grounded in the role, I worked hard to recruit new faculty colleagues who would bring excellence as scholars as well as collegial behaviors needed for effective programs; among the new faculty recruits, I was proud to attract outstanding exemplars of these attributes such as Robert Plomin, Judith Dunn, Lynne Vernon Feagans, along with many others including outstanding junior faculty. I learned so much from my colleagues at IFS (later Human Development and Family Studies) at Penn State, who covered development over the life course from infancy through old age, and across disciplines, including psychology, sociology, developmental statistics and research methodology, history, and behavior genetics. I won't mention all of my colleagues among the forty-plus faculty in the department plus many in other departments, as well as the outstanding students who were crucial in my scholarly and administrative development. It was an exciting and important time of my life!

Since I was 38 years old when I went there, had limited administrative experience, and had never been in a large public university, it is amazing to me that I survived the experience as Department Head (though there were certainly many rough spots!) and went on to become Dean of a new, larger college: the College of Health and Human Development. With benefit of hindsight, this role was my career favorite. Being a collegiate dean provides significant latitude in setting tone and direction, but at a more manageable scale than being President or in other university roles. Again with hindsight, relative to the administrative positions I held subsequently, I'm grateful that I had the opportunity to learn effective administration at a well-run university like Penn State; the budget process worked, administrative staff were outstanding (likely because Penn State provided the best positions within the entire region), and administrative systems mostly made sense. The biggest surprise, for me and my husband, was fundraising; it was a joy to make people so happy by investing their hard-earned money in university projects that I valued and knew made a difference to so many. Since this was a newly reconstituted college, merging two colleges and including units from a third, we could create the future we saw for the collection of units. It was a very exciting opportunity! Among the many new initiatives such as new College-wide centers, I am proudest of creating as a cornerstone of the College, the Program in Biobehavioral Health, an interdisciplinary unit intended to become a full department, a change that was completed just after my departure. Interdisciplinary research and education was valued at Penn State, and we were able to capitalize on this in developing the College. It was also a privilege to work with the other Deans as well as the Provost—Bill Richardson, with whom I worked again at the Kellogg Foundation.

While the decade at Penn State was largely a joy (and a relief to my husband who said he would go for "three to five years, with time off for good behavior"), I left to become the first Vice-President for Research (as well as the Dean of the Graduate School) at the University of Minnesota. We thought we were returning home to stay, but both my husband and I were surprised by how much we and our home state had changed in the 30 years since we'd left for college. I enjoy creating new structures and networks, and expected that the research VP role would provide ample creative opportunity. Unfortunately, I quickly learned that most of my faculty colleagues didn't want to change anything, so it was difficult to accomplish what I'd hoped, especially as a newcomer. It helped to have grown up in Minnesota in terms of knowing the geography, and some people, but it took time to develop the key relationships needed to accomplish change. I began working with the corporate sector to address some longstanding tensions in research development, and was also delighted to initiate some multidisciplinary research and education programs with my discretionary funds, with some of these programs sustaining to the present.

In addition to my administrative work, I arrived at Minnesota with research grants and one student but mostly had to recruit new research staff and students. There was lots of difficult ground work just to become established at the "U," and I was grateful to some of the research colleagues I knew previously for their important partnerships; Bob Blum and Geraldine Brookins were especially important colleagues and dear friends. My academic appointments at the University were in Pediatrics and the Institute of Child Development.

While at a University of Minnesota research retreat with colleagues from the corporate sector as well as the University, I was shocked to receive a phone call during a break (when I was out ice fishing!) informing me that I was being recruited to be the Deputy Director of the National Science Foundation (NSF). I was only in my third year at Minnesota, and had heard nothing previously about this possibility. I visited Washington and let them begin the process of vetting but didn't think seriously about the position until I was told that I had been nominated for the position by President Clinton. I thought that I could begin then to consider whether I was interested but learned quickly that that decision point had come far before, and that it was not possible to decline the Presidential nomination. So I left for Washington DC!

The Director of NSF with whom I worked in close partnership was Neal Lane, a physicist and wonderful human being. While these were difficult times in Washington during the 1990s, we were able to sustain funding for programs at NSF. I spent lots of time with members of Congress explaining how science worked, something I also had to explain to colleagues at the Office of Management and Budget during the times of wanting more immediate accountability for expenditures through the Government Performance and Results Act (GPRA). While my purview was all of science and engineering, I also was called upon to defend social sciences, to Congress as well as some other scientific disciplines. I quickly learned about science politics! And it was an exciting time to be in Washington—both positively and negatively! Most wonderful about the Clinton administration were the many outstanding women scientists recruited to serve the nation. Our regular meetings—most fittingly at the Cosmos Club where women for way too long had been admitted as guests required to enter through a side door and not as members—were a great source of energy and support. Dear friendships created or strengthened at that time included MRC Greenwood, France Cordova, Cora Marrett, Kitty Didion, among many others. Longtime friends from adolescent research also were engaged in some of the fun—including Karen Hein.

As we were approaching the election of 1996, I was recruited by Bill Richardson to leave government and join him at the W. K. Kellogg Foundation as Senior Vice President for Programs. It seemed like a good time to leave Washington, and I'd wanted to return to philanthropy ever since my earlier experience at the MacArthur Foundation. Kellogg was one of the largest U.S. foundations (now eclipsed by some of the newer foundations whose funding derived from technology firms, such as the Gates Foundation). I was responsible for all of Kellogg's programs in the United States, Latin America and the Caribbean, and Africa, where we were just launching a program in Southern Africa. It was a very exciting time, and I really valued many of my colleagues on the program staff. I enjoyed engaging strategic thinking to design and implement programs, and especially learned tremendously from the Africa program staff. With colleagues in the major foundations, I also started a group of lead program executives who met twice annually to share learning and provide mutual support. Both Bill and I had agreed at the outset to be there for a decade, so I "retired" and started a new philanthropic venture—Global Philanthropy Alliance to support young social entrepreneurs in Africa.

Global Philanthropy Alliance (GPA) was created legally before departing from Kellogg, but really took another year to begin to put the initial structures in place for an operating foundation. In the meantime I taught a course on global philanthropy at the University of Minnesota—where they'd had a global philanthropy center, just closed upon the death of the director. That course helped me organize my thoughts about what was known and what I wanted to do; in addition, one of my students became the first Executive Director.

Persuaded that I could more effectively develop the foundation from the Bay Area—a hub of global innovation, I agreed to join outstanding scholar and dear friend, Claude Steele at the Center for Advanced Study in the Behavioral Sciences (CASBS) and Stanford University. We worked hard to return the Center to its prior strengths, and accomplished some important changes. By 2008, it was clear that I needed to return home to Michigan to support my husband through some health issues. When Claude left for another position in 2009, I returned to spend more time on GPA and took an academic appointment at the University of Michigan.

One useful result of the experience at Stanford and CASBS is that I had no more interest in working on efforts at the periphery of my central interests. Reflecting on the lessons of adult development and aging, I more strongly focused on "time left" and doing only those things that were central to what I want to accomplish in my remaining years. These priorities start with family which now includes three wonderful grandchildren, and making a difference in Africa through Global Philanthropy Alliance and University of Michigan efforts. I have pruned other commitments (an endless chore!) but continue to serve some boards and scientific efforts that have global scientific or philanthropic components, often focused on adolescents or youth. Life is rich and rewarding!

None of what I have accomplished and enjoyed in my life was expected, contributing to the adventure it has been. Adolescent development continues to be an interest, and useful focal point for many other endeavors. For example, I often got through irritating administrative meetings by thinking about the emotional age of colleagues around the table, typically some more like adolescents. That was a useful perspective for productive management, as I'd always liked young adolescents—with their creativity and spirit. I am grateful for all the opportunities!

References

Abramowitz, R. H., Petersen, A. C., & Schulenberg, J. E. (1984). Changes in self-image during early adolescence. In D. Offer, E. Ostrov, & K. Howard (Eds.), *Patterns of adolescent self-image* (pp. 19–28). San Francisco: Jossey-Bass.

Baltes, P.B. (1968). Longitudinal and cross-sectional sequences in the study of age and generation effects. *Human Development. 11*, 145–171.

Barber, B. L., Jacobson, K. C., Miller, K. E., & Petersen, A. C. (1998), Ups and downs: Daily cycles of adolescent moods. *New Directions of Child Development, 82, 23–36.* (In R. W. Larson & A. C. Crouter (Eds.), *Temporal rhythms in adolescence: Clocks, calendars, and the coordination of daily life.* San Francisco: Jossey-Bass Publishers.)

Barker, R. G. & Gump, P. V. (1964). *Big school, small school: High school size and student behavior.* Stanford, CA: Stanford University Press.

Bingham, C. R., Stemmler, M., Petersen, A. C., & Graber, J. A. (1999). Imputing missing data values in repeated measurement within-subjects designs. *Methods of Psychological Research Online, 3*, 131–155.

Bock, R. D., & Petersen, A. C. (1975). A multivariate correction for attenuation. *Biometrika, 62*(3), 673–678.

Bock, R. D., Wainer, H., Petersen, A., Thissen, D., Murray, J., & Roche, A. (1973). A parameterization for individual human growth curves. *Human Biology, 45*(1), 63–80.

Brooks-Gunn, J., Auth, J. J., Petersen, A. C., & Compas, B. E. (2001). Physiological processes and the development of childhood and adolescent depression. In I. M. Goodyer (Ed.), *Mood disorders in childhood and adolescence* (2nd ed.).Cambridge: Cambridge University Press.

Brooks-Gunn, J., Graber, J. A., & Petersen, A. C. (1996). Introduction. In J. A. Graber, J. Brooks-Gunn, & A. C. Petersen (Eds.), *Transitions through adolescence: Interpersonal domains and context* (pp. ix–xi). Hillsdale, NJ: Lawrence Erlbaum.

Brooks-Gunn, J. & Petersen, A. C. (Eds.) (1983a). *Girls at puberty: Biological and psychosocial perspectives.* New York: Plenum.

Brooks-Gunn, J., & Petersen, A. C. (1983b). Introduction. In J. Brooks-Gunn & A. C. Petersen (Eds.), *Girls at puberty: Biological and psychosocial perspectives* (pp. xix–xxix). New York: Plenum.

Brooks-Gunn, J., Petersen, A. C., & Compas, B. E. (1995). Physiological processes in the development of childhood and adolescent depression. In I. M. Goodyer (Ed.), *The depressed child and adolescent: Developmental and clinical perspective* (pp. 81–109). New York: Cambridge University Press.

Brooks-Gunn, J., Petersen, A. C., & Eichorn, D. (1985a). The study of maturational timing effects in adolescence. *Journal of Youth and Adolescence, 14*(3), 149–161.

Brooks-Gunn, J., Petersen, A. C., & Eichorn, D. (Guest Eds.) (1985b). Time of maturation and psychosocial functioning in adolescence. Parts I and II. *Journal of Youth and Adolescence, 14*(3, 4).

Broverman, D. M., Broverman, I. K., Vogel, W., & Palmer, I. D. (1964). The automatization cognitive style and physical characteristics. *Child Development, 35*, 1343–1359.

Camarena, P., Sarigiani, P., & Petersen, A. (1997). Adolescence, gender, and the development of mental health. *The Narrative Study of Lives, 5*, 182–206.

Camarena, P. M., Stemmler, M., & Petersen, A. C. (1994). The gender differential significance of work and family: An exploration of adolescent experience and expectation. In R. K. Silbereisen & E. Todt (Eds.), *Adolescence in context: The interplay of family, school, peers, and work in adjustment* (pp. 201–221). New York: Springer.

Carey, S. (1980). Maturational factors in human development. In D. Caplan (Ed.), *Biological Studies of Mental Processes* (pp. 1–70). Cambridge, MA: MIT Press.

Carey, S., Diamond, R., & Woods, B. (1980). Development of face recognition – maturational component? *Developmental Psychology, 16*, 257–269.

Carnegie Council on Adolescent Development (1989). *Turning points: Preparing American youth for the twenty-first century.* Washington, DC: Carnegie Council on Adolescent Development.

Chodorow, N. (1978). *The reproduction of mothering.* Berkeley, CA: University of California Press.

Cohler, B. (1982). Personal narrative and the life course. In P. Baltes & O. G. Brim, Jr. (Eds.), *Life-span developmental and behavior*, Vol, 4. New York: Academic Press.

Conger, J. J., & Petersen, A. C. (1984). *Adolescence and youth: Psychological development in a changing world* (3rd ed.). New York: Harper & Row.

Crockett, L. J., Losoff, M., & Petersen, A. C. (1984). Perceptions of the peer group and friendship in early adolescence. *Journal of Early Adolescence, 4*(2), 155–181.

Crockett, L. J., & Petersen, A. C. (1987). Pubertal status and psychosocial development: Findings from the Early Adolescence Study. In R. M. Lerner & T. T. Foch (Eds.), *Biological–psychosocial interactions in early adolescence* (pp. 173–188). Hillsdale, NJ: Lawrence Erlbaum.

Crockett, L. J., & Petersen, A. C. (1993). Adolescent development: Health risks and opportunities for health promotion. In S. G. Millstein, A. C. Petersen, & E. O. Nightingale (Eds.), *Promoting the health of adolescents: New directions for the twenty-first century* (pp. 13–37). New York: Oxford University Press.

Crockett, L. J., Schulenberg, J. E., & Petersen, A. C. (1987). Congruence between objective and self-report data in a sample of young adolescents. *Journal of Adolescent Research, 2*(4), 383–392.

Ding, C. S., Davison, M. L., & Petersen, A. C. (2005). Multidimensional scaling analysis of growth and change. *Journal of Educational Measurement, 42*(2), 171–191.

Dorn, L. D., Crockett, L. J., & Petersen, A. C. (1988). The relations of pubertal status to intrapersonal changes in young adolescents. *Journal of Early Adolescence, 8*(4), 405–419.

Dorn, L. D., Dahl, R. E., Woodward, H. R., & Bro, F. (2006). Defining the boundaries of early adolescence; User's guide to assessing pubertal status and pubertal timing in research with adolescents. *Applied Developmental Science, 10*(1), 30–56.

Dubas, J. S., Graber, J. A., & Petersen, A. C. (1991a). A longitudinal investigation of adolescents' changing perceptions of pubertal timing. *Developmental Psychology, 27*(4), 580–586.

Dubas, J. S., Graber, J. A., & Petersen, A. C. (1991b). The effects of pubertal development on achievement during adolescence. *American Journal of Education, 99*(4), 444–460.

Dubas, J. S. & Petersen, A. C. (1996). Geographical distance from parents and adjustment during adolescence and young adulthood. In J. A. Graber & J. S. Dubas (Eds.), *Leaving home: Understanding the transition to adulthood. New directions for child development, 71* (pp. 3–19). San Francisco: Jossey-Bass Publishers.

Ebata, A. T. (1987). A longitudinal study of psychological distress during early adolescence. Unpublished doctoral dissertation, The Pennsylvania State University.

Eichorn, D. H. (1973). The Berkeley longitudinal studies: Continuities and correlates of behaviour. *Canadian Journal of Behavioural Science, 5*(4), 297–320.

Epstein, H. T. (1978). Growth spurts during brain development: Implications for educational policy and practice. In J. S. Chall & A. F. Monsky (Eds.), *Education and the brain.* Chicago, IL: Society for the Study of Education.

Epstein, J. L., & Petersen, A. C. (1991). Discussion and outlook: Research on education and development across the years of adolescence. *American Journal of Education, 99*(4), 643–657.

Erikson, E. H. (1968). *Identity: Youth and crisis.* New York: Norton.

Feinberg, M. E., McHale, S. M., Crouter, A. C., & Cumsille, P. (2003). Sibling differentiation: Sibling and parent relationship trajectories in adolescence. *Child Development, 74*(5), 1262–1274.

Fennema, E. & Sherman, J. (1977). Sex-related differences in mathematics achievement, spatial visualization, and affective factors. *American Educational Research Journal, 14*, 51–71.

Galambos, N. L., Almeida, D. M., & Petersen, A. C. (1990). Masculinity, femininity, and sex role attitudes in early adolescence: Exploring gender intensification. *Child Development, 61*, 1905–1914.

Galambos, N. L., Petersen, A. C., Tobin-Richards, M., & Gitelson, I. B. (1985). The Attitudes toward Women Scale for Adolescents (AWSA): A study of reliability and validity. *Sex Roles, 13*(5/6), 343–356.

Gilligan, C. (1977). In a different voice: Women's conceptions of self and of morality. *Harvard Educational Review, 47*(4), 481–517.

Gitelson, I. B., Petersen, A. C., & Tobin-Richards, M. H. (1982). Adolescents' expectancies of success, self-evaluations, and attributions about performance on spatial and verbal tasks. *Sex Roles, 8*(4), 411–419.

Graber, J. A., Brooks-Gunn, J., & Petersen, A. C. (Eds.) (1996). *Transitions through adolescence: Interpersonal domains and context.* Mahwah, NJ: Lawrence Erlbaum.

Graber, J. A., Petersen, A. C., & Brooks-Gunn, J. (1996). Pubertal processes: Methods, measures, and models. In J. A. Graber, J. Brooks-Gunn, & A. C. Petersen (Eds.), *Transitions through adolescence: Interpersonal domains and context* (pp. 23–53). Mahwah, NJ: Lawrence Erlbaum.

Grumbach, M. M., Grave, G. D., & Mayer, F. E. (Eds.) (1974). *The control of the onset of puberty.* New York: Wiley.

Guttentag, M. & Secord, P. (1983). *Too many women? The sex ratio question.* New York: Routledge.

Hamburg, D. A., Millstein, S. G., Mortimer, A. M., Nightingale, E. O., & Petersen, A. C. (1993). Adolescent health promotion in the twenty-first century: Current frontiers and future directions. In S. G. Millstein, A. C. Petersen, & E. O. Nightingale (Eds.), *Promoting the health of adolescents: New directions for the twenty-first century* (pp. 375–388). New York: Oxford University Press.

Herbst, L. & Petersen, A. C. (1979). *Timing of maturation, brain lateralization and cognitive performance in adolescent females.* Paper presented at the Fifth Annual Conference on Research on Women and Education, Cleveland, OH.

Herbst, L. & Petersen, A. C. (1980). *Timing of maturation, brain lateralization and cognitive performance.* Paper presented at the American Psychological Association meeting, Montreal, Canada.

Herman-Stahl, M. A., & Petersen, A. C. (1996). The protective role of coping and social resources for depressive symptoms among young adolescents. *Journal of Youth and Adolescence, 25*(6), 735–755.

Herman-Stahl, M. A. & Petersen, A. C. (1999). Depressive symptoms during adolescence: Direct and stress-buffering effects of coping, control beliefs, and family relationships. *Journal of Applied Developmental Psychology. 20*(1), 45–62.

Herman-Stahl, M. A., Stemmler, M. K., & Petersen, A. C. (1995). Approach and avoidant coping: Implications for adolescent mental health. *Journal of Youth and Adolescence, 24*, 649–665.

Hess, L. E., Petersen, A. C., & Mortimer, J. T. (1994). Youth unemployment and marginality: The problem and the solution. In A. C. Petersen & J. T. Mortimer (Eds.), *Youth unemployment and society* (pp. 3–33). New York: Cambridge University Press.

Hurtig, A. L., & Petersen, A. C. (1990). The relationship of sex role identity to ego development and self esteem at adolescence. In R. E. Muuss (Ed.), *Adolescent behavior and society* (4th ed., pp. 227–230). New York: McGraw Hill.

Hurtig, A. L., Petersen, A. C., Richards, M. H., & Gitelson, I. B. (1985). Cognitive mediators of ego functioning in adolescence. *Journal of Youth and Adolescence, 14*(5), 435–450.

Herman-Stahl, M. A., Stemmler, M. K. & Petersen, A. C. (1995). Approach and avoidant coping: Implications for adolescent mental health. *Journal of Youth and Adolescence, 24*, 649–665.

Inhelder, B., & Piaget, J. (1958). *The growth of logical thinking from childhood to adolescence.* New York: Basic Books.

Jacklin, C. N. (1981). Methodological issues in the study of sex-related differences. *Developmental Review, 1*(3), 266–273.

Jacklin, C. N. (1989). Female and male: Issues of gender. *American Psychologist, 44*(2), 127–133.

Jarcho, H. D., & Petersen, A. C. (1981). Cognitive development and the ability to infer others' perceptions of self. *Journal of Early Adolescence, 1*(2), 155–162.

Jones, M. C., & Mussen, P. H. (1958). Self-conceptions, motivations, and interpersonal attitudes of early- and late-maturing girls. *Child Development, 29*(4), 491–501.

Kagan, J., & Moss, H. A. (1962). *Birth to maturity*. New York: Wiley.

Kavrell, S. M., & Petersen, A. C. (1984). Patterns of achievement in early adolescence. In M. L. Maehr & M. W. Steinkamp (Eds.), *Woman and Science* (pp. 1–35). Greenwich, CN: JAI Press.

Keating, D. P. (1990). Adolescent thinking. In S. S. Feldman & G. R. Elliott (Eds.), *At the threshold: The developing adolescent* (pp. 54–89). Cambridge, MA: Harvard University Press.

Kellam, S. G., Ensminger, M. E., & Turner, R. J. (1977). Family structure and the mental health of children: Concurrent and longitudinal community-wide studies. *Archives of General Psychiatry, 34*(9), 1012–1022.

Kennedy, R. (1989, April). *The relationship of adjustment during early adolescence to sixth grade sex-role identification*. Paper presented at the biennial meeting of the Society for Research in Child Development, Kansas City, MO.

Kennedy, R. E., & Petersen, A. C. (1991). Stressful family events and adjustment among young adolescents. Unpublished manuscript, The Pennsylvania State University, University Park, PA.

Klaiber, E. L., Broverman, D. M., Vogel, W., Abraham, G. E., & Cone, F. L. (1971). Effects of infused testoterone on mental performance and serum L. H. *Journal of Clinical Endocrinology and Metabolism, 32*, 341–349.

Kohlberg, L. (1969). *Stages in the development of moral thought and action*. New York: Holt, Rinehart, and Winston.

Leffert, N., & Petersen, A. C. (1995). Patterns of development in adolescence. In M. Rutter & D. Smith (Eds.), *Psychosocial disorders of young people: Time trends and their causes* (pp. 67–103). Chichester: Wiley.

Leffert, N., & Petersen, A. C. (1996a). Healthy adolescent development: Risks and opportunities. In P. M. Kato & T. Mann (Eds.), *Handbook of diversity issues in health psychology* (pp. 117–140). New York: Plenum Press.

Leffert, N., & Petersen, A. C. (1996b). Biology, challenge, and adaptation: Effects on physical and mental health during adolescence. In M. Bornstein & J. Genevro (Eds.), *Child development & behavioral pediatrics* (pp. 129–154). Hillsdale, NJ: Lawrence Erlbaum.

Leffert, N., & Petersen, A. C. (1999). Adolescent development: Implications for the adolescent alone. In J. Blustien, N. Dubler & C. Levine (Eds.), *Adolescents alone: Ethics, law, and medical decisionmaking* (pp. 31–49). Piscataway, NJ: Rutgers University Press.

Linn, M., & Petersen, A. C. (1985a). Emergence and characterization of sex differences in spatial ability: A meta-analysis. *Child Development, 56*, 1479–1498.

Linn, M., & Petersen, A. C. (1985b). Facts and assumptions about the nature of sex differences. In S. S. Klein (Ed.), *Handbook for achieving sex equity through education* (pp. 53–77). Baltimore, MD: Johns Hopkins University Press.

Linn, M., & Petersen, A. C. (1986). A meta-analysis of gender differences in spatial ability: Implications for mathematics and science achievement. In J. S. Hyde, & M. Linn (Eds.), *The psychology of gender: Advances through meta-analysis* (pp. 67–101). Baltimore, MD: The Johns Hopkins University Press.

Maccoby, E. E., & Jacklin, C. N. (1974). *The psychology of sex differences*. Stanford University Press.

Meyerowitz, J. (2002). *How sex changed: A history of transsexuality in the United States*. Cambridge, MA: Harvard University Press.

Millstein, S. G., Nightingale, E. O., Petersen, A. C., Mortimer, A. M., & Hamburg, D. A. (1993). Promoting the healthy development of youth: Current frontiers and future directions. *Journal of the American Medical Association, 269*(11), 1413–1415.

Millstein, S. G., Petersen, A. C., & Nightingale, E. O. (1993a). Adolescent health promotion: Rationale, goals, and objectives. In S. G. Millstein, A. C. Petersen, & E. O. Nightingale (Eds.), *Promoting the health of adolescents: New directions for the twenty-first century* (pp. 3–10). New York: Oxford University Press.

Millstein, S. G., Petersen, A. C., & Nightingale, E. O. (Eds.) (1993b). *Promoting the health of adolescents: New directions for the twenty-first century*. New York: Oxford University Press.

Mussen, P. H., & Jones, M. C. (1957). Self-conceptions, motivations, and interpersonal attitudes of early- and late-maturing boys. *Child Development, 28*(2), 243–256.

Nesselroade, J. R., & Baltes, P. B. (1974). Adolescent personality development and historical changes: 1970–1972. *Monographs of the Society for Research in Child Development, 39* (Whole No. 154).

Newcombe, N., Bandura, N. M., & Taylor, D. G. (1983). Sex differences in spatial abilities and spatial activities. *Sex Roles, 9*(3), 377–386.

Nolen-Hoeksema, S. (1987). Sex differences in unipolar depression: Evidence and theory. *Psychological Bulletin, 101*, 259–282.

Offer, D., & Offer, J. B. (1975). *From teenage to young manhood: A psychological study*. New York: Basic Books.

Offer, D. & Petersen, A. C. (1977a). Adolescent development. In *Medical and Health Annual* (pp.189–190). Chicago: Encyclopedia Britannica.

Offer, D. & Petersen, A. C. (1977b). New directions in clinical psychiatric research. In *Medical and Health Annual* (pp. 318–319). Chicago: Encyclopedia Britannica.

Parsons, J. E. (Ed.) (1980). *The psychobiology of sex difference and sex roles*. New York: Hemisphere Publishing Co.

Petersen, A. C. (1973). The relationship of androgenicity in males and females to spatial ability and fluent production. Unpublished doctoral dissertation, University of Chicago.

Petersen, A. C. (1976). Physical androgyny and cognitive functioning in adolescence. *Developmental Psychology, 12*(6), 524–533.

Petersen, A. C. (Guest Ed.). (1977a). The measurement of adolescents' self-concept. *Journal of Youth and Adolescence, 6*(3).

Petersen, A. C. (1977b). The measurement of self among adolescents: An overview. *Journal of Youth and Adolescence, 6*(3), 201–203.

Petersen, A. C. (1979a). Can puberty come any earlier? *Psychology Today, 12*, 45–47.

Petersen, A. C. (1979b). Hormones and cognitive functioning in normal development. In M. A. Wittig & A. C. Petersen (Eds.), *Sex-related differences in cognitive functioning: Developmental issues* (pp. 189–214). New York: Academic Press.

Petersen, A. C. (1980). Biopsychosocial processes in the development of sex-related differences. In J. Parsons (Ed.), *The psychobiology of sex differences and sex roles* (pp. 31–55). New York: Hemisphere Publishing Corporation.

Petersen, A. C. (1981). The development of self concept in adolescence. In M. D. Lynch, A. A. Norem-Hebeisen, & K. J. Gergen (Ed.), *Self concept: Advances in theory and research* (pp. 191–202). Cambridge, MA: Ballinger Publishing.

Petersen, A. C. (1983a). Pubertal change and cognition. In J. Brooks-Gunn & A. C. Petersen (Eds.), *Girls at puberty: Biological and psychosocial perspectives* (pp. 179–198). New York: Plenum.

Petersen, A. C. (1983b). Menarche: Meaning of measures and measuring meaning. In S. Golub (Ed.), *Menarche: The transition from girl to woman* (pp. 63–76). Lexington, MA: Lexington Books.

Petersen, A. C. (1984). The Early Adolescence Study: An overview. *Journal of Early Adolescence, 4*(2), 103–106.

Petersen, A. C. (1987). The nature of biological–psychosocial interactions: The sample case of early adolescence. In R. M. Lerner & T. T. Foch (Eds.), *Biological–psychosocial interactions in early adolescence* (pp. 35–61). Hillsdale, NJ: Lawrence Erlbaum.

Petersen, A. C. (1988). *Coping with early adolescent challenge: Gender-related mental health outcomes*. Proposal funded by the W. T. Grant Foundation.

Petersen, A. C. (1999). *Ups and downs: Gender differences in adolescent mood variations*. Presentation at the Ninth European Conference on Developmental Psychology symposium: Longitudinal Studies on Gender Differences, Island of Spetses, Greece, September 1–5, 1999.

Petersen, A. C. (2000, March). *Biology, culture, and behavior: What makes young adolescent boys and girls behave differently?* Presentation in a symposium at the 8th Biennial Society for Research on Adolescence Conference, Fairmont Hotel, Chicago, IL.

Petersen, A. C. (2006). Conducting policy-relevant developmental psychopathology research. *International Journal of Behavioral Development, 30*, 39–46.

Petersen, A. C. (2009). Inconvenient truths: Behavioral research and social policy (pp. 229–245). In M. A. G. van Aken, R. E. Tremblay, & W. Koops (Eds), *Development of Behavior Problems*. New York: Psychology Press.

Petersen, A. C. (2011). Global issues in research and social policy. *Bulletin of the International Society for the Study of Behavioral Development, 2*(60), 20–22.

Petersen, A. C. (2013). Commentary: Engaging the majority world in research on adolescence. *Journal of Research on Adolescence, 23*(1), 185–186. (Special Issue: Adolescents in the Majority World.)

Petersen, A. C, Bingham, R., Stemmler, M., & Crockett, L. J. (1991, July). *Subcultural variations in development of depressed affect.* Poster presented at the biennial meeting of the International Society for the Study of Behavioral Development, Minneapolis, MN.

Petersen, A. C., Compas, B., & Brooks-Gunn, J. (1992). *Depression in adolescence: Implications of current research for programs and policy.* Report prepared for the Carnegie Council on Adolescent Development, Washington, DC.

Petersen, A. C., Compas, B. E., Brooks-Gunn, J., Stemmler, M., Ey, S., & Grant, K. (1993a). Depression in adolescence. *American Psychologist, 48*(2), 155–168.

Petersen, A. C., & Crockett, L. J. (1985). Pubertal timing and grade effects on adjustment. *Journal of Youth and Adolescence, 14*(3), 191–206.

Petersen, A. C., & Crockett, L. J. (1986). Pubertal development and its relation to cognitive and psychosocial development in adolescent girls: Implications for parenting. In J. B. Lancaster & B. A. Hamburg (Eds.), *School-age pregnancy and parenthood: Biosocial dimensions* (pp. 147–175). Hawthorne, NY: Aldine de Gruyter. Reprinted 2008, Transaction Publishers, New Brunswick, NJ.

Petersen, A. C., & Crockett, L. J. (1992). Adolescent sexuality, pregnancy, and child rearing: Developmental perspectives. In M. K. Rosenheim, & M. F. Testa (Eds.), *Early parenthood and coming of age in the 1990s* (pp. 34–45). New Brunswick, NJ: Rutgers University Press.

Petersen, A. C., Crockett, L. J., Richards, M. H., & Boxer, A. M. (1988). A self-report measure of pubertal status: Reliability, validity, and initial norms. *Journal of Youth and Adolescence, 17*(2), 117–133.

Petersen, A. C., & Dubas, J. S. (1992). Strategies for achieving sex equity in postsecondary education. In *Sex equity in educational opportunity, achievement, and testing: Proceedings of the 1991 ETS Invitational Conference* (pp. 119–135). Princeton, NJ: Educational Testing Service.

Petersen, A. C., & Ebata, A. T. (1986, March). *Effects of normative and non-normative changes on early adolescent development.* Paper presented in the symposium, Adolescent Adjustment to the Cumulation and Synchronization of Life Transitions, conducted at the biennial meeting of the Society for Research on Adolescence, Madison, WI.

Petersen, A. C., & Ebata, A. T. (1987a). Developmental transitions and adolescent problem behavior: Implications for prevention and intervention. In K. Hurrelmannand & F. X. Kaufmann (Eds.), *Social Intervention: Potential and Constraints.* New York: de Gruyter.

Petersen, A. C., & Ebata, A. T. (1987b, July). *Gender-related change in self-image during early adolescence.* Presentation at the International Society for the Study of Behavioral Development (ISSBD) IXth biennial meeting, Tokyo, Japan.

Petersen, A. C., Ebata, A. T., & Sarigiani, P. A. (1987, April). *Who expresses depressive affect in adolescence?* Paper presented in the symposium, The Development of Depressive Affect in Adolescence: Biological, Affective, and Social Factors, at the biennial meeting of the Society for Research in Child Development, Baltimore, MD.

Petersen, A. C., & Epstein, J. L. (1991). Development and education across adolescence: An introduction. *American Journal of Education, 99*(4), 373–378.

Petersen, A. C., Hurrelmann, K., & Leffert, N. (1993b). Adolescence and schooling in Germany and the United States: A comparison of peer socialization to adulthood. *Teachers College Record, 94*(3), 611–628. (Reprinted in R. Takanishi (Ed.), *Adolescence in the 1990s: Risk and Opportunity* (pp. 153–170). New York: Teachers College Press.)

Petersen, A. C., & Kellam, S. G. (1977). Measurement of the psychological wellbeing of adolescents: The psychometric properties of the How I Feel. *Journal of Youth and Adolescence, 6*(3), 229–247.

Petersen, A. C., Kennedy, R. E., & Sullivan, P. (1991a). Coping with adolescence. In M. E. Colten & S. Gore (Eds.), *Adolescent stress: Causes and consequences* (pp. 93–110). New York: Aldine de Gruyter.

Petersen, A. C., & Leffert, N. (1995). What is special about adolescence? In M. Rutter (Ed.), *Psychosocial disturbances in young people: Challenges for prevention* (pp. 3–36). Cambridge: Cambridge University Press.

Petersen, A. C., Leffert, N., & Graham, B. L. (1995). Adolescent development and the emergence of sexuality. *Suicide and life-threatening behavior, 25*(3), 4–17.

Petersen, A. C., Leffert, N., Graham, B. L., Alwin, J., & Ding, S. (1997). Promoting mental health during adolescent transitions. In J. Schulenberg, J. L. Maggs, & K. Hurrelmann (Eds.), *Health risks and developmental transitions during adolescence* (pp. 471–497). New York: Cambridge University Press.

Petersen, A. C., Leffert, N., Graham, B., Ding, S., & Overby, T. (1994). Depression and body image disorders in adolescence. *Women's Health Issues, 4*(2), 98–108.

Petersen, A. C., & Mortimer, J. (Eds.) (1994). *Youth unemployment and society.* New York: Cambridge University Press.

Petersen, A. C., Offer, D., & Kaplan, E. (1979). The self-image of rural adolescent girls. In M. Sugar (Ed.), *Female adolescent development* (pp. 141–155). New York: Brunner/Mazel.

Petersen, A. C., Sarigiani, P. A., & Kennedy, R. E. (1991). Adolescent depression: Why more girls? *Journal of Youth and Adolescence, 20*(2), 247–271.

Petersen, A. C., Schulenberg, J. E., Abramowitz, R., Offer, D., & Jarcho, H. (1984). A Self-Image Questionnaire for Young Adolescents (SIQYA): Reliability and validity studies. *Journal of Youth and Adolescence, 13*, 93–111.

Petersen, A. C., Silbereisen, R. K., & Sörensen, S. (1992). Adolescent development: A global perspective. In W. Meeus, M. de Goede, W. Kox, & K. Hurrelmann (Eds.), *Adolescence, careers and cultures* (pp. 1–34). New York: de Gruyter.

Petersen, A. C., & Taylor, B. C. (1980). The biological approach to adolescence: Biological change and psychological adaptation. In J. Adelson (Ed.), *Handbook of adolescent psychology* (pp. 117–155). New York: Wiley.

Petersen, A. C., Tobin-Richards, M., & Boxer, A. (1983). Puberty: Its measurement and its meaning. *Journal of Early Adolescence, 3*(1–2), 47–62.

Petersen, A. C., & Wittig, M. A. (1979). Sex-related differences in cognitive functioning: An overview. In M. A. Wittig, & A. C. Petersen (Eds.), *Sex-related differences in cognitive functioning: Developmental issues* (pp. 1–17). New York: Academic Press.

Rice, K. G., Herman, M. A., & Petersen, A. C. (1993). Challenge in adolescence: A conceptual model and psycho-educational intervention. *Journal of Adolescence, 16*, 235–251.

Richards, M. H., Boxer, A. M., Petersen, A. C., & Albrecht, R. (1990). Relation of weight to body image in pubertal girls and boys from two communities. *Developmental Psychology, 26*(2), 313–321.

Richards, M. H., Gitelson, I. B., Petersen, A. C., & Hurtig, A. L. (1991). Adolescent personality in girls and boys: The role of mothers and fathers. *Psychology of Women Quarterly, 15*, 65–81.

Richardson, R. A., Galambos, N. L., Schulenberg, J. E., & Petersen, A. C. (1984). Young adolescents' perceptions of the family environment. *Journal of Early Adolescence, 4*, 131–153.

Roberts, L. R., & Petersen, A. C. (1992). The relationship between academic achievement and social self-image during early adolescence. *Journal of Early Adolescence, 12*(2), 197–219.

Roberts, L. R., Sarigiani, P. A., Petersen, A. C., & Newman, J. L. (1990). Gender differences in the relationship between achievement and self-image during early adolescence. *Journal of Early Adolescence, 10*(2), 159–175.

Robertson, E. B., Skinner, M. L., Love, M. M., Elder, G. H., Jr., Conger, R. D., Dubas, J. S. et al. (1992). The Pubertal Development Scale: A rural and suburban comparison. *Journal of Early Adolescence, 12*(2), 174–186.

Sarigiani, P. A., Wilson, J. L., Petersen, A. C., & Vicary, J. (1990). Self-image and educational plans of adolescents from two contrasting communities. *Journal of Early Adolescence, 10*(1), 37–55.

Schulenberg, J. E., Asp, C. E., & Petersen, A. C. (1984). School from the young adolescent's perspective: A descriptive report. *Journal of Early Adolescence, 4*(2), 107–130.

Silbereisen, R. K., Petersen, A. C., Albrecht, H. T., & Kracke, B. (1989). Maturational timing and the development of problem behavior: Longitudinal studies in adolescence. *Journal of Early Adolescence, 9*(3), 247–268.

Spencer, M., & Dornbusch, S. (1990). Challenges in studying minority youth. In S. S. Feldman & G. R. Elliott (Eds.), *At the threshold: The developing adolescent* (pp. 123–146). Cambridge, MA: Harvard University Press.

Stemmler, M., & Petersen, A. C. (1999). Reciprocity and change within the affective family environment in early adolescence. *International Journal of Behavioral Development, 23*(1), 185–198.

Stemmler, M., & Petersen, A. C. (2005). Gender differential influences of early adolescent risk factors for the development of depressive affect. *Journal of Youth and Adolescence, 34*(3), 175–183.

Stemmler, M., & Petersen, A. C. (2011). Latent growth curve modeling and the study of problem behavior in girls. In T. Bliesener,

A. Beelmann, & M. Stemmler (Eds.), *Antisocial behavior and crime: Contributions of theory, methods, and evaluation research to prevention and intervention. Commemorative volume (Festschrift) in honor of Friedrich Losel* (pp. 315–332). Gottingen: Hogrefe.

Suresh, S. (2012). Cultivating global science. *Science, 336,* 959.

Tanner, J. M. (1969). Growth and endocrinology of the adolescent. In L. I. Gardner (Ed.), *Endocrine and genetic diseases of childhood.* Philadelphia: W. B. Saunders.

Tobin-Richards, M. H., Boxer, A. M., & Petersen, A. C. (1983). The psychological significance of pubertal change: Sex differences in perceptions of self during early adolescence. In J. Brooks-Gunn, & A. C. Petersen (Eds.), *Girls at puberty: Biological and psychosocial perspectives* (pp. 127–154). New York: Plenum.

Waber, D. P. (1976). Sex differences in cognition: A function of maturation rate? *Science, 143,* 212–218.

Waber, D. P. (1977). Sex differences in mental abilities, hemispheric lateralization, and rate of physical growth at adolescence. *Developmental Psychology, 13,* 29–38.

Wainer, H., & Petersen, A. C. (1972). *Grofit: A Fortran program for the estimation of parameters of a human growth curve.* Chicago: Statistical Laboratory, University of Chicago. (Research Memorandum No. 17.)

Wittig, M. A., & Petersen, A. C. (Eds.). (1979). *Sex-related differences in cognitive functioning: Developmental issues.* New York: Academic Press.

33

Self-Control at the Heart of Successful Development

Lea Pulkkinen

As a teenager I used to entertain myself by trying to imagine what kind of children the adults I knew had been in the past, and what kind of adults the children I knew were going to become in the future. I have remained interested in these imaginings, as is demonstrated by the longitudinal studies in which I have been involved for decades. These studies are introduced in the present chapter with a summary of selected results and the application of findings.

A Path to Study Psychology

The Start of My Studies There is a picture on the wall of my study which depicts a snowy winter landscape with a horse pulling a modest sleigh in which I often sat as a child. Cars and electricity were rare in the countryside where I lived in the 1940s. My father was away at war, defending Finland against the Soviet Union. In spite of the war, I had a safe childhood; my mother tried to protect me and my two sisters against adults' horrors and sorrows.

I graduated from high school in 1958 in Heinola, a small town in southern Finland. Since childhood, I had had two firm wishes for my future: not to become a housewife and not to become a farmer. My choices for what to study were, however, limited, because I was not interested in going to Helsinki or Turku, which were the old university towns in Finland. I did not know what to do, but then I heard that the Pedagogical Institute of Jyväskylä in Central Finland, which was established as a teachers' training school in 1863, was being expanded by establishing Liberal Arts Faculty. My telephone call to Jyväskylä was put through to the Rector (President) of the Institute. He regretted that the deadline for applications had closed two days earlier, but he asked me what I wanted to study. I asked, in turn, what it was possible to study in Jyväskylä. He was the professor

of Finnish language, and so he mentioned that first, then literature, psychology, history, languages … I replied by listing the first three of them. A week later I got a letter informing me that I had been accepted to start my studies at Jyväskylä: Finnish language, literature, and psychology.

The Content of Undergraduate Studies

It soon became clear that I was not a linguist, but I became enthusiastic about psychology. I attended an introductory course in psychology given by Martti Takala (1924–2012), a 33-year-old professor. He opened a completely new world to me as regards the content and methodology of psychology. I later became his collaborator and successor, and a life-time friend. After being paralyzed for 20 years, he passed away just when I was writing this chapter, which I dedicate to him with gratitude.

The first textbook I had to read was written in German by Rohracher (1947). However, I understood soon that English textbooks were more modern. I had studied only a short course in English at high school, but slowly with a dictionary I read a book by Olson (1949) on child growth and development. Other books which affected my orientation included a doctoral dissertation on deprived children in public care, a Swedish textbook on differential psychology by Ekman (1952), and the most interesting book by Hall and Lindzey (1957) on personality theories. In a research seminar held by Professor Takala we discussed a longitudinal study by Kagan and Moss (1962), and when it was my turn to introduce new literature, I chose a book by Bandura and Walters (1963). Social learning in children was new and inspiring.

My practical training for psychology at the Department of Psychology in the fall of 1960 included mainly calculating correlation coefficients and factor analyses using an electronic calculator (Monroe). In 1961, the first IBM computer in Jyväskylä was hired jointly by the state metal industry and the Pedagogical Institute; researchers could use the computer at night.

Career, Mentors, and Collaborators

I took my B.A. in 1961, my MA in 1963, my Licentiate Degree in 1966, and my PhD in 1970, all at the University of Jyväskylä. I never made a choice to become a psychologist, a profession which was then becoming established in Finland, as I have described in an article about psychology in Finland (Pitkänen, 1976; Pitkänen was my first married name[1]). I studied psychology because I was interested in it. My father, a businessman, who had been worried about my future employment as a psychologist, did not live to see that I had no difficulties with employment, because he died of a heart attack in 1961 at the age of 47. I had worked as a trainee in the university library from the first weeks of my studies, which gave me a good opportunity to learn about bibliographical systems and to get access to the newest literature for years after I had finished working there. In 1961 I was appointed part-time research assistant; in 1962 full-time teaching assistant; in 1966 lecturer; and in 1967 acting associate professor for 1 year. For the years 1968 and 1969 I received a much needed grant for my doctoral studies. I had married my teacher of psychometrics in 1960 and we had two daughters, born in 1961 and 1964. In 1970–72, I worked as an associate professor of education at Jyväskylä, and during the academic year 1972–73, I did my postdoctoral studies in social psychology at Sussex University, England, on a scholarship from the British Council. My supervisor was Professor Marie Jahoda (1907–2001). I participated in an interview study on Ugandan Asians expelled from Uganda by Idi Amin, and learned a new research method, the semi-structured interview. Marie Jahoda was the first model I had of a female researcher.

On my return to Jyväskylä in 1973 I got a tenure appointment as an associate professor of psychology. From 1982 to 1990 I worked as an acting full professor for Takala, who had been re-elected President of the University; his first period was from 1963 to 1967. On his retirement his professorship became open and I was appointed to it in 1990. In my roles of Head of the Department of Psychology and Dean of the Faculty of Social Sciences in the 1980s and 1990s, I was able to advance high-quality research on human development in our department. From 1996 to 2001 I was appointed Academy Professor, and from 1997 to 2005 (until my mandatory retirement) I served as Director of a national Centre of Excellence for research called Human Development and Its Risk Factors. At the same time I worked on the establishment of the Agora Center at the University of Jyväskylä for advancing a human-centered approach to information technology, and acted as its Vice-Director. Thereafter, I have continued my research at the university, which has provided me with office and other necessary facilities. Besides this academic career, I have had another, more domestic career with Finnish publications in the application of research findings (Pulkkinen, 2004; Rose, 2004), as explained later in this article.

I have found other important mentors in international conferences, in which I have participated actively since 1974, first within the International Society for Research on Aggression (ISRA) and later, particularly, within the International Society for the Study of Behavioural Development (ISSBD). Contacts also opened to me opportunities to visit other universities for a few months: the University of California, Berkeley; the Arizona State University; University of North Carolina, Chapel Hill; the Indiana University, Bloomington; and the University of Cambridge, UK.

From the mid-1970s on, Professor Paul Mussen (1922–2000), Director of the Institute of Human Development at the University of California, Berkley, was my good friend. I often stayed with his family. Paul Mussen enjoyed sunshine beside his swimming pool and there we had endless discussions which continued fresh after intervals of several years due to his incomprehensibly good memory. He encouraged my work on the longitudinal study and directed my interest in the application of research findings. Professor Urie Bronfenbrenner (1917–2005) from Cornell University, Ithaca, NY, encouraged me to continue my study within the ecological context of development. In 1984 when I was visiting him, he was the model who led me to purchase an Apple IIC, a personal computer. I thought that if he had learnt to use it, I would learn too. From this fall, a PC became my most important domestic appliance. Professor Paul Baltes (1939–2006), Director of the Max Planck Institute for Human Development, Berlin, encouraged me to advance scientific communication within the ISSBD. I organized its Tenth Biennial Meetings in Jyväskylä in 1989 and served as the President of ISSBD in the years 1991–96. While working on the ISSBD and, particularly, co-organizing and attending its workshops, I enjoyed seeing how working in this learned society could advance the study of childhood and adolescence in all continents.

In the early 1990s, Richard J. Rose, Professor of Psychology and Medical Genetics at Indiana University, Bloomington, invited me to collaborate with him and Jaakko Kaprio, Professor of Genetic Epidemiology at the University of Helsinki, in a longitudinal study with twin children. This collaboration added genetic factors to my conception of development, and created friendships. In 1999 I organized with Avshalom Caspi, then Professor at King's College, London, a conference on personality in life course in Finland, which anticipated a move toward the study of positive development (Pulkkinen & Caspi, 2002). I had got to know Avshalom as a bright student of Bronfenbrenner's in 1984. Local collaborators have mainly been my former students, who have continuously taught me new ideas through their works, most importantly, Dr. Katja Kokko. She is committed to continuing the longitudinal study which I initiated in 1968. Since 2003 we have been members of the Center for the Pathways from Childhood to Adulthood (CAPCA) established by the University of Michigan, USA, for comparative analyses of longitudinal data.

The Research Context in Jyväskylä in the 1960s

The first professorship chair of psychology in Finland was established in Jyväskylä in 1936 (Pitkänen, 1976). The Department of Psychology was small in 1958: one professor (Martti Takala, appointed in 1954) and three part-time assistants. At present there are ten professors and 22 PhD-level faculty, half of them on a tenure track. In a department with only one professor the professor's orientation to science affects students strongly. Takala had studied at Helsinki; his doctoral dissertation concerned asymmetries of visual space, but in Jyväskylä he turned his attention to psychological tests and personality research, and with his wife, to child-rearing attitudes.

My first tasks and publications as Takala's research assistant concerned an experiment measuring boys' aggression (Pitkänen, 1963), the effects of drug (chlorpromazine) intake on the level of motivation in men (Takala & Pitkänen, 1963), and a study on physical fitness in relation to motivational traits in schoolchildren. For conducting multitrait- multimethod analyses (Campbell & Fiske, 1959) we used several measures for each motivational trait. It gave me an opportunity to see similarities and differences between responses to different measures, and awakened my interest in the construct validity of personality variables.

Besides teaching and research, Takala was the President of the Pedagogical Institute in the period 1963–67. In 1966, the Institute became the University of Jyväskylä. The number of students at Jyväskylä has increased from a few hundred in 1958 to the present 15,000. Takala created an inspiring and expansive atmosphere which offered me good conditions for research and work. In the international evaluation of the University of Jyväskylä in 2011, our department received the highest ratings, an achievement based largely on what was created in the 1960s.

In 1969, the first professorship in Finland specifically defined for developmental psychology was established at the University of Jyväskylä; its occupant from 1971 to 2000 was Isto Ruoppila. Developmental psychological studies on intelligence, reading interests, social relationships, and dexterity had been conducted in Jväskylä since the 1940s under the supervision of professors in psychology and education. Until recently, this was the only chair of developmental psychology in Finnish-language universities.

The "Cone" and "Compass" Models

The first step in my independent research work, which I started in 1964, was the study of the conceptual construct of aggression in children. This work on aggression, which I defended for my licentiate degree (an intermediate academic degree between MA and PhD) in 1966, became the first part of my doctoral dissertation (Pitkänen, 1969). In the second part, I extended my interest into nonaggressive behavior. For both parts I devised visual models, as presented below, which Professor Kirsti Lagerspetz (1932–2001), the external reviewer of my doctoral dissertation, called the "cone" and "compass" models respectively.

A Descriptive Model of Aggression In a literature search I found thorough descriptive studies of children's aggression, but I also noticed that under the general rubric of aggression there were many kinds of behavior listed in different studies. I tried to conceptualize the relevant components of an aggressive act by the "cone" model (Figure 33.1). One dimension describes the motivational sequence of aggression: either the initiation of an aggressive act (offensive, also called proactive aggression) or a response to an aggressive act (defensive, also called reactive aggression). Another dimension describes the direction of aggression. This means a differentiation between targeting aggression directly at a recipient or expressing negative emotion indirectly, for example, by kicking furniture. There are also different modes of aggression such as verbal, physical, and facial, and differences in the intensity of aggressive acts. For example, an offensive, direct, and physical aggressive act may be a light push or knocking someone down. Richard Tremblay (2000) kindly called this analysis pioneering work on offensive and defensive aggression.

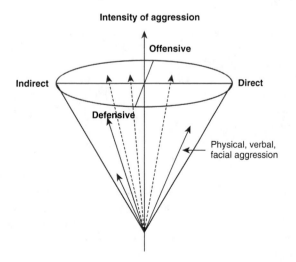

FIGURE 33.1 A descriptive model of aggression. (Modified from Pitkänen, 1969.)

The model was tested with kindergarten teachers' observations on boys' behavior. The results showed that the differentiations within the intensity, motivational sequence, and direction of aggression were more relevant than the differentiation between the physical, verbal, or facial modes of aggression, which correlated with each other. Offensive aggression accounted for the global rating of aggression more highly than defense-limited aggression, because offensively aggressive children also tended to defend themselves (Pitkänen, 1969, pp. 67–68).

A Descriptive Model for Aggression and Nonaggression

My studies on aggression generated questions about how children could avoid aggressive responses, that is, what sorts of alternative responses children had available to them to cope with frustrating situations. In the 1960s, the opposite of aggression (nonaggression) was generally referred to as the "inhibition of aggression," which implied either giving up or repressing emotions. Psychological research was oriented to psychopathology, anxiety, and aggression rather than to aspects of healthy functioning. Among a few exceptions were a study by Block and Martin (1955) on the constructive behavior manifested by children under conditions of frustration, and studies by the Feshbachs (e.g., N. Feshbach & Roe, 1968) on empathy as an alternative to aggression. Prosocial behavior started to emerge as a focus of study in the 1970s (Mussen & Eisenberg-Berg, 1977), and positive psychology at the beginning of this millennium (Seligman & Csikszentmihalyi, 2000).

In 1967, after an intensive period of reading and thinking, I got an insight into a way to describe differences in children's behavior covering also nonaggressive behaviors. I reasoned that the human brain allows for more variation in social behavior and learning than just the "fight or flight" (aggressive attack or fearful escape) studied in animal learning experiments. A characteristic of human beings is that they can observe their own behavior, intentions, and emotions and exercise control over their expression. Increasing attention was being paid to the importance of cognitive processes as determinants of emotional behavior (Pitkänen, 1969, p. 104), although the study of emotion regulation did not start until the early 1990s.

Several personality psychological investigations (see Pitkänen, 1969, p. 100) had shown that a large proportion of the common variance of individual differences in behavior could be described in terms of two orthogonal dimensions. One of the dimensions concerned differences in social activity/extraversion, and the other one differences in emotional stability versus lability/neuroticism. I devised a two-dimensional impulse control model (Pitkänen 1969; Pulkkinen, 1982) to depict children's behavior in conflict situations with behavioral activity and control of behavior as the basic dimensions. The model was renamed the model of emotional and behavioral regulation (Pulkkinen, 1995) and will be presented later (Figure 33.2).

I expected that human beings would be able to appraise the stimulus situations they encounter and make a decision between behavioral alternatives through cognitive control, which regulates both high and low activity. I identified four behavioral patterns as depicted in my "compass" model: the *uncontrolled expression of impulses* (high activity and low control, as in aggression); the *controlled expression of impulses* (high activity and high control, as in constructiveness); the *uncontrolled inhibition of impulses* (low activity and low control, as in anxiety); and the *controlled inhibition of impulses* (low activity and high control, as in compliance). The psychological processes involved were described in terms of neutralizing the emotional aspect and suppressing the behavioral aspect (Pitkänen, 1969, p. 112; Pulkkinen, 1982). The theoretical roots of impulse-control are found in psychoanalytic theory (Pulkkinen, 1986).

A Study of Individual Differences in Aggressive and Nonaggressive Behaviors

I tested the model with a random sample of 8-year-old children ($N = 369$; 53% boys). In the choice of measures, I wanted to focus on observable behavior. I used both teacher ratings and peer nominations on the same items (33) to secure the validity of the data (see Pitkänen, 1969, pp. 114–116). The items were targeted at behavioral activity (are always busy and play eagerly with other children) and passivity (are always silent, withdrawn); aggressive behavior (different types, see Figure 33.1); constructive behavior (try to act reasonably); compliant behavior (are peaceable and patient); anxious behavior (easily start crying); low control (moods change, lack concentration); and high control (always try to be friendly) (Pitkänen, 1969; Pulkkinen, 1987).

While formulating items I came across the study by Walder, Abelson, Eron, Banta, and Laulicht (1961) with children of the same age as my intended participants. I picked up some aggression items from their measure. The shared items made it possible for researchers in Finland and the USA to conduct comparative studies within the CAPCA collaboration decades later when both studies were continuing into middle age (Dubow, Huesmann, Boxer, Pulkkinen, & Kokko, 2006; Kokko, Pulkkinen, Huesmann, Dubow, & Boxer, 2009).

Other measures included two inventories then being standardized for children in Finland. Most of the scales had, however, low reliability and concurrent validity with teacher ratings and peer nominations (Pitkänen, 1969, pp. 119, 135). I was also interested in situational factors in boys' aggressive behavior, partly inspired by the criticism of personality traits presented by Mischel (1968). I developed a series of questions in which stimuli, targets (smaller, bigger, equal-sized boy; girl, teacher, father), and response types were systematically varied; and an "aggression machine" with corresponding variations. In the latter, attackers were pictured as well as attacks and responses differing by the intensity of the aggression. Participants responded by pressing a button (milder, equal, or stronger aggression) on their choice. Direct questions and attacks and the same-sized opponent resulted in the highest concurrent and predictive validity of aggressive behavior (Pitkänen-Pulkkinen, 1981a), also with the children of the participants 20 years later (Juujärvi, Kooistra, Kaartinen, & Pulkkinen, 2001).

The analyses of the data from 8-year-old children confirmed my expectations on behavioral differences between children. The two-dimensionality of individual differences was confirmed by the first two principal factors which could be rotated so that the two orthogonal axes depicted behavioral activity and control of behavior; they accounted for 57% to 72% of the total variance of teacher ratings and peer nominations (Pitkänen, 1969, pp. 122–123). The factors were stable across different informants (teachers, peers) and genders as shown by Tucker's coefficients of congruence. Other factors extracted were more specific and less stable.

Longitudinal Studies

The Jyväskylä Longitudinal Study of Personality and Social Development (JYLS)

I wrote in the discussion section of my dissertation (Pitkänen, 1969, p. 190): "A longitudinal study would make it possible to examine the stability of the individual patterns of behavior." An opportunity for the continuation of the study came in 1973 when I led a research seminar with six students for their Master's degree. We traced the participants at age 14 for a follow-up study. When the participants reached 20 years of age I collected a new data set with other students. Thereafter, major data collection waves have been conducted at ages 27, 36, 42, and 50 (in 2009). The participation rate at age 50 was 84% and the retention rate 73% without systematic attrition (Pulkkinen, 2009).

When the participants were 14, we succeeded in collecting teacher ratings and peer nominations for 96% of the initial sample using an abbreviated list of items for the same constructs as those assessed at age 8 (Pulkkinen, 1987, 2006). Semi-structured interviews, a technique with which I had become acquainted at Sussex, had to be limited to 43% of the participants and one of their parents due to an insufficient grant. The research grant at age 20 was also too small for the study of the whole initial sample. For data collection at age 27 I received grants for the study of the whole initial sample, and since then the Academy of Finland has supported this study generously up to the present. Measures in adulthood included a mailed questionnaire, a personal interview, inventories, and medical examinations (see https://www.jyu.fi/ytk/laitokset/psykologia/en/research/jyls/).

The Longitudinal Study of Health and Behavior in Twin Children (FinnTwin12)

A longitudinal study with twins was started in the early 1990s with Professor Richard J. Rose as the Principal Investigator and Jaakko Kaprio and Lea Pulkkinen as Co-PIs. The aim was to examine genetic and environmental determinants of health-related behaviors, with a particular focus on the use of alcohol. Major funding was obtained from the U.S. National Institutes of Health. As described by Rose (2006), there are many advantages in conducting longitudinal twin-family studies in this small Nordic country. One of them is a population-based Finnish Twin Register.

The study had a two-stage sampling design (Kaprio, 2006). Stage 1 was an epidemiological investigation of five consecutive and complete birth cohorts at age 12 years, including questionnaire assessments of both twins and parents at baseline, with the follow-up of all twins at age 14 and again at age 17.5 years. The questionnaires were returned by 2,724 families, with 87% participation. Stage 2 was an intensive assessment of a subsample of twin families nested within this epidemiological, population-based study. Of those families from whom permission was obtained for school contact, 1,035 were selected for intensive (Stage 2) study. For each twin in each pair we added a gender- and age-matched classmate control.

In-school assessments of the twins at age 12 included the administration of the Multidimensional Peer Nomination Inventory (MPNI) and its Teacher Rating Form. The MPNI was developed and expanded from the measure used in the JYLS at age 8 to cover aggression, hyperactivity-impulsivity, inattention, anxiety, depressive symptoms, constructiveness, compliance, and socially active behaviors (Pulkkinen, Kaprio, & Rose, 1999). At age 14, teacher ratings were made again. Several other measures were also included in the study (Kaprio, 2006). As a result of the common methodological basis and shared interests in research problems, results in the JYLS and FinnTwin12 are complementary (Pulkkinen, Kaprio, & Rose, 2006), as will be summarized below for socio-emotional behavior and the use of alcohol in adolescence. The impulse control model modified for socio-emotional behavior is first described.

A Model of Emotional and Behavioral Regulation

In the 1990s, when the study of emotion regulation started to flourish, I relabeled the impulse control model the model of emotional and behavioral regulation (Pulkkinen, 1995) without changing the process constructs of the impulse control model (Pulkkinen, 1982). The vertical axis of the model, *behavioral activity*, involves the suppression of behavioral aspect, whereas the horizontal axis, *self-control*, involves the neutralization of negative emotionality through the individual's cognitive processes. Emotion regulation in the name of the model refers to the redirection, control, and modification of negative emotional arousal to enable an individual to function adaptively in emotionally arousing situations (Cicchetti, Ganiban, & Barnett, 1991).

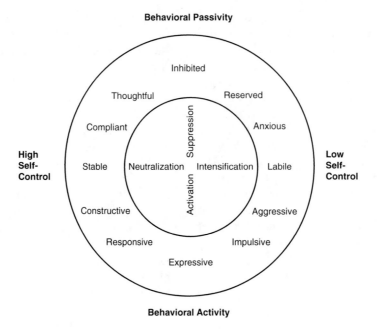

FIGURE 33.2 A model of emotional and behavioral regulation. (Modified from Pulkkinen, 1995.)

Self-control is one of the character strengths included under temperance which, in turn, is one of the core virtues in ancient philosophy and many religions (Peterson & Seligman, 2004). Temperance refers to strengths that protect against excess, and self-control (self-regulation) protects against destabilizing emotional extremes. Self-control balances or moderates activities and emotions between two extremes rather than suppressing them; excessive control is not optimal. This definition of self-control matches the idea of self-control in the model of emotional and behavioral regulation. The concepts of self-control and self-regulation have their own histories (Pulkkinen & Pitkänen, 2010), but they are currently often used interchangeably (Vohs & Baumeister, 2004).

I defined the coping behaviors depicted by the impulse control model as situation-specific, by which I meant that individuals may vary their behaviors according to their perceptions of situational demands, transitory states, and temperament reactivity. I expected, however, that more general behavioral habits would be formed as a result of social learning through parenting and other socializing experiences. Pulkkinen's (Pitkänen, 1969) definition of individual differences in coping behaviors bears some similarity to the definition of individual differences in temperament (Rothbart & Derryberry, 1981): they emerge when (re)activity is modulated by self-control (regulation) (Pulkkinen, Kokko, & Rantanen, 2012). I did not integrate coping behaviors with temperament and personality traits because at the time of collecting data from 8- and 14-year-old participants in the JYLS (in 1968 and 1974), modern temperament theories and measures were not available—neither the Big Five approach to personality nor measures for assessing these traits. In the light of present knowledge, temperament can be seen as the basis upon which both personality traits and coping styles

are built which are part of personality (McAdams & Pals, 2006). I currently use the term "socio-emotional behavior" to cover children's coping behaviors (Pulkkinen, Vaalamo, Hietala, Kaprio, & Rose, 2003), and refer by it to the integral role of emotions and emotion regulation in the process of socialization (Pulkkinen et al., 2012).

I described individual differences in socio-emotional behavior in the two-dimensional framework. The number of factors that adequately explain individual differences in personality is still being debated, but there are supporters of a two-factor structure of the Big Five personality traits identified by Digman (1997) as *alpha*—principally formed by agreeableness, conscientiousness, and emotional stability; and *beta*—covering extraversion and openness to experience. Rothbart and her colleagues identified three higher-order temperament traits for infants and toddlers: surgency (extraversion), negative affectivity, and effortful control (Rothbart & Derryberry, 2002), but two factors for adult temperament (Evans & Rothbart, 2009). They found that negative affectivity and effortful control tend to be polar opposites forming one factor, and the second factor is formed by extraversion/positive emotionality. These two factors resemble the two secondary factors of personality traits (Digman, 1997), which correlate highly with temperament traits, and the two dimensions in the model of emotional and behavioral regulation.

In the FinnTwin12 study, three factors extracted from variables for socio-emotional behavior were formed by externalizing problem behaviors (aggression, hyperactivity-impulsivity, inattention), internalizing problem behaviors (anxiety, depressive symptoms), and adaptive behaviors (constructiveness, compliance, socially active behaviors including leadership) (Pulkkinen et al., 1999). A factor structure is dependent on the composition of variables included in the analysis. The heuristic two-dimensional model helps, however, to understand relationships between constructs through, for instance, shared low self-control of negative emotions in externalizing and internalizing problem behaviors. The shared variance was demonstrated by a study in which recurrent pain in 11-year-old twin boys and girls was most strongly associated with internalizing and externalizing problem behaviors in cases of their co-morbidity, that is, occurring at the same time (Vaalamo, Pulkkinen, Kinnunen, Kaprio, & Rose, 2002). Interestingly, recurrent pain was also found in highly constructive girls, suggesting that they might have exceeded the optimal level of emotion regulation.

Empirical evidence of the model demands work on measurement techniques. It is a challenge to assess behavioral activity independent of its quality of high or low self-control, and to assess weak self-control of negative emotions independent of behavioral activity, covering both activity and anxiety. In the JYLS, ratings of girls' behavioral activity tended to correlate more positively with higher self-control than ratings of boys, and therefore girls' activity has been associated with more positive life paths (career success) than boys' activity (Pulkkinen, 2009).

Socio-Emotional Behavior

Factors Associated with Magnitude and Continuity The FinnTwin12 study provides consistent evidence across different contexts (home, school), child status (twin, singleton), informants (peers, teacher, parent, self), and age (12 and 14) of gender differences in socio-emotional behavior (Pulkkinen et al., 2003; Vierikko, Pulkkinen, & Rose, 2006). Boys exceeded girls in aggression and inattention, while girls scored higher in social anxiety and constructive behavior. In social activity, gender differences were less evident. Likewise in the JYLS, girls at ages 8 and 14 years exceeded boys in well-controlled behavior (covering both constructive and compliant behavior), whereas there were no gender differences in behavioral activity (Pulkkinen et al., 2012). For negative emotionality, boys exceeded girls in aggression; in social anxiety, gender differences were not significant.

Age changes in early adolescence were positive, because for both genders' externalizing and internalizing problem behaviors decreased from age 12 to age 14, while compliant behavior increased (Vierikko et al., 2006). There was significant relative stability in teacher-rated socio-emotional behaviors from age 12 to 14 (Vierikko et al., 2006), indicating that some children were consistently higher and some were consistently lower in these characteristics across time. When the interval was longer, from age 8 to 14 in the JYLS teacher ratings, the age-to-age correlations were lower. They were significant when boys and girls were combined (Pulkkinen, 1995), but correlations were often significant only for one gender (for aggressive and compliant behaviors among males and anxious behavior among females; Pitkänen-Pulkkinen, 1981b). It was also found that the magnitude of the correlations varied depending on the informant: continuity of aggression in females and anxiety in males were higher in peer nominations than in teacher ratings.

In the life course perspective, we found significant links from middle childhood to midlife for both extraversion and high self-control, but for negative affectivity continuity was less consistent (Pulkkinen et al., 2012). These findings agree with the results of Hampson and Goldberg (2006). Furthermore, we found that these links started at age 8 in males, but at age 14 in females, suggesting gender differences in socialization. The same observation was made with aggression (Kokko & Pulkkinen, 2005).

Environmental and Genetic Factors in Socio-Emotional Behavior We found that female twins had better social skills than female singletons; twins were higher in constructive and compliant behaviors but lower in inattention. Male twins, in turn, were higher in socially active behavior but lower in depressive symptoms (Pulkkinen et al., 2003). Thus, having a twin sister or brother advances self-control in girls and positive emotionality in boys. The smallest gender differences were obtained among opposite-sex twins, which suggests that reciprocal social interactions within brother–sister twin pairs lead them to model sex-typed behavior from one another.

Both genetic and environmental effects were found to be significant for socio-emotional behavior in boys and girls (Vierikko et al., 2006). However, genetic effects were found to be significantly larger for girls than for boys on aggression and, in contrast, larger genetic effects were found among boys than girls on depressive symptoms, anxiety, and social activity. Gender modulation of genetic and environmental effects was found neither for other aspects of externalizing problem behaviors (inattention and impulsivity-hyperactivity) nor for high self-control (constructiveness and compliance).

Developmental Paths In the JYLS, four developmental paths from age 8 to 20 were distinguished (Pulkkinen, 1982, 1983; Figure 33.3). One of them started from aggressive behavior and tended to lead to orientation to peers at age 14 and to a style of life at age 20 which can be identified as the *undercontrolled* lifestyle (called previously "Reveller"). Characteristics of this path are frequent contacts with others, aggressive behavior, poor concentration, early smoking and heavy drinking, orientation to entertainment, and conflicts with parents. Another path indicating low self-control started from anxious behavior and tended to lead to negativism toward school and other people and a lifestyle at age 20 which might be called the *overcontrolled* lifestyle due to the obvious neuroticism involved in it. At age 20, this lifestyle was characterized by low self-confidence, fear of the future, smoking, and risks of marginalization. The paths for high self-control started from constructive behavior leading to the *resilient* lifestyle, and from compliant behavior leading to the *reserved* lifestyle. The resilient lifestyle was characterized by optimism, satisfaction with choices, school success, and plans for the future, whereas the reserved lifestyle was characterized by social tension, abstinence, difficulty in making friends, and dependence on parents.

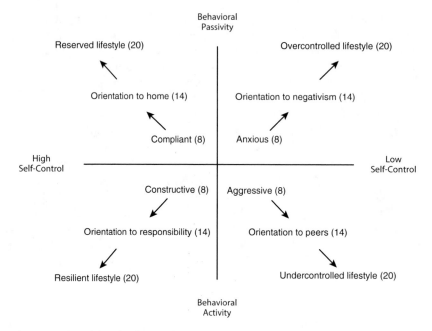

FIGURE 33.3 A schematic presentation of four developmental paths. (From Pulkkinen, 2012b. Reprinted by permission of L. Pulkkinen and the Association for Childhood Education International, 1101 16th St., N.W., Ste. 300, Washington, D.C. 20036. Copyright © 2012 by the Association.)

Aggression as an Antecedent of Problem Behaviors It has been shown in many studies that there is continuity of aggression across adolescence (Cairns & Cairns, 1994) and that aggression predicts criminal offenses (Farrington, 1991). The contributions of the JYLS to this literature specify these connections. First, the intensity of aggressive behavior in childhood predicts aggressiveness in adolescence and early adulthood (Pulkkinen & Pitkänen, 1993), and furthermore, in middle age (Kokko & Pulkkinen, 2005), but only when physical aggression in adulthood was used as the criterion; adulthood verbal aggression was not predictable (Kokko et al., 2009). The last mentioned comparative study conducted within the CAPCA also showed that continuity in aggression was higher in the USA than in Finland. Second, it is only offensive, proactive aggression in children which predicts criminal offenses (Pulkkinen, 1987, 1996); defensive, reactive aggression without offensive aggression may indicate assertiveness and be associated with well-controlled behavior (Pulkkinen, 1986). Aggression particularly predicts criminal offenses when it appears with other norm-breaking behavior in adolescence (Hämäläinen & Pulkkinen, 1996), and it predicts persistent offending, not adolescence-limited offending; the latter is associated with social activity, low anxiety, and early use of alcohol (Pulkkinen, Lyyra, & Kokko, 2009).

Childhood aggression and noncompliance correlate with vulnerability to accidents by age 27 in males (Pulkkinen, 1995). Aggression is also a risk for long-term unemployment (Kokko & Pulkkinen, 2000), and it predicts a higher divorce rate (Kinnunen & Pulkkinen, 2003), problem-drinking in middle age (Pitkänen, Kokko, Lyyra, & Pulkkinen, 2008); and a lower educational and occupational status both in Finland and the USA (Dubow,

Huesman, Boxer, Pulkkinen, & Kokko, 2006). Various processes are involved in these associations, such as the accumulation of problems in social functioning (Rönkä & Pulkkinen, 1995), low education (Dubow et al., 2006), and the formation of a cycle of maladaptation in adolescence including poor adjustment to school in adolescence, and heavy drinking and lack of occupational alternatives in young adulthood (Kokko & Pulkkinen, 2000).

Continuity exists not only in specific behaviors but also in the patterns of behaviors depicting either low self-control or high self-control, and their outcomes. Children who were high in aggression but low in constructiveness and compliance tended to be high in impulsivity but low in socialization and agreeableness in adulthood (Laursen, Pulkkinen, & Adams, 2002). As adults these individuals had more problem-drinking, had been arrested more often, had more unstable careers with periods of unemployment, and they were more depressed compared with individuals whose pattern depicted high self-control: low aggression but high constructiveness and compliance in childhood, and low impulsivity but high socialization and agreeableness in adulthood. A multi-problem pattern resulted in disruptive and antisocial behavior, low school success, and an unstable working career also in the comparative study between Finland and Canada (Pulkkinen & Tremblay, 1992).

High Self-Control as an Antecedent of Successful Development Historically, most studies of personality development have been biased by the goal of seeking to understand behavioral problems, and have tended to overlook the study of pathways to successful outcomes (Pulkkinen & Caspi, 2002). The study of successful development is more difficult, because success is more elusive and more difficult to operationalize than problem behaviors. Successful development in spite of risks has been conceptualized as resilience in problem-focused research, but it has also been defined in the literature as a successful resolution of psychosocial crises, the accomplishment of developmental tasks, the realization of one's potentials, social and psychological adaptation, and balancing an individual's resources against the social and physical environment (Pulkkinen, Nygren, & Kokko, 2002). We have defined successful development in terms of (1) external criteria, such as the accomplishment of age-graded developmental tasks and adaptation to society's norms (i.e., social functioning), and (2) internal criteria, such as subjective measures of well-being (i.e., psychological functioning).

We expected that high self-control in childhood would be associated with successful development, and found that it may be either a protective factor against negative outcomes in children with specific risks or a resource factor for positive development. For the former, we found that if aggressive children displayed some prosocial behavior indicating high self-control, the risk of long-term unemployment (Kokko & Pulkkinen, 2000) and criminal behavior (Hämäläinen & Pulkkinen, 1996) was reduced. Gottfredson and Hirschi (1990) argued that individuals possessing high self-control are less likely at all periods of life to engage in criminal acts. Our findings lent support to this crime theory. Non-offenders differed from persistent offenders by being more compliant and less aggressive in childhood (Pulkkinen et al., 2009).

High self-control, particularly constructive behavior, is associated with positive partnership (Kinnunen & Pulkkinen, 2003), higher educational and occupational status (Dubow et al., 2006; Pulkkinen, Ohranen, & Tolvanen, 1999), and higher income (Viinikainen, Kokko, Pulkkinen, & Pehkonen, 2010); a one standard deviation increase in the score for constructive behavior at age 8 was associated with a 10% increase in income at age 43. The connections of self-control in childhood are more direct with social functioning than with psychological functioning in adulthood (Pulkkinen et al., 2002). High self-control predicts career development which, in turn, is associated with psychological functioning at age 42 (Pulkkinen, Feldt, & Kokko, 2006). High self-control is associated with psychological functioning in adulthood also through social relationships (Pulkkinen, Lyyra, & Kokko, 2011). High self-control, particularly constructiveness, is one of the bases for the resilient lifestyle, whereas aggression is the basis for the undercontrolled lifestyle and anxiety for the overcontrolled lifestyle (Pulkkinen, 1996a; Pulkkinen, Feldt, & Kokko, 2005).

The Use of Alcohol in Adolescence

Behavioral Problems Are Associated with Alcohol Use The JYLS participants who took up drinking before the age of 14 scored significantly higher in all adult alcohol use indicators than individuals who began drinking at age 18 or later (the legal age limit) (Pitkänen, Lyyra, & Pulkkinen, 2005; Pitkänen et al., 2008). The likelihood of weekly drunkenness was 3.5 times higher among those who started alcohol use prior to age 14 than among those who were 16 or older when they began alcohol use. The results were in accordance with those obtained in the USA.

Antecedents of adult heavy drinking were found in the JYLS among male participants at age 8 in aggressiveness and among female participants at age 14 in aggressiveness, and for both genders in truancy at age 14 (Pitkänen et al., 2008). Conduct problems show considerable heritability, and the overlap between childhood conduct problems and later alcohol problems is due largely to shared genetic factors (Dick et al., 2009). Contemporaneous depressive symptoms and alcohol use are also genetically and environmentally correlated (Edwards et al., 2011).

The Changing Importance of Genetic and Environmental Factors in Drinking Shared environmental factors heavily influence alcohol use, and this is particularly true at age 14 (Edwards et al., 2010). In early adulthood, there was no evidence of shared environmental influences on alcohol problems; alcohol-related problems at ages 23–27 were largely influenced by genetic factors, and these overlapped with the genetic influences on frequency of use at earlier ages (Pagan et al., 2006). Once drinking has been initiated, hereditary factors influence drinking behavior more. Low parental monitoring was a risk factor for substance use at age 14, and girls were more vulnerable to the consequences of reduced parental monitoring than boys (Rose, Dick, Viken, Pulkkinen, & Kaprio, 2001). Furthermore, when monitoring was lower the influence of genetic factors was higher. Adolescents' reports on parenting practices were stronger predictors of adolescent drinking than parents' reports (Latendresse et al., 2009).

Environments shared by twin siblings at age 14 influence their decision to remain abstinent or to take up drinking (Rose et al., 2001). In a study which included both twins and the control classmates we found significant similarities between them in smoking and drinking patterns (Rose et al., 2003). The result demonstrates that also environmental influences outside the family affect children's behavioral development, and that important parts of shared environments are those shared by twin siblings with their peers and classmates. Adolescents who reported having friends who drink or smoke or are delinquent were more likely to drink themselves. The predictive value of each of these effects was greater among girls (Dick et al., 2007).

At age 18, genetic influences on drinking were higher in urban environments, whereas common environmental influences played a larger role in rural environments (Dick, Rose, Viken, Kaprio, & Koskenvuo, 2001). No evidence was found of socio-regional variables (urban/rural residency, migration rates, and the prevalence of young adults) moderating alcohol use at age 14, but their effects on female alcohol use at age 14 were significant (Dick et al., 2009). These socio-regional factors did moderate, however, the genetic influences on girls' behavioral problems (aggression, hyperactivity, inattention) at age 12. Genetic influences assumed greater importance in urban settings and in communities with a higher percentage of young adults.

Pubertal Maturation is Associated with Drinking   Pubertal maturation is a risk factor of early onset drinking (Dick, Rose, Pulkkinen, & Kaprio, 2001). We also found significant associations of higher testosterone levels with drinking (Eriksson, Kaprio, Pulkkinen, & Rose, 2005). After adjustment for pubertal maturation, these associations mostly disappeared. The association of pubertal development with testosterone is largely genetic in nature. Genetic influences made the largest contribution to variance of pubertal development, but secondary analyses found accelerated pubertal maturation in both boys and girls who at age 14 were reared in homes without a father. The result enriches our understanding of the elevated risk for substance use found among adolescents reared in single-parent households (Mustanski, Viken, Kaprio, Pulkkinen, & Rose, 2004).

From Science to the Application of Findings

My second career in the application of research findings started in the 1970s. When I worked at the Department of Education in Jyväskylä (1970–72), I came across the fact that education as a discipline was mainly oriented to institutional education, and that as the mother of two children I had learnt hardly anything about the influence of home and parenting on children in studies of psychology and education. As a consequence, in the semi-structured interviews with the 14-year-old JYLS participants and one of their parents, we tried to investigate the ecological context of the participants' lives as thoroughly as possible, covering, for instance, family constellation and relationships, housing, parents' work, parenting practices, and leisure activities. The results were striking. Children's socio-emotional behavior was highly associated with home conditions. For instance, constructive adolescents had received most encouragement for their activities from their parents; anxious adolescents had grown in the most unstable conditions; and aggressive adolescents had lived in the most selfish atmosphere (Pitkänen-Pulkkinen, 1980). These results were confirmed by analyses of data at age 20 (Pulkkinen, 1982) for instability of family life and parenting. A parenting factor associated with children's high self-control was identified as child-centered guidance which involved deliberate support for children's development, and a parenting factor associated with low self-control was identified as selfish treatment (more lately, parent-centered parenting style; Pulkkinen, 2011). Selfishness means that parents deal with the child more according to their own moods than according to the child's needs.

I wrote a book in Finnish (Pulkkinen, 1977) based on the data collected at age 14, and another book based on

data collected at age 20 (Pulkkinen, 1984), because I considered it important (and still do) that parents and educators can read about research results in their native language. The first book, particularly, was widely discussed and used as a text book in colleges. To support the development of children's self-control, we developed material for parents and daycare personnel (Pulkkinen, Heikkinen, Markkanen, & Ranta, 1977) by highlighting understanding one's own feelings and reactions, other people's feelings and reactions, and social skills (e.g., team work, sharing and taking turns, thinking of others, finding non-aggressive solutions to conflicts) (Pitkänen-Pulkkinen, 1977). Goleman (1995) later used the term *emotional intelligence* to refer to corresponding goals: self-awareness of the person in question, managing oneself emotionally, empathy, and as a result of these, skilled interaction.

My work and results were not in accordance with the political atmosphere of the social sciences in Finland in the 1970s. The role of the family in children's lives was then being downplayed. I was, however, invited to serve as an expert member on the Parliamentary Committee for Educational Goals in Day Care (Committee Report, 1980), and I managed to contribute to the emphasis of the parents' role in children's upbringing, and to educational objectives by introducing a framework, "The house of objectives." The grounds of the house are in the surrounding society. Its foundations are formed by the physical environment, care relationships, and the child's own activities. The latter penetrate all seven layers of the house of objectives: physical, social, emotional, aesthetic, intellectual, ethical, and religious education. In the daycare legislation (304/1983), educational objectives were defined on this basis and they have remained unchanged to this day.

In 1981 we established a Society for Home Upbringing for the support of parenthood, a society which I chaired for 7 years. As a result of its work and initiatives, the society soon achieved a position of respect and was listened to by committees of the Finnish Parliament on proposals for legislation concerning children. The society also started to develop the idea of a Family Research Unit, to be established at the University of Jyväskylä. This hope was realized in 1990, and I served as the Director of its Board until 1996. In 2004, the first professorship was established in the unit with donated funds, and the unit then received the status of Family Research Center.

The family as an institution is dependent on other institutions in society. For example, parents' work conditions affect family life. In the 1990s I became worried about children's loneliness after school hours when parents were working many more hours than children stayed at school, and children lacked supervision (Pulkkinen, 2004, 2012). With the support of Mrs. Eeva Ahtisaari, the wife of Mr. Martti Ahtisaari, Nobel Peace Prize Laureate, then President of Finland, we publicized this problem. Some members of the Finnish Parliament invited me to design a project for improving children's social skills which gave me an opportunity to consider also ideas about reducing children's loneliness. As a result, a 3-year *Integrated School Day (ISD) project* in seven schools. was conducted in the Agora Center and funded by the Finnish Innovation Fund (Sitra) in 2002–2005. The school day was restructured by including in it two types of voluntary activities. First, adult-supervised, mostly self-organized recreation, and indoor and outdoor activities, and second, clubs for hobbies which involved goal-oriented activities (e.g., team sports, cooking, arts, and music) (Pulkkinen & Launonen, 2005; Pulkkinen, 2012a).

The ISD program had positive effects on children's self-control (assessed using the Teacher Form of the MPNI). Children in the experimental group who had participated in the ISD program in grades 1–3 or 2–4 were lower in anxiety than children who had not attended the program (Metsäpelto, Pulkkinen, & Tolvanen, 2010). Participation in hobby clubs, particularly in arts and crafts clubs and music clubs in grades 3–5 or grades 4–6, improved self-control, academic achievements, and working skills such as concentration (Metsäpelto & Pulkkinen, 2012). The intervention contributed to a change in Finnish school legislation (2003/1136) which mandated that supervision of children's activities in the morning and afternoon should be available throughout the country for all first- and second-grade children and should be financially supported by the government.

In Conclusion

The goal of this chapter has been to describe the context and content of my studies. I have had wonderful mentors and colleagues who have given me the freedom to develop my ideas and have supported me in their fulfillment. I have worked hard with the vision in my mind that I got in 1967 concerning the role of self-control in successful development. Dozens of studies have confirmed it. Self-control as part of the virtue of temperance is a valuable resource in children and adolescents for their future. Its development should be nourished by parents, school, and all co-educators. Unfortunately, the individualism of our time often counteracts self-control. Environmental factors play an important role in adolescent drinking and other problem behaviors, and it is the responsibility of adults to create conditions which advance successful development in children and adolescents.

Science is highly respected in our present society, but I have become increasingly aware that its results are not well known and applied in everyday life. In the area of developmental science, knowledge about children's and adolescent's development has accumulated and many children and adolescents are doing better than ever before, but severe problems exist also in wealthy countries. Problems in families, such as selfishness, are reflected in society (Gerhardt, 2010). We need special efforts to improve the quality of childhood and adolescence.

Matthes (2012) has analyzed the process needed for an improvement of the quality of life as follows. We should discuss what kind of steps we can take and what strategies we need to develop. We need to increase awareness of problems, and in this process both research and the dissemination of knowledge play an important role. We need to establish organizations and institutions to highlight children's rights and perspectives. By working together and organizing ourselves more thoroughly and more professionally, action models can be developed to get the general public, politicians, and media involved. In addition to working on the national level, we need agreements on the international level, because problems in childhood and adolescence cannot be solved entirely in any one country. The process for improving the quality of childhood should be benchmarked with the environmental movement. A metaphor illustrates it beautifully:

> When fish are dying and start to float to the surface of a lake we all know something is wrong with the quality of the water in the lake or with some aspect of the environment of the fish species in question. Ecologists will work on identifying the pollution in the lake that caused the problem and try to remedy it.
>
> When things go wrong with human beings most of the time we follow another approach. To stay with the metaphor of the fish and the water: we take the fish (i.e., the child or the adolescent) out of the lake and put it into an aquarium (or in human terms prisons, institutions, remedial programs) and start to treat the fish with the aim of 'repairing' what has gone wrong.
>
> (Matthes, 2010, p. 15).

Acknowledgment

The preparation of this chapter has been supported by funding from the Academy of Finland (Grant No. 127125).

Note

1. I remarried in 1975, which caused me problems with a surname. Only in 1985 was Finnish legislation passed that allowed spouses more freedom in choosing their surname after marriage. My maiden name was Marttunen, my name after my first marriage was Pitkänen, and my name after my second marriage was Pulkkinen. I used the author name Pitkänen-Pulkkinen in international publications from 1976 to 1981 to maintain my identity, but gave it up later. The full list of Pulkkinen's (Pitkänen's) publications can be found on the following website: http://users.jyu.fi/~leapulkk.

References

Bandura, A., & Walters, R. H. (1963). *Social learning and personality development*. New York: Holt, Rinehart and Winston.

Block, J., & Martin, B. C. (1955). *Journal of Abnormal and Social Psychology, 51*, 281–285. doi:10.1037/h0047628

Cairns, R. B., & Cairns, B. D. (1994). *Lifelines and risks: Pathways of youth in our time*. Cambridge, U.K.: Cambridge University Press. doi:10.2277/0521481120

Campbell, D., & Fiske, D. (1959). *Psychological Bulletin, 56*, 81–105. doi:10.1037/h0046016

Cicchetti, D., Ganiban, J., & Barnett, D. (1991). In J. Garber & K. A. Dodge (Eds.),*The development of emotion regulation and dysregulation* (pp. 15–48). Cambridge, UK: Cambridge University Press. doi:10.1017/CBO9780511663963.003

Committee Report (1980). *Päivähoidon kasvatustavoitekomietean mietintö* [Educational objectives in day care]. Helsinki: Government Printing Centre.

Dick, D. M., Bernard, M., Aliev, F., Viken, R., Pulkkinen, L., Kaprio, J. et al. (2009). *Alcoholism: Clinical & Experimental Research, 33,* 1739–48. Epub 2009 Jul 15. PubMed PMID: 19624574. doi:10.1111/j.1530-0277.2009.01011.x

Dick, D. M., Rose, R. J., Pulkkinen, L., & Kaprio, J. (2001). *Journal of Youth and Adolescence, 30,* 385–399. doi:10.1023/A:1010471015102

Dick, D. M., Rose, R. J., Viken, R. J., Kaprio, J., & Koskenvuo, M. (2001). *Journal of Abnormal Psychology, 110,* 625–632.

Dick, D. M., Viken, R., Purcell, S., Kaprio, J., Pulkkinen, L., & Rose, R. J. (2007). *Journal of Abnormal Psychology, 116,* 213–218. doi:10.1037/0021-843X.116.1.213

Digman, J. M. (1997). *Journal of Personality and Social Psychology, 73,* 1246–1256. doi:10.1037/0022-3514.73.6.1246

Dubow, E. F., Huesmann, L. R., Boxer, P., Pulkkinen, L., & Kokko, K. (2006). *Developmental Psychology, 42,* 937–949. doi:10.1037/0012-1649.42.5.937

Edwards, A., Sihvola, E., Korhonen, T., Pulkkinen, L., Moilanen, I., Kaprio, J. et al. (2011). *Behavior Genetics, 41,* 476–487. doi:10.1007/s10519-010-9400-y

Ekman, G. (1952). *Differentiell psykologi.* Stockholm: Geber.

Eriksson, C. J. P., Kaprio, J., Pulkkinen, L., & Rose, R. J. (2005). *Behavior Genetics, 35,* 359–368. doi:10.1007/s10519-005-3228-x

Evans, D. E., & Rothbart, M. K. (2009). *Personality and Individual Differences, 47,* 565–570. doi:10.1016/j.paid.2009.05.010

Farrington, D. P. (1991). Childhood aggression and adult violence: Early precursors and later life outcome. In D. J. Pepler and K. H. Rubin (Eds.), *The development and treatment of childhood aggression* (pp. 5–29). Hillsdale, NJ: Lawrence Erlbaum.

Feshbach, N., & Roe, K. (1968). *Child Development, 39,* 133–145. doi:10.2307/1127365

Gerhadt, S. (2010). *The selfish society: How we all forgot to love one another and made money instead.* London: Simon & Schuster.

Goleman, D. (1995). *Emotional intelligence.* New York: Bantam Books.

Gottfredson, M. R., & Hirschi, T. (1990). *A general theory of crime.* Stanford, CA: Stanford University Press.

Hall, C. S., & Lindzey, G. (1957). *Theories of personality.* New York: Wiley. doi:10.1037/10910-000

Hämäläinen, M. & Pulkkinen, L. (1996). *Development and Psychopathology, 8,* 443–455. doi:10.1017/S0954579400007185

Hampson, S. E., & Goldberg, L. R. (2006). *Journal of Personality and Social Psychology, 91,* 763–779. doi:10.1037/0022-3514.91.4.763

Juujärvi, P., Kooistra, L., Kaartinen, J., & Pulkkinen, L. (2001). *Aggressive Behavior, 27,* 430–445. doi:10.1002/ab.1028

Kagan, J., & Moss, H. A. (1962). *Birth to maturity: A study in psychological development.* New York: Wiley.

Kaprio, J. (2006). In L. Pulkkinen, J. Kaprio, & R. J. Rose (Eds.), *Socioemotional development and health from adolescence to adulthood* (pp. 72–91). New York: Cambridge University Press. doi:10.1017/CBO9780511499784.006

Kinnunen, U., & Pulkkinen, L. (2003). *European Psychologist, 8,* 223–237. doi:10.1027//1016-9040.8.4.223

Kokko, K., & Pulkkinen, L. (2000). *Developmental Psychology, 36,* 463–472. doi:10.1037/0012-1649.36.4.463

Kokko, K., & Pulkkinen, L. (2005). *Aggressive Behavior, 31,* 485–497. doi:10.1002/ab.20063

Kokko, K., Pulkkinen, L., Huesmann, L. R., Dubow, E. F., & Boxer, P. (2009). *Journal of Research on Adolescence, 19,* 9–34. doi:10.1111/j.1532-7795.2009.00579.x

Latendresse, S. J., Rose, R. J., Viken, R. J., Pulkkinen, L., Kaprio, J., & Dick, D. M. (2009). *Journal of Clinical Child & Adolescent Psychology, 38,* 232–244. doi:10.1080/15374410802698404

Laursen, B., Pulkkinen, L., & Adams, R. (2002). *Developmental Psychology, 38,* 591–603. doi:10.1037//0012-1649.38.4.591

Matthes, M. (2010). How to improve the quality of childhood: Setting the scene. In C. Clouder, B. Heys, & M. Matthes (Eds.), *Improving the quality of childhood in the European Union: Current perspectives.* Brighton, UK: ECSWE. (www.ecswe.org/publications.php).

Matthes, M. (2012). Concluding chapter. Improving the quality of childhood: A learning process on the level of society. In C. Clouder, B., Heys, M., Matthes, M., & P. Sullivan (Eds.), *Improving the quality of childhood in Europe 2012* (pp. 199–219). Brighton, UK: ECSWE.

McAdams, D. P., & Pals, J. L. (2006). *American Psychologist, 61,* 204–217. doi:10.1037/0003-066X.61.3.204

Metsäpelto, R-L., & Pulkkinen, L. (2012). *Scandinavian Journal of Educational Research, 56,* 167–182. doi:10.1080/00313831.2011.581681

Metsäpelto, R.-L., Pulkkinen, L., & Tolvanen, A. (2010). *European Journal of Psychology of Education, 25,* 381–398. doi:10.1007/s10212-010-0034-5

Mischel, W. (1968). *Personality and assessment.* New York: Wiley.

Mussen, P., & Eisenberg-Berg, N. (1977). *Roots of caring, sharing, and helping: The development of prosocial behavior in children.* San Francisco: Freeman.

Mustanski, B. S., Viken, R., J., Kaprio, J., Pulkkinen, L., & Rose, R. J. (2004). *Developmental Psychology, 40,* 1188–1198. doi:10.1037/0012-1649.40.6.1188

Olson, W. C. (1949). *Child development.* Boston: D. C. Heath and Company.

Pagan, J. L., Rose, R. J., Viken, R. J., Pulkkinen, L., Kaprio, J., & Dick, D. M. (2006). *Behavior Genetics, 36,* 483–497. doi:10.1007/s10519-006-9062-y

Peterson, C., & Seligman, M. E. P. (2004). *Character strengths and virtues: A handbook and classification.* New York: Oxford University Press.

Pitkänen, L. (1963). *Scandinavian Journal of Psychology, 4,* 55–64. doi:10.1111/j.1467-9450.1963.tb01308.x

Pitkänen, L. (1969). *A descriptive model of aggression and nonaggression with applications to children's behaviour.* Jyväskylä, Finland: University of Jyväskylä. http://users.jyu.fi/~leapulkk/dissertation.html

Pitkänen, L. (1976). Finland. In V.S. Sexton & H. Misiak (Eds.), *Psychology around the world* (pp. 118–130). Monterey, CA: Brooks.

Pitkänen, T., Kokko, K., Lyyra, A.-L., & Pulkkinen, L. (2008). *Addiction, 103*(Suppl. 1), 48–68. doi:10.1111/j.1360-0443.2008.02176.x

Pitkänen, T., Lyyra, A-L., & Pulkkinen, L. (2005). *Addiction, 100,* 652–661. doi:10.1111/j.1360-0443.2005.01053.x

Pitkänen-Pulkkinen, L. (1977). Effects of simulation programmes on the development of self-control. In C.F.M. van Lieshout & D.J. Ingram (Eds.), *Stimulation of social development in school* (pp. 176–190). Amsterdam: Swets & Zeitlinger.

Pitkänen-Pulkkinen, L. (1980). The child in the family. *Nordisk Psykologi, 32,* 147–157.

Pitkänen-Pulkkinen, L. (1981a). *Aggressive Behavior, 7,* 97–110. doi:10.1002/1098-2337(1981)7:2<97::AID-AB2480070203>3.0.CO;2-1

Pitkänen-Pulkkinen, L. (1981b). Long-term studies on the characteristics of aggressive and non-aggressive juveniles. In P. F. Brain & D. Benton (Eds.), *Multidisciplinary approaches to aggression research* (pp. 225–243). Amsterdam: Elsevier/North-Holland Biomedical Press.

Pulkkinen, L. (1977). *Kotikasvatuksen psykologia.* [Psychology of upbringing.] Jyväskylä: Gummerus.

Pulkkinen, L. (1982). Self-control and continuity from childhood to adolescence. In B. P. Baltes & O.G. Brim, Jr. (Eds.), *Life-span development and behavior* (Vol. 4, pp. 63–105). Orlando, FL: Academic Press.

Pulkkinen, L. (1983). The search for alternatives to aggression. In A. P. Goldstein & M. Segall (Eds.), *Aggression in global perspective* (pp. 104–144). New York: Pergamon Press.

Pulkkinen, L. (1984). *Nuoret ja kotikasvatus.* [Youth and home environment.] Helsinki: Otava.

Pulkkinen, L. (1986). The role of impulse control in the development of antisocial and prosocial behavior. In D. Olweus, J. Block, & M. Radke-Yarrow (Eds.), *Development of antisocial and prosocial behavior: Theories, research, and issues* (pp. 149–175). New York: Academic Press.

Pulkkinen, L. (1987). *Aggressive Behavior, 13*, 197–212. doi:10.1002/1098-2337(1987)13:4<197::AID-AB2480130404>3.0.CO;2-E

Pulkkinen, L. (1995). *Child Development, 66*, 1660–1679. doi:10.2307/1131902

Pulkkinen, L. (1996a). *Journal of Personality and Social Psychology, 70*, 1288–1306. doi:10.1037/0022-3514.70.6.1288

Pulkkinen, L. (1996b). *Aggressive Behavior, 22*, 241–257. doi:10.1002/(SICI)1098-2337(1996)22:4<241::AID-AB1>3.0.CO;2-O

Pulkkinen, L. (2004). *European Psychologist, 9*, 125–141. doi:10.1027/1016-9040.9.3.125

Pulkkinen, L. (2006). In L. Pulkkinen, J. Kaprio, & R. J. Rose (Eds.), *Socioemotional development and health from adolescence to adulthood* (pp. 29–55). New York: Cambridge University Press. doi:10.1017/CBO9780511499784.004

Pulkkinen, L. (2009). *Scandinavian Journal of Psychology, 50*, 602–610. doi:10.1111/j.1467-9450.2009.00774.x

Pulkkinen, L. (2011). Family factors in the development of antisocial behavior. In T. Bliesener, A. Beelman, & M. Stemmler (Eds.), *Antisocial behavior and crime: Contributions of developmental and evaluation research to prevention and intervention* (pp. 89–108). Göttingen, Germany: Hogrefe.

Pulkkinen, L. (2012a). The Integrated School Day—improving the educational offering of schools in Finland. In C. Clouder, B., Heys, M., Matthes, M., & P. Sullivan (Eds.), *Improving the quality of childhood in Europe 2012* (pp. 41–65). Brighton, UK: ECSWE.

Pulkkinen, L. (2012b). Ten pillars of a good childhood: A Finnish perspective. *Childhood Education: Infancy through adolescence, 88*(5), 326–330.

Pulkkinen, L., & Caspi, A. (Eds.). (2002). *Paths to successful development: personality in the life course.* Cambridge, U.K.: Cambridge University Press. doi:10.2277/0521804833

Pulkkinen, L., Feldt, T., & Kokko, K. (2005). Personality in young adulthood and functioning in middle age. In S. Willis & M. Martin (Eds.), *Middle Adulthood: A lifespan perspective* (pp. 99–141). Thousand Oaks, CA: Sage.

Pulkkinen, L., Feldt, T., & Kokko, K. (2006). *Social Indicators Research, 77*, 171–195. doi:10.1007/s11205-005-5558-8

Pulkkinen, L., Heikkinen, A., Markkanen, T., & Ranta, M. (1977). *Näin ohjaan lastani: Lasten itsehallinnan harjoitusohjelma.* [Guiding my child: A program for developing self-control in children.] Jyväskylä: Gummerus.

Pulkkinen, L., Kaprio, J., & Rose, R.J. (1999). *Twin Research, 2*, 274–285. doi:10.1375/twin.2.4.274

Pulkkinen, L., Kaprio, J., & Rose, R. J. (Eds.). (2006). *Socioemotional development and health from adolescence to adulthood.* New York: Cambridge University Press. doi: 10.2277/0521846315

Pulkkinen, L., Kokko, K., & Rantanen, J. (2012). *Developmental Psychology, 48*, 1283–1241. doi: 10.1037/a0027463

Pulkkinen, L., & Launonen, L. (2005). *Eheytetty koulupäivä—lapsilähtöinen näkökulma koulupäivän uudistamiseen* [An integrated school day—a child-centered approach to the reform of a school day]. Helsinki: Edita.

Pulkkinen, L., Lyyra, A.-L., & Kokko, K. (2009). *Aggressive Behavior, 35*, 117–135. doi:10.1002/ab.20297

Pulkkinen, L., Lyyra, A-L., & Kokko, K. (2011). *International Journal of Behavioral Development, 35*, 475–481. doi:10.1177/0165025411422993

Pulkkinen, L., Nygren, H., & Kokko, K. (2002). *Journal of Adult Development, 9, 251–265.* doi:10.1023/A:1020234926608

Pulkkinen, L., Ohranen, M., & Tolvanen, A. (1999). *Journal of Vocational Behavior, 54*, 37–58. doi:10.1006/jvbe.1998.1653

Pulkkinen, L. & Pitkänen, T. (1993). *Aggressive Behavior, 19*, 249–263. doi:10.1002/1098-2337(1993)19:4<249::AID-AB2480190402>3.0.CO;2-I

Pulkkinen, L. & Pitkänen, T. (2010). Temperance and the strengths of personality: Evidence from a 35-year longitudinal study. In R. Schwarzer & P. A. Frensch (Eds.), *Personality, human development, and culture: International perspectives on psychological science* (Vol. 2, pp. 127–140). Hove, UK: Psychology Press.

Pulkkinen, L., & Tremblay, R. E. (1992). *International Journal of Behavioural Development, 15*, 527–553. doi:10.1177/01650254 9201500406

Pulkkinen, L., Vaalamo, I., Hietala, R., Kaprio, J., & Rose, R.J. (2003). *Twin Research, 6*, 106–118. doi:10.1375/twin.6.2.106

Rohracher, H. (1947). *Einführung in die Psychologie.* München: Psychologie-Verlag-Union.

Rönkä, A., & Pulkkinen, L. (1995). *Journal of Personality and Social Psychology, 69*, 381–391. doi:10.1037/0022-3514.69.2.381

Rose, R. J. (2004). *European Psychologist, 9*, 142–144. doi:10.1027/1016-9040.9.3.143

Rose, R. J. (2006). In L. Pulkkinen, J. Kaprio, & R. J. Rose (Eds.), *Socioemotional development and health from adolescence to adulthood* (pp. 1–25). New York: Cambridge University Press. doi:10.1017/CBO9780511499784.002

Rose, R. J., Dick, D. M., Viken, R. J., Pulkkinen, L., & Kaprio, J. (2001). *Alcoholism: Clinical & Experimental Research, 25*, 1594–1604. doi:10.1111/j.1530-0277.2001.tb02166.x

Rose, R. J., Viken, R. J., Dick, D. M., Bates, J., Pulkkinen, L., & Kaprio, J. (2003). *Psychological Science, 14*, 273–277. doi:10.1111/1529-1006.03434

Rothbart, M. K., & Derryberry, D. (1981). Development of individual differences in temperament. In M. E. Lamb & A. L. Brown (Eds.), *Advances in developmental psychology* (Vol. 1, pp. 37–86). Hillsdale, NJ: Erlbaum.

Rothbart, M. K., & Derryberry, D. (2002). Temperament in children. In C. Hofsten & L. Bäckman (Eds.), *Psychology at the turn of the millennium: Social, developmental, and clinical perspectives* (Vol. 2, pp. 17–35). Hove, UK: Psychology Press.

Seligman, M. E. P., & Csikszentmihalyi, M. (2000). *American Psychologist, 55*, 5–14. doi:10.1037/0003-066X.55.1.5

Takala, M., & Pitkänen, L. (1963). *Scandinavian Journal of Psychology, 4*, 115–122. doi:10.1111/j.1467-9450.1963.tb01315.x

Tremblay, R. E. (2000). *International Journal of Behavioral Development, 24*, 129–141. doi:10.1080/016502500383232

Vaalamo, I., Pulkkinen, L., Kinnunen, T., Kaprio, J., & Rose, R. J. (2002). *Journal of Pediatric Psychology, 27*, 245–257. doi:10.1093/jpepsy/27.3.245

Vierikko, E., Pulkkinen, L. & Rose, R. J. (2006). In L. Pulkkinen, J. Kaprio, & R. J. Rose (Eds.), *Socioemotional development and health from adolescence to adulthood* (pp. 176–196). New York: Cambridge University Press. doi:10.1017/CBO9780511499784.013

Viinikainen, J., Kokko, K., Pulkkinen, L., & Pehkonen, J. (2010). *Labour, 24*, 201–220. doi:10.1111/j.1467-9914.2010.00477.x

Vohs, K. D., & Baumeister, R. F. (2004). Understanding self-regulation: An introduction. In R. F. Baumeister & K. D. Vohs (Eds.), *Handbook of self-regulation: Research, theory, and application* (pp. 1–9). New York: Guilford Press.

Walder, L., Abelson, R., Eron, L., Banta, T., & Laulicht, J. (1961). *Psychological Reports, 9*, 497–556. doi:10.2466/pr0.1961.9.3.497

34

Lucking Out

A Career Shaped by Mentoring

JEAN E. RHODES

As a college freshman, I had the blind luck of enrolling in an introductory psychology course that was taught by the pioneering community psychologist, George Albee. It did not strike me as the least bit unusual that a world-renowned psychologist and former President of the American Psychological Association would staff this lowly course offering. Nor did I have the context to appreciate that Professor Albee's take on modern psychology was a radical departure from what was being taught in introductory courses across the country. Indeed, my first exposure to psychopathology was through the lens of social inequality, illuminating the pernicious effects on mental health of racism, sexism, homophobia, and poverty. Lectures on the Diagnostic and Statistical Manual of the American Psychiatric Association centered on its unreliability, and its intractable links with the economic interests of insurance companies. From Albee's vantage point, prevention—through political and social change—offered the only real hope of reducing the incidence of psychopathology. And the course mantra—"that no disorder has ever been treated out of existence"—rang from that lecture hall with a force that propelled George's students toward careers in public health, social policy, and community psychology.

My luck followed me back to my dorm, where I fell into a deep friendship with George's oldest daughter Marina, a young woman whose worldview and sardonic wit were unlike anything I had encountered in suburban New Jersey. I found myself magnetically drawn to Marina, George, and the entire cast of Albee characters, whose small farm overflowed with animals, exotic foods, and books, many books. By the time we were ready to graduate, Marina and I had moved onto the farm where, in exchange for room and board, I tended a flock of chickens.

George mixed his social commentary with irreverence and wit. He drove a checker cab, was frequently mistaken for Aleksandr Solzhenitsyn, and was known to rummage through grocery store trash bins in search of produce to feed his pigs. In other words, he was like no other professor at the University of Vermont. I took every course George had to offer and helped staff his annual Vermont Conference on the Primary Prevention of Psychopathology, anticipating each with the devotion equal to that of any Harry Potter fan.

I was drawn to George less for comfort than for his unrelenting commitment to social justice, his sense of humor, and his gently ironic approach to all things prosaic. But what really grabbed me, and has never let me go, was his belief in me. George seemed to hold the impression of me that, at my best, I hoped to convey. Over time, my sense of self shifted from a Jersey girl with modest ambition to someone who could and should try to make a difference in the world through community psychology. As an entering freshman, I had been surprised to learn that there existed non-medical "doctors." I had never heard of a PhD, much less met anyone who held such a degree. Within a few short years, I felt driven to obtain one.

George suggested that I pursue a degree in clinical-community psychology, a disciplinary alliance that still strikes me as somewhat paradoxical. Treating the victims of social injustice and stress, after all, does nothing to correct the basic causes. Indeed, George himself had written that, "Adherence to the medical model distracts attention from the social conditions that are far more important determinants of mental disturbance-and diverts resources from attempts to ameliorate these conditions" (Albee, 1986, p. 893). Even as I studied psychopathology in the clinical program at DePaul University, and learned to speak the language of psychiatry during three intensive years of psychodynamic training at the University of Chicago medical school, my commitment to social justice never wavered. Treating the casualties of Hyde Park's racial discrimination, poverty, and violence felt like trying to drain Lake Michigan with a cup.

As I was completing my degree, I was invited to join a lucrative private practice on Michigan Avenue. I did not feel the pull—a clinical route was never really an option.

George had written, in an article entitled "The Futility of Psychotherapy":

> Let us be clear that is it not sacrilegious, illegal or unconstitutional to choose a career as a psychotherapist in an affluent society. After facing the fact that doctoral level therapists serve primarily well-educated clients, that psychotherapy is rarely available to the poor, and is not much sought after by blue collar workers, the choice of the 'health profession' is no more blameworthy than the decision to become a dentist or a funeral director. . . . only when the findings of psychotherapists are translated into well formulated preventive actions to correct or change the social and economic structure will it have made a significant contribution to prevention.
>
> (Albee, 1990, p. 371)

So, in the fall of 1989, 10 years after taking that introductory psychology course, I began my academic career in the community/clinical psychology program at the University of Illinois, Champaign-Urbana (UIUC). Shaped by Ed Seidman and Julian Rappaport, it was an intellectually rich setting for community action and research. Rappaport's theory of empowerment, offered as alternative to preventing specific disorders, still shares much in common with the basic tenants of the field of positive youth development (PYD).

Early on in my independent research, I stumbled onto an intriguing and career-defining result. Chicago in the late 1980s had been swept into the worst crack epidemic in American history, and I had been exploring the strategies that impoverished youth were using to resist the overwhelming social and economic pressures to join the drug culture. Despite its allure, there remained some youth who kept a safe distance—their hearts and minds fixed on finishing high school and accomplishing more. Almost without exception, these so-called "resilient" youth had forged an important relationship with a caring nonparent adult. Sometimes this adult was an aunt or grandparent; in other cases it was coach, neighbor, or teacher. In all cases, this adult believed in and cared deeply about the youngster, who drew on the relationship to resist problems and achieve goals.

I had not set out with mentoring relationships as my academic field of specialty but, once discovered, the stage was set. As a community psychologist, I was taken in by the elegant logic of deploying volunteers to, in the words of psychologist George Miller, "give psychology away." And, as a clinical psychologist, my transference with George Albee was a vein that could be mined to the depths of the earth. I immersed in the literature on nonparent adults, beginning with the work of urban ethnographers. In their book *Growing Up Poor*, for example, sociologists Terry Williams and William Kornblum (1985, p. 108) described spending years on the streets with youth in poor New York City neighborhoods. They concluded that mentoring was a key difference between successful and unsuccessful teens. They wrote, "The probabilities that

teenagers will end up on the corner or in a stable job are conditioned by a great many features of life in their communities. Of these, we believe the most significant is the presence or absence of adult mentors." In *Tough Change*, sociologist Bernard Lefkowitz described supportive adults as a vital influence on at-risk youth:

> Again and again, I found that the same pattern was repeated: the kid who managed to climb out of the morass of poverty and social pathology was the kid who found somebody, usually in school, sometimes outside, who helped them invent a promising future.
>
> (1986, p. 107)

Yet I found that it was the field of developmental psychology that offered the strongest foundation for understanding the role of mentors in the lives of urban youth. Attachment researchers had identified the vital importance of caring connections, in infancy and beyond. Bowlby (1979, p. 103) wrote that humans seem "happiest and able to deploy their talents to best advantage when they are confident that, standing behind them, there are one or more trusted persons who will come to their aid should difficulties arise," and, although not the focus of their work, resilience scholars had made important observations about the role of caring adults in the lives of youth. Norman Garmezy (1985), for example, had observed that resilient children often had at least one significant adult. He reviewed the literature on children in war, looking at how boys and girls in Europe and Israel adapted. His studies pointed to non-family adults as prime factors in how children respond. Likewise, Michael Rutter (1979, p. 52) observed that vulnerable children with "one good relationship" were less prone to delinquency than others. The most ambitious of the "beating the odds" studies was Emmy Werner and Ruth Smith's (1982) 30-year survey of 500 children on the small Hawaiian Island of Kauai. Born into poverty, most were the children of sugar plantation workers in the rapidly declining sugar cane industry. Like the youth in Chicago, many grew up in fear of even greater poverty, struggling too through parental substance abuse. Children who became self-sufficient adults had had at least one adult—in addition to their parents—who provided guidance and support.

Although richly descriptive, this work did not seem to adequately explain *how* mentoring worked to protect youth, and why some adolescents were so much better able to attract and benefit from caring adult support than others. I wondered whether successful relationships with caring adults could simply be a proxy for healthy development. That is, youth with appealing dispositions and/or those who had enjoyed relatively strong relationships in the past may have been better equipped to elicit the support of nonparent adults and more willing to take healthy interpersonal risks within the relationships. From a community psychology perspective, the focus on this or any protective factors in isolation ran the risk of overlooking the larger social context in which mentoring relationships occur. An analysis of mentoring required a consideration not only of individual differences among youth but also of the family, community, and cultural circumstances that lead youth to mentoring relationships and help sustain them over time.

I thus launched a longitudinal research program aimed at understanding the role of natural mentoring relationships in the lives of urban adolescents. Working at a Chicago alternative school for pregnant and parenting teens, my students and I conducted a series of studies that explored the changing nature of relationships in vulnerable populations and their positive influence on a range of outcomes. These early studies delved into the role of the young mothers' attachment relationships in shaping subsequent mentoring relationships, and explored how mentors functioned within the broader social support network. Our findings suggested that mentors enhanced young women's capacity to elicit and appreciate the positive aspects of their social support networks and more effectively cope with relationship problems (Rhodes, Contreras, & Mangelsdorf, 1994; Rhodes, Ebert, & Fischer, 1992). This pattern was consistent with Patricia Hill Collins' observations concerning *othermothers*, who "often play a central role in defusing the emotional intensity between blood mothers and their daughters" (1987, p. 8). We also found that mentors helped youth achieve positive educational and vocational outcomes. (Klaw & Rhodes, 1995; Klaw, Rhodes, & Fitzgerald, 2003; Hellenga, Aber, & Rhodes, 2002).

Despite the promise of natural mentors, I was struck by the sheer number of teen mothers and other vulnerable youth who did not have networks of support, and had not readily found older adults to serve in that capacity. To help address the needs of such youth, volunteer mentoring programs, like Big Brothers Big Sisters, held particular promise. It seemed that, if those relationships could be understood and enhanced through clinical and developmental research, their full potential could be harnessed. Perhaps they could even be construed as an ecologically-valid alternative to psychotherapy.

A decade earlier, community psychologist Joseph Durlak had published an influential meta-analysis that showed that paraprofessionals could achieve clinical outcomes that were equal to or even better than those obtained by trained professionals. "In terms of measureable outcome," Durlak (1979, p. 80) had concluded that "professionals may not possess demonstrably superior clinical skills when compared with paraprofessionals. Moreover, professional mental health education, training, and experience do not appear to be necessary prerequisites for an effective helping person." I wondered whether this logic could be extended to mentors; with solid training, perhaps volunteer mentors could be as effective as paraprofessionals.

To gain a deeper knowledge of volunteer mentoring programs, I began to examine how, and under what circumstances, such relationships were most effective. This work led to collaborations, in the mid-1990s, with economist Jean Grossman and other researchers at the social policy organization, Public/Private Ventures (P/PV). Drawing on data that P/PV had collected as part of its large-scale, random assignment evaluation of Big Brother Big Sisters of America (Tierney, Grossman, & Resch, 1995), my students, colleagues, and I conducted a series of studies on the conditions under which assigned mentoring programs were most effective.

This work coincided with a growing public interest in mentoring programs. In fact, a remarkable two-thirds of all mentoring programs for teenagers in the United States had been launched in the mid-1980s through early 1990s, and public service campaigns were attracting ever-widening pool of volunteers. Former President, George W. Bush was touting mentoring in his speeches and recommending it for children whose parents were in prison, and his wife was promoting mentoring as an important way to combat illiteracy. Noteworthy mentoring initiatives for young people had been funded through the Office of Juvenile Justice and Delinquency Prevention (OJJDP), the Departments of Health and Human Services (HHS), Education (ED), and Labor, and the Corporation for National and Community Service. In response to the growing number of different federal agencies supporting youth mentoring, in 2003 the White House Task Force on Disadvantaged Youth called for the creation of a Federal Interagency Workgroup on Mentoring to coordinate all federally sponsored mentoring programs and activities. By 2004, HHS and ED were allocating a collective $100 million per year for mentoring programs to support children with parents in prison and to promote middle school students' academic outcomes, respectively (DuBois, Portillo, Rhodes, Silverthorn, & Valentine, 2011).

Momentum had come, as well, from shifts in the philosophical orientation of researchers and practitioners in the youth service sector, which was increasingly emphasizing the promotion of positive youth development as opposed to the prevention of specific disorders (Benson, Leffert, Scales, & Blyth, 1998; Eccles & Gootman, 2002; Lerner & Galambos, 1998; Larson, 2000). Within this context, mentoring seemed to hold a particularly strong appeal. It was easier to visualize than other approaches to youth service and, because it located the problem (a lack of role models) and solution (deployment of predominately middle-class volunteers) at the personal level, it fit neatly into American notions of upward mobility and the "pull-yourself-up-by-the-bootstraps" ideology (Walker, 2005). It is thus not surprising that BBBSA, the largest mentoring organization in the country, as well as other long-established organizations such as the Boys and Girls Clubs of America in which mentoring programs were often situated, were held as exemplars of a PYD model, conferring less-known programs with credibility and public support. Mentoring was playing a role as a gateway toward the public's expanding commitment to youth policies and programs and intuitions.

Despite my delight in the generous, bipartisan support of a social program for disadvantaged youth, I grew concerned with the rapid expansion of programs. Program administrators, working under the tacit assumption that mentoring programs were universally beneficial to youth (an assumption that was being countered in the research literature), were putting their limited resources into launching new matches rather than supporting existing ones.

As such, programs were being pressed to defer quality indicators in favor of growth. The cost of expanding the number of youth served was winning the battle in the competition with expenditures to enrich programs. And, in a climate of heightened pressure to show numbers, mentoring organizations were falling prey to trivializing what was at the very heart of their intervention: caring relationships. A "placeholder mentality" had emerged in some programs—a set of beliefs that the most important program goal is simply to get disadvantaged children off wait lists, that mentor–youth bonds are somewhat interchangeable and, more generally, that somehow if a relationship is formed through a program it does not adhere to the same set of rules as other close relationships (Rhodes, 2002).

Even more troubling, since volunteer recruitment was the rate-limiting factor in program growth, many programs were relaxing minimum volunteer screening, commitment, and training requirements. These trends reduced the burden that was placed on agencies and volunteers, but were at odds with the types of practices that my colleagues and I were finding were needed to establish and sustain high-quality mentoring relationships (see DuBois, Holloway, Valentine, & Cooper, 2002). Funding agencies were reinforcing this tendency, often using the number of new matches, as opposed to their sustainability, as the measure of program success. The only real danger associated with placing children in the care of unrelated adults, in the thinking of many agencies, was child molestation—a very troubling but comparatively infrequent occurrence. The disappointment and suffering of youth whose mentors failed them in more subtle ways going largely unattended. These children fade quietly from programs, and the troubled relationships they represent were completely overshadowed by the more compelling success stories of a subset of their peers (Rhodes & DuBois, 2006).

Yet, because a personal relationship is at the heart of mentoring interventions, inconsistencies, misunderstandings, and terminations can touch on youth's vulnerabilities in ways that other, less personal, approaches do not. To the extent that youth have identified with their mentors, and have begun to value the relationship, they could experience profound disappointment, rejection, and betrayal when problems arose. Such feelings, in turn, were thought to lead to a host of negative emotional, behavioral, and academic outcomes (Downey, Lebolt, Rincón, & Freitas, 1998). My contention, supported by research findings, is that vulnerable children would be better left alone than paired with volunteer mentors who do not recognize the responsibility they have been given. Thus, instead of adding another voice to the chorus of calls for more and bigger mentoring programs, I began advocating for a more measured approach

that built on research about the risks, as well as the rewards, of mentoring. It was clear to me that maintenance of minimum quality standards in the mentor–protégé relationships should be a primary concern, even at the expense of aggressive growth objectives.

Drawing on data from a national evaluation of BBBS (Tierney et al., 1995), Jean Grossman and I found that youth in prematurely terminating mentoring relationships showed increases in problem behaviors relative to randomly assigned control groups (Grossman & Rhodes, 2002). This finding was particularly concerning, given that as many as half of mentoring relationships in many mentoring programs were ending earlier than expected. Concerned with this trend, and wanting to reach a broader audience, I wrote a *New York Times* Op-Ed in which I described the lack of rigor in mentoring programs and the potential risks of early-terminated youth mentoring relationships. "Mentors." I argued, "must commit for the long haul; theirs can't be a half-hearted effort. And they need support from the programs that recruit them. The government, if it wants to push volunteer programs, must act in the same way. It must offer more than mere praise for volunteers. It must also commit for the long term and make sure these groups have the money they need to help their mentors succeed."

Within a week, the then-President and CEO of MENTOR: The National Mentoring Partnership, Gail Manza, was in my office, suggesting a partnership to enhance the quality of youth mentoring programs across the nation. Aligning practice and research in youth mentoring, she reasoned, would help improve the outcomes. Although critical of the uneven quality, I had not given up on mentoring programs and was eager to work with policy organizations to hold the field to a higher standard. Moreover, I was encouraged by the growing body of research that was providing an encouraging base of evidence for the benefits of high-quality mentoring relationships; nevertheless, the momentum for rapid expansion dominated the field of youth mentoring (e.g., Darling, Hamilton, Toyokawa, & Matsuda, 2002; DuBois et al., 2002; Spencer, 2005; DuBois & Karcher, 2005). Working with MENTOR, I felt better positioned to advocate for policies and quality programs that would give rise to transformative relationships.

In the late 1990s, my family moved to Boston, and I was fortunate enough to join the faculty of UMass Boston, a campus with both an urban undergraduate mission and a superb, social-justice-oriented graduate clinical psychology program. By 2002, I had written a book, *Stand by Me: The Risks and Rewards of Youth Mentoring*, in which I synthesized and made accessible the many studies that were emerging in the field, as a means of calling attention to the need for quality relationships and programs. Subsequent research and evaluation studies have continued to underscore the importance of relationship quality and endurance (Bernstein, Rappaport, Olsho, Hunt, & Levin, 2009;

Grossman, Chan, Schwartz, & Rhodes, in press; Herrera et al., 2007; Spencer, 2007)

Yet, because mentoring strikes deep emotional chords its constituents continue to look to our research and (typically modest) evaluation findings only to confirm what they intuitively hold to be true. Likewise, although research and evaluations tend to produce nuanced findings about the nature of the intergenerational relationships, practitioners value pure and simple findings that can be used directly for action. Consequently, the field of youth mentoring continues to have a public life of its own—a life that is, at times, removed from empirical and theoretical grounding. Despite expansive goals, there remains no clear road map for how to scale up this intervention approach in ways that provide all children with the high-quality mentoring relationships they deserve. Yet growth and quality are not necessarily incompatible. Bringing an intervention to scale while retaining fidelity is costly and challenging, but it can be done. Researchers are increasingly converging on a core set of practices in the field of youth mentoring that, when integrated into mentor training, can yield much larger effects (Kupersmidt & Rhodes, in press).

Along these lines, my colleagues and I recently used meta-analysis of 73 independent evaluations to take stock of the current evidence on the effectiveness of mentoring programs for youth (DuBois et al., 2011). Although the findings support the effectiveness of mentoring for improving outcomes across behavioral, social, emotional, and academic domains, gains were relatively modest (equivalent to a difference of 9 percentile points to scores of non-mentored youth on the same measures), comparable to those found more than a decade ago. Despite discernible improvements in our understanding of best practice, the inconsistent application of research-based approaches and the resulting variability in program effectiveness has attenuated mentoring effects. Importantly, the findings of this meta-analysis, as well as a growing body of peer-reviewed research, point toward particular practices that can dramatically raise (and in some cases double) the effects of mentoring. As we conclude, for investments in mentoring to yield optimal returns, there is a need for support to be directed toward several critical areas of concern: (1) ensuring adherence to practices (e.g., mentor screening and training) that both research and common sense dictate as essential elements of program quality; (2) facilitating the use of research to guide the development of the types of innovations that are likely to be required for substantial improvements in program effectiveness; and (3) fostering strong collaborations between practitioners and researchers in the design, implementation, evaluation, and ongoing refinement of interventions in ways that facilitate more measured and evidence-driven dissemination and growth within the field.

Concluding Thoughts

In retrospect, my career has been far more focused on individual relationships than anticipated. Despite initial ambivalence, I have come to appreciate my clinical training as instrumental to my understanding of youth mentoring. At the end of the day, youth mentoring is only a step or two removed from psychotherapy—an individualistic solution to income disparity, racism, or other disadvantage. Although there are limits to the clinical analogy, both mentoring and therapeutic relationships involve a human connection whose explicit goal is to foster the positive development of one of the partners. When positive change comes about in the protégé, it is often the result of an empathic bond with the therapist or mentor (Spencer & Rhodes, 2005). This does not, however, change the reality that we can never "treat disorders out of existence," that neither therapy nor mentoring can reach all the youth who need support (Albee, 2005, p. 38).

I sometimes worry that, rather than challenge the status quo, I have conspired with its supporters—powerful men and women who endorse a formulation that highlights individual frailty and redemption over structural impediments and change. Perhaps my research merely legitimizes mentoring as a substitute for a more equitable distribution of material resources or a concerted youth policy agenda. It may be pure rationalization, but I remain convinced that there are broader social and political implications to my work in this field. First, mentoring programs have provided an accessible context for growing numbers of American high-school and college students to perform public service and engage in a world that extends beyond their immediate family and friendship circles. Since early civic participation is the best predictor of lifelong commitment, mentoring can provide an important training ground for future volunteerism.

But, perhaps more importantly, I see benefits of connecting middle-class voters with at-risk youth. Mentoring provides a lens through which literally millions of middle-class adults have seen the ravages of poverty: decrepit schools with stressed teachers, unsafe neighborhoods, deteriorating housing, and other difficult circumstances. Although many Americans may already know that one in five children in our wealthy democracy live in poverty, this inequality somehow remains compartmentalized and largely ignored in our day-to-day lives. Yet, deeply connecting with one child in poverty through a mentoring relationship can illuminate its pernicious effects, potentially mobilizing more sustained authentic action. Support for a coordinated, public response to the out-of-school needs of school-aged youth is more likely to emerge when mentors see how their mentees' problems multiply during unsupervised hours. In doing so, mentoring programs are able to develop new constituencies' for PYD programs and policies. Mentors' negative stereotypes have also been challenged by the many sources of strength in low-income and minority neighborhoods. When middle-class mentors bear witness to caring that exists in families, religious institutions, and grassroots community organizations, and to the level of commitment that many low-income parents marshal in support of their children, it remains much more difficult to blame the victim.

Finally, there are the potential environmental benefits of mentoring. A growing number of environmentalists have suggested that, since each additional person puts new strains on the planet, smaller families could play an important role in slowing global warming. Although most adults are fiercely committed to their own children, only a small proportion connect in meaningful ways with young people outside their nuclear families (Scales, 2005). Limiting the size of families, while opening our hearts more fully to other people's children, would dramatically enrich the lives of countless young people while reducing our collective footprint (Weisman, 2007).

George remained my most important mentor until he passed away in 2006. As he got older, he would occasionally mail out cramped envelopes of his writings—a grab bag of scholarly articles, choice travelogues, recipes, and humor columns. Although impossible to limn a complex life from a single care package, it's worth a try. Just before his death in 2006, at the age of 86, he sent a collection of "odds and ends to show you that I keep busy" which contains an article in which he advises the mostly white, wealthy retirees of Longboat Key, Florida to visit London's Chinatown where "they will chop up half duck for you to take away for a midnight snack." Jammed beside a couple of humor columns, is an article on social justice that contains a personalized note enjoining me to "Keep up the struggle!" With the Marxist observation that "The ruling ideas of a society are those that support the ruling class" riffing in the background, George takes on everything from Protestants and Conservatives to patriarchs. He writes that, "I would love to see a coalition between psychology and the oppressed and exploited that would speak with one voice against the ruling elite who reject the idea of social equality."

Although cognitive neuroscientists currently rule the ideas of contemporary psychology, George reminds us that there is a more contextualized analysis of mental health—and that a just world is its own reward. Many of us still had work to share with George, stories to tell, and corny jokes to share. But his passions live on through his children and grandchildren, his students and grand-students. And, he will always be in our hearts, tapping our inner outrage, and reminding us to "Keep up the struggle!"

References

Albee, G. W. (1986). Toward a just society: Lessons from observations on the primary prevention of psychopathology. *American Psychologist, 41*(8), 891–897.

Albee, G. W. (1990). The futility of psychotherapy. In D. Cohen (Ed.), Challenging the therapeutic state: Critical perspectives on psychiatry and the mental health system [Special double issue]. *Mind and Behavior, 11*, 369–384.

Albee, G. W. (2005). Call to revolution in the prevention of emotional disorders. *Ethical Human Psychology and Psychiatry, 7*, 37–44.

Benson, P. L., Leffert, N., Scales, P. C., & Blyth, D. A. (1998). Beyond the 'village' rhetoric: Creating healthy communities for children and adolescents. *Applied Developmental Science, 2*(3), 138–159.

Bernstein, L., Rappaport, C. D., Olsho, L., Hunt, D., & Levin, M. (2009). *Impact evaluation of the U.S. Department of Education's Student Mentoring Program: Final report.* Washington, DC: U.S. Department of Education, Institute of Education Sciences, National Center for Education Evaluation and Regional Assistance. Retrieved from http://ies.ed.gov/ncee/pubs/20094047/pdf/20094047.pdf

Bowlby, J. (1979). *The making and breaking of affectional bonds.* New York: Brunner Routledge.

Collins, P. H. (1987). The meaning of motherhood in black culture and black mother/daughter relationships. *SAGE: A Scholarly Journal on Black Women, 4*, 3–10.

Darling, N., Hamilton, S. F., Toyokawa, T., & Matsuda, S. (2002). Naturally-occurring mentoring in Japan and the United States: Social roles and correlates. *American Journal of Community Psychology, 30*, 245–270.

Downey, G., Lebolt, A., Rincón, C., & Freitas, A. L. (1998). Rejection sensitivity and children's interpersonal difficulties. *Child Development, 69*, 1074–1091.

DuBois, D. L., Holloway, B. E., Valentine, J. C., & Cooper, H. (2002). Effectiveness of mentoring programs for youth: A meta-analytic review. *American Journal of Community Psychology, 30*, 157–197.

DuBois, D. L., & Karcher, M. J. (Eds.). (2005). *Handbook of youth mentoring.* Thousand Oaks, CA: Sage.

DuBois, D. L., Portillo, N., Rhodes, J. E., Silverthorn, N., & Valentine, J. C. (2011). How effective are mentoring programs for youth? A systematic assessment of the evidence. *Psychological Science in the Public Interest, 12*, 57–91.

Durlak, J. (1979). Comparative effectiveness of paraprofessional and professional helpers. *Psychological Bulletin, 86*, 80–92.

Eccles, J., & Gootman, J. A. (2002). *Community programs to promote youth development.* Washington, DC: National Academies Press.

Garmezy, N. (1985). The NIMH-Israeli high-risk study: Commendation, comments, and cautions. *Schizophrenia Bulletin, 11*, 349–353.

Grossman, J. B., Chan, C., Schwartz, S., & Rhodes, J. E. (In press). The test of time in school-based mentoring: The role of relationship duration and re-matching on academic outcomes. *American Journal of Community Psychology.*

Grossman, J. B., & Rhodes, J. E. (2002). The test of time: Predictors and effects of duration in youth mentoring programs. *American Journal of Community Psychology, 30*, 199–206.

Hellenga, K., Aber, M. S., & Rhodes, J. E. (2002). African American adolescent mothers' vocational aspiration-expectation gap: Individual, social, and environmental influences. *Psychology of Women Quarterly, 26*, 200–212.

Herrera, C., Grossman, J. B., Kauh, T. J., Feldman, A. F., McMaken, J., & Jucovy, L. Z. (2007). *Making a difference in schools: The Big Brothers Big Sisters school-based mentoring impact study.* Public/Private Ventures. Retrieved from http://www.ppv.org/ppv/publications/assets/220_publication.pdf

Klaw, E., & Rhodes, J. E. (1995). Natural mentors and the career activities on urban youth. *Psychology of Women Quarterly, 19*, 551–562.

Klaw, E. L., Rhodes, J. E., & Fitzgerald, L. F. (2003). Natural mentors in the lives of African-American adolescent mentors: Tracking relationships over time. *Journal of Youth and Adolescence, 32*, 223–232.

Kupersmidt, J., & Rhodes, J. (In press). Mentor training and support. In D. L. DuBois & M. Karcher (Eds.) *Handbook of youth mentoring* (2nd ed.). CA, Thousand Oaks, CA: Sage Publication.

Larson, R. (2000). Toward a psychology of positive youth development. *American Psychologist, 55*(1), 170–183.

Lefkowitz, B. (1986). *Tough change: Growing up on your own in America.* New York: Free Press.

Lerner, R. M., & Galambos, N. L. (1998). Adolescent development: Challenges and opportunities for research, programs, and policies. *Annual Review of Psychology, 49*, 413–446.

Rhodes, J. E. (2002). *Stand by me: The risks and rewards of mentoring today's youth*. Cambridge, MA: Harvard University Press.

Rhodes, J. E., Contreras, J. M., & Mangelsdorf, S. C. (1994). Natural mentor relationships among Latina adolescent mothers: Psychological adjustment, moderating processes, and the role of early parental acceptance. *American Journal of Community Psychology, 22*, 211–228.

Rhodes, J. E., & DuBois, D. (2006). Understanding and facilitating the youth mentoring movement. *Social Policy Report, XX*, 3–19.

Rhodes, J. E., Ebert, L., & Fischer, K. (1992). Natural mentors: An overlooked resource in the social networks of adolescent mothers. *American Journal of Community Psychology, 20*, 445–461.

Rutter, M. (1979). Protective factors in children's responses to stress and disadvantage. In M. W. Kent & J. E. Rolf (Eds.), *Primary prevention in psychopathology: Social competence in children* (pp. 49–74). Hanover, NH: University Press of New England.

Scales, P. C. (2005). Developmental assets and the middle school counselor. *American School Counselor Association, 9*(2), 104–111.

Spencer, R. (2007). "It's not what I expected": A qualitative study of youth mentoring relationship failures. *Journal of Adolescent Research, 22*(4), 331–354.

Spencer, R., & Rhodes, J. E. (2005). A counseling and psychotherapy perspective on youth mentoring. In D. L. DuBois & M. A. Karcher (Eds.), *Handbook of youth mentoring*. Thousand Oaks, CA: Sage.

Tierney, J. P., Grossman, J. B., & Resch, N. L. (1995). *Making a difference. An impact study of Big Brothers Big Sisters*. Philadelphia: Public/Private Ventures.

Walker, G. (2005). Youth mentoring and public policy. In D. L. DuBois & M. L. Karcher (Eds.), *Handbook of youth mentoring* (pp. 510–524). Thousand Oaks, CA: Sage.

Weisman, A. (2007). *The world without us*. New York: St. Martin's Press.

Werner, E. E., & Smith, S. (1982). *Vulnerable but invincible: A study of resilient children*. New York: McGraw Hill.

Willams, T. M., & Kornblum, W. (1985). *Growing up poor*. Lexington, MA: Lexington Books.

35

Growing Up in South Africa

Science, Politics, and Policy

LINDA M. RICHTER

Introduction

"Just a little girl from Welkom" was how my partner, Pat, described me over and over again when we got back home to South Africa, as he proudly recounted watching me deliver the first ever plenary paper on children to more than 20,000 delegates at the XVI International AIDS Conference in Mexico City in 2008 (Richter, 2008). While I was growing up, Welkom was a small frontier mining town whose hastily established primary schools added a grade each year to accommodate children as we progressed from the prior class, sometimes in the same room with children from one or more lower grades. My father was the shaft-sinker for one of the new gold mines and we lived in a settler community—much like Kimberley and Johannesburg were when they started at the beginning of the 20th century, but on a very much smaller scale—erected to extract from the ground some of the enormous mineral wealth found in this part of the world.

My paper at the 2008 Mexico AIDS Conference was heralded for bringing a much-needed new perspective to a field that had, until then, understood the challenges and fashioned international efforts largely in response to the grief and suffering of children whose parents had died from what is now a treatable disease. But this approach neglected the pre-existing and continuing backdrop to the HIV epidemic in the region. Besides the social injustice and misery that can result from corrupt governments and an unrestrained pharmaceutical market governed only by patents and profits, I drew attention to the pervasive, deep-rooted poverty of southern Africa, the region worst affected by HIV and AIDS, and the way in which destitution could grind the heart out of family commitment and parenting, and leave children unprotected and vulnerable to exploitation, loss of potential, and untold suffering. *AIDS orphans*, more accurately children who had lost one or more parents

presumptively to AIDS, were seldom worse off than their peers whose parents were alive. Some parents in southern Africa are separated from each other and their children for much of the year by hundreds of miles in their quest for any migrant work no matter how low paid; others are so poor that both hunger and shame pushes them to local drug use and alcohol, bringing on paralyzing demoralization or making them brutish and even cruel to their children (Wilson & Ramphele, 1989). Most so-called orphans have a surviving parent, usually their mother, and, those children who have lost both parents, live with close family and kin (Richter et al., 2009).. These families are vulnerable as a result of experiencing the illness and death of a parent, becoming impoverished in their efforts to pay for health care, and losing the income or livelihood of a breadwinner, with the uncertain prospect of infection and death of a surviving parent.

I argued that the solution lay not in trying to replace families by adopting children into the West or committing them to orphanages in their own villages and towns, or by ineffectually trying to offer Western models of play therapy or psychological counseling to the burgeoning numbers of affected children, but that a sustainable set of strategies had to be built on supporting extended families, who continued to try and protect the children of kin no matter how little there was to share. Vulnerable families include single mothers (many whose male partners died as a result of on-going wars and interpersonal violence, as well as the devastating effects of AIDS), as well as grandparents, adolescents and men left to raise children on their own (Richter, 2012). Supporting vulnerable families includes addressing their acute economic needs through a set of social welfare instruments, including social cash transfers (Richter, 2010a). Economic support needs to be supplemented by family-centered services for children affected by HIV and AIDS (Richter, 2010b).

It was a bold call, but two things made it easier. First, my husband of 25 years had died after a long illness, and I felt invulnerable, particularly to criticism. I felt as if nothing could hurt me as much. Second, it was a set of arguments I had honed in interaction with some of the most eminent thinkers on the topic through the Joint Learning Initiative on Children and AIDS (JLICA) (Bell & Binagwaho, 2006; Richter & Sherr, 2009). From 2007 to 2009, Jim Yong Kim, recently appointed head of the World Bank, Alex de Waal, who wrote about AIDS as a new variant of famine (de Waal & Whiteside, 2003), Agnes Binagwaho, now Minister of Health in Rwanda, Geoff Foster, Order of the British Empire for his pediatric work amongst children in Zimbabwe, myself, and others argued on how best to drive forward concerted and consensual action to address the critical situation of children affected by poverty and HIV/AIDS. It was an exciting process and I imagined it, quite humbly, as a little like participating in the meetings at the World Health Organization (WHO) following the world wars in Europe that I had researched while preparing a review for WHO on the importance of caregiver–child interactions for the survival and healthy development of young children (2004a). In response to the widespread dislocation and concern about the mental health of children orphaned, separated from their families or in institutional care, the Social Commission of the United Nations in 1948 authorized a study. Ronald Hargreaves employed John Bowlby at the WHO on a 6-month contract to review the evidence and interview people in the United States and Europe. WHO published Bowlby's monograph *Maternal Care and Mental Health* in 1951 and it was translated into 14 languages. Hargreaves maintained the momentum and, between 1951 and 1953, organized four meetings of the world's leading scholars in child development and related topics. Among those who attended these meetings were Jean Piaget, Margaret Mead, John Bowlby, Erik Erikson, Julian Huxley, Bärbel Inhelder, Konrad Lorenz, and Ludwig van Bertalanffy! WHO also commissioned Mary Ainsworth to take a re-look at Bowlby's work, published as *Deprivation of Maternal Care: A Reassessment of its Effects* (Ainsworth et al., 1962). Discovering these meetings and documents in the WHO library in Geneva was hugely influential in articulating the relationship between science and policy in my own career.

These recollections introduce several themes that are braided through my personal and professional life. My partner was referring to the fact that I "had come a long way." This has both figurative and literal connotations. This chapter describes part of the journey on the way. Figuratively, though, I go "a long way back," being a 6th-generation South African of mixed German, Polish, and English descent. My indignation at injustice and the courage to speak out was cooked in Eastern Europe and the cauldron of South Africa as many of us have experienced it, as well as the personal legacy I received from my parents and the people who influenced me along the way. Most importantly, it manifests in my continuing commitment not to separate my scholarly work from its consequential applications or praxis.

South Africa

I am rooted in South Africa, a country about which one can be as frustratingly ambivalent as I imagine feeling towards an addictive drug. Except for a post-doctoral fellowship in England and relatively short periods at Oxford, Harvard, and Melbourne Universities and at the Global Fund to Fight AIDS, Tuberculosis, and Malaria in Geneva, I live in South Africa as do all my children. I am White, female, and middle-class, and no outsider can imagine how complicated those descriptors can be and how perplexing they are to experience. An anecdote may help.

I grew up during *Apartheid*, when Black people were systematically excluded and oppressed through a vicious system of structural violence. Their land was taken from them, and their families were torn apart by taxes which forced men to work in the mines for cash income, at the same time preventing them from making their homes in town, and forcing them to leave wives and children in destitute rural areas but for a week or two of Christmas leave. We had servants. A gardener came after his morning shift underground ended. A maid lived in one room in our back garden. My parents allowed Martha and her husband to live together, against the law. This meant my tiny mother had to rush outside when the police regularly "raided" domestic premises late at night to "catch" couples together and come up with some excuse why the police couldn't enter our property. But my mother was also fluent in Xhosa and Zulu, having grown up in the Eastern Cape and worked in a rural magistrate's court. Every day I'd arrive home from school in the late afternoon to find my mother sitting at the dining-room table, with a mineworker respectfully on his haunches at her side, and a queue of four or five men waiting their turn. Most being illiterate, they came to ask her to write to their families and, when a reply came—written by a White woman very much like my mother at a trading store in some rural part of the Transkei—to read it to them. In retrospect, I giggle at the anomalies: Often my mom would argue with the man about some family matter, telling him he couldn't take his daughter out of school or threaten to beat his wife. And I imagine her similarly interfering in family affairs when letters came to be read!

I wanted, variously, to be a doctor, politician, and a gardener. I fiercely wanted to change things so they were less cruel for people, like Martha and Joseph, whom we loved and whose children we never met. Because of the restrictions of the *Apartheid* regime, their children lived in Lesotho with their granny and saw their parents only once a year. I also wanted to work in the garden, as my mother often did, because it is a quiet and reassuring occupation and South Africa is beautiful, abundant, and exotic.

From Schizophrenia to Early Child Development and Culture

Mid-way through my clinical psychology PhD in 1979, using a classical information-processing paradigm to study over- and under-inclusive cognitive functioning in acute schizophrenics, Colwyn Trevarthen, now Emeritus Professor of Child Psychology and Psychobiology at the University of Edinburgh, broke the academic boycott of South Africa and visited the University of Natal on a lecture tour. He showed me videotapes collected and discussed by the pediatrician Berry Brazelton, ethologist Martin Richards, anthropologist Gregory Bateson, and others at a summer school in 1967 at Harvard's Center for Cognitive Studies set up by Jerome Bruner. The videos showed the communicative capabilities of very young babies and of the exquisitely synchronized emotionally based interaction that takes place between a loving parent and a healthy child. I was completely entranced by the idea of "the amazing baby"—a term fondly associated with Colwyn's inspirational lectures on intersubjectivity and cooperation between adults and infants, and immediately made arrangements for a post-doctoral fellowship in the United Kingdom (Richter, 2004b).

When I returned home to South Africa after more than a year at Edinburgh University and, because of my continued "applied" bent, also with John and Elizabeth Newson at the University of Nottingham,[1] I set up a quasi-longitudinal study of communication between African mothers and their healthy babies covering the first year of life. What I captured and transcribed convinced me that unfolding human capacities in early development, and the generic parental responses to them, are universal at the level of what might think of as "deep structure" and, under most circumstances, perfectly matched to each other (Richter, 1995). As the Papoušeks (2002) described, the developing communicative, cognitive, and motor capacities of young children—themselves predictable within the normal range—stimulate what Trevarthen (1987) called a "syllabus" of broadly intuitive parental responses from engaged and loving caregivers, involving emotional attunement, increasingly elaborated language, social referencing, scaffolding and guidance, as well as containment and control of impulsive affect and behavior.

The notion that mother–infant interactions were universal in their general form, challenged the conclusion of the venerable anthropologist, Robert LeVine, on the basis of his study amongst the Gusii in Kenya (1990), that "mother-infant conversation is a population-specific pattern and is particularly rare among non-Western agricultural societies" (p. 108). I was confused by this statement. How could one of the mechanisms that was being proposed for the mental development of young children, for language and shared awareness, be thought to be rare among a particular cultural group of people? Of course, there are cultural differences between the ways in which African and American mothers interact with their children, just as there are differences between American and Japanese or French mothers and children. But these are differences of form, not fundamental structure or function. African mothers, for example, tend to touch their babies more frequently, especially on the face; Japanese mothers are reported to try and calm their babies

down more than American mothers and mothers in the UK, who often "hype" their babies up (Bornstein, 1989). While caregiving activities and values are strongly influenced by the social and cultural context, I hold that parental behavior with a young baby is primarily driven by common parental emotional states in response to characteristic infant signals (Dix, 1991).

I also realized that little attention had been given in this field to the problems of observing the behavior of people from a culture different from one's own, in comparison, for example, to extensive discussions regarding assessments of cognitive functioning among older children and adults. As Susan Goldberg (1977) articulated them, we need to understand how mothers from different cultural groups understand the context and intention of observational studies of their interactions with their babies; what they imagine the investigators are looking at; how best do they think they should behave; what are their conventions regarding public behavior, especially in the presence of men; and what influences how they describe and explain their behavior to "outsiders." We also need to reflect on why we think as we do, why differences versus similarities become figure or ground, and what the consequences of each perspective are.

Awareness of these distinctions, between "cultures of science" and the "cultures of people," and difference versus similarities being figure or ground stay with me and resurface periodically in my work. My policy-related activities have been driven by the conviction that, provided they are not mentally ill or abusing substances, all parents, even the poorest, want the same things for their children that I want for mine—survival, safety, friends and acceptance, achievements. The fact of resilience, that children from the most wretched circumstances do survive and thrive is testimony to the knowledge, skills, and resources in children, parents, families and communities (Richter, 1999).

Malnutrition, Maternal Depression, and the Promotion of Early Development

While I was observing children's early development in interaction with their intimate caregivers, for three decades my husband Dev Griesel and his colleagues had been studying rat models of protein-calorie malnutrition, testing etiological pathways, potential mechanisms, and rehabilitation (Cowley & Griesel, 1962). Dev often spoke about a design conundrum in their work—whatever method was used to malnourish rat pups, whether by limiting the nutrition of their mothers or restricting the amount that pups could feed, dams compensated for pup's undernutrition by increasing suckling, grooming, and retrieval of their pups. The impact of undernutrition on pup outcomes was confounded by maternal care. In the same way, reviews of studies of the impact of malnutrition on children generally conclude that the outcome depends to a large extent on the quality of the subsequent environment, and that deprived environments exacerbate the effects.

In addition, the rat work demonstrated that the effects of malnutrition are not limited to cognitive deficits, but impact also socio-emotional reactivity and behavior (Grantham-McGregor, 1995).

I interpreted these findings to mean that malnutrition affected children's development directly via altered physiology in response to nutritional deficiency, and also indirectly, through the quality of maternal compensatory behavior to support children's resilience to deprivation, as well as children's catch-up and recovery. At the time though, there had been no studies of how mothers feel and behave when their children are malnourished. I began to collect videotapes of mothers with their malnourished children under the same conditions I had used before—semi-naturalistic laboratory recording with two cameras, one behind the mother and one behind the child, which, when mixed, "opened" their interaction to detailed coding and analysis. The majority of mothers were inappropriate and intrusive with fractious children, resulting in disjointed, stilted communication. I couldn't understand why they looked so different from the "normal" mothers I filmed before. During a visit to the United Kingdom, I showed the videotapes to Lynn Murray at the University of Reading, who had worked with Colwyn Trevarthen at the same time as I did. She was studying postnatal depression at the time and immediately said that the mothers of malnourished children acted exactly like depressed mothers. Like us, Lynn and collaborators in South Africa subsequently found very high rates (39%) of postnatal depression among African women living in urban areas (Cooper et al., 1999).

I returned home from my visit with Lynn and together with students, undertook several studies to pursue the connection between infant malnutrition and maternal depression. In the first study, we found that 40% of women who lodged in hospital with their malnourished infants, reported feelings indicative of demoralization, preoccupation and depression (Richter & Mphelo, 1992). What we saw matched what Polansky and his colleagues (1972), working amongst poverty-stricken families in the Appalachians, called "an apathy–futility syndrome," strongly associated with emotional withdrawal from their children and subsequent neglect (Richter, 1993). At much the same time, several papers from other parts of the world were published, also reporting high rates of maternal depression associated with malnutrition (Salt, Galler, & Ramsey, 1988).

In a second study we examined the effect of attachment status of infants who were between 9 and 12 months of age at the time of admission to the hospital on catch-up growth measured around 2 years of age. During the 18 months follow-up period, securely attached children showed nearly twice the amount of catch-up growth as anxiously attached children, despite comparable initial weights at the time of admission (Richter, Bac, & Hay, 1990). We concluded that in order to promote children's development in the majority world where poverty, malnutrition, and AIDS affect large numbers, we needed to address the factors that affected parental emotional and motivational states, rendering them less sensitive and responsive to young children. Over the next two decades, work on the epidemiology and impact of postnatal depression burgeoned leading to its recognition as a global health and mental health threat to women and children (Wachs, Black, & Engle, 2009). The important of maternal well-being and its effects on care and the nutrition of children is also now widely recognized (Engle, Lhotska, & Armstrong et al., 1997).

As a result of these studies, I began to work closely with international organizations, the World Health Organization (WHO) and Karsten Hundeide from International Child Development Programmes (ICDP) in Norway, on feasible programs to promote caring relationships between parents and children. With experience gained in South Africa training health care staff and in Angola during the war working with relief volunteers, I began to collaborate with the WHO on ways to integrate psychosocial care into the health agenda and into services for children in developing countries. It is gratifying that some 20 years later WHO and UNICEF have produced a program, with guidelines and training manuals, for integration into the Integrated Management of Childhood Illness (IMCI), the syndromic treatment approach in low- and middle-income countries. Care for Child Development (CCD), the result of the work of many people, most especially Patrice Engle, incorporates the promotion of communication and playful learning into all encounters between health workers and mothers of young children, both during sick- and well-baby visits.[2]

What critically accelerated the development of CCD and other initiatives to raise awareness about and promote the development of young children in poor countries, was the formation of an International Child Development Steering Group. Together the group, of which I am a member, amassed evidence and reviewed data to produce several high-profile publications, including two special series in The Lancet on the loss of human potential as a result of poverty and childhood undernutrition and on effective interventions and strategies (Engle et al., 2007; Engle et al., 2011; Grantham-McGregor et al., 2007; Walker et al., 2011). What has also boosted interest in this field is the mounting scientific evidence on the long-term health and human capital outcomes of early development, including data from birth cohort studies.

Children, Youth, and Families—Birth to Twenty Plus

I've been tempted down too many rabbit holes to feel that I have achieved as much in my professional life as I could have. Apart from early child development, nutrition, and HIV, I've done studies on such different topics such as children who live on the street, palliative care for children, child abuse, men and fatherhood, and youth empowerment.

Two things drew me into these fields. The first was the policy and programmatic pull: The work was important, it could assist vulnerable people, actions needed to be taken, and there was the prospect to influence. The second was the opportunity to work with people in disciplines other than my own—neuropsychology, anthropology, epidemiology, demography, and economics. The boundary space always seemed more interesting to me than psychology on its own. So much so, that when the South African National Research Foundation conferred a top scientific rating on me, it was in the field of Health Sciences rather than Psychology.

There is one exception to the diversions in my career. I have been part of, and led, Birth to Twenty Plus (Bt20+), a birth cohort study of children in Soweto-Johannesburg, for 24 years.[3] It is now the largest and longest running birth cohort study in Africa and one of five such cohorts in low- and middle-income countries.

In 1989, Derek Yach, at the time an epidemiologist with the South African Medical Research Council (MRC), and Noel Cameron, an auxologist at the University of the Witwatersrand, asked me if I was interested in joining a multidisciplinary birth cohort study planned to begin in 1990. The rationale was that South Africa was entering several significant transitions that would have profound effects on child health, and that we should track them. The first was a demographic transition as infant mortality dropped and life expectancy increased; the second a nutritional transition as urbanization speeded up and, third, a social transition with the emergence of a free and democratic South African society. We planned to follow the birth cohort to 10 years and called the study Birth to Ten (Bt10).

I sprang at the opportunity and sketched out a biopsychosocial ecological model of child health and development, based on Bronbrenner's ideas (1977) to guide our start-up data collection. The study had all the elements that intrigue me—a big picture set of goals, over-ambitious in implementation, requiring minutely detailed methodologies, and presenting opportunities to learn about child and family development in unique ways (Yach et al., 1991). With start-up funds from the MRC, we began pilot studies to address the feasibility of what one South African epidemiologist at the time called "the biggest waste of time and money' he had ever heard of!

Working closely with the city's health department, we examined the number, type, and location of deliveries we could expect per annum in the demarcated geographical area; the seasonality of births; the accuracy of routinely collected delivery and administrative data; how miscarriages, still births, and neonatal deaths were managed and recorded, and the feasibility of following up women and babies 6–12 months after giving birth (Fonn et al., 1991). With this data we were forced to make a decision with long-reaching consequences. There was a marked racial division of birthing services reflective of South Africa's distorted social and political policies. Except for emergencies, all women in Soweto-Johannesburg delivered their babies in a health facility. But almost all White women[4] received antenatal and obstetrical services in the private sector while Black and so-called Colored women delivered their babies in public clinics and hospitals. Moreover, as indexed by Caesarean deliveries, there was marked over- and under-servicing in the private and public sectors, with a very high rate of White women having elective Caesarean sections, and corresponding under-servicing among Black women (Matshidze, Richter, Ellison, Levin, & Mcintyre, 1998).

As we didn't have the resources to liaise with tens of obstetricians and ensure our presence at the delivery of every woman in the private sector, we worried about the biasing effect on our enrolment. I visited Dr. Jean Golding, leader of the Avon Longitudinal Study of Parents and Children (ALSPAC),[5] which was starting up at much the same time as Bt10, and Sir Michael Rutter at the Institute of Psychiatry, King's College, London, to get their counsel. Both suggested that the most interesting findings from a birth cohort study in South Africa would be variations among the majority Black sample, rather than systematic comparisons between Black and White children because most differences found would likely be explained by socioeconomic factors. This is the approach we adopted, but with staggered enrolment from pregnancy to 6 months of age, our under-enrolment of White children and families was not as low as we feared. Nonetheless, at age 5 years, the group investigating bone density received funding to supplement the White sample and enrolled children now living in Soweto-Johannesburg who were born elsewhere between the same dates as Bt10, April 23 to June 8, 1990.

Our dates for enrollment were set and we carefully calculated the window in which we needed to enroll pregnant women in their third trimester in order for their baby to be born within the enrollment period. But South Africa was in tumult in 1990. The forces opposing *Apartheid* had momentum, civil disobedience against the government and oppressive laws was widespread, and political factions within Black society were contending for power. Soweto was at the heart of the struggle, riots were common, and army tanks daily rolled through Soweto in a bid to exercise control. With antenatal enrolment underway, Baragwanath Hospital,[6] the largest site for deliveries, experienced a 6-week paralyzing workers' strike, which led to a major misalignment of our antenatal and delivery data. Only 60% of women who we saw during pregnancy delivered their babies during the birth enrolment period (Richter et al., 1995).

Tragically, violence has remained an integral part of the lives of families in Soweto-Johannesburg. Political violence morphed into criminal violence and, in comparison with their pregnancy in 1989/1990, more mothers reported in 2001, when their children were 11 years old, that they or a household member were in real danger of being killed, were a victim of a violent crime, or had witnessed a violent crime (Barbarin, Richter, de Wet, & Wachtel, 1998). In our last round of data collection, when participants were 18–19 years old, the theme of violence endures with nearly a fifth of young people reporting having been a victim of crime.

We enrolled 3,273 families in 1990 and have maintained some 2,300 over a 24-year period, through almost yearly and, more recently, twice yearly data collection waves. We've put a lot of effort into retaining participants and our major losses occurred in the first 4 years of life (Norris, Richter, & Fleetwood, 2007), when urban children are often sent to be looked after by grannies and aunts in their rural home (Hill, Hosegood, & Newell, 2008). Retention of participants is now threatened as young people finish school, find work or leave home, making it harder to keep in touch. To remain in contact, in 2007–08, we issued all young people in the cohort with mobile phones, with the intention of delivering digital questionnaires (van Heerden, Norris, & Richter, 2010). This has proved more challenging than we thought it would be. Mobile phones are an integral part of the social world of young people. Some complete a questionnaire several times, perhaps because it's something to do or someone to communicate with, others send the questionnaires on to friends who are not part of the study but who nonetheless submit their responses.

The study covers biological, social, psychological, and economic issues, and we began Bt10 with a team of some 30 scientists. However, leadership in collaborative projects is critical and, by 1998 the study was floundering because everyone wanted "their" data, but no one took responsibility for resourcing core activities. I took the lead in 2000 and, together with my colleague, Shane Norris, have shaped the last decade and a half of the study. We changed our name to Birth to Twenty (Bt20) as we extended our time horizon. Shane and I share interests, his in obesity and mine in sexual and reproductive health. Puberty, and the transition from junior to senior school, is the fulcrum around which we see physical growth, self-esteem, and social position coming together with consequences for young people's health and wellbeing. We try and approach topics jointly, bringing physiology and psychology together. I am interested in adolescent smoking, and Shane added blood cotinine measures to self-reports (Richter, 2006). Shane is interested in obesity, and I added measures of body image to anthropometry.

It's been a fascinating scientific and personal journey, with my own son only 3 years older than the Bt20 sample. My interests have grown through the study—through infancy, early and middle childhood, to adolescence, young adulthood, and now parenting. In 2012, we embarked on Birth to Twenty Plus (Bt20+), the third major phase of the study, with the enrolment of more than 500 children born to our birth cohort and a follow-up study of chronic disease profiles among the mothers of the Bt20 cohort, who are now reaching middle-age. Both technology and ideas drive science, and our new measures make what we did in the 1990s seem quaint. Now we measure fetal growth during pregnancy using a Pea Pod, and measure neuropsychological development not only with psychometric tests but also Near Infrared Spectroscopy. As the social world has changed, and fathers are seen as an integral influence on children's development, we are attempting to enroll not only young Bt20 women who become pregnant but we also encourage young Bt20 men to enroll their non-Bt20 co-parents.

The long-term data is only now coming in to its own; it has taken much longer than we thought it would. I commonly joke that if you measure something once, you have a fact, but if you measure it six times you have confusion! But we have started to harvest the rewards of long term commitment as we explore relationships between birth weight, maternal stress or depression, blood lead levels at birth or early growth, and later educational achievement, behavioral problems, pubertal timing, or body mass index (Barbarin & Richter, 2001; Naicker, Norris, Mathee, Bekker, & Richter, 2010; Ramchandani, Richter, Norris, & Stein, 2010). A research network with the four other large, long-term cohorts in low- and middle-income countries[7] has also enabled us to reach a new level of scientific analysis. The Consortium of Health Oriented Research in Transitioning Societies (COHORTS) was formed in 2007 when Cesar Victora, now President of the International Epidemiological Society, brought together the principal investigators from the five cohorts to prepare a paper on the long-term effects of undernutrition (Victora et al., 2008). I have led the group for the last 3 years and through pooling our data we have achieved a sample of 11,000 people followed up from pregnancy or birth for a minimum of 20 years and, in the case of Guatemala and New Delhi, up to their mid-forties. This work has had a significant impact on the field, demonstrating for example, amongst other findings, that children who grow poorly in their first 2 years of life achieve roughly half a grade less of schooling in their lifetime than their better-nourished peers (Martorell et al., 2010).

Shane Norris is now the principal investigator of Bt20+, with me as his associate, effecting a seamless transition in management of a large research and field staff, multiple sources of local and international funding, postgraduate students, and collaborators all over the world. It's a privilege for me to support him as he comes into his own as a world-class researcher in the life-course study of obesity and chronic disease.

The Next Generation

I have alternated, in my employment, between being at a university and at a research institution, mainly because I've enjoyed the autonomy but not the isolation of a university department and the corollary at a research organization. But I have always had appointments at one or more universities and I have always had students. I was recounting the achievements my most prominent students when one of them quipped that it took four of them to replace me; I replied that, when I was their age, there was less to know and less to do. Because of the diversity of my interests, researchers I mentored as students work in many different fields.

Tamsen Rochat, who worked with me on early child development, is currently a recipient of a grant from Grand Challenges Canada Saving Brains: Unlocking Potential for Development[8] to follow up the development of children who participated 5 years earlier in an exclusive breastfeeding intervention with HIV-positive mothers. She has done ground-breaking work on antenatal depression amongst HIV-positive women (Rochat et al., 2006) and on psychosocial support for HIV-infected children (Richter, Chandan, & Rochat, 2009). She is expanding her work on postnatal depression in the context of HIV and has designed a study to test a community-based intervention to support women.

For nearly a decade Heidi van Rooyen, who I recruited 15 years ago, has project managed the South African arm of the largest community-based behavioral intervention trials yet mounted. Implemented in three African countries and Thailand, the aim of the study was to prevent HIV infection as assessed with a biological end-point. Project Accept tested the impact of community mobilization, mobile HIV counseling and testing, and post-test support clubs for HIV-positive people and their families on recent HIV infection (Khumalo-Sakutukwa et al., 2008). The post-intervention assessment in the KwaZulu-Natal site, involving interviews and blood draws was conducted amongst a cross-sectional sample of 13,500 18–32-year-olds recruited through household-level sampling techniques, demonstrated a significant reduction in recent HIV infection. During the study, Heidi established her own research program, first by investigating the impact of home-based HIV counseling and testing, then adding point-of-care diagnostics through CD4 testing and referral to treatment, and now self-, home- and community-based approaches (van Rooyen et al., 2012).

Chris Desmond, an economist, has worked with me for nearly 10 years on issues related to children and AIDS (Richter & Desmond, 2008). We collaborated in our thinking on the Joint Learning Initiative on Children and AIDS, as a result of which Jim Kim recruited Chris to the Center for Health and Human Rights at Harvard University to work jointly with Sudhir Anand, the Oxford-based economist, and Amartya Sen. The project, called the Cost of Inaction (Anand, Desmond, Marques, & Fuje, 2012), highlights the negative impacts of a failure to take action, in this case, to protect children affected by AIDS and poverty. Chris has returned to work with me at the Human Sciences Research Council and at Bt20+, and is initiating new projects on the long-term consequences of maternal mortality and scientific consensus on the consequences of HIV and AIDS for children.

I have mentioned Shane Norris in connection with Bt20+. He is a physiologist with a Master's degree in Business Administration and a post-graduate degree in Psychology. He is the recipient of a United Kingdom Medical Research Council and Department for International Development (DfID) African Research Leader award and the Director of the Developmental Pathways to Health Research Unit at the University of the Witwatersrand, in which Bt20+ is located. Shane is principally interested in life-course determinants of chronic diseases, particularly obesity and physical activity, as well as in interventions to improve health in childhood and adolescence.

I appreciate the fact that these four outstanding individuals and many of my other students and junior colleagues have chosen to stay in or return to South Africa and to invest their talents and energies in improving the health and wellbeing of children and youth in this country. After all, they could achieve well anywhere. In announcing the Business Journal Executive of 2012, Cromwell Schubarth, Senior Technology Reporter for the *Silicon Valley Business Journal,* wrote "This year's winner is definitely not South African," because the last four Silicon Valley executives who stood above the rest were originally from South Africa.[9]

Final Thoughts

I no longer think of infancy, child development, youth, or parenting as separate subjects but as part of the tapestry of the life course, just as I look back on my own life and see it whole, not one phase stopping and another starting. As in Birth to Twenty, the years passed and the kids just kept getting older. In an over-arching sense, I interpret the phases of development, as I do my own life, as involving different types of learning and different topics. The infant, in emotional communication with her mother, is learning how to learn in a human world; the junior school boy is learning about the objects in the world and how they work; the adolescent is learning how to contain their necessary recklessness—after all, great challenges face them as they leave home and become independent, and they need all the pluck they can muster.

I'm also no longer in a hurry. My experience has taught me that studies and projects, like children, bear fruit and ripen slowly, over time. Not only has Birth to Twenty taken so much longer than I thought to yield the data I intended 20 years ago, but a few weeks ago I attended a meeting at the WHO on their commitment to child development, as well as survival, as a goal of a holistic perspective on health. This is a long time after I first started to work with colleagues at the WHO on these issues in 1988.

Notes

1. Infant Care in an Urban Community (1963), Four Years Old in An Urban Community (1968), Seven Years Old in the Home Environment (1976), and Perspectives On School at Seven Years Old (1977).
2. Care for Child Development—see www.who.int/maternal_child_adolescent/documents/care_child_development/en/index.html
3. A comprehensive list of Bt20+ publications is available through a forthcoming publication, see Richter et al. (2013).
4. I use the terms White, Black, Colored, and Indian as the political categories denoted under the *Apartheid* regime.
5. www.bristol.ac.uk/alspac/

6. Now the Chris Hani-Baragwanath Hospital.
7. The cohorts are Pelotas in Brazil, INCAP in Guatemala, the New Delhi Birth Cohort, Cebu in the Philippines, and Birth to Twenty in South Africa.
8. www.grandchallenges.ca/grand-challenges/womens-childrens-health/saving-brains/
9. www.bizjournals.com/sanjose/news/2012/12/27/and-the-executive-of-the-year-for-2012.html

References

Ainsworth, M. D., Andry, R. G., Harlow, R. G., Lebovici, S., Mead, M., Prugh, D. G. et al. (1962). *Deprivation of maternal care: A reassessment of its effects.* Geneva: World Health Organization.

Anand, S., Desmond, C., Marques, N., & Fuje, H. (2012). *The cost of inaction: Case studies from Rwanda and Angola.* Cambridge, MA: Harvard University Press.

Barbarin, O., & Richter, L. (2001). *Mandela's children: Growing up in post-apartheid South Africa.* New York: Routledge,

Barbarin, O., Richter, L., de Wet, T., & Wachtel, A. (1998). Ironic trends in the transition to peace. Criminal violence supplants political violence in terrorizing South African Blacks. *Peace and Conflict: Journal of Peace Psychology, 4,* 283–305.

Bell, P., & Binagwaho, A. (2006). The joint learning initiative on children and HIV/AIDS. *The Lancet, 368,* 1850–1851.

Bornstein, M. (1989). Cross-cultural developmental comparisons: The case of Japanese-American infant and mother activities and interactions. What we know, what we need to know and why we need to know. *Developmental Review, 9,* 171–204.

Bowlby, J. (1951). *Maternal care and mental health.* Geneva: World Health Organization.

Bronfenbrenner, U. (1977). Toward an experimental ecology of human development. *American Psychologist, 32,* 513–531.

Cooper, P., Tomlinson, M., Swartz, L., Woolgar, M., Murray, L., & Molteno, C. (1999). Post-partum depression and the mother–infant relationship in a South African peri-urban settlement. *British Journal of Psychiatry, 175,* 554–558.

Crowley, J., & Griesel, R. (1962). Pre- and post-natal effects of a low protein diet on the behaviour of the white rat. *Psychologia Africana, 9,* 216–225.

De Waal, A., & Whiteside, A. (2003). New variant famine: AIDS and food crisis in southern Africa. *The Lancet, 362,* 1234–1237.

Dix, T. (1991). The affective organization of parenting: Adaptive and maladaptive processes. *Psychological Bulletin, 110,* 3–25.

Engle, P., Black, M., Behrman, J., Cabral de Mello, M., Gertler, P., Kapiriri, L. et al. (2007). Strategies to avoid the loss of developmental potential in more than 200 million children in the developing world. *The Lancet, 369,* 229–242.

Engle, P., Fernald, L., Alderman, H., Behrman, J., O'Gara, C., Yousalzai, A. et al. (2011). Strategies for reducing inequalities and improving developmental outcomes for young children in low-income and middle-income countries. *The Lancet, 378,* 1339–1353.

Engle, P., Lhotska, L., & Armstrong, H. (1997). *The care initiative: Guidelines for the analysis, assessment and action to improve nutrition.* New York: UNICEF.

Fonn, S., de Beer, M., Kgamphe, S., McIntyre, J., Cameron, N., Padayachee, G. et al. (1991). 'Birth to Ten': pilot studies to test the feasibility of a birth cohort study investigating the effects of urbanisation in South Africa. *South African Medical Journal, 79,* 449–454.

Goldberg, S. (1977). Ethics, politics and multicultural research. In P. Liederman, S. Tulkin, & A. Rosenfeld (Eds.), *Culture and infancy: Variations in the human experience* (pp. 587–598). New York: Academic Press.

Grantham-McGregor, S. (1995). A review of studies of the effect of severe malnutrition on mental development. *The Journal of Nutrition, 125,* 2233S–2238S.

Grantham-Mcgregor, S., Cheung, Y., Cueto, S., Glewwe, P., Richter, L., Strupp, L. et al. (2007). Developmental potential in the first 5 years for children in developing countries. *The Lancet, 369,* 60–70.

Hill, C., Hosegood, V., & Newell, M-L. (2008). Children's care and living arrangements in a high HIV prevalence area in rural South Africa. *Vulnerable Children and Youth Studies, 3,* 65–77.

Khumalo-Sakutukwa, G., Morin, S., Fritz, K., Charlebois, E., van Rooyen, H., Chingono, A. et al. (2008). Project Accept (HPTN 043): A community-based intervention to reduce HIV incidence in populations at risk for HIV in Sub-Saharan Africa and Thailand. *Journal of Acquired Immune Deficiency, 49,* 422–431.

LeVine, R. (1990). Enculturation: A biosocial perspective on the development of self. In D. Cicchetti & M. Beeghly (Eds.), *The self in transition: Infancy to early childhood* (pp. 99–117). Chicago: The University of Chicago Press.

Martorell, R., Horta, B., Adair, L., Stein, A., Richter, L., Fall, C. et al. (2010). Weight gain in the first two years of life is an important predictor of schooling outcomes in pooled analyses from five birth cohorts from low- and middle-income countries. *Journal of Nutrition, 140,* 348–354.

Matshidze, P., Richter, L., Ellison, G., Levin, J., & Mcintyre, J. (1998). Caesarean section rates in South African: Evidence of bias among different "population groups." *Ethnicity and Health, 3,* 71–79.

Naicker, N. Norris, S., Mathee, A, Bekker, P., &. Richter, L. (2010). Lead exposure is associated with a delay in the onset of puberty in South African adolescent females: Findings from the Birth to Twenty cohort. *The Science of the Total Environment, 408,* 4949–4954.

Norris, S., Richter, L., & Fleetwood, S. (2007). Panel studies in developing countries: Case analysis of sample attrition over the past 16 years within the Birth to Twenty Cohort in Johannesburg, South Africa. *Journal of International Development, 19,* 1143–1150.

Papoušek, H., & Papoušek, M. (2002). Intuitive parenting. In M. Bornstein (Ed.), *Handbook of parenting* (Vol. 2): *Biology and ecology of parenting* (2nd ed., pp. 183–206). Mahwah, NJ: Lawrence Erlbaum.

Polansky, N., Borgman, R., De Saix, C. (1972). *The roots of futility.* San Francisco: Jossey-Bass.

Ramchandani, P., Richter, L., Norris, S., & Stein, A. (2010). Maternal prenatal stress and later child behavioral problems in an urban South African setting. *Journal of the American Academy of Child and Adolescent Psychiatry, 49,* 239–247.

Richter, L.M. (1993). Protein-energy malnutrition and the psychological development of young children. *South African Journal of Clinical Nutrition, 6,* 28–32.

Richter, L.M. (1995). Are early adult-infant interactions universal: A South African view. *South African Journal of Child and Adolescent Psychiatry, 7,* 2–18.

Richter, L. (1999). Parenting in poverty: Young children and their families in South Africa. In L. Eldering & P. Leseman (Eds.), *Effective early education: Cross-cultural perspectives* (pp. 191–211). New York: Falmer Press.

Richter, L. (2004a). *The importance of caregiver–child interactions for the survival and healthy development of young children: A review.* Geneva: World Health Organization.

Richter, L. (2004b). Early child development in resource-poor settings: Balancing children's material and mental needs—A personal account. *Zero to Three,* November, 40–46.

Richter, L. (2006). Studying adolescence. *Science, 312,* 1902–1905.

Richter, L. (2008). No small issue: Children and families. Invited plenary presentation at the Seventeenth International AIDS Conference Universal Action Now, Mexico City, August 3–8. The Hague: Bernard van Leer Foundation.

Richter, L. (2010a). Social cash transfers to support children and families affected by HIV/AIDS. *Vulnerable Children and Youth Studies, 5,* 81–91.

Richter, L. (2010b). An introduction to family-centred services for children affected by HIV and AIDS. *Journal of the International AIDS Society, 13* (Suppl 2): S1 (June 23).

Richter, L. (2012). The central role of families in the lives of children affected by AIDS. In J. Heyman, L. Scherr, & R. Kidman (Eds.), *Protecting childhood in the AIDS pandemic: Finding solutions that work* (pp. 21–49). Oxford: Oxford University Press.

Richter, L., Bac, M., & Hay, I. (1990). Psychological aspects of the health care of young children. *South African Family Practice, 11*, 490–497.

Richter, L., Chandan, U., & Rochat, T. (2009). Improving hospital care for young children in the context of HIV/AIDS and poverty. *Journal of Child Health Care, 13*, 198–211.

Richter, L., De Kadt, J., Ginsburg, C., Makusha, T., & Norris, S. (2013). *The South African Birth Cohort Project.* Oxford Bibliographies Online.

Richter, L., & Desmond, C. (2008) Targeting AIDS orphans and child-headed households? A perspective from national surveys in South Africa, 1995–2005. *AIDS Care, 20*, 1019–1028.

Richter, L. M., & Mphelo, M. (1992). Enhancing mother-child relationships in undernutrition. *Proceedings: Child Health Priorities Conference, 1991.* Cape Town: University of Cape Town.

Richter, L., & Sherr, L. (2009). Editorial: Strengthening families: A key recommendation of the Joint Learning Initiative on Children and AIDS (JLICA). *AIDS Care, 21*, 1–2.

Richter, L., Sherr, L, Adato, M., Belsey, M., Chandan, U., Desmond, C. et al (2009). Strengthening families to support children affected by HIV and AIDS. *AIDS Care, 21*, 3–12.

Richter, L., Yach, D., Cameron, N., Griesel, R. D., & de Wet, T. (1995). Enrolment into Birth to Ten (BTT): Population and sample characteristics. *Paediatric and Perinatal Epidemiology, 9*, 109–120.

Rochat, T., Richter, L., Buthelezi, N., Tomkins, A., Doll. H., & Stein, A. (2006). Depression among pregnant rural African women undergoing HIV testing. *Journal of the American Medical Association, 295*, 1376–1378.

Salt, P., Galler, J., & Ramsey, F. (1988). The influence of early malnutrition on subsequent behavioral development. VII. The effects of maternal depressive symptoms, *Journal of Developmental and Behavioral Pediatrics, 9*, 1–5.

Trevarthen, C. (1987). Universal cooperative motives: How infants begin to know the language and culture of their parents. In G. Jahoda & I. Lewis (Eds.), *Acquiring Culture: Cross-Cultural Studies in Child Development* (pp. 37–90). London: Croom Helm.

United Nations Children's Fund, World Health Organization, The World Bank (2012). UNICEF-WHO-World Bank Joint Child Malnutrition Estimates, 2011 revision.

Van Heerden, A., Norris, S., & Richter, L. (2010). Using mobile phones for adolescent research in low and middle income countries: Preliminary findings from the Birth to Twenty cohort, South Africa. *Journal of Adolescent Health, 46*, 302–304.

Van Rooyen, H., Mcgrath, N., Chirowodza, A., Fiamma, A., Gray, G., Richter, L. et al. (2012). Mobile VCT: Reaching men and young people in urban and rural South African pilot studies (NIMH Project Accept, HPTN 043). AIDS and Behavior. http://link.springer.com/article/10.1007%2Fs10461-012-0368-x?LI=true

Victora, C., Adair, L., Fall, C., Hallal, P., Martorell, R., Richter, L., & Sachdev, H. (2008). Maternal and child undernutrition: Consequences for adult health and human capital. *The Lancet, 17*, 23–40.

Wachs, T., Black, M., & Engle, P. (2009). Maternal depression: A global threat to children's health, development, and behaviour and to human rights. *Child Development Perspectives, 3*, 51–59.

Walker, S., Wachs, T., Gardner, J., Lozoff, B., Wasserman, G., Pollitt, E. et al. (2007). Child development: Risk factors for adverse outcomes in developing countries. *The Lancet, 369*, 145–157

Walker, S., Wachs, T., Grantham-Mcgregor, S., Black, M., Nelson, C., Huffman, S. et al. (2011). Inequality in early childhood: Risk and protective factors for early child development. *The Lancet, 378*, 1325–1338.

Wilson, F., & Ramphele, M. (1989). *Uprooting poverty: The South African challenge.* A report for the Second Carnegie Inquiry into Poverty and Development in South Africa. Johannesburg: David Phillip.

Yach, D., Cameron, N., Padayachee, G. N., Wagstaff, L., Richter, L. M., & Fonn, S. (1991). Birth to Ten: Child health in South Africa in the nineties; Rationale and methods of a birth cohort study. *Paediatric and Perinatal Epidemiology, 5*, 211–233.

36

Clinical–Psychological Contributions to Adolescence Research

Hans-Dieter Rösler

My Own Development

Born in 1927 in Berlin, I had a sheltered upbringing in two Brandenburg villages as the only child of an elementary school teacher and his wife. For me, my early school years were dominated by the educational principles of the "Third Reich," and my youth by the Second World War, the beginning of which saw my father drafted into the *Wehrmacht* (German Army of the time), and to me suffering the same fate towards its end. Before this happened, however, I and my high-school classmates had already been deployed for air defence activities.

In the fall of 1945, I returned home, unharmed from British captivity, to my parents in the now Soviet-occupied zone. As my father, who had been released from Russian captivity due to his serious wounds, was not able to return to his previous work as a teacher, I took his place as a *Neulehrer* (literally, a "new teacher," meaning a teacher not tainted with the past Nazi ideology) and was thereby catapulted into adulthood at the age of 18. Without the support of any training, I became the sole teacher for the 200 pupils of the village, and remained so until a second teacher, and later another three, came to relieve me. These children, whose ages ranged from 6 to 14, had had their numbers increased by the influx of refugees from the eastern provinces of Germany then under Soviet control. At this time, and following the shocking revelations concerning the crimes of his regime, which had been vaguely suspected but were only now fully known, I also suffered from the loss of all youthful illusions about the "Führer." This made me a representative of the "sceptical generation," characterized by mistrust in politics and being freed from ideology, as described by Schelsky (1957).

The formal qualification of elementary school teacher, which I had acquired alongside my teaching career of four years, enabled me to enrol at the Humboldt University

of East Berlin in 1950 to study psychology. There I was introduced by Kurt Gottschaldt (1902–91) to the problems of neglect encountered by young people during the post-war period, and from which I progressed to the study of clinical developmental psychology. In 1954, after my graduation in psychology (holder of the German diploma degree), I followed the anthropologist and medical specialist in research on adolescence, Hans Grimm (1910–95), who was teaching biology at his Institute for Social Hygiene at the Academy for Advanced Medical Education in East Berlin. After he moved to the University Institute for Anthropology, I received an offer from the child psychiatrist Gerhard Göllnitz (1920–2003) to establish a "Laboratory for Clinical and Developmental Psychology" at the Rostock University Mental Hospital, of which he was Director, giving me the opportunity to cooperate with the departments of child neuropsychiatry, psychiatry and neurology. Starting in 1963 as an assistant professor, and continuing from 1975 as a full professor of psychology at the faculty of medicine, I directed the Laboratory for Clinical and Developmental Psychology until my retirement in 1992. After my retirement, I took the Chair of Developmental Psychology at the Justus-Liebig University of Giessen until 1994, although I have continued to observe all the research projects co-initiated by me, albeit from a distance. I have been married since 1950 and, together with my wife, can watch a third generation of descendants growing up.

Access Via Developmental Biology

Stimulated by Grimm's lecture on the "Constitutional biology of the ages," something I also taught when a visiting lecturer at the Psychological Institute of the Technical University of Dresden from 1958–67, I began investigating psychophysical development, which led to my interest in lifespan developmental psychology. Beforehand, I had taken my doctor's degree in anthropology at the Humboldt-University, dealing with studies on the basic types of the human hand, a relationship to psychology critically appreciated by Voracek, Dressler, and Loibl (2008) some 50 years later.

I was among the first psychologists within the public health service of the German Democratic Republic (GDR, more commonly referred to as East Germany) although our competences and role were largely undefined. In the 1950s, however, psychology as a scientific discipline was called into question by the authorities in the government and the communist party, resulting in priority being given to the Pavlovian "Teachings of the higher nervous function" taken from the Soviet Union. All this occurred before Pavlov's theses were corrected. Furthermore, psychological research and practice continued to be impeded by its defamation as "testology," which was adopted from the official doctrine of the Soviet Union. Although this doctrine was gradually undermined, the development and distribution of tests were not sanctioned before the founding of a psychodiagnostic center in 1981.

Secular Trends in Rates of Psychophysical Development

The increase in average body height of school beginners that had been observed during the first third of the 20th century led to secular changes in physical development becoming a much debated issue among medical specialists. This phenomenon was also seen when military recruits were measured, when developmental dates in early childhood were assessed, and by a trend toward earlier menarche in girls, particularly in the urban population. At first, there was a negative valuation of the causes and consequences of this phenomenon, whereby it was said that an "urbanization trauma" would lead to "hothouse growth" by "overstimulation" and finally to a discrepancy between premature physical and much later psychological maturation. This interpretation was based on the findings of studies concerning difficulties in raising children and the neglect of young people. However, by collecting evidence from specialized literature supporting a contrary view, I always opposed these pessimistic prognoses by writing papers presenting a more balanced stance (Rösler, 1963b, 1964, 1968, 1990).

With regard to earlier sexual maturation, the obvious issue was whether it affected the development of psychosexuality. This was approached by analyzing questions that girls and boys in elementary school-leaving classes in Halle and Berlin had written in the years 1950–56 concerning sexuality. This material had been collected by Grimm during lectures to students aged 13–15 years about the human reproduction process. Altogether, 835 questions were collected. These were compared with questions ($n = 87$) collected from pupils of the same age from Berlin in the years 1925–27 and showed that, over the period of almost 30 years, there had been a clear increase in direct questions about sexual intercourse and that the questions had been increasingly formulated in more concrete and less general terms. Furthermore, questions ($n = 276$) from same-age pupils in a rural Thuringian district, collected in 1951–53, allowed a comparison of the questions according to area of residence and showed the increase in questions about sexual intercourse to be greater in towns compared with villages (Grimm & Rösler, 1956).

In order to explain this time trend, we collected all articles with sexual content from a Berlin daily paper from 1955–57. During these 19 months, readers were provided with 128 separate articles and notices, including a total of 187 communications about sexual matters, of which, 159 topics concerned sexual offenses committed against children and adolescents. In 83%, children and their educators was the subject of discussion, possibly provoking sexual interest, but also increasing the knowledge of the juvenile reader (Rösler, 1969). Since then, modern mass media and sex education at school have further increased the level of information about sexual matters.

As to acceleration of psychophysical development, in Rostock we began to notice that some performance tests had become too easy for the test persons, suggesting that mental development was also accelerating. That was clarified by new standardized intelligence tests, such as the Colored Progressive Matrices by Raven (Kurth, 1969), the Working Test by Pauli (Thulesius & Teichmann, 1972), the Motometric Oseretzky Scale (Kurth, 1978), and the Hamburg–Wechsler Intelligence Test for the Preschool Age (Meyer-Probst, 1984), for which we gathered data and calculated norms ourselves. We also found evidence to show that, in Rostock, school beginners of the 1968 birth cohort had begun to walk and talk at an earlier age compared with those of the 1948 cohort. Likewise we noted accelerated performance in an infant test with Rostock crèche children (children of a day-nursery from infancy up to the age of 3 years) and school beginners (Rösler, 1969).

Our review of the existing empirical evidence on acceleration also led to the criticism of the so-called adolescence-maximum hypothesis of intelligence that is based on cross-sectional comparisons of age stages and which was refuted by the outcome of longitudinal studies. As a result of accelerated mental development, the younger cohorts achieved higher intelligence scores than the older ones, whose performance had remained constant since their youth (Rösler, 1967a, b).

Meanwhile a positive view of the acceleration of psychophysical development as a result of improved nutrition, education, and medical care has gained acceptance. The tendency of somatic and psychological development to co-vary has to be regarded as an exogenously conditioned correspondence in developmental speed as a result of common conditions of development (Rösler, 1964).

Juvenile Mothers

Due to the earlier sexual maturation of girls during the course of the 20th century, an increase of juvenile and mostly single mothers was to be expected; and indeed, births out of wedlock increased overall, as did the share of child-bearing women under 20 years (Rösler,

1959). To test the validity of this expectation, we carried out follow-up studies on the development of Rostock mothers who had been under 18 years when they gave birth, which had been in the period from 1952 to 1958, and on the development of their first-born children. For the purpose of pair comparison, we used 26 mothers of child-bearing age (from 22–26 years) who gave birth during the same period and had the same marital status at the time of the birth but who had been 18 years or older when they gave birth. They also had the same social background, and the sex, birth-year, and month of their first-born children were the same. The mothers were visited at home and were interviewed via a structured questionnaire. On the occasion of the mother's interview, the child was also interviewed about feelings and behaviors and asked to draw a picture of a man. Information on the child's behavior and performance at school was provided by the class teachers (Metzelthin & Rösler, 1970).

The study revealed that, of each maternal pair, the mothers who had given birth before the age of 18 had menstruated earlier, and were less socially and vocationally well developed than their female reference partners. Their children were smaller, showed a lower level of intelligence, failed more often at school, and demonstrated disruptive behavior in the classroom more often than the children of the reference partner mothers.

We also found that children of juvenile mothers received psychotherapeutic treatment more frequently. Among the cases of the Rostock Department for Child Neuropsychiatry (1957–68), the children of mothers under 22 years were overrepresented by 22.4% compared with 18% among all mothers. The children of young parents had also been admitted more often due to the consequences of inadequate upbringing (Rösler, Dudeck, Gebert, & Vehreschild, 1980). This was obviously related to the juvenile mothers having to try to educate and bring up children at an age when they themselves had not reached full maturity with regard to personality development, when for the majority their vocational training had not been completed, and where they had not established an own household. This was often compounded by the fact that their own upbringing had been deficient or burdened by poor home conditions. Today, in spite of oral contraception being readily available, and there being the option of legal abortion in many cases, these problems are still very relevant.

Clinical Formulation of Questions

From the psychological treatment of juvenile patients, and from consultations with their parents and educators, various research topics were developed that tackled the issues of suboptimal development and socialization from a pragmatic perspective as well as through clinical work. The advantage of this approach was that research questions could be largely dealt with free from ideology, but it had the disadvantage of a lack of structure. The Medical College and its infrastructure served as a space relatively protected from political interference, whereas educational and psychological research on adolescence was subject to politically motivated restrictions in the national higher education system. A documentation of the whole spectrum of research work on biosocial development of adolescents in the GDR (East Germany) is given by Silbereisen, Rösler, Kracke, and Reis (1993).

Of course, in the GDR, clinical developmental psychology also remained dependent on its academic mother discipline, which was part of Marxist-oriented psychology. The first attempt at a representation of child psychology by Clauß and Hiebsch (1958) was, however, criticized for "moving into a politically empty space" and had to be thoroughly revised because of a "lack of partiality" concerning the political aims of the government and communist party. Some 10 years later, Schmidt (1970) submitted a detailed concept of a general developmental psychology based on the philosophy of dialectical materialism. We took these basic works into account when conducting our studies, thereby complying with the principle of the dialectics between the biological, psychological, and social forces in personality development.

Causes and Consequences of Failure at School

Factors Inhibiting Achievement As, in the GDR, 22% of the 14-year-old school leavers in the school year 1957/58 had not attained the expected final-year level of achievement after 8 years of compulsory education, the Institute for Social Hygiene, which was still under the direction of Grimm, was instructed to investigate the causes of their failure. To this end, in a Berlin school preparing for practical vocations (non-college track), 107 students deemed to be at risk of failure and 107 age-matched reference partners with the best grades were medically examined, and were questioned by me about their family background, habits, and development at school. Their teachers filled out a student observation form. However, due to ideological reservations against the "bourgeois testing methodology" at that time, we had to do without an intelligence test.

The academically weak students clearly differed from their reference partners with good grades by more unfavorable family situations in many respects: unhealthy ways of living, a development beset with change of school and lack of family support, and by being held back by health problems (Rösler, 1963a). These results were received with astonishment by the officials responsible for school and health policy, because the findings did not comply with the optimism inherent in the model of a socialist society. Nevertheless, with this report I qualified as university lecturer at the Psychological Institute of the Technological University of Dresden.

The Subjective Importance of School Performance for Parents In our educational consulting practice, children were often presented by parents discontented with their children's scholastic achievements, although their children were not failing at school. To acquire a general overview of this phenomenon, we conducted a written survey with all parents of 13-year-old pupils of the 7th grade, in Rostock, in the school year 1963/64 (Teichmann, 1969a). According to this study, 42% of all parents were not satisfied with the performance of their children in school. This was true for 46% of parents whose children were achieving average grades (2.7–3.0, on a scale from 1 to 5) and even for 29% of those where the pupils were doing extremely well. With level of grades kept constant, the discontent increased with higher socio-economic status (SES), particularly in families with boys and in complete two-parent families. High educational demands on their offspring had become an epochal phenomenon, which already made children bearers of social expectations in an upward mobile society.

The likely consequences of this attitude were revealed by a pair comparison of 50 school students where the parents were either content or discontent with their offspring's attainment. In families with discontented parents, social relations had deteriorated and mental health was precarious. These results lead to attempts to change the attitudes and behaviors of parents and students through professional consultation (Teichmann, 1996b).

Gender Differences in School Performance As both the expectations of parents about school performance and school performance itself clearly differed between boys and girls at the beginning of adolescence, the age dependence of gender-specific school performance was analyzed. For this purpose, Bleck and Teichmann (1978) evaluated the reported final grades of the school year 1969/70 at Rostock schools providing general education, secondary and vocational schools, and from technical colleges and institutions of higher education ($n = 65,000$ grades). Gender differences in grades were found in favor of girls from the first to the 10th grade. Differences, which were particularly salient for languages and concerning conduct in class (also graded by teachers at that time), increased between the 5th and 7th grade and decreased thereafter. In our view, this result also justified the assumption that the gender differences were actually due to differences in the pace of psychological development. As the selection for attending a secondary school (high school, including college-bound track) was made around the time (ages 13/14) of the largest performance discrepancy in favor of female students, without taking into account the more equal performance expected later at the beginning of vocational training, a 1:1 gender-based admission policy was recommended, despite the initially lower grades of the male students. Possible biological and social causes of gender differences in mental capability were also considered (Rösler, Bleck, & Teichmann, 1976); a topic that is still discussed in the literature (Bischof-Köhler, 2006).

The Consequences of Minor Brain Defects from Early Childhood

For the treatment of students showing abnormalities in performance and behavior, the Rostock child psychiatrist Göllnitz had first pointed to the significance of a minor brain defect in 1954. Since then, the chronic cerebro-organic psycho-syndrome (encephalopathy) with hyperactivity and retarded motor behavior, weak concentration, affective instability, and quick fatigability, all corresponding with neurological findings, had been the main field of research of physicians and psychologists in the Rostock department.

Comparative and Follow-up Examinations up to Early Adolescence In a first step, under the direction of Göllnitz and Rösler (1975), 50 former patients of the Department for Child Neuropsychiatry, showing normal intelligence and with no cerebral paralysis, who had been treated for various mental disorders when aged between 6 and 10 years and diagnosed as encephalopathic on the basis of anamnestic and neurological criteria, were examined again 3–4 years after being discharged. Compared with the previous examination, they now displayed a reduced level of motor retardation, but were retarded in their mental development. Compared with a reference group of 50 non-patients of the same age, sex, and intelligence level, they showed lower academic achievements, and consequently their acquisition of experience was handicapped by the so-called psycho-syndrome. This syndrome was also indicated by their poorer achievements in concentration and stress tests, with general retardation due to a weakening of vitality. In the case of various cognitive demands concerning concept formation, classification and sorting of geometrical figures, they showed a delayed learning progress. In a personality test they demonstrated increased values for neuroticism, indicating emotional instability.

Follow-up and Comparative Examinations up to Post-Adolescence In a second step, encephalopaths assessed as of normal intelligence when young adults were re-examined. Richter (1986) examined 96 former patients of the Department for Child Neuropsychiatry who had been treated at approximately 12 years of age for various disorders diagnosed as a brain defect from early childhood, and who could be contacted again at a mean age of approximately 22 years. Compared with the earlier examination, results showed that the former patients had made up fully for their earlier motor retardation, but that their intelligence level had remained the same. Apart from micro-symptoms, no neurological findings could be recorded. However, their final school-leaving certificate results were lower than expected based on earlier intelligence measurements. There were no difficulties in their working- or family-life, or in their social integration.

Through a comparison of 18 of these former patients with 18 matched non-patients with a healthy brain development according to anamnestic findings, and of the same age and sex, the former patients were still distinguishable by less favorable self-assessments with regard to emotional stability and social resonance, whereas no differences remained with regard to intelligence, motor coordination, and concentration.

An association of the examined psychological target parameters could hardly be seen at the level of prenatal, perinatal, and postnatal risks, except for a retarded infantile development. Associations on the pathological organic level were not established, but could be well proved by features of the former patients' upbringing and educational milieu. This study demonstrated the high importance of favorable psychosocial developmental conditions, by which, as contributory factors, the prognosis of encephalopathy is mainly determined. These and other results were discussed on the basis of a comprehensive survey together with those of researchers from German-speaking countries (Rösler, 1989).

Over time, the concept of brain defect of early childhood has become obsolete, particularly as it happens more and more rarely due to an advanced neonatology. In many ways, it has been superseded by the nowadays frequently diagnosed attention-deficit hyperactive disorder (ADHD, in German ADHS) (Häßler, 1992).

Risks for Personality Development

The initiation of nationally coordinated, medical research projects in the GDR (East Germany) in the 1960s enabled a co-operation between gynecology and neonatology. Both of these disciplines were interested in the prognosis of high-risk-born children, with the suggestion of child psychiatric and psychological follow-ups. This led us to the planning of two longitudinal studies.

Prognoses from Infancy to Adolescence

Neonatal Erythroblastosis Morbus haemolyticus neonatorum (Mhn) means an immediate serious risk as a result of blood-group incompatibility between mother and child, which had disastrous consequences in the past. Most of the affected newborns died or suffered damage to their central nervous system. After the blood exchange transfusion had been adopted for the newborns, mortality and neurological–psychiatric defective states decreased considerably. However, in the early sixties, follow-up examinations, which were at that time carried out by us up until adolescence, were still missing over a longer period.

Together with a PhD candidate, who unfortunately died at an early age, we followed the psychological development of 124 surviving Mhn-children, who had been treated with an exchange blood transfusion in the Schwerin Children's Clinic after 1960 (Rösler & Springstein, 1988, 1990a, b). Compared with 124 children in the control group (matched for age, sex, mother's age, number of brothers and sisters, and father's level of occupation), their level of psychological development was lower by 19 development quotient (DQ) units in the first examination at the age from 7 months up to 3 years. At this age, relations to the social

milieu had yet not been assessed for the sample. Therefore the differences in level were exclusively interpreted as a consequence of Mhn.

Even in the second assessment at age 16.0 to 16.3 years, in which all participants took part, with the exception of one deceased in each group, those born with Mhn still showed deficits compared with those in the control group. The difference in IQ only was 9 units, but scholastic development of Mhn-children was clearly retarded: 33% of the Mhn-children compared with 15% of the control children had not completed grade 10, the final-year class, even after repeating the final class twice; their school grades—evaluated from the 1st to the 8th grade—had also remained low. Teachers judged Mhn-children as showing a generally lower intellectual capability; reduced activities at school, during extracurricular sport, and in leisure time; a lack of integration into social groups; and poor self-control.

In the second measurement, differences proved to be modified to a larger extent by psychosocial and additional perinatal factors. On the one hand, changes that may have occurred in the SES of parents were registered according to an 11-point scale which assessed the educational and upbringing milieu required by the state for people entitled to bring up and educate a minor (*Bildungs- und Qualifizierungsniveau*, BQN). The results showed that the conditions had deteriorated for the Mhn children from the first to the second assessment, mainly because their parents showed a lower level of occupational qualification activity than parents of the children in the control group, possibly due to the higher share of divorce in the Mhn group and the subsequent loss of a caretaker.

On the other hand, the Mhn-children did show a higher additional biological risk load, since the blood-group incompatibility between mother and child was followed by other concomitant factors, such as premature delivery or low birth weight, which in turn appeared more frequently at a lower level of the BQN of the parents. In contrast, neither the height of the serum bilirubin level at the time of the blood exchange transfusion, nor the time of treatment had an influence on the DQ in infancy or on the level of intelligence (IQ) in adolescence. In this respect, the neonatological treatment measures were optimal at that time. The differential courses of development resulted from the interaction of further biological and psychosocial developmental conditions, such as low birth weight or low parental occupational status. Since then, this birth risk occurs more rarely owing to a Rhesus immunization of the pregnant woman and is minimized by a blood exchange transfusion already carried out in the womb.

Multiple Perinatal Risks The interaction of biological and psychosocial risks for social and personality development became the basic principle of the Rostock Longitudinal Study (ROLS) on children at risk. Following the suggestion of neonatalogists, ROLS started as the work of a team of child psychiatrists and psychologists, and continued as a study on psychological development over the life-span.

In 1970/71, all high-risk births in Rostock were recorded by the government-funded research project "Perinatology" and complemented by a normative control group of the same size (every fourth normal birth of the same period). For these 1,000 newborns, pre-, peri-, postnatal and social data were collected, such as acute respiratory distress syndrome or family deviance. The development of these children was followed within the research project, "Defective child", under the direction of Professor Göllnitz. This was, however, only possible for a limited number of cases, so that we confined ourselves to the easily accessible crèche children (a day-nursery for babies and young children under the age of 3 years, often starting at a few weeks after birth in the GDR) of Rostock ($n = 294$) in 1972/73. That meant the exclusion of children mentally defective from birth, so a quasi "normal" random sample composed of high-risk children and matched control children in equal shares was formed.

A simple comparison of these groups had to be abandoned, however, as very few children were exposed to none of the 55 biological risks (e.g., gestosis, premature birth, nutritional diseases) and 42 psychosocial risks (e.g., mother without a school leaving certificate, father an alcoholic, cramped living conditions) coded at that time. Instead, cumulated individual risk indices were composed and correlated with psychological data, such as DQ, IQ, state of motor development (MQ), performance at school, and judgment of the children's behavior by mothers and caretakers. In the process of the ongoing study, the biological risk index remained the same at all waves of measurement, whereas the psychosocial index was recomputed at each measurement. In this way, the interactions of cerebral load factors of early childhood and environmental conditions during development were investigated.

As a result, over all waves studied (at the age of 2, 6, 10, and 14 years) the level of development declined together with increasing biological and psychosocial risk load, in the course of which the effects of both may intensify, but may also compensate each other. This has been demonstrated for cognitive ability in pre-schoolers (Meyer-Probst, Rösler, & Teichmann, 1983), for those of school age (Meyer-Probst & Teichmann, 1985) and for adolescents (Meyer-Probst, Teichmann, Hayes, & Rauh, 1991). Meyer-Probst, Piatkowski, and Teichmann (1988) exemplified this result with regard to performance at school, and Rösler et al. (1991) for motor skills. At first, these results triggered a protest by pediatricians, who did not want to believe that the psychological development of an infant may be adversely affected by the low level of education of the mother in the same way as the low birth weight exerts its influence. At this time, therefore, the study was in danger of being excluded from further financial support by the state. The fact that the study was meanwhile internationally recognized as relevant for issues of developmental psychiatry, however,

brought ROLS back to the interest of and promotion by the research authority within the Ministry of Health.

In the ROLS study, the assessment of 10- and 14 year-olds included measures of self-concept. With regard to their intellectual development, the interactive effects of biological and psychosocial risks were again demonstrated. In comparison with the total sample, children, who were exposed to four and more biological risks showed reduced levels of DQ or IQ that remained from 2 up to14 years. Of these children, however, those with an additional high psychosocial risk load were clearly retarded, whereas those raised under more favorable psychosocial conditions showed a developmental trajectory almost in accordance with the norm. The same pattern of compensation and intensification arose when looking at children with four and more psychosocial risks. Here, a more favorable intelligence development was associated with only a few biological risks, whereas a high load of early biological risks was followed by retarded patterns of intelligence development.

The self-concept of the children when they reached adolescence, however, proved to be rather independent of perinatal risks. Clear negative effects appeared only in the case of psychosocial risk load, deteriorating nervousness, aggressiveness, and neuroticism measured either as self-assessments or by mothers' ratings. A low level of the mother's school education, strains at the workplace, and parental divorce also had a negative effect. Furthermore, discipline problems at school, abnormalities in behavior, such as tics, enuresis, nail biting, and also early smoking were associated with adolescents' negative self-assessment. Taken together, it was not the objective risk factors as such but their subjective experience that was relevant for self-concept.

Transition to Adult Age During the time of German unification, around 1990, the study was reinvigorated on a low-budget base with the University of Rostock financing a PhD stipend for 3 years to Olaf Reis. With an extended inventory of methods and variables, a total of 199 (68%) of the original 294 test persons were assessed in a follow-up between May 1990 and June 1991. Detecting and motivating participants to remain involved in the study had become more difficult due to the possibility of mobility after the removal of borders between East and West Germany, and out-migration from the East for better employment opportunities became quite remarkable. In the detailed report by Reis (1997) the results were as follows: The cumulative risk concept, which has formed the basis of the study since its beginning, is confirmed with regard to intellectual development. Even at the age of 20 years, although in a lessened form, unfavorable intelligence test scores, level of overall lower school attainment, and final grades, still show the effect of perinatal difficulties and an even greater association with early and current psychosocial risk load. With an increasing number of risks, mental development seems to lag behind, but in this process, differences between perinatal and psychosocial risks appear. The biological risk effect decreases with advancing age; the social risk effect, however, increases in its size.

With regard to self-concept development, biological factors do not appear as risks at all, but psychosocial factors (measured at different times) predict differences in personality features, such as autonomy and self-worth. For the development of coping styles, which we examined for the first time along with mental health, results demonstrated the great importance of psychosocial, and the moderate contribution of biological risks. In combination with psychosocial load, biological factors hindered the development of effective coping strategies and had a detrimental effect on mental health.

Adolescence in Psychology of Life Span

Following my retirement, I have no longer been involved with the Rostock Longitudinal Study with regard to organization and advice, but I have not lost sight of it.

Mental Health in Post-Adolescence In 1993, soon after unification, the ROLS was deemed entitled to receive funding from the DFG (Deutsche Forschungsgemeinschaft), which not only helped to save the data from being lost during the radical changes of the universities and research centers, but also made it possible to investigate participants again at age 25.

Following a joint application, the study could be continued in cooperation with the Institute for Mental Health in Mannheim, where a similarly conceived longitudinal study on participants born in 1970 ($n = 361$) had taken place in West Germany. In 1995/96, at the age of 25, 212 participants from Rostock and 174 from Mannheim could be reexamined and their mothers interviewed. Thus, depending on the origin and socialization of the participants, an East-West German comparison of their earlier development became possible. However, a share of 41% of the Rostock sample were now living in West Germany, whereas their parents had remained in East Germany.

The ROLS research focused on mental health. Contrary to expectations, especially during the post-unification period, the Rostock participants showed less mental disorders than participants born in Mannheim. This referred equally to data from the previous examinations at the age of 6 years in Rostock and at the age of 8 years in Mannheim, and to data that had been collected up to the age of 25 years. These findings were despite the fact that the Rostock participants had all attended a crèche (traditionally not valued favorably in the West), and were later exposed to the stress of political change and the effects of related economic upheaval, such as rapidly growing unemployment. Understandably, participants from Rostock reported about more critical life events during the period

from 1989 until 1995 compared with the Mannheim sample (Ihle et al., 1999).

With the Rostock sample, we also checked the possibility of predicting mental health and behavior of adult participants based on childhood factors (Kruse, 2004). While doing so, the importance of family climate for social and personality development became evident. Data about social bonding, which had been collected as self-reported retrospective data at ages 14 and 25 years, showed positive relations to mental health (Meyer-Probst & Reis, 1999). A similar relation between previous and recent data was shown in predicting social integration and support at age 25 from various domains of early functioning (Reis, Eisermann, & Meyer-Probst, 2003).

Antecedents of Parenthood A follow-up investigation of the Rostock sample at age 38 ($n = 244$) by Reis, Dörnte, and von der Lippe (2011), funded again by the DFG, focused on parenthood: 73% of the Rostock sample reported already being parents. Women had experienced the birth of their first child when they were, on average, 27.3 years of age, and men at 29.5 years. To determine possible predictors for the timing of first parenthood, various criteria were probed. Level of education, measured by the final school-leaving grade and level of schooling (college-bound or not), was lower for women and men who had achieved parenthood at less than age 25, compared with those who became parents at an older age. An increased value of self-reported neuroticism at age 14 reduced the likelihood of parenthood between the age of 25 and 38 years, irrespective of gender. Social support from friends, colleagues, and the family, which was assessed at age 20, increased the likelihood of parenthood overall, but particularly among women. In this connection, those who had reported higher levels of neuroticism at age 14 had experienced less social support later on. It would seem that participants reporting higher neuroticism at age 14 were less likely to have built a supportive social network by the time they reached young adulthood, which in turn diminished the likelihood of their becoming parents. Finally, we can say that being in a partnership at the age of 25 favored the birth of at least one child, particularly among women. At this age, 10% of the total sample was married, 66% were living together with a partner, and 24% were still single.

Successful Aging At the end of my career, I was still involved in the planning of a large-scale gerontological research project, the "Interdisciplinary Long-Term Study of the Adult Age" (ILSE) examining conditions for healthy and contented aging. From 1992 onwards, we examined two birth cohorts—those born 1930/32 and those born 1950/52—in five German cities (Heidelberg, Bonn, Erlangen, Leipzig, Rostock). A biographical exploration was followed by performance and personality diagnostics, and then by a psychiatric screening. These were supported by a physical fitness test (conducted by a collaborating sports scientist) and a medical check-up. Since the surveys started after I had committed myself to being involved in Giessen after my retirement, Dorothea Roether took direction of the Rostock part. After my return to Rostock in 1994, I was once again involved in the project.

When evaluating the ILSE research findings—data were available for each of the five centers (Martin et al., 2000)—the following results are particularly noteworthy: Concerning the first survey on the cohort 1930/32, at age 62 to 64 years, cognitive capability ($n = 697$) at this age was still predicted by average final school grades. The better-educated participants also performed better in intelligence, particularly in the area of education-dependent crystalline intelligence, and also in concentration and attention tests (Oswald, Rupprecht, & Hagen, 1997).

Current satisfaction with life ($n = 500$) was classified into five styles of aging using cluster analyses of biographical data from childhood and youth and other socio-demographic, health and personality-psychological findings. The participants with the most favorable aging style "healthy, happy aging" (12% of the sample, women and men from East and West Germany in equal proportions) showed a high degree of satisfaction, good health, and prior experience of high competence and social integration as a result of favorable life circumstances. Minnemann, Schmitt, Sperling, and Jüchtern (1997, p. 253) give a résumé as follows:

> Although the members of this group hardly belonged to the level of the socially privileged (having rather a low level of education and thereby few occupational options), they experienced their childhood, school time, and vocational training as happy phases in their life.

Thus, the way for a positive attitude concerning one's own aging can be already started when young.

In my view the importance of adolescence in human development has to be viewed from different time perspectives: by looking back to childhood, by looking ahead to the adulthood, as well as looking back on life from old age. To do that longitudinally, and encompassing the whole life-span, remains the "silver bullet" of psychological research. However, results of such research apply only to the historical epoch experienced at the time in question. Adolescence, as the biologically defined period between sexual maturity and completion of growth, remains socially determined and varies along with cultural history and with regard to time and geography. Adolescence is a matter of context, as Silbereisen and Todt (1994) have shown.

Final Conclusions

Participation in adolescence research was an essential scientific aspect of my commitment to the establishment of clinical psychology in East Germany (Rösler, 2004). Its beginnings lie with the formation in 1962 of the

Gesellschaft für Psychologie of the German Democratic Republic (Society for Psychology of the German Democratic Republic), of which I was a founding member. I chaired its division of clinical psychology until 1980, convened national meetings, and, between 1981 and 1991, organized the state-licensed further education program "psychological specialist in medicine". During the *Wende* (political about-turn) in 1989, because I was the only board member who did not belong to the communist party, I was elected president of the Society. In this role I negotiated our joining with the German Psychological Society of former West Germany (DGPs), which later bestowed on me the rare acknowledgment of honorary member.

Over the course of 40 years, my activities helped to effect a change in neuropsychiatry from its earlier defect-psychological approach to that of a modern developmental-psychopathological one. My career also followed the international trend of a psychology of (early) childhood and adolescence extending to development over the life-span up to old age, although for the better part of my time in office we had access to the relevant international literature only after unification.

In this process, clinical-developmental psychology benefited greatly from the progress of psychological methodology and methods, whereby the initial limitation of scientific investigation to phenomenological description was overcome and opened up to include empirical surveys, inquiries, and experimental findings. Findings and test results could be examined with new methods of mathematical statistics for their various connections, going beyond a mere counting of frequencies. The transition from mechanical to electronic data processing made prospective longitudinal studies possible for the first time.

In East Germany, though, this process was slower in comparison with the West due to political and ideological barriers. Scientific exchange was obstructed by restrictions on attending international congresses and on visits to research labs abroad, even on procuring literature, tests, and technical equipment, as well as by the intrusive monitoring of all correspondence with colleagues outside the GDR. Openness was enhanced remarkably after the 22nd International Congress of Psychology in Leipzig in 1980, under the auspices of the International Union of Psychological Science (IUPsyS), but was only truly achieved with German reunification.

In preparation for the congress, and as a consequence of it, my collaborators and I could attend scientific meetings in the West, including workshops on longitudinal research. In 1974, 1978, and 1987 we organized the "Ostsee Symposium" (Baltic Sea Symposium) for clinical psychology with international attendance, of which the last one was devoted to clinical developmental psychology. Restrictions concerning participants from countries outside the Socialist Block became obsolete only after unification.

The final liberation from a dictatorship occurred unexpectedly for my generation, although our children had been actively involved, and it has already been forgotten by our grandchildren. May a stable democracy be maintained for them and for our great-grandchildren!

Of the colleagues and collaborators mentioned, only Olaf Reis is still working at the University of Rostock, as research coordinator in the child psychiatric clinic. He is also the PI of the further follow-ups of the Rostock Longitudinal Study. Joachim Kruse is a Professor at a University of Applied Science in Munich. Erich Kurth and Helfried Teichmann were Professors and Chairs of rehabilitation psychology in Rostock and Berlin, respectively. Bernhard Meyer-Probst was my successor as Professor and Chair of medical psychology, and Dorothea Roether collaborated with him as adjunct professor. They all still live in the city of Rostock and have been enjoying their retirement.

References

Bischof-Köhler, D. (2006). *Von Natur aus anders. Die Natur der Geschlechtsunterschiede* [Different by nature: the nature of gender differences]. Stuttgart: W. Kohlhammer.

Bleck, H. & Teichmann, H. (1978). Die Altersabhängigkeit geschlechtsspezifischer Schulleistungsunterschiede [The dependence on age in gender related differences of school performance]. *Probleme und Ergebnisse der Psychologie*, Heft 64, 31–42.

Clauß, G. & Hiebsch, H. (1958). *Kinderpsychologie* [Child psychology]. Berlin: Volk und Wissen.

Göllnitz, G. (1954). *Die Bedeutung der frühkindlichen Hirnschädigung für die Kinderpsychiatrie* [The importance of minimal brain damage to child psychiatry]. Leipzig: Georg Thieme.

Göllnitz, G. & Rösler, H.-D. (Eds.). (1975). *Psychologische Untersuchungen zur Entwicklung hirngeschädigter Kinder* [Psychological investigations to the development of brain damaged children]. Berlin: Deutscher Verlag der Wissenschaften.

Grimm, H. & Rösler, H.-D. (1956). *Kinder fragen nach dem Geschlechtsleben* [Children ask for sexuality]. Rudolstadt, Germany: Greifenverlag.

Häßler, F. (1992). The hyperkinetic child. A historical review. *Acta Paedopsychiatrica, 55*, 147–149.

Ihle, W., Esser, G., Schmidt, M. H., Blanz, B., Reis, O., & Meyer-Probst, B. (1999). Risk conditions and developmental patterns of mental disorders from childhood to early adulthood—results from two longitudinal studies in Rostock and Mannheim. In R. K. Silbereisen & A. v. Eye (Eds), *Growing up in times of social change* (pp.131–149). Berlin, New York: Walter de Gruyter.

Kruse, J. (2004). *Emotionale, kognitive und körperliche Entwicklung bis zum 25. Lebensjahr* [Emotional, cognitive, and somatic development until the age of 25 years]. Hamburg: Verlag Dr. Kovac.

Kurth, E. (1969). Erhöhung der Leistungsnormen bei den Farbigen Progressiven Matrizen [Raise of performance norms for progressive matrices]. *Zeitschrift für Psychologie,177*, 85–90.

Kurth, E. (1978). *Motometrische Entwicklungsdiagnostik* [Motometric developmental diagnostics]. Berlin: Deutscher Verlag der Wissenschaften.

Martin, P., Ettrich, K. U., Lehr, U., Roether, D., Martin, M., & Fischer-Cyrulis, A. (Eds). (2000). *Perspektiven der Entwicklung im mittleren und höheren Lebensalter: Ergebnisse der Interdisziplinären Längsschnittstudie des Erwachsenenalters (ILSE)* [Perspectives of development in middle and higher age: results of the Interdisciplinary Longitudinal Study of Adult Age]. Heidelberg: Steinkopff.

Metzelthin, U. & Rösler, H.-D. (1970). Katamnestische Untersuchungen zur Entwicklung jugendlicher Mütter und ihrer Kinder [Follow-up studies on the development of juvenile mothers and their children]. *Ärztliche Jugendkunde, 61*, 316–329.

Meyer-Probst, B. (1984). Erfahrungen mit dem Hannover-Wechsler-Intelligenztest für das Vorschulalter (HAWIVA) [Experiences with the Hannover-Wechsler-Intelligence test for the preschool age]. *Psychologie für die Praxis, 2*, 127–133.

Meyer-Probst, B., Piatkowski, J., & Teichmann, H. (1988). Der Zusammenhang zwischen Entwicklungsrisiken und Schulbewährung—Ergebnisse der Rosocker Längsschnittstudie [The connection between risks of development and school proof—Results of the Rostock Longitudinal Study]. *Psychologie für die Praxis, 6*, 195–214.

Meyer-Probst, B., & Reis, O. (1999). Von der Geburt bis 25: Rostocker Längsschnittstudie (ROLS) [From birth to 25: Rostock Longitudinal Study (ROLS)]. *Kindheit und Entwicklung, 8*, 59–68.

Meyer-Probst, B., Rösler, H.-D., & Teichmann, H. (1983). Biological and psychosocial risk factors and development during childhood. In D. Magnusson & V. L. Allen (Eds.), *Human development: An interactional perspective* (pp. 243–259). New York: Academic Press.

Meyer-Probst, B. & Teichmann, H. (1985). Effects of biological and psychosocial risks on personality development: Results of the Rostock Longitudinal Study after 10 years. *The German Journal of Psychology, 9*, 161–170.

Meyer-Probst, B., Teichmann, H., Hayes, A., & Rauh, H. (1991). Follow-up of a cohort of risk. children from birth into adolescence—The Rostock Longitudinal Study. *Internationa Journal of Disability, Development and Education, 38*, 225–246.

Minnemann, E., Schmitt, M., Sperling, U., & Jüchtern, J.-C. (1997). Formen des Alterns: Sozialer, gesundheitlicher und biogeiphischer Kontext [Patterns of life styles: Social, health—related and biographical context]. *Zeitschrift für Gerontopsychologie und biogeiphischer, 10*, 251–257.

Oswald, W. D., Rupprecht, R., & Hagen, B. (1997). Aspekte der kognitiven Leistungsfähigkeit bei 62-64jährigen aus Ost- und Westdeutschland [Aspects of cognitive performance of people aged 62–64 years from East and West Germany]. *Zeitschrift für Gerontopsychologie und -psychiatrie, 10*, 213–229.

Reis, O. (1997). *Risiken und Ressourcen der Persönlichkeitsentwicklung im Übergang zum Erwachsenenalter* [Risks and resources of personality development in transition to adulthood]. Weinheim, Germany: Beltz.

Reis, O., Dörnte, M., & von der Lippe, H. (2011). Neuroticism, social support, and the timing of first parenthood: A prospective study. *Personality and individual Differences, 50*, 381–386.

Reis, O., Eisermann, I., & Meyer-Probst, B. (2003). Soziale Verbundenheit im frühen Erwachsenenalter—Muster und Antezedentien [Social relatedness in early adulthood—patterns and antecedents]. *Zeitschrift für Familienforschung*, Sonderheft 3, 125–137.

Richter, G. (1986). Nachuntersuchung von Enzephalopathen normaler Intelligenz [Follow-up of normally intelligent encephalopathies]. In A. Herbst & H.-D. Rösler (Eds.), *Frühkindlich Hirngeschädigte als Erwachsene* (pp. 21–40). Leipzig: S. Hirzel.

Rösler, H.-D. (1957). Sexualthemen in der Tagespresse und ihre Bedeutung für das Kindes- und Jugendalter [Sexual themes in the daily press and their meaning for infancy and youth]. *Zeitschrift für ärztliche Fortbildung, 51*, 991–992.

Rösler, H.-D. (1959). Änderungen in der Entwicklung des nichtehelichen Kindes [Changes in the development of the illegitimate child]. *Das Deutsche Gesundheitswesen, 14*, 1630–1636.

Rösler, H.-D. (1963a). *Leistungshemmende Faktoren in der Umwelt des Kindes* [Achievement inhibiting factors in the environment of the child]. Leipzig: J. A. Barth.

Rösler, H.-D. (1963b). Zur Frage des psychischen Entwicklungswandels unserer Jugend [On the problem of the psychic developmental change in our youth]. *Psychiatrie, Neurologie und medizinische Psychologie,15*, 467–478.

Rösler, H.-D. (1964). Über psychophysische Korrelationen im Entwicklungsalter [On psycho-physic correlations in developmental age]. *Zeitschrift für Psychologie, 170*, 242–260.

Rösler, H.-D. (1967a). Akzeleration und Intelligenzleistung im Erwachsenenalter [Acceleration and intelligence performance in adult age]. In F. Klix, W. Gutjahr & J. Mehl (Eds),

Intelligenzdiagnostik—Probleme und Ergebnisse intelligenzdiagnostischer Forschungen in der DDR (pp. 223–227). Berlin: Deutscher Verlag der Wissenschaften.

Rösler, H.-D. (1967b). Säkulare Änderungen in der Entwicklung der Intelligenz [Secular changes in the development of intelligence]. *die heilkunst, 8*(11), 1–8.

Rösler, H.-D. (1968). Epochalpsychologische Probleme des Reifealters [Epoch-psychological problems of maturity age]. *Wissenschaftliche Zeitschrift der Universität Rostock, Mathematisch-Naturwissenschaftliche Reihe,17* (6/7), 513–516.

Rösler, H.-D. (1969). Generationsunterschiede in der geistigen Leistungsfähigkeit [Generation differences in intelligence performance]. In J. Siebenbrodt (Ed.), *Bericht über den 2. Kongreß der Gesellschaft für Psychologie in der DDR* (pp. 140–145). Berlin: Deutscher Verlag der Wissenschaften.

Rösler, H.-D. (1989). Psychological studies on children with minimal brain damage. *The German Journal of Psychology, 13,* 193–209.

Rösler, H.-D. (1990). Zur säkularen Akzeleration der psychischen und somatischen Entwicklung [Secular changes in mental and somatic development]. *Ärztliche Jugendkunde, 81,* 76–85.

Rösler, H.-D., Heider, B., Meyer-Probst, B., Langemann, I., Piatkowski, J., & Teichmann, H. (1991). Wirkungen biologischer und psychosozialer Risiken auf die motorische Entwicklung: Ergebnisse der Rostocker Längsschnittstudie nach 14 Jahren. [Effects of biological and psychosocial risks on motor development: Results of the Rostock Longitudinal Study after 14 years]. *Zeitschrift für Psychologie,* Suppl.11, 471–482.

Rösler, H.-D., Bleck, H., & Teichmann, H. (1976). Zum Problem des Geschlechtsunterschiedes in der geistigen Leistungsfähigkeit [The problem of gender differences in intellectual efficiency]. *Ärztliche Jugendkunde, 67,* 366–376.

Rösler, H.-D., Dudeck, A., Gebert, K., & Vehreschild, T. (1980). Pädagogische und soziale Bedingungen [Pedagogical and social conditions]. In G. Göllnitz, J. Külz & G. K. Uschakow (Eds.), *Zur Kompensation und Dekompensation in der kindlichen Entwicklung* (pp. 207–215). Jena: Gustav Fischer.

Rösler, H.-D. (2004). Hans-Dieter Rösler. In H. E. Lück (Ed.), *Psychologie in Selbstdarstellungen* (pp. 265–286), Lengerich, Berlin: Pabst Science Publishers.

Rösler, H.-D. & Springstein, H.-J. (1988). Differentielle Entwicklungsverläufe nach Morbus haemolyticus neonatorum [Differentiated development after fetal erythroblastosis]. *Zentralblatt für Gynäkologie, 110,* 25–34.

Rösler, H.-D. & Springstein, H.-J (1990a). Schulerfolg nach Morbus haemolyticus Neonatorum [School success after fetal erythtroblastosis]. *Pädiatrie und Grenzgebiete, 29,* 3–11.

Rösler, H.-D. & Springstein, H.-J. (1990b). Zur Spätprognose von Risikokindern am Beispiel des Morbus haemolyticus neonatorum [The late prognosis of children born at risk, for example fetal erythroblastosis]. *Wissenschaftliche Zeitschrift der Universität Rostock, Naturwissenschaftliche Reihe, 39,* 57–59.

Schelsky, H. (1957). *Die skeptische Generation* [The sceptical generation]. Düsseldorf: Eugen Diederichs.

Schmidt, H.-D. (1970). *Allgemeine Entwicklungspsychologie* [General developmental psychology]. Berlin: Verlag der Wissenschaften.

Silbereisen, R. K., Rösler, H.-D., Kracke, B., & Reis, O. (1993). Forschung zur biosozialen Entwicklung Jugendlicher in der DDR [Research on the biosocial development of adolescents in the GDR]. In L. A. Vaskovics & R. K. Silbereisen (Eds.), *Sozialforschung in der DDR—Sonderband* (pp. 71–158). Bonn: Informationszentrum Sozialwissenschaften.

Silbereisen, R. K. & Todt, E. (1994). Adolescence—a matter of context. In R. K. Silbereisen & E. Todt (Eds.), *Adolescence in context* (pp. 3–21). New York, Berlin: Springer Verlag.

Teichmann, H. (1969a). Die Ansprüche der Eltern an die Schulleistungen ihrer Kinder [The expects of parents to school performance of their children]. *Probleme und Ergebnisse der Psychologie,* Heft 31, 45–79.

Teichmann, H. (1969b). Belastungsfolgen bei Unzufriedenheit der Eltern mit den Schulleistungen ihrer Kinder [Load results after discontent of parents with the school performance of their children]. *Pädiatrie und Grenzgebiete, 8,* 301–313.

Thulesius, L. K. & Teichmann, H. (1972). Accelerative trends in intellectual development. *British Journal of social and clinical Psychology, 11,* 284–294.

Voracek, M., Dressler, S. G., & Loibl, L. M. (2008). The contributions of Hans-Dieter Rösler: pioneer of digit ratio (2D:4D) research. *Psychological Reports, 103,* 899–916.

37

Establishing Developmental Psychopathology

Michael Rutter

Childhood and Adolescence

I came from a very medical family, with both my father and grandfather working as general practitioners and then taking Public Health appointments. My interest in psychology was first stimulated at school by my physics master who introduced me to the writings of Sigmund Freud. I was intrigued by what Freud had to say on mental mechanisms but I thought that his account of psychosexual development was very unlikely to be correct (as shown later in the systematic review that I did on the topic). I trained myself to wake every time I had a dream and to write it down immediately before turning back to sleep. It was an interesting project that, although it produced no answers, excited my scientific curiosity. I left school at the age of 16 and went straight on to medical school (at an age below that which was officially allowed), with the intention of becoming a general practitioner. However, I became interested in the interconnections between brain and mind, both as a result of various readings and also my experience working on psychiatric, neurosurgical, and neurological units. An important turning point came with an elective with Professor Mayer-Gross who advised me to obtain a broad training in neurology and medicine before going on to psychiatric training at the Maudsley Hospital. He was the first person to emphasize the value of engaging in research and I knew that if I went to the Maudsley Hospital I would have to do that. Initially, I was somewhat put off because I thought I knew that I would not be interested in research and I would not be good at it. As it turned out, I was wrong on both counts because the voyage of discovery that is intrinsic to research proved quite compelling. Some developmental researchers have been very concerned that their research should confirm all their own hypotheses. That always seemed to me a bizarre aim because, if it proved to be the case, it would

mean that the whole of one's research career had been a waste of time. Instead, it is the discovery of the unexpected that makes research so addictive.

Psychiatric and Psychological Training

My psychiatric training at the Maudsley Hospital strongly fostered my interest in research. The then Head of the Institute of Psychiatry was Professor Sir Aubrey Lewis, a polymath with a towering intellect. Working with him was a little bit frightening but it was never anything other than hugely engaging and interesting. It prompted one to question and to try to understand. Each Saturday morning, trainees had to present at "journal clubs," Lewis having allocated them a particular paper. I was given a paper on experimentally induced sensory isolation and later an epidemiological paper looking at connections between illness in parents and psychiatric problems in children. The first provided the beginnings of my interest in maternal deprivation and the second provided the prompt for the comparable study that I undertook for my doctoral thesis. At that time, there was an immense amount of teaching on psychology as part of the course for the academic diploma in psychological medicine. This was led by Hans Eysenck, a wonderful teacher, who excited an interest in psychology among many trainees, including myself. However, he was not a good role model in that his psychology was somewhat idiosyncratic and was completely unquestioning, with his research findings sometimes suspect (Buchanan, 2010). Nevertheless, at that time, the amount of psychology was sufficient that successful completion of the course provided accreditation as a psychologist.

Lewis decided that I should become an academic child psychiatrist and that in order to do this I would have to go to the USA to work with psychologists who could teach me about development. I was not at all sure that I wanted to do child psychiatry and I noted that one of the conditions laid down by Lewis was that I should never undertake training in child psychiatry (because it was generally poor at that time and, most especially, because it was taught in a way that inhibited creativity and original thought). Indeed, I never have been formally trained in child psychiatry. I was excited by the possibility of training in developmental psychology and I chose to work with Herb Birch in New York (along with Alex Thomas and Stella Chess) on their developmental study of child temperament. Herb was also a polymath, who initially worked on studies of great apes but then moved to abnormal child development and, whilst a professor of psychology at Albert Einstein College of Medicine, went through medical school, alarming his teachers with the provocative and penetrating questions that he asked on everything.

Training and Research

Before going to New York, I worked in the MRC Social Psychiatry Unit (directed by Aubrey Lewis) and on my return from New York a year later I rejoined the Unit. The Unit was an immensely exciting place to be because of the extremely bright iconoclasts who helped me develop my research skills. Almost all of us were first appointed to the Unit before obtaining a doctorate and yet almost all went on to become international stars. The two members of the Unit with whom I worked most closely were Jack Tizard, a social psychologist initially from New Zealand, and George Brown, a medical sociologist. Although I never collaborated directly with her, I was also much influenced by Beate Hermelin and from her I learned to think experimentally. On one occasion, Jack asked Aubrey Lewis how on earth he was able to pick future stars so early in their careers. Aubrey thought for a moment and then said something along the lines of "Well, of course, they had to be very bright but I took the awkward ones that other people wouldn't have." Jack wasn't terribly pleased with that answer but Aubrey went on to explain that he wanted people who would not meekly accept the given wisdom of the day and who knew how to question constructively in order to develop new knowledge. That was very much the style in the Unit and it certainly influenced me in adopting a similar questioning style throughout my whole career.

My year in New York with Herb, Alex, and Stella was a hugely formative one, both from what I gained from them (and all three were immensely kind and supportive) and from the stars with whom they put me in touch. These are too many to list but they included Jerry Kagan, who later became a good friend; Lee Robins, the medical sociologist, who similarly became a close friend and a very important mentor; and Leon Eisenberg, the child psychiatrist, who also became a mentor and good friend. After I returned to London, I received a Belding Travelling Scholarship, entitling me, amongst other things, to spend some time in 1963 in St. Louis, getting to know Lee better and to appreciate what was required to undertake top quality longitudinal studies. Lee's own long-term follow-up of Child Guidance Clinic attendees has become the major classic in the field (Robins, 1966)

On my return to the social psychiatry unit in 1962, after learning a lot about development, I undertook a course in statistics at the London School of Hygiene and I initiated research in two rather different fields—studies of family interaction and studies of autism.

Autism

In moving into the field of autism, I decided to undertake a long-term follow-up of children with autism (at that time regarded as an infantile psychosis), using as a comparison a group of individuals referred over the same period of time to the same clinical center but with some psychiatric disorder of a different kind. Because autism involved substantial heterogeneity, the initial question was whether there was any unifying feature. The two groups were made comparable by stratification for age, sex, and IQ. The purpose was to determine whether there was anything meaningfully distinct about the diagnosis of autism and I thought about the study mainly as a "pot-boiler" while I got on with the planning of a family study. The autism study was later foolishly criticized because it did not have a normal control group, but that would have been absolutely pointless in that the differentiation from normality was the easy bit. The key query was whether autism differed from other psychiatric disorders arising in the same age period, and it was that consideration that determined the design. The findings were unexpected in two different respects. First, a substantial minority of the children with autism developed epileptic seizures during the period of adolescence, despite the fact that on the basis of the neurological assessments available at the time there had been no indication of abnormality (Rutter, 1970). This provided the first indication that autism represented a neurodevelopmental disorder and not a psychogenic psychosis. What was striking about the epilepsy was not so much its occurrence but rather the fact that it had its onset in adolescence, an unusual timing in individuals who did not have autism.

The second finding concerned the importance of both language impairments and cognitive deficits. The findings showed that good outcomes were most likely when the children gained useful language by the age of 5 years (a finding in keeping with Leon Eisenberg's similar observation earlier) and that poor outcomes were almost universal in those who had a nonverbal IQ below 50.

Autism and Specific Language Impairment The language findings suggested that autism might arise on the basis of a language deficit. My colleagues and I set out to test that hypothesis by comparing boys with autism but a nonverbal IQ within the normal range and a comparable group of boys with a severe developmental language disorder (now more usually called specific language impairment, SLI) also with a nonverbal IQ in the normal range. The initial findings showed such marked differences between the two groups that it was necessary to rule out the original hypothesis that autism represented an unusually severe degree of language impairment. Rather, the findings indicated that autism arose out of a much broader cognitive impairment that included language, but went well beyond it. The same two groups were then followed up into middle childhood and then on into early adult life. The findings were interesting in several different respects. First, a proportion of the individuals with SLI showed a drop in nonverbal IQ, whereas that was not found in the autism group. This meant that the cognitive comparisons were somewhat different in adult life as compared with those in early childhood. It was crucial to recognize the importance of developmental change—a point emphasized by Karmiloff-Smith in her arguments that modularity (with respect to either language or other cognitive functions) could not be assumed to be an innate "given" but rather represented a process that developed over time, albeit with biological constraints of one kind or another. The second key finding was that, although the groups did remain rather different, they were more similar in adult life than they had been in early childhood because so many of the individuals with SLI developed social problems that had not been manifest when they were young. Although there was no reason to doubt the original rejection of the language origin hypothesis, it was necessary to recognize that autism and SLI were more similar than had at first appeared to be the case (Rutter, 2008).

The key cognitive difference between autism and SLI concerned the profile or pattern of cognitive skills and weaknesses that was associated with autism. It was concluded that the language problems associated with autism arose out of a much broader cognitive deficit concerned with the meaning of language and communication—both verbal and nonverbal. During the 1960s, Hermelin and O'Connor took this much further in an ingenious program of experiments that showed the difficulties that autistic children had in a range of mentalizing skills (Hermelin & O'Connor, 1970). Moreover, the findings suggested that these might well underlie the social impairments that characterize autism. During the 1980s this led on to the identification (by Frith and Baron-Cohen) of "theory of mind" impairments in autism.

Claim that Autism Was Psychogenically Determined During the 1960s and 1970s some researchers were arguing that the cognitive impairment in autism was simply a consequence of social anxiety and social withdrawal and, therefore, did not have the usual meaning associated with intelligence. The arguments in favor of this proposition were not at all convincing but it seemed important that the ideas should be subjected to systematic testing (Rutter, 1979). The longitudinal study findings showed that IQs in children with autism had much the same predictive validity as those in any other group of children—contrary to what had been hypothesized on the social anxiety/withdrawal hypothesis. However, we tested the hypothesis more directly using experimental approaches. It was shown that IQ subtest scores (individual test items) went up and down according to task difficulty and not according to anxiety. On the other hand, it was shown that children with autism were particularly likely to adopt a stereotyped response pattern of some kind following task failure.

During this same time period, Bettelheim (1967) was arguing that autism arose as a result of parental rejection. We used a wide range of interview and questionnaire measures to examine this possibility. Our results, as well as those of others, were consistently negative. Some commentators were inclined to conclude that these negative findings provided a rejection of the psychogenicity hypothesis. However, that was going too far because, inevitably, all the research had to examine family functioning after autism had become manifest. Retrospective reports of earlier stresses and adversity were equally negative but it could not be completely ruled out that early stress or adversity had played some role in the origins of autism. The psychogenic origin theory faded away, nevertheless, because there was no supporting evidence for it and because of the growing evidence of neurodevelopmental impairment. Systematic comparisons of different forms of teaching or caring for children were also relevant in their finding that children did much better with structured teaching than with a permissive approach that allowed regression (which the psychogenic theorists had advocated).

Genetic Influences on Liability to Autism During the 1960s, I wrote a review paper that concluded that genetic influences were unlikely to be of major importance in autism because the rate of autism in siblings was so low (at that time estimated at about 2%). No sooner had the paper been published than I realized that my reasoning had been quite wrong. The key issue was not the absolute rate of autism but rather whether the rate in siblings was substantially higher than that in the general population—which it obviously was (the rate in the general population being estimated at that time was about 4 per 10,000). Accordingly, I decided that a systematic twin study was essential in order to determine the possible importance of genetic factors in the liability to autism. Two circumstances were crucial in taking things forward. First, I was asked whether I was interested in having the list of twin pairs accumulated over the years by the late Dr. M. Carter. Second, Dr. Susan Folstein came to my department to work for a period in the UK. It was particularly fortunate because she had more experience of genetics than I had at that time. Through a wide range of strategies we did as systematic a search as obtainable for all possibly autistic twin pairs in the UK. The spirit of cooperation among colleagues in the UK made that feasible in a way that would have been much more difficult in other countries. The sample was relatively small (21 pairs). Nevertheless findings clearly showed a high heritability and, moreover, showed that this liability extended beyond the traditional diagnostic boundary (Folstein & Rutter, 1977). During the 1970s, geneticists were reluctant to accept the concept of a broader phenotype but subsequent research has amply confirmed that it exists. A later extension of the twin sample by Tony Bailey and Ann Le Couteur (Bailey, Le Couteur, Gottesman, Bolton, & Simonoff, 1995: Le Couteur et al., 1996) enabled us to check whether the first study had missed relevant cases, with findings showing that very few had not been picked up. It provided strong confirmation of the high heritability and the extension of that liability to the broader phenotype. It was also quite striking how much heterogeneity there was within concordant monozygotic pairs.

The implication was that autistic-like abnormalities of a lesser degree were likely to be found in members of families having one or more children with autism. A systematic family study comparing families with a proband with autism and families with a Down syndrome child showed that this was indeed the case, as did a parallel study undertaken by Folstein and her colleagues in the USA.

Intervention Studies These relatively early studies led to several rather different developments. First, it was clear that systematic studies of intervention were required. Pilot studies showed that therapeutic gains tended to be relatively situation-specific unless particular steps were taken to ensure generalization. Accordingly, a treatment program was designed that used parents as cotherapists and which placed a high premium on trying to ensure that the approaches were used at school as well as at home and elsewhere (Howlin & Rutter, 1987). Efficacy was considered in relation to both short-term improvements and long term gains, using somewhat different strategies for the two. The findings from Patricia Howlin and Rosemary Hemsley (Hemsley et al., 1978) showed statistically significant and worthwhile reductions in behavioral problems but much more limited gains in both language and cognition. It was also striking, however, how much heterogeneity there was in children's responses. Nevertheless, the results of this home-based treatment were sufficiently striking that it became clear that they needed to be continued as part of a regular service now that efficacy had been shown. That was negotiated and achieved with the hospital services at that time.

Second, it was obvious from all the studies that we had undertaken that more systematic standardized methods of measurement were necessary and, in collaboration with Catherine Lord and Ann Le Couteur, we designed a diagnostic interview (Lord et al., 1989), a diagnostic observation schedule (Le Couteur et al., 1989), and, somewhat later, a questionnaire screening measure. The interview and observation measures have since become what is currently the "gold standard" set of measures for diagnosis. More recently, similar measures have been developed to assess, in dimensional terms, the broader phenotype of autism.

Molecular Genetics Technological, as well as conceptual, developments in molecular biology made possible the application of molecular genetics strategies designed to identify the actual genes underlying the liability to autism. An affected-relative study was established, based on an international consortium working together with the same methods. Despite the very high heritability of autism, it proved frustratingly difficult to identify the actual genes

responsible for the genetic influences. Important leads were found and were replicated but there is still quite a long way to go before the genetic basis of the liability to autism is properly sorted out. Recent findings have made it clear that pathogenic single gene mutations play some role, as well as the much more common polymorphic variations found more widely in the population (Rutter, 2010).

Quasi-Autism The last development was the most unexpected one. This involved the identification of quasi-autism in children who had experienced profound institutional deprivation lasting until at least the age of 6 months (Rutter & Sonuga-Barke, 2010). It would not have been likely that we would have included the relevant measures in our study of adoptees from Romania were it not for the fact that, by chance, at about the time we were planning the study, I had two separate clinical referrals of children, both of whom had suffered institutional deprivation and showed autistic-like features. It is clear that this does not constitute a usual causal factor for autism (because it is found so uncommonly in the field of autism) but the findings did suggest that autism-like patterns might arise on the basis of an external restriction of sensory processing as well as an internal deficit associated with a genetic liability.

Lessons from Autism Research I learned several research lessons in the course of this program of research that has extended for some half a century during which the concept of autism changed from that of a psychogenic psychosis requiring psychotherapy to a neurodevelopmental disorder best treated with developmentally oriented behavioral methods. First, there was the appreciation of the importance of undertaking research in a way that allowed the discovery of totally unexpected findings. The emergence of epilepsy in late adolescence was one example and the discovery of quasi-autism following institutional deprivation was another. Second, it is crucial to be alert to the occasions when you have been wrong in your inferences. The genetics of autism is the striking example of that kind. The need, however, is not to berate oneself for being wrong but rather to swiftly set about putting it right. Third, it is important to take seriously opposing views and to undertake research systematically to test their validity. The studies of family functioning and of the possibility that cognitive impairments derive from social anxiety/ withdrawal would be an example of this kind. Fourth, there is the need to look out for the opportunities presented by serendipity. The twin study exemplifies that well. Fifth, it is always desirable to examine the treatment implications of research findings and, wherever possible, to ensure that there is a two-way pathway from research to clinical work and back again. Sixth, when moving into a new territory, there may often be a need to develop new standardized measures, as was the case here. Seventh, it is always important to bear in mind the possibility of developmental change and its implications. The comparison of autism and specific language impairment exemplifies that. Eighth, there are many advantages to be derived from the parallel study of the normal and abnormal; the identification of "theory of mind" deficits constitutes a good example. Ninth, throughout the research, there were numerous examples of combining it with clinical work (as in the referral of children adopted from Romania who had autistic-like problems). Finally, it is necessary to train oneself in new skills when taking on research challenges that demand that. Obviously that was needed, so far as I was concerned, with the acquisition of expertise in genetics. The value of new technologies is also shown by the move from quantitative to molecular genetics.

Maternal Deprivation

As with the study of autism, my interest in maternal deprivation began at the start of my research career and continues to this day. My first approach involved a review of the literature, focusing on the difference between the short-term consequences and the long-term outcomes and also focusing on the differences among experiences encompassed by the broad term of maternal deprivation (Rutter, 1972). I learned all sorts of different things from this review, including the importance of a dispassionate balancing of the evidence and the value of considering what can be learned through animal studies. With respect to the last, the input from Robert Hinde was crucially important. I had met Robert whilst I was writing the first draft of my book on "maternal deprivation reassessed" and was bold enough to send him a copy of the draft asking for his comments, criticisms, and suggestions. It was a bit hopeful because I was still very much a fledgling scientist, whereas he was an international expert in the field of animal behavior. He wrote back a very long memo, extending over several pages. This started with some positive, friendly comments but then moved on to very detailed constructive criticisms that necessitated substantial rewriting. Once I had got over the shock of such a critical appraisal, I realized that actually it was very flattering that he had been willing to take the time and trouble going through my draft in such detail. Not only did I learn a lot from him on animal studies, I also learned the value of constructive criticism rather than bland comments of "marvelous." That constituted a model of feedback that I sought to follow. His input enabled me to greatly improve the book and he became, in effect, a mentor at a distance.

Some people are inclined to think that this interest must have been prompted by my evacuation to the USA between 1940 and 1944, during which time I was extremely well looked after by American foster parents (although they did not call themselves that). I was away from my biological parents and also separated from my sister but in no sense was I maternally deprived. Indeed, as it felt at the time, and still does today (I remained in touch with my American mother until her death this year). I was fortunate in having two sets of parents. My American parents had never met my British birth parents but, because we often spoke about them (weekly letters were regularly exchanged) both sets of parents were very much part of my life during the wartime years.

Because I was so struck with the heterogeneity of outcomes following maternal deprivation, in the book I raised the possibility of genetic influences on susceptibility to environmental experiences. That constituted the beginnings of my interest in gene–environment interaction, which later became a major research endeavor. It also got me thinking about the notion of resilience—namely a person's resistance to environmental stress or adversity, or a later overcoming of such effects. There were several studies over the years that examined the issue systematically. For example, studies undertaken with David Quinton examined children experiencing residential care because of a breakdown in parenting (Quinton & Rutter, 1988). We examined this both retrospectively and prospectively—two complementary research strategies that gave rise to very similar conclusions. One of the findings was that many of the young people taken into care as a result of parenting breakdown developed a mental set of thinking that they were unable to influence what happened to themselves. However, there were exceptions and it appeared that good experiences involving successes in other domains (such as at school) seemed to enable them to get a different mental set that involved planning in relation to key life decisions. Amongst other things, the findings led me to conceptualize resilience in terms of a process rather than a personality trait.

My review of maternal deprivation naturally led me to develop a major interest in children's development of selective attachments. Bowlby's theorizing and Mary Ainsworth's empirical studies were crucially important in differentiating attachments from other aspects of parent–child interactions. Many years later these notions played a major role in understanding the effects of institutional deprivation in children adopted from profoundly depriving Romanian institutions into U.K. adoptive families.

Study of Adoptees from Romanian Institutions During the early 1990s, the British Department of Health approached me to ask whether a study could be undertaken to determine what happened to children who had suffered such severe and pervasive institutional deprivation in early life and who were then adopted into what were, on average, well-functioning adoptive families. We were funded initially to undertake a pilot study and, when this showed that it was possible to trace and gain the cooperation of the families, a grant was provided for a systematic longitudinal study. This involved both adoptees from Romania and a comparison group of children who had not experienced such deprivation and who were adopted under the age of 6 months within the UK. Both groups were initially assessed at 4 years of age and then again at 6 years, 11 years, and 15 years. The assessments involved a mixture of qualitative and quantitative approaches, interviews both with the young people and their parents, psychological testing, and questionnaires. Without doubt, this constituted the most interesting and rewarding study that I have undertaken, because it threw up so many unexpected findings (Rutter & Sonuga-Barke, 2010). It constituted what came to be known as a "natural experiment" in which circumstances provided a means of testing the hypothesis about environmental causation. In the case of the study of Romanian adoptees, what was unique was that the children had been admitted to institutions at birth or in the first few weeks of life and, therefore, there was no opportunity for them to have been admitted because of handicap (a major confound in all previous studies of institutional care). It was also crucially important that the move from a profoundly depriving environment to a generally above-average family environment occurred at a defined moment and that there were longitudinal data that enabled the study of within-individual change, rather than having to rely on between-group differences.

The unexpected findings were of several different kinds. Thus, although the majority of the children had been severely subnourished, subnutrition played a surprisingly negligible role in individual differences in outcome. What proved to be crucially important was how long deprivation continued during the child's lifetime. There were no significant deficits when the children were aged less than six months at the time they left the institutions to go to their adoptive families. In sharp contrast, the rate of deficits rose to some 40–50% when the deprivation continued through the second half of the first year of life. At the time we started the study, the "given wisdom" was that recovery would occur quickly or not at all and the effects of deprivation would fade markedly over time. Those assumptions proved to be wrong. Whilst the greatest changes occurred during the first 2 years or so after adoption, they continued in many children right up to adolescence and beyond. Most strikingly, the effects of institutional deprivation were as marked at 15 years as they had been earlier. Our results also showed that deprivation in the absence of subnutrition nevertheless had marked effects on brain growth. These were not evident if the children left institutional care under the age of 6 months but were apparent if it continued after that age. It seemed that, as it were, it took a little while for the effects of deprivation to "kick in" biologically but they were then marked. The recovery of height and weight was mainly complete during the first 2 years but impairment in head growth, and by implication brain growth, as shown by a pilot brain-imaging study, continued right into adolescence. There was significant catch-up even during the period between 11 and 15 years, but it was incomplete. To a small, but statistically significant extent, the impairment in head growth accounted for some of the variance in psychological outcomes. Another assumption of virtually everyone in the field at the start of the study was that the main effects of institutional deprivation would be an increase in the rate of common forms of emotional and behavioral disturbance. That was not what we found at all. Rather, the effects were on unusual patterns such as disinhibited attachment, quasi-autism, and also on inattention/overactivity and cognition. It might have been thought that the extraordinarily strong and persisting effects of institutional deprivation would mean that changes for the better in adolescence were unlikely to occur. Certainly, there was remarkable persistence of the effects of deprivation, but this was not infrequently accompanied by important real life successes.

Although attachment theorists have been concerned to view the effects of institutional care in terms of an interference with the *security* of attachments, our findings provided no support for that view. Rather, experiences interfered with the *development* of selective attachments and did not bring about insecurity in selective attachments that had already been established.

We were able to maintain, over a period of many years, a very high level of cooperation from the families, and it appeared that one of the things that made a difference was the fact that I was available at the end of the telephone to give advice to the families when that was needed and also to see them personally if that was indicated. The families were perfectly well aware that this was a piece of research, and not a clinical service, but one of the ways of expressing our appreciation for their help was for us, in turn, to provide help when that was asked for. We provided newsletters throughout the study and after the 15-year follow-up we had two meetings with families in which both the young people and their parents spoke about participation in the study. Because of a commitment to view research in terms of policy and practice implications, we had two separate reports, one dealing with the science (Rutter & Sonuga-Barke, 2010) and one dealing with policy and practice (Rutter et al., 2009).

Stress, Coping, and Development During the 1970s, Norm Garmezy spent a sabbatical year in my Department and jointly we planned to establish a group to work together on "Stress, Coping, and Development," which took place in 1979/80 at the Center for Advanced Study in the Behavioral Sciences at Stanford. As it turned out, the final group of Fellows was more heterogeneous than we had envisaged initially, and that heterogeneity proved to be a strong advantage. Norm brought to the group his experience in running Project Competence, and thereby in studying stress and resilience, Jerry Kagan his knowledge of temperament, Jerry Patterson his unrivalled experience in studying parenting interventions, Judy Wallerstein her understanding of the effects of divorce, Lew Lipsitt his knowledge about stress in infancy, and Julius Segal his experience in using research to improve public policy (Garmezy & Rutter, 1983). All of us got on well together, and we learned a lot from each other. For me it was a hugely informative experience that influenced my research thereafter. Significantly, the friendships from that time have continued ever since. Norm and I wrote a chapter together on developmental psychopathology, emphasizing continuities and discontinuities over the course of development from infancy into adult life, and the continuities and discontinuities between normality and pathology (Rutter & Garmezy, 1983). My interest in the topic of resilience was also firmly established during my year at the Center.

The collaboration with Norm, by then a close friend as well as mentor, was cemented during the 1980s by participation in the MacArthur Foundation consortium in developmental psychopathology, chaired by Norm Garmezy. Once more, the opportunities for learning from world leaders were wonderful.

Lessons from Maternal Deprivation Research Although the subject matter was quite different, the lessons I learned about the science were broadly comparable with those that emerged from the autism studies. An iconoclastic skepticism about the wisdom of the day was important, as was a style of research that enabled sensitivity to the possibility of unexpected findings. Attention to the needs of participants in our research proved to be helpful in undertaking the research, as well as a necessary discharging of responsibilities to those who had helped us. Sometimes it is supposed that there is a sharp distinction between basic science and applied science but this field of research amply demonstrated that the dichotomy is false. The fact that the study of Romanian adoptees was both a hard-headed scientific natural experiment and also a study designed to produce policy implications proved a strength and not a weakness. Similarly, the combination of both quantitative and qualitative research methods also proved an asset. I concluded that both styles of research have an important place and that the supposed schism between the two is unnecessary, with combination often being the best way forward. Lastly, the sabbatical year free from administrative and clinical responsibilities was hugely beneficial, both because of the interactions with top-class developmental scientists and because it enabled me to think anew on research goals and strategies.

Epidemiology

After I returned from New York in 1962 to rejoin the Social Psychiatry Research Unit, I spent some time working as a junior member of the research team (led by Herb Birch) undertaking the Aberdeen epidemiological study. That provided me with useful experience in epidemiological approaches, and shortly after that Jack Tizard, my colleague in the Unit, was approached by the Department of Education with the question as to whether it would be possible to determine whether the physical ill health found to be associated with educational retardation some half a century earlier by Burt still applied today. The answer was that certainly that was possible but it would also provide the opportunity for a much wider ranging study to examine the interconnections among different forms of problems in childhood. The study could have both important policy

implications and also could provide knowledge on risk factors for different problems. Jack brought me in on these discussions and this led to a most productive set of meetings with the planning coming from both the government department and us as scientists. Back in the 1960s, the government in the UK recognized that it would be of value for them to have research that would provide information of broad use in planning but not necessarily answering questions in relation to specific government policies of that time. That totally changed in 1979 and, despite multiple changes of government since that time, it has never gone back to the cooperative planning approach that we enjoyed in the 1960s. The Department of Education not only provided a grant for the study but also seconded its senior medical officer, Dr. Kingsley Whitmore, to work part time, with a particular focus on providing a pediatric medical input.

Isle of Wight Study Initially, we planned to carry out a pilot study on the Isle of Wight (IoW), an island just off the south coast of England, but when we went to work there it dawned on us that this would be the ideal place for the main study, rather than in the broad region called Wessex on the mainland. Four features were crucial in taking that decision. First, the key players in the local government on the Isle of Wight were all situated in the same building and were very helpful in all that we wanted. Second, the IoW had a total population of about 100,000, which we reckoned was about right for studying common disorders. Third, the social class composition of the population on the Isle of Wight, at that time, was almost identical with that in the UK as a whole, and fourth its boundaries were defined by water so that there were no ambiguities as to who lived there and who did not. Jack was incredibly generous in asking me to take the main leadership of the study, although he remained very actively involved throughout, and his wisdom and guidance were crucially important in making a success of the study.

The large-scale field work for the study, involving the assessment of many hundreds of children, was undertaken in a way that, again, could not be done today. All those involved came down to the IoW on a Sunday evening and returned again on the Thursday. Friday and Saturday were spent undertaking all our usual work duties back in London and the next Sunday we went down to the IoW once again. Almost all the people who undertook the field work, for periods ranging from 2 weeks up to several months, had been trained either by Jack Tizard or myself. At that time both the Health Services and the universities were very flexible in allowing people to take time to do work of this kind, for which they were paid a rather modest nominal honorarium. This flexibility has long since gone. Each evening from Sunday through Wednesday we had a group meeting to discuss whatever issues had arisen during the day and after the meeting those of us who were involved in checking the interviews that had been undertaken that day worked hard for the hours leading up to midnight before retiring to bed. The whole team more or less took over one of the main hotels and, although we worked exceedingly hard, it was very much an enjoyable, friendly, cooperative enterprise. It is also noteworthy that, because those seeing children had to do so without knowing anything about them other than their age and sex, it proved a tremendously useful learning experience that would have been difficult to obtain any other way. Clinicians were used to undertaking assessments after interviewing parents and, when this was not possible for scientific reasons they had to focus their attention just on what the children said and how they behaved.

The IoW study included several important methodological innovations (Rutter, Tizard, & Whitmore, 1970; Rutter, 1989). First, multiple data sources were used to survey the entire population. Second, a two-stage research strategy was employed, beginning with a multiple source screen and following this with a much more detailed study of children whose problems were picked up on the screen. The detailed studies included standardized interviews with parents, children, and teachers, together with standardized neurodevelopmental and medical examinations and systematic individual psychological testing of the children. Third, the interviews used with both parents and children differed from what had been done previously in being both clinically oriented and standardized, with systematic testing of reliability and validity. Before the IoW study, most people had assumed that it was not useful to ask children direct questions about their psychopathology but the IoW study showed that it was useful. Fourth, psychiatric disorders were based on symptom patterns rather than assumptions about intra-psychic mechanisms (as had previously been the case). Fifth, longitudinal research strategies were used to examine the course of disorders and also to examine risk factors. Sixth, a range of research strategies were used to test causal hypotheses with respect to features as disparate as organic brain dysfunction and family discord. Seventh, standardized neurodevelopmental assessments were used to relate neurological findings to psychiatric measures. Eighth, use was made of longitudinal/epidemiological data to determine the ways in which nonresponders differed from subjects for whom data were available.

Several substantive findings of lasting importance were produced. There was a high rate of co-occurrence among all types of problem. It was also clear that the service needs were greatest for those who showed multiple problems, rather than those who showed just one. That had implications for U.K. policy because needs at that time tended to be based on which particular problem was present. The IoW findings showed that that was not a sensible way to proceed. This led on to the current situation whereby most patients have multiple diagnoses—so-called comorbidity. When we reviewed the issues it was found that there were many different explanations for this co-occurrence, and only a minority reflected true comorbidity in the sense of the co-occurrence of two completely different disorders. A second finding was the very substantial rise in

psychopathology, particularly involving depression, during the adolescent age period. This raised tricky questions on what features might be responsible for that change. The findings also brought out the rather different picture provided by reports from young people and from their parents (particularly with respect to depression).

The same rather modest level of agreement applied to reports from parents and from teachers. Some of this reflected the fact that children behave differently in different situations but, almost certainly, differences in part reflected differences in perception and in concept. Even today, there has not been a satisfactory study truly identifying the factors involved in differences among informants.

Against the prevailing views of the time, poor peer relations and inattention/overactivity were found to be the behaviors showing the strongest association with psychiatric disorder. This focused attention on the possible value of dimensional concepts that extended well beyond traditional diagnostic categories. Now, nearly half a century later, a long-term follow-up of the IoW sample into middle age (led by Barbara Maughan and Andrew Pickles) is showing that other features that had hitherto been dismissed as of no great interest actually constitute long-term risk factors— irritability being a good example of that kind.

The IoW studies highlighted the range of critical issues concerning depressive disorders arising in adolescence. In the 1960s, there was a general assumption that depression in young people had a quite different meaning from that in adult life but there was a need to test this systematically. The approach that we followed was a follow-up study led by Dick Harrington. The application to undertake this research was initially rejected and, for the one and only time in my career, I wrote back to the funding agency. In my letter I said that, of course, I accepted the decision but I thought I should point out that the reviewers had both misunderstood the design and that their logic led in the opposite direction to that they thought it did. I went on in a courteous fashion to point out the nature of the misunderstanding and its implications. To my surprise, the funding agency decided to send my reply back to the several reviewers who all responded by saying that, actually, I was quite right in what I said and that the study should be funded. So the study did go ahead. The findings were quite striking in showing that there was a strong risk of a recurrence of depressive disorders in adult life and, moreover, that the risk was diagnosis-specific. That is to say, depression was not associated with an increased rate of other disorders.

A later follow-up of a much larger sample by Eric Fombonne used a much tighter definition of depression (Fombonne, Wostear, Cooper Harrington, & Rutter, 2001). Similar outcome issues were investigated but there was a particular focus on whether depressive disorders that co-occurred with antisocial behavior had a different outcome. Findings confirmed the earlier investigation with respect to the high recurrence rate of depression but the outcome for depression was unaffected by the presence of antisocial behavior. On the other hand, this double diagnosis group had a much higher rate of suicidal behavior during the course of the 20-year follow up. The double group was also associated with greater social impairment in adult life. As in the earlier study, for those with antisocial behavior in childhood or adolescence, as well as depression, there was a high rate of criminality in adult life. These findings were associated with the general acceptance of the strength of continuities between childhood and adult life as well as with similarities between depressive disorders in the two age periods.

Similar issues led to further specific research looking at antisocial behavior. In line with other research, we found strong continuities between childhood and adult life but, in a follow up of a high-risk group, we paid particular attention to the unusual occurrence of antisocial behavior beginning for the first time in adult life without a previous occurrence in childhood. The findings showed that this occurrence was usually associated with either development of a new mental disorder (such as schizophrenia) or substance-abuse problems.

Organic Brain Dysfunction In addition to the main IoW survey in middle childhood (followed up into adolescence) there was a larger scale survey (led by Philip Graham, Bill Yule, and myself) of all school-age children in order to examine both the frequency and the patterns of neurological and neuropsychiatric disorders (Rutter, Graham, & Yule, 1970). A central question was whether organic brain dysfunction constituted a major risk factor for psychopathology. The alternatives were that the risks arose, not from brain dysfunction as such, but rather from low IQ or from physical handicaps. The epidemiological findings were clear-cut in showing that the main risk arose from organic brain dysfunction. For example, the rate of psychopathology was much increased in children of normal intelligence with epilepsy that was unassociated with neurological crippling. As always, however, it is important never to rely on just the findings of one study. Accordingly, we undertook a survey in North London, comparing the rates of mental disorder in children with a brain lesion above the brain stem (as for example with cerebral palsy) and those with a lesion below the brain stem (as for example with paralysis deriving from poliomyelitis). Again the psychopathological risk was greater in the group where the brain lesion was above the brain stem.

Naturally, that raised further questions as to whether the locus or laterality of the lesion or the presence of generalized brain pathology mattered. To answer that question, studies were undertaken with David Shaffer, Oliver Chadwick, and Gill Brown to examine in prospective fashion children with closed head injuries and those with penetrating head injuries leading to surgery (Rutter, Chadwick, & Shaffer, 1983). Obviously, it was not possible to assess the children before the head injury took place but it was possible to obtain a retrospective measure of behavior immediately after the accident before the

sequelae could be known. A 2½-year follow-up enabled within-individual change to be assessed. A marked difference was found between mild and severe head injuries.

The former showed a marked increase in the rate of behavioral disturbance prior to the accident, as compared with controls (who had suffered comparable severe accidents but with orthopedic rather than cranial injuries). This was not found in the severe group. The follow-up also indicated major differences in the course after the accident. Those with mild injuries showed no increase in disorder whereas those with severe injuries showed a marked increase. In both mild and severe injuries, new psychiatric disorders were associated with psychosocial adversity—indicating that as with any other group, multifactorial causation was the rule. A pattern of marked socially disinhibited behavior seemed to be specifically associated with brain damage but, this pattern apart, the effects of brain injury were not diagnosis-specific. The dose–response associations were much more marked for cognitive outcomes than they were for behavioral outcomes. Perhaps surprisingly, there were very few effects with respect to either the locus or laterality of the lesion. A review of studies of children with brain damage showed that some recovered to a substantial extent. That raised the query as to whether this was a consequence of psychological coping or adaptation based on the workings of undamaged parts of the brain, new brain growth in damaged parts, transfer of neural functioning from damaged to undamaged parts, or the take-up of functioning by a different part of the brain. Curiously, this vital question has, even now, not been adequately answered.

As occurred with several different research interests over the years, I regarded it as important to bring the clinical work and the science together. Accordingly, for quite a while I ran a clinic specifically for children with head injuries or other acquired brain lesions. This provided a much needed service but, in addition, it meant that I could check research findings against clinical experience and, vice versa, so that I could use the clinical experience to identify research needs.

In parallel with the brain injury studies, we also looked at a range of psychosocial risk factors, finding quite strong associations with psychopathology. Amongst other things, the research was also used to try to delineate better the nature of the specific psychosocial risk. For example, it was found that the psychopathological risks associated with parental divorce were much higher than those associated with bereavement—suggesting that the key feature derived from family discord rather than from parental loss as such.

Cycles of Deprivation In 1970, just after the IoW studies, I was appointed to the Educational Research Board of the Social Science Research Council, serving for 2 years before becoming vice-chairman. Committees of this kind can be very tedious but that was far from the case here. Jack Tizard was an excellent Chair of a highly talented but very diverse group that spanned psychology, sociology, and policy makers. It was a lively, somewhat argumentative, group but always good humored, cooperative, and problem-solving. I learned a lot from this service and gained experience in critically evaluating the work of other researchers, because decisions had to be made on which grant applications should be funded and which not. Also, between 1972 and 1980, I was vice-chairman of the Social Science Research Council and Department of Health and Social Security joint working party on "cycles of deprivation." This was a 7-year program prompted by Keith Joseph's argument (1972) that poor parenting was responsible for intergenerational transmission of deprivation in spite of a rising level of prosperity in the country as a whole. We aimed to establish a wide-ranging program of studies dealing with different aspects. A review by Nicola Madge and myself had shown the nature of the postulates and the dimensions involved in the inter-generational continuities in deprivation and disadvantage (Rutter & Madge, 1976). It was a challenging endeavor to build up research in a new area and, as probably was inevitable, the initial studies were much weaker than the much better ones that were supported towards the end of the program. Social scientists had done themselves a major disservice by attacking Keith Joseph on the grounds of his ideology rather than on the appropriate grounds of the extent to which his notions were empirically correct or incorrect. That unfortunate response played a major role in Keith Joseph, as Minister of State, deciding that the title of the Council would have to be changed to delete "science" and replace it with "research" (currently called the Economic and Social Research Council). This charge was accompanied by a downgrading of the importance of social science. I met with Keith Joseph several times during the course of this initiative and it is very much to his credit that he recognized good-quality research and also accepted that the findings of such research meant that some of his initial claims were mistaken. On the other hand, the research also showed that there were important inter-generational continuities (albeit involving a range of different mechanisms) and that these posed a challenge to both policy and practice.

Area Influences Although the IoW had a social composition that was more or less identical to that in the country as a whole, it was made up of small towns and included no major metropolitan conurbation. It was necessary, therefore to make a systematic study comparing inner London with the IoW—using the same team of investigators in both areas and the same standardized measures (Rutter & Quinton, 1977). The findings showed that the rate of both mental disorder and educational difficulties was about twice as high in inner London as it was on the IoW. As always, it was crucially important to check various methodological issues before inferring that this might represent a causal effect. Analyses showed that the measures had the same validity in both areas, that the area difference was just as marked for children born and bred in the area as for those who were

immigrants (showing that in-migration was not responsible), and that the area difference could not be accounted for by out-migration (i.e., that those without disorder were more likely to leave London). When the two areas were compared after standardizing for a composite measure of psychosocial disadvantage, it was found that most (but not quite all) of the difference was accounted for. That is, the higher rate of disorder in London was to a large extent due to adverse family circumstances. In addition, however, although the study had not particularly focused on school factors, we did find that there were important differences between the two areas in school problems of one kind or another, and the possibility arose that school functioning might account for some of the area differences.

Schools Studies It was our practice not only to let participants in our studies have newsletters reporting findings, but also to hold meetings to discuss findings and implications. At a meeting in London with school teachers, I received what felt at first to be hostile questioning on the school findings. To my surprise, at the end of the meeting the critical questioner, an experienced head teacher, came up to me and said that we definitely could not leave the findings there. It was crucially important for schools to know whether the differences among schools were a function of differences in the sort of children admitted to each school or, rather, whether the outcome differences were a function of how the schools performed. She went on to suggest that we set up a joint working group of researchers and teachers in order to plan what sort of study could answer this question and to provide support for the enterprise as a whole. The critical questioner had, quite reasonably, wanted to be sure that the findings were solid before doing anything further. As it turned out, she became our strongest supporter. She organized her colleagues to ensure that the study proposals were taken through the relevant committees and the school's enthusiasm undoubtedly made a real difference to our success in getting the study funded. At first, the powers that be were skeptical that schools would allow such a study, and then they queried whether the needed research could in fact be undertaken. In the end, they were persuaded and the study went ahead. Not only that, but when there was a teachers' strike in the middle of the study, the teachers' group persuaded their colleagues that they needed the findings from this study and that, therefore, whilst refusing to do any teaching during the strike, they should still nevertheless complete the questionnaires and the like that were asked for. It was an amazing experience.

At that time, I had no track record in education or schools research but what I did have was an effective design and a good record of developing the measures needed for innovative new studies. We had a very strong inter-disciplinary team of researchers, (Barbara Maughan, Peter Mortimore, and Janet Ouston), and the study was brought to a successful conclusion (Rutter, Maughan, Mortimore, Ouston, & Smith, 1979). In brief, a longitudinal study was undertaken in order that we might measure possible intake differences and so look at outcome variations after controlling for intake differences. The result showed quite substantial school effects and also indicated that these were associated with systematic differences in measured school functioning. Thus, we had interview and questionnaire measures but we also had detailed observations. The results showed that what mattered was not just what was done in the classroom but also the models of teacher behavior and the overall school ethos or climate. When the findings were published in 1979 they came under harsh attack from academic educationalists, although they were very well received by schools. The attacks partially came from those who were appalled that the possibility of improving things through school changes meant that the needed total political revolution might not happen. Others pointed to the possibility that unmeasured variables could account for the findings. In the event, not only did our internal analyses support our conclusions but other research undertaken subsequently broadly confirmed our findings and showed that, if anything, we slightly underestimated the importance of school effects.

It is always desirable to follow the finding of epidemiological associations with an intervention study to test for causal effects. Following the secondary school study in London, somewhat naively we attempted this in the less successful schools in our study, but this did not work because the schools did not see the need for change or did not appreciate how to bring about change. We then tried to look at the progress of secondary schools under threat of closure because of failing performance, followed by the appointment of a new head teacher who attempted to turn around the school's performance. As ill luck had it, it turned out that there were no such schools in that position at the time we needed them. Accordingly, we did the next best thing by looking at schools where that had been the situation, using new data to determine what happened. With respect to school attendance and pupils' exam performance, contemporaneous records allowed the study of longitudinal change. Barbara Maughan and Janet Ouston studied three such schools in detail. The findings showed that there had been the most dramatic turnaround in one of the schools, little change in another, and, in a third school, moderate improvements of a more limited kind. Comparisons of the strategies employed by the head teachers provided valuable leads on what might be the important factors in bringing about change. These highlighted the fact that what was needed to maintain good performance and those needed to bring about major change were not exactly the same (Rutter & Maughan, 2002).

Sex Differences During the early 1990s my colleague Terrie Moffitt (1993) proposed that antisocial behavior involved two markedly different sub-groups—namely one that began early in life, was associated with neurodevelopmental impairment, and which continued into adult life, and a second sub-group consisting of what she called adolescence-limited behavior. Findings from the Dunedin longitudinal study were used to examine antisocial behavior. There had been suggestions in the literature that, because it was so much less frequent in females than males, causal mechanisms in the two sexes might well differ. The new research used a variety of research strategies, all using epidemiological/longitudinal data, to determine whether or not this was the case Moffitt, Caspi, Rutter, & Silva, 2001). The findings were quite striking in showing that the risk factors worked very much the same way in males and females. What was different was that the neurodevelopmental risk factors were much more frequently present in males than females and that this led to a marked sex difference in the presence of antisocial behavior extending into adult life. It is well known that violent crime is much more commonly perpetrated by men than women and, hence, it was a surprise that it was found that domestic violence was actually similarly frequent in both sexes. This was so whether based on reports by the women or by their male partners. Other studies have shown much the same.

Natural Experiments As a result of these multiple studies of risk factors, I became increasingly aware of the need to use "natural experiments" as a means of testing hypotheses about environmentally mediated effects. At that time, many researchers either ignored this need or, alternatively, assumed that longitudinal data on their own would solve the problem, which it would not. My review noted the main methodological problems to be overcome and used examples from my own research, as outlined above, to illustrate the ways in which causal questions can be tackled. That has remained a major, indeed growing, interest. A paper in 2007 pulled together what is known (Rutter, 2007), and an Academy of Medical Sciences working party that I chaired looked at the issues more broadly in relation to medical conditions.

In the world of science, there is a general tendency to treat both books and reviews as less important contributions than empirical research papers. This is not wholly wrong in that most books are not subjected to peer review in the same systematic way, and many reviews are rather dreary recitals of findings without any kind of conceptual integration. In my opinion, however, rigorous conceptual overviews of the topic are useful provided they bring together research findings in order to provide new concepts or new ways of thinking about findings. As a result, the sex differences study was reported in book form and, together with colleagues, I undertook a book reviewing antisocial behavior (Rutter, Giller, & Hagell, 1998). It is also helpful for learned academies to set up working parties to look at particular issues. I have already mentioned the group on environmental causes (Academy of Medical Sciences, 2007), and I chaired a working party of the British Academy on the contributions of research for family policies (British Academy Working Group Report, 2010).

Lessons Gained from Epidemiological Research The lessons gained from epidemiological/longitudinal research are many. To begin with, it became obvious that epidemiology, like statistics, should be regarded as a basic science essential for psychology and for psychiatry. Provided that it was combined with judicious use of a range of natural experiments, it could do a great deal in sorting out which statistical associations might justify the causal inference, and which could not. At the time I started my career that was not a topic that was much discussed or considered, whereas now it is generally accepted as of crucial importance. The second lesson is the importance of a programmatic approach to problems. It is often the case that good research provides some solutions but it almost always opens up new questions. Scientists need to decide which of these new questions should be given priority in designing new research. My experience suggests that, when this is done, the findings from one often illuminate and add understanding to the findings in some other, apparently unrelated, topic. Third, there is often a need for an entirely new approach, as illustrated by the question of why there can be substantial recovery from the effects of brain damage. The fourth lesson is the importance of making maximum use of other people's leadership in particular studies. That constituted a key element in the planning of both the MRC research unit that I directed for many years (where, for example, there was a statistical section led by Andrew Pickles) and for the Social Genetic and Developmental Center that I set up much more recently in conjunction with Robert Plomin and then Peter McGuffin. Both were highly inter-disciplinary, both made extensive use of epidemiological/longitudinal research strategies, and both combined a focus on the effects of various risk factors and a focus on particular forms of psychopathology. Both, too, made strong use of genetic research strategies, the topic to be considered next.

Genetics

During my 1961–62 year working on the New York longitudinal study of child temperament, I undertook a very small preliminary twin study. One of the monozygotic pairs had been separated in infancy and were adopted into quite different families. When I interviewed them a few years later the circumstances in the two families were quite different. Although the temperamental features of the twins were fairly similar, their impact on the adoptive parents was utterly different. This first alerted me to the importance of examining gene–environment interplay. As noted above, my review of maternal deprivation about a decade later noted the marked heterogeneity in effects and I raised the possibility of genetic influences on susceptibility to the environment. The twin study of autism during the 1970s, undertaken with Susan Folstein, showed what could be done with a systematically analyzed twin study. It became clear to me that this was a topic that I would have to become seriously engaged with and that this would necessitate my training myself in genetics—initially in quantitative behavioral genetics and then later

in the use of molecular genetics. The first step in that direction was undertaken in relation to the genetics section of my research unit leading to papers on a review of research strategies and on empirical findings (Rutter, Silberg, O'Connor, & Simonoff, 1999).

At the beginning of the 1990s, I was invited to join the Virginia Twin Study of Adolescent Behavioral Development (VTSABD) working with Lindon Eaves and his team of very distinguished quantitative geneticists. This led to a variety of papers dealing with a range of issues including estimates of the heritability of different forms of psychopathology in young people (Eaves et al., 1997), the genetic analysis of patterns of comorbidity (Silberg et al., 1996), and the use of the twin design to examine environmental risk factors (Rutter et al., 1997) in the context of gene–environment correlations (rGE) and interactions (GxE). It was shown that, not only were there relatively low levels of agreement between the accounts of parents and children (as shown previously by others), but that the genetic findings were also different according to which informant was used. It was also shown that there were important age differences in genetic findings and that genes operated, not only through "main" effects on behavior but also indirectly through rGE and GxE. Once more, this led to reviews outlining the issues and indicating the research strategies that could be employed to investigate them (Rutter, 2006). From 1994 onwards, I was a member of the Social Genetic and Developmental Psychiatry center that I had set up and I learned even more about genetics from Robert Plomin and other colleagues.

During the 1990s, technological advances in molecular biology meant that it became feasible to seek to identify individual susceptibility genes using a full genome screen. Together with Tony Monaco, I was involved in planning, and then setting up, an International Molecular Genetic Study of Autism Consortium (IMGSAC). It was decided to adopt an affected relative pair linkage strategy (i.e., an examination of co-inheritance) and the findings showed linkage to a region on chromosome 7q (IMGSAC, 1998) Subsequent evidence confirmed the linkage and showed similar linkage to areas on chromosomes 2 and 16 (IMGSAC, 2001). Nevertheless, 12 years after the first linkage findings, we have still not identified the actual genes. In the meanwhile, research by others had shown that rare genes were associated with autism (usually accompanied by intellectual disability) in a tiny proportion of cases (1–2%). It had also been found that autism (in common with schizophrenia and attention deficit hyperactivity disorder, was associated with copy number variations (meaning sub-microscopic deletions and substitutions) (Pinto et al., 2010). The field of genetics was opening up in exciting ways, although the meaning of the findings remains uncertain (Rutter & Thapar, in press).

In the early part of this century, my colleagues Terrie Moffitt and Avshalom Caspi published a series of papers on the Dunedin study in which significant gene–environment interdependence was empirically shown. Although some traditional behavioral geneticists have resisted the evidence, it is clear that gene–environment interdependence is a real and important phenomenon, confirmed in multiple investigations. It had been suspected on the basis of quantitative behavioral genetic evidence (Rutter & Silberg, 2002), but the identification of individual genes and the interaction with measured environments has taken the field forward in a major way. I was not part of the research in Dunedin but I have played a substantial role in considering the operation of gene–environment interdependence (Rutter, 2006; Rutter, Thapar, & Pickles, 2009).

Lessons from Genetics The first lesson for me was a growing appreciation of the extent to which genetic factors were involved in virtually all behavior and in virtually all aspects of development. In order to come to terms with all of that, I had to do a lot of new learning, which was both exciting and quite challenging. That was particularly the case because the overall views about genetics have changed very considerably over the last 20 years as a result of genetic advances. To begin with, epidemiological and clinical, as well as genetic findings, have shown that most behavioral features arise as a result of multifactorial causation. That means that the effects of genes are probabilistic rather than deterministic, and that the causal process involves multiple genes and multiple environmental factors, with the particular features of the mix varying from individual to individual. Research has also shown that most risk factors operate dimensionally and most forms of common psychopathology also operate dimensionally. The boundaries between the normal and the abnormal have considerable fluidity. In addition, basic science research (not my own) has shown that although genes are present from birth, their effects are dependent on gene expression which is both developmental phase specific and tissue specific. Gene expression involves multiple DNA elements and also environmental influences and chance. What this means is that gene action needs to be considered as a dynamic process and not as a simple turning on of a switch. Genetic research findings have demonstrated the importance of environmental influences and have also shown the importance of the interplay between genes and environment. That is not how genes used to be thought about, and the change in view has huge implications for the consideration of developmental processes. Modern molecular genetic research, because it does require large samples, has meant that collaboration between research groups has become the norm rather than the exception, and close cooperation has been essential among multiple disciplines spanning both the laboratory and field work.

Other Issues

Psychiatric classification may not seem to be a topic of particular interest to developmental scientists, but actually it should be. One of the major advances in developmental studies has been the evidence of the strong continuities between childhood and adult life (Rutter, Kim-Cohen, & Maughan, 2006). As a consequence, it is now apparent that age-related variations in manifestation need to be considered with respect to all disorders at all ages (Rutter, 2011a). As a consequence it seems likely that the next major revision of the classification systems will no longer have a separate grouping of childhood-onset conditions.

As a developmental scientist, it was natural to pay attention to the changes over time in both societal and mental health patterns, as well as changes within individuals over the lifespan (Rutter & Smith, 1995). In the half century following World War II, the marked rise in prosperity in most industrialized countries was accompanied by a rise in many (but not all) forms of psychopathology in young people. The reasons why this was so have still not been adequately worked out.

The title of this chapter refers to the establishment of developmental psychopathology and it has been a privilege to have been able to participate in bringing about a paradigm shift regarding both normal and abnormal development across the lifespan. When I started my research career in the 1950s, adult psychiatrists totally dismissed developmental approaches as irrelevant, but from the 1980s onwards they have played a major role in showing their importance. Child psychiatrists, too, saw development entirely in terms of the psychoanalytic theory of psychosexual development, whereas now a more biologically informed concept has come to the fore. Most crucially, the approaches of developmental psychopathology have led to a new understanding of both the continuities and discontinuities in psychological development and the processes involved in risk mechanisms as they operate over the lifespan (Rutter, 2009).

Although my scientific interests have covered a wide field, they have nevertheless had a unity in the themes that brought them together. Science benefits from approaches that come from outsiders (see, for example, the influx of physicists into molecular biology), but progress needs a logical progression and not a scattergun involvement in disparate topics.

Overall Conclusions and Future Directions

Before drawing conclusions on both the achievements of developmental science and its future directions, it is necessary to pause to consider in what ways development differs from non-developmental change (Rutter, 2005). That has proved a surprisingly difficult question to answer and it must be accepted that development is an inherently "fuzzy" concept. A possible working definition was suggested some years ago as "systematic, organized, intra-individual change that is clearly associated with age-related progressions and which is carried forward in some way that has implications for a person's pattern of functioning at some later time" (Rutter & Rutter, 1993). Necessarily, it involves biology but the process is dynamic and probabilistic in its effects. It might be thought that it should involve reference to gains in skills or capacity but that would be misleading because development involves loss as well as gain (as shown for example by the loss of phonological discriminatory skills that are present in infancy but which disappear if the relevant sound differentiations are not part of the language of rearing). It is also clear that development does not necessarily involve more of the same because the whole concept of development comprises both continuity and change. The concept, too, has to span both normal and abnormal development as inherent in the concept of developmental psychopathology. Particularly in recent years, it has become evident that plasticity and adaptation to injury or stress is a key feature of normal development. It might be thought that development ought to have a fixed end point when maturity is reached but that would not work in relation to social development. Because many aspects of psychological and social development are dependent upon late-occurring experiences it is crucial to adopt a lifespan perspective. Key experiences in adult life have been shown through brain imaging techniques to involve structural changes in the brain.

There is a parallel need to consider what is meant by "good quality science" (Rutter, 2013). It is obvious that there is not, and could not be, a single best "scientific method." Some four decades ago Merton proposed that there were three main features that characterized good quality science: a search for laws or principles that could be generalized beyond the sample studied; an approach that involved conceptualizing the meaning or the mechanism underlying any set of findings or observations; and an attitude of questioning that involved looking for alternative counter-explanations to the proposition being put forward. Nearly three decades later the U.S. National Research Council, although using somewhat different language, put forward much the same message. There has been much fruitless posturing about supposed differences between qualitative and quantitative research methods but it is obvious that both have important contributions to make, although they are somewhat different. Both need to be concerned with the accuracy, precision, and breadth of their observations and interviews, as well as procedural issues of reliability and validity (Rutter, 2009).

With those concepts and considerations in mind, let me turn to the changes that have taken place in developmental sciences over the last 50 years or so, some of the key achievements, and the forward directions that are needed. There are several major changes that will have substantial implications for future directions. These include: a recognition of the need for longitudinal studies; an appreciation that it makes no sense to think of development only in terms of a particular age period; insofar as there is a focus on a particular period, both the antecedent development and subsequent circumstances have to be part of the picture; the antecedent development needs to consider prenatal, as well as postnatal, changes; a recognition that age is an ambiguous variable that indexes, not only biological maturation, but also changes in experiences; the testing of environmentally mediated effects

needs to include the use of natural experiments of several different kinds; the role of genetic effects on risk exposure and risk vulnerability means that there must be serious attention to gene–environment interplay; animal studies constitute one important means of examining mediating mechanisms; and there is huge heterogeneity in people's responses to all manner of experiences, both internal and external. All of these should shape future directions of developmental sciences, but a few developments warrant particular mention.

Theoretical physicists like to argue that the goal must be the establishing of rules (usually expressed in the form of equations) that are deterministic and which have universal application for all time. The big difference between physical and biological sciences is that the latter are unlikely to give rise to such deterministic conclusions; biology is essentially probabilistic in its effects. Nevertheless, it is a reasonable goal to want to derive principles that do have very broad applicability. That will necessarily involve a degree of acceptable reductionism. It will also be necessary for developmentalists to pay much more attention to biology than they have done in the past.

Some of the key challenges to be met are as follows. First, why do some experiences have a sensitizing effect whereas others have a "steeling" effect? What is different about the experiences, or what is different about the way the individual copes with them, or what is different about the basic biology? Second, although there is good evidence that the social context of experiences matters, we know relatively little about what this actually means with respect to mechanisms. Presumably a key issue is how individuals perceive and process the experiences, but new research will be required in order to test that out and also to look for alternative explanations. Third, insofar as some experiences have enduring effects that persist long after the experience itself, we need to ask how experiences become biologically embedded. A range of possibilities will need to be considered. At the moment, epigenetic mechanisms constitute a key interest but these need to be pitted against other alternatives such as the development of internal working models, the effects on neuroendocrine structure and functioning, biological programming, etc. Also, with each of these, the need is not so much to demonstrate that the mechanism operates but that it operates with respect to individual differences as well as group differences. Fourth, although it is well demonstrated that there are important continuities between normality and pathology, the details remain ill understood. It is accepted that many risks as well as many disorders operate dimensionally, but are the effects similar at all points on the distribution? Fifth, there are major transitions that take place during adolescence and adult life but what mechanisms are involved? For example, how does so-called prodromal schizophrenia become an overt psychosis? How does the broader autism phenotype become autism "proper"? How do the physiological changes associated with puberty have implications for psychopathology? Finally, what are the mechanisms involved in gene–environment interdependence? What is involved in the selection and shaping of environments? What is involved in individual differences in susceptibility to the environment? Do the individual differences apply just to risk environments or do they apply to environments that are both adaptive and maladaptive? In that connection, it will need to be accepted that neither genes nor environments can be divided up into those that are universally "bad" and universally "good." The effects of both tend to be pleiotropic. The challenges that lie ahead are immense but our understanding of both the concepts and the technologies available has grown greatly and we should feel confident that challenges not only can, but will, be met.

References

Academy of Medical Sciences. (2007). *Identifying the environmental causes of disease: How should we decide what to believe and when to take action?* London: Academy of Medical Sciences.

Bailey, A., Le Couteur, A., Gottesman, I., Bolton, P., Simonoff, E., Yuzda, E. et al. (1995). Autism as a strongly genetic disorder: evidence from a British twin study. *Psychological Medicine, 25*, 63–77.

Bettelheim, B. (1967). *The empty fortress: Infantile autism and the birth of the self.* London: Collier-Macmillan.

British Academy Working Group Report. (2010). *Social science and family policies.* British Academy Policy Centre, UK.

Buchanan, R. D. (2010). *Playing with fire: The controversial career of Hans J. Eysenck.* Oxford, UK: Oxford University Press.

Eaves, L. J., Silberg, J. L., Meyer, J. M,. Maes, H. H, Simonoff, E., Pickles, A. et al. (1997). Genetics and developmental psychopathology: 2. The main effects of genes and environment on behavioral problems in the Virginia Twin Study of Adolescent Behavioral Development. *Journal of Child Psychology & Psychiatry, 38*, 965–980.

Folstein, S., & Rutter, M. (1977). X Infantile autism: A genetic study of 21 twin pairs. *Journal of Child Psychology & Psychiatry, 18*, 297–321.

Fombonne, E., Wostear, G., Cooper, V., Harrington., R., & Rutter, M. (2001). The Maudsley long-term follow-up of child and adolescent depression: I. Psychiatric outcomes in adulthood. II. Suicidality, criminality and social dysfunction in childhood. *British Journal of Psychiatry, 17*(9), 210–217 & 218–223.

Garmezy, N., & Rutter, M. (Eds). (1983). *Stress, coping and development.* New York: McGraw-Hill.

Hemsley, R., Howlin, P., Berger, M., Hersov, L., Holbrook, D., Rutter, M. et al. (1978). Treating autistic children in a family context. In M. Rutter & E. Schopler (Eds.) *Autism: A reappraisal of concepts and treatment* (pp. 379–412). New York: Plenum Press.

Hermelin, B., & O'Connor, N. (1970). *Psychological experiments with autistic children.* Oxford, UK: Pergamon Press.

Howlin, P., & Rutter, M. (1987). *Treatment of autistic children.* Chichester: Wiley.

International Molecular Genetic Study of Autism Consortium (IMGSAC). (1998). A full genome screen for autism with evidence for linkage to a region on chromosome 7q. *Human Molecular Genetics, 7*, 517–578.

International Molecular Genetic Study of Autism Consortium (IMGSAC). (2001). A genomewide screen for autism: strong evidence for linkage to chromosomes 2q, 7q and 16p. *American Journal of Human Genetics, 69*, 570–581.

Joseph, K. (1972) *Speech to the Preschool Playgroups Association,* 29 June.

Le Couteur, A., Bailey, A. J., Goode, S., Pickles, A., Robertson, S., Gottesman, I. et al. (1996). A broader phenotype of autism: The clinical spectrum in twins. *Journal of Child Psychology & Psychiatry, 37*, 785–801.

Le Couteur, A., Rutter, M., Lord, C., Rios, P., Robertson, S., Holdgrafer, M. et al. (1989). Autism Diagnostic Interview: A standardized investigator-based instrument. *Journal of Autism and Developmental Disorders, 19*, 363–387.

Lord, C., Rutter, M., Goode, S., Heemsbergen, J., Jordan, H., Mawhood, L. et al. (1989). Autism diagnostic observation schedule: a standardized observation of communicative and social behavior. *Journal of Autism & Developmental Disorders, 19*, 185–212.

Moffitt, T. E. (1993) Adolescence-limited and life-course-persistent antisocial behavior: A developmental taxonomy. *Psychological Review, 100*, 674–701.

Moffitt, T. E., Caspi, A., Rutter, M., & Silva, P. A. (2001). *Sex differences in antisocial behavior: Conduct disorder, delinquency, and violence in the Dunedin Longitudinal Study.* Cambridge: Cambridge University Press.

Pinto, D., Pagnamenta, A. T., Klei, L., Anney, R., Merico, D., Regan, R. et al. (2010). Functional impact of global rare copy number variation in autism spectrum disorders. *Nature, 15*(466), 368–72.

Quinton, D., & Rutter, M. (1988). *Parenting breakdown: The making and breaking of inter-generational links.* Aldershot: Avebury.

Robins, L. (1966). *Deviant children grown up: A sociological and psychiatric study of sociopathic personality.* Baltimore: Williams & Wilkins.

Rutter, M. (1970). Autistic children: Infancy to adulthood. *Seminars in Psychiatry, 2*, 435–450.

Rutter, M. (1972). *Maternal deprivation reassessed.* Harmondsworth, Middx: Penguin Books.

Rutter, M. (1979). Language, cognition and autism. In R. Katzman (Ed.), *Congenital and acquired cognitive disorders.* New York: Raven Press, pp. 247–264.

Rutter, M. (1989). Isle of Wight revisited: Twenty-five years of child psychiatric epidemiology. *Journal of American Academy of Child & Adolescent Psychiatry, 28*, 633–653.

Rutter, M. (2005). Multiple meanings of a developmental perspective on psychopathology. *European Journal of Developmental Psychology, 2*, 221–252.

Rutter, M. (2006). *Genes and behavior: Nature–nurture interplay explained.* Oxford, UK: Blackwell Scientific.

Rutter, M. (2007). Proceeding from observed correlation to causal inference: The use of natural experiments. *Perspectives on Psychological Science, 2*, 377–395.

Rutter, M. (2008). Autism and specific language impairments: A tantalising dance. In V. Joffe, M. Cruice, & S. Chiate (Eds.), *Language disorders in children and adults* (pp. 122–137). London: Wiley.

Rutter, M. (2009). Understanding and testing risk mechanisms for mental disorders. *Journal of Child Psychology & Psychiatry, 50*, 44–52.

Rutter, M. (2010). Child and adolescent psychiatry: Past scientific achievements and challenges for the future. *European Journal of Child & Adolescent Psychology, 19*, 689–703.

Rutter, M. (2011a). Child psychiatric diagnosis and classification: Concept, findings, challenges and potential. *Journal of Child & Adolescent Psychiatry, 52*, 647–660.

Rutter, M. (2013). The role of science in understanding family troubles. In J. R. McCarthy, B. Gillies, & C.-A. Hopper (Eds.). *Family troubles? Exploring changes and challenges in the family lives of children and young people* (pp. 45–58). Bristol, UK: Policy Press.

Rutter, M., Beckett, C., Castle, J., Kreppner, J., Stevens, S., & Sonuga-Barke, E. (2009). *Policy and practice implications from the English and Romanian Adoptees (ERA) Study: Forty five key questions.* London: BAAF.

Rutter, M., Chadwick, O., & Shaffer, D. (1983). The behavioural and cognitive sequelae of head injury. In M. Rutter (Ed.), *Developmental neuropsychiatry* (pp. 83–111). New York: Guilford Press.

Rutter, M., Dunn, J., Plomin, R., Simonoff, E., Pickles, A., Maughan, B. et al. (1997). Integrating nature and nurture: Implications of person-environment correlations and interactions for developmental psychology. *Development and Psychopathology, 9*, 335–364.

Rutter, M, & Garmezy, N. (1983). Developmental psychopathology. In E. M. Hetherington (Ed.), *Socialization, personality, and social development,* Vol. 4 of *Mussen's handbook of child psychology* (4th ed., pp. 775–911). New York: Wiley.

Rutter, M., Giller, H., & Hagell, A. (1998). *Antisocial behaviour by young people*. New York and Cambridge: Cambridge University Press.

Rutter, M., Graham, P., & Yule, W. (1970). A neuropsychiatric study in childhood. *Clinics in Developmental Medicine, 35/36*. London: Heinemann/SIMP.

Rutter, M., Kim-Cohen, J., & Maughan, B. (2006). Continuities and discontinuities in psychopathology between childhood and adult life. *Journal of Child Psychology and Psychiatry, 163*, 1009–1018.

Rutter, M., & Madge, N. (1976). *Cycles of disadvantage: A review of research*. London: Heinemann Educational.

Rutter, M., & Maughan, B. (2002). School effectiveness findings 1979–2002. *Journal of School Psychology, 40*, 451–475.

Rutter, M., Maughan B., Mortimore P., Ouston, J., & Smith, A. (1979). *Fifteen thousand hours: Secondary schools and their effects on children*. Cambridge, MA: Harvard University Press.

Rutter, M., & Quinton, D. (1977). Psychiatric disorder—ecological factors and concepts of causation. In H. McGurk (Ed.), *Ecological factors in human development* (pp. 173–187). Amsterdam: North-Holland.

Rutter, M., & Rutter, M. (1993). *Developing minds: Challenge and continuity across the lifespan*. Harmondsworth, Middx: Penguin Books; New York: Basic Books.

Rutter, M., & Silberg, J. (2002). Gene-environment interplay in relation to emotional and behavioral disturbance. *Annual Review of Psychology, 53*, 463–490.

Rutter, M., Silberg, J., O'Connor, T., & Simonoff, E. (1999). Genetics and child psychiatry: I. Advances in quantitative and molecular genetics 2. Empirical research findings. *Journal of Child Psychology and Psychiatry, 40*, 3–18 & 19–56.

Rutter, M., & Smith, D. (Eds.). (1995). *Psychosocial disorders in young people: Time trends and their causes*. Chichester: Wiley.

Rutter, M., & Sonuga-Barke, E. J. (Eds.). (2010). Deprivation-specific psychological patterns: Effects of institutional deprivation. *Monographs of the Society for Research in Child Development, 75*, 1. Serial No. 295.

Rutter, M., & Thapar, A. (In press). Genetics of autism. In F. R. Volkmar, R. Paul, S. Rogers, & K. A. Pelphrey (Eds.), *Handbook of Autism and Pervasive Developmental Disorders, 4th Edition: Assessment, interventions, policy, the future*. Hoboken, NJ: Wiley press.

Rutter, M., Thapar, A., & Pickles, A. (2009). From JAMA commentary on paper by Risch et al.—Gene–environment interactions: Biologically valid pathway or artefact? *Archives of General Psychiatry, 66*, 1287–1289.

Rutter, M., Tizard, J., & Whitmore, K. (1970). *Education, health and behaviour*. London: Longmans; reprinted 1981, Melbourne, FA: Krieger.

Silberg, J. L,. Rutter, M., Meyer, J., Maes, H., Hewitt, J. K., Simonoff, E. et al. (1996). Genetic and environmental influences on the covariation between hyperactivity and conduct disturbance in juvenile twins. *Journal of Child Psychology & Psychiatry, 37*, 803–816.

38

Born in Clever[1]

RITCH C. SAVIN-WILLIAMS

Ritch's Early Life

Born in 1949 to Joy J. (Savin) and Francis C. Williams, Ritchie and his older sister, Pat, were raised in a Springfield apartment, a Kansas City rental property, and, eventually, a small Clever, Missouri, farm. Skimming lightly over his childhood, I am told that Ritchie appeared to others to be an unassumingly sedate, even placid, child who tried his best to please everyone. Growing up in an obedience-expecting family that rarely subsisted above the poverty line, Ritchie was by necessity temperamentally self-sufficient, gender-conforming, and content with his lot in life; it never occurred to him to ask his parents for help with his homework or to entertain him when bored. Indeed, if at 4 years of age Ritchie had been given the option by Professor Walter Mischel to eat one marshmallow now or two marshmallows in 15 minutes, Ritchie would have waited 15 minutes and then returned both marshmallows to Dr. Mischel.

Left to occupy himself after completing farm chores, Ritchie spent considerable time alone immersed in fantasies that frequently transcended small-town values and transported him beyond their geographic confines. Ritchie fully expected (a view shared by no one other than himself) a career in professional baseball as the centerfielder for the Kansas City A's or to become a Motown phenomenon. Perhaps the Supremes needed a fourth? Alternatively (or rather, additionally), Ritchie imagined himself as Superman's best friend, confidant, and eventual replacement. These fantasies of accomplishment and recognition intensified once Ritchie became fully aware that farming would never be his meal ticket—he would rather befriend than eat the family's animal stock. How to achieve his aspirations? Ritchie would have to leave Clever.

Adolescence: If Disappointed, Punt

Much of my early life was spent within the confines of Clever's red-brick school building—childhood on the first floor and adolescence on the second floor. This school had its advantages (I knew everyone) and its disadvantages (everyone knew me). Regardless, I loved my adolescence and its growing independence. What was presented to me at the time as education was not particularly challenging, though it did provide me with a unique, if not wholly deserved, identity as the "smart one." Consequently, it seemed only natural to befriend the cadre of teachers, who, for the most part, were consigned to Clever as either their first or last teaching job. I seldom had homework, although I do recall once producing a 20-page essay during the Cold War that noted the virtues of a "duck-and-cover" strategy in the Civil Defense Preparedness Kit. In the advent of a sudden flash of light or a siren warning of an impending nuclear attack (from the USSR), my fellow students would be best protected by assuming a fetal position under the school desk (hands covering the head). I also included, with pictures and arrows, the best escape routes if we needed to leave the school building.

Not uncommon for small-town America in which many residents are distantly related or hail from the same European (notably, Scandinavian) countryside, I had no mortal enemies. I count only a single brawl during those early impressionable years. It was the usual anarchistic 7th grade recess game of tag when, after being pushed to the ground by Jimmy, the class bully, I slugged him in the jaw (location determined by television). When, however, my adulating peers lifted me to their shoulders, Jimmy delivered his sucker punch, thereby saving face without causing me undue harm. I still knew I had won, but worried about whether I would be invited to Jimmy's 13th birthday party (I was). Perhaps this event sparked my research interest in dominance, bullying, and peer relations. Then again, the scuffle might simply have been an expression of an underlying impulsive streak (enhanced by puberty) that I have made great effort to shield from others.

This early adolescent victory was not, however, so easily or consistently achieved in other realms of my life. For example, the following year I was invited by the newly hired music teacher (who was fired a year later after a student found birth control pills in her purse) to leave mandatory Boys Glee Club with a simple, "Wouldn't you rather learn welding?" The replacement teacher was equally unimpressed with my nascent musical abilities and shrewdly, but considerately, inquired whether I might reconsider my decision to participate in the Junior High Band: "We've got enough drummers ($n = 1$), so wouldn't you rather take up the violin?" Unaccustomed as I was to school failure, these two votes of *no-confidence* stung; eventually in college they made sense when my musical ability test score was officially ranked "in the lowest 10th percentile" (in the nation!) during a Tests and Measurements course. Although a music career as the fourth Supreme or the fifth Beatle was now undeniably improbable, I had learned two valuable lessons: Criticism was tolerable because, I thought, critics really have my best interests at heart and "never-say-never" (but punt).

I now recognize that the first life lesson was naïve, even by Clever standards. The second lesson, however, has sustained me throughout my professional career—and within multiple realms. For example, one of my proudest collegiate moments arrived my junior year when I aced Introductory Piano with an inimitable rendition of "Home on the Range" (from memory). Buoyed beyond reason, I believed that I had conquered a musical deficit, although later I recognized that grades were largely determined by attendance (and I would never consider missing a class paid for by the State of Missouri). Nevertheless, the "A" proudly remains on my transcript. My smartest collegiate move was not to take Intermediate Piano.

Other childhood delusions similarly caved to adolescent clarity. Just as I was politely redirected from melodious pursuits, I began to suspect that the world of professional sports would not be the antidote to my flagging musical stardom. Besides being only slightly more athletic than musical, I had, shall we say, *difficult* relationships with organized sports—this in a school where we ran track on a dirt oval, used our shirts as bases for baseball, and occasionally forgot whether softball was a spring or fall activity. Although I adored sports (my first projected career as a Kansas City A's outfielder was shattered when the team sold out and moved to Oakland, California), the only celebrated game at Clever High was basketball. Unfortunately, basketball required a degree of coordination quite foreign to my body; independently I could run, bounce a ball, fake a shot, jump, and shoot—just not at the same time. This limitation was perceptively noted by Coach Smith who tactfully hinted, "Ritchie, might you more productively contribute to the team's overall effort if you kept score and did the charts?" Recalling my long stints on the far end of the bench, I could appreciate Coach Smith's point. Again, faced with failure, I punted (to maintain the sports analogy) and in

the process became an indispensable member of the team. In fact, I became so valuable (although I did not shave points, I did sketch elaborate diagrams with arrows and statistics that none of the players actually understood—but impressed them nonetheless) that Coach Smith expanded my role to that of team medic (no medical training necessary). Perhaps because it was 1964 and sexual diversity was rarely acknowledged (*although practiced*) in small-town Missouri, the excitement I experienced wrapping sprained, stressed, and disrobed body parts was understood by me at the time not as eroticism but as exhilaration that I was contributing to the team's success. It was School Spirit Supersized. Only later did memories of these medical interventions assume clearer meaning as I negotiated the messiness of my delayed sexuality.

Although these pivotal musical and athletic experiences did not inspire Ritchie to become a concert pianist, statistician, or medical doctor, they are prototypical examples of his ability, when confronted with looming odds imposed by powerful individuals, circumstances, or traditions, to refocus on that which he can accomplish and control. Indeed, as Ritchie exited adolescence and entered young adulthood, this propensity for making the best of fortuitous conditions and redefining possibilities became crucial when he moved 200 miles north and east to begin undergraduate studies at the University of Missouri. There, he lost his Ozark accent, sported a Beatles (not Supremes) haircut, and wore tie-dye shorts. In response to long-suppressed frustration from having grown up in an environment in which prevailing wisdom was seldom questioned, Ritchie experimented with expressing his discontents by challenging perceived truths and forsaking consensus while slowly establishing a reputation as someone who is willing to forgo the role of team player. Although he cherished this new role, it also proved to be personally taxing as it directly contradicted his Midwestern upbringing which mandated fitting in, knowing one's place, remaining a part of the status quo, and, perhaps above all else according to Ritchie, "faking niceness."

The College Years

When I finally escaped the confines of Clever to attend "the Big State University" in Columbia (1967–71), my high-school classmates predicted I would return to assume the role of preacher at the Clever Christian Church. Despite a history of giving "Youth Sunday" sermons, I knew they were wrong because of my waning commitment to organized religion as well as an overwhelming sense of restlessness that living in Clever could never resolve.

Once in college, I dabbled in several academic majors, beginning with Philosophy (ethics was fun; logic was anesthetizing), then Political Science (international relations opened a new world; language requirements shut it down), then Religion (critiquing traditional Biblical stories was a hoot; undergraduate religion majors were insufferable), and, finally, Psychology. My introduction to the latter, about which I knew nothing, came via the campus-renowned Fred McKinney Personality Show—a course that featured, courtesy of new video technology, Professor McKinney beamed directly into the classroom from his mysterious lab that no one could locate (I still believe he was sitting at home; wasn't that a martini in the background?).

My initial foray into research, though accidental, confirmed the suitability of the Psychology major decision. After working various jobs as a catering waiter, a youth minister at a local community church, and a dorm resident advisor, the campus Work Study office assigned me, apparently for no reason other than my new major, to typing psychology faculty manuscripts. After a month of uninspiring office drudgery, I overheard Professor Boice rail to departmental staff that his assigned work-study research assistant was unrelentingly and catastrophically dropping the lab's squeamish, slippery *Rana pipiens* (leopard frogs) onto the concrete floor.

Side note: I later verified the truthfulness of this claim when I located three of these ill-fated frogs and honored them by constructing a frog mobile, which remains (minus the 1½ eaten by my cat) a central attraction of my inspired office interior. The surviving dehydrated heroic corpses can be viewed (on request) when visiting my current faculty office.

Returning to Dr. Boice's tirade: Having grown weary of typing and then retyping manuscripts (there was no Microsoft Word, only White Out), I enthusiastically volunteered my rural history as demonstration of my familiarity and comfort with frogs, my acceptance of their lifestyle, and my love for all things crawling, leaping, and croaking. Hired on the spot, my life was dramatically and forever altered as I unexpectedly entered the world of research, becoming for my last three undergraduate years a near permanent resident of the Animal Behavior Lab. There I was known as the *frog guy* and the one who sometimes fed old research subjects to new research subjects. Memorizing their unique physical features (usually spot patterns), I assigned descriptive names (5-Spot, Dopey, Snake Eyes, etc.) to each frog; tempted them with a singular squirming, resistant mealworm; dropped the disenfranchised brunch into the pens; and recorded frog dyadic tongue lashing, mounting, and nipping/shoving (think World Federation of Wrestling—Raw).

Perhaps the most critical legacy of this early research experience was the tolerance, if not outright appreciation, Dr. Boice expressed when I shared unsolicited observations, alternative hypotheses, and novel research designs. Varying the number of frogs per pen (after a certain number, chaos reigned), grouping all dominant alphas in one pen and all meek omegas in another (some alphas became omega-like and some omegas became alpha-like), or repeatedly not excluding the frog who had previously snatched the mealworm (causing others to hibernate) yielded talking points between us, if not always publishable

findings. My reward (besides food money, a letter of recommendation, and banned and unlawful household pets) was three publications—which proved critical for my inauguration into Human Development (but only after a 2½-year religious detour; more on this hiatus later).

I also independently (and illicitly) tried my own hand at research. For a class assignment my budding developmental research interests (a retrospective supposition) inspired me to investigate an omission in the empirical literature on tonic immobility among frogs (when exposed to a predator, a frog feigns death by induction into a hypnotic state): the role of early experience (domestication) on normal frog behavior. The standard paradigm consists of holding an inverted frog on a table belly-side up so that movement of the head and limbs are arrested and the frog ceases to struggle and does not move for at least 10 seconds after being released. Testing whether familiarity with captivity and habituation to humans decreases susceptibility to tonic immobility necessitated the unlawful act of sneaking into my dorm room an assortment of wild frogs captured on my parents' Clever farm during a Thanksgiving break. Although not necessarily or explicitly forbidden by University policy, I highly suspected it was wrong and was thus deservedly plagued with the difficult task of muffling their dusk croaking.

Nevertheless, I was successful not only in wrestling frogs (I was alpha) but also in learning three lessons that would guide my scientific career:

1. It matters who you study (sample selection): The laboratory domesticated mail-order frogs took much longer to become immobile than the wild Clever frogs.
2. Direct observation is a preferred methodology for many psychological phenomena: Unable to interview or survey participant frogs (tame or wild) concerning their dominance status, I relied on their behavior as an indicator of peer interactions.
3. There are links between nonhuman and human behavior and observing the former offers insight into the latter (the similarity between frog tongue-lashing and adolescent bullying is not preposterous).

The field of comparative psychology ultimately proved less appealing to Ritchie than the intellectual stimulation derived from philosophical and theological debates about religion (it was, after all, the "God is Dead" era), his academic minor. Not inconsequential was the state of his country during this time. Of the handful of classes that Ritchie missed during his 4 years of college, one was to protest his government's "massacre" (his word) of the Vietnamese people. As the Vietnam War escalated and Ritchie's draft number approached, he grew increasingly worried and then alarmed for his life and those of others he was supposed to kill. He was advised by the campus anti-war draft board that an alternative to escaping to Canada or Sweden, claiming extreme back pain, or being psychiatrically diagnosed as a "homosexual," was attending seminary. Accordingly, in 1971 Ritchie accepted a scholarship for graduate studies at the University of Chicago Divinity School; there he pursued the intersection of religion, personality, and social interaction—a compatible tie-in with his still fleeting thoughts of becoming a youth minister (although not in Clever). After all, had not the best times of his young life been working with youth as a summer camp counselor and a youth minister?

Graduate School Part I: Divinity School

Once moving north and east to Hyde Park, Illinois, I became enamored with psychologist and practical theologian Professor Don Browning and historian of religion Professor Martin Marty. Despite his wise counsel that Divinity School might not be the best fit for me, Dr. Marty assumed a personal interest in my education, and through his generosity and guidance I learned enduring lessons about what it meant to be a scholar, how to make the best use of 7–11-minute appointments, and the value of feeding graduate students spaghetti dinners. Dr. Browning tried his best to convince me that a PhD in religious development during adolescence could be pursued in the Divinity School, even as I was being seduced by courses on human ethology and adolescent development offered by the Committee on Human Development. Until his very last days, Dr. Browning remained supportive and pointed out the links between our scholarly pursuits.

Ultimately, it was an ill-fit between the Divinity School and me as an increasing proportion of my coursework was taken in Human Development. I was awarded a Masters of Religious Studies after writing an unorthodox (because it was empirical) thesis on age changes in adolescent images of Jesus and how these developments were predicted by Nietzsche's anti-Christ theology (granted, it was a bit of a reach, but not forbidden).

Graduate School Part II: Human Development

As the military draft wound down (below Ritchie's #107), an internal transfer to Human Development in 1973 was secured with the publication of the early frog papers and his performance in human development courses. Although Ritchie was initially unaware that he needed a "Jewish mother," Professor Bernice Neugarten, Chair of Human Development, thought otherwise—and that was that. Dr. Neugarten, who combined intellectual rigor with a nurturing and supportive demeanor, applied these traits to Ritchie, who in turn prospered under her unrelenting nurturance, both financially (a research assistantship) and nutritionally (home-cooked meals). Even during holidays (and there are many Jewish holidays), Ritchie experienced the magic of sharing bread (and matzo) with some of the best minds in the social sciences. Although he usually thought it wise to keep counsel and to carefully choose his words when in the company of intellectual giants, on one embarrassing occasion he broke this rule and ventured to inquire what kind of animal was a lox.

It was during these social events that Ritchie first became aware of what a scholarly career could achieve, including the possibility that he could "think big and research narrowly." For her part, Dr. Neugarten confronted common myths about aging, such as the empty nest syndrome and the midlife crisis. In the years to come, her example emboldened Ritchie to contest common myths about homosexuality, such as the inevitability of gay youth suicidality and the assumptive, if not intractable, nature of sexual categories. By advocating for changes in public policy, Dr. Neugarten improved programs for the aged, fought ageism, and argued that social benefits should be based on personal economic conditions and not on age. Similarly inspired, Ritchie would fight homophobia by documenting the prevalence, normalcy, and positive attributes of same-sex-attracted individuals. Hoping to impact public policy, Ritchie would testify as an expert witness on court cases involving the Boy Scouts, same-sex marriage, and adoption because he strongly believed in the power of science to change lives. Dr. Neugarten taught one of the first courses in the nation on aging; Ritchie, on the science of homosexuality (1984). Dr. Neugarten stressed the value of interdisciplinary research, emphasized the diversity in socially constructed groups, and rejected age-divisiveness. So, too, Ritchie would publish across disciplines in the areas of biology, sociology, and various sub-fields of psychology (developmental, clinical, social, comparative, personality); argue for differential developmental trajectories by noting the vast diversity within same-sex-attracted populations; and integrate gay youth research with mainstream social/behavioral sciences and culture.

Before officially transferring from the Divinity School to Human Development, I took my first course in adolescence, a field of research still in its infancy, taught by Professor John Simms. I was immediately hooked, assuming at first that the material would assist me in becoming a youth minister (at least that was my justification to the Divinity School Registrar). I quickly discovered that the course consumed me far more than the death of God (and I understood youth better) and with greater passion—surely signs that transferring out of the Divinity School would be a wise decision. In the adolescence course I met fellow graduate student B. Bradford Brown, who came to Chicago straight from Princeton, and together we created an adolescent study group ($n = 4$) under the tutelage of Professor Bertram Cohler. Dr. Cohler's reading assignment was prototypical Chicagoan: Simply read everything ever written about adolescent development, create an annotated bibliography, synthesize, and suggest future research needs. Brad eventually became my best friend/mentor and was incalculably important for teaching me writing for scholarly audiences and how to comport myself in polite company, both painful but necessary lessons.

Also of critical significance was a course taught by Professor Daniel G. Freedman on human biology and behavior from the perspective of human ethology (an area also in its infancy). After viewing naturalistic films of nonhuman primate dominance behavior, I was struck by the similarities between these depictions and those of the (human) adolescents I encountered in summer camp and youth groups. Excited by this recognition, buttressed with recollections of how frog-like human adolescents often behave, and now equipped with the entire corpus of knowledge about adolescence, I experienced a first glimpse into my future: I would blend evolutionary psychology, naturalistic observation of behavior, and adolescent development. Agreeing to become my primary mentor, Dr. Freedman's disposition proved the perfect complement to that which I most needed: low-key and gently suggestive, open to wide-ranging discussions, theoretically and methodologically adventurous, and trusting of my instincts. I would later model this approach with my own PhD students and post-doctoral fellows.

Dominance and Altruism With few exceptions, previous adolescent research had generally failed to record the actual behavior of youth as they interact in naturalistic settings. Furthermore, with little conceptual understanding beyond the attribution of individual personality characteristics or the demands of the immediate social context to account for the existence of adolescent peer group structure, ethology offered both the methodological tools for conducting naturalistic observations of behavior and an evolutionary framework for making sense of dominance hierarchies.

The opportunity to correct this adolescent research deficit was rather fortuitous. During my Divinity School summers I was a camp counselor at Camp Wancaooah in upper Michigan. I had not considered collecting data in this setting until Dr. Freedman's course when it suddenly occurred to me: Why not blend work and pleasure? After reviewing everything known about primate dominance hierarchies and designing a multi-method research protocol for the Camp Wancaooah setting, I gathered observational, self-report, and peer rating data on early adolescent dominance behavior my third summer away from Chicago. My second master's thesis, published in a decidedly nonhuman-oriented journal (*Animal Behaviour*), was the result. Findings demonstrated that 13-year-old boys arranged themselves in a dominance hierarchy within days of meeting, the hierarchy remained stable over time, and the group structure provided guidance for interpersonal interactions. Once established, peer conflict was minimized and social roles were anticipated and enacted. Even the group's hierarchically lowest member (Omega) reported a positive experience; he might have been last but at least he had a place within the group.

These findings were sufficiently intriguing to Dr. Freedman that he encouraged me to conduct a more systematic study which included a diversity of groups, methods, and sexes. My dissertation was a three-summer project at Camp Wancaooah that incorporated observations of behavior,

self and peer ratings, adult evaluations, and physiological measurements. The goals were to explore sex differences in the development of group structure among eight groups of early adolescents, its stability over time, characteristics of different group rankings, and proximal functions of a dominance hierarchy. The result was two *Child Development* articles that bridged comparative and developmental psychology.

By the time I received the PhD in 1977, my publications spanned the gulf between frogs and Jesus and seemingly irreconcilable discipline fields by demonstrating that *humans behave like the animals that they are*. Thus, I had committed myself to studying normative youth development in their natural contexts; to using a variety of methodologies, especially observation of behavior; and to focusing on personality and social development. With an assist from Dr. Neugarten's encouraging phone call to Professor Urie Bronfenbrenner, I landed a job at the competition—Human Development at Cornell University beginning autumn 1977. It would be my first and only academic position; my migration north and east had ended.

Thus were planted the seeds for (newly renamed) Ritch's burgeoning reputation as an unconventional thinker. During his first several years at Cornell, he continued his ethological, multi-method, and multi-disciplinary approach to studying adolescent development. With graduate students Steve Small and Shep Zeldin observing adolescent prosocial (altruistic) behavior during co-ed biking and canoeing trips, Ritch expanded his focus to behavior other than dominance. They found that sex differences in helping behavior were striking: The sexes were equally prosocial, but in ways reflecting differences in instrumental and nurturance behavior. This research on dominance and altruism was the basis for Ritch's first book, Adolescence: An Ethological Perspective *(1987).*

Self-Esteem No longer sufficiently youthful to remain incognito and feign camp counselor status, I relocated my observational studies from summer camp to the day-to-day world of early adolescents in Ithaca, New York. Impressionistically, one salient characteristic of Camp Wancaooah's most dominant girls and boys was their high self-regard—something worthy of further investigation. I read the rather extensive self-esteem literature but could find few methodologies that incorporated a multi-method approach and none that included behavioral measures of self-esteem within naturalistic settings. To correct this, I developed a two-pronged strategy. First, while at Chicago I had become familiar with the experiential time-sampling technique employed by Professor Mihaly Czikszentmihalyi, a reader for my dissertation defense. Securing a grant from the Spencer Foundation, I purchased paging devices (beepers), gave them to a sample of local 7th graders, and asked them to record, when they were randomly paged (6–8 times daily for 1 week), their self-esteem and setting characteristics (time, location, others present, activity). Second, to directly assess self-esteem behavior I assigned an undergraduate student to each youth who acted as a big sister/brother; after each weekly visit with their adolescent, the research assistants recorded behavioral indices of self-esteem. Also included in the research design were peer-ratings of self-esteem (most youth knew each other) and a brief interview that I conducted with each youth about her/his self-regard.

In collaboration with post-doctoral fellow David Demo, this investigation grew into a 7-year longitudinal study of self-esteem. Self-report data collected when youth were paged with beepers allowed us to address a primary goal—to conduct ecologically valid research by gathering data during adolescents' normal daily routine. The findings countered conventional wisdom that adolescence is by definition a time of storm and stress, demonstrating that stability and continuity of self-esteem were more normative than exceptional for all measures and dimensions of self-esteem. Because I had examined intra-group variability over time, I was able to identify several *differential developmental trajectories*: Approximately 20% of adolescents was extremely stable in their self-esteem, 65% experienced mild and predictable contextual fluctuations in self-esteem (e.g., positive shifts coincided with Friday afternoons and hanging out with same-sex friends; negative shifts coincided with Monday mornings in school and with opposite-sex peers), and 15% oscillated unpredictably in their self-esteem. We suggested that discrepancies between common beliefs about adolescence and the actual lives they lead would diminish if behavioral and naturalistic approaches were more prevalent.

Thus, a second goal of the research project was to challenge the field's overwhelming reliance on self-report instruments for assessing adolescent self-esteem. With graduate student Gail Jaquish, I compared traditional measures with behavioral observations recorded by research assistants and school peers. We found striking disparities between these two methods which we explained by proposing two internally consistent, but not necessarily related, constructs: the presented self and the experienced self. Which should be believed? Both, we maintained, because they provide different but complementary information. Our inclination, however, was to favor the behavioral measures of self-esteem. Based on previous research, we reasoned that participant observers have access to processes unavailable to the actor and that actors are frequently unable to perceive their own personality or behavior apart from situational factors. Thus, on self-report tasks they may not be sensitive to their overall self-esteem level; instead, they report how they feel at that particular moment. Data derived from direct observation of behavior, however, may be more objective, accurate, and informed as well as less dependent on situational cues than self-report measures. This view was congruent with that of Dr. Mischel (1977, p. 248) who proposed that a necessary new direction for personality research can be achieved by moving "beyond our favorite pencil-and-paper and laboratory measures to include direct observation as well as unobtrusive nonreactive measures to study lives where they are really lived and not merely where the researcher finds it convenient to look at them."

Collectively, Ritch's research program resulted in two dozen journal articles and tenure in 1983. This event was not unexpected, although the dramatic shift in the content of his research that followed tenure was not anticipated by either Ritch or those closest to him. Two years earlier, Ritch introduced what might have been a major barrier to being awarded tenure: He disclosed to himself and others that his sexual and romantic interests were exclusively with men. He was admonished by his department chair to never mention this fact in class—which Ritch proudly and predictably disobeyed. The chair was dismissed (for other reasons) and soon thereafter Ritch began his career as a "professional gay," which would last beyond retirement.

Here, for Ritch, were new boundaries to challenge and, hence, transcend. His academic initiation into the lives of sexual-minority youth was launched in 1984 when Ritch taught one of the nation's first social science courses on homosexuality (which grew to over 100 students) and he began collecting data on what was at the time the largest study of gay, lesbian, and bisexual youth (n = 317). Not only was the sample large but, unlike previous investigations, it did not draw exclusively from youth who were runaways, prostitutes, criminals, or psychiatric patients. Even as the content of his teaching and research evolved, Ritch maintained his commitment to multi-method and multi-disciplinary approaches to studying personality and social development as well as to research that mattered for the lives of real adolescents and young adults. Based on the information derived from his research, Ritch grew increasingly incensed about existing beliefs concerning gay youth development because they distorted gay lives; he pledged to correct these misperceptions and provide sexual-minority youth a vocal opposition.

Sexual-Minority Youth During my earlier observational research on dominance, altruism, and social relations, I became aware of the peer ridicule visited on unprotected, vulnerable youth who were defenseless and with minimal peer support. At particular risk for peer abuse were those who did not act "appropriately" for their sex (that is, they were gender atypical) and were thus assumed to be lesbian or gay; transgendered youth were still largely invisible and undefined. Not surprisingly, initial studies on sexual minorities focused on these individuals because at the time research was dominated by clinicians, sociologists, and public health professionals whose agenda was to provide needed visibility and advocacy for disenfranchised youth. For the most part they recruited these gay youth from the streets, health clinics, support groups, and other locations in which the needy and vulnerable gather.

I did not disagree with the researchers' benevolent goals, but their overwhelming and exclusive focus on the pathology of sexual-minority youth simply did not ring true. First, the portrait inaccurately represented the many sexual-minority adolescents I had encountered who were quite healthy; indeed, many were thriving and behaving as if they were typical adolescents. Second, I feared that the resulting "suffering suicidal" scenario (suicide-attempting, drug-abusing, runaways adorned with body piercings and purple hair) being presented as normative gay adolescence might actually promote the very behavior it was intended to circumvent by causing vulnerable youth to relinquish hope for a happy and healthy future. It was time for a developmental psychologist to weigh in, to give voice to what I suspected were the majority of sexual-minority youth, and to provide a needed corrective to offset the existing pathological portrayal of same-sex-attracted youth.

To test the ubiquity of the suffering suicidal script prescribed to gays and lesbians, it would be necessary to sample a more normative, representative (*non-clinical*) population of sexual minorities. Wishing to debunk the popular myth of extreme levels of gay youth suicidality, depression, anxiety, and risky behavior, I recruited from numerous venues a more diverse and representative group of nonheterosexuals, dropped the assumption that all subgroups of nonheterosexuals were equally at risk, employed rigorous and standardized measures (especially of suicidality), and assessed not just negative but positive outcomes. The resulting data indicated that nonheterosexual youth experienced self-esteem levels comparable to heterosexual youth, young lesbians were especially healthy, and most sexual minorities did not unduly suffer negative parent and peer interactions (indeed, few were rejected by their family and most had good, supportive friends). Thus, despite their supposed sexual handicap, most nonheterosexual youth were experiencing ordinary lives as high-school and college students. The results were published in my second book, *Gay and Lesbian Youth: Expressions of Identity* (1990).

Graduate School Part III: Clinical Re-Specialization

Believing I needed to add to my arsenal a new research method and theoretical perspective that would deepen my understanding of the lives of same-sex-attracted individuals and thus more directly impact them, I returned to graduate school to re-specialize in clinical psychology. I commuted to the University of Massachusetts, Amherst (1989–93), served as a therapist in several community clinics, and completed a clinical residency in the Division of Psychiatry/Psychology at Children's Hospital of Michigan working with children and youth with attention deficit hyperactivity disorder, diabetes, spina bifida, or HIV infection. Increasingly thereafter, my research methodology included clinical interviews with personal narratives woven into the text. I was licensed as a Clinical Psychologist in New York State in 1995 and opened a limited clinical practice in Ithaca specializing in sexual-minority youth.

This clinical experience provided me with additional tools necessary for carrying out the next phase of my

research agenda: documenting the developmental experiences and clinical health of nonheterosexual adolescents. I conducted in-depth interviews with hundreds of youth and then embarked on an 8-year writing project that resulted in a book trilogy. These texts blended scientific data with life histories of lesbian, gay, bisexual, and questioning individuals and offered outreach suggestions for those who care about sexual-minority youth.

1. *". . .And Then I Became Gay." Young Men's Stories* (1998), based on intensive interviews with same-sex-attracted young men, indicated that development did not proceed in stages but through diverse developmental milestones and trajectories, and documented that, despite personal/social struggles, most same-sex-attracted young men were living happy and healthy lives.
2. *"Mom, Dad. I'm Gay." How Families Negotiate Coming Out* (2001) focused on the relationships young women and men had with family members; demonstrated that although most parents were not thrilled with having a gay child (for both selfish and child-protective reasons), many were not surprised and were perceived by their child to unconditionally love them; and offered suggestions for both youth and parents on how best to negotiate their lives together.
3. *The New Gay Teenager* (2005), my capstone book, summarized nearly everything I knew about sexual-minority youth and their development, including how best to define the population; gay youth in a historical perspective; developmental milestones (feeling different, first same-sex attraction, first sex, identity formation and synthesis); developmental diversity and resilience; and the normalization of same-sex desire among contemporary adolescents of all sexualities.

These books spoke of the tremendous diversity in developmental milestones and established that there was no one age of onset or invariant sequencing of first same-sex attraction, coming-out to self, disclosure to others, falling in love and dating, and self-acceptance. The data disputed widely held, but empirically unsubstantiated, beliefs about the linear and invariant progression of gay/lesbian development and the radical disparities between gays and heterosexuals; rather, data convincingly argued that identity, a primary development task during adolescence, unfolds along numerous pathways and corresponds in many respects to that which is experienced by heterosexuals.

The data also clearly supported the psychological normalcy of most same-sex-attracted youth, a finding that has been difficult for many to accept and hence remains controversial. Yet, what the youth have taught me is that most of them are content with their lives and would not change their sexual orientation even if they could. No magic pill for them; they simply want to be themselves. Thus, I have come to increasingly believe that it is necessary, even paramount, to cease pathologizing sexual-minority youth in favor of a greater focus on their diversity. Some clearly suffer extreme and chaotic lives, some are out-and-proud with amazing strength and fortitude, and some (most) are simply normal, ordinary adolescents with the same developmental needs and tasks as heterosexuals.

With these findings Ritch unwittingly, perhaps naively, entered the world of research politics. Initially, most investigations on gay youth were not conducted by developmental psychologists but by clinicians and public health advocates who, by definition, recruited abnormal populations of sexual-minority youth—those down and out. Even when Ritch presented an alternative perspective and justified it with science and suggested best practices, many ignored his findings or accused him of hindering their efforts to secure civil rights protection. In his most strident moments, Ritch accused these same individuals of placing sensationalism (research funding is available for studying what goes wrong rather than what goes right in the lives of marginalized populations) and political expedience above science. Not only was Ritch intolerant of the subservience of science to public policy (a lesson he learned at the Neugarten dinners) but also he questioned the wisdom of a "doom-and-gloom" strategy. Although Ritch seldom doubted the intent of its advocates (they wanted good things for gay youth), he believed that they might have inadvertently increased the negative plight of gay youth by reinforcing societal views of sexual minorities as weak and mentally ill and by misrepresenting their lives as especially suicidal which, he feared, might result in a self-fulfilling prophecy.

Ritch's research findings and his professional and clinical perspectives have been widely solicited by national and international media and his counsel is often sought by clinical, social, and political organizations concerned with improving the lives of sexual-minority youth. In addition to leading youth workshops on developing a positive identity, finding love, negotiating acceptance from family members, and staying healthy, Ritch has channeled his passion for improving the lives of sexual minorities into daylong clinical workshops for mental health professionals and those who care about the well-being of nonheterosexual youth.

Current Research

My research program continues to evolve and has recently included two new efforts. First, while exploring the sexual and romantic development of sexually marginalized youth I have become fascinated by those who fail to reside on the extreme poles of the sexual continuum (straights and gays) but rather reside somewhere in the middle—nonexclusive individuals who identify as mostly straight, bisexual, or mostly gay/lesbian. I am especially interested in *mostly straight* youth who are sufficiently inconspicuous that they could "pass" as straight, yet choose not to. For years I have wondered whether they are in transition to being gay, sexually attracted to one sex but romantically attracted to the other sex, or politically and socially

progressive straights who feel compelled to challenge hegemonic sexual assumptions. Perhaps, they are confused heterosexuals or members of a seldom studied and mostly disbelieved group who are truly sexually fluid. If the latter, I wonder whether such sexual fluidity impacts the stability of their sexual identity. I am currently exploring these issues in a longitudinal study of sexually nonexclusive adolescents and young adults.

A second ongoing research project addresses an issue that has plagued sex researchers for decades: the definition, and consequently, the assessment of sexual orientation. The resolution of this issue could well determine who is included in a given research sample. For example, I previously found that the population prevalence of sexual-minority youth varies from 1% to 20% depending on how sexual or romantic orientation is defined. Most investigators rely on self-report measures because they are quick and simple to collect; however, consistent with my approach toward dominance, altruism, and self-esteem, I assume a multi-discipline (especially biology and psychology), multi-method strategy that employs self-report (e.g., online survey, in-depth clinical interview) *and* behavioral (e.g., genital arousal, pupil dilation, eye-tracking) measures. Enhanced with novel tools for assessing sexual orientation and in collaboration with my post-doctoral fellow Gerulf Rieger and graduate students Zhana Vrangalova, Mathew Stief, and Sarah Merrill, my Sex & Gender Lab is attesting to the veracity of nontraditional methods for detecting a range of sexualities. For example, we are finding that a sexual continuum (rather than discrete sexual categories) characterizes males as well as females; that mostly straights exist both subjectively and objectively; and that some youth are inconsistent across sexual orientation measures. Regarding the latter, some youth claim to be of one sexual orientation (e.g., straight) yet respond physiologically (e.g., eye dilation and genital arousal) quite differently. Are they unaware of their sexuality or are they hiding it from themselves and others? We hope that by employing new technologies we will help the field answer such questions and, with the assistance of less intrusive devices that capture sexual responding, possibly broaden the scope of populations currently inaccessible to sex researchers, such as those of nontraditional ages (e.g., infants, children, elderly) and cultures (e.g., non-English speaking, societies with different conceptions of sexuality).

Final Comments

Ritch has dedicated his life to understanding adolescent development, and this focus has frequently meant discarding preconceived notions and distrusting conventional wisdom. Indeed, reflecting across a career that spans close to four decades, Ritch has remained predictably consistent in his questioning of established positions, especially when he believes they inaccurately portray the lives of youth. Whether it be the so-called ubiquity of adolescent storm and stress or the believed certainty that persecuted minorities suffer attenuated self-esteem and high rates of suicidality, it has never been easy for Ritch to passively accept over-reaching proclamations based on clinical observation, faulty research methodology, or historical precedent. Because he has been willing to view adolescents from unusual vantage points, especially in naturalistic settings, he has observed elements of development previously unrecognized or disavowed. It is his greatest wish that future generations of academics will embrace a similarly broad, multi-method, multi-discipline bias when seeking to understand the secrets of human development.

Rather than annihilating my career as some might have predicted, sexual minorities rescued it by providing the motivation necessary for me to remain in academe. I am fortunate to have lived long enough to witness a revolution in the lives of gay youth: Most contemporary youth of all sexual orientations believe, even if adults do not, that their same-sex-attracted peers are merely normal adolescents with the same developmental needs and accomplishments as heterosexuals. In this view, the current generation affirms its acceptance of sexual diversity. Perhaps before I give up research altogether I will witness the day when studying "gay youth" as a unique population will be considered unnecessary, even antiquated. I would welcome such professional obsolescence.

In closing, I add that re-specializing in clinical psychology instigated another, more profound life change—meeting my life partner and new Jewish nurturer, Kenneth Miles Cohen. In the last days of her life, Dr. Neugarten met Dr. Cohen and with an ever so slight smile completed the handoff. Dr. Cohen also became my collaborator, not only in this biography and other articles but also in writing a jointly edited life-course text, *The Lives of Lesbians, Gays, and Bisexuals: Children to Adults* (1996); co-teaching a course on gender and sexual minorities; and presenting day-long, research-based clinical workshops for healthcare professionals. Together we have demonstrated that two developmental/clinical psychologists can live happily (and unanalyzed) ever after.

Note

1. The *italicized* text was written by Kenneth M. Cohen, Ritch's long-term partner, because there are some things best said by someone other than the protagonist.

References

Mischel, W. (1977). On the future of personality measurement. *American Psychologist, 32,* 246–254.

Savin-Williams, R. C. (1987). *Adolescence: An ethological perspective.* New York: Springer/Verlag.

Savin-Williams, R. C. (1990). *Gay and lesbian youth: Expressions of identity.* Washington, DC: Hemisphere.

Savin-Williams, R. C. (1998). *". . .And then I became gay." Young men's stories.* New York: Routledge.

Savin-Williams, R. C. (2001). *"Mom, Dad. I'm gay." How families negotiate coming out.* Washington, DC: American Psychological Association.

Savin-Williams, R. C. (2005). *The new gay teenager.* Cambridge, MA: Harvard University Press. [Spanish edition (2009). *La nueva adolescencia homosexual.* Madrid, Spain: Ediciones Morata (Roc Filella Escola).]

Savin-Williams, R. C., & Cohen, K. M. (Eds.) (1996). *The lives of lesbians, gays, and bisexuals: Children to adults.* Fort Worth, TX: Harcourt Brace College.

39

If You Are Standing Around Just Watching, You Are Not Doing Your Job

JOHN SCHULENBERG

One of my favorite jobs over the past dozen years has been to serve as a baseball and softball coach for young people ages 5–17 in community and travel leagues. On a good day, I get to see development happening in real time, follow young people's thinking, and laugh with them. On a really good day, I get inspired by them, seeing their courage in action and being part of their in-the-moment experiences. When you do it right, there are no bad days in youth coaching. In our first age-10-girls' travel softball tournament, we lost every game by a lot, with some games ending because the other team made outs on purpose just to get it over with. Afterward, we had our team meeting where we highlighted the few good things that happened, especially the girls' wonderful sportsmanship. Nonetheless, I was in a foul mood, compiling a long mental list of the things we did wrong and thinking I had let down the girls and their families. I was following three of our players out to the parking lot and as I was catching up to them I could hear their laughter and excitement. One was saying ". . . being in a tournament is so cool!" and another one agreed and said "I can't wait' til our next tournament!" The other two immediately agreed with smiles on their faces.

All of this coaching has involved my own children (Clay and Franny), with me (and my wife Cathleen Connell) following more than leading our kids' interests in team sports. One thing I love about baseball and softball is that so much of it is about backing each other up. Baseballs and softballs have a mind of their own when hit and thrown, meaning that they often can get by you when you are trying to stop or catch them. So it is essential that everyone is backing each other up, never just standing around watching the play unfold. Thus the saying that all our players get to know by heart: "If you are standing around just watching, you are not doing your job." One

of the best responses over the years came from Delaney, an 8-year-old girl on our community league team: "Coach John, I get the feeling that you are trying to teach us about more things than just softball." All good coaches of young people know that they are teaching (and learning!) about far more than sports, but announcing this to the team tends to ruin all the fun, and ultimately the effectiveness. So, shhhh. Let them figure it out.

I am not entirely comfortable in writing this chapter. I believe the idea for this volume is an excellent one. I appreciate being included, and look forward to reading about the lives of my mentors and colleagues. Nonetheless, the self-focus is uncomfortable and I do not want to take myself all that seriously. But I take it as an opportunity to talk about the progression of research on adolescent development over the past three decades, giving attention to the ideas and personalities of scholars who have influenced my thinking and research direction, and more importantly, that of the field. So this is largely a story of people; my biggest fear in writing this is that I have left out someone dear and important to me—my apologies in advance!

To set the stage, I am currently at the University of Michigan, a professor of developmental psychology in the Department of Psychology, and a research professor at the Institute for Social Research and the Center for Human Growth & Development. I am fortunate to be working with many wonderful collaborators and students. My research covers quite a bit of ground regarding adolescence and the transition to adulthood, focusing especially on substance use, risky behaviors, and psychopathology; much of my research is longitudinal, following individuals across adolescence and into adulthood, and also cohort sequential, where we track historical change. Much of my conceptual work places substance use etiology and epidemiology within a developmental framework to consider the course, causes, and consequences of substance use during adolescence and the transition to adulthood.

One of my favorite novels is Ken Kesey's (1965) *Sometimes a Great Notion.* An appropriate quote from this book when looking back: "The past is funny . . . it never seems to let things lie, finished. It never seems to stay in place as it should" (p. 46). This chapter is non-linear, organized around key places, ideas, and groups in my life: Penn State HDFS, a developmental perspective, the University of Michigan, and the Society for Research on Adolescence. I conclude with a few observations about future hopes and directions.

Penn State HDFS

There is no doubt that the most significant 5 years of my life in terms of my current professional and personal life were at Penn State University in the Human Development and Family Studies (HDFS) graduate program. I arrived at Penn State in late August 1981, long on hair and short on money and confidence that I was on the right track. My most expensive possession was a beat-up 1968 VW bug, and the rest of my possessions barely filled the back seat.

Getting There The HDFS graduate program was the only non-clinical psychology program to which I had applied. I had been accepted into some good clinical psychology programs, but had begun to question my interest in and capacity for the front line. I had spent the previous 3 years working as a counselor at the Lighthouse Runaway Shelter in Cincinnati Ohio—a raw and inspiring experience with some very dedicated colleagues who did all they could to keep runaway youth off the streets and out of the juvenile justice system. In terms of intensity and clear sense of immediate purpose, nothing will ever beat that job. I often found myself admiring the young people we worked with, many who were leaving home due to abuse and neglect. The courage and resilience they often showed has remained inspiring. On the other hand, I could see the burnout growing in my more seasoned colleagues and started feeling some of it myself. We would only see our failures over and over again and we could only wonder about youth who did not return to us. The juvenile justice system was capricious, and yet often highly consequential for young people's chances in life. We sometimes lost young people to the streets, usually by their decision but once in a while by having them taken by force. I was facing the reality that most of the problems we saw were not due to faulty inner-workings. Becoming a clinical psychologist, as I imagined it then, was starting to lose its allure, disappointing given that that had been my dream for several years. I confided my misgivings to Professor David Ricks (who had trained with Henry Murray at Harvard, and gained fame by examining intra-individual covariation in mood and personality; e.g., Wessman & Ricks, 1966), my primary undergraduate mentor at the University of Cincinnati. He suggested I apply to the Penn State HDFS program. The more I learned about the program, especially the focus on life-span development and problem-focused interdisciplinary research, the more I liked it. I applied, was accepted, and invited to visit to help make my decision.

My visit to Penn State during the spring of 1981 started off badly—my VW broke down along the way, and I showed up late and grimy. My first meeting, for which I was several hours late, was with Professor Fred Vondracek (now retired) and it turned a bit antagonistic, with me questioning what one could do with a PhD in HDFS. He gruffly tossed a file on the table that listed where many HDFS students had gone with their PhDs. Later, we went to dinner with some other faculty, graduate students, and visiting students. It started off awkwardly, and I remember feeling tense and out of place, thinking I might as well cut my losses and leave. Then one of the other visiting students asked Fred where he was from and he answered in his obvious German accent, "West Virginia," which was true enough (he had spent time at West Virginia University), but his smile made it clear he was having fun with the person. This was my kind of humor; it broke the ice and Fred and I found an affinity for humor and beer that evening. I also met Mario Gaboury, the graduate student assigned to me (now at the University of New Haven), that evening; through our discussions and laughs late into the night, he made a convincing case for HDFS. Based on this visit, I decided I would give HDFS a shot. Fred became my primary advisor, friend, and dissertation Chair, and Mario became my friend and roommate. It is fair to say that had I not met Fred and Mario during that visit, I probably would have gone elsewhere.

Being There In the graduate student lounge, there was an old vacuum cleaner with a sign taped to it that said "No development happening here." It was funny at first, but then became an unremarkable part of the scenery. All of us in HDFS took for granted that of course development did not happen in a vacuum, that context mattered a whole lot. As a prelude to any argument today, this is a non-starter. No one would try to argue now that development is context-free. But at the time, this is exactly what much of the mainstream developmental psychology literature was effectively arguing, and this is part of the reason why HDFS was so different and so important to the field and to those of us who spent time there.

It is difficult to convey what an intense game-changing experience HDFS was for me. Part of it was me not having much of an academic background; neither of my parents went to college and no one we knew "wasted time" (my dad's phrase) in graduate school. So I had little idea about what to expect. But the large part of it was who was on the faculty at the time, and how interactive the faculty was. In addition to Fred Vondracek, the HDFS faculty members that I took courses from or worked with included: Jay Belsky, Bob Burgess, Linda Burton, Nan Crouter, Martin Ford, Jim Garbarino, Laurie Garduque, Gunhild Hagestad, Chris Hertzog, Jackie Lerner, Rich Lerner, Susan McHale, John Nesselroade, Anne Petersen, Michael Rovine, Warner Schaie, Hugh Urban, and Sheri Willis. Each, in their own right, was a fabulous scholar. Each was instrumental in helping to conceptually and empirically define the evolving sub-disciplines of life-span developmental psychology and life-course sociology. Together, they were revolutionizing how development was conceptualized and studied, advocating longitudinal research that crossed disciplines.

Also remarkable was how interactive this faculty was, with frequent large parties to which graduate students were invited. There were serious differences of opinion among some of the faculty, and it was highly instructive and entertaining to witness arguments at the parties. I have not seen this high level of faculty interaction since then, likely due to how unique this group of HDFS faculty was, as well as to changing times. This active engagement helped fuel the belief that something important was happening in HDFS.

As was typical for HDFS graduate students, I worked with several faculty over the years. Fred and I worked continuously together throughout the 5 years, focusing on adolescent career development. In addition to the substantive knowledge I gained from Fred, Fred's strong personality helped me gain confidence and direction. Most all of my early publications were with Fred (and much of this work was done at the Rathskeller bar across the street from the HDFS building). Fred's influence on my writing style ("If you don't know exactly what you're saying, no one else will!") and overall productivity ("Just get it done!") is still obvious to me today.

I worked with John Nesselroade, learning much about developmental methodology in general, and factor analysis in particular. John was the favorite of every single graduate student, and I do not think any of the other faculty minded this adoration we had for John because they all had it too. In working with Chris Hertzog, I gained some formative experience with LISREL (quite new at the time) that set the stage for much of my subsequent research. I also worked in Anne Petersen's research group that included several graduate students and post-docs including Rob Abramowitz, Elliott Asp, Phame Camarena, Lisa Crockett, Aaron Ebata, Nancy Galamos, Mike Losoff, Rhonda Richardson, and Pam Sarigiani. This was a highly interactive and productive group, and it was through Anne and this group of fellow students that I gained an appreciation for the clear benefits of larger-group collaborative work.

I took several seminars from Rich Lerner which were the most challenging and stimulating ones of my graduate career. Rich was intimidating as a professor, not because of his style (which is brash and big-hearted), but because of his encyclopedic knowledge of the field and command of developmental concepts and meta-theory. I too wanted that knowledge and command, and the meta-theory provided the big picture I needed regarding how and why life-span developmental psychology was evolving and how it related to the emerging fields of life course sociology, developmental science, and developmental psychopathology. When I consider my own evolving developmental perspective, discussed later in this chapter, much of it comes from Rich.

Nan Crouter was a new assistant professor, another clear favorite among the graduate students. Her influence on my career and life was pivotal. First, she exposed me to the work of Urie Bronfenbrenner and Glen Elder, bringing context to the forefront. Second, a paper I did for one of her seminars evolved, with her help, into my first first-authored publication (Schulenberg, Vondracek, & Crouter, 1984). Third, and most importantly, I met Cathleen Connell in one of Nan's seminars (prophetically, on work and family). Cathleen was a fellow graduate student in HDFS, but we did not have much contact until Nan's seminar. Sparks flew based on that contact, and the romance started (and is still happening).

What also has lasted from HDFS are some ongoing friendships and collaborations that started those many years ago. This is a common graduate school experience, no doubt, which is partly why conferences are so popular. I treasure these connections and lifelines built on the shared HDFS experience, and wish I had more time to keep more of them current. I still collaborate with Lisa Crockett, Lorah Dorn, and Lise Youngblade, and see many others at conferences and other professional meetings, including Aaron Ebata, Nancy Galambos, Karen Hooker, Michele Hostetler, Russ Isabella, Shelly MacDermid, Maureen Perry-Jenkins, and Michael Windle. Equally rewarding is to meet, and sometimes work with, the students of these lifelong colleagues. Finally, golf has kept some of these Penn State connections alive, especially with Todd Bartko, Adam Garfein, and Phame Camarena (as well as with John Nesselroade, Chris Herzog, and Scott Hofer). Todd and I make sure we play golf at least once a month in Michigan (yes, in the snow), with the streak now up to 134 months in a row.

A Developmental Perspective

The river of time eating away at its banks until it just

Crumbles.

Looks sudden.

Isn't.

Don Winslow (2012, p. 107)

At this point in my life, I cannot not take a developmental perspective. It has become my lens, good and bad, on all things family, work, and leisure. Seeing a behavior or characteristic at one point in time just seems less interesting and telling than seeing them vary or unfold over time. I can remember, as an adolescent, thinking that change was normal and stability was temporary. I was also drawn to the idea that what is really happening occurs below the surface. That there is some sort of natural time-structured rhythm that is hard to see but nonetheless creates order to the seemingly randomness of events over time was a notion that I took for granted—almost like a really good and intense novel. Of course, when I field-tested these ideas in real life, they did not work out so cleanly, thank goodness. Still, this affinity toward time-structure and underlying meaning has been with me for a while. So, my becoming a developmental scientist no doubt reflects selection and socialization, and a whole lot of luck.

One of the early lessons I learned about how social science "really works" for social scientists was from Rich Lerner in one of his seminars: We are humans studying humans; our science is beautiful and flawed because of this; as social scientists, we can and should take knowledge from every place we can get it including personal experience; and hopefully, the overlapping part of science and personal experience is not too large. I like to think that my own evolving developmental perspective reflects this lesson. Let me get the personal experience part into the mix, giving some details of my own adolescence, providing some lessons learned from my own children, and summarizing my evolving developmental perspective gained from personal and professional experiences.

My Adolescence and Transition to Adulthood I was born in Buffalo, New York. When I was 11, we (my parents, Gene and Barbara, older sister Sandy, younger sister Jane, and younger brother Rob) moved to St. Clairsville, Ohio, situated across the Ohio river and up a mountain from Wheeling, West Virginia. Moving from a metropolitan area of over 1 million people to a town of only 5,000 people (that was still the largest in the county), along with moving from the comfort of a large extended family to the starkness of no extended family, was quite a shock to the system. Few people moved to St. Clairsville, especially from a different state. As a fashion option for boys, long hair and bell-bottom pants, common in Buffalo in 1968, had not yet made it to St. Clairsville. Because of my Buffalo accent, compared to the eastern Ohio twang, people thought my name was Jan. Imagine my first day at school: Long-haired, bell-bottomed, funny-sounding Jan as the only new kid joining the 6th-grade class of 70 students. But my transition was nothing compared to that of my older sister Sandy. She was 14 and had lost her left leg to bone cancer 2 years earlier. When I saw her walk into high school her first day, head held up high, how could I not be inspired? She was and has remained my hero. Of course, over time, my family and I were made to feel quite welcomed, and I still have friends living in St. Clairsville. Nevertheless, this dramatic change in location and lifestyle had a large impact on my family and me. It took several years to no longer feel like an outsider. Of course, this switching of perspectives is not all bad, and I am sure some brooding insights, over and above what may typically happen during adolescence, were due to this transition.

No doubt, my siblings and I grew up faster in St. Clairsville than we would have in Buffalo. It was not uncommon for newly licensed 16-year-olds to drive down the mountain to Wheeling and spend the evening in a bar (at the time, a driver's license, regardless of age, was sufficient for being admitted into certain known bars). The main occupation in the county was coal-mining, which paid well enough to make college seem unnecessary for most. Less than a third of the high-school graduates went on to college. This was a fact of life in this town, and with the looming adulthood role of full-time employment immediately on the other side of high-school graduation, it was normal to experience the supposed fruits of adulthood sooner than did those living in more suburban college-going communities (e.g., see Ianni, 1998).

High-school sports was huge in the town, and athletics ran the school. I was not a great athlete—pretty good at best—but my school was small enough that I was able to participate in some high-school sports (football, wrestling, golf, and baseball). It did not take much deep thinking to see the clear benefits of team sports (versus the chess club, which I was also in) in terms of a wider circle of friends and girlfriends. I had always done well in school, and this continued on, encouraged by some outstanding high-school teachers who had high expectations for us and themselves. But what took up most of my focus was navigating and sometimes enjoying the social scene. It is easy for us to forget this as adults, that the main occupation for those going through high school is navigating their social life, avoiding missteps and loneliness, and finding comfort and validation in supportive friends. My friend and colleague, Rob Crosnoe (at University of Texas, Austin) wrote a wonderful book on this: *Fitting in and standing out* (2011). One of Rob's powerful points is that no matter how we as adults define school success and intervene to encourage it, our efforts will continue to fall short unless we also take into account how students view success, which clearly involves the social domain.

My father suffered, as did we along with him, from alcohol-use disorder. (In my father's side of the family, there is a long lineage of alcohol-use disorders and of mayors.) I certainly get the idea of steeling experiences, how good things can come from adversity, and I count on finding them in my research. But this notion only makes sense in retrospect and is little comfort when in the midst of the adversity. Growing up, there was a lot of love in my family and we tried our best to take care of each other. But this disorder, and all the individual and family difficulties that fed into and came out of it, was like a centrifugal force. I wanted to get away, and college was my way out.

My son Clay is now a junior in high school looking into colleges. Clay, Cathleen, and I make a formidable team in this time-consuming quest for the ideal college for him (and this will be repeated for Franny in a few years). In contrast, I made the decision to go to the University of Cincinnati because it met my two and only requirements: (a) It had to be inexpensive and thus in-state, and (b) it had to be as far away from my hometown as possible. In any event, it proved to be a great choice. I became a Psychology major during the first year, enjoyed nearly every class, and started aiming for a career in clinical psychology. Professors were accessible and research opportunities were plentiful. I benefitted very much from the teaching and mentorship of Professor Ricks (sadly, he passed away in 2004, shortly after retiring). I also worked with Professor John Steffen (now at University of Hawaii) and graduate student Michele Paludi (now at Union College). Among my friends was Joe Schumacher (now at

University of Alabama at Birmingham); we collaborated in a combined senior thesis on peer influences on drug use during adolescence.

Learning from My Children Probably like most parents, I feel I got lucky in the children department; and of course, equally lucky in the spouse department. At a most basic level, I am so grateful to be part of their lives and have them a part of mine. In addition to all else, I have enjoyed the developmental lessons I have learned from Clay and Franny. Of course, having someone—especially a developmental scientist—go on and on about their wonderful children is not one of life's most delightful experiences. So let me limit myself here and focus on two examples of a fundamental developmental lesson I learn from them again and again: The importance of looking at it from the developing person's perspective.

This lesson was when Franny was in pre-school. It was a rough morning with laundry and dry cleaning backed-up, and I had only a few clean shirts, none of which seemed to match my only clean suit jacket. Because I was running late, and I had to drop Franny off at pre-school, I just grabbed a shirt and asked Franny for help.

Me:	"Franny, does this shirt and jacket match?"
Franny (with certainty):	"Yes!"
Me:	"OK, let's go to school."
Me (in the car seeing in the daylight that the shirt and jacket do not match at all):	"Franny, I don't think these two match very well. Why do you think they match?"
Franny:	"They both have buttons, silly!"

And she was right. I was being silly, assuming she saw "a good match" the same way I did.

For this one, Clay was in middle school. After a school soccer game, I went and talked to Clay's coach, shook his hand, and gave my congratulations for a well-played game; a lot of other parents and players were still around. Clay and I were then walking back to the car.

Clay:	"Could you not do that again, talk to the coach like that?"
Me (a little surprised):	"What do you mean? Why?"
Clay:	"It's embarrassing."
Me (realizing that this is the first time he mentioned that I was publically embarrassing him, and seeing this as reflecting a milestone in his development and our parent–child relationship):	"Really! This is exciting! Tell me more. What made it embarrassing?"
Clay (seeing where this was going, and not wanting another	"This, right here, is embarrassing! Always asking me questions like this. It's
mini-lecture on adolescent development):	like we are in a stupid kid movie where you are the dorky professor dad. Can't we just be normal?"

(Both of us laughing.)

He was right, of course—we are probably not normal often enough, in part because I am a dorky professor dad. I sometimes step out of the experience, seeing it more abstractly and forgetting that important real moments are happening, not just great examples of developmental processes and milestones; probably we all suffer from that sometimes. Again, a matter of failing to truly see it from the developing person's perspective. Adolescence can be tough enough without having a parent who studies adolescence put a microscope on you. I hope Clay and Franny make it without too many scars from being used as interesting developmental examples; and I hope that they keep giving me great examples!

An Evolving Developmental Perspective "Development cannot be comprehended without the polar conceptualizations of continuity and discontinuity" (Werner, 1957, p. 137). In addition to the necessity of examining behaviors and characteristics as moving targets and highlighting the importance of looking at it from the developing person's perspective, another key aspect of my evolving developmental perspective is the tension between continuity and discontinuity across the life span. It is easy to pick out hints of what is to be, but only in retrospect (almost as good as Yogi Berra's "It's tough to make predictions, especially about the future"). In my research group, we like to think of development as being a contact sport, where any thoughts of predetermined pathways are quickly met with thoughts of powerful ongoing person–context interactions that can cause any number of diversions for ongoing trajectories. Ontogenetic continuity, whereby the distal past effectively "causes" the future (e.g., Schulenberg, Patrick, Maslowsky, & Maggs, in press), can sometimes be viewed as the default option in development—that is, if nothing out of the ordinary happens, we can and should expect this sort of continuity. But this is wrong in my view. Instead, ontogenetic continuity is just one possible pathway and reflects as much ongoing person–context interaction as we see in ontogenetic discontinuity. Ontogenetic discontinuity occurs when more proximal developmental influences—such as powerful life transitions that serve as turning points (Elder & Shanahan, 2006; Rutter, 1996)—neutralize or even over-ride the more developmentally distal ones (e.g., Schulenberg & Maggs, 2002; Schulenberg & Zarrett, 2006). When we see what looks like ontogenetic continuity (e.g., I did my senior thesis on peer influences on adolescent drug use and then years later, started a 20-year program of research on adolescent substance use), it only happened that way because a consistent direction was realized by the ongoing reciprocal effects between the changing person and changing context across the intervening interval. If something had gone a different way (e.g., say I stayed on track with clinical psychology and I entered private practice making millions as a sports psychologist with MLB players), then the initial developmentally distal "influence" (senior thesis topic) would have fallen away, having no effect into the future. I like to imagine that there are countless developmentally distal potential effects just waiting to be realized, but most fall away with little effect on the future because the ongoing person–context interaction took things in a different direction. In the quest for optimal development across the life span, the hope is that we can encourage the good kind of continuity and discontinuity alike.

Another component of my evolving developmental perspective worth noting here is heterogeneity in trajectories. Although I became enamored with psychology in college, a nagging concern could not be set aside. Over and over in our readings, we would confront the reality that findings typically applied to everyone in general and no one in particular, making us question the real-world relevance of the work (the work of my mentor, Professor Ricks, was an important exception). By holding up high the notion of invariant stages of development and failing to attend to interindividual differences, traditional developmental psychology was especially guilty of assuming homogeneity in course. But what was the alternative? "N of 1" stories and case studies were just as bad—describing one person in particular that may or may not relate to the general case.

Fast forward to today, and the concern is being addressed, with the understanding that development is multi-directional and that there usually is not one normative trajectory. There is now an abundance of multi-wave data sets and statistical strategies to identify heterogeneity in developmental trajectories. In-between now and then, the acceptance of heterogeneity in developmental course in the literature was not always smooth sailing. David Magnusson (1988) was instrumental in getting some in the field to start paying empirical attention to individual development, and helped usher in the long years of arguments regarding variable- versus person-centered approaches to research. My first empirical attempt to characterize differential developmental trajectories of binge drinking across the transition to adulthood with national longitudinal data (e.g., chronic and "fling" trajectories) was met with skepticism from respected colleagues at the University of Michigan (one advised me to abandon this line of inquiry) and elsewhere: A leader in the addictions field broke into laughter when he saw my poster at a conference—I believe it was laughter of surprise rather than of derision, but still, not much of a confidence boost for an assistant professor! Not everyone had this reaction of course, and my friend and colleague Bob Zucker (then at Michigan State, now at the University of Michigan) was especially helpful in encouraging this research, and it was eventually published in *Developmental Psychology* (Schulenberg, Wadsworth, O'Malley, Bachman, & Johnston, 1996). The key idea

here is that heterogeneity in course is essential to consider when attempting to understand adolescent development, an idea that places high value on larger and representative samples.

A final key aspect of my evolving developmental perspective is sensitive periods, a fairly ancient notion in developmental psychology. Erik Erikson's (1968) epigenetic theory highlights a series of critical periods across the life span. For example, the main developmental task of adolescence is forging an identity, and if one does not accomplish this task during adolescence, according to his theory, one is forever off track and will have trouble with accomplishing future tasks. Sensitive periods are viewed as more probabilistic and less harsh than critical periods, and refer to times across the life span when experiences are especially formative for biological and social reasons. Developmental psychology is built on the notion that early childhood experiences are indeed quite prognostic of future functioning (reflecting ontogenetic continuity discussed above), and our science is now progressing with long-term data and appropriate statistical strategies to test such notions (e.g., Fraley, Roisman, & Haltigan, 2013).

An essential set of questions for us to address is the extent to which adolescence is a sensitive period, whether it matters in the long run; more specifically, what experiences during adolescent matter the most, and for what sub-groups, in terms of adulthood functioning and adjustment? Several such questions are being pursued in our research group. Julie Maslowsky (now an RWJF Health and Society Scholar post-doc at Wisconsin who did her dissertation with me) is testing whether early adolescence matters more than later adolescence in terms of mental health influences on substance use. Justin Jager (now at Arizona State University who also did his dissertation with me) is comparing the impact of substance use during late adolescence versus during early adulthood on later substance-use difficulties. And in a research consortium described later, we are studying whether experiences during adolescence matter over and above childhood experiences in terms of adulthood psychosocial adjustment. Wouldn't it be great to have social policy based on an understanding of what mattered most during adolescence in terms of optimal development?

The University of Michigan

Getting Here My route to the University of Michigan (U of M) was not a direct one. After getting married and finishing graduate school in 1986, Cathleen and I went on a 4-year odyssey of finding two good academic positions in the same city. Times were different then in terms of dual career hires—then it was viewed as a clear problem, something to be avoided; now it is viewed more as an opportunity. I took a faculty position at Purdue University in the Child Development and Family Studies (CDFS) Department; Cathleen took a post-doc at Washington

University in St. Louis regarding health and aging. We had miserable weekdays and wonderful weekends, especially in St. Louis (a 5-hour commute from Purdue). I enjoyed my position at CDFS, and have remained friends with some colleagues and students from there, including Laura Gillespie (now DeHaan, at Calvin College); but there was not an imminent faculty position for Cathleen. After her post-doc, Cathleen took a faculty position at the University of Kentucky medical school in Lexington (another 5-hour commute from Purdue). She was there less than a year, both because a possible faculty position for me there fell through and because University of Michigan's School of Public Health offered her a faculty position. So she moved to Ann Arbor (again, 5 hours from Purdue!). She was circling me but not getting any closer, and after 4 years at Purdue, I decided to take a leave of absence and take a NIDA-funded post-doc to work with Ted Dielman (in the U-of-M medical school) and Lloyd Johnston (at the Institute for Social Research). After my first year at U of M, Purdue called with some good and bad news: (a) I was granted promotion with tenure; and (b) my request for another of year of leave of absence was denied (and by the way, still no position for Cathleen). ISR responded with a research faculty position offer, which I gladly took.

Institute for Social Research (ISR) and Survey Research Center (SRC) ISR is an interdisciplinary "soft-money" research institute. It thrives because grant-getting success and strong scholarship are equally important, and because the reigning management style is "bottom up," where the research faculty have full say in how it is run. This is in contrast to the "top down" management style of many academic departments, where administrators run the show, for better and worse. I am convinced that our administrative style is fundamental to our success as an organization and thus to the advancement of the scientific literatures to which we contribute. It is a wonderful place to be, provided one enjoys the challenges of funded research and is keenly interested in studying topics highly fundable. ISR is divided into five Centers, one of which is my main home, the Survey Research Center (SRC). SRC is home to several ongoing large-scale national studies including the Monitoring the Future study (described below), the Panel Study of Income Dynamics and the Health and Retirement Study. Keeping large-scale studies afloat and innovative is a constant challenge; it takes, among other things, a unique blend of strong scholarship, funding pragmatism, and a whole lot of expert help and dedication. Many of our colleagues in the Center are at the forefront of innovative data collection and analytic strategies, yielding a blend of substantive and methodological foci in most studies. One of the aspects I enjoy most is how interdisciplinary the SRC faculty are, including, for example, anthropologists, economists, epidemiologists, geographers, psychologists, psychiatrists, sociologists, and statisticians. Faculty meetings are never boring.

Department of Psychology The University of Michigan's storied Department of Psychology is one of the largest and most diverse departments at the University and across the country. One reason why it is so large is because many faculty, like me, have joint appointments. Having faculty with multiple appointments can create some chaos, but the clear advantage is increased cross-campus and cross-disciplinary collaboration. After a few years, my initial adjunct appointment with the Department was changed to a regular faculty appointment in the Developmental Area, joining in with a large group of other faculty with interests in adolescent and life-span development (e.g., Toni Antonucci, Jacque Eccles, John Hagen, Lois Hoffman, Vonnie McLoyd, Monique Ward). I have enjoyed teaching a graduate seminar on adolescence and the transition to adulthood for years, in part because I get as much if not more out of it than the pre- and post-docs that take it. Many new faculty joining in have enriched the Developmental area's emphasis on adolescence, including Rona Carter, Pam Davis-Kean, Dan Keating, and Chris Monk.

Shortly after I joined the department, Arnold Sameroff also joined in, bringing his well-known transactional approach to development and psychopathology along with his wicked humor and high interest in golf. We began a collaboration concerning wayward trajectories (of people and golf balls), leading to a successful NIMH center grant on developmental and ecological processes in mental health, which was housed in the Center for Human Growth and Development (a free-standing research center that houses many bio-psycho-social developmental studies from across the University). One emphasis of this NIMH Center was developmental psychopathology during the transition to adulthood, and we organized campus-wide seminars and a national workshop, resulting in a special issue of *Development & Psychopathology* (Schulenberg, Sameroff, & Cicchetti, 2004). Bringing needed attention to this critical life transition was important, and working with and learning from these two great scholars, Arnold and Dante Cicchetti, was a real benefit.

Substance Use Across Adolescence and the Transition to Adulthood I am convinced that substance use is best understood as a developmental phenomenon, and I examine the etiology and epidemiology of substance use from a developmental perspective. This means: (a) an emphasis on the age curve and heterogeneity of trajectories about the age curve (Schulenberg et al., 1996; in press); (b) concern with how adolescent and young adult substance-use trajectories are linked with upstream childhood characteristics and experiences and downstream adulthood functioning and adjustment (Schulenberg & Maggs, 2008), and with the complex array of risk and protective factors (Patrick & Schulenberg, 2011; Maslowsky & Schulenberg, in press) and developmental tasks and transitions of the second and third decades of life (Jackson & Schulenberg, in press; Staff et al., 2010); and (c) viewing adolescent and young adult substance-use trajectories as embedded within the socio-demographic and broader historical context (Jager, Schulenberg, O'Malley, & Bachman, in press; Keyes et al., in press).

I joined the Monitoring the Future (MTF) study in 1991. MTF is an ongoing national study regarding the epidemiology and etiology of substance use across adolescence and adulthood. It was started by Lloyd Johnston and Jerry Bachman in the early 1970s, with Patrick O'Malley joining shortly thereafter (all three are Research Professors at ISR). It was not initially designed as a drug-use study, but rather a more general "monitoring" study to follow historical and developmental change in behaviors and attitudes among the nation's youth. At the time that they were searching for the appropriate funder, the National Institute on Drug Abuse (NIDA) was established, and the match was made. Through a series of investigator-initiated R01s, MTF has been funded by NIDA ever since. The design of MTF is cohort-sequential longitudinal, starting with high-school seniors—i.e., new nationally representative cohorts of high-school seniors are added each year and random samples of each cohort are followed longitudinally into adulthood. In fact, we studied the MTF study in graduate school in John Nesselroade's course as one of the few ongoing studies that permits separation of age, period, and cohort (APC) effects on behavior/attitudes. Indeed, to get at the broad array of individual and society mechanisms of adolescent drug use, the separation of age, period, and cohort effects is essential and is a unique capacity that MTF brings to the field (Johnston, O'Malley, Bachman, & Schulenberg, 2012; Keyes et al., 2012).

Much of my work over the past two decades has been with MTF data. And all of my work on substance use during adolescence and the transition to adulthood has been with a long list of great colleagues and students. I have learned much about "big science" from Lloyd, Jerry, and Patrick and I continue to enjoy working on MTF with them. Shortly after I started at U of M, Jennifer Maggs (a student of Nancy Galambos, a Penn State HDFS graduate school friend and colleague) took a post-doc in ISR with Jacque Eccles, and Jennifer and I started a collaboration to examine how developmental transitions relate to substance use and other health risks (Schulenberg, Maggs, & Hurrelmann, 1997). Jennifer is now a Professor in HDFS and Penn State (there it is again), and I continue to benefit from our ongoing collaboration. I have had a great run with pre-doc students (from the U-of-M Developmental Psychology area, Combined Program in Education and Psychology, and School of Public Health) and post-doc students that worked with me on MTF and other projects over the years, including: Bridget Ammon (Lehigh University), Justin Jager (Arizona State University), Deb Kloska (University of Michigan), Alison Bryant (College of Holy Cross), Meghan Martz (current student), Julie Maslowsky (University of Wisconsin), Jamaal Matthews (Montclair State), Sean McCabe (University of Michigan), Alicia Merline (American Pediatric Association), Emily Messersmith (Arbor Research Collaborative), Sherri Wynne (Washington University), Colleen Pilgrim (Schoolcraft College), Deborah Safron (Michigan State), Kenny Steinman (Ohio State), Susan Sy (Cal State Fullerton), Kate Wadsworth (University of Puget Sound), and Nicole Zarrett (University of South Carolina). Several internal and external colleagues have joined in on MTF studies as well, to the benefit of us all, including Philippa Clarke (University of Michigan), Kerry Keyes (Columbia University), Jeremy Staff (Penn State), and Laura Wray-Lake (University of Rochester). Most of these collaborations have continued, and I hope they go on for a long time. Recently, Megan Patrick joined us on MTF as a part of the SRC research faculty. Megan was a graduate student of Jennifer Maggs at Penn State (making Megan a "grand-daughter" of Nancy Galambos!), and she has been a perfect addition, illustrating well the entrepreneurial-scholar qualities that will help her thrive in MTF and SRC. Finally, very few of these successful collaborations over the years would have happened without much appreciated funding, especially from NIDA, as well as NIAAA, NIMH, NICHD, RWJF, and NSF.

PDRP and Vicki Levin Being part of an ongoing NIH grant review panel is akin to going through a shared crisis every 4 months, and colleagues with whom one has this experience become friends for life. One of the primary review committees for many NIH grant applications concerning development and psychopathology is the Psychosocial Development, Risk and Prevention (PDRP) study section. In 2005, I was very fortunate to get a call from Vicki Levin, the consummate Scientific Review Officer of PDRP, to come and effectively "try out" for PDRP. Vicki, who had unparalleled social skills, treated the committee like it was her family (including providing us with home-baked snacks), and insisted that every application be evaluated thoroughly, fairly, and with vision. I apparently passed the test, part of which was whether one "played well with others," and served as a member 2005–07, and then as Chair 2007–09. Three times a year, we would hole up in a hotel conference room for 2 days and intensively work through all our reviews of the applications. One important reviewer lesson learned early on was from Ann Masten (at University of Minnesota and current President of SRCD): One can and should advocate for applications that are highly significant for the field despite some flaws, but only once in a while. I made many good friends through these years, especially Pamela Cole (Penn State), Rand Conger (UC Davis), Jennie Noll (Cincinnati Children's Hospital Medical Center), Bonnie Leadbeater (University of Victoria), Seth Pollack (University of Wisconsin), Helene White (Rutgers), Lise Youngblade (Colorado State University, and fellow Penn State graduate), and Xiaojia Ge (University of Minnesota, who, sadly, passed away in 2009).

Vicki and I worked closely together when I became Chair, and I had the pleasure of meeting her husband, Sandy Levin (Congressman from Michigan). Sadly, Vicki became quite ill and had to retire in early 2008, and then passed away in the fall of 2008. Before her passing, Pamela, Seth,

Elena Grigorenko (Yale), and I organized a tribute to Vicki including presenting her with a painting commissioned in her honor ("The Moon" by Vladimir Shpitalnik, a photo of which many of us still have as our screen saver). Amazing, but not surprising, over 100 scholars from across the country joined in this tribute, offering support and very similar stories about how much a difference Vicki made in their lives and careers. After she passed, we had a memorial for Vicki at the 2009 SRCD conference in Denver, which was packed with researchers, NIH people, and Vicki's family. In part stimulated by the outpouring of support, the Levin family decided to set up an award for early career scholars to fund their time to develop outstanding grant applications and also to visit NIH and talk with people in advance, one of Vicki's strong beliefs in how things should work. Pamela, Sandy, Seth, and I worked together to seek funding and establish the SRCD Victoria S. Levin Award for Early Career Success in Young Children's Mental Health Research. Through this whole experience, in addition to learning a great deal more about the world of NIH funding, my life was enriched by Vicki and her two families.

Consortium on the Analysis of Pathways from Childhood to Adulthood (CAPCA) Pam Davis-Kean, a Professor in Psychology and Research Professor in ISR, in collaboration with Jacque Eccles, initiated CAPCA in 2003. CAPCA is a National Science Foundation funded international consortium housed in ISR that includes over 25 long-term data sets from Canada, Finland, Sweden, UK, and USA, and of course the scholars who work on them. Under Pam's excellent leadership, we meet three times a year, finding common interests and common ground across the different data sets. The simple notion here is that similar findings across numerous studies are far more compelling than findings from a single study. The group has done well along many dimensions including collaborative publications (e.g., Schulenberg & Maggs, 2008; Schulenberg & Schoon, 2012), grant spin-offs, and graduate student and advance training on longitudinal methods. And a real benefit is forging new collaborations and friendships, for me including Aprile Benner, Rob Crosnoe, Kate Duckworth, Katja Kokko, Jen Lansford, Greg Pettit, and Ingrid Schoon. We join others in the field, such as Patrick Curran and Andrea Hussong (2009), believing that this is a needed direction for our science, seeking ways to combine studies to replicate findings and increase our scientific yield and credibility.

Future of SRC I am currently Associate Director of SRC (Bill Axinn is current SRC Director, another Penn State connection), focused largely on faculty recruitment and mentoring. I coordinate our Faculty Research Fellows (FRF) program, which is now our primary way for recruiting early career scholars. SRC is sufficiently unique and the mix of needed talents and motivations to be a successful early career entrepreneurial scholar is sufficiently opaque that we decided on a faculty try-out program,

thus the FRF program. We have been quite successful in attracting outstanding early career scholars from multiple disciplines (so far, economics, psychology, sociology, and statistics) and connecting them up with appropriate senior mentors regarding grantsmanship (and other matters of course), with several FRFs already making the successful transition to SRC research faculty (including Megan Patrick, mentioned above, our first successful FRF). There are many exciting aspects of this, but for me, the real excitement is working with these bright scholars as a group and seeing how they are viewing the science, especially in terms of mixing methods and crossing disciplines. Many of us more senior researchers in SRC are now having an easier time imagining the wonderful future of SRC.

The Society for Research on Adolescence (SRA)

SRA was launched while I was a graduate student, and the editors of this volume were all heavily involved in SRA's launching and successful development over the years. Because of a job interview for a faculty position, I missed the very first conference in 1986 in Madison, Wisconsin. Given how the interview went (not well) and how well SRA's first conference went, I obviously made the wrong choice. But I have attended every SRA conference since then. Imagine the idea of this group for a moment—scholars from across the world who are fully focused on trying to get a better understanding of all aspects of adolescence meet to share and advance their research. It is that simple and that grand all at once.

In addition to my affinity to the idea of SRA, my interest was stimulated by Penn State HDFS mentors; I too wanted to be involved as much as possible and volunteered often. My first chance was provided by Jeanne Brooks-Gunn—she invited me to help organize the first "meet the professor luncheons" (now called "meet the scientist luncheons") for the 1990 SRA conference in Atlanta. It went well. An important lesson in all this was just how happy people were to be involved; not a single invitee turned us down. Conferences like SRA serve multiple purposes, perhaps the two most important ones being conveying advances in the science and providing the opportunity for people to get together—old friends and new ones. I enjoyed both purposes tremendously over the years. I continued to volunteer and served on numerous committees and review panels. Diane Scott-Jones, editor of SRA's *Journal of Research on Adolescence* (*JRA*), invited me to serve as a Co-Editor of JRA, to which I happily agreed. I served in this role 1995–2001, sharing the experience with other Co-Editors during that period including Liz Susman and Lisa Crockett (both representing Penn State connections). It was exciting to be involved in helping to move along a broad range of some of the best research on adolescence, the learning curve had to be sharp, and being a journal editor is one of the biggest contributors to frequent late nights.

In 2006, Vonnie McLoyd (then President of SRA) invited me to serve as SRA Program Co-Chair for the 2008 conference in Chicago. I was happy to accept and joined in with Karen Rudolph, the other Program Co-Chair. I very much enjoyed working with Karen and we both took our job quite seriously, worrying through a lot of decisions and details. Our job was to organize the program including deciding on the invited speakers (with Vonnie), setting up the review system for the submitted program, making final decisions on the submitted program, and about 100 other things. Among lessons learned, it was once again refreshing to see how happy people were to say yes and get involved when asked; equally important was learning how professional and amazing the SRA staff was in terms of working through the details and making sure all went smoothly. For a volunteer organization, SRA works incredibly well, both because people want to join in and because SRA staff are so good. By all indications, the 2008 Chicago conference was a success. I was then fortunate to be elected to SRA Executive Council, the decision-making body of SRA (2008–2012). Before this, I felt pretty much in the know about how SRA worked, but gained much new insight into the inner-workings and true dedication of those involved. Reed Larson was President 2008–10 and Niobe Way was President 2010–12. The two are quite different in their styles, with Reed attending to details and advancing SRA's infrastructure; Niobe is more of a big-picture person, and focused on making SRA more international; nonetheless, the two exemplified clear dedication to SRA and served as important role models for the organization.

I was then fortunate to be elected SRA President, and will follow the current President, Stephen Russell and serve 2014–16. Stephen is an inspiring leader and consensus builder. I am looking forward to my turn, dedicated to keeping the key qualities of SRA front and center: emphasis on early career scholars, emphasis on increasing diversity in our samples and ranks, and keeping us attractive to multiple disciplines and especially to those who wish to cross disciplines in their own work. I believe we ought to be at the forefront of identifying and guiding the future of our science and advising funding agencies and Foundations about the likely and possible future of research on adolescence. SRA has been a central part of the fast evolution of research on adolescence over the past three decades; we are now benefitting from the hard work, leadership, and scholarship of our predecessors, and I believe we pay them back by working hard for the future SRA scholars and leaders. A lot of people gave me the chance to be involved in SRA over the years, and I want to return the favor to others coming along.

Conclusions: A Hoped-For Future

There can be an implied notion in an autobiography that the end, or at least the best stuff, has already happened. I do not believe that is the case here, for I think the best is yet to come regarding the research I am conducting with my students and colleagues, and definitely regarding the scientific understanding of adolescence.

There used to be a common belief that theory was way ahead of our research, that our methodological and statistical strategies were not able to capture the complexity explicit in many grand theoretical frameworks. We do not hear this belief much now because methods and statistics have been fast catching up. Crossing disciplines is starting to be commonplace. NIH is now giving high priority to innovation in funded research, with an advantage being shifting norms toward, for example, multi-modal data collections (e.g., combining fMRI and survey research) and merging levels of analysis (e.g., focusing on biological, social, and cultural mechanisms within the same study). Fears of neurological hegemony and biological reductionism are still voiced by some, but more and more, scholars are understanding that focusing on just a single level of explanation is not only insufficient, it can be misleading (Crone & Dahl, 2012). Increasingly, the broader context in which the developing individual is embedded is getting serious empirical attention in terms of how it alters developmental trajectories. For example, the recent MTF work of Justin Jager shows that although substance use has been declining for recent cohorts of high-school students compared with past cohorts, the more recent cohorts have a faster rate of increase in post-high school substance use compared with past cohorts (Jager, et al., in press). This relatively more rapid post-high school escalation suggests shifts in etiologic mechanisms and intervention targets, and more generally the power of changing cultural effects on individual trajectories. Such new insights come from integrating breadth and depth in our science, allowing us to gain empirical footholds on the grand and beautifully complex ecological (Bronfenbrenner, 1979), developmental-contextual (Lerner, 2006), bio-psycho-social (Zucker, 1994), and systems (Sameroff, 2010) frameworks of human development.

In many ways, we are now realizing the earlier hopes of programs like Penn State's HDFS in terms of cross-disciplinary problem-focused research ascending. Luke Hyde, a new Assistant Professor who joined our Department of Psychology, could be described as a neuro-psych researcher who also focuses on psycho-social mechanisms, or a psycho-social researcher who also focuses on neuro-psych mechanisms (e.g., Hyde, Gorka, Manuck, & Hariri, 2011). Luke recently mentioned that such labels do not matter much to him—the main point is that the most telling discoveries are now coming from the intersection of neurological and psycho-social mechanisms and he wants to be part of this discovery process. From what I am seeing, Luke's perspective represents the welcomed new guard.

Our understanding of adolescence has progressed incredibly over the past three decades, and it has been a joy to be witnessing and be a part of it all. I am optimistic about the future of our science for many reasons, but mainly because of the early career scholars that I have met and worked with and whose articles and grants I have read. As a group, they are far more research- and funding-savvy than I was starting out. I have heard some concerns among my senior colleagues that the newer cohorts of researchers are too self-focused, not interested enough in, for example, volunteering their time to SRA. I disagree with them. I see a lot of desire to be involved among the early career scholars I know. And I do not see any of them standing around just watching.

References

Bronfenbrenner, U. (1979). *The ecology of human development: Experiments by nature and design.* Cambridge, MA: Harvard University Press.

Crone, E. A., & Dahl, R. E. (2012). Understanding adolescence as a period of social-affective engagement and goal flexibility. *Nature Reviews Neuroscience, 13*, 636–650.

Crosnoe, R. (2011). *Fitting in, standing out: Navigating the social challenges of high school to get an education.* New York, NY: Cambridge University Press.

Curran, P. J., & Hussong, A. M. (2009). Integrative data analysis: The simultaneous analysis of multiple data sets. *Psychological Methods, Special Issue: Multi-Study Methods for Building a Cumulative Psychological Science, 14*, 81–100.

Elder, G. H., Jr., & Shanahan, M. J. (2006). The life course and human development. In R. M. Lerner (Ed.), *Theoretical models of human development*, Vol. 1 of the *Handbook of child psychology* (6th ed.). W. Damon & R. M. Lerner, Editors-in-chief. Hoboken, NJ: John Wiley & Sons.

Erikson, E. H. (1968). *Identity: Youth and crisis.* New York: Norton.

Fraley, R. C., Roisman, G. I., & Haltigan, J. D. (2013). The legacy of early experiences in development: Formalizing alternative models of how early experiences are carried forward over time. *Developmental Psychology, 49*, 109–126.

Hyde, L. W., Gorka, A., Manuck, S. B., & Hariri, A. R. (2011). Perceived social support moderates the link between threat-related amygdala reactivity and trait anxiety. *Neuropsychologia, 49*, 651–656.

Ianni, F. (1998). *The search for structure: A report on American youth today.* New York: Free Press.

Jackson, K. M., & Schulenberg, J. E. (In press). Alcohol use during the transition from middle school to high school: National panel data on prevalence and moderators. *Developmental Psychology.*

Jager, J., Schulenberg, J. E., O'Malley, P. M., & Bachman, J. G. (In press). Historical variation in rates of change in substance use across the transition to adulthood: The trend towards lower intercepts and steeper slopes. *Development and Psychopathology.*

Johnston, L. D., O'Malley, P. M., Bachman, J. G., & Schulenberg, J. E. (2012). *Monitoring the Future national survey results on drug use, 1975–2011:* Vol. I, *Secondary school students.* Ann Arbor, MI: Institute for Social Research, University of Michigan.

Kesey, K. (1965) *Sometimes a great notion.* New York: Bantam Books.

Keyes, K. M., Schulenberg, J. E., O'Malley, P. M., Johnston, L. D., Bachman, J. G., Li, G. et al. (2012). Birth cohort effects on adolescent alcohol use: The influence of social norms from 1976–2007. *JAMA Psychiatry, 69*, 1304–1313.

Lerner, R. M. (2006). Developmental science, developmental systems, and contemporary theories of human development. In W. Damon & R. M. Lerner (Eds.), *Theoretical models of human development*, Vol. 1 of the *Handbook of child psychology* (6th ed.). Hoboken, NJ: Wiley.

Magnusson, D. (1988). *Individual development from an interactional perspective: A longitudinal study.* Hillsdale, NJ: Erlbaum.

Maslowsky, J., & Schulenberg, J. E. (In press). Interaction matters: Quantifying conduct problem by depressive symptoms interaction and its association with adolescent alcohol, cigarette, and marijuana use in a national sample. *Development & Psychopathology.*

Patrick, M. E., & Schulenberg, J. E. (2011). How trajectories of reasons for alcohol use relate to trajectories of binge drinking: National panel data spanning late adolescence to early adulthood. *Developmental Psychology, 47*, 311–317.

Rutter, M. (1996). Transitions and turning points in developmental psychopathology: As applied to the age span between childhood and mid-adulthood. *International Journal of Behavioral Development, 19*, 603–626.

Sameroff, A. (2010). A unified theory of development: A dialectic integration of nature and nurture. *Child Development, 81*, 6–22.

Schulenberg, J. E., & Maggs, J. L. (2002). A developmental perspective on alcohol use and heavy drinking during adolescence and the transition to young adulthood. *Journal of Studies on Alcohol. Supplement, 14*, 54–70.

Schulenberg, J. E., & Maggs, J. L. (2008). Destiny matters: Distal developmental influences on adult alcohol use and abuse. *Addiction, 103*, 1–6.

Schulenberg, J. E., Maggs, J., & Hurrelmann, K. (Editors) (1997). *Health risks and developmental transitions during adolescence.* New York: Cambridge University Press.

Schulenberg, J. E., Patrick, M. E., Maslowsky, J., & Maggs, J. L. (In press). The epidemiology and etiology of adolescent substance use in developmental perspective. In M. Lewis & K. Rudolph (Eds.), *Handbook of developmental psychopathology.* New York: Springer.

Schulenberg, J. E., Sameroff, A. J., & Cicchetti, D. (2004). Editorial: The transition to adulthood as a critical juncture in the course of psychopathology and mental health. *Development and Psychopathology, 16*, 799–806.

Schulenberg, J. E., & Schoon, I. (2012). The transition to adulthood across, time and space. Overview of special issue, *Longitudinal and Life Course Studies, 3*, 164–172.

Schulenberg, J. E., Vondracek, F. W., & Crouter, A. C. (1984). The influence of the family on vocational development. *Journal of Marriage and the Family, 46*, 129–143.

Schulenberg, J. E., Wadsworth, K. N., O'Malley, P. M., Bachman, J. G., & Johnston, L. D. (1996). Adolescent risk factors for binge drinking during the transition to young adulthood: Variable- and pattern-centered approaches to change. *Developmental Psychology, 32*, 659–674.

Schulenberg, J. E., & Zarrett, N. R. (2006). Mental health during emerging adulthood: Continuity and discontinuity in courses, causes, and functions. In J. J. Arnett & J. L. Tanner (Eds.), *Emerging adults in America: Coming of age in the 21st century* (pp. 135–172). Washington, DC: American Psychological Association.

Staff, J., Schulenberg, J. E., Maslowsky, J., Bachman, J. G., O'Malley, P. M., Maggs, J. L. et al. (2010). Substance use changes and social role transitions: Proximal developmental effects on ongoing trajectories from late adolescence through early adulthood. *Development and Psychopathology, 22*, 917–932.

Werner, H. (1957). The concept of development from a comparative and organismic point of view. In D. B. Harris (Ed.), *The concept of development: An issue in the study of human behavior* (pp. 125–148). Minneapolis: University of Minnesota Press.

Wessman, A., & Ricks, D. F. (1966). *Mood and personality.* New York: Holt, Rinehart & Winston.

Winslow, D. (2012). *The kings of cool.* New York: Simon & Schuster.

Zucker, R. A. (1994). Pathways to alcohol problems and alcoholism: A developmental account of the evidence for multiple alcoholisms and for contextual contributions to risk. In R. A. Zucker, J. Howard, & G. M. Boyd (Eds.), *The development of alcohol problems: Exploring the biopsychosocial matrix of risk* (pp. 255–289). Rockville, MD: National Institute on Alcohol Abuse and Alcoholism.

40

Contributing to Adolescent Research in Non-Typical Ways

Pursuing the Many Faces of Social Cognition

Lonnie R. Sherrod

 I have followed an unusual career path, with most of my positions being non-academic. However, I begin my professional career, even at the undergraduate level, with an interest in social cognitive development, and that interest has remained with me, although it has assumed many faces. Hence, despite having many different types of jobs at varied organizations, there has been considerable consistency in my academic interests. The interest in adolescence entered later; my initial work was on infancy.

Beginnings: An Early Concern for Academics

I guess it is appropriate to start at the beginning, since it is relevant to my lifelong path. I was born in Northeastern Tennessee. I was a premature baby, which in 1950 was non-trivial, and got pneumonia shortly after coming home from the hospital. As a result, my mom had an image of me as being sickly, and since I was an only child that meant considerable overprotection. Since I was not allowed to do much outdoors activity or engage in rough-and-tumble play, I settled on quiet, school-type pastimes, which meant I was destined to be a good student, and never really considered any career other than academics. Hence it is quite ironic that I ended up in non-academic jobs. But that happened unexpectedly and by chance. Young scientists interested in alternate career routes often look to me for advice, but I can offer little advice because my career route was neither planned nor strategically designed. Serendipity certainly played a role in my career path.

I was interested in science as well as art from an early age. Until my undergraduate years, I felt some tug between these two interests. My undergraduate mentor, Peter Klopfer, was a Zoologist and a Quaker. One of his many accomplishments was founding an independent Quaker or Friends school in Durham, NC. When visiting his house on one occasion, I mentioned I had always felt some tension between art and science (or specifically Biology), and one of his school-age daughters said that was totally unfounded. She then proceeded to tell me about a course she was taking at the Friends school on "design in nature." Since that day, I have felt much less regret on choosing a single career path. I appreciate that art and science are each different types of truth seeking which differ mainly in their methods, and across my career I have tried to maintain some familiarity with the methods of both. In recent years, many researchers have made the point that about 95% of our knowledge of children is based on 5% of the world's children. As a result, our knowledge is based on WEIRD (Western, Educated, Industralized, Rich, and Democratic) populations (Arnett, 2008). Science, in my opinion, is at least in part a search for universals, which is why WEIRD samples are not considered to be a fatal flaw. But these international researchers question whether this is correct. So I may have been right in the first place; science and art may have more in common than we typically acknowledge.

Nonetheless, I stopped my school-based pursuit of art in high school and instead settled on biology. Being a "good," I would even say "goody two shoes," teenager, I did a lot of school age activities (except for sports, which was always an anathema to everyone at my school) but the science fair was the one at which I shone. And this solidified my career path as a scientist.

Ethology and Development

I was an undergraduate at Duke University, which did not have a biology department but had Botany and Zoology departments. I chose Zoology because I had always been interested in animals, and aligned myself, as I have said, with Peter Klopfer, an ethologist. I had already read Konrad Lorenz and his contemporaries. I served as an undergraduate TA in Dr. Klopfer's introductory Biology course and did my senior thesis with him. So my fate was sealed.

I did my undergraduate thesis on imprinting. I had read Lorenz's account and it made perfect sense to me that nature would build in such a failsafe system to increase the survival chances of species born mobile by having them fixate on and attach to the mother so that they then followed and stayed close. However, even then, it did not make sense to me that early fixation experiences determined the life path; hence the potential for a life-span view on development was already present. So my thesis asked about the relative importance to mate selection of imprinting versus the subsequent socialization experience. I used two varieties of ducks, white Pekings and wild mallards. Each duckling was imprinted to their own kind or to the other variety of duck. They were then reared with the same or the different species of ducks. I did use hormone injections to speed up the interest in choosing a mate but otherwise the study was relatively naturalistic. And I found that having both imprinting and socialization experience of the same kind, which is the typical and natural way, resulted in the strongest preference for a type of mate. However, when the experiences differed, the more recent socialization experience was more important than the early imprinting experience to final mate selection (Sherrod, 1974). This little study was the first of a series of studies and experiences that underscored the lifelong nature of development and the accumulation of experiences in generating developmental outcomes. Hence it set the stage for my interest in adolescence and the life span.

Graduate school was the next step of course, and I knew I wanted to continue with the same line of work. It was an incredibly messy time for me personally. I was breaking up with my college girlfriend and on the verge of being drafted during the Vietnam War. The personal stories are as interesting and important as the professional one. For example, I was the first cohort to be subject to a lottery to determine your eligibility for the draft. My number was 7! Klopfer, being a Quaker, convinced me to apply for Conscientious Objector (CO) status. And that delayed my being drafted long enough to begin graduate study. However, I didn't give a lot of thought to the next step. At Klopfer's suggestion, I went to the University of Rochester to study with Jerram Brown who investigated song learning in Red Winged Blackbirds. This move was based largely on my interest in development which had clearly entered my mindset. I still have a view of the importance of fate for one's life choices; as I will describe, going to Rochester was the right choice for me—although Biology was not. I also totally lucked out in that the draft ended before my local draft board ruled on my CO application.

At Rochester, I quickly realized that Biology was not the field for me. The Duke program was founded in evolution, ecology, and animal behavior. The Rochester Biology department better reflected the center of the field which was Biochemistry and Molecular Biology. So I sought out the Rochester Psychology department. Michael Chandler, David Elkind and Arnold Sameroff were the developmental faculty. I audited a course with each of them, but found

my way to Sameroff in part because I audited his introductory developmental course. I still remember in the first class, he said he became a developmental psychologist because he had always "considered the process of becoming inherently more interesting than simply being." That hit home, solidifying my interest in development and targeting Sameroff as a potential mentor. I audited several of his courses but more importantly met with him on a regular basis to discuss development. I read most of Piaget and discussed the readings with Sameroff. Referring again to the importance of fate and serendipity, Arnold Sameroff, as then President of SRCD, was one of the people who hired me for my current position as Executive Director of SRCD. And given my age, this position will probably end my career. So I have begun and ended my career as a developmental psychologist with Sameroff's help.

Delving into Psychology from Zoology was not that difficult because I had had a joint undergraduate major in Psychology and Zoology at Duke. While most of my psychology had been comparative, it nonetheless exposed me sufficiently to the field that it was not difficult to make the shift. So I finished a master's degree in Biology at Rochester and applied to graduate school in Developmental Psychology. Sameroff, of course, recommended his alma mater Yale and his mentor William Kessen. I also applied to Minnesota since it was the top program in the country and to Hopkins to work with Mary Ainsworth because of her ethological orientation. In the end, I chose Yale for lots of reasons, both personal and professional. Although by this time, the personal issues in my life had satisfactorily resolved themselves.

Biology, in terms of evolution and ecology, still has an important influence on both my interests and my theoretical orientation, and this was strengthened in my first position after graduate school.

Infant Social Cognition

Since I had had 2 years of graduate study already, I arrived at Yale knowing exactly what I wanted to do. Having been intellectually starved for 2 years, except for my time with Sameroff, Yale was a dream come true for me. The intellectual richness of the program was amazing, and Kessen was the perfect mentor for me—smart and directive but allowing for independence.

My dissertation was analogous in several ways to my undergraduate thesis. At that time, there was an argument in the infant face perception literature that the human facial configuration served as an innate releasing stimulus for infant looking behavior. As with imprinting, this made sense ecologically; it was clear why this might have evolved, but I did not think this could be the whole story. So my dissertation examined the characteristics of the human face that elicited infants' attention or looking behavior. I showed babies of 1, 3, and 5 months of age five stimuli: their mother's non-interactive face, the non-interactive face of a stranger female, a mannequin's head, a diagrammatic face (two-dimensional), and the diagrammatic face scrambled. The idea was that this collection of stimuli represented the main features that might capture infants' attention: mother versus stranger index familiarity; stranger versus mannequin animation; mannequin versus schematic face three-dimensionality; and regular versus scrambled schematic face facial configuration. I also used five exemplars of each stimulus to control for any single feature of a particular stimulus capturing babies' attention (this was Kessen's idea and really served to distinguish the study).

Again the results were analogous to those for the undergraduate thesis. Facial configuration made a difference. Babies looked longer at the schematic face than at the scrambled version. But the more features the stimulus possessed, the more babies looked. They looked more at mom than the stranger, more at the stranger than at the mannequin, more at the mannequin than the schematic face, and more at the regular than scrambled face. And the role of these features increased with age. Hence, the conclusion was that the human face is incredibly effective at eliciting infants' visual attention, but it is the full array of features, no single one, that accounts for this (Sherrod, 1979).

By now I had recognized social cognition, cognition of the social world, as my interest. Michael Lamb, who entered graduate study at Yale at the same time, and I edited a volume (Lamb & Sherrod, 1981; Sherrod, 1981), and this interest continued even after my concern for adolescence developed (Sherrod, 1990, 1991). Interestingly, Ed Zigler has become as much a mentor as Kessen as my interest in social policy has grown, but I actually had little contact with him at Yale; my interests were then very basic. I was very keenly aware of the biological basis of behavior, from an evolutionary perspective, but did not think very much about the social relevance of my work.

Dramatically Expanding Horizons

Like all new PhDs I looked mainly for academic jobs and post-docs upon completing my degree. At Yale I had worked quite a bit with Dorothy and Jerome Singer on their television-viewing research. TV viewing is of course another form of social cognition, and I was especially interested in the characteristics of TV that captured and held young children's attention. For the same reason, I became interested in make-believe play, another topic of the Singers' work. This was the time of *Mr. Rogers* and *Sesame Street* and which approach was best for children, the slow socially oriented style of *Mr. Rogers' Neighborhood* or the more hectic academic type presentation of *Sesame Street,* which was very controversial. I have several publications with the Singers and this interest lasted past graduate school (Sherrod & Singer, 1979, 1989; Singer, Singer & Sherrod, 1980). This was also the first instance of an applied orientation to my interests, although I am not sure I realized it at that time. I had also

been very interested in Michael Lamb's concern with father attachment and was interested in the stimulus features babies used to differentiate the mothers and fathers; he was then at University of Michigan. So continuing to work with the Singers or with Lamb were the main two postgraduate endeavors I considered.

Then one day Kessen came to me saying he had received a call from Eleanor Sheldon, then President of the Social Science Research Council, and they were looking for a staff person, probably in psychology, with an interest in biology and in cognition. Kessen replied he had just the person for her in the form of me. So I applied, was interviewed, and took the job as Staff Associate (that was the title used for staff who worked with research planning committees) at SSRC. I took the job with the idea that I would use it as a 2-year post-doc to learn about grant-writing, the social institutional structure of science, and other disciplines' approaches to topics that interested me. But I liked the work and the organization, and modesty aside, I thought I was good at it, at least better than I thought my other friends in academia would be. Working at the SSRC with the top senior people in their field was of course just an incredible amount of fun. So I ended staying at SSRC about 8 years, which meant that non-academic jobs were certainly a viable option if not the only option available to me.

Broadened Perspectives on Science

At SSRC, I worked with three main programs: Biosocial Science (BSS), Giftedness, and Life Course Perspectives on Human Development (LCP). At that time, SSRC did what was described as "research planning," which meant that each program organized workshops, conferences, training institutes, and publications whose goal was to change the face of research in that field. Each program was led by an 8–12 person committee which I staffed. Committees were fully multidisciplinary and involved the most distinguished scholars in the field.

LCP was the largest and most active of my three programs but it was also the one I felt least qualified to staff. My own work had been with babies and very young children with the Singers. I was also already active in the Society for Research in Child Development (SRCD), which further verified for me that development was a childhood phenomenon. After all, the major theories of development such as Piaget had development ending in early adolescence. So the idea that development continues throughout life was really quite novel to me. Of course the idea that the potential for change continues across the full span of life was only one small piece of the overall life-course or life-span perspective. Equally important was the idea of multiple influences on development including history. I still use in talks and papers the diagram illustrating the relative influences on development of age-graded (what developmental psychologists study), history-graded (the LCP contribution), and non-normative influences (Baltes, Reese, & Lipsitt, 1980).

One point I am fond of making is that this is a theoretical diagram; it was never tested empirically. So, for example, out of home child care is a history graded influence; yet it has a lot of influence on infants.

The top scholars in adult development and aging worked with the LCP Committee: Paul Baltes , Orville G. Brim, Jr., Glen Elder, David Featherman, and Matilda Riley, to mention a few. I quickly came to appreciate the merits of the LCP approach, including its implications for child development, so we formed a subcommittee on child development in life-span perspective (involving folks like Judith Dunn, Mavis Hetherington, Richard Lerner, and Ross Parke). Both groups produced edited volumes to which I contributed, either co-editing or a co-authoring a chapter (Dunn & Sherrod, 1988; Hetherington, Lerner, & Perlmutter, 1988; Sherrod & Brim, 1986; Sorensen, Weinert, & Sherrod, 1986). Understandably the LCP group was interested in longitudinal research, and we did two inventories of datasets available at that time (Migdal, Abeles, & Sherrod, 1981; Verdonik & Sherrod, 1984). This work also dramatically reinforced my commitment to studying development with all its complexity (Brim & Kagan, 1980). Baltes, Brim, and Lerner became lifelong mentors. Because Brim had also followed a non-traditional career, he became an especially important mentor and role model (Sherrod, 2009).

One other SSRC activity was the Committee on Biosocial Science. This group involved scholars such as Jean Altman and Jane Lancaster, both primatologists, as well as Melvin Konner, an anthropologist who had studied with Robert Levine and Alice Rossi, a sociologist. It arose during the time of Sociobiology as promoted by E. O. Wilson among others. The BSS project was intended to address some of the tenets of a sociobiological approach but with a strong multidisciplinary scientific basis. Its major idea was that genetics changes more slowly than the environment so that our genetic makeup is selected for functioning in earlier, probably different environments. One needs then to ask about the organism's range of reaction to the environment in which it finds itself. Jane Lancaster, an anthropologist and chair of the committee, uses the example of the human female reproductive lifeline to illustrate the approach. People such as the !Kung, probably similar to our ancestors, reach puberty late and nurse newborn offspring for 4–5 years after birth. This builds in birth control so that across a !Kung woman's reproductive lifeline, she might have 4–5 births separated by 4–5 years, the typical nursing period. Contrast this with the modern female who may have a total of 2 births and a lifetime of artificial birth control, meaning a 10-fold increase in experienced menstrual periods. The BSS approach asks what is the human female's range of reaction to this dramatic change in reproductive lifeline, regarding issues such as cervical or breast cancer as well as social relations with partners.

The BSS approach can of course be applied to numerous topics of relevance to human development and psychology. We chose three applied topics: child abuse, teenage pregnancy, and parenting behavior. Conferences and books were organized on each of these topics (Gelles & Lancaster, 1987; Lancaster & Hamburg, 1986; Lancaster, Rossi, Altmann, & Sherrod, 1986). This was my first direct contact with applied research and social policy; it was also my first direct focus on adolescence. It also allowed me to return to my interest in social cognition, and I became very interested in how adolescent cognitive abilities in, for example, decision making influenced the particular decisions teens made about real-world issues such as having sex, doing drugs, and so forth. I did not publish in this area but it served to fulfill my intellectual interest in social cognition. I also realized that adolescence was as interesting as infancy because the extent and rate of change was equally great in both periods but adolescents were actually more interesting because they were aware of the changes.

The third SSRC activity focused on giftedness and involved Mihaly Csikszentmihalyi, David Feldman, and Howard Gardner, for example. It examined the conceptualization of giftedness across domains and how this interacts with early identification. This group was of course closest to my background and interests because of its relevance to social cognition. Colby and Damon's work on moral exemplars reflects the type of concern pursued by this group (Colby & Damon, 1992).

The work at SSRC exposed me to the best science in the field, to the leaders of developmental science across disciplines, and it dramatically broadened my perspective on science and the areas of most interest to me. It indicated to me the critical importance of longitudinal research, reinforced my belief in the significance of development beyond early life, and initiated my interest in adolescence and social policy.

SSRC was also my first exposure to international research. SSRC then had Area Committees which represented studies of regions of the world such as Latin America or Southeast Asia. I learned a lot from these groups. One, the Japan Committee, was especially interested in the LCP because of their aging population and their veneration of the elderly. This collaboration, which also was applied, opened new vistas regarding the importance of an international perspective. The LCP Committee was also fully collaborative with Europe, especially the Max Planck Institutes in Germany. The giftedness committee also had an international focus and held one major conference in Jerusalem examining the early identification of musical talent. These opportunities not only allowed for considerable international travel which opened up the world for me but they also illustrated how important cross national comparisons were to developmental science.

I have said that one reason for joining SSRC was to learn about the social institutional structure of science. During most of my tenure at SSRC, Kenneth Prewitt was president. As a political scientist, he was especially interested in science policy and science politics. Early in my tenure, the Reagan administration attacked the

National Science Foundation. This led to the formation of the Consortium of Social Science Associations, COSSA, which just celebrated its 30th anniversary. Prewitt was instrumental in making this happen, and there were multiple staff discussions of what was happening. I was squarely in the midst of Washington science politics and I learned a lot which has served me well in subsequent positions. It was so gratifying for me that Prewitt was President of COSSA when the 30th anniversary was celebrated. Since SRCD is a Board member of COSSA, I was able to attend the event.

Also, one of the most formative experiences for me in graduate school was participating in a summer institute at the University of Colorado at Boulder on biological training for developmental scientists. Robert Plomin as a young investigator was Director and Gerald McClearn and John DeFries were strong participants. Since I had the masters in Biology, the content was not as novel for me as for some other participants, but it was a most noteworthy graduate experience. I still have contact with several participants, including my wife who was a participant. At any rate, my first job at SSRC was to evaluate this program of summer institutes of which ours was just one. And the evaluation showed that our group had maintained the most contact of all the institutes.

But after 8–9 years, I felt the need to explore new horizons. Plus the world was changing. It was increasingly difficult to get funding, especially for research planning. The MacArthur Foundation Networks emerged which functioned a lot like SSRC committees but with their own funding. Hence, I decided it was time to explore new horizons.

A former SSRC staff member had moved to the Graduate Faculty of the New School for Social Research. They were interested in an Assistant Dean with a background in Psychology, for various reasons we need not elaborate. So I took a position as Assistant Dean of the Graduate Faculty. In large part, I wanted to explore university administration as one career option. I quickly learned that I was not fond of university administration. It was not as substantive as the SSRC work had been; I did and still do consider myself a scholar despite my non-academic positions. And I preferred working at a national level on issues of field development rather than local institutional issues. After 2–3 years the option arose of going to the William T. Grant Foundation as Vice President for Program, and I grabbed it.

The New School experience was, however, very useful. It was interesting to see a university in operation, to learn of the types of issues they confront and how they are handled. The six social science departments of the Graduate Faculty were each distinctive in their own way so I learned even more about disciplinary perspectives. Ira Katznelson, a political scientist, was Dean, and Jonathan Fanton university president, and I learned a lot from each.

The Importance of Funding

The BSS Committee at SSRC had a grant from the William T. Grant Foundation, so I knew Robert Haggerty, Foundation President, and a pediatrician. He felt a need for more program staff than were available to him. He coined the idea of Senior Program Associates or part-time program staff. He would buy a day a week of a scholar's time with the idea that they then spent 20% of their time on Foundation program activities such as reviewing grants and presenting them to the board. I was one of the early program associates he hired, if not the first one. I did this during my last year or two at SSRC and my full stay at the Graduate Faculty. So, when his Vice President for Program retired, he asked me if I would be interested. I responded affirmatively and began a 10-year period at the Foundation, first as Program VP, then as Executive VP. The work at the Foundation was more like that at SSRC, being substantive and scholarly as well as nationally focused. Although we did fund research outside the United States, international work was not, however, an important aspect of the Foundation's mission.

At the Foundation I learned the power of money. If you really want to shape a field, putting money into the directions you wish to promote is one way of doing it. Most people assume giving away money is easier than raising it; this is not the case. There is far more intellectual talent than a small to mid-size foundation can fund. So making decisions about what to fund is agonizing. Grant functioned a lot like the National Science Foundation when I was there, funding what we called investigator-initiated research. The idea is that scholars in the field are more qualified to decide what needs to be done than a small foundation staff. However, we did of course announce funding initiatives, which is one way of shaping the field. Even SRCD uses this mechanism in its small Request for Proposals (RFP) program to encourage more international and multidisciplinary research in the field.

When I arrived at the Foundation, President Haggerty had organized the program around stress and coping in school-age children. The idea was that school-age children had not been well studied and we needed to understand the challenges to healthy development during this period. Since we were investigator initiated we could only fund what came to us, so most grants went to topics like divorce, parental mental illness, childhood bereavement, child abuse or neglect, and teen problem behaviors (Haggerty, Sherrod, Garmezy & Rutter, 1994). The field of adolescence was rapidly growing during this time; the Society for Research on Adolescence was, for example, formed. Again since we were investigator initiated, much of what we funded was in fact on adolescence because the field was growing so fast. Hence I think that the Grant Foundation contributed considerably to the growth of what was in fact a new field in developmental science. And as a result, my interest in adolescence fully bloomed.

Since we had funded numerous longitudinal studies of adolescence, we decided we would encourage these investigators to pursue their samples through young adulthood. The LCP had promoted the idea of developmental embeddedness; this was the idea that to understand any one developmental period, you had to examine what came before and after that period. Hence these studies of young adulthood were intended to maximize the gains from the studies we funded on adolescence (Sherrod, Haggerty & Featherman, 1993; Sherrod, 1996). But again in my immodest view I think we contributed to the emergence of a new field, the transition to and the study of young adulthood. Of course this is now as much a focus of developmental research as is adolescence.

One of the more successful Grant Foundation programs was Faculty Scholars, which offered 5 years of stable funding to young investigators. The idea was to allow them to buy out courses or fulfill other needs that allowed them to make a commitment to research in order to strengthen their case for tenure and thereby allow them to stay in research. When I arrived at the Foundation, almost all applications came from psychology, pediatrics, and psychiatry. We recognized that there was developmental science in other fields and we wanted to use the program to diversify the field. So we added to the selection committee scholars from disciplines such as Anthropology, Economics, and Sociology. Jane Lancaster, an anthropologist, with whom I had worked at SSRC, was one example. Immediately we began to get applications from these other fields and began offering faculty scholar grants. Hence, again modesty aside, the Foundation contributed to increasing the disciplinary diversity of developmental science (Sherrod, 2003a). There is still work to be done; SRCD is currently continuing to promote disciplinary breadth in the field. At this writing, SRCD's past president was an economist, Greg Duncan, so we have made progress. The Faculty Scholars program is still ongoing at the Foundation but is now entitled the Scholars Program, recognizing that important developmental science now occurs in settings other than universities.

Applied Research and Social Policy

It has always interested me that every field has its own professional development networks. As a developmental scientist I had participated in SRCD since graduate school. But for foundation staff, these were the Council on Foundations and the New York Regional Association of Grantmakers. I interpreted that part of my role as VP was to represent the Grant Foundation in these circles. Since Grant was one of the few foundations, if not the only one, to fund research, this meant promoting the importance of research to efforts to help children and families, which is what most other foundations did (with an interest in children and families). It was of course a bit of a hard sell but folks were receptive, and I became involved in numerous program activities of the respective grant-making associations.

When I was in graduate school, the Yale Developmental Program had a training grant from the Carnegie Corporation of New York. It supported graduate students like me, as well as post-docs, and in large part accounted for the incredible richness of the program. Hence when I encountered this lack of funding for research by present-day foundations, I of course had to ask what happened and looked into the history of philanthropy.

Most current large foundations such as Ford, Carnegie, and Rockefeller, were started early in the 20th century by these self-made businessmen. At the transition from the 19th to 20th century there were numerous charities that offered help to folks that needed it. But these new philanthropists saw these charities as treating symptoms and they wanted to address the "causes" of social problems thereby "curing" them. And they saw science with its ability to separate cause and effect as one means of doing this. They did not necessarily directly fund a lot of research (although they did fund more research than present-day foundations) but they did value science as being useful to their efforts (which is not true today) (Sherrod, 2002b).

The Grant Foundation was founded during this era. The Grant stores were rather like five-and-dime operations, so that many of their employees were working-class people. Mr. Grant noticed that many of them confronted challenges such as mental illnesses and other stresses that compromised their development. So he established the foundation to understand "how to help young people live up to their full potential." Since the 1930s this has been interpreted to mean funding research. It is interesting that SRCD was founded at about the same time (Sherrod, 1998, 2002b).

It is not clear how foundations lost their connection to research. It happened in the last half of the 20th century and happened foundation by foundation. Carnegie, for example, was one of the last to abandon research. It may be that they saw few social problems as being solved, so concluded that science had not been helpful to philanthropy. Foundation leadership increasingly came to consist of folks outside science. The new philanthropists such as Gates and Soros do not share the appreciation of science held by those founders from the early 20th century.

Applied Research and Social Policy

As a result of the activities promoting research to foundations, I also became involved with SRCD, making the opposite argument, that researchers should be interested in social policy. In many ways, this was actually a harder sell. Because of the visibility of my work on social policy, SRCD asked me to join its Committee on Child Development, Public Policy, and Public Information (now Committee on Policy and Communication) in 1991. I was chair from 1993 to 1995 and co-chair from 1995 to 1999. I also joined APA's Committee on Children, Youth, and Families from 1998 to 2001 and was chair my final year.

SRCD, being a scientific organization, was unsure how much of its attention should be devoted to social policy. Science policy had been on the agenda for a long while and the "social policy" committee and congressional science fellowship program had both started in the 1970s (see Hagen, 2008, for the full history of social policy at SRCD). Nonetheless in the 1990s, SRCD did not have its own presence in Washington DC. Committee chairs Richard Weinberg, Sharon Ramey, and most importantly Aletha Huston, and I labored to put social policy on SRCD's agenda. A turning point was reached in the mid-1990s when the Republican congress was elected in the middle of the Clinton administration. I was taking over as chair of the social policy committee and even SRCD members who had previously argued policy was not appropriate for SRCD were approaching me as committee chair, arguing that the Society could not allow Congress to eliminate all we had built for children, such as the school lunch program. So SRCD joined three other developmental societies in producing four research briefs that addressed issues key to pending legislation (e.g., the importance of nutrition for development in defense of the school lunch program). It was smooth sailing after that, and in her presidential address Aletha Huston argued that science and social policy are just different sides of the same coin (Huston, 2008). SRCD now has a vibrant and active office of Policy and Communication in Washington DC.

Of course communication is a critical component of attention to policy, so that I also developed an interest in communication (Rosenberg & Sherrod, 1994; Sherrod, 1997, 1999) and I became editor with Jeanne Brooks-Gunn of SRCD's Social Policy Report (which disseminates research information of relevance to policy) around 2000.

It is interesting that my work in social policy and communication led to my first straightforward academic job as Professor of Psychology in Fordham University's Program in Applied Developmental Psychology, beginning in 2000. Fordham wished me to bring my interests in social policy and program evaluation to their applied program, and these were the courses I taught. Fordham also solidified and enhanced my understanding of and commitment to applied research (Sherrod, 2002a ; Sherrod, Busch, & Fisher, 2004).

Civic Engagement in Youth

In the 1990s Constance Flanagan applied to the Grant Foundation for a faculty scholars grant to study youth civic engagement in seven nations varying by the amount of social change they were undergoing. She got the grant and her seven-nation study is now a landmark in the field (Flanagan, Bowes, Jonsson, Csapo, & Sheblanova, 1998). This topic intrigued me. I clearly saw it as an example of social cognition although it was not always viewed from that perspective. And given its importance I could not understand why it did not receive more attention from both research and policy. It is as important in adulthood as working and raising a family yet all of our research focuses on cognitive development into schooling and work or social development into relationships and families. So I began to pursue the topic. Flanagan and I edited a special issue

of the *Journal of Social Issues* on the topic (Flanagan & Sherrod, 1998). And I began to orient foundation funding to the topic so that we funded certain particular important ventures, such as Torney-Purta's analyses of the large IEA study (Torney-Purta, Lehmann, Oswald, & Schulz, 2001). At Fordham, with students I also attended to the definition and conceptualization of civic engagement from a social cognitive perspective (Sherrod & Lauckhardt, 2008a, b).

So when I moved to Fordham as a faculty member, this became my research topic. Since we were already doing program work on the topic, the Foundation gave me a small grant to organize a multidisciplinary consortium to deliberate and advise them about program. The consortium lasted for about 10 years, my full tenure at Fordham. And although the Foundation lost interest in the topic under new leadership, the Consortium produced three significant publications including the first handbook in the area which I finished at SRCD (Sherrod, Flanagan, &Youniss, 2002; Sherrod, Flanagan, Kassimir, & Syvertsen, 2005; Sherrod, Torney-Purta, & Flanagan, 2010).

At Fordham my research centered squarely on the social cognitive side of youth civic engagement. We were interested in young people's political attitudes and understanding of civic engagement, producing several papers on youth's understanding of the rights and responsibilities of citizenship; youth see rights in terms of freedoms and entitlements and responsibilities as being political or civic (Bogard & Sherrod, 2008; Sherrod, 2008). We also looked at youth's responses to September 11, 2001 and found that their political views provided a filter through which they reacted (Sherrod, Quinones & Davila, 2004). I developed my interest in the topic just as Putnam published his two theses arguing for low levels of civic engagement in youth; we did not believe this, and our first project was to hold focus groups to discuss young people's political interests. This led to an interest in activism (Sherrod, 2006; Sherrod, Flanagan, Kassimir, & Syvertsen, 2005).

We were also especially interested in civic engagement in diverse youth, which can share differentially in the rights and responsibilities of citizenship in this country. Youth's individual social address as represented by SES, ethnicity, religion, and immigrant status provides lens through which they understand citizenship (Bogard & Sherrod, 2008; Sherrod, 2003b). In fact, studies of civic engagement provide a means for using research to address social issues of inequities and social justice (Fisher, Busch, Jopp & Brown, 2012). SRCD has just formed a new Committee on Equity and Justice to address how research may play a role in the larger socio-political nature of society.

Given the nature of Fordham, we also examined community service and religion and spirituality as contributors to youth civic engagement (Sherrod & Spiewak, 2008; Spiewak & Sherrod, 2010). Finally since one of the 6 C's of positive youth development (PYD) is contribution, civic engagement and PYD are very intertwined; civic engagement is both an expression of PYD and contributes to it (Sherrod, 2005, 2007).

This work on youth civic engagement represents the last rendition of my interest in social cognition. It and Fordham also allowed me to function fully as a scholar for the first time in my career. I had always pursued scholarly interests, published, and served as adjunct faculty but Fordham provided the first opportunity for me to do this full time. Then when the opportunity arose to take a leadership role as Executive Director of SRCD, I just could not say no despite how much I loved my scholarly life at Fordham. SRCD has played an important role in my professional life and development since graduate school. And I have worked with the organization in numerous capacities, so it seemed a fitting end to a career in developmental science. And I maintain my relationship with Fordham continuing to teach my social policy course.

In Conclusion

Although this chapter has not really addressed how a scholar goes about pursuing an "alternative career," I hope I have illustrated how one can make as much of a contribution to the field in these non-academic jobs as you can do as an independent research scholar. It is this self-realization that has kept me on this career track and made me satisfied with my career choices. I hope the chapter also illustrates the many faces of social cognition, indicating what an important topic it is to the field.

References

Arnett, J. (2008). The neglected 95%: Why American psychology needs to become less American. *American Psychologist, 63*, 602–614.

Baltes, P., Reese, H., & Lipsitt, L. (1980). Life span developmental psychology. *Annual Review of Psychology, 31*, 65–110.

Bogard, K., & Sherrod, L. (2008). Citizenship attitudes and allegiances in diverse youth. *Cultural Diversity and Ethnic Minority Psychology, 14*(4), 286–296.

Brim, O. G., & Kagan, J. (Eds.). (1980). *Constancy and change in human development*. Cambridge, MA: Harvard University Press.

Colby, A., & Damon, W. (1992). *Some do care: Contemporary lives of moral commitment*. New York, NY: Free Press.

Dunn, J., & Sherrod, L. R. (1988). Changes in children's social lives and the development of Social understanding. In E. M. Hetherington, M. Perlmutter, & R. Lerner (Eds.), *Child development in life-span perspective* (pp. 143–158). Hillsdale, NJ: Lawrence Erlbaum Associates.

Fisher, C., Busch-Rossnagel, N., Jopp, D., & Brown, J. (2012). Applied developmental science, social justice, and socio-political well-being. *Applied Developmental Science, 16*(1), 54–64.

Flanagan, C., Bowes, J., Jonsson, B.. Csapo, B., & Sheblanova, E. (1998). Ties that bind: Correlates of male and female adolescents' civic commitments in seven countries. *Journal of Social Issues, 54*, 457–476.

Flanagan, C., & Sherrod, L. R. (1998). Political development: Growing up in a global community. *Journal of Social Issues, 54*, 447–456 .

Gelles, R., & Lancaster, J. (1987). *Child abuse and neglect: Biosocial dimensions*. New York, NY: Aldine de Gruyter.

Hagen, J. (2008). SRCD and social policy 1976–2008. Unpublished manuscript.

Haggerty, R. J., Sherrod, L. R., Garmezy, N., & Rutter, M. (1994). *Stress, risk, and resilience in children and adolescents: Processes, mechanisms, and interventions*. New York, NY: Cambridge University Press.

Hetherington, M., Lerner, R., & Perlmutter, M. (1988). *Child development in life-span perspective*. Hillsdale, NJ: Lawrence Erlbaum Associates.

Huston, A. (2008). From research to policy and back. *Child Development, 79*(1), 1–12.

Lamb, M., & Sherrod, L. (Eds.). (1981). *Infant social cognition: Empirical and theoretical considerations*. Hillsdale, NJ: L. Erlbaum Associates.

Lancaster, J., & Hamburg, B. (1986). *School age pregnancy and parenthood: Biosocial dimensions*. New York, NY: Aldine de Gruyter.

Lancaster, J., Rossi, A., Altmann, J., & Sherrod, L. (Eds.). (1986). *Parenting across the life span: Biosocial dimensions*. New York, NY: Aldine de Gruyter.

Midgal, S., Abeles, R., & Sherrod, L. R. (1981). *An inventory of longitudinal studies of middle and old age*. New York: Social Science Research Council.

Rosenberg, S., & Sherrod, L. R. (1994). *A directory of organizations concerned with dissemination of research in child development*. New York: W. T. Grant Fd. and SRCD.

Sherrod, L. R. (1974). The role of sibling associations in the formation of social and sexual companion preferences in ducks, *Anas playtyrhychos. Zeitschrift für Tierpsychologie, 34*, 247–264.

Sherrod, L. R. (1979). Social cognition in infants: Attention to the human face. *Infant Behavior and Development, 2*, 279–294.

Sherrod, L. R. (1981). Issues in cognitive and perceptual development: The special case of social stimuli. In M. Lamb & L. R. Sherrod (Eds.), *Infant social cognition: Empirical and theoretical considerations*. Hillsdale, NJ: L. Erlbaum Associates.

Sherrod, L. R. (1990). How do babies know their friends and foes? *Human Nature, 1*(4), 331–353.

Sherrod, L. R. (1991). Studying infants' lives: Competency, context, and variability. In F. Kessel, M. Bornstein, & A. Sameroff (Eds.), *Contemporary constructions of the child: Essays in honor of William Kessen*. Hillsdale, NJ: L. Erlbaum.

Sherrod, L. R. (1996). Leaving home: The role of individual and familial factors. *New Directions in Child Development, 71*, 111–119.

Sherrod, L. R. (1997). Promoting youth development through research-based policies. *Applied Developmental Science, 1*(1), 17–27.

Sherrod, L. R. (1998). The common pursuits of modern philanthropy and the proposed outreach university: Enhancing research and education. In R. Lerner & L Simon (Eds.), *Creating the new outreach university for America's youth and families: Building university–community collaborations for the 21st century*. New York, NY: Garland Press.

Sherrod, L. R. (1999). Giving child development knowledge away: Using university-community partnerships to disseminate research on children, youth and families. *Applied Developmental Science, 3*, 228–234.

Sherrod, L. R. (2002a) Philanthropy, science, and social change: Corporate and operating foundations as engines of applied developmental science. In R. Lerner, F. Jacobs, & D. Wertlieb (Eds.), *Promoting child, adolescent and family development: A handbook of program and policy*. Thousand Oaks, CA: Sage Publications.

Sherrod, L. R. (2002b) The role of psychological research in setting a policy agenda for children and families. In A. Higgins-D'Alessandro & K. Jankowski (Eds.), *Science for society: Informing policy and practice through research in developmental psychology. New directions for child development*. San Francisco: Jossey-Bass.

Sherrod, L. R. (2003a) The William T. Grant Foundation: Building leaders in the science of human development. In J. Miller, R. Lerner, & L. Schiamberg (Eds.), *Human ecology: An encyclopedia of children, families, communities, and environments*. Santa Barbara, CA: ABC-Clio.

Sherrod, L. R. (2003b) Promoting the development of citizenship in diverse youth. *PS: Political Science and Politics*, April, 287–292.

Sherrod, L. R. (2005). Ensuring liberty by promoting youth development. *Human Development, 303*, 1–6.

Sherrod, L. R. (2006). Promoting citizenship and activism in today's youth. In S. Ginwright & R. Watts (Eds.), *Beyond resistance! Youth activism and community change: New democratic possibilities for practice and policy for America's children*. New York: Routledge.

Sherrod, L. R. (2007). Civic engagement as an expression of positive youth development. In R. Silberisen & R. Lerner (Eds.), *Approaches to positive youth development*. Thousand Oaks, CA: Sage Publications.

Sherrod, L. R. (2008). Youth's Perceptions of Rights as reflected in their views of citizenship. In M. Ruck & S. Horn (Eds.), Young people's perspectives on the rights of the child. *Journal of Social Issues, 64*(4), 771–790.

Sherrod, L. R., (2009). Special Issue: A tribute to Orville Gilbert Brim. *Research in Human Development, 6*(4), 195–266.

Sherrod, L. R., & Brim, O. G., Jr. (1986). Retrospective and prospective views of life_course research on human development. In A. Sorensen, F. Weinert, & L. R. Sherrod (Eds.), *Human development and the life course: Multidisciplinary perspectives.* Hillsdale, NJ: L. Erlbaum.

Sherrod, L. R., Busch, N. & Fisher, C. (2004). Applying developmental science: Methods, visions, and values. In R. Lerner & L. Steinberg (Eds.), *Handbook of adolescent psychology* (pp. 747–780). New York, NY: Wiley and Sons.

Sherrod, L. R., Flanagan, C., Kassimir, R., & Syvertsen, A. (Eds.). (2005). *Youth activism: An international encyclopedia.* Westport, CT: Greenwood Publishing Group.

Sherrod, L. R., Flanagan, C., & Youniss, J. (Eds.) (2002). Growing into citizenship: Multiple pathways and diverse influences. *Applied Developmental Science, 6*(4).

Sherrod, L. R., Haggerty, R. J., & Featherman, D. L. (Eds.). (1993). Late adolescence and the transition to adulthood. *Journal of Research on Adolescence, 3*(3).

Sherrod, L., & Lauckhardt, J. (2008a) The development of citizenship.. In R. Lerner & L. Steinberg (Eds.), *Handbook of adolescent psychology* (3rd ed.), Vol. 2 (pp. 372–408). New York: Wiley.

Sherrod, L., & Lauckhardt, J. (2008b) Cultivating civic engagement. In J. Rettew (Ed.), *Positive psychology: The science of human flourishing*, Vol . 4. Greenwood Publishing Group.

Sherrod, L. R., Quinones, O., & Davila, C. (2004). Youth's political views and their experience of September 11, 2001. *Applied Developmental Psychology, 25*, 149–170.

Sherrod, L. & Singer, J. (1979). The development of make-believe play. In J. Goldstein (Ed.), *Sports, games, and play*. Hillsdale, NJ: L. Erlbaum Associates.

Sherrod, L. R. & Singer, J. (1989). The development of make-believe play. In J. Goldstein (Ed.), *Sports, games, and play* (2nd ed.). Hillsdale, NJ: Erlbaum.

Sherrod, L. R., & Spiewak, G. (2008). Assessing spiritual development in relation to civic and moral development during adolescence. In R. Roeser, R. Lerner, & E. Phelps (Eds.), *On the study of spirituality and development during adolescence* (pp. 322–338). West Conshohocken, PA: Templeton Fd Press.

Sherrod, L., Torney-Purta, J., & Flanagan, C. (Eds.). (2010). *Handbook of research on youth civic engagement.* Hoboken, NJ: Wiley.

Singer, J., Singer, D., & Sherrod, L. R. (1980). A factor analytic study of preschoolers' play behavior. *Academic Psychology Bulletin, 2*, 143–56.

Sorensen, A. B., Weinert F. E., & Sherrod, L. R. (Eds.) (1986*). Human development and the life course: Multidisciplinary perspectives.* Hillsdale, NJ: L. Erlbaum.

Spiewak, G., & Sherrod, L. R. (2010). The shared pathways of religious/spiritual engagement and positive youth development. In A. Warren, R. Lerner, & E. Phelps (Eds.), *Positive youth development and spirituality: Research perspectives and future possibilities.* Hoboken, NJ, Wiley.

Torney-Purta, J., Lehmann, R., Oswald, H., & Schulz, W. (2001). *Citizenship and education in 28 countries: Civic knowledge and engagement at age fourteen.* Amsterdam: IEA.

Verdonik, F., & Sherrod, L. R. (1984). *An inventory of longitudinal research on childhood and adolescence.* New York, NY: Social Science Research Council.

41

Development as Action in Context

Rainer K. Silbereisen

When I started working on this chapter, I was attending a workshop in the Caribbean aimed at increasing the capacity of psychologists and psychology organizations to utilize culture-appropriate scientific standards of the discipline and thereby to meet the needs of the general population more closely. I was impressed by the variety of cultural and ethnic backgrounds, by the pressing challenges of precarious economies and migration waves presented, and by the enthusiasm of the participants. It was obvious that young people made up a huge portion of the population in the islands of the Caribbean, affected by all the problems of globalization in this part of the world. Research and teaching on adolescence in the region, however, is in its very beginnings, and the challenge is to adjust knowledge from Western countries to fit local circumstances and regional opportunities. This scenario reminded me of my own complex pathway to psychology as a field of academic training, and from there to my place in today's developmental science.

Origins

I was born shortly before the end of World War II as the first child of a couple from the South-West of Germany, close to the region of the Black Forest that till today I deem my spiritual home. My father, a research and development specialist in engineering was the co-inventor of a new technology in metallurgy that enabled a faster and more cost-effective production of gear wheels and other complicated devices. After the end of the war, this new process ("powder metallurgy," Silbereisen et al., 1992), which was a typical dual-use technology relevant for car manufacturing and other machinery, led him to leading positions in industry and to extensive international collaboration. His expectations for his son, therefore, were quite clear—I should also study an engineering discipline! To that end, I attended a high school specializing in mathematics and natural sciences, but, to his dismay, in the end I decided to become a psychologist. However, when in 1987 I happened to call him from Beijing, China, thereby demonstrating it was not only the top brass of German industry that could make it to this emerging hotspot of modernization, but also someone in psychology, which was a discipline he had difficulties seeing as a real science, he accepted—albeit reluctantly—this waste of what he saw as my technological talents. This event happened when I was attending a satellite workshop in China that was held in parallel to the biennial congress of the International Society for the Study of Behavioral Development (ISSBD) in Tokyo, Japan. As such, this meeting was a first in breaking new ground for the opening-up of Chinese science to the world and to collaboration with Western institutions (Harold Stevenson's early activities in China were very important in this regard).

When, after many years away from home, I visited my old bedroom (kept untouched) in my parent's house, I found evidence of why I had probably chosen psychology—there were the books by Karl Marx, Sigmund Freud, and Konrad Lorenz, all heavily used, next to the technology hype of my youth, such as cybernetics. After a short internship in an industrial plant, which provided me with unmissable work experience, I began studying psychology in Muenster, Germany, rather far away from home according to the custom of the time. Initially, I had considered medicine as a compromise to my father's wishes, but I turned it down almost as soon as I was accepted.

The books were not the only indication of my interests: There was also evidence of my work as a student companion and supervisor of troubled kids from the industrial heart land of Germany on a recreational vacation to the Italian Alps (a location I have been enjoying ever since), meant to support their economically challenged parents. This work had been my first experience with the reality of life beyond my middle-class background, and it left its mark in my emerging concept of the causes of social inequality. Being a first-generation academic also contributed to this growing awareness. It was not easy in Germany at that time for me to feel at home in a classical university environment, when it was still the norm for a very small percentage of the population to attend such institutions. Indeed, compared with many of my fellow students I lacked a lot of intellectual preparation. For example, we had had no classes in philosophy at school, and our family was not part of the general social network of the others. Although my father had had a reasonable education for the time, and although his talents in technology had led him to an appointment as collaborator in the forerunner of one of today's Max Planck Institutes, nobody in our family had attended university or was familiar with university life.

Soon after I started my studies in Muenster, however, I underwent a particular initiation ritual that changed my self-concept as a student. Professor Wolfgang Metzger, the great old man of the famous Gestalt psychology and on the faculty at Muenster, maintained the custom of inviting students who had presented him with a particularly good seminar paper to his home. To my surprise, I received such an invitation: the "young man" was interviewed about his career plans and, as a special gimmick, was given a personal tour of his wife's world-renowned children's doll collection. This experience was as close to receiving a knighthood as was possible, and from that moment on I seriously studied psychology as a science. I also started to tick "Professor" every year in the students' statistics survey as my strived-for future career. Another immediate consequence that on reflection I attribute to the Metzger episode was that I accepted an invitation to enroll at the Technical University of Berlin as part of a founder-cohort of a new psychology program. Perhaps it is important to note that the establishment of a department of psychology at this German equivalent of the MIT, with a history in war science, was a product of the British postwar re-education policy in Germany. This move to Berlin brought me unexpectedly into contact with two contrasting elements: with the very traditional representative of psychology, Robert Kirchhoff, who was both challenging and supportive at the same time; and with a very nontraditional city that represented the physical and ideological border between East and West.

From the point of view of my psychology studies, I soon became involved as student research assistant and wrote my master's thesis on the effect of electronic bandwidth manipulation on the perception of the human voice (Silbereisen, 1974). This research was reminiscent of my technology-oriented upbringing, and reflected first steps towards the audiovisual voice generation now in universal use whenever you call overseas via satellite. I should also add that I owe a lot of my stimulation for scientific work to the younger faculty members at the department, particularly Juergen Bortz, whose textbook of psychological statistics formed how German psychologists handled data

for generations. Nevertheless, given the escalating political situation of the late 1970s (especially protests against the Vietnam War) I felt guilty because I saw my topic as irrelevant for societal reform—how short-sighted that was given the later relevance for communication via the internet! As a first response, I also studied how such bandwidth manipulation influenced characteristics in favor of or against a "therapeutic voice" supporting client-centered self-exploration in therapeutic settings.

This work did not, however, go far enough to suit my political activism (I was the representative of socialist and reform groups in various elected university bodies during my career from student to professor) or my growing identity that was obviously characterized by "existential guilt." This term was used by Martin Hoffman (whom I met later and was very much impressed) particularly in reference to middle-class American youth during the Vietnam War era who felt guilty because they were so well off in contrast to the majority of the world.

First Steps

After a long search, and under the influence of the writings by people like John Flavell, Michael Chandler, and Robert Selman, I came up with the idea of studying perspective-taking (its conceptual relationship to person perception, my old topic, also played a role) because it seemed to be relevant for prosocial and altruistic behavior that I deemed important for the functioning of civil society. My particular interest was to investigate the role of parenting in promoting the development of perspective-taking. At that time, as far as I remember, there were only two other young scientists in Germany who specialized in this field. One (Monika Keller) pursued it in a cognitive-structural fashion; the other (Hans Bertram) from the tradition of symbolic interactionism. My personal motive was to study the role of the micro system, particularly the family. I conducted two studies, one of which became my doctoral dissertation, where I found that authoritative parenting, as one would call it now, was positively related to higher levels of perspective-taking in school-aged children (Silbereisen, Heinrich, & Trosiener, 1975). But my advisor, Klaus Eyferth, found another aspect of my results much more impressive—namely, that parents differed in their own perspective-taking level as a function of whether their occupation and job required direct interaction with people. This finding meant that social background and its developmentally instigative characteristics were highly relevant, and given my social and political interest, this implication was important to me.

Although I eventually moved away from the topic (in hindsight, given the importance this socio-cognitive skill has been receiving in social neuroscience and in research on intergroup relationships, this change was perhaps also a mistake), it played a major role in personal and substantive transitions in my life. Given my research expertise and methodological training (I worked as research associate in the methods group), I received an offer to go as post-doc (a term that was unknown in Germany at that time) to the University of Saarbrucken. Here I not only learned a lot more about Lawrence Kohlberg, moral judgment, and perspective-taking, but I was also initiated into cultural and cross-cultural psychology by Lutz Eckensberger and his academic teacher Ernst Boesch, himself the founder of a particular symbolic action theory (a topic to which I will return). The time in Saarbrucken was a formative experience in style and content of interaction, which was very different from that of the "gruff" Berliners, being more elegant in behavior, and thereby reflecting its connection to France and French culture. In particular, it helped to elaborate my interest in the role of contexts and action for development, especially concerning migration and acculturation, although this focus only came later to the fore of my research.

In Saarbrucken I studied perspective-taking again, but now in real life contexts. Earlier I had already supervised work on how to promote perspective-taking in kindergarten settings and had co-edited a book with Eckensberger that summarized the Saarbrucken action approach to the development of social cognition (Eckensberger & Silbereisen, 1980). At this time I also formed a group located at my new university that trained administrative personnel and social workers in a "citizen-oriented" approach to dealing with public welfare clients. I found this field very difficult but it satisfied my wish to make a difference by pursuing science-based practice. Moreover, it meant I was able to show my mentors in Saarbrucken, who often complained it was impossible to get research funds for such applied endeavors that it was, in fact, quite easy. We not only trained officials in perspective-taking, but did so based on good empirical evidence for its need. We had sent pseudo-clients instructed by us with a fake case history to the offices, and had video-taped the interaction with the case workers. The somewhat paradoxical result was that those who received more financial support (at the first meeting) were those who were better in "taking the perspective" of the welfare agents—they could be convinced by arguments offered in their own conceptual framework and in their own way of communicating. Most clients, however, were not able to show this functioning and often misunderstood the official situation, approaching it like an informal talk with a possibly helpful family member: They received less financial support (Silbereisen & Schuhler, 1985). This style is known in linguistics as conversational narrative, and a protagonist in the field, Uta Quasthoff, helped in framing the results in a bigger picture.

The research on perspective-taking and its relevance for pro-social behavior resulted in contacts with Nancy Eisenberg (Eisenberg, Boehnke, Schuhler, & Silbereisen, 1985). We were both invited to Poland to a conference that brought together leaders in this field. In the early 1980s, still during the Cold War, it was interesting to see that such a topic of personal conditions for peaceful interpersonal and intergroup relationships was particularly welcome by the authorities of this socialist society. I was known to the organizer, Janusz Reykowski, from an earlier workshop in Torun that had been sponsored by ISSBD. The Polish conference was in general an amazing "East meets West" experience but, most importantly, it brought me into contact with future research partners in East Germany, some of whom were associated with the leading psychologist, Friedhart Klix. The conference was also a strong demonstration of Polish independence: Contrary to common practice at that time, "East and West" even shared rooms, which would certainly have resulted in a lot of reporting to authorities. Although unrecognized by me at the time, this event was already a sign that the winds of political change were starting to blow.

Settled in Berlin

The next major phase in my career took me back to Berlin, although getting into the university scene in Berlin was not easy in general, and for a young post-doc in particular. As is typical of the German system, I first needed an appointment offer as professor somewhere in Germany, and in order to promote this appointment I had secured a visiting professor position at the Technical University of Darmstadt, which is close to Frankfurt in the West. However, my earlier political activism as a student and then young researcher in Berlin had earned me a reputation as oppositional, and during the time of the Cold War any activities possibly indicative of leftist leanings were reported and filed. This was known as the Black List, and I soon realized that my name was probably included. First, despite being placed in first position for a full professorship in a South Western state of Germany, my appointment was blocked. At the time it was difficult to know whether it was due to my previous activities in Berlin—there were many rumors—but my suspicions were confirmed years later when I met the politically conservative minister of science who had turned down the university's request to appoint me. She confessed what had happened, even in front of others, and apologized, which I found very honorable. Indeed, I hold her memory in the highest esteem and only use this example to show how times were, and the impact they had on my career. In the end, I made it back to Berlin, but this return would never have happened without the courage of a social psychologist, Martin Irle. When I was about to be turned down again for a different position, he wrote a letter on my behalf, promoting me to a follower of "critical rationalism" in the Popper tradition. This letter impressed the 1977 incoming social-democratic minister of science of Berlin (Peter Glotz) and I received an offer to join the faculty of the Technical University. It is significant that his letter was franked to show that it had been sent from a private address and not through the channels of the ministry, probably to save time. I did my utmost to fulfill the high expectations I felt he had of me, and I am also very happy to note that this minister was one of the most profound reformers of the German educational system (he built a new university with social sciences as the focus, and later, after unification, became a professor of management in Switzerland).

A Drug Epidemic as Trigger for Developmental Research

Somewhat ironically, I had the good luck that a huge problem related to health and societal cohesion, previously unknown in Germany, was making itself known and obviously requiring a forceful scientific initiative: Berlin and Germany in general experienced a surge of drug addiction among young people, and I became part of a team working on the fate of very young, untreated heroin addicts. They were the so-called "Children of Zoo Station," named after the main railway station in the middle of the city where they lived as runaways under conditions of exploitation and prostitution (the situation was covered in a book and became an international, provocative movie in the late 1970s). Later, after the breakdown of the Soviet Union, there were similar reports concerning Moscow and Saint Petersburg, illustrating the severity of the problem we had observed in Berlin many years earlier. The Technical University rented research space next to the railway station, and we did a then unusual "mixed-methods" combination of street work and in-field research. We were also one of the first research groups with our own terminal connected to the mainframe computer at a center of technological research, an unheard of privilege for psychologists at that time. Interestingly, my former PhD advisor, Klaus Eyferth, was my promoter and elder statesperson who helped to open doors at this time.

This time was when an explanation of substance abuse was sought by subsuming it under the umbrella of well-established theories of antisocial behavior. I realized, however, that this approach did not say much about how such behaviors develop, and I came to the tentative conclusion that abuse of hard drugs had a biographical history of early risk factors and lesser problems, and that its precursors were related to failure in resolving the age-typical tasks of adolescence. I subsequently introduced the psychological concepts of developmental tasks and of coping with stress into our debates, and took another look at our qualitative interviews with young addicts by using this framework. To my surprise, their past lives—in all their current misery—had not differed much from that of many other troubled young people, and I gradually formed the idea that a better understanding of their drug history would require the identification of the "break points" from the normative to the deviant, and what kind of experiences and contexts thereby play a role. This insight actually predates a more modern concept propagated by Moffitt et al. (2011), where they refer to "snares" that derail normative development.

The Berlin Youth Longitudinal Study

It is a bit difficult to organize what happened next in any systematic way, because so much occurred simultaneously. Nevertheless, with the idea of looking for the break points from normative to deviant development, I broadened my reading and became familiar with concepts and research of Richard Jessor, Denise Kandel, and Eric Labouvie. The "problem behavior proneness" in Jessor's approach, in particular, convinced me that I was on the right track. At this time (as happened repeatedly in my career life), the German National Science Foundation (DFG) was a major enabler through their competitive funding resources. I wanted to study youth development in a prospective longitudinal fashion, because only in this way could one understand the possible diversity and overlap of different pathways to normative and deviant development I had seen in the lives of the young heroin addicts we had studied. The Berlin Youth Longitudinal Study (BYLS) was funded for several years and brought me into cooperation, and in part into conflict, with other stakeholders in the field of research on youth problems, from sociology and education.

Early in the course of the project, together with a very talented post-doc (Peter Kastner, later on a playwright and innovative culture manager), I developed a taxonomy of pathways to the use and abuse of psychoactive substances that focused on the "purpose" of substance use for the user. To define purpose, we (Silbereisen & Kastner, 1987) distinguished, for instance, between use that was expected to offer relief from difficulties in resolving developmental tasks and use as a replacement for unachievable normative aims. If substance use was seen as making good things even better and bad things less harmful to the self, then our idea was to look for "functional equivalence" as way of prevention. This idea is still around in many prevention and intervention programs against substance use in Germany and elsewhere. Years later, John Schulenberg published similar developmental typologies based on the Monitoring the Future studies (Schulenberg, Maggs, Steinman, & Zucker, 2000).

Planning and carrying out the BYLS was supported by an international workshop we held in 1983 in Berlin. It brought all the core scientific actors together that I had identified in the field; beyond those already mentioned, this group also included people like Peter Bentler, Glen Elder, Richard Lazarus, and Urie Bronfenbrenner. It was not a workshop on substance use but, as the title of the resultant book reveals, namely "Development as Action in Context—Problem Behavior and Normal Youth Development" (Silbereisen, Eyferth, & Rudinger, 1986), we worked to establish the view that young people negotiate their own development through their interaction with age-typical personal and by physical encounters of their own choosing. This workshop was also the opportunity to bring my young collaborators into contact with leaders in the field.

Two participants and their work were especially relevant for my thoughts in planning research at that time and for my future endeavors. First, Urie Bronfenbrenner and his concept of developmental contexts and developmentally instigative personal attributes matched well with our own analyses of the biographies of young addicts. In an associated part of the prospective BYLS, we had conducted a series of systematic observations in various leisure locales of young people, such as discotheques and the then new shopping mall, "Forum Steglitz" in downtown Berlin. Peter Noack, since his student times, was highly involved in this work (Noack, 1990). In fact, this idea predated influence by Bronfenbrenner and was more reminiscent of the early work of the Muchows in the 1920s (Muchow & Muchow, 1935/1998). They had studied how youngsters utilized the displays in the first German department store in Leipzig as props in order to "rehearse" the new roles as grown-ups, including fake consumption and making impressions on others through role play. We found that the young Berliners basically did the same—they went to discotheques to be part of the "scene" to learn about what was "in" and how they should behave to be "cool" and not specifically in order to take drugs. We identified a typical behavioral pattern of watching others, evaluating their behavior by chatting with friends, and trying to mimic what they had seen. In particular, behaving against the rules of conduct was not so much an indication of deviancy but a carefully orchestrated demonstration of one's persona and assets. This behavior was especially done for the benefit of the other sex, who watched it all with interest, themselves utilizing facilities at the settings as a showcase (Noack & Silbereisen, 1988). Exploiting our longitudinal survey data, we also found that going to such places indeed promotes resolving age-typical developmental tasks, and that the young seem to pursue a clear plan—once they found new intimate friends, they retired from the public to the private (Silbereisen, Noack, & von Eye, 1992). This research led me and some other German scientists, such as Klaus Hurrelmann, to visit Cornell University, in Ithaca, where we learned more about the research there. Urie Bronfenbrenner was a wonderful host and set up all kinds of introductions for his guests. One I remember particularly was a discussion with Stephen Hamilton, who happened to be a fan of European welfare state institutions, such as the apprenticeship system. This system, he felt, gave young people skills and responsibility, which led to a solid standing in society, rather than letting them flounder around until deemed senior enough for real work, as was the case in the United States.

Second, Glen Elder was also important for the evolvement of my research. In the mid-1980s, in Germany there was one of the first economic recessions after World War II, resulting in an increase of unemployment from 3% to 8% within a few years (it climbed to 11% in the 1990s). This change was alarming, and I looked for an approach that would help to understand the role of economic hardship for adolescent development. It was here that Elder,

and in particular his exceptional student, Avshalom Caspi (who worked with us for some time in Berlin later on), was decisive: We subsequently added a component on how youth and their families dealt with the economic situation to our BYLS questionnaires (Galambos & Silbereisen, 1987).

All in all, the BYLS brought a group of very talented graduate students to my lab (many of whom, such as Klaus Boehnke, Sabine Walper, Peter Noack, and Sabine Zank have been professors themselves for many years now), and we were able to use our data to coin another "buzz" term—"the constructive role of substance use" (Silbereisen & Noack, 1988). What we wanted to convey with the term was that learning how to use culture-typical psychoactive substances in a "responsible" way is part of growing up. Trying to avoid consumption totally would possibly do harm to normative activities that are characteristic of adolescence in a particular culture, such as forming peer-groups and initiating romantic relationships that often involve opportunities for alcohol consumption (Silbereisen & Reitzle, 1992). Moreover, abstinence has its own problems, as was convincingly shown by Block (Shedler & Block, 1990). These results also gave us a rationale for the notion of responsible use of legal and non-use of illegal substances to be utilized later in our own prevention programs.

Cumulating Evidence in Poland

The BYLS had another consequence for my life and career paths. It led me into cross-national (and cross-cultural) research in earnest, as already instigated by the Saarbrucken experience. Janusz Reykowski, together with his colleague Adam Fraczek, offered us the opportunity to replicate our study in Warsaw, Poland. The fact that a research group from capitalist West Berlin would team up with researchers in socialist Poland on such a sensitive issue as substance use was extraordinary, as I knew then, and as I learned in more detail after the borders became fully open. This research situation also allowed me to experience at first hand one of the first real cracks in the Eastern Bloc; the imposition of Martial Law on the people of Poland in response to the activities of the Solidarnosc trade union movement, which resulted in a heavy military presence on the streets and to some of my friends being interned in camps. When we analyzed the Polish data I made two observations of relevance for my thinking about adolescent development in general. First, we found a timing difference between the Polish and Berlin samples; compared with the young Berliners, the age-mates in Warsaw showed lower levels of familiarity with and a later onset of substance use (Silbereisen & Smolenska, 1991). From a naïve ethnocentric perspective, when I presented our research findings during an invited speech at a congress in the United States, I referred to this as "delayed" rather than different. To this, I received a wonderful one-liner from Arnold Sameroff—"I like your data but I dislike your interpretation." Due to my research background in the then still rather homogeneous Germany I was simply not as sensitized to the improper meaning of terms such as delayed when referring to ethnic groups, but I quickly learned my lesson, and was thankful for it.

Another experience with the German–Polish comparison was more benign but nevertheless provocative. We had demonstrated with the BYLS that Elder's approach concerning the role of economic hardship for adolescent development was valid in Berlin, and had also shown that education moderated the effect of economic hardship, with very little effect among the better educated. Basically we found that the same applied to Warsaw, but with an interesting exception that seemed plausible, although our view was ad hoc. In the Polish sample, experience of hardship led to the expected adjustments of the household economy, but in contrast to Berlin (and to what was found in the United States) these adjustments had no costs related to parents' negative affect (Silbereisen, Walper, & Albrecht, 1990). We interpreted this finding as a consequence of the strength of the traditionally closely knit Polish family, accustomed over generations to overcome hard times: We know the same "hardening" applies to people today living in areas that are confronted periodically with natural disasters.

Giving Back

My tenure in Berlin in the late 1970s and during the first half of the 1980s was very exciting professionally. I had established a very good relationship with Paul Baltes, the newly appointed director of the Max Planck Institute for Human Development and Education (they later omitted "education" in the name of the institute), and one outcome of this relationship was a multi-site program "Promotion of Postgraduates in Developmental Psychology," funded by the Volkswagen Foundation. This program was the first of many later initiatives in Germany that combine fellowships with a structured training program. I should add that the study of human development in Germany was hampered by the fact that many eminent researchers and university teachers had left the country before the war due to the Nazi regime. The Volkswagen Foundation had planned a new start by providing young scientists with financial means to attend international congresses and to invite established foreign scientists to such events in Germany, which is how I myself came to the field. I was invited by Heinz Heckhausen and Hellgard Rauh to apply at the Foundation for a grant to organize an international workshop on social cognition. I was successful, the workshop assembled the up-and-coming young scientists in German developmental psychology, and there I met Michael Chandler and James Youniss for the first time.

Our postgraduate program brought many interesting visiting scientists to Berlin, and we also had some joint appointments with research scientists at the Max Planck Institute. In terms of qualification and networking, it was a tremendous success and provided a head start for many young scientists who enjoyed the chance to work with a group of excellent advisors, including Margret Baltes. The program socialized many young scientists, such as Jutta Heckhausen, Ursula Staudinger, and Ulman Lindenberger, who now belong to the leading echelon in the discipline. Meanwhile I was elected to Department Head and later Dean of the college, and in fulfilling these responsibilities I was able to provide support for the various exchanges. A particular highlight at this time was when, upon my suggestion, the university bestowed the degree of honorary doctor of philosophy on Urie Bronfenbrenner.

Up to New Horizons

Although I had a comfortable position in Berlin, in German academic life, one has to move in order to get promoted or to increase one's research assets (in-house promotion through ranks is virtually impossible). For this reason, in 1986 I relocated to the University of Giessen in the former West Germany, where there was a group specializing on adolescence, which I found attractive. The irony was that I had been asked to recommend somebody for a position opening, which I did, but they came back and said they wanted me. During my tenure there, I received intellectual support from Anne Petersen and her group at the Pennsylvania State University, probably based on her experience of me as visiting professor for 6 months in 1987, and rooted in a joint interest in the role of puberty in adolescent development. Fred Vondracek was also involved and stayed in Giessen for some time. We had data on pubertal timing in the BYLS (Silbereisen & Kracke, 1997), thanks to the good advice of one of the elders of German developmental psychology, Otto Ewert, and we indeed found some interesting differences with U.S. samples in the role of early maturation in depressive mood among girls (less negative in Germany, which we related to the more liberal sexual education and public habit in Germany) (Silbereisen, Petersen, Albrecht, & Kracke, 1989). Later, other researchers found similar results in other European countries.

Period Comparisons of Social Change

The main focus of my time in Giessen, however, was a different one, and this focus turned out to be as important as my experience in Berlin. I and a new group of talented graduate students, among them Baerbel Kracke and Beate Schwarz (both hold professor positions now) were part of a team that carried out a new phase of the so called Shell Youth Study. It was to be the latest in a series of studies with the aim of documenting the situation of young people, the diversity of their background and chances, and their future-time perspectives. Previous results of the Shell Youth Study had been rather useful for debates on relevant public policies, but were not well reputed for producing basic scientific insights. We wanted to change this situation. Then, in the middle of preparation for the field work, in 1989, the Berlin Wall fell! When it actually happened, I was at a conference in Portugal, and my colleagues there found it difficult to understand my somewhat confused feelings—happy about the fall of the wall, but concerned about the lack of a "blue print" for how to rebuild a civil society. However, following the activities of the late Juergen Zinnecker, a leading German youth researcher, the study was redesigned to include a sample from East Germany. The logistical difficulties of having to implement this change so shortly after the political *Wende* (meaning, "turn-around" or "about turn") were tremendous, but the social change offered a truly unique research opportunity. My idea was to study differences and commonalities in the timing and sequencing of developmental tasks between the two parts of the country, thereby demonstrating the role of large-scale socioecological contexts.

Why? Some developmental tasks are more or less shaped by biological processes, such as the timing of puberty and its physiological underpinnings, whereas others are under the strong influence of societal institutions and expectations, such as the timing of first occupational interests that are triggered by the school system and its cultural and political aims. Such conditions differed between the two Germanys before unification (and in part still do) in terms of the guiding influence of the state versus the role of personal decisions, including differences in the range of training and job opportunities. Other developmental tasks, however, such as dealing with puberty, are not "institutional," so that we did not expect to find any East/West differences. Indeed we found differences where we had expected to, even after controlling for various other conditions, with young East Germans reporting earlier timetables for socio-institutional tasks, reflecting the stronger state supervision and the restricted choices given to the young.

Naturally, the political changes also had consequences regarding scientific contacts and networks. Due to pre-*Wende* personal connections and to research funds from the Humboldt Foundation, we were able to host young scientists from East Germany for collaborative work. One outcome was that we produced a systematic documentation of East German research projects and results of relevance for the study of human development (Silbereisen, Roesler, Kracke, & Reis, 1993); the other outcome was that we were able to extend the Shell Youth Study originally carried out in 1991 by a new same-aged cohort in 1996. This work enabled us to investigate the potential effects of the dramatic social change (represented as time periods in the design) that took place during the first 5 years following German unification. To cut a long story short—the differences between East and West that we had observed in 1991 either remained or had begun to disappear, depending on whether the social institutions providing the "social clocks" had changed or not in the course of unification. For instance, the timing of first vocational interests in the East in 1996 were as late as those in the

West in 1991 and 1996 (no change in the West), but obviously were now later than they had been in 1991, when the influence of the old regime had not yet totally waned. The question was, of course, whether the differences between the periods were indeed due to the societal changes that had taken place. The intuitive evidence was that the structural changes and their manifestation in individuals' life had affected the changes in the timing of developmental tasks. In one of our studies on the timing of financial independence, we could indeed show that it was the extension of education—whereby a much higher share of the young in the East was able to attend college-bound tracks after unification—that triggered the period difference we found (Reitzle & Silbereisen, 2000). In my view, the much more comprehensive series of publications of our studies, particularly on young people, clearly revealed how contextual change affected individual development, and identified the rapid economic restructuring of a centrally planned economy to a capital system as a driving force behind the differences we found in peoples' behavior (Silbereisen & Wiesner, 2000; Silbereisen, Reitzle, & Juang, 2002). Jim Youniss edited with me a Special Issue of the American Behavioral Scientist (Silbereisen & Youniss, 2011) which was devoted to further research on families and development in Germany before and after unification. It included several studies that taken together revealed what unification implied for youth development.

Open Borders and Migration

Another major and rather dramatic change that occurred in the aftermath of German unification was that Germany experienced a huge new wave of immigration after the breakdown of the socialist bloc. It had already become a country of immigration before unification; in the early 1960s labor migrants from Turkey and Spain were encouraged. Now, ethnic Germans from the countries of the former Soviet Union were able to immigrate to Germany under privileged conditions, such as financial support and the instantaneous granting of citizenship upon their arrival. They belong to a German Diaspora which had in part moved to Eastern Europe centuries earlier when conditions were particularly advantageous. During and after World War II, however, these people became a discriminated against minority and were forcefully relocated to poorer, usually remote areas of the Soviet Union. When the borders to the West were opened after 1989, they immigrated to Germany, partly because of the discrimination they had experienced, but also pulled by presumed chances for an economically more prosperous life for themselves and their children. Their welcome in Germany, however, was rather lukewarm among the local population and other ethnic minorities, who perceived them as competitors (their level of education and occupational training was high). Cultural differences between these rather traditional people and local Germans were also much bigger than imagined.

We formed an interdisciplinary research group that comprised sociologists and psychologists and studied samples of these *Aussiedler* families from the former Soviet Union, Poland, and Romania. At that time, i.e., in the late 1990s, with beginnings still in Giessen, there was not much knowledge on the acculturation of diaspora migrants outside Israel, and so our main effort initially was to demonstrate that these privileged immigrants were no different to other immigrants in terms of difficulties related to acculturation and integration (Silbereisen, Lantermann, & Schmitt-Rodermund, 1999). Again studying the timetabling of developmental tasks, we found that the young adapt more quickly than the parents and that even after several years a discrepancy between the generations within the families remained (Schmitt-Rodermund & Silbereisen, 1999, 2009). Nevertheless, both parties had much later individual autonomy expectations than was found to be usual among natives, thereby reflecting the differences in cultural background, and probably reflecting the fact that *Aussiedler* are rather collectivist in orientation.

At this point I should add that studying the topic of changing developmental timetables in the context of migration and in the context of political and economic change alike was very instructive. While it showed the obvious range and limits of plasticity of such aspects of human development, it also revealed a deeper structure of commonality: Whereas the ethnic German immigrants moved to a new institutional order in Germany, the East Germans stayed put (except for the two million out of 16 million that moved to former West Germany even after unification). Nevertheless they were also confronted with a new institutional order, that is, the Western mold of representative democracy and market economy that was transferred to them during the process of unification. Interestingly, my familiarity with both versions of this system change told me early on that German unification would not be an issue of just a few years, as most politicians at that time claimed, but a task that would take at least one generation to complete, as is found in other ordinary migration settings. Such similarities of two modes of social change share adaptive mechanisms, as was shown later by Greenfield (2009).

The differences from what we were used to in the West concerning the economy and other aspects of social life, such as the greater gender equality in the East before unification, sensitized us to investigate whether such conditions have an influence possibly overlooked in analyses using samples from Western countries. Indeed, in collaboration with a young Indian fellow of the Humboldt Foundation, we found that the correlates of divorce for adults and children in the East appeared to be less negative than often found in previous research. We attributed this difference to the financial implications of divorce for the remaining single parent, typically the wife, that were less negative in East Germany due to equal income opportunities, even when caring for small children (Sharma & Silbereisen, 2007). Likewise, when analyzing how people in the East

dealt with economic hardship, results were similar to those of the earlier Polish study. Although people responded with the same cost-saving adaptations of the family economy as we found in the parallel sample from the West, the negative effects of these undertakings on the well-being of the parents were less pronounced. We interpreted this finding as arising as a consequence of economic hardship following unification being a rather collective experience, and that people conceived it as a failure of the state rather than of their own behavior, which given their past experience with a highly protective society was understandable (Forkel & Silbereisen, 2001). The role of the larger context into which economic hardship is embedded was not known from the earlier U.S. research.

Overall, these and other observations helped form my view on hidden constraints in our models of how people deal with strains related to work and family. In pursuing this research, I came closer to understanding how contexts actually operated rather than simply claiming that they have an effect, as is so often the case in research.

The Pennsylvania Dream

In 1992, following an internationally announced job offer, I moved to the Department of Human Development and Family Studies at the Pennsylvania State University in the United States. According to my memory, this position was meant to strengthen research on adolescence following the departure of Richard Lerner to take up a position at Michigan State University. For me, this job was a dream came true, and based among other things on my feeling, like many more of the younger generation, that Germany was not oriented enough toward innovation and science. At that time, very few Germans made it to U.S. universities (an exception was a friend and colleague at Penn State, Alexander von Eye). I did not stay for long, however, against my original intentions to go for good. The main reason for returning to Germany was that I had received several attractive offers by German universities to go on with my research on social and political change; but a personal transition in my life also played a role in my return. An exchange program for graduate students between Penn State and my new institution in Germany kept the collaboration going until 2012. This successful cooperation was supported by foundation funding (International Study and Training Partnerships, German Academic Exchange Service DAAD) and was particularly strengthened through my contact with Fred Vondracek and his work on vocational development; we both have been on each other's university faculty as honorary or adjunct professors.

Although the actual time in the United States was short, it had a long-reaching effect through the vocational development emphasis (Silbereisen, Vondracek, & Berg, 1997; Reitzle, Vondracek, & Silbereisen, 1998; Vondracek, Silbereisen, Reitzle, & Wiesner, 1999). Without the experience there I would not have become interested in and gone on to investigate entrepreneurship; here I am thankful for the many good suggestions and real support from Fred Vondracek and also from his student Vladimir Skorikov, now a professor at the University of Hawaii. Penn State had so much to offer, such as an excellent methods group, Lisa Crockett, then a younger colleague of Anne Petersen's, specialized in adolescent risk behavior and ethnic differences, and Constance Flanagan who introduced me to research on civic engagement (she was also well-traveled across Eastern Europe). I was also very impressed by Warner Schaie and Sherry Willis as world-renowned experts in psycho-gerontological research. Robert Plomin made me familiar with behavioral genetics, and Susan McHale made me more curious to study family processes.

Developmental Science in Jena

Returning to Germany was not easy because of the several options I was offered. At the end, I chose the 450-year-old Friedrich Schiller University of Jena. The founding of the University was related to the religious reformation by Martin Luther and his followers, and it certainly had its heyday during the German Romantic period (typically said to be from 1820 to 1850). The time was obviously ripe for developmental thinking in history and social science. Karl Marx did his dissertation at the University of Jena, and in biology one of the most outspoken protagonists of Darwin's thinking, Ernst Haeckel, was also at the university. Most importantly, however, was William Thierry Preyer, a professor of physiology at the University of Jena and author of *The Mind of a Child* (1882). This book was a record of systematic physiological and psychological observations collected during the first 3 years of the life of his son, and is seen by many as the actual invention of developmental psychology in the more modern sense. In his memory, my university and I donated the William Thierry Preyer Award for Excellence in Research on Human Development to the European Association of Developmental Psychology (EARA). The first award went to Cigdem Kagitcibasi. Her research on the consequences of rapid social change in Turkey on mothers' behaviors (reflecting the demands of modernization) gave me a lot of inspiration. So, going to Jena was after all a good thing with particular historical meaning for a developmentalist. It was also a wonderful opportunity to help build a new department and college of social and behavioral sciences almost from scratch. I went there in 1994, and for years after unification the possibility of resentments against those from the West of the country was still a reality. They were called derogatively the *Besserwessis,* that is a game with words meaning those who claim to know everything better because they come from the West. The fact that I had moved from the United States and had chosen to leave a full professorship there in favor of Jena gave me a wonderful head start. In other words, I owe Penn State a lot.

The Jena Model of Social Change

Upon my return to Germany and joining Jena University, I was almost immediately involved in the establishment of a new DFG-funded graduate college, as Baltes and colleagues had done in the past, but this time the program was focused on the social and developmental psychology of intergroup relations. Soon after, however, I was asked to join a multi-site and multi-discipline Collaborative Research Center (SFB 580), also funded by the DFG on "Social Development in Post-Socialist Societies—Discontinuity, Tradition, Structural Formation." This work gave me the opportunity to pursue my earlier research on unification in a new framework of collaboration and with a fresh theoretical approach.

The SFB research was based on a "challenge-response" model of social change in the tradition of Arnold Toynbee (Toynbee, 1947). The idea was that challenges on the societal level, such as a discrepancy between the declared humanistic aims of the East German society and the reality of very limited personal freedoms, would lead to a collective response by the population. The nature of this response would be based on the particular circumstances and definitely not be in any predetermined direction. It could, therefore, include open protest leading to system change by those subdued, or arrangements between old elites and emerging new powers (Schmidt, 2010; Silbereisen, Reitzle, & Pinquart, 2005). One knows from recent experimental research that such variability between groups of people, and even entire countries, in part stems from the fact that people stop complying with the rules and start to resist in earnest once they see the grip of the authorities beginning to crumble (Laurin, Kay, & Fitzsimons, 2012), which is exactly what happened in East Germany and in other former socialist countries. This approach by sociologists, like my Jena colleague Heinrich Best, was seen as a counter position to the prevalent view according to which communist East Germany was doomed to fail because of its lack of modernization—the old regime with its top-down governing style had no answer to the requirements of modern production with distributed responsibilities and higher individual autonomy, and consequently the political answer had to be an accelerated modernization.

In our own 8-year project, "Psychosocial Resources and Coping with Social Change," we had the idea to depart from a structurally equivalent model for the individual level, thereby providing an answer to the unresolved problem of how to connect the macro and micro levels (Oishi & Graham, 2010). Our "Jena Model of Social Change and Human Development" starts with what we call "demands," that is, the experience of recent (often negative) changes (i.e., over the past 5 years) at the individual level in domains such as work and family. These demands can be traced back to structural changes of the political and economic system on the macro level, and are likely to interrupt or disturb the resolving of age-typical developmental tasks because of the changed external conditions for their accomplishment (Silbereisen, Pinquart,

& Tomasik, 2010). One example is growing perceived uncertainties in the labor market and the manifestation of these uncertainties in one's own job or concerning one's future planning. In order to make sure that the reports of participants in our representative surveys do not reflect normative change in people's career, we controlled for the effects of job promotions and also avoided obviously age-related topics. The load of such demands indeed differed, as expected, between the East (higher) and West of Germany in the mid-2000s; it also differed across smaller administrative units, reflecting the economic situation as indicated by the rate of unemployment or the internal migration balance. Furthermore, supports implicit in a stable employment situation or an intact family were mirrored in lower demand loads (Tomasik & Silbereisen, 2009; Tomasik, Silbereisen, & Heckhausen, 2010; Silbereisen, Ritchie, & Overmier, 2010).

In a number of essay reviews with Martin Tomasik, we looked at the existing data in publications on changes in adolescent development in post-socialist Eastern Europe and other regions of the world such as India, Vietnam, and China. Here we also found changes concerning the timing and content of the development of personal autonomy, but to expect a change of the entire set of developmental task (except for social-institutional tasks) would be misleading. The most important factor behind such changes across a range of countries was distortions concerning the participation in the economy due to high rates of youth unemployment (Silbereisen & Tomasik, 2011; Tomasik & Silbereisen, in press).

The demands people report are not only a mirror of the current situation but also reveal traces of the past. We found that those affected by high demand loads often report precocious behavioral autonomy during adolescence, which probably led them away from concentrating on education and thus interfered with providing a solid base for future economic success (Haase, Tomasik, & Silbereisen, 2008), especially in times of turmoil. Furthermore, in a prospective longitudinal study from childhood to young adulthood in Italy, which utilized our measures of demands, we found that higher competence in adolescence was related to lower demand loads in early adulthood (Blumenthal, Silbereisen, Pastorelli, & Castellani, unsubmitted manuscript). This research underscored the importance of adolescence as constituting formative years.

Our model has two more unique features. First, the actual demand load is conceived as the effect of a filtering of societal change through a number of contexts, representing the effect of societal institutions, such as the kind of welfare system that a country has established to protect its citizens from undue social change. The interesting fact is that young people are often less shielded against negative effects of economic downturns than older workers with high job seniority. This concept of filtering was also used successfully in cross-national research on the consequence of globalization by Hofaecker, Buchholz, & Blossfeld (2010). Second,

we used a particular approach to assess how people deal with the demands, namely, the use of developmental self-regulation strategies, as suggested by Heckhausen and colleagues (Heckhausen, Wrosch, & Schulz, 2010). For instance, people may engage with and attempt to resolve uncertainties by actively dealing with them, or they may disengage by discounting any harm experienced or abandoning a particular task entirely and trying something else (Tomasik, Silbereisen, & Pinquart, 2010). In our analyses we used psychological well-being as the criterion of adjustment and found that, on average, people chose engagement over disengagement; that engagement had positive effects on well-being and disengagement had negative effects; and that level of well-being was highest when control beliefs and control strategies matched, such as believing in one's own capability to deal with the demands in concordance with engagement (Grümer, Silbereisen, & Heckhausen, under revision).

Obviously, the political and economic change of the 1990s in Germany not only entailed negative changes, as reported above, but also positive changes, such as increased self-determination. Concerning well-being, we found that negative demands could be balanced out by resourceful positive new experiences, such as a larger scope for own decision-making at the workplace (Obschonka & Silbereisen, 2012).

From the point of view of contextualized developmental science, the most provocative finding related to the moderation of the relationship between demands and well-being by features of the context. Taking the unemployment rate in the region as an example, we found that, on average, the negative relationship was less negative, and in some cases even positive, when the unemployment rate was high (Pinquart, Silbereisen, & Koerner, 2010). This relation is also known from economic research by the term "social norm effect." According to this, aggregate unemployment moderates the effects of individual unemployment on health ideas (Clark, Knabe, & Raetzel, 2010) in exactly the same way that we found, except that we had gathered data on uncertainties instead of on actual unemployment (and at closer scrutiny, even in economic data, the prospect of becoming unemployed rather than actual unemployment had the biggest effect).

We also observed that people's demands helped to explain adjustments of the family economy above and beyond financial hardship. The fact that we studied economic hardship following the Elder tradition and always found some deviations from results in the United States (reflective of the contextual circumstances) was reported in an essay with the title "Berlin-Warsaw-Jena: A Journey with Glen H. Elder through Sites of Social Change" (Silbereisen & Tomasik, 2009). This work demonstrated that, in order to understand the range of possible influences of economic circumstances on behavioral development more clearly, we need to carry out carefully planned cross-national comparisons.

Check on Generalizability

With this view in mind, and capitalizing on the old connection to Polish scientists, we had the good luck to be able to replicate our German study on social change in Poland. Following the careful translation of all questionnaires, the new study was carried out with the help of our colleagues, under the leadership of Jacek Wasilewski from the University of Social Sciences and Humanities in Warsaw, and with the use of a professional survey institute. Although the analyses are still ongoing, we know already that the level of the demands did not vary much from the German sample, and that the role of engagement and disengagement when dealing with the demands was also about the same. We also found that, in both countries, the intra-individual patterns of positive demands (e.g., increasing job-related learning tasks) and negative demands (e.g., increased labor market uncertainties) were rather equally distributed in the population (Obschonka, Silbereisen, & Wasilewski, 2012). For example, a personal pattern of higher levels in positive demands and lower levels in negative demands (a group one may call "winners" of the political change) was particularly prevalent among the most privileged in terms of psychological resources and adjustment, socio-economic status, autonomy and self-determination at work, and high job positions. A negative pattern of social change demands, in turn, was particularly prevalent among the least-privileged group.

Nevertheless, we also found differences between Germany and Poland in the association between demands and regulation strategies that in our understanding reflect divergences between the standards of welfare in the two countries. In Germany, how the demands were appraised was relevant, that is, as challenge or threat and as gain or loss, with engagement always being higher if the valuation was more positive. Beyond this relation, it was also relevant whether people believed they could overcome these strains that were rooted in uncertainties in their work life. The role of this belief was also true in Poland, but the appraisals had almost no effect. In our view, this difference reflected the fact that the welfare support of people in precarious jobs, or who were unemployed, was only a fraction of what is usual in Germany. In other words, when confronted with demands, Poles had to deal with them irrespective of if they were seen as a challenge or a threat (Tomasik, Silbereisen, Lechner, & Wasilewski, 2012). Whether the effect of demands and coping on well-being is also moderated by regional structure of opportunity (and thus the social norm) where people live is a step in the analyses we still have to undertake.

Our investigation of demands of social change took another turn when we had the opportunity to team up with research in China led by Xinyin Chen. He had shown in past research, by comparing periods only a few years apart, that the change of the economic system in the big urban centers had resulted in a change in the aims of parental socialization toward more appreciation of individual responsibility and to more proactive interpersonal behavior, which was very much in contrast to the tradition of "withdrawn" values and behaviors common in China. That these changes took only a decade or so was especially remarkable (Chen & Chen, 2010). Against the backdrop of these results, we investigated how people evaluated changes in their life that reflect the economic reforms toward allowing more private enterprises as partial replacement of the traditional state-controlled industries. Compared with our data on Germany and Poland, various domains of change (uncertainties related to work, new opportunities for education, advanced technologies, and modern lifestyles) were seen more positively among parents of adolescents in China, especially in urban compared with rural regions. Not surprisingly, given the earlier research, there was also a relationship between positive attitudes toward social change and more appreciation of autonomy in their children's behavior (Chen, Bian, Xin, Wang, & Silbereisen, 2010).

Active Aging

Given the historical background of the SFB research program, we were interested in the difficulties resulting from social change subsequent to the political and economic transformation after German unification, including the consequences of globalization. We were, however, also interested in other changes affecting the population, particularly growing life expectancy and the resulting call for "active aging" from the European Union (Avramov & Maskova, 2003) and the World Health Organization (WHO, 2002). We collected a large sample covering the age span from 56 to 75 years and developed a list of relevant demands, all related to expectations for people to contribute to the public good by maintaining their health and fitness, and to take responsibility for their own welfare even at an advanced age. The European Commission propagated 2012 as the year of active aging. We also gathered data on the appraisal of these demands and controlled for health status, socioeconomic background, and various other variables. According to our results, the demands of active aging were mainly perceived as challenges rather than threats—quite in contrast to what many social scientists had expected. Interestingly, on average the East German participants perceived more pressures to stay active than their West German counterparts, but once we looked only at those who were retired the differences were gone. This result is again proof that the institutional context, in this instance the common pension system for the entire country, plays a moderating role in how people perceive social change. Beyond the overall positive attitude toward the expectations of active aging, there are of course groups that have difficulties, such as those with lower education and/or health problems. A major policy conclusion is to offer targeted activation strategies that pay tribute to personal circumstances (Pavlova & Silbereisen, 2012a).

Civic Engagement

In all analyses mentioned thus far, we had looked especially at psychological well-being as a criterion—not only because this focus is an outcome of adaptation and development in its own right, but also because well-being is itself a precondition for productivity and life success (Lyubomirsky, King, & Diener, 2005). But, of course, social change affects many more facets of psychosocial outcomes for the individual. In our Jena Model we had stated explicitly that some outcomes are likely to feed back to the macro level: We deemed civic engagement a prototype of such behaviors. From our research, and contrary to our initial expectations, we soon learned that civic engagement was not a likely response to the experience of uncertainties. Overall, civic engagement seemed rather to require stability in one's career life, a good education, and interpersonal skills. Indeed, our research suggests that experiencing the demands of social change primarily directs people to focus on their own fate rather than pointing them towards dealing with problems of the collective. Recently, we investigated different profiles of civic engagement in an independent sample of East Germans, aged 20–40 years, which led to a further differentiation of our approach (Pavlova & Silbereisen, 2012b). Concerning occupational uncertainty, we found an interesting contrast between younger and older participants. Whereas engaged coping with difficulties in the work domain was related to higher civic engagement among the younger participants, the opposite was found among the older group. We interpreted this difference as reflecting an age-typical distinction between growth goals among the younger and maintenance goals among the middle-aged adults.

The aging of the population and structural change, especially in industries in the East, resulted in a reduction in services in rural areas, with public transport as a prime example. This situation was accompanied by the collapse of many small businesses that had provided work in the past. The resulting internal migration to regions offering better opportunities has meant that few people are willing to take over responsibility for administrative and political offices in their communities, although civic engagement outside traditional institutions may be more appreciated. Our research attempts to provide a better understanding of the commonalities and differences between the two kinds of activities.

Center for Applied Developmental Science (CADS)

The almost 20 years I have spent in Jena allowed me to settle down after a rather unstable life of commuting between different cities and countries, moving to new places and universities. This new-found stability lead to my developing the Center for Applied Developmental Science (CADS), occupying a refurbished building with a wonderful art deco façade, all with the help and support of colleagues like Richard M. Lerner, Wolfgang Schneider, Christiane Spiel, and Verona Christmas-Best (who has

been collaborating with me on basically all international matters since the early beginnings in Jena). The aim was to have extra lab and office space for my more applied research endeavors and a hub for young investigators in exchange programs. This center was negotiated because I had been offered the post of Vice President at the international Jacobs University in Bremen, and my wife, Eva Schmitt-Rodermund, also had an offer there. However, the University of Jena provided the CADS and gave her also an attractive new appointment, combining research and administration (and meanwhile she was appointed as professor), so instead of moving, we stayed in Jena (and were able to raise our child Julian in this wonderful city with its 450-year-old university).

The common theme of the research at the CADS was to demonstrate that developmental thinking can enrich various fields of research and application that are not often studied with this vein. An instance reminiscent of my earlier research on substance use and abuse is the development of prevention programs against alcohol and nicotine consumption among adolescents. Lead by Karina Weichold, and with my support, we developed a new universal prevention program, called IPSY (an acronym for Information and Psychosocial Competence), which was carefully evaluated with samples of German school populations against control groups, including parallel smaller studies in Italy and Austria. The results showed that the program was able to delay initiation and/or reduce the rate of increase concerning alcohol and nicotine use; the program has been implemented in secondary schools in many areas in Germany. Concerning IPSY, we were also able to demonstrate the limits of involving peers as facilitators (their selection has to be done much more carefully than reported in past literature). Furthermore, we were able to show that the program worked for male and female students alike (Weichold, Brambosch, & Silbereisen, 2012), and that those who were already involved in substance use at an early age (probably Moffitt's life-course cases), although not affected by the program, at least did not show any additional increases in usage (Spaeth, Weichold, Silbereisen, & Wiesner, 2010). Characteristic of our particular combination of basic, applied, and translational research at the CADS is that we identified differential trajectories of substance use (Spaeth et al., 2010) and investigated mechanisms of how program-increased life skills have a diminishing effect on substance use.

Another line of research within the CADS addressed a weak spot in the German economy. Compared with other countries, the share of entrepreneurs is way too small, and this fact became especially evident following German unification because any form of self-employment had been strongly discouraged under the old socialist regime in the East. Small businesses are known to be at the heart of innovation, but people in the East were not used to taking initiative due to lacking experience. We, in collaboration with the economist, Uwe Cantner, and his colleagues started an interdisciplinary research project, the Thuringian Founder

Study, where we used various large data sets capturing the process of founding an innovative business, and where we conceived models to explain both intentions to start an own business and the economic success of these new businesses. The theoretical rationale used concepts such as Icek Ajzen's "theory of reasoned action," and combined it with variables suggested by various economic approaches. Furthermore, we gathered retrospective assessments of early entrepreneurial activities (selling toys, organizing events, etc.) during adolescence, as well as a concurrent measure of entrepreneurial personality, based on the Big Five personality factors. The main result was that early adolescent entrepreneurial behavior played a substantial role in predicting the process of starting an innovative business (Obschonka, Silbereisen, & Schmitt-Rodermund, 2011). These early competences and activities appeared as a central mechanism through which the individual personality structure and early stimulating contexts such as helpful parental role models may affect an entrepreneurial career. We further found that the economic variables, such as expected benefits or human and social capital, were relevant for entrepreneurial intentions in that they mainly worked through attitudes, norms, and control beliefs, as indicated by our model. In collaboration with Ingrid Schoon and her colleagues, we could compare these results on early competencies and activities with those gained by prospective longitudinal data in a normative population sample (British Cohort Studies). This work showed that early social competencies were relevant for future self-employment (Obschonka, Duckworth, Silbereisen, & Schoon, 2012). Taken together, it was very clear that our life-span perspective with early behaviors as the starting point is relevant. The results provide advice as to how entrepreneurial competences and interests can be fostered from early in life. In this context, Eva Schmitt-Rodermund and Elke Schroeder developed an intervention program that helps young people find out whether they have entrepreneurial talent (Schröder & Schmitt-Rodermund, 2006).

By far the largest study conducted within the CADS, however, was related to the topic of immigration and acculturation, departing from the earlier study on the adaptation of ethnic migrants in Germany. Research on migration allowed my colleagues and me another perspective on social change, as the transition to another country can be seen as prompting a change in the social context in which the immigrating individuals develops. Note that migrants often move to countries better adjusted to new global challenges. A consequence was that normative development needs to be differentiated from the effects of acculturative processes. Pursuing this aim called for longitudinal research comparing immigrants with natives. Another consequence was to investigate a variation in the receiving context and thereby to compare ethnic Germans from the former Soviet Union with another highly similar group in another country—Russian Jewish Diaspora immigrants in Israel. Two large research projects were conducted in this regard. The first was titled "Impact of social and cultural adaptation of

juvenile immigrants" focused on adolescents. Two general results stand out in this line of research. First, in contrast to what many believe, a substantial share of the changes in adolescent immigrants can be attributed to normative development rather than to acculturation (Titzmann & Silbereisen, 2012); second, the receiving context does have an effect on the long-term adjustment of immigrants, as a higher segregation in Israel as compared to Germany resulted in different experiences (Titzmann, Silbereisen, Mesch, & Schmitt-Rodermund, 2011) and subsequently a slower social integration (Titzmann, Silbereisen, & Mesch, 2012).

These comparisons of various immigrant groups in two countries turned out to be highly informative with regard to how a societal or ethnic context can affect the development of individuals. Therefore, this idea was developed further and led to establishment of the German–Israeli research consortium on "Migration and Societal Integration," carried out by interdisciplinary teams from various universities in both countries. Our own research group studied the role of biographical/ecological transitions for different aspects of positive development in childhood, adolescence, and young adulthood. We took the model of positive development propagated by Richard Lerner and others, and assessed manifestations of the Five Cs—competence, confidence, character, connection, and caring. The idea was that transitions, for instance from home to kindergarten, provide opportunities and experiences that should help ethnic minorities (Turks in Germany, Arabs in Israel) and immigrants (in Germany: ethnic German immigrants from countries of the former Soviet Union and Russian Jewish immigrants; in Israel: Russian Jewish immigrants) to overcome disadvantages possibly related to the foreign language spoken at home or the non-integrative acculturation orientation of the families. We compared the effects of transitions in these groups with the respective effects in native German and Israeli samples. As expected, we found some ethnic differences in positive outcomes among children that could not be explained away by socio-economic factors, and thus seemed to be cultural in nature. The experiences related to the transition also seemingly promoted psychosocial growth in some areas of positive development. In spite of the promoting effect, however, the differences between the groups stayed about the same and did not diminish in the majority of outcomes studied (Silbereisen, Titzmann, Michel, Sagi-Schwartz, & Lavee, 2012). In other words, some cultural differences in psychosocial functions did not change through the transition, which could be an indication that, depending on the specific cultural niche, different levels in psychosocial functioning may be adaptive. We also found that transitions in adolescence and young adulthood seem to enhance normative psychosocial development. Adolescents after the transition to a romantic relationship in Israel and Germany, for example, found it less important that their partner has a similar ethnic background or a good economic standing. Instead, other characteristics become more important in partnerships, such as mutual understanding, opportunities for disclosure, or relationship quality. Note, however, that we cannot be sure whether the ethnic differences found are crucial for future academic or social success. Interestingly, the results for Germany and Israel, with its much more elaborated regime of immigrant integration, did not differ much.

Serving the Discipline

Over the years of my career as scientist, I had the opportunity to work with and learn from many especially talented students and colleagues from Germany and from various other regions of the world. They convinced me that offering opportunities for others is a responsibility and a duty for somebody who was lucky enough to be able to get it all. Against this backdrop, I have collaborated with the Jacobs Foundation for more than a decade, and with the help of wonderful reviewers, such as Terrie Moffitt and Ype Poortinga, I have supported young scholars from less well-off countries with seed research grants. I have also found resources from other foundations to establish a series of workshops on disasters and their impact in various regions of the world. This topic is close to my heart because disasters, whether natural or man-made, have the potential to derail human development and to change life trajectories. The developmental science viewpoint, with its distinction of different periods and its belief in the path dependency of psychosocial adjustment, is very important for the better understanding of how we can help people in need.

I count my involvement and leadership in structured fellowship programs for young scholars, funded by research foundations and philanthropies, as another instance of activities aimed at the next generation of developmentalists. The program with Paul Baltes and colleagues mentioned earlier and the Graduate School on Intergroup Relations were followed years later by the "Graduate School of Human Behavior in Social and Economic Change" (GSBC, www.gsbc.uni-jena.de), which is still active. This organization gave me mentoring responsibilities for an entire cohort of young scholars from around the world, working in an interdisciplinary setting. This program for PhD students and post-docs is, in my understanding, the sister program to the "Pathways to Adulthood" Consortium, also funded by the Jacobs Foundation (www.jacobsfoundation.org) and co-chaired by Ingrid Schoon, Jacquelynne Eccles, myself, and others.

I undertook such initiatives often inspired by experiences gained in my role as Officer and President of international learned societies, such as the International Society for the Study of Behavioral Development (ISSBD) or the International Union of Psychological Science (IUPsyS, www.iupsys.net). Without the many suggestions and challenges by my friends and fellow officers, I would not have been able to serve my scientific discipline and its community of scholars. Lea Pulkkinen, Ken Rubin, Anne Petersen, Wolfgang Schneider, Bruce Overmier, and Pierre Ritchie are among those who liked to challenge me with their perspectives on various aspects of the science of human behavior and its application, and were a

source of inspiration for my own thinking. I was involved in the editing of several journals, such as Editor of the *International Journal of Behavioral Development* (*IJBD*) and Editor of *European Psychologist*. I have also served on many committees of various learned societies, such as the Society for Research on Adolescence (SRA). All this work broadened my scope and horizons, as well as, I hope, serving these organizations well.

Others, outside these circles and not yet mentioned, were as important. Concerning my interest in contexts, I was much impressed by Jeanne Brooks-Gunn's ideas of how neighborhoods influence an individual's development—as a matter of fact we have interesting data not yet analyzed that will give more substance to the notion of "social norm." I should also mention that the entire idea of utilizing large-scale changes outside the individual and on the level of entire societies, as a quasi-experimental approach with which to study the ecological causes for human behavior and development, was inspired by the writings of Michael Rutter (e.g., Rutter, 2007).

Conclusions

In hindsight, and from a mere career point of view, I have the feeling I should perhaps have reduced the diversity of my interests and concentrated on fewer issues. It probably would have given me and the research work more visibility but, I believe, less pleasure and satisfaction. I have enjoyed studying individuals' strivings to pursue their goals in various contexts, and I am very thankful that I could experience and study the role of radical changes in the institutional order and other major conditions of life for adjustment and development. I may not have achieved any historically lasting breakthrough, but I think I have played a strong role in showing how developmental contexts work and how people interact with them across the life span, which is a topic to which others now refer more often than in the past (Oishi & Graham, 2010). And indeed, when the German Psychological Society (DGPs) bestowed on me the Franz-Emanuel-Weinert Award, which recognizes research that has helped to improve societal conditions for people's lives, I felt that ultimately I had arrived where I had always wanted to be. To my delight, in 2012, ISSBD validated this conclusion by giving me the Distinguished Scientific Award for the Applications of Behavioral Development Theory and Research.

I belong to a generation in Germany that began to strive for international collaboration and recognition (becoming a fellow of the American Psychological Association (APA) and the Association for Psychological Science (APS) was personally very important), but the academic scene in my younger years was still characterized by the tremendous hiatus due to the Nazi period. German developmental psychology had lost almost all reputed scientists due to enforced emigration and without a "head start" program by the Volkswagen Foundation, we would have had no chance to specialize in human development (Heinz

Heckhausen, Franz-Emanual Weinert, Hellgard Rauh, Leo Montada, and Rolf Oerter worked hard to improve the situation with the support of the foundation). Due to the model of my late PhD advisor Klaus Eyferth (himself a student of a German emigrant, Curt Werner Bondy), whose funeral I attended with colleagues and former students while finishing this chapter in the summer of 2012, I became very much engaged in applied fields from early in my career and enjoyed social and political responsibility, which is, if I really need one, my excuse for the diversity of my research interests.

Nevertheless, I hope the common denominator in my life career is clear—people's actions in context that help to pursue their development. "Action" indeed is a European and particularly German concept (Jochen Brandtstaedter, a gerontological psychologist, is one of the most well-known representatives today) that can be translated as purposeful, goal-directed behavior (Silbereisen, 1984). Its study, however, requires combining quantitative and qualitative research methodologies, and must be open to interdisciplinary work. In this regard, I would like to mention again the late Paul Baltes; he was the extremely talented mediator between the scientific cultures around the globe, and for that, if for no other reason, we all owe him a great deal.

References

Avramov, D., & Maskova, M. (2003). *Active ageing in Europe* (Population Studies, No. 41). Strasbourg Cedex, France: Council of Europe Publishing. Retrieved from www.coe.int/t/e/social_cohesion/population/D%C3%A9mographie%20n%C2%B041%2016x24%20En.pdf

Best, H. (2007). Der Challenge-Response-Ansatz als forschungsleitende Perspektive für die Transformationsforschung. In D. de Nève, M. Reiser, & K.-U. Schnapp (Eds.), *Herausforderung-Akteur-Reaktion. Diskontinuierlicher sozialer Wandel aus theoretischer und empirischer Perspektive* (pp. 11–23). Baden-Baden, Germany: Nomos.

Blumenthal, A., Silbereisen, R. K., Pastorelli, C., & Castellani, V. (Unsubmitted manuscript). Concurrent socio-economic characteristics and adjustment during adolescence as precursors of work-related uncertainties in early adulthood.

Chen, X., Bian, Y., Xin, T., Wang, L., & Silbereisen, R. K. (2010). Perceived social change and childrearing attitudes in China. *European Psychologist, 15*, 260–270.

Chen, X., & Chen, H. (2010). Children´s socioemotional functioning and adjustment in the changing Chinese society. In R. K. Silbereisen & X. Chen (Eds.), *Social change and human development: Concept and results* (pp. 209–226). London: Sage.

Clark, A., Knabe, A., & Raetzel, S. (2010). Boon or bane? Others' unemployment, well-being and job insecurity. *Labor Economics, 17*, 52–61.

Eckensberger, L. H., & Silbereisen, R. K. (eds.) (1980). *Entwicklung sozialer Kognitionen: Modelle, Theorien, Methoden, Anwendung* [Development of social cognition: Models, theories, application]. Stuttgart: Klett-Cotta.

Eisenberg, N. H., Boehnke, K., Schuhler, P., & Silbereisen, R. K. (1985). The development of prosocial behavior and cognition in German children. *Journal of Cross-Cultural Psychology, 16*, 69–82.

Forkel, I., & Silbereisen, R. K. (2001). Family economic hardship and depressed mood among young adolescents from former East and West Germany. Special issue on families and development in childhood and adolescence: Germany before and after reunification

(R. K. Silbereisen & J. Youniss, Eds.) of the *American Behavioral Scientist, 44*, 1955–1971.

Galambos, N. L., & Silbereisen, R. K. (1987). Income change, parental life outlook, and adolescent expectations for job success. *Journal of Marriage and the Family, 49*, 141–149.

Greenfield, P. M. (2009). Linking social change and developmental change: Shifting pathways of human development. *Developmental Psychology, 45*, 401–418.

Grümer, S., Silbereisen, R. K., Heckhausen, J. (in press). Subjective well-being in times of social change: Congruence of control strategies and perceived control. *International Journal of Psychology*.

Haase, C. M., Tomasik, M., & Silbereisen, R. K. (2008). Premature behavioral autonomy: Correlates in late adolescence and young adulthood. *European Psychologist, 13*, 255–266.

Heckhausen, J., Wrosch, C., & Schulz, R. (2010). A motivational theory of life-span development. *Psychological Review, 117*, 32–60.

Hofaecker, D., Buchholz, S., & Blossfeld, H.-P. (2010). Globalization, institutional filters and changing life course. Patterns in modern societies: A summary of the results from the GLOBALIFE-Project. In R. K. Silbereisen & X. Chen (Eds.), *Social change and human development: Concepts and results* (pp. 101–124). London: Sage.

Laurin, K., Kay, A. C., & Fitzsimons, G. J. (2012). Reactance versus rationalization: Divergent responses to policies that constrain freedom. *Psychological Science, 23*, 205–209.

Lyubomirsky, S., King, L., & Diener, E. (2005). The benefits of frequent positive affect: Does happiness lead to success? *Psychological Bulletin, 131*, 803–855.

Moffitt, T. E., Arsenault, L., Belsky, D., Dickson, N., Hancox, R. J., Harrington, H. et al. (2011). A gradient of childhood self-control predicts health, wealth, and public safety. *Proceedings of the National Academy of Science of the United States of America, 108*, 2693–2698.

Muchow, M., & Muchow, H. H. (1998). *Der Lebensraum des Großstadtkindes*. Weinheim: Juventa. (Original work published 1935.)

Noack, P. (1990). *Jugendentwicklung im Kontext. Zum aktiven Umgang mit sozialen Entwicklungsaufgaben in der Freizeit*. Munich: Psychologie Verlags Union.

Noack, P., & Silbereisen, R. K. (1988). Adolescent development and choice of leisure setting. *Children's Environments Quarterly, 5*(2), 25–33.

Obschonka, M., Duckworth, K., Silbereisen R. K., & Schoon (2012). Social competencies in childhood and adolescence and entrepreneurship in young adulthood: A two-study analysis. *International Journal of Developmental Science, 6*(3–4), 137–150.

Obschonka, M., & Silbereisen R. K. (2012). The positive side of change: The psychological role of gains in self-determination associated with today´s social and economic change. Unpublished manuscript. University of Jena, Germany.

Obschonka, M., Silbereisen, R. K., & Schmitt-Rodermund, E. (2011). Successful entrepreneurship as developmental outcome: A path model from a lifespan perspective of human development. *European Psychologist, 16*(3), 174–186.

Obschonka, M., Silbereisen, R. K., & Wasilewski, J. (2012). Constellations of new demands concerning careers and jobs: Results from a two-country study on social and economic change. *Journal of Vocational Behavior, 80*, 211–223.

Oishi, S., & Graham, J. (2010). Social ecology: Lost and found in psychological science. *Perspectives on Psychological Science, 5*, 356–377.

Pavlova, M. K., & Silbereisen, R. K. (2012a). Perceived level and appraisal of the growing expectations for active ageing among the young-old in Germany. *Research on Aging, 34*, 80–99.

Pavlova, M., & Silbereisen, R. K. (2012b). Dispositional optimism fosters opportunity-congruent coping with occupational uncertainty. *Journal of Personality, 81*, 76–86.

Pinquart, M., Silbereisen, R. K., & Koerner, A. (2010). Coping with family demands under difficult economic conditions: Associations with depressive symptoms. *Swiss Journal of Psychology, 69*, 53–63.

Reitzle, M., & Silbereisen, R. K. (2000). The timing of adolescents' school-to-work transition in the course of social change: The example of German unification. *Swiss Journal of Psychology, 59,* 240–255.

Reitzle, M., Vondracek, F. W., & Silbereisen, R. K. (1998). Timing of school-to-work transitions: A developmental-contextual perspective. *International Journal of Behavioral Development, 22,* 7–28.

Rutter, M. (2007). Proceeding from observed correlation to causal inference. The use of natural experiments. *Perspectives on Psychological Science, 2,* 377–395.

Schmidt, S. (2010). A Challenge-Response-Model in research on social change. In R. K. Silbereisen & X. Chen (Eds.), *Social change and human development: Concepts and results* (pp. 31–49). London: Sage.

Schmitt-Rodermund, E., & Silbereisen, R. K. (1999). Determinants of differential acculturation of developmental timetables among adolescent immigrants to Germany. *International Journal of Psychology, 34*(4), 219–233.

Schmitt-Rodermund, E., & Silbereisen, R. K. (2009). Immigrant parents' age expectations for the development of their adolescent offspring: Transmission effects and changes after immigration. In U. Schönpflug (Ed.), *Cultural transmission: Psychological, developmental, social, and methodological aspects* (pp. 297–313). New York: Cambridge University Press.

Schröder, E., & Schmitt-Rodermund, E. (2006). Crystallizing enterprising interests among adolescents through a career development program: The role of personality and family background. *Journal of Vocational Behavior, 69*(3), 494–509.

Schulenberg, J., Maggs, J., Steinman, K., & Zucker, R. (2000). Developmental matters: Taking the long view on substance abuse etiology and intervention during adolescence. In P. Monti, S. Colby, & T. O'Leary (Eds.). *Adolescents, alcohol and substance abuse: reaching teen through brief interventions* (pp. 19–57). New York: Guilford Press.

Sharma, D., & Silbereisen, R. K. (2007). Revisiting an era in Germany from the perspective of adolescents in mother-headed single-parent families. *International Journal of Psychology, 42,* 46–58.

Shedler, J., & Block, J. (1990). Adolescent drug use and psychological health: A longitudinal inquiry. *American Psychologist, 45,* 612–630.

Silbereisen, H., Zapf, G., Dalal, K., Thümmler, F. Beuers, J., Schulten, R. (1992). *Powder metallurgy.* Shrewsbury, UK: European Powder Metallurgy Association.

Silbereisen, R. K. (1974). Untersuchungen zur Wirkung von Daempfungsverzerrungen auf den Expressivgehalt von Sprechstimmen. *Zeitschrift fuer experimentelle und angewandte Psychologie,* 637–661.

Silbereisen, R. K. (1984). Action-theory perspectives in research on social cognition. In M. Frese & J. Sabini (Eds.), *Goal-directed behavior: The concept of action in psychology* (pp. 215–227). Hillsdale, NJ: Erlbaum.

Silbereisen, R. K., Eyferth, K., & Rudinger, G. (Eds.). (1986). *Development as action in context: Problem behavior and normal youth development.* Heidelberg, New York: Springer.

Silbereisen, R. K., Heinrich, P., & Trosiener, H. J. (1975). Untersuchung zur Rollenuebernahme: Die Bedeutung von Erziehungsstil, Selbstverantwortlichkeit und soziooekonomischer Struktur. *Zeitschrift fuer Sozialpsychologie, 1,* 62–75.

Silbereisen, R. K., & Kastner, P. (1987). Jugend und Problemverhalten. In R. Oerter & L. Montada (Eds.), *Entwicklungspsychologie* (Neuauflage, pp. 882–919). Munich: Psychologie Verlags Union.

Silbereisen, R. K., & Kracke, B. (1997). Pubertal timing and adjustment in adolescence. In J. Schulenberg, J Maggs, & K. Hurrelmann (Eds.), *Health risks and developmental transitions during adolescence* (pp. 85–109). Berlin: de Gruyter.

Silbereisen, R. K., Lantermann, E. D., & Schmitt-Rodermund, E. (Eds.) (1999). *Aussiedler in Deutschland. Akkulturation von Persoenlichkeit und Verhalten.* Opladen, Germany: Leske und Budrich.

Silbereisen, R. K., & Noack, P. (1988). On the constructive role of problem behavior in adolescence. In N. Bolger, A. Caspi, G. Downey, & M. Moorehouse (Eds.), *Person and contexts: Developmental processes.* Cambridge, UK: Cambridge University Press.

Silbereisen, R. K., Noack, P., & von Eye, A. (1992). Adolescents' development of romantic friendship and change in favorite leisure contexts. *Journal of Adolescent Research, 7*(1), 80–93.

Silbereisen, R. K., Petersen, A. C., Albrecht, H. T., & Kracke, B. (1989). Maturational timing and the development of problem behavior: Longitudinal studies in adolescence. *Journal of Early Adolescence, 9,* 247–268.

Silbereisen, R. K., Pinquart, M., & Tomasik, M. J. (2010). Demands of social change and psychosocial adjustment: Results from the Jena study. In R. K. Silbereisen & X. Chen (Eds.), *Social change and human development: Concepts and results* (pp. 125–147). London: Sage.

Silbereisen, R. K., & Reitzle, M. (1992). On the constructive role of problem behavior on adolescence: Further evidence on alcohol use. In L. P. Lipsitt & L. L. Mitnick (Eds.), *Self-regulatory behavior and risk taking: Causes and consequences* (pp. 199–217). Norwood, NJ: Ablex Publishing.

Silbereisen, R. K., Reitzle, M., & Juang, L. (2002). Time and change: Psychosocial transitions in German young adults 1991 and 1996. In L. Pulkkinen & A. Caspi (Eds.), *Paths to successful development: Personality in the life course* (pp. 227–254). Cambridge, UK: Cambridge University Press.

Silbereisen, R. K., Reitzle, M., & Pinquart, M. (2005). Social change and individual development: A challenge-response approach. In K. W. Schaie & G. E. Elder, Jr. (Eds.), *Historical influences on lives and aging* (pp. 148–165). New York: Springer.

Silbereisen, R. K., Ritchie, P., & Overmier, B. (2010). Psychology at the vortex of convergence and divergence: The case of social change. In UNESCO International Social Science Council (Eds.), *World social science report: Knowledge divides* (pp. 2013–217). Paris: UNESCO Publishing.

Silbereisen, R. K., Roesler, H. D., Kracke, B., & Reis, O. (1993). Forschung zur biopsychosozialen Entwicklung Jugendlicher in der ehemaligen DDR. In Informationszentrum Sozialwissenschaften, L. Vaskovics, & R. K. Silbereisen (Eds.), *Sozialforschung in der DDR, Sonderband, Forschungsprojektdokumentation "Familie und Jugend"* (pp. 73–158). Bonn: Informationszentrum Sozialwissenschaften.

Silbereisen, R. K., & Schuhler, P. (1985). *Buergernaehe der Sozialhilfeverwaltung: Interaktion zwischen Sachbearbeiter und Klient.* Schriftenreihe des Bundesministers fuer Jugend, Familie und Gesundheit, Bd. 174 (pp. 221–361). Stuttgart: Kohlhammer.

Silbereisen, R. K., & Smolenska, Z. (1991). Überlegungen zu kulturellen Unterschieden der Jugendentwicklung: Werte und Freizeitverhalten in Berlin (West) und Warschau. In W. Melzer, W. Heitmeyer, L. Liegle, & J. Zinnecker (Eds.), *Osteuropäische Jugend im Wandel. Ergebnisse vergleichender Jugendforschung in der Sowjetunion, Polen, Ungarn und der ehemaligen DDR* (pp. 86–100). Weinheim/Munich: Juventa.

Silbereisen, R. K., Titzmann, P. F., Michel, A., Sagi-Schwartz, A., & Lavee, Y. (2012). The role of developmental transitions in psychosocial competence: A comparison of native and immigrant young people in Germany. In A. S. Masten, K. Liebkind, & D. J. Hernandez (Eds.), *Capitalizing on migration: The potential of immigrant youth* (pp. 324–358). New York: Cambridge University Press.

Silbereisen, R. K., & Tomasik, M. (2009). Berlin-Warsaw-Jena: A Journey with Glen H. Elder through sites of social change. *Research in Human Development, 5,* 244–258.

Silbereisen, R. K., & Tomasik, M. J. (2011). Psychosocial functioning in the context of social, economic, and political change. In K. H. Rubin & X. Chen (Eds.), *Socioemotional development in cultural context* (pp. 305–331). New York: Guilford Press.

Silbereisen, R. K., Vondracek, F. W., & Berg, L. A. (1997). Differential timing of initial vocational choice: The influence of early childhood family relocation and parental support behaviors in two cultures. *Journal of Vocational Behavior, 50,* 41–59.

Silbereisen, R. K., Walper, S., & Albrecht. H. T. (1990). Families income loss and economic hardship: Antecedents of adolescents' problem behavior. In V. McLoyd & C. Flanagan (Eds.), *Risk and protective factors in children and adolescents' response to economic crises and deprivation* (pp. 27–47). New Directions in Child Development. San Francisco: Jossey-Bass.

Silbereisen, R. K., & Wiesner, M. (2000). Cohort change in adolescent developmental timetables after German unification: Trends and possible reasons. In J. Heckhausen (Ed.), *Motivational psychology of human development: Developing motivation and motivating development* (pp. 271–284). Amsterdam: Elsevier.

Silbereisen, R. K., & Youniss, J. (2001). Families and development in childhood and adolescence: Germany before and after reunification. Special Issue of *American Behavioral Scientist, 44.*

Spaeth, M., Weichold, K., Silbereisen, R. K., & Wiesner, M. (2010). Developmental pathways of alcohol use in early adolescence: Examining the differential effectiveness of a Life Skills Program (IPSY). *Journal of Consulting and Clinical Psychology, 78,* 334–348.

Titzmann, P. F., & Silbereisen, R. K. (2012). Acculturation or development? Autonomy expectations among ethnic German immigrant adolescents and their native German age-mates. *Child Development, 83,* 1640–1654.

Titzmann, P. F., Silbereisen, R. K., & Mesch, G. (2012). Change in friendship homophily: A German Israeli comparison of adolescent immigrants. *Journal of Cross-Cultural Psychology, 43*(3), 410–428.

Titzmann, P. F., Silbereisen, R. K., Mesch, G., & Schmitt-Rodermund, E. (2011). Migration-specific hassles among adolescent immigrants from the Former Soviet Union in Germany and Israel. *Journal of Cross-Cultural Psychology, 42*(5), 777–794.

Tomasik, M. J., & Silbereisen, R. K. (2009). Demands of social change as a function of the political context, institutional filters, and psychosocial functioning. *Social Indicators Research, 94,* 13–28.

Tomasik, M. J., & Silbereisen, R. K. (In press). Social change and adolescent developmental tasks: The case of post-communist Europe. *Child Development Research.*

Tomasik, M., Silbereisen, R. K., & Heckhausen, J. (2010). Is it adaptive to disengage from demands of social change? Adjustment to developmental barriers in opportunity-deprived regions. *Motivation and Emotion, 34,* 384–398.

Tomasik, M. J., Silbereisen, R. K., Lechner, C. M., & Wasilewski, J. (2012). Negotiating demands of social change in adolescents and young adults from Poland. (Manuscript submitted for publication.)

Tomasik, M. J., Silbereisen, R. K., & Pinquart, M. (2010). Individuals negotiating demands of social and economic change: A control theoretical approach. *European Psychologist, 15,* 246–259.

Toynbee, A. J. (1947). *A study of history: Abridgement of Volumes I–VI by D. C. Somervell.* Oxford, UK: Oxford University Press.

Vondracek, F. W., Silbereisen, R. K., Reitzle, M., & Wiesner, M. (1999). Vocational preferences of early adolescents: Their development in social context. *Journal of Adolescent Research, 14,* 267–288.

Weichold, K., Brambosch, A., & Silbereisen, R. K. (2012). Do girls profit more? Gender-specific effectiveness of a Life Skills Program against alcohol consumption in early adolescence. *Journal of Early Adolescence, 32*(2), 200–225.

Wiesner, M., Weichold, K., & Silbereisen, R. K. (2007). Trajectories of alcohol use among adolescent boys and girls: Identification, validation, and sociodemographic characteristics. *Journal for Psychology of Addictive Behaviours, 21*(1), 62–75.

World Health Organization (2002). *Active aging: A policy framework.* Geneva.

42

Studying Adolescent–Parent Relationships

A Personal History

JUDITH G. SMETANA

Early Beginnings

I first fell in love with psychology as a high-school student. Beyond an array of Advanced Placement classes, my high school offered the opportunity to take Introductory Psychology at the junior college (San Francisco City College) just a few streetcar stops away from my high school. Perhaps it was the allure of taking a college course, but I was immediately hooked. I became a psychology major at the University of California, Berkeley. I attended Berkeley during some turbulent times, but between protests against the Vietnam War, being tear-gassed on the way to class, and student strikes, I managed to take a wide range of courses. Several (such as a wonderful two-semester course in Black History and a sociology course taught by Robert Bellah) had great resonance later in my career. In my major, I was especially attracted to courses in developmental and social psychology.

Like many psychology majors, I had vague plans of a career as a clinician, but two experiences disabused me of that notion. I spent a semester volunteering at what was then the California School for the Blind and Deaf, working with a (partially) deaf and (mostly) blind teenage girl. After that experience, I decided I didn't have "the right stuff" to be a clinical psychologist. (My ignorance of the field led me to assume that all clinical situations would be as challenging as my volunteer experience had been, but regardless, it was the right call. I don't have the patience to be a good clinician!) And more importantly, I discovered that I was fascinated by research.

Many of the psychology classes at Berkeley were large lectures, but I enrolled in the Honor's Program in Social and Personality Psychology. This afforded me the opportunity to participate in small seminars with faculty and gave me my first real insights into research. My instructors were Christina Maslach (new to Berkeley at the time) and Jack Block, who was beginning his famous longitudinal study of personality development (Gjerde, Block, & Block, 1993; Shedler & Block, 1991). I was searching for an Honors thesis topic, and social psychologist Tom Crawford allowed me to analyze data from his research on attitude–behavior linkages. I was excited about research but unsure as to whether my future lay in studying developmental or social psychology. I vacillated between them before I found my home.

I began graduate school in Human Development and Family Studies at Cornell University, under the mentorship of Barbara Koslowski. But a boyfriend and acceptances to graduate programs on the West Coast, as well as the cold, snowy winter in Ithaca drew me back to California before I had a chance to really settle in at Cornell. With admission to the graduate program in hand, I moved to Santa Cruz and matriculated into the social psychology doctoral program at the University of California at Santa Cruz. (Of course, the irony is that I've spent my career 75 miles from Ithaca in an even snowier setting than Cornell and, once again, studying developmental psychology.) The first-year social psychology seminar was taught by Elliot Aronson, an inspired teacher and brilliant researcher who had just arrived from the University of Texas, and Ted Sarbin, who was famous for his insights in developing role theory (a contextualist approach to social behavior). My advisor was Nancy Adler, a new Assistant Professor at that time, who was doing research on attitudes regarding abortion and who later helped to create the field of health psychology.

The faculty at UC Santa Cruz was amazing, but the field of social psychology was in shambles. As a 1975 *American Psychologist* article stated, "Whether they [social psychologists] are experiencing an identity crisis, a paradigmatic crisis or a crisis of confidence, most seem agreed that a crisis is at hand" (Elms, 1975, p. 967). M. Brewster Smith, an eminent social psychologist and one of my mentors at UC Santa Cruz, concurred. As Elms went on to state, "M. Brewster Smith has repeatedly registered his agreement; for example: 'Our best scientists are floundering in the search for a viable paradigm. It is hard to tell the blind alleys from the salients of advance'" (p. 967). The consensus was that social psychology was "clearly in need of new and better theories" (p. 972). This was not exactly the type of message that an eager young graduate student wanted to hear. In the midst of this theoretical void, several graduate students (myself included) had advocated for the hiring of a young assistant professor to come to Santa Cruz in developmental psychology.

"If You Want to Get Ahead, Get a Theory"

This admonition, the title of a 1974 article by Karmiloff-Smith and Inhelder, has been true for me. Elliot Turiel had been a colleague of Lawrence Kohlberg's at Harvard. Kohlberg (1969) had developed his highly influential stage model of moral judgment development during the 1960s, and his theory was in full flower at that time. Kohlberg had proposed that moral judgments develop through a sequence of six qualitatively distinct, universal, and invariant stages of thought. Turiel (1974, 1977a) had conducted several key studies that provided support for Kohlberg's model, but his research also led him to challenge Kohlberg's differentiation theory of development. Kohlberg had proposed that more fully developed (principled) moral judgments develop out of a global confusion of moral and nonmoral concepts. Instead, Turiel's research suggested that rather than an immature form of moral thinking, social conventions (the arbitrary regularities and norms that provide expectations for appropriate behavior in different social contexts) are a qualitatively distinct mode of thinking from prescriptive moral judgments. The proposition was that morality and social convention are distinct domains of social knowledge that develop in tandem because they emerge from qualitatively different types of social experiences and social interactions (Nucci & Turiel, 1978; Turiel, 1977b, 1983; Weston & Turiel, 1980).

During his first semester at Santa Cruz, Turiel taught a popular graduate seminar on moral development. The syllabus was heavily theoretical and focused on grand theories—Freud, Skinner, Piaget, Kohlberg, and others. If social psychology in the 1970s was theoretically challenged, here was theory in spades! I quickly became convinced that my future lay in developmental, not social, psychology. Unfortunately, there was no formal developmental psychology doctoral program at UC Santa Cruz at the time and very few developmental faculty. (Patricia Greenfield was there, along with various visiting developmental faculty.) Luckily, the ethos at Santa Cruz was to encourage students to "do their own thing," and I did. Along with several other graduate students, I decided to work with Turiel and focus on social development.

My doctoral dissertation integrated social-psychological and developmental issues. I focused on adolescent and young adult women's reasoning and decision-making about abortion. My interest in this topic came from research Nancy Adler was doing on attitudes about contraception and abortion, as well as my own experiences as a volunteer crisis pregnancy counselor at the local Planned Parenthood clinic (which I had helped to establish, and I served on its first Board of Directors). I was struck by the very different ways that women talked about their choices. I believed that the theoretical distinctions Turiel was elaborating in terms of different forms of social knowledge might be useful in understanding young women's thinking.

My dissertation was also informed by the research my fellow graduate student, Larry Nucci, was conducting for his doctoral dissertation (Nucci, 1977, 1981). Nucci proposed that children develop an understanding of personal issues as distinct from concepts of morality and social convention. In his view, personal issues involved preferences and choices over such issues as control over one's body, privacy, and choice of friends or activities. To define and describe children's thinking about personal issues as a distinct domain of thought, Nucci had conducted semi-structured interviews with children and adolescents across a wide age range to obtain their judgments and justifications. In listening to young women talk about their decision-making, it seemed to me that for some women, moral issues loomed large, whereas for others, reasoning focused more on personal choice. Although these different ways of thinking about abortion were very much part of the political discourse about abortion, women's reasoning seemed to get at deeper issues.

Thus, I interviewed 70 young women aged 13–31 who were in the process of making decisions about unplanned pregnancies. I had written and received a National Science Foundation dissertation grant for this research, so with funds available to offer women honoraria, I recruited a diverse sample of women who were referred from different agencies, from Planned Parenthood to Birthright, and I was able to interview them within a week of their learning about their pregnancies. I also included a non-pregnant control group of young women, matched in age and sociodemographic background. My interview included a detailed analysis of their thinking about their choices, as well as two Kohlbergian moral judgment dilemmas (which were scored at Harvard by one of Kohlberg's colleagues), and a sorting task derived from social domain theory and Nucci's dissertation. I followed up with participants several weeks after their interviews to find out what they had chosen to do, and I also re-interviewed them a year later.

I puzzled for a long time over my interview transcripts, trying to make sense of the complex responses, but eventually it became clear to me that women were drawing a bright line between what they viewed as personal issues of privacy, personal choice, and control over their bodies and moral judgments that entailed a weighing and consideration of two equal human lives. For some women, the issue of control over their bodies extended through pregnancy, other women focused solely on moral considerations, and some women coordinated these two sets of concerns, drawing the line at different times during the pregnancy based on various criteria (more or less informed by biological facts). Not surprisingly, their mode of reasoning was strongly associated with their decisions. Women who viewed abortion as a personal issue for all or the early period of their pregnancy were more likely to have an abortion, whereas women who viewed abortion as a moral decision tended to continue their pregnancies (Smetana, 1981b; 1982). Moral judgment data supported the distinctions I had drawn, as moral reasoning on Kohlberg's hypothetical moral judgment dilemmas was significantly correlated with moral reasoning about abortion only for those who I had identified as treating abortion (during part or all of a pregnancy) as a moral issue. Both the attempt to unravel the complex associations between judgments and actions and the focus on the criteria women used to decide whether abortion was moral or personal (e.g., informational assumptions) were new to social domain theory.

I had written and been awarded an NICHD post-doctoral fellowship to study with Lois Hoffman at the University of Michigan. But after the fellowship was awarded, Hoffman went on sabbatical (as did Martin Hoffman, whose work also was of interest to me). Because my fellowship was funded through the Population Division of NICHD, there were restrictions on who could serve as a mentor. I finally settled on a faculty member at Michigan (who subsequently left academia) who was doing research on women and sex roles. She agreed to be my post-doc sponsor—as long as I did not make many demands on her time. I had no idea that this was an unconventional arrangement for a post-doctoral fellowship, but it worked out very well. I was largely on my own, but Michigan was a friendly and hospitable place. There were several research groups who welcomed me (including Libby Douvan's and Joe Adelson's), several developmental courses I decided to audit, and many wonderful faculty (Jacquelynne Eccles in particular) who were encouraging. Although my training in developmental psychology at UC Santa Cruz had been unorthodox to say the least, I left Michigan with much greater confidence in my grounding as a developmentalist.

Transitions to Adulthood

When I interviewed for a job in adolescent development at the University of Rochester's Graduate School of Education and Human Development (GSEHD), however, my choice of a dissertation topic and the inclusion of young adult women in my sample led a couple of faculty members to question whether I was "really" a developmental psychologist. So when I arrived at Rochester, I resolved to prove my "bona fides" by studying young children. Until that point, research on children's moral and conventional thinking had mostly concentrated on school-age children and adolescents, and I was convinced that research with young children was necessary to substantiate the claim that children's moral and social concepts were separate strands of development. The challenge was to develop interview questions that translated complex theoretical criteria into questions that were understandable but tapped young children's competence. Thus, my first few years at the University of Rochester were spent developing those methods and conducting research on preschool children's moral and conventional judgments (Smetana, 1981a, 1985; Smetana & Braeges, 1990; Smetana, Kelly, & Twentyman, 1984). My focus on young children plus a Foundation for Child Development Young Scholar Award in Social and Affective Development helped to assuage my colleagues' concerns about whether I was truly a developmentalist.

My interest in studying adolescent–parent relationships emerged from numerous sources—my dissertation, of course, but also my teaching. I regularly taught a course on Adolescent Development at GSEHD. The literature on adolescent–parent relationships was rife with references to the "generation gap," adolescent alienation from adult society (Keniston, 1960), and, from the neo-psychoanalytic perspective, notions of adolescent storm and stress.

Although the results of several large-scale survey studies did not support these notions, they consistently demonstrated that adolescents had conflicts and minor disagreements with parents over the mundane issues of everyday life, such as doing homework and choice of music, clothes, and hairstyle (Douvan & Adelson, 1966; Offer, 1969; Rutter, 1980). Although researchers generally viewed these conflicts as unimportant, some (Offer, 1969) reported that parent–adolescent clashes contributed to parents' perceptions that the teenage years were the most difficult period they had experienced as a parent. Also influential at the time, Montemayor (1983, 1986) had conducted several studies describing the types of conflicts adolescents had with their parents. For the most part, however, the available research was largely descriptive and atheoretical.

The available findings resonated, because it seemed to me that researchers had expected to find conflicts over big (that is, moral) issues, whereas the descriptive findings showed that conflicts occurred over more minor issues. To my way of thinking, these were largely social-conventional issues. My background in social-cognitive development led me to ask questions and adopt methods that were not common in research on adolescent–parent relationships at the time. I wanted to go beyond a description of what parents and teens argued about to consider adolescents' and parents' interpretations and thinking about the issues. Thus, I employed semi-structured clinical interviews (standard methods in moral judgment research) to examine how adolescents and parents reason about their conflicts. I added a classification task, drawn from methods used in my (and Larry Nucci's) dissertation, to identify how individuals classify different social events in terms of the legitimacy of parental authority.

This approach led to a very fruitful program of research on adolescents' and parents' reasoning about conflicts. I initially studied a sample of 102 primarily middle- and upper middle-class European American adolescents and their married parents, as well as a small additional sample of divorced mothers and adolescents (Smetana, 1988a, 1989; Smetana, Yau, Restrepo, & Braeges, 1991). We interviewed mothers, fathers, and teens to obtain their reasoning about conflicts, which were coded using categories derived from social domain theory. Like others, I found that adolescent–parent conflict occurs over the everyday issues of family life but, more importantly, I identified the different types of reasons parents and adolescents used to justify their perspectives on disputes. I had hypothesized that adolescent–parent conflict would occur over the social-conventional rules and standards of the family, and this hypothesis was supported—but only for parents.

I had initially expected that adolescents, too, would appeal to social conventions—but to peer group rather than family conventions. Thus, it was unexpected (but perfectly obvious in retrospect) that adolescents primarily justified their perspectives on conflicts with claims to personal jurisdiction and personal choice. Adolescents clearly understood but rejected their parents' conventional positions on disputes. Likewise, parents understood that adolescents desired personal choice and fulfillment, but parents rejected this view (Smetana, 1989). Thus, I proposed that adolescent–parent conflict reflects age-related increases in adolescents' attempts to claim broader areas of personal control (Smetana, 1988b). Moderate levels of conflicts are functional in that they reflect adolescents' attempts to expand their autonomy, construct a coherent self-identity, and assert a subjective sense of agency by claiming an arena of personal discretion and choice.

Because our individual interviews had focused on issues of family conflict that were salient to each family member, the classification task examining concepts of legitimate parental authority provided a useful, more standardized assessment of how individuals distinguish between conventional regulation and moral concern, on the one hand, and issues of personal choice and autonomy, on the other (Smetana, 1988a). This task has proved to be extremely useful in understanding transformations in adolescent–parent relationships in different ethnic and cultural contexts (Assadi, Smetana, Shahmansouri, & Mohammadi, 2011; Cumsille, Darling, Flaherty, & Martinez, 2009; Fuligni, 1998; Smetana, 2000; Smetana & Asquith, 1994), as well as judgments of legitimate adult authority in different settings and contexts (Smetana & Bitz, 1996). My students and I expanded on these findings in various ways. For instance, we compared justifications obtained in individual interviews and in the context of a structured, videotaped family interaction task (Smetana, Braeges, & Yau, 1991), and we also examined discussion of conflicts and their resolution (Smetana, Yau, & Hanson, 1991).

"Most of the Subjects Were White and Middle Class"

But as we proceeded with these studies, concerns with culture (Shweder & Sullivan, 1993) and ethnicity (Graham, 1992; McLoyd, 1990; Spencer & Dornbusch, 1990) were coming to the fore in the developmental sciences. My interest in culture was piqued when my graduate student, Jenny Yau, proposed to conduct her doctoral dissertation on cultural conflicts between Chinese-American adolescents and their parents (Yau & Smetana, 1993). With her dissertation completed, Jenny returned to her native Hong Kong for a job, and we resolved to collaborate on a study examining reasoning about conflict among Chinese youth in Hong Kong. The first of our studies focused on a sample of lower- to lower-middle-class Chinese adolescents (Yau & Smetana, 1996), and a later study compared youth in Hong Kong and Shenzhen, an industrial city in close proximity to Hong Kong. Unlike Hong Kong, which was still a British colony at that time, Shenzhen was in the People's Republic of China (Yau & Smetana, 2003).

Chinese culture has been described as prototypically collectivist (Markus, Mullally, & Kitayama, 1997) and strongly influenced by Confucian values (Chao, 1995). Thus, we were particularly interested in whether and how appeals to personal jurisdiction would be expressed in this context. Our interview was similar to the one used in our previous studies with European American youth. That is, adolescents were asked to generate a list of issues that caused conflicts with parents, rate their frequency and intensity, provide justifications for their positions on the disputes, and describe how conflicts were and ideally should be resolved.

We found that Chinese adolescents had conflicts with their parents, although somewhat lower in frequency and intensity than among European American youth. Chinese youth, like their European American counterparts, also treated conflicts primarily as issues of personal jurisdiction. As among European American youth, conflicts were resolved primarily in terms of the parents' point of view. Although Chinese adolescents wanted their views to prevail, there appeared to be more joint decision-making and less of a transfer of power (that is, children getting their way) than among our primarily European American samples. These findings are consistent with research from the social domain theory view suggesting that characterizations of cultures as individualistic or collectivist are too broad and stereotypical; rather, cultures are heterogeneous and include a coexistence of different orientations, including concerns with justice, welfare and rights (moral issues), conventions, and autonomy and personal choice.

Sandra Graham's (1992) article, "Most of the subjects were white and middle class" had also struck a chord with me, as the sample for my initial study of adolescent–parent relationships was mostly European American, suburban, and middle class (Smetana, 1989). In reading the literature on ethnicity, I was struck with how much of the research on African American youth focused on problem behavior rather than normative developmental issues and on samples of urban youth of lower socioeconomic status. Indeed, it seemed to me that when researchers wanted to study normative development, they studied White, middle-class youth. When they wanted to study problem behaviors, they (too often) focused on poor, ethnic minority youth. My initial research on adolescent–parent relationships had been funded by the National Institute of Mental Health (NIMH), and in seeking further support to follow my sample longitudinally, I also proposed to conduct a pilot study of African American middle-class families. Unfortunately, despite a couple of submissions, the continuation grant to NIH was not funded.

The William T. Grant Foundation was not interested in the longitudinal extension of my original work, but they were excited about my proposal to study African American families. What was initially proposed as a small pilot study turned into a multi-method, multi-informant longitudinal study of middle-class African American families. This was my first experience conducting research in the African American community in Rochester, but I hired a part-time project coordinator to help me recruit (and retain) families into the study. My course work in Black History at UC Berkeley proved very useful in understanding the long history of oppression and the many historical, economic, and sociological challenges African American families face. I was extremely fortunate to hire Cheryl Gaines, a lawyer who came to Rochester to study for the ministry in the highly regarded Black Church program at Colgate Rochester Divinity School. Cheryl knew the Black church community in Rochester, was excited about the research, and was a natural community organizer. We ran focus groups to find out what families thought about various aspects of the research, we formed a community Advisory Board for advice and help with community "buy-in," and I found myself attending Black churches on Sundays, and speaking to pastors and congregations about the need for Black families—not just those dealing with adversity and with issues of drugs and violence—to be visible and represented in research on adolescent social development in family contexts.

With the ongoing support of the William T. Grant Foundation, we were able to follow our families for 5 years, from early to late adolescence. We focused on many of the same issues I had investigated in my previous studies, such as adolescents' and parents' reasoning about issues of conflict and the legitimacy of parental authority (Smetana, 2000; Smetana, Daddis, & Chuang, 2003; Smetana & Gaines, 1999), but we also extended the research in several ways.

I had long been interested in parenting beliefs and practices (Smetana, 1995), but this project brought these issues to the fore. Whereas my earlier research had focused more on describing normative developmental patterns, this research led to a shift towards considering adaptive and maladaptive adolescent outcomes. For instance, we considered the implications of parental family decision-making and parents' overcontrol of the personal domain for adolescent adjustment (Smetana, Campione-Barr, & Daddis, 2004; Smetana & Daddis, 2002). In addition, with Alexis Abernethy, a clinical psychologist in the Psychiatry Department at the Medical School, we developed a culturally sensitive coding system for coding Black family interactions (Smetana, Abernethy, & Harris, 2000). And although the findings were not published as empirical papers, we also collected extensive data on racial socialization and adolescents' and parents' feelings about prejudice and discrimination, which I have described more recently (Smetana, 2011).

During these years, I also moved from the GSEHD (renamed the Warner Graduate School of Education & Human Development) to the Department of Clinical and Social Sciences in Psychology. Although I valued the interdisciplinary perspectives reflected in the Warner School and had many wonderful colleagues there, support for developmental psychology (and quantitative research more generally) had waned. Moving to Psychology afforded me colleagues with shared interests, the opportunity to (re)create the developmental psychology graduate program at the University of Rochester, and access to graduate students explicitly interested in developmental research (which had not always been the case in a school of education).

And my graduate students were pushing the research in exciting new directions. For instance, our data consistently showed that adolescents claim more authority than parents are willing to grant and that autonomy is, in part, child-driven and emerging "from the bottom up." My graduate student, Chris Daddis, and I had found that although adolescents push for more autonomy, parents are the ones to grant it (Daddis & Smetana, 2005). Nevertheless, Chris kept asking how adolescents go about developing their beliefs about appropriate levels of autonomy. The answer, for him, was in peer relationships. Therefore, for his dissertation, he examined similarities in close friends' evaluations of legitimate parental authority (Daddis, 2008a, b) and, subsequently, the role of crowd membership in parental authority evaluations (Daddis, 2010). Meanwhile, Nicole Campione-Barr focused on another family subsystem, asking how siblings influence perceptions of autonomy and the role of sibling ordinal status and gender composition in these processes (Campione-Barr & Smetana, 2009, 2010). Aaron Metzger was intrigued by adolescents' community involvement and focused on domain differences in adolescents' civic engagement (Metzger & Smetana, 2009). These different ways of linking the parent–child relationships subsystems in the family and to the broader context of peer relationships and community involvement have proved to be exciting and fruitful extensions of the research.

Don't Ask, Don't Tell (Your Mother or Father)

In 2000, Stattin and Kerr's influential papers questioning the interpretation of measures of parental monitoring appeared (Kerr & Stattin, 2000; Stattin & Kerr, 2000). This research showed that parental knowledge stems not from parents' attempts to monitor and surveil their children, but rather from adolescents' willingness to disclose information about their activities to their parents. Indeed, they found that only child disclosure, and not parental control or solicitation, led to increased parental knowledge and in turn, to reductions in juvenile delinquency, conduct problems, and substance and alcohol use. Their research called into question decades of research on the effects of parental monitoring on adolescent adjustment. I found Kerr and Stattin's research interesting because it was consistent with my notions of "child-driven" processes in adolescent autonomy development. Moreover, it reminded me of some of the anecdotes that arose in interviews with Chinese youth in Hong Kong. In talking about how they managed conflict with parents, some Chinese youth reported that rather than confront their parents directly, they used more devious tactics to get their way. I had found those anecdotes interesting, but in the context of Kerr and Stattin's findings, they took on new meaning in terms of how teens actively manage information to gain greater autonomy from parents. And with my own children reaching middle adolescence, the issues seemed extremely germane!

My students and I embarked on an initial questionnaire study of disclosure and secrecy in adolescent–parent relationships (Smetana & Metzger, 2008; Smetana, Metzger, Gettman, & Campione-Barr, 2006). This research expanded prior work on disclosure in adolescent–parent relationships by separating disclosure and secrecy, a distinction that Finkenauer and her colleagues had shown to be important (Finkenauer, Engels, & Meeus, 2002), and by considering the domain of the activity disclosed or concealed. Since then, we have elaborated on our initial research by employing different methods, including a sorting task (Smetana, Villalobos, Tasopoulos-Chan, Gettman, & Campione-Barr, 2009) and daily diaries (Smetana, Villalobos, Rogge, & Tasopoulos-Chan, 2010), as well as more diverse samples (Nucci, Smetana, Araki, Nakaue, & Comer, 2012; Villalobos & Smetana, 2012; Yau, Tasopoulos-Chan, & Smetana, 2009). As with our research on adolescent–parent conflict, the findings of these studies show that although the developmental processes seem to be similar among diverse groups and serve similar developmental functions (e.g., autonomy development), there are important contextual differences.

Along with others, our research has shifted to a broader consideration of information management (that is, the different strategies that adolescents use to keep information from parents), as well as the strategies that parents use to keep informed about where their adolescents are, who they are with, and what they are doing. We continue to bring a social-cognitive perspective to these issues by examining associations between adolescents' and parents beliefs—about the acceptability of different strategies as well as parents' right to know about different activities—and their behaviors.

In addition, throughout my career I have continued to do research on young children's moral judgments. But completing the circle from my early studies, I have begun

to consider how adolescents weigh and coordinate moral and other social concepts in their thinking about different social issues and situations such as illegal music downloading (Jambon & Smetana, 2011), harassment in dating situations (Shaw, Wainryb, & Smetana, 2012), and secrecy and lying to parents (Rote & Smetana, under review). This more recent research, along with other research from the social domain theory perspective, has more explicitly adopted a relational, developmental systems approach to social development (Lerner, 2006; Overton, 2006).

Final Thoughts

I have been fortunate to have had so many wonderful colleagues and graduate students who have collaborated with me and challenged my thinking. It has been exciting to be part of the growth of the field of adolescent development and to see interest in this developmental period flourish. As I look back on my career, my interests have been influenced by trends in the field—for instance, the increased focus on ethnic and cultural diversity and the emphasis on how contexts constrain and influence adolescent development. At the same time, it is gratifying to see that at least in a very small way, my approach to understanding how adolescents' active agency influences their development has had some influence on the direction of research on adolescent–parent relationships and on how adolescents (and parents) construct, interpret, and make meaning of their social worlds.

References

Assadi, S., Smetana, J. G., Shahmansouri, N., & Mohammadi, M. R. (2011). Beliefs about parental authority, parenting styles, and adolescent-parent conflict among Iranian mothers of middle adolescents. *International Journal of Behavioral Development, 35*, 424–431. doi:10.1177/0165025411409121

Campione-Barr, N., & Smetana, J. G. (2009). The impact of sibling ordinal status on adolescents' expectations for and actual behavioral autonomy. Unpublished manuscript, University of Missouri–Columbia.

Campione-Barr, N., & Smetana, J. G. (2010). "Who said you could wear my sweater?" Adolescent-sibling conflict and associations with relationship quality. *Child Development, 81*, 463–471. doi:10.1111/j.1467-8624.2009.01407.x/

Chao, R. (1995). Chinese and European American cultural models of the self reflected in mothers' child rearing beliefs. *Ethos, 23*, 328–354. doi:10.1525/eth.1995.23.3.02a00030

Cumsille, P., Darling, N., Flaherty, B. P., & Martinez, M. L. (2009). Heterogeneity and change in the patterning of adolescents' perceptions of the legitimacy of parental authority: A latent transition model. *Child Development, 80*, 418–432.

Daddis, C. (2008a). Influence of close friends on the boundaries of adolescent personal authority. *Journal of Research on Adolescence, 18*, 75–98. doi:10.1111/j.1532-7795.2008.00551.x

Daddis, C. (2008b). Similarity between early and middle adolescent close friends' beliefs about personal jurisdiction. *Social Development, 17*, 1019–1038. doi:10.1111/j.1467-9507.2008.00471.x

Daddis, C. (2010). Adolescent peer crowds and patterns of belief in the boundaries of personal authority. *Journal of Adolescence, 33*, 699–708. doi:10.1016/j.adolescence.2009.11.001

Daddis, C., & Smetana, J. G. (2005). Middle class African American families' expectations for adolescents' behavioral autonomy.

International Journal of Behavioral Development, 29, 371–381. doi:10.1080/01650250500167053

Douvan, E., & Adelson, J. (1966). *The adolescent experience*. New York: Wiley.

Elms, A. C. (1975). The crisis of confidence in social psychology. *American Psychologist, 30*, 967–976. doi:10.1037/0003-066X.30.10.967

Finkenauer, C., Engels, R. C. M. E., & Meeus, W. (2002). Keeping secrets from parents: Advantages and disadvantages of secrecy in adolescence. *Journal of Youth and Adolescence, 2*, 123–136. doi:10.1023/A:1014069926507

Fuligni, A. J. (1998). Authority, autonomy, and parent-adolescent conflict and cohesion: A study of adolescents from Mexican, Chinese, Filipino, and European backgrounds. *Developmental Psychology, 34*, 782–792.

Gjerde, P. F., Block, J., & Block, J. H. (1991). 45. The preschool family context of 18 year olds with depressive symptoms: A prospective study. *Journal of Research on Adolescence, 1*, 63–91.

Graham, S. (1992). Most of the subjects were white and middle class: Trends in published research on African-Americans in selected APA journals, 1970–1989. *American Psychologist, 47*, 629–639. doi: 10.1037/0003-066X.47.5.629

Jambon, M. M., & Smetana, J. G. (2012). College students' moral evaluations of illegal music downloading. *Journal of Applied Developmental Psychology, 33*, 31–39. doi:10.1016/j.appdev.2011.09.001

Karmiloff-Smith, A., & Inhelder, B. (1974). If you want to get ahead, get a theory. *Cognition, 3*, 195–212. doi:10.1016/0010-0277(74)90008-0

Keniston, K. (1960). *The uncommitted: Alienated youth in American society*. New York: Harcourt, Brace.

Kerr, M., & Stattin, H. (2000). What parents know, how they know it, and several forms of adolescent adjustment: Further support for a reinterpretation of monitoring. *Developmental Psychology, 36*, 366–380. doi: 10.1037/0012-1649.36.3.366

Kohlberg, L. (1969). Stage and sequence: The cognitive-developmental approach to socialization. In D. Goslin (Ed.), *Handbook of socialization theory and research* (pp. 347–480). Skokie, IL: Rand McNally.

Lerner, R. M. (2006). Developmental science, developmental systems, and contemporary theories of human development. In W. Damon & R. M. Lerner (Series Ed.) & R. M. Lerner (Vol. Ed.), *Handbook of child psychology:* Vol. 1. *Theoretical models of human development* (6th ed., pp. 1–17). Hoboken, NJ: John Wiley & Sons.

Markus, H. R., Mullally, P. R., & Kitayama, S. (1997). Diversity in modes of cultural participation. In U. Neisser & D. Jopling (Eds.), *The conceptual self in context: Culture, experience, and self-understanding* (pp. 13–61). Cambridge, UK: Cambridge University Press.

McLoyd, V. (1990). Minority children: Introduction to the special issue. *Child Development, 61*, 263–266. doi:10.1111/j.1467-8624.1990.tb02777.x

Metzger, A., & Smetana, J. G. (2009). Civic and political engagement: Associations between domain-specific judgments and behaviors. *Child Development, 80*, 433–441.

Montemayor, R. (1983). Parents and adolescents in conflict: All families some of the time and some families most of the time. *Journal of Early Adolescence, 3*, 83–103. doi:10.1177/027243168331007

Montemayor, R. (1986). Family variation in storm and stress. *Journal of Adolescent Research, 1*, 15–31. doi:10.1177/074355488611003

Nucci, L. P. (1977). The personal domain: A domain distinct from morality and social convention. Unpublished doctoral dissertation, University of California, Santa Cruz.

Nucci, L. P. (1981). Conceptions of personal issues: A domain distinct from moral or societal concepts. *Child Development, 52*, 114–121.

Nucci, L. P., Smetana, J. G., Araki, N., Nakaue, M., & Comer, J. (2012). Japanese adolescents' disclosure to parents: Family decision-making, domain of activity, and well-being. Unpublished manuscript, University of California, Berkeley.

Nucci, L. P., & Turiel, E. (1978). Social interactions and the development of social concepts in preschool children. *Child Development, 49*, 400–407. doi: 10.2307/1128704

Offer, D. (1969). *The psychological world of the teenager*. New York: Basic Books.

Overton, W. F. (2006). Developmental psychology: Philosophy, concepts, methodology. In W. Damon & R. M. Lerner (Series Ed.) & R. M. Lerner (Vol. Ed.), *Handbook of child psychology:* Vol. 1. *Theoretical models of human development* (6th ed., pp. 18–88). Hoboken, NJ: John Wiley & Sons.

Rote, W. M., & Smetana, J. G. (Under review). Adolescents' and parents' judgments of the acceptability of information management strategies and their correlates.

Rutter, M. (1980). *Changing youth in a changing society*. Nuffield Provincials Hospital Trust.

Shaw, L. A., Wainryb, C., & Smetana, J. G. (2012). Early and middle adolescents' reasoning about moral and personal concerns in opposite sex interactions. Unpublished manuscript, Weber State University.

Shedler, J., & Block, J. (1991). Adolescent drug use and psychological health: A longitudinal inquiry. *American Psychologist, 45*, 612–630. doi:10.1037/0003-066X.45.5.612

Shweder, R. A., & Sullivan, M. A. (1993). Cultural psychology: Who needs it? *Annual Review of Psychology, 44*, 497–523. doi:10.1146/annurev.ps.44.020193.002433

Smetana, J. G. (1981a). Preschool children's conceptions of moral and social rules, *Child Development, 52*, 1333–1336. doi:10.2307/1129527

Smetana, J. G. (1981b). Reasoning in the personal and moral domains: Adolescent and young adult women's decision-making about abortion. *Journal of Applied Developmental Psychology, 2*, 211–226. doi:10.1016/0193-3973(81)90002-2

Smetana, J. G. (1982). *Concepts of self and morality: Women's reasoning about abortion*. New York: Praeger.

Smetana, J. G. (1985). Preschool children's conceptions of transgressions: Effects of varying moral and conventional domain-related attributes. *Developmental Psychology, 21*, 18–29. doi: 10.1037/0012-1649.21.1.18

Smetana, J. G. (1988a). Adolescents and parents' conceptions of parental authority. *Child Development, 59*(2), 321–335. doi:10.2307/1130313

Smetana, J. G. (1988b). Concepts of self and social convention: Adolescents' and parents' reasoning about hypothetical and actual family conflicts. In M. R. Gunnar & W. A. Collins (Eds.), *21st Minnesota Symposium on child psychology: Development during the transition to adolescence* (pp. 77–122). Hillsdale, NJ: Erlbaum.

Smetana, J. G. (1989). Adolescents' and parents' reasoning about actual family conflict. *Child Development, 60*, 1052–1067. doi:10.2307/1130779

Smetana, J. G. (1995). Parenting styles and conceptions of parental authority during adolescence. *Child Development, 66*, 299–316. doi:10.2307/1131579

Smetana, J. G. (2000). Middle class African American adolescents' and parents' conceptions of parental authority and parenting practices: A longitudinal investigation. *Child Development, 71*, 1672–1686. doi:10.1111/1467-8624.00257

Smetana, J. G. (2011). *Adolescents, families, and social development: How teens construct their worlds*. Malden, MA: Wiley-Blackwell.

Smetana, J. G., Abernethy, A., & Harris, A. (2000). Adolescent-parent interactions in middle-class African American families: Longitudinal change and contextual variations. *Journal of Family Psychology, 14*, 458–474. doi:10.1037/0893-3200.14.3.458

Smetana, J. G., & Asquith, P. (1994). Adolescents' and parents' conceptions of parental authority and adolescent autonomy. *Child Development, 65*, 1147–1162. doi: 10.2307/1131311

Smetana, J. G., & Bitz, B. (1996). Adolescents' conceptions of teachers' authority and their relations to rule violations in school. *Child Development, 67*, 1153–1172. doi:10.2307/1131885

Smetana, J. G., & Braeges, J. L. (1990). The development of toddlers' moral and conventional judgments. *Merrill-Palmer Quarterly, 36*, 329–346.

Smetana, J. G., Braeges, J. L., & Yau, J. (1991). Doing what you say and saying what you do: Reasoning about adolescent–parent conflict in interviews and interactions. *Journal of Adolescent Research, 6*, 276–295. doi:10.1177/074355489163002

Smetana, J. G., Campione-Barr, N., & Daddis, C. (2004). Developmental and longitudinal antecedents of family decision-making: Defining health behavioral autonomy for African American adolescents. *Child Development, 75*, 1418–1434. doi: 10.1111/j.1467-8624.2004.00749.x

Smetana, J. G., & Daddis, C. (2002). Domain-specific antecedents of psychological control and parental monitoring: The role of parenting beliefs and practices. *Child Development, 73*, 563–580. doi:10.1111/1467-8624.00424

Smetana, J. G., Daddis, C., & Chuang, S. S. (2003). "Clean your room!": A longitudinal investigation of adolescent-parent conflict in middle class African American families. *Journal of Adolescent Research, 18*, 631–650. doi:10.1177/0743558403254781

Smetana, J. G., & Gaines, S. (1999). Adolescent-parent conflict in middle-class African-American families. *Child Development, 70*, 1447–1463. doi: 10.1111/1467-8624.00105

Smetana, J. G., Kelly, M., & Twentyman, C. T. (1984). Abused, neglected, and nonmaltreated children's conceptions of moral and conventional transgressions. *Child Development, 55*, 277–287. doi: 10.2307/1129852

Smetana, J. G., & Metzger, A. (2008). Don't ask, don't tell (your mother or father): Disclosure and nondisclosure in parent-adolescent relationships. In M. Kerr, H. Stattin, & R. Engels (Eds.), *What can parents do: New insights into the role of parents in adolescent problem behavior* (pp. 65–87). New York: Wiley.

Smetana, J. G., Metzger, A., Gettman, D. C., & Campione-Barr, N. (2006). Disclosure and secrecy in adolescent–parent relationships. *Child Development, 77*, 201–217. doi: 10.1111/j.1467-8624.2004.00749.x

Smetana, J. G., Villalobos, M., Rogge, R. D., & Tasopoulos-Chan, M. (2010). Keeping secrets from parents: Daily variations among poor, urban adolescents. *Journal of Adolescence, 33*, 321–331. doi: 10.1016/j.adolescence.2009.04.003

Smetana, J. G., Villalobos, M., Tasopoulos-Chan, M., Gettman, D. C., & Campione-Barr, N. (2009). Early and middle adolescents' disclosure to parents about their activities in different domains. *Journal of Adolescence, 32*, 693–713. doi: 10.1016/j.adolescence.2008.06.010

Smetana, J. G., Yau, J., & Hanson, S. (1991). Conflict resolution in families with adolescents. *Journal of Research on Adolescence, 1*, 189–206. doi: 10.1207/s15327795jra0102_5

Smetana, J. G., Yau, J., Restrepo, A., & Braeges, J. L. (1991). Adolescent–parent conflict in married and divorced families. *Developmental Psychology, 27*, 1000–1010. doi: 10.1037/0012-1649.27.6.1000

Spencer, M., & Dornbusch, S. M. (1990). Challenges in studying minority youth. In S. S. Feldman & G. R. Elliot (Eds.) *At the threshold: The developing adolescent* (pp. 123–146). Cambridge, MA: Harvard University Press.

Stattin, H., & Kerr, M. (2000). Parental monitoring: A reinterpretation. *Child Development, 71*, 1072–1085. doi: 10.1111/1467-8624.00210

Turiel, E. (1974). Conflict and transition in adolescent moral development. *Child Development, 45*, 14–29. doi: 10.2307/1127745

Turiel, E. (1977a). Conflict and transition in adolescent moral development II: The resolution of disequilibrium through structural reorganization. *Child Development, 48*, 634–637. doi:10.2307/1128665

Turiel, E. (1977b). Distinct conceptual and developmental domains: Social convention and morality. In C. B. Keasey (Ed.), *Nebraska symposium on motivation* (pp. 77–116). Lincoln: University of Nebraska Press.

Turiel, E. (1983). *The development of social knowledge: Morality and convention.* Cambridge, UK: Cambridge University Press.

Villalobos M., & Smetana, J. G. (2012). Latino values and Puerto Rican adolescents' disclosure and lying to parents. *Journal of Research on Adolescence, 35*, 875–885.

Weston, D., & Turiel, E. (1980). Act-rule relations: Children's concepts of social rules. *Developmental Psychology, 16*, 417–424. doi: 10.1037/0012-1649.16.5.417

Yau, J., & Smetana, J. G. (1993). Chinese-American adolescents' reasoning about cultural conflicts. *Journal of Adolescent Research, 8*, 419–438. doi:10.1177/074355489384005

Yau, J., & Smetana, J. G. (1996). Adolescent-parent conflict among Chinese adolescents in Hong Kong. *Child Development, 67*, 1262–1275. doi: 10.2307/1131891

Yau, J., & Smetana, J. G. (2003). Adolescent-parent conflict in Hong Kong and Shenzhen: A comparison of youth in two cultural contexts. *International Journal of Behavioral Development, 27*, 201–211. doi: 10.1080/01650250244000209

Yau, J. Y., Tasopoulos-Chan, M., & Smetana, J. G. (2009). Disclosure to parents about everyday activities among American adolescents from Mexican, Chinese, and European backgrounds. *Child Development, 80*, 1481–1498. doi: 10.1111/j.1467-8624.2009.01346.x

43

Pursuing Identity-Focused Resiliency Research
Post-*Brown v. Board of Education 1954*

MARGARET BEALE SPENCER

During my preschool years and most certainly evident during the early primary grades, I consistently experienced an unusual level of awareness of diverse perspectives. As a second-generation, northern-born, city-dwelling, youngest sibling of three, this propensity to be critically aware was magnified at particular historical moments. For example, exposure to discussions concerning the Supreme Court's 1954 opinion and determination of the *Brown v. Board of Education* Decision mattered to members of my community.

I grew up in an African American family and neighborhood within Philadelphia, Pennsylvania and was socialized by parents and extended kin. Specifically, an early divorce meant that childrearing was primarily provided by my mother, two older sisters, actively involved kin of both parents, as well as a host of engaged and "ever-observing and monitoring" neighbors (!). We lived in a working-class community when the Brown Decision as national policy took effect. By the point of its determination I was completing the last few primary school grades at a school located outside my home neighborhood. The policy change had no impact on my schooling experience; however, it was certainly a critical ingredient of adult discussions in my home and neighborhood. Accordingly, the experiences of these "personally unknown" African American students and families occupied "center stage" in our community and family and mattered a great deal.

I left my neighborhood school at the end of 3rd grade. The remaining three primary grades were completed at an uncommonly diverse school. At the time, neither my family nor I anticipated that leaving my neighborhood school meant that I would not have another African American teacher/educator until many years later as a doctoral student at the University of Chicago. On many levels, the move was life changing and introduced foundational

perspectives about race, ethnicity, and equity. The experience demonstrated the potential for all to practice impartiality, and ingrained the insight that no group took primacy over intellectual prowess.

Students at the new elementary school differed by race, ethnicity, nativity, and faith community. The elite demonstration school was located in the near downtown central area of the City. It required testing for admission, provided unusually progressive curriculum innovations (e.g., a host of interesting "elective" classes) although a public school and, as noted, represented broad cultural diversity. In fact, as opposed to Christmas dominating the major annual school holiday tradition, instead, we sang and learned the customs associated with Hanukkah and the Jewish faith. My values and views concerning cultural pluralism were established early and affected my own identity processes. The educational programming, academic opportunities, and social experiences continue to buttress my commitment to equity, honesty, and the critical function of equal educational opportunity.

My mother always had questions about the attendant "lessons learned" from my culturally diverse primary-grade experiences and generally "checked facts" with an aunt and uncle who happened to be Black Jews. In fact, my uncle was the cantor in their home synagogue; our family members always enjoyed attending his performances at synagogue-sponsored musical events. The similarities and differences from home and neighborhood perspectives juxtaposed against this particular primary-school experience provided numerous illustrations of diverse points of view. Thus, in addition to learning traditional "academic facts," inferring and connecting myriad perspectives; observing cautions, beliefs and meanings about life and liberty; and being made aware of behavioral expectations for excellence, I was provided with critical insights which shape my philosophical foundation as a developmental scientist.

Although I was totally unaware of the behavioral sciences in any formal way at the time, nonetheless, the cumulative experiences were preparing me for a future in developmental science. They fomented the practice of a tradition of scholarly resistance, as needed, and intellectual risk-taking (i.e., having the confidence and sense of responsibility to ask uncomfortable questions and to pursue knowledge-imbued answers to same). It is this set of basic experiences and ethical attributes which, for me, continue to represent a source of personal satisfaction. More specifically, I have learned that without the inherent intellectual and ethical strengths accrued, I may have been likely to take the easy and safe route of not questioning but, instead, maintaining "intellectual traditions of the behavioral sciences" or failing to question the status quo. Too frequently, behavioral science custom, in fact, continues to accept pathology or a problem-assuming posture about the human development of phenotypically or linguistically "different" (i.e., non-White) individuals (i.e., if their humanity is acknowledged at all). In my case, the basis for questioning such short-sighted assumptions began early and was part of my basic cultural socialization and childhood family and schooling experiences.

My fourth grade teacher and first instructor at the new, non-neighborhood school was Ms. Sharp. She went out of her way to insure that I felt comfortable. I concluded long ago that every student needs a "Ms. Sharp" in their academic lives. Particularly during periods of extra challenge (e.g., being the "new kid"), such individuals communicate high expectations, function as authentic supports, and thus, provide consistent opportunities for inferring positive self- appraisals. Given the foundational comfortableness provided, one of my first observations and indelible lessons learned about academic expectations and performance outcomes is that *no particular group* has a "corner" on intellectual prowess and more general talent.

Absolutely everyone was expected to perform at a consistently high level. In fact, anyone could be sent to the rear of one's row in Ms. Allen's 5th grade classroom if one was ill-prepared or failed to perform to criterion. Without exception, *anyone* could suffer the immediate demand to clear one's desk drawer and to move to the back of the row. The "public command" to move to the rear also required that everyone else in back of you in the row had to move forward by one desk, as well (thus, making room for you at the rear[!]). Relatedly, and most importantly, finding yourself at the front of the row did not mean that you were better than anyone else. The position suggested and required consideration of the fact that others had failed to perform to standard and had been moved to the rear.

Mr. Kushner's 6th grade classroom also provided important lessons as preparation for a career in psychology and developmental science specifically. His class was a constant crucible for demonstrations of integrity which were linked with academic performance expectations, achievement outcomes, and honest self-assessments. Specifically and uniquely, he insisted on an honest self-appraisal of performance. Students were required to submit their own report card grades. His one and only ineradicable two-part rule was straightforward, tough, and consistently enforced.

When asked for the grades by subject to be submitted for report card dissemination, if a student over-estimated an "earned grade," the report card reflected one grade lower. On the other hand, if a student under-estimated performance, the report card grade reflected the lower grade! Earnest and accurate self-appraisal was the expectation; thus, the consequences were harsh if the straightforward, unbiased, and *justly implemented* rule was violated. Tears, pink cheeks, intense anger, and "flushed faces" were the obvious "data" observable to all for rule infractions. Accordingly, a critical multifaceted lesson learned was the importance of excelling academically, appraising performance outcomes accurately, taking responsibility for personal assessments, coping with consequences for falling short, and observing (and learning from) practiced "justice." Thus, the consequences of articulated values and sustained academic effort were an ever-present part of my early life not only at school but in our family and community.

Family, school, and neighborhood inputs were generally the same relative to expectations for academic excellence, integrity, and good behavior. An awareness of psychology was not a part of my consciousness in any way. Instead, and generally taking a range of forms and emanating from a variety of sources, "information of social and cultural salience" constantly swirled about me—for ready access and analysis. About a decade later, the various context-associated experiences noted prepared me to ask quite specific and candid human-development-relevant questions about diverse humans.

The referenced inputs and insights became progressively more complex and evident given discussions about the implementation of the *Brown v. Board of Education* Decision of 1954. I never found the subliminal messages concerning race either dissonance-producing or perplexing. Instead, they were experienced as a curious part of everyday life and another important source of information for analysis: I understood quite early that there were lots of very confused people. The possibility that some suggested malevolence, at best as well, was not hypothesized until much later.

In fact, even more so than the 1954 Brown Decision, the particularly salient history-making event prominent during this period was the brutal killing of Emmett Louis Till on August 28, 1955. Given the community's discussion of this heinous incident it was unavoidable that I would "sneak" a look at periodicals. They described the crime and provided pictures of the handsome, healthy, happy-appearing adolescent victim. The circuitous perusal of my mother's periodicals and review of the published stories and pictures of Emmett Till's kidnapping and murder were shocking. It was my first time actually seeing an image of a dead body laid out in a coffin. Most significant, of course, was the fact that he was a 14-year-old boy and African American, like me, who also lived in the north but was visiting relatives in Mississippi when his kidnapping and murder occurred. The shocking contrast of seeing him pictured in a jaunty hat with an attractive smile and then displayed in a coffin horribly mutilated afforded vivid contrasts which became indelibly etched in my memory.

Not surprising, the Emmett Till murder was never a current events topic discussed or presented in our racially and culturally diverse school. However, overhearing adult discussions of this tragedy provided a vivid understanding that brown children raised in the north could be easily savaged and disposed of without justice. At the time I was unaware that this event motivated the African American Civil Rights Movement; however, it was a period which heightened my awareness of the imposed *invisibility* of common occurrences of injustice. Of course, within a half-dozen years, these were themes which would trigger my own very deep commitment to and engagement in the American Civil Rights Movement as well as global liberation efforts (i.e., with particular emphases regarding African nations). Years later, these occurrences served a foundational role, which encouraged my question-asking pattern as a psychology student. The lack of human development thinking when considering the experiences of minority youth represent examples of insufferable intolerance which I continue to find impossible to ignore. At the same time, my interest in White privilege and human vulnerability, more generally, emanates from my awareness of the consistent silencing of the histories of individuals and their contextual experiences of physical and psychological violence. Given the "ghosts" or attitudinal residuals of the Brown Decision (as well as other historical writings), which suggested the superiority of Whites, my attempts to bring attention to the complexities of life in America, particularly for individuals of color, have been consistently noted in my own scholarship. However, along with parallel other behavioral and social scientists, the perspective concerning coping, health and resiliency—too frequently—have been stridently ignored.

At the start of the 20th century, the essentialness and necessity for Black people to develop and make use of double consciousness or simultaneous levels of awareness was stated quite eloquently in 1902 with the classic statement by W. E. B. Du Bois avowed in his exemplary publication, *The Souls of Black Folk* (Du Bois, 1902). The perspective has been elaborated and stated by a variety of scholars during the interim (e.g., Boykin, 1986). It is unclear whether or not Du Bois intended that his remarks be applied to very young children. Nevertheless the heightened levels of social cognitive processes and analysis orientation noted as very prominent in my early life have persisted and are fundamental aspects of my own identity formation and coping processes, which continue as salient both personally and professionally. Dr. Du Bois' perspective as well as many others contributes to a philosophical orientation, which undergirds my theoretical stance vis-à-vis developmental science as applied to diverse humans.

Early Years

Communicated as inputs both from my older siblings and multiple significant adults in my life, I understood both formally and informally that I was the youngest of three girls from whom exceedingly high behavioral standards and academic habits and outcomes were expected. We were not unique. These anticipated values were modeled and enforced, first, by my highly talented older sisters as well as shared by parents, neighbors, and extended kin. Our parents were hardworking adults whose early divorce made life more complex than ideal, particularly given our community's long-term character. At varying periods, our neighborhood represented different levels of economic challenge as well as exemplary models of impressive family and individual adaptive coping and developmental task success. For example, not only have contemporary Philadelphia leaders, local Ivy League scholars, business forerunners, and professional models of accomplishment launched their successful careers in our community, but nationally, well-known individuals such as Bill Cosby began their lives or spent considerable time there, although exiting after varying periods. Accordingly, quite early in my own development, appreciating the variability within and between individuals, families, and communities was an essential part of my considerable social knowledge base and data for reflection purposes. In our community, my sisters and I were known as "the Beale girls" and children for whom, as suggested, high behavioral expectations was the norm. I knew that informal monitoring by invested neighborhood adults was a part of my daily life. In fact, as an adult, I learned that my mother received unsolicited weekly "reports" about our after-school activities and behaviors while she was away at work. As children, my sisters and I were unaware of the sources of my mother's "monitoring data" but were aware that it was timely and *always accurate*. Accordingly, years later as a psychology student, it came as a shock that textbooks narrowly viewed particular neighborhoods only in pathological terms and implied that they were bereft of strengths and resources. On the other hand, and given these not unusual experiences, as a developmental science researcher decades later reporting findings from our program of developmental research, it was not surprising to obtain research findings which indicated that high-achieving youths' reported beliefs of parental monitoring were predictive of academic excellence (Spencer, Dupree, Swanson, & Cunningham, 1996). Although it was difficult to recognize that developmental scientists were unwilling to believe otherwise, parental monitoring can occur through neighbor monitoring and have the same powerful effect. Given the frequently supportive role of neighbors, such situations are not unusual.

My mother, Mrs. Beale, was a voracious reader whose major goal in high school was to pursue the study of all things French and to live in France at some point. Given that she and her four siblings were orphaned by both parents' untimely deaths—separated by one month—when my mother was just 13, her post-secondary educational goals were not realized. That significant loss and significant challenge did not mar her fundamental values about education, effort, and excellence. Her father was the first Black civilian deep-sea diver working off the Philadelphia wharf. He died on Mother's Day, 1 month following his wife's untimely death. Nonetheless, even with such huge challenges, my mother maintained her incredibly significant achievement orientation, always read to us, and maintained an interesting library, which she enjoyed throughout life, in fact—well into her 9th decade of life. Not surprisingly, there were always literacy messages modeled and affect inferred and stated about the joys of reading, the critical importance of schooling, and the significance of communication acts more generally. I remain confident that this context influenced my motivation level which resulted in my being a self-taught reader by age three. Highly engaged uncles were supplemental and core socializing agents in my life.

Particularly from my father's brothers, there were always strongly shared perspectives about the significance of debate. Both had some post-secondary educational training and had government jobs. One of the two completed college on scholarship. This set of uncles provided opportunities and modeled consistent messages about the necessity of analyzing events, asking questions from multiple perspectives, sharing observations, and defending all conclusions shared. No allowances were made for age; they expected the same analysis quality from each of us. I savored and, in fact, loved every moment of each shared opportunity. Others shared parallel instructions about life and behavioral expectations.

My mother's two brothers provided critical lessons about the importance of learning, behaving like "a lady," showing concern beyond the self, laughing at oneself … and having fun, as well. These uncles attended high school but did not have post-secondary educational training; yet given the early loss of parents and the need to earn a living, they accrued lots of "street smarts." Lessons from the four uncles were critically important to my future. Particularly the values of having an inquiring mind (manifested without dissonance); engaging in analysis, debate, and inquiry; showing sensitivity for others; and feeling confident standing alone, as needed, in the defense of salient perspectives and ideals. All were base-line expectations. All four had served in the military during World War II. Each had something to say about racial socialization matters, the problem of inequality and injustice, communicated lessons about American citizenship, and the fact of our family's contributions to the nation's growth and development. The latter was pointedly restated to me during my college years of student activism and Nationalist leanings. This background—particularly as a girl interested in math and science—prepared me to be open to and to adopt non-traditional professional interests during an era when most young women in my all-girls high-school class were aspiring to careers in primary grade teaching, nursing, medical technology, or administrative support careers. Of course, at the time, I would not have understood the work of a psychologist and, accordingly, it was not an interest on my list of long-term career commitments. On the other hand, becoming a chemist or pediatrician were serious intellectual interests. Thus, studying pharmacy seemed

to offer a reasonable compromise, given my academic strengths, and one step further in pursuit of a math/science career. Plus I knew several pharmacists. That particular career ladder reinforced my interests and well-developed academic prowess; it also afforded work opportunities needed in the future while contemplating (and paying for!) medical school pursuits.

However, upon enrollment in a 5-year undergraduate pharmacy program of study, in addition to the lack of minority presence, there emerged an unanticipated gender "story." I did not anticipate that using my coveted 4-year scholarship to pursue the 5-year pharmacy curriculum would include an implicit message to the very few women enrolled in the program of study. The stated message was that their seats should be occupied by men who would support a family one day. The variously communicated message was reinforced by the fact that the one woman in a science lab with a PhD performed the job of distributing glassware; that is, she was responsible for overseeing glassware checked out for use in the day's experiments. Needless to say, given my all-female high-school academic success experiences, diverse leadership opportunities (Student Association President, Vice President, Treasurer and Fencing Team Captain, etc.), and consistent feedback that we could accomplish anything while valuing our femininity, I did not find college an "inspiring" chapter in my academic life. The mainly male professional program experience was disappointing because of its implicit message suggesting the second-class citizenship of women (!). Except for the one English course and an uninspiring introductory sociology class, both taken during the first year of the 5-year math/science-emphasizing program of study, overall, college functioned as an "interesting" math and science strength-reinforcing program of study, which guaranteed employment following graduation.

Nonetheless, the primary-, middle-, and high-school, and undergraduate professional curriculum exposures, collectively considered, provided formal and informal insights about race and gender. As described, primary-school experiences aided an understanding that no one group had a "corner" on intellectual prowess. Teachers made it clear that you were graded based upon performance. However, perceptiveness accrued during junior high as well as high school and college provided many growth stimulating opportunities. The insights assisted in acknowledging and understanding the subtle forms of resistance to the implementation of the Brown Decision and an ongoing call for national reflections about race, class, and gender, as well as social change more generally. My civil rights activities during college were particularly instructional given my well-developed meta-cognitive "social antennae" honed and groomed throughout childhood and adolescence.

Moreover, in addition to profiting from significant activities as a civil rights activist during my college and emergent adulthood period, a totally unexpected event occurred. The extraordinarily good news is that I met my future husband, Charles, on a blind date: a brilliant chemistry graduate student (also with a pharmacy undergraduate degree) from a local rival College of Pharmacy. We bonded immediately and married when I completed course work for the BS Degree in Pharmacy and he was awarded an MS Degree in Organic Chemistry. We headed to the University of Kansas where Charles chose to commence his doctoral studies in the Department of Organic Pharmaceutical Chemistry. Leaving the east coast and launching our lives together during that first year in Kansas, I worked full-time as a hospital pharmacist. The experience in the large teaching and research hospital did not make my field of study any more interesting. Nonetheless, I completed the required hours for my licensure examination, informally observed chronically ill children with their families (which actually sparked an interest in resiliency), and became licensed as a registered pharmacist. The second year we decided that the 1-hour drive each way was too challenging given my newly acquired driver's license. Thus, I began working part-time at the hospital pharmacy and enrolled in a course each semester at the University of Kansas while we implemented family formation goals. I did not have a plan of study in mind. In candor, and although I enjoyed their company, I was not interested in spending flexible time playing bridge with the other graduate student wives. Thus, taking courses was a way of figuring out what might be interesting to me as potential "next steps," and the timing of the courses fit in with my part-time hospital pharmacy work. Also relevant is that "the Movement" (i.e., the American Civil Rights struggle) was late arriving to the Midwest and we were meeting very interesting fellow students from around the country. As noted, I enjoyed a very active life as a participant of the east coast Civil Rights Movement. Given parallel movements igniting in various regions of Africa, I explored significant questions having to do with liberty, justice, freedom, and responsibility. Being part of university life allowed for a continuing engagement with these themes. Totally unexpected, of course, is that the two courses selected while working part-time in the hospital pharmacy while observing very ill but emotionally resilient children, in fact, changed my life, and I have happily never looked back.

Introduction to Psychology: Awareness of Ghosts of *Brown v. Board of Education 1954* and the Need for Conceptual Resistance

In addition to providing foundational aspects of my meaning-making orientation and personality, ideally, the introduction to psychology at the University of Kansas afforded an explanation as to why some American students of color may develop highly honed antennae for discerning inequality. That is, as a function of normal social cognitive development in the family, community, and American schooling experiences as cultural contexts, it would be difficult to not notice the many illustrations of social inequities in 20th century America.

These thoughts remained with me as I completed two courses—Introduction to Psychology and a Research Methods course—at the University of Kansas. The methods

course was taught by Grace Heider, the wife of renowned balance theory author and scholar, Dr. Fritz Heider. Although I had taken only those two courses, she recruited me into the doctoral program in social psychology, and with full federal funding. It was housed within the Department of Psychology. At the start of the program, while speaking with the departmental chair, Dr. Anthony Smith, he thought that I described my interests in developmental terms and suggested that I speak with Dr. Frances Horowitz, Chair of the Human Development Program and a renowned infant researcher. She became an amazing mentor.

My most memorable courses were with Dr. Fritz Heider, who taught a systems and theories course which was life-changing. Courses with ecological psychologists Drs. Herbert Wright and Paul Gump were highly interesting, as well as a child development course with Dr. Frances Horowitz who agreed to direct my thesis project: "The effects of systematic social (puppet) and token reinforcement on the modification of racial and color concept-attitudes in preschool aged children." I chose the topic because psychology at KU at the time was also heavily influenced by behavior modification scholars such as Dr. Donald Baer (e.g., Baer, 1962; Baer & Sherman, 1964). The issue of race was very much a part of the daily fare at KU because the Civil Rights Movement, as acknowledged, was late in its arrival to the Midwest.

I was not only a new doctoral student in psychology but was pregnant with our first child. Thus, I was very interested in discerning what the psychology experts had to say about the development of Black children. Not surprisingly, I was highly invested in thinking about the best strategies for supporting the development of our child. However, reviewing psychology texts to see what researchers had to say about minority child development was, at minimum, shocking. Negro or minority children were listed primarily under categories such as deviancy, pathology, problems, aggression, or deficits. Given my own and others' "child development histories," I not only found the portrayals strange, but the consistency also seemed, at best, deliberate. A lot of the published reports referenced social psychologist Dr. Thomas Pettigrew and psychoanalysts Drs. Kardiner and Ovesey. The research conducted by Drs. Kenneth and Mamie Clark which had been cited as a footnote in the *Brown v. Board of Education* Decision of 1954 was also consistently referenced. After reading the studies by the Clarks and taking several course offerings, I decided that another methodological approach might represent a contribution to the literature. As stated, in addition to my science program at the secondary level, I had enjoyed 5 years implementing scientific studies as an undergraduate. At the same time, one of my jobs was working part-time in a gastroenterology lab in the medical school which provided other models of basic research.

Graduate School Research

Charles was completing his coursework in organic pharmaceutical chemistry very quickly, thus I knew that although I was enrolled as a doctoral student, there would be time only for a Master's Thesis project. Given my review of the relevant literature, I decided that another approach to the findings by the Clarks was needed. Therefore, given the mentoring and support of Dr. Frances Degen Horowitz, I designed a replication and extension of what had become known as The Doll Studies implemented by Drs. Kenneth and Mamie Clark (Clark & Clark, 1940, 1950, 1963; Clark, K. B. 1963), and which could be completed in my 1 year (i.e., the limited time available for the completion of a Master's Thesis). In addition to the design and construction of a mechanized reinforcement system, the project required a thorough review of the literature. The review exercise made apparent quite strident assumptions about the psychopathology of minority people (e.g., Kardiner & Ovesey, 1951; Pettigrew, 1964). Others conducting empirical research in this area at the time included Dr. John Williams (Williams, 1964, 1966, 1967; Williams & Roberson, 1967).

One very important opportunity enjoyed while a student at Kansas was an in-person meeting with Dr. Thomas Pettigrew. He was invited by our department to give a talk, and as the graduate student representative, I volunteered to pick him up from the airport. Given that the Kansas City Airport is a solid hour away from Lawrence, Kansas, the drive provided an opportunity both to discuss Dr. Pettigrew's work and underlying assumptions, as well as to share my study and findings available at that point. I haven't the foggiest idea if my study mattered to him given that he was incredibly polite and patient; however, it was critically important to me that I share another perspective different from his own thesis provided in his broadly read book, *A Profile of the Negro American* (Pettigrew, 1964). My interest as a newcomer to psychology was to better understand underlying influences for the broadly communicated assumptions of Black pathology, deviance, and problem-imbued individuals and families (i.e., all stated without culturally sensitive and knowledgeable perspectives and grounded research evidence). My 5 years as a lab science student, as well as observations made while at the same time working in a medical school gastroenterology lab, as noted, all made a significant impact on my thought process concerning the conduct of scientific research. However, as a new behavioral science student, I inferred that the research questions, assumptions, and conduct of methods too frequently seemed flawed in some way when reporting on research with minorities.

Among others, a major flaw of the Doll Studies, which the Clarks' work came to be called, was their need to paint commercially available White dolls Black (see Cross, 1991). Thus, one methodological concern was the inherent unattractiveness of painted-over White dolls to make them represent people of African descent. Thus, in replicating the work, there was a need to design a methodology without this inherent shortcoming. In addition, given what I was learning about child development and children's learning, it appeared important to determine if children actually internalized what they experienced in a White-dominated society; in other words, were other socializing experiences in the family and community salient for psychological well-being? In this case, for example, children's views about racial groups might be linked to color biases and connotations. Accordingly, given my exposure to social reinforcement scholars such as Dr. Donald Baer (see Baer, 1965; Baer et al., 1965; Baer & Sherman, 1964), it appeared prudent to question whether social and puppet reinforcement would be effective in changing the prior learning for samples of preschool Black and White children. Thus, one goal was to determine if social and token reinforcement might impact preschool children's naturally learned racial and color concept attitudes. The methodology used was effective in demonstrating that social (mechanized puppets) and token (reinforcement) feedback were effective for obtaining new ideas and evaluative judgments about color concepts and racial groups.

Thus, over a 10-week period with 2- to 4-week intervals, the research strategy was an attempt to convert the naturally formed color-racial concept attitudes of 48 Black and White preschoolers between the ages of 3 years, 3 months and 5 years, 11 months. On a scale of 0–100 with lower scores suggesting Black (positive) bias and higher scores indicating a White (positive) bias, the findings indicated a change from an approximate 70–80% White bias or preference to a 20–35% Black bias or preference. Although not significant, data trends suggested that the Caucasian experimenter was more reinforcing than the Black experimenter for the new learning (i.e., obtaining a positive Black color bias for White and Black children). Findings for Caucasian preschool-aged children indicated more negativity about the color black and Black persons than was the case in the responses from Black children. The experimental manipulation caused a significant difference in the responses of control versus experimental participants (i.e., those exposed to the reinforcement condition). In sum, the experiment was successful in teaching Black and White children that Blacks and the color black were positive and the color white and White individuals were negative (Spencer, 1970; Spencer & Horowitz, 1973).

A major conceptual flaw in the thesis project submitted was my own "buy in" of the view that children's racial and color concepts represented race pride or self-esteem. Thus, upon the completion of the thesis and my enrollment at the University of Chicago in the Committee on Human Development as a NIMH Child Development Traineeship student, my Chicago mentor and ultimate dissertation advisor, the Marshall Field IV Professor of Urban Education, Dr. Edgar Epps (e.g., see Epps, 1969), wanted to hear about the Kansas thesis project. He requested a copy and dutifully read my thesis. He immediately corrected my flawed assumption about the links between racial attitudes and color connotations with Black children's racial pride and self-esteem. In fact, Dr. Epps very patiently explained that my thesis project measured only children's racial attitudes, preferences, and color connotations. His work examining achievement patterns of northern and southern youth provided important insights for my work (Epps, 1969). He patiently and sensitively stated that the project and findings said *absolutely nothing about children's self-esteem or degree of race pride (!)*. This epiphany was both mind-boggling and life-changing. What he communicated to me was that through my interpretation of the findings and conceptual framing of the need for the work, inadvertently, I had bought into the social science "hype." He shared that I had been influenced by the social science assumptions about Black psychopathology (!). In a sensitive and thoughtful manner, this brilliant scholar informed me that the very biases which I attempted to conceptualize differently, in fact, at one level, were impactful for me, as well (!!).

Although I believed that my intellectual inquiry and research strategy formulated resistance against a priori deviancy assumptions, in fact, the social science literature represented an exceedingly powerful conceptual vehicle. It quite effectively framed Blacks as the "deviant other" and Whites as the "standard" of normalcy. Thus, even though I was conceptually prepared to offer scholarly resistance to stereotypes, aspects of the rhetoric, in fact, had been influential as represented in my thesis. Professor Epps served as my source of real conceptual resistance and I remain extraordinarily grateful for his *intellectually brilliant conceptual intervention* in my professional training. Moreover, he delivered the incredible insights in a psychologically sensitive manner. To this day, he remains my "scholar hero."

Thus, to currently hold the endowed chair—Marshall Field IV Professor of Urban Education—for which he was the inaugural chair-holder, remains a source of special pride. In fact, I remain sincerely indebted to him for reigniting and reestablishing all of the dispositions and values introduced in my childhood by my several uncles (e.g., the critical importance of honest debate, resistance, and thoughtful dialogue and analysis). Without question, I am exceedingly appreciative of his role in my doctoral training and generous support of my becoming a responsible professional, behavioral scientist with integrity, and a serious scholar not hesitant to ask "uncomfortable" questions.

At the same time, while planning my doctoral research strategy, I took courses during that first year in child development with Dr. Diana Slaughter (Defoe), a faculty member in the Committee on Human Development. It was for her class that I reconceptualized and reframed the thesis project. I co-authored, in article format, the thesis project with my former KU advisor, Dr. Frances Horowitz. The paper was published in the American Psychological Association flagship journal, *Developmental Psychology* (1973). During that inaugural first year at U Chicago, I was also introduced to another methods professor, Dr. Susan Stodolsky. Given the experiences had at KU with ecologists Drs. Herbert Wright and Paul Gump, her methods course provided opportunities to test out strategies for examining whether or not there are direct linkages between self-esteem, self-concept, and children's racial attitudes and color connotations during the preschool period of development.

In planning for the pilot work for Sue Stodolsky's methods class, I became enthralled with the research of Dr. John Flavell (*The Development of Role-Taking and Communication Skills in Children*, 1968) and advanced U Chicago doctoral student, Robert Marvin (*Attachment, Exploratory, and Communicative Behavior of Two, Three and Four Year Old Children*, 1973). My reading of Piaget had commenced while still a student at KU, thus the new addition to my exposure to Piagetian theorizing and cognition, more generally, was the affect and context-acknowledging work of Drs. Robert DeCharms (*Personal Causation*, 1968), Robert White (competence and effectance motivation, 1959, 1960), and Melvin Feffer (Feffer, 1959, 1967; Feffer & Gourevitch, 1960). This body of theorizing aided my foundational appreciation of human development as representing the several domains of human functioning: cognitive/intellectual, biological, and affective/psychosocial. I should add that 14 months after the birth of our first child while completing the Master's at KU, we added a second daughter to our family. Thus, I actually began my doctoral studies at U Chicago with a new 4-month-old daughter and the Lawrence, Kansas-born 18-month-old (i.e., our first daughter). Accordingly, like Piaget, our children provided a daily source of stimulation, pride, and thirst for understanding the processes of human development as linked to cultural and socializing contexts. Because I was parenting two children at the time, my new experiences as a parent provided daily reminders that having a narrow concern with cognition alone would be inadequate for understanding the processes and unfolding character of human development of children, generally, and youth of color in particular, given the many under-acknowledged challenges remaining following the *Brown v. Board of Education* Decision of 1954.

The very exciting influences of some of the behavioral scientists I have noted aided my rapid movement through the program. Thus, I was able to complete my coursework and qualifying examination, present my dissertation proposal, and collect my dissertation data in the first 2 years at U Chicago. However, it took 3 years to actually analyze the data and to complete the writing of the dissertation primarily in the evenings while benefiting from work experiences during the day. Specifically, while my husband moved from university teaching to medical school, I benefitted from clinical experiences at Chicago Read Mental Health Hospital and the Institute for Juvenile Research (IJR). I also learned a great deal while directing the NICHHD Research Study as the Research Project Director for Dr. Diana Slaughter (Defoe), as noted, a professor in the Committee on Human Development and one of my dissertation committee members along with Dr. Sue Stodolsky and committee chair, Dr. Edgar Epps. Interestingly, my outside reader was the new Committee on Human Development faculty member, Dr. Martha McClintock. Years later, Martha became the mentor and MD–PhD advisor to our younger daughter's program of study at U Chicago (!). Although the dissertation writing process took longer than desired, none-theless, the clinical insights accrued and research project director insights learned were exceedingly helpful.

The applied clinical experiences afforded opportunities to interact with clinicians, psychiatrists, social work-ers and public school personnel. The diversely grounded experiences afforded options for understanding how the lessons gleaned from University of Kansas psychologi-cal ecologists (Drs. Wright and Gump) meshed with the insights obtained from University of Chicago cognitive (language) psychologist Dr. Carol Feldman and the affec-tive domain-emphasizing clinicians and psychiatrists with whom I worked in the several applied settings.

At the same time, I was embattled with the narrow bio-logical perspective promulgated by my U Chicago Human Development professor, Dr. Daniel G. Freedman. In fact, we argued animatedly and incessantly; moreover, I did not trust to take his courses for a grade but instead audited them. That is, I wanted to "consider and understand" what I viewed as his overly deterministic views but declined to be graded for my unavoidable critique of same. Alternatively, the anthropology versus the biology curriculum option was selected. Ultimately and interestingly, in an informal way, some of his ideas have become contributors to my broad theoretical orientation; as noted, at the time, I could see only the race-linked biases in his perspectives. Overall, my 3-year period of work, dissertation writing, conceptual syn-thesis process, and parenting were nothing less than highly stimulating (and yes, frequently stressful) times, as well. As noted, the period also included toddlerhood and parent research experiences as a research project director.

Conceptualizing how issues of power, race, and class contribute to the complex process of human development for children and families happened mainly through my project director role for Dr. Diana Slaughter's research project. The U Chicago research project, totally independ-ent of my own dissertation research, was a collaborative project with a large Chicago service provider: United Charities of Chicago. Our only son was born while direct-ing Dr. Slaughter's collaborative project which focused on the parenting practices of low-income mothers living in one of three public housing projects in Chicago (Slaughter & Spencer, 1976). The project examined their parenting knowledge and emotional support provided either through a Toy Demonstration approach to toddler development or as a function of a parental group model. Parallel with my virtual yearlong clinical experiences at Chicago Read Mental Hospital and the Institute of Juvenile Research, this project and research leadership experience provided opportunities for understanding the "art of collaboration" and insights required for applying psychological knowl-edge and human development perspectives to diversely resourced communities.

Five years into my doctoral studies in the Committee of Human Development at the University of Chicago and the several work opportunities noted, I defended my dis-sertation. With the unique training and program of research

behind me, I launched my professional career as a devel-opmental psychologist with basic and applied interests in the development of diverse youth (i.e., minorities as well as Caucasian children and youth). My dissertation findings were salient for establishing important links between young children's early identity processes and their social cognitive development. Extending the Master's Thesis, the dissertation established that preschool children's normal and appropri-ate cognitive limitations, in fact, provided protection against the internalization of color and racially linked biases. The project established that a majority of the study's African American preschool children enjoyed quite positive and healthy self-images, although they had effectively learned biases concerning dark skin tones and the color black. The study employed multiple measures of social cognition (i.e., affectual, conceptual and perceptual measures). The work ascertained that children's affectual social cognition devel-oped first, perceptual role-taking, second, and conceptual social cognitive tasks, third (Spencer 1976, 1982a, 1982b). In fact, while a student at U Chicago, I met Dr. Jeanne Block (wife of Dr. Jack Block), who made some of her measures available. She was always exceedingly helpful in addition to being an amazing role model. Along with many other findings, the dissertation completion prepared me to think through next-steps for the work's replication and extension up the developmental ladder and into adolescence.

Launching a Career as a Developmental Psychologist

A critical downside for a minority graduate student launching a career in the mid-1970s as a professor and psychologist was the paucity of role models of color. In fact, from the time when I left my neighborhood school at the end of 3rd grade until graduate school at the University of Chicago, I did not have as a teacher or have access to a single Black educator or professor until arriving at the University of Chicago (!). Accordingly, as African Americans, Drs. Epps and Slaughter were extraordinar-ily useful on multiple levels as teachers, mentors, role models, and professionals of immense integrity and moral strength of character. I was, indeed, quite fortunate.

Unfortunately and too frequently for minority scholars, a newly minted graduate will be without mentors, models, or just a "warm body" with whom one has shared his-tory as a function of gender, race, or ethnicity. Too often, a new graduate will find him/herself in a situation where basic sensitivity to acknowledging the human develop-ment of ethnically or racially diverse citizens, including their capacity for resiliency, is absent. Although usu-ally unacknowledged, this absence is a source of chronic stress that Caucasian professionals are spared. Everyone is vulnerable and possesses both supports and challenges (Spencer 2006, 2008a, 2008b). However, lacking a con-text of support represents a significant source of stress. It potentially moves one from a normative vulnerable status instead to an invisible, not acknowledged but *significantly high vulnerability level*. Chronic stress has consequences.

Dueling with other assistant professors or just pursuing successful role performance, in general, does not happen on an "even playing field." The high stress of minority status is made worse when one asks uncomfortable questions that more senior people do not believe represent "worthy" scientific research trajectories. Colleagues frequently advise that particular questions lack objectivity since the inquiry is viewed to suggest "applied interests," or they communicate that a particular topic implies "advocacy." No one would generally acknowledge that behavioral science, too frequently, represents advocacy of the status quo as suggested in the *Brown v. Board of Education* Decision of 1954, i.e., the superiority of Whites over Blacks (see Spencer 2005, 2006). The problem of maintaining the status quo is evident in very simple ways such as the nature of the "scientific questions" posed (or ignored) and the selection of participants or comparison groups for analysis (see Fisher et al., 1995).

For example, the most heinous research design flaw continues to be the evaluation of White middle-income children as compared against impoverished minority youth (!). In fact, it makes behavioral scientists "uncomfortable" when such flaws are acknowledged. The excuse is that it is impossible to get individual level data; thus, school-level socioeconomic status (SES) data is used. However, because of housing discrimination patterns, minority schools are frequently mixed SES; minority students from middle-income families attend schools that may be labeled as lower-income. Not being burdened in the same way, middle-income schools that Whites attend are more homogeneous by SES. This difference represents a research opportunity itself. That is, no one questions relentless and subtle discriminatory housing policies on schooling experiences, resource allocation, teacher assignment, and the learning and development of diverse students. Of course, this questioning of the status quo would never happen. Additionally, many established scholars fail to note that their very strident mindset and limited views about the context-linked human development of diverse persons, in fact, insure chronic struggle and stress for those young scholars who understand differences as representing only *different—not deficit—realities.* The fact of different realities and everyday experiences suggests the need for more informed research methods (see Fisher et al., 1995).

For example, "colleagues" may believe that asking questions about healthy minority youth development lacks credibility, since the "consensus" has been established that the White standard is the norm. Accordingly, such individuals assume that differences of any kind must suggest deviancy and deficit as opposed to the problem of contextual differences. With a few exceptions, there is frequently an absence of senior faculty presence with enough moral courage to consider an alternative analysis of issues. The noted situation thwarts support for alternative questions about development. Most unfortunate and not surprising is that minority individuals themselves may choose to ignore "the conceptual battle" by agreeing with White

stereotypes and joining efforts which support the maintenance of the status quo. As an unstated "arrangement," not resisting the status quo and, instead, participating in the conceptual farce makes colleagues feel "comfortable." Making oneself "invisible" to the conceptual and methodological issues noted by Fisher et al. (1995) and others has benefits. It insures mentoring, diverse support, invitations to participate on prestigious committees, the procurement of fair and less reactive evaluations of article submissions and federal and foundational research submissions, and diminishes levels of chronic psychological assaults and micro-aggressions.

Over my multi-decades career, I have experienced *extraordinary exceptions* to the characterization and shortcomings noted and, thus, enjoyed many opportunities; that is, I have enjoyed and continue to enjoy relationships with non-minority colleagues who claim their full humanity: Whiteness does not define their identity. That fact alone has been the only way that any scholarly successes could have been accrued. Unfortunately, at the same time and like many other scholars of color, I continue to be victim to many biases, as well. Although rephrased, the old adage still applies that a minority scholar with a doctoral degree . . . is still a devalued American. Color and identifiability mattered in the mid-late 20th century and continue to make a difference in 21st-century America (Fegley, Spencer, Goss, Harpalani, & Charles, 2008; Spencer et al., 2011).

At one level, I was cognizant of the situation described when accepting my first academic position. However, in truth, upon the completion of my doctoral degree, I was extraordinarily excited about moving my program of research forward. And I was *equally naïve,* and most certainly blinded by my enthusiasm about the research opportunities ahead. The combination of these qualities obfuscated my common sense. I had grown up as a northerner with neither firsthand experience nor relationships in the southern region of the United States. My experiential base with southern culture emanated from periodicals, novels, and conversations with acquaintances and fellow students.

My first faculty appointment was situated in the Deep South and lacked diversity of any kind. I was not political in the least when contemplating my first appointment. As indicated, I was just excited about moving my developmental science forward. Of course, another consideration was the need to match my job options with internship/ residency opportunities needed by my husband, who had completed medical school as I defended my dissertation. I followed the advice of my Master's Degree mentor, Dr. Frances Horowitz, who suggested that I apply for a vacancy at Emory University in psychology due to the sudden demise of Dr. Boyd McCandless. It is indeed interesting that Dr. McCandless, I found out later, was the action editor of my first publication. I applied and was offered a position as an assistant professor. I did not consider nor think twice about the fact that Emory was in the Deep South. It did not register at the time that during the interview process with members of the departmental faculty, I did not meet a single woman nor person of color.

The problem of American racism had not abated during my graduate training years, thus I should have considered the fact that the psychology department at the time comprised 20 White men, *period*. I was focused on the replication and extension of my dissertation research, and I accordingly gave other highly relevant themes short shrift. Nonetheless, I arrived and obtained a university small grant to begin grant writing. My U Chicago research training and project director activities paid off. My first NIMIH grant was secured by the end of my first year as an assistant professor. At the same time, the success was also the beginning of professional adversity since the work focused on minority children and required that I buy out some of my teaching requirements. The Chair was unhappy with my decisions (i.e., to focus on minority children and to buy out part of my teaching). However, some of the adverse consequences were offset by non-psychology department relationships. Exploring the role of spirituality in human development and resiliency, more generally, was augmented through my valued relationship with theologian scholar and theorist, Dr. James Fowler, who provided leadership for the Center for the Study of Faith and Human Development. The roles of religion and spirituality continue as important conceptual insights in my current program of research and theorizing (e.g., Spencer, 2006, 2008; Brittian & Spencer 2011).

My research agenda situated in educational and neighborhood settings was facilitated and supported in the Educational Studies Division, which included opportunities to emphasize gender. Specifically, the period provided the opportunity to examine the unique experiences of African American boys given the awful occurrence of the missing and murdered child crisis of Atlanta which stretched over a virtual 20-month period (Spencer, 1986; Slaughter-Defoe, Spencer & Oyemade, 2006). The work had a significant impact on my interest in the character of vulnerability and resiliency of boys (Spencer, Cunningham, & Swanson, 1995).

At the same time, significant relationships with psychologists were forged outside of the University through organizations such as the Society for Research in Child Development (SRCD) and colleagues such as Dr. Richard Lerner with whom multiple collaborations continue. A much-needed writing collaboration was planned with my sociology colleague from graduate school at U Chicago, Dr. Walter Allen (UCLA) and Dr. Geraldine Brookins (Harvard-trained developmental psychologist). The outcome was the publication of the 1985 volume, *Beginnings: The Affective and Social Development of Black Children* (Spencer, Brookins, & Allen, 1985), which was supported by two SRCD-financed study group meetings. The volume's publication attained our goal to move forward new ways of thinking about Black children's development that were developmentally sensitive, culturally non-pathologizing, and theoretically grounded. The volume became one of Erlbaum's major publications. The foundational

resources from the two study group meetings were used for framing the issues to be addressed in the volume and, specifically, came from the Study Group Committee of the Society for Research in Child Development (SRCD). As a product, the volume contributed to the positive shift in the direction of culturally inclusive programs of research, and supported a new generation of young scholars in need of alternative ways of conceptualizing youth development. The volume provided a needed referral source for young scholars looking for alternative strategies for framing their questions about the human development of youth of color.

Although these efforts appeared to assist in moving the field forward, there were always, at least, an equal number of steps of "retreat." In many ways, it continued to be very difficult to acknowledge the downside of the Brown Decision, i.e., its articulating of a superior status for White children and a problem-oriented research agenda for diverse youth of color (see Spencer, 1985, 1990, 2008a, 2008b; Spencer & Markstrom-Adams, 1990). This situation influenced my thinking that perhaps new ways of theorizing about human development inclusive of race, ethnicity, social class, and nativity status was needed. Thus, in addition to publishing papers and the 1985 edited volume and achieving multiple sources of funding, I began working on new identity-focused, cultural ecological sensitive theorizing about human development for diverse citizens (i.e., all humans varying by race, ethnicity, class, nativity, and faith group).

The Phenomenological Variant of Ecological Systems Theory (P-VEST) became a reality over the course of several years as I transitioned to the University of Pennsylvania as the Board of Overseers Professor of Human Development (Spencer 1995, 2006, 2008a, 2008b; Spencer, Dupree, & Hartmann 1997; Spencer et al., 2006). Utilizing long-term theoretically oriented research and valued training, as well as personal and professional challenges and opportunities, collectively, was helpful in the conceptualization, synthesis, and application of P-VEST (see Spencer, 2006, 2008a, 2008b for a synthesis of research and findings).

On the one hand, there were multiple challenges in my first job. However, the important accomplishments achieved during my combined several decades at Emory and the University of Pennsylvania were noteworthy. In addition to producing a theoretical framework applicable in the design and testing of qualitative and quantitative research, other scholarly outcomes included the successful replication and extension of identity processes acknowledging and resiliency focused research to the middle childhood years and through to late adolescence (e.g., see Spencer, 2001; Spencer, Cunningham & Swanson, 1995; Spencer & Dornbusch, 1990; Spencer & Markstrom-Adams, 1990; Spencer & Swanson, 2000; Swanson & Spencer, 1991). In addition to the mentoring and collegial relationships noted (e.g., with Drs. Frances Horowitz, Fritz and Grace Heinder, Edgar Epps, Diana Slaughter, Jeanne Block, Richard Lerner, Walter Allen, Geraldine Brookins, and U Chicago student cohort members), I enjoyed and continue to value amazing relationships with colleagues and post-docs. Among others they include former students, post-docs, and research colleagues (e.g., U Penn post-docs Drs. Dena Swanson, Michael Cunningham, Davido Dupree, Elaine Cassidy, as well as faculty and research colleagues Drs. Howard Stevenson, Doug Frye, and Suzanne Fegley). All were always collaborative, collegial, innovative, thoughtful and resourceful.

At U Penn, in addition to serving as the program director of the Interdisciplinary Studies of Human Development (ISHD) Program in the Graduate School of Education (GSE), it was gratifying, at the same time, to Direct the Center for Health Achievement Neighborhoods Growth and Ethnic Studies (CHANGES) as well as the W. E. B. Du Bois Collective Research Institute. With support from fellow psychologist and colleague Dr. Howard Stevenson, together with other colleagues, post-docs, and graduate students within GSE and throughout the University and beyond, we were able to accomplish amazing and innovative studies together.

Returning to the University of Chicago as the Marshall Field IV Professor of Urban Education in the Department of Comparative Human Development continues to represent a good experience with old as well as valued new colleagues (particularly Drs. Susan Stodolsky, Richard Taub, Steven Raudenbush, Martha McClintock, Lauren Rich, and Micere Keels). As a stimulating context, it fosters unique collaborations and valued exchanges which extend my identity-focused resiliency theorizing, basic science, as well as serving to stimulate applied research efforts to new levels.

I continue to be as conceptually grounded and analysis oriented, as was evident in my childhood described initially. In many ways, and although I was unaware of it at that time, my entire childhood and youthful history prepared me to engage in efforts which acknowledge societal challenges to understand identity processes and their significance for achieving life-span resiliency.

The various collaborative options which I have enjoyed and experienced both as challenges and opportunities have aided my appreciation of the impact of a developmental perspective both as basic science and as applied to myriad settings. However, its salience can be enjoyed and function as a benefit to diverse individuals only if freed from the limited and tainted views concerning some of America's diverse citizenry. It is interesting that my career will end where the majority of my training actually began. I continue to feel exceedingly pleased that my "accidental psychologist" path happened and that the work trajectory appears to be of help to the current and next generation of psychologists and colleagues who dare to look beyond "the accepted" and to push the conceptual envelop. Ideally, the questions pursued and conceptual strategies introduced and synthesized do and will encourage us to not so quickly accept "the status quo" so persuasively presented. Alternatively, encouraging and fostering the exploration of thoughtful (and uncomfortable to some) questions increases the probability of making a difference in the

resiliency promotion and the authentic support and development of all citizens. I believe that goal is possible if we can earnestly examine "the self" both individually and collectively (see Spencer, 2011).

In many ways, the wording of the *Brown v. Board of Education* Decision of 1954 set the stage for reinforcing assumptions about the superior status of White Americans. The fallacy of White superiority continues to function as an "elephant in the room" apparition both in the design of research, the interpretation of findings, and its myriad imputations in foundational roles in policy and professional training. The broad consequence impacts the conduct and interpretation of behavioral science. Erik Erikson's theorizing is correct in postulating that it is possible to embrace our polar opposites (e.g., speculating about the experience of all humans) only when we first confront and analyze the self (see Spencer, 2011). I am hopeful that developmental science, in facing and analyzing itself and its research trajectories, will lead the way for positive change in the support of all citizens' positive life-course trajectories. This path is different from the current pattern of stereotyping groups given research findings of reported group difference. Ideally the field might contribute to the scholarly resources and insights needed for guaranteeing authentic opportunities available to the nation's diverse citizenry as a global model. Perhaps, as too overly optimistic, it may be a naïve perspective. Nevertheless, I believe the noted goal can be achieved because people may be better than their behaviors would suggest.

References

Baer, D. M. (1962). A technique of social reinforcement for the study of child behavior: Behavior avoiding reinforcement withdrawal. *Child Development, 33*, 847–858.

Baer, D. M., Peterson, R. F., & Sherman, J. A. (1965). *Development of generalized imitation by reinforcing behavioral similarity to a model.* Paper presented at the Society for Research in Child Development Meetings, Minneapolis MN, March 1965.

Baer, D. M., & Sherman, J. A. (1964). Reinforcement control of generalized imitation in young children. *Journal of Experimental Child Psychology, 1*, 37–49.

Boykin, A. W. (1986). A triple quandary and the schooling of Afro American children. In U. Neisser (Ed.), *The school achievement of minority children* (pp. 57–92). Hillsdale, NJ: Erlbaum.

Brittian, A. S., & Spencer, M. B. (2011). Assessing the relationship between ethnic and religious identity among and between diverse American youth. In A. E. A. Warren, R. M. Lerner, & E. Phelps (Eds.), *Thriving and spirituality among youth: Research perspectives and future possibilities* (pp. 205–230). Hoboken, NJ: John Wiley & Sons.

Brown v. Board of Education of Topeka, 347 U.S. 483 (1954).

Clark, K. B. (1963). *Prejudice and your child.* Boston: Beacon Press.

Clark, K. B., & Clark, M. K. (1939). The development of consciousness of self and the emergence of racial identification in Negro preschool children. *Journal of Social Psychology, 10*, 591–599.

Clark, K. B., & Clark, M. K. (1940). Skin color as a factor in racial identification of Negro preschool children. *Journal of Social Psychology,* SPSSI Bulletin, *11*, 159–169.

Clark, K. B., & Clark, M. K. (1950). Emotional factors in racial identification and preference in Negro children. *Journal of Negro Education, 19*, 341–350.

DeCharms, R. (1968). *Personal causation: The internal affective determinants of behavior.* New York: Academy Press.

Cross, W. E. Jr. (1991). *Shades of Black: Diversity in African American identity*. Philadelphia: Temple University Press.

Du Bois, W. E. B. (1902). *The souls of black folk*. Greenwich, CT: Fawcett Publications.

Epps, E. G. (1969). Correlates of academic achievement among Northern and Southern urban Negro students. *Journal of Social Issues, 25*, 55–70.

Feffer, M. H. (1959). The cognitive implications of role taking behavior. *Journal of Personality, 27*, 152–168.

Feffer, M. H. (1967). Sympton expression as a form of primitive decentering. *Psychological Review, 74*, 16–28.

Feffer, M. H., & Gourevitch, V. (1960). Cognitive aspects of role taking in children. *Journal of Personality, 28*, 384–396.

Fegley, S. G., Spencer, M. B., Goss, T. N., Harpalani, V., & Charles, N. (2008). Colorism embodies: Skin tone and psychosocial well-being in adolescence. In W. Overton & U. Mueller (Eds.), *Body in mind, mind in body: Developmental perspectives on embodiment and consciousness* (pp. 281–312). Mahwah, NJ: LEA Inc.

Fisher, C. B., Murray, J. P., Dill, J. R., Hagen, J. W., Hogan, M. J., Lerner, R. M. et al. (1993). The national conference on graduate education in the applications of developmental science across the life span. *Journal of Applied Developmental Psychology, 14*, 1–10.

Flavell, J. H. (1968). *The development of role-taking and communication skills in children*. New York: Wiley.

Kardiner, A., & Ovesey, L. (1951). *The mark of oppression: Explorations in the personality of the American Negro*. New York: Norton.

Marvin, R. (1973). Attachment, exploratory and communicative behavior of two, three and four year old children. Unpublished doctoral thesis, University of Chicago.

Pettigrew, T. F. (1964). *A profile of the Negro American*. Princeton, NJ: Van Nostrand.

Slaughter, D. T., & Spencer, M. B. (1975, April). Modernization through education of mother-child dyads: Description of research strategy. Paper presented at the Biennial Meeting of the Society for Research in Child Development, Denver, CO. Retrieved from ERIC database. (ED115372).

Slaughter-Defoe, D. T., Spencer, M. B. and Oyemade, U. J. (2006). Our children too: A history of the first 25 years of the Black Caucus of the Society for Research in Child Development, 1973–1997: VI. The Atlanta child murders and the Black Caucus of the SCRD. *Monographs of the Society for Research in Child Development, 71*(1), 75–83.

Spencer, M. B. (1982a). Personal and group identity of Black children: An alternative synthesis. *Genetic Psychology Monographs, 106*, 59–84.

Spencer, M. B. (1982b). Preschool children's social cognition and cultural cognition: A cognitive developmental interpretation of race dissonance findings. *Journal of Psychology, 112*, 275–286.

Spencer, M. B. (1985). Cultural cognition and social cognition as identity factors in Black children's personal-social growth. In M. B. Spencer, G. K. Brookins, & W. R. Allen (Eds.), *Beginnings: The social and affective development of Black children* (pp. 215–230). Hillsdale, NJ: Erlbaum.

Spencer, M. B. (1986). Risk and resilience: How Black children cope with stress. *Social Science, 71*(1), 22–26.

Spencer, M. B. (1990). Parental values transmission: Implications for the development of African-American children. In J. B. Stewart, & H. Cheathan (Eds.), *Interdisciplinary perspectives on Black families* (pp. 111–130). Atlanta, GA: Transactions.

Spencer, M. B. (1995). Old issues and new theorizing about African American youth: A phenomenological variant of ecological systems theory. In R. L. Taylor (Ed.), *Black youth: Perspectives on their status in the United States* (pp. 37–69). Westport, CT: Praeger.

Spencer, M. B. (2001). Identity, achievement orientation and race: "Lessons learned" about the normative developmental experiences of African American males. In W. H. Watkins, J. H. Lewis, & V. Chou (Eds.), *Race and education: The roles of history and society in educating African American students* (pp. 100–127). Needham Heights, MA: Allyn & Bacon.

Spencer, M. B. (2005). Crafting identities and accessing opportunities post-Brown. *American Psychologist, 60*(8), 821–830.

Spencer, M. B. (2006). Phenomenology and ecological systems theory: Development of diverse groups. In R. M. Lerner, & W. Damon (Eds.), *Handbook of child psychology*, vol. 1: *Theoretical models of human development, 6th ed.* (pp. 829–893). New York: Wiley.

Spencer, M. B. (2008a). Lessons learned and opportunities ignored post-Brown v. Board of Education: Youth development and the myth of a colorblind society. *Educational Researcher, 37*(5), 253–266.

Spencer, M. B. (2008b). Phenomenology and ecological systems theory: Development of diverse groups. In W. Damon and R. Lerner (Eds.), *Child and adolescent development: An advanced course* (pp. 696–735). New York: Wiley.

Spencer, M. B. (2011). American identity: Impact of youths' differential experiences in society on their attachment to American ideals. *Applied Developmental Science, 15*(2), 61–69.

Spencer, M. B., Brookins, G. K., & Allen, W. R. (Eds.) (1985). *Beginnings: Social and affective development of Black children*. Hillsdale, NJ: Erlbaum.

Spencer, M. B., Cunningham, M., & Swanson, D. P. (1995). Identity as coping: Adolescent African American males' adaptive responses to high risk environments. In H. W. Harris, H. C. Blue, & E. H. Griffith (Eds.), *Racial and ethnic identity* (pp. 31–52). New York: Routledge.

Spencer, M. B., & Dornbusch, S. (1990). Challenges in studying minority youth. In S. Feldman & G. Elliot (Eds.), *At the threshold: The developing adolescent* (pp. 123–146). Cambridge, MA: Harvard University Press.

Spencer, M. B., Dupree, D., & Hartmann, T. (1997). A phenomenological variant of ecological systems theory (PVEST): A self-organization perspective in context. *Development and Psychopathology, 9*, 817–833.

Spencer, M. B., Dupree, D., Swanson, D. P., & Cunningham, M. (1996). Parental monitoring and adolescents' sense of responsibility for their own learning: An examination of sex differences. *Journal of Negro Education, 65*(1), 30–43.

Spencer, M. B., Dupree, D., Tinsley, B., McGee, E. O., Hall, J., Fegley, S. G. et al. (2011). Resistance and resiliency in a color-conscious society: Implications for learning and teaching. In K. R. Harris, S. Graham, & T. Urdan (Eds.), C. B. McCormick, G. M. Sinatra, & J. Sweller (Assc. Eds.), *APA educational psychology handbook: Vol. 1. Theories, constructs, and critical issues* (pp. 461–494). Washington, DC: American Psychological Association.

Spencer, M. B., Harpalani, V., Cassidy, E., Jacobs, C., Donde, S., Goss, T. N. et al. (2006). Understanding vulnerability and resilience from a normative development perspective: Implications for racially and ethnically diverse youth. In D. Chicchetti & E. Cohen (Eds.), *Handbook of developmental psychopathology*, Vol. 1 (pp. 627–672). Hoboken, NJ: Wiley.

Spencer, M. B., & Horowitz, F. D. (1973). Racial attitudes and color concept-attitude modification in Black and Caucasian preschool children. *Developmental Psychology, 9*, 246–254.

Spencer, M. B., & Markstrom-Adams, C. (1990). Identity processes among racial and ethnic minority children in America. *Child Development, 61*(2), 290–310.

Spencer, M. B., & Swanson, D. P. (2000). Promoting positive outcomes for youth: Resourceful families and communities. In S. Danziger & J. Waldfogel (Eds.), *Securing the future* (pp. 182–204). New York: The Russell Sage Foundation Press.

White, R. W. (1959). Motivation reconsidered: The concept of competence. *Psychological Review, 66*, 297–333.

White, R. W. (1960). Competence and the psychosexual stages of development. In M. R. Jones (Ed.), *Nebraska symposium on motivation* (pp. 97–140). Lincoln: University of Nebraska Press.

Williams, J. E. (1964). Connotations of color names among Negroes and Caucasians. *Perceptual and Motor Skills, 18*, 721–731.

Williams, J. E. (1966). Connotations of racial concepts and color names. *Journal of Personality and Social Psychology, 3*, 531–540.

Williams, J. E., & Roberson, J. K. (1967). A method for assessing racial attitudes in preschool children. *Educational and Psychological Measurement, 27*, 671–689.

44

The Importance of Serendipity

LAURENCE STEINBERG

Two psychopathic killers persuaded me to abandon my dreams to someday become a comedy writer and study psychology instead.

I did not enter college in 1970 intending to become either a psychologist or a professor. I majored in English when I began my freshman year at Johns Hopkins, hoping to study creative writing. (Although Hopkins is well known for its medical school, it also has one of the best undergraduate writing programs in the country.) I became interested in psychology during the second semester of my freshman year, because of an introductory course in personality theory taught by Bob Hogan. Our final assignment in the course was to analyze Dick and Perry, the sadistic murderers in Truman Capote's book, *In Cold Blood*, and Hogan, in his comments on my paper, was very complimentary about my psychoanalytic skills. Hogan was an exceptionally charismatic and popular instructor, who bore a striking resemblance to one of the Smothers Brothers, in both physical appearance and comedic skill. I cannot recall whether it was his manner, the course content, his ten written words of encouragement at the bottom of my paper, or the combination of all three that hooked me, but by the end of the semester I was ready to abandon the study of Victorian literature and Romantic poetry. One of my best friends from high school eventually became a writer on *Seinfeld*, so I experienced my dream career vicariously.

Hogan's class was one of the few high points in an otherwise unhappy year at Hopkins. I hated the large lecture classes, and I especially hated the fact that Hopkins had only just gone co-ed that year, and women were in short supply. Seeking to remedy both of these deficiencies, I transferred to Vassar after two semesters of anonymity and celibacy. This was an enormously important turning point in my life, for Vassar was where I was introduced to academics as a profession. Hopkins afforded few opportunities for undergrads to actually get to know any professors. (What a shame, in retrospect, considering that my first psychology professor was Mary Ainsworth.) In much the same as I was drawn to psychology because of my fascination with Bob Hogan as a person, I was drawn to a career in academics because of the personal relationships I formed with several of my professors at Vassar, most importantly, Anne Constantinople, who was my advisor, and Vicki Raeburn, for whom I worked as a research assistant. I had never known college professors before—growing up, none of my friends' parents nor any of my parents' friends were professors—and I envied the life they led, or at least the life I thought they led. To be sure, much of what I imagined the professorial life to be was my own romanticized version of how professors lived. But as a naive and impressionable 20-year-old, I identified intensely with what I imagined the academic life to be. I started smoking a pipe and wearing a lot of tweed.

My interest in a career in academic psychology conflicted with my upbringing, which was decidedly polyester, and not tweedy. Which is why, shortly after arriving at Vassar, I decided to go pre-med. I can only explain this by saying that I was raised to believe that there were only two professions that were appropriate for nice Jewish boys, and I had no interest in becoming a lawyer. The truth of the matter was that I had no real interest in becoming a doctor, either. Still, I completed the pre-med curriculum while majoring in psychology, and at the beginning of my senior year, I applied to about a dozen medical schools. I started going on interviews for admission, which I came to dread. My ambivalence about a career in medicine must have been apparent to the people interviewing me, because, despite a strong academic record and respectable test scores, I was repeatedly rejected. Maybe the interview committees could tell from the greenish hue my face would take on during the obligatory tour of the teaching hospital that the idea of coming into contact with actual physical maladies, much less cadavers, made me nauseated. The rejection letters rolled in, and I began to worry about my future, or the lack of one. I used the letters to wallpaper my apartment's bathroom.

At the time I was sharing an apartment with three other classmates, one of whom was Jay Belsky, who would go on to become one of the leading psychologists in the study of infant development. Jay suggested that I consider applying to graduate school in psychology as a fall-back position, since I majored in it, enjoyed it, and seemed to have some talent for it. And, of course, there was my interest in living the life of a professor. I applied to just two programs: one at Cornell, and one at Florida. The logic behind these choices was odd, to say the least. I applied to Cornell because Jay was applying there, and he told me that it was a good program. I applied to Florida because one of my other apartment-mates was the son of a professor who taught there, which was reason enough for me. I was admitted to both schools and selected Cornell because I had no desire to live in Florida. Late that spring I was also admitted, finally, to medical school, but, against my relatives' advice—or perhaps in spite of it—turned down the offer and went off to graduate school in Human Development and Family Studies. Had I been accepted into med school earlier in the year, I would be practicing medicine today.

Graduate School

Cornell in the mid-1970s was an exciting place to be for those interested in human development. Urie Bronfenbrenner—who would later become a close friend and mentor, but only after I left Cornell—was just then developing the "ecological perspective," a movement, of sorts, that would dramatically change the field of developmental psychology over the next decade. All of us, even those of us who did not work with Urie, were influenced by his point of view, whether we knew it or not.

When I arrived at Cornell in the fall of 1974 I knew little about what I wanted to study other than the fact that I was still interested in personality, an interest left over from my Dick and Perry days. The closest match on the faculty was John Hill, the department chair. I was assigned to John as his advisee, and began attending his research meetings. It was this bit of serendipity that got me involved in the study of adolescence. It also got me my first job, as I'll explain.

I may be one of the first developmental scientists who was specifically trained in adolescence. When I got to Cornell, John was one of the only scholars in the field of developmental psychology who specialized in the age period. It is hard to believe, given the popularity of research on adolescence today, but in 1974, there was virtually no scientific literature on adolescent development. Most of what was written was based on clinical anecdote, and any serious scholar of development looked upon the study of adolescence as an empirical wasteland, which it more or less was. John had been asked by the National Institute of Education to develop a research framework for studying adolescence, and he had finished a draft of this the summer before I got to Cornell. It was one of the first comprehensive models for the study of adolescence, and still to this day, it influences the way I teach adolescent development, both in the classroom and in my textbook on the topic (Steinberg, 2014).

John's own research at the time was on the development of social cognition in adolescence. I could not think of anything less interesting. I wanted to study personality development, and although I didn't tell John, I was flirting with the idea of becoming a family therapist and combining an academic career with a clinical practice. Family therapy was all the rage at this time. Cornell did not have a clinical program, though, and there was no way for me to gain any expertise in clinical psychology through my graduate program. I contacted Dan Matusiewicz, a family therapist at a local clinic who had studied with Sal Minuchin, the structural family therapy guru, explained my situation, and somehow convinced Dan to take me on as an apprentice. My first case was a married couple that was having sexual problems. During our first session, the husband said to me, "She doesn't like it when I kiss her cupcakes." I could feel myself about to start laughing. I decided I wasn't cut out to be a therapist. People were just too weird. As my friend Mavis Hetherington once said about herself when asked why she never became a clinician, I am incapable of unconditional positive regard.

Although I was not interested in John's research on person perception, I remained in his research group because he was a great advisor. To John's credit, he permitted me to branch off on my own and pursue my interest in family systems theory. I began to think about taking some of the procedures used to study family interaction in the therapeutic context and using them to study "normal" families. Given John's interest in adolescence, it made sense for me to focus my interest in family dynamics on this age period.

Serendipity struck again during my second semester of school. One afternoon, during my second semester of graduate school, I was thumbing through journals and came across a study by Ted Jacob, comparing patterns of interaction in families with 11- versus 16-year-olds from working- and middle-class households. As I read and reread the article, I began to envision a similar study that bridged this work with John's conceptual framework. I thought it would be interesting to see if the changes in family interaction that took place at this time were linked somehow to changes in the child. Rather than look at interaction patterns as a function of age, though, like Jacob did, I decided to look at them as a function of the adolescent's biological, cognitive, and social maturation. That night, I began designing a study to look at changes in family interaction as children entered puberty, developed formal operations, and moved from elementary to secondary school, a study that eventually became my dissertation. It is the little random events, like discovering Jacob's study at a time I was ready to assimilate it, that make individual careers what they are.

I started the study during my second year of graduate school, although it took some persuading on my part to do so. John was skeptical of a second-semester graduate student's plan to start his dissertation research this early in grad school. I made a deal with him: I would analyze the first wave of cross-sectional data for my predissertation project. If the results looked promising, I would conduct more data collection and analyze the longitudinal data for my dissertation. After recruiting a team of Cornell undergraduates to help—we were doing home observations and microcoding audiotapes of mother–father–son interaction—I started collecting data in the fall of 1975. The cross-sectional analyses proved interesting (Steinberg & Hill, 1978), and I conducted observations of the same families the next spring and again, the following fall.

I found that family interaction patterns were closely linked not to the child's chronological age, school grade, or cognitive maturation, but to his pubertal status (Steinberg, 1981). Perhaps the most important finding was that conflict between adolescents and their parents peaked during the apex of pubertal development. Up until this point, almost all that had been written about puberty and adolescent development examined the effects of early or late maturation. My dissertation demonstrated that puberty played an important role in the adolescent's social relationships even when it occurred on time. Understanding the links between biology and behavior in adolescence was to become a major focus of my career, drawing me into the study of hormone-behavior relationships, sociobiology, and, eventually, developmental neuroscience.

UC Irvine and the Adolescent Work Project

Although I finished my doctorate in 3 years—in part because John was leaving Cornell in 1977 to go to Boys Town, and I did not want to have to get a new advisor—I had no job offer in hand as late as May of my last year. I had traveled to Washington to interview for a position as a researcher at a nonprofit organization with a government contract to study day care centers, which was not what I wanted to do, and I returned to Ithaca late one night after a long drive home during which I became depressed over the fact that I wasn't going to get to be a professor after all. On my desk in the communal office, shared by graduate teaching assistants, was a message for me to call someone from the Program in Social Ecology at the University of California, Irvine. I had never heard of Irvine, much less the field of "social ecology." They were looking at the last minute for someone who could teach developmental psychology the next fall, and the head of their search committee had placed calls to the department chairs of three or four well-known graduate programs. Because John was Cornell's department chair at the time, he got the search committee's call, and he suggested that they contact me. I called the search committee chair back the next day and was interviewed over the phone by him and by the head of Social Ecology, Ellen Greenberger, who offered me the job. After I accepted the offer, I looked on a map to see where Irvine was. I defended my dissertation in August, 1977 and drove that next week across the country to take a one-year replacement faculty position. Fortunately,

the position turned into a tenure-track job the following year, and I interviewed for, and got, the job.

I would return to the study of family relations later in my career, but by the time I left Cornell, in 1977, I was ready for a change. My years at UC Irvine were dominated by my involvement in a large-scale research project that Ellen Greenberger and I launched, on the impact of employment on adolescent development and adjustment (Greenberger & Steinberg, 1986). This study, which was stimulated by a debate Ellen and I had over whether her 16-year-old daughter should be permitted to take an after-school job (I was for it, but Ellen disagreed), led to the surprising conclusion that working a lot during the school year had deleterious consequences for adolescents' development. This project was an important component of my development as a scientist, for through my collaboration with Ellen, who was a very experienced researcher, I learned how to write grant proposals, manage a large-scale field study, develop and carry out policy-relevant research, and, most importantly, have an insane amount of fun while doing good work. Several years ago, at an event honoring Ellen's retirement from full-time teaching, I told stories describing how she and I would work together in her living room, interrupting our writing to draft fake papers poking fun at the silly things psychologists study, and to make sure we watched our favorite show, *The Newlywed Game*, which never failed to throw us into hysteria (albeit after a couple of martinis). One afternoon, instead of doing what we had planned, we worked on a new self-report measure to assess individuals' tendency to complain, which we called the "K scale," because we were convinced that the reason peoples' reports of stress were correlated with their reports of mental health symptoms was simply that they were kvetches who whined about everything.

The Madison Study of Families

In 1982, I was tenured and promoted to Associate Professor at UC Irvine—news I received in the form of a telegram I received when my wife, Wendy, and I were honeymooning in Paris. The next year, I was offered a job at the University of Wisconsin–Madison, which offered me a 50% raise and a promotion to Full Professor. I was ambivalent about leaving my job at Irvine, but we decided that we wanted to try living outside of California.

Our years in Madison were good ones. Our son, Ben, was born there in 1984, and life was calm and simple. I was able to work at home often, and even when I had to go in to the office, my "commute" was a 10-minute bike ride. I was able to be much more involved in caring for Ben than would have been the case had we been living in Southern California and fighting the constant freeway traffic.

Ellen and I continued to write up pieces of the adolescent work study. We decided to write *When Teenagers Work* (Greenberger & Steinberg, 1986), in which we were able to take the time and space we needed to really flesh out our ideas about adolescent employment in detail. By now I had enjoyed enough of a break from family research to revisit some of the issues I had explored in my dissertation. In 1984, I started a new study of family relationships at adolescence that extended my earlier work in several ways. In addition to studying how family relationships changed during adolescence, I was also interested in understanding how different approaches to parenting affected adolescents' psychosocial development.

At the time I began working on the research design, I took on Susan Silverberg (now Susan Koerner) as a graduate advisee. I had supervised a couple of graduate students while at Irvine, but Sue was really the first doctoral student I worked with who shared my specific interests in family relations during adolescence. Sue was especially interested in looking at the transition into adolescence from the parents' point of view, which had not been done before. Although I had planned all along on collecting data from parents, the questions I intended to ask concerned child-rearing. Sue thought we were missing an important opportunity to learn about parents' psychological development and how this was affected during the transition. And, indeed, what we learned from Sue's portion of the study turned out to be far more interesting than what we learned from the part that I had designed.

My collaboration with Sue was the first in what would become a series of fabulous working relationships with graduate students, at Wisconsin and, later, at Temple. I realized throughout the course of these collaborations how much I had learned from my relationship with John about the importance of the mentor–student relationship. John knew when to be supportive and when to be critical. (I can still recall, in its entirety, his written reaction to first draft of my dissertation proposal: "This is not good enough for me to comment on.") He was able to balance my dependence on him as an advisor with my growing needs for autonomy as an independent investigator. I've tried to model John in the way in which I supervise my students. Working with graduate students has been, and probably will always be, my favorite part of the job.

The Madison study revitalized my interest in studying adolescent family relationships. My students and I were enormously productive, and we published numerous articles on the impact of parents on adolescent development (Steinberg, Elmen, & Mounts, 1989), on the development of autonomy (Steinberg & Silverberg, 1986), on parents' mental health during the adolescent transition (Silverberg & Steinberg, 1990), and, of course, on the impact of puberty on family relationships (Steinberg, 1987).

I've noted that serendipity has played a major role in my development as a researcher, and something that happened at this point in my career is a perfect illustration. I got a call one day from John asking me to pinch-hit for him as a speaker on a panel examining similarities and differences between the social relations of humans and other primates. Jane Goodall, the eminent primatologist, was going to be the featured speaker, and two other scholars

(one of whom was to have been John) were asked to contribute to the symposium. In John's place, I was supposed to give a talk on parent–adolescent relationships in humans and nonhuman primates. Not knowing the first thing about primate development, I made an appointment with Chris Coe, the director of the Wisconsin Primate Center (where Harry Harlow had done his famous studies of infant monkeys and surrogate mothers), who was able to point me to the relevant literature. I steeped myself in this work for the next week, and came away with enough of an understanding of family relations among monkeys and apes to at the very least avoid embarrassing myself in front of Goodall. I started to think about parent–adolescent relationships in an evolutionary perspective.

Around this same time, I was visiting my old Vassar apartment-mate, Jay Belsky, at Penn State, where he was on the faculty. One afternoon, while driving around the Pennsylvania countryside, we started discussing my findings on puberty and parent–child conflict. Jay asked how I was so sure that it was puberty that was causing the increase in conflict, rather than the reverse; perhaps, he suggested, conflict between parents and adolescents stimulated pubertal maturation. My initial reaction was to laugh at what I believed to be an absurd proposition, but I said that it was easy enough to look at with our data, since we had assessed both puberty and parent–child conflict among all of our Madison families twice over a 1-year period. I ran the analyses as soon as I got home.

Sure enough, the analyses suggested that pubertal maturation seemed to be stimulated by conflict and distance in the parent–child relationship, at least among girls. I published an article showing that preadolescent girls who fought with their parents were more likely to go through menarche earlier than girls whose family relationships were not as conflicted, and that the conflict preceded pubertal development (Steinberg, 1988). Most other researchers were highly skeptical of the finding, but this paper drew enough attention to the issue of social influences on pubertal maturation in humans to stimulate other researchers to examine their data in similar ways. The finding has now been replicated at least a dozen times, including an analysis that Jay and I published with our collaborators from the NICHD Study of Early Child Care and Youth Development (Belsky et al., 2007).

Intrigued by the finding, I made another appointment with the Wisconsin Primate Center director to ask if what we had found in our study made sense in terms of what we knew about puberty among primates. He informed me that the timing of pubertal maturation in many species of monkeys and apes was linked to the quality of the juvenile's family relationships, in exactly the same way as we had found among humans. Closeness between parents and offspring inhibited pubertal maturation, whereas distance accelerated it. I developed an evolutionary model of adolescent family relationships to try to explain these findings, in which I suggested that parent–adolescent conflict was an adaptive mechanism that had evolved to avoid inbreeding within family groups (Steinberg, 1989). I sent an early draft of the paper to John, who called late one night to tell me how proud he was of the cross-disciplinary work I was doing, which meant the world to me. Later, Jay, Pat Draper, and I used this finding as a jumping-off point for the development of a sociobiologically informed theory of socialization (Belsky, Steinberg, & Draper, 1991) and of adolescent psychopathology (Steinberg & Belsky, 1996). Still today, I remain interested in evolutionary approaches to the study of adolescence and have written about adolescent brain development in evolutionary perspective (Steinberg, 2008).

Most of my work during my tenure at Madison focused on variations in parenting practices and their impact on adolescent development and adjustment. Since graduate school, I had maintained a strong interest in the work of Berkeley psychologist Diana Baumrind, and I was especially interested in looking at her notions about "authoritative" parenting in samples of families with adolescents. I was eager to see if the psychological benefits Baumrind had found to be associated during childhood with parenting that was warm yet firm were present among teenagers as well. In a series of papers, we showed that this was indeed the case (Steinberg et al., 1989).

As I began to publish more in the area of adolescent–family relationships, and, more specifically, on effective parenting during the adolescent years, I began to receive phone calls from journalists interested in writing about family life with teenagers. One day, on a lark, I dropped into the local bookstore to see what had been written on the subject for parents of teenagers. I was shocked to discover that there was very little on the shelves, and that what was there was usually incorrect hyperbole. I had not written for popular audiences before, but I felt confident that I could produce a useful book for parents that was grounded in the science of adolescent development. (OK, it wasn't *Seinfeld*, but at least it was writing for a popular audience.) I called Ann Levine, an acquaintance who was an accomplished social science writer, and asked if she was interested in working together on an advice book for parents of adolescents. Our collaboration resulted in *You and Your Adolescent*, which has now been revised several times (Steinberg, 2011).

Beyond the Classroom

In 1987, serendipity struck again. Out of the blue I received a call from Fred Newmann, a colleague at Wisconsin's School of Education, who invited me to join a team of researchers studying high-school reform, at a newly formed research center established at Wisconsin by the federal government. Fred had experts at the Center who specialized in secondary education, but there was no one at the Center with special expertise in the study of adolescent development. Fred invited me to play this role and join the Center's team. In return for my time and input, I would have access to a portion of the Center's budget,

which I could use to support my work on adolescent family relationships. The only catch was that the work had to have relevance for the study of high-school reform.

One of the fabulous things about being on the faculty of a top-notch university like Wisconsin is the access one has to the best scholars in their respective fields. Brad Brown, who was in the department of Educational Psychology, is one of the world's leading experts in the study of peer relationships in adolescence. I called Brad and asked if he would be interested in collaborating on a new project, one designed to look at the joint influences of parents and peers on school achievement. Brad was enthusiastic, and we agreed to spend the next few months reading and discussing the relevant literature. It looked to us as if this was an area that was ripe for empirical attention, and we set about designing a study. I would take primary responsibility for the family component, and Brad would lead up the portion of the study on peers.

I was in my office one day when one of my graduate students came in with an unpublished paper by a sociologist at Stanford named Sanford Dornbusch, who had been studying the impact of parents on adolescent achievement. From the looks of the paper, it appeared as if he had already done exactly what I had hoped to do in the new study with Brad. My first reaction was that it was more or less pointless to do what someone had already done, and I called Brad with the bad news that we had been scooped. Later that day, though, I decided to call this Dornbusch fellow and ask a few detailed questions about what he had studied. I introduced myself over the phone and explained what Brad and I were interested in doing.

Sandy could not have been happier. He suggested that we pool our efforts and our funding and work together. I hung up the phone and called Brad, who agreed that it was worth looking into. The next day I flew out to California to meet with Sandy in person.

I don't think I've ever met a more generous colleague than Sandy—or one who talked faster. We sat in his office and discussed what a collaboration might look like. By the end of the day, we had drafted a written understanding of the proposed collaboration and planned a series of meetings to bring the Stanford and Wisconsin research teams together. Over the next year, Sandy, Brad, and I, along with our research staffs, met several times and designed an enormous study—one that ultimately would involve 3 years of data collection and more than 20,000 adolescents in Wisconsin and Northern California.

New Directions at Temple

In 1988, we moved from Madison to Philadelphia, where I joined the Psychology Department at Temple University. Although I had been exceptionally happy at Wisconsin, as a family we had grown tired of small-town Midwestern living, not to mention the rough Wisconsin winters. Wendy wanted to pursue graduate study in creative writing, and whereas Temple had a graduate program in writing, Wisconsin did not. By this time, Brad, Sandy, and I had started data collection, and the research teams were up and running. We had hired postdoctoral fellows at both Stanford and Wisconsin to manage the day-to-day workings of the project, and this made it possible (if not ideal) for me to move to Philadelphia and co-direct the project from a distance.

Because I was not intimately involved in the actual data collection for this study, I had time during my first years at Temple to take on another writing project. Having successfully co-authored *You and Your Adolescent*, I felt emboldened enough to try writing another book for the general public. My intent was to write a book on the parent–adolescent relationship based on the Madison study, but as I sifted through the questionnaire data we had collected as well as transcripts of the hundreds of interviews we had conducted with teenagers and their parents, I drew a blank, literally. I stared at an empty computer screen for the better part of a year. It was the first extended writing block that I had ever experienced.

Part of my block stemmed from some awful news I had received. John Hill had become very ill, and late in 1988, he died. I felt as if I had lost a father, an older brother, and a best friend, all folded into one person. Every time I tried to read or write anything about adolescence, I thought of John. I began to feel the sort of irrational guilt that one feels when a parent dies. Had he known how much I was influenced by him? Had he known how important a role he had played in my development? It was an eerie feeling, and one that was far more powerful than I could ever have expected.

Eventually, I came out of my funk. It occurred to me that what was most interesting about the study we had done in Madison was the parents' perspective on the transition of the family into adolescence. Perhaps this realization had something to do with my own development as a father. Although Ben was still a young child, I could already feel how profoundly his own development was affecting the way that Wendy and I saw ourselves. (Watching Ben develop as a teenager would later be a constant source of stimulation for my research.) I returned to the data and the interviews with an eye toward using them to tell the story of adolescence from the parents' point of view. Building on the ideas that Sue Silverberg and I had developed when we first designed the project, I began to sketch out an outline for a book that would examine the intersection of adolescence and midlife. After struggling for many months to find the right voice for the book, I turned to my wife for help. This resulted in *Crossing Paths* (Steinberg, 1994), an exploration of the ways in which the child's entry into adolescence affects the mental health, social relationships, and self-conceptions of mothers and fathers as they negotiated their own transition into midlife.

Once the manuscript for *Crossing Paths* was handed over to the publisher, I turned my attention to the tidal wave of data that was coming in from our California and Wisconsin samples. I became very interested in exploring ethnic differences in parenting and its relation to adolescent adjustment. Our Madison study, which produced numerous papers on the benefits of authoritative parenting,

had been almost exclusively White. With the demography of American adolescence changing as rapidly as it was, many social scientists began asking whether the "truths" about parenting derived from studies of White adolescents generalized to other populations as well. The massive data set we had collected allowed us to look at this in detail. I was asked to give an invited address at the 1990 meetings of the American Psychological Association, and I decided to focus on ethnic differences in family socialization.

This work proved to be extremely interesting. Although there were important exceptions to the rule, our findings suggested that authoritative parenting was beneficial for all teenagers, regardless of their race, family structure, or socioeconomic status (Steinberg et al., 1991). The most important exception to this pattern concerned academic achievement, though, where we found that authoritative parenting did not seem to have the same advantages for Black or Asian youngsters as it did for Whites or Hispanics. Subsequent analyses of the data indicated that this was probably the case because of different levels of peer group support for achievement in different ethnic groups, a finding that served to remind me that one could not study parenting without taking other aspects of adolescents' lives into account (Steinberg, Dornbusch, & Brown, 1992). Bronfenbrenner's ecological perspective, to which I had been exposed in my early days of graduate school, proved invaluable in helping me to make sense out of our findings.

Drawing heavily on Urie's perspective, and consulting with him frequently as I looked at our data, I began to look at "parenting in context." I asked Nancy Darling, a former student of Urie's, to come to Temple to work as my postdoctoral fellow, to help analyze the large data set. We wrote several empirical papers based on these data (e.g., Lamborn, Mounts, Steinberg, & Dornbusch, 1991; Steinberg, Lamborn, Darling, Mounts, & Dornbusch, 1994; Steinberg, Lamborn, Dornbusch, & Darling, 1992) as well as a long conceptual piece on socialization in the family (Darling & Steinberg, 1993). In 1993, I had a chance to pay tribute to Urie, as a speaker and contributor to a festschrift honoring his career, and I tried pulling together a lot of what I had been thinking about concerning families, peer groups, neighborhoods, and ethnic differences in adolescent development. During 1995, with the assistance of Sandy and Brad, I fleshed out these thoughts in *Beyond the Classroom* (Steinberg, 1996).

The MacArthur Projects

I experienced another writing block after finishing *Beyond the Classroom*, and couldn't figure out what I wanted to do next. Once again, a phone call from out of the blue provided an answer. I heard from, John Monahan, a former colleague of mine from my early days at UC Irvine, who had become a law professor at Virginia. We hadn't spoken in years. John was directing a research network for the MacArthur Foundation, on mental health and the law. He called to ask if I was interested in writing a white paper for his network, on adolescent judgment and decision-making, focusing on the implications of this research for the treatment of adolescents under the law. I wasn't particularly interested in the legal issues, but I wasn't working on anything else at the time, so I agreed to do the paper and asked Beth Cauffman, one of my graduate students at the time, to help (Steinberg & Cauffman, 1996). I went to one of John's network meetings and discussed some of these ideas with the group, which included Tom Grisso and Ed Mulvey, with whom I would end up working closely. Soon, and purely coincidentally, I was invited to join one of the foundation's other research networks, on psychopathology and development, headed by David Kupfer. And later that year, I got a call from MacArthur asking if I would head up a new research network for the foundation, on adolescent development and juvenile justice. I jumped at the opportunity.

Directing the MacArthur Foundation Research Network on Adolescent Development and Juvenile Justice was one of the high points of my career. We assembled an outstanding group of social scientists, legal scholars, and legal practitioners, and launched several large-scale studies at the intersection of developmental science and legal policy, on adolescents' competence to stand trial (Grisso et al., 2003), on the factors that lead juvenile offenders to desist from crime (Mulvey et al., 2010), and on age differences in capacities that are relevant to judgments of criminal responsibility, such as impulsivity, risk assessment, and susceptibility to peer influence (Steinberg, Cauffman, Woolard, Graham, & Banich, 2009). The Network's research and theorizing, I'm proud to say, has had a considerable and wide-reaching impact on legal policy both in the United States and abroad. I helped draft the amicus briefs submitted by the American Psychological Association in several key Supreme Court cases, and our work influenced the Court's opinions in cases that abolished the juvenile death penalty and placed limits on sentencing juveniles to life without the possibility of parole. In fact, in Justice Kennedy's majority opinion in the juvenile death penalty case, an article I co-authored with Elizabeth Scott, a law professor at Columbia and member of our network, was cited and quoted several times (Steinberg & Scott, 2003).

Partly as a result of my involvement in the MacArthur networks on mental health and the law, psychopathology, and juvenile justice, I became interested in adolescent brain development. Several other members of the psychopathology network and I co-authored a chapter for a handbook on developmental psychopathology, in which we examined the ways in which neurobiological and contextual factors interact to make adolescence an especially vulnerable period for the onset of various forms of psychopathology (Steinberg et al., 2006). Around this time, popular interest in adolescent brain development was taking off, and I was increasingly being asked by journalists and juvenile justice practitioners about the implications of new research on the adolescent brain for legal policy. I quickly realized that I was going to have to acquire more than a cursory familiarity with developmental neuroscience. Fortunately, through my various MacArthur collaborations, I had

developed close friendships with some of the best developmental neuroscientists in the country, including Marie Banich, Ron Dahl, Chuck Nelson, and Danny Pine, and, drawing on their recommendations, I began reading the burgeoning literature on the topic. Thanks to a sabbatical leave from Temple, I was able to spend the better part of a year steeping myself in adolescent neuroscience.

My modest, but developing, understanding of adolescent brain science proved to be especially important as my work on adolescent psychopathology came to intersect with my work in the area of juvenile justice, mainly around the issue of adolescent risk-taking. By the end of my sabbatical, I had come to see adolescent risk-taking as the result of the different developmental timetables of the maturation of brain systems implicated in sensation-seeking and reward-seeking, on the one hand, and those important for the development of self-regulation, on the other (Steinberg, 2010). Middle adolescence turns out to be a time of heightened sensation-seeking and sensitivity to reward but still immature self-regulation—a combination that often produces risky decision-making. This framework has guided several analyses of the MacArthur juvenile justice network's study of capacities relevant to criminal responsibility. We showed that scores on measures of sensation-seeking and reward sensitivity follow an inverted U-shaped function, peaking around age 15 or so, whereas measures of self-regulation and foresight show a gradual increase from preadolescence through the mid-20s (Cauffman et al., 2010; Steinberg et al., 2008; Steinberg et al., 2009). With the support of a prize I won from the Jacobs Foundation in 2009, my colleagues and I are now in the field, replicating this research project in 11 other countries, in Europe, Asia, Africa, and South America. So far, it looks like we are seeing the same patterns in these countries as we did in the United States.

Adolescent Brain Development and Behavior

During the past several years, in collaboration with my Temple colleague Jason Chein, I began a series of studies of the neural underpinnings of adolescent risk-taking in the presence of peers. In 2005, my former student Margo Gardner and I had published a paper showing that adolescents, but not adults, took more risks during a video driving game when they were being observed by the peers than when alone (Gardner & Steinberg, 2005). Jason, who is a cognitive neuroscientist, and I began discussing why this might be. We replicated the study that Margo and I had done, this time with brain imaging, and found that when adolescents playing the driving game were being observed by their friends, they showed stronger activation of reward circuitry in the brain, and that this heightened activation was correlated with risky decision-making (Chein, Albert, O'Brien, Uckert, & Steinberg, 2011). As in the previous study, we found no such effect among adults. My colleagues and I are now beginning several new studies to further understand why this is, some of which are being conducted under the auspices of yet another MacArthur Foundation research network—on Law and Neuroscience.

When I teach graduate seminars, I often ask students to look at an individual scholar's career and try to make sense of it. I'm not sure what I would say about my own. I suppose the three most consistent themes are that adolescent development is driven in large part by biology, that it is essential to understand the broader context in which adolescent development takes place, and that it is possible to do rigorous science on social problems in a way that informs policy and practice. As I've looked back by writing this essay, though, what is most striking to me is how much of my career was shaped by events that could not have been predicted. Woody Allen had it absolutely right when he said that "Eighty percent of success is just showing up." It's a hard thing to explain to someone just starting out, but among all of the factors that shape a career, nothing is probably as important as being in the right place at the right time, and being able to take advantage of opportunities when they are handed to you.

References

Belsky, J., Steinberg, L., & Draper, P. (1991). Childhood experience, interpersonal development, and reproductive strategy: An evolutionary theory of socialization. *Child Development, 62*, 647–670.

Belsky, J., Steinberg, L., Houts, R., Friedman, S., DeHart, G., Cauffman, E. et al. (2007). Family rearing antecedents of pubertal timing. *Child Development, 78*, 1302–1321.

Cauffman, E., Shulman, E., Steinberg, L., Claus, E., Banich, M., Woolard, J. et al. (2010). Age differences in affective decision making as indexed by performance on the Iowa Gambling Task. *Developmental Psychology, 46*, 193–207.

Chein, J., Albert, D., O'Brien, L., Uckert, K., & Steinberg, L. (2011). Peers increase adolescent risk taking by enhancing activity in the brain's reward circuitry. *Developmental Science, 14*, F1–F10.

Darling, N., & Steinberg, L. (1993). Parenting style as context: An integrative model. *Psychological Bulletin, 113*, 487–496.

Gardner, M., & Steinberg, L. (2005). Peer influence on risk-taking, risk preference, and risky decision-making in adolescence and adulthood: An experimental study. *Developmental Psychology, 41*, 625–635.

Greenberger, E., & Steinberg, L. (1986). *When teenagers work: The psychological and social costs of adolescent employment.* New York: Basic Books.

Grisso, T., Steinberg, L., Woolard, J., Cauffman, E., Scott, E., Graham, S. et al. (2003). Juveniles' competence to stand trial: A comparison of adolescents' and adults' capacities as trial defendants. *Law and Human Behavior, 27*, 333–363.

Lamborn, S., Mounts, N., Steinberg, L., & Dornbusch, S. (1991). Patterns of competence and adjustment among adolescents from authoritative, authoritarian, indulgent, and neglectful homes. *Child Development, 62*, 1049–1065.

Mulvey, E., Steinberg, L., Piquero, A., Besana, M., Fagan, J., Schubert, C. et al. (2010). Trajectories of desistance and continuity in antisocial behavior following court adjudication among serious adolescent offenders. *Development and Psychopathology, 22*, 453–475.

Silverberg, S., & Steinberg, L. (1990). Psychological well-being of parents at midlife: The impact of early adolescent children. *Developmental Psychology, 26*, 658–666.

Steinberg, L. (1981). Transformations in family relations at puberty. *Developmental Psychology, 17*, 833–840.

Steinberg, L. (1987). The impact of puberty on family relations: Effects of pubertal status and pubertal timing. *Developmental Psychology, 23*, 451–460.

Steinberg, L. (1988). Reciprocal relation between parent-child distance and pubertal maturation. *Developmental Psychology, 24*, 122–128.

Steinberg, L. (1989). Pubertal maturation and parent-adolescent distance: An evolutionary perspective. In G. Adams, R. Montemayor, & T. Gulotta (Eds.), *Advances in adolescent development*, Vol. 1 (pp. 71–97). Beverly Hills, CA: Sage.

Steinberg, L. (with W. Steinberg). (1994). *Crossing paths: How your child's adolescence triggers your own crisis.* New York: Simon & Schuster.

Steinberg, L. (in collaboration with B. Brown & S. Dornbusch) (1996). *Beyond the classroom: Why school reform has failed and what parents need to do.* New York: Simon & Schuster.

Steinberg, L. (2008). A social neuroscience perspective on adolescent risk-taking. *Developmental Review, 28*, 78–106.

Steinberg, L. (2010). A dual systems model of adolescent risk-taking. *Developmental Psychobiology, 52*, 216–224.

Steinberg, L. (2011). *You and your adolescent: The essential guide for ages 10 to 25.* New York: Simon & Schuster.

Steinberg, L. (2014). *Adolescence* (10th ed.). New York: McGraw-Hill.

Steinberg, L., Albert, D., Cauffman, E., Banich, M., Graham, S., & Woolard, J. (2008). Age differences in sensation seeking and impulsivity as indexed by behavior and self-report: Evidence for a dual systems model. *Developmental Psychology, 44*, 1764–1778.

Steinberg, L., & Belsky, J. (1996). A sociobiological perspective on psychopathology in adolescence. In D. Cicchetti & S. Toth (Eds.), *Rochester Symposium on Developmental Psychopathology*, Vol. 7, pp. 93–124.

Steinberg, L., & Cauffman, E. (1996). Maturity of judgment in adolescence: Psychosocial factors in adolescent decisionmaking. *Law and Human Behavior, 20*, 249–272.

Steinberg, L., Cauffman, E., Woolard, J., Graham, S., & Banich, M. (2009). Are adolescents less mature than adults? Minors' access to abortion, the juvenile death penalty, and the alleged APA flip-flop. *American Psychologist, 64*, 583–594.

Steinberg, L., Dahl, R., Keating, D., Kupfer, D., Masten, A., & Pine, D. (2006). Psychopathology in adolescence: Integrating affective neuroscience with the study of context. In D. Cicchetti & D. Cohen (Eds.). *Developmental psychopathology*, Vol. 2: *Developmental neuroscience* (pp. 710–741). New York: Wiley.

Steinberg, L., Dornbusch, S., & Brown, B. (1992). Ethnic differences in adolescent achievement: An ecological perspective. *American Psychologist, 47*, 723–729.

Steinberg, L., Elmen, J, & Mounts, N. (1989). Authoritative parenting, psychosocial maturity, and academic success among adolescents. *Child Development, 60*, 1424–1436.

Steinberg, L., Graham, S., O'Brien, L., Woolard, J., Cauffman, E., & Banich, M. (2009). Age differences in future orientation and delay discounting. *Child Development, 80*, 28–44.

Steinberg, L., & Hill, J. (1978). Patterns of family interaction as a function of age, the onset of puberty, and formal thinking. *Developmental Psychology, 14*, 683–684.

Steinberg, L., Lamborn, S., Darling, N., Mounts, N., & Dornbusch, S. (1994). Over-time changes in adjustment and competence among adolescents from authoritative, authoritarian, indulgent, and neglectful families. *Child Development, 65*, 754–770.

Steinberg, L., Lamborn, S., Dornbusch, S, & Darling, N. (1992). Impact of parenting practices on adolescent achievement: Authoritative parenting, school involvement, and encouragement to succeed. *Child Development, 63*, 1266–1281.

Steinberg, L., Mounts, N., Lamborn, S., & Dornbusch, S. (1991). Authoritative parenting and adolescent adjustment across various ecological niches. *Journal of Research on Adolescence, 1*, 19–36.

Steinberg, L., & Scott, E. (2003). Less guilty by reason of adolescence: Developmental immaturity, diminished responsibility, and the juvenile death penalty. *American Psychologist, 58*, 1009–1018.

Steinberg, L., & Silverberg, S. (1986). The vicissitudes of autonomy in early adolescence. *Child Development, 57*, 841–851.

45

Lives in Transition

A Hormones and Behavior Odyssey

Elizabeth J. Susman

The history of science covers thousands of years, and every moment of our conscious existence is enriched by the scientific advances made by those who preceded us. I am honored beyond words to be asked to present my autobiography as a scientist along with the many distinguished colleagues who are also contributing to this volume. But the question prior to sitting down to write became, how can an autobiography help to build a science? Autobiographies are fraught with biases. Skepticism is pervasive regarding the credibility of autobiographies. In the history of science, skepticism about science has been both encouraged and somewhat dissipated by the perspective of famous philosophers of science like Paul Feyerabend (1975, as cited by Schick) in his writings on the end of science. Feyerabend suggested that science is much closer to a myth than a scientific philosophy. He goes on to suggest that science can be viewed as a religion because it rests on certain dogmas that cannot be rationally justified. Accepting science requires a leap of faith. So please read the work that follows with the knowledge that my science of the psycho- and neurobiology of stress and development and my role in this field may be based on partial myths. But most of the history of my research requires only one major assumption dating back to the 19th-century thinking that testosterone and other hormones really do have transformative effects on a person's behavior and emotions.

Of course, such weighty philosophical considerations were not the basis of my career choice. My interest in biological issues had much more primitive beginnings. From my earliest memory, my interest in domestic and wild animals, plants (flowers and gardening), weather patterns, and my larger nonsocial environment has been enduring. My love of cats and their independent and subtle behavior has been a lifetime passion. Having had as many as 16 cats simultaneously provided limitless opportunities

for studying feline behavior. When my mother decided to get rid of some of the outdoor cats and anticipating much grief with the loss of the cats, my solution was to keep a few of the cats in a dresser drawer, preventing my mother from finding them. An older sister helped me to understand that this was not a good solution but she also was instrumental in convincing my parents to allow the cats to live out their natural lives. A highlight of my love for felines was stalking a leopard in the bush in Africa; seeing its skillful-beyond-belief hunting and eating habits and how this leopard protected her young was a highlight of my love for felines. My interest in cats exists today but my interest has moved on from understanding the nuances of feline behavior to the ever-so-subtle dimensions of adolescent behavior.

As a high-school student my interest in the life and natural sciences (biology, physics, and chemistry) was molded by one exceptional teacher who made these topics come alive. Sadly, my interest in math was suppressed by peers and others who viewed math as an area where girls were less skilled: Math was only for the boys. So what were my choices for a career post high school in this small town Eastern Canada environment: teacher, librarian, banking (the employer of choice for my two older sisters), or nursing? The latter was an obvious choice given my interest in biology and the lack of career choices for women. So off I went to nursing school in Toronto. After graduating I headed off to California with two life-long friends to pursue a job prior to beginning a program in advanced nursing at University of Western Ontario. University of California, Los Angeles (UCLA) was my first stop where my pediatric nursing experience was interesting and provided a launching point for my interest in children. Abandoning my plan to return to Canada and University of Western Ontario I left pediatrics and obtained a position at the Neuropsychiatric Institute (NPI) at UCLA. At the NPI my interest in research germinated. Working in a psychiatric, clinical research setting with severely disturbed and autistic youth from two very different theoretical perspectives was indeed challenging. The NPI child psychiatry therapy program at the time was primarily "milieu" therapy derived from psychoanalytic theory. Shortly after beginning to work at the NPI the unit became behavioral in orientation under the influence of stimulus–response theory and the operant conditioning approach of Dr. Ivar Lovaas. He was a clinical psychologist at UCLA who is considered to be one of the fathers of applied behavior analysis (ABA) therapy for autism. Lovaas was the first to provide evidence that the behavior of autistic children can be modified through teaching. Experiencing a paradigm shift from milieu to applied behavior analysis on a daily basis was both a challenge and a reward. The shift in the NPI environment was especially instrumental and enlightening as it was my first organized research experience. My life-long interest in research began to take shape along with a great appreciation for the importance of an underlying theory in guiding research.

Simultaneous with being a psychiatric nurse at NPI, I was working on a bachelor's degree in psychology at UCLA. The impetus for returning to school was motivated partially on increasing possible career options based on having a degree from the prestigious UCLA psychology department. As a psychology major I could pursue my inherent interest in biological basis of development. Some of my favorite classes were in anthropology and biology, where I developed a keen interest in the migratory patterns of Pacific salmon. Now what did this interest have to do with human development? My interest was sparked by an outstanding teaching assistant and professor whose research was on understanding the reproductive signals that influence Pacific salmon to travel hundreds of miles to return to their birthplace to spawn their young. Could this seemingly nonadaptive migratory pattern of behavior be a result of genetic influences related to hormone signaling?

In spite of my fabulous position at the NPI and my interest in being a psychology major at UCLA, I married the continuing love of my life and moved to Pennsylvania and Penn State. To make a long story short I finished a BS at Penn State and was fortunate to get to know one of the most influential child developmental psychologists of the last several decades, Aletha Huston. This fabulous mentor, friend, and adviser sparked in me a life-long interest in aggressive behavior. At the time I met Aletha, she and her colleagues were conducting an influential study on the effects of television aggression on children's aggressive and prosocial behavior. The study used stories and teacher training combined with prosocial television, *Mr. Rogers' Neighborhood,* to increase prosocial behavior in preschool settings.

My role on the project took on many graduate assistant duties, but in the process of working with Aletha she suggested I enroll in graduate school at Penn State, which I did, and I received a PhD 4 years later. The PhD program in Human Development and Family Studies (HDFS) was undergoing drastic changes at my entry into the program in the 1970s. The Department of HDFS was chaired by Paul Baltes who, along with John Nesselroade, Jack

Wohlwill, Richard Lerner, and others gave a new face to developmental psychology. Other great developmental psychologists, including Warner Schaie and Sherry Willis, came to Penn State during this era as well. These scholars articulated theories and methods for explaining developmental processes using a new perspective, the life-span developmental theory (e.g., Baltes, Reese, & Nesselroade, 1977; Wohlwill, 1973). The life-span perspective focuses on understanding changes that occur in every period of human development. These multidimensional changes in social-emotional functioning are viewed as a product of experiential history of individuals, life history, culture, and of the immediate contexts in which individuals find themselves. Innovative and novel designs and analytic techniques for assessing developmental changes grew out of this era as well. The designs extended longitudinal methodologies to include cohort sequential, cross-sequential, and other designs that considered both intra-and interindividual differences in developmental changes from birth to death. My research has been heavily influenced by a life-span way of thinking about how individuals develop over time, specifically, how adolescents navigate the biological transitions and how these changes affect both aggressive behavior and emotions. My dissertation in HDFS was on a quite different topic. It focused on the work of my mentor, Aletha Huston, on how young children use different cognitive, visual, and verbal processing strategies to learn prosocial behavior and regulate aggressive behavior and prosocial behavior from viewing television. Yes, this dissertation topic was a far distance from the biology of development and behavior.

The influence of biology on psychological and behavioral processes was not a popular topic during my graduate school era in the 1970s. I would have been an extreme outlier to consider biological influences on aggression, as biology was considered deterministic at that time. Contextual influences on behavior were the sine qua non of developmental psychology. Yes, life-span developmentalists focusing on the aging process did consider biological influences on cognition and behavior, but this interest did not filter down the age continuum to children and adolescents.

From Molecular Biology to Social Behavior

After receiving my PhD I dealt with the problems faced by the majority of dual-career families. The academic career opportunities were nonexistent at PSU and Central PA, my husband was content with his blooming academic career at Penn State, and being a stay-at-home person was not for me. So my only choice was to have a commuter marriage. As a place-holding strategy I looked for post-doc positions. At that point in the history of developmental psychology a post-doctoral fellowship was viewed as something one did if he/she could not get an academic position, rather than the current perspective of a post-doc as an opportunity to gain more in-depth knowledge and to generate publications in one's area of expertise. I interviewed for two post-doc positions and accepted a post-doc at the National Institute of Mental Health (NIMH). Accepting a post-doc position at the National Institutes of Health (NIH) was a magnificent career opportunity. My official position was in the Laboratory of Developmental Psychology (LDP), NIMH, but my research project was in the National Cancer Institute (NCI). What a scary but exciting opportunity I had laid in my lap. A collaboration on the psychological consequences of childhood cancer was just beginning between the intramural programs in NIMH and NCI. The concern of the NCI was the effects of an innovative treatment program on the psychological outcomes of children and youth who participated in an intensive chemotherapy treatment regimen. First, I should point out that my excitement about the opportunity was that it would get me back into research on biological underpinnings of social behavior. The aim of the overall study that I designed, with the help of Marian Radke-Yarrow then Chief of LDP, Phillip Pizzo (past Dean of the School of Medicine at Stanford), and Arthur Levine (then Chief of Pediatric Oncology), was to assess how children's behavior changed as a result of receiving intensive chemotherapy for recurrent cancers. The design consisted of an experimental study whereby children were randomly assigned to receive chemotherapy in either a laminar air flow (LAF) room or a regular hospital room. A LAF is a relatively germ-free room wherein air flows in layers so as not to stir up particles from the floor or other contaminated areas. Anyone entering the room must be gowned and gloved in sterile attire. See-through plastic separated the patients from others. The rationale behind this specialized environment was that individuals are at high risk for infection related to immune suppression while receiving intensive chemotherapy. The LAF rooms were expected to reduce the high risk for infection. But the isolation for the patient imposed by the LAF was great and the effects of social isolation on children had been documented for over a century. So who were the patients and why did they receive chemotherapy in a LAF? The patients were children and teenagers, as young as age four and as old as 17, who had cancers that failed to respond to conventional cancer treatments. These were children and youth who conventionally are known as "terminally ill" as all other treatment had failed to stop the progression of their tumors. The comparison group consisted of youth who received the same chemotherapy in a regular hospital room setting.

The aim was to identify changes in emotions and social behavior prior to, during, and after receiving chemotherapy. The framework used to conceptualize the study was the early work of Rene Spitz, John Bowlby, and others on the effects of isolation on social behavior of animals and humans. The primary methodology used to assess changes in behavior and emotions was systematic observation based on categories developed by primatologists and psychologists to observe social behavior. Five days a week, trained observers visited the participants in the LAF or regular hospital room and observed activity every 30 seconds for one half-hour. Observational categories included type of physical activity, emotions, verbalizations, and type of interaction with others (e.g. nurse, doctor, family member). Multiple biological measures were obtained by the medical staff every day of LAF treatment. The analytic strategy consisted of linking observational data and immune function markers, which are an indication of the side-effects of chemotherapy, to establish effects of the chemotherapy. The group-difference findings showed that there were few differences in the emotions, physical activity, or verbalizations between the LAF and comparison youth. In contrast, there were major changes in behavior that paralleled changes in immune functioning; social behavior declined as immune functioning became compromised. What was most surprising and clinically significant was that as immune function returned to pre-chemo levels, positive emotions, verbalizations, and physical activity did not always return to pre-chemo levels (Susman et al., 1981). These findings had major significance for how the nursing and medical staff interacted with the participants before leaving the hospital. Prior to our findings the staff had a party to celebrate the end of chemo and discharge from the hospital. Based on our observational findings, and interview data, the celebration was no longer held, given that the adolescents were not in a celebratory mood post chemo. For these children and youth, going through the intensive chemotherapy was the first recognition of the seriousness of their illness (Susman, Pizzo, & Poplack, 1981; Susman et al., 1982). Some expressed feelings of depression and sadness. Based on our findings rather than celebrating post chemo, the staff took on a supportive role that sometimes included a recommendation for psychotherapy.

To summarize, let me begin by answering a question that readers likely have at this point. Was this not a depressing experience working with terminally ill children and adolescents? No. First, most of these children did not die while receiving chemotherapy or during the immediate short term post chemo. I was in contact with one of the participants in the study until January 2012, when he died of other causes. Second, the children and youth view cancer differently than do adults. Their primary aim was to get back to a normal life with friends, family, and school, and they rarely mentioned fears of death. Third, the NCI had a support system for the staff, including my research assistants and me, which included a psychiatrist with whom we met as a group monthly. A second question is likely, how did this unique experience contribute to your career in developmental psychology? First, the experience of working at NCI gave me a view of coping with adversity that has not nearly been replicated in any other aspect of my life. The strength of families and youth is impressive in enduring these painful health problems. Second, working with first-rate scientists whose specialties ranged from the molecular biology of cancer (oncology clinicians, biochemists, and social workers) to psychiatrists gave me an appreciation and keen interest for interdisciplinary research that has been enduring. For instance, my co-mentor, Dr. Arthur Levine, a molecular biologist and oncologist, taught me how to write for an interdisciplinary audience. His mentoring remains with me today as I remember to reduce psychological jargon and make every effort to write in a simplified manner to explain complex scientific information to an interdisciplinary audience. Third, the roots of my last 25+ years of research were concretized while I was a post-doc at NCI where I decided to continue a research career.

As I worked with collaborators at NIC I became aware of another problem faced by children with leukemia. What were the psychological effects of failure to be on time in growth in children with cancer? Children who were treated for leukemia with central nervous radiation appeared to have shorter stature or other delayed puberty-related problems (Oberfield et al., 1996), especially if they received radiation during the pubertal years. Questions regarding growth and puberty led me to pursue studies of the neuro- and psychobiology of puberty that continue today.

And Now on to the Puberty Eras

After completing my post-doc I was offered a tenure track position at PSU in the School of Nursing. My wish was to stay at NIH, but given my dual career situation it was best for my personal and family life. It was difficult to settle into a faculty position after the experience at NIH, where my interest in health and biological issues could bloom. Biological influences were still not quite accepted in developmental research. After 2 years I was offered a position at NIH in 1980 in the same lab where I had done my post-doc, Developmental Psychology, NIMH. My invitation was to start a program of research that included biological aspects of development in youth. At the time NIMH was becoming increasingly biologically oriented. The offer was one that offered my dreams on a silver, or maybe even gold, platter; the dream was to have one foot in psychology and one foot in biological sciences. Shortly after arriving back at NIMH I pursued the first of a series of short-term longitudinal studies on the effect of hormone changes on psychological and behavioral parameters during puberty. My collaborators are too many to enumerate here but one was particularly influential in helping to initiate the study on hormone changes and psychological development of children and their families. George Chrousos, M.D. was an excellent collaborator and is now an internationally noted endocrinologist and pediatrician with his primary research contributions in the study of stress. He and his colleagues were becoming in the 1980s to be recognized for their work on the interaction between the endocrine, stress system and depression (Chrousos & Gold, 1992). Dr Chrousos not only provided substantive content to framing the aims and hypothesis but also assisted with carrying out the study and made funding available for massive numbers of hormone assays.

The product of the initial collaboration was a short-term longitudinal study of hormone changes at puberty and emotions, cognition, behavior including aggression, family–adolescent interaction, and other constructs of interest. The study produced multiple publications in journals and presentations at professional meetings (e.g., Susman et al., 1987; Nottelmann et al. 1987) and these publications continue to be forthcoming even in 2012 (Marceau, Dorn, & Susman, 2012). The publications describe in detail the interconnectedness of pubertal hormones and aggression. As anticipated testosterone was associated with externalizing problems but not as consistently as is true in male adults. One finding that was particularly unique was the inverse association between hormones (testosterone, estrogen, and adrenal androgens) and externalizing and internalizing behavior problems. That is, young adolescents with more behavior problems had lower levels of hormones. Our hypothesis was that there would be consistent positive relations between androgens like testosterone and externalizing behavior. The finding was especially true for young adolescents who were later in their pubertal development. This finding was puzzling to the psychologists in the research group. Thanks to the interdisciplinary nature of our team these inverse relations were intuitively interpretable; when the stress system is activated there is a down-regulation of the reproductive system, hence the pattern of higher stress system hormones (e.g., androstenedione) and lower reproductive system hormones (e.g., testosterone). With regard to puberty, stressors during puberty may suppress ever so slightly the production of reproductive hormones even at a time when reproductive hormones are normatively increasing.

The findings regarding stress and the reproductive system led to reports of the stress-related hormone, cortisol, and helped to launch the now blossoming field of the psychobiology of stress in adolescents. The influence of one's research is hard to evaluate, but if the popularity of studies on cortisol is an indication of the impact then our early studies did have an influence on the field. The number of published reports and oral and poster presentations of basal and reactivity cortisol at professional meetings has grown exceedingly fast in the last two decades. An exciting aspect of the growth of studies of cortisol (Fisher, Stoolmiller, Gunnar, & Burraston, 2007) is that investigators are now showing how changing behavior is related to changes in hormones (Dorn, Kolko, Shenk, Susman, & Burkstein, 2011) like testosterone (Shenk et al. 2012). The cause–effect relation between these changes is yet to be determined.

The recent upsurge in reports of cortisol has shown that cortisol levels are not always in the predicted direction with behaviors such as aggression. Cortisol is not always elevated in depressed children as it is in adults. Disruptive behaviors are sometimes related to suppression of basal or reactivity cortisol. This inconsistency in findings led me to spend part of a sabbatical in Sweden reviewing the psychophysiology and other literatures on arousal and stress and disruptive behavior. Adrian Raine's work was particularly instrumental in my writing a theoretical paper on the underpinnings of low arousal and disruptive behavior. Dr Raine and colleagues showed that children as young as three with low arousal (e.g., low heart rate) exhibited more aggression than high-arousal children at age 11 (Raine, Venables, & Mednick, 1997). The result of my sabbatical work is a theoretical paper (Susman, 2006) proposing that early adverse experiences affect the development of the neurobiology of the stress system. These early adverse experiences were hypothesized to affect the stress system such that chronic exposure to an unpredictable, chaotic, or harsh childrearing environment leads to down-regulation of the stress system when confronted with acute stressors. Otherwise known as the *attenuation hypothesis*, this perspective is now used to explain lower cortisol reactivity following an acute stressor. An empirical example of confirmation of this hypothesis is a study of the effects of the stress experience of sexual abuse in girls. Girls who were sexually abused initially showed higher basal cortisol than comparison girls who were not abused but, over time, sexually abused girls became lower on cortisol levels (Trickett, Noll, Susman, Shenk, & Putnam, 2010). The explanation of down-regulated cortisol is that it is an adaptive response to chronic stressors. Continued stress-arousal eventually could lead to physiological damage to various organ systems (e.g., cardiovascular system). Therefore, individuals in chronic stressful environments down-regulate hypothalamic-pituitary-adrenal (HPA) activity as opposed to continuing to react to chronic stressors, thereby preserving organ systems.

Now, this report goes back to 1986, the year of my second return to Penn State from NIMH. I was offered a tenure-track position in the School of Nursing. The decision to return to Penn State was made based on two considerations. The first reason was that after 8 years of a commuter marriage I tired of living at a distance from my husband and home. Second, Anne Petersen was then the department head of HDFS. Anne Petersen's presence at PSU was a huge motivation for me to return, as her interest in combining biology and behavior was at the heart of her research. Since 1980, Anne has been my friend, mentor, and colleague. Her leadership over the last few decades was instrumental in making adolescent development a methodologically rigorous, important, and visible field of inquiry. Anne was, and remains, a truly interdisciplinary scientist and academic leader. She strongly supported my interest in biobehavioral issues to flourish. Anne became my Dean shortly after returning to PSU and in that role was very supportive of my developing a lab at Penn State that provided the expertise and equipment for doing endocrine assays for faculty and students at a cost that was reasonable. That lab was the forerunner of Salimetrics, Inc. which was later developed by Dr. Douglas Granger.

Dr. Petersen's sage perspective on the future of health and behavior led her to create the Department of Biobehavioral Health, focused entirely on the integration of biology and behavior. Faculty was recruited with the criterion that their research and scholarship must be interdisciplinary and include biological or health issues and some aspect of behavior. I have been a contented member of that department since its inception in 1991. In brief, Penn State provided the perfect context for research on the endocrine aspects of adolescent behavior.

Of note is that Richard Lerner also was at Penn State in the 1980s; he was, and continues to be, a recognized leader on adolescent development. Dr. Lerner organized a conference on integrating biological, psychological, and contextual issues. Prior to that time a small group of us labored to integrate biological processes, hormones in my case, into developmental psychology. During those times there was a great deal of skepticism among developmental psychologists regarding biological issues. To many psychologist colleagues, biology was still determinism. Rich's conference was confidence-building for me as it was legitimizing that biology was important in adolescent development. In addition to Rich, two other scholars were instrumental in convincing me to pursue hormone biological issues, Robert Cairns and David Magnusson. Bob was an intellectual giant in traversing research barriers between biology and psychological theory and research; he conducted both animal-model and human-model research, he believed in the power of genes and was a master theoretician. Writing this report brings tears to my eyes (because of his too-early death) as I hear Bob coaching me to pursue my hormone-behavior research, "Come on Liz. You can do it." David Magnusson was my international mentor for bringing about theoretical synthesis of biology and behavior. He was a mentor and supporter across at least three decades. A highlight of my career was being a Senior Research Scholar in his department at University of Stockholm in 1999.

After the Lerner conference, now armed with confidence that the biology of stress was a critical influence in developmental outcomes, my first RO1 NICHD grant was to assess the impact of stress in the lives of pregnant teens and outcomes for themselves and their infants. This study was novel as it assessed cortisol, testosterone, estrogen, and adrenal androgens in mothers from the first trimester to the postpartum period (e.g. Susman, Granger, Murowchick, Ponirakis, & Worrall, 1996). An age- and SES-matched group of nonpregnant girls formed the comparison group. A key report from the study was the relation between corticotrophin hormone (CRH) and antisocial behavior, as well as depression and anxiety. CRH is the hormone that precipitates the HPA axis stress response for which cortisol is the final step in the response. It is secreted in the brain and the placenta and is high during pregnancy. We found that lower CRH during early pregnancy predicted a greater number of depression symptoms in late pregnancy. Lower concentrations of CRH also were related to a greater number of conduct disorder symptoms in early pregnancy and predicted depression in the postpartum period. These findings were important as they support the long-standing hypothesis that CRH, an initiator of the stress response, is related to depression and antisocial behavior during and post pregnancy. CRH also is implicated in the onset of labor and delivery and fetal lung maturation. Lower CRH levels may be a risk for neonatal respiratory problems. The extent to which an adolescent's behavior affects CRH as suggested by our correlational findings is unknown and has not been examined in subsequent research. The lower CRH findings were instrumental in my thinking and motivated research to explain why under stressful conditions some individuals are characterized by lower CRH and cortisol. The *attenuation hypothesis* partially was derived from these findings.

A reward of one's academic and research career is engaging in government policy making efforts. During the era when I was doing a study on stress and pregnancy I was asked to participate in an NIH Consensus Development Conference in 1994 on the effects of glucocorticoid administration on delaying the onset of labor in women at risk for premature delivery. The purpose of a Consensus Development Conference is to use existing research to develop guidelines for clinical practice. To participate in a Consensus Conference is a tremendous honor as one's interpretation of empirical findings helps to mold medical practice. The consensus panel concluded that a single course of corticosteroids to pregnant women at risk for preterm delivery reduced the risk of death, respiratory distress syndrome, and intraventricular hemorrhage in preterm infants. However, repeat courses of antenatal corticosteroids had become into common usage, which was not the recommendation of the panel. Given this practice of giving repeat doses, I was asked to participate in a *second* Consensus Conference on the effects of repeat doses of corticosteroids on fetal and neonatal development. The results of the second conference were more complicated and recommended future clinical trials research. Participating in these conferences was a challenging and almost frightening endeavor as lives are at stake if incorrect inferences are drawn from the existing literature. Yes, participating in these two NIH interdisciplinary conferences was a highly meaningful and educational experience.

Other studies in the last decade further advanced our science of the psycho-and neurobiology of stress, emotions and behavior, and puberty. One highly interdisciplinary study is noteworthy. With two pediatric endocrinologists, a biostatistician, and other disciplines, we obtained an RO1 from NICHD to assess the effect of sex hormone (testosterone or estrogen) replacement therapy on aggression, cognition, and behavior problems on boys and girls. The adolescents in the study all were delayed in progressing through puberty and required medical intervention. We capitalized on this clinical experiment to assess the effects of sex steroids on aggression, cognition, and behavior problems. The study used the ultimate in experimental designs: a randomized, double-blinded, placebo-controlled, and cross-over clinical trial. The design provided the opportunity to assess the effect of sex steroids independent of physical morphological changes

on our parameters of interest without the adolescent or family knowing whether treatment or placebo was being received. The findings, highly summarized, were that testosterone or estrogen increased self-reported aggression in boys and girls (Finkelstein et al., 1997), sexual fantasies in boys (Finkelstein et al., 1998), and perceived self-confidence (Schwab et al., 2001) but had few effects on cognition (Liben et al., 2002) or parent reports of behavior problems (Susman et al., 1998). These findings were well received by some groups but were received with skepticism by others. A primary criticism of the design was that we had no comparison group of adolescents who were progressing through puberty at a normal pace. A control sample of healthy comparison adolescents was impossible to include. Human subjects' ethical issues prevent giving hormone replacement to normally developing adolescents. The importance of the study was that it showed that testosterone and estrogen did have effects on self-reported human aggressive behavior and other aspects of development- like competencies. The sex differences in response to treatment are noteworthy. For instance, girls responded to a lower dose of estrogen and increased in their aggressive behavior faster than boys responded to testosterone. Overall, these results are the first to causally relate the administration of physiological doses of sex steroids to changes in aggressive and other behaviors.

Finally, other recent past and current studies of puberty and development further assess emotions and antisocial behavior. These studies broadened an approach to the assessment of the stress system by incorporating an index of autonomic nervous system activity, salivary alpha amylase (sAA). A new marker of sympathetic, stress reactivity, sAA is considered a surrogate marker of sympathetic adrenomedullary (SAM) activity (Granger, Kivlighan, El-Sheikh, Gordis, & Stroud, 2007). SAA is an enzyme produced in the oral mucosa and is an assumptive marker of the adrenergic component of the stress response. SAA levels are associated with SAM activity and increase under stressful conditions that are also associated with increases in plasma catecholamines, heart rate, systolic blood pressure, preinjection period (PEP), and cardiac output. In a recent study of boys and girls at puberty, for boys, timing of puberty moderated the association between cortisol and sAA reactivity and antisocial behavior. Higher cortisol reactivity in later-timing boys was related to a composite index of antisocial behavior and rule-breaking behavior problems. In contrast, lower sAA reactivity and earlier timing of puberty in boys was related to rule-breaking and conduct-disorder symptoms. The interaction between timing of puberty and HPA or SAM regulation and timing of puberty in boys suggests that reproductive, neuroendocrine mechanisms are involved in the extensively documented adverse consequences of off-time pubertal development.

Finally, a long-term interest is the effects of child abuse and neglect on the development of children and youth. This interest grew out of collaboration with Penelope K. Trickett beginning in 1980. Across the last two decades

Penny has maintained a strong record of funding and scholarship on the short- and long-term effects of abuse and neglect on children. My contribution to this collaboration focuses on the neurobiology of abuse; gonadal and adrenal hormones, cortisol, sAA, and body mass index (BMI). Not only have I advanced in my understanding of exposure to violence and trauma but my students have also benefitted greatly from this collaboration. One of my students recently published a paper showing that even nonmalatreated children in community settings experience neurobiological effects of exposure to violence on their development. Peckins and I (see below) showed that young adolescents exposed to higher levels of community violence in nonurban settings had lower (attenuated) cortisol reactivity compared with those with lower exposure. We are now pursuing similar questions in nonmaltreated youth in inner city neighborhoods where exposure to violence is a common occurrence.

Now and the Future

So what are my goals and directions for the future? The goals are not lofty but of great importance for my personal well-being. My aspiration is to continue to ask good questions and pursue rigorous methods to advance the neurobiology of adolescent health and development. I should be ending my career in research about now by U.S. professorial and cultural norms. But research is my passion and a life time of doing research does not fade away quickly. In addition, important new questions are just too intriguing not to pursue. For instance, I have a collaboration with Tomas Paus that is very exciting. To make a very long and complicated research project summary short, the longitudinal study combines brain development, endocrinology, emotions, behavior, and health. My interest is in tracking endocrine changes with structural changes in the brain at puberty. The endocrine component of the study in combination with the MRI structural brain changes data present the possibility for answering enduring questions about simultaneous brain development, puberty and behavior.

Continuing to do research with my past undergraduate and graduate students and long-term colleagues is highly rewarding. Mentoring students and post-docs is one of the most rewarding aspects of doing interdisciplinary research. Introducing a bit of biochemistry into a student's struggle to interpret a complicated hormone-behavior finding is especially rewarding, as doing biobehavior research is more difficult than doing traditional behavioral or social science research. Students and colleagues bound for a career in hormone-behavior research should learn some basic physiology and spend some time in an endocrine laboratory. Parenthetically, I regret not spending more time in the lab.

And a related point for budding scientists in biobehavioral research; ignore the warnings that one cannot go into fields wherein one was not trained like endocrinology,

genetics, or neuroscience. A key to success in doing good biobehavioral research is to find good collaborators who are not just collaborators on research but collaborators who are willing to share their knowledge with you and your students. My experience at NIH gave me an unprecedented opportunity to learn endocrinology from senior collaborators. In addition, ignore the warnings that human subjects will not participate in studies that require giving blood, spit, and urine, exposing their brains to a scanner, or other perceived invasive research methods. My philosophy has been that it is not what one asks research participants to do but how it is asked and who is doing the asking that is important. A well-conceived and important research question that is presented in a clear fashion to a potential participant rarely receives a negative response.

In conclusion, my participation in my scientific societies is a primary source of continuing professional rewards. As president of the Society for Research on Adolescence I learned the complexities of managing and growing a scientific, intellectual effort. My membership on Governing Council (GC) of Society for Research on Child Development is a highly rewarding experience as SRCD is an institution with a long history where novel scientific initiatives are possible primarily for young scholars. For instance, the new "Off Year" meetings that began during my time on GC have received great praise for their focused topics and smaller attendance.

But there is one new initiative that I hope to undertake, and that is writing a book on puberty for parents and children. The longstanding myths about the negative aspects of puberty need to be dismissed, and parents and adolescents need to view puberty as a new opportunity for experiencing the richness of adolescent life.

References

Baltes, P. B., Reese, H. W., & Nesselroade, J. R, (1977). *Life-span developmental psychology: Introduction to research methods.* Hillsdale, NJ: Lawrence Erlbaum Associates.

Chrousos, G. P., & Gold, P. W. *(*1992). The concepts of stress and stress system disorders: Overview of physical and behavioral homeostasis. *Journal of the American Medical Association, 267,* 1244–1252.

Dorn, L. D., Kolko, D. J., Shenk, C. E., Susman, E. J., & Burkstein, O. (2011). Influence of treatment for disruptive behavior disorders on adrenal and gonadal hormones in youth. *Journal of Clinical Child and Adolescent Psychology, 40,* 562–571.

Feyerabend, P. (1975). *Against method: Outline of an anarchistic theory of knowledge.* New York: Verso Books.

Finkelstein, J. W., Susman, E. J., Chinchilli, V. M., Kunselman, S. J., D'Arcangelo, M. R., Schwab, J. et al. (1997). Estrogen or testosterone increases self-reported aggressive behaviors in hypogonadal adolescents. *Journal of Clinical Endocrinology and Metabolism, 82,* 2423–2438.

Finkelstein, J. W., Susman, E. J., D'Arcangelo, M. R., Kunselman, S. J., Schwab, J., Demers, L. et al. (1998). Effects of estrogen or testosterone on self-reported sexual responses and behaviors in hypogonadal adolescents. *Journal of Clinical Endocrinology and Metabolism, 83,* 2281–2285.

Fisher, P. A., Stoolmiller, M., Gunnar, M. R., & Burraston, B. O. (2007). Effects of a therapeutic intervention for foster preschoolers on diurnal cortisol activity. *Psychoneuroendocrinology, 32,* 892–905.

Granger, D. A., Kivlighan, K. T., El-Sheikh, M., Gordis, E., & Stroud, L. R. (2007). Salivary α-amylase in biobehavioral research. *Annals of the New York Academy of Science, 1098*, 122–144.

Liben, L. S., Susman, E. J., Krogh, H. R., Chinchilli, V. M., Kunselman, S., D'Arcangelo, R. et al. (2002). The effects of sex steroids on spatial cognition during induced puberty. *Developmental Psychology, 38*, 236–253.

Marceau, K., Dorn, L. D., & Susman, E. J. (2012). Stress and puberty-related hormone reactivity, negative emotionality, and parent-adolescent relationships. *Psychoneuroendocrinology, 37*, 1286–1298.

Nottelmann, E. D., Susman, E. J., Inoff-Germain, G. E., Cutler, G. B., Jr., Loriaux, D. L., & Chrousos, G. P. (1987). Developmental processes in American early adolescence: Relations between adolescent adjustment problems and chronologic age, pubertal stage and puberty-related serum hormone levels. *Journal of Pediatrics, 110*, 473–480.

Oberfield, S. E., Soranno, D., Nirenberg, A., Heller, G., Jeffrey, R. D., Levine, L. S. et al. (1996). Age at onset of puberty following high-dose central nervous system radiation therapy. *Archives of Pediatrics and Adolescent Medicine, 150*, 589–592.

Peckins, M. E., Dockray, S., Eckenrode, J., Heaton, J. & Susman, E. J. (2012). The longitudinal impact of exposure to violences on cortisol reactivity in adolescents. *Journal of Adolescent Health, 51*, 366–372.

Raine, A., Venables, P. H., Mednick, S. A. (1997). Low resting heart rate at age 3 years predisposes to aggression at age 11 years: evidence from the Mauritius Child Health Project. *Journal of the Academy of Child and Adolescent Psychiatry, 36*, 1457–1464.

Schick, T. Jr. (1997). The end of science? *The Skeptical Inquirer, 21*(2), 36. www.best.com/~dolphin/scimyth.html.

Schwab, J., Susman, E. J., Finkelstein, J. W., Chinchilli, V. M., Kunselman, S. J., D'Arcangelo, R. M. et al. (2001). The role of sex hormone replacement therapy on self-perceived competence in adolescents with delayed puberty. *Child Development, 72*, 1439–1450.

Shenk, C. E., Dorn, L. D., Kolko, D. J., Susman, E. J., Noll, J. G., & Bukstein, O. G. (In press). Predicting treatment response for oppositional defiant disorder and conduct disorder using pre-treatment adrenal and gonadal hormones. *Journal of Child and Family Studies*.

Susman, E. J. (2006). Psychobiology of persistent antisocial behavior: Stress, early vulnerabilities and the attenuation hypothesis. *Neuroscience and Biobehavioral Reviews, 30*, 376–389.

Susman, E. J., Dockray, S., Granger, D. A., Blades, K. T., Randazzo, W., Heaton, J. A. et al. (2010). Cortisol and alpha amylase reactivity and timing of puberty: Vulnerabilities for antisocial behavior in young adolescents. *Psychoneuroendocrinology, 35*, 557–569.

Susman, E. J., Finkelstein, J. W., Chinchilli, V. M., Schwab, J., Liben, L. S., D'Arcangelo, M. R. et al. (1998). The effect of sex hormone replacement therapy on behavior problems and moods in adolescents with delayed puberty. *Journal of Pediatrics, 33*, 521–525.

Susman, E. J., Granger, D. A., Murowchick, E., Ponirakis, A., & Worrall, B. K. (1996). Gonadal and adrenal hormones: Developmental transitions and aggressive behavior. *New York Academy of Sciences, 794*, 16–30.

Susman, E. J., Hollenbeck, A. H., Hersh, S. P., Levine, A. S., Pizzo, P. A., Nannis, E. D. et al. (1981). The impact of an intensive medical regimen on the social behavior of child and adolescent cancer patients. *Journal of Applied Developmental Psychology, 2*, 29–47.

Susman, E. J., Inoff-Germain, G. E., Nottelmann, E. D., Cutler, G. B., Loriaux, D. L., & Chrousos, G. P. (1987). Hormones, emotional dispositions and aggressive attributes in young adolescents. *Child Development, 58*, 1114–1134.

Susman, E. J., Nannis, E. D., Strope, B. E., Hersh, S. P., Levine, A. S., & Pizzo, P. A. (1982). Conceptions of cancer: The perspectives of children and their family. *Journal of Pediatric Psychology, 7*, 253–261.

Susman, E. J., Pizzo, P. A., & Poplack, D. (1981). Coping with adolescent cancer: Living with the aftermath. In P. Ahmed (Ed.), *Coping with cancer* (pp. 99–117). New York: Elsevier North Holland.

Trickett, P. K., Noll, J. G., Susman, E. J., Shenk, C. E., & Putnam, F. W. (2010). Attenuation of cortisol across development for victims of sexual abuse. *Developmental Psychopathology, 22*, 165–175.

Wohlwill, J. F. (1973). *The study of behavioral development*. New York: Academic Press.

46

War, Family Secrets, Sports, and the Developmental Origins of Aggression

RICHARD E. TREMBLAY

In the Beginning

I am tempted to start this autobiographical chapter with the present: I am 68 years old, I am starting a study of environmental effects on gene expression with newborn monozygotic twins, and I am immersed in the pleasures of interacting with my newborn son. However, I will follow Aristotle's wise suggestion in his book on Politics: "He who considers things in their first growth and origin ... will obtain the clearest view of them."

I was conceived towards the end of the Second World War when the mathematician John von Neumann and other very bright European immigrants to North America were creating game theory, the first modern computer, and the atomic bomb (Heims, 1980). These historical events at the time of my birth are important because they still have a profound impact on the way I perceive humans and try to understand the developmental origins of aggression. Pure science, such as mathematics, has always been an instrument that can be used to create wellbeing as much as destruction. For example, the advent of the computer clearly changed my world for the better, but my social and moral development was also marked by the horrors of the Second World War and the fear of the Atomic Bomb being used by the Russians against the Western world. That fear was intense to the point that many people were building expensive fallout shelters. The Bomb was conceived by geniuses as a means of defense, but it was used twice by the Western world with the specific aim of killing at least 100,000 civilians. Over the years I learned that physical force was an instrument used by the bad as well as good guys to achieve their aims.

At the time of my birth, other European immigrants to North America were making major contributions to a completely different human endeavor, the study of children's development. The work of two of these immigrants would eventually be central to my professional education:

Fritz Redl, a student of Anna Freud in Vienna, was creating Pioneer House in Detroit to treat aggressive children (Redl & Wineman, 1951), and Erik H. Erikson was gathering information to write *Childhood and Society* (Erikson, 1950).

Although I was born in Canada, far away from the horrors of the war, I learned the true date of my birth only when I was 37 years old! It was a bit unsettling from a personal perspective, but the story that I describe below gives a good idea of the socio-cultural environment which molded the development of my brain. It is also of interest to those who, like me, rely on official records to study human development.

My father was in the army during the war. I was conceived when, on a furlough, he went to see his longtime girlfriend. She was 25, he was 27, and they had known each other for almost 10 years. They decided to marry when my mother discovered she was pregnant. However, they did all they could to hide the fact that I was conceived out of wedlock, since they were living at a time when moral behavior was strictly controlled by the Catholic Church in the Canadian province of Québec. After their marriage they went to live near the army camp where my father was a physical education trainer of the soldiers who were being sent to liberate France and The Netherlands from the German occupation. The camp was in the neighboring province of Ontario, approximately 600 km from my parent's home town. I was born on the 23rd of November, but my parents waited until the 23rd of December to announce the birth to their family, explaining that I was born prematurely because my mother had fallen down stairs. A few months later they went back to their home town with a baby supposedly premature and had me baptized with my maternal grandparents as godparents. The official document (the baptism certificate) signed by my parents, my maternal grandparents, and the priest declared that I was born on December 23, 1944. At that time baptism certificates recorded in the church archives were official birth records used for numerous purposes, including registration at school, obtaining a driver's license or a passport. However, by my 20th birthday a huge cultural revolution had occurred in Québec. We, the baby boomers, had stopped going to church, stopped becoming priests or nuns, and, with the help of "the pill," were going to have one of the lowest reproductive rates in the world.

The state eventually took over many of the responsibilities of the church, and church documents became obsolete. So, by age 37, when I had to renew my passport to take a sabbatical leave in France, I was required for the first time to present an official birth certificate rather than a baptism certificate. From that official birth certificate, which I obtained from the province of Ontario, I learned my real birth date and learned that I was not the premature baby so often described by my mother's younger sisters as needing careful attention. I don't know how I would have dealt with this secret if my mother had still been alive (she died when I was 12 years old), but on the 23rd of November following the discovery of my real birth date I invited my father for dinner at his club restaurant and ordered a bottle of champagne. Why the champagne he asked? It's my birthday Dad! He answered timidly: I told your mother that you would eventually find out.

At the end of the war my father returned to the main occupation he had held since he was 18, football player for the National Capital of Canada team, the Ottawa Rough Riders. He was an excellent football player and I spent my childhood with a father who was celebrated in the newspapers, the sport magazines, and on radio for his dazzling punt returns and accurate placement kicks. I started organizing football games with cousins and friends probably when I was around 7 years old. My success in creating research teams for longitudinal and experimental studies is possibly due to the long experience I had in getting friends together to play American football, a game where each player has a very specific role in achieving success.

Compared with other team sports such as soccer, baseball, cricket, basketball, and volleyball, football is a game that involves much physical aggression. You have to learn complex skills, but also learn to hit and get hit as hard as possible while maintaining control of your emotions. The fear and anger of being hit, as well as the pleasure of hitting becomes a way of life. Your bleeding nose, sore knees, and broken ribs are warrior trophies. I realized during my academic career that it probably hurts less to be hit by an opponent when you are running with the football towards his goal line than when you receive an aggressive anonymous review for a grant proposal or a paper submitted to a scientific journal. During a football game you know who hit you and you learn how to run away from that person on the next play or in the next game. To survive in academia you have to learn to dodge unknown aggressors.

Adolescence

My adolescence was a continuation of my sporting childhood and a preparation for a sporting adulthood. My father coached the hockey team in which my younger brother and I learned to excel. My brother eventually became a professional hockey player. Being less talented and more intellectually oriented, I eventually played hockey for the University of Ottawa where I majored in physical education.

I had a somewhat atypical adolescence. Because my mother had died and my father travelled a lot, adult supervision was minimal. I did many foolish things, but my main goals were to excel in football and hockey while surviving in school. I must also have had some form of leadership because I ended up being president and vice president of my class a few times in high school and during my undergraduate studies. My brother's adolescence was very different. Although he was very successful in school when he decided to study, he was strongly peer oriented. In hindsight, he probably suffered more from our mother's death because he was younger and more emotionally sensitive. Being a very good hockey player he left high school when he was offered a contract from a professional hockey organization. This meant that his peers became similarly talented hockey players who had also left high school in the hope of becoming professional players. For most of these young men, including my brother, the professional hockey career did not last long. They were not educated enough to find lucrative jobs and their lifestyle was rather tumultuous. I had very few contacts with my brother during early adulthood and I still do not understand what led him to commit suicide when he was 32 years old. The differences between my brother's life and mine has always puzzled me and has helped me understand that family environments do not have the same impact on children of a given family, hence the importance of studying siblings. I also learned that even if two siblings are brought up together until adolescence they know very little of each other's motivations, possibly because we know little of our own motivations even in late adulthood.

I believe that I was kept in line by two powerful motivations, my academic interests and my high school sweetheart, whom I married in my 21st year. Although sports had been the center of my life, I was also strongly attracted to the pleasure of learning, in the sense of getting to the root of things. When I started learning to count in early primary school I took a notebook and started to write the numbers from 1 onwards with the aim of getting to the end of numbers. I realized recently that this experience must be common when I read that a famous modern painter, Roman Opalka, had spent the last 46 years of his life doing this on canvas. I was also very much attracted by philosophy, literature, and psychology. By the end of my 3rd year as a major in physical education (I was 20) it became clear that I did not have the talent nor the desire to become a professional hockey or football player. I could very well see from my father's long and famous football career that long careers in sports ended at best in the early thirties, and that meant having to establish a second career. I also realized that I was not very much attracted by the prospect of becoming a high school physical education teacher, as did most of most of those who majored in physical education. Thus, by age 20 I had no clear idea where I was going.

Graduate Studies and Other Experiences

Mental Hospital In the fall of my last year of my major in physical education I started looking at the job offers on the billboard of the department. One of them especially caught my attention: A newly built psychiatric hospital was looking for a physical education graduate to take responsibility for the patients' recreational program. The reason I was attracted to this offer was serendipitous. During the summer break I had read a novel (*Lilith*) by J. R. Salamanca in which a young man who was a recreational therapist in a mental hospital fell in love with a seductive and bright female patient. I had bought that novel because the nickname of my high-school sweetheart, whom I was marrying that September, happened to be Lilith.

I eventually took that job. It involved organizing the recreational activities of 2,000 patients and directing a team of a dozen recreational technicians. I was turning 21 and had absolutely no training in recreational therapy. The first thing I did when I arrived at the hospital was to go to the library and read on recreational therapy. It did not take long for me to realize that I had to go back to university to do graduate training in this field if I wanted to do something useful for the patients. The head of the hospital totally agreed and offered to sponsor me for a scholarship from the newly created medical research training fund of the Health Ministry.

Residential Center for Juvenile Delinquency I eventually chose to do a master degree in psycho-education in the department of psychology at the University of Montreal. The program had been specifically designed to train professionals for residential treatment of children and adolescents. The theoretical training was largely based on psychoanalytic ego psychology and Piaget's cognitive development psychology. One of the basic intervention models was taken from Fritz Redl and David Wineman's work published in the two volumes titled *The Aggressive Child* (1951). The life-span developmental model rested mainly on the work of Erik H. Erikson, and practical training involved field work in residential centers for children or adolescents. I was sent to a residential treatment center for juvenile delinquents. My career as an adolescent specialist was starting! Having majored in physical education I eventually became involved in the physical education and sport activities of the residential center. For my master degree thesis I choose to study, through direct observation, how juvenile delinquents who were in different phases of their residential treatment approached the learning of gymnastics. This was a very labor-intensive enterprise that started to teach me that you can very easily lose track of where you are going when you dig very deeply into a narrow topic or a technique, a frequent beginner's mistake in science and one that a good supervisor can help prevent.

Maximum Security Mental Hospital After finishing this 3-year master degree funded by the Ministry of Health I had to work for at least 3 years in a state hospital facility. To keep as close as possible to my newly gained expertise with juvenile delinquents I chose to work in a new maximum security mental hospital, where most patients had committed violent crimes. The head of the hospital had decided to experiment the Therapeutic Community approach (Jones, 1953) to treat this assembly of psychopaths, drug addicts, schizophrenics, and mentally deficient adults who were now at the end of the line, since everything else had failed. The physical environment was spectacularly modern and the staff was composed mainly of young 1970s idealists who believed that theory, good faith, and hard work would help these unfortunate humans return to a "normal" life. I learned much about the limits of psychiatry during these 3 years thanks especially to Henri Ellenberger, who had just published his monumental book on the discovery of the unconscious (Ellenberger, 1970) and participated in our weekly case studies. I also learned that many of these dangerous patients were humans with whom it was good to play and talk.

University of London

One year after I finished my master degree and started to work with mentally ill offenders the University of Montreal created a school of psycho-education, separate from the department of psychology, and offered me a half-time position that could become a full-time tenure track position if I did a PhD. I accepted the offer and two years later went to do my PhD at the University of London's Institute of Education in the department of educational and developmental psychology. When I arrived in London I was told that the supervisor I had chosen had moved to Leeds University. I was offered to follow him or to be supervised by Robert Andry, who was directing a training program in forensic psychology and worked as a consultant in the Hong Kong prisons. His PhD research had focused on juvenile delinquency and parental pathology (Andry, 1960). Because of his frequent trips to Hong Kong I was given a co-supervisor, Daisy Penfold, a statistician who had worked with Cyril Burt (1925) and was close to retirement.

I had decided that I would do my PhD thesis on the impact of residential treatment for juvenile delinquents, and more specifically its impact on body image. The body image idea was an attempt to bridge my undergraduate training in physical education and my master degree training, which was strongly influenced by psychoanalytical thinking. I was using Seymour Fisher's attempt to operationalize Freudian concepts (Fisher & Cleveland, 1968). However, clinical psychology at the University of London was dominated by Hans Eysenck, whom my psychodynamically oriented professors at the University of Montreal referred to as the devil in person because of his behavioral orientation. The clash between psychoanalysis and behaviorism during most of the 20th century was in my mind very similar to the clash between Catholicism and Protestantism. Having liberated myself from my Catholic education during my adolescence, I was now ready to liberate myself from psychoanalytic theory. I read Eysenck's book *Crime and Personality* (1964) soon after I arrived. Although I first reacted to his ideas with the criticism of my previous professors, I rapidly realized that I understood the logic of his arguments much better than I ever did the logic of most of the psychoanalytic ideas I had read over the past 10 years. One way to summarize this is that I had the impression I was intelligent enough to understand Eysenck's reasoning, an impression I did not have when I read most of the psychoanalysts, especially the French psychoanalysts. This did not prevent me from having friends who were being trained at Anna Freud's Hampstead clinic. Interestingly, some 20 years later I was ask by Peter Fonagy, who had recently become director of the Hampstead clinic, to be on their International Advisory Board.

The second major influence during my PhD was the developmental psychology influence. Professor Lindley, who was in charge of the weekly graduate research seminar, introduced us to the importance of the developmental perspective. He had been one of the initiators of the series of birth cohort longitudinal studies which started in the early 1950s in Belgium, England, France, Sweden and Switzerland (Sand, 1966; Stattin & Klackenberg-Larsson, 1993). A few months after I started my PhD, I was given a newspaper clipping of a book review on juvenile delinquency by my upstairs neighbour, a Canadian postdoctoral student in cancer genetics who eventually became President of the Canadian Institutes of Health Research (Alan Bernstein). He knew that my thesis was on the treatment of juvenile delinquents and wondered if I had heard of the study described in the book. At that time I was far from realizing that the study I discovered in *Who becomes delinquent?* (West & Farrington, 1973) would have such a profound impact on my career. Indeed, my PhD research on the effects of residential treatment for delinquent boys made me realize the importance of understanding the early development of antisocial behaviour, and the Cambridge Study in Delinquent Development (Farrington, 2003) was a model.

The third major influence was my co-supervisor, the statistician Daisy Penfold, whom I met every month in her office at the end of the afternoon, so that we could have a glass of sherry and talk about the challenges of gardening in a cold country like Canada. I attended a few of her lectures on statistics, but her main influence was through her questions during our meetings. They forced me to spend large amounts of time reading on statistical analyses to find answers to her questions. I knew I had earned my PhD when I presented to Daisy my statistical analyses strategy for longitudinal data based on Wohlwill's (1973) work for developmental stages. She said: I have never heard of this type of analysis but it makes sense. My

principal supervisor, Robert Andry, was instrumental in forcing me to think about family impact on juvenile delinquency, but more importantly he helped open the doors to the four residential institutions for juvenile delinquents in the London area.

Eventually the main thrust of my PhD was to assess the impact of the residential units' social climate on the changes in behavior of juvenile delinquents over an 8-month period in six residential institutions, four in the London area and two in Canada (Tremblay, 1976). I used the adolescents' and educators' ratings (Moos, 1975) to assess social climate of the residential units and educator ratings to assess the adolescent's behavior.

The study was an excellent training in planning a longitudinal study as well as collecting and analyzing longitudinal data. However, the most important impact of the study was in the realm of scientific frauds! At the end of the study I presented the results to each residential institution and gave each headmaster a copy of the data. A few years later I was alerted by a former staff member of one of the London residential centers that the headmaster had published a book with my data. The book (Mayers, 1980) claimed that an experiment had been done in his residential institution and had shown significant beneficial effects on the behavior of the boys. I eventually sent an article to the *British Journal of Criminology* showing that my data had been falsified to demonstrate beneficial effects in that residential center. The editor hesitated to publish the article because he was afraid the headmaster would sue the journal. The article was eventually published (Tremblay, 1984) and, from what I was told, the headmaster was fired, apparently for an accumulation of deceptive behaviors. Almost a decade later Mark Lipsey published a meta-analysis of treatment effects for juvenile delinquency (Lipsey, 1992) which included the forged data. He deleted them from his data bank after I sent him my article, but one wonders how many fraudulent data sets are still undiscovered. Having spent a decade working in residential settings with deviant adolescents and adults I could understand why a brazen headmaster would manipulate data to "save" his institution and become famous. Residential treatment of juvenile delinquents and criminals at the time was under strong attack (Lipton, Martinson, & Wilks, 1975). Daily work to rehabilitate juvenile delinquents is probably impossible if you think that there are no beneficial effects. This is one of the reasons why it is so difficult to convince clinicians to use randomized controlled trials to assess treatment effectiveness.

There were two other important influences during my PhD. While reviewing the literature on the treatment and prevention of juvenile delinquency I found a fascinating book that that had been published 20 years earlier and that I had never seen cited. It was the first report sponsored by the World Health Organization (WHO) after its creation in 1948: *Psychiatric aspects of juvenile delinquency* by the Swiss child psychiatrist Lucien Bovet (1951). The aim of the report was to describe the best practices to deal with the juvenile delinquency problem that many countries faced after the Second World War. In this synthesis of the state of research on juvenile delinquency, Bovet summarized the work of Sheldon and Eleonore Glueck and the Cambridge–Somerville study. He emphasized Thorsten Sellin's comments on the lack of observed effects of the Cambridge–Somerville experiment 3 years after the end of this amazing preventive experiment which had started in the 1930s (Powers & Witmer, 1951). One of Sellin's comments was that the boys were probably too old (mean: 10.5 years) when the preventive intervention started. Written at the same time as Bowlby's (1951) famous report to the WHO on maternal care and mental health, Bovet concluded: "Any rational prophylaxis must, therefore, attack the basic disorders of which delinquency is a sign. Its form and scope will be that of a vast mental health campaign" (p. 45). He even went on to add: "Treatment of the non-delinquent little girl or teen-age girl might perhaps have been the most efficacious prophylaxis for the delinquency which a few years later will break out in her sons" (p. 46). To this day I am convinced that if Bovet's 1951 report had been taken seriously, the science of preventing chronic antisocial behavior during childhood and adolescence would be much more advanced. Unfortunately, he could not promote his book because he died with his wife in a car accident not long after its publication, and hardly anyone referred to the first ever WHO monograph, not even the latest report on violence by the WHO (Krug, Dahlberg, Mercy, Zwi, & Lozano, 2002)!

Assistant Professor at the University of Montreal

At the end of my PhD, in the summer of 1976, I went back to the University of Montreal as an assistant professor. I was told that in 4 years I would be asked to replace the head of the department who had reluctantly accepted the job for one term and that I needed to quickly gain experience by taking the responsibility of the undergraduate and graduate programs. Naively, I thought that it was normal to do this administrative work, teach, and start a funded research program in a department created 5 years earlier with psycho-dynamically oriented clinicians who did not particularly appreciate quantitative research. Fortunately, I decided to link my research program to my administrative responsibilities. I created a research team on the training of educators for maladjusted children and the study of adult–child interactions. The later enabled me to focus on my growing interest in nonverbal communication and ethology. I created a graduate course on the use of nonverbal communication and ethology for the reeducation of maladjusted children and eventually published a book on ethology and child development (Tremblay, Provost, & Strayer, 1985).

Kindergarten Cohort Studies to Understand Adolescent Behavior In 1980 the largest school board of Montreal asked me to help them assess the behavior problems of kindergarten children. It did not take me long to realize that this

was a wonderful opportunity to start a longitudinal study with a large sample of kindergarten males from low socioeconomic areas of Montreal and study the development of juvenile delinquency. The original aim of the longitudinal study was to follow the most disruptive kindergarten children up to adolescence to understand which factors explain why some would become juvenile delinquents and others not. I was clearly influenced here by West and Farrington's (1973) study of delinquency development in London. I eventually decided to randomly choose a group of these disruptive kindergarten boys for a prevention experiment. Forty years after the start of the Cambridge–Somerville study (McCord, 1978), starting an intervention based on parent training and social skills training of 7-year-old boys appeared to be a step forward towards Bovet's 30-year-old recommendation. I invited a number of international investigators to help plan this study. The enthusiastic support of Joan McCord, David Farrington, Lea Pulkkinen, and Rolf Loeber was extremely encouraging during the early stages of our work. Joan McCord made annual visits to help plan the assessments and work on data analyses. We eventually published an edited volume on early prevention of antisocial behavior (McCord & Tremblay, 1992). Rolf Loeber convinced me of the importance to focus on physical aggression. Lea Pulkkinen was greatly helpful in sorting out the different personality approaches to longitudinal research and played an important role in my association with the International Society for the Study of Behaviour Development (see Pulkkinen, Chapter 33 this volume). David Farrington was convinced that we needed longitudinal-experimental studies such as the one we started and systematically invited me to take part in different committees, including the NIJ–MacArthur foundation planning committee for the study that eventually became the Project on Human Development in Chicago Neighborhoods (Xue, Leventhal, Brooks-Gunn, & Earls, 2005). The intensive 2 years of work on this committee introduced me to the world of American Criminology. I had the pleasure of working with a very large group of American criminologists including Al Blumestein, Al Reiss, Felton Earls, Lee Robins, Rob Sampson, Denise Kandel, Del Elliott, Joan McCord, Malcolm Klein, David Rowe, David Hawkins, Terry Thornberry, Lloyd Ohlin, Michael Tonry, and James Q. Wilson (Farrington et al., 1990; Tonry et al., 1991). I believe that David Farrington and I were the only non-American participants.

The Montreal Longitudinal-Experimental study is now in its 28th year (Arseneault, Tremblay, Boulerice, & Saucier, 2002; Gatti, Tremblay, & Vitaro, 2009; Kerr, Tremblay, Pagani-Kurtz, & Vitaro, 1997; Mâsse & Tremblay, 1997; Petitclerc, Gatti, Vitaro, & Tremblay, 2013; Tremblay, Pihl, Vitaro, & Dobkin, 1994). The experimental intervention for the disruptive kindergarten boys has shown long-term impacts on substance use, school achievement, and criminal behavior up to age 24 years (Boisjoli, Vitaro, Lacourse, Barker, & Tremblay, 2007; Tremblay, Kurtz, Mâsse, Vitaro, & Pihl, 1995; Vitaro,

Barker, Brendgen, & Tremblay, 2012). We also initiated a longitudinal study of a population-based representative sample of kindergarten children (Québec Longitudinal Study of Kindergarten Children) to be able to compare the development of the Montreal boys from low socio-economic areas with a random sample of the population (Broidy et al., 2003; Côté, Tremblay, Nagin, Zoccolillo, & Vitaro, 2002; Fontaine et al., 2008).

In 1995, I was invited to participate in the creation of the National Consortium on Violence Research (NCOVR) funded by the US National Science Foundation and National Institute of Justice in 1995. This led to an extremely productive and stimulating collaboration with Daniel Nagin of Carnegie-Mellon University to describe the different developmental trajectories of antisocial behavior. The initial results (Nagin & Tremblay, 1999; see Figure 46.1) clearly showed that the large majority of boys from the poorest inner city areas of Montreal were using physical aggression less frequently as they grew older. Only a very small group of boys (4%) did not show the declining trend; these were the boys who had the highest level of physical aggression in kindergarten and remained at the highest level until adolescence. When interviewed at ages 15 and 17, they were the boys who reported the highest frequency of physical violence, and they were the ones most frequently found guilty of infractions before 18 years of age. These results were showing that there was a serious problem with social learning theory concerning the development of aggression from school entry to adulthood. Frequency of physical aggression was not increasing while they were increasingly exposed to aggression from the media and their peers (DHHS, 2001; Tremblay, 2000, 2006). The developmental trajectories were also indicating that the increasing arrest rate for physical aggressions during

adolescence appears to be due to a change in adults' reactions to youths' aggressions with age. Because puberty leads to an increase in height, weight, strength, and cognitive skills, it also leads to a dramatic change in the negative consequences of a physical aggression. Adults are much more fearful of being aggressed by a 16-year-old than by a 10-year-old. This leads the police and judicial system to start arresting and convicting individuals who had been physically aggressive with others at least since kindergarten. Within the NCOVR collaboration we replicated these findings using five other longitudinal studies in Canada, New Zealand, and the USA (Broidy et al., 2003).

Figure 46.1 clearly shows that all the boys tended to be at their peak level in frequency of physical aggression at 6 years of age, when they were at the end of their kindergarten year. This observation made me wonder when children start to use physical aggression if they are at their peak frequency of use in kindergarten. When I reviewed the literature on physical aggression during early childhood in the early 1990s I realized that there were very few studies and essentially no longitudinal studies tracing the development of physical aggression from infancy to adolescence. One of the factors that limited the study of aggression in young children was the idea that the physical aggressions of children were not "true" aggressions because young children could not intend to aggress (Kagan, 1974). I also remembered that in the early 1980s I had assessed the PhD thesis of a French ethologist who had filmed a huge amount of social interactions in a daycare center and had specifically studied the frequency of aggressions and prosocial behaviors (Restoin et al., 1985). He reported that the ratio of physically aggressive social interactions to other type of social interactions increased from 9 to 24 months and then decreased.

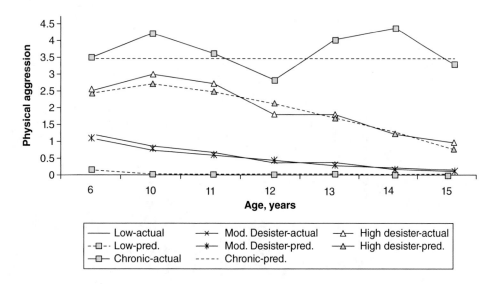

FIGURE 46.1 Trajectories of physical aggression from 6 to 15 years (Nagin & Tremblay, 1999).

Studies of Birth Cohorts to Understand the Developmental Origins of Aggression I was now convinced that Aristotle was wiser than most modern developmental criminologists, psychiatrists, or psychologists when he said that an investigation of causes needed to start at the beginning. So, following his advice we finally started to study large cohorts of children from birth to understand how and why children learn to use physical aggression. It took me close to 10 years to find the resources to start these studies, and it took all my power of conviction to get my colleagues to accept the inclusion of physical aggression items in the parent rating questionnaires before the children were 2 years of age. Their argument was that children do not aggress before 2 years of age, and parents would be shocked to be asked if their child had physically aggressed against someone. Results eventually showed that from 9 to 42 months of age the frequency of physical aggressions increases substantially and then starts decreasing (see Figure 46.2) (Alink et al., 2006; Côté, Vaillancourt, LeBlanc, Nagin, & Tremblay, 2006; NICHD, 2004; see also Tremblay et al., 1999; Tremblay et al., 2004). These studies show that the downward trend observed in Figure 46.1 started in the preschool years. The same general developmental picture is drawn whether we use data from different period, different countries, different reporting sources, or different methodologies. Frequency of anger outbursts and physical aggression increase rapidly from the first year after birth to approximately the third, and then the frequency decreases. The longitudinal studies tracing the developmental trajectories during early childhood will soon be old enough to report on trajectories of physical aggression during adolescence and adulthood. However, we know from predictive studies that aggression during childhood is the best predictor of aggression during adolescence and adulthood (Broidy et al., 2003; Loeber, Lacourse, & Homish, 2005). Thus, although physical aggressions by very young children appear qualitatively different from physical aggressions by adolescents and

adults, the trajectory of the former appears to lead to the trajectory of the latter.

Present and Future Directions: Early Bio-Psycho-Social Developmental Mechanisms Leading to Chronic Physical Aggression and Other Mental Health Problems

Much of the work we have done with our longitudinal studies was "simply" to describe development from birth to adulthood. Surprisingly, reviewers of papers we sent to "developmental" journals over the years often criticized these papers by saying that they were "only descriptive", as if taking 5, 10, 15, 20 years to describe intra-individual change in behavior was not crucial for the science of human development. My response to the PhD students we supported to write many of these papers and who received these criticisms is that their descriptive work was as important for understanding human development as the descriptive work Columbus and Magellan did to understand the geography of our planet and the descriptive work Copernicus and Galileo did to understand our solar system. We need to have a precise idea of the long-term developmental trajectories of human behavior to identify the mechanisms that drive development.

But we did not limit our work to describing development. We also made numerous attempts to use longitudinal data to identify potential bio-psycho-social mechanisms which could be manipulated to prevent or correct the development of chronic aggression (e.g., Barker et al., 2007; Booij et al., 2010; Côté et al., 2007; Fontaine et al., 2008; Van Bokhoven et al., 2005; Wang et al., 2012).

We are studying these bio-psycho-social mechanisms with two strategies that are more appropriate than longitudinal studies of singletons: twin studies and experimental preventive studies. In the mid-1990s we initiated a longitudinal study of a large sample of twins followed from birth. With reference to the development of physical aggression,

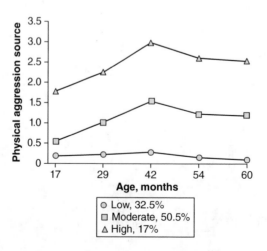

FIGURE 46.2 Trajectories of physical aggression from 17 to 60 months (Côté et al., 2007).

we showed that at 17 months of age, when children start to substantially increase the frequency of these aggressions, 80% of the variance in frequency was explained by genetic factors (Dionne, Tremblay, Boivin, Laplante, & Pérusse, 2003). This does not mean that the developmental trajectories of physical aggression are determined only by genetic factors. It means that at the beginning of life there are strong genetic differences in how we react to our environment. However, as we have seen above, the frequency of physical aggression decreases with age. As we grow older we acquire experience from our interactions with the environment. Our early genetically determined behavior creates environmental reactions which impact on our gene expression (epigenetic development) and on our brains (brain development) so that we can survive in that environment (Hackman, Farah, & Meaney, 2010; Tremblay, 2010). As Francis Galton showed more than a century ago, use of identical and fraternal twins helps to roughly quantify the contribution of genes and environment in a given population at a given point in time, but we are now also using twins who share the same genes (monozygotic twins) to study the impact of the environment on gene expression, brain, and behavior development (Guimond et al., 2012; Tremblay, 2010; Tremblay & Szyf, 2010; Vitaro et al., 2011).

Experimental preventive interventions with long-term follow-ups are probably the best means to study developmental mechanisms in humans. The approach is similar to experiments with animals, for example those who study the impact of early caring environments on development (Suomi, 2005). These animal studies usually deprive individuals of the normal caring environment to investigate the negative impact on normal development (e.g., Provençal et al., 2012; Weaver et al., 2004). Obviously this can't be done with humans, but we can enrich the environment of individuals who would be brought up in adverse environments (e.g., Olds et al., 1998; Tremblay, 2010).

We used our original preventive intervention with aggressive kindergarten boys to study these mechanisms (for example, the impact of parents and friends) that lead to behavior problems during adolescence, school achievement, and criminal behavior during adulthood (Tremblay et al., 1995; Vitaro et al., 2012). We also started preventive interventions during pregnancy to prevent serious behavior problems during childhood, adolescence, and adulthood, but also to study the mechanisms that are involved. The new technologies can now help identify the impact of prenatal and early postnatal interventions on gene expression, brain development, and behavior from birth to adolescence (Provençal et al., 2012). In order to take full advantage of the twin natural experiment to advance our understanding of developmental mechanisms and identify preventive interventions we can randomly modify monozygotic twins' environments, for example by enriching nutrition, giving parenting support, and enriching child-care environments and school experience. This research strategy will provide control for genetic effects while enabling experiments of different combinations of interventions from the prenatal period to adolescence.

Developmental research on human behavior is becoming more interdisciplinary, more intergenerational, and more international. I envy those who will be around over the next century to study human development. The field will most certainly make leaps and bounds. However, I consider myself lucky to have lived at a time when the opposition between social learning of aggression and genetics of aggression slowly but surely led to some form of integration of these perspectives. I am now even luckier to take part in the unforeseen leap to intergenerational environmental effects on gene expression (Provençal et al., 2012; Tremblay & Szyf, 2010; Wang et al., 2012). I expect a major acceleration of our understanding of bio-psycho-social mechanisms in the next few decades.

My new challenge, at the end of my 7th decade, is to find time to keep up with this acceleration and two other forms of acceleration. First, during my adolescence I was training to run the length of a football field (100 yards) as fast as possible. Over the past 4 years I have been training to run marathons (42 km) as fast as possible. I have learned that running marathons is like doing longitudinal studies, it's a matter of endurance. Second, as I mentioned at the beginning of this chapter, I am the proud father of a newborn son. Having had two children when I was much younger, I am fascinated by the difference in the intensity of my emotional, cognitive, and physical involvement. I want to be present to understand and enjoy every step this newborn makes. At a time when most of my peers are retiring to "enjoy a leisurely life," I find myself doing more than I ever did and hoping that I can do more. We have only one life and I hope to end it in full stride. Thanks to my younger son's mother, I have all the support and motivations I need to achieve this aim.

References

Alink, L. R., Mesman, J., van Zeijl, J., Stolk, M. N., Juffer, F., Koot, H. M. et al. (2006). The early childhood aggression curve: Development of physical aggression in 10- to 50-months-old children. *Child Development, 77*(4), 954–966.

Andry, R. G. (1960). *Delinquency and parental pathology: A study in forensic and clinical psychology.* London: Methuen.

Arseneault, L., Tremblay, R. E., Boulerice, B., & Saucier, J.-F. (2002). Obstetrical complications and violent delinquency: Testing two developmental pathways. *Child Development, 73*(2), 496–508.

Barker, E. D., Séguin, J. R., White, H. R., Bates, M. E., Lacourse, E., Carbonneau, R. et al. (2007). Developmental trajectories of male physical violence and theft: Relations to neurocognitive performance. *Archives of General Psychiatry, 64*(5), 592–599. doi: 10.1001/archpsyc.64.5.592

Boisjoli, R., Vitaro, F., Lacourse, E., Barker, E. D., & Tremblay, R. E. (2007). Impact and clinical significance of a preventive intervention for disruptive boys: 15-year follow-up. *British Journal of Psychiatry, 191*, 415–419.

Booij, L., Tremblay, R. E., Leyton, M., Seguin, J. R., Vitaro, F., Gravel, P. et al. (2010). Brain serotonin synthesis in adult males characterized by physical aggression during childhood: A 21-year longitudinal study. *PloS One, 5*(6). doi: 10.1371/journal.pone.0011255

Bovet, L. (1951). *Psychiatric aspects of juvenile delinquency.* Geneva, Switzerland: World Health Organization.

Bowlby, J. (1951). *Maternal care and mental health.* Geneva, Switzerland: World Health Organization.

Broidy, L. M., Nagin, D. S., Tremblay, R. E., Bates, J. E., Brame, B., Dodge, K. A. et al. (2003). Developmental trajectories of childhood disruptive behaviors and adolescent delinquency: A six site, cross national study. *Developmental Psychology, 39*(2), 222–245.

Burt, C. L. (1925). *The young delinquent.* London: University of London Press.

Côté, S. M., Boivin, M., Nagin, D. S., Japel, C., Xu, Q., Zoccolillo, M. et al. (2007). The role of maternal education and non-maternal care services in the prevention of children's physical aggression. *Archives of General Psychiatry, 64*(11), 1305–1312.

Côté, S. M., Tremblay, R. E., Nagin, D. S., Zoccolillo, M., & Vitaro, F. (2002). Childhood behavioral profiles leading to adolescent conduct disorder: Risk trajectories for boys and girls. *Journal of the American Academy of Child and Adolescent Psychiatry, 41*(9), 1086–1094.

Côté, S. M., Vaillancourt, T., LeBlanc, J. C., Nagin, D. S., & Tremblay, R. E. (2006). The development of physical aggression from toddlerhood to pre-adolescence: A nation wide longitudinal study of Canadian children. *Journal of Abnormal Child Psychology, 34*(1), 71–85.

DHHS. (2001). *Youth violence: a report of the Surgeon general.* Washington, DC: United States Department of Health and Human Services.

Dionne, G., Tremblay, R. E., Boivin, M., Laplante, D., & Pérusse, D. (2003). Physical aggression and expressive vocabulary in 19 month-old twins. *Developmental Psychology, 39*(2), 261–273.

Ellenberger, H. F. (1970). *The discovery of the unconscious: The history and evolution of dynamic psychiatry.* New York, NY: Basic Books.

Erikson, E. (1950). *Childhood and society.* New York, NY: W.W. Norton.

Eysenck, H. J. (1964). *Crime and personality.* London: Routledge and Kegan Paul.

Farrington, D. (2003). Key results from the first forty years of the Cambridge study in delinquent development. In T. P. Thornberry, & M. D. Krohn (Eds.), *Taking stock of delinquency: An overview of findings from contemporary longitudinal studies* (pp. 137–183). New York, NY: Kluwer Academic/Plenum Publishers.

Farrington, D. P., Loeber, R., Elliott, D. S., Hawkins, D., Kandel, D. B., Klein, M. W. et al. (1990). Advancing knowledge about the onset of delinquency and crime. In B. B. Lahey, & A. E. Kazdin (Eds.), *Advances in clinical child psychology*, Vol. 13 (pp. 283–342). New York, NY: Plenum.

Fisher, S., & Cleveland, S. E. (1968). *Body image and personality* (2nd ed.). Mineola, NY: Dover Publications.

Fontaine, N., Carbonneau, R., Barker, E. D., Vitaro, F., Hébert, M., Côté, S. M. et al. (2008). Girls' hyperactivity and physical aggression during childhood and adjustment problems in early adulthood. *Archives of General Psychiatry, 65*(3), 320–328.

Gatti, U., Tremblay, R. E., & Vitaro, F. (2009). Iatrogenic effect of juvenile justice. *Journal of Child Psychology and Psychiatry, 50*(8), 991–998. doi: 10.1111/j.1469-7610.2008.02057.x

Guimond, F.-A., Brendgen, M., Forget-Dubois, N., Dionne, G., Vitaro, F., Tremblay, R. E. et al. (2012). Associations of mother's and father's parenting practices with children's observed social reticence in a competitive situation: A monozygotic twin difference study. *Journal of Abnormal Child Psychology, 40*(3), 391–402. doi: 10.1007/s10802-011-9573-8

Hackman, D. A., Farah, M. J., & Meaney, M. J. (2010). Socioeconomic status and the brain: Mechanistic insights from human and animal research. *Nature Reviews Neuroscience, 11*(9), 651–659. doi: 10.1038/nrn2897

Heims, S. J. (1980). *John von Neumann and Norbert Wiener, from mathematics to the technologies of life and death.* Cambridge, MA: MIT Press. ISBN 0-262-08105-9.

Jones, M. (1953). *The therapeutic community: A new treatment method in psychiatry.* Oxford, England: Basic Books.

Kagan, J. (1974). Development and methodological considerations in the study of aggression. In J. de Wit & W. W. Hartup (Eds.), *Determinants and origins of aggressive behavior* (pp. 107–114). The Hague, Netherlands: Mouton.

Kerr, M., Tremblay, R. E., Pagani-Kurtz, L., & Vitaro, F. (1997). Boys' behavioral inhibition and the risk of later delinquency. *Archives of General Psychiatry, 54*(9), 809–816.

Krug, E. G., Dahlberg, L. L., Mercy, J. A., Zwi, A. B., & Lozano, R. (2002). World report on violence and health, from: www.who.int/violence_injury_prevention/violence/world_report/wrvh1/en

Lipsey, M. W. (1992). Juvenile delinquency treatment: A meta-analytic inquiry into the variability of effects. In T. D. Cook, H. Cooper, D. S. Cordray, H. Hartman, L. V. Hedges, R. J. Light et al. (Eds.), *Meta-analysis for explanation* (pp. 83–127). New York, NY: Russell Sage Foundation.

Lipton, D., Martinson, R., & Wilks, J. (1975). *The effectiveness of correctional treatment: A survey of treatment evaluation studies.* New York, NY: Praeger.

Loeber, R., Lacourse, E., & Homish, D. L. (2005). Homicide, violence and developmental trajectories. In R. E. Tremblay, W. W. Hartup, & J. Archer (Eds.), *Developmental origins of aggression* (pp. 202–219). New York, NY: Guilford Press.

Mâsse, L. C., & Tremblay, R. E. (1997). Behavior of boys in kindergarten and the onset of substance use during adolescence. *Archives of General Psychiatry, 54*, 62–68.

Mayers, M. O. (1980). *The hard-core delinquent.* Farnborough, Hants: Saxon House.

McCord, J. (1978). A thirty-year follow-up of treatment effects. *American Psychologist, 33*(3), 284–289.

McCord, J., & Tremblay, R. E. (Eds.). (1992). *Preventing antisocial behavior from birth through adolescence: Experimental approaches.* New York, NY: Guilford Press.

Moos, R. H. (1975). *Evaluating correctional and community settings.* London: John Wiley & Sons.

Nagin, D., & Tremblay, R. E. (1999). Trajectories of boys' physical aggression, opposition, and hyperactivity on the path to physically violent and nonviolent juvenile delinquency. *Child Development, 70*(5), 1181–1196.

NICHD. (2004). The developmental course of gender differenciation. *Monographs of the Society for Research in Child Development.*

Olds, D., Henderson, C. R., Cole, R., Eckenrode, J., Kitzman, H., Luckey, D. et al. (1998). Long-term effects of nurse home visitation on children's criminal and antisocial behavior: 15-year follow-up of a randomized controlled trial. *Journal of the American Medical Association, 280*(14), 1238–1244.

Petitclerc, A., Gatti, U., Vitaro, F., & Tremblay, R. E. (2013). Effects of juvenile court exposure on crime in young adulthood. *Journal of Child Psychiatry and Psychology, 54*(3): 291–297.

Powers, E., & Witmer, H. (1951). *An experiment in the prevention of delinquency: The Cambridge-Somerville Youth Study.* Montclair, NJ: Columbia University Press.

Provençal, N., Suderman, M. J., Guillemin, C., Massart, R., Ruggiero, A., Wang, D. et al. (2012). The signature of maternal rearing in the methylome in Rhesus Macaque prefrontal cortex and T cells. *Journal of Neuroscience, 32*(44), 15626–15642.

Redl, F., & Wineman, D. (1951). *The aggressive child: Children who hate.* Glencoe: Free Press.

Restoin, A., Montagner, H., Rodriguez, D., Girardot, J. J., Laurent, D., Kontar, F. et al. (1985). Chronologie des comportements de communication et profils de comportement chez le jeune enfant. In R. E. Tremblay, M. A. Provost, & F. F. Strayer (Eds.), *Ethologie et développement de l'enfant* (pp. 93–130). Paris: Editions Stock/Laurence Pernoud.

Sand, E. A. (1966). *Contribution à l'étude du développement de l'enfant. Aspects médico-sociaux et psychologiques.* Brussells, Belgium: Éditions de l'Institut de sociologie de l'Université libre de Bruxelles.

Stattin, H., & Klackenberg-Larsson, I. (1993). Early language and intelligence development and their relationship to future criminal behavior. *Journal of Abnormal Psychology, 102*(3), 369–378.

Suomi, S. J. (2005). Genetic and environmental factors influencing the expression of impulsive aggression and serotonergic functioning in Rhesus monkeys. In R. E. Tremblay, W. W. Hartup, & J. Archer (Eds.), *Developmental origins of aggression* (pp. 63–82). New York, NY: Guilford Press.

Tonry, M., Ohlin, L. E., Farrington, D. P., Adams, K., Earls, F., Rowe, D. C. et al. (1991). *Human development and criminal behavior: New ways of advancing knowledge*. New York, NY: Springer-Verlag.

Tremblay, R. E. (1976). *A psycho-educational study of juvenile delinquents during residential treatment*. London: University of London.

Tremblay, R. E. (1984). Treatment of hard-core delinquents in residential establishments: The Ardale Case. *British Journal of Criminology, 24*(4), 384–393.

Tremblay, R. E. (2000). The development of aggressive behaviour during childhood: What have we learned in the past century? *International Journal of Behavioral Development, 24*(2), 129–141.

Tremblay, R. E. (2006). Prevention of youth violence: Why not start at the beginning? *Journal of Abnormal Child Psychology, 34*(4), 481–487.

Tremblay, R. E. (2010). Developmental origins of disruptive behaviour problems: The 'original sin' hypothesis, epigenetics and their consequences for prevention. *Journal of Child Psychology and Psychiatry, 51*(4), 341–367. doi: 10.1111/j.1469-7610.2010.02211.x

Tremblay, R. E., Japel, C., Pérusse, D., McDuff, P., Boivin, M., Zoccolillo, M. et al. (1999). The search for the age of "onset" of physical aggression: Rousseau and Bandura revisited. *Criminal Behavior and Mental Health, 9*(1), 8–23.

Tremblay, R. E., Kurtz, L., Mâsse, L. C., Vitaro, F., & Pihl, R. O. (1995). A bimodal preventive intervention for disruptive kindergarten boys: Its impact through mid-adolescence. *Journal of Consulting and Clinical Psychology, 63*(4), 560–568.

Tremblay, R. E., Nagin, D., Séguin, J. R., Zoccolillo, M., Zelazo. P. D., Boivin, M. et al. (2004). Physical aggression during early childhood: Trajectories and predictors. *Pediatrics, 114*(1), e43–e50.

Tremblay, R. E., Pihl, R. O., Vitaro, F., & Dobkin, P. L. (1994). Predicting early-onset of male antisocial-behavior from preschool behavior. *Archives of General Psychiatry, 51*(9), 732–739.

Tremblay, R. E., Provost, M. A., & Strayer, F. F. (Eds.). (1985). *Ethologie et développement de l'enfant*. Paris: Stock.

Tremblay, R. E., & Szyf, M. (2010). Developmental origins of chronic physical aggression and epigenetics. *Epigenomics, 2*(4), 495–499. doi: 10.2217/epi.10.40

Van Bokhoven, I., Van Goozen, S. H. M., van Engeland, H., Schaal, B., Arseneault, L., Séguin, J. R. et al. (2005). Salivary cortisol and aggression in a population-based longitudinal study of adolescent males. *Journal of Neural Transmission, 112*(8), 1083–1096. doi: 10.1007/s00702-004-0253-5

Vitaro, F., Barker, E. D., Brendgen, M., & Tremblay, R. E. (2012). Pathways explaining the reduction of adult criminal behaviour by a randomized intervention for disruptive kindergarten children. *Journal of Child Psychology and Psychiatry, 53*(7) 748–756.

Vitaro, F., Brendgen, M., Boivin, M., Cantin, S., Dionne, G., Tremblay, R. E. et al. (2011). A monozygotic twin difference study of friends' aggression and children's adjustment problems. *Child Development, 82*(2), 617–632. doi: 10.1111/j.1467-8624.2010.01570.x

Wang, D., Szyf, M., Benkelfat, C., Provençal, N., Caramaschi, D., Côté, S. M. et al. (2012). Peripheral SLC6A4 DNA methylation is associated with in vivo measures of human brain serotonin synthesis and childhood physical aggression. *PLoS ONE, 7*(6), 39501.

Weaver, I. C. G., Cervoni, N., Champagne, F. A., D'Alessio, A. C., Sharma, S., Seckl, J. R. et al. (2004). Epigenetic programming by maternal behavior. *Nature Neuroscience, 7*(8), 847–854. doi: 10.1038/nn1276

West, D. J., & Farrington, D. P. (1973). *Who becomes delinquent*. London: Heinemann.

Wohlwill, J. F. (1973). *The study of behavioral development*. New York, NY: Academic Press.

Xue, Y., Leventhal, T., Brooks-Gunn, J., & Earls, F. J. (2005). Neighborhood residence and mental health problems of 5- to 11-year-olds. *Archives of General Psychiatry, 62*(5), 554–563.

47

My Career Trajectory in Understanding the Ecological Realities of Adolescence in India

SUMAN VERMA

In a country as large and diverse as India, adolescent experiences differ widely according to social and cultural contexts. For those from the upper social strata, schooling may be equated with competition and stress. In the lower social strata, meanwhile, poor access to schooling, gender disparities, and the early arrival of adult responsibilities (entering the workforce, marriage, and child-bearing, to name just three) are more often the reality. Given this scenario, some of the key themes that have guided my work on adolescence are school stress, risk, and resilience among working children, family life experiences amidst social change, and life-skills education for empowering the youth. I also share some of the inner dilemmas and challenges of working in this field along with my efforts in advocacy that have shaped my experiences of engaging in research, practice, and policy.

The invitation to write this chapter came at a time when I was at the threshold of retiring from government service (but certainly not from academia). With considerably less work pressure ahead of me, I was excited to finally have time for the things I've always wanted to do, including writing my autobiography. Working on this chapter was also a golden opportunity to retrospect, to take stock of the past 36 years of work in my discipline of human development, and to look forward to the future. In the coming pages, I will reflect on my varied academic and professional experiences and mentors that influenced and impacted my career trajectory. First, I'll provide a brief snapshot of my own childhood and education before examining the different aspects of developmental experiences of adolescents in different behavior settings that have guided my research throughout the years.

Early Years and Family Ties

I grew up in a family with a defense background, which required relocating nearly every other year. Army life

was fun (at least for me), as it presented the opportunity to travel across the country, change schools often, make new friends, and learn new languages. These experiences enabled me to develop adaptability and versatility in my personality, and also inspired my love for travel and exploration. My happily married parents (now for 68 years) provided a safe, secure environment for their four children. We were disciplined, of course, but also groomed to depend on ourselves and make our own decisions. For my parents, education was of the highest priority and freedom of expression was among their cherished values. To this day, they are my role models and source of support.

My father was commissioned as an officer in the British army in 1943. I grew up listening to anecdotes of his army experiences, including the Indo-Pakistan partition and the freedom struggle. From my parents, I learned more about Gandhi, Bose, Ambedkar, Tagore, Patel, Nehru, and other freedom fighters than at school. Nehru's famous "Tryst with Destiny" speech, given on India's Independence Day in 1947, stirred patriotic emotions within me with a glimpse of the independence fever that gripped the country. My mother is also a gifted storyteller who blessed us with a deep understanding of Indian mythology through the epics—*Ramayana*, *Mahabharata*, and *Gita*—which she read to us as children. Piety, positive actions, and good deeds were always emphasized. And though we did not strictly observe the rituals, the celebration of festivals was always a high point.

Being the eldest son, my father was highly respected and was consulted on most issues, even by his own father. We had a large extended family whom we would meet every summer at my grandfather's house; my cousins were my extended peer network, and I always looked forward to these yearly reunions. I have particularly fond memories of playing "dark room" with them (this game is like playing hide-and-seek in a pitch-dark room where cues are given by hurling cushions, pillows, and footwear at the person giving the den). Deserving a special word is Kiran, my multi-faceted and talented sister, who was just a couple of years older than me. She was a little bossy when we were children, but always helpful in school-related tasks and projects. During adolescence, we disagreed on almost everything, but as we made the transition into our twenties, we became the best of friends. I sought out and valued her advice, and she supported me both personally and professionally, despite having settled in the United States. She would schedule appointments, facilitate meetings with scholars in Washington, DC and Maryland, and host my colleagues in her artistically styled home. When I lost Kiran in a tragic incident in 2005, I lost my soul mate. Parental bonding and submerging in work were the only solace. Her daughters, my nieces Karishma Kadian and Neena Koyen—professionals in their own right—continue to be interested in my research pursuits and often provide very meaningful feedback. Our deep emotional connection is invaluable.

Education

In 1974, I graduated from Delhi University with a degree in Home Science. I then moved to the highly reputed Department of Human Development and Family Studies (HDFS), Maharaja Sayajirao University of Baroda, to complete my master's in Child Development. Realizing a love for working with children, I chose to specialize in this field. This is where I met my guru, T. S. Saraswathi, an incredible teacher and great scholar whose mentorship was equal parts challenge and reward. Perhaps more than anyone else, it was T.S. Saraswathi who instilled in me the critical thinking skills and sensitivity required of researchers. She was a hard taskmaster to be sure, but I owe much to her.

I must acknowledge other great minds at the HDFS department in Baroda who were a great source of inspiration and motivation. First, the vivacious Amita Verma who spearheaded the department. As a student, I remember her as a visionary with a nonjudgmental perspective ever willing to entertain our crazy, mad ideas. Then there was Veena Mistry and Rumy Mistry, the campus' most popular and accessible couple. We spent countless memorable evenings together, stimulated by grand discussions and delicious home-cooked Parsi meals.

The curriculum was challenging, as it involved both course- and fieldwork. As I mentioned, I'd been exposed to some of the world's great literature growing up, but discovering Freud, Piaget, Vygotsky, Bandura, Bronfenbrenner, and other theorists opened up my eyes. I spent many sleepless nights discussing their theories with my roommate, Meena Mathur, and our mutual friend, Chandra Schanz (nee Arora). Although Meena and I settled in different cities after graduation, we continued to collaborate on academic activities; in fact, we were instrumental in starting Child Development departments in our respective universities. When Chandra finished her master's degree, she stayed in Baroda for a number of years working with children. Those late nights may have happened decades ago, but we remain best friends—and continue to serve as sounding boards for each other, no matter the madness of our ideas and dreams.

Ultimately, I left the HDFS department with a stronger zeal for fieldwork over academics. Twenty days after receiving my masters in May 1976, I started my first job with the Indian Council for Child Welfare (ICCW) in Jind, a backward district in the state of Haryana.

Child Welfare: A Reality Check

Starting in June 1976, I worked for the Haryana Branch of the ICCW, where as a district Child Welfare Officer I was responsible for implementing and supervising day care centers, *balwadis* (preschools), special nutrition programs, and supervised homework classes. During the initial months, I was disheartened by the wide gap between what I had expected and the on-the-ground reality. The quality of Early Childhood Education (referred to hereafter as "ECE") services was poor; the teachers' skills and preparedness were outdated. There was no program planning, let alone a vision for the goals of the services being provided. To make things worse, my co-workers had a biased attitude towards rural children and lacked any notion of child rights.

I knew I would have to start from scratch. But I needed to be cautious: Most of the teachers were my seniors who regarded me as a novice. I realized my best path forward was to approach them as a co-worker on equal footing, with a personal goal of becoming a role model. To earn their trust, I spent most of my time traveling to the village ECE centers, where I worked with each teacher (called *balsevika*) to plan (and hopefully implement!) the new programs. I was struck by the poor working conditions. The *balsevikas* had minimal educational materials, makeshift school buildings, and zero motivation. There was a crucial need for an intensive in-service teacher-training program with ongoing feedback mechanisms.

In early 1977, I introduced the peer-feedback system and conducted a series of workshops on ECE-related issues such as child development, program planning, and low-cost educational aids. Greater responsibility coupled with greater recognition worked wonders for the teachers' self-esteem and motivation. Crucially, I was always careful to work alongside them—as a peer. It was a long and arduous process, but I ultimately managed to raise funds, equip the centers and crèches with equipment, and train senior teachers to conduct their own workshops and supervise *balwadis* in adjacent villages.

The message of our progress spread, and I started getting requests from other district child welfare officers to run similar workshops for their teachers. Within 18 months, my district was named best in the state of Haryana (1977–78). During this time, I also started the Bal-Bhawan, an after-school recreation center for children offering dramatics, sports, creative arts, science, music, dance, and other extracurricular activities.

While I was enjoying my professional work, my personal life presented its own challenges. Jind is a very conservative region with minimal social offerings for a young 22-year-old. To stave off the loneliness, I spent much of my time reading and learning to play the sitar. I also began a serious practice of yoga and meditation, and found myself inspired by books about philosophy, mysticism, and a spiritual understanding of life. I delved into the work of Plato, Aristotle, David Hume, Immanuel Kant, Jean-Paul Sartre, Simone de Beauvoir, Albert Camus, and Fritjof Capra. One quote from de Beauvoir remains fresh in my mind: "I wish that every human life might be pure transparent freedom."

On the spiritual front, I was deeply impressed with the teachings of Jiddu Krishnamurti. To this day, I ponder some of his subtle concepts, such as "When the observer is the observed." I would also like to cite Krishnamurti on this concept:

> When man becomes aware of the movement of his own consciousness he will see the division between the thinker and the thought, the observer and the observed, the experiencer and the experience. He will discover that this division is an illusion. Then only is there pure observation which is insight without any shadow of the past. This timeless insight brings about a deep radical mutation in the mind.
>
> (Krishnamurti, 1980, 2008)

In March 1978, I was offered a job as Principal of the training wing of the Haryana State Council for Child Welfare in Chandigarh, a beautiful city I'd visited a few times in the past year. I happily accepted. For the next 5 years, I trained teachers to work in rural areas under the state welfare schemes and the Integrated Child Development Services Scheme (ICDS), one of the world's largest integrated child development systems. My work focused on the standardization of teaching modules, teaching aids in ECE centers, and parent awareness programs for promoting child health and development. The Indian Association for Preschool Education (IAPE) provided a good opportunity to network with professionals from different states on issues related to ECE. It also provided a forum to discuss theoretical issues related to skill development and training component.

In this new position, I was confronted with many of the same issues I'd seen in the field for years: lack of follow-up, poor monitoring of the workers, and a gap between teacher training and their expectations. But I was also faced with a new, more profound challenge: the organization's top-down bureaucracy. It wasn't long before I found myself in an ideological dilemma: Working within a system so defined by waste and inefficiency—to say nothing of institutional stubbornness—could I make any concrete improvements in the lives of children? I soon realized that I could not change the system. My only options were to accept the conditions or quit. I chose the latter.

By this time, I had enrolled for my PhD at the Panjab University. In November 1983, I was selected for a teaching post in Child Development in the Government Home Science College in Chandigarh. Thus began my transition to academics.

Becoming an "Academic Activist"

When I joined the college, there was only one subject of Child Development at the under-graduate level—and I was the only faculty member. Within a year, I started the department's lab nursery school, *Chaitanya* ("to create awareness"), which I designed and furnished. At the same time, I was designing a new post-graduate program in Child Development. In 1986, I started an MSc in Child Development and increased the number of department faculty.

These early years were difficult. For starters, getting new posts sanctioned by the government was nothing less than arduous. I was also teaching upwards of 26 hours each week, plus supervising the nursery. I loved teaching and enjoyed spending time with my students, whom I took to conferences and seminars—especially those organized by the Indian Association for Preschool Education—in an effort to bolster their field experience. I drew on my own time at the Indian Council for Child Welfare in Haryana, and was able to connect theory and real-world practice. In 1986, my own education reached its apex when I was awarded my PhD, working under Vidhu Mohan from the Psychology department at Panjab University. I will be forever grateful to Mohan for being a mentor and championing the academic activities I organized in the college.

Driven by my own experiences connecting theory, research, and fieldwork, I had a vision for an interdisciplinary curriculum for the Child Development department at the Government Home Science College. I also sought to introduce an ethno-cultural perspective among the faculty and students.

In these first years, I concentrated on strengthening the department by starting the master's and doctoral programs, a diploma in child guidance and family counseling, updating the syllabi, and appointing faculty. Other priority areas were to: (a) improve the quality of research with a thrust on documentation and dissemination; (b) establish strong networks with non-government organizations and other professionals in planning community outreach activities for students; (c) keep our faculty at the forefront of their fields through refresher courses; and (d) augment departmental resources with labs for counseling, psychological tools and testing, books, journals, and resource files for subjects taught.

Once again, I struggled with innovating in an institution where the academic culture thrived on perpetuating stereotypes and promoting mediocrity. I cannot be sure if my vision was fulfilled completely, but I do believe that I did my best. This professional lethargy among my colleagues was always bothersome to me but I did not allow it to bog me down. My past experience in the ICCW had strengthened my resolve to keep moving forward. Although sense of alienation prevailed, I continued to move on, sometimes with a smile, but sometimes with deep anguish and frustration. Often, I would take comfort in Tagore's song *Ekla Chalo Re*:

If they answer not to thy call walk alone.

If they are afraid and cower mutely facing the wall,
O thou unlucky one,
open thy mind and speak out alone.

If they turn away, and desert you when crossing the wilderness,
O thou unlucky one,
trample the thorns under thy tread,
and along the blood-lined track travel alone.

If they do not hold up the light when the night is troubled with storm,
O thou unlucky one,
with the thunder flame of pain ignite thy own heart
and let it burn alone.

                              (Rabindranath Tagore)

During these years, advocacy became the defining factor of my work. I also came to understand that, at core, I'm an academic activist. I organized seminars and workshops, and wrote about issues affecting the lives of children and youth, such as: improving the status of the girl child in India (Verma, 1991); alleviating pressures of the burdened preschooler (Verma, 1993); child-friendly cities (1997a); academic stress among adolescents (Verma & Gupta, 1990, 1994); life-skills education to deal with adolescent problem behaviors (Verma, 2000b, 2006); adolescents in single-parent families (Kaur, Sharma & Verma, 2003; Sharma & Verma, 2004); and child abuse and neglect (Kaur & Verma, 2006).

As a professor, field training was a top priority; my students were placed in child welfare agencies across the city. One, Mother Teresa's Missionaries of Charity, remains near and dear to my heart. I'd begun working with the home's differently abled children in 1981, and I saw that the Sisters took great care to address their physical needs. But I saw a great opportunity to help the children with their emotional, social, and cognitive needs as well. I designed and opened a play center specifically for these children with special needs and ran it three times a week after work. This laid the foundation of my relationship with them for the next 22 years. The Sisters were devoted and supportive, and made it possible for me to arrange operations for kids with polio and cerebral palsy; to aid recovery, I founded a physiotherapy unit. We also successfully placed children in regular schools. To foster a greater sense of community among the residents, I made a point of celebrating all religious and national festivals with them. My students joined the festivities—and our times together soon became grand familial celebrations.

It wasn't just the children and students who benefited from these experiences. Spending time with these resilient, wonderful kids helped me confront society's harsh realities. I still remember Salim, a child with cerebral palsy who, one day while he was painting, suddenly looked straight into my eyes and said: "You know, my father thought I was asleep when he abandoned me in the garbage dump." My heart skipped a beat, but Salim only paused, smiled, and continued with his work. My real-life training in resiliency started here, with these children who were living with painful memories—yet rising up with dignity to life's challenges.

Perhaps driven by my frustration with the bureaucracies around to me, I made great efforts to network with other agencies. Through the United States India Educational Foundation (USIEF) in New Delhi, I was able to host two Fulbright scholars for a semester of teaching and collaborative research. With Douglass Abbot from the University of Nebraska, I studied the family life experiences of children of daily wagers at construction sites in the city (Abbot, Sharma, & Verma, 2004); with Reed Larson from the University of Illinois, I initiated a time-use study of Indian adolescents, conducted a national-level seminar on research methodology, and collaborated on various articles.

Yet institutional challenges remained. In 1991, I initiated a project for mainstreaming street children by involving a number of NGOs at the city level. Despite having a sanctioned grant from UNICEF, the Education department refused to grant me permission. (They believed that academicians should not involve themselves with applied work with children; that was work for the NGOs.) These were frustrating moments, but such is the rigidity of the bureaucratic system. Spending time in my garden nurturing my plants was a great stress-buster.

That being said, I had positive experiences working with certain other institutions, including the National Council for Educational Research and Training (NCERT), where my work on the stress experienced by young children received a lot of support. The following sections contain brief discussions of select research themes and areas of work.

The Early Childhood Education Initiative

In the mid-1980s, the issue of academic stress among preschool children was only just beginning to gain importance. Fortunately, some of my colleagues at the IAPE and NCERT—most notably, Rajalakshmi Murlidharan and Venita Kaul—were, like me, studying the effect of stress on early cognitive abilities and classroom adjustment.

In 1989, NCERT initiated a nationwide drive to bring awareness to ECE-related issues in India. Workshops were held across the country, focusing in part on academic stress among preschoolers. At that time, ECE was seen as a downward extension of primary school philosophies and methodologies; the needs of very young students were being disregarded or ignored. Outreach efforts were made to the nation's top schools, widely considered to be the pacesetters, and policy-makers. At the workshops, recommendations were made to put preschool education back on sound footing—not just at the elite schools, but also in public environments.

Back in *Chaitanya* lab nursery, the faculty and I worked on a curriculum that took into account the developmental level of children. We hoped to see an increased focus on activity- and play-based instruction. As the Chandigarh chapter coordinator for IAPE, I helped organize several workshops for the city school preschool teachers to educate them on issues related to ECE program planning and stress among young children. In 1992, we also conducted a baseline survey in schools across the city to study the status and quality of ECE in the schools.

Results were not very encouraging. Most schools interviewed children as young as 2–3 years for admission and had a formal reading and writing curriculum for children 3–5 years. The children were carrying heavy school bags, spending hours doing their homework, and were made to take written exams on a monthly basis. The particular needs of young children were widely disregarded in favor of obsolete but long-standing academic processes. For example, when asked, it was commonplace for nursery school teachers to identify counting from 1 to 100 (forward and backward) and reciting the alphabet as their benchmarks of student achievement. In many schools, young children were punished for expressing themselves in Hindi or their native language. Meanwhile, these same students were interviewed—in English—as part of the admissions process. This blind obsession with spoken English at the preschool level (when the children were barely learning to express their myriad colored thoughts and ideas) was repressive. To make things worse, the teacher-to-pupil ratio was commonly one-to-fifty. What chance did students have in such a rigid, crowded environment? And what of the teachers? With such large classes, it was little wonder that I met teachers who had completely lost the ability to relate to children (not to mention play with them!). The communication gap between the teachers and the children was glaringly stark and painful to see.

In 1993, I worked with the NCERT to organize a regional seminar on "The Burdened Preschooler: Issues and Alternatives" to provide a forum for discussing the content and methodology in ECE, admission criteria, and universalization of the curriculum at the preschool level. We also launched the *Basta Hatao Bachpan Bachao* ("Shed School Bags, Save Childhood") campaign to alleviate academic stress on preschool children and improve the quality of ECE in Chandigarh.

I'm happy to say that our campaign spread throughout the country. The report (Verma, 1993) was circulated nationwide among government institutions, schools, and teachers, and it was instrumental in highlighting stress among young children in urban ECE centers. The campaign also drew the attention of the Chandigarh Education department, which agreed to a citywide implementation of the report's recommendations. I convened a core group of members from the management committees of various schools, teachers, and the government to work on action plans for the schools. We ran several workshops for government and private schools, helped revise curriculum and admission criteria,

and implemented the recommendations. I consider this one of my most successful initiatives in advocacy.

Despite the positive outcome, this campaign posed several challenges that I had not anticipated. For instance, since this issue of reducing academic burden on preschoolers involved multiple stakeholders, I realized that the nexus between the schools and the publishers was strong. As a team, we worked hard to convince the principals that children do not need textbooks at this age and that they should shed school bags for them. This meant that the books supplied by the publishers had to be stopped, which was not acceptable to the school authorities for several reasons (including a strong publisher lobby). Finally, as a compromise, we substituted the 3-Rs books by replacing them with story books and activity books for children. Also, there was the challenge of balancing the theory of developmental appropriateness of curriculum with the entrenched attitudes and practices in the system. Despite the workshops, we had to work with the teachers at the individual level, taking them to attend the IAPE conferences, inviting them to the college for various functions at *Chaitanya* lab nursery, and sharing resource materials to mention a few. These strategies worked with some schools whereas they failed to make an impact on others. On reflecting back, I feel this indeed was a theory versus situational reality challenge wherein as a team we had to tread carefully given the complexity of the problem.

Five years after launching *Basta Hatao Bachapan Bachao*, I conducted an impact evaluation study to examine the campaign's lasting effects (Verma, 1997b). The findings were mixed:

- Although admission tests had been banned for young children, schools were instead interviewing their parents.
- The development-oriented curriculum we had developed with the teachers was accepted by the majority of the schools, but implementation was weak among government schools.
- The mindset of the teachers was still rigid; they preferred to teach the 3 Rs.
- While we found greater awareness among both teachers and parents of the ill-effects of academic pressure on young children, formal schooling pressure continued to increase expectations on kindergarten children.

The silver lining was that the media supported us all along and widely covered these issues effectively. On Republic Day, January 26, 1994, the Chandigarh Administration presented me with a certificate of commendation for services rendered in the field of education, which I humbly accepted.

Social Deprivation and Adolescent Development

My doctoral work focused on problem-solving abilities among socially deprived and non-deprived adolescents (Verma & Mohan, 1990, 1993). I continued to work in this area, examining cognitive aspects such as concept formation, creativity, attention span, and moral judgment among socially deprived children (Verma & Chawla, 1989; Verma & Chodha, 1990; Verma & Loomba, 1990; Verma & Singh, 1990). The studies revealed that fragmented thinking, erratic and disruptive shifts in communication, faulty language, and poor cognitive and problem-solving skills were some of the outcomes of social deprivation. Differences between socially deprived and non-deprived children were evident in their learning experiences, language codes, verbal and non-verbal communication, goals, skills, and values.

In terms of cultural practices, parents of the deprived children were predominantly authoritarian in their orientation. Children were treated as subordinates with minimal involvement in family decision-making. Children in non-deprived families, on the other hand, were often treated as peers. They actively participated in the decision-making process; they initiated conversations and made demands. These differences in socialization fostered the development of information-processing in children. It was clear that, due to the detrimental effects of prolonged physical, social, and cognitive deprivation, impoverished children were unable to meet the educational demands—resulting in failures and dropouts. These children also reported harsh parenting practices, lack of motivational experiences, and limited exposure to educational materials and resources, games, and recreational activities. This proved the need to work on an enrichment program to foster problem solving abilities among socially deprived children.

In 1993, using a pre-post test design, I conducted along with a student a 16-week program (Verma & Verma, 1994) of 10-to-12-year-olds based on the theoretical assumptions of De Bono (1986). The goal was to foster lateral thinking in socially deprived children. In other words, we wanted children to solve problems through unorthodox methods that are normally ignored by logical thinking. The objectives of the intervention were to:

- develop skills in lateral thinking;
- introduce flexibility in thought processes;
- develop creative thinking ability through deliberate generation of alternatives;
- enhance the ability to apply appropriate strategies for solving problems;
- provide exposure to a variety of problem solving tasks to facilitate the availability of concepts and transfer of learning.

The techniques included generation of alternatives, brainstorming, and hypothetical problem-solving through creative expression such as drama, drawing, and storytelling. We held evaluation sessions to discuss problem-solving strategies with the children, teaching them how to apply new, more effective strategies. The results revealed a significant improvement in the problem-solving scores of the experimental group as compared to the control.

This study served as a pilot for a larger study conducted in different schools in Chandigarh for deprived children. Vidhu Mohan and I were the co-investigators of this study, sponsored by the University Grants Commission in New Delhi. The premise was to help children develop certain perceptual skills and logic that are essential for thinking and learning. To have this incorporated into the educational system would enable socially deprived children to acquire crucial skills and effectively manage their environmental demands, whether it's learning, problem-solving, or interpersonal relationships. School teachers were actively involved in the implementation to facilitate integration into the school curriculum.

The positive impact of the intervention was evident from the improved academic performance of children, their greater ability to solve problems successfully, and the positive transfer of learning to cognitive tasks.

Time-Use Studies of Adolescents and Life-Skills Education

Over the years, I continued to stay connected with my alma mater; the department of HDFS, Baroda. In 1990, T.S. Saraswathi initiated a national research network project, sponsored by the International Development Research Centre and Human Development and Family Studies department, M.S. University, Baroda. I was part of this project. She was already working on establishing the reliability and validity of time-use methods (Saraswathi & Sridharan, 1991) and I decided to study time-use among university students (Verma & Saraswathi, 1992).

For our methodology, we compared and evaluated three methods of time-use data collection. The first was the 24-hour concurrent record (by diary) wherein the respondents provided information on activities, locations, other persons present, and accompanied by their thoughts and feelings at the time. They also recorded their level of motivation for the particular activity. The time for the whole day (24 hours) was divided into 15-minute lots (except for midnight to 6 a.m.). The second was the 24-hour global recall by diary wherein the respondents recalled an average day and filled in the diary with the same format as in the first method. Whereas the concurrent scheme required hourly recordings, this method asked participants to recall the day's events (and thoughts and feelings) largely in hindsight. In the third method, 24-hour global recall by interview, respondents' recollections of an average day were gathered via interview, using the same data format as the previous two methods (Verma, Kaur, & Saraswathi, 1995).

We found that the first method—the 24-hour concurrent diary—yielded the most accurate data. In terms of the actual findings, we found significant variations among student time-use across activities, locations, companions, and feelings. We found significant differences according to gender, type of academic program, and type of day (e.g., a college day, Sunday, a pre-examination day). It was evident that, for youth in an Indian setting, most difficulties arise when their ability to dictate how to spend their time is limited. Primarily, restrictions came from organizational, cultural, social, and personal factors; access to goods and motivation also impacted student time-use (Verma & Saraswathi, 1992).

The time-use profiles provided insights into the developmental experiences across life settings of the youth, how differences in conceptions of time affect time spent, how societal priorities and gender socialization determine time-use, and how time use might be modified to improve individual development and well-being among the youth.

Qualitative analysis of the data also revealed an absence of a clear concept of time management among the youth. They voiced a need to be oriented, initiated, and sensitized to the value of time and individual time-structuring strategies for a successful future. This led to the planning of a 5-year longitudinal intervention study on expanding time awareness and life-skills education for the psychosocial competence in the youth. This study was funded from 1992 to 1997 by the Jacobs Foundation in Zurich, under the young investigators research grant award.

Initially, this research was envisioned as a 3-year longitudinal study, to be conducted in three phases with a quasi-experimental design (Verma, 1995a). The rationale was that behavior could be changed by providing a strong knowledge base, special skills, and effective strategies (which alone can bring about changes in time perspective, effective time utilization, and the development of various time management skills to achieve personal goals and aspirations). The emphasis was on the usage of creative techniques such as brainstorming, generation of alternatives, creative drama, and simulation exercises to make the sessions lively, meaningful, and participatory.

The sample comprised first-year female students from my college (mean age: 18.78) who were followed longitudinally. In the first phase, they were pre-tested for their ability to organize and structure time; their time-use patterns were recorded using time diaries. In the second phase, the Treatment group ($n = 44$) was exposed to a 5-month intervention program on time sensitization, whereas the Control-1 group ($n = 39$) was exposed to a non-experimental program focused on issues unrelated to time structuring. A post-test was conducted with the groups using the same assessment measures from the pre-test.

In phase three, both groups were again exposed to a 5-month program. A Control-2 group was selected from a different college matched for age, gender, and academic background for post-test analysis. This group was not exposed to any treatment. A final post-test was conducted with the three groups using the same assessment measures from phase one. In addition, peer feedback, parent feedback, teacher rating, and a final evaluation schedule were administered to study the impact of the intervention on certain daily life skills related to effective time utilization.

Relative to untrained subjects (Control-1 and Control-2 groups), the Treatment group demonstrated improvements in their ability to structure time with a greater sense of purpose. We found significant gains in their time planning with regard to individual study and maintenance activities, leading to higher academic achievement and productive work output. They showed greater ability to shoulder responsibility, be punctual, use effective coping strategies, and follow a systematic and methodical work pattern. Compared with the two Control groups, the Treatment group also demonstrated greater efficiency in organizational abilities in household chores, meeting deadlines, and spending more time on meaningful activities. They had higher academic grades, were more regular in assignment submissions, and worked better on teams. They also displayed a higher frequency in taking stock of time wasters, interruptions, prioritizing tasks and charting goals (Verma, 1995a , 1995b; Verma & Sekhon, 1995).

I have firmly believed that an effective program needs to translate conceptual models of intervention into developmentally and culturally appropriate curricula, operationalize guidelines for implementation, and specify associated teaching tools and materials. Based on this study, I developed a handbook entitled *Time Pressures of Growing Up: Perspectives for the Youth* (Verma, 1995c) to connect education with life experiences. Most existing literature on time management addressed a 25-plus-year-old population engaged in executive jobs or other work situations. With help from four college-age team members, my handbook instead addressed the real-world needs of students. The goal was to create a dialogue around time-use among young people. It also encouraged parents and teachers to sensitize children to the importance of time organization.

Given the proven efficacy of the time sensitization program for youth, my next challenge was its dissemination. In the early 1990s, integrating programs on time sensitization or life skills into the educational system was still novel. I shared my work with various NGOs, schools, and college heads in the city, and conducted workshops for teachers and students. I received positive feedback from many institutions about teachers using the handbook.

At the end of phase three in 1994, we conducted in-depth interviews and program appraisals with the subjects. The majority lauded the program for its uniqueness and suggested it continue, however, with a shift in focus to wider issues related to the future. They expressed the need for guidance in areas pertaining to career goals, life planning, personal development, and stress management. Some also drew attention to the lack of family support for realization of personal goals due to gender stereotypes. Looking at the need-based demand and the longitudinal input in the intervention, the fourth and fifth phases of the study were planned for the next 2 years. These would involve an 8-month life-skills program on a wider range of skills for adjustment to future challenges. While there was some sample attrition, most of the treatment group students continued to pursue their master's in the college.

At phase four, in addition to time structure, the three groups were now pre-tested for future expectations, reactions to difficulties, well-being, self-esteem, and life perspective. Following the theoretical orientation of the social cognitive theory and based on the concepts of modeling, behavioral rehearsal, and social reinforcement (Bandura, 1986), a skill-oriented approach was adopted for the program. The premise was that the optimal route for the development of personal, social and cognitive skills is to enhance the self-perceived level of psychosocial competence. The specific skills targeted in the program were self-awareness, stress management, coping with emotions, decision-making, problem solving, communication, assertiveness, and interpersonal relations.

The skill-building procedures included:

- circulating resource material that provided the knowledge base, principles, and strategies for skill acquisition using application questions, self-assessment inventories, skill practice exercises, and case studies to facilitate skill competency;
- conducting workshops and interactive sessions with the participants;
- holding individual counseling sessions to discuss the subjects' need-based problems.

The implementation of a formal needs assessment served to guarantee the relevance and usefulness of the training. The curriculum was based on continuous feedback from the subjects, inclusion of peer mentors in the development of resource material, and a combination of elements from past life-skills programs. By doing this, the intervention joined theory-based and empirically tested approaches to behavior change and culturally sensitive content.

The results revealed improved knowledge, attitudes, perceptions, and behavioral intentions. Youths' pre-test to post-test scores revealed improvement in self-esteem and self-efficacy beliefs, a greater sense of well-being, higher scholastic achievement, greater awareness of strategies for skill acquisition, and enhanced motivation for skill competence following participation in the life-skills curriculum. Interviews and feedback from the subjects showed that they perceived a substantial benefit from the program in skill awareness and acquisition, personal initiative, motivation, self-confidence, life planning, and interpersonal relations. The absence of comparable gains among control subjects further substantiated the efficacy of life-skills training for youth.

In a nutshell, this study provided convincing empirical evidence for promoting self-efficacy beliefs and personal development in youth and finding space for life-skills education in schools and colleges. Issues related to the program's reproducibility, methodological concerns (timing, duration, skill transfer), lessons learnt, as well as implications for research, program, and policy were examined to foster mental health and well-being in young people (Verma, 2000b, 2003).

Longitudinal studies are not easy to implement, especially if they have an intervention component. For instance, retaining the students for 5 years was an uphill task. Maintaining a close bond with the girls meant dedicating long hours to individual counseling sessions, taking them on outings, and even a seemingly simple task like making small talk in the college's corridors. On the plus side, working with young creative minds was stimulating and helped me understand the adolescent psyche and issues with greater insight.

It is now heartening to note that a number of noteworthy agencies—including the WHO, UNESCO, and UNICEF—have implemented programs to enhance social and cognitive skills among children and adolescents. These efforts have translated into holistic programs and culturally sensitive strategies to promote health and well-being among adolescents through schools (Verma & Konantambigi, 2011).

Capturing Cultural Change and Adolescents' Daily Life Experiences

Reed Larson (the Fulbright Scholar from the University of Illinois) and I exchanged our work on time use at the International Society for the Study of Behavioral Development (ISSBD) biennial meetings. I was impressed with his work using the Experience Sampling Method (ESM, Csikszentmihalyi & Larson, 1987). We decided to collaborate on a project to examine the daily lives of middle-class Indian adolescents and their families.

This was the first study of its kind in India. Using ESM, we focused on family members' daily use of time to understand patterns of time and emotion in relation to other sources of information about traditional Indian society, as well as other parts of the world. We collected data from 100 middle-class families following the ESM procedures. In each family, eighth graders and their mothers and fathers wore alarm watches for 1 week. When signaled by the watches, they filled out reports on their activities and subjective states. In total, they provided 13,674 ESM self-reports. Because the signals and subsequent reports occurred randomly, they provided a representative sample of the typical activities and states experienced by the family members.

The findings suggested many ways in which middle-class Indian family life had and hadn't changed, relative to traditional Indian life. We found that adolescents spent large portions of their waking hours engaged with schoolwork, yet family remained a high priority in their lives. A substantial number of mothers were employed, yet they continued to assume nearly all responsibility for housework and childcare. Fathers appeared to be less of an authority figure and more involved in their children's daily lives than in the past, yet they still held a privileged position in the family.

Analyses of the adolescents' data focused on four topics: their daily range of emotions, schoolwork, time with family, and TV viewing.

The findings on daily emotions were consistent with international stereotypes of adolescents. The eighth graders reported wider emotional swings—both positive and negative—than their parents (Verma & Larson, 1999). The negative emotions were often attributable to stress. When examining the school experience of these students (Verma, Sharma, & Larson, 2002) relative to data from ESM studies in Korea and Japan, we found that Indian youth spent larger portions of their time on schoolwork—studying and being tutored. The emotional states associated with schoolwork and adult monitoring were quite often negative. Unhappiness, boredom, and anxiety were common, and individuals who spent more time doing schoolwork experienced more negative emotions. These findings highlighted the major role that competition for college admission had assumed in the lives of middle-class Indian adolescents.

At the same time, we found that Indian adolescents were very involved with their families (Larson, Verma, & Dworkin, 2002). They spent more time with family than friends (unlike their American counterparts). When compared with Americans, Indian adolescents reported more positive emotional states when with families. They spent twice as much time talking to their families—with more time talking to their fathers—indicating that time with family was, on average, developmentally beneficial for Indian adolescents. Contrary to parent–adolescent relationships in the West, which are often characterized by distancing, individuation, and renegotiation, the developmental task of Indian adolescents was not to disengage from family, but to reduce impulses that might set them apart and strengthen emotional bonds (Larson, Verma, & Dworkin, 2003).

Indian adolescents spent much of their time with family watching TV (Verma & Larson, 2002a). Our data indicated that TV viewing occupied about 12 hours per week for these youth, a rate similar to that for middle-class youth around the world. Television viewing in India was often a family activity, whereas American adolescents were more prone to watching TV alone, choosing a program that suits their own interests. While there was plenty of research about the negative influences of television, our findings indicated the need to understand this activity occurring within a context of parental consent and participation.

In terms of the parents, we found that mothers spent four to seven times more of their day on household labor and childcare than their husbands, with approximately half of this time spent on food preparation (Verma & Larson, 2000, 2002b). The husband's contribution to household labor only slightly increased when the wife was employed. In contrast to ESM data from an American study, however, Indian women did not report markedly negative emotions when they were doing housework; they also reported more choice and control. We interpreted these results in terms of a traditional division of labor that clearly demarcates wives' and husbands' roles. While these findings suggested that middle-class Indian mothers—80% of whom had domestic help—did not feel oppressed by their large load of daily labor, we emphasize that there are large numbers of poorer women in India for whom conditions of household labor are less favorable.

Likewise, our findings on the fathers' data showed interesting trends (Larson, Verma, & Dworkin, 2001). While fathers did relatively little family work, they spent substantial amounts of time with their children and these interactions were not perceived as authoritarian. Indian fathers spent more time talking with their children, particularly their daughters, than American fathers with teenagers. And unlike American families, Indian father's emotions were less likely to be transmitted to their wives and children. These findings indicated that, while Indian middle-class fathers were still typically viewed as the head of the family, they tend to interact with family members in a democratic fashion; and, while some commentators have suggested that men have traditionally been peripheral to Indian family life, middle-class fathers were very much a part of their families' daily activities.

Conducting this ESM study was rewarding as well as labor intensive. The study provided rich time-use data on daily life experiences without relying upon recall, with an added advantage of additional data on subjective states of the respondents at each time sample. Despite an intensive pilot study conducted to examine the reliability of the questionnaires, cultural dissonance in terminologies, and using alarm watches; data collection posed its own set of challenges: cooperation of the subjects, novelty of using the watches and wearing them for a week, dealing with mechanical failure of the watches, repeated reminders and visits to respondents for regular filling of the ESM forms, dealing with incomplete forms, and drop outs. Adolescent respondents were very excited wearing these watches and often tampered with the settings, thus having to restart the data collection. Very often we left the watches with the family for a week and let them get used to them before starting the study. Adults, especially the fathers were more apprehensive about wearing the watches to office. Finally, when we did finish the data collection and found ourselves with thousands of ESM reports, the analyses itself was mind-boggling (Sharma & Verma, 2010). Working with a fine scholar like Reed was wonderful. One learnt much about the analyses of this complex ESM data from him and his student Jodi Dworkin. Reed was very curious and interested in learning about the cultural realities of Indian life and often we had great discussions on adolescent developmental issues including their attitude towards marriage and gender roles.

Larson and I worked on two other collaborative writings on adolescents' time use across cultures. The first was a review article for *Psychological Bulletin* on the similarities and differences in children's work, play and developmental opportunities across nations (Larson & Verma, 1999). We found that industrialization and schooling were linked to declines in time children spent in household and wage labor. This labor was more often unchallenging, though sometimes hazardous; developmental benefits were limited, and reduction in these activities would allow time for more developmentally beneficial activities. East Asian adolescents from postindustrial societies spent this freed-up time in schoolwork, a use associated with lower intrinsic motivation but high academic achievement and economic productivity. North American adolescents spent more time in leisure, associated with greater self-direction but of an uncertain relation to their development. These contrasting patterns of time use present alternatives that developing nations may choose between as they make the transition to an industrial and postindustrial society.

For our second joint work, Reed and I focused on adolescents' use of leisure time across cultures for the *New Directions for Child and Adolescent Development* series (Verma & Larson, 2003). Leisure time provides a developmentally enriching context for adolescents to experiment with roles and develop adaptive strategies and interpersonal skills that impact socialization and the transition to adulthood. To illuminate these diverse developmental opportunities—as well as the potential risks—this volume explored the varied facets of everyday leisure across the world and the cultural patterns that shape these experiences. We found significant differences across nations in how youth spend their free time, with major implications for their well-being and mental health.

Across the regional diversity of the chapters, a series of common themes also emerged, with distinct patterns of adolescent leisure that reflected diverse cultural values and practices. Some of these have a direct impact on resources and access to leisure alternatives, while others have effects that are mediated through cultural notions about appropriate social behavior.

Understanding Cross-Cultural Perspectives on Adolescence in the 21st Century

Another experience that expanded my worldview of adolescent development across cultures was joining a study group chaired by Larson. In 2000, the Study Group on Adolescence in the 21st Century brought together an international panel of scholars to reflect on how wider societal changes are likely to affect adolescents' experiences over the next three to five decades. How will likely social, economic, and technological changes alter the preparation of adolescents in becoming competent adults?

The timing was perfect. Using the recent turn-of-the-century to command the attention of educators and other professionals concerned with adolescents, the group sought to recast basic issues within a global framework. Group members worked on regional papers and specific societal trends, with Saraswathi and me handling the India chapter (Verma & Saraswathi, 2002a). Ours was an uphill task: accessing published and unpublished literature. But the experience was at least a familiar one for both of us. Using multi-pronged strategies—which were

both time- and labor-intensive—we eventually compiled a wealth of information on all aspects of adolescent development in India from the last 30 years. In addition to writing the chapter "Adolescence in India: Street Urchins or Silicon Valley Millionaires?," we published an annotated bibliography on Adolescence in India (Verma & Saraswathi, 2002b). This compilation of research examines the trends shaping adolescence in different developmental domains.

I also developed a paper with some of the study group members on changes in adolescents' interpersonal experiences and how they're being prepared for adult relationships in the 21st century, if at all (Larson, Wilson, Brown, Furstenberg, & Verma, 2002). The study group's work, published in three volumes, provided an excellent resource for students and faculty on adolescent development across nations. The volumes not only present a set of projections about emerging opportunities and concerns, they also inform research, policy, and practice. We also highlighted the emergence of new "adolescences" across countries, due to globalization, diversity between and within societies, and urbanization, with a greater separation from the adult world that was affecting their transition to adulthood (Larson & Verma, 2002).

At-Risk Children and Their Socialization for Survival

My work with street children started in 1990 when my students and I conducted a situational analysis of the condition of street kids in Chandigarh (Verma & Dhingra, 1993). The study revealed that while the majority of the children were living with families, they were also spending most of their time on the street doing odd jobs. Most were not attending school, or they had dropped out. Their numbers ranged from 3,000 to 3,500 in different parts of the city.

My utopian ideas about a child labor-free Chandigarh motivated me to gather the city's NGOs. I proposed mainstreaming the city's street children through home-based intervention, which ran contrary to the prevailing norm of institutionalization of these children (to my mind, a repressive alternative). The plan would be implemented jointly by my college department and the participating agencies. As previously mentioned, the proposal was very well-received by UNICEF, and was even approved. The Education department, however, issued their veto.

I shared some of this work at the preconference workshop on street children at the 1993 ISSBD biennial meeting in Recife, Brazil, as organized by Harold Stevenson, Urie Bronfenbrenner, and Analucia Schliemann. This was my first and most memorable ISSBD conference, partly because I had the pleasure of meeting Bronfenbrenner, a remarkable developmental psychologist. Our first encounter was actually at the airport in Rio de Janeiro, aboard a packed shuttle en route to the aircraft. While placing my carry-on bag in the crammed luggage space, I noticed a similar bag next to mine. Someone suddenly asked, "What if I walk off with your suitcase? It looks so much like mine." I looked up, saw a tall gentleman, and answered, "You will only be disappointed since there are only conference papers in mine."After a pause, he said, "I am Urie Bronfenbrenner, what brings you here?"

You can imagine what followed. I was shaking his hand so hard while prattling on about how I teach his theory, what a big fan I am of his work, and how I have used it in my own research.

With this great omen, the preconference workshop proved a great success. But the next day, we were confronted with a shocking headline: "Seven Street Children Shot by the Police while Sleeping on the streets of Rio." There we were, a group of international experts, discussing ways to improve the lives of street children. Just miles away, the atrocities against them were ongoing. They were seen as parasites and criminals. This type of apathy toward homeless and working children was not unique to Brazil (which is exactly why we had convened in the first place), but it's prevalent in most countries where the concentration of street children is high.

It's these headlines and the indifferent attitude of civil society that inspired me to work with at-risk street children in the first place. To get a sense of their experiential realities, I studied the daily life activities of street children using the time diaries. In addition to collecting time-use statistics, we studied the quality of their family life experiences, work-related problems, peer networks, schooling experiences, abuse and victimization, coping responses, preference for social support in stressful situations, and the impact of informal social control and neighborhood violence on involvement in anti-social activities and risky health behaviors (Gupta & Verma, 1997; Verma, 1994a, 1994b, 1995d, 1999; Verma & Mehta, 1994; Verma & Sharma, 2006).

Our findings concluded that the streets do indeed make children "street smart." Caught in the complexities of hostile street life, they develop an intuitive street intelligence that sensitizes them to lurking dangers, the need for self-preservation and how to conform to group dynamics for survival. Initiated early into family responsibilities and street trades—essentially, left with few options but to behave like "little adults"—they become resilient, resourceful, self-reliant, and independent. They develop practical living and personal safety skills by observing and modeling, often by trial and error (and often to their detriment). These are some of the survival strategies that are way beyond their developmental maturity and certainly at the cost of their well-being. Fragile communities that lack cohesiveness with poor, informal social control mechanisms results in the child's involvement in violence and health risk behaviors, with unique social stresses and personal challenges. Due to physical and socio-economic disadvantages, the street child is socialized to learn roles, competencies, and adaptive skills essential to survive competently on the streets. Children who fail to develop these skills are at a greater risk of exploitation at the hands of the drug mafia or other criminal gangs active on the streets.

Given their migratory nature and heavy time schedules, it's always challenging to work with street and working children. There's also the issue of data collection: What works with college students may not be practical for these un- or undereducated subjects. For example, while working on the time-use study, I decided to use the time diary that I had effectively used with college students. While pilot testing it with the street children, we realized how wrong we were. We found that many street children didn't even have a "clock concept" of time. This led to intensive work over the next 6-8 months devising time-exposure games. We used pictorial representations of the movement of the sun, sequencing of activities, and recall of the previous day's activities. We standardized these pre-exposure games before collecting data on time-use using the yesterday recall method with parent and peer crosschecks on activities done together. By the end of the study, all the children understood the clock concept and could tell the time. A multi-method approach worked best with this group. Similarly, for the study on coping and social support preferences, we used observation, creative drama, peer feedback, and focus group discussions with the children to identify the situations and standardize the questionnaire.

But successful fieldwork is more than just collecting solid data. To understand a community, one must often be immersed in that community. In the case of street kids, one must earn their trust. But as I've learned, these experiences proved to be very meaningful, providing a greater understanding of the world in which children lived and forming a close connection with them. I was able to solicit friends to sponsor education for many of these children whom we placed in schools through NGOs. It also created a forum for children to share their problems and parental counseling. I recollect two situations that reflect how responsive and loyal the children are once you win their trust.

One day, I was interviewing some beggar children along with my students in a posh market area. Suddenly, we were surrounded by adult beggars accusing us of informing the police. (Begging is illegal.) They were angry and could not be placated. Just as the situation became troublesome, I saw a familiar face: one of our subjects, an adolescent. He stepped in, pacified the group, and escorted us out of the mob. In another incident, my car broke down one hot afternoon near a marketplace. Before I could figure out what to do, my car started to move. I looked out to see some of my street children subjects pushing the car toward the mechanic. They recognized my black Peugeot from the joy rides we had taken and knew exactly how to help. I was so happy to treat them to samosas and ice cream for coming to my aid.

These are the types of responsive connections that develop while working diligently and positively with a group, and it's an experience I have always valued.

In the area of child work, I was influenced by the late Inderjit Khurana, an educator and social activist who was the first to start the railway platform schools for beggar children in Bhubaneswar, Orissa. I remember one conversation with her, wherein she stated: "If children do not come to schools, then let schools go to them."

I conducted interviews with 12 youths from her organization who had successfully made their transition from the streets to mainstream, to document their life histories. One common theme that emerged from their stories was the intervention of a "trustworthy" and "compassionate" person in their lives who respected their decision to make life choices. In their case it was Inderjit.

Another person with exemplary work in the area of child labor is Shantha Sinha from the M. Venkatarangaiya Foundation in Secunderabad, Andhra Pradesh. Her laudable initiatives include efforts to eliminate child labor, introduce universal schooling, bridge gender disparities, and encourage community leadership to protect child rights. She currently heads the National Commission for the Protection of Child Rights in New Delhi, overseeing cases of societal intolerance with regards to child rights.

My most recent street children research project was a collaborative cross-cultural study sponsored by the Center for Advanced Study in the Behavioral Sciences at Stanford and funded by the Jacobs Foundation. This study examined pathways of risk, protection, and well-being among street youth across four countries. The other team members were Deepali Sharma from India, Laurike Moeliono from Indonesia, Madelene Sta. Maria from the Philippines, and Neo Morojele from South Africa. In this study, we examined:

- To what extent do the dimensions of individual attributes, peers activities, family context, and schooling determine pathways of risk and protection that impact the health and well-being of street youth groups in select urban areas across India, Indonesia, the Philippines, and South Africa?
- What are the differences in risk and opportunity experiences across these countries among youth who are family-based, street-based, or shelter-based?
- How can children's cultural contexts explain the similarities and differences in experienced risk and opportunities?

Within the child rights framework (UNICEF, 2002), the conceptual model was based on the theory of risk and protection by Jessor (1993) and the realities of street children across the four countries (which are comparable on many demographic indicators related to child work and existing child protection mechanisms). This model emphasized the important linkages between the domains of individual attributes, family/significant others, peers, and school. The focus was on the factors within each of these domains that predict risk and protection outcomes that impact the

well-being of an individual (Verma & Morojele, 2008; Verma & Sta. Maria, 2008).

Using a multi-method and child participation approach, we collected quantitative and qualitative data from 478 street children ages 12 to 18 who were family-, street-, or shelter-based. In addition to the interviews, focus group discussions, narratives and personal accounts from the children and other key informants, we conducted validation sessions with the respondents after computing the results to better understand some of the observed trends. Using Structural Equation Modeling, the results revealed the significant role peers and significant others played in predicting risky outcomes across countries, with some variations.

In some countries, protective outcome was predicted by self-efficacy, family resilience, and peer support. Except in India, family support did not predict protective outcome and well-being among children. Across the countries, a positive school climate reduced engagement in risky behaviors with significant gender differences in experiences of abuse and victimization on the streets. Girls were more vulnerable to exploitation and sexual abuse, whereas boys reported bullying from street gang members. Parental and community safety nets regulated the work of family-based children, whereas the role of peer networks was paramount for involvement in health risk behaviors in the case of street-based children. For shelter-based children, the quality of care and monitoring available at the shelter was a crucial predictor of engagement in non-risk activities.

Street experiences challenge ideas of transition to adulthood leading to "altered pathways" (Verma, 2010). Street children began these life transitions even before they acquired requisite skills, learning experiences, resources, social support, and other assets that increase the likelihood of success. For many, these transitions were compromised by the many risks that characterize street living, such as affiliation with gangs or street subculture leading to extended or fractured transitions.

Thus, limiting contact with the justice system is a crucial micro-system-level factor (per Bronfenbrenner's model) for street youth to preserve their prospects of successfully leaving the street and pursuing work. Cultural variations in social welfare and law enforcement policies introduced a further macro-system-level determinant of the risks of vulnerability and prospects of resilience for street youth (Woodhead, 2004). In terms of Jessor's model, the qualitative analyses revealed several typologies of resilience-enhancing factors across the four countries (Sharma & Verma, 2009; Verma, Sta. Maria, & Morojele, 2011). While the children voiced their desire for change, they still felt the pull of their street identity and sources of security beckoning them back to the streets.

The real challenge lies in how we can arrest and prevent a child's transition to the streets. Once they're incorporated into street culture, they become "almost inaccessible." The one lesson I learned from my years of working with this group is their need for positive public acceptance and respect for their work. If we want to change their lives, we have to walk the extra mile hand-in-hand with them—and with dignity.

So what comes next? As a researcher with an orientation toward advocacy, I have always tried to engage those in policy and practice. Collectively, we need to continue working, despite heartbreaks along the way, to evolve strategies that make us more effective (Petersen, 2011). We must focus on crucial social issues and join hands with key stakeholders to reduce the gap between developmental science and social policy (Silbereisen, 2011).

In the above sections, I have tried to summarize my work and outstanding concerns in the area of adolescent psychology. I now briefly share some of the experiences that have helped me grow as a scholar: the first as a fellow at the Center for Advanced Study in the Behavioral Sciences (CASBS) and the second, from my association with the International Society for the Study of Behavioral Development (ISSBD) over the last two decades.

The CASBS Experience and Meeting Great Minds

I was a two-times fellow at the Center for Advanced Study in the Behavioral Sciences, Stanford—first from 2001 to 2002, and again from 2007 to 2008. My image of the Center was that of Rabindranath Tagore's *Shantineketan*, where you are one with nature, deeply immersed in meditation, self-study, and self-reflection. The physical surroundings were indeed breathtaking, with excellent views of the Bay Area and surrounding mountains. It was thrilling to watch deer, birds, and even snakes, and one quickly learns to share lunch with the bees. It was a delight to watch and study the behavior of my favorite of all: the humming birds. Inside the facility was no less amazing: The library facilities at the Center provided access to scientific materials at the click of the button. Things that once took several months to collect could be gathered in a matter of weeks. The joy of availability of information was immense.

Amidst all this, the 9/11 attacks on the World Trade Center in 2001 were deeply disturbing. However, the rich discussions with scholars that followed sensitized me to world political issues, especially that of U.S. foreign policies. My understanding of this global phenomenon of terrorism was markedly increased, and I better understood the role of religion. Some of these issues were already affecting lives across nations, including India. Like the daily dish walk and volleyball games, Wednesday seminars were a high point. I learned about a wide range of interdisciplinary topics, and the discussions that followed were always intellectually stimulating. I received meaningful feedback on my own work on street and working youth in India, including different ways of looking at the issue of child work. I also realized the need to develop life histories of these children in order to document the life trajectories that shape their adulthood.

This period also proved beneficial in networking with scholars within and outside the Center. Within the Center, I met Allan Badley, Bob Scott, Carlos M. Benavides, Carlos Costa-Ribeiro, Claude Steele, Dave Messik, Doug McAdams, Donald Brenneis, Manuela Cunha, Patrick Heuveline, Richard Swedberg, Robert Crosnoe, Rogers Hall, Shirley Heath, Susan Hanson, Silvia E Giorguli Saucedo, and Susan Rose-Ackerman; they were generous enough to offer their insightful feedback on my works-in-process. Outside the Center, I developed close professional links with William Damon and was a regular at the seminars held at the Center of Adolescence at Stanford. This connection not only gave me the opportunity to present my work on adolescence in India, but also understand the current issues of research in the field.

Additionally, my interactions with Albert Bandura over the years have been immensely rewarding. We first met in November 1992 at the Jacobs Foundation conference on "Youth in the Year 2000: Psycho-Social Issues and Intervention," organized by Michael Rutter at the Marbach Castle in Germany. Even before meeting Bandura, I had been using his Social Cognitive Theory as a theoretical basis in my research with youth. Another career stalwart I met at the conference is Anne Petersen, who over the years has been a mentor and great source of inspiration, and has provided rich input for many of my academic activities. I also remain deeply impressed by Eleanor Maccoby, whose input has been invaluable to my work. I visited other universities and met scholars such as Lewis Aptekar and Bill Myers, whose work dovetails with my own.

During my first fellowship, after reading my proposal on cross-cultural street youth, Doug McAdams, Director, CASBS, suggested I apply for a special project. Taking his advice, and alongside Marlis Buchmann, we secured Center sponsorship for a special project on "Comparative Perspectives on Adolescent Development in a Globalizing World: Changing Opportunities, Constraints, and Pathways of Risk." In August 2005, with help from Reed Larson, we held a conference at CASBS, bringing together close to 25 young scholars from around the world, each engaged in research on youth issues in developing countries. Our primary objective was to advance comparative cross-national research on adolescent development in developing countries, with a special focus on at-risk youth, and also establish an international network of youth researchers and scholars. Our analytical research centered on mechanisms of marginalization (i.e., the determinants of these marginalized pathways) and impacts of marginalization (i.e., the experience and behavioral outcomes associated with different pathways of marginalization).

Against this intellectual background, the conference goals were twofold: identify salient research topics and promising research questions regarding at-risk youth issues from a comparative perspective, and identify groups of participants from different countries with common research interests and research questions, willing to pursue these questions in their future work.

The conference deliberations resulted in three projects, two of which were convened by Marlis Buchmann: "Structural Change, Institutional Settings and the Transition from School to Work in Three Latin American Cities: Buenos Aires, Lima, and Mexico City" and "Adolescent Regimes in the Developing World: A Comparative Perspective." I was responsible for the third, "Pathways of Risk and Protection Among Street Children in India, Indonesia, the Philippines, and South Africa." In 2007, three members of the special project team and the two conveners spent the fellowship year at CASBS working on the project.

My time spent at CASBS has been memorable in many ways, not least being the opportunity to connect to myself, to find more meaning in life, and to discover clarity in my own thought processes. Working on the street children project with team members from across the globe provided insights and perspectives unexplored, and also taught me the challenges of a cross-national project. The opportunity to share one's work with other fellows and respond to their queries helped remove mental blocks from my own mind and posed challenges to my core ideas and concepts.

Unexpectedly, the Center proved to be a retreat where the spirit of international solidarity is strong. The psychological foundation for achievement and sharing, the power of motivation, the compulsions of a curious mind—all of these are nurtured in a space that grants freedom of thought, action, and expression. I emerged with greater confidence and greater appreciation for my own work. The sense of belonging to a community of scholars from diverse backgrounds and disciplines helped widen my perspective, delve on unconventional issues, connect to diverse cultures, and drop barriers across disciplines. Dropping initial inhibitions, this connectivity and shared vision proved very challenging. Sharing of thought frames, shedding long-standing views and mindsets, confronting self-doubt, and emerging through self-reflection were some of the memorable developmental processes that I encountered.

The ISSBD Connection

I have been involved with the ISSBD since 1993. Its interdisciplinary membership and life-span perspective helped connect me to an international community of scholars, while also broadening me as a researcher and teacher. The ISSBD biennial meetings have long served as my preferred platform for disseminating research to an international audience.

More than once, ISSBD gatherings have led to collaborations. I was a part of the multi-country project organized by Ken Rubin on parenting beliefs and socio-emotional development among toddlers (Rubin et al., 2006). I collaborated with Eugene C. Roehlkepartain, from the Center for Spiritual Development in Childhood and Adolescence, Search Institute, Minneapolis on an exploratory study of Indian adolescents' spiritual development. Using focus groups and interviews with adolescents, parents, and teachers, I examined the different dimensions of spirituality, its definition and factors facilitating its development among Indian adolescents. The results revealed that in India, spiritual development went hand-in-hand with religious activities. Families were the primary context and parents fostered spirituality through various parenting practices. Teachers also considered it an important dimension of development. Given the changing global context of adolescent experiences, there is a redefining of spiritual principles within the family context. Peer and school experiences profoundly affected the patterns of spiritual development, and religion and spirituality, coupled with civic engagement, are the resources youth used to contribute meaningfully to the world (Verma & Sta. Maria, 2006).

As a teacher, I always invested in my students and mentoring them was a high priority. Over the years, many of my students have presented at and attended the biennial meetings of ISSBD. Deepali Sharma and I started the first young scholars' initiative at the 2004 ISSBD biennial meetings in Ghent, Belgium. In the years since, our initiative has grown—and there is now a young scholar representative in the ISSBD Executive Committee. Currently, the young scholars are screening several new and exciting proposals on need-based workshops exclusively for their community, as well as other opportunities for collaboration and mentorship.

As the India Coordinator for ISSBD for 15 years and an EC member, I focused on promoting greater visibility for the Asia region in the Society, organizing activities in the region and encouraging young scholar participation in ISSBD activities. For many years, India's membership has been among the top four in the Society. As the Society's Liaison Officer with the World Health Organization (WHO), I shared mutually beneficial information on various health issues, including expertise from a panel that gave guidance on strengthening the work of WHO at the global level, and I organized conjoint symposia at the ISSBD meetings. I organized two Asia region workshops in Chandigarh (in 1995, with Rajalakshmi Muralidharan, and in 2011, with Deepali Sharma) and two national-level workshops, on scientific writing in Baroda (in 1998, with T.S.Saraswathi) and qualitative research methods in Mumbai (in 2003, with Rajani Konantambigi). I am currently working with Deepali Sharma on an edited volume based on the 2011 regional workshop on "Risk, Protection, and Resilience among Children At-Risk: Research and Action Plans."

These activities have been made possible by working with key members of the Society, including Lea Pulkkinen, Rainer Silbereisen, Anne Petersen, Wolfgang Schneider, Arnold Sameroff, Ann Sanson, Robert Serpel, August Flammer, Leni Verhofstadt-Deneve, Marcel van Aken, Peter Smith, Toni Antonucci, Adarsh Sharma, Venita Kaul, Meena Mathur, and Rajalakshmi Sriram. Reviewing articles for scientific journals, mentoring young scholars, serving on program committees for various biennial meetings, and organizing preconference workshops for young scholars have not just proved to be enjoyable, but also an opportunity to serve the discipline. The connections I've made through these activities have expanded my knowledge of the work of other scholars, while also enhancing my sense of belonging and understanding of developmental social science.

I valued working with Catherine Cooper, another reputed scholar. Her work on "Bridging Multiple Worlds" examines issues of migration, ethnic minorities, and cultural diversities in the development of identity and educational pathways for youth in American society (Cooper, 2011). Our similar concerns and shared purpose are reflected in our work, despite approaching the issues from different cultural settings. In 2007, ISSBD launched a study to examine ways to make regional workshops more impactful and effective. Cooper and I undertook this study and presented the findings at the ISSBD 2008 Executive Committee Meeting in Wurzburg, Germany.

We also convened an invited symposium, with insights from respondents from 19 nations, to build on the findings. Across the regions, the respondents' recommendations converged on four steps:

1. Facilitate regional collaborations by forming research groups and creating opportunities for resource sharing.
2. Build capacity among young scholars by providing avenues for professional growth, greater interconnectivity, and institutional placements.
3. Identify senior scholars for mentoring at the regional and global levels.
4. Form regional centers of excellence that respond to cultural needs and move beyond training to developing collaborations.

It became clear that the discipline needs a *multilevel IT project* to build regional empowerment, human resource sharing, and research infrastructure to facilitate cross-cultural comparative projects. Strategies for supporting regional teams include networking, capturing regional perspectives, taking steps to overcome financial constraints, and developing an online data bank to build research infrastructure (Cooper & Verma, 2009, p. 41). I am now working with Cooper and Anne Petersen to make this concept of a research platform a reality.

The lack of IT infrastructure greatly impedes research collaborations in the developing world. There is significant need for an innovative, thoughtfully designed web-based IT tool for scholars in developing countries to carry out cross-national research within the context of a multidisciplinary framework. A major focus for this project is to ensure the platform provides opportunities, dialogs across cultural boundaries, and best practices for research capacity building and professional development from an international perspective.

Other project components include establishing criteria for ongoing evaluations of the IT platform to ensure the tools are culturally appropriate, as well as creating a detailed dissemination plan designed to highlight project implications for scholars. Currently, this is one of my high priority projects.

Looking Forward While Looking Back

With Krishnamurti in mind—"the observer is the observed"—reflecting on these past decades has been intense. I've been able to analyze my work and appreciate the time I've spent trying to understand adolescent issues from an international perspective and realize the efforts made to make a difference through innovative methodologies and longitudinal intervention studies, with the advocacy component an integral part of my work. For all the decades of hard work, one experience is most humbling above all: receiving the Alumni Achievement Award for the year 2000-01 from Amita Verma, department of HDFS, Baroda, my alma mater.

While looking forward I see several issues and challenges that will confront the coming generation of young scholars of adolescent psychology in India. The fluctuating economy in the country continues to alter the social pathways from childhood to adulthood. Newly emerging transitions patterns are distinct and diverse, offering new opportunities for some groups of young people and confronting others with tremendous risks. The challenge is how we can put in place effective mechanisms that will ensure a social and cultural milieu with psychological resources for our children and adolescents congenial for their holistic development and transition to a productive adulthood. As researchers, our efforts need to focus on reducing knowledge gaps, provide opportunity for developing new theoretical perspectives, while refining and extending existing ones. If as researchers we want our voices to be heard, then we need to generate creative solutions through convincing empirical data on protective approaches to positive youth development that feeds into social policy. This socially responsible reciprocity between theory, practice, and policy will foster development and dissemination of innovative strategies and culturally sensitive mechanisms to enhance mental health, resilience, and well-being in our future generation.

Today, having retired from my full-time position—with its administrative responsibilities and heavy teaching loads—I no longer must "live within deadlines." I am the master of my own time. With such a luxury, it should be easier to work on issues crucial to my work with marginalized children. Yet I still find myself very busy. I plan to work closely with the Chandigarh chapter of the National Commission for Protection of Child Rights to provide developmental options and choices for the socially disadvantaged. Additionally, there's the book on risk and resilience among children at-risk—plus the IT research platform under the aegis of ISSBD.

I've been cautioned that, upon retirement, there's a danger of over-enthusiastically engaging in self-created deadlines. Hopefully, I will not fall into that trap. At least, not too much. All I need is a little time for my garden, my yoga, and my daily walks along Chandigarh's Sukhna Lake.

Acknowledgment

I thank the following for their valuable feedback on this chapter: Anne Petersen, Rainer Silbereisen, Catherine Cooper, Neena Koyen, Jeff Koyen, Karishma Kadian, Meena Mathur, Venita Kaul, Chandra Schanz, Deepali Sharma, and Gurmeet Singh.

References

Abbott, D. D., Sharma, S., & Verma, S. (2004). The emotional environment of families experiencing chronic poverty in India. *Journal of Family & Economic Issues, 25*(3), 387–409.

Bandura, A. (1986). *The social foundations of thought and action: A social cognitive theory.* Englewood Cliffs, NJ: Prentice Hall.

Cooper, C. R. (2011). *Bridging multiple worlds: Cultures, identities, and pathways to college.* New York: Oxford University Press.

Cooper, C. & Verma, S. (2009). The ISSBD workshop study: Insights from 19 nations. *ISSBD Bulletin, 2*(56), 41–44.

Csikszentmihalyi, M., & Larson, R. (1987). The experience sampling method. *Journal of Nervous and Mental Disease, 175*, 526–536.

De Bono, E. (1986). *The CoRT thinking programme.* Oxford, UK: Pergamon Press.

Gupta, A., & Verma, S. (1997). Preference for social support by Indian street children and adolescents in stressful life situations. *Resources in education*, ERIC, University of Illinois.

Jessor, R. (1993). Successful development among youth in high-risk settings. *American Psychologist, 48*(32), 117–126.

Kaur, I., Sharma, D., & Verma, S. (2003). Experiences of adolescents in single parent families. *Journal of Family Welfare, 49*(1), 10–20.

Kaur, S., & Verma, S. (2006). *Parents as perpetrators of abuse among rural Indian adolescents.* Paper presentation for the symposium "Adolescent abuse across cultures: Perpetrators, psychosocial outcomes and treatments measures" (Convenors Verma, S. & Kambouridis, H.), *XIXth Biennial Meetings of the International Society for the Study of Behavioral Development*, July 2–6, 2006, Melbourne, Australia.

Krishnamurti, J. (1980). *The core of the teachings.* Retrieved on October 2, 2012 from: http://www.kfa.org/coreofteachings.php

Krishnamurti, J. (2008). *The observer and the observed: A selection of passages from the teachings of J. Krishnamurti.* New Delhi, India: Motilal Banarsi Das.

Larson, R., & Verma, S. (1999). How children and adolescents spend time across the world: Work, play and developmental opportunities. *Psychological Bulletin, 125*(6), 701–736.

Larson, R., & Verma, S. (2002). Globalization and the emergence of new adolescences: Findings from the work of an interdisciplinary study group on "Adolescence in the 21st century." *International Society for the Study of Behavioral Development Newsletter, 1*(4), 23.

Larson, R., Verma, S., & Dworkin, J. (2001). Men's work and family lives in India: The daily organization of time and emotion. *Journal of Family Psychology, 15*(2), 206–224.

Larson, R., Verma, S., & Dworkin, J. (2002). Adolescents' family relationships in India: The daily lives of Indian middle-class teenagers. In J. Arnett (Ed.), *Readings on adolescence and emerging adulthood.* Abington, MA: Prentice Hall.

Larson, R., Verma, S., & Dworkin, J. (2003). Adolescence without family disengagement: The daily family lives of Indian middle class teenagers. In T. S. Saraswathi (Ed.), *Cross-cultural perspectives in human development.* New Delhi, India: Sage Publications.

Larson, R., Wilson, S., Brown, B. B., Furstenberg, F. F., & Verma, S. (2002). Changes in adolescents' interpersonal experiences: Are they being prepared for adult relationships in the 21st century? *Journal of Research in Adolescence*, special issue, "Adolescence in the 21st century", *12*(1), 31–68.

Petersen, A. C. (2011). Global issues in research and social policy, *ISSBD Bulletin, 2*(60), 20–22.

Rubin, K. H., Hemphill, S. A., Chen, X., Hastings, P., Sanson, A., LoCoco, A. et al. (2006). Parenting beliefs and behaviors: Initial findings from the international consortium for the study of social and emotional development. In K. H. Rubin (Ed.) *Parental beliefs, parenting, and child development in cross-cultural perspective.* New York: Psychology Press.

Saraswathi, T. S., & Sridharan, A. (1991). Time use by college students: A methodological study. *Perspectives in Education, 7*(1), 41–54.

Sharma, D. & Verma, S. (2004). Family life experiences and psychosocial well-being among adolescents in single parent families. Poster presentation at *XVIIIth Biennial Meetings of the International Society for the Study of Behavioral Development*, July 11–15, Ghent, Belgium.

Sharma, D. & Verma, S. (2009). Typologies of protection in a risky world: Narratives by marginalized street children. *The Indian Journal of Home Science, 28*(1), 64–77.

Sharma, D. & Verma, S. (2010). Experience sampling method: Profiling Indian families. *ISSBD Bulletin, 1*(57), 29–32.

Silbereisen, R. K. (2011). Developmental science and social policy: Living together apart, and how one can. *ISSBD Bulletin, 2*(60), 18–20.

UNICEF (2002). *A world fit for children.* New Delhi, India: UNICEF.

Verma, S. (1991). *Status of the girl child and gender related issues in our cultural context: Action Strategy.* Chandigarh, India: Department of Child Development, Government Home Science College, Panjab University.

Verma, S. (1993). *The burdened preschooler: Issues and alternatives.* A report submitted to National Council for Educational Research & Training, New Delhi, India.

Verma, S. (1994a). Struggle for survival: A profile of street children in India. *Newsletter International Society for Study of Behavioural Development, 1*(25), 3.

Verma, S. (1994b). The working child in India. *Child Workers in Asia, 10*(3), 7–9.

Verma, S. (1995a). *Expanding time awareness: A short-term longitudinal intervention study on time sensitization in the youth.* A research report submitted to the Johann Jacobs Foundation, Zurich.

Verma, S. (1995b). Stirring the ripples: Feelings experienced by university students. *Current Research in Family and Community Sciences, III*(1), 6–13.

Verma, S. (1995c). *Time pressures of growing up: Perspectives for the youth.* A research report submitted to the Johann Jacobs Foundation, Zurich.

Verma, S. (1995d). In defence of children. *International Journal of Early Years Education, 3*(1), 70–73.

Verma, S. (1997a). *Towards child friendly cities: A study of the slum child in Amritsar city.* A research report sponsored by and submitted to the National Institute of Urban Affairs, New Delhi, India and UNICEF.

Verma, S. (1997b). An impact evaluation of the *Basta Hatao Bachpan Bachao* campaign in the city of Chandigarh, paper presented at the NCERT seminar *Early childhood education initiatives*, March 3–4, New Delhi, India.

Verma, S. (1999). Socialization for survival: Developmental issues among working street children in India. In M. Raffaelli and R. Larson (Eds.), *Developmental issues among homeless and working street youth.* San Francisco: Jossey-Bass.

Verma, S. (2000a). The Indian social reality of passage to adulthood. *ISSBD Newsletter, 2*(37), 6–9.

Verma, S. (2000b). Convenor, WHO symposium, "Life skills education initiatives to promote psychosocial well-being in adolescents across cultures," *XVIth Biennial Meetings of the International Society for the Study of Behavioral Development*, July 11–14, Beijing, China.

Verma, S. (2003). Life skills program for psychosocial competence in the youth. In Bhagbanprakash (Ed.), *Adolescents and life skills.* Commonwealth Youth Program Centre, Chandigarh, India.

Verma, S. (2006). Life skills for psychosocial competence in youth: Intervention initiatives in India. *ISSBD Newsletter, 2*(50), 7–10.

Verma, S. (2010). Invited Speaker: "Altered pathways: Risk, protection and well-being among street youth in India, Indonesia, the Philippines and South Africa." *XXIst Biennial Meetings of the International Society for the Study of Behavioral Development,* (ISSBD), July 18–22, 2010, Lusaka, Zambia.

Verma, S., & Chawla, S. (1989). Concept formation in socially deprived and non-deprived children. *Asian Journal of Psychology and Education, 22*(3–4), 18–28.

Verma, S., & Chodha, R. (1990). The impact of preschool education on cognitive abilities of 6 year old children from upper and lower social class groups. *Home Science, 20*(1), 5–12.

Verma, S., & Dhingra, G. (1993). Who do they belong to? A profile of street children in Chandigarh. *Peoples' Action, 8*(1), 22–25.

Verma, S., & Gupta, J. (1990). An exploratory study on some aspects of high academic stress and symptoms in 12–15 years old students. *Journal of Psychology and Clinical Studies, 6*(1), 7–12.

Verma, S., & Gupta, J. (1994). Measuring academic stress of school children. *Third Handbook of Social and Psychological Instruments.* New Delhi, India: ICSSR.

Verma, S., Kaur, S., & Saraswathi, T. S. (1995). Measuring time use by university students. *The Indian Journal of Social Science, 8*(1), 79–88.

Verma, S., & Konantambigi, R. (2011). Interventions for the development of social skills among children in select developing countries. In P. K. Smith & C. H. Hart (Eds.), *Wiley-Blackwell Handbook of Childhood Social Development* (2nd ed.). Oxford, UK: Wiley.

Verma, S., & Larson, R. (1999). Are adolescents more emotional? A study of the daily emotions of middle class Indian adolescents. *Psychology and Developing Societies, 11*(2), 179–194.

Verma, S., & Larson, R. (2000). Indian women's experience of household labour: Oppression or personal fulfillment? *The Indian Journal of Social Work, 62,* 46–66.

Verma S., & Larson, R. (2002a). Television in adolescents' lives: A member of the family. *Journal of Youth and Adolescence, 31*(3), 177–183.

Verma, S., & Larson, R. (2002b). Indian women's experience of household labour. *Women and Gender in Global Perspectives, 22*(1), 1.

Verma, S., & Larson, R. (2003) *Adolescent leisure across cultures: Time, experience and developmental risk,* New Directions in Child and Adolescent Development, San Francisco: Jossey-Bass.

Verma, S., & Loomba, S. (1990). Learning abilities as a function of creativity and attention span in children. *Asian Journal of Psychology and Education, 23*(5–6), 16–25.

Verma, S., & Mehta, M. (1994). Resilience and dignity of the street girl child: Some profiles. In V. R. Dhoundiyal, N. C. Dhoundiyal, & A. Shukla (Eds.), *The Indian girls.* Almora, India: Sri Almora Book Depot.

Verma, S., & Mohan, V. (1990). Social deprivation, intelligence and personality correlates in children. *Indian Journal of Community Guidance Service, 7*(3), 25–36.

Verma, S., & Mohan, V. (1993). Problem solving as related to intelligence and personality in socially deprived and non-deprived children. *Researches in child and adolescent psychology:* Seminar Readings, NCERT, New Delhi, India.

Verma, S., & Morojele, N. (2008). Convener, symposium "Pathways of risk and protection among street youth in India, Indonesia, the Philippines and South Africa," *International Congress of Psychology,* July 20–25, Berlin, Germany.

Verma, S., & Saraswathi, T. S. (1992). *At the crossroads: Time use by university youth.* A research report submitted to IDRC, New Delhi, India.

Verma, S., & Saraswathi, T. S. (2002a). Adolescence in India: Street urchins or Silicon Valley millionaires? In B. Bradford Brown, R. W. Larson, & T. S. Saraswathi (Eds.), *The world's youth: Adolescence in eight regions of the globe* (pp. 105–140). Cambridge, UK: Cambridge University Press.

Verma, S., & Saraswathi, T. S. (2002b). *Adolescence in India: An annotated bibliography,* Jaipur, India: Rawat Publications.

Verma, S., & Sekhon, P. (1995). The effect of personality and time structure on time use by college students. *Journal of Community Guidance and Research, 13*(1), 1–12.

Verma, S., Sharma, D., & Larson, R. (2002). School stress in India: Effects on time and daily emotions. *The International Journal of Behavioral Development, 26*(6), 500–508.

Verma, S., & Sharma, D. (2006). Cultural dynamics of family relations among Indian adolescents in varied contexts. In K. H. Rubin (Ed.), *Parental beliefs, parenting, and child development in cross-cultural perspective.* New York: Psychology Press.

Verma, S., & Singh, V. (1990). Moral judgement as related to intelligence in socially deprived and non-deprived children. *Asian Journal of Psychology and Education, 23*(1–2), 39–52.

Verma, S., & Sta. Maria, M. (2006). The changing global context of adolescent spirituality. In E. C. Roehlkepartain, P. E. King, L. Wagener, & P. L. Benson (Eds.), *The Handbook of Spiritual Development in Childhood and Adolescence.* New Delhi, India: Sage Publications.

Verma, S., & Sta. Maria, M. (2008). Conveners, symposium "Mapping typologies of risk and protection among street children in developing countries," *XXth Biennial Meetings of the International Society for the Study of Behavioral Development,* (ISSBD), July 13–17, Wurzburg, Germany.

Verma, S., Sta. Maria, M., & Morojele, N. (2011). A cross-cultural view to the study of resilience among street children, *ISSBD Bulletin, 1*(59), 11–14.

Verma, S., & Verma, G. (1994). Children solve problems: Impact of an enrichment programme on the problem solving abilities of deprived children. *Childhood, 2,* 122–128.

Woodhead, M. (2004). Psychosocial impacts of child work: A framework for research, monitoring and intervention, *The International Journal of Children's Rights, 12,* 321–377.

48

Yesterday's and Today's Adolescents

Different Contexts, Same Challenges?

Bruna Zani

Introduction: A Swirl of Emotions

I was first annoyed. That was my initial reaction as I read the editors' e-mail. I thought it was one of those *spam* e-mails, or maybe a joke from a colleague trying to be funny. I was about to delete it.

Then surprised. It turned out it was neither a spam e-mail nor a joke, but a serious proposal coming from distinguished colleagues for a noteworthy project.

I started feeling curious. But why me? Alongside so many internationally renowned names, and one of only two Italians—the other one being Augusto Palmonari, my own *boss* for so many years, and the one with whom I started to study adolescence.

And full of doubts. Does this mean I, too, have entered the world of *seniors*? After all, I am in my sixties . . . The emotions I am feeling and the difficulties I am still having in writing this chapter today, days away from the deadline for its submission, must be rooted in a certain inability on my part to think of myself as old enough to write an autobiography. It must be because Italy's retirement age for full professors is 70 . . .

So I accepted the task—and now I have to do it.

Autobiographical Sketch I started studying adolescence when I was in my twenties, the period that is sometimes called "emerging adulthood" thanks to Arnett—but at that time we were simply considered "adults." I continued my research when my first children, the twins, become adolescents. I tried to follow their development "in vivo" and to learn how to behave as a mother of adolescent boys. As you know, every parent of adolescent children has to learn how to manage the adolescence of their child, and so I learnt. Just as that period was over—I was 40—I became pregnant again. "Same husband" I would tell my often bemused colleagues. And if one dared ask, "but why?," I would reply, in true adolescent-speak: "It happens, you know?" And so the story started again, a second time, with a girl who became adolescent. Of course the dynamics of her development and of our mother–daughter relationship but also of the entire family have been quite different from the previous one with the two boys. And I continued my research with the adolescents, trying to understand what was different and what stayed the same in the psychology of adolescents, in a period of great social changes like those we are living through today.

My Academic and Professional Career

My academic background is in Political Sciences with a major in Sociology, and this strongly influenced my subsequent work in the field. My theoretical framework has always been characterized by a particular attention for the social aspects of a phenomenon, both as structural elements and as contexts within which people's life was to be studied and with which human behavior interact. My Sociology dissertation was centered on participant observation within an institute for orphaned girls. I studied both the behaviors of adolescent girls within the institute and the relationships between the institute and the local community.

The "official" transition towards Psychology came a few years later when I won several scholarships which enabled me to work at university with some continuity. I became part of the Social Psychology team at the University of Bologna, headed by Augusto Palmonari. After a specialization in Psychology at the University of Turin, over the years I took over different positions at different faculties—always at the University of Bologna. I started as a researcher at Political Sciences, then moved to Pedagogy Faculty, then became associate professor in 1989 at the Education Sciences faculty. In 2000 I became full professor in Social Psychology at the Faculty of Psychology where I still work today.

I served as Dean of the Faculty of Psychology (2002–08), President of the Deans of the Italian Faculties of Psychology (2005–06), President of the Teaching Committee of the University of Bologna (2005–09), and Member of the Academic Senate of the University of Bologna (2002–12). My teaching and research focused on Community Psychology, and I am President of the Italian Society of Community Psychology (SIPCO) and a member of the Executive Committee of the European Community Psychology Association (ECPA). I am also member of the Editorial Board of Journal of Community and Applied Social Psychology and of the Italian *Rivista di Psicologia di Comunità* (*Journal of Community Psychology*).

The Beginnings

This is the first time I have described the entirety of my work. *Adolescence* occupies a central place in my work. My different research interests have crossed and developed over the years, sometimes in response to external requests coming from local agencies seeking informed advice in order to develop policies aimed at adolescents and young people. My scientific approach has always been characterized by a close attention to the link between the university and the needs of society as I firmly believe—with Holzkamp (1972)—in the importance of carrying out research with external validity (i.e. not only methodologically correct, but also related to and benefiting society at large). My research on Community Psychology focused on intervention projects, are conducted upon request, and in collaboration with other partners in the community (i.e. Local Health Services and other associations and centers working with young people in school and community contexts). These collaborative projects take into account the perspectives and needs of the different research partners, instead of adopting a "top-down" (researcher-led) perspective.

Other research interests were developed in response to research questions, developed in conjunction with the network of colleagues belonging to the European Association for Research on Adolescence (EARA, I was one of the founding members in 1988). EARA has played—and continues to play—a key role for the development of adolescent research in Europe through its biennial conferences which enable regular meetings and exchanges among colleagues to take place as well as fostering the creation of scientific bonds for joint research projects.

My major contributions to EARA were the organization in 1992—together with Augusto Palmonari-of the 3rd EARA Conference in Bologna and the participation as a teacher in the 1st EARA Summer School organized by Monique Bolognini in Switzerland. From 1998–2002, I was also member of its Executive Committee. In the same period (1998–2001), I was member of the Editorial Board of the *International Journal of Behavioral Development*.

Thanks to EARA I have been involved in two major European projects. The first project, in the mid-1990s,

involved the Groningen (Sandy Jackson and Harke Bosma) and Cardiff (Terry Honess) teams and was centered on parent–adolescent relationships (decision making, acquisition of autonomy, communication, conflict) in our three European countries (The Netherlands, UK, and Italy). More recently, the second project was conducted, under the scheme of the 7th Framework Programme of the European Commission, on the Processes Influencing Democratic Ownership and Participation (PIDOP) (2009–12)—more on that later.

From the start my theoretical background has been strongly influenced by Kurt Lewin and his analysis of "the person-in-the-context," with a particular attention to three aspects: field theory, group work and action-research. Drawing on this epistemological and methodological basis, other authors, like Bronfenbrenner (1979) and his ecological theory of human development, (Rappaport, 1977; Sarason , 1974), provided further elements for my research.

Research Areas

In the last 30 years I have followed at least four main lines of research, writing mostly in Italian, often in English and some in French (and just once, this year, in Spanish). The four areas are briefly described below.

Adolescents and Family Relationships: Communication, Acquisition of Autonomy, Conflict
This topic has been deeply investigated in a research program started in 1993–94 and never formally finished! A final publication on some data has still to be written, but time has passed and life events have taken their toll, with the death of a dear colleague, Sandy Jackson, and the retirement of another, Harke Bosma, which resulted in an unfinished task.

The program was designed to explore adolescent and parental constructions of adolescence in three European countries (Groningen, The Netherlands; Cardiff, UK; and Bologna, Italy). It was a longitudinal cross-national study on 13–15- (first wave) and 15–17- (second-wave) year-olds and their parents (both fathers and mothers). A great enterprise, very demanding, difficult like each cultural collaboration, with misunderstanding at the beginning, discovery and surprise for some cultural differences, sometimes very marked even if all countries were in Europe, but also a very stimulating and enjoyable task. One (not secondary) benefit of multiple-country studies is the possibility for the teams involved to travel across the countries. In fact, we had many meetings respectively, in Groningen, Cardiff and Bologna, and as you know, the exchanges favor the reinforcement of interpersonal links.

Autobiographical Comment. I remember the long discussions with my Dutch and English colleagues about the adolescent's autonomy and the differences in parental styles across the countries.

We choose as our targets the 13- and 15-year-olds, to be contacted again two years later, at 15 and 17: we wanted to study the developmental trajectory of autonomy and discovered the substantial influence of context. In Holland, 17 represents a turning point, because it's the year just before for the majority of adolescents leave home, which has an impact on parents, especially mothers' role in preparing children to leave home and live independently. In Italy at that time no 17-year-old boy or girl—in their 4th and penultimate year of high school—would dream of leaving their parents' home, but more importantly no Italian mother of a 17-year-old child thought it necessary to educate their child to live independently.

This phenomenon is often referred to in terms of *mammoni* (attached to mother) children, initially noted as being typically Italian but which then started to be seen in other European countries, partly due to the economic crisis and the related financial difficulty of setting up a household. I recall my Dutch colleagues' surprise as I described the fact the adolescents and young people would live with their parents until the age of 23–25 (this is now 30–33!). But then it was my turn to be surprised when one of them asked "And what about sex?" Easy: in Catholic Italy, adolescents' sexuality officially does not exist! Adolescents are always "small children" in the eyes of their parents.

An important product of this cooperation was the construction and validation of two instruments: the Perspectives on Adolescent Decision Making (PADM) and the When We Disagree (WWD) scales, that have been shown suitable for application with large groups of adolescents and parents. These two instruments facilitate the exploration of adolescent and parental construction of adolescence, the development of adolescent autonomy within the family, and the changing patterns of interaction between adolescents and parents.

The first instrument, the *Perspectives on Adolescent Decision Making (PADM)* questionnaire, was designed to study adolescents' and parents' ideas about adolescent decision making, and to obtain information concerning how the adolescent and the parent are seen to approach specific issues of potential conflict (a list of 21 issues was presented, concerning, for example, smoking, drinking, but also chores, bedtime, appearance, go out, time at home, friends), whether conflict occurs and whether the behavior involved is regarded as "normal" for adolescents of the same age-group. For each of the 21 issues, four standard questions were addressed:

- Whether the adolescent decides for him/herself on… (Adolescent choice).
- Whether the parents feel the adolescent should or should not… (Parental feeling).
- Whether there are often arguments between parents and adolescent about… (Arguments).
- Whether it is normal for someone of the adolescent's age to decide for him/herself (Normality).

The form of the quartet of questions remains the same for all the 21 issues. For example:

- I decide myself whether I smoke or not.
- My parents feel I shouldn't smoke.
- I often have arguments with my parents about smoking.
- I think it's normal for someone of my age to decide for him/herself about smoking.

The first common article (Bosma et al., 1996) reported the data on a representative sample of 500 Italian adolescents aged 13 and 15. Results showed the sensitivity of the instrument to the age-grading of normative expectations with regard to adolescence and provide evidence of the validity of the instrument (also, in comparison with the Olson measures on Parent–Adolescent Communication Scale and the Family Satisfaction Scale, Olson et al., 1982) for the research into adolescent decision making within the family. In general, the patterns found for boys and girls separately were highly similar, contrary to other findings in the literature showing clear differences between the sexes. Changes in adolescents' conceptions of parental authority were seen, regarding issues such as choice of friends, clothing and personal appearance, considered matters for personal choice, whereas issues such as "Time in at night" and "Where to go when going out" were seen as matters still under the parental control.

A second common publication (Zani, Bosma, Zijsling, & Honess, 2001) discussed two waves of longitudinal results concerning Italian and Dutch adolescents and their parents, focusing on what each group thinks is normal for adolescents. A strong concordance between parent and youth constructions of adolescence, while at the same time showing systematic differences based on timing, emerged. Gender differences were also found. It was "normative" to grant girls more autonomy inside the family home and boys more autonomy outside the home Anyway, these differences were found for Italian but not for Dutch families. The scores for boys tended to be higher for some "hot" topics, like "time in," "going out," and "sex": girls are given more room in private matters and are more strictly controlled than boys when they enter public spaces.

The second instrument, the *When We Disagree (WWD) scales* (Honess et al., 1997) was developed as a multidimensional measure of conflict with the aim to assess both conflict styles and outcomes, from the point of view of both adolescents and their parents, and including both self-perceptions and perceptions of the other member of the dyad. The instrument measures two styles of conflict: aggression (involving sarcasm, anger, and shouting), and compromise (involving reasoning, listening, compromising, and caring for the other), and three outcomes: frustration (feelings of resignation, ending up feeling hurt), escalation (involving more confrontation), and intimacy (feeling that conflict helped to better understand each other). In our research the When We Disagree scales were used to examine conflicts between adolescents and their parents in a sample of 13- and 15-year-old children. Results of the first study on Cardiff adolescents confirmed the intensification of conflict with age. Older children reported more aggression from parents, more frustration, and lower intimacy outcomes. Moreover, female adolescents experienced higher levels of frustration than males (Honess et al., 1997). In the analysis of Italian data (involving three groups, adolescents, fathers, and mothers) we found an increase in a more aggressive style, with outcome of frustration and escalation from 13 to 15 years. Parents (especially mothers) described their relationship with female adolescents as more conflictual. Moreover, adolescents are described by all family members as more aggressive than their parents (Zani & Cicognani, 1999).

More recently, Elvira Cicognani and I analyzed our data trying to overcome the existing studies which are focused on frequency and intensity of disagreements, and include only one informant (adolescent or parent). We then conducted a "family study" in order to investigate conflict styles and outcomes using the When We Disagree scales, involving a large sample of intact families (302 Italian families, for a total of 906 participants, adolescents, their mothers and fathers (Cicognani & Zani, 2010a, b). The families tended to face disagreements using compromise strategies to a higher extent than aggression; moreover, conflict episodes generally ended with intimacy outcomes rather than frustration, further supporting theoretical explanations of conflict emphasizing its role in facilitating transformations of family relationships across the adolescent years (Steinberg, 1990). Results confirmed the intensification of conflict from early to middle adolescence already reported in the literature (Honess et al., 1997), providing a multifaceted but consistent picture. In particular, the evidence from adolescents' answers indicated that mothers of older adolescents were perceived as more aggressive than mothers of 13-year-old children, and older female adolescents described themselves as more aggressive toward both parents than all other subgroups. Fathers' perceptions seemed to confirm the more difficult position of older female adolescents; however, from their experience, relationships with male children seemed to improve as they grow older. The perceived worsening of mother-adolescent relationship with age found support in mothers' self-described lower tendency to compromise with 15-year-old children than with younger ones. Finally, even though the hypothesis on the increase with age of frustration outcomes was not confirmed, the lower perceived intimacy outcomes by older adolescents did support the conclusion that conflict processes within the family are more difficult during middle adolescence than early adolescence. The data also confirmed the more difficult position of older female adolescents, consistently with theoretical explanations emphasizing the role of gender socialization processes and their impact on the quality of family relationships (Laursen, Coy, & Collins, 1998).

I can now say that the When We Disagree scales filled an important gap in the literature, from both a theoretical and methodological point of view, by providing a multifaceted instrument capable of disentangling different dimensions of conflict processes and shedding more light on developmental pathways, as well as on differences according to other participants' characteristics.

Other works related to these topics were conducted over time, trying to explore the ever more problematic relationship between parents and their adolescent children. I received—and still receive—several requests for advice and training from associations of parents, teachers and educators. The most frequent remark parents—and especially mothers—would make is "I can't recognize my child any longer," followed unsurprisingly by a request for a behavioral recipe: "How should I behave? What should I do?"

Comment. Italian mothers' (and I'm one of them!) characteristics are well known abroad, perhaps also due to films and novels on Italian families: their key role in raising children, their protectiveness and their difficulty in recognizing their children's autonomy and striving for independence. Even if adolescence is no more than the traditional "storm and stress" period of the past, the great majority of parents with adult children, if asked, would not hesitate to indicate their children's adolescence as the most critical period in their relationships with them.

It should be noted that the process of separation applies to both parties, i.e., not just the adolescent but also their parents. They, too, have to detach themselves from their youth, accept that they are becoming adults and help them in their process of emancipation. The way in which parents experience this process will have a huge impact on future development and autonomy of their children. Difficulties arise because adolescents are ready for adult life 2 years after they believe they are, which is two years before their parents think they should be.

I have repeatedly tackled these issues (Cicognani & Zani, 2003; Zani, 1993, 2005, 2011a, 2011b). If we wanted to succinctly define the main characteristic of parent–adolescent relationship we could say that it is a "very long process of negotiation." This is hardly surprising to anyone who has experienced—or is experiencing—this relationship as a parent. This has been verified in research on different contexts and countries—even if, it must be acknowledged, Western countries.

Important Comment. I would like to emphasize that action research or intervention research has always been my favorite and privileged methodology, in that it combines the collaboration and involvement of the "target" persons with the carrying out of the empirical research. We made many formal and informal interviews with parents (mothers and fathers, individually and together as a couple) collecting qualitative data, together with quantitative data from questionnaires and scales. My idea is that a *multi-method approach* is the most appropriate to conduct studies and research.

Perception of Risk and Risk Behaviors in Adolescence In an invited lecture in 2007 at the 13th European Conference on Developmental Psychology in Jena, thanks to Rainer Silbereisen, I presented a summary of my research on "Risk seeking and wellbeing in adolescents and young adults." Over the years, theoretical perspectives guiding our research on determinants of risk behaviors shifted from social cognitive models focusing on intra-individual cognitive processes as the basis of risk behavior (Zani & Cicognani, 1998), to more "ecological" models (Bronfenbrenner, 1979), emphasizing the role of the different contexts in which adolescents are embedded (e.g., the family, the peer group, the school, other community contexts) and their complex interconnection as both risky and protective factors (Zani & Cicognani, 2002a, b). The topic is really complex and intriguing, and it is important to question some commonsense ideas, and to underline the need of continuing research and maintaining the attention of adolescents and adults on the issue.

Adolescence is commonly depicted in the literature as a time of "risk taking." Research studies have consistently shown that during this phase of the life cycle the tendency to take risks by adopting health-detrimental habits, like smoking, drinking, using substances, having unprotected sex, is strong and very common. Taking risks is considered as a natural, almost inevitable phenomenon (Jessor, 1998). As regards the interpretation of such behaviors, recent theoretical frameworks emphasize that taking risks may have positive functions in the development of adolescents (at personal and social levels): it is a way to test one's abilities and competences, it allows one to satisfy the needs associated with autonomy, and to master one's environment. Moreover, taking risks may have important social functions (i.e., gaining admission to the peer group, and achieving a more mature "adult" status). These needs are often satisfied by experimentation, which implies the evaluation of one's limits and taking risks. However, this makes the adolescent particularly vulnerable to situations of high risk (Steinberg, 2002). At the same time, adolescents are not homogeneous. Male adolescents appear more prone to take risks than females. Risk behaviors increase from early to middle and late adolescence. Adolescents and youngsters living in disadvantaged contexts (e.g., out-of-school adolescents, adolescents from low cultural and social backgrounds) exhibit more risk taking.

Some possible explanations of risk taking during adolescence which have been advanced in the literature are the following:

1. Adolescents do not understand the risks they are taking (e.g., there is a lack of knowledge about the dangers associated with risk behaviors; many educational and preventive interventions are based on this assumption).
2. Adolescents actually understand the risks but choose to ignore them (e.g., according to such a position, risk taking is a consequence of the adoption of dysfunctional coping strategies, like denial, when facing problems).
3. Adolescents are aware of the risks they are taking but consider them to be acceptable (given the attendant benefits). In this case, risk taking is seen as the end

result of a cost–benefit analysis, the result of deliberate choices from alternative courses of action.
4. Adolescents derive benefits from risky behavior (e.g., they enjoy the thrill or social status that comes with it).
5. Adolescents underestimate the likelihood of bad outcomes (the adolescent invulnerability hypothesis). According to such hypotheses, risk taking is the result of a faulty judgmental process, leading adolescents to underestimate the likelihood of negative outcomes for themselves in comparison with their peers.

Such explanations can be broadly grouped into individual level variables (e.g., personality, like sensation seeking, cognitive processes involved in risk perception) and environmental variables (e.g., peer group influences, family influences, school influences). Among social variables, a distinctive role has been attributed to peer group influences, generally conceptualized under a negative light as a source of social influence (or pressure) toward the adoption of detrimental health behaviors (Zani & Cicognani, 2000). The impact of the peer group has recently been discussed for what concerns its causal role, and it is still an open question whether adolescents are influenced by the group or they simply choose to belong to a particular group (more or less involved in risky practices) because such membership provides support and acknowledgement to their needs. The mechanisms by which the group affects adolescents' involvement in risk behaviors need further attention.

In the light of this theoretical framework, our research questions were the following:

1. How widespread are the risk behaviors in adolescence?
2. Who are the risk takers?
3. Why do adolescents engage in risk behaviors? Antecedents and motivations
4. What is the impact of risk behaviors on adolescents' life?

1. Concerning the diffusion, we can consider the main domains of risky activities as parts of constellations that according to Jessor (1998) are called Problem behaviors (smoking, drinking, drug use, driving at high speed, unprotected sex are highly correlated) (Zani & Cicognani, 2002a).

Many adolescents adopt some risk behaviors, but for the majority the experience does not become an habit or a lifestyle, as data repeatedly collected by national and European agencies have shown . Data from the European School Survey Project on Alcohol and Other Drugs (ESPAD, 2007) involving more than 100,000 students for 35 countries (average age 15.8 years) showed that in nearly all ESPAD countries, 50–80% of the students had smoked cigarettes at least once in their lifetime. In eight of the 35 ESPAD countries, more boys than girls had smoked 40 times or more in their lifetime. In two-thirds of the ESPAD countries, the vast majority (90% or more) of the students have drunk alcohol at least once in their lifetime. However, most of these students do not drink on a regular basis. More boys than girls report high levels of alcohol consumption.. The vast majority of students in all ESPAD countries that have tried any illicit drug have used marijuana or hashish. Thus, the number of students reporting cannabis use is almost identical with the total illicit drug prevalence.

2. Who are the risk takers? In general, and consistently over time, the findings of our research confirm that "at risk adolescents" are more likely to be older: the 16–18-year-olds smoke, drink alcohol (except wine), get drunk, and use more drugs. Males drink wine, beer, and spirits more often than girls; they get drunk and use more drugs than females. Students from technical/vocational school smoke and get drunk more often than students of other schools, like lyceums. Italian adolescents smoke and drink alcohol (wine) more than immigrant adolescents. What we found at the beginning of the year 2000 was that "the first time" was earlier; risk was "gendered"; and differences between school types were constant. Much less is known about the "invisible adolescents" (the out-of-school) (Zani & Cicognani, 2002b).

More recently we conducted a research (Sanza, Cicognani, Zani, & Nasuelli, 2011) on about 5,000 high school and about 4,000 university students, from five Italian regions, research funded by the Italian Ministry of Health. Findings confirmed the importance of considering the interrelation of demographic, individual and contextual factors in the explanation of risky behavior. Alcohol consumption among Italian university students is a widespread phenomenon, similar to other national contexts. In particular, alcohol use is higher among males than females, it increases with entry to university and shows a decline as the end of university studies approaches; and it is higher among students living on campus (and particularly among students belonging to fraternities and sororities) than those living with their parents. The latter result is particularly interesting since the role of such contextual variable has not been investigated extensively, outside of the North American context. For example, students who decided to attend university far from home (still a lower number in Italy versus other contexts owing to the importance of family bonds in Italy) might be a "special" group of individuals in terms of personality characteristics (e.g., more eager to seek new experiences, and to become independent from their families) as our data on sensation-seeking differences seem to confirm. Alternatively, we should consider the importance and salience of peer group norms for students living far from the family, especially when attempting to construct a supportive network of friends in the absence of perceive parental control. Moreover, this residential condition may increase the availability of alcohol both at home and through the attendance of recreational places where alcohol is commonly used; data on recreational habits of students might help clarify this. The increase in alcohol consumption at the beginning of university, which confirms the pattern found in studies in other countries suggests the importance of developmental factors and psychosocial transitions, as indicated by studies on risk behaviors among adolescents. Studies have also shown a natural decline in drinking toward the end of university, as young people are approaching new roles and responsibilities, and this trend also indicates the partial dependence of this behavior on contextual and environmental factors. Other important results of this study concern the role of *sensation seeking*, perceived frequency of drinking by peers and self-efficacy in resisting peer group pressures in explaining frequency of drinking and drunkenness. We know that the perception of group norms supporting drinking behaviors is one of the strongest predictors of drinking, whereas self-efficacy in refusing peers' proposals to drink has been found as a protective factor. The important result emerging from our study concerns the indirect effect of sensation seeking on drinking patterns; specifically, students with higher sensation seeking are more likely to drink alcohol also because they tend to congregate with peers who drink more frequently and because they have lower levels of self-efficacy in resisting their pressures. Altogether, these variables explain a considerable portion of the variance in drinking frequency (Cicognani & Zani, 2011).

3. The exploration of the motivations given by the adolescents as the basis of their behavior: besides the classic motivations (management of emotions, search for new and stronger sensations, have fun), there are also social motivations, linked to the belief that the alcohol consumption favors the social relationships and make the situations more enjoyable. Survey data collected in different national contexts confirm that the degree of involvement in risk behaviors differs and that distinct motives for taking risks can be distinguished. For example, from a research conducted on French adolescents (Le Quéau & Olm, 1999), it appears that over one-third of the adolescent population does not take risks and an equivalent proportion is capable of establishing limits to their attempts to experiment with transgressive behaviors. The remaining third includes "at risk" adolescents, which can be distinguished into three groups according to their risk profile: those adolescents who are involved in a difficult process of separation/individuation from their parents, who take risks in order to attract the attention of parents or for compensatory motives, those who are pushed by hedonistic motives (e.g., sensation seekers) and truly "problematic" youth, the latter being a minority (about 6%).

4. Results have different implications for preventative interventions. It is possible to incorporate sensation seeking into interventions; in particular, partly different approaches may be adopted for students showing patterns of stability versus increase in sensation-seeking levels. The former might benefit from interventions aimed at modifying the ways sensation seeking is expressed (e.g., offering opportunities for healthy and productive expression of such tendencies). Interventions minimizing unhealthy

expression of sensation seeking would be useful also for students showing a pattern on increase in sensation seeking; the latter would also benefit from interventions aimed at the factors responsible for such increase (e.g., socialization processes). Similarly, results suggest the usefulness of preventative interventions targeting peer group norms (e.g., peer education interventions), as well as interventions focused on enhancing students' skills and self-efficacy (e.g., life skills, assertiveness training); such programs should focus on students in the university context (especially those students living in student residences) including also the local community, and should be paralleled by interventions in collaboration with community stakeholders, focused on alcohol policies (e.g., collaborations with sellers in pubs and other recreational places attended by students in order to set limits to the amount of alcohol consumed).

Important Comment. The characteristics of the different profiles of consumers must be determined, in order to focus the preventative actions: very often the target of the interventions is "the young population," without further specifications, as if the young people were a homogeneous group. It is necessary to consider factors, like the social context, personality variables, motivations in the choice of places of fun, the expectations of the substance use and the modalities of having fun: all these variables allow to plan prevention projects "tailored" with respect to the target, and to the goals, instruments and messages of the interventions.

In the nineties, "the AIDS era" began in Italy and we started a series of research on the perception of AIDS risk in adolescence and also a series of interventions in schools, under the pressure and the request of teachers, educators, parents, local authorities, and organizations for the fight against AIDS. It was possible to teach about sex to all children at different levels of schooling, but not about condom or contraceptive methods other than abstinence!

The results from our research on the AIDS risk (Cicognani & Zani,1998; Zani & Cicognani, 1995) showed the negative effect of religious opinions and values concerning sexual behavior (especially among girls). Individuals with more traditional opinions about sexual intercourse, for example being in favor of the possibility of having intercourse only within the frame of stable relationships, are not safe from contagion, especially at this age, where relationships, while intended to be stable, not always prove to be so in the end. Another matter of concern comes from data showing that individuals with more traditional opinions (such as practicing Catholics) are also the least informed. Opinions may represent a sort of coping strategy that might impair a realistic assessment of personal risk, with the effect of exposing these individuals to greater risk under given circumstances.

In that context, given the particular situation, we decided to focus also on a category of young people almost totally neglected in the empirical literature on

HIV risk behaviors: adolescents and young adults who are not attending school after completion of compulsory education ("out-of-school," Cerchierini, Cicognani & Zani, 2000; Cicognani & Zani, 1998; Zani & Cicognani, 2006a,b). Even if the focus was mainly exploratory and descriptive, given the paucity of existing data, results confirmed that these adolescents and young adults are an "at-risk" population from the point of view of HIV contagion. The non-students' level of knowledge on HIV/AIDS appeared strongly deficient on several issues (concerning means of transmission of the virus and the effectiveness of the pill as protection). As expected, knowledge is lower among "out-of-school" youngsters, compared with the students, even though it increases with age. Females (both "out-of-school" and students) have better information than males, presumably because they are more active in their search for information (using all the sources to a greater extent than males) and also because the sources they use are more reliable. Preferred sources of information differ in the two groups: "out-of-school" adolescents turn to informal and proximal sources, such as family, friends, and partners, which are not always reliable because they mostly rely on commonsense and often erroneous beliefs. Students prefer school and media sources, which are certainly more reliable from the point of view of correctness of the information provided. These preferences might be a potential explanation of the differences found in levels of knowledge, and suggest the importance of addressing preventive interventions also to significant persons which belong to the network of primary relationships for "out-of-school" youngsters. Risk perceptions are overall low, both for oneself and for a peer. Optimistic bias (perceptions of risk for a peer are higher in comparison with personal risk) also exists. It is noteworthy that these "out-of-school" perceive a higher personal risk and are more worried about getting HIV compared with students, suggesting that they are realistic in their self-assessment. Considering attitudes toward precautions, "out-of-school" youngsters show more negative attitudes toward condoms than students (they think that condoms reduce pleasure and interfere with the attempt to establish confidence in their partner). Sexually experienced "out-of-school" adolescents and young adults use condom less frequently. They tend to leave the decision about contraception to their partner to a higher extent than students (who show a stronger tendency to reach a joint decision). Further, they have a higher number of sexual partners. Considering intentions to use condoms in the future, "out-of-school" youngsters show lower intentions to use condoms with a casual partner and as a regular means of contraception. These results suggested that "out-of-school" adolescents and young adults are a vulnerable population to the risk of HIV; however, they have also less opportunities to be involved in prevention programs which mostly concern students in schools. Although the proportion of teenagers not in schools is low, it is remarkable that so little effort is being expended to reach and impact them. Among the possible reasons is their low visibility and practical difficulties in reaching them (they do not attend schools; if they are employed, they are scattered across firms of different sizes, mostly small-scale, they have part-time jobs or work only for some months during the year; if they are unemployed, they are at home or most often in the street). Moreover, they are less willing than students to participate to research and prevention interventions (owing to difficulties in language comprehension and expression). The difficulties we found in contacting out-of-school adolescents for the purpose of research should be taken into account when devising interventions. This points to the need of choosing specific contexts and places to reach them and devising specific instruments for doing research and interventions for such population. The only places where we can reach a considerable number of adolescents belonging to our target are vocational courses and musical events. These are the context were we can devise group interventions. In other contexts (e.g., especially work, but also sports associations) we needed to think at different forms of interventions (e.g., directed at adults who work with adolescents, like coaches). Moreover, we should consider also the role of other factors like refusals to participate owing to diffidence, interpersonal and linguistic difficulties. This requires the adoption of a multi-level approach, including: (1) different types of interventions, addressed at different levels (individual, group, community) , (2) other partners in the intervention (in some context it was impossible to reach "out-of-school" youngsters without the support of other referent persons), and (3) different methods and techniques, more suited to this particular target (e.g., music). For what concerns the contents of interventions, the data suggest that they should focus on : (1) the provision of better information on the nature of AIDS, the means of transmission and prevention (in order to make more informed choices in their sexual behaviors); such information should be provided also to the people belonging to their network of relationships (to whom they tend to address for information); (2) the provision of interpersonal skills and abilities (which are necessary to negotiate the use of precautions with their partners) (Cerchierini, Cicognani, & Zani, 2000).

Adolescence and the Life Contexts: Feelings of Insecurity, Sense of Community, and Wellbeing Another research topic in which I was involved in the last two decades concerns the psychosocial processes that are relevant in characterizing the association between the adolescents and their community. The concept of "community" introduces a level of analysis of the developmental processes in adolescence less investigated in the literature. The ecological perspective (from Bronfenbrenner on) is the classical and well-known framework in studying the context-specific nature of developmental processes. However, it is also true that the systems more investigated by the researchers are still the family, the school, the peer groups (alone or in their interaction) and in a very limited way the neighborhood and the local community (Shinn & Toohey, 2003; Silbereisen & Todt, 1994). One reason could perhaps refer to the difficulty of operationalizing such contexts and their links with the individual processes. Our work was based on the theoretical-methodological perspective of Community Psychology (Zani, 2012; Zani & Palmonari, 1996), and has been focused on the construct of Sense of Community (SoC) , considered as a subjective indicator of the quality of relationships with the local community. Thanks to the grants received by the Ministry of Research and University in the PRIN (PRojects of National Interests) program, I had the opportunity to coordinate national studies on some new (at the time) topics.

The first project was "Psychosocial Factors of Risk Perception and of Unsafety in the Urban Context" (PRIN 1999–2000), aimed toward analyzing the community in its local/residential dimension , that is the town/neighborhood where the adolescents live, a level of belonging considered superordinate and more inclusive than the other contexts of ordinary life. In this analysis two constructs were used, the feelings of urban insecurity and the Sense of Community, which have been extensively studied in adult populations, but very little in adolescence. This position was abandoned when scholars started to investigate the development of identity processes in adolescence in relation to the environment (*place identity*) and the community (*community identity*) (Pretty, 2002). Our research questions initially were embedded in another theoretical framework, the "stress and coping" framework (Moos, 2002). The idea was that the insecurity could be considered as a form of chronic stress linked to the ever more complex conditions of urban living. We wanted to explore the psychological feeling and the behaviors of adolescents associated with insecurity, and the role of Sense of Community together with other personal (sociodemographic, direct experience of victimization), structural (dimension of urban context), and psychosocial (social support) factors in influencing the feeling of insecurity. The hypothesis was that the Sense of Community, considered according to the literature (Shinn & Toohey, 2003) an environmental coping resource, would reduce the perceived insecurity. The results were fully reported in a edited book (Zani, 2003). Main findings (Cicognani, Zani, & Albanesi, 2004; Zani, Cicognani, & Albanesi, 2001) confirmed that the level of insecurity is higher in girls than in boys, and in the adolescents living in bigger cities compared with those living in smaller towns.. We found also the subjective feeling of insecurity is increased by the negative experiences in some parts of the town, whereas the resources of social support and sense of belonging have a more complex role, in that they seem to amplify the fears through the processes of social interactions and of social constructions of risks. The nature of these links between sense of belonging to a place and the feeling of insecurity is still an open debate.

The second project was "Sense of Community, Psychosocial Wellbeing and Forms of Participation" (PRIN

2001–2002). The aims were to investigate the meanings of community for the adolescents, and the construction of a scale adequate to measure the Sense of Community in adolescence. We started studying adolescents' sense of belonging to territorial community (e.g., country or city), considering it not only as a geographical context, but as the locus of meaningful social relations (Puddifoot, 1996). Using a qualitative (focus groups) and quantitative approach (Albanesi, Cicognani, & Zani, 2005; Cicognani, Albanesi, & Zani, 2006), it was possible to detect the various meanings of community for adolescents, and subsequently develop a 20-item scale for assessing Sense of Community with adolescents (Chiessi, Cicognani, & Sonn, 2010). Our data suggested the usefulness of a model of adolescent Sense of Community which is consistent with McMillan and Chavis's (1986) perspective, even though it articulates the concept and its dimensions according to needs and experiences of this developmental phase. Specifically, research confirmed that adolescents' Sense of Community includes: Sense of Belonging, Support and Emotional Connection in the Community, Support and Emotional Connection with Peers, Satisfaction of Needs and Opportunities for Involvement, and Opportunities for Influence. Focus group research confirmed the usefulness of distinguishing emotional connection referred to the community and to the peer group, the latter being a more significant context for the construction of meaningful emotional relationships during this developmental period. Moreover, we found that, even though adolescents perceive that they have limited influence over their community, they would be interested in having more opportunities for exerting influence. The subscale Opportunities for Influence obtained the highest scores, confirming the importance of providing youngsters more circumstances where they can experience an active involvement in their community contexts. This picture was consistent with data collected by Da Silva, Sanson, Smart, and Toumbourou (2004), who found that 50% of the adolescents of their sample would participate in volunteer and political activities if more opportunities existed. Therefore, youngsters' Sense of Community should be on the agenda of policy makers.

Differences emerged in Sense of Community scores according to gender and school and year-level interactions. These differences reflect differential participation in settings and activities and point to the need to examine Sense of Community beyond territorial community, and to look at the specific settings for participation and how this mediates and moderates Sense of Community. The same observation can be made in relation to schools. That is, how is Sense of Community experienced within different school settings and what are the implications for belonging to territorial communities? Again, the broader representations of community including how gender and social class are intertwined with these representations will influence Sense of Community. Therefore, as we wanted to enhance Sense of Community, we needed to consider the everyday settings in which people participate and

the broader social, cultural, and political contexts within which Sense of Community is experienced..

In our research (Albanesi, Cicognani, & Zani, 2007; Cicognani, Albanesi, & Zani, 2008) conducted on high-school students living in two cities in North Italy, we found that involvement in formal groups increases Sense of Community. However, this effect seems to be specific for groups in which young people have the opportunity to play specific roles (like in sport teams) or in groups in which members are actively involved, as it happens in religious groups. The kind of group to which one belongs seems to affect also specific dimensions of Sense of Community: sport group members score higher on all dimensions of Sense of Community except for opportunity for influence, while members of religious groups perceive that they have more opportunities for influence, suggesting that the values shared within the group are critical in defining to what extent one can consider community trustworthy and open to young people initiatives and influence.

As regards the relation between group membership and civic engagement, it appears that even if levels of personal engagement in prosocial-oriented activities are moderately low, belonging to formal groups seems to act as a catalyst for it: the more the group has an explicit prosocial orientation, the more often young people show altruistic behaviors.

Considering the relation between Sense of Community, prosocial-oriented civic engagement and wellbeing, on the one hand, Sense of Community appears to be a mediator of the relation between group membership and social wellbeing, and to be the main predictor of social wellbeing, confirming the results obtained by Pretty (2002). On the other hand, we found that its effect increases social wellbeing through the partial mediation of prosocial-civic engagement, suggesting that behaviors that reflect the affective and cognitive component of Sense of Community (doing things for other members of the community, participation in events that reflect the culture and the traditions of the community) increase young people's perception of their social wellbeing.

Protest-oriented civic engagement does not play a significant role on levels of social wellbeing, contrasting some of the results of research on social activism. This could be related to a limited interest of adolescents in exerting influence on institutions. An alternative explanation could be based on the analysis of the different costs and benefits of protest and prosocial activities: costs implied in protest engagement against formal institutions are high compared with the chances to affect power relationships and to produce real local changes. Prosocial behaviors, on the other hand, produce desirable outcomes with less effort because they are primarily devoted to alleviating someone else's suffering by providing personal resources (time, money), and are not devoted to changing community power relationships. Our preliminary conclusion was that promoting Sense of Community is an instrument to increase young people's social participation and wellbeing.

The third project was "Life Contexts, Social Inequalities and Wellbeing" (PRIN 2003–2004). This study provided evidence of the significant impact of the residential context on adolescents' Subjective Wellbeing, adding to the existing literature on the role of neighborhood and community contexts in young people welfare (Leventhal & Brooks-Gunn, 2000; Shinn & Toohey, 2003). In particular, our research (Zani & Cicognani, 2005) provided a contribution for what concerns the type of context investigated (less common in the research literature, which focuses especially on urban youth), and the dimensions of wellbeing considered (Emotional and Psychological). Our adolescents and young adults experience low levels of Residential Satisfaction, and especially those youngsters living in towns, who can be considered as relatively more deprived on the basis of objective indicators. This result confirmed the correspondence between "objective" measures of residential quality (e.g., services and facilities available in the territory) and subjective perceptions by residents. The lowest scores concern satisfaction for transport and school facilities, that is services that are directly relevant for adolescents' needs on a daily basis (since they are used every day, particularly by adolescents). This result is particularly interesting if we consider that, in order to test the role of the residential context, we did not choose to contrast a small versus a large town, where it would be much easier to find significant differences. On the contrary, the two towns considered share many environmental characteristics (e.g., are located in the same valley in the North of Italy, along a river) and differ in terms of structural resources available (e.g., services and recreational opportunities; distance from larger towns). Such peculiarities allow us to keep constant some parameters of the residential context and to identify more clearly which structural characteristics are relevant in affecting youngsters' perceptions.

A second question addressed by this research concerned the possible mediation role of personal and social resources in the relationship between residential context and Stress and Wellbeing outcomes (Cicognani, Zani, & Albanesi, 2010). A personal resource considered is Self-efficacy, which is considered an indicator of youngsters' coping competence. Among social resources, both proximal (family, friends) and distal (Sense of Community) factors were included. Considering differences according to demographic variables, results showed that young adults perceive greater support from the family than adolescents, whereas gender differences were found in perceived support from friends and Sense of Community, showing that females rely more on proximal sources of support (friends), whereas males rely on more distal sources (relationships within the community). These results are consistent with other research in the literature (Colarossi & Eccles, 2003). Moreover, both Self-efficacy and Family Support are higher among participants who are more satisfied of the economic situation of their family, indicating that economic resources increase both personal and social resources. Overall, results confirmed the important role of perceived Social Support in buffering the negative impact of a deprived residential context, and indicate that different sources of support (friends versus family) play a significant role for different dimensions of wellbeing. Self-efficacy has a significant direct impact on wellbeing outcomes, independently of the characteristics of the living context.

Civic and Political Participation in Young People Finally, I would like to mention the last (by now!) project, "Processes Influencing Democratic Ownership and Participation" (PIDOP), a multidisciplinary research project funded by the European Commission under the 7th Framework Programme. It has involved nine research teams, across European Universities: Surrey (UK), Liège (Belgium), Masaryk University, Brno (Czech Republic), Jena (Germany), Bologna (Italy), Porto (Portugal), Örebro (Sweden), Ankara (Turkey), and Queen's University, Belfast (UK).

The project ran for 3 years from 2009 to 2012 and formally ended on April 30, 2012. As you can imagine, a very impressive amount of data (at the theoretical and empirical level) was collected and it is not easy to account for all the findings that emerged (because the teams are still analyzing the data). Just to give an idea, I will briefly delineate the main points.

The focus was on three different levels of factors, to see how they impact on civic and political participation: macro-level contextual factors (e.g., political, institutional and electoral factors); social factors (e.g., family, educational and media factors); psychological factors (e.g., motivational, cognitive, attitudinal and identity factors). Four groups of individuals were identified by the European Commission as being at risk of political disengagement: young people, women, minorities, and migrants. In practice, the main focus of the project was on youth, with the data being explored for differences between women *vs.* men, and differences between ethnic majority *vs.* ethnic minority/migrant individuals. The project examined the differences, as well as the relationship, between *political* and *civic* participation in these populations (Barrett, 2012).

The project had five main objectives:

1. to audit existing theory and research on civic and political participation in the disciplines of Politics, Sociology, Social Policy, Psychology and Education;
2. to audit and analyze existing policies on civic and political participation within Europe;
3. to identify empirically the factors and processes which drive civic and political participation within Europe;
4. to develop a theoretical understanding of the factors and processes responsible for civic and political participation;
5. to formulate new evidence-based policy and practice recommendations for key stakeholders at regional, national, and European levels.

The theoretical and empirical work in the project was broken up into several separate work packages, concerning a variety of tasks: collation and analysis of current policies; development of a political theory of participation; development of a psychological theory of participation; modeling of existing survey data; collection of new data; theoretical integration and practical recommendations; dissemination activities.

As regards the new data, each team in the consortium collected data from both their own local national group and from at least two ethnic minority or migrant groups living in their country (for a total of 27 national and ethnic groups). In all of these groups, data were collected from two age groups:16–17-year-olds (pre-voting age), and 18–26-year-olds (post-voting age). There were three phases in data collection: In phase one, focus groups were conducted with girls and boys in both age ranges from all 27 national and ethnic groups, The focus groups explored the young people's perceptions of citizenship and participation as they viewed them across a wide range of different life contexts In total, 117 focus groups were conducted involving 740 participants from various national, ethnic, or migrant communities). In phase two, interviews were conducted with some of the individuals who had been identified during the focus groups as important sources of influence by the focus group participants. These interviews primarily involved parents, teachers and youth workers, as these were the most frequently cited sources of influence. (In total, 96 in-depth interviews were conducted.) In phase three, a quantitative survey was conducted involving a total collected data from 8197 participants, with an approximately even gender balance within each of the 27 ethnic groups. This is an exceptionally large data set from majority and minority/immigrant groups in nine different countries that enabled the project to construct cross-nationally valid and reliable measures of political attitudes and behaviors. However, the data also reflected large variations between different national contexts, as well as between different immigrant/minority groups. Across the whole sample, young people from minority groups reported higher levels of political attentiveness, and higher levels of civil disobedience, economic participation, and political participation on the net. Young people from majority backgrounds were more likely to vote and report personal enhancement as a motivation for participating in politics. A preliminary presentation of some data is given in a special issue of the journal *Human Affairs* (Zani & Barrett, 2012), but currently all the teams are involved in a series of "dissemination" proposals.

The most ambitious goals of the project were twofold: (1) to develop an integrated multi-level theory of how and why different forms and interpretations of participation develop or are inhibited, incorporating reference to macro-level contextual factors, proximal social factors and psychological factors, drawing on the theoretical work conducted by political scientists and psychologists members of the teams, and the findings of empirical data we collected; and (2) to formulate new evidence-based policy and practice recommendations for key stakeholders at regional, national, and European levels—these recommendations were presented in April 2012 in Brussels to policy makers and members of the European Commission and are reported in five Policy Briefing papers (all documents can be downloaded from www.fahs.surrey.ac.uk/pidop).

Autobiographical Comment. I am particularly proud of this project, because I considered it one of my more successful ideas. I worked hard to realize this enterprise. A group of us were in Antalya, Turkey, in 2006, at the end of the EARA Conference, exchanging the final greetings with a group of "friends and colleagues," and I suggested: "Why don't we make a common proposal to the next European Commission call?" Of course all agreed, and then everybody went back to regular academic life, as usually each of us is involved in important but ordinary tasks. I tried to link together all the friends, making a network, asking for practical and efficient involvement, trying to face the variety of problems in the path. This is my only merit, but without the invaluable and incredible energy and talent of my colleague and friend, Martyn Barrett, the Project Coordinator, and of course of the active contributions and efforts of all of the participant teams, this dream would have not been realized. The other point to be mentioned is that we had fun being and working together in these 3 years, hosting and being hosted by all the countries involved.

The specific contribution given by the Bologna team to the project is the focus on the relationship between political and civic participation and psychological Sense of Community and social wellbeing among adolescents and young adults. The aim is to discuss the role of Sense of Community in affecting young people's participation in civic life and the effects of their involvement in the community on social wellbeing. In this case we referred to the concepts and relevant theories drawing from Community Psychology perspectives (Cicognani & Zani, 2009; Zani, Cicognani, & Albanesi, 2011).

The relation between Sense of Community and the different forms that participation can take during adolescence has been a relatively understudied topic. Da Silva et al. (2004) found that community attachment plays a role, even if smaller compared with the role of peers' pressure and attachment, in the adoption of behaviors that reflect civic responsibility.

The exact direction of the association between Sense of Community and social participation is not clear, however. Many authors suggested that opportunities to exert power (Prilleltensky, Nelson, & Peirson, 2001) and to be involved in school activities (Bateman, 2002) or having places to congregate outside school (Pretty, 2002) increase adolescents' Sense of Community development. As regards the effect of social participation on wellbeing, in the literature there is a general recognition that during adolescence, contributing to community life through social participation increases adolescents' self-efficacy and personal control and enhances positive developmental outcomes and wellbeing (Sherrod, Torney-Purta & Flanagan, 2010;

Smetana, Campione-Barr, & Metzger, 2006). Most indicators consider psychological wellbeing; less attention has been given to social wellbeing. A result that is consistent throughout all our studies is the significant role of Sense of Community in influencing young people's social wellbeing: Sense of Community increases social wellbeing directly when studied in deprived context, and mediates the relation between group membership and social wellbeing when studied in connection with civic engagement. Sense of Community exerts its positive effect increasing the adoption of active coping strategies, especially among female adolescents.

Among psychological factors, internal political efficacy systematically predicts actual participation, mediating the impact of sociodemographic and social factors, and indicating the importance of perceived competences for motivating youths to participate. This result suggests the need to provide youths with opportunities to experience feelings of competence and effectiveness in order to motivate them to action (Zani, Cicognani, & Albanesi, 2012).

Different Contexts, Same Challenges? Some Lines for Future Research

Looking at the program of the 13th Biennial Conference of the European Association for Research on Adolescence (EARA, September 2012), one can realize that all the "traditional" issues on adolescence are still on the agenda. Identity formation, risky behaviors, family relationships, academic motivations and achievement, cognitive, moral, sexual development, peer relations, migration experiences and integration, etc. Does it mean that we are falling into a loop, studying for decades the same topics? I don't think so: well, to be honest, much research is sadly repeating the same schemata and replicating the same findings. As already said, we learned a lot, but many problems have still to be solved.

In order to delineate future lines of research we can learn from the limitations of the previous studies. In the area of family relations, for example, there are a lot of cross-sectional research, but less longitudinal research. Both are important, of course depending on the aims of the studies. In the case of the analysis of parent–adolescent conflict relationships, longitudinal research is necessary to establish the role of developmental factors as distinct from cohort effects. Consider that the gap between the generations is largely a myth. When parents and adolescents disagree, it tends to be over mundane, day-to-day issues, not over major values. Many disagreements between parents and teenagers stem from different perspectives that they bring to the discussion. Parents typically see the issues as matters of right or wrong, whereas adolescents see them as matters of personal choice. Thus fighting is not a central feature of normative family relationships, but bickering is (Steinberg, 2002). It is important to consider not only the frequency of conflict or the topics around

which it occurs, but the different ways or styles in which it may be expressed, to better define the possible outcomes, and to give a picture of the strategies used in facing conflicts. Further research is needed in order to test the instruments in different contexts and with different family constellations (not only the intact families), because cultural differences might impact on parenting styles affecting family members' behaviors during conflict episodes. Such a study would be extremely important to clarify the often inconsistent findings of the literature on this crucial topic of research.

In the area of risky behavior, I would like to mention a specific problem: Today, at least in the Italian context, HIV/AIDS is no longer a priority issue, socially or culturally. Other issues (female bullying; "well-educated" adolescents from "good" families that are increasingly involved in aggressive and deviant actions; deaths of youngsters due to traffic accidents on Saturday evenings, etc.) are considered to be more worrying for our society and require explanation and intervention. New generations of adolescents feel very distant from the HIV issue and are less cautious. It is important to keep this issue on top of the research and prevention agenda, and at the same time, our instruments and theoretical models should take into account the influence of life contexts, culture, and values on young people.

It is useful to implement prevention policies at a very early stage, particularly before the start of a sexually active life, taking into account the differences due to age and the level of sexual experience. Primary prevention implies talking about daily life, about various experience contexts, about the social actions that act upon risk factors, internal and external, before these factors have a chance to create forms of unrest. Sometimes inadequate prevention may become a further risk factor, that is it can either be indifferent or, worst, produce effects contrary to those that were expected. Consider, for example, information or discouraging campaigns providing correct medical data which, however, do not have any effect on personal growth or psychological processing. The educational aspects of prevention may provide the emotional and intellectual resources needed for self-defense and self-protection, and stimulate the choice of positive attitudes and behaviors, so as to increase personal empowerment, without replacing individuals in their choices. The important thing, whichever way you look at it, is to show adolescents that they are not alone, but that there exist in their immediate context available resources, among adults and in the community, able to provide multiple forms of support in relational and social terms.

Some experiences of intervention with the aim to increase adolescents' Sense of Community and social participation need to be conducted and improved, both in territorial and school community contexts. Following the Community Psychology perspective, most promising interventions are those that involve the whole contexts and not only adolescents (e.g., in the school context, school principals, teachers, students, parents), and extend also to the neighborhood and community context where the school is located, consistently with "ecological" frameworks, and follow "community development" approaches. These "bottom-up" approaches attempt to involve members of local communities in a collective process of need assessment and search for possible solutions. Their aim is to empower individuals by offering them opportunities to influence the conditions that affect their lives. A considerable body of evidence demonstrates that young people who are afforded opportunities for meaningful participation within their communities are more likely to achieve a healthy development and to realize particular goals in their lives. A developed community is therefore one that allows all its members, including the youngest ones, to participate.

Another important and "new" issue for the European context, and especially for Italy, is the growing number of immigrant adolescents coming from countries with different cultural norms concerning patterns of relationships during adolescence and with different styles of socialization. The psychological processes of acquisition of autonomy and identity formation for these adolescents, in particular the "second generations," are the same as their Italian peers, but they have to complete these developmental tasks facing not only the often contradictory requests coming from their parents and Italian society, but also their condition of socio-economic disadvantage and social vulnerability. Moreover, risky behaviors among immigrant adolescents are of growing concern. Practitioners and social workers are currently experiencing the urgency of doing preventive interventions for such youngsters, searching for specific and "tailored" intervention approaches and methods. Again, we need to think of interventions involving community settings where such adolescents might be approached, through the involvement of other significant adult figures. Considering trends in immigrant population growth in Italy, this is undoubtedly one of the main challenges for future research and intervention programs.

And finally, I would underline the importance of analyzing the topic of participation: we are observing the renaissance of desire of participation in Europe (and also in other parts of the world), and of forms of commitment in civic and social experiences that seem to be popular, and effective, even if unexpected. Many questions are facing the researchers who are interested in understanding whether the traditional political participation has definitely declined among young people in Europe, what are the new forms of participation, whether there is still a gender gap in the form of participation, what are the most important psychosocial factors that can promote youth participation, and what are the psychosocial implications of these forms of participation.

Moreover, among adolescents belonging to ethnic minority groups, the participatory experiences in civic and political domain are linked to the citizenship conceptions.

Participation among migrant groups is crucially dependent on the political institutions and opportunities that are available to them in their country of residence. Actually the situation in Europe concerning rights associated with citizenship (the voting right) and possibilities to have access to alternative arenas in public domain (civic, social, volunteering) varies considerably in the extent to which these different forms of participation are supported or inhibited. Many factors operate at the macro, social, and psychological levels which are related to active citizenship. So it is important to analyze how these problems impact on migrant adolescents, what it means to be a "citizen" for them, and what are the relevant factors that facilitate or hamper their representation of citizenships.

To Conclude

So, what have I learnt from my adolescent children? I've learnt how to become a mother, negotiating roles and rules on a daily basis, taking firm stands and gradually granting them greater spaces of autonomy. I recall mothers of my children's friends who would say, in a slightly envious tone, "You are a psychologist, so you have a better understanding of what's going on," thus implicitly attributing me a greater parental competence. Truth is, I, too, like many other mothers, have made some clumsy errors. I have never "studied" my children; on the contrary, I would sometimes be surprised at what was happening to our intrafamily relationships and I would find myself saying out loud "It's a textbook example!" (i.e., this is exactly what psychology of adolescence textbooks describe). It was as if I was verifying "on the ground" that what had been analyzed and written by researchers—including me!—was indeed happening. I remember my strong relationship with my sons (the one with their father being more troubled) and the—I believe very specific—experience with twin children who were very different from each other, yet strongly linked in their being "a couple" and claiming their rights versus us parents. I recall a high level of conflict with my daughter which reached its peak—as textbooks say!—when she was 15, and then a slow but steady building of *female complicity* in the following years.

Have my thoughts about adolescence changed over the years? My personal experience—of being a young mother with twin boys and then a "mature" mother with a girl—has been deeply intertwined with my reflections on adolescence and my analyses of different cohorts of adolescents in two different historical periods, the 1980s and the 2000s. Cultural and social changes have obviously had a profound effect on socialization, family relations, and gender roles. To mention just a few examples: the lengthening of adolescence with the invention of additional categories—the emergent adulthood—is perpetuating a stand-by situation for young generations who are not recognized as having skills, competencies, and responsibilities in the public life, especially in the "gerontocratic" Italian context.

The "gender gap" in adolescent behavior which was apparent in the 1970s and questioned in the 1980s is nowadays gradually diminishing; few are the differences noted in their adoption both of at risky behavior and of virtuous civic engagement behavior. There is a diminution of the differentiation between male and female roles, by means of a reduction in stereotypic patterns of both roles and the adoption of certain characteristics of the opposite role.

Parents' greater permissiveness, which followed a more authoritarian approach, has contributed to raise a generation of "fragile" adolescents with few secure reference points. They may feel freer, but they are also more or less implicitly looking for rules and adult role models. What may be lacking today are, indeed, adult role models. As usual, adolescents rely on their peer group, but continue to relate to—and place hope in—their family, which represents the source of security and stability, especially in these difficult times of economic crisis and increasing youth unemployment.

References

Albanesi, C., Cicognani, E., & Zani, B. (2005). L'uso dei focus group per la costruzione di una scala di misurazione del senso di comunità in adolescenza [The use of focus group for the construction of a scale to measure the sense of community in adolescence]. *Sociologia e ricerca sociale, 76–77*, 159–171.

Albanesi, C., Cicognani, E., & Zani, B. (2007). Sense of community, civic engagement and social wellbeing in Italian adolescents, *Journal of Community and Applied Social Psychology, 17*, 387–406.

Barrett, M. (2012). *The PIDOP Project: Achievements and recommendations*. Plenary address presented at the 2nd International Multidisciplinary Conference, organized by the PIDOP consortium on "Political and Civic Participation', University of Surrey, Guildford, UK, April 16–17. Downloadable from: www.surrey.ac.uk/cronem/files/MartynBarrett.pdf

Bateman, H. V. (2002). Sense of community in the school: Listening to students' voices. In A. Fisher & C. Sonn (Eds.), *Psychological sense of community: Research applications, and implication*s (pp. 161–179). New York: Plenum Publishers.

Bosma, H., Jackson, S., Zijsling, D. H., Zani, B., Cicognani, E., Xerri, M. C. et al. (1996). Who has the final say? Decisions on adolescent behaviour within the family. *Journal of Adolescence, 19*, 277–291.

Bronfenbrenner, U. (1979). *The ecology of human development: Experiments by nature and design*. Cambridge, MA: Harvard University Press.

Cerchierini, L., Cicognani, E., & Zani, B. (Eds.) (2000). *L'HIV non va a scuola. Una ricerca intervento con gli adolescenti e i giovani non studenti a Bologna*. [The HIV does not go to school. A research intervention with non-student adolescents in Bologna.] Bologna, Italy: CLUEB.

Chiessi, M., Cicognani, E., & Sonn, C. (2010). Assessing sense of community in adolescents: Validating the brief version of the brief scale of sense of community in adolescents (SoC-A). *Journal of Community Psychology, 38*, 276–292.

Cicognani, E., Albanesi, C., & Zani, B. (2006). Il senso di comunità in adolescenza: Uno strumento di misura [Sense of community in adolescence: a measurement instrument]. *Bollettino di Psicologia Applicata, 250*, 13–30.

Cicognani, E., Albanesi, C., & Zani, B. (2008). The impact of residential context on adolescents' and young adults' well being. *Journal of Community and Applied Social Psychology, 18*, 558–575.

Cicognani, E., & Zani, B. (1998). Chi ha paura dell'AIIDS? Uno studio sulle componenti della valutazione del rischio in adolescenza [Who is afraid of AIDS? A study on the components of risk evaluation in adolescence]. *Bollettino di Psicologia Applicata, 226*, 47–60.

Cicognani, E.& Zani, B. (2003). *Genitori e adolescenti* [Parents and adolescents]. Rome: Carocci.

Cicognani, E., & Zani, B. (2009). Sense of community and social participation among adolescents and young adults living in Italy. In D. Dolejsiova & M. Garcia Lopez (Eds.), *European citizenship—In the process of construction. Challenges for citizenship, citizenship education and democratic practice in Europe* (pp. 100–113). Strasbourg: Council of Europe Publishing.

Cicognani, E., & Zani, B. (2010a). An instrument for measuring parents' perceptions of conflict style with adolescents: The "When We Disagree" scales. *The European Journal of Developmental Psychology, 7*(3), 390–400.

Cicognani, E., & Zani, B. (2010b). Conflict style and outcomes in families with adolescent children. *Social Development, 19*(2), 427–436.

Cicognani, E., & Zani, B. (2011). Alcohol use among Italian university students: The role of sensation seeking, peer group norms and self-efficacy. *Journal of Alcohol and Drug Education, 55*(2), 17–36.

Cicognani, E., Zani, B., & Albanesi, C. (2004). Adolescents et sentiment d'insécurité: dimensions et antécédents, *Psychologie et société, 7*, 25–45.

Cicognani, E., Zani, B., & Albanesi, C. (2010). Il contesto socio-ambientale come fattore di stress. Effetti sulle strategie di coping e sul benessere in adolescenza [Socio-environmental context as a source of stress. Impact on coping strategies and on well being in adolescence]. *Rassegna di Psicologia, XXVII*, 43–62.

Colarossi, L. G., & Eccles, J. (2003). Differential effects of support providers on adolescents' mental health. *Social Work Research, 27*, 19–30.

Da Silva, L., Sanson, A., Smart, D., & Toumbourou, J. (2004). Civic responsibility among Australian adolescents: Testing two competing models. *Journal of Community Psychology, 32*(3), 229–255.

ESPAD (2007). *The 2007 ESPAD Report. Substance use among students in 35 European countries*. Available at: www.espad.org

Holzkamp, K. (1972). *Kritische Psychologie* [Critical psychology]. Frankfurt: Fischer.

Honess, T., Charman, E., Zani, B., Cicognani, E., Xerri, M. L., Jackson, S. et al. (1997). Conflict between parents and adolescents: Variation by family constitution. *British Journal of Developmental Psychology, 15*, 367–385.

Jessor, R. (1998). *New perspectives on adolescent risk behaviour*. New York: Cambridge University Press.

Laursen, B., Coy, K., & Collins, W. A. (1998). Reconsidering changes in parent–child conflict across adolescence: a meta-analysis. *Child Development, 69*, 817–832.

Le Quéau, P., & Olm, C. (1999). *Les accidents de la route: une minorité de jeunes prend le risques*. Paris: Credoc.

Leventhal, T., & Brooks-Gunn, J. (2000). The neighbourhoods they live in: The effects of neighbourhood residence on child and adolescent outcomes. *Psychological Bulletin, 126*, 309–337.

McMillan, W. D., & Chavis, M. D. (1986). Sense of community: A definition and a theory. *Journal of Community psychology, 14*, 6–22.

Moos, R. H. (2002). The mystery of human context and coping: An unraveling of clues. *American Journal of Community Psychology, 30*, 67–88.

Olson, D. H., McCubbin, H. I., Barnes, H., Larsen, A., Muxen, M., & Wilson, M. (Eds.) (1982). *Family inventories: Inventories used in a national survey of families across the family life cycle*. St. Paul, MN: University of Minnesota.

Pretty, G. M. H. (2002). Young people's development of the community-minded self: Considering community identity, community attachment and sense of community. In T. Fisher & C. C. Sonn (Eds.), *Psychological sense of community: Research, applications, and implications* (pp. 183–203). New York: Kluwer Academic/Plenum Publishers.

Prilleltensky, I., Nelson, G., & Peirson, L. (2001). The role of power and control in children's lives: an ecological analysis of pathways toward wellness, resilience, and problems. *Journal of Community and Applied Social Psychology, 11*(2), 143–158.

Puddifoot, J. E. (1996). Some initial considerations in the measurement of community identity. *Journal of Community Psychology, 24*(4), 327–337.

Rappaport, J. (1977). *Community psychology. Values, research, and action.* New York: Holt, Rinehart & Winston.

Sanza, M., Cicognani, E., Zani, B., & Nasuelli, F. (Eds.) (2011). *Le rotte del divertimento e il consumo di sostanze psicoattive. Nuovi comportamenti, interventi di prevenzione e di riduzione dei rischi* [The route of entertainment and the substance use]. Milano: Franco Angeli.

Sarason, S. B. (1974). *The psychological sense of community: Prospects for a community psychology.* San Francisco: Jossey-Bass.

Silbereisen, R., & Todt, E. (1994). *Adolescence in context.* New York: Springer-Verlag.

Sherrod, L., Torney-Purta, J., & Flanagan, C. (Eds.) (2010). *Handbook of research on civic engagement in youth.* Hoboken, NJ: Wiley.

Shinn, M., & Toohey, S. M. (2003). Community contexts of human welfare. *Annual Review of Psychology, 54*, 427–459.

Smetana, J. G., Campione-Barr, N., & Metzger, A. (2006). Adolescent development in interpersonal and societal contexts. *Annual Review of Psychology, 57*, 255–284.

Steinberg, L. D. (1990). Interdependency in the family: Autonomy, conflicts and harmony in the parent-adolescent relationship. In S. S. Feldman & G. R. Elliot (Eds.), *At the threshold. The developing adolescent* (pp. 833–840). Cambridge, MA: Harvard University Press.

Steinberg, L. D. (2002). *Adolescence* (6th ed.). New York: McGraw-Hill.

Zani, B. (1993). Dating and interpersonal relationships in adolescence. In S. Jackson & H. Rodriguez-Tomé (Eds.), *Adolescence and its social worlds* (pp. 95–119). Hove, UK: Erlbaum.

Zani, B. (Ed.) (2003). *Sentirsi in/sicuri in città* [Feeling un/safe in town]. Bologna, Italy: Il Mulino.

Zani, B. (2005). Il senso di autoefficacia nei genitori di adolescenti [The feeling of self efficacy in parents of adolescents]. In E. Cicognani, L. Cerchierini, & M. Baldazzi (Eds.), *Lavorare con genitori di adolescenti* (pp. 105–118). Rome: Carocci.

Zani, B. (2011a). Le relazioni affettive e sessuali. [The affective and sexual relationships] In A. Palmonari (Ed.), *Psicologia dell'adolescenza* (pp. 229–251). Bologna, Italy: Il Mulino.

Zani, B. (2011b). *Le relazioni familiari* [The family relationships]. In A. Palmonari (Ed.), *Psicologia dell'adolescenza* (pp. 187–208). Bologna, Italy: Il Mulino.

Zani, B. (Ed.) (2012). *Psicologia di comunità. Prospettive, idee, metodi* [Community psychology. Perspectives, ideas, methods]. Rome: Carocci.

Zani, B., & Barrett, M. (2012). Introduction: Engaged citizens? Political participation and social engagement among youth, women, minorities, and migrants. *Human Affairs, 22*(3), 273–282.

Zani, B., Bosma, H., Zijsling, D., & Honess, T. (2001). Family context and the development of adolescent decision making. In J. E. Nurmi (Ed.), *Navigating through adolescence: European perspectives* (pp. 199–225). New York: Routledge Falmer.

Zani, B., & Cicognani, E. (1995). Il problema dell'AIDS nei giovani: credenze, percezione del rischio e strategie di "coping" [The AIDS problem in young people: beliefs, risk perception and coping strategies]. *Giornale Italiano di Psicologia, 5*, 827–852.

Zani, B., & Cicognani, E. (1998). Adolescenti e precauzioni nei confronti dell'AIDS: un'applicazione della teoria del comportamento pianificato [Adolescents and precautions towards AIDS: an application of the theory of planned change]. *Psicologia della Salute, 2–3*, 81–98.

Zani, B., & Cicognani, E. (1999). La gestione del conflitto nelle famiglie con adolescenti: le prospettive di genitori e figli [Conflict management in families with adolescent children: the perspectives of parents and adolescents]. *Giornale Italiano di Psicologia, XXVI*(4), 791–815.

Zani, B., & Cicognani, E. (2000). *Psicologia della salute* [Health psychology]. Bologna, Italy: Il Mulino.

Zani, B., & Cicognani, E. (2002a). Peer group relationships and risk behaviours in adolescence. *Revista de Psihologie Aplicata* [*Journal of Applied Psychology*], *4*(1), 29–42.

Zani, B., & Cicognani, E. (2002b). I "non studenti" e l'AIDS: comportamenti a rischio e strategie di prevenzione ["Out-of-school" youngsters and AIDS: risk behaviors and precautionary strategies]. *Psicologia della Salute, 4*(1), 67–83.

Zani, B., & Cicognani, E. (2005). Contesti di vita e benessere negli adolescenti [Life contexts and wellbeing in adolescents]. In G. Sarchielli & B. Zani (Eds.), *Persone, gruppi e comunità* (pp. 281–306). Bologna, Italy: Il Mulino.

Zani, B., & Cicognani, E. (2006a). Sexuality and intimate relationships in adolescence. In S. Jackson & L. Goossens (Eds), *Handbook of adolescent development* (pp. 200–222). London: Psychology Press.

Zani, B., & Cicognani, E. (2006b). Autoefficacia e comportamenti a rischio [Self-efficacy and risk behaviors]. *Psicologia della Salute, 3*, 9–26.

Zani, B., Cicognani, E., & Albanesi, C. (2001). Adolescents' sense of community and feeling of unsafety in the urban environment. *Journal of Community and Applied Social Psychology, 11*(6), 475–489.

Zani, B., Cicognani, E., & Albanesi, C. (2011). *La partecipazione civica e politica dei giovani: discorsi esperienze, significati* [Civic and political participation of young people: discourses, experiences, meanings]. Bologna, Italy: CLUEB.

Zani, B., Cicognani, E., & Albanesi, C. (2012). The perspective of social and community psychology for a model of political and civic participation. Unpublished paper. The Pidop project.

Zani, B., & Palmonari, A. (Eds.) (1996). *Manuale di psicologia di comunità* [Handbook of community psychology]. Bologna, Italy: Il Mulino.

Appendix
Synopses of the Contributions of Deceased Colleagues to the Developmental Science of Adolescence

A1
Paul B. Baltes[1]

LISETTE M. DESOUZA

Paul B. Baltes (1939–2006) was a developmental psychologist who focused on the theoretical and methodological study of the life span, often in collaboration with his wife, Margaret M. Baltes, and colleagues John R. Nesselroade and K. Warner Schaie. Paul Baltes completed his PhD in 1967 at the University of Saar in Saarbrucken. Upon completion of his doctorate, he became an assistant professor at the University of West Virginia. Baltes and Baltes then moved to the Pennsylvania State University, and then to Germany in 1980, where Paul Baltes became the director of the Max Planck Institute for Human Development. He remained in this position until 2004. In 2004, he founded the Max Planck International Research Network on Aging (MaxNetAging), an interdisciplinary "virtual institute for the advancement of research on the causes, patterns, processes, and consequences of aging" (MaxnetAging).

Baltes and Baltes are well regarded for their selective optimization with compensation (SOC) model of development (Baltes & Baltes, 1990). This model elucidates processes of developmental regulation through goal selection, goal pursuit, and goal maintenance. Their work is grounded within a life-span approach to the study of development and focuses on the potential for plasticity and positive development, even in aged populations. Paul Baltes's interest in the aged population included cognitive functioning and aging as it related to functional losses and gains in wisdom. Baltes, Baltes, and colleagues applied theoretically predicated and methodologically sound interdisciplinary research in the Berlin Aging Study (BASE) (Baltes, Lindenberger, & Staudinger, 2006). With John Nesselroade, he conducted the first cohort sequential study of adolescent development (Nesselroade & Baltes, 1974). This work established that sources of variation other than those associated with age (e.g., variation linked to the historical moment and to birth cohort) contribute to change trajectories in adolescence.

Baltes was a member of the U.S. Social Science Research Council, the German-American Academic Council, the Berlin-Brandenburg Academy of Sciences and of the European Academy of Sciences, the Royal Swedish Academy, and of the American Academy of Sciences. He was also Vice President of the German Academy Leopoldina. He held honorary doctorates from the universities of Jyväskylä, Stockholm, Geneva, and Humboldt University (in Berlin). He received the German Order Pour le Mérite for Arts and Sciences in 2000 and the Great Federal Cross of Merit in 2001.

Baltes's career as a developmental scientist was esteemed in the academy and also in social and political realms. His methodological rigor and theoretical perspective continue to be applied to the contemporary study of life-span development.

Note

1. Information was derived from the Max Planck Institute for Human Development and the Margaret M. and Paul B. Baltes Foundation.

Selected References

Baltes, P. B., & Baltes, M. M. (1990). Psychological perspectives on successful aging: The model of selective optimization with compensation. *Successful Aging: Perspectives from the Behavioral Sciences, 1,* 1–34.

Baltes, P. B., Lindenberger, U., & Staudinger, U. M. (2006). Lifespan theory in developmental psychology. In R. M. Lerner (Ed.), *Theoretical models of human development.* Vol. 1: *Handbook of child psychology* (6th ed., pp. 569–664). Editors-in-chief: W. Damon & R. M. Lerner. Hoboken, NJ: Wiley.

Nesselroade, J. R., & Baltes, P. B. (1974). Adolescent personality development and historical change: 1970–1972. *Monographs from the Society for Research in Child Development, 9*(154), 1–80.

A2

Peter L. Benson[1]

Mary H. Buckingham

Peter Lorimer Benson, PhD (1946–2011) was CEO and president of Search Institute, a community-based research institute aimed at promoting and discovering the resources youth need to thrive. Benson's work focused on positive adolescent development, specifically in the domains of spiritual development and thriving. In particular, Benson pioneered the "Developmental Assets" framework, a research-based conception that remains a key approach to studying positive youth development. In addition, Benson's work focused on the importance of building "sparks," i.e., the passions of youth. His approach to studying positive youth development has been applied in numerous youth-serving systems.

Benson attended Augustana College, where he majored in psychology. He then attended Yale University, where he received an MA in the psychology of religion (1970). After completion of this degree, Benson moved to Denver, where he studied at the University of Denver and earned an MA (1972) and PhD (1973) in experimental social psychology. His research at the University of Denver and dissertation focused on the development of altruism.

Benson began his career in academia at Eastern Michigan University, where he worked from 1973 to 1975. He then moved to a faculty position at Earlham College. In 1978, after several years in academia, Benson took a position at Search Institute and became the president of Search Institute in 1985. Benson was awarded the American Psychological Association's William James Award for career achievement in the scientific study of religion.

Benson's focus on the role of developmental assets in the healthy development of youth involved advocating for the scientific study of adolescent thriving. Later in his career, he focused his research on "sparks" and what it takes to help youth thrive. Benson played a key role in connecting the academic and applied communities. "Sparks," i.e., what gives youth hope, focus, and joy in their lives, and the importance of sparks in the thriving of youth, was widely communicated to communities, youth-serving organizations, and to the Dalai Lama, who spoke with Benson about the importance of this concept. The individual resources, ecological resources, and positive experiences and opportunities, known as the 40 Developmental Assets, along with Benson's contributions to the field with regard to spiritual development, altruism, and thriving in adolescence can be found in over 220 articles, books, and other publications authored and co-authored by Benson including *All Kids Are Our Kids* (Benson, 2006), *What Kids Need to Succeed* (Benson, Galbraith, & Espeland, 1994), and *Sparks* (Benson, 2008).

Note

1. Information for this brief biography was derived from the Search Institute and Lerner, R. M., & Fisher, C. B. (2012). A tribute to Peter L. Benson and his contributions to applied developmental science: Editors' introduction. *Applied Developmental Science, 16*(1), 1–2.

Selected References

Benson, P. L. (2006). *All kids are our kids: What communities must do to raise caring and responsible children and adolescents*, 2nd ed. San Francisco: Jossey-Bass.

Benson, P. L. (2008). *Sparks: How parents can help ignite the hidden strengths of teenagers*. San Francisco: Jossey-Bass.

Benson, P. L., Galbraith, J., & Espeland, P. (1994). *What kids need to succeed*. Minneapolis: Free Spirit.

A3

Daniel B. Elkonin[1]

MARIA K. PAVLOVA

Daniel Borisovich Elkonin, PhD (1904–84) was a Soviet psychologist who elaborated on Lev Vygotsky's cultural historical theory and Aleksei Leontiev's and Piotr Galperin's activity theory to study child development. His major contributions to developmental and educational psychology include research on child play and learning, developmental education programs for primary school, and mixed-methods research on adolescent development.

Elkonin graduated from the Herzen Leningrad State Pedagogical Institute in 1927. From 1929 until 1937, he worked there at the Department for Pedology. Between 1931 and 1934, he established a close collaboration with Lev Vygotsky and launched his research on child play and on the relation between education and psychological development.

However, in 1936, pedology was banned in the USSR. Elkonin's doctoral degree was revoked, and he lost his position. In 1940, he earned another doctoral degree with a thesis addressing the development of speech in school children.

In 1941, Elkonin joined the Soviet Army to fight against the Nazi invasion. After the war, which claimed the lives of his wife and two daughters, Elkonin moved to Moscow to teach psychology at one of military education institutions. After Stalin's death in 1953, Elkonin's academic career finally received a boost. He changed to the Psychological Institute of the RSFSR Academy of Pedagogical Sciences, in Moscow, where he sequentially directed the Primary School Psychology Lab, the Adolescent Psychology Lab, and the Lab for the Assessment of Psychological Development in Schoolchildren. In 1962, he received his second doctorate (similar to German habilitation), and in 1968, was elected a corresponding member of the U.S.S.R. Academy of Pedagogical Sciences. For many of these years, he was also teaching at the Lomonosov Moscow State University.

His major book on adolescence, *Vozrastnyje i individualnyje osobennosti mladshikh podrostkov* [Age-Related and Individual Characteristics of Early Adolescents] (Elkonin & Dragunova, 1967), reported on a short-term but labor-intensive longitudinal study where participative observations and unstandardized interviews were combined with standardized assessments of pubertal status, cognitive development, and sociometric status. In this work, Elkonin emphasized the great variability and heterogeneity of individual developmental trajectories. In his seminal theoretical article "Toward the Problem of Stages in the Mental Development of the Child" (1971/1972), Elkonin argued that child development progresses through the intermittent, discontinuous advances in motivational and cognitive/instrumental domains and that leading activities of each developmental stage serve to advance development in the currently dominant domain. He suggested that in early adolescence, close interpersonal interactions in peer groups foster the understanding of self and other, and facilitate the acquisition of group norms. However, in late adolescence, preparation for career choice and further education become more salient.

During more than 50 years of his scientific career, Elkonin published over 100 books and articles in Russian, including the famous *Psykhologija igry* [Psychology of Play] (1978); some of them were translated into English, German, and other languages. He was a very energetic and truly kind person who was a wonderful companion and colleague. His work was highly influential and attracted many followers in the USSR and its satellite countries.

Note

1. Information was partly derived from: Elkonin, B. D. (2004). Predislovije [Preface]. In D. B. Elkonin, *Detskaja psikhologija* (2nd ed.). Moscow: Academia; Elkonin Daniel Borisovich (2013). Retrieved from: www.psy.msu.ru/people/elkonin.html; Zinchenko, V. P. (1994). Shtrikhi k portretu D. B. Elkonina [Drawing a portrait of D. B. Elkonin]. *Voprosy psykhologiji, 94*(1), 43–47.

Selected References

Elkonin, D. B. (1971/1972). Toward the problem of stages in the mental development of the child. *Soviet Psychology, 10*(3), 225–251. doi:10.2753/RPO1061-04051003225

Elkonin, D. B. (1978). *Psykhologija igry* [Psychology of play]. Moscow: Pedagogika.

Elkonin, D. B., & Dragunova, T. V. (Eds). (1967). *Vozrastnyje i individualnyje osobennosti mladshikh podrostkov* [Age-related and individual characteristics of early adolescents]. Moscow: Prosveshenije.

A4

Stuart T. Hauser[1]

Santiago Gasca

Stuart T. Hauser, MD, PhD (1938–2008) was the former President of the Judge Baker Children's Center, Professor of Psychiatry at Harvard Medical School, and the Co-Director of the Clinical Research Training Program in Social and Biological Psychiatry. Hauser was internationally known for his research on adolescent development and personality development.

Hauser grew up in the Bronx as an only child and attended Antioch College for his bachelor's degree in philosophy and physics. He then pursued a master's degree in Social Anthropology at Harvard University. He then received his MD from Yale University in 1966 and, soon after his residency, began research training in adolescent development, adolescent psychopathology, and family process at the National Institute of Mental Health. Hauser returned to Harvard in 1977 to receive his PhD in Developmental Psychology and Personality. He completed his psychoanalytic training at the Boston Psychoanalytic Institute a year later.

Hauser was a major contributor to the emerging field of developmental science. He published widely on a variety of subjects, ranging from resilience to developmental pathways, and published more than 100 journal articles, 37 chapters, and 8 books during his career, including *Adolescents and Their Families* (1991) and *Black and White Identity Formation* (1971). Hauser's books and chapters also targeted general audiences, seeking to disseminate research findings on subjects such as risk and resilience, family processes, and psychosocial development. Hauser is also remembered as an outstanding mentor. The Stuart T. Hauser Harvard Clinical Research Training Program in Biological and Social Sciences is named in his honor.

While his research spanned many topics and had positive impacts on the field of adolescent development, the longitudinal studies he conducted during his time at Harvard may be his most influential work. His first study focused on the psychosocial determinants and consequences of adolescents with diabetes. His second project, Paths over Time and Across Generations, is ongoing and focuses on the identity development of high-school students and of psychiatric patients. The original participants are now in their forties and the project has contributed to the increased understanding of a developmental pathways, resilient outcomes, and personality development, among other areas.

Note

1. Sources were derived from the Judge Baker Children's Center and the Harvard Medical School.

Selected References

Fonagy, P., Jabobson, A. M., McCarly, R. W., & Reiss, D. (2010). Reflections on the legacy of Stuart T. Hauser: Scientist, colleague, and mentor. *Research in Human Development, 7*(4), 307–321.

Hauser, S. T. (1971). *Black and white identity formation: Studies in the psychosocial development of lower socioeconomic class adolescent boys.* New York: John Wiley.

Hauser, S. T. (1991). *Adolescents and their families: Paths of ego development.* New York: Free Press.

McCarley, R.C., Allen, J., Hauser, B.B., Kirshner, L.A., & Waldinger, R. (2011). Stuart T. Hauser: Harvard Medical School—Memorial minute. *Harvard Gazette.* Retrieved from: http://news.harvard.edu/gazette/story/2011/03/stuart-t-hauser/

A5

John P. Hill[1]

ROBEY B. CHAMPINE

The seminal contributions of John P. Hill, PhD (1936–88) to the field of adolescent development underscored the importance of examining the biological, psychological, and social changes that take place during adolescence. His landmark research on pubertal change and transformations in family relationships advanced the understanding of contextual influences on social development and adjustment.

Hill attended Stanford, and earned his PhD in clinical psychology from Harvard in 1964. He then joined the Institute of Child Development at the University of Minnesota, where he taught a course on adolescence and created the Minnesota Symposia on Child Psychology, a series that publishes developmental science essays. In 1970, he became Professor of Human Development and Family Studies at Cornell, where he held other appointments, including Associate Dean for Graduate Education and Research. During this time, he authored "Some Perspectives on Adolescence in American Society" (Hill, 1973), a paper that emphasized the importance of understanding the psychosocial changes that take place during adolescence.

While at Cornell, Hill collaborated with then graduate student, Laurence Steinberg, on a well-known study that examined the impact of pubertal change among adolescent boys on family interactions (Steinberg & Hill, 1978). Their findings suggested the influence of physical and intellectual maturation on the adolescent–parent relationship (Steinberg & Hill, 1978), and inspired follow-up studies that explored the impact of puberty on individual and familial adaptational processes.

In 1977, Hill left Cornell and joined the Center for the Study of Youth Development in Boys Town, Nebraska as Senior Research Scientist and Director of a Research Program on Social Relations in Early Adolescence. From 1981 until his passing in 1988, he was Professor of Psychology at Virginia Commonwealth University (VCU). During this time, he authored "Early Adolescence: A Research Agenda" (Hill, 1983), in which he made recommendations to advance the understanding of psychosocial development during adolescence, including fostering applied research to inform policies and programs.

Throughout his 24-year career, Hill's insightful scholarship was captured in the more than 60 articles he published. He was one of the first associate editors of *Developmental Psychology*, President of the Society for Research on Adolescence, served as department chair at Cornell and VCU, and was a consultant to various commissions and agencies. He was named a Fellow of the American Psychological Association and an Outstanding Researcher in Early Adolescence by the Center for Early Adolescence, and he received other honors in recognition of his scientific contributions.

Note

1. Information was derived from: Holmbeck, G. N. & Blyth, D. A. (1991). Introduction. *The Journal of Early Adolescence, 11*(1), 6–19.

Selected References

Hill, J. P. (1973). Some perspectives on adolescence in American Society. Paper prepared for the Office of Child Development, U.S. Department of Health, Education, and Welfare, Washington, DC.

Hill, J. P. (1983). Early adolescence: A research agenda. *Journal of Early Adolescence, 3*(1–2), 1–21.

Stenberg, L. D. & Hill, J. P. (1978). Patterns of family interaction as a function of age, the onset of puberty, and formal thinking. *Developmental Psychology, 14*(6), 683–684.

A6

Roberta G. Simmons[1]

ROBEY B. CHAMPINE

The scholarship of Roberta G. Simmons, PhD (1937–93) in the field of adolescent development, and her research on the emotional effects of organ transplants among donors and recipients, advanced the understanding of individual and contextual influences on social-psychological adjustment. Throughout her 29-year career, she was an innovative and insightful scholar, who integrated research in human development, psychiatry, and medical sociology.

Simmons attended Wellesley College, and earned her PhD in sociology from Columbia in 1964. She worked for 2 years at the National Institute of Mental Health (NIMH), where she collaborated with the late Morris Rosenberg on a study of the relationship between race and self-esteem among urban school children. In their book, *Black and White Self-Esteem*, Rosenberg and Simmons (1972) presented findings that challenged the assumption that Black children have lower self-esteem than White children, and suggested the impact of social-contextual factors on personal beliefs and attitudes.

She held faculty appointments in sociology and psychiatry at the University of Minnesota for 18 years, and was a Research Associate in Surgery. In 1987, she became professor of psychiatry and sociology at the University of Pittsburgh. Her books and more than 85 scholarly articles and chapters document her seminal contributions to understanding development and psychological well-being. In *Moving Into Adolescence* (Simmons & Blyth, 1987), she presented findings from her longitudinal examination of the impact of school transition on self-image and adjustment during early and middle adolescence. She was also known for her groundbreaking research on the social-psychological impacts of kidney transplants, which she undertook in collaboration with her husband, Dr. Richard L. Simmons. In *Gift of Life,* Simmons, Marine, and Simmons (1987) examined the costs and gains of organ donation, and explored the psychological consequences of altruism and stressful decision-making.

Simmons was esteemed for her professional leadership as a founding member of the Society for Research on Adolescence, as President of the Midwestern Sociological Society, Vice President of the Eastern Sociological Society, Chair of the medical sociology section of the American Sociological Association, and as a member of numerous other professional committees. She was a 15-year recipient of the NIMH Research Scientist Career Development Award, a Guggenheim Fellow, and a Fellow at the Center for Advanced Study in the Behavioral Sciences.

Note

1. Information was derived from: Blyth, D. A. (1993). In honor of Roberta G. Simmons (1937–1993): Scholar, mentor, friend. *Journal of Research on Adolescence, 3*(4), 445–447.

Selected References

Simmons, R. G., & Blyth, D. A. (1987). *Moving into adolescence: The impact of pubertal change and school context.* Hawthorne, NY: Aldine de Gruyter.

Simmons, R. G., Marine, S. K., & Simmons, R. L. (1987). *Gift of life: The effect of organ transplantation on individual, family, and social dynamics.* New Brunswick, NJ: Transaction Books.

Rosenberg, M., & Simmons, R. G. (1972). *Black and white self-esteem: The urban school child.* Washington, DC: American Sociological Association.

A7

Hershel D. Thornburg

KATHLEEN N. GREENMAN[1]

Hershel D. Thornberg, PhD (1936–87) was an educational psychologist who dedicated his career to the study of early adolescence, school reform, and minority youth. Thornberg is most known for his impact on the fields of adolescent and child development, sex education, teacher preparation, and psychiatry.

Thornberg's career went through several phases. After completing his bachelor's degree at Friends University in Wichita, Kansas, he was ordained as an Evangelical Quaker Minister. Soon after being ordained, Thornberg began teaching high school and went on to serve as an assistant principal. Thornberg earned a Master's of Education in counseling and guidance while pursuing his Doctorate in Education from the University of Oklahoma in Norman. Upon receiving his PhD in Education in 1967, he immediately joined academia in a tenure-track position at the University of Arizona. During his time at the University of Arizona, Thornberg served as the Department Head of Educational Psychology and collaborated with colleagues to establish a doctoral program focused specifically on early adolescence.

Thornberg met and married his wife Ellen Branson Muench during his time at the University of Oklahoma. She shared his passion for middle-school education reform. As academic entrepreneurs, Thornberg and his wife teamed up to meet the need for a research journal on early adolescence and launched the *Journal of Early Adolescence* in 1981. In 1985, they also started the *Journal of Adolescent Research*, which united the literature on all adolescent populations. In response to the momentum surrounding these journals, the Thornbergs started the Biennial Conference on Adolescence Research, which paved the way for the creation of the Society for Research on Adolescence (SRA), of which Thornberg was elected founding president. The SRA and the Biennial Conference were the first formal groups to unite professionals across many disciplines to discuss adolescent development and well-being.

Across his career, Thornberg developed the two journals, a conference series, a society and a doctoral program. In addition, he published 80 articles and 11 books. Among his books are: *Preadolescent Development: Readings* (1974), *Introduction to Educational Psychology* (1984), and *You and Your Adolescent* (1977). His publications led to various other chapters, monographs, and speeches as well as to a variety of consultation engagements and instruction workshops for students, teachers, schools and government groups. Thornberg's scholastic contributions and initiatives continue to encourage dialogue across academia and positively influence the study of adolescent development.

Note

1. Information was derived from: Adams, G. R. (1986). In memory of Hershel D. Thornburg (1936–1987). *The Journal of Early Adolescence, 6*, 5–8; Adams, G. R. (2004). In memory of Dr. Ellen Thornburg (September 13, 1934–October 3, 2002). *The Journal of Early Adolescence, 24*, 9–11.

Selected References

Thornberg, H. (1974). *Preadolescent development: Readings.* Tucson: University of Arizona Press.

Thornberg, H. (1977). *You and your adolescent.* Tuscon, AZ: Help Books.

Thornberg, H. (1984). *Introduction to educational psychology.* University of Michigan/West Publishing Co.

Index

Note: *italic* page numbers indicate tables; **bold** indicate figures.

1970 British Birth Cohort Study 72
4-H 213, 295–6, 303
9/11 532

A Developmental Study of Adolescent Mental Health (Peterson) 358–9
A History of Experimental Psychology (Boring) 1, 2
Abbot, Douglass 523
Aber, J. Lawrence 33
Aberdeen epidemiological study 418–19
Abernethy, Alexis 478
abuse and neglect research 507–8
academic stress, in preschool children 523–4
academics, religious socialization 100, 102
Academy of Experimental Criminology 160
access to resources 73
achievement, and socialization 237–8
achievements, in developmental science 425
Act 48, Vermont 228
action, and development 459
action grammar **337**
action research 216–17, 540
action theories 283
active aging 467
adaptation: to stress 425; and transformation 328
adaptive developmental regulations 283, 298
adjustment: academic and social 136; emotional and behavioral 89
Adler, Nancy 474, 475
adolescence: as area of study 2; emergence of 170; lengthening 206, 233; phases 192, 194, 197–8; use of term 1–2
adolescence-maximum hypothesis 403
Adolescent Development: A Life-Span Perspective (Lerner and Spanier) 292
adolescent medicine, status 25
adolescent–parent relationships 476–7; Chinese youth 477, 479; disclosure and secrecy 479; India 528
adolescent psychiatry *see* Hamburg, Beatrix
adolescent psychology, bias 99
Adolescent Risk Reduction Program 219
Adolescent Storm and Stress: An Evaluation of the Mead-Freeman Controversy (Côté) 99
adolescents: as consumers 202; disclosure of information 51
adulthood: markers of 236; understandings of 336
Affordable Care Act 28
African-American families 478

African-Americans, assumptions of pathology 487
African Population and Health Research Center 252
after-school care 382–3
age: normative expectations 539; Sense of Community (SoC) 545
age-based policies 75
age-graded behaviors 245
age norms 245
age-related variation 424
age-segregation 204
agency 55, 76, 82
aggregates, of youth 170
aggression 80, 375; adolescent–parent relationships 540; as antecedent of problem behaviors 380; bio-psycho-social development 516; birth cohort studies 516; compass model 376; cone and compass models 375; cone model **375**; descriptive model 375–6; experimental preventive studies 517; genetics and environment 516–17; individual differences in aggression/non-aggression 376; longitudinal studies 514–15; measures of 376–7; and non-aggression 376; offensive and defensive 375–6; and pubertal hormones 505–6; and sex hormone replacement therapy 507; trajectories **515**, **516**
aging 408–9, 467
aging society 189–90
agricultural depression, Iowa 91–2
Ahtisaari, Eeva 382–3
"AIDS in Adolescence: A Rationale for Concern" 220
AIDS: Trading Fears for Facts—A Guide for Young People (Hein and Foy DiGeronimo) 225
Ainsworth, Mary 258, 394, 416
Albee, George 386–7, 391
Albee, Marina 386
alcohol use 202, 381–2, 440, 542
Allen, Ms. 483
Allen, Walter 491
Allport, Gordon 200, 201
altruism 127
American Board of Pediatrics 312
American Lives (Clausen) 145
American Society of Criminology 156
Amerika Häuser 332
An Intensive Study of Factors related to Sex Differences in Cognition (Gittelson et al.) 361

Anand, Sudhir 399
And Then I Became Gay: Young Men's Stories (Savin-Williams) 434
Anderson, Pam 301
Andersson, Tommy 324
Andrews, Frank 68
Andry, Robert 512, 513
Anglo-American pragmatism 170–1
anomie 241
anti-smoking 196
antisocial behavior 203
apartheid 394
apathy–futility syndrome 396
applied behavior analysis 503
applied research, and social policy 451, 453–4
apprentice/student research 348–9
apprenticeship 71
area influences, in deprivation 421
Argyris, Chris 212
Aristotle 2
Arnett, Jeffrey Jensen 5–14, 73; as author and editor 11–12; Bermuda 7; Clark University 12; concept of emerging adulthood 11; critique of psychology 12–13; cultural psychology 12; Denmark 9; disillusionment with traditional methods 6, 7; dissertation 7; early aspirations 5; expert witness 9–10; first research 6; graduate school, University of Virginia 6–7; heresy 5; independent scholarship 10–12; interviewing 7–8; marriage and family 8, 12; Michigan State University 5–6; music 6, 7; neuropsychology 6; Northwestern University 8; Oglethorpe University 7–8; papers 11, 12; perspective on development 12; place in psychology 12; pleasure of work 13–14; postdoc 8; psychology of religion 6; San Francisco 9–10; stepfamilies study 6; teaching 7; tenure 10; textbook writing 10–11; transition to adulthood 9; University of Chicago 8; University of Missouri 9
Aronson, Elliot 474
Asch, Solomon 47
Asher, Steve 90
assets-based approach 84, 221, 227, 228; *see also* positive youth development movement; strengths-based approach
attachment 82, 387, 396, 416, 417
attenuation hypothesis 506
attitude-behavior linkages 474